Biographical Dictionary of
American Sports

BASEBALL,
REVISED AND EXPANDED EDITION

Biographical Dictionary of American Sports

BASEBALL, REVISED AND EXPANDED EDITION

G–P

Edited by David L. Porter

GREENWOOD PRESS
Westport, Connecticut • London

Library of Congress Cataloging-in-Publication Data

Biographical dictionary of American sports. Baseball / edited by
    David L. Porter.—Rev. and expanded ed.
        p. cm.
    Includes bibliographical references (p.   ) and index.
    Contents: [1] A–F — [2] G–P — [3] Q–Z.
    ISBN 0–313–29884–X (set : alk. paper). — ISBN 0–313–31174–9 (A–F
: alk. paper). — ISBN 0–313–31175–7 (G–P : alk. paper). — ISBN
0–313–31176–5 (Q–Z : alk. paper)
    1. Baseball—United States Biography Dictionaries.   2. Baseball—
United States—History.   I. Porter, David L., 1941–   .
II. Title: Baseball.
GV865.A1B55   2000
796.357'092'273—dc21   99–14840
    [B]

British Library Cataloguing in Publication Data is available.

Library of Congress Catalog Card Number: 99–14840
ISBN: 0–313–29884–X (set)
        0–313–31174–9 (A–F)
        0–313–31175–7 (G–P)
        0–313–31176–5 (Q–Z)

First published in 2000

Greenwood Press, 88 Post Road West, Westport, CT 06881
An imprint of Greenwood Publishing Group, Inc.
www.greenwood.com

Printed in the United States of America

The paper used in this book complies with the
Permanent Paper Standard issued by the National
Information Standards Organization (Z39.48–1984).

10 9 8 7 6 5 4 3 2 1

Cover photographs: National Baseball Hall of Fame Library, Cooperstown, NY.

Unless otherwise credited, all photographs appearing in this volume are courtesy of the National
Baseball Hall of Fame Library, Cooperstown, NY.

Every reasonable effort has been made to trace the owners of copyright materials in this book,
but in some instances this has proven impossible. The editor and publisher will be glad to
receive information leading to more complete acknowledgments in subsequent printings of the
book and in the meantime extend their apologies for any omissions.

Contents

Illustrations

VOLUME 3

Photos for Volume 3 follow page 1509.

Preface

The *Biographical Dictionary of American Sports (BDAS)* series began because of a need for a scholarly, comprehensive biographical dictionary of notable American athletic figures. Sports encyclopedias typically had concentrated on statistical achievements of notable American athletic figures and contained comparatively little biographical background data. Sports biographies, meanwhile, usually featured just the greatest or most prominent athletic figures.

The *BDAS* series, consisting of six volumes published between 1987 and 1995, has profiled 3,383 notable American sports figures. To date, 973 entries have featured major league baseball players, managers, umpires, and/or executives. A majority appeared in a 1987 volume devoted exclusively to baseball, while the remainder were included in either the 1992 or 1995 supplemental volumes.

This three-volume book, arranged alphabetically, features 1,450 baseball entries. It contains revised and updated entries for all 973 figures included in the earlier volumes. These figures typically compiled impressive career statistical records as players, managers, coaches, umpires, and/or executives. One quarter are members of the National Baseball Hall of Fame in Cooperstown, New York. The position players often batted above .300 lifetime with at least 2,000 career hits and/or 300 career home runs. In some instances, they demonstrated remarkable fielding and/or running abilities. Starting pitchers typically compiled at least 175 major league victories with outstanding win–loss percentages and excellent earned run averages, while relief pitchers ranked among career save leaders.

An additional 477 baseball luminaries who have helped shape the development of the national pastime from the mid–nineteenth century to the present are also profiled. Roberto Alomar, Jeff Bagwell, Albert Belle, Dante Bichette, Craig Biggio, Kevin Brown, Ken Caminiti, David Cone, Andres

Galarraga, Tom Glavine, Juan Gonzalez, Ken Griffey, Jr., Randy Johnson, David Justice, Chuck Knoblauch, Barry Larkin, Kenny Lofton, Greg Maddux, Edgar Martinez, Pedro Martinez, Tino Martinez, Mike Mussina, Mike Piazza, Ivan Rodriguez, Garry Sheffield, John Smoltz, Sammy Sosa, Frank Thomas, Jr., Mo Vaughn, Larry Walker, Matt Williams, and other current stars with several years of major league experience are featured for the first time.[1] A vast majority of the new entries are former major league players, managers, umpires, and executives. New baseball entries also include 31 Negro League and 33 All-American Girls Professional Baseball League (AAGPBL) stars. The AAGPBL operated from 1943 to 1954. Jean Faut Eastman, Betty Weaver Foss, Dottie Kamenshek, Sophie Kurys, Dottie Schroeder, Joanne Weaver, Connie Wisniewski, and other AAGPBL players are profiled.

The selection of the new baseball entries proved very challenging. Before making final choices, the editor thoroughly researched several baseball encyclopedias and histories.[2] Frederick Ivor-Campbell assisted in the selection of nineteenth-century personalities, while Rick Center suggested many AAGPBL entries. Other contributors also suggested subjects worthy of inclusion. Of course, the editor assumes ultimate responsibility for any significant baseball figures inadvertently excluded from this volume.

The additional baseball entries met three general criteria. First, they either were born in or spent their childhood years in the United States. Foreigners who made exceptional impacts on the national pastime are also covered. Second, they typically compiled impressive statistical records. Major leaguers, for example, batted above .275 with at least 1,000 hits and/or 100 home runs, recorded at least 100 major league victories with fine win–loss percentages and/or earned run averages, demonstrated fine fielding and/or running abilities, or excelled as managers, coaches, umpires, or executives. Third, they made a major impact on professional baseball, earning significant awards or performing for championship teams.

Biographies usually indicate the subject's full given name at birth; date and place of birth and, when applicable, date and place of death; parental background; formal education; spouse and children, when applicable; and major personal characteristics. Entries feature the subject's baseball career through December 1999 and typically include information about his or her entrance into professional baseball; positions played; teams played for with respective leagues;[3] lifetime batting, fielding, and/or pitching records and achievements; individual records set, awards won, and All-Star and World Series appearances; and impact on baseball. Biographical and statistical data frequently proved elusive for Negro Leaguers and early major leaguers. Entries on managers usually cover their teams guided, with inclusive dates; major statistical achievements; career win–loss records with percentages; premier players piloted; and managerial philosophy, strategy, and innovations.

Biographies of club executives, league officials, umpires, sportswriters, and sportscasters describe their various positions held, notable accomplishments, and impact on baseball.

Brief bibliographies list pertinent sources for each biographical entry. Authors benefited from interviews or correspondence with biographical subjects, relatives, or acquaintances. Former major leaguers and AAGPBL players proved especially cooperative in furnishing information. The National Baseball Library in Cooperstown, New York, *The Sporting News* in St. Louis, MO, the Northern Indiana Historical Society in South Bend, IN, college, university, and public libraries, radio and television networks, newspapers, and magazines also provided invaluable assistance. When an entry cites a subject covered elsewhere in this book, an asterisk follows the person's name. Appendices list biographical entries by place of birth and players alphabetically by main position played. Other Appendices list major league managers, executives, and/or umpires, National Baseball Hall of Fame members, Negro Leaguers, and AAGPBL players.

One hundred fifty-two contributors, mostly members of the Society for American Baseball Research or North American Society for Sport History, contributed baseball entries for this revised and expanded volume. Sixty-seven people contributed new baseball entries for this volume. Most authors are university or college professors with baseball expertise. School teachers, administrators, writers, publishers, editors, journalists, librarians, businessmen, government employees, clergymen, consultants, and others also participated. Contributors are cited alphabetically with occupational affiliation following the index.

The editor deeply appreciates the enormous amount of time, energy, and effort expended by contributors in searching for biographical information. I am especially grateful to William E. Akin, Dennis S. Clark, Scott A.G.M. Crawford, John L. Evers, John R. Hillman, Frederick Ivor-Campbell, William J. Miller, Frank J. Olmsted, Frank V. Phelps, James A. Riley, Duane A. Smith, Luther W. Spoehr, Robert E. Weir, and Jerry J. Wright, each of whom wrote at least 10 new baseball entries. Akin, Evers, David Fitzsimmons, James N. Giglio, Hillman, George W. Hilton, Miller, Scot E. Mondore, Olmsted, Riley, Victor Rosenberg, William M. Simons, Edward J. Tassinari, Sarah L. Ulerick, and Weir kindly agreed to write additional entries when contributor Stan W. Carlson died in December 1996 and when other last-minute cancellations occurred. Mondore, Bill Deane, and Richard Topp supplied family information on numerous players. Biographical subjects, relatives, or acquaintances often furnished data. Richard H. Gentile and Thomas C. Eakin sent biographical material on Massachusetts and Ohio entries, respectively. William Penn University librarians again provided considerable assistance. Cynthia Harris gave adept guidance and helped in the planning and writing of this volume, while Elizabeth Meagher furnished valuable assistance in the production stage. As always, my wife, Marilyn, demonstrated considerable patience, understanding, and support throughout the project.

NOTES

1. Several other promising stars are not included because they are still in the early phases of their major league careers.

2. The principal baseball reference sources examined for major league baseball players included *The Baseball Encyclopedia*, 10th ed. (New York, 1996); John Thorn et al., eds., *Total Baseball*, 5th ed. (New York, 1997); David Nemec, *The Great Encyclopedia of 19th Century Major League Baseball* (New York, 1997); David Neft et al., eds., *The Sports Encyclopedia: Baseball* (New York, 1997); Charles F. Faber, *Baseball Ratings: The All-Time Best Players at Each Position*, 2d ed. (Jefferson, NC, 1995); *The Complete 1998 Baseball Record Book* (St. Louis, MO, 1998); *The Sporting News Official Baseball Register, 1998* (St. Louis, MO, 1998); *The Sporting News Official Baseball Guide, 1998* (St. Louis, MO, 1998); and Mike Shatzkin, ed., *The Ballplayers* (New York, 1990). James A. Riley, *The Biographical Encyclopedia for the Negro Baseball Leagues* (New York, 1994) and W. C. Madden, *The Women of the All-American Girls Professional Baseball League: A Biographical Dictionary* (Jefferson, NC, 1997) proved invaluable sources for Negro League and AAGPBL players, respectively.

3. Professional major leagues represented include the National Association (1871–1875), National League (1876–), American Association (1882–1891), Union Association (1884), Players League (1890), American League (1901–), Federal League (1914–1915), Negro National League (1920–1931, 1933–1948), Eastern Colored League (1923–1928), East-West League (1932), Negro Southern League (1932), Negro American League (1933–1950), and All-American Girls Professional Baseball League (1943–1954).

Abbreviations

The abbreviations, listed alphabetically, include associations, baseball terms, conferences, journals, leagues, organizations, and reference sources mentioned in the text and bibliographies.

AA	American Association
AAGPBL	All-American Girls Professional Baseball League
AAGPBLPA	All-American Girls Professional Baseball League Players Association
AAU	Amateur Athletic Union
ABA	American Basketball Association
ABC	American Broadcasting Company
ABCA	American Baseball Coaches Association
ABL	American Basketball League
AC	Athletic Club
ACAB	*Appleton's Cyclopaedia of American Biography*
ACBC	American College Baseball Coaches
ACC	Atlantic Coast Conference
ACFL	Atlantic Coast Football League
AFL	American Football League
AH	*American Heritage*
AHI	*American History Illustrated*
AIL	Arizona Instructional League
AL	American League
AlFL	Alabama-Florida League
AlL	Alaskan League

AlSL	Alaska Summer League
AM	*American Mercury*
AmBC	American Bowling Congress
AMeL	Arizona-Mexico League
AML	Arkansas-Missouri League
AmLit	*American Literature*
AmM	*American Magazine*
ANL	American Negro League
AOA	American Olympic Association
AP	Associated Press
ApL	Appalachian League
ArSL	Arizona State League
ArTL	Arizona-Texas League
AS	*American Scholar*
ASL	Alabama State League
AtA	Atlantic Association
AtL	Atlantic League
AtM	*Atlantic Monthly*
AV	*American Visions*
BA	*Baseball America*
BAA	Basketball Association of America
BBM	*Beckett's Baseball Monthly*
BBWAA	Baseball Writers Association of America
BC	Business College
BD	*Baseball Digest*
BDAC	*Biographical Dictionary of the American Congress*
BEaC	Big East Conference
BEC	Big Eight Conference
BeL	Bethlehem Steel League
BGL	Blue Grass League
BH	*Baseball History*
BHR	*Baseball Historical Review*
BL	Border League
BL	*Boy's Life*
BM	*Baseball Magazine*
BNC	Big Nine Conference
BoM	*Boston Magazine*

BPBP	Brotherhood of Professional Baseball Players
BPRA	Bowling Proprietory Association of America
BPY	Baseball Players of Yesterday
BQ	*Baseball Quarterly*
BR	*Boston Referee*
BRJ	*Baseball Research Journal*
BRL	Blue Ridge League
BRQ	*Baseball Research Quarterly*
BRS	Bottomley Ruffing Schalk
BRuL	Babe Ruth League
BS	*Black Sports*
BSC	Big Six Conference
BSL	Bi-State League
BStL	Big State League
BT	*Biography Today*
BTC	Big Ten Conference
BUDS	Baseball Umpire Development School
BVL	Blackstone Valley League
BW	*Baseball Weekly*
CA	Central Association
CA	*Contemporary Authors*
CAB	*Cyclopedia of American Biography*
CAD	*Coach and Athletic Director*
CaL	California League
CAL	Canadian-American League
CaPL	Canadian Provincial League
CarA	Carolina Association
CaSL	California State League
CB	*Current Biography Yearbook*
CBCA	College Baseball Coaches of America
CbL	Cumberland League
CBS	Columbia Broadcasting System
CC	Community College
CCNY	City College of New York
CCo	*Cooperstown Corner*
CCSL	Copper Country Soo League
CdL	Colorado League

CH	*Chicago History*
ChNL	Chicago National League
CIF	California Interscholastic Federation
CIL	Central Interstate League
CKAL	Central Kentucky Amateur League
CL	Central League
ClL	Colonial League
CmA	Commercial Association
CML	Connie Mack League
CnL	Canadian League
CNL	Cuban National League
CNN	Cable News Network
CntL	Continental League
CoC	Country Club
CoPL	Coastal Plain League
CPL	Central Pennsylvania League
CPrL	Canadian Provincial League
CQR	*Congressional Quarterly Researcher*
CrA	Carolina Association
CrL	Carolina League
CRL	Cocoa Rookie League
CSC	*Canadian Sports Collector*
CSL	Cotton States League
CSSL	California State Semipro League
CtL	Connecticut League
CtSL	Connecticut State League
CUL	Cuban League
CUSL	Cuban Summer League
CUWL	Cuban Winter League
CWL	California Winter League
DAB	*Dictionary of American Biography*
DaM	*Dawn Magazine*
DH	designated hitter
DIB	*Dictionary of International Biography*
DL	Dakota League
DM	*Dodgers Magazine*
DRWL	Dominican Republic Winter League

DSM	*Diamond Sports Memorabilia*
DT	*Delaware Today*
EA	Eastern Association
EaIL	Eastern Intercollegiate Athletic League
ECA	Eastern Championship Association
ECAC	Eastern Collegiate Athletic Association
ECaL	Eastern Carolina League
ECL	Eastern Colored League
EDL	Eastern Dixie League
EIL	Eastern Interstate League
EL	Eastern League
EPL	East Penn League
ERA	earned run average
ESL	Eastern Shore League
ESPN	Eastern Sports Network
ESUTS	Eastern States Umpire Training School
ETL	East Texas League
EvL	Evangeline League
EWL	East-West League
FBC	Fox Broadcasting Network
FCA	Fellowship of Christian Athletes
FECL	Florida East Coast League
FIL	Florida International League
FInL	Florida Instructional League
FL	Federal League
FlL	Florida League
FSL	Florida State League
FWL	Far West League
GAL	Georgia-Alabama League
GC	Golf Club
GCL	Gulf Coast League
GCRL	Gulf Coast Rookie League
GFL	Georgia-Florida League
GML	Green Mountain League
GQ	*Gentlemen's Quarterly*
GSL	Georgia State League
HAF	Helms Athletic Foundation

HB	*Harper's Bazaar*
HR	home run(s)
HRL	Hudson River League
IA	International Association
IAD	*Italian-American Digest*
IAL	Inter-American League
IaL	Iowa League
IBA	International Baseball Association
ID	*In Dixieland*
IdSL	Idaho State League
IIAC	Illinois Intercollegiate Athletic Conference
IIL	Illinois-Iowa League
IInL	Illinois-Indiana League
IlML	Illinois-Missouri League
IlSL	Illinois State League
IL	International League
Ind	Independent
InL	Instructional League
IOBL	Idaho-Oregon Baseball League
IOL	Iron and Oil League
IoSL	Iowa State League
IS	*Inside Sports*
ISA	Interstate Association
ISDL	Iowa and South Dakota League
ISL	Interstate League
IVL	Imperial Valley League
IvL	Ivy League
JAC	*Journal of American Culture*
JC	Junior College
JCL	Japan Central League
JEE	*Journal of Economic Education*
JeSH	*Jewish Sports History*
JPC	*Journal of Popular Culture*
JPL	Japanese Pacific League
JSH	*Journal of Sport History*
JSS	*Jewish Social Studies*
JW	*Journal of the West*

KL	Kitty League
KOML	Kansas-Oklahoma-Missouri League
KSL	Kansas State League
LCS	League Championship Series
LD	*Literary Digest*
LL	Longhorn League
LM	*Lippincott's Magazine*
LPGA	Ladies Professional Golfers Association
LSL	Lone Star League
LSU	Louisiana State University
MAC	Mid-American Conference
MAL	Middle Atlantic League
MasL	Massachusetts League
MD	*Magazine Digest*
MEL	Mexican League
MEWL	Mexican Winter League
MH	*Men's Health*
MISL	Michigan State League
MiVL	Mississippi Valley League
MkL	Mandak League
ML	Midwest League
MLPA	Major League Players Association
MLPAA	Major League Players Alumni Association
MLUA	Major League Umpires Association
MM	*Mariners Magazine*
MnL	Manila League
MOL	Michigan-Ontario League
MOVL	Mississippi-Ohio Valley League
mph	miles per hour
MSA	Massachusetts State Association
MSL	Middle States League
MtL	Montana League
MtnSL	Mountain State League
MtSL	Montana State League
MUL	Muny League
MVC	Missouri Valley Conference
MVL	Missouri Valley League

MVP	Most Valuable Player
MWL	Minnesota-Wisconsin League
NA	National Association
NaBC	National Baseball Congress
NAIA	National Association of Intercollegiate Athletics
NAL	Negro American League
NAML	National Association of Minor Leagues
NAPBL	National Association of Professional Baseball Leagues
NASSH	North American Association for Sport History
NAtL	North Atlantic League
NBA	National Basketball Association
NBBC	National Baseball Congress
NBC	National Broadcasting Company
NCAA	National Collegiate Athletic Association
NCAB	*National Cyclopedia of American Biography*
NCBWA	National Collegiate Baseball Writers Association
NCC	North Central Conference
NCL	North Carolina League
NCSL	North Carolina State League
NEA	Newspaper Enterprise Association
NEAL	Northeast Arkansas League
NECSL	Northeastern Connecticut State League
NEL	New England League
NeL	Northeastern League
NEQ	*New England Quarterly*
NeSL	Nebraska State League
NFL	National Football League
NGBL	National Girls Baseball League
NHL	National Hockey League
NIFL	Negro Independent Football League
NL	National League
NLe	*New Leader*
NNL	Negro National League
NoA	Northern Association
NoL	Northern League
NR	*New Republic*
NSD	*National Sports Daily*

NSL	Negro Southern League
NTL	North Texas League
NWL	Northwestern League
NY	*New York*
NYJ	*New York Journal*
NYNJL	New York-New Jersey League
NYPL	New York-Pennsylvania League
NYSBC	New York State Boxing Commission
NYSL	New York State League
NYT	*New York Times*
NYU	New York University
NYWT	*New York World Telegram*
OAB	*Oberlin Alumni Bulletin*
OHQ	*Ohio Historical Quarterly*
OIL	Ohio-Indiana League
OKSL	Oklahoma State League
OL	Ohio League
OPL	Ohio-Pennsylvania League
OrL	Oregon League
OSL	Ohio State League
OTBA	Old Timers Baseball Association
OTBN	*Oldtyme Baseball News*
PAPBP	Protective Association of Professional Baseball Players
PCC	Pacific Coast Conference
PCL	Pacific Coast League
PEC	Pacific Eight Conference
PIL	Pacific International League
PiL	Piedmont League
PL	Players' League
PNL	Pacific Northwest League
PoL	Pony League
POML	Pennsylvania-Ohio-Maryland League
PPAA	Pittsburgh Pirates Alumni Association
PPVL	Panhandle-Pecos Valley League
PrL	Pioneer League
PRL	Puerto Rican League
ProL	Provincial League

PRWL	Puerto Rican Winter League
PSA	Pennsylvania State Association
PSL	Pennsylvania State League
PT	*Psychology Today*
PTC	Pac-Ten Conference
PW	*People Weekly*
RAL	Rookie Appalachian League
RB	*Ragtyme Baseball*
RBI	runs batted in
RD	*Readers Digest*
RR	*Reds Report*
RRVL	Red River Valley League
RS	*Ragtyme Sports*
SA	Southern Association
SABR	Society for American Baseball Research
SAL	South Atlantic League
SBC	Sun Belt Conference
SC	Southern Conference
SCD	*Sports Collectors Digest*
SCQ	*Southern California Quarterly*
SDL	South Dakota League
SEAL	*The Scribner Encyclopedia of American Lives*
SEC	Southeastern Conference
SEL	Southeastern League
SEP	*Saturday Evening Post*
SeS	*Senior Scholastic*
SH	*Sports Heritage*
SI	*Sports Illustrated*
SIAA	Southern Intercollegiate Athletic Association
SIC	*Sports Illustrated Canada*
SIL	Southwest International League
SL	Southern League
SL	*Sport Life*
SML	Southern Michigan League
SMU	Southern Methodist University
SN	*Saturday Night*
SNEL	South New England League

SPBA	Senior Professional Baseball Association
SpL	Sophomore League
SpL	*Sporting Life*
SR	*Saturday Review*
SS	*Sports Scoop*
SSBM	*Street & Smith Baseball Magazine*
SSL	Sooner State League
ST	*Sporting Times*
STL	South Texas League
SuL	Sunset League
SW	*Sport World*
SWaL	Southwestern Washington League
SWC	Southwest Conference
SWL	Southwestern League
TAC	*The American Chronicle*
TAI	*The Annals of Iowa*
TBA	*The Berean Alumnus*
TBR	*The Baseball Review*
TCU	Texas Christian University
TD	*The Diamond*
TF	*The Fan*
3IL	Three I League
TL	Texas League
TM	*Texas Monthly*
TNP	*The National Pastime*
TNY	*The New Yorker*
TOL	Texas-Oklahoma League
TP	*This People*
TPI	Total Pitcher Index
TrM	*Trenton Magazine*
TSL	Tri-State League
TSN	*The Sporting News*
UA	Union Association
UCLA	University of California at Los Angeles
UIL	Utah-Idaho League
UL	Union League
UP	United Press

UPI	United Press International
USAT	*USA Today*
USC	University of Southern California
USL	United States League
USOC	U.S. Olympic Committee
UtA	Utah Association
VaL	Valley League
VL	Virginia League
VSL	Virginia State League
VVL	Virginia Valley League
VWL	Venezuelan Winter League
WA	Western Association
WAC	Western Athletic Conference
WC	Western Conference
WCAC	West Coast Athletic Conference
WCaL	Western Canadian League
WCL	West Carolinas League
WeIL	Western International League
WIBC	Women's International Bowling Congress
WIL	Wisconsin-Illinois League
WL	Western League
WM	*World Monitor*
WNABA	Women's National Adult Baseball Association
WPL	Western Pennsylvania League
WSC	Western State Conference
WSJ	*Wall Street Journal*
WSL	Wisconsin State League
WTL	Western Tri-State League
WTNML	West Texas-New Mexico League
WTxL	West Texas League
WWA	*Who's Who in America*
WWE	*Who's Who in the East*
WWIB	*Who's Who in Baseball*
WWM	*Who's Who in the Midwest*
WWWA	*Who Was Who in America*
YM	*Yankee Magazine*
YMCA	Young Men's Christian Association

CROSS-REFERENCE TO BIOGRAPHICAL DICTIONARY VOLUMES

*	Current Volume
FB	Football Volume
IS	Basketball and Other Indoor Sports Volume
OS	Outside Sports Volume

G

GAETTI, Gary Joseph (b. August 19, 1958, Centralia, IL), player, is the youngest of two children born to Bill Gaetti and Jackie Gaetti and excelled in football and baseball at Centralia High School. Following graduation in 1976, Gaetti continued his baseball career while attending Lakeland JC in Matton, IL in 1977 and Northwest Missouri State University in Maryville, MO in 1978. The Chicago White Sox (AL) and St. Louis Cardinals (NL) selected him in separate amateur drafts in 1978. After spending one more year at Northwest Missouri, Gaetti signed as a third baseman with the Minnesota Twins (AL) in June 1979 and played for Elizabethton, TN (ApL). The Twins promoted Gaetti to Wisconsin Rapids, WI (ML) in 1980 and Orlando, FL (SL) in 1981.

The 6-foot, 200-pound Gaetti joined the Minnesota Twins in September 1981 and hit a HR in his first major league at bat. With Minnesota from 1981 to 1990, the right-handed–hitting Gaetti ranked among the AL stars. As a Minnesota Twin, he batted .256 in 1,361 games, powered 201 HR, and produced 758 RBI. He won four consecutive Gold Gloves from 1986 to 1989 and enjoyed the unique experience of participating in two triple plays in one game against the Boston Red Sox in 1990. Gaetti performed in the 1988 and 1989 All-Star games. In the 1987 AL Championship Series against the Detroit Tigers, he batted .300, became the first player to hit HR in his first two at bats in a League Championship Series contest and was named its MVP. Gaetti played in the 1987 World Series against the St. Louis Cardinals, helping Minnesota win in seven games.

In January 1991, free agent Gaetti signed a four-year contract with the California Angels (AL). For the California Angels, Gaetti divided his time between third base and first base. In June 1993, California released him unconditionally. The Kansas City Royals (AL) signed him the same month as a utility infielder/DH. He led AL third basemen with a .982 fielding percentage in 1994 and made the *TSN* Silver Slugger Team in 1995 with 35 HR and 96 RBI. In December 1995, he joined the St. Louis Cardinals (NL) as a free agent. Gaetti batted .274 with 23 HR and 80 RBI to help St. Louis win the NL Central in 1996. He clouted a three-run HR in the Division Series against the San Diego Padres and batted .292 with one HR and four RBI in the NL Championship Series against the Atlanta Braves. The Chicago Cubs (NL) signed Gaetti in August 1998 after the St. Louis Cardinals released him. He clouted 19 HR, including eight after joining the Chicago Cubs, and belted a two-run HR to help defeat the San Francisco Giants in a playoff to determine the NL wild card, but struggled in the NL Division Series against the Atlanta Braves. The Cubs released Gaetti in October 1999. Through 1999, he had a .255 career batting average with 443 doubles, 360 HR, and 1,340 RBI.

Gaetti and his wife, Debbie, have two sons, Joseph and Jacob, and reside in Raleigh, NC.

BIBLIOGRAPHY: Gary Gaetti file, National Baseball Library, Cooperstown, NY; *The Baseball Encyclopedia*, 10th ed. (New York, 1996); Hank Hersch, "The Gospel and Gaetti," *SI* 71 (August 21, 1989), pp. 42–44; *Minnesota Twins Yearbook*, 1990; James E. Welch, telephone conversation with Randy List, sports editor, Centralia (IL) *Sentinel*, July 2, 1993.

James E. Welch

GALAN, August John "Augie" (b. May 25, 1912, Berkeley, CA; d. December 28, 1993, Fairfield, CA), player, demonstrated admirable versatility at bat, in the field, and on the bases. After completing four years at Berkeley High School, he entered professional baseball with the San Francisco, CA Seals (PCL) in 1932. He joined the Chicago Cubs (NL) two years later as a second baseman, but soon blossomed into one of the NL's better outfielders. A switch-hitting leadoff man with six seasons above .300, he also led the NL in stolen bases in 1935 and 1937 and was selected an All-Star three times in 1936, 1943, and 1944.

The Cubs tried the 6-foot, 175 pounder at three infield positions before stationing him in left field in 1935. He played every inning of 154 games in 1935, making 203 hits, leading the NL with 133 runs scored, batting .314, and not hitting into one double play in 646 at-bats. At Wrigley Field on June 25, 1937 against the Brooklyn Dodgers, he matched Wally Schang's* record as the first two switch-hitters to clout HR from both sides of the plate in one game. The left-handed HR came off Fred Fitzsimmons,* while the right-handed HR was blasted off Lefty Birkhofer.

Injuries in 1940–1941 caused Galan's release to the PCL. Galan protested, was recalled, and was sold in August 1941 to the Brooklyn Dodgers (NL), where he lent stability to the patchy lineups of the World War II years. He twice led the NL in walks in 1943 and 1944 and achieved a career-high .318 batting average in 1944. Brooklyn also used Galan at first and third base.

The Dodgers traded Galan to the Cincinnati Reds (NL) for pitcher Ed

Heusser in December 1946. Galan enjoyed one fine season for the Reds before reinjuring his arm and played mainly as a pinch hitter until 1949. In 1,742 major league games covering 16 years, he made 1,706 hits, hit 100 HR, and averaged .287 at the plate. He appeared without distinction for the Chicago Cubs in the 1935 and 1938 World Series and the Brooklyn Dodgers in the 1941 World Series. His first All-Star game saw him contribute a HR off "Schoolboy" Rowe.*

Off-seasons, Galan helped his French-speaking father, Gratian Galan, operate the family-owned commercial laundry. He married Shirley Ann Boyle in 1953 and had four children.

BIBLIOGRAPHY: Warren Brown, *The Chicago Cubs* (New York, 1946); August Galan file, National Baseball Library, Cooperstown, NY; Eddie Gold and Art Ahrens, *The Golden Era Cubs, 1876–1940* (Chicago, IL, 1985); William F. McNeil, *The Dodgers Encyclopedia* (Champaign, IL, 1997); Frank Graham, *The Brooklyn Dodgers* (New York, 1945); Walter M. Langford, *Legends of Baseball* (South Bend, IN, 1987); David Nemec, *Great Baseball Feats, Facts and Firsts* (New York, 1987); *NYT*, December 30, 1993, p. B6; John Thorn et al., eds., *Total Baseball*, 5th ed. (New York, 1997).

A. D. Suehsdorf

GALARRAGA, Andres Jose "Big Cat" (b. June 18, 1961, Caracas, Venezuela), player, is the son of Francisco Galarraga, a house painter, and Juana Galarraga, a domestic maid. The 6-foot 3-inch, 235-pound first baseman, who bats and throws right-handed, attended Enrique Felmi High School in Caracas. Galarraga and his wife, Eneyda, have two daughters, Andrea and Katherine.

The Montreal Expos (NL) signed Galarraga in 1979 and assigned him to West Palm Beach, FL (FSL). After spending seven games there, he completed the 1979 season at Calgary, Canada (PrL) and remained there the following year. Galarraga played for Jamestown, NY (NYPL) in 1981 and returned to West Palm Beach the following two seasons. He earned MVP honors with Jacksonville, FL (SL) in 1984 and led the AA in runs scored with Indianapolis, IN in 1985. Galarraga joined the Montreal Expos for 24 games in 1985 and played for the Expos until traded to the St. Louis Cardinals (NL) in November 1991 for pitcher Ken Hill. His best year with the Expos came in 1988, when he scored 99 runs, made 184 hits, and posted 42 doubles, 29 HR, and 92 RBI. He led the NL in hits and doubles. Galarraga finished among the major league's leaders in 12 different offensive categories, becoming only the second Montreal player to post consecutive 90-RBI seasons. He was named to the All-Star and *TSN* Silver Slugger teams in 1988 and won Gold Glove awards the following two seasons.

After suffering a broken wrist in April 1992, Galarraga spent an 11-game rehabilitation assignment with Louisville, KY (AA). He experienced a subpar season with a .243 batting average and was granted free agency by the St. Louis Cardinals. The Colorado Rockies (NL) signed him in November 1992. In his first season there, Galarraga led the NL in batting with a .370

average and clouted 31 HR. No expansion player had accomplished this feat previously. The .370 batting average marked the highest percentage by a righthanded major league batter since 1939. He batted .400 as late as July 5th, making the All-Star team and earning Comeback Player of the Year honors. In 1995, Galarraga again belted 31 HR and ranked third in the NL with 106 RBI. He led the Rockies to the NL Division Series. Although Galarraga collected five base hits for a .278 batting average, Colorado lost to the Atlanta Braves in the NL Division Series. His best season came in 1996, when he led the NL with career-high 47 HR and 150 RBI. In 1997, Galarraga batted .318 with 41 HR and 140 RBI and produced career bests with 120 runs and 191 hits. The Atlanta Braves (NL) acquired Galarraga as a free agent in November 1997. His .305 batting average, 44 HR, and 121 RBI helped Atlanta capture the NL East with a franchise-best 106 victories in 1998. Galarraga batted .250 with 3 doubles in the NL Division Series against the Chicago Cubs. Although clouting a grand slam HR in the NL Championship Series against the San Diego Padres, he made an uncharacteristic four errors. Galarraga missed the 1999 season with lymphoma.

In 14 major league seasons, Galarraga has played in 1,794 games, scored 1,011 runs, made 1,921 hits, and compiled a .290 batting average. He has posted 364 doubles, 30 triples, 332 HR, 1,172 RBI, 467 walks, 1,615 strikeouts, and 121 stolen bases.

BIBLIOGRAPHY: *Colorado Rockies Media Guide*, 1997; M. Farber, "Cat Quick," *SI* 86 (June 2, 1997), pp. 68–70; Andres Galarraga file, National Baseball Library, Cooperstown, NY; Richard Hoffer, "Strokes of Luck," *SI* 78 (June 28, 1993), pp. 22–24, 26; Hank Hersch, "Cat's Meow in Montreal," *SI* 69 (August 3, 1988), pp. 50–52; *TSN Official Baseball Register*, 1998; *USAT Baseball Weekly*, October 4–10, 1995, p. 43.

John L. Evers

GALBREATH, John Wilmer (b. August 10, 1897, Derby, OH; d. July 20, 1988, Columbus, OH), baseball executive, horse breeder, and sportsman, was the son of farmer Francis Hill Galbreath and Belle (Mitchell) Galbreath. After graduating from Mt. Sterling High School, he worked his way through Ohio State University by washing dishes, waiting tables, and photographing fellow students. After his college graduation on 1920, he formed a real estate business. During the 1930s, he amassed a fortune by buying company-owned towns from U.S. Steel, Westinghouse, the Erie Mining Company, and other corporations. After renovating the houses, he sold them back to the workers. He made a second fortune by building, leasing, and managing skyscrapers. He married Helen Mauck on September 14, 1921 and had two children, Joan Hill and Daniel Mauck Galbreath. After Helen died in 1946, Galbreath married Dorothy Bryan Firestone on February 17, 1955.

Galbreath invested considerable money in two racing stables named Darby Dan Farms near Columbus, OH and at Lexington, KY. In 1955, he paid a world record $2 million for 1955 Kentucky Derby winner Swaps. In 1959, he leased the undefeated Italian horse Ribot for five years at $1.35 million. When the animal's contrary disposition prevented its return to Italy, Galbreath leased the horse for life. Darby Dan Farms produced several notable horses, including Chateaugay (1963 Kentucky Derby and Belmont Stakes winner), Proud Clarion (1967 Kentucky Derby), Little Current (1974 Preakness and Belmont Stakes), and Graustark. When his horse Roberto (named for baseball player Roberto Clemente*) won the 1972 English Epsom Derby, Galbreath became the only person to win derbies on both sides of the Atlantic. Galbreath, among the most influential American horse racing figures, headed the committees building the Belmont and Aqueduct race tracks and modernizing the Saratoga racing plant in New York. He formed the group that bought up shares in the Kentucky Derby when a business conglomerate threatened to take it over.

In 1946 Galbreath joined a four-man syndicate, including singer–entertainer Bing Crosby, that purchased the Pittsburgh Pirates (NL). Four years later, he bought 70 percent of the club, named himself president, and hired Branch Rickey* as general manager to reverse the Pirates' dismal fortunes. During the next 15 years, Galbreath lost an estimated $2 million. The 1952 Pirates, who lost 112 games and finished last in the NL by 54½ games, rank among the worst baseball teams ever. Galbreath's patience, however, paid off. Led by outfielder Roberto Clemente and manager Danny Murtaugh,* the Pirates upset the powerful New York Yankees, four games to three, in the 1960 World Series. As baseball owner, Galbreath helped to formulate the 1957 players' pension plan and to choose a successor to Commissioner Ford Frick.* By the late 1970s, Galbreath's honesty and even-handedness made him among America's most respected elder sportsmen.

His son, Daniel, executive, graduated from Amherst College in 1950 and earned a Masters degree in business administration from Ohio State University in 1952. He married Elizabeth Lind on July 17, 1954 and has three children, Laurie Lind, Lizanne, and John Wilmer II. He assumed many of his father's business interests in the 1950s and 1960s and was named president of the Pittsburgh Pirates in 1970. Under his leadership, the Pirates reached the NL Championship Series in 1970, 1971, 1974, 1975, and 1979. Pittsburgh captured the 1971 and 1979 World Series, defeating the Baltimore Orioles both times. Following the 1979 season, the club's fortunes and quality of play declined markedly. In 1985, the Galbreath family sold its majority interest in the Pirates to a unique public-private coalition consisting of the city of Pittsburgh and several local corporations and individuals.

BIBLIOGRAPHY: John Galbreath file, National Baseball Library, Cooperstown, NY; Richard L. Burtt, *The Pittsburgh Pirates, A Pictorial History* (Virginia Beach, VA, 1977); "Down the Mountain," *Time* 76 (August 22, 1960), p. 56; Jack Mann, "Superfan and Super Achiever," *SI* 24 (January 24, 1966), pp. 53–60; *NYT*, July 21, 1988,

p. D-22; *WWA*, 3 (1982–83), pp. 1, 149; Bob Smizik, *The Pittsburgh Pirates: An Il-lustrated History* (New York, 1990).

John Hanners

GALVIN, James Francis "Pud," "Gentle Jeems," "The Little Steam Engine"
(b. December 25, 1856, St. Louis, MO; d. March 7, 1902, Pittsburgh, PA),
player and umpire, grew up in the Irish section of St. Louis known as Kerry
Patch. He married Bridget Griffin on February 20, 1878 and had 11 children. Galvin began his professional pitching career in 1875 for the St. Louis
Brown Stockings (NA). In 1876 he pitched for the St. Louis Red Stockings,
an independent club, hurling no-hit, no-run games against independent Philadelphia Philles on July 4 and the Cass Club of Detroit on August 17. The
latter no-hitter probably was the first perfect game (no batters reaching base)
ever by a pro pitcher. In 1877 Galvin pitched four shutouts in 19 games for
Allegheny, PA (IA), part of baseball's first minor league. For the 1878
pennant-winning Buffalo, NY Bisons (IA), Galvin pitched 106 of the team's
116 games, winning 72, losing 25, and tying three. In addition, he recorded
17 shutouts, hurled 96 complete games, and won 10 of 15 games against NL
clubs.

In 1879, Buffalo joined the NL. With Buffalo from 1879 to 1885, Galvin
became one of the game's premier pitchers, winning 37, 20, 28, 28, 46, 46,
and 13 games for a team never finishing above third place. Galvin pitched
no-hit, no-run games against the Worcester, MA Ruby Legs on August 20,
1880 and against the Detroit Wolverines on August 4, 1884. In 1884, Galvin
shut out the Providence, RI Grays 2–0 to end their 20-game winning streak
and stop Providence pitcher Hoss Radbourne,* who had won 18 consecutive
contests. A workhorse of legendary reputation, Galvin pitched 593 innings
in 1879, 656 innings in 1883, and 636 innings in 1884.

In June 1885, Buffalo sold Galvin to the Pittsburgh Alleghenies (AA) for
$2,500 and gave him $750 of the sale price. His $3,000 contract with the Al-
legheny club exceeded by $1,000 his salary at Buffalo. He hurled for the
Pittsburgh Alleghenies (NL) from 1887 to 1889 and in 1890 jumped to the
Pittsburgh Burghers (PL). When the PL folded after one season, Galvin returned to the Pittsburgh Nationals for the 1891 season and part of the 1892
season and completed his major league career with the St. Louis Browns
(NL) in 1892. He failed in a comeback attempt with Buffalo, NY (EL) in
1894 and umpired briefly in the NL. After his baseball career, Galvin resided
in Pittsburgh, operated an unsuccessful saloon, and worked for a contractor
and as a bartender. When he died, the impoverished Galvin left his wife and
six surviving children, including Marie and Walter.

He was nicknamed "Gentle Jeems" for his placid nature, "Pud" for making pudding out of opposing batters, and "The Little Steam Engine" for his
vigorous pitching style. The 5-foot 8-inch, 190-pound Galvin proved a superb fielder and strong hitter and often played in the outfield when not

pitching. Besides using an intimidating fastball and a devastating change of pace, he developed a brilliant pickoff move. In an 1886 contest for Pittsburgh, he walked three batters and then picked each one off first base. During his 14-year major league career, Galvin won 360 games to share seventh place among all pitchers. He ranks second only to Cy Young* in complete games (639), innings pitched (5,941.1), and games lost (308). He notched 1,799 strikeouts and recorded 57 shutouts. Despite these imposing credentials, he was not elected to the National Baseball Hall of Fame until 1965.

BIBLIOGRAPHY: James Galvin file, National Baseball Library, Cooperstown, NY; James F. Galvin, correspondence with Buffalo Baseball Club, 1877, 1878, Joseph M. Overfield Collection, Tonawanda, NY; Frederick Ivor-Campbell et al., eds., *Baseball's First Stars* (Cleveland, OH, 1996); George Moreland, *Balldom* (New York, 1914); Joseph Overfield, "A Memorable Performer-Jim Galvin," *BRJ* 11 (1982), pp. 80–83; Joseph Overfield, "First Great Minor League Club," *BRJ* 6 (1977), pp. 1–6; Pittsburgh *Gazette*, March 8, 1902; Lowell Reidenbaugh, *Baseball's Hall of Fame-Cooperstown* (New York, 1993); *TSN*, February 13, 1965.

Joseph M. Overfield

GAMBLE, Oscar Charles (b. December 20, 1949, Ramer, AL), player, married Juanita Kenner and has one daughter, Sheena. The oft-traveled Gamble began his professional baseball career as a sixteenth round draft choice of the Chicago Cubs (NL) in 1968 and appeared in 24 games with the Cubs in 1969 at age 19. In November 1969, the Chicago Cubs traded him to the Philadelphia Phillies (NL). The 5-foot 11-inch, 177-pound Gamble, who batted left and threw right, struggled with southpaw pitching and shuttled between the major and minor leagues.

In November 1972, the Philadelphia Phillies sent Gamble to the Cleveland Indians (AL) for Del Unser. He performed mostly a DH role with the Indians, clouting 20 HR in 1973. After spending two more seasons with Cleveland, Gamble was traded in November 1975 to the New York Yankees (AL) for Pat Dobson. He enjoyed New York's media attention, while his wife, Juanita, sang the national anthem before several games. In 1976, his powerful swing produced 17 HR mostly over Yankee Stadium's short right field fence. Gamble helped the New York Yankees win the 1976 AL pennant, but batted only .125 in the World Series against the Cincinnati Reds. The New York Yankees in April 1977 sent Gamble, LaMarr Hoyt,* and $200,000 to the Chicago White Sox (AL) for Bucky Dent. In 1977, Gamble attained career highs with 31 HR and 83 RBI.

Gamble joined the San Diego Padres (NL) via free agency in November 1977. Although batting a solid .275 in 1978, he furnished only seven HR and 47 RBI. In October 1978, San Diego traded Gamble to the Texas Rangers (AL). The Rangers in August 1979 shipped him to the New York Yankees for Mickey Rivers.* His finest major league season came in 1979 with a career-best .358 batting average, but his 274 at bats did not qualify him for the batting crown. Gamble spent the next five seasons with New York as an outfielder and DH, appearing in the 1980 and 1981 AL Championship Series and batting .333 in the 1981 World Series against the Los Angeles Dodgers. He rejoined the Chicago White Sox in March 1985 and clouted four HR that campaign, giving him 200 career HR. During 17 major league seasons, he batted .265 with 666 RBI.

BIBLIOGRAPHY: *Microsoft Complete Baseball*, CD-ROM (Redmond, WA, 1994); Mark Gallagher, *The Yankee Encyclopedia*, vol. 3 (Champaign, IL, 1997); Oscar Gamble file, National Baseball Library, Cooperstown, NY; *The Baseball Encyclopedia*, 10th ed. (New York, 1996); Mike Shatzkin, ed., *The Ballplayers* (New York, 1990).

Chad Israelson

GANDIL, Arnold "Chick" (b. January 19, 1887, St. Paul, MN; d. December 13, 1970, Calistoga, CA), player, instigated the Chicago Black Sox scandal and remains the single most lurid figure in baseball history. His personal iniquities obscure a career as a solid first baseman for three AL clubs.

His parents were Christian Gandil and Louise (Bichel) Gandil, both Swiss immigrants. Gandil left school at age 16 to play semiprofessional baseball at Amarillo, TX and in mining towns in Arizona and New Mexico, suiting his rough-and-ready personality. The 6-foot 2-inch 195 pounder also boxed there as a heavyweight. He entered professional baseball with Shreveport, LA (TL) in 1908 and was drafted by the St. Louis Browns (AL). Gandil never played for the St. Louis Browns, being purchased by owner Charles A. Comiskey* for the Chicago White Sox (AL) in 1910. He fielded adeptly with a two-handed style suitable to the era's small gloves, but Comiskey believed Gandil could not hit a curve ball and sent him to Montreal, Canada (IL). Gandil returned to the major leagues with the Washington Senators (AL), hitting .305 in 1912 and .318 in 1913. He played there for two additional seasons and with the Cleveland Indians (AL) in 1916. Comiskey reacquired him for the 1917 world championship Chicago White Sox as regular first baseman.

Gandil also started on the 1919 AL championship Chicago White Sox, but late that season joined with gambler Joseph "Sport" Sullivan in conceiving the plot to throw the World Series against the Cincinnati Reds. He lined up the only dependable White Sox pitchers, Eddie Cicotte* and Claude Williams,* and, unnecessarily, five other position players. His own play in the Series remained strong. Gandil sought a $6,000 salary for 1920, but failed to get it and vowed never again to play for Comiskey. He began playing and managing in independent baseball leagues. Revelation of the plot in September 1920 caused his permanent banishment from organized baseball. In 1,147 games, he batted .277 with 1,176 hits and 557 RBI. Gandil maintained his innocence and petitioned for reinstatement three times, but secured no response from Commissioner Kenesaw Mountain Landis.* He admitted to gathering funds from teammates in 1917 to pay the Detroit Tigers to lose consecutive doubleheaders to the Chicago White Sox, but Landis did not accept his affidavit. In a 1956 *SI* article, Gandil published his interpretation of the 1919 scandal: Gamblers had originated the plot. The players initially agreed to join, but withdrew and did not throw any games. When this version did not achieve acceptance, Gandil reverted to protesting his complete innocence.

Gandil worked as a plumber in Los Angeles, CA and Oakland, CA until 1952 and then retired to Calistoga, CA, where he died of emphysema and smoking-related cardiac disease. He had smoked heavily for 70 years. He was survived by his wife, Laurel F. (Kelly) Gandil, whom he had married at age 19, and by a son-in-law.

BIBLIOGRAPHY: Eliot Asinof, *Eight Men Out* (New York, 1963); Arnold "Chick" Gandil, as told to Melvin Durslag, "This Is My Story of the Black Sox Series," *SI* 5 (September 17, 1956), pp. 62–68; Chicago *Tribune*, February 26, 1971, Sec. 3, p. 6; *TSN*, March 6, 1971, p. 47; Arnold "Chick" Gandil file, National Baseball Library, Cooperstown, NY; Shirley Povich, *The Washington Senators* (New York, 1954); Warren Brown, *The Chicago White Sox* (New York, 1952); Dan Gutman, *Baseball Babylon* (New York, 1992); Daniel E. Ginsburg, *The Fix Is In* (Jefferson, NC, 1995).

George W. Hilton

GANT, Ronald Edwin "Ron" (b. March 2, 1965, Victoria, TX), player, is the son of George Gant and graduated in 1983 from Victoria High School, where he played baseball and football. The Atlanta Braves (NL) selected the 6-foot, 200-pound Gant, who bats and throws right-handed, as an infielder in the fourth round of the June 1983 free agent draft. He spent nearly five minor league seasons with the Gulf Coast, FL Braves (GCL) in 1983, Anderson, SC (SAL) in 1984, Sumter, SC (SAL) in 1985, Durham, NC (CrL) in 1986, Greenville, SC (SL) in 1987, and Richmond, VA (IL) in 1989. Gant led major league rookies in HR (19), RBI (60), and errors with Atlanta in 1988. The Braves optioned him in 1989 to become an outfielder.

Gant starred with the Atlanta Braves from 1990 through 1993, attaining career highs in batting average (.303) and hits (174) in 1990. He clouted 32 HR and stole 33 bases in 1990, earning NL Comeback Player of the Year honors. In 1991, he made *TSN* All-Star and Silver Slugger teams after clouting 32 HR, stealing 34 bases, and knocking in 105 runs. Gant homered with three RBI in the NL Championship Series against the Pittsburgh Pirates, setting a series record with seven steals and sharing the single game mark for most thefts (3). In the World Series setback to the Minnesota Twins, he batted .267 with four RBI. Gant made the 1992 NL All-Star team and belted two HR, including a grand slam HR, with six RBI in the NL Championship Series against the Pittsburgh Pirates. He sat out much of the World Series against the Toronto Blue Jays. His best major league season came in 1993, when he batted .274 with career highs in HR (36) and RBI (117) and belted three doubles with three RBI in the NL Championship Series against the Philadelphia Phillies.

The Atlanta Braves released Gant in March 1994 after he shattered his right leg in a dirt motorcycle accident. The Cincinnati Reds (NL) signed him in June 1994. *TSN* gave Gant NL Comeback Player of the Year honors in 1995 for batting .276 with 29 HR, 88 RBI, and a .554 slugging percentage. After homering with two RBI in the Division Series against the Los Angeles Dodgers, he struggled in the NL Championship Series against the Atlanta Braves. In December 1995, Gant joined the St. Louis Cardinals (NL) as a free agent. His 30 HR in 1996 marked the most for a Cardinal since 1987. He hit .400 with one HR and four RBI in the Division Series against the San Diego Padres and just .240 with one HR and four RBI in the NL Championship Series loss to the Atlanta Braves. In November 1998, the Philadelphia Phillies (NL) acquired him in a trade.

Through the 1999 season, Gant has batted .257 with 1,393 hits, 257 doubles, 266 HR, 856 RBI, and 228 stolen bases. He holds the NL Championship Series record for most strikeouts (26) and shares the mark for most runs (17). The Smyrna, GA resident and his wife, Heather, have one son, Ryan.

BIBLIOGRAPHY: Ronald Gant file, National Baseball Library, Cooperstown, NY; Gary Caruso, *The Braves Encyclopedia* (Philadelphia, PA, 1995); Paul M. Johnson, "Ron Gant," *Sport* 87 (July 1996), pp. 16, 18, 20; Franz Lidz, "Right Off the Bat," *SI* 82 (June 1995), pp. 44–48; Tom Verducci, "Mr. Clutch," *SI* 79 (September 27, 1993), pp. 28–29; *TSN Baseball Guide*, 1998; *St. Louis Cardinals Media Guide*, 1998.

David L. Porter

GANTNER, James Elmer "Jim," "Gumby" (b. January 5, 1953, Eden, WI), player and coach, is the son of Elmer Gantner, a field supervisor at a canning corporation, and Erma (Cappozzo) Gantner and graduated in 1971 from Campbellsport, WI High School, where he participated in track and field, golf, baseball, and basketball. The 5-foot 11-inch, 175-pound Gantner attended the University of Wisconsin–Oshkosh and played in the NAIA baseball World Series in 1973 and 1974, earning All-Tournament honors both years. The Milwaukee Brewers (AL) signed him in 1974 and assigned him to Newark, NY (NYPL) that season and to Thetford Mines, Canada (EL) and Berkshire, MA (EL) the following two seasons. In 1977, Gantner played third base and batted .281 for Spokane, WA (PCL).

After brief trials with the Milwaukee Brewers in 1976 and 1977, Gantner became the team's top utility infielder in 1978 and won the starting second base job in 1981. In 1982, the left-handed hitter compiled his highest batting average (.295) while helping the Brewers win their first AL pennant. In the World Series against the St. Louis Cardinals, Gantner hit .333. The following season, he batted .282 and recorded career-highs in runs scored (85), HR (11), and RBI (74).

Gantner, not blessed with natural talent, performed with mental toughness and heart. A solid, dependable fielder, he possessed a strong arm, excelled at turning the double play, and remained tough with runners sliding into second base. Gantner led AL second basemen in total chances (613) in 1981, (900) in 1983, and (844) in 1984, double plays (95) in 1981 and (128) in 1983, assists (512) in 1983, and putouts (362) in 1984 and (325) in 1988. He shares the major league record for playing the longest errorless game by a second baseman (25 innings) and the AL single-game mark for most innings played by a second baseman (25), both set on May 8–9, 1984. Gantner holds the second highest lifetime fielding average by an AL second baseman (.985). In his 17 year major league career, he played in 1,801 games with 1,696 hits, 726 runs scored, 262 doubles, 47 HR, and 568 RBI and compiled a .274 batting average.

Gantner, who enjoys hunting and fishing, married Sue Ann Crofts in November 1975 and has two daughters, Jaime and Sarah, and two sons, Mark and Matthew. The Heartland, WI resident rejoined the Milwaukee Brewers as a coach in 1997. Milwaukee switched to the NL in 1998.

BIBLIOGRAPHY: James Gantner file, National Baseball Library, Cooperstown, NY; James Gantner, letter to Edward J. Pavlick, March 1996; Chuck Carlson, *True Blue* (Dallas TX, 1993); *Milwaukee Brewers Media Guide*, 1990; M. Sullivan, ed., *The Scouting Report* (New York, 1986); *TSN Baseball Register*, 1993; Milwaukee *Journal-Sentinel*, August 10, 1995.

Edward J. Pavlick

GARBER, Henry Eugene "Gene" (b. November 13, 1947, Lancaster, PA), player, spent his boyhood on the family farm that had been tilled by his paternal ancestors for over a century. Although later describing himself as "a farmer who plays ball," he starred in football, basketball, and baseball in high school and college. The graduate of nearby Elizabethtown College earned a bachelor's degree in history and political science.

In 1965, the 5-foot 10-inch, 175-pound right-handed pitcher was drafted by the Pittsburgh Pirates (NL) in the 13th round of the first rookie draft. Over the next decade, Garber started as a pitcher for seven different teams in five minor leagues and briefly appeared with the Pittsburgh Pirates in 1969, 1970, and 1972. He was voted the IL's Pitcher of the Year in 1972, but the Pirates dealt him that October to the Kansas City Royals (AL) for pitcher Jim Rooker. After posting a 9–9 win–loss record and recording 11 saves with the 1973 Royals, Garber was returned to the minors and then sold in July 1974 to the Philadelphia Phillies (NL).

From 1974 to 1988, Garber established himself as a major league relief pitcher. Although overshadowed by other Phillies relievers, the quiet, bearded Garber became the workhorse of their relief corps. Using a corkscrew motion and a partial underhand delivery, he led the NL in appearances (71) in 1975 and tied a NL record by winning three consecutive games in relief. After spending five seasons with the Phillies, Garber was traded in

June 1978 to the Atlanta Braves (NL) for starting pitcher Dick Ruthven. The club's stopper led the Braves staff in saves for four seasons. His 30 saves in 1982 set a team record, but his 16 losses in 1979 established a NL record in futility. In August 1987, the Braves sent Garber to the Kansas City Royals (AL) for a minor league catcher. With the Royals, he notched 8 saves in 1987 and 6 saves in 1988.

The 40-year-old Garber and Dan Quisenberry,* the club's longtime stopper, were released on July 5, 1988. In 19 major league seasons, Garber appeared in more games than Cy Young* (931), notched 218 saves, and compiled a 96–113 win–loss record with 940 strikeouts, 445 bases on balls, and a lifetime 3.34 ERA. His 108 relief losses rank first all-time while his 94 relief victories rank seventh. Despite such consistency, however, Garber toiled in obscurity. He never appeared in an All-Star game or a World Series and never won an award as a reliever. After leaving baseball in 1988, he returned to his Elizabethtown 500 acre dairy farm and works there with his brother, Herb.

BIBLIOGRAPHY: Gene Garber file, National Baseball Library, Cooperstown, NY; Ross Forman, "Former Baseball Players Reminisce at Fan Fest," *SCD* 21 (August 12, 1994), pp. 60–61; Gary Caruso, *The Braves Encyclopedia* (Philadelphia, PA, 1995); Rich Westcott and Frank Bilovsky, *The New Phillies Encyclopedia* (Philadelphia, PA, 1993); John Thorn, *The Relief Pitcher* (New York, 1979); John Thorn et al., eds., *Total Baseball* (New York, 1997); *TSN*, July 18, 1988.

David Q. Voigt

GARCIA, Edward Miguel "Mike," "Big Bear" (b. November 17, 1923, San Gabriel, CA; d. January 13, 1986, Fairview Park, OH), player, came from a poor Mexican-American background, the sixth of nine children. He began his professional baseball career as a pitcher in 1942 following high school graduation in Visalia, CA. The Cleveland Indians (AL) sent him to Appleton, WI (WSL). Garcia spent the next three years in the U.S. Army Signal Corps and played in the minor leagues from 1945 to 1948. The Cleveland Indians summoned Garcia in September 1948, enabling him to pitch two scoreless innings of the season's last game. In his rookie season, Garcia compiled a 14–5 record and led the AL with a 2.36 ERA in 1949. A slump to an 11–11 mark came the following season.

Garcia's best major league years occurred in the 1951–1954 period. Cleveland finished second in the AL for three consecutive years and then won the 1954 AL pennant in record-breaking fashion. During that span, Garcia averaged nearly 20 wins per season and recorded the lowest overall ERA and highest winning percentage on a superb starting staff which included Bob Feller,* Bob Lemon,* and Early Wynn.* The 6-foot 1-inch, 225-pound Garcia relied on a devastating sinking fastball, particularly effective in the shadow-laden second game of doubleheaders. Although wielding a 19–8 record and winning the ERA championship with 2.64 in 1954, Garcia lost on the final day of the season and dropped the third game of the World Series against the New York Giants. He led the AL in shutouts with 6 in 1952 and 5 in 1954.

Injuries plagued Garcia for the remainder of his baseball career. He won 38 games from 1955 to 1961, the last two years being spent with the Chicago White Sox (AL) and Washington Senators (AL). He finished with a 142–97 record and a 3.27 ERA. Subsequently, Garcia operated a dry cleaning establishment in the Cleveland, OH area and became the local little league commissioner. He died on the thirty-fifth anniversary of his marriage to Gerda Martin, a union that produced one son, Mike, and two daughters, Lisa and Celeste.

BIBLIOGRAPHY: Mike Garcia file, National Baseball Library, Cooperstown, NY; Cleveland (OH) *Plain Dealer*, March 3, 1959, January 14, 1986; John Phillips, *Winners* (Cabin John, MD, 1987); Bob Feller with Bill Gilbert, *Bob Feller Now Pitching* (New York, 1990); John Thorn et al., eds., *Total Indians* (New York, 1996).

James N. Giglio

GARDNER, Floyd "Jelly" (b. September 27, 1895, Russellville, AR; d. 1977, Chicago, IL), player, starred as a defensive outfielder with great range and a good arm. A speedy baserunner adept at drawing walks, the left-handed Gardner proved an ideal lead-off batter for manager Rube Foster's* champion Chicago American Giants (NNL) of the 1920s.

Gardner learned to play baseball while attending Arkansas Baptist College and starred with the Longview Giants in Dallas, TX during the summers of 1916–1917. His summer 1917 performance with the Texas All-Stars impressed the top black ballclubs. In 1919, he moved to Chicago and worked odd jobs while playing baseball. Gardner began his professional baseball career as an outfielder with the Detroit Stars in 1919, but joined Foster's Chicago American Giants the following season. During the next seven seasons, the American Giants won four NNL pennants and the Negro World Series over the ECL champion Atlantic City, NJ Bacharach Giants in 1926. That year, the line-drive hitter led Chicago with a .376 batting average. The American Giants repeated as champions the next year, but Gardner departed earlier that season.

The 5-foot 7-inch, 160 pounder, a tough, scrappy, and argumentative player, usually prevailed in frequent arguments and fights. Gardner's heavy drinking, night life, and feisty disposition created tension in the clubhouse. Foster coped with Gardner's temperament, but trouble developed when Dave Malarcher* became manager. Gardner jumped to the New York Lincoln Giants in 1927. Gardner also played with the Homestead, PA Grays before ending his career with the Chicago American Giants in 1933. He worked in the Post Office and on the Gulf, Mobile, and Ohio Railroad as a porter and waiter, retiring in 1965.

BIBLIOGRAPHY: *Afro-American*, 1927–1932; Chicago *Defender*, 1919–1933; Kansas City *Call*, 1920–1933; New York *Age*, 1927–1932; Robert W. Peterson, *Only the Ball Was White* (Englewood Cliffs, NJ, 1970); Philadelphia Tribune, 1927–1932; Pittsburgh *Courier*, 1927–1932; James A. Riley, *The All-Time All-Stars of Black Baseball* (Cocoa, FL, 1983); James A. Riley, *The Biographical Encyclopedia of the Negro Baseball Leagues* (New York, 1994); James A. Riley, interviews with former Negro League players, James A. Riley Collection, Canton, GA; *The Baseball Encyclopedia*, 10th ed. (New York, 1996).

James A. Riley

GARDNER, William Lawrence "Larry" (b. May 13, 1886, Enosburg Falls, VT; d. March 11, 1976, St. George, VT), player, coach, and administrator, was signed from the University of Vermont campus by the Boston Red Sox (AL) in 1908. After being sent to Lynn, MA (NEL) for seasoning, he started from 1910 to 1917 as the Boston Red Sox third baseman. The New Englander by birth and temperament felt more comfortable playing for Boston, especially after University of Vermont friend Ray Collins joined the Red Sox. Although few players from that era had attended college, the Boston Red Sox fielded more college players than any other major league team. Bill Carrigan,* Duffy Lewis,* Harry Hooper,* Chris Mahoney, and Marty McHale had attended college and welcomed Gardner.

In the dead ball era, Gardner hit over .300 five times and retired with a .289 lifetime batting average. In 1,923 games, he made 1,931 hits, slammed 301 doubles, and knocked in 934 runs. Gardner, a good fastball hitter, always batted well against Walter Johnson.* Ty Cobb* alleged that he never beat out a bunt against Gardner. Years later Gardner told Cobb, "You clenched your jaw and clamped your lips together when you intended to bunt." Gardner shrewdly never told others how Cobb telegraphed the bunt, keeping the information secret. In 1914 Babe Ruth,* a raw, untutored youth, joined the Red Sox. Ruth's behavior shocked Gardner and the more cultivated team members, but his immense talent impressed them. Gardner starred on the AL championship teams of 1912, 1915, and 1916 and drove in the winning run in the final game of the 1912 World Series against the New York Giants. In the fourth game of the 1916 World Series against the Brooklyn Dodgers, his three-run HR off Rube Marquard* proved the deciding blow and the turning point.

In January 1918 Gardner was traded to the Philadelphia Athletics (AL), but manager Connie Mack* the next year gave his position to promising rookie Jimmy Dykes.* Gardner ended his career from 1919 to 1924 with the Cleveland Indians (AL). Although not excelling in the 1920 World Series, he was involved peripherally in its most celebrated play. A photo showed Gardner and a Brooklyn runner at third watching Bill Wambsganss* making the final out of his unassisted triple play. Subsequently, Gardner coached baseball at the University of Vermont for 25 years and served as athletic director there for eight years. An articulate, well-read man who enjoyed campus life, he and Jack Coombs* were considered among the nation's finest collegiate coaches. Although respecting the players he coached, Gardner maintained that the players of his era were superior.

BIBLIOGRAPHY: Larry Gardner file, National Baseball Library, Cooperstown, NY; Frederick G. Lieb, *The Boston Red Sox* (New York, 1947); Robert Redmount, *The Red Sox Encyclopedia* (Champaign, IL, 1998); Franklin Lewis, *The Cleveland Indians* (New York, 1949); Ty Cobb with Al Stump, *My Life in Baseball* (New York, 1961); Lawrence Ritter, *The Glory of Their Times* (New York, 1966); *TSN*, March 27, 1978.
                                                            Anthony J. Papalas

GARNER, Philip Mason "Phil," "Scrap Iron," "Gar" (b. April 30, 1949, Jefferson City, TN), player and manager, is the son of Drew Garner, a Baptist minister, and Mary Frances (Helton) Garner and graduated from Beardon High School in Knoxville, TN, where he played baseball, basketball, and football. He attended the University of Tennessee, earning a B.S. degree in business. Garner played baseball three years for the Volunteers, twice making the All-SEC team.

The Oakland Athletics (AL) selected Garner in the January 1971 free agent draft secondary phase. The 5-foot 10-inch, 180-pound right-handed infielder played both second base and third base. During his minor league career, he made the All-Star teams at Burlington, IA (ML), Birmingham, AL (SL), and Tucson, AZ (PCL).

After brief appearances with the Oakland A's in 1973 and 1974, Garner replaced Dick Green at second base in 1975. The veteran Oakland club won the World Series in 1972, 1973, and 1974. Garner made the 1975 AL All-Star team. Financial reasons forced A's owner Charlie Finley* to dismantle his club, trading Garner in March 1977 to the Pittsburgh Pirates (NL).

Garner enjoyed his best years with the Pittsburgh Pirates, twice making the NL All-Star team (1980, 1981) and helping the Pirates capture the 1979 World Series. His hard play earned him the support of the blue-collar Pittsburgh Pirates fans. During 1979, he batted a career high .293 in the regular season and .417 in the NL Championship Series against the Atlanta Braves. In the seven-game World Series against the Baltimore Orioles, his .500 batting average tied a fall classic record.

The Pittsburgh Pirates traded Garner to the Houston Astros (NL) in August 1981. Garner helped the Houston Astros to the 1981 Division Series and the 1986 NL Championship Series. He was traded to the Los Angeles Dodgers (NL) in June 1987 and finished his playing career the following year with the San Francisco Giants (NL). During 16 major league seasons, Garner batted .260 with 1,594 hits, 109 HR, 738 RBI, and 780 runs scored.

From 1989 to 1991, Garner returned to the Houston Astros as first base coach. From 1992 to August 1999, he has managed the Milwaukee Brewers (AL) to a 563–617 record. Milwaukee joined the NL Central Division in 1998. The Detroit Tigers named him manager in October 1999.

Garner and his wife, Carol, have three children, Eric, Bethany, and Ty, and reside in Kingwood, TX. Garner enjoys hunting, fishing, and trapshooting.

BIBLIOGRAPHY: Phil Garner file, National Baseball Library, Cooperstown, NY; *The Baseball Encyclopedia*, 10th ed. (New York, 1996); Richard L. Burtt, *The Pittsburgh Pirates, A Pictorial History* (Virginia Beach, VA, 1977); Dan Donovan, "Phil Garner: Best No. 8 Hitter in the Majors," *BD* 39 (July 1980), pp. 60–62; Phil Garner file, *TSN*, St. Louis, MO; *Milwaukee Brewers 1998 Media Guide*; Billy Reed, "Garner Got His Start Selling Cookies to Jailbirds," Louisville *Courier-Journal*, October 11, 1979; Bruce Markusen, *Baseball's Last Dynasty* (New York, 1998); Bob Smizik, *The Pittsburgh Pirates: An Illustrated History* (New York, 1990); Paul White, "Big Risks for Big Returns," *BW*, June 19–25, 1996.

Frank W. Thackeray

GARR, Ralph Allen "Roadrunner" (b. December 12, 1945, Monroe, LA), player and scout, is the son of Jesse Garr, Sr. and Annie (Lyons) Garr and grew up in Ruston, LA. Garr earned a B.S. degree in Physical Education in 1967 from Grambling State College, where he starred in football and baseball. The Atlanta Braves (NL) selected the second baseman–outfielder in the third round of the June 1967 draft. The speedy 5-foot 11-inch, 185-pound Garr, who switch hit and threw right-handed, spent nearly four minor league seasons with Austin, TX (TL) in 1967, Shreveport, LA (TL) in 1968, and Richmond, VA (IL) in 1969 and 1970. He twice led the IL in batting and in 1970 batted a record .457 in the DRWL.

After three brief trials, Garr started for the Atlanta Braves from 1971 through 1975. As a lead-off hitter, he in 1971 batted .343, established career-highs with 100 runs scored and 219 hits, and led the NL with 18 sacrifice hits. Garr tied a major league extra inning record on May 17, 1971 by clouting HR in the 10th and 12th innings against the New York Mets. A fine .325 batting average followed in 1972. In a 20-inning May 1973 contest against the Philadelphia Phillies, he tied another major league record with 11 at bats. Garr's best major league season came in 1974, when he paced the NL with a career-high .353 batting average and 17 triples, led the senior circuit with 214 hits, and made the NL All-Star team. In 1975, his 11 triples topped the NL.

The Atlanta Braves traded Garr to the Chicago White Sox (AL) in December 1975. Garr batted .300 in both 1976 and 1977, but saw diminished playing time thereafter. In September 1979, the Chicago White Sox sold him to the California Angels (AL). His major league career ended with California in 1980.

During his major league career, Garr batted .306 with 1,562 hits, 212 doubles, 64 triples, 408 RBI, and 172 stolen bases and seldom struck out. His blazing speed enabled him to leg out numerous infield hits. Fans squeaked, "Beep! Beep!" when Garr reached first base. He stole home plate

in his initial attempt. Players remembered his squeaky voice, Hank Aaron*
imitations, and non-stop comic monologues. After being a minor league
hitting and base running instructor, Garr has scouted for the Atlanta Braves
since 1985. He married Ruby Mack in February 1968 and has four children,
Keisha, Shonta, Ralph, Jr., and Rae Alysia.

BIBLIOGRAPHY: Ralph Garr file, National Baseball Library, Cooperstown, NY;
Ralph Garr, letter to David L. Porter, December 9, 1997; *TSN Baseball Register*, 1980;
Don Delliquanti, "Two Beeps, A Cloud of Dust," *SI* 34 (May 10, 1971), pp. 58–59;
"Beep! Beep!," *Time* 98 (July 5, 1971), p. 43; John Thorn et al., eds., *Total Braves*
(New York, 1996); Gary Caruso, *The Braves Encyclopedia* (Philadelphia, PA, 1995).

David L. Porter

GARVER, Ned Franklin (b. December 25, 1925, Ney, OH), player, is the
son of Arl H. Garver, a farmer, and Susie L. (Connelly) Garver and started
playing baseball at age 14 on the sandlots of Ney, a rural hamlet of 300
people in northwestern Ohio. He starred in baseball and basketball at Washington Township School, where he graduated in 1943. Garver married his
high school sweetheart, Dorothy Sims, on June 4, 1943. The couple have
two children, Donnie and Cheryl.

His professional baseball career began in 1944 with Newark, OH (OSL),
where he compiled a 21–8 win–loss record as a pitcher and hit .407. He
pitched at Elmira, NY (EL) and Toledo, OH (IL) in 1945 and San Antonio,
TX (TL) in 1946 and 1947 before joining the St. Louis Browns (AL).

The boyish-looking 5-foot 10-inch, 190-pound right-hander fast became
a mainstay of the St. Louis Browns' staff. A seven-game winner in his rookie
1948 season, Garver led the AL in losses with 17 the following season. In
1950, he finished 13–18 and led the AL for the first time with 22 complete
games. In June 1950, Garver won the final game of a three-game series, 10–
5, at Fenway Park in Boston after the Boston Red Sox had trounced the
Browns, 20–4 and 29–4. Garver's 20–12 record in 1951 made him the only
20th-century pitcher to win 20 games for a team that lost at least 100 contests and finished in last place. Garver, whose 24 complete games led the
AL, also pitched in the All-Star Game that year. His outstanding skill with
a bat kept him in so many games. In 1951, he compiled the highest average
on the St. Louis Browns with a .305 mark in 95 at bats and occasionally
batted sixth. He lost his zest for hitting after Early Wynn* beaned him
midway through his career and finished with a lifetime .218 batting average.

Later known as the "Mayor of Ney," Garver signed a $25,000 contract
in 1952. The contract amount tied him with immortal George Sisler* as the
highest paid player in St. Louis Browns history. In August 1952, owner–
president Bill Veeck* traded him to the Detroit Tigers (AL) in a multiplayer
deal. Garver endured three straight fifth-place finishes with the Detroit Tigers from 1952 to 1956. Detroit shipped him to the Kansas City Athletics
(AL), where he suffered through three straight seventh-place finishes be-

tween 1957 and 1959. In 1960, Garver's dream of playing for a winner faded, as the Kansas City Athletics finished last. As a member of the eighth-place expansion Los Angeles Angels (AL) in 1961, finished his 14-year major league career. Besides having the unique career statistic of 881 walks and 881 strikeouts, he compiled a composite record of 129–157 and .451 winning percentage. He pitched in 2,477.1 innings with a 3.73 ERA and 18 shutouts.

Garver subsequently worked as personnel and industrial relations director for a food company in his native Ney. A cerebral player who still likes to discuss his philosophy of pitching, Garver was inducted into the St. Louis Browns Hall of Fame in 1985.

BIBLIOGRAPHY: Ned Garver file, National Baseball Library, Cooperstown, NY; William M. Anderson, *The Detroit Tigers* (South Bend, IN, 1996); Richard Bak, *A Place for Summer* (Detroit, MI, 1998); Bill Borst, ed., *Ables to Zoldak*, vol. 1 (St. Louis, MO, 1988); Bill Borst, ed., *The Brown Stockings*, vol. 1 (St. Louis, MO, 1986); Bill Borst, *Still Last in the American League* (West Bloomfield, MI, 1992); Arthur Doranzo, Detroit (MI) *Free Press*, January, 18, 1953, p. 12; Gene Karst and Martin Jones, Jr., *Who's Who in Professional Baseball* (New Rochelle, NY, 1973); Brent P. Kelley, *Baseball Stars of the 1950s* (Jefferson, NC, 1992); Fred Smith, *995 Tigers* (Detroit, MI, 1981); Mike Shatzkin, ed., *The Ballplayers* (New York, 1990).

William A. Borst

GARVEY, Steven Patrick "Steve" (b. December 22, 1948, Tampa, FL), player, is the only child of Greyhound bus driver Joseph Patrick Garvey and Mildred (Winkler) Garvey. He graduated from Chamberlain High School in Tampa, where he starred in baseball and football. For the Michigan State University Spartans, he excelled as an All-American baseball player and starting defensive halfback in football. In 1971, he graduated from Michigan State with a Bachelor of Science degree in education. He married Cyndy Truhan on October 29, 1971 and had two children before their divorce.

Garvey was the first draft choice of the Los Angeles Dodgers (NL) in 1968 and assigned to Ogden, UT (PrL). After a three-game tryout the following year, he spent most of the season at Albuquerque, NM (TL) and hit .373. In 1970, he rejoined the Los Angeles Dodgers. Originally a third baseman, he was switched to first base in 1973 and starred in the remarkable Dodgers infield with Davey Lopes,* Bill Russell,* and Ron Cey* for a decade.

A steady, durable right-handed power hitter, Garvey batted .294 with 2,599 career hits, 440 doubles, 272 HR, and 1,308 RBI in 19 major league seasons from 1969 through 1987. He led the NL in hits with 202 in 1978 and 200 in 1980. Besides having six 200-hit seasons, he accumulated five with over 100 RBI and 20 HR. His 33 HR in 1977 established a record for Dodgers first basemen. The same year, he tied an NL mark with five extra-base hits (two HR and three doubles) in one game. In 1982, he batted a consistent .285 at home and .279 away, .280 on grass and .285 on artificial turf.

Garvey played the entire Dodgers schedule for seven seasons, breaking the NL consecutive game record. His streak ended in 1983 at 1,207 games, the fourth longest in major league history. An impeccable fielder with a .996 career average, Garvey earned four Gold Gloves. In 1976, he set a league record for fewest errors (3) by a first baseman handling at least 1,500 chances. In the strike-shortened 1981 season, he missed a perfect 1.000 average by the margin of one error in 1,075 chances. Garvey did not make an error in 1,319 chances in 1984.

These performances earned him 11 All-Star Game appearances, including eight in the starting lineup, and two awards as its MVP. In 1977, he became the first National Leaguer to get over 4 million votes in the All-Star balloting. In 1974, he was chosen NL MVP. A reliable clutch hitter, Garvey batted .393 in All-Star competition, .368 in one Division Series, .356 in five NL Championship Series, and .319 in five World Series. After 13 seasons with the Dodgers, he elected free agency in 1982 and negotiated a five-year, $6.6 million contract with the San Diego Padres (NL). He spent the final five seasons of his major league career with the Padres.

In 1977, a junior high school in Lindsay, CA was named after him. He serves as honorary chairman of the Multiple Sclerosis Foundation. An enterprising businessman, he founded and chaired Professional Athletes Career Enterprises, Inc. (PACE) of Barrington, IL. A national career counseling and placement service, PACE helps athletes adjust to the job market outside the world of sports. He broadcast for XTRA in San Diego and served as an executive for *Sport*. Garvey operates a marketing management consultant company.

BIBLIOGRAPHY: Steve Garvey with Skip Rozin, *Garvey* (New York, 1986); M. S. Goodman, "A Swinger No More," *PW* 40 (December 6, 1993), pp. 99–102; John Heins, "Stepping Into the Vacuum," *Forbes* 123 (April 30, 1984), p. 134; Tom Hultman, "Destined to be a Dodger," *SCD* 24 (June 20, 1997), pp. 170–172; Peter C. Bjarkman, ed., *Encyclopedia of Major League Baseball Team Histories: National League* (Westport, CT, 1991); Gene Karst and Martin J. Jones, Jr., *Who's Who in Professional Baseball* (New Rochelle, NY, 1973); Robert E. Kelly, *Baseball's Best* (Jefferson, NC, 1988); Los Angeles *Times*, September 11, 1977; Steve Garvey file, National Baseball Library, Cooperstown, NY; David L. Porter, Interview with Steve Garvey, July 27, 1989; *The Baseball Encyclopedia*, 10th ed. (New York, 1996); Rick Reilly, "America's Sweetheart," *SI* 71 (November 27, 1989), pp. 92–96; William F. McNeil, *The Dodgers Encyclopedia* (Champaign, IL, 1997); Tommy Lasorda and David Fisher, *The Artful Dodger* (New York, 1985); San Diego Padres *Media Guide, 1987.*

David L. Porter

GASTON, Clarence Edwin "Cito" (b. March 17, 1944, San Antonio, TX), player, coach, and manager, graduated from Holy Cross High School in

Corpus Christi, TX. The Atlanta Braves (NL) signed Gaston in March 1964 and assigned him to Binghamton, NY (NYPL). The outfielder–first baseman spent five seasons in the minor leagues with stops at Greenville, SC (WCL), West Palm Beach, FL (FSL), Batavia, NY (NYPL), Austin, TX (TL), Richmond, VA (IL), and Shreveport, LA (TL).

The 6-foot 4-inch, 210-pound outfielder debuted with the Atlanta Braves on September 14, 1967. The San Diego Padres (NL) selected Gaston as their 30th pick in the 1969 expansion draft. The towering outfielder played six seasons for the San Diego Padres, appearing in over 100 games each year. He made the NL All-Star squad in 1970, when he batted a career-high .318.

The Atlanta Braves reacquired Gaston in November 1974 for pitcher Danny Frisella. The Braves used him as a pinch hitter and reserve outfielder. The Atlanta Braves sold him to the Pittsburgh Pirates (NL) in September 1978. After the Pittsburgh Pirates released him in November 1978, Gaston signed with Santa Domingo, DR (IAL). When the new IAL folded, he joined Leon, Mexico (MEL) for the 1979 and 1980 seasons. In 11 major league seasons, he batted .256 with 799 hits, 91 HR, and 387 RBI.

Hank Aaron* convinced Gaston to become a roving hitting instructor for the Atlanta Braves in 1981. Two seasons later, Gaston joined the Toronto Blue Jays (AL) organization in the same capacity. The Blue Jays named Gaston manager on May 15, 1989, replacing Jimy Williams. Toronto's record stood at 12–24 when Gaston took over, but the Blue Jays finished 77–49 under his leadership and won the AL East Division championship.

The Blue Jays repeated as AL East Division champions from 1991 through 1993 and won consecutive AL pennants in 1992 and 1993. Toronto defeated the Atlanta Braves in the 1992 World Series and the Philadelphia Phillies in the 1993 World Series. TSN named Gaston and fellow Toronto executive vice president Pat Gillick Sportsmen of the Year in 1993. Gaston's managerial record stood at 681–635 when fired in September 1997. Toronto named him batting coach in October 1999. The Dunedin, FL resident and his wife, Denise, have two children, Adrian and Carly.

BIBLIOGRAPHY: *CB* (1993), pp. 198–202; Cito Gaston file, National Baseball Library, Cooperstown, NY; W. Leavy, "Baseball's Minority Managers: Taking Charge on the Field," *Ebony* 48 (May 1993), pp. 110–112ff; W. Leavy, "Cito Gaston on Top of the Baseball World," *Ebony* 49 (May 1994), pp. 144ff; *NYT Biographical Service* 20 (June 1989), pp. 547–548; *TSN Baseball Register*, 1997; *Toronto Blue Jays Media Guide*, 1997.
                                                                                                       John Hillman

GEHRIG, Henry Louis "Lou," "The Iron Horse," "Columbia Lou" (b. June 19, 1903, New York, NY; d. June 2, 1941, Riverdale, NY), player, was the son of skilled mechanic Heinrich Gehrig and Christina (Flack) Gehrig, both German immigrants who settled in New York City. They had four children, but only Lou survived. Gehrig attended Public School No. 132 and New York's High School of Commerce, excelling in baseball, football, swimming, and other sports. Although entering Columbia University in 1921, Gehrig was barred from athletic competition for one year because he had played baseball briefly that summer for Hartford, CT (EL). The next year he participated in both football and baseball at Columbia, starring in the latter sport. In June 1923, the New York Yankees (AL) signed him to a baseball contract. Gehrig played most of the 1923 and 1924 seasons at Hartford, where he won acclaim as a power-hitting first baseman. He did not become a regular player for the Yankees until June 1, 1925, when he began the 2,130 consecutive game streak which ran to the end of his career in 1939.

Gehrig experienced moderate success in 1925–1926, leading the AL with 20 triples the latter season. In 1927, he blossomed as a major slugging star and challenged teammate Babe Ruth* most of the season in HR. Gehrig ended the season with 47 HR, while Ruth slugged a then record 60 HR. He bested Ruth in most other departments, however, by batting .373, leading the AL with 52 doubles and 447 total bases, and setting a then major league record with 175 RBI. Besides being voted the AL's MVP, Gehrig helped the 1927 Yankees (whom most baseball authorities consider the greatest team of all time) sweep the World Series from the Pittsburgh Pirates in four games.

Gehrig continued playing exceptional ball, scoring and knocking in over 100 runs for 13 consecutive seasons. In 1931 he slugged 46 HR and became baseball's top run producer by scoring 163 and knocking in 184. He led the league in RBI five times, runs scored and total bases four times, slugging percentage twice, and batting average once. Gehrig won the triple crown (HR, RBI, and batting average) in 1934, and in 1927 and 1936 he won AL MVP awards.

The left-handed slugger became the first AL player to hit four HR in one game, connecting against the Philadelphia Athletics on June 3, 1932. Gehrig also compiled a career record of 23 grand slam HR. The powerfully built 6-foot, 210-pound slugger ran the bases well, stole home 15 times, and fielded adequately. Although quiet and modest off the field, Gehrig exhibited very competitive characteristics during game situations. His impressive career batting statistics included 534 doubles, 493 HR, 1,888 runs scored, 1,995 RBI, 1,508 walks, and a .340 batting average.

During spring training in 1939, Gehrig appeared to lack power and coordination. Shortly after the season started, he removed himself from the lineup on May 2, after playing in 2,130 consecutive games. A thorough examination at the Mayo Clinic in Rochester, MN indicated that the 35-year-old star had contracted a rare muscle disease called amyothropic lateral sclerosis and had a slim chance for survival. He continued as non-playing captain of the Yankees until the season's end. At Yankee Stadium on July 4, 1939, over 62,000 fans and a grateful nation honored the modest hero. In December 1939, he was elected to the National Baseball Hall of Fame.

Mayor Fiorello LaGuardia named Gehrig New York City Parole Commissioner, a position he held until his health failed. Gehrig married Eleanor Twitchell of Chicago in September 1933. They had no children. Lou Gehrig

Plaza in the Bronx was named for him. Gehrig made Major League Baseball's All-Century Team and ranked 34th among ESPN's top century athletes.

BIBLIOGRAPHY: Lou Gehrig file, National Baseball Library, Cooperstown, NY; B. Anderson, "Just a Pipp of a Legend," *SI* 66 (June 29, 1987), pp. 78–82; Richard Bak, *Lou Gehrig* (Dallas, TX, 1995); Mark Gallagher, *The Yankee Encyclopedia*, vol. 3 (Champaign, IL, 1997); Dave Anderson et al., *The Yankees* (New York, 1979); Bob Broeg, *Super Stars of Baseball* (St. Louis, MO, 1971); *CB* (1940), pp. 330–332; *DAB*, Supp. 3 (1941–1945), pp. 294–295; Raymond J. Gonzalez, "The Gehrig Streak Reviewed," *BRJ* 4 (1975), pp. 34–37; Raymond Gonzalez, "Larrupin' Lou and 23 Skidoo," *BRJ* 12 (1983), pp. 22–26; Raymond Gonzalez, "Lou Who? Stole Home 15 Times," *BRJ* 7 (1978), pp. 109–111; Raymond Gonzalez, "Still the Greatest One-Two Punch," *BRJ* 6 (1977), pp. 98–101; Frank Graham, *Lou Gehrig, A Quiet Hero* (New York, 1942); Ray Robinson, *Iron Horse* (New York, 1990); Donald Honig, *The Power Hitters* (St. Louis, MO, 1989); B. Kashatus, "Pride of the Yankees," *AHI* (July/August 1991), pp. 42–43; John P. McCarthy, *Baseball's All-Time Dream Team* (Cincinnati, OH, 1994); A. W. Laird, *Ranking Baseball's Elite* (Jefferson, NC, 1990); D. Noonan, "Double Legacy of the Iron Horse," *SI* 68 (April 4, 1988), pp. 112–116; Peter Schmuck, "A Matter of Record," *Sport* 83 (May 1992), pp. 22–24ff; Joseph J. Vecchione, ed., *The New York Times Book of Sports Legends* (New York, 1991); *TSN Baseball Register, 1942*.

L. Robert Davids

GEHRINGER, Charles Leonard "Charlie," "The Mechanical Man" (b. May 11, 1903, Fowlerville, MI; d. January 21, 1993, Bloomfield Hills, MI), baseball and football player, coach, and executive, grew up on a farm near Lansing, MI and played baseball with his brother, Al. Gehringer starred as a third baseman for his Fowlerville High School and town teams and played both baseball and football at the University of Michigan. After one year there, he entered professional baseball with the Detroit Tigers (AL) organization. Former Tigers outfielder Robert Veach* arranged Gehringer's tryout at Detroit's Navin Field. Gehringer impressed Tigers manager Ty Cobb,* who assigned him to London, OH (MOL). At London, Gehringer was shifted to second base and batted .292 in 1924. After Gehringer hit .462 in five games with the Tigers at season's end, he in 1925 batted .325 with 25 HR and 108 RBI at Toronto, Canada (IL) and led IL second basemen in fielding. He rejoined the Tigers for the final eight games of the season as a replacement for Frank O'Rourke.

The 5-foot 11½-inch, 185-pound Gehringer, who batted left-handed and threw right-handed, played his entire 19-year major league career (1926–1942) with Detroit and started at second base for 16 seasons. An outstanding fielder, he possessed quick hands and proved graceful and virtually flawless with a glove. He paced AL second basemen in fielding percentage seven times, led or tied for the lead in assists seven times, and prevailed in putouts three years. Gehringer, a fine .320 lifetime batter, hit .277 his rookie year and batted at least .300 from 1927 to 1940 except for a .298 mark in 1932. His best marks included .356 in 1934, .354 in 1936, and .371 and an AL batting title in 1937. A consistent hitter, he possessed some power, with 1,427 career RBI. He made over 200 hits in each of seven seasons, including five in succession from 1933 through 1937. In 2,323 career games, Gehringer stroked 2,839 career hits, including 574 doubles (12th), 146 triples, and 184 HR. He scored 1,774 runs and recorded seven 100-plus RBI seasons.

With Gehringer at second base, Detroit often finished well and won AL flags in 1934, 1935, and 1940. He batted .379 in the 1934 World Series and .375 in the 1935 classic to help the Tigers win the world championship, but hit only .211 in the 1940 classic. Overall, Gehringer's .321 post-season batting average was one point above his career mark. Nicknamed "The Mechanical Man" because of his calm, consistent, superior play, Gehringer received many honors. He was named to *TSN* Major League All-Star team in 1933, 1934, 1936, 1937, and 1938 and was selected AL MVP in 1937. Gehringer played every inning of the first six All-Star games and hit .500, a record for players participating in at least five midseason classics. In 1949 he was named to the National Baseball Hall of Fame.

When his playing skills deteriorated in 1942, Gehringer became a Detroit Tigers coach. He then joined the U.S. Navy, serving in the Fitness Program for the duration of World War II. After the war, he became a manufacturer's agent until being named vice-president and general manager of the Detroit Tigers in 1951. He held both posts until the end of the 1953 season, when he hired Muddy Ruel* as general manager. Gehringer, a bachelor, retired from the Detroit front office in 1959 and resided in Birmingham, MI.

BIBLIOGRAPHY: Charles Gehringer file, National Baseball Library, Cooperstown, NY; Lee Allen and Tom Meany, *Kings of the Diamond* (New York, 1965); Martin Appel and Burt Goldblatt, *Baseball's Best: The Hall of Fame Gallery* (New York, 1977); Richard Bak, *Cobb Would Have Caught It* (Detroit, MI, 1991); John Benson et al., *Baseball's Top 100* (Wilton, CT, 1997); Donald Honig, *Baseball When the Grass Was Real* (New York, 1975); Craig Carter, ed., *TSN Daguerreotypes*, 8th. ed. (St. Louis, MO, 1990); *NYT*, January 23, 1993, p. 28; Fred Smith, *995 Tigers* (Detroit, MI, 1981); *The Baseball Encyclopedia*, 10th ed. (New York, 1996); Ken Smith, *Baseball's Hall of Fame* (New York, 1978).

Douglas D. Martin

GENTILE, James Edward "Diamond Jim" (b. June 3, 1934, San Francisco, CA), player, is the son of Peter and Zona Gentile and graduated from the local Sacred Heart College. He signed with the Brooklyn Dodgers (NL) in 1952, spending seven seasons as a first baseman in their farm system. The muscular 6-foot 3½-inch, 215-pound left-hander clouted 235 HR in the minor leagues and batted a career best .314 with Pueblo, CO (WA) in 1954. The "Ted Williams shift" was used occasionally against him. Dodger executive Fresco Thompson lauded Gentile as our "best young prospect," but the latter sometimes became angry with himself when he did not achieve what he wanted. The Los Angeles Dodgers sold him to the Baltimore Orioles (AL) in October 1959.

Paul Gallivan, Baltimore Orioles scout formerly with the Dodgers who recommended Gentile, explained, "He's only sore at himself, the way Ted Williams* gets." Manager Paul Richards* encouraged him, while teammate Gene Woodling* helped him level his swing. Gentile batted .292 with 21 HR in 1960 in his first year with the Baltimore Orioles. Richards accurately observed, "he's going to get better and better." In 1961, Gentile batted .302 with 147 hits, 46 HR, and 141 RBI and clouted two consecutive grand slam HR in successive innings against the Minnesota Twins on May 9, 1961. Overall, he belted five grand slam HR that year to tie a major league record. Enthusiastic Baltimore Orioles fans honored him at Jim Gentile Day with a new Corvette. Gentile made the AL All-Star teams three consecutive times from 1961 to 1963.

Baltimore traded Gentile to the Kansas City Athletics (AL) for Norm Siebern* in November 1963. The Houston Astros (NL) acquired him from the Kansas City Athletics in June 1965, briefly re-uniting him with Richards. His major league career ended with the Cleveland Indians (AL) in 1966. He spent the next two seasons as player–coach with San Diego, CA (PCL), a Philadelphia Phillies (NL) farm club. He played the 1969 season in Japan before retiring from baseball. Oriole fans reminisce about Gentile's 1961 season, when he incredibly clouted eight HR in just nine games at Wrigley Field in Los Angeles, CA. The same year, Roger Maris* broke Babe Ruth's* single season HR record. Gentile's 141 RBI trailed Maris by just one. In 936 career major league games, Gentile batted .260 with 179 HR and 549 RBI.

Gentile married Carole June Housman in September 1952. He later married Paula Nance and has five children, Steve, Scott, Tori, James Jr., and Tony. Gentile worked in the retail business for 20 years, retiring at age 57. For several years, he has participated in the Baltimore Orioles Fantasy Camp and the Tom Belcher Baseball Camp in Chandler, OK. He also golfs and "enjoys life."

BIBLIOGRAPHY: Jim Gentile file, National Baseball Library, Cooperstown, NY; Zander Hollander, "Gentile Called Best Prospect at Dodgertown," TSN, April 22, 1953; Dick Young, "The Young Dodgers, Part III," Sunday News (Brooklyn), February 24, 1957, p. B10; Larry Klein, "Gentile Just Wanted a Chance," Sport 30 (November 1960), pp. 38–39, 96–97; "Orioles Slugging Gentile No Gent to Rival Pitchers," New York Herald Tribune, June 8, 1960; John F. Steadman, "Gentile Hoping for Another Lucky Year," Baltimore News Post, May 24, 1962, p. 5B; Mike Shatzkin, ed., The Ballplayers (New York, 1990); John Thorn et al., eds., Total Baseball, 5th ed. (New York, 1997); TSN Official Baseball Register, 1966; Ted Patterson, The Baltimore Orioles (Dallas, TX, 1995); James H. Bready, Baseball in Baltimore (Baltimore, MD, 1998).

William J. Miller

GIAMATTI, Angelo Bartlett "Bart" (b. April 4, 1938, Boston, MA; d. September 1, 1989, Edgartown, MA), executive, headed the NL, served as commissioner, and left an unchallenged reputation for dedication and integrity. The son of Valentine Giamatti and Mary Claybaugh (Walton) Giamatti, he grew up in Holyoke, MA. His father taught at Mt. Holyoke College. After receiving his doctorate in 1964 from Yale University, Giamatti became a popular professor of English there and specialized in Renaissance literature. He was named president of Yale in 1978 at age 40, despite admitting that "all I ever wanted was to be president of the American League." A devoted Boston Red Sox (AL) fan, he especially admired Bobby Doerr.* His occasional baseball articles included one for the *NYT* during the strike of 1981. Giamatti took the fan's perspective and termed the strike "utter foolishness. . . . The people of America care about baseball, not about your squalid little squabbles."

After being named NL president in 1986, Giamatti strove to enhance the game's respectability. Giamatti, who cracked down on both corked bats and doctoring of the ball and proceeded against rowdyism in the stands, saw himself as a "trustee" of the game's "fundamental values" which were derived from its American heritage. He viewed baseball as an example of individual interaction with the community, a constitutional ideal. No one should spoil it, for the game was a vital institution born of American history.

After being appointed commissioner on April 1, 1989, Giamatti met a severe test deriving from gambling allegations leveled against Pete Rose.* A documented report asserted that the Cincinnati Reds (NL) manager had bet on baseball games, including those of his own team between 1985 and 1987. Rose's attorneys tried to challenge the commissioner's authority by maneuvering the case into court, but Giamatti stood his ground. In a dramatic public announcement on August 24, 1989, the commissioner banned Rose for life and stated that "no one is bigger than the game."

Only a week later, Commissioner Giamatti suffered a sudden fatal heart attack at his summer home after having served only 154 days. No other commissioner had died in office. Many commentaries proclaimed the high esteem in which he was held. New York Yankees (AL) owner George Steinbrenner maintained that Giamatti "loved baseball more than anyone I ever knew," while President George Bush commended him for defending the "highest possible ethical standards." Giamatti's own words, "Baseball will break your heart," expressed much of the game's sorrowful reaction to the death of this "man of principle" at age 51.

BIBLIOGRAPHY: A. Bartlett Giamatti file, National Baseball Library, Cooperstown, NY; Roger Angell, "Celebration," *NY* 64 (August 22, 1988), pp. 50–60; Frank Deford, "A Gentleman and a Scholar," *SI* 70 (April 17, 1989), pp. 86–90, 94–98, 100; A. Bartlett Giamatti, "The Green Fields of the Mind," Boston (MA) *Globe*, December 22, 1977; A. Bartlett Giamatti, *Take Time for Paradise* (New York, 1989); P. Gray,

"Egghead at the Plate," *Time* 132 (September 26, 1988), pp. 72–74; *NYT*, September 2, 3, 1989; Kenneth S. Rabson, ed., *A Great and Glorious Game* (Chapel Hill, NC, 1998); James Reston, Jr., *Collision at Home Plate* (New York, 1991); Jerome Holtzman, *The Commissioners* (New York, 1998); Pete Rose and Roger Kahn, *Pete Rose: My Story* (New York, 1989); Charles Siebert, "Baseball's Renaissance Man," *NYT Magazine*, September 4, 1988, pp. 36–38, 46–48; *TSN*, September 11, 1989; *USAT*, August 24, 1989; *WWA*, 45th ed. (1988–1989), p. 1,119; Anthony Valerio, *Bart: A Life of A. Bartlett Giamatti* (San Diego, CA, 1991).

William J. Miller

GIBSON, George C. "Moon" (b. July 22, 1880, London, Canada; d. January 25, 1967, London, Canada), player and manager, spent 12 seasons as the Pittsburgh Pirates' (NL) catcher and established a club record by playing 1,113 games at that position. He entered professional baseball with Buffalo, NY (EL) in 1903 and spent two seasons with Montreal, Canada (EL). Gibson first experienced major league baseball as a 25-year-old rookie with the Pittsburgh Pirates in 1905, when he caught 44 games. In 1906, the right-handed Gibson shared catching duties with Heinie Peitz.

Gibson, a large player for his era, stood nearly six feet tall and weighed 190 pounds. He failed, however, to generate the batting statistics one might expect from a man of his physical stature, batting a season best .285 in 1914. Gibson never made more than 34 extra-base hits in any one season and hit only 15 career HR. Although Gibson's major league playing career spanned 14 seasons, he played on just one pennant winner. With the 1909 Pirates, Gibson caught every game in Pittsburgh's seven-game World Series triumph over the Detroit Tigers. He batted .240 and hit two doubles in the World Series. In 1909, Gibson set a NL record for most games caught in a season (150) and a major league mark for most consecutive games caught (133). He also accepted the most chances by a catcher in a season (847). He led NL catchers in fielding percentage in 1909, 1910, and 1912.

After Gibson played just 33 games for the Pittsburgh Pirates in 1916, the New York Giants (NL) acquired him on waivers that August. He caught 39 games over the next two seasons before retiring. In 1919, he managed Toronto, Canada (IL).

Pirates' owner Barney Dreyfus* hired Gibson as Pittsburgh's manager in 1920. His notable players included Walter Maranville,* Max Carey,* and Charlie Grimm.* In 1920, Pittsburgh sported a 79–75 record and finished fourth in the NL standings. The following season, the Pirates challenged for the NL pennant until fading in September to a disappointing second. Pittsburgh floundered in fifth place in 1922, when Gibson resigned in frustration. He coached for the Washington Senators (AL) in 1923 and Chicago Cubs (NL) in 1925 and 1926, serving as the Cubs' interim manager in September 1925. Gibson rejoined the Pittsburgh Pirates as manager in 1932. Pittsburgh posted consecutive second-place finishes in 1932 and 1933, but started poorly in 1934. Gibson, who married Margaret McMurphy, was fired 51 games into the season, reputedly for not maintaining team discipline.

Gibson's major league career spanned 1,213 games with a lifetime .236 batting average and .977 fielding average. His managerial record featured 413 wins and 344 losses and a .565 winning percentage.

BIBLIOGRAPHY: George Gibson file, National Baseball Library, Cooperstown, NY; Frederick G. Lieb, *The Pittsburgh Pirates* (New York, 1948); Mike Shatzkin, ed., *The Ballplayers* (New York, 1990); Dennis De Valeria and Jeanne Burke De Valeria, *Honus Wagner: A Biography* (New York, 1996); William Hageman, *The Life and Times of a Baseball Hero* (Champaign, IL, 1996); Richard L. Burtt, *The Pittsburgh Pirates, A Pictorial History* (Virginia Beach, VA, 1977); Bob Smizik, *The Pittsburgh Pirates: An Illustrated History* (New York, 1990); *The Baseball Encyclopedia*, 10th ed. (New York, 1996); Thomas Aylesworth and Benton Minks, *The Encyclopedia of Baseball Managers* (New York, 1990).

John G. Robertson

GIBSON, Joshua "Josh" (b. December 21, 1911, Buena Vista, GA; d. January 20, 1947, Pittsburgh, PA), player, was the son of sharecropper and mill-worker Mark Gibson and Nancy (Woodlock) Gibson. Josh had a brother, Jerry, who pitched for the Cincinnati Tigers, and a sister, Annie. Gibson attended public school through grade five in Buena Vista and studied at Allegheny Pre-Vocational School in Pittsburgh, where he began learning the electrician's trade. In 1930 he married Helen Mason, who later died giving birth to their twin children, Josh, Jr., and Helen.

In 1927, Gibson joined the semipro Pittsburgh Crawfords. Three years later, the powerfully built 6-foot 1-inch, 215-pound Gibson joined the Homestead, PA Grays (ANL) at midseason. His HR at Yankee Stadium in New York and Forbes Field in Pittsburgh were the longest hit in each park. In 1931, the 19-year-old Gibson hit 75 HR and quickly became a star of the first magnitude. From 1932 to 1936, he excelled for the Pittsburgh Crawfords (NNL) and caught for the legendary Satchel Paige.* He slugged 69 HR in 1934 and 84 HR in 1936. From 1937 to 1940, he starred for the Grays and dominated the NNL in hitting. In 1940, he signed a contract for $6,000 (a $2,000 raise) with Vera Cruz, Mexico (MEL). After returning to the Grays in 1942, he developed a brain tumor. Since Gibson refused to be operated on, the brain tumor contributed to his early death.

From 1933 to 1945, Gibson played winter baseball in Puerto Rico, Cuba, Mexico, and Venezuela. In 1941, he compiled a remarkable .480 batting average and earned the MVP Award in Puerto Rico. During the early 1940s, Gibson earned $6,000 in the NNL and $3,000 in Puerto Rico annually. Gibson's salary was surpassed only by that of Paige among black players. In contrast, Babe Ruth* earned a peak salary of $80,000 in the 1930–1931 era.

From 1937 to 1946, Gibson and Buck Leonard* were considered the NNL's Babe Ruth and Lou Gehrig* and helped the Grays win nine consecutive NNL titles. Gibson never played for a losing team. Due to poor record keeping, his HR hitting prowess cannot be fully documented. Estimates place his total HR around 960 and his lifetime batting average over .350 for his 17-year career. He hit four HR in one game in 1938 in Washington's spacious Griffith Stadium and in 1943 hit 11 HR to left field there, a feat never duplicated by major leaguers.

Gibson batted .483 as a starting catcher in nine Negro East-West All-Star games played before large crowds at Comiskey Park in Chicago. Walter Johnson* rated Gibson superior to Bill Dickey,* while Roy Campanella* considered him an all-time great catcher. According to Johnson, Gibson combined superb defensive skills with impressive power hitting. In exhibition contests, he batted well against star major league pitchers Grover Cleveland Alexander,* Dizzy Dean,* and Bob Feller.* As a batter, he turned up his cap bill, rolled up his left sleeve, and hit from a flat-footed stance. Joe DiMaggio,* emulating Gibson's style, did not take a stride into the pitch. In 1972, Gibson became the second player from the Negro Leagues elected to the National Baseball Hall of Fame. Many baseball experts regard Gibson as the sport's greatest HR hitter in numerical and power terms.

BIBLIOGRAPHY: Joshua Gibson file, National Baseball Library, Cooperstown, NY; James Bankes, *The Pittsburgh Crawfords* (Dubuque, IA, 1991); Martin Appel and Burt Goldblatt, *Baseball's Best: The Hall of Fame Gallery* (New York, 1977); William Brashler, *Josh Gibson* (New York, 1978); John Holway, *Josh and Satch* (Westport, CT, 1991); James A. Riley, *The All-Time All-Stars of Black Baseball* (Cocoa, FL, 1983); Robert W. Peterson, *Only the Ball Was White* (Englewood Cliffs, NJ, 1970); Pittsburgh *Courier*, January 25, 1947; David L. Porter, ed., *African-American Sports Greats* (Westport, CT, 1995); Mark Ribowsky, *The Power and the Darkness* (New York, 1996); James A. Riley, *The Biographical Encyclopedia of the Negro Baseball Leagues* (New York, 1994); Andrew S. Young, *Great Negro Baseball Stars* (New York, 1953); Andrew S. Young, *Negro Firsts in Sports* (Chicago, IL, 1963).

                                                          Robert T. Bowen, Jr.

GIBSON, Kirk Harold "Gib" (b. May 28, 1957, Pontiac, MI), player and sportscaster, is the son of Robert Gibson and Barbara (Schell) Gibson and starred as an All-American at Michigan State University at flanker in football and outfielder in baseball. After Gibson set several school football records, the St. Louis Cardinals (NFL) drafted him in the seventh round in 1979. In 1978, the Detroit Tigers (AL) had made him a first round draft selection and signed him for a $200,000 bonus after his only season of college baseball. After beginning professional baseball with Lakeland, FL (FSL) in 1978, he played a final season of college football that fall and joined Evansville, IN (AA) in 1979. Despite suffering a knee injury, he helped Evansville to a title in the AA playoffs with a .429 batting average. In September, the Detroit Tigers promoted him.

A natural all-around athlete, Gibson exhibited power, speed, leadership, intensity, raging moods, and competitiveness. Injuries, however, plagued him throughout his major league career. He paced the Detroit Tigers with a career high .328 batting average and stole 17 bases in the strike-shortened 1981 season. In 1984, Gibson helped guide Detroit to the AL title with 27 HR, 91 RBI, and 29 stolen bases. He was voted MVP of the 1984 AL Championship Series after batting .417 against the Kansas City Royals. Gibson clouted two HR with five RBI in the decisive fifth game of the World Series for the victorious Tigers against the San Diego Padres. In 1985, he logged a career high 29 HR and 97 RBI while stealing 30 bases in 34 attempts. Although injured early in the 1986 season, Gibson led the Tigers with a career best 34 stolen bases and produced 86 RBI and 28 HR. A new injury sidelined him in April 1987. He returned in May to post 24 HR and 79 RBI in just 128 games, helping the Tigers capture the AL Eastern Division.

After an arbitrator awarded Gibson free agency status, the Los Angeles Dodgers (NL) acquired him in January 1988. He hit .290 with 25 HR, 76 RBI, 106 runs scored, and 31 stolen bases in 35 attempts in 1988, earning NL MVP honors and helping the Los Angeles Dodgers win the NL pennant. Hobbled by injuries, Gibson did not start the first game of the World Series against the Oakland Athletics. As a pinch hitter against relief ace Dennis Eckersley* in the bottom of the ninth inning, he belted a two-out, two-run HR on a 3-2 pitch to give the Dodgers a 5-4 victory. The Dodgers swept the Athletics, marking the pinnacle of his long career. Injuries limited his batting average to a career low of .213 in 1989. Gibson began the 1990 season on the disabled list and joined the Albuquerque, NM Dukes (PCL) on rehabilitation assignment. He rejoined the Los Angeles Dodgers and batted .260 in only 89 games. He also stole 26 bases in 28 attempts for a .929 success rate, the best in the major leagues.

Gibson demanded to be traded at season's end and signed with the Kansas City Royals (AL), batting only .236 in 1991. Kansas City traded him to the Pittsburgh Pirates (NL) for pitcher Neal Heaton in March 1992, but he was released unconditionally after just 16 games. Gibson rejoined the Detroit Tigers as a free agent in 1993. Although initially used strictly as the DH, he later started in center field and hit .261 with just one error in 116 games. Gibson appeared in only 98 games with the Tigers in 1994, but improved his batting average to .276 with 23 HR. He batted .260 as Detroit's DH in 1995, but an injured shoulder forced him to retire that August.

In his 17-year major league career, Gibson batted .268, stole 284 bases, scored 985 runs, recorded 870 RBI, clouted 255 HR, and compiled a .976 fielding average. In February 1998, he joined Fox Sports as an analyst for Detroit Tigers games. He married JoAnn Sklarski on December 21, 1985. They reside in Grosse Pointe Shores, MI with their daughter, Colleen, and two sons, Kirk and Kevin.

BIBLIOGRAPHY: Kirk Gibson with Lynn Henning, *Bottom of the Ninth* (Chelsea, MI, 1997); *The Baseball Encyclopedia*, 10th ed. (New York, 1996); *Detroit Tigers Media Guides*, 1979–1987, 1994; Donald Dewey and Nicholas Acocella, *The Biographical*

History of Baseball (New York, 1995); Kirk Gibson file, National Baseball Library, Cooperstown, NY; Lloyd Johnson and Brenda Ward, *Who's Who in Baseball History* (Greenwich, CT, 1994); *Kansas City Royals Media Guide*, 1991; *Los Angeles Dodgers Media Guides*, 1988–1990; G. Richard McKelvey, *Fisk's Homer, Willie's Catch and the Shot Heard Round the World* (Jefferson, NC, 1998); Richard Miller, "Gibson's Series Heroics Highlight Bottom of the Ninth," SCD 24 (June 13, 1997), p. 190; Fred Smith, *995 Tigers* (Detroit, MI, 1981); Sparky Anderson with Dan Ewald, *They Call Me Sparky* (Chelsea, MI, 1998); William M. Anderson, *The Detroit Tigers* (South Bend, IN, 1996); John Thorn et al., eds., *Total Baseball*, 5th ed. (New York, 1997); Ken Valenti, *Clout! The Top Home Run Hitters in Baseball History* (Lexington, MA, 1989).

                                                                            Jack C. Braun

GIBSON, Robert "Bob," "Hoot," "Gibby" (b. November 9, 1935, Omaha, NE), player, coach, and executive, is the seventh child of Pack Gibson, a millworker who died before Robert's birth, and Victoria Gibson. Despite suffering from rickets, asthma, pneumonia, hay fever, and a rheumatic heart as a child, Gibson starred in basketball and baseball at Omaha Technical High School from 1949 to 1953. After rejecting an offer from the Kansas City Monarchs (NAL), he accepted a basketball scholarship at Creighton University in Omaha in 1953 and broke numerous scoring records there. He married high school sweetheart Charline Johnson in April 1957 and has two daughters, Renee and Annette.

In 1957, Gibson signed as a pitcher with the St. Louis Cardinals (NL) and was sent to Omaha (AA). In the autumn of 1957, he played basketball with the Harlem Globetrotters. Gibson displayed increased speed and better control at Rochester, NY (IL) and saw action with the Cardinals in 1959 and 1960, compiling 3–5 and 3–6 win–loss marks. After having respectable 13–12 and 15–13 seasons in 1961 and 1962, he posted 18, 19, 20, and 21 victories with St. Louis from 1963 to 1966, respectively. Between 1962 and 1966, he averaged 230 strikeouts per year. Gibson's 9–2 mark the final six weeks of the 1964 season paced the St. Louis Cardinals to their first NL pennant since 1946.

Although suffering a broken ankle in a July 15, 1967 contest, Gibson returned in September to win three games to help the Cardinals win another NL pennant. In 1968, the 6-foot 1-inch, 193-pound right-hander enjoyed an extraordinary 22–9 season with 15 consecutive wins, 13 shutouts, 268 strikeouts, and a 92-inning stretch yielding only 2 runs. He compiled a 1.12 ERA, the lowest ever in the major leagues for at least 300 innings pitched. The season proved even more remarkable given the arthritis and chipped bone in Gibson's right elbow. Gibson set numerous World Series records in 1964, 1967, and 1968, including eight consecutive complete games pitched, seven consecutive victories, 17 strikeouts in a game (1968), and three complete-game wins in a World Series (1967).

In 1969 and 1970, Gibson won 20 and 23 games, respectively, and averaged over 300 innings and 270 strikeouts per season. A torn thigh muscle slowed him to a 16–13 mark in 1971, but he hurled his 50th career shutout and on August 14 tossed an 11–0 no-hitter against the Pittsburgh Pirates. After rebounding to a 19–11 log in 1972, he missed two months of the 1973 campaign with a torn cartilage and finished at 12–10. Arthritis and knee injuries took a heavy toll, causing Gibson to finish his playing career with 11–13 and 3–10 marks. Gibson completed a 17-year Cardinals career with a 251–174 record, 56 shutouts, 3,117 strikeouts, and a 2.91 ERA. A good hitter, "Gibby" slugged 24 career HR and batted .303 in 1970. His honors included two Cy Young* awards (1968, 1970), NL MVP (1968), nine Gold Gloves, and overwhelming election to the National Baseball Hall of Fame in 1981. Gibson, pitching coach for the New York Mets (NL) in 1981, the Atlanta Braves (NL) from 1982 to 1984, and St. Louis Cardinals in 1995, is part-owner of a bank and a radio station in Omaha and served as an athletic director at Creighton University. He works as a special advisor to AL president Gene Budig.* Gibson made Major League Baseball's All-Century Team.

BIBLIOGRAPHY: Bob Broeg, "Fire-Breathing Gibby Was Cool," *TSN 1981 Baseball Yearbook* (1981), pp. 85–89; Bob Broeg, *Redbirds: A Century of Cardinals' Baseball* (St. Louis, MO, 1981); *CB* (1968), pp. 145–148; Bob Gibson file, National Baseball Library, Cooperstown, NY; John Benson et al., *Baseball's Top 100* (Wilton, CT, 1997); J. Buckley, Jr., "World Series: Kings of the Hill," *SI* 75 (October 7, 1991), pp. 45ff; John Devaney, *The Greatest Cardinals of Them All* (New York, 1968); Bob Gibson with Phil Pepe, *From Ghetto to Glory* (Englewood Cliffs, NJ, 1968); Bob Gibson with Lonnie Wheeler, *Stranger to the Game* (New York, 1994); Peter Gordon, "Bob Gibson in 1968," *BRJ* 17 (1988), pp. 41–44; Jack Lang, "Gibby a Shoo-in with 84% of Vote," *TSN*, January 31, 1981, p. 43; David Lipman and Ed Wilks, *Bob Gibson: Pitching Ace* (New York, 1975); Larry Moffi and Jonathan Kronstadt, *Crossing the Line* (Jefferson, NC, 1994); David L. Porter, ed., *African-American Sports Greats* (Westport, CT, 1995); Rob Rains, *The St. Louis Cardinals* (New York, 1992); Bob Broeg and Jerry Vickery, *St. Louis Cardinals Encyclopedia* (Grand Rapids, MI, 1998); Ken Young, *Cy Young Award Winners* (New York, 1994); Steve Rushin, "The Season of High Heat (1968)," *SI* 79 (July 19, 1993), pp. 30–37.

Frank J. Olmsted

GILES, George Franklin (b. May 2, 1909, Junction City, KS; d. March 3, 1992, Manhattan, KS), player and manager, was the son of John F. Giles and Charlotte (Gossard) Giles and began his baseball career in 1925 with the Kansas City Royal Giants. He remained in baseball through the 1939 season, playing first base and the outfield for twelve different Negro League clubs. His longest stints came with the Kansas City Monarchs (NNL, NAL) for the 1927–1928, 1932–1934, and 1939 campaigns and the New York Black Yankees (NNL) from 1936 to 1938. Giles also played for Gilkerson's Chicago, IL Union Giants in 1926 and 1929, St. Louis Stars (NNL) in 1930–1931, Philadelphia Stars (NNL) in 1932 and 1938, Detroit Wolves (EWL) in 1932, Homestead, PA Grays (EWL) in 1932, Baltimore Black

Sox (NNL) in 1933, Brooklyn Eagles (NNL) in 1935, and Pittsburgh Crawfords (NNL) in 1938. He never got the opportunity to play in white organized baseball.

Giles ended a successful Negro League career with a .309 lifetime batting average. Others described him as "exceptionally skilled," a "great hit and run man," and an "all-around hitter." Giles contributed to his teams in numerous ways. He helped the St. Louis Stars win the NNL title in 1930, and served as player–manager of the Brooklyn Eagles in 1935, when he hit .365 and made the All-Star squad. Giles, nicknamed the "Black Bill Terry*" after the New York Giants (NL) outstanding first baseman of the 1930s, also played for various Latin American clubs, including Cienfuegos, Cuba and San Juan, PR during the winter seasons. He barnstormed against major league All-Stars Lefty Grove* and Dizzy Dean* and played for Satchel Paige's* All Stars in 1939.

Giles married Helen E. Miller on January 11, 1929 in Manhattan, KS and had four children. His grandson, Brian Giles, played from 1981 through 1986 with the New York Mets (NL), Milwaukee Brewers (AL), and Chicago White Sox (AL). After retiring from the Negro Leagues, Giles worked a civil service job in Fort Riley, KS and operated a motel and tavern in Manhattan, KS.

BIBLIOGRAPHY: James A. Riley, *The Biographical Encyclopedia of the Negro Baseball Leagues* (New York, 1994); John Coates II, "Historically Speaking: George Giles," *BS* (January 1974), pp. 58–59; John B. Holway, *Blackball Stars* (Westport, CT, 1988); John B. Holway, *Black Diamonds* (Westport, CT, 1989); Janet Bruce, *The Kansas City Monarchs* (Lawrence, KS, 1985).

Leslie Heaphy

GILES, Warren Crandall (b. May 28, 1896, Tiskilwa, IL; d. February 7, 1979, Cincinnati, OH), executive, was the son of William F. Giles and Isabelle S. Giles, who owned a contracting company. Giles graduated from high school in Moline, IL and attended Staunton, VA Military Academy from 1914 to 1916 and Washington and Lee University for one semester before joining the U.S. Army in 1917. An infantry officer wounded in France, he returned to Moline to join his father's business. Giles' suggestions on how to improve the Moline (3IL) team earned him the club presidency in 1919 and started a 50-year career in baseball administration.

Giles proved an able minor league executive. After winning the 1921 3IL pennant, he took a front office post with St. Joseph, MO (WL), became part owner, and aided Branch Rickey* of the St. Louis Cardinals (NL) in searching for young players. When Rickey organized his farm system, Giles headed his top team at Syracuse, NY (IL) in 1926–1927 and Rochester, NY (IL) from 1928 to 1936. In nine years, Rochester won four IL pennants and two IL championships. Several Rochester managers, including Billy Southworth* and Bill McKechnie,* later piloted major league clubs. Giles' junior assistant,

Gabe Paul,* became a major league executive. Giles married Mabel Skinner in October 1932 and had one child, William, who became an executive with the Philadelphia Phillies (NL).

Challenged to save a debt-ridden team, Giles joined the Cincinnati Reds (NL) as general manager from 1937 to 1947 and as president until 1952. Under the leadership of the stocky, convivial executive, the Reds regained financial strength and improved on the field with manager McKechnie and stars like Ernie Lombardi* and Bucky Walters.* Cincinnati won NL pennants in 1939 and 1940 and the 1940 World Series, but declined during World War II. Giles, who believed ballplayers should serve in the military even if it hurt the sport, resorted to playing 15-year-old pitcher Joe Nuxhall* for one game in 1944.

In voting for a new baseball commissioner in 1951, owners stalemated between NL president Ford Frick* and Giles. After the 17th ballot, the Reds' president withdrew from contention. In 1952, Giles became the 11th NL president and held that position until 1969. An active president, he thought that teams not well supported in one city could go elsewhere. Giles facilitated the move of the Braves from Boston to Milwaukee in 1953 and then to Atlanta in 1966, and the shift of the Brooklyn Dodgers and New York Giants to California in 1957. He added new franchises in New York, Houston, San Diego, and Montreal and favored the construction of new stadiums. In a strategy with long-range implications, Giles cooperated with efforts of NL teams to sign black and Latin American players, jumping ahead of the rival AL. During his 18-year presidency, the NL won 10 world championships and 15 All-Star games. A principal figure in shaping modern baseball administration, the affable, strong-willed Giles was inducted in 1979 to the National Baseball Hall of Fame.

BIBLIOGRAPHY: Lee Allen, *The National League Story* (New York, 1967); Warren Giles file, National Baseball Library, Cooperstown, NY; Jerome Holtzman, *The Commissioners* (New York, 1998); Gene Karst and Martin J. Jones, Jr., *Who's Who in Professional Baseball* (New Rochelle, NY, 1973); Paul McFarlane, ed., *Hall of Fame Fact Book* (St. Louis, MO, 1983); *NYT*, February 8, 1979.

Joseph E. King

GILLIAM, James William "Junior," "Jim" (b. October 17, 1928, Nashville, TN; d. October 8, 1978, Inglewood, CA), player and coach, joined the Baltimore Elite Giants (NNL) upon graduation from Pearl High School in 1946. Teammates nicknamed him "Junior" because at age 17 he was the youngest player on the Elite Giants. From 1947 to 1950, he and shortstop Tom "Pee Wee" Butts* formed one of the best double play combinations in the Negro Leagues. Besides having fine defensive skills, the 5-foot 11-inch, 175-pound Gilliam proved a good switch-hitter and base stealer and was named to the NNL East All-Star team each year from 1948 to 1950.

In 1951, the Brooklyn Dodgers (NL) tried to buy the contract of pitcher

Leroy Farrell from the Baltimore Elite Giants. Baltimore asked $10,000, which the Dodgers thought too high. The Brooklyn Dodgers agreed to the price when the Elite Giants included Gilliam and pitcher Joe Black. Gilliam reported to the Montreal, Canada Royals (IL), batting .287 in 1951 and .301 in 1952. He led the IL in runs scored both seasons with 117 and 111 and second basemen with a .987 fielding average in 1952.

In 1953, the Brooklyn Dodgers moved Jackie Robinson* to the outfield and third base and installed Gilliam at second base. Gilliam responded with a rookie record 100 bases on balls. He led the NL in triples (17) and scored 125 runs, winning the NL Rookie of the Year honors. Gilliam scored more than 100 runs per season from 1953 to 1956 and batted a career-high .300 in 1956. Writer Roger Kahn* described Gilliam as "a black deer, lovely to behold as he turned the bases." Gilliam drew over 90 walks in a season five times, being the toughest Brooklyn and Los Angeles Dodger in history to strike out. He teamed with shortstops Pee Wee Reese* and Maury Wills* to anchor the Dodgers' middle infield for more than a decade. Don Drysdale* claimed that Wills became such a great base stealer because Gilliam batted behind him. On July 21, 1956, Gilliam set a major league record by making 12 assists in a game. In 1957, he led NL second basemen in putouts (416) and fielding average (.986).

In his only All-Star game, Gilliam homered for the NL in 1959. He batted .211 in seven World Series with the Brooklyn and Los Angeles Dodgers. The Los Angeles Dodgers named Gilliam coach after the 1964 season, but he came out of retirement in 1965 and 1966 to play third base. He returned to coaching full-time for the Los Angeles Dodgers from 1967 until his death. He died of a cerebral hemorrhage two days before the Los Angeles Dodgers entered the 1978 World Series. Los Angeles retired his uniform number 19. Dodgers manager Tommy Lasorda* called Gilliam "one of the greatest human beings I could ever come across."

Gilliam, an avid billiards players, married Gloria White in 1949. After their divorce, he married Edwina Fields in April 1959. His major league career totals included 1,956 games, 1,163 runs, 1,889 hits, 65 HR, 558 RBI, 203 stolen bases, and a .265 batting average.

BIBLIOGRAPHY: Stanley Cohen, *Dodgers! The First 100 Years* (New York, 1992); Don Drysdale with Bob Verdi, *Once a Bum, Always a Dodger* (New York, 1990); James Gilliam file, National Baseball Library, Cooperstown, NY; Richard Goldstein, *Superstars and Screwballs* (New York, 1991); Peter Golenbock, *Bums* (New York, 1984); Roger Kahn, *The Boys of Summer* (New York, 1973); Gene Karst and Martin J. Jones, Jr., *Who's Who in Professional Baseball* (New Rochelle, NY, 1973); Larry Moffi and Jonathan Kronstadt, *Crossing the Line* (Jefferson, NC, 1994); Dan Riley, ed., *The Dodgers Reader* (New York, 1992); James A. Riley, *The Biographical Encyclopedia of the Negro Baseball Leagues* (New York, 1994); Richard Whittingham, *The Los Angeles Dodgers: An Illustrated History* (New York, 1982).

Frank J. Olmsted

GLASSCOCK, John Wesley "Jack," "Pebbly Jack" (b. July 22, 1859, Wheeling, WV; d. February 24, 1947, Wheeling, WV), player and manager, was the son of carpenter Thomas Glasscock and Julia (Carrol) Glasscock. He married Rhoda Rose Dubula (or Deubal), who died in 1925, and had four children. Glasscock, generally rated the best shortstop of the 1880s, possessed great range, sure hands, and a strong, accurate right arm and fielded barehanded until 1890. In 17 major league seasons, the 5-foot 8-inch, 160-pound right-handed Glasscock made 2,040 hits and batted .290, high for a shortstop. Glasscock's best performance on September 27, 1890 saw him hit singles in all six at bats. He led the NL in 1890 with a .336 hitting average and 172 hits and in 1889 with 205 hits.

After playing sandlot baseball, he performed with the semipro Evening Standards of Wheeling, WV in 1876, the Champion City Club of Springfield, OH, in 1877, and Forest City of Cleveland in 1878 as a third baseman. When the Cleveland Blues joined the NL in 1879, Glasscock played second base and then switched to shortstop the next year. After jumping to the Cincinnati Outlaw Reds (UA) in 1884, he played for the St. Louis Maroons (NL) in 1885 and 1886. When the team moved to Indianapolis as the Hoosiers in 1887, he became field captain and then managed them to a 34–33 record in 1889. Allegedly he discovered pitcher Amos Rusie* at that time. When Indianapolis folded, Glasscock was sold to New York (NL) and played the 1890–1891 seasons for the Giants. He joined the St. Louis Browns (NL) in 1892 and was traded in June 1893 to the Pittsburgh Pirates (NL) for shortstop Frank Shugart. The Pirates released Glasscock, who had suffered arm and finger injuries, after the 1894 season. He played briefly with the Louisville Colonels (NL) and Washington Senators (NL) in 1895, and finished that season at first base for the Wheeling, WV Stogies (ISL). Glasscock then performed at first base for St. Paul, MN (WL) in 1896, 1897, and 1898, Fort Wayne, IN (ISL) in 1899 and early 1900, and Sioux City, IA (WL) in 1900, managing the last two clubs. Following his baseball career, he worked as a carpenter in Wheeling.

BIBLIOGRAPHY: Wheeling (WV) *Intelligencer*, February 24, 1947; John B. Glasscock file, National Baseball Library, Cooperstown, NY; Harold W. Lanigan, "Jack Glasscock, 81, Recalls His Days of Fun and Fame as Barehanded Shortstop on Pebbly Diamonds," *TSN*, April 24, 1941, March 5, 1947; Paul MacFarlane, ed., *TSN Daguerreotypes of Great Stars of Baseball* (St. Louis, MO, 1981), pp. 108–109; *The Baseball Encyclopedia*, 10th ed. (New York, 1996); Robert L. Tiemann and Mark Rucker, eds., *Nineteenth Century Stars* (Kansas City, MO, 1989); John Phillips, *The Spiders—Who Was Who* (Cabin John, MD, 1991); United States Census, 1860, 6th Ward, Wheeling, Ohio County, VA, 423, Microfilm M-653, Roll 368.

Frank V. Phelps

GLAVINE, Thomas Michael "Tom" (b. March 25, 1966, Concord, MA), player, is the son of Fred Glavine, a building contractor, and Millie Glavine.

His younger brother, Michael, plays minor league baseball. Glavine, a four-time all-league baseball player and a three-time all-league hockey player at Billerica, MA High School, was a fourth-round draft pick of the Los Angeles Kings (NHL) in June 1984, following his high school graduation. The Atlanta Braves (NL) selected him as a left-handed pitcher in the second round of the free-agent June 1984 draft and signed him for an $80,000 bonus.

Glavine pitched for Bradenton, FL (GCL) in 1984 and Sumter, SC (SAL) in 1985, leading the SAL with a 2.35 ERA. In 1986, he made the All-Star team for Greenville, SC (SA) and was promoted to Richmond, VA (IL). Despite winning only six of 18 decisions for Richmond in 1987, he joined the Atlanta Braves for nine games. In 1988, Glavine lost a NL-leading 17 games and won just seven of 34 starts. After developing a new change-up, he established himself in 1989 with 14 wins, only eight defeats, and a 3.68 ERA. Glavine slipped to a 10–12 mark in 1990, but blossomed in 1991 with a 20–11 record, a 2.55 ERA, and 192 strikeouts in 246.2 innings. He shared the league lead in wins and led the NL with nine complete games, as the young Braves players topped the NL West division in 1991. Glavine lost two games in the Braves' 1991 NL Championship Series against the Pittsburgh Pirates (NL) despite boasting a 3.21 ERA and split two decisions in the Braves' losing effort against the Minnesota Twins in the World Series. He won the NL's Cy Young* Award and garnered *TSN* Pitcher of the Year honors.

In 1992, Glavine won 20 games and suffered only eight setbacks with a 2.76 ERA. His 20 victories and five shutouts paced the NL. He lost two games in the NL Championship Series against the Pirates and split two decisions with a 1.59 ERA in Atlanta's World Series loss to the Toronto Blue Jays. In 1993, he recorded an NL best 22 victories and lost only six, combining with newly acquired Greg Maddux* to lead the powerful Braves to another NL West division title. Although Glavine won his only decision against the Philadelphia Phillies in the 1993 NL Championship Series, the Braves failed to reach the World Series. The shrewd, unflappable, 6-foot 1-inch, 190-pound southpaw had become perhaps the finest left-hander in baseball and performed with the strongest group of starting pitchers in baseball.

Glavine won 13 and lost nine in the strike-shortened 1994 season. In 1995 he finished with 16 victories, only seven setbacks, and a 3.08 ERA. He was not involved in any decisions in either the NL Division Series against the Colorado Rockies or the NL Championship Series against the Cincinnati Reds. In the World Series, Glavine recorded two victories (including the final game), gave up only two runs in 14 innings, and was named the World Series' MVP. The Braves defeated the Cleveland Indians for their first world title since 1958. In 1996, Glavine won 15 games and lost only 10 with a 2.98 ERA, as the Braves again won the NL East. In the NL Division Series, he won his only decision against the Los Angeles Dodgers. Glavine split two decisions as the Braves defeated the St. Louis Cardinals in the NL Championship Series. He allowed just one earned run in his only World Series outing against the New York Yankees, but the Braves lost the fall classic in six games. But he lowered his career World Series ERA to 1.75, sixth on the all-time list. In 1997, his 14–7 record and 2.96 ERA helped the Braves capture another NL East title. He won Game 2 of the NL Division Series against the Houston Astros and pitched brilliantly to defeat the Florida Marlins, 7–1, in Game 2 of the NL Championship Series, but lost the crucial Game 6. In 1998, Glavine helped spark the Braves to another NL East title with a 20–6 record and 2.47 ERA, earning his second NL Cy Young Award. He gave up only one run and struck out eight Chicago Cubs in his only NL Division Series start, but lost twice to the San Diego Padres in the NL Championship Series. He finished 14–11 in 1999, as Atlanta won another NL East title. Glavine started Game 3 of the NL Division Series and hurled seven shutout innings in the NL Championship Series. He had no decision in Game 3 of the World Series.

A poker-faced, relentless competitor, Glavine won more games (106) than any other major league pitcher from 1991 through 1996. He consistently threw his fastball and change-up with pinpoint precision on the outside corner of the plate. Glavine made the NL All-Star team in 1991, 1992, 1993, 1996, 1997, and 1998. Except in the strike-shortened 1994 and 1995 seasons, he always pitched over 200 innings per campaign and almost never missed a turn. He fielded his position well and even supplied some offensive punch. *TSN* named him the NL's best-hitting pitcher in 1991, 1995, 1996, and 1998. Through 1999, Glavine has compiled a 187–116 record with 18 shutouts, a 3.38 ERA and 1,659 strikeouts in 2,659.2 innings. He ranked second in wins (164) in the 1990s.

Glavine has participated in the MLPA since succeeding Dale Murphy* as the Braves' Player Representative in 1992. He and his wife, Carri, were married on November 2, 1992 and live in Alpharetta, GA with their daughter, Amber.

BIBLIOGRAPHY: Tom Glavine file, National Baseball Library, Cooperstown, NY; Gary Caruso, *The Braves Encyclopedia* (Philadelphia, PA, 1995); *TSN Baseball Guide*, 1998; *TSN Official Baseball Register*, 1998; Tom Glavine with Nick Cafardo, *None But the Braves* (New York, 1996); Tim Kurkjian, "A Good Skate," *SI* 74 (June 10, 1991), pp. 63–64; Ed Lucas and Paul Post, "Fast Track to Cooperstown," *SCD* 26 (January 22, 1999), p. 20; Dan Schlossberg, "Tom Glavine," *SCD* 23 (May 10, 1996), pp. 80–81; John Thorn et al., eds., *The Total Braves* (New York, 1996); Leigh Montville, "A Gripping Tale," *SI* 77 (July 13, 1992), pp. 42–45;

Luther W. Spoehr

GLEASON, William J. "Kid," "Bill," "Youngster" (b. October 26, 1866, Camden, NJ; d. January 2, 1933, Philadelphia, PA), player, coach, and manager, attracted attention as a curveball pitcher in Camden, NJ while a teenager. Despite Gleason's losing minor league record, manager Harry Wright* of the Philadelphia Phillies (NL) signed the enthusiastic 5 foot 7 inch, 150 pound right-hander in 1888. Although winning only 16 games in his first two seasons, Gleason led Philadelphia in 1890 with a 38–17 win–loss mark. He finished second in the NL in wins and percentage (.691), third in complete games (54) and shutouts (6), and fourth in strikeouts (222) and ERA (2.63). In 1891, he paced the Phillies with 24 victories. Philadelphia dealt Gleason in 1892 to the St. Louis Browns (NL), where the switch-hitter also performed part-time as a fielder. The Browns traded him to the Baltimore Orioles (NL) during the 1894 season. His 15–5 pitching performance and .325 batting average helped the Orioles capture the 1894 NL pennant. Gleason batted .309 and played 85 games at second base in 1895, helping the Orioles repeat as NL titlists.

Baltimore sent Gleason in 1896 to the New York Giants (NL), where the team captain led the NL in assists (468) in 1898 and in both assists (465) and putouts (403) in 1899. Gleason, who reputedly suggested the first intentional base on balls about 1897, jumped to the Detroit Tigers of the new AL in 1901 and played for two seasons there. The Philadelphia Phillies acquired him for the 1903 season, utilizing his familiarity with the tricks of the game and his natural teaching skills as a player–coach until 1908. Four minor league seasons followed, with Gleason retiring as an active player in 1911.

In 22 major league seasons, Gleason compiled a .261 batting average, made 1,944 hits, slugged 216 doubles, and stole 328 career bases. During only eight pitching seasons, he recorded 138 wins, 131 losses, a 3.79 ERA, and 240 complete games.

The Chicago White Sox (AL) hired him as a coach from 1912 to 1914 and in 1916 and 1917. In 1919, he managed the infamous "Black Sox." Chicago won the 1919 AL pennant, but lost the World Series against the Cincinnati Reds because several players had become involved in a scandal. Gleason managed Chicago through the 1923 season, compiling a 392–364 overall win–loss record. He joined the Philadelphia Athletics (AL) as coach in 1926, helping guide them to three AL pennants and two World Championships. Gleason became seriously ill with a heart ailment after the 1932 season and died at the home of his daughter, with whom he had lived since the 1927 death of his wife. He was survived by his brother, Harry, who also played professional baseball.

BIBLIOGRAPHY: Thomas Aylesworth and Benton Minks, *The Encyclopedia of Baseball Managers* (New York, 1990); *The Baseball Encyclopedia*, 10th ed. (New York, 1996); Joseph C. De Luca, "William J. 'Kid' Gleason, Camden, New Jersey's Human Pepper Box," unpublished ms., 1990; William Gleason file, National Baseball Library, Cooperstown, NY; "In Picking Out Living Monuments to Baseball Gleason Stands Out Boldest," Philadelphia (PA) *Inquirer*, circa 1915; Frederick Ivor-Campbell et al., eds., *Baseball's First Stars* (Cleveland, OH, 1996); Rich Westcott and Frank Bilovsky, *The New Phillies Encyclopedia* (Philadelphia, PA, 1993); Allen Lewis, *The Philadelphia Phillies: A Pictorial History* (Virginia Beach, VA, 1981); Gene Karst and Martin J. Jones, Jr., *Who's Who in Professional Baseball* (New Rochelle, NY, 1973); Eliot Asinof,

Eight Men Out (New York, 1963); Dan Gutman, *Baseball Babylon* (New York, 1992); Daniel E. Ginsburg, *The Fix Is In* (Jefferson, NC, 1995); Garrett J. Kelleher, "Kid Gleason," *BRJ* 17 (1988), pp. 79–81; Frederick G. Lieb and Stan Baumgartner, *The Philadelphia Phillies* (New York, 1953); John Thorn et al., eds., *Total Baseball*, 5th ed. (New York, 1997).

Gaymon L. Bennett

GOLDSMITH, Fred Ernest (b. May 15, 1856, New Haven, CT; d. March 28, 1939, Berkley, MI), player and umpire, married Rowena Rooks. He did not become a printer like his father, but started pitching semiprofessionally for baseball teams in Bridgeport, CT and New Haven. In 1877, the 6-foot 1-inch, 195-pound right-hander hurled the Tecumsehs of London, Canada to the IA championship. After spending another season with Tecumseh, he in 1879 joined the Springfield, MA team and tried out with the Troy, NY Trojans (NL). Goldsmith pitched for the Chicago White Stockings (NL) from 1880 to 1884. Chicago released him because of an arm injury. He finished the 1884 season with the Baltimore Orioles (AA) before retiring. His major league career included 112 wins, 68 losses, .622 winning percentage, and a 2.73 ERA. After umpiring in the AA in 1888–1889, he tended bar and farmed near Detroit, MI.

Goldsmith and Larry Corcoran* pitched the Chicago White Stockings to three NL pennants between 1880 and 1883, with the former winning 98 games and losing 52. His 21–3 record and .875 winning percentage in 1880 remained a club record until broken by Rick Sutcliffe* in 1984. Goldsmith, the first White Stockings pitcher to hit two HR in a game, performed that feat against the Buffalo, NY Bisons on May 27, 1884. He claimed to have invented the curveball, although Candy Cummings* supposedly threw it in 1867. Goldsmith first demonstrated the pitch. On the Capitoline Grounds in Brooklyn, NY, on August 16, 1870, three poles were laid out on a 45-foot chalkline. According to a Brooklyn *Eagle* article by Henry Chadwick,* Goldsmith's pitches curved right of the center pole and then left of the far pole.

BIBLIOGRAPHY: Fred Goldsmith file, National Baseball Library, Cooperstown, NY; Adrian C. Anson, *A Ball Player's Career* (Chicago, IL, 1900); Eddie Gold and Art Ahrens, *The Golden Era Cubs, 1876–1940* (Chicago, IL, 1985); Frederick Ivor-Campbell et al., eds., *Baseball's First Stars* (Cleveland, OH, 1996); Warren Wilbert and William Hageman, *Chicago Cubs: Seasons at the Summit* (Champaign, IL, 1997); Warren Brown, *The Chicago Cubs* (New York, 1946); *Spalding-Reach Official Baseball Guide 1940* (New York, 1940).

William E. McMahon

GOMEZ, Vernon Louis "Lefty," "Goofy," "The Gay Castillion," "El Gomez" (b. November 26, 1908, Rodeo, CA; d. February 17, 1989, Greenbrae, CA), player and manager, is the son of Manuel Gomez and Mary Gomez, of Spanish and Irish ancestry, respectively, and owners of a cattle ranch. After completing grammar school in Rodeo, Gomez attended high school in nearby Richmond, CA. Gomez married stage actress June O'Dea on February 26, 1933, and had four children. Gomez signed as a pitcher with San Francisco, CA (PCL) in 1928 and was optioned to Salt Lake City, UT (UIL) that year. Gomez pitched for San Francisco in 1929, when the New York Yankees (AL) purchased his contract. After spending part of the 1930 season at St. Paul, MN (AA), Gomez played with New York through 1942 and pitched briefly in 1943 for the Boston Braves (NL) and Washington Senators (AL).

Gomez, one of the premier left-handed pitchers of the 1930s, pitched 2,503 innings, won 189 contests, and lost 102 games for a .649 percentage. During his career, he struck out 1,468 batters, compiled a 3.34 ERA, and registered 28 shutouts. In his best season (1934), Gomez recorded a 26–5 won–lost record, a 2.33 ERA, and six shutouts. Gomez played on seven AL pennant winners and won six World Series games without a loss. He led the AL in victories (1934, 1937), winning percentage (1934, 1941), and ERA (1934, 1937) twice, in shutouts (1934, 1937, 1938) and strikeouts (1933, 1934, 1937) three times, and in innings pitched (1934) and complete games (1934) once.

Eccentric, engaging, witty, friendly, voluble, and colorful, the 6-foot 2-inch, 175-pound left-hander became a favorite of the press and was nick-named "Lefty," "Goofy," and "El Gomez." Journalists frequently wrote vignettes featuring his offbeat humor. Sportswriters, for example, recounted the following story: "My first name was Quits. The day I was born my Dad came in and looked at me, and then said to my mother, " 'Let's call it Quits.' " Despite his self-deprecating badinage, the handsome, gray-eyed, brown-haired Gomez possessed shrewd intelligence.

From June 1946 through the 1947 season, Gomez pitched four innings and managed the Binghamton, NY Triplets (EL) to last place finishes. In 1948, he began a three-decade association as a spokesman with the Wilson Sporting Goods Company and resided in Fairfax, CA during his later years.

Gomez's 1972 election to the National Baseball Hall of Fame attests to his ability and reflects the favorable circumstances under which he played. Players on New York or pennant-winning teams attract more publicity than those on less successful franchises in smaller localities. Moreover, the abundant anecdotes attributed to Gomez by the press demonstrate that baseball is both entertainment and sport.

BIBLIOGRAPHY: Vernon Gomez file, National Baseball Library, Cooperstown, NY; Martin Appel and Burt Goldblatt, *Baseball's Best: The Hall of Fame Gallery* (New York, 1977); John Benson et al., *Baseball's Top 100* (Wilton, CT, 1997); Frank Graham, *The New York Yankees* (New York, 1943); Mark Gallagher, *The Yankee Encyclopedia*, vol. 3 (Champaign, IL, 1997); Oscar Kahn, "Lefty Gomez—King of Diamond Comics," *TSN*, January 17, 1948, pp. 7–8; Howard Liss, *Baseball's Zaniest Stars* (New York, 1971); Tom Meany, *Baseball's Greatest Pitchers* (New York, 1951); Joseph J. Vecchione, *The New York Times Book of Sports Legends* (New York, 1991); *NYT*, February 18, 1989, p. 10.

William M. Simons

GONZALEZ, Juan Alberto (Vazquez) "Igor" (b. October 16, 1969, Vega Baja, PR), player, is the son of Juan Gonzalez, a high school mathematics teacher, and Lelé Gonzalez. Gonzalez played baseball at Vega Baja High School, from which he graduated in 1987, and also participated in the American Legion baseball program. Texas Rangers (AL) scout Luis Rosa signed him to a professional contract at age 16.

Gonzalez hit .240 for the Gulf Coast, FL Rangers (GCL) in 1986 and batted .265 with 14 HR for Gastonia, NC (SAL) in 1987. He played for Charlotte, FL (FSL) in 1988 and Tulsa, OK (TL) in 1989. At Tulsa, he belted 21 HR with a .293 batting average, leading the TL in total bases with 254. The Texas Rangers promoted him to the major leagues in September 1989, but he managed only nine hits in 60 at bats. In 1990, the 20-year-old Gonzalez, the youngest AA player, played with Oklahoma City. He led the AA in HR (29), RBI (101), and total bases (252), and was named the AA MVP. The Texas Rangers called him up in August 1989 for 22 games as an outfielder and DH. He went hitless in his first 11 at bats, but rebounded to hit .289 for the Rangers.

In 1991, the 6-foot 3-inch, 220-pound Gonzalez performed in his first full major league season and paced the Texas Rangers in HR with 27. He hit 43 HR in 1992 to lead the AL at age 22, making him the sixth youngest league HR titlist in in major league history. The following winter, he played for Santurce, PR, being named the PRWL's MVP. He batted .333 with a league-leading seven HR and 14 RBI in 21 games. Gonzalez paced the AL in HR (46) and slugging percentage (.632) in 1993. He played in the 1993 and 1998 All-Star Games. In 1996, Gonzalez batted .314 with 47 HR and 144 RBI to help Texas win the AL West and hit .438 with 5 HR and 9 RBI in the AL Division Series against the New York Yankees. He led Texas with 42 HR and 131 RBI in 1997.

In 1998 Gonzalez became the first major leaguer to knock in over 100 runs before the All-Star Game and led the AL with 157 RBI and 50 doubles, earning his second AL MVP award. He also ranked second in slugging percentage (.630) and fourth in HR (45) and total bases (382). His .318 batting average and 193 hits helped Texas win the AL West, but New York Yankees pitchers held him to just one hit in the AL Division Series. He made *TSN* AL Silver Slugger teams (1992–1993, 1996–1998) and *TSN* AL All-Star teams (1993, 1996, 1998). Gonzalez batted .326 with 39 HR, 128 RBI, and a .601 slugging percentage to help Texas repeat as AL West titlists, but hit only .182 with one HR in the 1999 AL Division Series.

His 340 HR through the 1999 season remain the most in Texas Rangers history. He produced 3-HR games on June 7, 1992, and August 28, 1993.

Gonzalez, who participates in charity work in his native Puerto Rico during the off-season, has purchased several thousand dollars of tickets to Rangers' games for underprivileged children. His son, Juan Igor, was born in February 1992. In November 1998, the Detroit Tigers acquired him. Through 1999, he has a .294 career batting average with 340 HR and 1,075 RBI. He ranked fifth in RBI (1,068) in the 1990s.

BIBLIOGRAPHY: Juan Gonzalez file, National Baseball Library, Cooperstown, NY; Nicholas Dawidoff, "The Not-Really Rookies," *SI* 74 (April 1, 1991), pp. 46–51; Phil Rogers, "Lone Ranger," *Sport* 84 (May 1993), pp. 61–63; Dennis Tuttle, *Juan Gonzalez* (Alexandria, VA, 1995); Tom Verducci, "Puerto Rico's New Patron Saint," *SI* 78 (April 5, 1993), pp. 60–67; Rick Weinberg, "Texas Terror," *Sport* 83 (May 1992), pp. 38–40.

David A. Goss

GOODEN, Dwight Eugene "Doc," "Doctor K" (b. November 16, 1964, Tampa, FL), player, is the youngest of six children of Dan Gooden and Ella Mae Gooden. Upon encouragement from his parents, he began pitching baseball at age 12 and starred as a senior hurler for Hillsboro High School. His professional baseball career began in 1982, when the New York Mets (NL) signed him for $600 a month plus an $85,000 bonus. After spending 1982 in the lower minor leagues, he compiled an outstanding 19–4 record and 300 strikeouts in just 191 innings for Little Falls, NY (NYPL) in 1983.

The rangy, 6-foot 3-inch, 190-pound moundsman with a fluid pitching motion joined the New York Mets in 1984 and became an instant sensation. His great poise, crackling 95-mph fastball, and good curveball enabled the 19-year-old Gooden to win 17 games and lead the NL with 276 strikeouts in just 218 innings. Gooden's ratio of 11.39 strikeouts per nine innings marked the best in major league history to that point for a starter. Gooden, an excellent batsman, won NL Rookie of the Year honors and became the youngest player to appear in an All-Star Game. In 1985, NL batters found him almost unhittable, as he led the senior circuit in wins (24), complete games (16), strikeouts (268), and ERA (1.53). The unanimous NL Cy Young* Award selection seemed ready to dominate the game, but the 1986 campaign marked a different story. Although Gooden helped the New York Mets reach the World Series with a 17–6 record, his performance dropped off noticeably. He began to experience off-the-field problems, including a bout with drugs. Gooden no longer dominated games, as his fastball lost much of its natural movement, his strikeouts declined, and his ERA ballooned. Subsequent seasons saw him frequently on the disabled list. Nevertheless, Gooden maintained winning records and in 1991 signed a three-year contract with the New York Mets for $15.45 million.

From 1992 through 1994, Gooden lost more games than he won. The erosion of the New York Mets as a team and the possible overuse of his pitching arm at too young an age may have contributed to his declining performance. In June 1994, Gooden was suspended for substance abuse. The suspension was extended to include the entire 1995 season. In February 1996, the New York Yankees (AL) signed Gooden as a free agent. He hurled a 2–0 no-hit victory against the Seattle Mariners on May 14, 1996 and finished with an 11–7 record, but did not appear in the playoffs. Injuries limited him to a 9–5 record in 1997. In December 1997, he joined the Cleveland Indians (AL) as a free agent. Gooden compiled on 8–6 mark in 1998, helping Cleveland capture the AL Central Division. Gooden maintains an outstanding 188–107 mark, a .637 winning percentage, and 2,238 strikeouts and only 910 walks in 2,695.2 innings. He has compiled a 0–1 record and 2.04 ERA in the 1986 and 1988 NL Championship Series and a 0–2 mark and 8.00 ERA in the 1986 World Series against the Boston Red Sox. He hurled one game without a decision and compiled a 1.59 ERA in the 1997 AL Division Series against the Cleveland Indians. Gooden pitched less than one inning of Game 2 in the 1998 AL Division Series against the Boston Red Sox, being ejected by umpire Joe Brinkman when John Valentin was called safe at home plate. He lost one decision in the AL Championship Series against the New York Yankees with a 5.79 ERA in 4.2 innings. Despite his decline, the tall, handsome flamethrower remains a formidable presence in the game. In November 1999, he filed for free agency.

Gooden married Monica Colleen Harris in November 1987 and has three children, Dwight, Jr., Ashley, and Ariel.

BIBLIOGRAPHY: John Benson et al., *Baseball's Top 100* (Wilton, CT, 1997); Tom Callahan, "Doctor K Is King of the Hill," *Time* 127 (April 7, 1986), pp. 54–58+; *CB* (1986), pp. 177–180; M. Geffner, "Nothing Special," *Sport* 82 (June 1991), pp. 61–66; Jordan A. Deutsch, *Dwight Gooden* (New York, 1986); C. Horowitz, "Undamned Yankee," *NY* 29 (August 12, 1996), pp. 22–29; Barry Jacobs, "Baseball's Youngest Legend," *SEP* 258 (July–August 1986), pp. 54–55; J. S. Kunen, "Say it Ain't Show Doc!," *PW* 27 (April 20, 1987), pp. 123–124; Mike Lupica, "Fear Strikes Out Again," *Esquire* 113 (May 1990), pp. 71–73; W. Nack, "The Good Doctor Has a Bad Scrape," *SI* 66 (January 5, 1987), pp. 28–30; Dwight Gooden file, National Baseball Library, Cooperstown, NY; Craig Neff, "Doctor K: Awesome and Then Some," *SI* 63 (September 2, 1985), pp. 14–19; E. M. Swift, "So Good, So Young," *SI* 62 (April 15, 1985), pp. 28–32+; Tom Verducci, "From Phenom to Phantom," *SI* 78 (March 22, 1993), pp. 34–37; Tom Verducci, "The High Price of Hard Living," *SI* 82 (February 27, 1995), pp. 16–24; Tom Verducci, "A New High," *SI* (May 27, 1996), pp. 32–34; Ralph Wiley, "Doc and Darryl," *SI* 69 (July 11, 1988), pp. 70–74+; Steve Wulf, "A Crash Landing for an Ace," *SI* 66 (April 13, 1987), pp. 32–34; Ken Young, *Cy Young Award Winners* (New York, 1994).

Frank P. Bowles

GOODMAN, Ival Richard "Goody" (b. July 23, 1908, Northview, MO; d. November 25, 1984, Cincinnati, OH), player, scout, and manager, participated in four sports in Poteau, OK. The St. Louis Cardinals (NL) signed him and optioned him to WA clubs at Shawnee, OK, Ft. Smith, AZ, and Bartlesville, OK from 1930 to 1932. After being promoted to Columbus, OH (AA) in 1932, Goodman played for Houston, TX (TL) in 1933 and

Rochester, NY (IL) in 1933 and 1934. His .331 batting average with 19 HR interested the Cincinnati Reds (NL), who purchased his contract for $20,000. During the off-season, he worked in the Oklahoma oilfields and found his exceptional footspeed aided him in some risky assignments.

From 1935 to 1942, the left-handed hitting, 5-foot 10-inch, 170-pound Goodman started in right field for the Cincinnati Reds. The consistent hitter and excellent outfielder helped the Reds win the 1939 and 1940 NL pennants and 1940 World Series against the Detroit Tigers. He led the NL in triples in 1935 and 1936, set a Cincinnati team record for HR with 30 in 1938, and batted .323 in 1939 to help the Reds capture their first NL crown since 1919. Goodman batted .295 in his two World Series appearances and made the NL All-Star team in 1938 and 1939.

Injuries hindered Goodman's career. Once he was beaned while running to first base by catcher Mickey Owen. In the 1939 All-Star game, he injured a shoulder diving for a ball and never again played with his former ability. Goodman ended his major league career with the Chicago Cubs (NL) in 1943 and 1944, quiting after another beaning and brain concussion. His major league career included a .281 batting average, 85 triples, 95 HR, and 525 RBI in 1,107 games. In 1959 he was inducted into the Cincinnati Reds Hall of Fame.

Goodman managed Portsmouth, VA (PiL) to its first pennant in 30 years in 1945 and served as player–manager at Dayton, OH (OSL) in 1946. Goodman worked for the Rinaldi Chemical Company in Cincinnati for the next 25 years and scouted for the Chicago Cubs. Goodman married Harriet Cook in October 1939 and had a son, Ival, Jr., and two daughters, Janet and Carol Ann. He was survived by his second wife, Rose.

Blood clots caused the amputation of Goodman's right leg in 1970, but he still donated his time to the BPY organization and threw out the first pitch for the sixth game of the 1972 World Series.

BIBLIOGRAPHY: Ival Goodman file, National Baseball Library, Cooperstown, NY; *Cincinnati Reds Yearbook, 1960*; Lee Allen, *The Cincinnati Reds* (New York, 1948); *Cincinnati Enquirer*, November 27, 1984.

Richard D. Miller

GOODMAN, William Dale "Billy" (b. March 22, 1926, Concord, NC; d. October 1, 1984, Sarasota, FL), player, manager, coach, and scout, was the son of Fred Grady Goodman and Margie (Barringer) Goodman. He played textile league baseball around Concord, NC and graduated from Winecoff High School in 1944. He married Margaret Little on October 25, 1947 and had two children, Kathy and Robert.

The left-handed-hitting Goodman entered professional baseball with the Atlanta, GA Crackers (SL), batting .336 in 1944. After serving in the U.S. Navy, he returned to the Atlanta Crackers and batted .389 in an abbreviated 1946 season. The Boston Red Sox (AL) acquired him prior to the 1947 season for an estimated $70,000, but he spent most of the year at Louisville, KY (AA) and hit .340. Goodman made the major leagues permanently in 1948 and batted .310 for Boston, sharing fourth place in the voting for Major League Rookie of the Year.

Goodman overcame some limitations to become a Red Sox mainstay for almost a decade. The 5-foot 11-inch, 165 pounder possessed little power, only average speed, and a mediocre throwing arm. Nonetheless, he proved a skillful hitter who could spray singles and doubles all over the field and a sure-handed and versatile fielder. Goodman, the consummate utility player, demonstrated competence at second base, first base, third base, and the out-field. His best season occurred in 1950. Pressed into full-time duty when outfielder Ted Williams* was injured in the All-Star game, Goodman led the AL with a .354 batting average and finished second to Phil Rizzuto* in the AL MVP race. Goodman placed third in AL batting in 1953 with a .313 average and made the AL All-Star team in 1949 and 1953.

Goodman was traded to the Baltimore Orioles (AL) in June 1957 and Chicago White Sox (AL) in December 1957. Although past his peak, he helped the White Sox win the 1959 AL pennant and batted .231 in his only World Series against the Los Angeles Dodgers. Goodman finished his major league career in 1962 with the expansion Houston Colt 45s (NL). He retired with a lifetime .300 batting average, 1,691 hits, and 591 RBI, but only 19 HR.

Goodman continued in baseball as the player–manager of the Durham, NC Bulls (CrL) in 1963 and 1964 and the manager of Cocoa, FL (FSL) in 1965. His three-year managing record included 184 wins and 228 losses. He also scouted and coached for the Boston Red Sox, Kansas City Athletics (AL), and Atlanta Braves (NL) minor league systems in the late 1960s. Goodman, who died at his longtime off-season Sarasota, FL home after a year-long bout with cancer, is a member of the North Carolina Sports Hall of Fame.

BIBLIOGRAPHY: William Goodman file, National Baseball Library, Cooperstown, NY; Al Hirshberg, "This Modest Young Guy in the Outfield," *SEP* 223 (March 17, 1951), pp. 34, 141–144; Donald Honig, *Baseball Between the Lines* (New York, 1976); "Solid Substitute," *Time* 56 (September 18, 1950), pp. 59–60; Jim L. Sumner, "Billy Goodman," *TNP* 13 (1993), pp. 87–89; *TSN*, February 19, 1947, p. 11, August 9, 1950, p. 11, September 13, 1950, p. 3, April 1, 1953, p. 3, February 22, 1956, p. 7, December 24, 1958, p. 21; Rich Westcott, *Diamond Greats* (Westport, CT, 1988); Peter Golenbock, *Fenway* (New York, 1992); Robert Redmount, *The Red Sox Encyclopedia* (Champaign, IL, 1998).

Jim L. Sumner

GORDON, Joseph Lowell "Joe," "Flash" (b. February 18, 1915, Los Angeles, CA; d. April 14, 1978, Sacramento, CA), player, scout, coach, and manager, was a right-handed–hitting second baseman. He and his older brother, Jack, were brought up by their widowed mother, Louise (Evans) Gordon. He graduated from the University of Oregon in 1939 and married Dorothy Crum on June 3, 1938. They had two children, Judy and Joseph.

Gordon played for Oakland, CA (PCL) in 1936 and Newark, NJ (IL) in 1937. He advanced to the New York Yankees (AL) in 1938 and played seven years there through 1946 except for two years in wartime military service. The Yankees traded Gordon in October 1946 to the Cleveland Indians (AL), for whom he played from 1947 to 1950. The 5-foot 10-inch, 175-pound Gordon, a spectacular, acrobatic second baseman, led the AL four times in double-play participation and assists and once in putouts. Gordon's wide range partly caused him to lead the AL four times in errors and to average 24 miscues per season for 11 major league years.

Gordon hit very hard for a middle infielder and ranked among the first five AL batters in several statistics, including finishing second in HR with 29 in 1947 and 32 in 1948 and fourth in batting with .322 in 1942. The winner of the 1942 AL MVP Award, he played in six World Series and nine All-Star games and hit .500 in the 1941 World Series against the Brooklyn Dodgers. Overall, Gordon batted .268 with 264 doubles, 52 triples, 253 HR, and 975 RBI. His .970 fielding average included 264 career errors. He played for Sacramento, CA (PCL) in 1951 and 1952 and made a token appearance with San Francisco, CA (PCL) in 1953.

Gordon managed Sacramento (PCL) in 1951 and 1952 and San Francisco (PCL) in 1957, finishing first there. After scouting for the Detroit Tigers (AL) from 1953 to 1955, he coached for them in 1956. He piloted the Cleveland Indians (AL) from 1958 to 1960, with his club finishing second to the Chicago White Sox in 1959. General Manager Frank Lane* found Gordon incompatible and traded him in August 1960 for manager Jimmy Dykes* of the Detroit Tigers. Gordon managed the Kansas City Athletics (AL) in 1961, but impatient new owner Charles Finley* soon jettisoned him. From mid-1961 through 1968, he scouted for the Los Angeles Angels (AL). He piloted the 1969 Kansas City Royals (AL) in their inaugural season and resumed scouting for the Los Angeles Angels until 1972. In five years at the helm of major league clubs, Gordon compiled a 305–308 win–loss mark. Subsequently, he became a very successful land salesman for the California-based Joe French Realty Company and sold over a $1 million worth of mostly ranch land.

BIBLIOGRAPHY: *The Baseball Encyclopedia*, 10th ed. (New York, 1996); Joseph Gordon file, National Baseball Library, Cooperstown, NY; Thomas Aylesworth and Benton Minks, *The Encyclopedia of Baseball Managers* (New York, 1990); Franklin Lewis, *The Cleveland Indians* (New York, 1949); John Thorn et al., eds., *Total Indians* (New York, 1996); Russell Schneider, *The Boys of Summer of '48* (Champaign, IL, 1998); John Phillips, *Winners* (Cabin John, MD, 1987); Mark Gallagher, *The Yankee Encyclopedia*, vol. 3 (Champaign, IL, 1997); Dave Anderson et al., *The Yankees* (New York, 1978); Joseph Gordon file, *TSN* Archives, St. Louis, MO; *TSN Official Baseball Register, 1960*.
Lowell L. Blaisdell

GORDON, Sidney "Sid" (b. August 13, 1917, New York, NY; d. June 17, 1975, New York, NY), player and coach, was the son of Jewish parents, Morris Gordon and Rose Gordon. His father worked as a plumber and owned a coal business. Gordon grew up in the New York City borough of Brooklyn, graduating from Samuel Tilden High School. A high school and semiprofessional baseball star, he signed a professional contract in 1938 with the New York Giants (NL) organization. Gordon spent from 1938 to 1941 in the minor leagues with Milford, DE (ESL), Clinton, IA (3IL), and Jersey City, NJ (IL).

At the end of the 1941 season, Gordon joined the New York Giants for nine NL games. After spending most of the 1942 season at Jersey City, he played in a few games for New York that year. In 1943 Gordon appeared in 131 games for the Giants, dividing his time between third base, first base, and the outfield, but he missed the 1944 and 1945 seasons due to U.S. Coast Guard service. From 1946 to 1949, he performed again as a Giants regular. Although primarily used in the outfield in 1946 and 1947, he moved to third base for the 1948 and 1949 seasons. A multiplayer trade sent Gordon to the Boston Braves (NL) in December 1949. Gordon returned to the outfield in Boston and accompanied the Braves when they moved to Milwaukee (NL) in 1953. In December 1953, Milwaukee traded Gordon to the Pittsburgh Pirates (NL). Gordon remained at Pittsburgh until May 1955 and finished his major league career that season with the Giants.

A left fielder–third baseman, Gordon compensated for a lack of speed with hustle. He led NL outfielders in fielding average in 1952 and third basemen in 1948. Gordon's hitting, rather than defensive skills, earned him All-Star Game selections in 1948 and 1949. The muscular 5 foot 10 inch, 185 pound, right-handed Gordon hit with power and consistency. He slugged 25 or more HR five times and surpassed 100 RBI in three different seasons. In 1950, Gordon tied the then major league record with 4 grand-slam HR in a season. During 13 major league campaigns covering 1,475 games, Gordon achieved a .283 career batting average, amassed 220 doubles, connected for 202 HR, knocked in 805 runs, and scored 735 times. Gordon recorded more than twice as many walks (731) as strikeouts (356).

Gordon married Mary Goldberg in November 1940. After serving as a player–coach for the Miami, FL Marlins (IL) during the 1956 season, he became a life insurance underwriter for Mutual of New York. Gordon assisted the Jewish Education Committee and other Jewish groups. From Hank Greenberg's* retirement to Sandy Koufax's* ascent to stardom, Gordon and Cleveland Indians (AL) third baseman Al Rosen* were baseball's most prominent Jewish standard bearers.

BIBLIOGRAPHY: Sidney Gordon file, National Baseball Library, Cooperstown, NY; Bernard Postal et al., *Encyclopedia of Jews in Sport* (New York, 1965); Harold Ribalow, *The Jew in American Sports*, rev. ed. (New York, 1954); Robert Slater, *Great Jews in Sports* (Middle Village, NY, 1983); Frank Graham, *The New York Giants* (New York, 1952); Noel Hynd, *The Giants of the Polo Grounds* (New York, 1988); Fred Stein,

570   GORE, GEORGE

Under Coogan's Bluff (Glenshaw, PA, 1978); Gary Caruso, *The Braves Encyclopedia* (Philadelphia, PA, 1995).

William M. Simons

GORE, George "Piano Legs" (b. May 3, 1857, Saccarappa, ME; d. September 16, 1933, Utica, NY), player and manager, grew up in Hartland, ME, where he attracted attention as a hard-hitting, left-handed batting ballplayer. The 5-foot 11-inch, 195-pound Gore entered organized baseball in the early years of the professional game as an outfielder with the Fall River, MA and New Bedford, MA teams in 1877–1878. His lusty hitting and strong throwing arm interested Albert G. Spalding,* co-owner of the Chicago White Stockings (NL), who signed Gore to a $1,900 contract.

After batting .263 with the 1879 Chicago White Stockings, Gore posted an NL-leading .360 batting average as leadoff man in 1880 for the first of three consecutive NL pennant-winning clubs. He also led the NL with a .399 on-base percentage and .463 slugging percentage. Gore paced the NL in runs scored twice (1880, 1881) and walks three times (1882, 1884, 1886). Chicago's title reign ended in 1883. The 1885–1886 White Stockings won two more NL titles, as Gore batted .313 and .304. Although Gore had compiled five consecutive .300-plus batting efforts, Chicago released him for excessive drinking and womanizing.

After the New York Giants (NL) signed him, Gore batted .290 in 1887 and helped the club land consecutive pennants for the next two seasons. In 1890 he played for the New York Giants (PL), batting .318 with a .499 slugging average. On rejoining the New York Giants (NL) in 1891, Gore batted .284. The following year New York dealt the fading star to the St. Louis Browns (NL), where he batted .205 and briefly managed that hapless team. Gore retired from the major leagues after the 1892 season, having played with seven champion NL squads in his 14-year career.

The versatile Gore posted a lifetime .301 batting average and set several long-standing records, including five assists, seven stolen bases, and five extra base hits in particular games. Between 1879 and 1891, he averaged over 100 hits a season and ranked among the premier base stealers and run scorers of his era. Indeed, modern statisticians list the leadoff batter among the dozen best offensive players of his era. He worked in a paper mill near Hartland, ME and later resided at the Masonic Home in Utica, NY.

BIBLIOGRAPHY: Will Anderson, *Was Baseball Really Invented in Maine?* (Portland, ME, 1992); Eddie Gold and Art Ahrens, *The Golden Era Cubs, 1876–1940* (Chicago, IL, 1985); Warren Brown, *The Chicago Cubs* (New York, 1946); Warren Wilbert and William Hageman, *Chicago Cubs: Seasons at the Summit* (Champaign, IL, 1997); Noel Hynd, *The Giants of the Polo Grounds* (New York, 1988); James D. Hardy, Jr., *The New York Giants Baseball Club* (Jefferson, NC, 1996); George Gore file, National Baseball Library, Cooperstown, NY; Adrian C. Anson, *A Ball Player's Career* (Chicago, IL, 1900); Albert G. Spalding, *America's National Game* (New York, 1911); John

Thorn et al., eds., *Total Baseball*, 5th ed. (New York, 1997); Robert L. Tiemann and Mark Rucker, eds., *Nineteenth Century Stars* (Kansas City, MO, 1989); vol. 2 David Quentin Voigt, *American Baseball*, vol. 2 (University Park, PA, 1983).

David Q. Voigt

GOSLIN, Leon Allen "Goose" (b. October 16, 1900, Salem, NJ; d. May 15, 1971, Bridgeton, NJ), player and manager, was the son of James Goslin, a farmer and trapper, and Rachel (Baker) Goslin and grew up on a New Jersey dairy farm. He developed his strength and size through performing various farm chores. His father sold the farm in 1917 and moved to Salem, NJ where Goslin attended high school. In 1917, Goslin joined the semipro Salem, NJ All-Stars as a 16-year-old pitcher for $3 a game. The next year, Goslin pitched for an industrial league team and impressed professional scouts with his baseball skills. The talented pitcher entered pro baseball with the Columbia, SC club (SAL) in 1920. Goslin, who threw right and batted left-handed, often pinch-hit and played the outfield when not pitching. In 1921, he was switched permanently to the outfield and led the SAL in runs scored, hits, RBI, and .390 batting average. At age 21, the 5-foot 11-inch, 180-pound Goslin was purchased for $7,000 by the Washington Senators (AL). He in 1922 enjoyed a .324 batting average, his first of 11 seasons with at least a .300 mark. Two years later, he batted .344 and led the AL with 129 RBI. Eleven times Goslin knocked in at least 100 runs in a season. Goslin led the AL in triples in 1923 and 1925 and saw his batting average climb to .354 in 1926 and a .379 peak in 1928, stroking a single in his final at bat to edge Heinie Manush* by one point for the AL batting title. In 1928, he injured his arm in spring training by trying to throw a medicine ball like a baseball. The injury nagged him all season, causing him to experiment throwing left-handed and nearly ending his baseball career.

After being traded to the St. Louis Browns (AL) in June 1930, Goslin returned to the Senators in December 1932. Goslin slugged three HR in one game three times and led the Senators to three AL pennants (1924–1925, 1933) and a world championship (1924). He belted three HR in both the 1924 and 1925 World Series and another in the 1933 classic. In 1924, he made four hits in Game 4 and set a record for most consecutive hits in one series (six). Goslin was traded to the Detroit Tigers (AL) in December 1933 and helped lead the Tigers to two straight pennants (1934–1935). Goslin in 1935 drove home Mickey Cochrane* with a ninth-inning single in the sixth and decisive game to win the championship over the Chicago Cubs. In 32 World Series games, Goslin collected 37 hits and a .287 batting average. When Detroit released him in 1938, he signed with the Senators and played in only 38 games. Goslin served as player–manager (1939–1941) for Trenton, NJ (ISL), leading his teams to second, third, and fourth place finishes. Following his retirement from baseball, Goslin operated a boat and fishing tackle rental business in the Salem, NJ area. Goslin, who married Marian

Wallace in December 1940, was elected to the National Baseball Hall of Fame in 1968.

An AL outfielder for 18 seasons, Goslin ranks high on the all-time major league lists in several categories. He recorded 2,735 hits, 4,325 total bases, 1,609 RBI (20th), 500 doubles, and 173 triples (22nd), and in 1934 hit safely in 30 consecutive games. In 2,287 career games, he scored 1,483 runs, slugged 248 HR, and compiled a .316 lifetime batting and .500 slugging average. The free-spirited Goslin devised a striped bat in 1932 to confuse opposition pitchers and fielders, but the "zebra bat" caused such heated controversy that AL president Will Harridge* ruled it illegal.

BIBLIOGRAPHY: Goose Goslin file, National Baseball Library, Cooperstown, NY; Bill Borst, ed., *Ables to Zoldak*, vol. 1 (St. Louis, MO, 1988); Frederick G. Lieb, *The Detroit Tigers* (New York, 1946); Gene Karst and Martin J. Jones, Jr., *Who's Who in Professional Baseball* (New Rochelle, NY, 1973); Craig Carter, ed., *TSN Daguerreotypes*, 8th ed. (St. Louis, MO, 1990); A. W. Laird, *Ranking Baseball's Elite* (Jefferson, NC, 1990); New York *World*, July 29, 1928; *The Baseball Encyclopedia*, 10th ed. (New York, 1996); Lowell Reidenbaugh, *Baseball's Hall of Fame-Cooperstown* (New York, 1993); Shirley Povich, *The Washington Senators* (New York, 1954); Fred Smith, *995 Tigers* (Detroit, MI, 1981); Lawrence S. Ritter, *The Glory of Their Times* (New York, 1966); Salem (NJ) *Sunbeam*, May 17, 1971; *TSN Official Baseball Record Book 1998*.

David S. Matz and John L. Evers

GOSSAGE, Richard Michael "Goose" (b. July 5, 1951, Colorado Springs, CO), player, is the son of landscaper Jack Gossage and Sue Gossage. At Wasson High School in Colorado Springs, Gossage starred in baseball and basketball. After his father died, Gossage signed as a pitcher with the Chicago White Sox (AL) in the 1970 free agent draft following graduation instead of accepting a college basketball scholarship. The 6-foot 3-inch, 180-pound right-hander subsequently attended Southern Colorado State College and entered pro baseball with Sarasota, FL (GCL) in 1970. With Appleton, WI (ML) in 1971, Gossage compiled an 18–2 win–loss record and was named Player of the Year. In 1972 for the White Sox, he finished with a 7–1 record as a relief pitcher. After pitching with average success for Des Moines–based Iowa (AA) and Chicago in 1973 and 1974 mostly in the minor leagues, Gossage was named Fireman of the Year in 1975 by earning 26 saves for the White Sox. He slumped to a 9–17 record as a starter in 1976 and was traded that December to the Pittsburgh Pirates (NL). He responded with 26 saves and established an NL record for most strikeouts by a relief pitcher in one season (151). Unable to agree on contract terms, Gossage signed with the New York Yankees (AL) as a free agent in November 1977.

With the Yankees between 1978 and 1983, Gossage compiled a 41–28 record and saved 150 games. He led the AL in saves in 1978 and 1980 and was named 1978 Fireman of the Year. Gossage compiled a 1–0 record in six World Series appearances for the Yankees (1978, 1981) and did not allow a single run. A nine-time All Star (1975–1978, 1980–1982, 1984–1985), Gossage was the losing pitcher for the AL in 1978 and gained the save for the NL in 1984. Granted free agency in 1983, Gossage signed a multimillion dollar contract with the San Diego Padres (NL) in January 1984. He led the Padres to the NL pennant with a 10–6 regular season record and 25 saves, but his team lost to the Detroit Tigers in the World Series. In 1985, he compiled a 5–3 mark, 1.82 ERA, and 26 saves in 50 appearances. The Padres suspended Gossage for a portion of the 1986 season, but he still recorded 21 saves.

His saves totals steadily declined thereafter. In February 1988, the San Diego Padres traded him to the Chicago Cubs (NL). Gossage split 1989 between the San Francisco Giants (NL) and New York Yankees (AL), spent 1991 with the Texas Rangers (AL), played 1992 and 1993 with the Oakland A's (AL), and ended his major league career in 1994 with the Seattle Mariners (AL).

During his 22 year major league career, Gossage pitched 1,809 innings in 1,002 games, allowed 732 walks, and struck out 1,502 batters. He compiled a 3.01 ERA, a 124–107 win–loss record, and 310 saves.

Gossage's greatest assets as a pitcher included fear and intimidation. He threw a baseball upwards of 100 miles per hour and the batter knew it, making Gossage fully confident he could get the batter out. Although deadly serious and mean when pitching, he was mild, meek, and friendly around the clubhouse and at home with his wife, Cornelia, and sons, Jeff and Keith.

BIBLIOGRAPHY: Goose Gossage file, National Baseball Library, Cooperstown, NY; G. Castle, "The Goose Again," *Sport* 80 (March 1989), pp. 38–40; Mark Gallagher, *The Yankee Encyclopedia*, vol. 3 (Champaign, IL, 1997); Bob Cairns, *Pen Men* (New York, 1993); Tom Cushman, "Going with Goose," *TSN*, April 9, 1984, p. 3; A. W. Laird, *Ranking Baseball's Elite* (Jefferson, NC, 1990); Phil Pepe, "Golden Goose-Gossage Is Yanks' Bird of Paradise," *TSN*, August 22, 1981, pp. 2, 30; Phil Pepe, "The Goose Fires Golden Eggs for Yankees," *TSN*, September 30, 1978, p. 3; *TSN Official Baseball Register, 1994*, Tom Verducci, "Making Hay," *SI* 81 (September 12, 1994), pp. 68–70.

John L. Evers

GOWDY, Henry Morgan "Hank" (b. August 24, 1889, Columbus OH; d. August 1, 1966, Columbus, OH), player, coach, scout, and manager, was the son of Horace "Harry" Gowdy and Caroline (Burkhart) Gowdy and played football, basketball, and baseball at North High School in Columbus. After playing minor league baseball in 1908 and 1909 with Lancaster, OH (OSL), he in 1910 led the TL with a .312 batting average at Dallas. His first major league experience came briefly at first base for the New York Giants (NL) in 1910 and 1911. In July 1911, Gowdy was traded to the Boston Braves (NL). Manager Johnny Kling* made him a catcher in 1912 and optioned him to the Buffalo, NY Bisons (IL) in 1913. He returned to the Boston

Braves from 1914 until 1923, rejecting a $30,000 offer to jump to the FL. After moving back to the New York Giants from 1923 to 1925, Gowdy rejoined the Boston Braves for 1929 and 1930. He finished his major league career with a .270 batting average in 1,050 games, playing in over 100 games only from 1914 through 1916.

Gowdy, a popular after-dinner speaker, was the leading star of the 1914 World Series for the "Miracle Braves" against the Philadelphia Athletics, hitting .545 (then a World Series record) with a 1.182 slugging average, three doubles, a triple, a HR, and five walks in four games. Along with manager George Stallings,* Pat Moran,* and Johnny Evers,* he pioneered in using combination signals behind the plate. He met less fortune for the New York Giants in the 1924 World Series against the Washington Senators. Besides batting only .259 with one RBI, Gowdy in the 12th inning of the seventh game stumbled over his mask after Muddy Ruel* hit a pop foul. Ruel then doubled and scored the winning run on Earl NcNeely's bad-hop single over third baseman Fred Lindstrom's* head.

Gowdy coached baseball at several colleges and also managed Columbus, OH (AA) in 1926, Minneapolis, MN (AA) in 1926 and 1927, Rochester, NY (IL) in 1928, Dayton, OH (CL) in 1949, and Oklahoma City, OK (TL) in 1950. He coached for several NL clubs, including the Boston Braves (1929–1937), Cincinnati Reds (1938–1942, 1945–1946), and New York Giants (1947–1948), managing Cincinnati for four games in 1946. Gowdy also served briefly in the Cleveland Indians (AL) farm system and scouted in both the major and minor leagues in the 1950s. His last organized baseball assignment came as a scout for the New York Giants in 1958. He married Pauline Emma Walsh of Columbus, OH on May 26, 1920. They had no children.

Gowdy, the first professional baseball player to serve in World War I, enlisted as a private and soon rose to sergeant. He was sent to France in October 1917, fighting at Château-Thierry, St. Mihiel, Champaigne, Lorraine, and the Argonne Forest. After the armistce, he served with the occupation army. In March 1925, Gowdy experienced the proudest moment of his life. The baseball field at Fort Benning, GA, the site of a school for infantry officers, was named Gowdy Field.

In 1942, Gowdy volunteered for duty in World War II at age 53. He was assigned to Fort Benning in special services and conducted the baseball program for the infantry school.

BIBLIOGRAPHY: Hank Gowdy file, National Baseball Library, Cooperstown, NY; John Thorn et al., eds., *Total Baseball*, 5th ed. (New York, 1997); Mike Shatzkin, ed., *The Ballplayers* (New York, 1990); John D. Stevens, "Hero of the AEF: Hank Gowdy," *Timeline* (March–April 1996), pp. 51–54; "How My Career Has Been Uncommonly Lucky: From an Interview with 'Hank' Gowdy," *BM* 33 (July 1924), pp. 344, 374; *BM* 20 (January 1918), pp. 266, 302; *BM* 22 (December 1918), pp. 76–78, 112; *BM* 18 (May 1917), pp. 507, 530; John Thorn et al., eds., *Total Braves* (New

York, 1996); Gary Caruso, *The Braves Encyclopedia* (Philadelphia, PA, 1995); Harold Kaese, *The Boston Braves* (New York, 1948); Noel Hynd, *The Giants of the Polo Grounds* (New York, 1988).

Victor Rosenberg

GRACE, Mark Eugene (b. June 28, 1964, Winston-Salem, NC), player, is the son of Gene Grace and Sharon (Cloe) Grace and grew up in California. After graduating from Tustin, CA High School in 1982, he attended Saddleback College in Mission Viejo, CA and majored in Business Administration at San Diego State University. The Minnesota Twins (AL) drafted Grace in 1984, but he did not sign a contract. The following year, the Chicago Cubs drafted him in the 24th round. Grace turned professional this time and began his playing career at Peoria, IL (ML) in 1986, winning the ML batting title with a .342 mark. In 1987, he played for Pittsfield, MA (EL) and was voted the EL's MVP. He started the 1988 season for Des Moines–based Iowa (AA), but was promoted by the Cubs in early May.

Through the 1999 season with Chicago, Grace has compiled a .310 batting average with 415 doubles, 137 HR, and 922 RBI in 1,767 games. In 1995, he led the NL in doubles with 51 and batted .326. He paced the Cubs with a career-high .331 batting average in 1996 followed by .319 in 1997. His .309 batting average, 39 doubles, 17 HR, and 89 RBI helped the Cubs reach the NL Division Series as a wild card. Atlanta Braves hurlers held Grace to just one hit in the NL Division Series. In 11 seasons, Grace has finished among the top ten NL batters eight times. An excellent fielding first baseman, the 6-foot 2-inch, 190-pound left-hander has compiled a career .995 fielding average and won Rawlings Gold Glove awards in 1992, 1993, 1995, and 1996. He made All-Star appearances in 1993, 1995, and 1997. In the 1989 NL Championship Series, he made 11 hits for a .647 batting average with 8 RBI. After the 1992 season, he traveled to Japan with a Major League All-Star team and was named tour MVP. Grace ranked first in hits (1,754) and doubles (364) and third in games played (1,491) in the 1990s.

Grace filed for free agency in 1994 and 1995, but the Cubs resigned him both times. A great fan favorite, he attributes his popularity to his "old fashioned, dirty uniform" style of play. He is divorced from his wife, Michelle, and lives in Chicago during the off-season. He participates in several charitable activities, including the Amyotrophic Lateral Sclerosis Foundation and Easter Seals.

BIBLIOGRAPHY: Mark Grace file, National Baseball Library, Cooperstown, NY; G. Castle, "Beers with . . . Mark Grace," *Sport* 81 (July 1990), pp. 21–23; *Chicago Cubs Media Guide, 1998*; Chicago *Tribune*, February 28, 1988, March 14, 1989, November 9, 1992, April 9, 1995, September 17, 1995; John Thorn et al., eds., *Total Baseball*, 5th ed. (New York, 1997); *The Baseball Encyclopedia*, 10th ed. (New York, 1996); Warren Wilbert and William Hageman, *Chicago Cubs: Seasons at the Summit* (Champaign, IL, 1997).

John E. Findling

GRANT, James Timothy "Mudcat" (b. August 13, 1935, Lacoochie, FL), player, is the son of James Grant, who died when Grant was a child, and Viola Grant, a domestic who reared seven children. Grant began working as a 13 year old in a lumber mill in Lacoochie and attended segregated Moore Academy, where he starred in all major sports. Florida A&M University awarded him a football scholarship, but he soon left there to help support his family. Grant's first break came when scout Fred Merkle,* who had seen him play third base in high school, invited him to attend a Cleveland Indians (AL) minor league camp in 1954. Nothing pleased Grant more for his childhood hero was Indian Larry Doby.*

In 1954, the Cleveland Indians made the 18-year-old, powerful 6-foot 1-inch, 186-pound right-hander a pitcher and optioned him to Fargo, ND–Moorhead, MN (NoL), where he won 21 games. Three years later for San Diego, CA (PCL), he compiled an 18–7 record with a 2.32 ERA. From 1958 to 1964, Grant won 67 contests and lost 63 for the Indians. In 1961, he led Indians pitchers with a 15–9 mark and a 3.86 ERA. After Grant suffered two consecutive losing seasons, the financially strapped Indians traded him in June 1964 to the Minnesota Twins (AL) for Lee Stange, George Banks, and about $100,000.

Benefiting from the instruction of pitching coach Johnny Sain,* Grant achieved his most productive years with the Minnesota Twins. The 1965 campaign marked by far his best season. He carried the Twins to the AL pennant, leading the AL with 21 victories, a .750 winning percentage and six shutouts. Grant reserved his top performances against the AL's four best teams, whom he defeated 11 times. He also pitched in the 1965 All-Star game. In the 1965 World Series against the Los Angeles Dodgers, Grant earned two of the Twins' three victories and hit a HR in the sixth game. No AL pitcher had homered in a World Series since 1920. Grant remained with the Minnesota Twins through the 1967 season. He hurled for the Los Angeles Dodgers (NL) in 1968, Montreal Expos (NL) and St. Louis Cardinals (NL) in 1969, Oakland Athletics (AL) in 1970, Pittsburgh Pirates (NL) in 1970 and 1971, and Oakland in 1971. In 1970, Grant contributed substantially as a reliever to the Pirates' quest for the NL pennant. The lateness of his joining Pittsburgh, however, kept him out of the NL Championship Series. During his major league career, the good hitting and fielding Grant won 145 and lost 119 with a 3.63 ERA in 571 games.

The genial, community oriented, and talented stage performer became a television broadcaster of Cleveland Indians games in the 1970s. Grant organized Slugout, a private company, in the 1980s to overcome illiteracy and drugs in the Los Angeles area. He married Lucille Teamor on October 20, 1962, but that marriage ended in divorce. His personal life has undergone undeterminable changes, leaving Grant with 12 grandchildren.

BIBLIOGRAPHY: James Grant file, National Baseball Library, Cooperstown, NY; *TSN*, February 1, 1964, October 9, 1965; Larry Moffi and Jonathan Kronstadt, *Crossing the Line* (Jefferson, NC, 1994); Jack Torry, *Endless Summers* (South Bend,

IN, 1995); Terry Pluto, *The Curse of Rocky Colavito* (New York, 1994); David S. Neft and Richard M. Cohen, *The Sports Encyclopedia: Baseball*, 15th ed. (New York, 1995); Bill Deane, letter to James N. Giglio, April 24, 1996.

James N. Giglio

GRANT, Ulysses F. "Frank" (b. August 1, 1865, Pittsfield, MA; d. May 27, 1937, New York, NY), player, was the son of Franklin Grant and was probably the best of the black players in organized baseball during the 19th century before the color line was drawn. Grant, whose father died in 1865, was primarily a second baseman, but played all infield positions and the outfield during six years in the minor leagues. As a teenager, he pitched and caught for amateur clubs in Pittsfield, MA, and Plattsburg, NY. He began his professional career with Meriden, CT (EL) in 1866, but the club folded in mid-season. Grant was then signed by Buffalo, NY (IA) and led the Bisons with a .344 batting average. The following year, he again led Buffalo batters with a .353 mark. Despite his small stature, the 5-foot 7½ inch, 155 pounder led the IA in slugging with 27 doubles, 10 triples, and 11 HR in 105 games.

In 1888 Grant topped the Bisons again by batting .346 in 95 games, mostly as an outfielder. The next year he could not reach contract terms with the Bisons and signed with the Cuban Giants, the preeminent 19th century black team. The Giants represented Trenton, NJ (MSL) that summer. Grant spent 1890 with Harrisburg, PA (EIL, AtA).

In his last year in white leagues (1891), he again played for the all-black Cuban Giants, who represented Ansonia, CT (CtSL). After the circuit dissolved in July, Grant and the Cuban Giants returned to barnstorming. Grant starred as a second baseman for the Cuban Giants for several years and spent his last year as a professional (1903) with the Lansing, MI Colored Capital All-Americans.

Like the handful of other black players in white leagues during the 19th century, Grant suffered much discrimination on and off the field. Some white pitchers consistently threw at him, while base runners often tried to spike him at second base. Grant, whose Buffalo teammates refused to be photographed with him in 1888, sometimes was refused service at hotels and restaurants. Despite these handicaps, he earned the complimentary sobriquet "the black Dunlap." (Fred Dunlap* of the St. Louis Browns was acknowledged as the best second baseman during the 1880s.) He worked as a waiter for a catering service for 36 years in New York City until his death of arteriosclerosis.

BIBLIOGRAPHY: Jerry Malloy, "Out at Home," *TNP* 2 (Fall 1982), pp. 14–28; Robert W. Peterson, correspondence with Merl Kleinknecht, Raymond J. Nemec, and Joseph M. Overfield, Robert W. Peterson Collection, Ramsey, NJ; Robert W. Peterson, *Only the Ball Was White* (Englewood Cliffs, NJ, 1970); Frank Grant file, National Baseball Library, Cooperstown, NY; James A. Riley, *The Biographical Encyclopedia of the Negro Baseball Leagues* (New York, 1994); Robert L. Tiemann and Mark Rucker, eds., *Nineteenth Century Stars* (Kansas City, MO, 1989); Sol White, *History of Colored Base Ball* (Philadelphia, PA, 1907).

Robert W. Peterson

GRANTHAM, George Farley "Boots" (b. May 20, 1900, Galena, KS; d. March 16, 1954, Kingman, AZ), player, performed as a versatile infielder for 13 NL seasons with a .302 career batting average. A left-handed hitter, he primarily played the unusual combination of first base and second base.

Grantham attended grammar and high school in Flagstaff, AZ and made his minor league baseball debut with Tacoma, WA (PIL) in 1920. After playing in 1921 with Portland, OR (PIL), he batted .359 and recorded 160 RBI as third baseman for Omaha, NE (WL) in 1922. His major league debut came with the Chicago Cubs (NL) on September 22, 1922. Grantham led the NL in strikeouts in 1923 and 1924. In October 1924, Chicago traded Grantham in a controversial deal to the Pittsburgh Pirates (NL) for shortstop Rabbit Maranville,* first baseman Charley Grimm,* and others. With the Pirates, the 5-foot 10-inch, 170-pound infielder appeared in the 1925 World Series against the Washington Senators and the 1927 World Series against the New York Yankees. Grantham batted over .300 in each of his seven seasons with Pittsburgh. Pittsburgh sold him to the Cincinnati Reds (NL) in February 1932. Grantham concluded his major league career with the New York Giants (NL) in 1934.

In 1,444 major league games, Grantham compiled a .461 slugging average. His appearances included 848 games at second base, 502 at first base, and the remainder at third base and in the outfield. Grantham's best year came in 1925, when he batted .326 for the world champion Pirates. He stole 43 bases for the 1923 Cubs in his first full major league season, but proved erratic defensively. Grantham subsequently lived in Kingman, AZ.

BIBLIOGRAPHY: George Grantham file, National Baseball Library, Cooperstown, NY; *The Baseball Encyclopedia*, 10th ed. (New York, 1996); Eddie Gold and Art Ahrens, *The Golden Era Cubs, 1876–1940* (Chicago, IL, 1985); Frederick G. Lieb, *The Pittsburgh Pirates* (New York, 1948); Richard L. Burtt, *The Pittsburgh Pirates, A Pictorial History* (Virginia Beach, VA, 1977); John Thorn et al., eds., *Total Baseball*, 5th ed. (New York, 1997); *WWIB*, 1927, 12th ed.

Robert B. Van Atta

GREEN, George Dallas, Jr. (b. August 4, 1934, Newport, DE), player, manager, scout, and executive, is the son of George Dallas Green, Sr. and Mayannah Sealy (Jones) Green. After graduating from Conrad High School in Wilmington, DE, Green in 1981 earned a Bachelor of Science degree from the University of Delaware. He married Sylvia Lowe Taylor on January 31, 1958 and has two daughters, Dana and Kim, and two sons, John, a minor league pitcher, and Douglas.

The Philadelphia Phillies (NL) signed the 6-foot 5-inch, 210-pound right-handed pitcher in 1955. He began his professional baseball career that season with Reidsville, NC (CrL) and Mattoon, IL (MOVL). Green hurled for Salt Lake City, UT (PrL) in 1956, Miami, FL (IL) and High Point-Thomasville, NC (CrL) in 1957, Miami in 1958, and Buffalo, NY (IL) in 1959 and 1960 before being promoted to the Philadelphia Phillies. He pitched parts of eight seasons in the major leagues, compiling a 20–22 lifetime record in 185 games. He hurled for Philadelphia from 1960 to 1964 and in 1967, the Washington Senators (AL) in 1965, and the New York Mets (NL) in 1966. Green also performed minor league stints with Little Rock–based Arkansas (PCL) in 1964 and 1965, San Diego, CA (PCL) in 1966, and Reading, PA (EL) in 1967 as a player–coach. During his minor league career, he compiled a 90–54 record in 201 games.

Green began his managerial career with Huron, SD (NoL) in 1968 and guided Pulaski, VA (ApL) to an ApL championship in 1969, garnering Manager of the Year honors. In 1970, he became assistant director of minor leagues for the Philadelphia Phillies. Philadelphia promoted Green to director of the minor leagues in 1972 and field manager in 1979. In 1980 he guided the Phillies to a 91–71 mark and the NL title, becoming the fourth rookie manager to lead his club to a World Series Championship. The Phillies defeated the Kansas City Royals in six games. Green in 1982 joined the Chicago Cubs (NL) organization, spending six years as general manager and serving as president from 1985 to 1987. *TSN* named him Baseball Executive of the Year in 1984, as he helped shape the first Chicago Cubs squad since 1945 to compete in post-season play. The San Diego Padres defeated Chicago in the NL Championship Series. The New York Yankees (AL) appointed Green manager in 1988, but fired him during the season. Green scouted for the New York Mets (NL) organization from 1991 to 1993 and was named their field manager in 1993. Green, who compiled a career 454–478 major league managerial record, was replaced by Bobby Valentine in August 1996. He rejoined the Phillies in 1999 as senior advisor to the general manager.

BIBLIOGRAPHY: Dallas Green file, National Baseball Library, Cooperstown, NY; Elliot Asinof, "On the Spot," *NYT Magazine*, March 26, 1989, pp. 28–31ff; Eddie Gold and Art Ahrens, *The New Era Cubs, 1941–1985* (Chicago, IL, 1985); *New York Mets Information Guide*, 1995; *TSN Official Baseball Register*, 1996; WWA, 42nd ed. (1982–1983), p. 1292; Rich Westcott and Frank Bilovsky, *The New Phillies Encyclopedia* (Philadelphia, PA, 1993); Allen Lewis, *The Philadelphia Phillies: A Pictorial History* (Virginia Beach, VA, 1981).

John L. Evers

GREENBERG, Henry Benjamin "Hank," "Hammerin' Hank" (b. January 1, 1911, New York, NY; d. September 4, 1986, Beverly Hills, CA), player and executive, was the son of Rumanian Jewish immigrants David Greenberg and Sarah Greenberg. His father owned a cloth-shrinking business. After graduating from New York City's James Monroe High School in 1929, he

attended New York University for a semester. Greenberg married Carol
Gimbel, the department store heiress, in February 1946. The couple had
three children before divorcing. He married Mary Jo Tarola in 1966.

Four varsity high school letters, an athletic scholarship from New York
University, and overtures from professional baseball teams resulted less from
natural grace than from size, strength, constant practice, and applied intelligence. Regarding Lou Gehrig* as a permanent fixture at first base, the 6-
foot 4-inch, 215-pound Greenberg rejected an offer from New York Yankees
scout Paul Krichell and instead signed with the Detroit Tigers (AL) organization. Aside from two seasons in the outfield later in his career, Greenberg
remained at first base throughout his playing days. He spent from 1930
through 1932 in the minor leagues, playing sequentially for Hartford, CT
(EL), Raleigh, NC (PiL), Evansville, IN (3IL), and Beaumont, TX (TL).
Greenberg appeared in a single game for Detroit in September, 1930, and,
except for U.S. Army duty from 1941 to 1945, starred for the Tigers from
1933 to 1946. During World War II Greenberg served in the China-Burma-
India theater with the first B-29 unit to go overseas. In 1947, he concluded
his playing career with the Pittsburgh Pirates (NL).

Hired by Cleveland Indians (AL) owner Bill Veeck* for the front office
in 1948, he soon became the Indians' general manager. Leaders in the campaign to integrate baseball racially, the Indians won AL pennants in 1948
and 1954 and set attendance records. Following Veeck to Chicago (AL),
Greenberg joined the White Sox in 1958 as part-owner and vice-president.
In 1959, the White Sox won their first AL pennant in 40 years. After severing his relationship with the White Sox in 1961, he became a successful
investment banker in New York City and later moved to Beverly Hills, CA.

Due to four and one-half seasons lost to military service during World
War II at the peak of his talents, Greenberg's career 331 HR and 1,276 RBI
do not fully reflect his stature as a player. Despite the relative brevity of his
career (the equivalent of 10 full seasons), Greenberg became baseball's original "Hammerin' Hank" and ranks with the most powerful sluggers who
ever played the game. After sharing the AL HR title with Jimmie Foxx* in
1935, he won the AL HR crown outright in 1938, 1940, and 1946. No right-
handed batter surpassed his 1938 total of 58 HR until Mark McGwire* and
Sammy Sosa* in 1998. Greenberg drove in more runs than any other AL
player four times (1935, 1937, 1940, and 1946). His 1937 183 RBI came
within one of the AL record. In addition, he led the AL in doubles twice
(1934, 1940) and runs scored once (1938). The generally steady but unspectacular fielder compensated for limited range through diligence and determination. Greenberg, nevertheless, paced first basemen in putouts twice,
fielding average once, and assists twice. He also led the AL in errors twice,
once each as a first baseman and an outfielder. In 1935 and 1940 he received
the AL MVP Award. Only four players have exceeded Greenberg's career
.605 slugging percentage. Besides playing on four AL pennant-winning

teams (1934–1935, 1940, 1945), he compiled a career .313 batting average. In 1,394 games, he made 1,628 hits and slammed 379 doubles.

Greenberg, elected to the National Baseball Hall of Fame in 1956, helped institutionalize the power hitting popularized by Babe Ruth* in the 1920s as a major element of strategy and promotion. He also served as an ethnic standard-bearer for co-religionists seeking assurance that Judaism and American secularism were compatible. Amid the rising anti-Semitism of the 1930s, Greenberg's baseball heroics took on symbolic meaning for many Jewish Americans.

BIBLIOGRAPHY: John Benson et al., *Baseball's Top 100* (Wilton, CT, 1997); Seymour Brody, *Jewish Heroes in America* (New York, 1991); Hank Greenberg file, National Baseball Library, Cooperstown, NY; Bob Broeg, *Super Stars of Baseball* (St. Louis, MO, 1971); Arthur Daley, *Kings of the Home Run* (New York, 1962); Jack Drees and James Miller, *Where Is He Now?* (New York, 1973); Hank Greenberg, *Hank Greenberg* (New York, 1989); Zander Hollander and Larry Fox, *The Home Run Story* (New York, 1966); Donald Honig, *The Power Hitters* (St. Louis, MO, 1989); Ralph Kiner, "Unforgettable Hank Greenberg," *RD* 133 (October 1988), pp. 83–87; Erwin Lynn, *The Jewish Baseball Hall of Fame* (New York, 1987); *NYT*, September 5, 1986, p. A-1; Frederick G. Lieb, *The Detroit Tigers* (New York, 1946); Fred Smith, *995 Tigers* (Detroit, MI, 1981); William M. Anderson, *The Detroit Tigers* (South Bend, IN, 1996); Richard Bak, *A Place for Summer* (Detroit, MI, 1998); John Thorn et al., eds., *Total Indians* (New York, 1996); William Simons, "The Athlete as Jewish Standard Bearer," *JSS* 44 (Spring 1982), pp. 95–112; Joseph J. Vecchione, *The New York Times Book of Sports Legends* (New York, 1991).

William M. Simons

GREENLEE, William Augustus "Gus," "Big Red" (b. 1897, Marion, NC; d. July 10, 1952, Pittsburgh, PA), baseball executive and boxing promoter, was known by nearly everyone in black Pittsburgh. Some patronized his nightclubs, others drank his bootleg liquor, while many more spent money on his numbers operations. Above all, they recognized Greenlee as black Pittsburgh's leading sportsman of the 1930s. They cheered his stable of boxers, especially John Henry Lewis (IS), and witnessed numerous sporting events that he promoted at Greenlee Field. During the 1930s, black Pittsburgh knew Greenlee as owner of the Pittsburgh Crawfords (NNL). Although two of his brothers became doctors and a third practiced law, Greenlee left college after one year and became black Pittsburgh's "Mr. Big." With over 200 pounds padding his 6-foot 3-inch frame, he commanded attention both in the rackets and in local politics.

The son of a masonry contractor, Greenlee was born in a log cabin and joined the migration north in 1916. Greenlee settled in Pittsburgh, where he shined shoes, worked at a steel mill, and drove a taxi. After serving overseas during World War I, Greenlee bootlegged liquor and operated nightclubs. His best-known establishment, the world-renowned Crawford Grill, became a mecca for jazz afficionados and the hub of his numbers operation.

The Crawfords, one of the area's top sandlot teams, asked Greenlee in 1931 to become their owner. Before Greenlee arrived, the team relied mainly on local black youths. Greenlee built the club into one of the finest ever assembled and champions of the NNL by 1935. Between 1931 and 1938, Greenlee owned the Crawfords with future Hall of Famers Oscar Charleston,* Judy Johnson,* Cool Papa Bell,* Satchel Paige,* and Josh Gibson.* In 1932 Greenlee constructed one of the nation's finest black-controlled stadiums in the city's Hill District.

Greenlee not only promoted the Crawfords, but resurrected the NNL. The NNL broke ground for black professional sport in the 1930s, achieving financial stability and public presence unprecedented for a black sporting venture. Greenlee served as NNL architect and president during the league's first five seasons. His biggest contribution may have been the creation in 1933 of an annual All-Star game, the East-West classic, in which black baseball's best players displayed their talents.

In 1937 Paige, Bell, and several other teammates decimated the Crawfords by jumping to the Dominican Republic to play for General Trujillo. Greenlee quit the NNL a season later, disbanded the Crawfords, and razed Greenlee Field, which never had become solvent. Greenlee, as promoter, sponsored Lewis, who became the first American black light-heavyweight champion by defeating Bob Olin in St. Louis, MO on October 31, 1935.

Greenlee reentered black baseball in 1945 by forming the USL, a rival black circuit linked with Brooklyn Dodgers general manager Branch Rickey.* Considered by many a stalking horse for Rickey's plans to integrate baseball, the USL folded after two seasons. Greenlee then retreated to the Crawford Grill, which was destroyed by fire in 1951. White numbers men cut into his numbers operations, while the federal government pursued him over unpaid income taxes.

BIBLIOGRAPHY: James Bankes, *The Pittsburgh Crawfords* (Dubuque, IA, 1991); Janet Bruce, *The Kansas City Monarchs* (Lawrence, KS, 1985); John B. Holway, *Blackball Stars* (Westport, CT, 1988); John N. Ingham and Lynne B. Feldman, *African-American Business Leaders* (Westport, CT, 1994); Robert W. Peterson, *Only the Ball Was White* (Englewood Cliffs, NJ, 1970); James A. Riley, *The Biographical Encyclopedia of the Negro Baseball Leagues* (New York, 1994); Donn Rogosin, *Invisible Men: Life in Baseball's Negro Leagues* (New York, 1983); Robert L. Ruck, *Sandlot Seasons: Sport in Black Pittsburgh* (Champaign, IL, 1986); M. Santa Maria, "King of the Hill," *AV* 6 (June 1991), pp. 20–24.

Robert L. Ruck

GREENWELL, Michael Lewis "Mike" (b. July 18, 1963, Louisville, KY), player, graduated in 1982 from North Fort Myers, FL High School, where he starred in baseball. The Boston Red Sox (AL) drafted Greenwell in the third round in June 1982 and assigned the 6-foot, 205-pound infielder to

Elmira, NY (NYPL). Greenwell, who batted left-handed and threw right-handed, played the outfield at Winston-Salem, NC (CrL) in 1983 and 1984 and spent the next two seasons at Pawtucket, RI (IL) with two brief stints with the Boston Red Sox. His first three major league hits were HR, the initial blast winning a 13-inning September 1985 game against the Toronto Blue Jays. The Boston Red Sox used Greenwell as a pinch hitter against the California Angels in the 1986 AL Championship Series and New York Mets in the World Series.

Greenwell, among baseball's best hitters, swung smoothly like George Brett* and exhibited patience, seldom striking out. In 1987 he finished third in the AL Rookie of the Year balloting, batting a career-best .328 with 31 doubles, 19 HR, and 89 RBI. He replaced left fielder Jim Rice* in 1988, hitting .325 and attaining career highs in hits (192), doubles (39), triples (8), HR (22), RBI (119), walks (87), and stolen bases (16). Boston captured the AL East Division crown, as Greenwell led the AL with 23 game-winning RBI and made the first of two consecutive AL All-Star appearances. The Oakland A's defeated the Boston Red Sox in the AL Championship Series, limiting Greenwell to one HR and three RBI. Greenwell's postseason honors included making the *TSN* AL All-Star and Silver Slugger teams. In 1989, he batted .308 with 14 HR and 95 RBI.

Greenwell's power production declined thereafter because a foot injury forced him to stop using his rear foot as a springboard during his swing. In 1990, his .297 batting average, 14 HR, and 73 RBI helped the Boston Red Sox garner another AL East Division title. The Oakland A's held Greenwell hitless in the AL Championship Series. Greenwell hit .300 with 83 RBI in 1991, but belted only nine HR. Elbow and knee surgery sidelined him much of 1992, but Greenwell batted .315 with 38 doubles, 13 HR, and 72 RBI in 1993. The Boston Red Sox finished second in the AL East Division for the wild card in 1995, with Greenwell batting .297 with 15 HR and 76 RBI. The Cleveland Indians limited him to a .200 batting average in the 1995 AL Division Series. His last major league season came in 1996, when injuries limited him to 77 games.

In 12 major league seasons, Greenwell batted .303 with 275 doubles, 130 HR, and 726 RBI. He struck out in only seven percent of his at bats, but possessed a weak arm and lacked speed. He and his wife, Tracy, have one son, Bo, and reside in Cape Coral, FL.

BIBLIOGRAPHY: Mike Greenwell file, National Baseball Library, Cooperstown, NY; Peter Golenbock, *Fenway* (New York, 1992); Robert Redmount, *The Red Sox Encyclopedia* (Champaign, IL, 1998); John Hough, *A Player for a Moment* (San Diego, CA, 1988); *1994 Baseball Almanac*; Mike Shatzkin, ed., *The Ballplayers* (New York, 1990); Dan Shaughnessy, *The Curse of the Bambino* (New York, 1990); Dan Shaughnessy, *One Strike Away* (New York, 1987); *TSN Official Baseball Register*, 1997.

David L. Porter

GRICH, Robert Anthony "Bobby" (b. January 15, 1949, Muskegon, MI), player, grew up in Long Beach, CA and starred in baseball, basketball, and football at Woodrow Wilson High School there. As a senior in 1967, Grich earned All-CIF first team honors as a shortstop. Additionally, he was selected first team All-City quarterback, second team All-City on the basketball team, and Long Beach, CA Player of the Year. Grich led his American Legion baseball team to a second-place finish in the 1966 California state tournament.

Following Grich's high school graduation, he attended the University of California at Los Angeles (UCLA) and Fresno State University. The University of Southern California and UCLA both offered Grich football scholarships. He opted for baseball, however, when the Baltimore Orioles (AL) drafted him in the first round. After being signed by scouts Al Kubski and Bobby Mattick, the 6-foot 2-inch, 190-pound Grich soon showed signs of greatness. In 1969 with Dallas–Ft. Worth, TX, he shared the TL's MVP award. The following year, he appeared with the Baltimore Orioles (AL) in 30 games and contributed to that club's East Division championship. Although ineligible to play in postseason competition, Grich was rewarded with a championship ring by his Orioles teammates following their 1970 World Series victory over the Cincinnati Reds. Grich returned to the minor leagues with Rochester, NY (IL) the following year and won the IL's MVP Award and the *TSN* Minor League Player of the Year trophy. In 1971 he also married Martha "Marty" Johnston, his high school sweetheart.

Grich returned to the Baltimore Orioles in 1972 and made a considerable impact as an all-around player for the next 15 years. Grich set a major league record by committing the fewest errors in a season five times. During the 1974 season, he also established a modern record for most putouts by a second baseman (484). He paced AL second basemen in fielding percentage with .995 in 1973. In 1985, he led the AL second basemen in fielding percentage (.997) and committed only 2 errors in 606 chances. Grich held the major league record for career fielding percentage at second base (.984) and holds season marks for fielding percentage for 150 games or more (.995) and 100 games or more (.997). During the 1985–1986 seasons, Grich played 77 consecutive games without committing an error. Four Gold Glove awards were won by Grich.

Grich also honed his batting skills after joining the California Angels (AL) as a free agent in November 1976. In 1979, Grich hit 30 HR and drove in 101 runs. Following his 1980 selection as Century Club Athlete of the Year, Grich hit 22 HR to rank among the four AL leaders during the strike-shortened 1981 season. No second baseman had led the AL in HR since National Baseball Hall of Famer Nap Lajoie* had accomplished it for the Philadelphia Athletics (AL) in 1901. Also during 1980, Grich paced the AL with a .543 slugging percentage. Overall, he hit 320 doubles, 224 HR, batted .266, and made 1,833 hits.

Following his retirement from baseball in 1986, Grich pursued downhill skiing and golf and collected automobiles. The former four-time All Star also chaired the Orange County Chapter for Cystic Fibrosis and participated in fund-raisers for handicapped children.

BIBLIOGRAPHY: Robert Grich file, National Baseball Library, Cooperstown, NY; Ted Patterson, *The Baltimore Orioles* (Dallas, TX, 1995); James H. Bready, *Baseball in Baltimore* (Baltimore, MD, 1998); Joe Jares, "The Back Is Better Than Ever," *SI* 51 (July 16, 1979), p. 50; Dick Miller, "Grich, as in Rich, New Angel Money Man," *TSN*, June 30, 1979, p. 23; Dick Miller, "Never Be as Good as I Was," *TSN*, March 31, 1979, p. 38; Leigh Montville, "The First to Be Free," *SI* 72 (April 16, 1990), pp. 98–108; Tracy Ringolsby, "Bobby Grich: From Pits to Peaks," *TSN*, October 13, 1979, p. 21; Loel Schrader, "Grich Comes Back—For a Night," Long Beach (CA) *Press Telegram*, May 1, 1987; John Thorn et al., eds., *Total Baseball*, 5th ed. (New York, 1997).

Samuel O. Regalado

GRIFFEY, George Kenneth, Jr. "Ken" (b. November 21, 1969, Donora, PA), player, is a 6-foot 3-inch, 205-pound outfielder–DH who bats and throws left-handed. He is the son of George Kenneth Griffey, Sr.* and Alberta (Littleton) Griffey. His father served as the hitting coach for the Seattle Mariners (AL), Colorado Rockies (NL), and Cincinnati Reds (NL) and played outfield with four major league teams between 1973 and 1991. Griffey graduated from Moeller High School in Cincinnati, OH, where he played football and baseball. He and his wife, Melissa, have one son, Trey, and one daughter, Taryn.

The Seattle Mariners selected Griffey as the first overall pick of the June 1987 free-agent draft. He spent his first professional baseball season with Bellingham, WA (NWL) and split the 1988 campaign with San Bernadino, CA (CaL) and Burlington-based Vermont (EL). Griffey joined the Seattle Mariners in 1989 and on August 24, 1990 became part of the first father-son duo to play simultaneously in the major leagues. He and his father hit consecutive singles for the Seattle Mariners. Griffey batted a career-high .327 in 1991, scored 113 runs and made 180 hits in 1993, and clouted 49 HR with 146 RBI in 1996. He led the AL with 359 total bases in 1993 and 40 HR in 1994 and holds the Seattle franchise records for most runs, hits, HR, and RBI. Griffey, who tied the major league record for most consecutive games with one or more HR (8) in 1993, in 1996 agreed to a four year contract for $34 million to become the then highest paid player in baseball. Griffey, considered by many as the best all-around baseball player, became the third youngest player to reach 150 HR and has homered in every AL park.

After being sidelined between May 27 and August 15, 1995, Griffey led the Seattle Mariners over the New York Yankees in the AL Division Series. He batted .391 and belted five HR to tie a single series record for most HR. Seattle lost the AL Championship Series to the Cleveland Indians, but Griffey batted .333 with seven hits. His best season came in 1997, when he batted .304, led the AL with a career-high 56 HR and 147 RBI, and recorded a career-best 185 hits. In the AL Division Series against the Baltimore Orioles, he hit only .133 with two RBI. In 1998, he again paced the AL with 56 HR and finished third with 146 RBI. In 1999, he led the AL with 48 HR and shared third with 134 RBI. He has been selected for 10 All-Star games and was chosen MVP in 1992. Griffey, who has batted .476 in All-Star games through 1999, received the most votes in four All-Star games and holds the all-time record with 6,079,688 votes in 1994. Griffey, a Gold Glove winner for 10 consecutive years (1990–1999), made six *TSN* AL All-Star and Silver Slugger Teams (1991, 1993–1994, 1997–1999). In 1997, he was named BRWAA AL MVP and *TSN* Major League Player of the Year. He made the AP All-Star Team in 1999.

In 11 major league seasons through 1999, Griffey has scored 1,063 runs and made 1,742 hits in 1,535 games. He has batted .299 with 320 doubles, 30 triples, 398 HR (including 10 grand slam clouts), produced 1,152 RBI, and recorded 747 walks, 984 strikeouts, and 167 stolen bases. Griffey made Major League Baseball's All-Century Team.

BIBLIOGRAPHY: Ken Griffey, Jr. file, National Baseball Library, Cooperstown, NY; Barry Bloom, "Off the Record," *Sport* 88 (October 1997), pp. 70–74; *CB* (1996), pp. 175–179; D. Dieffenbach, "Ken Griffey, Jr.," *Sport* 85 (March 1994), pp. 20ff; D. Dieffenbach and Darryl Howerton, "The Strike Zone," *Sport* 87 (May 1996), pp. 26–30; "The Griffeys: Major League Baseball's First Father-Son Pair," *Ebony* 44 (September 1989), pp. 78ff; Hank Hersch, "Born to be a Big Leaguer," *SI* 68 (May 16, 1988), pp. 64ff; Ed Lucas and Paul Post, "Griffey, the King of Cardboard," *SCD* 25 (May 29, 1998), pp. 132–133; David L. Porter, ed., *African-American Sports Greats* (Westport, CT, 1995); Steve Ryan, "Chasing Maris' Home Run Record," *SCD* 24 (September 12, 1997), pp. 90–91; C. Smith, "Hey, Junior!" *Sport* 82 (March 1991), pp. 38–42; E. M. Swift, "Bringing Up Junior," *SI* 72 (May 7, 1990), pp. 38–42; Alan Shipnuck, "Junior Comes of Age," *SI* 81 (August 8, 1994), pp. 24–30; *TSN Official Baseball Register*, 1998; *USAT Baseball Weekly Almanac*, 1997; Tom Verducci, "Hitting His Prime," *SI* 86 (May 12, 1997), pp. 86–88.

John L. Evers

GRIFFEY, George Kenneth, Sr. "Ken" (b. April 10, 1950, Donora, PA), player and coach, was a 5-foot 11-inch, 190-pound outfielder–first baseman who threw and batted left-handed. Cincinnati sportswriter Earl Lawson had observed that Stan Musial* had put Donora, PA on the map, but Griffey kept it there. His father, "Buddy," had played on Musial's high school team. Griffey was also the son of Ruth (Bailey) Griffey. He made the All-State football team at the end position. Griffey's seeming preference for football, however, delayed his selection by the Cincinnati Reds (NL) until the 29th round of the June 1969 draft. Griffey reached the Cincinnati Reds permanently in 1974.

Griffey, a fast runner, batted consistently and lacked power. Reds manager Sparky Anderson* pressured Griffey to use his speed to fullest advantage, comparing him to Lou Brock.* Griffey batted between Pete Rose* and Joe Morgan* and starred for the Cincinnati Reds, winners of two consecutive world championships in 1975 and 1976. Griffey was selected six times for the All-Star Game and achieved his best batting average (.336) in 1976, being edged out for the championship on the last day. Unfortunately, Griffey sustained a severe injury to his left knee in 1979. The Reds, who refused to sign Griffey to a five-year contract, traded him to the New York Yankees (AL) in November 1981.

Griffey had played right field regularly for seven years with Cincinnati, but he joined a bedlam of mismatched players in New York. Manager Billy Martin* insisted on platooning him at first base and in the outfield. A disagreement with George Steinbrenner* resulted in Griffey being fined for missing a game. Griffey was traded to the Atlanta Braves (NL) in June 1986 and was reduced to a reserve role, although attaining the 2,000-hit level in July 1988. He was released by Atlanta and signed with the Cincinnati Reds in August 1988.

Griffey and his wife, the former Alberta Littleton, saw their oldest son, Ken, Jr.,* selected first in the baseball draft and achieve major league status as an outfielder with the Seattle Mariners (AL) by 1989. Griffey joined the Seattle Mariners in August 1990, making them the first father–son team to play simultaneously on the same major league team. Griffey batted .377 with 3 HR and 18 RBI in 21 games with Seattle in 1990 and saw limited action in 1991. Griffey retired after the 1991 season with a .296 batting average, 2,143 hits, 364 doubles, 152 HR, 859 RBI, and 200 stolen bases. He coached for the Seattle Mariners in 1993 and 1994, Colorado Rockies (NL) in 1996, and Cincinnati Reds since 1997.

BIBLIOGRAPHY: Ken Griffey, Sr. file, National Baseball Library, Cooperstown, NY; *The Baseball Encyclopedia*, 10th ed. (New York, 1996); *Cincinnati Reds Media Guide*, pp. 34–35; "The Griffeys: Major League Baseball's First Father-Son Pair," *Ebony* 44 (September 1989), pp. 78ff; Hank Hersch, "Born to be a Big Leaguer," *SI* 68 (May 16, 1988), pp. 64ff; Robert E. Kelly, *Baseball's Best* (Jefferson, NC, 1988); Greg Rhodes and John Erardi, *Big Red Dynasty* (Cincinnati, OH, 1997); Robert H. Walker, *Cincinnati and the Big Red Machine* (Bloomington, IN, 1988); Mark Gallagher, *The Yankee Encyclopedia*, vol. 3 (Champaign, IL, 1997); John Thorn et al., eds., *Total Baseball*, 5th ed. (New York, 1997); *TSN*, March 10, 1973, September 1, 1986, August 15, 1988; *TSN Baseball Register*, 1992; *WWIB*, 1990, 74th ed.

William J. Miller

GRIFFIN, Michael Joseph "Mike" (b. March 20, 1865, Utica, NY; d. April 10, 1908, Utica, NY), player and manager, generally was considered the best major league center fielder from 1887 to 1898. The son of an Irish-American cigarmaker, Griffin attended the Maryst School, spent four years in the Advanced School, and married Margaret Esther Barney in 1890. According to his sons, Griffin began his professional baseball career in 1884 and helped Utica, NY win an IL pennant in 1886. He played in three major leagues, with the Baltimore Orioles (AA) from 1887 to 1889, Philadelphia Quakers (PL) in 1890, and Brooklyn Bridegrooms (NL) from 1891 to 1898. Griffin led his position in fielding in 1892, 1894, 1895, and 1898 and combined outstanding defensive ability with speed and a potent bat. He led the AA in runs scored (152) in 1889, and the NL in doubles (36) in 1891. While captain for Brooklyn in 1898, he managed four games. He retired following the 1898 season, when Brooklyn sold him to the St. Louis Browns (NL) without his consent and under unacceptable conditions.

Griffin, who weighed 160 pounds, stood 5-feet 7-inches tall, and batted and threw right-handed, hit a HR on April 16, 1887 in his first major league at bat and may have been the first player to accomplish that feat. After hitting the HR in the first inning, Griffin made two more extra-base hits. He hit at least .300 five seasons, including .301 (1887), .358 (1894), .333 (1895), .308 (1896), and .316 (1897). His lifetime statistics included a .296 batting average, 1,753 hits, 313 doubles, 108 triples, .407 slugging average, and 1,405 runs scored in 1,511 games. Despite these achievements, he never played on a major league championship team. An early players' rights advocate, Griffin in 1892 protested the terms of his contract. *SL* on February 27, 1892 reported, "Griffin has already received the ultimatum of the club [Brooklyn] and must take the Southern trip or look for center field honors elsewhere." After voluntarily retiring in his prime, he became a part owner and vice president of the Consumers Brewery Company and was a salesman for the Gulf Brewing Company in Utica, NY and remained there until his death from pneumonia.

BIBLIOGRAPHY: Michael Griffin file, National Baseball Library, Cooperstown, NY; Al Kermisch, "From a Researcher's Notebook," *BRJ* 7 (1978), pp. 47–48; Craig Carter, ed., *TSN Daguerreotypes*, 8th ed. (St. Louis, MO, 1990); *The Baseball Encyclopedia*, 10th ed. (New York, 1996); Alfred H. Spink, *The National Game* (St. Louis, MO, 1911); *SL*, February 27, 1892, April 16, 1908; *TSN* undated supplement, 1899; Robert L. Tiemann and Mark Rucker, eds., *Nineteenth Century Stars* (Kansas City, MO, 1989); Frank Graham, *The Brooklyn Dodgers* (New York, 1945); William F. McNeil, *The Dodgers Encyclopedia* (Champaign, IL, 1997); James H. Bready, *Baseball in Baltimore* (Baltimore, MD, 1998); David Nemec, *The Beer and Whisky League* (New York, 1994).

Mark D. Rucker

GRIFFITH, Calvin Robertson, Sr. *See* Clark Calvin Griffith.

GRIFFITH, Clark Calvin "The Old Fox" (b. November 20, 1869, Clear Creek, MO; d. October 27, 1955, Washington, DC), player, manager, and owner, was the son of Isaiah Griffith, a commercial hunter and trapper, and Sarah (Wright) Griffith. He married Addie Ann Robertson in December 1900 and had no children. Upon the death of Mrs. Griffith's brother, they brought up seven nephews and nieces in their home. They officially adopted several of the children, including baseball executive **Calvin Robertson Griffith, Sr.** (b. December 11, 1911, Montreal, Canada; d. October 20, 1999, Melbourne, FL). Calvin's sister, Thelma, married Joe Cronin,* while his brother, Sherry Robertson, played with the Washington Senators (AL). His brothers, William and James Robertson, served as executives in the Senators organization.

Griffith spent his youth near America's prairie country in a log cabin and became a professional trapper by age 10. He contracted malaria at age 13, precipitating a family move to more urban Bloomington, IL. By age 18, he pitched professionally in Illinois and signed his first professional contract in 1888. Griffith, his era's premier pitcher, spent three seasons with Milwaukee, WI (WL) and jumped in 1891 to the newly formed AA with the St. Louis Browns and Boston Reds. When the AA folded, he compiled a 13–7 record for Tacoma, WA (PNL) in 1892 and a 30–18 mark for the Oakland, CA Oaks (PCL) in 1893. He led a players' strike against Oaks owners for back pay and joined other Oakland team members briefly as actors in San Francisco's Barbary Coast district. Griffith, nicknamed "The Old Fox," was signed by Adrian "Cap" Anson* for the Chicago Colts (NL) in 1893, remained there well into the 1900 season, and experienced many excellent years there. In 1900, he became a principal participant in the formation of the AL.

As vice-president of the BPPA, Griffith in 1900 led the National Leaguers in a revolt. Players demanded raising the salary ceiling to $3,000 a year and uniforms paid for and supplied by team owners. Griffith obtained a strict pledge from all BPPA members not to sign contracts without the group's advice and consent, leading to the availability of high quality players for the AL. Griffith helped AL president Ban Johnson* secure 39 major league stars and served as player–manager of the Chicago White Stockings franchise in 1901 and 1902. Although an excellent pitcher who compiled the AL's best winning percentage in 1901, Griffith appeared mainly in relief roles thereafter. He started 30 of 35 games in 1901, but relieved in 18 of his 25 appearances by the 1905 season. His celebrated, revolutionary reliance on relief pitching, a new pitching/managing philosophy shared by Griffith's staunchest rival, John McGraw,* had begun. Griffith subsequently developed baseball's first great relievers, Allan Russell and Fred Marberry,* with the Washington Senators (AL). During his 20-year pitching career, he won 237 games, lost only 146 contests, and compiled a 3.31 ERA.

From 1903 to 1908, Griffith served as player–manager of the New York Highlanders (AL) and was mistreated by the owners, press, and fans. Griffith managed the Cincinnati Reds (NL) from 1909 through 1911, taking with him a lifelong animosity toward the New York Yankees. AL president Johnson coaxed him back to manage the Washington Senators, an ailing franchise in the standings and at the bank. Griffith mortgaged some property and used all his available cash to rescue the club. Besides receiving 10 percent of the team's stock, he was elected to its board of directors in 1912. After three consecutive losing seasons and resultant arguments with other stockholders, Griffith bought a controlling share of the stock in 1920, resigned as field manager, and became club president. Financial strife did not end for Griffith, although the Senators won the AL pennant in 1924 and 1925. He shrewdly maneuvered players via the trading block and guided the club to the 1933 pennant, but thereafter never fielded contenders. His clubs won 1,491 of 2,916 games, for a .522 winning percentage.

Griffith developed outstanding post–World War I baseball talent, including Walter Johnson,* Joe Cronin, Fred Marberry, Bucky Harris,* and Leon "Goose" Goslin.* He welcomed any publicity and controversy, continually baiting umpires and utilizing a flamboyant, cunning "spitball" delivery. During his windup, he hid the ball with his body by bringing his leg up high and then cut the ball's hide on his spikes. Nevertheless, he led the movement in 1920 to enforce the ban of all forms of illegal pitches. Griffith's best pitch, the sinker, was learned from Charles "Old Hoss" Radbourne* before he signed his first contract. Griffith also helped invent the screwball with Christy Mathewson,* who called the pitch a "fadeaway." In 1894, as a publicity stunt, he became the first of many to "pitch" a baseball from the top of the Washington Monument. The first to use professional on-field entertainers, he hired former players Al Schact and Nick Altrock as baseball clowns. In 1934, he signed a pitcher from the House of David team so that he could claim the only bearded major league player. His administrative and scouting philosophies revolutionized baseball. He helped change the waiver rule governing the release and movement of players and establishing a single, base waiver claim fee. He signed the first modern-era player of Cuban descent (Armando Marsans) and imported several Latin Americans before and during World War II. He initiated use of a "speed gun" to time fastball pitcher Bob Feller* in a 1946 pre-game exhibition and frequently juggled Washington's pitching rotation to ensure weekend appearances for Walter Johnson,* his biggest gate attraction.

During both world wars, Griffith raised money to provide baseball equipment and related materials to American servicemen abroad, and converted the club's ballfield in Charlotte, NC into a camp for soldiers on weekend leave from boot camp. He befriended government officials and became baseball's permanent liaison with President Franklin Roosevelt. In 1918 he appealed the drafting of his star catcher, Eddie Ainsmith, creating a flood of anti-Griffith sentiment. During World War II, he lunched weekly with the Selective Service head and received short-term deferments for many better players. His clubs played 21 night games yearly during the war, although other teams were restricted to fourteen because of blackout requirements. In 1945 he signed pitcher Bert Shepard, who had lost his leg during the war after a promising minor league career. Although Shepard pitched in only one game for the Senators, Griffith believed that he could be an inspiration to other disabled veterans.

Calvin, Griffith's nephew and adopted son, played baseball at Staunton Military Academy and George Washington University. As a youngster, he served as Senators mascot and batboy. After selling peanuts and running errands for the front office staff, he quickly learned the baseball business and was hired by Clark as team secretary of the Chattanooga, TN Lookouts (SA) in 1935. In a surprise move, 25-year-old Calvin was named team president only two years later. During the early 1940s, he played semi-professional ball on a team organized by Joe Cambria, the Senators' chief Latin American scout. In 1942 he became head of the Senators' concessions. As his uncle grew older, Calvin assumed more responsibility for team operations. Upon Clark's death in 1955, Calvin became president of the Senators.

After several losing seasons and continued deficits inherited from his uncle, Calvin moved the AL team to Minnesota before the 1961 campaign and changed its name. Under Calvin, the Minnesota Twins became a powerful club with hitters Harmon Killebrew* and Tony Oliva.* The retirement of his better players, divisional reorganization, and the advent of free agency, however, renewed the club's money problems. Griffith continually sold his better players and prospects and ultimately fielded the youngest, least experienced team in either league. The last team organized by Griffith before he sold the franchise to Minneapolis banker Carl Polhad in 1984 managed an inspiring challenge for the divisional title before finishing second. Griffith remained with the franchise, coordinating and developing talent throughout the organization.

BIBLIOGRAPHY: Clark Griffith file, National Baseball Library, Cooperstown, NY; Calvin Griffith file, National Baseball Library, Cooperstown, NY; Anthony J. Connor, *Baseball for the Love of It* (New York, 1982); Glenn Dickey, *The History of American League Baseball* (New York, 1980); Richard Goldstein, *Spartan Seasons* (New York, 1980); Frederick Ivor-Campbell et al., eds., *Baseball's First Stars* (Cleveland, OH, 1996); John Kerr, *Calvin: Baseball's Last Dinosaur* (Dubuque, IA, 1990); Eddie Gold and Art Ahrens, *The Golden Era Cubs, 1876–1940* (Chicago, IL, 1985); Warren Brown, *The Chicago Cubs* (New York, 1946); Warren Wilbert and William Hageman, *Chicago Cubs: Seasons at the Summit* (Champaign, IL, 1997); Mark Gallagher, *The Yankee Encyclopedia*, vol. 3 (Champaign, IL, 1997); Frank Graham, *The New York Yankees* (New York, 1943); Gene Karst and Martin J. Jones, Jr., *Who's Who in Professional Baseball* (New Rochelle, NY, 1973); Craig Carter, ed., *TSN Daguerreotypes* (St. Louis, MO, 1990); William B. Mead, *The Worst Ten Years of Baseball* (New York, 1978); *NYT*, December 29, 1943, October 23–26, 28–29, November 1, 1955; Shirley Povich, *The Washington Senators* (New York, 1954); *NYT Biographical Service* 25 (September 1994), pp. 1412–1421; *The Baseball Encyclopedia*, 10th ed. (New York, 1996); Steven A. Reiss, *Touching Base* (Westport, CT, 1980); John Thorn, *The Relief Pitcher* (New York, 1979); *Time* 66 (November 7, 1955), p. 110; *TSN*, January 21, 1937.

                                                            Alan R. Asnen

GRIMES, Burleigh Arland "Ol' Stubblebeard" (b. August 18, 1893, Emerald, WI; d. December 6, 1985, Clear Lake, WI), player, manager, and scout, was the last legal major league spitball pitcher. He was the son of Nick Grimes, a dairy farmer, and Ruth (Tuttle) Grimes and attended Black Brook School in Clear Lake. He began his professional career with Eau Claire, WI (MWL) in 1912. Grimes also pitched at Ottumwa, IA (CA) in 1913, Chattanooga, TN (SA) in 1913–1914, Birmingham, AL (SA) from 1914 to 1916, and Richmond, VA (VL) in 1914. The Pittsburgh Pirates (NL) signed Grimes in 1916, but he lost 13 straight games for the last place club in 1917. With the Brooklyn Dodgers (NL) from 1918 to 1926, he enjoyed fine records of 23–11 (1920), 22–13 (1921), 21–18 (1923), and 22–13 (1924). Grimes pitched for the New York Giants (NL) in 1927 and the Pittsburgh Pirates in 1928 and 1929, compiling a 25–14 record in 1928. After joining the St. Louis Cardinals (NL) in 1930, he recorded 17 wins in 1931. He also hurled for the Chicago Cubs (NL) in 1932–1933, St. Louis (NL) in 1933–1934, and Pittsburgh (NL) in 1934.

His four World Series (1920, 1930–1932) resulted in a 3–4 overall record. Grimes defeated the Cleveland Indians in the second game of the 1920 World Series and the Philadelphia Athletics twice in the 1931 classic despite a severely inflamed appendix. His major league record included 270 career wins against 212 losses, 35 shutouts, 497 games started, 314 games completed, 1,512 strikeouts in 4,179.2 innings pitched, and a 3.53 ERA. Grimes led the NL four times in complete games (1921, 1923–1924, 1928), three times in games started (1923–1924, 1928) and innings pitched (1923–1924, 1928), twice in wins (1921, 1928), appearances (1918, 1928), and hits surrendered (1923–1924), and once each in winning percentage (1920) and strikeouts (1921).

After ending his major league career in 1934 with the New York Yankees (AL), he pitched and managed for Bloomington, IL (3IL) in 1938. He managed Louisville, KY (AA) in 1936, the Brooklyn Dodgers (NL) to a 130–171 record in 1937–1938, Montreal, Canada (IL) in 1939, Grand Rapids, MI (MISL) in 1940, Toronto, Canada (IL) in 1942–1944, 1947, and 1952–1953, and Rochester, NY (IL) in 1945–1946. Grimes also scouted for the New York Yankees (AL, 1947–1952), Kansas City Athletics (AL, 1956–1957), and Baltimore Orioles (AL, 1960–1971) and coached for Kansas City in 1955. Grimes served one year in the U.S. Navy (1918) and was elected to the National Baseball Hall of Fame in 1964. He married five times and had no children. His wives included Florence (1913–1931), Laura (1931–1939), Inez Martin (1940–1964), Zerita Brickell (1965–1974), and Lillian Gosselin (1975–1985).

BIBLIOGRAPHY: *SEAL*, vol. 1 (1981–1985), pp. 339–340; Burleigh Grimes Museum, Clear Lake, WI; Burleigh Grimes file, *TSN*, St. Louis, MO; Burleigh Grimes file, National Baseball Library, Cooperstown, NY; Donald Honig, *The Man in the Dugout* (Lincoln, NE, 1995); Frank Graham, *The Brooklyn Dodgers* (New York, 1945); Tom Meany, *Baseball's Greatest Pitchers* (New York, 1951); Richard Goldstein, *Superstars and Screwballs* (New York, 1991); William F. McNeil, *The Dodgers Encyclopedia*

(Champaign, IL, 1997); Gene Karst and Martin J. Jones, Jr., *Who's Who in Professional Baseball* (New Rochelle, NY, 1973); Eddie Gold and Art Ahrens, *The Golden Era Cubs, 1876–1940* (Chicago, IL, 1985); Tom Knight, "Burleigh Grimes," *TNP* 16 (1996), pp. 72–73; *The Baseball Encyclopedia*, 10th ed. (New York, 1996); *NYT*, December 7, 1985.

Horace R. Givens

GRIMM, Charles John "Charlie," "Jolly Cholly" (b. August 28, 1898, St. Louis, MO; d. November 15, 1983, Scottsdale, AZ), player, manager, coach, sportscaster, and executive, played sandlot baseball and worked as a batboy in Sportsman's Park in St. Louis. He entered professional baseball with the Philadelphia Athletics (AL), batting .091 in 12 games as an outfielder and pinch hitter in 1916. After performing with Durham, NC (NCL) as an outfielder, pitcher, and first baseman in 1917, he played 50 games the next year with the St. Louis Cardinals (NL) before being sent to Little Rock, AR (SA) for seasoning at first base. In 1919, he hit .285 and led SA first basemen in putouts and fielding average. Near the end of the season, Grimm was sold to the Pittsburgh Pirates (NL) for $3,500 and hit .318 in 12 games. From 1920 through 1924, the left-handed, 5-foot 11½-inch, 173 pounder started at first base for Pittsburgh and continued excelling defensively. He led NL first basemen in fielding in 1920, 1923 and 1924 and eventually improved his hitting, batting a career-high .345 with 99 RBI in 1923.

In October 1924, Grimm joined the Chicago Cubs (NL) in a six-player trade and spent the rest of his playing career (1925–1936) there. He led NL first basemen in fielding in 1928, 1930, 1931, and 1933, setting a major league record by leading seven seasons in fielding average. Although lacking power, he batted over .300 in four seasons for the Cubs (1925, 1927, 1931–1932), and hit .331 in 1931. Grimm played in two World Series with Chicago, hitting .389 and one HR in the 1929 loss to the Philadelphia Athletics and .333 in the New York Yankees' sweep in 1932. Grimm's .290 career batting average included 2,299 hits, 394 doubles, 108 triples, 79 HR, 908 runs scored, and 1,078 RBI. His .993 fielding percentage proved even more impressive, as his 20,711 putouts and 22,087 chances accepted remain close to major league records.

Grimm enjoyed a long managerial career. He served as player–manager of the Chicago Cubs from 1932 through 1936 and continued as bench pilot until July 1938. Chicago won NL pennants with 21 consecutive victories in 1932 and 100 triumphs in 1935. Grimm was replaced by Gabby Hartnett* as Cubs manager in July 1938 and spent the next two and one-half seasons in the broadcast booth. He returned to the Cubs as a coach briefly in 1941 and then managed Bill Veeck's* Milwaukee, WI club (AA) through 1943, capturing a pennant and the Little World Series that year. He returned as Cubs manager from 1944 through 1949 and won another pennant in 1945, but lost the World Series to the Detroit Tigers. Grimm moved to the Chicago Cubs front office in 1949, but a dispute with the club business manager caused him to quit. After managing Dallas, TX (TL) in 1950, he piloted Milwaukee again in 1951 and 1952 and won another AA pennant and Little World Series in 1951. In May 1952, he became manager of the Boston Braves (NL) and kept the job when the Braves moved to Milwaukee in 1952. Grimm's Braves finished as contenders from 1953 through 1955, but did not win an NL pennant. In 1956, Grimm was fired and returned to the Chicago Cubs. He served as vice-president from 1957 through 1959, managed for 17 games in 1960, shifted to the broadcast booth, and coached on the field in 1961. He rejoined the front office, serving in various capacities until 1981. During retirement, he worked as a special consultant to General Manager Dallas Greed.* Grimm, one of the baseball's most colorful and fun-loving figures and a highly competent player and manager (1,287 wins, 1,069 losses for a .547 winning percentage over 19 years), died of cancer.

BIBLIOGRAPHY: Charles Grimm file, National Baseball Library, Cooperstown, NY; Bob Buege, *The Milwaukee Braves: A Baseball Eulogy* (Milwaukee, WI, 1988): Thomas Aylesworth and Benton Minks, *The Encyclopedia of Baseball Managers* (New York, 1990); Eddie Gold and Art Ahrens, *The Golden Era Cubs, 1876–1940* (Chicago, IL, 1985); Warren Brown, *The Chicago Cubs* (New York, 1946); Craig Carter, ed., *TSN Daguerreotypes*, 8th ed. (St. Louis, MO, 1990); Gary Caruso, *The Braves Encyclopedia* (Philadelphia, PA, 1995); *NYT*, November 17, 1983; *The Baseball Encyclopedia*, 10th ed. (New York, 1996); *TSN*, November 1983.

Douglas D. Martin

GRIMSLEY, Ross Albert, II (b. January 7, 1950, Topeka, KS), player, was a 6-foot, 3-inch, 200-pound pitcher who threw and batted left-handed. His father, Ross Grimsley I, pitched minor league baseball for 16 years and appeared in seven games for the Chicago White Sox (AL) in 1951. Grimsley graduated from Frayser High School in Memphis, TN in 1968 and pitched American Legion Post No. 1 to the 1968 national championship.

The Cincinnati Reds (NL) selected Grimsley first in the free-agent draft. His rookie 1971 season with the Cincinnati Reds brought a 10–7 mark. Catcher Johnny Bench* proclaimed: "Man, does his fast ball move. . . . It jumps . . . right by 'em." Grimsley achieved a 14–8 record with a 3.05 ERA in 1972 and threw a two-hitter to defeat the Pittsburgh Pirates, 7–1, in the NL Championship Series. Manager Sparky Anderson* claimed that Grimsley pitched as fast as Steve Carlton* on certain days. Grimsley also won two games against the Oakland A's in the 1972 World Series. The Cincinnati Reds traded him to the Baltimore Orioles (AL) in December 1973. Grimsley in 1974 responded with an 18–13 mark and 3.07 ERA. He seemingly mastered the change-up, but unexpected control problems dropped him to a 10–13 mark in 1975 for his first losing record. Grimsley, who married Merriam G. Judy, compiled a 14–10 mark for the Orioles in 1977 and opted for free agency.

After signing with the Montreal Expos (NL), Grimsley achieved "one of those years where everything goes right." The 1978 campaign marked the pinnacle of Grimsley's career, as he boasted a 20–11 record with a 3.05 ERA. His 20th victory came against the Cardinals at St. Louis on the last day of the season. He made the 1978 NL All-Star team for the only time in his career. The city of Montreal designated him Player of the Year. Grimsley recorded just 10 wins in 1979, witnessing his zenith and his nadir in successive seasons. He was traded to the Cleveland Indians (AL) in July 1980 and returned to the Baltimore Orioles for 1982, spending his final major league season mostly as a reliever. During his major league career, Grimsley compiled a 124–99 career mark with a 3.81 ERA.

BIBLIOGRAPHY: Ross Grimsley file, National Baseball Library, Cooperstown, NY; John Thorn et al., eds., *Total Baseball*, 5th ed. (New York, 1997); *The Baseball Encyclopedia*, 10th ed. (New York, 1996); David S. Neft et al., eds., *The Sports Encyclopedia: Baseball*, 16th ed. (New York, 1996); Mike Shatzkin, ed., *The Ballplayers* (New York, 1990); *WWIB, 1981*; *TSN*, May 29, 1971, p. 41, October 28, 1972, June 23, 1973, June 21, 1975, p. 12, May 13, 1978, p. 3; *TSN Official Baseball Register, 1983*; Ted Patterson, *The Baltimore Orioles* (Dallas, TX, 1995); James H. Bready, *Baseball in Baltimore* (Baltimore, MD, 1998); Greg Rhodes and John Erardi, *Big Red Dynasty* (Cincinnati, OH, 1997); Robert H. Walker, *Cincinnati and the Big Red Machine* (Bloomington, IN, 1988).

William J. Miller

GRISSOM, Marquis Deon (b. April 17, 1967, Atlanta, GA), player, is the 15th of 16 children of a Ford plant assembly worker and graduated from Lakeshore High School in College Park, GA. Grissom majored in Business Communication at Florida A&M University, where he played baseball two seasons. The Montreal Expos (NL) selected the 5-foot 11-inch, 190-pound center fielder, who bats and throws right-handed, in the third round of the June 1988 draft. He spent under two minor league seasons with Jamestown, NY (NYPL) in 1988 and Jacksonville, FL (SL) and Indianapolis, IN (AA) in 1989 before joining the Montreal Expos.

Grissom, who remained with the Montreal Expos through 1994, led the NL in stolen bases (76) and outfield assists (15) in 1991 and with a career-high 78 stolen bases in 1992. His top season with the Expos came in 1993, when he batted .298 with 188 hits, 27 doubles, 19 HR, and a career-best 95 RBI. He appeared in the 1993 and 1994 All-Star Games, clouting a HR in the latter.

Grissom starred two seasons with the Atlanta Braves. In 1995, he batted .524 with 5 runs, 11 hits, two doubles, three HR, and four RBI in the NL Division Series against the Colorado Rockies and .263 in the NL Championship Series against the Cincinnati Reds. In the World Series triumph over the Cleveland Indians, he batted .360 with nine hits, a HR, and three stolen bases. His best major league campaign came in 1996, when he achieved career highs in batting average (.308), runs (106), hits (207), triples (10), and HR (23) and earned his fourth consecutive Gold Glove. He batted .286 with 10 hits, one HR, and three RBI in the NL Championship Series against the St. Louis Cardinals. His stellar World Series performance against the New York Yankees featured a .444 batting average with 12 hits, two doubles, a triple, and five RBI.

A blockbuster March 1997 deal sent Grissom and David Justice* to the Cleveland Indians (AL). Cleveland captured the AL Central Division in 1997, as Grissom batted .262 with 12 HR and 66 RBI. He hit .261 with one HR and four RBI in the AL Championship Series against the Baltimore Orioles. In the World Series, he batted .360 with two RBI and sparkled defensively against the Florida Marlins. Marlin pitchers halted his consecutive game World Series hitting streak at 15, two shy of the record. Cleveland traded him to the Milwaukee Brewers (NL) in December 1997.

In 11 major league seasons through 1999, Grissom has batted .277 with 1,550 hits, 131 HR, 601 RBI, and 382 stolen bases. The Fairburn, GA resident married Tia Bolden and has two children, D'Monte and Tiana.

BIBLIOGRAPHY: Marquis Grissom file, National Baseball Library, Cooperstown, NY; Leigh Montville, "We Are Family," *SI* 77 (September 28, 1992), pp. 38–41; *Atlanta Braves Media Guide*, 1997; *TSN Baseball Register*, 1998; John Thorn et al., eds., *Total Braves* (New York, 1996).

David L. Porter

GROH, Henry Knight "Heinie" (b. September 18, 1889, Rochester, NY; d. August 22, 1968, Cincinnati, OH), player, manager, and scout, attended local schools. From 1908 through 1910, Groh played shortstop with Oshkosh, WI (WSL). After subsequent minor league stops at Decatur, IL (3IL) and Buffalo, NY (EL), he in 1912 joined the New York Giants (NL). Although debuting in the major leagues at age 22, the 5-foot 8-inch, 158-pound Groh looked so young that many spectators believed manager John McGraw* had signed the team's batboy. Groh appeared in 27 games as a substitute infielder for the 1912 Giants. During May 1913, he was traded to the Cincinnati Reds (NL) with Red Ames,* Josh Devore,* and $20,000 for Art Fromme and Eddie Grant and immediately became the Reds' regular second baseman. After being shifted to third base in 1915, he led the NL a record six times in double plays and fielding average and had a .967 lifetime fielding average. His .983 percentage in 1924 bettered the previous record by six points.

Groh, who starred for Cincinnati for nine years, managed the Reds the last 10 games of 1918 and then returned to a playing role to help lead the 1919 squad to the world championship. In December 1921, Giants manager McGraw shipped center fielder George J. Burns,* catcher Mike Gonzalez, and $100,000 to the Reds for the coveted Groh. With Groh at third base, the Giants won the NL pennant the next three years. Groh batted .474 in the 1922 World Series and later proudly displayed this figure on his auto license plate. Sidelined with a bad knee in late 1924, he lost his third base position to Fred Lindstrom.* After finishing his major league career with the NL pennant-winning Pittsburgh Pirates in 1927, Groh played for and managed minor league teams in Charlotte, NC (PiL), Canton, OH (CL), and Binghamton, NY (EL). He later scouted for several major league teams, invested in bowling alleys, and worked as a cashier at River Downs Race Track in Cincinnati.

A dangerous right-handed hitter with his unique "bottle bat," Groh batted .292 lifetime. In 1,676 games, he made 1,774 hits, slugged 308 doubles, and knocked in 566 runs. He led the NL twice in doubles (1917–1918) and once each in runs (1918) and hits (1917). McGraw in 1912 suggested that Groh use a heavier bat to raise his batting average, but the latter could not find one he could grip comfortably. Finally, he whittled down the handle of a Spalding bat to his satisfaction and used a similarly altered cudgel the rest of his career. Groh married Marguerite "Ruby" Bender in Cincinnati on February 24, 1915. The popular, highly newsworthy Groh had engaged in a whirlwind three-week courtship with Ruby that became the talk of Cincinnati. Groh's brother, Lew, played briefly for the 1919 Philadelphia Athletics (AL).

BIBLIOGRAPHY: Henry Groh file, National Baseball Library, Cooperstown, NY; *The Baseball Encyclopedia*, 10th ed. (New York, 1996); Lawrence S. Ritter, *The Glory of Their Times* (New York, 1966); Lee Allen, *The Cincinnati Reds* (New York, 1948); Donald Honig, *The Cincinnati Reds* (New York, 1992); Noel Hynd, *The Giants of the Polo Grounds* (New York, 1988); Frank Graham, *The New York Giants* (New York, 1952).

Dennis T. "Tom" Chase

GROMEK, Stephen Joseph "Steve" (b. January 15, 1920, Hamtramck, MI), player, is the son of Adam Gromek and Josephine Gromek. His involvement in baseball began in the American Legion program because St. Ladislas High School in Hamtramck had no baseball team. Following his graduation, the Cleveland Indians (AL) signed the Polish-American and sent him to Logan, UT (MtnSL) in 1939. That season, the 6-foot 1-inch, 145-pound shortstop damaged his left shoulder while overswinging at the plate. The pain persisted the following spring at Fargo, ND–Moorhead, MN (NoL), preventing him from hitting with power. Gromek considered quitting because his chronically ill father and sister needed more financial support than minor league baseball could provide.

At Flint, MI (MISL), manager Jack Knight converted the right-hander to a pitcher. In 1941, Gromek won his first nine starts with Flint and compiled a 14–2 record. He joined the Cleveland Indians later that season and remained there until July 1942, winning three and losing one. Cleveland returned him to the minor leagues for more seasoning. In 1943, Gromek won

16 games for the Baltimore, MD Orioles (IL). Cleveland Indians coaches altered his delivery from overhand to sidearm, giving his fastball more movement. Gromek also developed a good curve, sinker, and change of pace pitch.

Gromek became the Cleveland Indians most effective pitcher during the late World War II years while Bob Feller* served in the military. In 1944, he compiled a 10–9 record with a club-leading 2.56 ERA for starting pitchers. Gromek led the staff for the fifth-place Indians with a 19–9 mark in 1945, completing 21 out of 30 starts with a 2.55 ERA. Although the Indians expected much of Gromek in the postwar period, he never fulfilled his potential. In 1946, Gromek slipped to a 5–15 effort and a 4.33 ERA. He severely injured his left knee the following spring, resulting in a lackluster 3–5 season. In 1948, Gromek fashioned a 9–3 mark as a spot starter and reliever. He outdueled Johnny Sain* of the Boston Braves, 2–1, in the fourth game of the World Series. He considered the victory his "greatest moment" especially since the Indians won the fall classic. Gromek's best performance for the pitching-rich Indians in the next four seasons came in 1950 with a 10–7 mark.

The Indians traded him to the second division Detroit Tigers (AL) in June 1953, fulfilling his childhood dream. He enjoyed his second most productive season in 1954, when he led Detroit Tigers pitchers with an 18–16 record and a 2.74 ERA in a career-high 252.2 innings. His major league career, which ended in 1957, included 123 wins, 108 losses, and a 3.41 ERA in 447 appearances. Gromek married Jeanette Kayko in 1946. They have two sons, Carl and Gregory. Bryan, a third sibling, died in 1969. Gromek spent much of his post baseball career as a salesman in Detroit, MI, retiring from AAA Michigan in 1980.

BIBLIOGRAPHY: Steven Gromek file, National Baseball Library, Cooperstown, NY; Steven Gromek to James N. Giglio, November 28, 1995; Cleveland (OH) *Plain Dealer*, February 28, 1948; *TSN*, August 10, 1944, March 29, 1945, July 19, 1945, June 9, 1954; Russell Schneider, *The Boys of Summer of '48* (Champaign, IL, 1998); Fred Smith, *995 Tigers* (Detroit, MI, 1981); John Phillips, *Winners* (Cabin John, MD, 1987); Jack Torry, *Endless Summers* (South Bend, IN, 1995); David S. Neft et al., *The Sports Encyclopedia: Baseball*, 16th ed. (New York, 1996).

James N. Giglio

GROVE, Robert Moses "Lefty," "Mose" (b. March 6, 1900, Lonaconing, MD; d. May 22, 1975, Norwalk, OH), player, was the son of coal miner John Grove and homemaker Emma (Beeman) Grove. Grove, who left Lonaconing public school in eighth grade, married Ethel Gardner on January 30, 1921, and had two children, Robert G. and Doris. The shy, taciturn, gruff country lad distrusted and feared city strangers, but generously provided young area boys with baseball equipment. A dedicated, highly competitive pitcher, he occasionally displayed strong temper. On August 21, 1931 after 16 consecutive wins, he lost a 1–0 decision to the St. Louis Browns, denying him the

AL consecutive win record. The infuriated Grove attributed his defeat to the authorized absence of batting star Al Simmons.* Grove, a master psychologist, used his personal traits (6-foot 3-inch frame, scowl, stare, speed, and wildness) to his pitching advantage. Teammates' occasional costly errors and failure to produce timely runs drew Grove's ire.

The strong-armed Grove played first base in 1917 for a Midland, MD team. In early 1920, he began his professional career pitching six games for Martinsburg, WV (BRL) at a monthly $125 rate. Jack Dunn,* owner of the Baltimore Orioles (IL), bought his contract for $2,000. With the Orioles from 1920 to 1924, he compiled an outstanding 109–36 record and led the IL four times in strikeouts. By 1924, he earned a $7,500 annual salary. Philadelphia Athletics (AL) manager Connie Mack* persuaded Dunn to sell him for a record $100,000. He pitched for the Athletics from 1925 to December 1933, when the Boston Red Sox (AL) bought him, Max Bishop,* and Rube Walberg* for two players and $125,000. After pitching for Boston from 1934 to 1941, Grove retired and operated a bowling alley in Lonaconing. Following his wife's death, he spent his remaining years in Norwalk, OH at his daughter-in-law's home.

Grove holds the AL record for four consecutive seasons as ERA leader, shared the mark of 16 consecutive wins, and compiled the second highest AL career winning percentage (.680). With the Athletics, he topped the AL seven consecutive seasons in strikeouts, five times in ERA, four times each in wins and winning percentage, and once in shutouts. At Boston, he led the AL four times in ERA and once in winning percentage. During nine years with the Athletics, he appeared in 402 games, pitched 2,401 innings, compiled a 195–79 record, a .711 won-lost percentage, and a 2.87 ERA, struck out 1,523 batters, and walked 740 hitters. With the Red Sox for eight seasons, he appeared in 214 games, pitched 1,539 innings, and compiled a 105–62 record, a .629 won-lost percentage, and a 3.34 ERA, struck out 743 batters, and walked 447 hitters.

During his 17-year major league career, he appeared in 616 games, pitched 3,940.2 innings, compiled a 300–141 record, a .680 won-lost percentage, and a 3.06 ERA, struck out 2,266 batters, and walked 1,187 hitters. On TSN All-Star teams from 1928 to 1932, he won the AL MVP Award in 1931. He starred on the AL champion Athletics teams from 1929 to 1931 and hurled four World Series victories, helping his club win the 1929 and 1930 World Series. Grove was elected to the National Baseball Hall of Fame in 1947 and was chosen by Boston fans in 1982 as the second left-hander on the Red Sox "dream team." Grove also made Major League Baseball's All-Century Team.

One of baseball's greatest left-handed pitchers, Grove was called "my best one" by manager Mack. According to manager Joe Cronin,* "He was all baseball. We all admired him and his dedication to the sport." Grove increased the popularity of baseball because of his skill and feisty character and drew large crowds whenever he pitched. An intelligent athlete constantly improving his effectiveness, he lengthened the time between pitches to improve his rhythm. His sore arm at Boston caused him to develop craftiness, a curve, a change-of-pace forkball, and better control, while his temper continually sparked teammates to play harder both in the field and at bat.

BIBLIOGRAPHY: Lefty Grove file, National Baseball Library, Cooperstown, NY; John Benson et al., *Baseball's Top 100* (Wilton, CT, 1997); Bob Broeg, "Grove's Badges: Hot Temper, Blazing Fast Ball," *TSN*, July 12, 1969, pp. 28–29; Ellery H. Clark, Jr., *Boston Red Sox: 75th Anniversary History* (Hicksville, NY, 1975); Ellery H. Clark, Jr., *Red Sox Fever* (Hicksville, NY, 1979); Ellery H. Clark, Jr., *Red Sox Forever* (Hicksville, NY, 1977); Ellery H. Clark, Jr., interviews with Lefty Grove, April 1927, June 1935, Cy Perkins, April 1927, Howard Ehmke, December 1944, Connie Mack, December 1944, Max Bishop, January 1950, Mrs. Robert Grove, May 1983, Joe Cronin, July 1983; Paul Doherty, "300 for Lefty," *TNP* 11 (1992), pp. 38–39; Peter Golenbock, *Fenway* (New York, 1992); John P. McCarthy, *Baseball's All-Time Dream Team* (New York, 1994); Joseph J. Vecchione, *The New York Times Book of Sports Legends* (New York, 1991); Robert Redmount, *The Red Sox Encyclopedia* (Champaign, IL, 1998); Frederick G. Lieb, *Connie Mack* (New York, 1945); Frederick G. Lieb, *The Boston Red Sox* (New York, 1947); Jim Kaplan, "The Best Pitcher Ever," *BRJ* 27 (1998), pp. 62–65; Donald Honig, *Baseball When the Grass Was Real* (New York, 1975); *The Baseball Encyclopedia*, 10th ed. (New York, 1996).

Ellery H. Clark, Jr.

GUERRERO, Pedro "Pete" (b. June 29, 1956, San Pedro de Macoris, DR), player, is the son of Francisco Sanchez and M. Guerrero. His brother, Luis, played minor league baseball in 1977. Major leaguers Joaquin Andujar, George Bell,* Mariano Duncan, Tony Fernandez,* Julio Franco,* and Juan Samuel also came from San Pedro de Macoris. The Cleveland Indians (AL) signed Guerrero in January 1973 at age 16 after he led the entire Dominican Republic Legion with a .438 batting average. Guerrero played third base and shortstop for the Sarasota, FL Indians (GCL) before being traded to the Los Angeles Dodgers (NL) for pitcher Bruce Ellingsen. Guerrero batted .327 in six seasons with the Los Angeles Dodgers farm system and led the PCL in RBI at Albuquerque, NM with 116 in 1978 and 103 in 1979. His best position, first base, was occupied by perennial All-Star first baseman Steve Garvey.*

From 1980 to 1987 with the Los Angeles Dodgers, the 6-foot, 195-pound Guerrero compiled a .310 batting average and exceeded 30 HR three times while dividing time between third base and left field. In June 1985, the right-handed power hitter was selected NL Player of the Month, tying the then major league record for HR in June with 15. He led the NL with a .425 on-base percentage and a .577 slugging percentage. He batted .196 in three NL Championship Series with Los Angeles, but was named co-MVP in the Los Angeles Dodgers' 1981 World Series Championship over the New York Yankees (AL) when he batted .333, belted two HR, and drove in seven tallies.

On August 16, 1988, the Los Angeles Dodgers traded Guerrero to the St. Louis Cardinals (NL) for pitcher John Tudor.* In 1989, Guerrero enjoyed his finest overall season. After moving to first base, he played every game, batted .311, drove in a career-high 117 runs, and led the NL with 42 doubles. Guerrero hit .406 with runners in scoring position and drove in one of every five St. Louis Cardinal runs.

Guerrero was hounded by injuries much of his career, suffering back spasms, a pinched nerve in the neck, pulled hamstrings, strained wrists, a fractured leg, and knee surgery. After spending most of 1992 on the disabled list, Guerrero was granted free agency. He played for the Jalisco, Mexico Charros (MEL) in 1993, but was released in June. His 15-year major league career included 1,536 games, 1,618 hits, 267 doubles, 215 HR, 898 RBI, and a .300 batting average.

Guerrero married Denise Chavez in 1980 and has a daughter, Ashley Maria. They reside in Rio Rancho, NM, but return often to the Dominican Republic. Guerrero enjoys playing the drums, Latin music, and fishing.

BIBLIOGRAPHY: Pedro Guerrero file, National Baseball Library, Cooperstown, NY; *St. Louis Cardinals 1991 Media Guide*; John Dewan, ed., *The Scouting Report: 1990* (New York, 1990); Rick Hummell, "At Age 36, Guerrero Looks for Another Job as Hitter," St. Louis (MO) *Post-Dispatch*, June 13, 1993, p. F3; Richard Justice, "Pedro Guerrero: Making the Grade to Stardom," *BD* 42 (November 1983), pp. 46–48; Robert E. Kelly, *Baseball's Best* (Jefferson, NC, 1988); Dan Schlossberg, *Baseball Stars: 1986* (Chicago, IL, 1986); Larry Whiteside, "How Pedro Guerrero Joined the Majors' Home Run Elite," *BD* 44 (October 1985), pp. 65–66; William F. McNeil, *The Dodgers Encyclopedia* (Champaign, IL, 1997).

Frank J. Olmsted

GUIDRY, Ronald Ames "Ron," "Louisiana Lightning," "Gator" (b. August 28, 1950, Lafayette, LA), player, is the son of railroad conductor Roland Guidry and Mary (Grace) Guidry. At Northside High School in Lafayette, Guidry starred in football, basketball, and track and field. He developed his pitching skills playing American Legion ball because his school did not field a team. The 5-foot 11-inch, 160-pound Guidry in 1971 resigned his scholarship at the University of Southwest Louisiana to enter the professional baseball free agent draft and was signed by the New York Yankees (AL) as their third selection. The next few years in the Yankees farm system proved unspectacular. Guidry pitched with only moderate success with Johnson City, TN (ApL) in 1971, Fort Lauderdale, FL (FSL) in 1972, Kinston, NC (CrL) in 1973, and West Haven, CT (EL) in 1974. In 1975 and 1976, Guidry divided time between the Yankees and their top Syracuse, NY (IL) farm team.

With a sound arm and superior athletic ability, Guidry was destined to succeed. His incredible ability to throw hard (over 95 miles per hour) with sheer power defied his scant 160 pounds. In 1977, Guidry won 16 games and helped the Yankees win the AL pennant. He won one game in the 1977

World Series, as the Yankees defeated the Los Angeles Dodgers in six games. In 1978, the Cajun left-hander became the ace of the Yankees pitching staff. Guidry's 25–3 record ranked as the highest winning percentage (.893) in major league baseball history for pitchers winning at least 20 games. He compiled the lowest ERA for a left-hander in the AL since 1941 (1.74), most strikeouts by a Yankees pitcher (248), most strikeouts in one game by an AL left-hander (18), a major league high shutouts (9), and a Yankees record for victories at the start of the season (13). The Yankees again captured the AL pennant and World Series over the Dodgers in six games, with Guidry winning Game 3. For his efforts, Guidry was named *TSN* Man of the Year, Major League Player of the Year, AL Pitcher of the Year, and AL Cy Young* Award winner.

The mainstay of the pitching staff, Guidry made a 1–1 record in the 1981 World Series loss to the Dodgers. In 1985, Guidry compiled a 22–6 mark and 3.27 ERA, led the AL in victories, finished fourth in complete games (11), struck out 143 batters in 259 innings, and placed second in the Cy Young Award balloting. Guidry suffered three consecutive losing seasons with the Yankees, retiring after the 1988 campaign. In 14 major league seasons, he won 170 games and lost only 91 decisions for a .651 winning percentage and a 3.29 ERA and struck out 1,778 batters in 2,392 innings. He was named to five All-Star teams (1978–1979, 1982–1983, 1985) and All-Star fielding teams (1982–1986). Guidry married his hometown sweetheart, Bonnie Lynn Rutledge, in September 1972 and has two children, Jamie Rachael and Brandon. Hunting dominates Guidry's life.

BIBLIOGRAPHY: Ronald Guidry file, National Baseball Library, Cooperstown, NY; Mark Gallagher, *The Yankee Encyclopedia*, vol. 3 (Champaign, IL, 1997); Maury Allen, *Ron Guidry* (New York, 1979); John Benson et al., *Baseball's Top 100* (Wilton, CT, 1997); *NYT Biographical Service* 20 (July 1989), pp. 668–670; *TSN Official Baseball Register, 1989*; Robert Obojski, "Guidry's Popularity Still Strong in New York," *SCD* 25 (February 20, 1998), pp. 140–141; Paul Post, "Rapport with Martin Helped Guidry in '78," *SCD* 23 (October 4, 1996), pp. 150–151.

John L. Evers

GULLETT, Donald Edward "Don" (b. January 6, 1951, Lynn, KY), player and coach, was an outstanding high school athlete. His hard throwing made him the first choice of the Cincinnati Reds (NL) in the 1969 rookie draft. A brief stint with Sioux Falls, SD (NoL) included a 7–2 pitching record and an NoL-leading 1.96 ERA. The left-handed, 6-foot, 190-pound farm boy joined the Cincinnati Reds as a 19-year-old rookie in 1970. Used mainly in long relief situations, Gullett compiled 5 wins and 6 saves in 44 games. Gullett's remarkable promise showed in an August relief effort fanning the first six New York Mets batters that he faced to tie an NL record for relievers. In the NL Championship Series against the Pittsburgh Pirates, he saved two of the three victories for the triumphant Reds.

Gullett augmented his fastball with a curveball, becoming a full-time starter with the Reds in 1970. In the next seven seasons, Gullett led the pitching staff to help the Reds win five divisional titles, four NL championships (1970, 1972, 1975–1976), and two World Series (1975, 1976). Gullett compiled a 2–3 record in NL Championship Series play and recorded victories in two World Series games. He led the NL in winning percentage in 1971 and 1975 and was named to the 1974 *TSN* All-Star team. His only losing season came in 1972 with a 9–10 record. By the end of the 1976 season, the 25-year-old Gullett's 91–44 career win-loss record caused Cincinnati manager Sparky Anderson* to compare him with Whitey Ford* and predict eventual National Baseball Hall of Fame honors. Gullett's career, however, was marred by nagging injuries, including a chronic sore shoulder that frequently sidelined him.

In 1976, Gullett played out his option with the Reds and entered the first reentry draft that November. The ensuing bidding made Gullett the first free agent signed by the New York Yankees (AL). He was signed to a six-year contract for $2.1 million. Gullett's 14–4 mark with the 1977 Yankees paced AL hurlers in winning percentage, but he lacked effectiveness in postseason play. Gullett's ailing shoulder sidelined him in 1978 after he had compiled a 4–2 record. After failing to recover from rotator cuff surgery, the 29-year-old Gullett was released by the Yankees in 1980. His 109–50 lifetime record in 1,390 innings pitched included 921 strikeouts, 14 shutouts, and a 3.11 ERA. Such performances underscored the tragedy of his forced early retirement. He has coached for the Cincinnati Reds since 1993. Gullett resides on a Maloneton, KY farm, having recovered from his 1986 heart attack.

BIBLIOGRAPHY: Donald Gullett file, National Baseball Library, Cooperstown, NY; Boston (MA) *Sunday Globe*, October 31, 1982; New York *Daily News*, February 6, 1986; *NYT*, October 25, 1980; John Thorn, *The Relief Pitcher* (New York, 1979); John Thorn et al., eds., *Total Baseball*, 5th ed. (New York, 1997); *TSN Baseball Register, 1981*; Donald Honig, *The Cincinnati Reds* (New York, 1992); Greg Rhodes and John Erardi, *Big Red Dynasty* (Cincinnati, OH, 1997); Robert H. Walker, *Cincinnati, and the Big Red Machine* (Bloomington, IN, 1988).

David Q. Voigt

GULLICKSON, William Lee "Bill" (b. February 20, 1959, Marshall, MN), player, is the son of Donald Gullickson and Nancy Gullickson, who owned a tire store in Joliet, IL. Gullickson graduated from Joliet Catholic High School, where he compiled a 23–1 record in baseball his junior and senior years and made all-conference in basketball. His six no-hitters set the Illinois record for most no-hitters.

Gullickson, the second player taken in the June 1977 draft behind Harold Baines,* began his professional baseball career at West Palm Beach, FL (FSL) in 1977. After stops at Memphis, TN (SL) and Denver, CO (AA), he made his major league debut on September 26, 1979 for the Montreal Expos (NL). Gullickson started the 1980 season with Denver, but was promoted to Montreal after a 6–2 start with a 1.91 ERA. He finished 10–5 with a 3.00 ERA for the Montreal Expos in 1980 and set a major league rookie record for strikeouts in a game with 18 against the Chicago Cubs in Montreal, Canada on September 10. *TSN* named him NL Rookie Pitcher of the Year, while he placed second to Steve Howe in the BBWAA NL Rookie of the Year balloting.

The right-handed throwing Gullickson played for the Montreal Expos (NL) from 1979 to 1985, Cincinnati Reds (NL) in 1986 and 1987, New York Yankees (AL) in 1987, Houston Astros (NL) in 1990, and Detroit Tigers (AL) from 1991 to 1994 during a 14-year major league career, compiling a 162–136 record with a 3.93 ERA. Shortly after Gullickson made the major leagues, doctors diagnosed him with diabetes. He required insulin shots and a rigid eating pattern, often eating between innings during pitching assignments. In 1987, Gullickson recorded his sixth consecutive season with 10 or more wins. He received $2 million to pitch for the Yomiuri Giants in Japan, notching 14–9 and 7–5 records in 1988 and 1989.

In 1991, the 6-foot 3-inch, 225-pound Gullickson shared the AL lead in triumphs (20) and games started (35) for Detroit, marking his only 20 victory season. He led the NL with 27 HR allowed in 1984 and the AL with 35 HR surrendered in 1992. On April 10, 1982, Gullickson tied the modern major league mark with six wild pitches in a single game. He finished 1–0 with a 1.17 ERA for Montreal against the Philadelphia Phillies in the 1981 NL Division Series, and 0–2 with a 2.51 ERA against the Los Angeles Dodgers in the 1981 NL Championship Series. He and his wife, Sandy Leslie, have four children, Cassie, Carly, Craig, and Chelsey.

BIBLIOGRAPHY: Bill Gullickson file, National Baseball Library, Cooperstown, NY; Peter C. Bjarkman, *Encyclopedia of Major League Baseball Team Histories National League* (Westport, CT, 1991); Ian MacDonald, "Sun Always Shines for Expos' Gullickson," *TSN*, September 6, 1980, p. 41; Ron Rappoport, "A Shot in the Arm for the Expos," Chicago *Sun-Times*, September 25, 1980.

David A. Goss

GUMBERT, Harry Edward "Gunboat" (b. November 5, 1909, Elizabeth, PA; d. January 4, 1995, Wimberley, TX), player and executive, was the son of Arthur Addison Gumbert and Elizabeth (Wilson) Gumbert and graduated from Bentleyville High School. He did not play interscholastic baseball because his school had no team and began his career pitching semiprofessional baseball in rural Pennsylvania.

Gumbert asked Charleroi, PA (MAL) for a tryout in 1930 and compiled a 13–12 season. The Baltimore Orioles (IL) purchased his contract and assigned him to York, PA (NYPL) in 1931. The 6-foot 2-inch, right-handed pitcher spent the 1932 season at Binghamton, NY (NYPL) and 1933 at

Williamsport, PA (NYPL). After being traded to Galveston, TX (TL) in 1934, Gumbert won 18 games and lost only 12 decisions for the TL champions. The Philadelphia Phillies (NL) purchased his contract, but optioned him to Baltimore before the 1935 season.

Gumbert won 20 and lost 10 for the Baltimore Orioles before the New York Giants (NL) acquired him for $15,000 in September 1935. He made his major league debut on September 12 against the Chicago Cubs and posted a 1–2 record in his abbreviated rookie season. The Pennsylvania native performed solidly for the New York Giants the following five seasons, winning 66 games and losing 52 contests and recording a career-high 18 victories in 1939. The Giants captured consecutive NL pennants in 1936 and 1937 and used Gumbert briefly against the New York Yankees in both World Series.

The New York Giants traded Gumbert, Paul Dean, and cash to the St. Louis Cardinals (NL) for William McGee in May 1941. Gumbert provided strong pitching support for the St. Louis Cardinals and made his third World Series appearance against the New York Yankees in 1942. The Cincinnati Reds (NL) purchased Gumbert from St. Louis in June 1944. He finished the 1944 season with the Cincinnati Reds and missed the 1945 campaign due to military service. Gumbert returned to Cincinnati in 1946, the last season he worked primarily as a starter. He led the NL in saves with 17 in 1948 and relief wins with 10 in both 1947 and 1948. The Reds waived him to the Pittsburgh Pirates (NL) in July 1949. The Pirates released Gumbert after just one relief appearance in 1950. He concluded his playing career with Sacramento, CA (PCL). Gumbert finished with a lifetime major league record of 143 wins, 113 losses, 48 saves, and a 3.68 ERA.

Gumbert served as general manager at Galveston, TX (GCL) in 1951 before moving to Houston, TX to sell insurance and electrical equipment. He retired to Wimberley, TX near Austin. Gumbert married Rachel House on October 28, 1935. They had a son, H. E. "Eddie," and two daughters, Melinda and Lisa.

BIBLIOGRAPHY: Harry Gumbert file, National Baseball Library, Cooperstown, NY; Noel Hynd, *The Giants of the Polo Grounds* (New York, 1988); Peter Williams, *When the Giants Were Giants* (Chapel Hill, NC, 1994); Frank Graham, *The New York Giants* (New York, 1952); Bob Broeg and Jerry Vickery, *St. Louis Cardinals Encyclopedia* (Grand Rapids, MI, 1998); Richard L. Burtt, *The Pittsburgh Pirates, A Pictorial History* (Virginia Beach, VA, 1977); *The Baseball Encyclopedia*, 10th ed. (New York, 1996).

John Hillman

GURA, Lawrence Cyril "Larry" (b. November 26, 1947, Joliet, IL), player, received a B.A. degree in physical education from Arizona State University in Tempe, where he won 19 of 20 games and received All-America baseball honors his senior year. Gura pitched no-hitters three days apart at the NBC Tournament in 1968. He pitched for the U.S. Olympic baseball team that won the gold medal in Mexico City, Mexico in 1968. A boyhood dream was fulfilled when the Chicago Cubs (NL) selected him in the second round of the June 1969 free agent draft, gave him a $50,000 signing bonus, and assigned him to Tacoma, WA (PCL). The 6-foot 1-inch, 185-pound southpaw pitched at Tacoma from 1969 to 1971 and at Wichita, KS (AA) in 1972 and 1973. Chicago recalled Gura, who displayed good control and some strikeout capability annually from 1970 to 1973. In November 1973, Chicago traded Gura to the Texas Rangers (AL) for pitcher Mike Paul. Texas swapped him in May 1974 to the New York Yankees (AL) for catcher Duke Sims. In 1974, for Syracuse, NY (IL), Gura split 14 decisions and led the IL with a 2.14 ERA. After joining the New York Yankees, he took five of six decisions and posted a 2.41 ERA. Gura won seven and lost eight the next season, but got into manager Billy Martin's* doghouse. The New York Yankees traded him to the Kansas City Royals (AL) in May 1976 for catcher Fran Healy.

Kansas City Royals manager Whitey Herzog* moved Gura to the bullpen, where he won all four decisions and recorded a stingy 2.30 ERA. In 1977, Gura saved 10 games and finished 8–5, pitching mostly in relief. Herzog moved him into the starting rotation with Dennis Leonard,* Paul Splittorff,* and Rich Gale in 1978. Gura responded by triumphing 16 of 20 times with a 2.72 ERA. His .800 winning percentage ranked third in the AL, with only Ron Guidry* and Nolan Ryan* giving up fewer hits per nine innings. Gura, a mainstay of the Royals' starting rotation from 1978 to 1984, won 99 games, including career best 18 victories in 1980 and 1982. An excellent fielder, he did not make an error in 1980, 1981, 1983, and 1984. The Royals' Pitcher of the Year in 1978 and 1981, Gura made the 1980 AL All Star pitching staff. He hurled for the Kansas City Royals in the AL Championship Series in 1976, 1977, 1978, and 1980, splitting four decisions. In the 1980 World Series, Gura recorded no decisions and allowed only three earned runs in 12.1 innings against the victorious Philadelphia Phillies. He attributed much of his success to a rigid conditioning program and strict diet. Gura traveled with health foods and a blender to maintain his regimen.

In 1983, Gura led the AL with 18 losses. He experimented in September with a knuckleball, one of his pitches at Arizona State, in an attempt to regain his edge. Although Gura posted a winning record in 1984, his ERA ballooned to 5.18. When the Kansas City Royals released him in May 1985, Gura returned to the Chicago Cubs organization. After winning seven of 10 starts for Des Moines–based Iowa (AA), Gura lost three decisions for Chicago and was released in August. The Joliet, IL resident compiled a major league record of 126 victories, 97 defeats, 14 saves, 801 strikeouts, and a 3.76 ERA in 2,047 innings and 403 games. He and his wife, Cindy, have one daughter, Kristina.

BIBLIOGRAPHY: Larry Gura file, National Baseball Library, Cooperstown, NY; Sid Bordman, *Expansion to Excellence* (Marcelline, MS, 1981); Zander Hollander, ed., *The*

Complete Handbook of Baseball, 14th ed. (New York, 1984); Kansas City Royals, *Grandslam* (Kansas City, MO, 1978, 1981, 1982); *TSN Official Baseball Register, 1986*.

Frank J. Olmsted

GUSTAFSON, Clifford Lincoln "Cliff," "Coach Gus" (b. February 12, 1931, Kenedy, TX), coach, is the son of Oscar Elmer Gustafson, a farmer, and Wendla (Rolf) Gustafson and has excelled as a baseball mentor at the University of Texas. The Texas Longhorns have been coached by three legendary figures for the last eight decades. Billy Disch began the great baseball tradition there in 1911 and was followed 29 years later by Bibb Falk.* Falk's clubs won 20 SWC titles in 25 years from 1940 to 1967, excluding four years of military service during World War II. Despite following two legends, Gustafson far surpassed the win–loss records of these outstanding coaches.

Gustafson, known as "Coach Gus" when he was hired by Texas in 1967, had won nearly 80 percent of his games and seven State Championships while coaching baseball at South Antonio, TX High School. His final high school squad triumphed in all 39 games. In 29 seasons at Texas, Gustafson's teams have won 21 SWC Championships and appeared in 16 College World Series. Texas captured National Championships in 1975 and 1983, with Gustafson being named ABCA Coach of the Year both times. Over 30 of his players, including Roger Clemens,* Kelly Gruber, Burt Hooten,* Spike Owen, Greg Swindell, and Brooks Kieschnick, have appeared in the major leagues.

On February 2, 1988, the Longhorns defeated University of Texas-Arlington, 9–3, giving Gustafson his 1,000th collegiate coaching victory. Rod Dedeaux* and Ron Fraser* remain the only other major college baseball coaches to surpass 1,250 victories. In 29 seasons, Gustafson compiled 1,427 wins, 373 losses, and two ties for a .792 winning percentage. He ranks first among NCAA Division I coaches in career victories and third in winning percentage. Gustafson retired following the 1996 season. He married Jane Elizabeth (Davenport) Gustafson.

BIBLIOGRAPHY: *Official NCAA Baseball Records*, 1968–1991; *University of Texas Baseball Media Guide*, 1968–1991; Tim Kurkjian, "Cliff Gustafson," *SI* 80 (May 2, 1994), p. 65; *The 1999 CSPN Information Please Sports Almanac*.

Cappy Gagnon

GWYNN, Anthony Keith "Tony" (b. May 9, 1960, Los Angeles, CA), player, is the second of three sons of Charles A. Gwynn and Vandella (Douglas) Gwynn and grew up with two baseball-playing brothers. Charles, Jr., was drafted by the Cleveland Indians (AL), while Chris played with three major league clubs. Gwynn starred in both baseball and basketball at Long Beach, CA Poly High School and attended San Diego State University on a basketball scholarship. After being requested to play baseball in his sophomore year, he hit .301, .423, and .416 in his last three seasons for the Aztecs. The San Diego Padres (NL) selected the 5-foot 11-inch, 200-pound outfielder in the third round of the June 1981 free agent draft. The San Diego Clippers (NBA) drafted him the same day.

In 1981, Gwynn, who bats and throws left-handed, led Class A Walla Walla, WA (NWL) with a .331 batting average and finished the season with Class AA Amarillo, TX (TL). The next season, he hit .328 for Honolulu-based Hawaii (PCL). San Diego promoted him in July 1982, and he finished the season with a .289 batting average. After just 17 games in 1983 at Las Vegas, NV (PCL), he completed the campaign with the Padres and batted .309 in 86 games.

Gwynn led the NL in both batting average (.351) and hits (213) in 1984, his first full major league season. He again led the NL in hits (218) in 1986 as well as in runs scored (107). His .370 batting average led both major leagues in 1987, while his 218 hits topped the NL. A .313 batting average the next season enabled him to repeat as NL champion, and he led the NL again in both batting average (.336) and hits (203) in 1989. Gwynn believes that conflict with a few teammates hampered his performance in 1990, but he still batted .309 and tallied 177 hits. His superlative .358 batting average in 1993 trailed only Andres Galarraga* of the expansion Colorado Rockies. On August 4, 1993, he collected six hits in a 12 inning game. In the strike-shortened 1994 season, Gwynn batted a career-high .394 with 165 hits and 64 RBI. He led the NL in batting average (.368) and hits (197) in 1995 and batting average (.353) in 1996, helping the Padres capture the NL West. Gwynn tied a NL record by winning his eighth NL batting title (.372) in 1997, when he established career-highs in hits (220), doubles (49), HR (17), and RBI (119). In 1998, he batted .321 with 16 HR and 69 RBI to help San Diego win the NL West. Gwynn hit .338 with 62 RBI in 1999 and became the 22nd member of the 3,000 hits club on August 6.

Since 1983, Gwynn's season batting average has not fallen below .300. He has accomplished this feat with a 32½ inch, 31-ounce bat, one of the smallest in the major leagues. He holds the San Diego all-time records for highest batting average (.339), runs scored (1,361), hits (3,067), doubles (522), triples (84), RBI (1,104), and even stolen bases (318). He has clouted 133 HR and holds the NL record for most years leading the league in singles with seven. In 9,059 at bats, he has struck out only 421 times.

Gwynn, admired for his work ethic, has combined video technology with hours of extra drill to transform his natural batting talent into consistent efficiency at the plate and his suspect fielding ability into above-average skill. He has received Gold Glove honors five times and has also been named to the NL All-Star team 15 times in the past 16 years.

In the 1984 NL Championship Series, Gwynn batted .368 and made key hits in the final two games to help the San Diego Padres defeat the Chicago Cubs. He hit .263 against the Detroit Tigers, as the Padres lost the World Series, four games to one. He hit .308 in the NL Division Series against the

St. Louis Cardinals in 1996. After struggling in both the 1998 Division Series against the Houston Astros and Atlanta Braves in the 1998 Championship Series, he feasted on New York Yankees pitching for a .500 batting average, six hits, a HR, and three RBI in the World Series.

Gwynn remains a model of consistency and stability and ranks among the game's most complete players. He lives in Poway, CA, northeast of San Diego, with his wife, Alicea, and their two children, Anthony II and Anisha.

BIBLIOGRAPHY: Tony Gwynn file, National Baseball Library, Cooperstown, NY; Tony Gwynn and Jim Geschke, *Tony!* (Chicago, IL, 1986); *CB* (1996), pp. 185–189; *The Baseball Encyclopedia*, 10th ed. (New York, 1996); Barry Bloom, "Tony Gwynn," *Sport* 85 (September 1994), pp. 26–27; Ron Fimrite, "Small Stick, Tall Stats," *SI* 64 (April 14, 1986), pp. 50–52; Bill Gutman, *Baseball's Hot New Stars* (New York, 1988); Richard Hoffer, "Fear Of Failure," *SI* 83 (September 18, 1995), pp. 66–70; Kevin Kernan, "The Sport Q & A: Tony Gwynn," *Sport* 82 (July 1991), pp. 34–38; Danny Knobler, "Pssst . . . Heard About Tony Gwynn?" *Newsweek* 80 (August 1989), pp. 22–28; Tim Kurkjian, "Beginning Again," *SI* 74 (March 11, 1991), pp. 44–47; Ivan Maisel, "He's a Hefty Problem for Pitchers," *SI* 60 (May 14, 1984), pp. 70–71; Malcolm Moran, "Gwynn Finds Camera Doesn't Lie," *NYT Biographical Service* 15 (May 1984), p. 660; David L. Porter, ed., *African-American Sports Greats* (Westport, CT, 1995); Mike Shatzkin, ed., *The Ballplayers* (New York, 1990); Samantha Stevenson, "Tony Gwynn: A Portrait of the Scientist in the Batter's Box," *NYT Biographical Service* 22 (June 1991), pp. 616–617; John Thorn et al., eds., *Total Baseball*, 5th ed. (New York, 1997); George Vecsey, "Tony Gwynn: Just Arriving," *NYT Biographical Service* 15 (October 1984), pp. 1323–1324.

Gaymon L. Bennett

H

HACK, Stanley Camfield "Stan," "Smiling Stan" (b. December 6, 1909, Sacramento, CA; d. December 15, 1979, Dixon, IL), player, manager, and coach, was a 6-foot, 175-pound third baseman who threw right-handed and batted left-handed. He played his entire major league baseball career with the Chicago Cubs (NL) from 1932 through 1947. Hack graduated from high school in Sacramento, where he participated in baseball. He worked as a bank clerk in Sacramento and played on a local city league team when the Sacramento, CA Solons (PCL) offered him a tryout in 1931. Initially he was reluctant to surrender the security of his bank position for the uncertainty of a baseball career, but took a two-week vacation in March 1931 to attend the tryout camp. The Solons were very impressed with Hack's performance and persuaded him to resign his bank post and sign a baseball contract. The 21-year-old Hack started for the PCL club and enjoyed a .352 batting average in 164 games. After being purchased by the Cubs (NL) for $40,000 in 1932, Hack opened the season as regular Cubs third baseman before being benched because of weak hitting. In 1933, he batted .299 in 137 games for Albany, NY (IL) and hit .350 in 20 games for the Cubs later that season. Hack started at third base for the Cubs for the rest of his playing career and led Chicago to four World Series (1932, 1935, 1938, 1945), collecting 24 base hits in 18 games. Hack tied the fall classic record for most singles in four games (7) and most hits in one game (4) and compiled a .348 overall batting average. In Game 6 of the 1945 World Series, he doubled home the winning run in the bottom of the 12th inning.

Selected the all-time Cubs third baseman, Hack recorded at least a .300 batting average during seven seasons, scored over 100 runs a season seven times, and paced the NL in hits (1940–1941) and stolen bases (1938–1939) twice. Always among the defensive standouts, Hack topped NL third basemen in putouts five times (including 1937–1940), double plays three times, and twice each in assists and fielding average. He set a World Series record (since broken) by making 12 putouts in the 1945 fall classic. In four All-Star games (1938, 1939, 1941, 1943), Hack made six hits with a .400 batting average. During 16 seasons with the Cubs, Hack played in 1,938 games, compiled 2,193 hits, 363 doubles, 81 triples, 57 HR, 642 RBI, and a .301 batting average. He also enjoyed a walk/strikeout ratio of better than two to one.

Hack in 1948 began managing in the Cubs farm system with stops at Des Moines, IA (WL), Springfield, MA (IL), and Los Angeles, CA (PCL). Named manager of the Chicago Cubs (NL) in 1954, Hack experienced little success with seventh-, sixth-, and eighth-place finishes. After coaching for the St. Louis Cardinals (1957–1958), Hack piloted the NL club for the remainder of the 1958 season when manager Fred Hutchinson* was fired. In four managerial seasons, Hack's clubs won 199 and lost 272 for a .423 mark. Hack also performed managerial stints at Denver, CO (AA), Salt Lake City, UT (PCL), and Dallas-Fort Worth, TX (TL) before retiring from baseball in 1966. After divorcing his first wife, Dorothy Alice Weisel, Hack married Glennyce Mary Graf on November 30, 1957. He had one son and two daughters and owned and operated a restaurant in Grand Detour, IL.

BIBLIOGRAPHY: Thomas Aylesworth and Benton Minks, *The Encyclopedia of Baseball Managers* (New York, 1990); Bob Broeg and Jerry Vickery, *St. Louis Cardinals Encyclopedia* (Grand Rapids, MI, 1998); Stanley Hack file, National Baseball Library, Cooperstown, NY; Jim Enright, *Chicago Cubs* (New York, 1975); Eddie Gold and Art Ahrens, *The Golden Era Cubs, 1876–1940* (Chicago, IL, 1985): Eddie Gold and Art Ahrens, *The New Era Cubs, 1941–1985* (Chicago, IL, 1985); Gene Karst and Martin J. Jones, Jr., *Who's Who in Professional Baseball* (New Rochelle, NY, 1973); Craig Carter, ed., *TSN Daguerreotypes* (St. Louis, MO, 1990); Brent P. Kelley, *The Case For: Those Overlooked by the Baseball Hall of Fame* (Jefferson, NC, 1992); *The Baseball Encyclopedia*, 10th ed. (New York, 1990).

David S. Matz and John L. Evers

HADDIX, Harvey "The Kitten" (b. September 18, 1925, Medway, OH; d. January 8, 1994, Springfield, OH), player and coach, was the son of Harvey Haddix and Nellie Mae (Greider) Haddix. His father, a farmer and semi-professional pitcher, taught his son the curveball that launched his career. Two of his three brothers, Ben and Fred, played professional baseball at the minor league level. Haddix, who graduated from Catawba High School in 1943, found that farm life taught him to work hard and kept him in good shape in the off-season. He married Marcia Williamson on December 10, 1955 and had three children.

Haddix was known throughout his career as a versatile, durable, and highly competitive player. A strikeout pitcher with sharp control, he also proved a fine hitter and base runner and an excellent fielder. His accomplishments remain especially noteworthy in light of his diminutive 5-foot 9-inch, 160-pound physical stature and his years lost to military service. Having played baseball "ever since I can remember," he traveled at his own expense to a St. Louis Cardinals (NL) tryout camp in 1943. Shortly after signing with the St. Louis Cardinals, he was deferred from World War II military service to work on the family farm. He resumed his baseball career in 1947, promptly winning 19 games for Winston-Salem, NC to take the CL's MVP. He also acquired his nickname, "The Kitten," for his physical and stylistic resemblance to St. Louis Cardinals left-hander Harry "The Cat" Brecheen.* After three All-Star seasons at Columbus, OH (IL) from 1948 through 1950, Haddix was drafted into the U.S. Army and missed the entire 1951 season and most of the 1952 campaign.

In his first full major league season, Haddix won 20 games for the 1953 St. Louis Cardinals and hurled an NL-leading 6 shutouts. In 1954 his 18 wins, including 10 straight victories and 36 consecutive scoreless innings, made him the first St. Louis southpaw ever to triumph in 38 games in two years. Haddix was traded to the Philadelphia Phillies (NL) in May 1956, Cincinnati Reds (NL) in December 1957, and Pittsburgh Pirates (NL), the team of his greatest victories, in January 1959. On May 26, 1959, Haddix accomplished what no pitcher had ever done. He pitched 12 perfect innings against the Milwaukee Braves, only to lose in the 13th frame, 1–0. In the 1960 World Series, he won two games in the Pirates' triumph over the New York Yankees. In 1987, Pittsburgh fans elected him as the all-time best left-handed pitcher of the Pirates.

Haddix joined the Baltimore Orioles (AL) in December 1963 and retired following the 1965 season with a major league career record of 136 wins, 113 losses, and a 3.63 ERA. He had also earned three Gold Glove awards for outstanding fielding and been named to the NL All-Star team three times from 1953 to 1955. Haddix then served as pitching coach with the New York Mets (NL) in 1966 and 1967, Cincinnati Reds (NL) in 1969, Boston Red Sox (AL) in 1971, Cleveland Indians (AL) from 1975 to 1978, and Pittsburgh Pirates (NL), where he contributed to the World Championship in 1979. After his 1984 pitching staff had recorded the best ERA in baseball, he retired to his farm in South Vienna, OH.

BIBLIOGRAPHY: Harvey Haddix file, National Baseball Library, Cooperstown, NY; Bob Broeg and Jerry Vickery, *St. Louis Cardinals Encyclopedia* (Grand Rapids, MI, 1998); Jim O'Brien, *Maz and the 1960 Pirates* (Pittsburgh, PA, 1994); Dick Groat and Bill Surface, *The World Champion Pittsburgh Pirates* (New York, 1961); Richard L. Burtt, *The Pittsburgh Pirates, A Pictorial History* (Virginia Beach, VA, 1977); Les Biederman, "Kitten Carves History with Left Paw," *TSN*, June 3, 1959, p. 5; Bob Broeg, "Haddix Hungry Pitcher, Goal 60 Grand," *TSN*, November 3, 1954, pp. 5–6; Ray Gillespie, "Kitten Knitting Knuckler to Key Up Cards," *TSN*, February 24, 1954, pp. 3–4; Omer Johnson, "On Haddix Farm, Pop and the Boys All Played

Game," *TSN*, January 14, 1953, p. 13; Ronald A. Mayer, *Perfect!* (Jefferson, NC, 1991); Steve Stout, "The Greatest Game Ever Pitched," *TNP* 14 (1994), pp. 3–60; *NYT*, January 10, 1994, p. B8.

Allen E. Hye

HAFEY, Charles James "Chick" (b. February 12, 1903, Berkeley, CA; d. July 2, 1973, Calistoga, CA), player, was one of five sons and three daughters of sewer contractor Charles Hafey and May Hafey. Hafey graduated from St. Mary's High School and at age 17 signed with the St. Louis Cardinals (NL). Hafey claimed to be age 18, thinking it would improve his chances. A right-handed pitcher, he excelled for the Shattuck Avenue Merchants team. In 1922, Hafey pitched batting practice for the St. Louis Cardinals. He married Bernice Stigliano on December 1, 1922 and had one son. In 1923, Cardinals manager Branch Rickey* switched the strong-armed, erratic pitcher to the outfield to utilize his powerful bat. Hafey already had demonstrated major league hitting potential by lashing line drives into the outfield. He batted .284 in 1923 for Fort Smith, AR (WA), .253 for St. Louis, and .350 for Houston, TX (TL) the next year. After appearing in 21 games for Syracuse, NY (IL) in 1925, the Cardinals promoted him.

Hafey enjoyed a great career with the Cardinals, despite ill health, poor eyesight, and salary disputes. After Hafey was beaned several times in 1926, Dr. Robert Hyland told him to wear glasses. Hafey, one of the first outfielders to wear lenses, used three different pairs because his eyesight varied. A chronic sinus infection compounded his vision problems, requiring many operations the next few seasons. After hitting .336 in 1930, Hafey held out for $15,000. The Cardinals offered him only $12,000, causing him to report ten days late to spring training. Hafey eventually signed for $12,500, but Rickey fined him $2,100 for not being in playing condition. After winning the NL batting title in 1931 with a .349 mark, Hafey demanded a $17,000 salary, including a return of the $2,100 fine. Rickey traded Hafey to the Cincinnati Reds (NL) in April 1932 for $50,000 (a percentage of which he banked for himself), Bennie Frey, and Harvey Hendrick. From 1932 to 1935, Hafey saw limited service with the Reds. The quiet, soft-spoken Hafey became quite a practical joker, once tying the hands and feet of his roommate Ernie Lombardi* to the bedposts while he slept. A sinus condition forced him to retire after the 1935 season. He attempted a brief comeback with the Reds in 1937, but hit only .261.

Hafey batted with considerable power, slugging 82 HR and knocking in 343 runners from 1928 to 1930. During his career, he played in 1,283 games, scored 777 runs, made 1,466 hits, slugged 164 HR, knocked in 833 runs, and compiled a .317 batting average. Although hitting only .205 in four World Series, he set a record for the most doubles (5) in a six-game set. Hafey, one of the game's best right-handed hitters, in 1929 made 10 consecutive hits. In 1971, the Veterans Committee elected him to the National

Baseball Hall of Fame. Hafey's older brother and three nephews also played professional baseball. Hafey raised sheep and cattle on his ranch, but suffered from emphysema and a disabling stroke.

BIBLIOGRAPHY: Charles Hafey file, National Baseball Library, Cooperstown, NY; Bob Broeg, "Hafey's Dilemma," St. Louis *Post Dispatch*, July 8, 1973; Gene Karst and Martin J. Jones, Jr., *Who's Who in Professional Baseball* (New York, 1973); Frederick G. Lieb, *Comedians and Pranksters of Baseball* (St. Louis, MO, 1958); Craig Carter, ed., *TSN Daguerreotypes* (St. Louis, MO, 1990); Lawrence Ritter and Donald Honig, *The 100 Greatest Baseball Players of All Time* (New York, 1981); *TSN* (July 21, 1973); Frederick G. Lieb, *The St. Louis Cardinals* (New York, 1945); John Thom, *Champion Batsman of the 20th Century* (Los Angeles, CA, 1992); Rob Rains, *The St. Louis Cardinals* (New York, 1992); Bob Broeg and Jerry Vickery, *St. Louis Cardinals Encyclopedia* (Grand Rapids, MI, 1998).

William A. Borst

HAHN, Frank George "Noodles" (b. April 29, 1879, Nashville, TN; d. February 6, 1960, Candler, NC), player, was a 5-foot 9-inch, 160-pound, left-handed pitcher who married Salome Stevens. Hahn's brief career with the Cincinnati Reds (NL) featured him as one of the most effective pitchers ever for second-division clubs. He appeared in the major leagues at age 20, with his 23 wins in 1899 ranking him behind only Kid Nichols,* Bob Feller,* and Dwight Gooden* for victories by a pitcher under age 21. Although enduring a losing season in 1900, he hurled the first 20th-century no-hitter on July 12 against the Philadelphia Phillies and led the NL with 145 strikeouts.

Hahn's most successful season came with 22 wins in 1901, although he suffered 7 losses because his last-place Reds were shut out. He paced the NL with 132 strikeouts and 4 shutout. Hahn recorded 42.3 percent of his cellar team's victories, a record that stood until Steve Carlton* won 27 contests for the last-place Philadelphia Phillies (NL) in 1972. No previous pitcher had triumphed 20 times for a last-place team. He finished 41 of his 42 starts, a record for most complete games by a left-hander and for most games started without relief, and led the NL in strikeouts with 239. His modern mark for strikeouts in a single game (16 on May 22, 1901) stood until Dizzy Dean* fanned 17 batters in 1933. The 16 strikeouts remained a Reds record until Jim Maloney* broke it in 1965. He led the NL in 1901 in innings pitched with 375 and walked only 69 batters, a ratio of 1.65 walks per 9 innings. Cincinnati newspapers frequently described him as "The Great Hahn," but he usually was nicknamed "Noodles." He won 23 games in 1902 and 22 games in 1903, compiling ERAs of 1.76 and 2.52. In 1903, he appeared in 34 games and had 34 complete games.

Hahn hurt his arm learning the spitball in 1905, causing the Reds to release the 26-year-old hurler. A brief tenure with the New York Highlanders (AL) in 1906 ended his major league career. During his major league career, the control pitcher walked only 1.70 batters per 9 innings, a record for a left-handed pitcher. He issued only 381 walks in 2,029 innings. He completed 212 of his 231 starts, producing 130 wins, 94 losses, and a 2.55 ERA for perennial second-division teams.

Following his baseball career, he became a Doctor of Veterinary Medicine and served as a government meat inspector in Cincinnati, OH. He regularly attended Cincinnati games, often working out with the Reds and serving as their nonsalaried assistant in charge of batting practice. However, younger players were not regaled with stories of his past glories. He moved to North Carolina in 1953 and resided there until his death.

BIBLIOGRAPHY: Frank Hahn file, National Baseball Library, Cooperstown, NY; Donald Honig, *The Cincinnati Reds* (New York, 1992); Lee Allen, *The Cincinnati Reds* (New York, 1948); Bob Rathgeber, *Cincinnati Reds Scrapbook* (Virginia Beach, VA, 1982); Lonnie Wheeler and John Baskin, *The Cincinnati Game* (Wilmington, OH, 1988).

David B. Merrell

HAINES, Jesse Joseph "Pop" (b. July 22, 1893, Clayton, OH; d. August 5, 1978, Dayton, OH), player and coach, was the son of auctioneer Elias Haines. He married Carrie M. Weidner in 1915 and had one daughter. After attending public schools in Phillipsburg, OH, he pitched for Dayton, OH (CL), Saginaw, MI (SML), Fort Wayne, IN (CL), Springfield, OH (CL), Topeka-Hutchinson, KS (WL), Tulsa, OK (WL), and Kansas City, MO (AA) from 1914 through 1919 and had brief tryouts with the Detroit Tigers (AL) in 1915 and 1916 and Cincinnati Reds (NL) in 1918. His record of 21 victories against only five defeats with Kansas City in 1919 induced St. Louis Cardinals (NL) manager Branch Rickey* to persuade several community stockholders to borrow $10,000 from a bank to buy Haines' contract. Haines represented a big gamble for the financially troubled club.

The 6-foot, 180-pound Haines excelled for the St. Louis Cardinals. From 1920 through 1937, the right-hander won 210 games, lost only 158 (.571 winning percentage), and helped his club win NL pennants in 1926, 1928, 1930, 1931, and 1934. Besides recording at least 20 victories three times (1923, 1927–1928), he pitched a no-hit, no-run game against the Boston Braves in 1924. In 1927, he led the NL in complete games (25) and shutouts (6). In six World Series games (1926, 1928, 1930, 1934), he won three of four decisions and compiled a low 1.67 ERA. His stellar .444 career World Series batting average included one HR. During his major league career, he pitched 3,208.2 innings, struck out 981 batters, and compiled a 3.64 ERA. Haines, who relied on a blazing fastball and knuckleball, coached in 1938 with the Brooklyn Dodgers (NL). He served seven terms from 1938 through 1965 as auditor for Montgomery County, OH.

BIBLIOGRAPHY: Jesse Haines file, National Baseball Library, Cooperstown, NY; Rob Rains, *The St. Louis Cardinals* (New York, 1992); Frederick G. Lieb, *The St. Louis*

Cardinals (New York, 1945); Robert Gregory, *Diz* (New York, 1992); Robert E. Hood, *The Gashouse Gang* (New York, 1978); Bob Broeg and Jerry Vickery, *St. Louis Cardinals Encyclopedia* (Grand Rapids, MI, 1998); Harold (Speed) Johnson, *Who's Who in Major League Baseball* (Chicago, IL 1933); Gene Karst and Martin J. Jones, Jr., *Who's Who in Professional Baseball* (New Rochelle, NY, 1973); *NYT*, July 26, 1978.

Gene Karst

HALE, Arvel Odell "Chief," "Bad News" (b. August 10, 1908, Hosston, LA; d. June 9, 1980, El Dorado, AR), player, was the son of James M. Hale, a farm laborer, and Ella Hale. Hale, of Irish and American Indian ancestry, was nicknamed "Chief." He graduated from high school in Hosston and married Mabel Rainwater of El Dorado, AR in 1930. They had a daughter, Dorinda, and son, Odell, Jr.

Hale began his professional baseball career in 1929 as an infielder with Alexandria, LA (CSL). Sportswriters there dubbed him "Bad News" out of respect for his hitting. When Hale batted, reporters observed, "here came 'Bad News.' " He hit .324 for Alexandria with 23 HR and 24 stolen bases. Hale was promoted to Decatur, IL (3IL) in 1930 and New Orleans, LA (SA) in 1931. After a brief trial with the Cleveland Indians (AL) in September 1931, he was optioned to Toledo, OH (AA) for a final year of seasoning. At Toledo, Hale was helped by manager Bibb Falk.* His .333 batting average included 206 hits, 36 doubles, and 12 triples in 1932 and earned him a spot with the Cleveland Indians in 1933.

Hale played with the Cleveland Indians eight years before concluding his major league career in 1941 with the Boston Red Sox (AL) and New York Giants (NL). He hit .276 in 98 games in 1933 and batted over .300 four of the next six years, achieving a career-high .316 in 1936. Although not a longball threat, Hale belted 10 or more HR four times and averaged 39 doubles and seven triples from 1934 through 1938. He drove in 101 runs in both 1934 and 1935, scored 126 runs in 1936, and appeared in 150 or more games for three consecutive years from 1935 through 1937. Hale led the AL in pinch-hit appearances in 1940 with 40. The infielder split his duties between second base (518 games) and third base (439 games), compiling a .959 lifetime fielding average. He kept in shape during the off-season by hunting and fishing.

Hale's best day as a hitter came on July 12, 1938, when he hit for the cycle against the Washington Senators. His most unusual experience as a fielder occurred at third base on September 7, 1935 against the Boston Red Sox. A line drive off Joe Cronin's* bat bounced off Hale's head to Cleveland shortstop Bill Knickerbocker, who caught it and threw to second baseman Roy Hughes to catch the runner off second. Hughes fired to first baseman Hal Trosky* to complete the triple play. During 10 major league seasons, Hale batted .289 with 1,071 hits, 70 HR, and 573 RBI.

BIBLIOGRAPHY: Arvel Hale file, National Baseball Library, Cooperstown, NY; *TSN Baseball Register*, 1940; Harold "Speed" Johnson, *Who's Who in Major League Baseball*

(Chicago, IL, 1933); Franklin Lewis, *The Cleveland Indians* (New York, 1949); John Thorn et al., eds., *Total Indians* (New York, 1996).

Michael J. McBride

HALL, George William "Gentleman George" (b. March 29, 1849, Stepney, England; d. June 11, 1923, Ridgewood, NY), player, was the son of George R. Hall, an engraver, and Ida (Taylor) Hall. Hall began his major league baseball career in 1871 as an outfielder with the Washington Olympics (NA), batting .294 in 32 games. He played all five NA seasons, including stints with the Lord Baltimores in 1872 and 1873, the champion Boston Red Stockings of 1874, and the Philadelphia Athletics in 1875. Hall's five NA seasons saw him rank second in the circuit in triples in 1875 and bat an overall .311 in 244 games.

In 1876, the Philadelphia Athletics joined the newly established NL. The same year, Hall reached a career-high .366 batting average with a NL-leading five HR. When the Philadelphia Athletics were dropped from the NL, the 5-foot 7-inch, 142-pound, left-handed swinger joined the Louisville, KY Grays (NL) in 1877. Hall batted .323 and led NL outfielders with a .900 fielding average. At the close of that campaign, he agreed to play with the St. Louis Browns (NL). His admitted involvement in a game-fixing scheme, however, led to his subsequent expulsion from the NL and ended his playing career.

The notorious game-fixing scandal caused the 1877 Louisville Grays to blow a commanding lead, enabling the Boston Red Caps to win the NL pennant. Hall, Jim Devlin,* Bill Craver, and Al Nichols were found guilty of conspiring with gambler James McCloud to throw games for money, causing the expulsion of all four players from the NL. The scandal also prompted the Louisville Colonels and St. Louis Browns, which had signed Hall and Devlin to contracts for 1878, to resign from the NL.

Hall's appeals for reinstatement were rejected, ending his seven-year major league career ignominiously. He batted a gaudy .322 with 377 runs scored, 13 HR, and 149 RBI. Hall worked as an engraver and as a clerk in an art museum in New York City.

BIBLIOGRAPHY: John Thorn et al., eds., *Total Baseball*, 5th ed. (New York, 1997); A. H. Tarvin, "75 Years on Louisville's Diamonds," Louisville Public Library Report, 1940; John E. Findling, "The Louisville Grays' Scandal of 1877," *JSH* 3 (Summer 1976), pp. 176–187; George Hall file, National Baseball Library, Cooperstown, NY; James D. Smith III, "Bowing Out on Top," *TNP* 2 (Fall 1982), pp. 73–80; Philip Von Borries, *Legends of Louisville* (West Bloomfield, MI, 1993); Philip Von Borries, *Louisville Diamonds* (Paducah, KY, 1997); Dan Gutman, *Baseball Babylon* (New York, 1992); Daniel E. Ginsburg, *The Fix Is In* (Jefferson, NC, 1995); Robert L. Tiemann and Mark Rucker, eds., *Nineteenth Century Stars* (Kansas City, MO, 1989); David Q. Voigt, *American Baseball*, vol. 1 (University Park, PA, 1983).

David Q. Voigt

HALLER, Thomas Frank "Tom" (b. June 23, 1937, Lockport, IL), player, coach, and executive, is the son of Frank Haller, a crane operator for US Steel Company, and Julia (McGee) Haller. Bill, his older brother, umpired in the AL from 1963 to 1982. At Lockport High School, he was an all-conference football quarterback, basketball guard, and baseball first baseman.

Haller entered the University of Illinois on a football scholarship in the fall of 1955, but also played basketball and baseball for two years. He began catching during the summer of 1957 and started at quarterback in football in 1957. Haller married Joan Alexander on April 13, 1958 and has two sons, Tom, Jr., and Tim.

After signing with the San Francisco Giants (NL) baseball club in February 1958, Haller batted .228 for Phoenix, AZ (PCL) with 16 HR and 54 RBI in 105 games. He hit .276 for Springfield, MA (EL) in 1959 and .251 for Tacoma, WA (PCL) in 1960 before joining the San Francisco Giants in 1961. Haller, the Giants' regular catcher from 1962 through 1967, enjoyed his most productive year in 1966 by batting .240 with 27 HR and 67 RBI. He played in the 1962 World Series against the New York Yankees and made three consecutive NL All-Star game squads from 1966 to 1968.

The San Francisco Giants traded Haller to the Los Angeles Dodgers (NL) in February 1968. He spent four seasons with Los Angeles, compiling a career-best .286 batting average with 10 HR and 47 RBI in 1970. Haller was traded to the Detroit Tigers (AL) in December 1971 and closed out his playing career there in 1972. In 1,294 major league games, he batted .257 with 134 HR and 504 RBI.

After spending four years in the insurance business, Haller rejoined the San Francisco Giants as bullpen coach in 1977 and was promoted to field director of player development for their minor league system in the fall of 1979. He served as Executive Vice President of Baseball Operations and general manager from July 1981 through 1985. The Chicago White Sox (AL) hired Haller to manage their Birmingham, AL (SL) team in the fall of 1985 and promoted him to the front office in June 1986 as assistant to Vice President Ken Harrelson.

Following the 1986 season, Haller moved to the Palm Springs, CA area and worked as an agent for a mortgage company until becoming owner/general manager of Reliable Building Maintenance Services in February 1991. The company name was changed to Total Allegiance Maintenance Services in August 1995, with Haller as vice president and his wife, Joan, as president.

BIBLIOGRAPHY: Tom Haller file, National Baseball Library, Cooperstown, NY; *TSN Baseball Register, 1973*; *San Francisco Giants 1985 Media Guide*; Tom Haller file, Varsity I Association, University of Illinois, Urbana, IL; Jay Langhammer, telephone interview with Tom Haller, April 1996; David Plaut, *Chasing October* (South Bend, IN, 1994); William F. McNeil, *The Dodgers Encyclopedia* (Champaign, IL, 1997).

Jay Langhammer

HALLMAN, William Wilson (b. March 31, 1867, Pittsburgh, PA; d. September 11, 1920, Philadelphia, PA), player and manager, began his professional baseball career as a 19-year-old for Wilkes-Barre, PA (PSL). Wilkes-Barre signed Hallman as a pitcher, but used him as a catcher in an exhibition game against Lehigh University. He fielded the position well and hit a grand slam HR, causing Wilkes-Barre to make him an everyday player. In 1887, his second year with Wilkes-Barre (now IA), Hallman was moved to shortstop. His .333 batting average led the Philadelphia Phillies (NL) to acquire him.

In a 14-year major league career, Hallman played for three Philadelphia teams, the Phillies (NL) from 1888–1889, 1892–1897, 1901–1903; the Quakers (PL) in 1890; and the Athletics (AA) in 1891. His other clubs included the St. Louis Cardinals (NL) in 1897, the Brooklyn Superbas (NL) in 1898, and the Cleveland Blues (AL) in 1901. After joining St. Louis in 1897, Hallman became their manager and produced a 13–36 win-loss record. He was demoted to the minor leagues in 1899 and spent two years with Buffalo, NY (WL). The 1901 expansion to 16 clubs enabled him to play a few more major league seasons. Hallman's baseball career ended with Denver, CO (WL) in 1904. He worked as a comedian with a burlesque show.

The 5-foot 8-inch, 160-pound right-hander played mainly at second base and often performed a utility role. His .272 batting average and 1,634 hits in 1,503 major league games included four consecutive .300 seasons from 1893 to 1896. Defensively, he compiled an above-average fielding percentage (.940) with below-average range. His best defensive season perhaps came as a shortstop in 1889, when he led the NL in total chances per game.

BIBLIOGRAPHY: William Hallman file, National Baseball Library, Cooperstown, NY; Donald Dewey and Nicholas Acocella, *Encyclopedia of Major League Baseball Teams* (New York, 1993); George L. Moreland, *Balldom* (New York, 1914); Rich Westcott and Frank Bilovsky, *The New Phillies Encyclopedia* (Philadelphia, PA, 1993); Allen Lewis, *The Philadelphia Phillies: A Pictorial History* (Virginia Beach, VA, 1981); Frederick G. Lieb and Stan Baumgartner, *The Philadelphia Phillies* (New York, 1953); John Phillips, *Who Was Who in Cleveland Baseball, 1900–10* (Cabin John, MD, 1989); *TSN*, September 23, 1920, p. 4.

William E. McMahon

HAMILTON, William Robert "Sliding Billy," "Good Eye Billy" (b. February 16, 1866, Newark, NJ; d. December 16, 1940, Worcester, MA), player, manager, scout, and executive, was the son of Samuel Hamilton and Mary (McCutchin) Hamilton. Hamilton grew up in Clinton, MA, where he and his father worked in a cotton mill. Reputedly Hamilton signed with Waterbury, CT (EL) during 1886, but their box scores do not include his name. He batted .380 for Lawrence, MA (NEL) in 1886 and Salem, MA (NEL) in 1887 and .352 for Worcester, MA (NEL) in 1888 before being sold in midseason to Kansas City, MO (AA). Hamilton's brilliant major league career saw him with Kansas City in 1888 and 1889, the Philadelphia Phillies (NL) from 1890 through 1895, and the Boston Beaneaters (NL) from 1896 through 1901. At Philadelphia, Hamilton, Ed Delahanty,* and Sam Thompson* formed one of baseball's all-time great outfields. The Phillies unwisely traded Hamilton to Boston for third baseman and field captain Billy Nash,* who fizzled in Philadelphia. At Boston, he played with NL pennant winners in 1897 and 1898.

A left-handed batter and thrower, the stumpy, 5-foot 6½-inch, 165-pound Hamilton was selected for the National Baseball Hall of Fame in 1961. His outstanding 14-season major league statistics included 2,158 hits in 1,591 games, 1,690 runs (over one per game, an all-time record), 912 stolen bases (a record until recent years), 1,187 bases on balls, and a .344 batting average—despite shortened seasons in 1893 (typhoid fever) and 1898 and 1899 (knee injuries). He led his league once in batting championships, four times in runs scored, five times in walks, and five times in stolen bases. An ideal leadoff man, Hamilton hit many singles, batted for high average, and exercised sharp judgment and patience in waiting out pitchers for walks. Hamilton seldom struck out, earning him a second nickname, "Good Eye Billy." His ability to get on base resulted in a .455 on-base average, second only to John McGraw* among nineteenth-century regulars.

Hamilton proved the bane of infielders with his extreme speed and elusiveness on the basepaths and daringly hurtled himself at bases. Hamilton stole 111 bases in 1889 and 1891. Since these totals included extra bases taken by the base runner on batters' singles and doubles per scoring rules of that time, Hamilton's numbers are not comparable with those of Ty Cobb* and other notable twentieth-century base stealers. Nevertheless, the popular "Sliding Billy" was the best base runner of his day. A superlative ball hawk, Hamilton became an ideal center fielder by combining extreme speed and sure-handedness with his uncanny crack-of-the-bat judgments of the direction and depth of batted balls and an acrobatic instinct for catching balls off-balance. Consequently, he ran down every possible catch and made spectacular grabs commonplace. His best single season came in 1894, when he batted .404 with 220 hits, led the NL in runs scored (an all-time season record, 192), bases on balls (126), on-base average (.523), and stolen bases (98), and sustained a 46 consecutive game hitting streak. His .344 lifetime batting average is seventh best in major league history.

Hamilton played outfield and managed with Haverhill, MA (NEL) from 1902 through 1908, except 1905; Lynn, MA (NEL) in 1909 and 1910; and Harrisburg, PA (outlaw TSL) in 1905 and 1906. He scouted for the Boston Rustlers-Braves (NL) during 1911 and 1912 and bench managed at Fall River, MA (NEL) in 1913, Springfield, MA (NEL) in 1914, and Worcester, MA (EL, as part-owner) in 1916. He married Rebecca Jane Carr in 1888 and had four daughters: Ethel (Mrs. Leroy E. Fields), Mildred (Mrs. Howard

Prior), Ruth (Mrs. John C. Miller), and Dorothy (Mrs. H. P. Starr). Having invested earnings wisely and bought property, the Hamiltons lived comfortably in Clinton, MA until his death.

BIBLIOGRAPHY: Martin Appel and Burt Goldblatt, *Baseball's Best: The Hall of Fame Gallery* (New York, 1977); William Hamilton file, National Baseball Library, Cooperstown, NY; Craig Carter, ed., *TSN Daguerreotypes* (St. Louis, MO, 1990); Jerrold Casway, "The Best Outfield Ever?" *BRJ* 27 (1998), pp. 3–7; Harold Kaese, *The Boston Braves* (New York, 1948); Gary Caruso, *The Braves Encyclopedia* (Philadelphia, PA, 1995); Frederick Ivor-Campbell et al., eds., *Baseball's First Stars* (Cleveland, OH, 1996); David Pietrusza, "Sliding Billy Hamilton: Prince of Thieves," *BRJ* 20 (1991), pp. 30–32; *The Baseball Encyclopedia*, 10th ed. (New York, 1996); John Thorn and Pete Palmer, *The Hidden Game of Baseball* (New York, 1984); *TSN*, December 26, 1940, January 25, 1961; United States Census 1880, Massachusetts, Worcester County, T-9, Roll 565, 352; Worcester (MA) *Telegram*, December 16, 1940; John Thorn et al., eds., *Total Braves* (New York, 1996); Rich Westcott and Frank Bilovsky, *The New Phillies Encyclopedia* (Philadelphia, PA, 1993); Frederick G. Lieb and Stan Baumgartner, *The Philadelphia Phillies* (New York, 1953).

Frank V. Phelps

HAMNER, Granville Wilbur "Granny" (b. April 26, 1927, Richmond, VA; d. September 12, 1993, Philadelphia, PA), player, manager, and coach, was of Scotch-Irish ancestry and grew up in Richmond, where he attended Benedictine High School. After signing for an $8,000 bonus in 1944, he joined the Philadelphia Phillies (NL) and hit .247 in 21 games as a shortstop. Hammer spent most of the 1945 season with Utica, NY (EL), but appeared briefly with the Philadelphia Phillies as a teammate of his brother, Garvin. He appeared in two games with Philadelphia in both 1946 and 1947, spending most of 1946 in the U.S. Army Medical Corps. He returned to Utica in 1947, fielding well and improving markedly at the plate.

Hamner stayed with the Philadelphia Phillies in 1948 and started at shortstop in 1949. The following year, he hit .270 and set a club record (since broken) by starting 157 games at shortstop for the Phillies. Philadelphia startled the baseball world by edging out the powerful Brooklyn Dodgers for the NL title on the last day of the 1950 season. No Phillies team had won a NL pennant since 1915. The Yankees swept Philadelphia in the World Series, but Hamner hit .429. Despite the efforts of Hamner, outfielders Richie Ashburn* and Del Ennis,* and pitcher Robin Roberts,* the Phillies played mediocre baseball thereafter. Hamner started for the NL at shortstop in the 1952 All-Star game and at second base two years later, making him the first player in All-Star game history to start at two different positions. He subsequently played primarily at second base, but returned to shortstop when needed. Hamner's peak years at bat came from 1952 to 1954 when he averaged nearly 90 RBI and joined Ennis in providing the club much of its offensive power.

Hamner declined rapidly as a hitter his last three seasons as a regular and was relegated to the bench in 1958. The Philadelphia Phillies traded him to the Cleveland Indians (AL) in May 1959, but he struggled there. The strong-armed Hamner, who had appeared in four games as a pitcher in 1956 and 1957, made an unsuccessful comeback as a pitcher with the Kansas City Athletics (AL) in 1962. He managed in the minor leagues and served as an infield instructor in the Philadelphia Phillies minor league system. Hamner died while attending a baseball memorabilia show and a reunion of the 1950 Whiz Kids. He played in 1,531 major league games, compiling a .262 batting average with 104 HR and 708 RBI. Hamner lost both decisions as a pitcher and compiled a 5.40 ERA. He married Shirley Wiltshire in 1945 and had four children.

BIBLIOGRAPHY: *WWIB, 1951*, 36th ed.; *Who's Who in the Big Leagues, 1955*; Rich Marazzi and Len Florito, *Aaron to Zuverink* (New York, 1981); Granville Hamner file, National Baseball Library, Cooperstown, NY; Harry Paxton, *The Whiz Kids* (New York, 1950); Rich Westcott and Frank Bilovsky, *The New Phillies Encyclopedia* (Philadelphia, PA, 1993); Allen Lewis, *The Philadelphia Phillies: A Pictorial History* (Virginia Beach, VA, 1981); Frederick G. Lieb and Stan Baumgartner, *The Philadelphia Phillies* (New York, 1953); Robin Roberts and C. Paul Rogers III, *The Whiz Kids and the 1950 Pennant* (Philadelphia, PA, 1996).

Lloyd J. Graybar

HANLON, Edward Hugh "Ned" (b. August 22, 1857, Montville, CT; d. April 14, 1937, Baltimore, MD), player, manager, and executive, was the son of a housebuilder and began his career as a pitcher for the Montville, CT town team. After signing his first professional contract in 1876 with Providence, RI (NEL), he played for Fall River, MA in 1877, Rochester, NY in 1878, and Albany, NY in 1879. His third base play for Albany earned a berth with the Cleveland Blues (NL) for the 5-foot 9½-inch, 170-pounder. Hanlon played left field for Cleveland in 1880, leading the NL in errors and hitting .246. Cleveland sold Hanlon in 1881 to the Detroit Wolverines (NL), where he was installed in center field. Hanlon quickly became a solid fielder, pacing NL outfielders in putouts in 1882 and 1884, total chances per game in 1882 and 1883, and double plays in 1883. He batted above .300 only in 1885, when he hit .302 and was named Detroit team captain. The Wolverines won the NL championship in 1887, but fell apart the next year and were sold.

In the 1888–1889 off-season, Hanlon joined an All-Star team that barnstormed against Adrian Anson's* Chicago White Stockings. The 32,000 mile tour included the United States, Hawaii, New Zealand, Australia, Ceylon, Arabia, Egypt, Europe, England, Scotland, and Ireland, bringing baseball to several countries for the first time. In 1889 Hanlon signed with the Pittsburgh Alleghenys (NL) and assumed managerial responsibilities late in the season. In 1890 he joined the player revolt against the owners known as the Brotherhood War. Hanlon jumped to the Pittsburgh Burghers of the new

PL as center fielder and manager and batted .278 for his sixth-place team. When the NL owners crushed the upstart league, Hanlon in 1891 returned to the Pittsburgh Pirates and batted .266 for his last-place squad. He joined the Baltimore Orioles (NL) franchise the next year, but an injury ended his playing career after 11 games. The Hanlon-led Orioles finished last in 1892 and climbed to eighth in 1893. A .260 lifetime hitter, he proved a good, fast, strong-armed outfielder. In 13 major league seasons, he made 1,317 hits, 159 doubles, and 79 triples, scored 930 runs, and stole 329 bases.

By trading shrewdly and often, Hanlon quickly built a championship team in Baltimore. He acquired John McGraw,* Joe Kelley,* and Wilbert Robinson* in 1893 and added Willie Keeler,* Hugh Jennings,* Dan Brouthers,* and others the next season to vault the Orioles into first place. Nine Orioles batted over .300, while eight drove in at least 92 runs. For three straight seasons (1894–1896), Baltimore won the NL championship. In 1897 and 1898, the Orioles finished second. The Orioles fielded one of the best teams in baseball history. Although the pitching staff lacked outstanding performers, the Orioles offense required only adequate hurlers. Triumphant Baltimore drove the opposition to distraction by executing "inside baseball" better than any team of that era. Scholars and contemporaries disagree as to who originated and refined the techniques, but Hanlon's Orioles implemented the strategy with relentless precision and verve. They hit and ran, used the squeeze play, and platooned right-handers versus left-handed pitchers and vice-versa. Hanlon also became the first Orioles manager to take his team south for spring training.

When the Baltimore franchise moved to Brooklyn (NL) as the Superbas in 1899 without McGraw and Robinson, Hanlon's team won pennants the next two years. Of ten pennants contested from 1891 through 1900, Hanlon's clubs won five. The Brooklyn move made Hanlon baseball's highest paid manager. He retained that distinction upon joining the Cincinnati Reds in 1906, but met little success in two years there. Hanlon, who had lived in Baltimore since 1892, left Cincinnati in 1907 and became president of the Baltimore Orioles (EL). After selling the team to Jack Dunn,* he tried unsuccessfully to buy the Boston Red Sox in 1911 and invested much of his savings in the Baltimore Terrapins franchise (FL) in 1914 and 1915. A civic leader, Hanlon served for 21 years as member of the City Park Board and from 1931 on as its president. He and Ellen Jane Kelly had five children, including three daughters and a son, Edward. Another son, Joseph, died in World War I. Hanlon's substantial contributions to baseball are not well recognized. His managerial contributions included five pennants in seven years, a 1,313–1,164 career record (.530), the building of one of baseball's legendary teams, and the use of innovative techniques. Several of Hanlon's players, including McGraw, Jennings, Kelley, Robinson, and Fielder Jones,* enjoyed successful managerial careers. In 1996, the Veterans Committee elected him to the National Baseball Hall of Fame.

BIBLIOGRAPHY: Ned Hanlon file, National Baseball Library, Cooperstown, NY; Lee Allen, *The National League Story* (New York, 1961); Baltimore *Sun*, April 15, 1937; James H. Bready, *The Home Team* (Baltimore, MD, 1979); Frank Graham, *McGraw of the Giants* (New York, 1944); *NYT*, April 15, 1937; Edwin Pope, *Baseball's Greatest Managers* (Garden City, NY, 1960); *The Baseball Encyclopedia*, 10th ed. (New York, 1996); Robert Smith, *Baseball* (New York, 1947); Robert L. Tiemann and Mark Rucker, eds., *Nineteenth Century Stars* (Kansas City, MO, 1989); Thomas Aylesworth and Benton Minks, *The Encyclopedia of Baseball Managers* (New York, 1990); James H. Bready, *Baseball in Baltimore* (Baltimore, MD, 1998); Frank Graham, *The Brooklyn Dodgers* (New York, 1945); William F. McNeil, *The Dodgers Encyclopedia* (Champaign, IL, 1997).

Douglas D. Martin

HARDER, Melvin Leroy "Mel," "Chief" (b. October 15, 1909, Beemer, NE), player and coach, is the son of a Nebraska Power Company machinist. After his parents, Claus H. Harder and Clara (Skala) Harder, moved to Omaha, NE, Harder attended Druid Hill grade school and Omaha Technical High School from 1924 to 1927. As a high school sophomore, he pitched his team to the city championship. During the spring of 1927, he signed with Omaha, NE (WL) and was optioned to Dubuque, IA (MOVL). After Harder returned to Omaha, the Cleveland Indians (AL) purchased his contract.

Harder hurled for the Cleveland Indians from 1928 to 1947, but the 18-year-old right-hander pitched only 49 innings his rookie season. At midseason the following year, the Indians briefly sent him to the New Orleans, LA Pelicans (SA). Harder blossomed after developing a curveball to complement his fastball and adding weight to his 6-foot 1-inch, 150-pound frame. From 1930 to 1933, he averaged 13 wins a season. On July 31, 1932, he pitched the inaugural game at Cleveland Municipal Stadium, losing 1–0 to Lefty Grove* of the Philadelphia Athletics. Harder married Hazel Claire Schmidt of Omaha in 1932 and has two daughters, Kathryn Gay and Penny Lyn.

Harder enjoyed his finest seasons in the mid-1930s, winning 20 games in 1934 and 22 games in 1935 against the likes of Lou Gehrig,* Charles Gehringer,* and Jimmie Foxx.* His 2.61 ERA in 1934 comprised the AL's second lowest. Nicknamed "Chief" and "Wimpy" by teammates, Harder earned national recognition by pitching five scoreless innings in the 1934 All-Star game. He participated in the 1935, 1936, and 1937 All-Star games, hurling 13 scoreless innings against National Leaguers.

After an impressive 12–3 start in 1936, Harder injured his arm and finished the season in pain with a disappointing 15–15 record. Harder won between 12 and 17 games annually for the next four years, but arm problems continued to plague him. Following a mediocre 5–4 season in 1941, he underwent surgery and hurled 13 victories in 1942. He pitched with Cleveland until retirement in 1947, amassing 223 career wins and 186 defeats and compiling more triumphs than any Indian except Bob Feller.* In 582 games, he pitched 3,426.1 innings, struck out 1,161 hitters, and posted a 3.80 ERA.

Harder returned to the Indians as a first base coach for the 1948 pennant-winning season and served as pitching coach there from 1949 through 1963. A mild-mannered, patient teacher, he contributed immensely to the pitching successes of Bob Lemon,* Early Wynn,* Mike Garcia,* and Feller during the 1950s. The bespectacled Harder was said to possess a camera in his head, enabling him to spot a pitching flaw immediately. After wearing an Indians uniform longer (36 years) than any other ballplayer, the Chardon, OH resident ended his coaching career with the New York Mets (1964), Chicago Cubs (1965–1966), and Cincinnati Reds (1967–1968), all of the NL, and the AL Kansas City Royals (1969).

BIBLIOGRAPHY: Mel Harder file, National Baseball Library, Cooperstown, NY; Bob Becker, *Pride of the Indians* (Lakewood, OH, 1997); Cleveland *News*, September 10, December 6, 1941; Cleveland *Plain Dealer*, June 23, 1935, May 18, July 2, 1947, December 24, 1961, January 21, 23, October 24, 1962, June 26, 1963, February 17, 1974, March 26, 1976; James N. Giglio, correspondence with Mel Harder, February 4, 1984; Paul Green, "Mel Harder" (interview), *SCD* 11 (June 22, 1984), pp. 64–78; Brent P. Kelley, *The Case For: Those Overlooked by the Baseball Hall of Fame* (Jefferson, NC, 1992); Brent P. Kelley, *The Early All-Stars* (Jefferson, NC, 1997); Bob Feller and Bill Gilbert, *Now Pitching Bob Feller* (New York, 1990); Franklin Lewis, *The Cleveland Indians* (New York, 1949); Ted Taylor, "Does Doc Cramer Belong in the Hall of Fame?" *SCD* 25 (June 11, 1998), pp. 90–91; John Thorn et al., eds., *Total Indians* (New York, 1996); John Phillips, *Winners* (Cabin John, MD, 1987).

James N. Giglio

HARGRAVE, Eugene Franklin "Bubbles" (b. July 15, 1892, New Haven, IN; d. February 23, 1969, Cincinnati, OH), player and manager, remains one of two 20th-century catchers to win an NL batting title and was the son of Franklin Hargrave and Rebecca (Davis) Hargrave. His first job came in the upholstery business.

The 5-foot 11-inch, 170-pound, right-handed hitter signed with Terre Haute, IN (3IL) in 1911 and joined the Chicago Cubs (NL) for three games in 1913. Hargrave played sparingly with the Chicago Cubs in 1914 and 1915 and returned to the minor leagues in 1916. In 1921, he joined the Cincinnati Reds (NL). In eight seasons with the Reds, Hargrave batted over .300 six times. In 1926, he ended Rogers Hornsby's* six-year reign as the NL batting champion with a sparkling .353 average. No NL catcher won another batting title until Cincinnati's Ernie Lombardi* hit .342 in 1938. Hargrave also led NL catchers in fielding in 1926. The Cincinnati Reds released him after the 1928 season. He starred for St. Paul, MN (AA) as a player–manager in 1929, batting .369. He hit .278 in his final major league season with the New York Yankees (AL) in 1930.

Hargrave operated restaurants in St. Paul, MN and Cincinnati, OH and retired in 1966 as a supervisor for the William Powell Valve Company. Hargrave, who married Hester Wolf on May 20, 1918 and had one son,

Eugene, Jr., was nicknamed "Bubbles" because of a speech impediment. His younger brother, William "Pinky," caught in the major leagues from 1923 to 1933. Hargrave hit .310 with 155 doubles, 29 HR, and 376 RBI in 852 major league games.

BIBLIOGRAPHY: *The Baseball Encyclopedia*, 10th ed. (New York, 1996); Peter J. Cava, Indiana-born Major League Player files, Peter J. Cava Collection, Indianapolis, IN; Bubbles Hargrave file, National Baseball Library, Cooperstown, NY; James K. Skipper, *Baseball Nicknames* (Jefferson, NC, 1992); Paul MacFarlane, ed., *TSN Daguerreotypes* (St. Louis, MO, 1981); John Thom, *Champion Batsman of the Twentieth Century* (Los Angeles, CA, 1992); Lee Allen, *The Cincinnati Reds* (New York, 1948); Donald Honig, *The Cincinnati Reds* (New York, 1992).

Peter J. Cava

HARGROVE, Dudley Michael "Mike" (b. October 11, 1949, Perryton, TX), player, coach, and manager, is the son of Dudley Hargrove and Rita Ann Hargrove. He married Sharon Rupprecht, his junior high school sweetheart, on December 27, 1970 and has five children, Kim, Melissa, Pam, Andy, and Cynthia. As a youth, he played American Legion baseball. A graduate of Perryton, TX High School, he lettered in football, basketball, and golf. Hargrove played baseball at Northwestern State College in Alva, OK and completed a bachelor's degree in physical education and social science. Simultaneously, he played semiprofessional baseball in Kansas. Hargrove planned to teach until the Texas Rangers (AL) selected him in the 25th round of the 1972 draft. He signed for $2,000 and played two years in the minor leagues. After jumping to the major leagues, he became the BBWAA and *TSN* AL Rookie of the Year in 1974 and batted .323 and 131 games as a first baseman for the Texas Rangers. Trades followed to the San Diego Padres (NL) in October 1978 and the Cleveland Indians (AL) in June 1979. His first three seasons with the Cleveland Indians saw him have a 23-game hitting streak in 1980 and hit .325, .304, and .317.

In his 12-year major league career, the 6-foot, 195-pound first baseman compiled a .290 batting average and .400 on-base percentage and batted over .300 six times. He twice led the AL in walks (1976, 1978) and set the Cleveland Indians season record for walks (111) in 1980. Four times, he drew over 100 walks in a season. In the early 1980s, Hargrove's rituals at the plate earned him the nickname of "the human rain delay." His antics clearly bothered opposing pitchers. In 1,666 major league games, he drew 965 walks and made 1,614 hits. A line-drive hitter, he belted only 80 career HR. The Oakland A's (AL) signed Hargrove as a 1986 free agent, but released him during spring training. Since then, he has coached and managed in the minors and majors.

The Cleveland Indians, struggling in last place with a 25–52 win–loss record, named Hargrove manager in July 1991. Hargrove guided Cleveland to a 32–53 mark, but the Indians still finished last with the most losses in club history. The Cleveland Indians struggled the next two seasons, but attained a 66–47 record in the strike-shortened 1994 campaign. The Cleveland Indians captured the AL Central Division in 1995 with a 100–44 mark, swept the Division Series against the Boston Red Sox, and won the AL Championship Series against the Seattle Mariners. The Atlanta Braves defeated the Indians 4–2 in the World Series. Hargrove guided the Cleveland Indians to another Central Division title in 1996, but the Baltimore Orioles eliminated them in the AL Division Series. The Cleveland Indians took a third consecutive AL Central Division crown in 1997. They triumphed in the AL Division Series against the New York Yankees and the AL Championship Series against the Baltimore Orioles, but the Florida Marlins edged them in the seven-game World Series. Hargrove's club finished first again in the AL Central Division with an 89–73 mark. In 1998 Cleveland defeated the Boston Red Sox 3–1 in the AL Division Series, but the New York Yankees eliminated them in the six-game AL Championship Series. Cleveland won a fifth straight AL Central Division Title in 1999 with a 97–65 record, but dismissed Hargrove as manager after losing the AL Division Series. Through 1999, Hargrove piloted Cleveland to a 721–591 record and .550 winning percentage. In November 1999, the Orioles named him manager.

Hargrove was All-State in football in 1967 and All-District in basketball in 1968 as a high school student. At Northwestern State College, he made All-Conference twice and was named to *Who's Who*. His honors include being twice selected as Cleveland Indians' Man of the Year (1980, 1981) and winning the Frank Gibbons Good Guy Award (1985). He was chosen the CrL's Manager of the Year at Kingston, NC in 1987, PCL Manager of the Year at Colorado Springs, CO in 1989, and *TSN* AL Manager of the Year in 1995.

BIBLIOGRAPHY: Mike Hargrove file, National Baseball Library, Cooperstown, NY; John Thorn et al., eds., *Total Indians* (New York, 1996); Terry Pluto, *The Curse of Rocky Colavito* (New York, 1994); Jack Torry, *Endless Summers* (South Bend, IN, 1995); Russell Schneider, *The Glorious Summer of 1995* (Cleveland, OH, 1996); *The Baseball Encyclopedia*, 10th ed. (New York, 1996); Sharon Hargrove and Richard Hauer Costa, *Safe at Home* (College Station, TX, 1989); Mike Shatzkin, ed., *The Ballplayers* (New York, 1990).

David B. Merrell

HARPER, Tommy (b. October 14, 1940, Oak Grove, LA), player, scout, coach, and executive, is the son of Ulysses Harper and Louetta (Weir) Harper and moved with his family to California at age four. After starring in several sports at and graduating in 1958 from Ecinal High School in Alameda, CA, he attended Santa Rosa, CA JC in 1958 and San Francisco State University in 1959. Harper batted .507 at San Francisco State in 1960. In 1960, the Cincinnati Reds (NL) signed him as a shortstop–second baseman. The 5-foot 9-inch, 160-pound Harper, who batted and threw right-handed, spent three minor league seasons with Topeka, KS (3IL) in 1960 and 1961 and San Diego, CA (PCL) in 1962, appearing briefly with the Cincinnati Reds in 1962.

The quiet, introspective Harper blended speed and power as a major league leadoff batter and outfielder from 1962 through 1967. His best season with the Cincinnati Reds came in 1965, when he batted .257 with 18 HR, 64 RBI, and 35 stolen bases and led the NL with a career-high 126 runs scored. In November 1967, the Cincinnati Reds traded Harper to the Cleveland Indians (AL). The Seattle Pilots (AL) selected Harper in the October 1968 expansion draft. He in 1969 led the major leagues with a career-best 73 stolen bases, the highest AL total since Ty Cobb's* 96 in 1915.

Harper became a more aggressive hitter when the Seattle franchise shifted to Milwaukee as the Brewers in 1970. In 1971, he established career highs in batting average (.296), hits (179), doubles (35), HR (31), and RBI (82), stole 38 bases, and made the AL All-Star team. Only four major leaguers had attained 30 HR and 30 stolen bases the same season.

In October 1971, the Milwaukee Brewers traded Harper to the Boston Red Sox (AL). Harper enjoyed his best season with Boston as team MVP in 1973, leading the AL and breaking Tris Speaker's* club record with 54 stolen bases and batting .281 with 17 HR and 71 RBI. The California Angels (AL) acquired him in December 1974 and sold him to the Oakland Athletics (AL) in August 1975. His major league playing career ended with the Baltimore Orioles (AL) in 1976.

During 14 major league seasons, Harper batted .257 with 256 doubles, 36 triples, 146 HR, 567 RBI, and 408 stolen bases in 1,810 games. His 1,609 hits and 753 walks gave him more opportunities to steal bases. He once scored on a foul ball between third base and home plate. The Sharon, MA resident, who married Bonnie Jean Williams in October 1962, served as a minor league instructor–scout with the New York Yankees (AL) from 1977 to 1979 and minor league instructor–coach with the Boston Red Sox in 1980. He coached with the Boston Red Sox from 1981 through 1984 and served as assistant to the general manager in 1985. After spending two years with the Boston City Parks, he joined the Montreal Expos (NL) organization as a base running instructor in 1987 and has coached with the Montreal Expos since 1990.

BIBLIOGRAPHY: Tommy Harper file, National Baseball Library, Cooperstown, NY; Bill Ballew, "Tommy Harper: 30–30 Man and Pilots Only Most Valuable Player," *SCD* 21 (September 16, 1994), pp. 152–153; Robert Redmount, *The Red Sox Encyclopedia* (Champaign, IL, 1997); Peter Golenbock, *Fenway* (New York, 1992); *TSN Baseball Register*, 1977; *WWA*, 39th ed., vol. 1 (1976–1977), p. 1338; Bill Libby, *Heroes of the Hot Corner* (New York, 1972); Peter Carry, "Baseball's Week," *SI* 30 (May 19, 1969), p. 95; Larry Keith, "Leading Man without a Voice," *SI* 37 (September 7, 1970), p. 44; Jack Lautier, *Fenway Voices* (Camden, ME, 1990); Rich Marazzi, "Tommy Harper," *SCD* 25 (February 27, 1998), pp. 80–81.

David L. Porter

HARRAH, Colbert Dale "Toby" (b. October 26, 1948, Sissonville, WV), player and coach, was a 6-foot, 185-pound infielder who threw and batted right-handed. The son of Burton Harrah and Glenna Harrah, he grew up in Marion, OH and lettered in baseball, basketball, football, and track and field at Elgin, OH High School. Ohio Northern University offered Harrah a football scholarship, but he signed a free agent baseball contract with the Philadelphia Phillies (NL) in December 1966. Harrah, who attended Texas Wesleyan University, married Janet Beane on October 27, 1979 and has four children, Toby, Haley, Katie, and Thomas.

The Washington Senators (AL) selected Harrah in the 1967 minor league draft. After joining the Washington Senators in 1969, he became a regular shortstop in 1971 and moved with the franchise to Texas in 1972. The Texas Rangers traded their 1975 Player of the Year to the Cleveland Indians (AL) for Buddy Bell* in December 1978. In 1982, Cleveland named him Co-Player of the Year. The New York Yankees (AL) acquired Harrah in February 1984 and returned him to the Texas Rangers in February 1985. Harrah's major league career ended there as a second baseman in 1986. Harrah managed Oklahoma City, OK (AA) to a 69–71 mark in 1987 and a 67–74 record in 1988 and coached for the Texas Rangers from 1989 through 1992. He coached for the Cleveland Indians in 1996 and for the Detroit Tigers (AL) since 1998.

Known as a hard worker, Harrah played shortstop in 813 games, third base in 1,099 contests, and second base in 244 games. His good batting eye resulted in 1,153 walks to only 868 strikeouts. A lifetime .264 hitter, Harrah made 1,954 hits, 307 doubles, 175 HR, 918 RBI, and 238 stolen bases. He retired as the Texas leader in several offensive categories. His Rangers season records, set in 1985, include most walks (113), best on-base percentage (.437), and highest fielding percentage by a second baseman (.989).

Harrah, a four-time AL All-Star (1972, 1975–1976, 1982), led the AL in walks (109) in 1977. One of his five career grand-slam HR came against the Baltimore Orioles on August 8, 1977, when he hit a club record three round-trippers. In 1989, he batted .318 with 44 RBI for the West Palm Beach, FL Tropics (SPBA). He participated in charities, auctions, and charity golf and established a reputation as a loyal, respectful, hard-working, aggressive player. The Texas Baseball Hall of Fame enshrined him.

BIBLIOGRAPHY: Toby Harrah file, National Baseball Library, Cooperstown, NY; Phil Rogers, *The Impossible Takes a Little Longer* (Dallas, TX, 1991); Jack Torry, *Endless Summers* (South Bend, IN, 1995); Terry Pluto, *The Curse of Rocky Colavito* (New York, 1994); Russell Schneider, *The Glorious Summer of 1995* (Cleveland, OH, 1996); *The Baseball Encyclopedia*, 10th ed. (New York, 1996); Robert E. Kelly, *Baseball's Best* (Jefferson, NC, 1988); Mike Shatzkin, ed., *The Ballplayers* (New York, 1990); *TSN Official Baseball Register, 1987*.

David B. Merrell

HARRELL, Dorothy. *See* Dorothy Harrell Doyle "Snooky."

HARRIDGE, William "Will" (b. October 16, 1883, Chicago, IL; d. April 9, 1971, Evanston, IL), executive, was born to poor English immigrant parents on Chicago's south side. He graduated from high school, attended night classes to learn stenography, and was employed by the Wabash Railroad in Chicago. Harridge's skill at scheduling transportation for AL teams and umpires impressed AL founder and president Ban Johnson.* Johnson made arrangements with the railroad in 1911 to hire the surprised railway clerk, who had never exhibited an interest in baseball, as his private secretary. Harridge married Maude Hunter in June 1911 and had one child, William, Jr.

The quiet, reliable Harridge served the occasionally tempestuous Johnson as personal secretary from 1911 to 1927. In 1927, Johnson's conflicts with team owners and Commissioner Kenesaw Mountain Landis* led to his ouster from the AL presidency and his replacement by Ernest S. Barnard* of the Cleveland Indians (AL). Club owners, perhaps recognizing that Harridge had handled many league matters during the difficult transition in AL presidents, appointed him AL secretary. When Barnard died in March 1931, Harridge was chosen interim president. With the strong support of owners Charles Comiskey* of the Chicago White Sox and Philip Ball of the St. Louis Browns, he was unanimously elected the third AL president two months later. Harridge was reelected president three times and remained the AL's chief executive for a record 28 years. After resigning in 1958, he chaired the AL board until his death in 1971. A year later, Harridge was inducted into the National Baseball Hall of Fame.

Throughout his long tenure as AL head, Harridge concentrated on administrative matters and avoided publicity for himself and his office. When appearing before the public, Harridge spoke briefly, acted dignified and reserved, and represented the solemn, business orientation of the sport. His penchant for discreetly handling AL matters behind closed doors with little fanfare won him the respect and loyalty of team owners. Harridge actively promoted AL participation in the first All-Star game in 1933 and championed the annual spectacle during his presidency. Besides firing and suspending players and managers for "baiting" umpires, he stopped Bill Veeck* from further using a midget pinch-hitter for the 1951 St. Louis Browns (AL) and in 1948 dismissed umpire Ernest Stewart for trying to unionize AL umpires. Harridge also established new departments within his office to promote attendance at AL games. Harridge was inclined to let club owners rule the AL and proved a steady, cautious administrator, content with the daily routine of business at league headquarters in Chicago.

BIBLIOGRAPHY: Lee Allen, *The American League Story* (New York, 1965); William Harridge file, National Baseball Library, Cooperstown, NY; Jerome Holtzman, *The Commissioners* (New York, 1998); Paul MacFarlane, ed., *TSN Hall of Fame Fact Book* (St. Louis, MO, 1982); Eugene C. Murdock, *Ban Johnson: Czar of Baseball* (Westport, CT, 1981); *NYT*, April 10, 1971.

Joseph E. King

HARRIS, Anthony Spencer "Spence" (b. August 12, 1900, Duluth, MN; d. July 3, 1982, Minneapolis, MN), player, manager, and scout, enjoyed a 28-year professional baseball career, setting minor league records for runs scored (2,287), hits (3,617), doubles (743), and total bases (5,434) and compiling a .318 overall batting average. The 5-foot 9-inch, 160-pound left-hander may also have led in bases on balls, recording a high on-base percentage. The son of Wilfred Harris and Helen (Ronan) Harris, he attended schools in Duluth, MN, Milwaukee, WI, and Seattle, WA. A graduate of Seattle's Broadway High School, Harris in 1921 signed with nearby Tacoma, WA (PIL). Most of the outfielder's next three seasons were spent with Bay City, MI (MOL). Although rarely a league leader, Harris won admiration as a talented, durable, hustling ballplayer. His .319 batting average with 35 stolen bases for Bay City in 1924 earned him an outfield reserve spot with the 1925–1926 Chicago White Sox (AL). Despite a two-season .261 batting average, Harris was sent to Shreveport, LA (TL) in 1927 and batted .354 with a TL-leading 60 doubles.

Harris joined Minneapolis, MN (AA) in 1928 and spent the next decade there except for brief stays with the Washington Senators (AL) and Philadelphia Athletics (AL). In 1928, he led the AA with 32 HR, 41 doubles, and 133 runs. From 1928 to 1937, Harris batted at least .300 annually (reaching .363 in 1930), surpassed 100 RBI six times (including 127 in 1928), and hit most of his 258 career HR. In 1938 he joined San Diego, CA (PCL), when Ted Williams* came to the Minneapolis Millers. Through 1945 Harris also played for three other PCL clubs, including Hollywood, CA, Seattle, WA, and Portland, OR. In 1946, the veteran began three seasons with Yakima, WA (WeIL) and closed his professional baseball career with Marysville, CA (FWL) in 1948, batting .361 in 11 games. Harris retired to the Midwest with Olivia (Henriksen) Harris, his wife since 1935. Although a manager in North Platte, NE (NeSL) in 1956 and scout for the New York Mets (NL) in 1962, the personable Harris mainly worked in men's furnishings in Minneapolis, MN.

BIBLIOGRAPHY: Spencer Harris file, National Baseball Library, Cooperstown, NY; SABR, *Minor League Baseball Stars* (Cooperstown, NY, 1978), pp. 52–53; John Thorn et al., eds., *Total Baseball*, 5th ed. (New York, 1997).

James D. Smith III

HARRIS, Ellander Victor "Vic" (b. June 10, 1905, Pensacola, FL; d. February 23, 1978, Mission Hills, CA), player, coach, and manager, was the son of William Harris and attended school in the South. After moving to Pittsburgh, PA, he attended McKelvy Grade School from 1914 to 1919 and Schenley High School from 1919 to 1922. Harris entered professional baseball in 1923 with the Cleveland Tate Stars and was signed the following year by Rube Foster* of the Chicago American Giants (NNL). He joined Cum

Posey's* Homestead, PA Grays (ANL) in 1925 and played there through 1948, except for spending 1934 with the Pittsburgh Crawfords (NNL) and working in 1943 and 1944 in a defense plant. He married Dorothy Smith on October 14, 1936 and had two children, Judith Victoria and Ronald Victor.

Although quiet and soft-spoken, Harris played with determination and aggressiveness. The left-handed batter and right-handed thrower became a fearsome base runner, formidable hitter, and a sure-handed outfielder. Available statistics indicate that Harris batted around .300 during his Negro League career. He participated in six East–West (Negro League) All-Star games, including the 1933, 1935, and 1939 classics, and played winter ball primarily in Puerto Rico and Cuba.

Harris, better remembered as a manager, was named Homestead field leader in 1935 and piloted the Grays to eight NNL pennants. From 1937 through 1945, Hall-of-Famers Josh Gibson* and Buck Leonard* paced the Grays to nine straight flags. The 1943 and 1944 titles came under James Taylor.* Harris guided the Homestead Grays to NNL crowns from 1937 to 1942 and in 1945 and 1948 and managed the 1948 team to the Negro World Series championship. In 1949 he coached the Baltimore Elite Giants, winners of the NAL title. Harris finished his managerial career in 1950, directing the Birmingham, AL Black Barons (NAL) to a 51–24 record. He also managed in the CUWL in 1938 and PRWL in 1936 and from 1947 to 1950.

During his era, Harris was considered the top Negro League manager. His teams posted a 382–238 mark in regular season play from available records and a 10–10 mark during post-season play. An excellent motivator, he was well liked and respected by his players.

BIBLIOGRAPHY: Baltimore *Afro-American*, September 20, 1947; William Brashler, *Josh Gibson* (New York, 1978); Vic Harris with John B. Holway, "Vic Harris Managed Homestead Grays," *DaM* (March 8, 1975); *Negro Player Reports* (Baseball Hall of Fame #1, courtesy of Cliff Kachline, January, 1972); Robert W. Peterson, *Only the Ball Was White* (Englewood Cliffs, NJ, 1970); James A. Riley, *The Biographical Encyclopedia of the Negro Baseball Leagues* (New York, 1994); James A. Riley, *The All-Time All-Stars of Black Baseball* (Cocoa, FL, 1983).

Merl F. Kleinknecht

HARRIS, Joseph "Joe," "Moon" (b. May 20, 1891, Coulters, PA; d. December 10, 1959, Renton Township, PA), player, was a hard-hitting first baseman–outfielder who batted .317 over 10 major league seasons between 1914 and 1928. Harris lived his entire life on western Pennsylvania farms and played on town baseball teams before signing with McKeesport, PA (OPL) in 1912. It took him five years to reach the major leagues, although the New York Yankees (AL) gave him a two-game trial in 1914.

The Cleveland Indians (AL) drafted the 5-foot 9-inch, 170-pound Harris from Chattanooga, TN (SA) in 1917. Harris hit .304 in 1917 before joining the U.S. Army and serving in France. He batted .375 for Cleveland in 1919, but the Indians refused to give him the raise he expected. Harris, thus, held out for the 1920 and 1921 seasons. The local independent Franklin, PA team matched Cleveland's offer, but the holdout cost him the opportunity to play in the 1920 World Series.

The Cleveland Indians traded Harris to the Boston Red Sox (AL), for whom he batted over .300 for three seasons. His best power production came with 13 HR in 1923 and 36 doubles and 77 RBI in 1924. The Boston Red Sox dealt him to the Washington Senators (AL) in April 1925. After batting .313 in 1925, Harris was the outstanding player of the 1925 World Series. He homered in his first at bat to pace the Washington Senators to a 4–1 win over the Pittsburgh Pirates. Harris knocked in the winning run and homered in Game 3 and tied Game 5 with his third World Series HR, but Washington lost. He walked, scored, and doubled in two runs in Game 6. The Washington Senators dropped the World Series to Pittsburgh, but Harris batted a resounding .440 with two doubles, three HR, and six RBI.

In February 1927, the Pittsburgh Pirates (NL) purchased Harris to bolster its pennant run. He batted .326, hitting over .300 for the ninth straight year. In the World Series loss to the New York Yankees, Harris batted a meager .200. He never regained his batting stroke, hitting just .236 for Pittsburgh and the Brooklyn Robins (NL) in 1928.

After spending three minor league seasons with Sacramento, CA (PCL), Toronto, Canada (IL), and Buffalo, NY (IL), Harris quit the game to devote his energies to his fruit farm in Renton Township, PA. He married Pearl Hepner in 1921 and resided in Renton Township until his death from colon cancer.

BIBLIOGRAPHY: Joseph Harris file, National Baseball Library, Cooperstown, NY; Morris A. Bealle, *The Washington Senators* (Washington, DC, 1947); Donie Bush, "Did a Road Roller Strike Us?" *BM* 41 (November 1928), pp. 537–39; Joe Harris, "The Castoff Who Became a Star," *BM* 39 (October 1927), pp. 494–95; Shirley Povich, *The Washington Senators* (New York, 1954); Henry W. Thomas, *Walter Johnson* (Washington, DC, 1995); Franklin Lewis, *The Cleveland Indians* (New York, 1949); Frederick G. Lieb, *The Boston Red Sox* (New York, 1947); Robert Redmount, *The Red Sox Encyclopedia* (Champaign, IL, 1998); Charles Einstein, *The Fireside Book of Baseball* (New York, 1956).

William E. Akin

HARRIS, Stanley Raymond "Bucky" (b. November 8, 1896, Port Jarvis, NY; d. November 8, 1977, Bethesda, MD), player, manager, and scout, was of Swiss-Welsh descent and the son of Thomas Harris, a coal miner, and Katherine (Rupp) Harris. Harris grew up in Pittstown, PA and ended his formal education at age 13. The 5-foot 9½-inch, 156 pounder began his professional baseball career in Muskegon, MI (CL) in 1916 and played for Norfolk, VA (VL) the next season until the club disbanded. Harris, who batted and threw right-handed, completed 1917 with Reading, PA (NYSL) and spent the 1918 and 1919 seasons with Buffalo, NY (IL). In late 1919, the Washington Senators promoted Harris to their AL club.

During a 12-year major league career, the slick-fielding second baseman compiled a .274 batting average, made 1,297 hits, knocked in 506 runs, and stole 167 bases. Besides setting a major league record in 1922 for most put-outs (479) by a second baseman, he led his position in fielding (1927), put-outs (1922–1923, 1926–1927), errors (1923), and double plays (1923, 1925). In 1924, Washington Senators owner Clark Griffith* named the youthful Harris player–manager. The 27-year-old "Boy Wonder" promptly led Washington to its first AL pennant and World Series title. In the seven-game World Series against the New York Giants, Harris batted .333 with two HR and handled 54 fielding chances. He established records for most putouts and assists by a second baseman in a series game (8 each) and for a seven-game series (26, 28). Harris the next year led Washington to the World Series and continued as Senators player–manager until October 1928, when he was traded to the Detroit Tigers (AL) for infielder Jack Warner. In October 1926 Harris married Elizabeth Sutherland, daughter of the U.S. Senator from West Virginia. They had three children.

The perennial "available man," Harris managed in five different decades and piloted more major league games than anyone except Connie Mack* and John McGraw.* Harris, who ranks as the third winningest manager (2,157) and second in games lost (2,218), piloted the Detroit Tigers (1929–1933), Boston Red Sox (AL, 1934), Washington Senators (AL, 1935–1942), and Philadelphia Phillies (NL, 1943). After serving the 1944–1945 seasons as bench manager and front office executive with Buffalo NY, (IL), Harris in 1947 joined the New York Yankees (AL) as manager. He led the Bronx Bombers to a 1947 World Series triumph over the Brooklyn Dodgers and was named *TSN* Major League Manager of the Year, but was replaced by Casey Stengel* after New York finished third in 1948. From 1950 to 1954, Harris managed the Washington Senators (AL) to five second-division finishes. He closed his managerial career on a winning note at the Detroit Tigers (AL) in 1956. After being assistant to the general manager of the Boston Red Sox (AL, 1956–1960), he scouted for the Chicago White Sox (AL, 1962) and Washington Senators (AL, 1963–1971). In 1975 Harris was elected to the National Baseball Hall of Fame.

BIBLIOGRAPHY: *DAB*, Supp. 10 (1976–1980), pp. 313–315; Stanley Harris file, National Baseball Library, Cooperstown, NY; Mark Gallagher, *The Yankee Encyclopedia*, vol. 3 (Champaign, IL, 1997); Robert Redmount, *The Red Sox Encyclopedia* (Champaign, IL, 1998); William M. Anderson, *The Detroit Tigers* (South Bend, IN, 1996); Frederick G. Lieb, *The Detroit Tigers* (New York, 1946); Thomas Aylesworth and Benton Minks, *The Encyclopedia of Baseball Managers* (New York, 1990); Fred Smith, *995 Tigers* (Detroit, MI, 1981); Henry W. Thomas, *Walter Johnson* (Washington, DC, 1995); Shirley Povich, *The Washington Senators* (New York, 1954); Morris Bealle, *The Washington Senators* (Washington, DC, 1947); Paul MacFarlane, ed., *TSN Hall of Fame Fact Book* (St. Louis, MO, 1983); Edwin Pope, *Baseball's Greatest Managers* (New York, 1960).

William Ivory

HART, James Ray "Jim Ray" (b. October 30, 1941, Hookerton, NC), player, grew up in rural eastern North Carolina and signed with the San Francisco Giants (NL) organization. He began his professional baseball career in 1960 with Quincy, IL (ML) and Salem, VA (ApL) and advanced through the San Francisco Giants chain at Fresno, CA (CaL) in 1961, Springfield, MA (EL) in 1962, and Tacoma, WA (PCL) in 1963. Hart batted .355 with Fresno in 1961 and an EL-leading .337 for Springfield in 1962, earning EL Player of the Year honors.

Hart reached the major leagues with the San Francisco Giants in 1963, but was hit in the head by a pitch from Bob Gibson* in his first game. He soon suffered a second beaning and played only seven games in his rookie campaign. Hart became San Francisco's regular third baseman in 1964, when he batted .286 with a club rookie record 31 HR. A steady power hitter, he averaged almost 28 HR per season from 1964 through 1968. Hart reached his career high in HR in 1966 with 33, making the NL All-Star team, and drove in over 90 runs in 1965, 1966, and 1967. A shoulder injury reduced his effectiveness thereafter.

Hart spent parts of 1970, 1971, and 1972 with Phoenix, AZ (PCL) while recovering from injuries. The San Francisco Giants traded him to the New York Yankees (AL) in April 1973. He finished his career as DH there in 1974, ending his major league career with a .278 batting average, 148 doubles, 170 HR, 518 runs, and 578 RBI in 1,125 games. The 5-foot 11-inch, 185-pound right-hander hit for the cycle against the Cincinnati Reds on September 8, 1970 and tied a then major league record with six RBI in one inning. He married Bobby Jean Moore in December 1963.

BIBLIOGRAPHY: Jim Ray Hart file, National Baseball Library, Cooperstown, NY; *TSN Official Baseball Register*, 1970; Nick Peters, *Giants Almanac* (Berkeley, CA, 1988); Peter C. Bjarkman, *Encyclopedia of Major League Baseball Team Histories National League* (Westport, CT, 1991); Fred Stein and Nick Peters, *Giants Diary* (Berkeley, CA, 1987).

Jim L. Sumner

HARTNETT, Charles Leo "Gabby" (b. December 20, 1900, Woonsocket, RI; d. December 20, 1972, Park Ridge, IL), player, coach, and manager, was the eldest of 14 children. He grew up in Millville, MA, where he finished elementary school and attended Dean Academy for two years. Hartnett played baseball for Dean Academy and a semipro team while working in a local factory. After Hartnett began his professional career with Worcester, MA (EL) in 1921, the Chicago Cubs (NL) purchased his contract for $2,500. During spring training of his rookie year (1922), he said nothing to reporters, who tagged him with the ironic nickname "Gabby." A right-handed catcher, the durable Hartnett played 19 seasons for Chicago (1922–1940) and appeared in over 100 games 12 seasons. A solid hitter, he compiled a .297 lifetime batting average and achieved a career-high .354 mark in 1937. His most noteworthy hit, the "homer in the gloamin'," came in the bottom of the ninth inning on September 28, 1938 and enabled the Cubs to defeat the Pittsburgh Pirates and win the NL pennant. Hartnett once held the career HR mark for catchers with 236, made 1,912 hits and 396 doubles, and knocked in 1,179 runs.

An excellent defensive catcher and handler of pitchers, Hartnett helped lead the Chicago Cubs to NL pennants in 1929, 1932, 1935, and 1938. Hartnett paced NL catchers six times each in fielding percentage and assists and four times in putouts. He appeared in five All-Star games and was catcher for the NL when a line drive broke pitcher Dizzy Dean's* toe, effectively ending the latter's career. Dean had shaken off Hartnett's sign and thrown another pitch. During the 1938 season, Hartnett replaced Charlie Grimm* as Cubs manager. He directed the team to a 203–176 won–loss record through the 1940 season and spent 1941 as a player–coach with the New York Giants (NL). Minor league managing stints followed in Indianapolis, IN (AA) in 1942, Jersey City NJ (IL) in 1943, and Buffalo, NY (IL) in 1946. After leaving baseball in 1947, he became successful in the insurance business and owned a bowling alley. Hartnett briefly returned to baseball as a coach in 1965 and scout in 1966 for the Kansas City Athletics (AL). On his 72nd birthday, he died of cirrhosis of the liver. Described as a "beefy man with a tomato-red face who talked a lot," the 6-foot 1-inch, 218-pound Hartnett spearheaded the successful Cubs teams of the 1930s. He was named MVP by the BBWAA in 1935 and was elected to the National Baseball Hall of Fame in 1955.

BIBLIOGRAPHY: Gabby Hartnett file, National Baseball Library, Cooperstown, NY; Bob Broeg, *Super Stars of Baseball* (St. Louis, MO, 1971); Warren Brown, *The Chicago Cubs* (New York, 1946); Jim Enright, *Chicago Cubs* (New York, 1975); Charlie Grimm, *Jolly Cholly's Story* (Chicago, IL, 1968); Gene Karst and Martin J. Jones, Jr., *Who's Who in Professional Baseball* (New Rochelle, NY, 1973); *The Baseball Encyclopedia* 10th ed. (New York, 1996); *NYT*, December 21, 1972; Lowell Reidenbaugh, *Baseball's Hall of Fame-Cooperstown* (New York, 1993); Dan Valenti, *Clout! The Top Home Run Hitters in Baseball History* (Lexington, MA, 1989); Warren Wilbert and William Hageman, *Chicago Cubs: Seasons at the Summit* (Champaign, IL, 1997); Thomas Aylesworth and Benton Minks, *The Encyclopedia of Baseball Managers* (New York, 1990); Eddie Gold and Art Ahrens, *The Golden Era Cubs, 1876–1940* (Chicago, IL, 1985).

John E. Findling

HARTSEL, Tully Frederick "Topsy" (b. June 26, 1874, Polk, OH; d. October 14, 1944, Toledo, OH), player, was nicknamed "Topsy" because of its similarity to his real name. Hartsel, who batted and threw left-handed, stood only 5-feet 5-inches tall and weighed just 155 pounds. With his tiny strike zone, he led the AL five times in walks with 87 in 1902, 121 in 1905, 88 in 1906, 106 in 1907, and 93 in 1908.

In September 1898, Hartsel debuted professionally in baseball with the Louisville, KY Colonels (NL). He played with Louisville for two years until traded to the Cincinnati Reds (NL). In April 1901, the Cincinnati Reds sold the left fielder to the Chicago Cubs (NL). In 1901, Hartsel led the Cubs in HR with seven and tied the major league record for most putouts by a left fielder in a 9-inning game with 11. After being traded to the Philadelphia Athletics (AL) in 1902, he paced the AL in stolen bases (47) and runs scored (109). Hartsel remained with Philadelphia until his retirement following the 1911 season, helping the A's win four AL pennants. He batted over .300 four times (1898, 1900–1901, 1903) during his 14-year career. From 1900 to 1909, Hartsel ranked 12th in stolen bases (233), ninth in triples (88), and 13th in runs (754). He batted .276 lifetime with 1,336 hits, 837 walks, and 247 stolen bases. Hartsel played in the 1905 and 1910 World Series, batting .273 in six games. During the 1905 World Series against the New York Giants, Hartsel led off and paced the Philadelphia A's with a .294 batting average. In 1906, he played in the longest game in AL history, a 24-inning victory against the Boston Red Sox.

In an era before outfield fences, Hartsel was a victimized by fan intervention during a game at Philadelphia. He attempted to catch a long fly into left field. As Hartsel ran toward the ball, he went into an unmoving wall of spectators rooting for the other team. He could not penetrate the crowd while the ball fell safely for a HR.

Hartsel, who married Angie May Goodwin, remained active in the OTBA and managed teams in the junior amateur leagues. He piloted a Junior Boys League team, the Toledo Mud Hens, to second place in 1912. He also worked for the Community Traction Company in Toledo, OH.

BIBLIOGRAPHY: Tully Hartsel file, National Baseball Library, Cooperstown, NY; "Tully Hartsel," *Microsoft Complete Baseball*, CD-ROM (Redmond, WA, 1994); John Thorn et al., eds., *Total Baseball*, 5th ed. (New York, 1997); Ralph Hickok, *Who Was Who in American Sports* (New York, 1971); David Nemec and Pete Palmer, eds., *Fascinating Baseball Facts* (Lincolnwood, IL, 1994); Robert Smith, *Baseball* (New York, 1947); "Great Umpire Calls Last Strike on Toledo Diamond Star of Yore," Toledo (OH) *Times*, October 16, 1944; Eddie Gold and Art Ahrens, *The Golden Era Cubs, 1876–1940* (Chicago, IL, 1985); Frederick G. Lieb, *Connie Mack* (New York, 1945); Connie Mack, *My 66 Years in the Big Leagues* (Philadelphia, PA, 1950).

                                                                    Lowell D. Smith

HARVEY, Bryan Stanley (b. June 2, 1963, Soddy-Daisy, TN), player, graduated in 1981 from Bandys High School in Catawba, NC, lettering in baseball, basketball, and football. After attending the University of North Carolina at Charlotte for one year, he married Lisa Ann Martin on March

26, 1983. They have three children, Kristopher, Whitney, and Hunter. Harvey owns a 900-acre Catawba, NC horse, cattle, and ostrich ranch. He played on the nationally known Howard's Furniture slow-pitch softball team with his father, Stan, a welder and legendary slow-pitch slugger.

A California Angels (AL) scout saw Harvey in a 1984 American Legion state tournament. The 6-foot 2-inch, 212-pound right-hander began his professional baseball career with the Davenport, IA based Quad Cities (ML) in 1985 and joined the California Angels in 1988, earning *TSN* Rookie Pitcher of the Year award. Elbow surgery shortened his season and he began a career-long struggle with arm problems. His pitching strengths included an unflappable manner, a 92-mph fastball, and, when working, a virtually unhittable forkball. In 1989, he and Rob Dibble of the Cincinnati Reds (NL) established a new major league record by averaging 12.9 strikeouts per 9 innings. Two years later, he made the AL All-Star Team and was selected both the AL Rolaids Relief Man and *TSN* AL Co-Fireman of the Year while saving 46 games for last-place California. Arm problems returned in 1992. The Florida Marlins (NL) risked assuming his large salary and chose him in the November 1992 expansion draft.

Harvey's amazing 1993 season confirmed the Florida Marlins' hopes. He played in the All-Star game and saved 45 of the Marlins' 64 victories, winning or saving a record 71.9 percent of their games. Injuries sidelined him in 1994 and 1995. He returned to the California Angels in December 1995, after transplant surgery, but missed the entire 1996 season. In December 1997, the Houston Astros (NL) signed him to a minor league contract. He enjoyed a fine career average of 10.4 strikeouts per 9 innings. Other major league career totals included 17 wins against 25 losses, a 2.49 ERA, and 177 saves.

BIBLIOGRAPHY: Bryan Harvey file, National Baseball Library, Cooperstown, NY; Bill Ballew, "Bryan Harvey Reemerges Among Game's Top Closers," *SCD* 20 (July 16, 1993), pp. 100–101; *California Angels 1996 Media Guide; The Scouting Report*, 1990, 1994 (New York, 1990, 1994).

John T. English

HARVEY, Harold Douglas "Doug," "Silver Fox" (b. March 13, 1930, Southgate, CA), umpire, is the son of Harold Wollen, a part-time minor league umpire, and Margaret Mae (Teters) Harvey. His mother came from Cherokee-Choctaw descent, making Harvey the first major league umpire of Native American ancestry. An all-around athlete, Harvey attended El Centro JC and San Diego State College and played baseball, basketball, and football. The former collegiate catcher worked as a construction representative for the Southern California Gas Company. Harvey's interest in umpiring came while watching New York Yankees (AL) pitcher Don Larsen* hurl a perfect game against the Brooklyn Dodgers in the 1956 World Series on television. A "natural," Harvey rose rapidly through the umpiring ranks and reached the NL in 1962 after only four minor league campaigns. These included three CaSL seasons (Class C) from 1958 to 1960 and one PCL campaign (Class AAA) in 1961.

Harvey's prematurely gray hair earned him the nickname "Silver Fox," adding an aura of distinction to his authoritative on-field demeanor. The 6-foot 2-inch, 195-pound Harvey ranked among his era's best, most respected umpires. A 1974 MLPA poll named Harvey the best NL umpire and the only arbiter to receive an "Excellent" rating. Harvey, who retired after the 1992 season, umpired five All-Star games (1963–1964, 1971, 1977, 1982), 31 games in a record 9 League Championship Series (1970, 1972, 1976, 1980, 1983–1984, 1986, 1989, 1991), and 28 games in 5 World Series (1968, 1974, 1981, 1984, 1988). He stirred up a controversy in 1978 by ejecting Don Sutton* for deliberately scuffing baseballs. The Los Angeles Dodgers pitcher went unpunished after threatening to sue Harvey and the NL if he was given the mandated 10-day suspension for defacing balls.

Harvey married Joan Manning in 1951 and then Joy Ann Glascock in 1960, having three sons, Douglas, Scott, and Todd, by his second marriage. Harvey's automobile bore personalized license plates, "NL UMP," indicating pride in his chosen profession.

BIBLIOGRAPHY: Doug Harvey file, National Baseball Library, Cooperstown, NY; Doug Harvey file, *TSN* Archives, St. Louis, MO; Doug Harvey, letter to Larry R. Gerlach, December 8, 1988; St. Louis (MO) *Post-Dispatch*, July 16, 1978; *TSN Baseball Register*, 1964, 1969–1979, *Green Book*, 1962–1990.

Larry R. Gerlach

HAUSER, Joseph John "Unser Choe" (b. January 12, 1899, Milwaukee, WI; d. July 11, 1997, Sheboygan, WI), player and manager, remains the only professional baseball player to register two 60-plus HR seasons. One of eight children born to Andrew Hauser, a blacksmith, and Mary (Hautsinger) Hauser, both German immigrants, Hauser left St. Michael's School at age 14 for mill work to help the family. He pitched for the local champion "Zunker Comers" and semiprofessional baseball in Waupun, WI. In 1918, manager Connie Mack* contracted Hauser for the Philadelphia Athletics (AL). After Hauser played at Providence, RI (EL) in 1918–1919 and Milwaukee, WI (AA) in 1920–1921, Mack paid $25,000 and traded four players for the promising first baseman.

As a 5-foot 10½-inch, 175-pound rookie in 1922, Hauser hit .323 in 111 games. The following season, Hauser batted .307 with 17 HR and 94 RBI. In 1924, the left-hander trailed only Babe Ruth* in HR with 27 and plated 115 runners. At spring training in 1925, however, Hauser was sidelined by a split right kneecap and missed that entire season. He was stiff-kneed the next season and was sent to Kansas City, MO (AA) in 1927, where he enjoyed a comeback with a .353 batting average, 91 extra-base hits, and 134 RBI and belted 500-foot HR on consecutive days. In 1928, his fast start with the Philadelphia Athletics was stalled by overcoaching from Ty Cobb* and the emergence of first baseman Jimmie Foxx.* A brief June 1929 stop with the Cleveland Indians (AL) ended Hauser's major league career with a .284 composite batting average, 79 HR, and 356 RBI.

In 1930, "pulling the ball" with a lighter bat, Hauser hit a professional baseball record 63 HR and garnered 175 RBI for Baltimore, MD (IL). He joined Minneapolis, MN (AA) in 1932 and the next year clouted 69 HR with a recorded 182 RBI and batted .332. A broken left kneecap in July ended his fine 1934 campaign with 33 HR. Hauser's five great seasons from 1930 through 1934 saw him average 49 HR and 134 RBI and win acclaim as "home-run king of the minors." Gradually slowed by injuries, Hauser moved with his wife, Irene (Kaye), in 1937 to Sheboygan, WI (WSL). At Sheboygan, he ended his playing career in 1942 with a .302 batting average and 14 HR, managed four pennant winners, and opened a successful sporting goods store. Hauser, who belted 399 career HR, also piloted Union City, TN (KL) and Duluth, MN (NoL) in the 1950s and was elected to the Wisconsin Athletic Hall of Fame in 1967 and the Wisconsin Old-Timers State Hall of Fame in 1988. Decades earlier, Hauser had left his mark on Cooperstown, NY. As the AA representative to the unique 1939 NA (minor league) All-Star game dedicating the National Baseball Library, Hauser contributed a towering HR. He died four days after being notified by Major League Baseball that he would be eligible for a pension.

BIBLIOGRAPHY: Joseph Hauser file, National Baseball Library, Cooperstown, NY; *Minor League Baseball Stars* (Cooperstown, NY, 1978); Jim Krenz, "An Unforgettable Evening with 'Unser Choe' Hauser," *SCD* 24 (August 8, 1997), pp. 120–121; Frederick G. Lieb, *Connie Mack* (New York, 1945); Eugene Murdock, "They Called Him Unser Choe," *BRJ* 6 (1977), pp. 37–46; *NYT*, July 21, 1997, p. B9; John Thorn et al., eds., *Total Baseball*, 5th ed. (New York, 1997); Stew Thornley, " 'Unser Choe' Hauser: Double 60," *BRJ* 20 (1991), pp. 20–22.

James D. Smith III

HAYES, Frank Witman "Blimp" (b. October 13, 1914, Jamesburg, NJ; d. June 22, 1955, Point Pleasant, NJ), player, impressed umpire Frankie Marshall officiating games of Pennington Prep High. The umpire sent the 6-foot, 190-pound Hayes to Philadelphia Athletics (AL) manager Connie Mack.* After noting his size, the fatherly Mack advised Hayes to catch and optioned him to Albany, NY (IL) and Buffalo, NY (IL) for seasoning in 1933. Although still a rookie, Hayes joined Babe Ruth* and other major league All-Stars on their 1934 trip to the Orient. His first full season with the Philadelphia Athletics in 1936 saw Hayes hit .271 in 144 games. Hayes developed a reputation for durability. He tied a major league mark by hitting four doubles in one game on July 25, 1936, always batting right-handed.

Hayes, well liked for his work ethic, exhibited some defensive weaknesses, especially on pop fouls. Coach Russell "Lena" Blackburne successfully drilled Hayes hard on improving his defensive skills. Hayes enjoyed his best year in 1940, batting .308 and being compared with Bill Dickey.* Hayes' trade in June 1942 to the St. Louis Browns (AL) caused his career to take a downturn. Rick Ferrell,* the regular St. Louis Browns catcher, prevented Hayes from getting enough work. Fortunately, the Philadelphia Athletics reacquired Hayes in February 1944. Hayes caught all 155 games for the Philadelphia Athletics during the 1944 season. Short of playing talent during wartime baseball, Connie Mack asked Hayes to catch as many games as he could. Hayes replied, "That is all right with me." His 312 consecutive game streak set a major league record for catchers covering the 1943–1946 seasons. During that span, Hayes caught for the St. Louis Browns, Philadelphia Athletics, and Cleveland Indians (AL). After the Cleveland Indians acquired Hayes in May 1945, the streak ended in bitterness on April 21, 1946. Cleveland manager Lou Boudreau* removed Hayes from the starting lineup without telling him, causing the catcher to react angrily. Hayes caught Bob Feller's* no-hitter nine days later, winning the game 1–0 on his solo HR. Nevertheless, the estrangement between manager Boudreau and Hayes remained irreparable. In July 1946, the Cleveland Indians sold Hayes to the Chicago White Sox (AL) for the waiver price. Ironically, the news leaked out the day of the 1946 All-Star game, for which Hayes was the starting AL catcher. An All-Star being sold for the $7,500 waiver price seemed strange. Hayes also had performed in the 1940, 1941, and 1944 All-Star games and had been chosen for the 1939 team. His major league career ended in 1947 after five games with the Boston Red Sox (AL). In 14 major league seasons, he batted .259 with 119 HR and 628 RBI.

Hayes, who married Helen Morton in February 1942, earned the respect of many baseball authorities. Sportswriter Frank Gibbons called Hayes "a good fellow, proud of his ability . . . and record," while sportswriter Franklin Lewis praised "his courage . . . strength, and . . . steadiness [as] . . . a real big leaguer." Hayes remained the true professional.

BIBLIOGRAPHY: Frank Hayes file, National Baseball Library, Cooperstown, NY; Stan Baumgartner, "A Durable Hayes Ready to Take Up Where 'Iron Man' Mueller Left Off," TSN, March 22, 1945; Ed Burns, "What Will People Say? Chisox Get All-Star Hayes on Waivers," TSN, July 17, 1946; Frank Gibbons, "The Hayes Misunderstanding," BD 5 (November 1946); Franklin Lewis, "Rain in Philly Led to Hayes Deal, New Champ Hailed," Cleveland (OH) Press, June 29, 1945; Franklin Lewis, The Cleveland Indians (New York, 1949); Frederick G. Lieb, Connie Mack (New York, 1945); Connie Mack, My 66 Years in the Big Leagues (Philadelphia, PA, 1950); Bill Borst, ed., Ables to Zoldak, vol. 1 (St. Louis, MO, 1988); Red Smith, "Prodigal Pappy: Frankie Hayes," BD 3 (May 1944); John Thorn et al., eds., Total Baseball, 5th ed. (New York, 1997); The Baseball Encyclopedia, 10th ed. (New York, 1996).
                                                                  William J. Miller

HAYLETT, Alice M. "Al," "Sis" (b. April 2, 1923, Coldwater, MI), player, starred as a pitcher–outfielder. She grew up in a farm family of English, Pennsylvania Dutch, and Indian ancestry and graduated from Coldwater High School in 1940. After taking a summer job in Battle Creek, Haylett worked full-time for five years and played softball for different local teams. She was playing for Van's Sports Shop in Battle Creek when she heard about the AAGPBL from Betty Whiting, a fellow softball player who had played in the AAGPBL in 1944.

The 5-foot 6-inch, 155-pound, right-handed Haylett pitched four AAGPBL seasons with the Grand Rapids, MI Chicks from 1946 through 1949 and played the outfield, batting .221 her first season. The Chicks fielded some great teams, finishing second in 1946, taking AAGPBL championships in 1947 and 1949, and compiling the best won–lost record during 1948.

Haylett won 19 of 30 decisions in 1947 and ranked as the AAGPBL's premier pitcher in 1948 with 25 victories against only five losses, leading the AAGPBL with a .833 winning percentage and a 0.77 ERA. She changed to overhand pitching and baffled hitters with remarkably accurate fastballs and curve balls. She was named Pitcher of the Year and an All-Star team member, helping Grand Rapids win a pennant. The shy, quiet hurler let her pitching speak for itself. Her career 70–47 win–loss record included a cumulative 1.92 ERA. Haylett's career ended prematurely when she developed a sore arm.

Haylett, who never married, worked at the Kellogg Cereal Company in Grand Rapids for 30 years and retired to Florida in 1981. She returned to softball briefly, likes to bowl, and took up golf at age 45.

BIBLIOGRAPHY: Barbara Gregorich, *Women at Play* (San Diego, CA, 1993); W. C. Madden, *The Women of the All-American Girls Professional Baseball League* (Jefferson, NC, 1997); AAGPBL files, Northern Indiana Historical Society, South Bend, IN.

Dennis S. Clark

HEATH, John Geoffrey "Jeff" (b. April 1, 1915, Ft. William, Canada; d. December 9, 1975, Seattle, WA), player and sportscaster, recorded more major league hits, doubles, triples, and RBI than any other Canadian-born player.

Heath's father, Harold, moved the family to Seattle, WA during the Great Depression. Heath starred in football and baseball at Garfield High School, where he graduated in 1934. His professional baseball career began in 1936, when he set the MAL record by knocking in 187 runs for Zanesville, OH. He also batted .383 with 28 HR. For Milwaukee, WI (AA) in 1937, he hit a resounding .367.

In 1938, the sturdy 5-foot 11-inch, 185-pound Heath played left field for the Cleveland Indians (AL), leading the AL with 18 triples, belting 21 HR, driving in 112 runs, and batting a career-high .343. After Heath's outstanding rookie season, his batting average slipped to .292 in 1939 and .219 in 1940.

Heath enjoyed his finest major league year in 1941, when he batted .340, drove in 123 runs, and hit 32 doubles, 20 triples, and 24 HR. His feat of becoming the first major league player to collect more than 20 doubles, triples, and HR in one season went unnoticed. The same season, he became the first player to hit a HR into the upper deck of Cleveland's Municipal Stadium.

By the end of World War II, Heath had worn out his welcome in Cleveland. The press labeled him a "trouble-maker" and "Peck's Bad Boy," with Heath later admitting to being "temperamental, a cry baby and hard to handle." The Cleveland Indians dealt him to the Washington Senators (AL) in December 1945 for George Case.* In June 1946, the Washington Senators traded Heath to the St. Louis Browns (AL) for Joe Grace.

Sold to the Boston Braves (NL) after batting only .251 in 1947, Heath helped the Braves capture the 1948 NL pennant. Heath batted .319 and finished second on the Boston Braves in HR (20) and RBI (76). Tragically, Heath broke his ankle sliding into home shortly before the 1948 season ended and lost his only chance to play in a World Series. He saw limited service with the Boston Braves in 1949, but an injured leg and advancing age forced him to retire. In 14 major league seasons, he batted .293 with 279 doubles, 102 triples, 194 HR, and 887 RBI.

Heath resided in Seattle, WA, where he had attended the University of Washington in off-seasons. A sportscaster in Seattle, he did color commentary for baseball games and made commercials. He married Theabelle Callard in January 1939 and had two daughters and a son. His death came from a heart attack in 1975.

BIBLIOGRAPHY: Jeff Heath file, National Baseball Library, Cooperstown, NY; Gordon Cobbledick, "Heath Hustles—In His Own Way!" *BD* 2 (October 1943), pp. 60–63; Stan Grosshandler, "Heroes of the Middle Atlantic League," *BRJ* 2 (1973), pp. 56–58; John G. "Jeff" Heath, "I Did It the Wrong Way," *BD* 12 (January 1953), pp. 5–8; Franklin Lewis, *The Cleveland Indians* (New York, 1949); John Thorn et al., eds., *Total Indians* (New York, 1996); John Phillips, *Winners* (Cabin John, MD, 1987); Bill Borst, ed., *Ables to Zoldak*, vol. 1 (St. Louis, MO, 1988); Gary Caruso, *The Braves Encyclopedia* (Philadelphia, PA, 1995).

William E. Akin

HEBNER, Richard Joseph "Richie" (b. November 26, 1947, Boston, MA), player, coach, and manager, of Irish-German descent, is one of five sons of William Hebner, a cemetery superintendent, and Margaret (Kinkenny) Hebner, a native of Ireland. His brother, William, umpired in the IL. At Norwood Senior High School, he played ice hockey and baseball for four years. The Boston Bruins (NHL) hockey club selected him as a left wing in the first round of the 1966 NHL draft and offered a $10,000 bonus. He accepted a $40,000 bonus from the Pittsburgh Pirates (NL), however, mainly because he "just liked baseball better."

Although originally signed as a shortstop, Hebner became a third baseman in the minor leagues. He hit .359 for Salem, VA (ApL) in 1966 and served six months on active duty in the U.S. Marines. Hebner batted .336 for Raleigh, NC (CrL) in 1967 and .276 for Columbus, OH (IL) in 1968, being called up to the Pittsburgh Pirates at the season's end.

Hebner hit .301 for the Pittsburgh Pirates in 1969. The 6-foot 1-inch, 190 pounder helped supply left-handed power for Pittsburgh's "Lumber Company," belting 17 HR in 1971, 19 in 1972, and 25 in 1973. Pittsburgh won Eastern Division championships in 1970, 1971, 1972, 1974, and 1975 and the World Series title in 1971. His two World Series hits against the Baltimore Orioles included a HR in the third game.

Hebner's batting average declined in 1975 and 1976. When the Pittsburgh Pirates tried to cut his salary, he signed as a free agent with the Philadelphia Phillies (NL). Hebner's batting average rebounded to .285 in 1977 and .283 in 1978, as he played mostly first base and helped the Phillies win two straight Eastern Division crowns. After Philadelphia signed Pete Rose,* he was traded to the New York Mets (NL) in March 1979.

The free-spirited New Englander strongly disliked New York City. Although he shared the team lead with 79 RBI, the New York Mets traded him to the Detroit Tigers (AL) in October 1979. He hit .290 with 12 HR and a career-high 82 RBI in 104 games as a first and third baseman in 1980, but missed the last six weeks with an injured ankle. Hebner struggled in the split 1981 season and was sold to the Pittsburgh Pirates in August 1982. He batted .265 in 1983 and joined the Chicago Cubs (NL) as a free agent in January 1984. Hebner spent the 1984 and 1985 seasons as a pinch-hitter and utility player, batting only once against the San Diego Padres in the 1984 NL Championship Series. The Cubs released him in March 1986 partly because teams then carried only 24 players on their rosters.

In 18 major league seasons, Hebner hit .276 with 273 doubles, 57 triples, 203 HR, and 890 RBI. He batted .284 in 26 games in eight NL Championship Series. Crouched deep in the left-handed batter's box, the devastating low-ball hitter connected very effectively to the opposite field. The right-handed thrower possessed limited range at third base especially when slowed by injuries, but adeptly charged bunts and slow-hit, topped balls and threw well on the run to first.

The outgoing, personable Hebner remained popular with fans and the press almost everywhere he went. Two confrontations with manager Bill Virdon* in Pittsburgh and his noisy dissatisfaction with New York City alone disrupted his happy-go-lucky approach to life. He maintained a large supply of one-line jokes about his off-season job as a grave-digger ("It's quiet work") and often made news as the proverbial eligible young bachelor. He married Patricia Downing on November 4, 1979.

Hebner managed Myrtle Beach, SC (SAL) in 1988 for the Toronto Blue Jays (AL) and served as batting coach from 1989 through 1991 for the Boston Red Sox (AL), managed by his friend, Joe Morgan. From 1993 through 1995, he worked as a roving hitting instructor for the Toronto Blue Jays (AL). In 1995 and 1996, Hebner managed the Toronto affiliate in Syracuse, NY (IL). He served as batting coach in 1997 for Lynchburg, VA (CrL) and since 1998 for Nashville, TN (AA, PCL).

BIBLIOGRAPHY: Richie Hebner file, National Baseball Library, Cooperstown, NY; *The Baseball Encyclopedia*, 10th ed. (New York, 1996); Richard L. Burtt, *The Pittsburgh Pirates, A Pictorial History* (Virginia Beach, VA, 1977); Eddie Gold and Art Ahrens, *The New Era Cubs, 1941–1985* (Chicago, IL, 1985); Rich Westcott and Frank Bilovsky, *The New Phillies Encyclopedia* (Philadelphia, PA, 1993); Fred Smith, *995 Tigers* (Detroit, MI, 1981); Chuck Greenwood, "After Leaving the Bucs Twice Via Free Agency, Hebner Has Returned as a Coach," *SCD* 26 (January 15, 1999), pp. 110–111; Bob Smizik, *The Pittsburgh Pirates: An Illustrated History* (New York, 1990).

Luther W. Spoehr

HECKER, Guy Jackson (b. April 3, 1856, Youngsville, PA; d. December 3, 1938, Wooster, OH), player, umpire, and manager, was the only player to lead a major league in both pitching victories and batting. During his youth in Oil City, PA, he grew into a 6-foot, 190-pound, handsome, blond, mustached right-hander. He demonstrated little interest in formal education and worked for a business house in Oil City. He preferred instead to play for local amateur and semiprofessional baseball teams in Oil City from 1875 to 1882, except for a stint in 1877 with Springfield, OH.

Tony Mullane,* former Oil City teammate, persuaded Hecker to sign with the Eclipse Club of Louisville, KY when it entered the newly formed AA in 1882. Hecker, the regular first baseman, pitched a no-hitter against the Pittsburgh Alleghenys toward the end of his first season. In 1883, he hurled 28 victories and alternated as a first baseman. Hecker set AA pitching records in 1884, pitching 72 complete games, hurling 670.2 innings, and winning an incredible 52 games. He also paced the AA in strikeouts (385) and ERA (1.80) while batting .297. "His combined skill as a pitcher, a batsman, a fielder and a base-runner," the New York *Clipper* concluded, "renders him the most effective all-round player in the professional fraternity." John Thorn and Pete Palmer reached the same conclusion in *Total Baseball*.

Although never again pitching as well, Hecker triumphed 30 times in 1885 and 26 times in 1886. As Hecker's pitching declined, his hitting improved. In 1886 he led the AA in hitting with a .341 batting average. In a game against the Baltimore Orioles, he set major league records (since tied numerous times) with six hits and seven runs scored. He also became the first pitcher to hit three HR in a game. At the peak of his career with Louisville, Hecker was well known around town. His reputation abounded as a "great ladies man" who "always wore a close fitting shirt that set off his figure in great style." In the late 1880s, he opened a popular saloon in Louisville, KY.

Louisville released Hecker in 1889, but he remained in baseball for several more years. After umpiring in the AA in 1889, he managed and played for the Pittsburgh Alleghenys (NL) in 1890. Both roles went awry, as his team finished last and he batted only .226. His major league career concluded with a .282 batting average, 175 pitching victories, and a 2.93 ERA. After managing minor league baseball teams in Fort Wayne, IN (WL) and Jacksonville, IL (IIL), Hecker returned to Oil City and piloted amateur, semiprofessional, and professional teams through 1898. He operated a grocery store in Oil City and then moved to Wooster, OH, working there for the Ohio Fuel Gas Company. He retired after sustaining a serious injury in a 1931 automobile accident. He was survived by his wife, Martha, and one son, Guy Clifford Hecker.

BIBLIOGRAPHY: Guy Hecker file, National Baseball Library, Cooperstown, NY; Bob Bailey, "A Pitcher Winning a Batting Title? Ridiculous!" *BRJ* 16 (1987), pp. 83–84; New York *Clipper*, 1884; A. H. Tarvin, *Seventy Years on Louisville Diamonds* (Louisville, KY, 1940); John Thorn et al., eds., *Total Baseball*, 5th ed. (New York, 1997); Robert L. Tiemann and Mark Rucker, eds., *Nineteenth Century Stars* (Kansas City, MO, 1989); Philip Von Borries, *Legends of Louisville* (West Bloomfield, MI, 1993); Philip Von Borries, *Louisville Diamonds* (Paducah, KY, 1997); David Nemec, *The Beer and Whisky League* (New York, 1994).

William E. Akin

HEGAN, James Edward "Jim" (b. August 3, 1920, Lynn, MA; d. June 17, 1984, Swampscott, MA), player, coach, and scout, came from an Irish-Catholic background. The 6-foot 2-inch, 195-pound Hegan, who neither drank nor smoked, played American Legion and public school baseball before graduating from Lynn English High School. The Cleveland Indians (AL) signed him to a contract in 1938 and sent him to Springfield, OH (MAL). As a catcher, he advanced to Wilkes-Barre, PA (EL) and Oklahoma City, OK (TL) before reaching the Cleveland Indians in late 1941. That season, he batted a career-high .319 in a 16-game major league stint. He married Clare Helen Kennedy in November 1941 and had two sons, with Mike becoming a major league first baseman. The backup catcher slumped to .194 at the plate for Cleveland in 1942 before enlisting in the U.S. Coast Guard from December 1942 to December 1945.

In the postwar era, the handsome, modest Hegan emerged as one of baseball's premier catchers. He caught one of the greatest pitching staffs ever, including Bob Feller,* Gene Bearden, Bob Lemon,* Early Wynn,* Mike Garcia,* and Herbert Score,* and played on AL pennant winners in 1948 and 1954. Hegan caught 18 20-game winners from 1946 to 1957, establishing a record that may never be broken. No one surpassed Hegan in handling pitchers, running down foul balls, and throwing out runners. He led the AL in putouts from 1947 to 1949 and in assists from 1948 to 1950. In 1948, Satchel Paige* named him "big catch" and compared him with the legendary Josh Gibson.* No Cleveland Indian during this period enjoyed more popularity with the fans and teammates. Hegan caught 1,666 major league games, including no-hitters by Feller, Lemon, and Don Black. His mediocre hitting alone has denied Hegan election to the National Baseball Hall of Fame. His best season came in 1948, when he hit .248 with 14 HR and 61 RBI. His fly balls frequently were caught just short of the fence. His 17 major league seasons included 14 with the Indians and brief stops with the Detroit Tigers (AL) and Philadelphia Phillies (NL) in 1958, San Francisco Giants (NL) in 1959, and Chicago Cubs (NL) in 1960. Hegan finished his career with a .228 batting average, 92 HR, and 525 RBI. After his playing career ended in 1960, Hegan coached for the Detroit Tigers from 1974 through 1978 and New York Yankees (AL) from 1960 through 1973 and 1979 and 1980 and scouted for the latter team.

BIBLIOGRAPHY: Jim Hegan file, National Baseball Library, Cooperstown, NY; Franklin Lewis, *The Cleveland Indians* (New York, 1979); John Thorn et al., eds., *Total Indians* (New York, 1996); John Phillips, *Winners* (Cabin John, MD, 1987); Bob Feller and Bill Gilbert, *Now Pitching Bob Feller* (New York, 1990); Russell Schneider, *The Boys of Summer of '48* (Champaign, IL, 1998); Cleveland (OH) *Plain Dealer*, April 20, 1978, June 19, 1984, July 17, 1984, July 21, 1984.

James N. Giglio

HEILMANN, Harry Edwin "Slug" (b. August 3, 1894, San Francisco, CA; d. July 9, 1951, Southfield, MI), player, coach, and sportscaster, attended St. Mary's High School in Oakland, CA and Sacred Heart College. Portland, OR signed him as an outfielder–first baseman out of college in 1913 for their NWL farm club. The Detroit Tigers (AL) drafted the 6-foot 1-inch, 200-pound Heilmann in 1914, but he could not break into the stellar hitting outfield of Ty Cobb,* Sam Crawford,* and Bobby Veach.* He was sent in 1915 to San Francisco, CA (PCL), where his hard hitting overcame weak fielding and lack of speed. From 1916 to 1929, he played for the Detroit Tigers. Since the Tigers had a plethora of slugging outfielders, Heilmann occasionally played first base. In 1919 and 1920, he led AL first baseman in errors. On October 5, 1920, he married Harriet Maynes.

Cobb, who became manager in 1921, permanently moved Heilmann to the outfield and markedly improved his batting average by changing his batting stance and grip. Nicknamed "Slug," Heilmann led the AL that year with 237 hits and a sparkling .394 batting average. In 1923, 1925, and 1927, he also won batting titles and attributed the strange sequence of dates to his two-year contracts. He particularly valued his 1921 title because he narrowly edged his close friend Cobb for that championship. Although not a HR hitter, Heilmann usually led his hard-hitting team in RBI and eight times hit 40 or more doubles. After hitting .344 in 1929, Heilmann was sent that October to the Cincinnati Reds (NL). He batted .333 and hit 43 doubles in 142 games in 1930, but arthritis forced him to miss the next season. Heilmann retired in 1932 at age 37, finishing the year as club coach.

One of baseball's greatest hitters with a lifetime .342 batting average, Heilmann batted and threw right-handed. In 2,148 games, Heilmann made 2,660 hits, 542 doubles, and 183 HR and knocked in 1,539 runs. A fair fielder, he led the AL in outfield assists in 1924 with 31. Heilmann made three errors in one inning to tie a major league record for first basemen. His championship batting averages of .394, .403, .393, and .398 came within nine hits of giving him a nearly unprecedented .400 average for those four years. In 1925, he made six hits in nine at bats on the last day to surpass Tris Speaker* for the batting title. Two years later, he recorded seven for nine on the final day to narrowly edge Al Simmons.* Heilmann, who could have won either title by remaining on the bench, rarely beat out infield hits. His maximum HR production was 21 in 1922, while his best RBI mark was 139 in 1921. Despite Heilmann's hitting skills, the Tigers did not win an AL pennant. His career was interrupted by military service in 1918, a broken collarbone in 1922, sinus surgery in 1924, and arthritis in 1931, the latter ending his career. In 1952, he was elected to the National Baseball Hall of Fame.

Unlike many baseball players, Heilmann moved successfully into a second career. After an unsuccessful experience in the insurance business, he entered radio broadcasting and from 1933 until 1951 announced the Detroit Tigers' games. Although other announcers vied with one another in their shrillness, Heilmann told droll, low-key stories, demonstrated his superb knowledge of the game, and even took elocution lessons. Extremely popular with Michigan fans, he attracted a large following among younger listeners who had not known him as a player.

As player and announcer, Heilmann served the Detroit club for nearly 34 years. During spring training in 1951, Heilmann was found to have cancer and was hospitalized in Florida and Detroit. He died the day before the annual All-Star game, held in Detroit that year. Thousands of his fans crowded the Shrine of the Little Flower for the final services. He left his wife, Mae, and one son and one daughter.

BIBLIOGRAPHY: Harry Heilmann file, National Baseball Library, Cooperstown, NY; Lee Allen, *The American League Story* (New York, 1962); Martin Appel and Burt Goldblatt, *Baseball's Best: The Hall of Fame Gallery* (New York, 1977); John Benson et al., *Baseball's Top 100* (Wilton, CT, 1997); Joe Falls, *Detroit Tigers* (New York, 1975); *NYT*, 1916–1951, June 12, 1924, July 10, 1951; Marc Okkonen, "Harry Heilmann, Announcer," *TNP* 10 (1990), pp. 33–36; Lowell Reidenbaugh, *Baseball's Hall of Fame-Cooperstown* (New York, 1993); Charles C. Alexander, *Ty Cobb* (New York, 1984); Richard Bak, *Ty Cobb: His Tumultuous Life and Times* (Dallas, TX, 1994); William M. Anderson, *The Detroit Tigers* (South Bend, IN, 1996); Frederick G. Lieb,

The Detroit Tigers (New York, 1946); Fred Smith, *995 Tigers* (Detroit, MI, 1981); Jamie Selko, "Harry Heilmann's Batting Races," *TNP* 15 (1995), pp. 45–50.

Thomas L. Karnes

HELD, Woodson George "Woodie" (b. March 25, 1932, Sacramento, CA), player, is the son of Frederick George Held, a telephone lineman and semi-professional baseball player, and Julia Agnes (Chapman) Held. Of German, Irish, and Dutch descent, Held played sandlot baseball and served as batboy for Sacramento (PCL) from 1945 to 1947. An all-around athlete, Held starred on the Sacramento High School baseball team. Held met his wife, Nadine Mast, when they were high school students. They married February 1, 1952.

A versatile player with good power and a strong arm, Held received a $6,000 bonus from New York Yankees (AL) scout Joe Devine in 1951 as an outfielder. He advanced in the New York Yankees organization between 1951 and 1954 and appeared briefly with New York in September 1954. The New York Yankees optioned him in 1955 to Denver, CO (AA), where he hit .276 with 35 HR and 125 RBI and made the All-Star team at third base in 1956. The New York Yankees traded Held to the Kansas City Athletics (AL) in June 1957 in an eight-player deal. Held played in 1,390 AL games over 14 major league seasons with New York, Kansas City, the Cleveland Indians, Washington Senators, Baltimore Orioles, and Chicago White Sox, hitting .240 with 179 HR and 559 RBI. His best year came in 1959, when he batted .251 for Cleveland with a career-high 29 HR and 71 RBI in 143 games mostly at shortstop (103) and third base (40). Two years later, he recorded a career-best .267 batting average and 78 RBI with 23 HR in 146 games while playing second base (96 games) and outfield (35 games). The likeable, hot-tempered free swinger struck out often. Held, whose versatility may have hindered his development as a fielder, ended his baseball career with the Chicago White Sox in 1969.

After leaving baseball, the free-spirited Held has worked as a pizza parlor proprietor, electrician, lumber yard owner, bartender, construction worker, iron welder, Yellowstone Park tourist guide, and professional snowmobile racer. Snowmobiling remained his self-professed love despite a serious accident in 1971. He resides in Dubois, WY.

BIBLIOGRAPHY: Woody Held file, National Baseball Library, Cooperstown, NY; Edward Kiersh, *Where Have You Gone, Vince DiMaggio?* (New York, 1983); Hal Lebovitz, "Held Haunts Foes and Boss With Homers: Smashes Bring Joy to Frankie, Who Tried to Deal Woodie," *TSN*, April 29, 1959, pp. 3–4; *The Baseball Encyclopedia*, 10th ed. (New York, 1996); John Thorn et al., eds., *Total Baseball*, 5th ed. (New York, 1997); Jack Torry, *Endless Summers* (South Bend, IN, 1995); Terry Pluto, *The Curse of Rocky Colavito* (New York, 1994); John Thorn et al., eds., *Total Indians* (New York, 1996).

Edward J. Tassinari

HEMUS, Solomon Joseph "Solly," "Mighty Mouse" (b. April 17, 1923, Phoenix, AZ), player, coach, and manager, was signed by the St. Louis Cardinals (NL) in 1946. The 5-foot 9-inch, 163-pound Hemus batted .363 at Pocatello, ID (PrL) in 1946. He played shortstop, second base, and third base, throwing from the right side but batting left-handed. The St. Louis Cardinals recalled him in both 1949 and 1950.

Hemus replaced star shortstop Marty Marion* when the latter became St. Louis Cardinals' manager in 1951. He batted .281 and played a steady shortstop. His small size fueled his determination to be a complete player. Hemus' batting average dipped to .268 in 1952, but he socked a career-high 15 HR and scored an NL-leading 105 runs. The following season, Hemus compiled career highs with 32 doubles, 11 triples, 61 RBI, and 110 runs scored. He recorded a .279 batting average while playing every game for the St. Louis Cardinals. In 1954, St. Louis started rookie Alex Grammas at shortstop and used Hemus as a reserve shortstop, third baseman, and second baseman. Hemus played 124 games in his new capacity and produced a career-best .304 batting average. Throughout his career, he walked often and led the NL in being hit by a pitch three times. After Hemus hit .243 in 1955, the St. Louis Cardinals swapped him to the Philadelphia Phillies (NL) for infielder Bobby Morgan in May 1956. Hemus struggled in 1957, but rebounded 99 points in 1958 to bat .284 in 105 games.

The St. Louis Cardinals fired manager Fred Hutchinson* late in 1958. After Hemus was dealt in 1955, he wrote a flattering letter to Cardinals owner Gussie Busch* thanking him for letting him play with a great Cardinals organization. Busch remembered the letter and admired the tenacity and hustle of the "Mighty Mouse." St. Louis reacquired him from the Philadelphia Phillies for Gene Freese in September 1958 and named him player–manager in 1959. Hemus, only 35 years old, guided St. Louis to 71 wins, 83 defeats, and a seventh-place finish. In 1960, he piloted the Cardinals to third place with 86 victories and 68 defeats. St. Louis started slowly in 1961 and plodded along to mid-season. With the team at 33–41 in July, general manager Bing Devine replaced Hemus with Cardinals coach Johnny Keane.* Critics contend Cardinals teams might have accomplished more if Hemus had not limited the playing time of 39-year-old Stan Musial,* had utilized black players Curt Flood* and Bob Gibson,* and had not tangled so often with the umpires. Musial reported that Hemus also lost respect by "taking a strong stand, only to back down while trying to be a nice guy." Hemus' major league record as a manager included 190 wins, 192 losses, and two ties. As a major league player, he batted .273 with 736 hits, 51 HR, 459 runs, and 263 RBI in 969 games.

Casey Stengel* hired Hemus as a coach for the expansion New York Mets (NL) in 1962. Hemus coached for the Cleveland Indians (AL) in 1964 and 1965 and left baseball for the oil and gas leasing business in Houston, TX. He married Margeurite Maguire in November 1942 and has one daughter.

BIBLIOGRAPHY: Solly Hemus file, National Baseball Library, Cooperstown, NY; Bob Broeg and Jerry Vickery, *St. Louis Cardinals Encyclopedia* (Grand Rapids, MI, 1998); Thomas Aylesworth and Benton Minks, *The Encyclopedia of Baseball Managers* (New York, 1990); Bob Broeg, *Redbirds: A Century of Cardinals' Baseball* (St. Louis, MO, 1981); Stan Musial as told to Bob Broeg, *Stan Musial: The Man's Own Story* (Garden City, NY, 1964); Curt Flood with Richard Carter, *The Way It Is* (New York, 1971); Bob Gibson with Phil Pepe, *From Ghetto to Glory* (New York, 1968); Rob Rains, *The St. Louis Cardinals* (New York, 1992); James Toomey, *St. Louis Cardinals 1961 Yearbook* (St. Louis, MO, 1961); Rich Westcott and Frank Bilovsky, *The New Phillies Encyclopedia* (Philadelphia, PA, 1993).

Frank J. Olmsted

HENDERSON, Arthur Chauncey "Rats" (b. August 29, 1897, Richmond, VA; d. April 11, 1981, Wilmington, DE), player, was the son of Curtis Henderson, a laborer, and had 11 brothers and sisters. To assist the family, he and his siblings worked from an early age and sacrificed a formal education. He acquired his nickname "Rats" as a teenager when someone hid a rat in his lunch box while he was working at a local glass factory. Henderson began playing baseball in an adult neighborhood league at age 15. As a right-handed, sidearm hurler, the 5-foot 7-inch, 180-pound Henderson combined a fine curveball with an intimidating fastball.

In 1922, Henderson joined the first-year Richmond Giants and quickly became their ace pitcher. During an exhibition game, Henderson handily defeated the Atlantic City, NJ Bacharach Giants. The Bacharach Giants immediately signed the young hurler, who won 16 games against five losses. In 1923, the Bacharach Giants joined the newly organized ECL. Henderson quickly became Atlantic City's ace, compiling 8–6, 8–1, and 13–5 records from 1923 to 1925. Several clubs sought the ECL's best young pitcher's services. Henderson jumped briefly to Chappie Johnson's* New York Stars for $280 a month in 1924, but returned to the Bacharach Giants after six games. During the winter of 1924–1925, Henderson compiled an 8–5 record in Cuba. He returned to the Bacharach Giants in 1925 as one of the highest paid Eastern players at $375 per month.

In 1926, the Bacharach Giants won the ECL pennant behind Henderson's 15–5 performance and made the World Series against the Chicago American Giants. Henderson started four games with one shutout, two losses, and a 1.45 ERA. The Bacharach Giants lost the World Series five games to three, with two ties. Henderson finished 19–7 in 1927, leading the Bacharach Giants to a second ECL pennant and another World Series against the Chicago American Giants. He suffered a late season injury and missed the World Series rematch. In 1928, Henderson fared 13–2 before developing arm problems at mid-season. His disappointing 6–10 record in 1929 stemmed partly from considerable weight gain. After resting his ailing arm in 1930, Henderson lost both decisions with the Detroit Stars (NNL) in 1931.

Over the next decade, Henderson played with John Henry Lloyd's* Johnson Stars and sold rugs on the Atlantic City, NJ boardwalk to support his wife, Wilmae, and family. After leaving organized baseball in 1941, Henderson worked with Continental Can Company from 1947 to 1965. During an impressive nine-year career, Henderson won 107 games and lost 53 decisions before suffering arm trouble.

BIBLIOGRAPHY: Dick Clark and Larry Lester, eds., *The Negro Leagues Book* (Cleveland, OH, 1994); Phil Dixon, *The Negro Baseball Leagues* (Mattituck, NY, 1992); John B. Holway, *Black Diamonds* (Westport, CT, 1989); Neil Lanctot, *Fair Dealing and Clean Playing* (Jefferson, NC, 1994); Arthur Henderson file, National Baseball Library, Cooperstown, NY; Negro Leagues Baseball Museum, Kansas City, MO; Robert W. Peterson, *Only the Ball Was White* (New York, 1970); Mark Ribowsky, *A Complete History of the Negro Leagues, 1884 to 1955* (New York, 1995); James A. Riley, *The Encyclopedia of the Negro Baseball Leagues* (New York, 1994).

Jerry J. Wright

HENDERSON, David Lee "Dave," "Hendu" (b. July 21, 1958, Merced, CA), player, is the son of William Henderson and attended Dos Palos schools, where he played football as running back and linebacker and was recruited by over 100 colleges. His brother, Joe, pitched in 16 games with two major league teams during his three-year career. Henderson signed for a $100,000 bonus with the Seattle Mariners (AL) after being selected in the first round of the June 1977 amateur draft. He married Loni Lee Smith on February 9, 1980 and has two children, Chase and Trent.

Henderson played with four different minor league teams in three different Northwestern leagues before joining the Seattle Mariners (AL) in 1981. The 6-foot 2-inch, 210-pound right-hander wore Jackie Robinson's* number 42 and remained popular with fans: "I'm just a big kid playing baseball," he said.

The Boston Red Sox (AL) in August 1986 acquired Henderson and Spike Owen. They both helped Boston win the Eastern Division. In Game 5 of the 1986 AL Championship Series, Henderson's two-out HR in the top of the ninth inning gave the Red Sox a 6–5 lead over the California Angels, while his sacrifice fly scored the winning run in the 11th inning. In the 1986 World Series against the New York Mets, he hit .400 with HR in Games 2 and 6 and knocked in five runs.

Henderson was traded to the San Francisco Giants (NL) in September 1987 and signed with the Oakland Athletics (AL) in December 1987 as a free agent. His best major league season came in 1988, when he batted .304 with 100 runs, 154 hits, 38 doubles, 24 HR, and 94 RBI. He hit .375 against the Boston Red Sox in the 1988 AL Championship Series and batted .300 in the World Series against the Los Angeles Dodgers as a leadoff batter. In 1988, he was voted AL Comeback Player of the Year and received 28 MVP votes.

Henderson hit a HR against the Toronto Blue Jays in the 1989 AL Championship Series and two HR in Game 3 (the earthquake-postponed game) of the World Series against the San Francisco Giants, batting .308. He remained with the Oakland A's from 1990 through 1993, appearing against the Cincinnati Reds in the 1990 World Series. His major league career ended with the Kansas City Royals (AL) in 1994. The crowd pleaser often ate pizza after games with the Oakland fans who sat in the "Hendoland" section of the bleachers. In 14 major league seasons, Henderson batted .258, belted 197 HR, and knocked in 708 runs. He clouted three HR and knocked in 10 runs in AL Championship Series. He batted 66 points higher during World Series play, belting four HR and driving in 10 runs.

BIBLIOGRAPHY: David Henderson file, National Baseball Library, Cooperstown, NY; Dan Shaughnessy, *One Strike Away* (New York, 1987); Robert Redmount, *The Red Sox Encyclopedia* (Champaign, IL, 1997); John Mickey, "One on One With . . . Dave Henderson," *Sport* 82 (October 1991), pp. 23–24; *NSD*, June 12, 1991; Steve Rushin, "The Fans' Man," *SI* 74 (May 6, 1991), pp. 22–24; *TSN*, January 5, 1980, April 18, 1981; *NYT*, July 10, 1991.

Thomas H. Barthel

HENDERSON, Rickey Henley (b. December 25, 1958, Chicago, IL), player, is the fourth of seven children of John Henderson and nurse Bobby Henderson. His father left when Rickey was two months old, after which his family moved to Arkansas and then Oakland, CA. An All-American running back at Oakland Technical High School, Henderson was recruited by several football powers. Henderson, however, signed with the hometown Oakland Athletics (AL), who selected him in the fourth round of the 1976 draft.

With Modesto, CA (CaL) in 1977, Henderson developed his batting stance and stole 95 bases. At Ogden, UT (PCL) in 1979, he perfected his head-first slide. In his 89 games with the Oakland Athletics that year, he stole 33 bases. In his first full major league season (1980), the 5-foot 10-inch, 180-pound speedster surpassed Ty Cobb's* 65-year-old AL stolen base record of 96 with 100 thefts. He also stole 130 bases in 1982, 108 in 1983, 80 in 1985, 87 in 1986, and 93 in 1988. His 130 stolen bases in 1982 erased Lou Brock's* major league single season record of 118.

Henderson's base-stealing reputation overshadows his other accomplishments. Henderson's .409 plus on-base percentage makes him this century's best leadoff hitter. Batting from a crouch to reduce his strike zone, he receives many walks. Henderson, whose 116 bases on balls in 1982, 103 in 1983, and 126 in 1989 led the AL, does not wait for walks. In 1981 Henderson, who throws left but bats right, paced the AL with 89 runs on 135 hits and batted a solid .319. Although usually batting for base hits, he demonstrates considerable power. In 1985, he led the AL in runs scored (146) and stolen bases (80) and finished fourth in batting average (.314) and on-base percentage (.419). Henderson also made 172 hits, 28 doubles, 24 HR, and 72 RBI, finishing third in the MVP balloting. In 1986 the leadoff batter paced the AL in runs scored (130) and stolen bases (87) and slugged a career-high 28 HR.

From 1979 to 1982, Henderson teamed with Dwayne Murphy and Tony Armas* to form one of baseball's most effective outfields. Many ranked Henderson the best left fielder in the majors. He consistently stood among the leaders in chances and putouts, leading the AL in the latter category with 327 and winning the Gold Glove award in 1981. The long-time Oakland resident and fan favorite was traded to the New York Yankees (AL) in December 1984 for five players.

In 1988, Henderson batted .305 and led the AL with 93 stolen bases. In June 1989, the Yankees traded him to the Oakland A's (AL). He paced the AL in runs scored (72), walks (70), and stolen bases (52) in 1989. Henderson batted .400 with two HR and five RBI in the AL Championship Series against the Toronto Blue Jays and .474 with three RBI against the San Francisco Giants in the World Series. In 1990, he led the AL in runs scored (119) and stolen bases (65) and knocked in three runs in the AL Championship Series against the Boston Red Sox. Henderson batted .333 in a losing cause against the Cincinnati Reds in the World Series. The BBWAA awarded him the AL MVP that year. In 1992, he helped the Oakland A's reach the AL Championship Series against the Toronto Blue Jays. The Oakland Athletics traded him in July 1993 to the Toronto Blue Jays. Henderson struggled in both the AL Championship Series against the Chicago White Sox and the World Series against the Philadelphia Phillies. Henderson returned to the Oakland A's in 1994 and 1995 and joined the San Diego Padres (NL) as a free agent in December 1995. He helped the San Diego Padres win the NL West in 1996 and batted .333 in the NL Division Series against the St. Louis Cardinals. He divided 1997 between San Diego and the Anaheim Angels (AL) and rejoined the Oakland A's in 1998. In December 1998, the New York Mets (NL) acquired him as a free agent. Henderson batted .315 with 37 stolen bases to help the Mets win the wild card in 1999 and hit .400 in the NL Division Series, setting a series record with six stolen bases. He won TSN NL Comeback Player of the Year honors.

Through 1999, Henderson has batted .284 with 2,103 runs, 2,816 hits, 472 doubles, 278 HR, 1,020 RBI, and 1,334 stolen bases. He holds major league records for most stolen bases, HR as a leadoff batter (73), and years leading his league in stolen bases (12) and AL career records for most stolen bases (1,231), HR as a leadoff batter (69), and years with 50 or more stolen bases (8). He made the TSN AL All-Star and TSN Silver Slugger teams in 1981, 1985, and 1990 and made the AL All-Star teams in 1980, 1982 through 1988, 1990, and 1991. He holds Oakland A's career records for most runs scored (1,270), hits (1,768), doubles (289), stolen bases (867), and batting average (.288). He ranked second in stolen bases (463) in the 1990s.

BIBLIOGRAPHY: Rickey Henderson file, National Baseball Library, Cooperstown, NY; John Benson et al., *Baseball's Top 100* (Wilton, CT, 1997); *CB Yearbook* (1990), pp. 293–297; Ron Fimrite, "He Finally Bagged It," *SI* 57 (September 6, 1982), pp. 14–19; Ron Fimrite, "A Well Matched Set," *SI* 56 (May 10, 1982), pp. 88–102;

Peter Gammons, "Man of Steal," *SI* 73 (October 1, 1990), pp. 60–68; R. Kroichick, "Rickey Henderson: Man of Steal," *Sport* 82 (March 1991), pp. 52–56; Peter Gammons, "Light Years Ahead of the Field," *SI* 65 (July 28, 1986), pp. 34–36; Peter Gammons, "Who's the Fastest Man in Baseball?" *Sport* 73 (May 1982), pp. 44–48; Rickey Henderson with John Shea, *Off Base: Confessions of a Thief* (New York, 1992); Mark Gallagher, *The Yankee Encyclopedia*, vol. 3 (Champaign, IL, 1997); Bill James, "So What's All the Fuss," *SI* 57 (September 6, 1982), pp. 30–34; Jim Kaplan, "No Slouch in the Crouch," *SI* 55 (September 14, 1981), pp. 52–54; Robert E. Kelly, *Baseball's Best* (Jefferson, NC, 1988); Danny Knobler, "Baseball's Best Leadoff Hitters," *Sport* 81 (July 1990), pp. 40–42; R. Kroichick, "Stealing Time," *Sport* 84 (May 1993), pp. 46–50; David L. Porter, ed., *African-American Sports Greats* (Westport, CT, 1995); *TSN Official Baseball Register, 1998; TSN*, October 15, December 3, 17, 1984; C. Wolff, "Yankee Maverick Sets the Pace," *NYT Biographical Service* 17 (August 1986), pp. 990–992.

Gaymon L. Bennett

HENDRICK, George Andrew, Jr. "Silent George" (b. October 18, 1949, Los Angeles, CA), player and coach, is the son of George Hendrick, Sr., graduated from Samuel Gompers High School in Los Angeles, and attended East Los Angeles JC. He married Carol Threatt and had one son, Brian, who played basketball at the University of California. Hendrick, the first player selected in the January 1968 free-agent draft, signed with the Oakland Athletics (AL). At Burlington, IA (ML) in 1968, he led the ML with a .327 batting average. The 6-foot 3-inch, 195-pound Hendrick batted .307 at Lodi, CA (CaL) the following season and continued to hit well in 1970 at Burlington, IA (ML) and Birmingham, AL (SL), connecting for 18 HR. In 1971, his 21 HR and 63 RBI in 63 games at Des Moines-based Iowa (AA) earned Hendrick a promotion to the Oakland Athletics. In 42 games for Oakland, he batted .237 with only 8 RBI.

After an eight-game stint with Iowa in 1972, Hendrick was recalled by the Athletics and struggled with a .182 batting average in 58 games. He replaced the injured Reggie Jackson* in five World Series games against the Cincinnati Reds, hitting just .133. Oakland outfielder Joe Rudi* worked with Hendrick on his hitting and defensive play. Hendrick was traded to the Cleveland Indians (AL) in March 1973 and started in center field. He delivered 21 HR and batted .268, but conflicted with Indians manager Ken Aspromonte and asked to be traded the next season. The Indians, however, did not trade Hendrick, who produced a season that was virtually a carbon copy of the previous year. Others criticized Hendrick at times for an easygoing style, but he responded, "What difference does it make how you do something as long as you get the job done?" Hendrick hit 24 HR in 1975 and 25 HR in 1976 and continued to bat around .260. Cleveland traded him to the San Diego Padres (NL) for three players in December 1976. In 1977, Hendrick responded by belting 23 HR and batting .311. The Padres in May 1978 shipped him to the St. Louis Cardinals (NL) for pitcher Eric Rasmussen, a deal that proved a steal for the Cardinals.

With St. Louis, Hendrick played center field and right field and moved to first base in June 1983 when Keith Hernandez* was traded to the New York Mets (NL). From 1978 to 1984, Hendrick provided power and clutch hitting for the Cardinals. He batted at least .300 three times and exceeded 100 RBI twice. A key ingredient in the 1982 St. Louis World Championship, Hendrick batted .308 in the NL Championship Series against the Atlanta Braves and hit .321 in the World Series versus the Milwaukee Brewers. He drove in the winning run in Game 7. Hendrick shunned the press in Cleveland and St. Louis because sportswriters earlier had misquoted him but was comfortable with manager Whitey Herzog* and popular with Cardinals players and fans. Herzog called Hendrick "a smart hitter and one of the best defensive right fielders in the game." The Cardinals traded the aging Hendrick to the Pittsburgh Pirates (NL) for hurler John Tudor* in December 1984. In August 1985, Hendrick was dealt to the California Angels (AL) in a six-player trade. From 1986 to 1988, Hendrick served as DH, pinch-hitter, and occasional outfielder for the Angels. His last major league season came in 1988 with the California Angels. Hendrick played outfield for the Gold Coast, FL Suns (SPBA) for the 1989–1990 inaugural season and batted .331 with 23 RBI.

Hendrick won *TSN* Silver Slugger awards as an outfielder in 1980 and at first base in 1983 and was selected twice as an All-Star in each league. His major league career totals included 1,980 hits, 941 runs, 343 doubles, 267 HR, 1,111 RBI, and a .278 batting average in 2,048 games. The West Mills, CA resident coached for the St. Louis Cardinals in 1996 and 1997 and Anaheim Angels in 1999.

BIBLIOGRAPHY: George Hendrick file, National Baseball Library, Cooperstown, NY; Whitey Herzog and Kevin Horrigan, *White Rat* (New York, 1987); Zander Hollander, ed., *The Complete Handbook of Baseball, 1977* (New York, 1977); *St. Louis Cardinals 1982 Scorebook*; Mike Shatzkin, ed., *The Ballplayers* (New York, 1990); Marybeth Sullivan, ed., *The Scouting Report: 1986* (New York, 1986); Jack Torry, *Endless Summers* (South Bend, IN, 1995); Terry Pluto, *The Curse of Rocky Colavito* (New York, 1994); John Thorn et al., eds., *Total Indians* (New York, 1996); Bob Broeg and Jerry Vickery, *St. Louis Cardinals Encyclopedia* (Grand Rapids, MI, 1998); Rob Rains, *The St. Louis Cardinals* (New York, 1992).

Frank J. Olmsted

HENDRIX, Claude Raymond (b. April 13, 1889, Olathe, KS; d. March 22, 1944, Allentown, PA), player, was one of the major leagues' best hitting pitchers with the Pittsburgh Pirates (NL), Chicago Whales (FL), and Chicago Cubs (NL) from 1911 through 1920. The right-hander made his major league debut on June 11, 1911 with the Pittsburgh Pirates and compiled a 24–9 win–loss record for the 1912 Pirates before jumping to a newly formed "third major league," the FL, in 1914. He enjoyed an FL-leading 29–10 mark and 1.69 ERA with the Chicago Whales in 1914, pacing the FL in appearances and complete games. A 16–15 record followed in 1915 before the Chicago Cubs purchased him in February 1916. He pitched a no-hitter for the Whales against the Pittsburgh Rebels on May 15, 1915.

His 144–116 major league pitching record resulted in a 2.65 career ERA. The 6-foot, 195 pounder also excelled as a hitter, batting .241 with 13 HR and 97 RBI. In 1912, his .322 batting average and 6 triples led all major league pitchers. He tied George "Babe" Ruth* with 4 HR to pace all 1915 hurlers and led all 1918 pitchers with 3 HR, one ahead of Ruth. In 1918, his 20–7 record enabled him to share the NL lead in winning percentage and helped the Cubs to win the NL pennant.

Hendrix relieved in the 1918 World Series Game 6 for the Chicago Cubs against the Boston Red Sox, making one hit in his only at-bat. The Cubs released him in February 1921 for having supposedly bet against his teammates in an August 1920 contest he was originally scheduled to pitch.

BIBLIOGRAPHY: Claude Hendrix file, National Baseball Library, Cooperstown, NY; *The Baseball Encyclopedia*, 10th ed. (New York, 1996); Robert Davids, ed., *Great Hitting Pitchers* (Cooperstown, NY, 1979); Mark Okkonen, *Federal League of 1914–15* (Garrett Park, MD, 1989); Emil H. Rothe, "Was the Federal League a Major League?" *BRJ* 10 (1981), p. 1; John Thorn et al., eds., *Total Baseball*, 5th ed. (New York, 1997); Frederick G. Lieb, *The Pittsburgh Pirates* (New York, 1948); Eddie Gold and Art Ahrens, *The Golden Era Cubs, 1876–1940* (Chicago, IL, 1985); Warren Wilbert and William Hageman, *Chicago Cubs: Seasons at the Summit* (Champaign IL, 1997); Warren Brown, *The Chicago Cubs* (New York, 1946); Jim Enright, *Chicago Cubs* (New York, 1975).

                                                                Robert B. Van Atta

HENKE, Thomas Anthony "Tom" (b. December 21, 1957, Kansas City, MO), player, is the son of Frederick Henke and Mary Jane (Grothoff) Henke. He graduated from Blair Oaks High School in Jefferson City, MO and attended East Central JC in Union, MO. Henke was drafted by the Seattle Mariners (AL) in 1979 and the Chicago Cubs (NL) in 1980, but did not sign until the Texas Rangers (AL) selected him in the secondary phase of the June 1980 draft. The 6-foot 5-inch, 215-pound right-hander pitched for the Gulf Coast Rangers, FL (GCL) and Asheville, NC (SAL) in 1980 and Asheville and Tulsa, OK (TL) in 1981. In 1982 at Tulsa, Henke led the TL with 52 appearances and recorded 100 strikeouts in 87.2 innings to earn a September trial with the Texas Rangers. He divided the 1983 and 1984 seasons between Oklahoma City, OK (AA) and the Texas Rangers.

Henke's break came in 1985, when the Texas Rangers signed free agent DH Cliff Johnson. The Toronto Blue Jays (AL) took Henke from Texas as compensation. At Syracuse, NY (IL) in 1985, he surrendered runs in only two of 39 appearances, recorded a 0.88 ERA, and allowed only 13 hits in 51.1 innings to earn IL Pitcher of the Year honors. After Toronto recalled him during a pennant drive, Henke won three games, saved 13, and recorded a 2.02 ERA to help the Blue Jays edge the New York Yankees for the AL

East title. He won two games in the AL Championship Series, but the Kansas City Royals prevailed in seven games.

From 1985 to 1992, Henke ranked among the premier closers in major league baseball. He used a 94-mph fastball, hard slider, and split-finger fastball to set the Toronto team record for career saves with 217 while averaging 1.14 strikeouts per inning. Left-handed and right-handed batters alike found him formidable to face. In 1987, Henke led the AL with 34 saves and 12.3 strikeouts per nine innings and pitched 2.2 scoreless innings in the All-Star game. Two years later, he recorded a sparkling 1.92 ERA in 64 games. Opponents did not score against him in nine relief appearances in the 1989, 1991, and 1992 AL Championship Series. Henke saved three games, as Toronto defeated the Oakland Athletics in six games to win the 1992 AL pennant. He then preserved two more victories in the Blue Jays' World Series Championship over the Atlanta Braves.

In 1993, the Texas Rangers signed Henke as a free agent for two years at $8 million. He responded with a career-high 40 saves in 1993. Time on the disabled list, coupled with the season-ending baseball strike on August 12, left him with just 15 saves for the 1994 campaign.

Henke signed with the St. Louis Cardinals (NL) to be close to his family in Taos, MO. In 1995 he produced what may have been his best season, earning 36 saves in 38 opportunities with a career-best 1.82 ERA and an All-Star game appearance. His honors included the Rolaids Relief Award and the St. Louis Sportswriters Man of the Year Award. At the pinnacle of his profession, Henke decided to put his wife, Kathy, and their four children first. He considered the money not as important as time with his family. Henke handles chores around their farm, helps the children with their homework, and visits his parents. His major league career included 642 games, all in relief, 41 victories, 42 losses, 311 saves, a 2.67 ERA, and 861 strikeouts in 789.2 innings.

BIBLIOGRAPHY: Thomas Henke file, National Baseball Library, Cooperstown, NY; John Dewan, ed., *The Scouting Report: 1994* (New York, 1994); Zander Hollander, *The Complete Handbook of Baseball 1995* (New York, 1995); Rick Hummel, "Still Unofficial, But Chances Slim Henke Will Pitch," St. Louis *Post-Dispatch*, December 20, 1995, Sect. D, p. 6D; Dan O'Neill, "Family Ties Make Henke a Homebody and Liking It," St. Louis *Post-Dispatch*, March 19, 1996, Sect. C, pp. 1, 5; Marybeth Sullivan, ed., *The Scouting Report, 1986* (New York, 1986); Bob Cairns, *Pen Men* (New York, 1993).

Frank J. Olmsted

HENRICH, Thomas David "The Clutch," "Tommy," "Old Reliable," "The Great Debater" (b. February 20, 1916, Massillon, OH), player, coach, and sportscaster, excelled as an outfielder and first baseman. He is one of six children of a plastering contractor and attended St. John's Catholic High School in Canton, OH. The 6-foot, 180-pound left-handed Henrich ranked among the most respected power clutch hitters in New York Yankees (AL) history and teamed with Joe DiMaggio* and Charlie Keller* to form one of the greatest outfields of the 1940s. Broadcaster Mel Allen nicknamed him "Old Reliable" after a train. Henrich started organized baseball with the Cleveland Indians (AL) organization in 1934 and enjoyed three consecutive brilliant minor league seasons, batting .326 in 1934 with Monessen, PA (PSL), .337 in 1935 with Zanesville, OH (MAL), and .346 in 1936 with New Orleans, LA (SL). Henrich thought his performance entitled him to a major league promotion, but his contract was sold to Milwaukee, WI (AA) in 1936. Henrich appealed to Commissioner Kenesaw Mountain Landis,* who ruled against Cleveland and declared him a free agent.

Eight different major league teams expressed interest, after which he signed with the New York Yankees (AL) for a $25,000 bonus. Henrich started 1937 with Newark, NJ (IL) and batted .320 the New York Yankees in 67 games. He performed regularly in right field from 1938 to 1942, hitting 22 HR in 1938 and 31 HR in 1941. Following the 1942 regular season and before the World Series, he joined the U.S. Coast Guard and missed the next three seasons. Upon returning to the New York Yankees in 1946, he starred in right field and at first base the next four seasons. His retirement followed a broken back bone in 1949 and a knee injury in 1950.

Sportswriter Red Smith observed that Henrich "got more pure joy out of baseball than any player I ever knew." A member of seven Yankees World Championship teams, he batted .282 lifetime with 269 doubles, 183 HR, and 795 RBI. Henrich led the Yankees three times in doubles and twice in triples, runs scored, games played, at bats, and RBI. In perhaps his best seasons, he in 1947 and 1948 starred as the team leader and a superb defensive player renowned for delivering in pressure situations. His four grand-slam HR in 1948 tied a club record. Perhaps his most memorable moments involved World Series play against the Brooklyn Dodgers. In the fourth game of the 1941 classic, he struck out to end the game. He reached first base on Mickey Owen's passed ball, after which the Yankees rallied to win the contest and eventually the World Series. After posting his best World Series statistics with a .323 batting average and 10 hits in 1947, he delivered the HR in the bottom of the ninth inning that enabled Allie Reynolds* to best Don Newcombe* in the 1949 World Series opener. After coaching with the Yankees in 1951 and helping launch the outfielding career of Mickey Mantle,* Henrich broadcast sports and coached for the New York Giants (NL) in 1957 and the Detroit Tigers (AL) in 1958 and 1959. Henrich, an accomplished musician, married Eileen O'Reilly on July 7, 1942, and belongs to the Ohio Sports Hall of Fame. He lists ice hockey and music as important side interests and lives in Prescott, AZ.

BIBLIOGRAPHY: Dom Forker, *The Men of Autumn* (Dallas, TX, 1989); David Halberstam, *Summer of '49* (New York, 1989); Tommy Henrich with Bill Gilbert, *Five O'Clock Lightning* (Chicago, IL, 1992); New York Yankees Sports Information Bureau; Paul Post, " 'Old Reliable' Always Came Through in Clutch," *SCD* 24 (January 10, 1997), pp. 120–121; Mike Shatzkin, ed., *The Ballplayers* (New York, 1990); Frank Graham, *The New York Yankees* (New York, 1943); Mark Gallagher, *The Yankee Encyclopedia*, vol. 3 (Champaign, IL, 1997); Tom Henrich file, National Baseball Library, Cooperstown, NY; Donald Honig, *Baseball Between the Lines* (New York, 1976); *TSN Baseball Register, 1938–1950*; Frank Waldman, ed., *Famous Athletes of Today*, 11th Series (Boston, MA, 1949).

Leonard H. Frey

HENTGEN, Patrick George "Pat" (b. November 13, 1968, Detroit, MI), player, is a 6-foot 2-inch, 200-pound pitcher who throws and bats right-handed. He is the son of Pat Hentgen, an insulator, and Marcia Hentgen and graduated in 1986 from Fraser High School in Detroit, where he played baseball and football. Hentgen captained the baseball team and was offered a baseball scholarship at Western Michigan University. He and his wife, Darlene, have one daughter, Taylor Renee.

The Toronto Blue Jays (AL) selected Hentgen in the fifth round of the 1986 free-agent draft and assigned him to St. Catharines, Canada (NYPL). In 1987, he posted an 11–5 won–lost record for Myrtle Beach, SC (SAL). Hentgen pitched the following two seasons for Dunedin, FL (FSL), leading the FSL in games started in 1988 and finishing second in games started and strikeouts in 1989. After posting a 9–5 pitching record at Knoxville, TN (SL) in 1990, he led the IL in strikeouts at Syracuse, NY (IL) in 1991. Called up by Toronto in September 1991, Hentgen appeared in three games for the Blue Jays. He started the 1992 season with the Toronto Blue Jays and notched his first major league victory on April 10th.

After becoming a full-time starting pitcher in 1993, Hentgen helped lead the Toronto Blue Jays to the World Series title. He compiled a 19–9 record during the regular season, but lost Game 3 to the Chicago White Sox in the AL Championship Series. In the World Series, he won Game 3 against the Philadelphia Phillies. Hentgen recorded 13–8 and 10–14 records the following two seasons and made the AL All-Star Team for the second straight time in 1994. He enjoyed a banner year in 1996, compiling a 20–10 record and establishing career bests in victories (20), ERA (3.22), games and games started (35), complete games (10), innings pitched (265.2), and strikeouts (177). Hentgen led the major leagues in complete games and innings pitched, finished second in the AL in wins and ERA, and matched his career best and shared the major league lead with three shutouts. He was selected the BBWAA AL Cy Young* Award winner, *TSN* AL Pitcher of the Year, and a *TSN* AL All-Star team member. His 1997 campaign featured a 15–10 record and 3.68 ERA. In November 1999, the St. Louis Cardinals acquired him.

In nine major league seasons through 1999, Hentgen has compiled a 105–76 won–lost record with a 4.14 ERA. He has appeared in 250 games, completing 31 of 222 starts with nine shutouts. Hentgen has allowed 1,587 hits and 557 walks in 1,555.2 innings pitched while striking out 995 batters. He did not miss a regular assignment in his career until 1998, making 159 consecutive starts through 1997. Hentgen, only the second Blue Jay to win 20 games in one season, ranks among the all-time team leaders in victories, shutouts, starts, complete games, and strikeouts. He held the club record for most season wins on the road (12) in 1993 and most strikeouts in a nine-inning game (14) in 1994.

BIBLIOGRAPHY: Pat Hentgen file, National Baseball Library, Cooperstown, NY; *TSN Official Baseball Register*, 1998; *Toronto Blue Jays Official Guide*, 1998.

John L. Evers

HERMAN, Floyd Caves "Babe" (b. June 26, 1903, Buffalo, NY; d. November 27, 1987, Glendale, CA), player, coach, and scout, was the son of Charles Herman and Rose Etta (Caves) Herman and attended Glendale, CA High School. Herman wanted to play football for the University of California, but signed as a first baseman and outfielder with the Brooklyn Dodgers (NL).

Nicknamed "Babe," the youthful Herman in 1921 hit .330 for Edmonton, Canada (WCaL). In 1922 he played for Reading, PA (IL) and Omaha, NE (WL), where he hit .416. Herman batted .300 or better from 1923 to 1925 for other minor league teams, including Atlanta, GA, Memphis, TN, San Antonio, TX, Little Rock, AR, and Seattle, WA. He married Anna Merriken on November 9, 1923 and had three sons and one daughter.

The very superstitious Herman played first base and later outfield for the famous NL "Daffy Dodgers" of manager Wilbert Robinson.* He laid his glove up in the field if facing a left-handed pitcher and face down if opposing a right-hander. He crowded the plate and could hit to all fields. A left-handed batter, the 6-foot 4-inch, 190-pound Herman once doubled into a double play when three Dodgers runners wound up on third base in 1926. Herman was never hit on the head by a fly ball, but once was hit on the shoulder. He excelled at the plate, hitting .381 in 1929. Although batting .393 the following year, Herman lost the NL batting title to Bill Terry.* That same season, he clouted 35 HR and knocked in a career-high 130 runs. Though Herman looked ungainly in the field, his lifetime .961 fielding average ranked the same as Ty Cobb.*

On March 14, 1932, the Dodgers traded Herman, Ernie Lombardi,* and Walt Gilbert to the Cincinnati Reds (NL) for Joe Stripp,* Tony Cuccinello,* and Clyde Sukeforth. Although he hit .326 and led the NL with 19 triples with Cincinnati, the Reds sent him to the Chicago Cubs (NL) in a multi-player deal in November 1932. After Herman had two fair seasons, including a .304 batting mark in 1934, the Cubs traded him to the Pittsburgh Pirates (NL) in November 1934. With Herman struggling at .235 in June 1935 the Pirates sold him back to the Reds. The Reds sent Herman to the Detroit

Tigers (AL) in April 1937 after he posted a .279 batting average in 1936. The Tigers released him following 17 games, after which he spent several seasons in the minor leagues with Toledo, OH (AA), Jersey City, NJ (IL), and Hollywood, CA (PCL). In 1945 the Dodgers recalled Herman, who hit .265 in 37 games.

During his major league career, Herman played in 1,552 games, compiled a .324 batting average, hit 399 doubles and 181 HR, and knocked in 997 runs. In one 1933 game, he belted three HR against the Philadelphia Phillies. On July 10, 1935 with the Reds, Herman slugged the first HR hit during a night game against the Brooklyn Dodgers. Herman subsequently scouted for the NL Pittsburgh Pirates (1947–1950), AL New York Yankees (1953–1954, 1962–1963), NL Philadelphia Phillies (1955–1959), NL New York Mets (1961), and NL San Francisco Giants (1964) and coached for the Pirates (1951) and Seattle, WA Reindeer (PCL) in 1952. He lived in Glendale, CA, where he raised turkeys, owned an orange grove, and grew prize-winning orchids.

BIBLIOGRAPHY: Frank Graham, *The Brooklyn Dodgers* (New York, 1945); William F. McNeil, *The Dodgers Encyclopedia* (Champaign, IL, 1997); Floyd Herman file, National Baseball Library, Cooperstown, NY; Maury Allen, *Baseball's 100* (New York, 1981); Harold H. Horowitz and Ralph Tolleris, *Big Time Baseball* (New York, 1950); Gene Karst and Martin J. Jones, Jr., *Who's Who in Professional Baseball* (New Rochelle, NY, 1973); Brent P. Kelley, *The Case For: Those Overlooked by the Baseball Hall of Fame* (Jefferson, NC, 1992); Richard Goldstein, *Superstars and Screwballs* (New York, 1991); John Lardner, "Unbelievable Babe Herman," *Sport Magazine's World of Sport* (New York, 1962); *NYT*, November 30, 1987, p. B-13; Ira Smith, *Baseball's Famous Outfielders* (New York, 1954); Red Smith, "Holy Name in Brooklyn," *NYT Biographical Service*, November 1979; Pete Williams, "Stealing First and Fielding with Your Head," *BRJ* 19 (1990), pp. 39–44; Eddie Gold and Art Ahrens, *The Golden Era Cubs, 1876–1940* (Chicago, IL, 1985).

William A. Borst

HERMAN, William Jennings "Billy," "Bryan" (b. July 7, 1909, New Albany, IN; d. September 5, 1992, West Palm Beach, FL), player, coach, manager, and scout, attended New Albany High School and pitched his church team to a league championship. As a minor leaguer, the 5-foot 11-inch, 195-pound Herman played second base for Vicksburg, MS (CSL) and Louisville, KY (AA) in 1928, Dayton, OH (CL) in 1929, and Louisville (AA) from 1929 through 1931. After joining the NL, the right-handed batter and thrower performed as a second baseman for the Chicago Cubs (1931–1941), Brooklyn Dodgers (1941–1946), and Boston Braves (1946). In 1,922 major league games, he made 2,345 hits, slugged 486 doubles, scored 1,163 runs, and knocked in 839 runs. Herman, the second baseman on *TSN* Major League All-Star team in 1943, compiled a .304 lifetime batting average. Besides batting .433 in 10 All-Star games, he starred on NL pennant-winning clubs with Chicago, 1932, 1935, and 1938 and Brooklyn in 1941. The stellar defensive second baseman holds NL records at his position for most years leading in putouts (7), putouts in a doubleheader (16, June 28, 1933), and seasons accepting at least 900 chances (1932–1933, 1935–1936, 1938).

Herman subsequently served as player–manager for the Pittsburgh Pirates (NL) in 1947 and Minneapolis, MN (AA) in 1948 and played for Oakland, CA (PCL) in 1950. He also managed Richmond, VA (PiL) in 1951, the Boston Red Sox (AL) from 1964 to 1966, Bradenton, FL (GCRL) in 1968, and Tri-City, WA (NWL) in 1969. Herman's major league clubs won 189 games and lost 274, perennially finishing in the second division. His major league coaching assignments included stints with the Brooklyn Dodgers (NL) from 1952 to 1957, Milwaukee Braves (NL) in 1958 and 1959, Boston Red Sox (AL) from 1960 to 1964, California Angels (AL) in 1967, and San Diego Padres (NL) in 1978 and 1979. The Oakland Athletics (AL) hired him as a scout from 1968 through 1974.

An expert at stealing opponents' signals, Herman was lauded by Casey Stengel* as "one of the . . . smartest players ever to come into the National League." Herman, who resided in Palm Beach Gardens, FL, married Hazel Jean Steproe on August 31, 1927 and later wed Frances Ann Antonucci on May 23, 1961. In 1975 he was elected to the National Baseball Hall of Fame.

BIBLIOGRAPHY: Thomas Aylesworth and Benton Minks, *The Encyclopedia of Baseball Managers* (New York, 1990); William J. Herman file, National Baseball Library, Cooperstown, NY; Donald Honig, *Baseball When the Grass Was Real* (New York, 1975); Donald Honig, *The Man in the Dugout* (Lincoln, NE, 1995); Warren Wilbert and William Hageman, *Chicago Cubs: Seasons at the Summit* (Champaign, IL, 1997); Warren Brown, *The Chicago Cubs* (New York, 1946); Jim Enright, *Chicago Cubs* (New York, 1975); Eddie Gold and Art Ahrens, *The Golden Era Cubs, 1876–1940* (Chicago, IL, 1985); Peter Golenbock, *Bums* (New York, 1984); Frank Graham, *The Brooklyn Dodgers* (New York, 1945); Richard Goldstein, *Superstars and Screwballs* (New York, 1991); Paul MacFarlane, ed., *TSN Hall of Fame Fact Book* (St. Louis, MO, 1983); *NYT*, September 7, 1992, p. 20.

Brian R. Kelleher

HERNANDEZ, Guillermo (Villanueva) "Willie" (b. November 14, 1954, Aguada, PR), player, is the son of Dionicio Hernandez and Domingo Hernandez and entered professional baseball in 1974 with Spartanburg, SC (WCL) in the Philadelphia Phillies (NL) organization, leading the WCL in innings pitched, complete games, and strikeouts. He was drafted by the Chicago Cubs (NL) in 1976 and played the next seven seasons there. The slender, 6-foot 2-inch, 183-pound left-hander quickly became a mainstay relief pitcher, teaming with Bruce Sutter* to give the Chicago Cubs a strong bullpen. Chicago used him as a set-up man during these years. With an 8–7 record, 3.03 ERA, and four saves, he was selected Chicago Rookie of the

Year in 1977. His best year for the Cubs came in 1978 with his 8–2 record and three saves.

In May 1983, Hernandez was traded to the Philadelphia Phillies and appeared in three World Series games against the Baltimore Orioles. The Philadelphia Phillies sent him in March 1984 to the Detroit Tigers (AL), where he enjoyed his greatest seasons. With 32 saves, a 9–3 record, and AL-leading 80 games in 1984, he was named the AL MVP and the AL Pitcher of the Year and also won the AL Cy Young* Award. The Detroit Tigers defeated the San Diego Padres in the five-game World Series, as Hernandez saved two games with a 1.69 ERA. A 31-save season followed in 1985, but his saves and game appearances dropped steadily thereafter. The 1989 season, his last major league campaign, saw him injured much of the second half. The Detroit Tigers released him in December 1989.

Hernandez appeared in 744 major league games, boasting a 70–63 record, 3.38 ERA, and 147 saves during his 13-year career. His achievements included an over two-to-one strikeout-to-walk ratio and selection to AL All-Star teams from 1984 to 1986. He married Carmen Rivera and has three children.

BIBLIOGRAPHY: Willie Hernandez file, National Baseball Library, Cooperstown, NY; *TSN Baseball Register*, 1990; *Chicago Cubs Media Guide*, 1977, 1982; Eddie Gold and Art Ahrens, *The New Era Cubs, 1941–1985* (Chicago, IL, 1985); Bob Cairns, *Pen Men* (New York, 1993); Ken Young, *Cy Young Award Winners* (New York, 1994); Rich Westcott and Frank Bilovsky, *The New Phillies Encyclopedia* (Philadelphia, PA, 1993); William M. Anderson, *The Detroit Tigers* (South Bend, IN, 1996); Sparky Anderson and Dan Ewald, *Sparky* (New York, 1990); Richard Bak, *A Place for Summer* (Detroit, MI, 1998).

Duane A. Smith

HERNANDEZ, Keith (b. October 20, 1953, San Francisco, CA), player, is the son of fireman John Hernandez and Jacquelyn (Jordan) Hernandez. Hernandez's father, his number one fan and adviser, formerly played infield in the St. Louis Cardinals (NL) farm system. Hernandez, a 6-foot, 185-pound all-around athlete, quit the Capucino High School baseball team his senior year. Consequently, he was drafted only 42nd by the St. Louis Cardinals (NL) in 1971 and was the 783rd player selected. He attended the College of San Mateo and is an avid history buff.

Hernandez, who signed with the Cardinals for a $30,000 bonus despite his low selection, played first base for St. Petersburg, FL (FSL) and Tulsa, OK (AA) in 1972, and for Arkansas (TL) and Tulsa (AA) in 1973. He joined St. Louis permanently at midseason in 1975 and led the Cardinals defensively with a .996 fielding average. From 1976 to 1983, Hernandez played first base for the Cardinals and paced the NL in many defensive categories. He consistently ranked among the leaders in total chances and led in assists in four seasons. Besides topping the NL in putouts two times and double plays six times, he earned Gold Glove awards from 1978 through 1988.

Hernandez, a left-handed batter, also posed an offensive threat. The .296 lifetime hitter led the NL in intentional walks received in 1982 (19) and ranked among leaders in on-base percentage and game-winning RBI. In 1979 he led the NL with 116 runs, 48 doubles, .344 batting average, and a .421 on-base percentage, being named *TSN* NL Player of the Year and NL Co-MVP. Three years later, Hernandez played in the NL Championship Series and World Series. Hernandez made five All-Star teams, hitting .300 with a 1.000 fielding average.

In June 1983, Hernandez was traded to the New York Mets. Although initially upset with the trade, he led the Mets in 1984 to a second-place finish in the NL East. In 1985 he paced the NL in game-winning RBI (23), placed sixth in hitting (.309), and tied for fifth in doubles (34). On July 4, he hit for the cycle in a 16–13 victory over the Atlanta Braves in 19 innings. In 1986 Hernandez finished fifth in the NL in batting (.310) and tied for first in on-base percentage (.413), helping the Mets to capture the NL pennant. In the NL Championship Series against the Houston Astros, Hernandez hit .269 and knocked in three runs. He batted .231 and knocked in four runs as the Mets defeated the Boston Red Sox in the World Series. He appeared in the NL Championship Series against the Los Angeles Dodgers in 1988. His major league career ended with the Cleveland Indians (AL) in 1990.

During 17 major league seasons, Hernandez recorded 2,182 hits, 426 doubles, 162 HR, and 1,071 RBI. He led the NL in runs and fielding average twice and doubles and batting average once. He ranks tenth in lifetime fielding percentage (.994) among first basemen and holds major league records for most seasons leading first baseman in double plays (6) and career assists by a first baseman (1,682). He made the *TSN* All-Star team in 1979, 1980, and from 1984 to 1986 and the *TSN* Silver Slugger team in 1980 and 1984. Commissioner Peter Ueberroth* in February 1986 suspended Hernandez for one year for his involvement with drugs. Hernandez avoided the suspension by donating 10 percent of his salary to a drug rehabilitation program, contributing one hundred hours of community service, and agreeing to periodic testing. Hernandez is separated from his wife, Sue, has three daughters, Jessica, Melissa, and Mary, and lives in New York City.

BIBLIOGRAPHY: Robert Obojski, "Former Mets Prove Popular Signers at NYC Area Shows," *SCD* 25 (December 18, 1998), pp. 126–127; Bob Broeg and Jerry Vickery, *St. Louis Cardinals Encyclopedia* (Grand Rapids, MI, 1998); John Thom, *Batting Champions of the 20th Century* (Los Angeles, CA, 1992); Keith Hernandez file, National Baseball Library, Cooperstown, NY; *CB* (1988), pp. 238–241; Keith Hernandez and Mike Bryan, *If at First; a Season with the Mets* (New York, 1987); "Hernandez: First Baseman without Peer," *NYT Biographical Service* 17 (August 1986), pp. 1069–1070; *Idaho Statesman*, December 15, 1984, p. 1B; Joe Jares, "KHrnnz Is Dng Jst Grt," *SI*

51 (September 17, 1979), pp. 50–51; Robert E. Kelly, *Baseball's Best* (Jefferson, NC, 1988); *The Baseball Encyclopedia*, 10th ed. (New York, 1996); William Nack, "He's Still Not Home Free," *SI* 65 (October 13, 1986), pp. 104–108; Rob Rains, *The St. Louis Cardinals* (New York, 1992); *TSN Baseball Register*, 1990; *TSN*, July 24, 1984, p. 11, October 15, 1984, p. 35, December 3, 1984, p. 54; C. S. Smith, "The Afterlife," *NY* 27 (April 4, 1994), pp. 56–57; H. Stein, "The Extra Innings of Keith Hernandez," *MH* 8 (June 1993), pp. 68–71; George Vecsey, "Keith Hernandez, Historian at First Base," *NYT Biographical Service* (August 1983), pp. 946–947; *WWA*, 42nd ed. (1982–1983), p. 1419.

Gaymon L. Bennett

HERSHISER, Orel Leonard, IV "Bulldog" (b. September 16, 1958, Buffalo, NY), player, is the first of four children of Orel Leonard Hershiser III and Mildred Hershiser. Small for his age, he did not make the varsity baseball team at Cherry Hills, NJ East High School until his junior year.

In 1976, Hershiser received a partial baseball scholarship from Bowling Green, OH State University (MAC), where he compiled a 6–2 record in his third season. The Los Angeles Dodgers (NL) selected the 6-foot 3-inch, 192-pound right-hander in the 17th round of the 1979 free agent draft and signed him for a $10,000 bonus. The Los Angeles Dodgers assigned him to Clinton, IA (ML) in 1979, San Antonio, TX (TL) in 1980 and 1981, and Albuquerque, NM (PCL) the next two seasons before he made his major league debut in September 1983.

His pitching success began in 1984 after Los Angeles Dodger manager Tom Lasorda* dubbed him "Bulldog" to inspire aggressiveness. Shortly afterward, Hershiser compiled a season-best 33-inning scoreless streak. In 1985, he won 19 of 22 decisions to lead the NL with an .864 winning percentage. From 1984 to 1987, he tallied 60 wins, nine more than Don Sutton* and Don Drysdale,* the Dodgers' all-time victory leaders, won in their first four major league seasons. His success depends on a full arsenal of pitches, including an outstanding sinking fastball, all delivered with deadly accuracy. He studies opposing batters carefully, recording their performance on a personal computer and pitching them accordingly.

Hershiser's finest major league season came in 1988, when he led the NL in wins (23), innings pitched (267), and shutouts (8) and shared the lead in complete games (15). He surpassed Drysdale's record of 58 consecutive scoreless innings in his final regular season start, shutting out the San Diego Padres for 10 innings to raise his total to 59.

Hershiser appeared in four of the seven 1988 NL Championship Series games, recording a win and a save. He shutout the Oakland Athletics in the second game of the World Series and clinched the series for the underrated Los Angeles Dodgers in the fifth contest, going the distance for a 4–2 victory. Hershiser, who enjoys batting, tied a World Series record in Game 2 with three hits in three at bats. He hit two doubles and a single, as many hits and more total bases than he allowed. In 1993, Hershiser batted .356, making 26 hits.

In 1988, Hershiser was honored as the MVP in both the NL Championship Series and the World Series, received the NL Cy Young* Award, and was named the *SI* Sportsman of the Year, *TSN* Major League Player of the Year, and AP Male Athlete of the Year. Hershiser signed a three-year, $7.9 million contract, the highest at the time in major league baseball.

Shoulder surgery forced him to miss most of the 1990 season, diminishing his pitching effectiveness. The Los Angeles Dodgers released him following the 1994 season.

In April 1995, the Cleveland Indians (AL) signed Hershiser. He compiled a 16–6 record with a 3.87 ERA in 1995 and hurled a shutout in the AL Division Series against the Boston Red Sox. Hershiser was named AL Championship Series MVP in 1995 after boasting a 2–0 mark and 1.29 ERA against the Seattle Mariners. He split two decisions with a 2.57 ERA in the World Series against the Atlanta Braves. After finishing 15–9 with a 4.24 ERA in 1996, Hershiser started one game in the AL Division Series against the Baltimore Orioles. He fared 14–6 with a 4.47 ERA in 1997 and started two games without a decision in the AL Division Series against the New York Yankees. Hershiser appeared in one game against the Baltimore Orioles in the 1997 AL Championship Series, but lost two decisions with an 11.70 ERA in the World Series against the Florida Marlins. In December 1997, the San Francisco Giants (NL) acquired him. He finished 11–10 in 1998, before being released that October. After trying out with the Cleveland Indians (AL), he joined the New York Mets (NL) in March 1999. After compiling a 13–12 record in 1999, he hurled nearly 10 scoreless innings in the NL Division Series and NL Championship Series and rejoined the Dodgers in December 1999.

Through the 1999 season, Hershiser compiled a 203–145 win–loss record with 2,001 strikeouts, 25 shutouts, and a 3.41 ERA. He was named to the NL All-Star team in 1987, 1988, and 1989.

An outspoken Christian and model family man, Hershiser resides in Winter Park, FL with his wife, Jamie, and two sons. He enjoys golf and baseball card collecting.

BIBLIOGRAPHY: Orel Hershiser file, National Baseball Library, Cooperstown, NY; William F. McNeil, *The Dodgers Encyclopedia* (Champaign, IL, 1997); John Thorn et al., eds., *Total Indians* (New York, 1996). *CB* (1990), pp. 297–301; *The Baseball Encyclopedia*, 10th ed. (New York, 1996); Peter Gammons, "A Case of Orel Surgery," *SI* 69 (October 31, 1988), pp. 36–37; Orel Hershiser with Jerry B. Jenkins, *Out of the Blue* (Brentwood, TN, 1989); Ross Newhan, "King of the Hill," *Sport* 79 (September 1988), pp. 51–56; Bruce Newman, "A Big-Name Pitcher," *SI* 64 (May 5, 1986), pp. 36–42; Joseph Nocera, "The Man with the Golden Arm," *Newsweek* 113 (April 10, 1989), pp. 42–48; Scott Ostler, "Orel in Wonderland," *Sport* 80 (March 1989), pp. 32–34; Mike Shatzkin, ed., *The Ballplayers* (New York, 1990); John Thorn et al., eds., *Total Baseball*, 5th ed. (New York, 1997); Steve Wulf, "Destiny's Boys," *SI* 69 (October 31, 1988), pp. 32–36; Steve Wulf, "Sportsman of the Year," *SI* 69 (December 19, 1988), pp. 60–76.

Gaymon L. Bennett

HERZOG, Charles Lincoln "Buck" (b. July 9, 1885, Baltimore, MD; d. September 4, 1953, Baltimore, MD), player, played infield for the New York Giants (NL) on several pennant-winning clubs. New York Giants manager John McGraw* traded him twice, but later reacquired him to fill the team's immediate needs.

The 5-foot 11-inch, 160-pound right-handed Herzog, a graduate of the University of Maryland, began his professional baseball career with York-Reading, PA (ISL) in 1907 and got his first taste of major league baseball by batting .300 with the 1908 New York Giants. He appeared in 64 games that season, mostly as a shortstop. Herzog became a reserve outfielder in 1909, batting .185 in 42 games. In December 1909, New York traded Herzog to the Boston Doves (NL) for Beals Becker. For the Doves in 1910, Herzog played solely as a third baseman with a .915 fielding percentage and .250 batting average. In July 1911, the New York Giants reacquired Herzog from Boston for Al Bridwell and Hank Gowdy.* Splitting his time between shortstop and third base, Herzog played an instrumental role on three consecutive NL pennant winners from 1911 through 1913. In the 1912 World Series against the Boston Red Sox, Herzog batted .400 and delivered five extra-base hits.

Herzog was traded to the Cincinnati Reds (NL) in December 1913 and played shortstop there until 1916. In July 1916, Cincinnati returned Herzog to the New York Giants. As New York's second baseman, he helped the Giants win the 1917 NL pennant. Herzog was shipped to the Boston Braves (NL) in January 1918 for the second time in his career. Between 1918 and 1920, Herzog played every infield position for the Boston Braves and the Chicago Cubs (NL). His 13-year major league career consisted of 1,493 games with 1,370 hits, 20 HR, a .259 batting average, and respectable .954 regular-season fielding average. He played in 25 World Series games, batting .245.

In 1921, Herzog batted .295 with Columbus, OH-Louisville, KY (AA). After leaving baseball, Herzog worked for the B&O Railroad. As athletic passenger agent, he made the travel arrangements for numerous professional baseball clubs.

BIBLIOGRAPHY: Buck Herzog file, National Baseball Library, Cooperstown, NY; Noel Hynd, *The Giants of the Polo Grounds* (New York, 1988); Lee Allen, *The Cincinnati Reds* (New York, 1948); Gary Caruso, *The Braves Encyclopedia* (Philadelphia, PA, 1995); Harold Kaese, *The Boston Braves* (New York, 1948); Eddie Gold and Art Ahrens, *The Golden Era Cubs, 1876–1940* (Chicago, Il, 1985); Charles C. Alexander, *John McGraw* (New York, 1988); Ray Robinson, *Matty: An American Hero* (New York,

1993); Frank Graham, *The New York Giants* (New York, 1952); Mike Shatzkin, ed., *The Ballplayers* (New York, 1990); *The Baseball Encyclopedia*, 10th ed. (New York, 1996).

John G. Robertson

HERZOG, Dorrell Norman Elvert "Whitey," "White Rat," "Rellie" (b. November 9, 1931, New Athens, IL), player, scout, coach, manager, and executive, is the second of three sons of Edgar Herzog, an employee for Mound City Brewing Company and the Illinois Highway Department, and Lietta (Fanke) Herzog. He attended New Athens High School, whose ballpark now is named Whitey Herzog Field. His older brother, Herman, played two years of minor league baseball. The 5-foot 11-inch, 180-pound Herzog signed with the New York Yankees (AL) in 1949 for $1,500 and played center field with farm clubs in McAlester, OK (SSL), Norfolk, VA (PiL), Joplin, MO (WA), Beaumont, TX (TL), Quincy, IL (3IL), and Kansas City, MO (AA). Herzog, who spent 1953 and 1954 in the U.S. Army, married Mary Lou Sinn in February 1953 and has three children, Debbie, David, and Jimmy.

The Washington Senators (AL) organization acquired Herzog in February 1956. Herzog, a left-hander, played at Denver, CO (AA) before becoming a regular center fielder for the Washington Senators in 1956. From 1957 to 1963, he substituted at first base and in the outfield for the Washington Senators, Kansas City Athletics (AL), Baltimore Orioles (AL), and Detroit Tigers (AL). He compiled a .257 career batting average with 25 HR and 172 RBI in 634 games.

Herzog scouted and coached for the Kansas City Athletics in 1965 before joining the New York Mets (NL) as third base coach in 1966 and, later, director of player development. His managerial debut came in 1973 with the Texas Rangers (AL). After coaching with the California Angels (AL) in 1974 and 1975, Herzog was hired in 1975 to pilot the Kansas City Royals (AL). In 4½ seasons there, he led the Royals to three AL West titles and two second-place finishes. Kansas City, however, lost all three AL Championship Series to the New York Yankees.

Herzog became St. Louis Cardinals (NL) skipper in 1980 and later general manager. He engineered numerous trades to overhaul the Cardinals completely, helping lead St. Louis to the best overall record in the NL East for the 1981 split season and win the 1982 World Championship against the Milwaukee Brewers. Under his field direction, St. Louis won NL pennants again in 1985 and 1987. On July 6, 1990, Herzog resigned as Cardinals manager.

Herzog, who was considered a civic treasure in St. Louis, was widely regarded as a genius for his grasp of baseball at every level. He compiled 1,281 wins and 1,125 losses as a major league pilot and was selected UPI Manager of the Year (1976), UPI and *TSN* Manager of the Year (1982), *TSN* Man of the Year (1982), BBWAA NL Manager of the Year (1985), and Executive of the Year (1981, 1982). In August 1991, Herzog joined the California Angels (AL) as senior vice president of player personnel. He served as senior vice president and general manager of the Angels in 1994. Herzog's autobiography, *White Rat: A Life in Baseball*, sold well.

BIBLIOGRAPHY: Whitey Herzog file, National Baseball Library, Cooperstown, NY; Bob Broeg, *Redbirds: A Century of Cardinals' Baseball* (St. Louis, MO, 1981); Bob Broeg and Jerry Vickery, *St. Louis Cardinals Encyclopedia* (Grand Rapids, MI, 1998); Ron Fimrite, "Buck and the Singing Cowboy," *SI* 76 (April 13, 1992), pp. 60–62; Whitey Herzog and Kevin Horrigan, *White Rat* (New York, 1987); Kansas City Royals, *Grandslam, 1979*; Leonard Koppett, *The Man in the Dugout* (New York, 1993); Rob Rains, *The St. Louis Cardinals* (New York, 1992); T. Ringolsby, "Sport Interview," *Sport* 77 (April 1986), pp. 25–27; Thomas Aylesworth and Benton Minks, *The Encyclopedia of Baseball Managers* (New York, 1990).

Frank J. Olmsted

HEYDLER, John Arnold (b. July 10, 1869, Lafargeville, NY; d. April 18, 1956, San Diego, CA), umpire, sportswriter, and executive, became a printer's apprentice at age 14 in Rochester, NY and worked for the Bureau of Printing and Engraving in Washington, DC. He reportedly recited "Casey at the Bat" to President Grover Cleveland, to whom he was presenting a draft of a printed document for approval. Heydler, an avid fan and amateur player, became involved in the sport as an occupation almost by accident when asked to umpire a game in 1895 because the regular official did not show up. He served as an assistant umpire in the NL from 1895 to 1898 and covered the game as a sportswriter from 1898 to 1903. His first important executive activity came in 1903, when he was named private secretary to NL president Harry Pulliam.* His principal responsibility comprised compiling statistics, thus preserving much of the game's early history.

After being selected NL secretary-treasurer in 1907, Heydler served as acting NL president in 1909 and as NL president in his own right in 1918. His tenure came after the sport had established itself as America's pastime and was experiencing its most difficult, disreputable period, culminating with the Chicago Black Sox scandal in 1919. As NL president, Heydler did not exhibit aggressive leadership or rigorously investigate suspected wrongdoing. In 1919 he exonerated Hal Chase* from charges of betting on and throwing games in previous seasons. This action resulted in heavy criticism. Nonetheless, Heydler became one of the last presidents to stand up to the owners. In 1920, he actively backed the selection of Judge Kenesaw Mountain Landis* as Commissioner of Baseball. Heydler clearly recognized the importance of creating a strong Commissioner's Office to tame the owners. His support of this move proved critical in changing the direction which baseball underwent thereafter.

The innovative Heydler, well regarded in the sport, helped establish the

National Baseball Hall of Fame to honor the sports heroes and fix the sport of baseball in the national consciousness. He also proposed in 1929 that pitchers should not bat and suggested that a tenth man hit for them. He thus fathered the DH system currently used in the AL. Upon retiring as president because of ill health in 1934, Heydler served as NL chairman of the board until his death. Heydler, a lifetime Lutheran, married Nancy Humphrey of Franklin, PA on September 18, 1894 and apparently had no children.

BIBLIOGRAPHY: John Heydler file, National Baseball Library, Cooperstown, NY; Gene Karst and Martin J. Jones, Jr., *Who's Who in Professional Baseball* (New Rochelle, NY, 1973); *NYT*, April 19, 1956; Marshall Smelser, *The Life That Ruth Built* (New York, 1975); *Time* 67 (April 30, 1956), p. 80; David Q. Voigt, *American Baseball*, vol. 2 (Norman, OK, 1970).

Charles R. Middleton

HICKMAN, Charles Taylor "Charlie," "Piano Legs," "Handsome Charlie" (b. March 4, 1876, Dunkard, PA; d. April 19, 1934, Morgantown, WV), player and scout, was the son of Issac N. Hickman and Josephine N. Hickman, prominent Green County, PA citizens. Hickman, who had a brother, Guy, and a sister, Mary, was educated in Greene County schools and attended West Virginia University in 1895–1896. In 1896, the 5-foot 9-inch, 215-pound right-handed Hickman, whose massive leg structure earned him the nickname "Piano Legs," entered professional baseball as a pitcher with New Castle, PA (ISL).

From 1897 through 1899, Hickman saw limited action with the Boston Beaneaters (NL) as a pitcher, first baseman, and outfielder. He starred in 1900 with the New York Giants (NL), hitting .313 with a .482 slugging percentage his first full season. Hickman also enjoyed a 27-game hitting streak, but his 91 errors at third base set a NL record and resulted in his shift to first base and the outfield thereafter. After performing for New York through 1901, Hickman played for the Boston Pilgrims (AL) in 1902, Cleveland Blues (AL) from 1902 to 1904, Detroit Tigers (AL) in 1904 and 1905, Washington Senators (AL) from 1905 to 1907, Chicago White Sox (AL) in 1907, and Cleveland Naps (AL) in 1908. With the Cleveland Blues in 1902, Hickman, Nap Lajoie,* and Bill Bradley* hit successive HR off Jack Harper of the St. Louis Browns. No one in the AL had accomplished this feat before. Hickman came close to winning the AL triple crown in 1902, finishing second in HR with 11, second in RBI with 110, and third in batting average with .361. With the Washington Senators from 1905 to 1907, Hickman befriended President Theodore Roosevelt and frequently visited the White House. A knee injury in 1908 ended his major league career. The 1909–1911 seasons found Hickman playing with Toledo, OH (AA). After finishing up with Milwaukee, WI (AA) in 1911, Hickman scouted for the Cleveland Naps and Indians (AL) every summer until 1926.

Hickman married Pearl Taylor in 1913 and had a son, Charles, Jr., and a daughter, Harriet. He was elected Morgantown, WV city recorder in 1918 and served as mayor for three terms until 1921. From 1921 to 1928, Hickman engaged in merchandising. He served as magistrate for the Morgantown District from 1928 until 1930, when he resigned due to ill health. He was elected sheriff of Monogalia County in 1933, but died of heart failure at his home.

The fair, modest, and compassionate Hickman was known for his judicial wisdom and understanding. In his 12-year major league career, Hickman played in 1,081 games with 1,176 hits, a .295 batting average, and a then remarkable .440 slugging percentage. He hit 217 doubles, 91 triples, 59 HR, scored 478 runs, and knocked in 614 runs. As a pitcher, Hickman compiled a 10–8 record in 185 innings over six seasons with a 4.28 ERA.

BIBLIOGRAPHY: Charles Hickman file, National Baseball Library, Cooperstown, NY; *Dominion-News*, April 20, 1934, pp. 1–2; *TSN*, April 26, 1934; John Phillips, *Who Was Who in Cleveland Baseball, 1901–10* (Cabin John, MD, 1989); Fred Smith, *995 Tigers* (Detroit, MI, 1981); Gary Caruso, *The Braves Encyclopedia* (Philadelphia, PA, 1995); Mike Shatzkin, ed., *The Ballplayers* (New York, 1990); Morgantown *Post*, April 19, 1934, pp. 1–2.

John H. Ziegler

HIGGINS, Michael Franklin, Jr. "Pinky" (b. May 27, 1909, Red Oak, TX; d. March 21, 1969, Dallas, TX), player, manager, scout, and executive, was the son of Dallas police officer Michael Higgins, Sr. The three Higgins sons, all talented high school athletes, played college sports. Clen played football at the University of Texas, while Jimmy performed for Southern Methodist University. Mike played football and baseball at the University of Texas. After graduating from there in 1930, Higgins signed with Connie Mack's* Philadelphia Athletics (AL) and played in only 14 games, mainly at third base, on their world championship team. After spending 1931 with Dallas, TX and San Antonio, TX (TL) and 1932 with Portland, OR (PCL), he played third base for the Athletics from 1933 through 1936. He was traded in December 1936 to the Boston Red Sox (AL), where he hit .302 and .303 his next two seasons and drove in 106 runs each season. From 1939 to 1944, the right-hander performed as the regular third baseman with the Detroit Tigers (AL). In February 1935, he married Hazel French of Dallas, TX. They had two daughters, Diane and Elizabeth. During World War II, he served in the U.S. Navy. He played in 18 games with Detroit in 1946 and in May was traded back to Boston (AL), where he finished his last season as a player. A clutch hitter and a solid fielder, the 6-foot 1-inch, 185-pound Higgins compiled a .292 lifetime average with 1,941 hits, 374 doubles, 140 HR, and 1,075 RBI. In his first full season, Higgins batted .314, had eight hits in a June 1933 doubleheader, and hit for the cycle in an August game. During the 1938 season with Boston, he hit safely in 12 successive times at bat to break the AL record of 10 straight hits. In the 1940 World Series with the Detroit Tigers, he batted .333, made 8 hits and 6 RBI, recorded 30 composite putouts, and handled a record 10 chances in one game. In 64 games with Boston in 1946, Higgins helped the Red Sox win an AL pennant by batting .275 and delivering some clutch hits.

After his playing career ended, Higgins spent eight years managing in the Red Sox minor league system and developed a reputation as a winner and a patient, skillful handler of talent. After moving steadily up from Class B to AAA clubs, he became manager of the Red Sox in 1955. In his first year, he was named *TSN* Manager of the Year and guided Boston to an 84–70 fourth-place finish. Although not producing a pennant winner in eight seasons as Red Sox manager, he steered his teams to third place finishes in 1958 and 1959. As manager, Higgins gave players the benefit of the doubt when struggling with slumps or problems and earned their respect and loyalty with his easygoing, approachable manner. His last three years at Boston were spent as Red Sox executive vice-president and general manager. After being dismissed in 1965, he scouted for the Houston Astros (NL).

His car struck and killed a Louisiana state highway worker and injured three others in February 1968. Pleading guilty to drunk driving, he was sentenced to four years in prison. After serving less than two months of his sentence, he was paroled and died of a heart attack one day after his release.

BIBLIOGRAPHY: Pinky Higgins file, National Baseball Library, Cooperstown, NY; Gene Karst and Martin J. Jones, Jr., *Who's Who in Professional Baseball* (New Rochelle, NY, 1973); Howard Liss, *The Boston Red Sox* (New York, 1982); Thomas Aylesworth and Benton Minks, *The Encyclopedia of Baseball Managers* (New York, 1990); Frederick G. Lieb, *Connie Mack* (New York, 1945); Frederick G. Lieb, *The Detroit Tigers* (New York, 1946); Frederick G. Lieb, *The Boston Red Sox* (New York, 1947); Robert Redmount, *The Red Sox Encyclopedia* (Champaign, IL, 1997); Fred Smith, *995 Tigers* (Detroit, MI, 1981); Tom Meany et al., *The Boston Red Sox* (New York, 1956); *NYT*, March 22, 1969, p. 33.

                                                                Douglas A. Noverr

HIGHAM, Richard "Dick" (b. July 24, 1851, Ipswich, E. Suffolk, England; d. March 18, 1905, Chicago, IL), player, manager, and umpire, immigrated to New York City in 1853 with his parents, James Higham, an innkeeper in England and restaurant owner in New York, and Mary Hart (Langley) Higham. He played cricket and baseball for several leading metropolitan clubs in his teens and joined New York's professional Mutuals in 1870.

Higham remained with the New York Mutuals when they joined the newly formed NA in 1871. After playing outfield a season with the Baltimore Lord Baltimores (NA), he returned to the New York Mutuals in 1873 for two seasons. Part way through the 1874 season, he replaced Tom Carey as manager and lifted the Mutuals into second place with a 29–11 finish. The Chicago White Stockings (NA) signed Higham for 1875, but suspended him briefly in late June on suspicion of game fixing. Chicago released him in mid-August when he was found wagering against his team. He completed the season with the Mutuals.

In 1876 Higham played in the new NL with the Hartford, CT Dark Blues, where he hit .327 and shared the NL lead in doubles (21). After a season with the independent Syracuse, NY Stars, he returned to the NL with the Providence, RI Grays and led the NL in doubles (22) and runs (60). In 1879, he played for Albany, NY and Rochester, NY in the minor league NA. His major league playing career ended after one game with the Troy, NY Haymakers (NL) in 1880.

Higham, who had substituted as an umpire in the original NA, joined the NL umpiring staff in 1881. In June 1882, however, the NL expelled him permanently for advising a gambler to bet against the Detroit Wolverines, whose games he umpired.

Higham married Clara Learned on September 8, 1888 in Kansas City, MO, where he worked as a bookkeeper. They had two sons, Harold and Langley. By 1896, Higham lived in Chicago and worked in a restaurant.

The 5-foot, 8½-inch Higham weighed 171 pounds, threw right-handed, and batted left. He alternated mostly between catcher and right field, but also played second base and all other positions but pitcher. In 372 major league games, he batted .307 with 85 doubles, 15 triples, and four HR among his 549 hits. He declined to wear a mask as a catcher, but became the first major league umpire to wear one.

BIBLIOGRAPHY: Richard Higham file, National Baseball Library, Cooperstown, NY; Daniel E. Ginsburg, *The Fix Is In* (Jefferson, NC, 1995); Harold V. Higham, correspondence with Larry R. Gerlach, 1997; Frederick Ivor-Campbell et al., eds., *Baseball's First Stars* (Cleveland, OH, 1996); William J. Ryczek, *Blackguards and Red Stockings* (Jefferson, NC, 1992); *Spalding's Base Ball Guide*, 1883; John Thorn et al., eds., *Total Baseball*, 5th ed. (New York, 1997).

Frederick Ivor-Campbell

HILL, J. Preston "Pete" (b. 1880; d. 1951, Buffalo, NY), player and manager, ranked among the finest hitters in Negro baseball's early years. In 1904, the left-handed–hitting Hill began his baseball career with the Philadelphia Giants. Hill, a line-drive hitter with occasional HR power, teamed five years at Philadelphia with stars Rube Foster,* Grant "Home Run" Johnson,* Pete Booker, Charlie Grant, and Dan McClellan.* The Philadelphia Giants played against all-white teams in the Philadelphia City League. The white teams fielded "Turkey Mike" Donlin,* Harry McCormick, Jake Stahl,* "Topsy" Hartsel,* and other major leaguers.

After jumping in 1909 to the Leland Giants of Chicago, Hill captained and was assistant manager of the incredible 123–6 1910 team. The Giants, managed by Rube Foster, included stars John Henry Lloyd,* Bruce Petway,* and Frank Wickware.* In the fall of 1910, he played a three-game series against his friend Frank Chance's* Chicago Cubs (NL). Hill, a part Indian who was known as Foster's "money hitter," played for the Chicago American Giants from 1911 to 1918. For six seasons, he participated in winter baseball in Cuba and compiled a .307 composite batting average. He produced a league-leading .365 mark in the 1910–1911 campaign and hit safely in 115 of 116 games in 1911. He batted four for four in 1909–1910 against 21-game winner Ed Willett of the Detroit Tigers (AL) and four for nine in 1910–1911 against Eddie Plank* and Chief Bender* of the Philadelphia Athletics (AL). In recorded games against white ballplayers, he batted an even .300.

From 1919 to 1921, he became player–manager of the Detroit Stars. The Stars entered the NNL in 1920. He played for and managed the Milwaukee Bears (NNL) in 1923 and returned to Detroit in 1924. After moving in midseason 1924 to the Baltimore Black Sox (ECL), he performed occasionally and served as club business manager through the 1925 season. Hill formed the Buffalo Red Caps and later worked at the Ford Motor Company in Detroit. His career spanned two distinct eras of black baseball. After participating on the great barnstorming teams of the century's first two decades, he starred in the early NNL years. Hill and the era's other great players gave relative stability to the Negro leagues. In 1952 the Pittsburgh *Courier* selected him on the second All-Time All-Star team.

BIBLIOGRAPHY: Terry A. Baxter, correspondence with Jorge Figueroda, 1984, Cuban League statistics, Terry A. Baxter Collection, Cedar Rapids, IA; John B. Holway, "Pete Hill," John B. Holway Collection, Alexandria, VA; John B. Holway, *Rube Foster* (Alexandria, VA, 1981); Joseph M. Overfield, correspondence with John B. Holway, December 26, 1983, John B. Holway Collection, Alexandria, VA; Robert W. Peterson, *Only the Ball Was White* (Englewood Cliffs, NJ, 1970); James A. Riley, *The All-Time All-Stars of Black Baseball* (Cocoa, FL, 1983); James A. Riley, *The Biographical Encyclopedia of the Negro Baseball Leagues* (New York, 1994); *Sol White's Official Baseball Guide* (1907; reprint, Columbia, SC, 1984).

                                                                                                                            Terry A. Baxter

HILLER, John Frederick (b. April 8, 1943, Toronto, Canada), player, achieved one of the most memorable comebacks in major league baseball history. The oldest of two sons of Donald Hiller, a car collision shop owner, and Ethel (Cassis) Hiller, he attended David and Mary Thompson High School in Toronto before being signed by the Detroit Tigers (AL) as a free agent in 1962. The 6-foot 1-inch, 190-pound right-handed–hitting southpaw spent around 4½ years in the minor leagues, interrupted by brief stints with the Detroit Tigers in 1965 and 1966. Partway through the 1967 season, Hiller joined the parent club and became an effective reliever and spot starter in the Detroit Tigers' "near miss" drive for the 1967 AL pennant and on their 1968 world championship team. Hiller, who compiled nine wins, two saves, and a 2.39 ERA in 1968, saw action in two World Series games against the St. Louis Cardinals.

After experiencing mediocre performances in 1969 and 1970, Hiller suffered a heart attack in 1971 and underwent bypass surgery. He retired with his baseball career seemingly over. Hiller, however, made excellent progress, being resigned as a Detroit Tigers batting practice pitcher in June 1972 and as an active player in July. He pitched in 24 games with a 2.03 ERA that season and hurled 3½ scoreless innings in three games of the 1972 AL Championship Series against the Oakland A's, winning Game 4 in extra innings. Over the next four years, Hiller established himself as one of the premier major league closers. He led the AL in games pitched (65) in 1973 and established a since-eclipsed major league record for saves (38), winning 10 games, losing five, and sporting a 1.44 ERA! That year, he was named *TSN* Comeback Player of the Year, *TSN* Fireman of the Year, and Fred Hutchinson Award recipient. The following year, his 17 wins and 14 losses both tied AL records for relief pitchers. He also was selected an AL All-Star.

In 15 major league seasons through 1980, Hiller pitched in 545 games, still a Tigers record, with 125 saves, 1,036 strikeouts, and a 2.83 ERA. Several peers, surveyed in the mid-1980s, cited Hiller as having the best "change up" they had ever seen.

Hiller married Janis Baldwin in September 1965 and had three children, Wendy, Joseph, and Danielle, and a stepson, Joseph Sabatini. After retiring in 1980, he lived in Iron Mountain, MI and married his second wife, Linette Lynn LaChapelle, on March 23, 1985.

BIBLIOGRAPHY: John Hiller file, National Baseball Library, Cooperstown, NY; Maury Allen, *Baseball: The Lives Behind the Seams* (New York, 1990); *Detroit Tigers Media Guides*, 1968–1980; *TSN Official Baseball Register*, 1981; John Hiller, letter to Sheldon Appleton, January 1993; Eugene and Roger McCaffrey, *Players' Choice* (New York, 1987); John Thorn et al., eds., *Total Baseball*, 5th ed. (New York, 1997); Bob Cairns, *Pen Men* (New York, 1993); Fred Smith, *995 Tigers* (Detroit, MI, 1981); William M. Anderson, *The Detroit Tigers* (South Bend, IN, 1996); Richard Bak, *A Place for Summer* (Detroit, MI, 1998); Joe Falls, *Detroit Tigers* (New York, 1975).

Sheldon L. Appleton

HINES, Paul A. (b. March 1, 1852, Washington, DC; d. July 10, 1935, Hyattsville, MD), player, starred as an outfielder in the NA, NL, and AA from 1872 to 1891. During his career he played with the Washington Nationals (NA, 1872–1873), Chicago White Stockings (NA, 1874–1877), Providence, RI Grays (NL, 1878–1885), Washington Statesman (NL, 1886–1887), and Indianapolis, IN Hoosiers (NL, 1888–1889). Although only 5-feet 9-inches tall and 173 pounds, Hines possessed quickness afoot and remained a good base runner even in his late thirties. Hines played center field adequately throughout his career, effectively using his above-average speed.

Hines' record as a right-handed batter made him a leading player of his generation. A consistently hard hitter, he compiled a lifetime .302 batting average in the NA and .301 marks in the NL and AA. Hines, who 11 times hit at least .300, only twice batted below .270. His best performances came in his first two years (1878, 1879) with the powerful Providence team. In 1878 Hines became the first Triple Crown winner in major league history by leading the NL with four HR, 50 RBI, and a .358 batting average. That feat was not duplicated until Hugh Duffy* performed it in 1894. In 1879, Hines finished second in batting (.357) and led the NL with 146 hits. He paced the NL in doubles in 1876 (21), 1881 (27), and 1884 (36), slugging average (.486) in 1878, and fielding average in 1876 and 1880. He also was credited with the first unassisted triple play against the Boston Red Caps on May 8, 1878.

Hines starred on championship teams with the Chicago White Stockings in 1876 and the Providence Grays in 1879 and 1884. As his skills deteriorated, Hines split the 1890 season with the Pittsburgh Alleghenys and Boston Beaneaters (NL) and concluded his playing career as a substitute for the Washington Statesmen (AA) in 1891.

Hines played and managed minor league baseball for five seasons in Mobile, AL and Burlington, IA. He resided in Washington, DC and served many years as postmaster in the Department of Agriculture. He died deaf and blind at the Sacred Heart Home in nearby Hyattsville, MD.

BIBLIOGRAPHY: Paul Hines file, National Baseball Library, Cooperstown, NY; Eddie Gold and Art Ahrens, *The Golden Era Cubs, 1876–1940* (Chicago, IL, 1985); Frederick Ivor-Campbell, "1884; Old Hoss Radbourne and the Providence Grays," *TNP* 4 (Spring 1985), pp. 33–38; *The Baseball Encyclopedia*, 10th ed. (New York, 1996); Robert L. Tiemann and Mark Rucker, eds., *Nineteenth Century Stars* (Kansas City, MO, 1989).

Gordon B. McKinney

HISLE, Larry Eugene (b. May 5, 1947, Portsmouth, OH), player and coach, was orphaned and brought up by relatives. At Portsmouth High School, he excelled in basketball, baseball, and academics. Hisle, a high school All-American basketball player, belonged to the National Honor Society. Hisle spent one weekend touring the University of Michigan campus with basketball stars Lew Alcindor (Kareem Abdul-Jabbar) and Cazzie Russell, but accepted a basketball scholarship at Ohio State University (BTC). Before Hisle attended Ohio State, however, the Philadelphia Phillies (NL) selected him in the second round of the June 1965 free agent draft and gave him a $40,000 bonus. In 1966, he was assigned to Huron, MI (NoL), where he batted .433, knocked in 13 runs, and belted three HR in 21 games. The following year found Hisle in Tidewater, VA (CrL) with a .302 batting average, 23 HR, and 74 RBI. He spent the majority of the 1968 season with

San Diego, CA (PCL), hitting .303. In September 1968, Hisle batted .364 in seven games for the Philadelphia Phillies.

Hisle spent the 1969 and 1970 full seasons and part of the 1971 campaign with the Philadelphia Phillies. His best year with Philadelphia came in 1969, when he hit .266 and stroked 20 HR. He finished the 1971 season with Eugene, OR (PCL) and batted .325 with 91 RBI and 23 HR for Albuquerque, NM (PCL) in 1972. Following the 1972 season, Hisle changed clubs three times within 40 days. On October 22, he was traded to the Los Angeles Dodgers (NL) for first baseman Tommy Hutton. Four days later, the Los Angeles Dodgers sent him to the St. Louis Cardinals (NL) for pitchers Rudy Arroyo and Greg Millikan. The following month, the St. Louis Cardinals shipped him with pitcher John Cumberland to the Minnesota Twins (AL) for pitcher Wayne Granger. Hisle played five seasons from 1973 to 1977 with the Minnesota Twins and enjoyed his best performance there in 1977, when he led the AL with 119 RBI, batted .302, slammed 28 HR, and played in the All-Star game at New York's Yankee Stadium. Minnesota granted him free agency following the 1977 season. Hisle signed that November with the Milwaukee Brewers (AL), where he played from 1978 until his retirement in 1982. His best Brewer performance occurred in 1978 with a .290 batting average, 115 RBI, 34 HR, and an All-Star game appearance. During 14 major league seasons, Hisle hit .273 with 193 doubles, 166 HR, and 674 RBI.

From 1983 to 1984, Hisle served as an outfield instructor in Milwaukee's minor league system. In 1989, the Houston Astros (NL) appointed him minor league hitting instructor. The next two years, he held the same title with the Toronto Blue Jays (AL). Toronto utilized Hisle as a hitting coach from 1992 through 1995 and won World Series championships in 1992 and 1993. Hisle lives in Mequon, WI with his wife, Sheila, and their son, Larry, Jr., and has served as a minor league hitting instructor for the Toronto Blue Jays in 1996 and 1997 and Milwaukee Brewers in 1998.

BIBLIOGRAPHY: Larry Hisle file, National Baseball Library, Cooperstown, NY; *The Baseball Encyclopedia*, 10th ed. (New York, 1996); Mark Mulvoy, "Money in the Phillies' Bank," *SI* 28 (April 22, 1968), p. 55; *TSN Official Baseball Register*, 1983; James E. Welch, telephone conversation with Toronto Blue Jays Public Relations Office, Toronto, Canada, April 28, 1994; Rich Westcott and Frank Bilovsky, *The New Phillies Encyclopedia* (Philadelphia, PA, 1993); Jeff Everson, *This Date in Milwaukee Brewers History* (Appleton, WI, 1987); Peter C. Bjarkman, ed., *Encyclopedia of Major League Team Histories American League* (Westport, CT, 1991).

James E. Welch

HOBLITZELL, Richard Carleton "Dick," "Doc," "Hobby" (b. October 26, 1888, Waverly, WV; d. November 14, 1962, Parkersburg, WV), player, manager, and umpire, played solidly at first base in the early 20th century for the Cincinnati Reds (NL) and Boston Red Sox (AL), performing for the world champions of 1915 and 1916.

His parents, Henry Hoblitzell and Laura (Alcock) Hoblitzell, moved to Parkersburg, WV when he was only eight years old. He starred as a football runningback for Parkersburg High School in 1903–1904, Marietta, OH Academy in 1905–1906, and Western University of Pittsburgh in 1907.

Hoblitzell started playing baseball summers while still in school. Under the name Hollister, he joined a semiprofessional baseball club in Jackson, OH in 1906 and moved to Clarksburg, WV (WPL) in 1907. In 1908 Hoblitzell played briefly for Reading, PA (TSL) and Newark, NJ (EL) before it was discovered that Clarksburg had not released him. Clarksburg assigned him to Wheeling, WV (CL). He batted .357 there before Clarksburg sold him to the Cincinnati Reds for $1,000.

Hoblitzell played parts of seven seasons with Cincinnati, ranking among the top NL first basemen for five campaigns. His best offensive seasons came in 1909, when he batted .308 for his only year over .300, and 1911, when he batted .289 with 11 HR, 91 RBI, 180 hits, and 32 stolen bases. The durable performer led the NL in at bats in 1910 and 1911. He completed a degree at the Ohio College of Dental Surgery while with Cincinnati and in 1912 married Constance Olinda Henderson, also a West Virginia native.

Hoblitzell's hitting dropped off sharply in the first half of the 1914 season, causing the Cincinnati Reds to sell him to the Boston Red Sox (AL) for the waiver price. He regained his batting eye in Fenway Park, batting .319 the second half of 1914. Hoblitzell started at first base for the 1915 and 1916 AL pennant winners and World Series champions, batting .313 in the 1915 fall classic against the Philadelphia Phillies. As the Red Sox clean-up hitter in 1916, he hit a disappointing .235 in the 1916 World Series against the Brooklyn Robins and yet set a record with four walks in Game 2. He missed out on a third championship ring by enlisting in the U.S. Army Dental Corps in May 1918.

When released from service in 1920, Hoblitzell signed as a player–manager in the minor leagues. For most of the 1920s, he made Charlotte, NC his home, played and managed for the Charlotte, NC Hornets (SAL), worked in real estate and scouted for the Cincinnati Reds.

During the Depression, Hoblitzell moved his family back to West Virginia and raised dairy cattle on a farm outside Williamstown. He managed Columbus, OH (AA) and Charleston, WV (MAL) in 1931 and umpired in the PiL in 1932 and IL in 1933 before devoting full attention to his farm.

In 11 major league seasons, Hoblitzell batted .278 with 1,310 hits and 593 RBI in 1,318 games. His statistics resemble those of Frank Chance,* his contemporary and National Baseball Hall of Fame first baseman.

BIBLIOGRAPHY: Richard Hoblitzell file, National Baseball Library, Cooperstown, NY; William E. Akin, "West Virginia, Mother of Big Leaguers," Charleston (WV) *Gazette-Mail State Magazine*, September 17, 1971, pp. 2–4; Lee Allen, *The Cincinnati Reds* (New York, 1948); Frank C. Lane, "The Red Sox and the Phillies," *BM* 16 (November 1915), pp. 28–33; Frederick G. Lieb, *The Boston Red Sox* (New York, 1947); John J. Ward, "The Castoff Who Became a Star," *BM* 16 (December 1915), pp. 67–68; Robert Redmount, *The Red Sox Encyclopedia* (Champaign, IL, 1998).

William E. Akin

HODGE, Gilbert Ray. *See* Gilbert Raymond Hodges.

HODGES, Gilbert Raymond "Gil" (b. Gilbert Ray Hodge, April 4, 1924, Princeton, IN; d. April 2, 1972, West Palm Beach, FL), player and manager, was the son of coal miner Charles Hodges and Irene (Horstmeyer) Hodges. He won varsity letters in four sports at Petersburg, IN High School and played summer American Legion baseball. The Brooklyn Dodgers (NL) scouted and signed him in mid–1943 after Hodges spent three years at St. Joseph's College in Rensselaer, IN. Brooklyn used him as a third baseman in the season finale. Drafted into the U.S. Marine Corps, he served in the Pacific theater during World War II.

Discharged as a sergeant in February 1946, Hodges spent a season at Newport News, VA (PiL) learning to be a catcher. Hodges was recalled for 1947 and remained with the Dodgers in Brooklyn from 1947 through 1957 and Los Angeles from 1958 through 1961. He became regular catcher in 1948, but was shifted to first base when Roy Campanella* was acquired. Hodges quickly mastered that position and subsequently won Gold Glove awards for defensive excellence there. After being taken by the New York Mets (NL) in the 1961 expansion draft, he finished his playing days there in 1963. In May 1963, he was traded to the Washington Senators (AL) to be the manager. Hodges led the Senators from tenth place in 1963 to sixth in 1967 and then returned to the Mets in November 1967 as manager. New York finished ninth in 1968, but won the world championship in 1969 and came in third in 1970 and 1971. During the 1972 spring training season, Hodges suffered a fatal heart attack following a round of golf.

Despite some problems hitting the curveball and enduring prolonged slumps, the powerful 6-foot 1½-inch, 200-pound Hodges batted .273, slugged .487, hit 370 HR, and drove in over 100 runs per season during seven consecutive years in his career. Hodges compiled 1,921 hits, 295 doubles, 1,105 runs, 1,274 RBI, and 1,137 strikeouts in 2,071 games. On August 31, 1950, he knocked four HR into the left field stands at Ebbets Field to tie a major league record. As a manager, Hodges compiled a 660–753 record (.467 winning percentage). Frequently called the physically strongest baseball player, Hodges possessed unusually huge hands. Each hand measured almost twelve inches from thumb tip to little finger tip. The devout Catholic was an even-tempered, soft-spoken, gentle person, courageous in overcoming a fear of the tight pitch, and astute and meticulous in managerial operations. Hodges, who made Brooklyn his permanent home, married Joan Lombardi in December 1948 and had four children, Irene, Barbara, Cindy, and Gilbert Ray II.

BIBLIOGRAPHY: Gil Hodges file, National Baseball Library, Cooperstown, NY; Thomas Aylesworth and Benton Minks, *The Encyclopedia of Baseball Managers* (New York, 1990); Marino Amuroso, *Gil Hodges* (Middlebury, VT, 1991); Tom Fox, "Every Day Is Father's Day to Hodges," *TSN*, June 15, 1963, p. 3; Gil Hodges, player questionnaire, Washington Senators, 1964; Roger Kahn, *The Boys of Summer* (New York, 1972); Joe King, "Diamond Dossier . . . Gil Hodges," *TSN*, June 6, 1951, p. 13; Brent P. Kelley, *The Case For: Those Overlooked by the Baseball Hall of Fame* (Jefferson, NC, 1992); Joe King, "Homer Festival Puts Hodges in Famed Society," *TSN*, September 13, 1950, p. 5; Roscoe McGowan, "Gil's Capable Hands Make Job Look Easy," *TSN*, March 13, 1957, p. 3; *NYT*, April 3, 1972, pp. 1, 52; *The Baseball Encyclopedia*, 10th ed. (New York, 1996); Tom Meany et al., *The Artful Dodgers* (New York, 1954); *TSN*, April 15, 1972, p. 5; Joseph J. Vecchione, *The New York Times Book of Sports Legends* (New York, 1991); William F. McNeil, *The Dodgers Encyclopedia* (Champaign, IL, 1997); Peter Golenbock, *Bums* (New York, 1984); Richard Goldstein, *Superstars and Screwballs* (New York, 1991); James R. Hartley, *Washington's Expansion Senators (1961–71)* (Germantown, MD, 1998).

Frank V. Phelps

HOFFER, William Leopold "Bill," "Chick," "The Wizard" (b. November 8, 1870, Cedar Rapids, IA; d. July 21, 1959, Cedar Rapids, IA), player and manager, helped pitch the Baltimore Orioles (NL) to three Temple Cup appearances in his first three major league seasons. The son of railroad engineer Louis Hoffer, a German immigrant, he debuted professionally for hometown Cedar Rapids (IlaL) in 1890. Hoffer divided 1892 between Joliet, IL (IlnL), Grand Island, NE (NeSL), Toledo, OH (WL), and Marinette, WI (WSL), as each club folded during the season. In 1893, he compiled a 14–17 won–lost record for Nashville, TN (SL) before the club disbanded and finished 3–4 at Buffalo, NY (EL). After a 28–17 season at Buffalo in 1894, the 5-foot 9-inch, 155-pound right-hander signed with NL champion Baltimore Orioles.

Hoffer's 31–6 record in 1895 produced a NL-leading .838 winning percentage and four shutouts and helped the Baltimore Orioles earn another NL pennant. In the Temple Cup Series, though, Hoffer lost two games as the Orioles fell to the NL runner-up Cleveland Spiders. In 1896, Hoffer again led the NL in winning percentage (.781) with a 25–7 record. The Baltimore Orioles once more won the NL pennant. In Temple Cup play, Hoffer's two victories helped the Orioles sweep Cleveland. In 1897, Hoffer compiled a 22–11 record for second-place Baltimore and led the Orioles to another Temple Cup victory with two wins over the Boston Beaneaters.

The Baltimore Orioles released Hoffer because of an injured arm and a 0–4 record in 1898. He signed with the Pittsburgh Pirates (NL), completing the year 3–0. After Hoffer's 8–10 season in 1899, Pittsburgh released him. Hoffer enjoyed a 16–12 record with then-minor league Cleveland Blues (AL) in 1900. When the AL became a major league in 1901, his record fell to 3–8. He finished the season with Sacramento, CA (CaL). After spending three years with Des Moines, IA (WL) as manager, pitcher, and outfielder and two years away from the game, Hoffer played for Quincy, IL (IaL) in 1907, Oklahoma City, OK (WA) in 1908, and Cedar Rapids (3IL) in 1909.

Hoffer worked for the U.S. Postal Service and spent 27 years as an engineer and conductor on the interurban Crandic Railroad between Cedar Rapids and Iowa City, retiring in 1940. He and his wife, Emily, were married 67 years.

In six major league seasons, Hoffer pitched 1,254.1 innings in 161 games and compiled a 92–46 record with a .667 winning percentage and 3.75 ERA.

BIBLIOGRAPHY: Jerry E. Clark, *Anson to Zuber: Iowa Boys in the Major Leagues* (Omaha, NE, 1992); William Hoffer file, National Baseball Library, Cooperstown, NY; David Nemec, *The Great Encyclopedia of 19th Century Major League Baseball* (New York, 1997); John Thorn et al., eds., *Total Baseball*, 5th ed. (New York, 1997); Robert L. Tiemann and Mark Rucker, eds., *Nineteenth Century Stars* (Kansas City, MO, 1989); John Phillips, *Who Was Who in Cleveland Baseball 1901–10* (Cabin John, MD, 1989); James H. Bready, *Baseball in Baltimore* (Baltimore, MD, 1998).

Frederick Ivor-Campbell

HOLLIDAY, James Wear "Bug" (b. February 8, 1867, St. Louis, MO; d. February 15, 1910, Cincinnati, OH), player, grew up in St. Louis and began playing baseball with local amateur teams in 1881. In 1885, using the name "Hall," he played right field for the Chicago White Stockings (NL) for four games in the World Series against the St. Louis Brown Stockings in St. Louis. In 1886, he still played professionally under the name of Hall for St. Joseph, MO (WL). In 1887, performing under his own name, he helped Topeka, KS (WL) win the pennant. Holliday moved to Des Moines, IA of the new WA in 1888. His .311 batting average helped Des Moines win the league championship. Holliday played for the Cincinnati Red Stockings (AA) in 1889 and batted .321 as a rookie. From 1890 to 1898, he played with the Cincinnati Reds (NL) and compiled a career .311 batting average. A power hitter in his era, he stroked 65 HR among his 1,134 hits and led the AA with 19 HR in 1889 and the NL with 13 HR in 1892. His best all-around season came in 1894, when he batted .372 with 13 HR and 119 RBI.

Almost exclusively an outfielder, Holliday started as the Cincinnati Reds' center fielder from 1889 through 1894. During his major league career, he also appeared in 18 games as an infielder and two as a pitcher. His career fielding average was .935.

After his playing career, Holliday umpired in the NL in 1903 and later in the AA. He worked in a Cincinnati poolroom and also covered horse racing for a local newspaper. Holliday had contracted rheumatism by 1907 and died in 1910 after a long bout with locomotor ataxia, a convulsive affliction brought on by syphilis. The right-handed 5-foot 7-inch, 165-pound Holliday hit from a crouched stance and reputedly possessed the quickest swing of his time. His obituary in the St. Louis, MO *Post-Dispatch* called him "once one of the best known and most popular of ballplayers."

BIBLIOGRAPHY: James Holliday file, National Baseball Library, Cooperstown, NY; *The Baseball Encyclopedia*, 10th ed. (New York, 1996); Peter C. Bjarkman, ed., *Encyclopedia of Major League Baseball Team Histories National League* (Westport, CT, 1991); New York *Clipper*, September 22, 1889; Frederick Ivor-Campbell et al., eds., *Baseball's First Stars* (Cleveland, OH, 1996); Lee Allen, *The Cincinnati Reds* (New York, 1948); St. Louis (MO) *Post-Dispatch*, February 15, 1910; St. Louis (MO) *Republican*, October 18, 1885; Mike Shatzkin, ed., *The Ballplayers* (New York, 1990); John Thorn et al., eds., *Total Baseball*, 5th ed. (New York, 1997); *TSN*, March 17, 1886.

John E. Findling

HOLLOCHER, Charles Jacob "Charlie" (b. June 11, 1896, St. Louis, MO; d. August 14, 1940, Frontenac, MO), player, was the son of Jacob L. Hollocher and Annie M. (Engel) Hollocher, of German and Irish descent. He married Jane Ellen Gray on October 6, 1918 and had one child, Jane Ann. A second marriage to Ruth Fleming produced no children. Hollocher, who batted left-handed and threw right-handed, began his professional baseball career with the Muscatine, IA Muskies (CA) and dazzled fans at minor league parks until his major league debut on April 16, 1918.

The 5-foot 7½-inch, 158-pound Hollocher, considered by peers among the premier shortstops of his era, starred with the Chicago Cubs (NL) from 1918 through 1924. He led the NL with 161 hits and 509 at-bats in 1918 and fielding averages of .963 in 1921 and .965 in 1922. Hollocher, however, batted only .190 with one triple in the 1918 World Series against the Boston Red Sox. His .340 batting average on a career-high 201 hits in 1922 marked the highest for a shortstop since Honus Wagner's* .354 batting average in 1908. After holding out for more money in 1924, Hollocher signed a two-year contract reportedly worth $12,000 per year. He never fulfilled his promise due to recurrent illness and refused to report to training camp in 1925 because of chronic pains in his abdomen. When doctors could find nothing wrong, he ended his major league career. Newspaper accounts for over a decade indicated that Hollocher suffered from shaky nerves.

During seven major league seasons, Hollocher batted .304 with 894 hits, 145 doubles, 241 RBI, and a .954 fielding average in 760 games. He batted second, hitting over .300 four times and seldom striking out. Hollocher also participated in two triple plays. After leaving the Cubs, he operated a tavern, was employed as a night watchman, and worked as an investigator for the Prosecuting Attorney's office in Des Peres, MO. At age 43, Hollocher committed suicide. When Constable Arthur C. Mosley and Deputy Charles Gordon noticed a parked car on a driveway leading to a partly wrecked house, they found a suicide note and a shotgun still containing the price tag.

BIBLIOGRAPHY: Arthur Ahrens, "Tragic Saga of Charlie Hollocher," *BRJ* 15 (1986), pp. 6–8; Charles Hollocher file, National Baseball Library, Cooperstown, NY; Peter Filichia, *Professional Baseball Franchises* (New York, 1993); John Thorn et al., eds., *Total Baseball*, 5th ed. (New York, 1997); Mike Shatzkin, ed., *The Ballplayers* (New

York, 1990); Warren Wilbert and William Hageman, *Chicago Cubs: Seasons at the Summit* (Champaign, IL, 1997); Eddie Gold and Art Ahrens, *The Golden Era Cubs, 1876–1940* (Chicago, IL, 1985); Warren Brown, *The Chicago Cubs* (New York, 1946); Jim Enright, *Chicago Cubs* (New York, 1975).

Scot E. Mondore

HOLMES, Thomas Francis "Tommy," "Kelly" (b. March 29, 1917, Brooklyn, NY), player, manager, scout, and executive, attended New York City public schools. On January 5, 1941, he married high school sweetheart Lillian Helen Petterson. They have a son and daughter and reside in Woodbury, NY. Following his high school career, he excelled as a strong-armed outfielder and left-handed hitter with the Brooklyn Bay semiprofessional team. In 1937 the New York Yankees (AL) assigned outfielder Holmes to Norfolk, VA (PiL), where he batted .320 and did not miss a game. At Binghamton, NY (EL) in 1938, he paced the EL with a .368 batting percentage, 200 hits, and 41 doubles. He played with Kansas City, MO (AA) in 1939 and with Newark, NJ (IL) from 1939 through 1941, hitting consistently above .300. In 1940 and 1941, he led the IL in hits with 211 and 190, respectively.

Since the Yankees possessed an all-star outfield of Joe DiMaggio,* Tommy Henrich,* and Charlie Keller,* manager Joe McCarthy* dealt Holmes in February 1942 to the Boston Braves (NL). From 1942 through 1950, he started as regular left fielder for the Braves. In 1951, the Braves assigned him as player–manager of their Hartford, CT (EL) team. At Boston, Holmes set a then NL record by hitting in 37 consecutive games from June 6 to July 11, 1945. Named the NL's MVP in 1945, he had a sparkling .352 batting average and led the NL with 28 HR, 47 doubles, 224 hits, and .577 slugging percentage. His consecutive game hits record was surpassed by Pete Rose* of the Cincinnati Reds with 44 in 1978. The Braves recalled Holmes in 1951 to succeed manager Billy Southworth.* As player–manager, he lifted the Braves to a fourth-place finish and briefly served as pilot the following season. Holmes, however, preferred to manage in the minor leagues, helping to develop young players' batting techniques.

Holmes, who finished his 11-year career with the Brooklyn Dodgers (NL) for the remainder of the 1952 season, compiled a .302 lifetime batting average with 1,507 hits, 292 doubles, and 581 RBI. In 1948, he batted .325 and excelled in left field to help the Braves win the NL pennant. The Cleveland Indians stilled Holmes' bat in baseball's only "Indian Summer" World Series, besting Boston in six games. In 1952, Holmes earned a second World Series ring with brief appearances against the New York Yankees. His subsequent minor league managerial assignments included Toledo, Canada (AA), 1953; Elmira, NY (EL), 1954; Fort Worth, TX (TL), 1955; Portland, OR (PCL), 1956; and Montreal, Canada (IL), 1957. After serving as a Los Angeles Dodgers (NL) scout in 1958, he returned to New York to be third director of the Greater New York Sandlot Baseball Foundation. Holmes became a sales executive at Hi-Temp Wires and Teflon Products and later manufacturer's representative for various metal products.

From 1973 through 1994, the New York Mets (NL) employed Holmes as community relations director of the metropolitan area youth sandlot program. Sixty-five youngsters enrolled in the program made the major leagues. With the Mets, he established sandlot clinics, developed youth baseball programs, and created a goodwill program between New York City and Tokyo. Holmes also served as an executive of Kenko Sports, manufacturers of rubberized baseballs for young players. Holmes maintained a heavy speaking and public appearance schedule with the Mets and participated in many community endeavors on Long Island.

BIBLIOGRAPHY: Thomas Holmes file, National Baseball Library, Cooperstown, NY; *American League Red Book* (New York, 1941); Craig Carter, ed., *TSN Daguerreotypes* (St. Louis, MO, 1990); *National League Green Book* (New York, 1942); Donald Honig, *Baseball Between the Lines* (New York, 1976); Gary Caruso, *The Braves Encyclopedia* (Philadelphia, PA, 1995); Harold Kaese, *The Boston Braves* (New York, 1948); *TSN World Series Record Book*, 1948, 1952 (St. Louis, MO, 1948, 1952); John Thorn et al., eds., *Total Braves* (New York, 1996); Rich Westcott, *Masters of the Diamond* (Jefferson, NC, 1994).

Carl Lundquist

HOLTZMAN, Kenneth Dale "Ken" (b. November 3, 1945, St. Louis, MO), player, is the son of Henry Holtzman, a machinery salesman. Holtzman began pitching at the age of seven in University City, MO and compiled an unbelievable 255–5 record in nine amateur seasons. At University City High School, the southpaw posted a 31–3 record and was named MVP for helping his team win the 1963 Missouri state baseball championship. At the University of Illinois, he in 1965 was named the Illini's Sophomore Athlete of the Year and was chosen by major league scouts as the nation's best collegiate left-hander. In June 1965 the 6-foot 2-inch, 175-pound hurler was selected in the fourth round of baseball's first free-agent draft by the Chicago Cubs (NL), who gave him a reported $65,000 bonus.

Holtzman began his professional baseball career in 1965 with Treasure Valley, ID (PrL) and soon was promoted to Wenatchee, WA (NWL). In September 1965, he made his major league debut for the Chicago Cubs. He started for Leo Durocher's* Cubs in 1966 and remained a fixture through 1971. Dubbed the "next Sandy Koufax,*" he posted a club-high 11 victories and 171 strikeouts for the 1966 tenth-place Cubs. His fast start in 1967 ended in late May when he was called to active duty with the Illinois National Guard. He appeared in only four more games the rest of the season, finishing with a 9–0 win–loss record. In 1968 his record fell to 11–14, as he served intermittent National Guard duty. He compiled a 17–13 mark with 6 shutouts in 1969 and finished 17–11 with 15 complete games and 202 strikeouts in 1970.

In 1971, Holtzman suffered through a disappointing 9–15 season and disagreed with the Chicago Cubs management. Chicago traded Holtzman to the Oakland A's (AL) in November 1971 for outfielder Rick Monday.* He never won fewer than 18 games in four seasons with Oakland from 1972 through 1975 and compiled an overall 77–55 mark and .583 winning percentage in helping the A's capture four straight AL Western Division titles and three consecutive World Series championships from 1972 through 1974. Holtzman, who pitched in the 1973 All-Star game, posted a combined 2–3 record in five AL Championship Series games and finished 4–1 in eight World Series games. After contract problems with A's owner Charles O. Finley,* Holtzman and Reggie Jackson* were traded to the Baltimore Orioles (AL) for Mike Torrez* and Don Baylor* in April 1976. He compiled a 5–4 record with Baltimore before being swapped in mid-June to the New York Yankees (AL). With the Yankees, he finished 9–7 in 1976 and 2–3 in 1977 and did not appear in any of the Yankees' AL Championship Series or World Series games in either season. In June 1978, New York sold him to the Chicago Cubs (NL). Holtzman finished his career there with a 0–3 record in 1978 and a 6–9 mark in 1979.

In 14 major league seasons, the fine fastball, curve, and change-up pitcher compiled a 174–150 mark and 3.49 ERA, hurled 31 shutouts, and struck out 1,601 players in 2,867.1 innings. He pitched a 3–0 no-hitter against the Atlanta Braves in 1969 and a 1–0 no-hitter against the Cincinnati Reds in 1971, becoming only the fifth modern-day left-hander to hurl multiple no-hitters. Holtzman, who today works as an insurance executive, married Michelle Collins on February 7, 1971. They reside with their three daughters in Buffalo Grove, IL, a suburb of Chicago.

BIBLIOGRAPHY: Bruce Markusen, *Baseball's Last Dynasty* (New York, 1998); *The Baseball Encyclopedia*, 10th ed. (New York, 1996); *Chicago Cubs Official Press, Radio, and TV Roster Book*, 1966, 1967, 1979; Jim Enright, *Chicago Cubs* (New York, 1975); Eddie Gold and Art Ahrens, *The New Era Cubs, 1941–1985* (Chicago, IL, 1985); Kenneth Holtzman file, National Baseball Library, Cooperstown, NY; Erwin Lynn, *The Jewish Baseball Hall of Fame* (New York, 1987); Jim Langford, *The Game Is Never Over* (South Bend, IN, 1980); John Thorn et al., eds., *Total Baseball*, 5th ed. (New York, 1997); *TSN*, February 20, 1971.

Raymond D. Kush

HONOCHICK, George James "Jim" (b. August 19, 1917, Oneida, PA; d. March 10, 1994, Allentown, PA), player and umpire, was the son of George Honochick and Susan (Klima) Honochick, Czechoslovakian immigrants. His father, a coal miner, died when he was six years old. A star football and baseball player in high school at West Hazelton, PA, Honochick transferred his senior year to the New Mexico Military Academy and graduated from there in 1936. He played fullback in football and the outfield in baseball at

Temple University, receiving in 1940 a Bachelor of Science degree in education.

Honochick played professional baseball as an outfielder with Baltimore, MD (IL) from 1941 to 1943, when he began three years of military service as an ensign in charge of a gunnery crew on a U.S. Navy patrol boat. He rejoined the Baltimore Orioles upon discharge in 1946, but in June became interested in umpiring. Upon the recommendation of his manager Tommy Thomas, Honochick began his professional umpiring career in the Class D ESL in July 1946. He spent the next two seasons umpiring in the Class AA IL, and with just two years and six weeks of umpiring experience, reached the AL in 1949. Besides having the "size" favored by the AL, the 6-foot 1-inch, 230-pound Honochick demonstrated quick and accurate judgment and an ability to control players and managers. During his 25-year major league career, he umpired five All-Star games (1951, 1954, both games in 1960, 1966), six seven-game World Series (1952, 1955, 1960, 1962, 1968, 1972), and the final two games of the strike-marred 1970 AL Championship Series.

Honochick retired after the 1973 season and worked in public relations. In 1978, he signed with the Miller Brewing Company to do television commercials. Although proud of his near 20–20 vision, Honochick appeared frequently until the mid-1980s as a near-sighted umpire in a series of extremely popular Lite beer commercials featuring former baseball players. As Honochick later recalled, "I received more recognition and money from those beer commercials than for my entire 25 years as a big league umpire." Honochick married Anita Renes in 1946 and had a son and a daughter. In 1993, a section of a street near his Allentown home was renamed "Honochick Drive."

BIBLIOGRAPHY: Jim Honochick file, National Baseball Library, Cooperstown, NY; Larry R. Gerlach, ed., *The Men in Blue: Conversations with Umpires* (New York, 1980; Lincoln, NE, 1994); Allentown (PA) *Morning Call*, March 12, 1994; *Referee* 19 (June 1994), p. 15.

Larry R. Gerlach

HOOPER, Harry Bartholomew (b. August 24, 1887, Bell Station, CA; d. December 18, 1974, Santa Cruz, CA), player, manager, and coach, was the son of Joseph Hooper, a farmer, and Kathleen (Keller) Hooper. He married Esther Henchy on November 26, 1912 and had three children, Harry Jr., Marie, and John. After graduating in 1907 with a B.S. degree in civil engineering from St. Mary's College in Oakland, CA, he played outfield in 1907 and 1908 for Alameda, CA and Sacramento, CA (outlaw CaSL). Manager Charles Graham recommended him to Boston Red Sox (AL) owner John I. Taylor, who signed Hooper in 1909 for $2,850.

Hooper, one of the most intelligent, observant, dedicated, and innovative baseball players, performed for fun and placed winning far above money. Popular with players and fans alike, he became the only Red Sox player to participate on four world championship teams. Hooper played with Boston from 1909 to 1920 and for the Chicago White Sox (AL) from 1921 to 1925. In 1927, he served as player–manager for San Francisco (PCL). As baseball coach at Princeton University in 1931 and 1932, he compiled a mediocre 22–29–1 win–loss record. Subsequently he sold real estate in Santa Cruz, CA and worked as a U.S. postmaster of Capitola, GA.

During 17 major league seasons, he batted .281 in 2,309 games and hit 1,842 singles, 389 doubles, 160 triples, and 75 HR. Hooper walked 1,136 times, stole 375 bases, knocked in 817 runs, and scored 1,429 times. From 1910 to 1915, he played alongside strong-armed outfielders Duffy Lewis* and Tris Speaker.* The fast, aggressive Hooper still leads the Red Sox with 130 triples and 300 stolen bases.

Hooper relied on his own judgment and devised a signal system for teammate base runners. He credited Jesus Christ with answering his prayer in the deciding game of the 1912 World Series, when he made his famous bare-handed catch of Larry Doyle's* drive to prevent the New York Giants from winning in regular innings. A member of the world champion Red Sox in 1912, 1915, 1916, and 1918, he starred in the fifth 1915 game by becoming the first player to hit two HR in a single World Series contest. In 1971, he was elected to the National Baseball Hall of Fame.

Hooper, a remarkable leadoff batter for Boston, made 1,707 hits and walked 826 times for a .403 on-base percentage there. Defensively, he became the best outfielder to play the sunfield in Boston and made 344 assists, a record for right fielders. Hooper invented the "rump-slide," wherein he slid on one hip with feet forward and knees bent to catch many short fly balls. As Boston captain, he persuaded Red Sox manager Ed Barrow* to play Babe Ruth* in the outfield when he was not pitching. Hooper continually improved his batting, base-running, and outfield strategy and exemplified personal leadership in stressing combined individual effort to produce team successes. He greatly enhanced baseball's popularity by suggesting Ruth's timely move to the outfield.

BIBLIOGRAPHY: Harry Hooper Diaries, St. Mary's College, Moraga, CA; Lawrence Ritter, *The Glory of their Times* (New York, 1966); Harry Hooper file, National Baseball Library, Cooperstown, NY; Ellery H. Clark Jr., *Boston Red Sox: 75th Anniversary History* (Hicksville, NY, 1975); Ellery H. Clark, Jr., correspondence with Harry Hooper, Duffy Lewis, Harry Hooper, Jr., John Hooper, Red Sox Analytical Letter Collection, Ellery H. Clark, Jr. Papers, Annapolis, MD; Ellery H. Clark, Jr., *Red Sox Fever* (Hicksville, NY, 1979); Ellery H. Clark, Jr., *Red Sox Forever* (Hicksville, NY, 1977); *The Baseball Encyclopedia*, 10th ed. (New York, 1996); Frederick G. Lieb, *The Boston Red Sox* (New York, 1947); Robert Redmount, *The Red Sox Encyclopedia* (Champaign, IL, 1998); Paul J. Zingg, *Harry Hooper* (Urbana, IL, 1993).

Ellery H. Clark, Jr.

HOOTON, Burt Carlton (b. February 7, 1950, Greenville, TX), player and coach, is the son of James Vernon Hooton, an Exxon employee, and Mary

(MacHam) Hooton, a school teacher. At Richard King High School in Corpus Christi, TX, he compiled a 15–1 record for the 1967 state championship team as a junior. After an off-season knee injury limited his pitching performance as a senior, Hooton was selected fifth by the New York Mets (NL) in the June 1968 free agent draft. He instead entered the University of Texas on a baseball scholarship.

As a freshman in 1969, Hooton earned the first of three straight All-American selections with a 12–0 record, 136 strikeouts, and 0.88 ERA. He led the 1970 Longhorns to third place at the College World Series, posting a 12–1 mark, 97 strikeouts, and 1.46 ERA. As a junior, he enjoyed an 11–2 record, 153 strikeouts, and 1.11 ERA. He threw a 7-inning no-hitter against Sam Houston State University and a 1–0, 13-inning shutout (including eight perfect innings) with a school record 19 strikeouts versus Texas Tech University.

The Chicago Cubs (NL) selected Hooton in the first round of the free agent draft secondary phase in 1971. Hooton signed a $50,000 bonus contract and joined the Cubs immediately. He appeared three innings in one game against the St. Louis Cardinals, but suffered tendonitis problems and missed a month. Hooton was assigned to Tacoma, WA (PCL) and equalled a PCL record with 19 strikeouts against Eugene, OR. After posting a 7–4 record with Tacoma in 1971, he returned to Chicago. Hooton struck out 15 New York Mets in his second major league start and pitched a two-hit shutout against the Mets in his next start. He began the 1972 season with a no-hitter against the Philadelphia Phillies on April 16 and finished with an 11–14 record and 2.80 ERA as a rookie.

Hooton, considered the originator of the knuckle curve, suffered two more sub-.500 seasons with the Chicago Cubs and was traded to the Los Angeles Dodgers (NL) in May 1975. He compiled an 18–9 record, 153 strikeouts, and 3.07 ERA in 1975 and remained a key member of the Los Angeles Dodgers staff through 1984, appearing in the 1977, 1978, and 1981 World Series and the 1981 All-Star game. Hooton reached a career-high 19–10 mark with a 2.71 ERA during 1978. Hooton pitched for the Texas Rangers (AL) in 1985, but was released following spring training in 1986. He retired with a 151–136 career major league record, 3.38 ERA, and 1,491 strikeouts in 480 appearances.

Hooton, who married Ginger Northington on December 30, 1972, has one son, Eugene Carlton, and one daughter, Virginia Lane. He returned to the University of Texas to earn a Bachelor's degree in broadcast journalism following his playing days and served as a minor league pitching coach for the Dodgers at Salem, OR (NWL) in 1988 and 1989, San Antonio, TX (TL) from 1990 to 1994, and Albuquerque, NM (PCL) in 1995 and 1996.

BIBLIOGRAPHY: Bert Hooton file, National Baseball Library, Cooperstown, NY; Eddie Gold and Art Ahrens, *The New Era Cubs, 1941–1985* (Chicago, IL, 1985); Jim Enright, *Chicago Cubs* (New York, 1985); William F. McNeil, *The Dodgers Encyclopedia*

(Champaign, IL, 1997); Tommy Lasorda and David Fisher, *The Artful Dodger* (New York, 1985); Jim Langford, *The Game Is Never Over* (South Bend, IN, 1980); Gary Herron, "Happy Hooton," *SCD* 22 (July 28, 1995), pp. 166–68; *Texas Rangers 1985 Media Guide*; *TSN Baseball Register*, *1986*; Jay Langhammer, phone interview with Virginia Hooton, April 1996.

Jay Langhammer

HOPP, John Leonard, Jr. "Johnny," "Cotney" (b. July 18, 1916, Hastings, NE), player, is the son of John Hopp, Sr., and Alice (Shreiner) Hopp and grew up in a sports family with five brothers and three sisters. His father, a Russian native of German descent and educated through the fourth grade, migrated to a Nebraska farm and worked in the poultry business. He and his brother, Henry, sometimes were nicknamed "Hippity" by the press. The cotton-white–haired Hopp was more often called "Cotney," "Johnny," or "Old Motorboat."

In high school, Hopp pitched and played outfield for an American Legion team and appeared in the 1932 state championship. His first attempt at semi-professional baseball at the age of 18 failed. In 1935, the 5-foot 9¾-inch, 170-pound Hopp spent a year at Hastings College and played football at right halfback. In 1937, the St. Louis Cardinals (NL) signed Hopp after noticing him excel for Norfolk, NE (NeSL) in 1936. Soreness in his left throwing arm kept him in the minor leagues in 1937 and 1938. In September 1939, the stocky Hopp was called up to pinch-hit for the St. Louis Cardinals. The left-handed batter's first time at the plate resulted in a single that drove in two runs. He married his former high school girlfriend, Marion Simpson, on October 19, 1935. On the same day as Hopp's first professional hit, his wife delivered a daughter, Terrill. A son, Johnny, was later born. His first wife died of cancer in 1968. His second wife, Sarah, produced a daughter, Patricia, and son, George.

Hopp, an outfielder–first baseman, remained with the St. Louis Cardinals until 1946 and played in the 1942, 1943, and 1944 World Series. During 1944, he improved his batting average over 100 points to .336, led NL outfielders with a .997 fielding percentage, and hit .185 in the World Series against the St. Louis Browns. In February 1946, Hopp was traded to the Boston Braves (NL) and made the All-Star team. He later played briefly with the Pittsburgh Pirates (NL), New York Yankees (AL), and Detroit Tigers (AL), retiring after 16 seasons in 1952. In 1950, Hopp batted a career-high .339 for the Pittsburgh Pirates and New York Yankees and enjoyed a stretch of eight straight hits. He briefly appeared in the 1950 and 1951 World Series for the Yankees. During his major league career, Hopp batted .296 with 1,262 hits and 458 RBI. The Scottsbluff, NE resident worked as public relations representative for a Nebraska natural gas company and officiated basketball games, retiring at age 53.

BIBLIOGRAPHY: Al Hirshberg and Joe McKenney, eds., *Famous American Athletes of Today*, 10th series (Boston, MA, 1947); "Johnny Hopp," *Microsoft Complete Baseball*,

CD-ROM (Redmond, WA, 1994); John Thorn et al., eds., *Total Baseball*, 5th ed. (New York, 1997); John Hopp file, National Baseball Library, Cooperstown, NY; Fred Smith, *995 Tigers* (Detroit, MI, 1981); Harold Kaese, *The Boston Braves* (New York, 1948); Gary Caruso, *The Braves Encyclopedia* (Philadelphia, PA, 1995); Frederick G. Lieb, *The St. Louis Cardinals* (New York, 1945); Rob Rains, *The St. Louis Cardinals* (New York, 1992); Bob Broeg and Jerry Vickery, *St. Louis Cardinals Encyclopedia* (Grand Rapids, MI, 1998); Jerry E. Clark, *Nebraska Diamonds* (Omaha, NE, 1991).

Lowell D. Smith

HORLEN, Joel Edward "Joe" (b. August 14, 1937, San Antonio, TX), player and coach, is of German descent and attended Oklahoma State University, where he helped the Cowboys win the 1959 NCAA College World Series. In 1959, the Chicago White Sox (AL) signed Horlen for a $50,000 bonus. The 6-foot, 170-pound pitcher, who batted and threw right-handed, spent under three minor league seasons with Lincoln, IL (3IL) in 1959, Charleston, SC (SAL) in 1960, and San Diego, CA (PCL) in 1961 before joining the Chicago White Sox in 1961.

Horlen pitched nearly his entire major league career with the Chicago White Sox, posting a 113–113 record from 1961 through 1971. He combined with Gary Peters* to lead the Chicago White Sox staff, finishing 11–7 with a 3.27 ERA in 1963, 13–9 with a career-best 1.88 ERA in 1964, 13–13 with a 2.88 ERA in 1965, and 10–13 with a 2.43 ERA in 1966. His 1966 ERA trailed just Peters among AL hurlers. On July 29, 1963, the hard-luck Horlen carried a no-hitter into the ninth inning against the Washington Senators at JFK Stadium. With one out, Chuck Hinton bounced a single to center field. One out later, Don Lock drilled Horlen's hanger for a HR to defeat Chicago 2–1.

Horlen's major league career peaked in 1967, when he boasted a 19–7 record and made the AL All-Star team. Horlen led AL hurlers with the lowest ERA (2.06) and highest winning percentage (.731) and shared the AL lead in shutouts (6). He started 35 games for the first of three consecutive seasons. On September 10, Horlen pitched a 6–0 no-hit victory against the Detroit Tigers. Despite Horlen's record, Jim Lonborg* of the pennant-winning Boston Red Sox won the AL Cy Young* Award.

Although boasting an impressive 2.37 ERA in 1968, Horlen lost 14 of 26 decisions and led the AL in hit batsmen (14). He already had paced AL moundsmen in wild pitches with 14 in 1966. His record declined to 13–16 with a 3.78 ERA in 1969 and 6–16 with a 4.87 ERA in 1970. Chicago released Horlen in April 1972. His major league career ended that year with a 3–4 record and 3.00 ERA as a reliever for the Oakland A's (AL). He lost one decision to the Detroit Tigers in the 1972 AL Championship Series and pitched briefly against the Cincinnati Reds in the 1972 World Series.

During 12 major league seasons, Horlen compiled a 116–117 record with a 3.11 ERA, 18 shutouts, and 1,065 strikeouts in 2,002 innings. He batted just .134 and shares with Bob Feller* the season record for most 1–0 victories with seven. He married Catherine Louise Zinsmeister in January 1959 and had one daughter. The San Antonio, TX resident built houses from 1973 through 1976, served as a roving pitching instructor for the Cleveland Indians (AL) in 1977 and 1978, and started a roofing company and helped start a golf program at the University of Texas-San Antonio from 1979 through 1986. After serving as a pitching coach with the New York Mets (NL) from 1987 through 1991, he worked as a pitching coach with Omaha, NE (AA) in 1992 and Phoenix, AZ (PCL) in 1993 and 1994.

BIBLIOGRAPHY: Joel Horlen file, National Baseball Library, Cooperstown, NY; Gary Herron, "Horlen Was a Classic Good-Pitch/No-Hit Hurler," *SCD* 22 (March 17, 1995), pp. 138–139; Bob Vanderberg, *Sox: From Lane and Fain to Zisk and Fisk* (Chicago, IL, 1982); Richard Lindberg, *Who's on Third?* (South Bend, IN, 1983); *Chicago White Sox 1968 Yearbook; TSN Baseball Register*, 1973.

David L. Porter

HORNER, Robert James "Bob" (b. August 6, 1957, Junction City, KS), player, is the son of Jimmy Horner, a salesman of internal engines, and Elaine Horner. Horner made All-State in baseball and lettered in basketball at Apollo (AZ) High School. His baseball honors included being named College All-American at Arizona State University in 1977 and 1978 and College Player of the Year in 1978. Horner married Christine Berry on October 21, 1978 and has two sons, Trent and Tyler.

In 1978, Horner debuted with a HR in his first game for the Atlanta Braves (NL) after being the nation's first draft pick. The 6-foot 1-inch, 215-pound right-handed third baseman earned NL Rookie of the Year honors in 1978 by hitting a HR once every 14.04 at-bats, a better average than that of any previous honoree. "Another Harmon Killebrew,*" said Montreal Expos Manager Dick Williams.* Within two full seasons, Horner ranked among the top sluggers in baseball. He placed fifth in the NL with a .314 batting average in 1979 and finished second in the NL behind Mike Schmidt* with 35 HR in 1980. After leading the Braves in HR for the fourth consecutive year in 1981, Horner began experiencing major injuries that would plague him for the rest of his career. In 1984, he was sidelined after May 30 because of a broken navicular bone in his right wrist. The next season, he reported to spring training early and appeared in the Braves' line-up on opening day. Later that season he switched to first base, fielded a perfect 1.000 in 950 total chances, and participated in 105 double plays. In 1986 he appeared in at least 130 games for a second straight season while belting 27 HR. He was voted to the NL All-Star team in 1982.

In November 1986, Horner was granted free agency by Atlanta after several celebrated disputes with owner Ted Turner (OS). The Yakult, Japan Swallows (JCL) signed him in May 1987. Horner became an instant fan favorite in Japan and led all U.S. players with a .327 batting average, 31 HR, and 73 RBI. He returned to major league baseball by joining the St. Louis Cardinals (NL) in January 1988. Horner developed soreness in his left shoulder and underwent surgery in early August. St. Louis released him in December 1988. He did not return to the major leagues. His career major league totals included a .277 batting average, 1,047 hits, 218 HR, and 685 RBI. The Irving, TX resident worked with Bar Code Promotions, a computer company, for several years.

BIBLIOGRAPHY: *The Baseball Encyclopedia*, 10th ed. (New York, 1996); Albert J. Figone, interview with Bob Horner, September 27, 1989; Bob Horner file, National Baseball Library, Cooperstown, NY; Robert E. Kelly, *Baseball's Best* (Jefferson, NC, 1988); John Thorn et al., eds., *Total Braves* (New York, 1996); Gary Caruso, *The Braves Encyclopedia* (Philadelphia, PA, 1995); Los Angeles (CA) *Times*, June 7, 1978; New York *Post*, March 10, 1989; Phoenix (AZ) *Gazette*, November 21, 1978; Fluffy Saccucci, "Horner Was a Fixture at the Hot Corner," *SCD* 25 (June 19, 1998), p. 76; Joseph M. Schuster, "Return of the Red Devil," *Sport* 79 (June 1988), pp. 57–60; E. M. Swift, "No Yen to Play in Japan," *SI* 68 (March 28, 1988), pp. 62ff; *St. Louis Cardinals Media Guide, 1988*; *USAT*, April 16, 1987; A. Wolff, "A New Kind of Orient Express," *SI* 66 (May 18, 1987), pp. 28–29.

Albert J. Figone

HORNSBY, Rogers "Rajah" (b. April 27, 1896, Winters, TX; d. January 5, 1963, Chicago, IL), player, manager, coach, and scout, is ranked by many as the greatest right-handed hitter of all time. Hornsby, the son of cattle rancher and farmer Edward Hornsby and Mary Dallas (Rogers) Hornsby, moved to a farm near Austin, TX, when his father died. The Hornsbys later moved to Fort Worth, TX, where he attended school and excelled in baseball.

Hornsby began playing baseball professionally in 1914 at age 18 with Hugo, OK (TOL) and Denison, TX (WA). After being purchased by the St. Louis Cardinals (NL), he played in his first major league game on September 1, 1915. An aggressive, driving player with a fierce will to win, Hornsby played as a regular infielder (primarily a second baseman) for the Cardinals from 1916 through 1926 under managers Miller Huggins* and Branch Rickey.* From 1920 through 1925, Hornsby set an NL record by winning six consecutive batting titles. Batting above .400 three times, Hornsby holds the modern season record for highest average, hitting .424 in 1924. He led the NL in HR (1922, 1925), RBI (1920–1922, 1925), hits (1920–1922, 1924), runs scored (1921–1922, 1924, 1927, 1929), doubles (1920–1922, 1924), triples (1917, 1921), walks (1924, 1927–1928), on-base percentage (1920–1925, 1927–1928), and slugging percentage (1917, 1920–1925, 1928–1929). One of the finest fielding infielders of his time, Hornsby led NL second basemen in 1922 with a .967 fielding average and completed his career with a .965 fielding average.

In June 1925, Hornsby succeeded Rickey as manager of the St. Louis Cardinals. He led St. Louis to the 1926 pennant and world championship over the New York Yankees, the first club flag of the twentieth century. The NL's MVP in 1925, the successful manager was idolized by St. Louis fans and demanded a three-year contract from Cardinals owner Sam Breadon* for $50,000 annually. When Breadon declined and an impasse followed, Hornsby on December 20, 1926 was traded to the New York Giants (NL) for Frankie Frisch* and Jimmy Ring. Protesting St. Louis fans, stunned at the trade of their hero, tried to get the trade cancelled. Many vowed to boycott the team, but the trade stood.

Controversy and adversity continually plagued Hornsby. Known for his unpredictable mood changes, the generally quiet Hornsby argued strenuously. His relations with team owners showed intolerance, suspicion, belligerence, and a lack of diplomacy. Hornsby's compulsive gambling on horse races caused him constant financial setbacks and home problems, with two of his three marriages ending in divorce. His first wife, Sarah, divorced him in 1923. Hornsby married Jeannette Pennington Hine in February 1924, but they were later divorced. In January 1957, he married Marjorie Bernice Frederick. He had two sons, Rogers, Jr., a U.S. Air Force pilot, and William, who played minor league baseball briefly.

The outspoken Hornsby lasted only one season with John McGraw's* New York Giants. Although he hit 26 HR, drove in 125 runs, and batted .361 in 1927, he was traded in January 1928 to the Boston Braves (NL). He became manager of the Braves in May 1928 and led the NL in hitting with a .387 average, but was traded that November to the Chicago Cubs (NL) for five players and $200,000. Named the NL's MVP in 1929, Hornsby batted .380 and led the Chicago Cubs to the pennant. He managed the Cubs from September 1930 until August 1932, when unconditionally released because of problems with the front office. By this time, Hornsby was finished as a regular player and in considerable debt because of gambling losses.

In 1933, Hornsby returned to the Cardinals as a substitute infielder and signed that July as the manager of the St. Louis Browns (AL). He remained there until July 1937, when fired because of his gambling activities. He managed the St. Louis Browns again briefly in 1952 and the Cincinnati Reds (NL) later that same season and most of 1953. Between 1938 and 1943, Hornsby managed several minor league teams. These included Chattanooga, TN (SA) in 1938, Baltimore, MD (IL) in 1939, Oklahoma City, OK (TL) in 1940 and 1941, and Fort Worth, TX (TL) in 1942. In 1944 after taking over a last place team and leading them to 40 victories in 74 games, Hornsby was named Manager of the Year with Oklahoma City, OK (TL). Between 1944 and 1949, Hornsby supervised a baseball school sponsored by the Chicago *Daily News*. He managed minor league teams in Beaumont, TX (TL) in 1950 and Seattle, WA (PCL) in 1951, winning the league championship both seasons. He served as a coach with the Chicago Cubs (NL) in 1958 and 1959 and scouted and coached for the New York Mets (NL) in 1961 and 1962.

During his major league career, Hornsby won seven batting titles and compiled a lifetime .358 batting average, ranking second only to Ty Cobb's* .366. In 2,259 games, Hornsby made 2,930 hits, 541 doubles, 169 triples, 301 HR and 1,584 RBI, and scored 1,579 runs. His managerial record spanned 13 seasons, producing 701 wins in 1,530 games, one pennant, and one world championship. In 1942, he was elected to the National Baseball Hall of Fame. Hornsby made Major League Baseball's All-Century Team.

BIBLIOGRAPHY: Thomas Aylesworth and Benton Minks, *The Encyclopedia of Baseball Managers* (New York, 1990); John Benson et al., *Baseball's Top 100* (Wilton, CT, 1997); Charles C. Alexander, *Rogers Hornsby: A Biography* (New York, 1995); Bob Broeg, *Super Stars of Baseball* (St. Louis, MO, 1971); Gene Karst and Martin J. Jones, Jr., *Who's Who in Professional Baseball* (New Rochelle, NY, 1973); *DAB*, Supp. 7 (1961–1965), pp. 364–366; Rogers Hornsby, *My Kind of Baseball*, J. Roy Stockton, ed. (New York, 1953); Rogers Hornsby and Bill Surface, *My War With Baseball* (New York, 1962); Noel Hynd, *The Giants of the Polo Grounds* (New York, 1988); Bob Broeg and Jerry Vickery, *St. Louis Cardinals Encyclopedia* (Grand Rapids, MI, 1998); Warren Wilbert and William Hageman, *Chicago Cubs: Seasons at the Summit* (Champaign, IL, 1997); Tom Murray, *Sport Magazine's All-Time All Stars* (New York, 1977); Rob Rains, *The St. Louis Cardinals* (New York, 1992); Eddie Gold and Art Ahrens, *The Golden Era Cubs, 1876–1940* (Chicago, IL, 1985); Rogers Hornsby file, National Baseball Library, Cooperstown, NY; Gary Caruso, *The Braves Encyclopedia* (Philadelphia, PA, 1995).

John L. Evers

HORTON, Willie Watterson (b. October 18, 1942, Arno, VA), player and coach, is the youngest of 21 children of James Thomas Clinton Horton and Lillian (Watterson) Horton. He led Detroit Northwestern High School to a city championship in 1959 and signed with the Detroit Tigers (AL) in August 1961 for a $50,000 bonus. On December 18 of that year, he married Patricia Strickland. After their divorce, he married Gloria Kendrick in 1981. These marriages produced three sons and four daughters.

Horton spent the 1962–1964 seasons in the minor leagues with Duluth, MN-Superior, WI (NoL) in 1962, Syracuse, NY (IL) and Knoxville, TN (SAL) in 1963, and Syracuse, NY (IL) in 1964, briefly appearing with the Detroit Tigers in 1963 and 1964. In his first full major league season in 1965, the 5-foot 11-inch, 200-pound right-handed left fielder batted .273, belted 29 HR, and knocked in 104 runs. These statistics resembled his standard performance the next decade, as Horton compiled a .273 lifetime batting average. Although a mediocre fielder, Horton exhibited physical strength widely respected around the league. In the Tigers' world championship 1968 season, Horton led the team in batting average (.285—fourth highest in the AL), slugging percentage (.543), and HR (36). He batted .304 in the seven-game World Series against the St. Louis Cardinals.

When traded to the Texas Rangers (AL) in April 1977, Horton ranked among the top ten Tigers in HR (262), total bases (2,549), and RBI (886). Horton, who played in the 1965, 1968, 1970, and 1973 All-Star games, hit three HR in one game in June 1970 and May 1977. In 1977 and 1978, Horton played briefly for the Texas Rangers (AL), Cleveland Indians (AL), Oakland Athletics (AL), and Toronto Blue Jays (AL). As a DH for the Seattle Mariners (AL) in 1979, he batted .279, slammed 29 HR, made 106 RBI, and was named Comeback Player of the Year. He finished his major league career with the Mariners in 1980, seven hits short of the 2,000 mark. In 2,028 major league career games, he slugged 284 doubles and 325 HR and knocked in 1,163 runs. He played for the Portland, OR, Beavers (PCL) in 1981 and 1982 and in the MEL (1983), served as a minor league batting instructor for the Oakland Athletics (1984, 1985) and coach for the New York Yankees (AL) in 1985 and the Chicago White Sox (AL) in 1986. He worked with the Police Athletic League in Detroit and serves as national sales representative for the Orr Tool & Dye Corporation of Erie, MI.

BIBLIOGRAPHY: Reid Creager, "Willie Horton: A Detroit Tiger for Life," *SCD* 24 (September 19, 1997), pp. 160–161; Joe Falls, *Detroit Tigers* (New York, 1975); William M. Anderson, *The Detroit Tigers* (South Bend, IN, 1996); Richard Bak, *A Place for Summer* (Detroit, MI, 1998); *The Baseball Encyclopedia*, 10th ed. (New York, 1996); Fred Smith, *995 Tigers* (Detroit, MI, 1981).

Sheldon L. Appleton

HOUGH, Charles Oliver "Charlie" (b. January 5, 1948, Honolulu, HI), player and coach, is the son of Richard Hough, a minor league third baseman in 1933, and married Sharon Ann O'Brien. Hough was drafted out of Hialeah (FL) High School by the Los Angeles Dodgers (NL) in 1966 and began playing baseball professionally at Ogden, UT (PrL), where he won five of 12 decisions. A good all-around athlete, the 6-foot 2-inch, 190-pound right-hander finished 15–5 the next season with Santa Barbara, CA (CaL) and Albuquerque, NM (TL). Hough pitched for Albuquerque in 1968 and 1969, hurled for Spokane, WA (PCL) in 1970 and 1971, and returned to Albuquerque (PCL) in 1972, where he was selected Pitcher of the Year. Throughout his minor league tenure, he occasionally was employed at first base, third base, or in the outfield. Hough learned to throw the knuckleball in 1969 to alleviate the strain on his sore arm. He later perfected the pitch with instruction from Hoyt Wilhelm* and Jim Brewer. Hough pitched each September for the Los Angeles Dodgers from 1970 to 1972 before making the club permanently in 1973. Managers Walter Alston* and Tom Lasorda* cast him in a relief role at Los Angeles from 1973 to 1980. Hough's best season with the Dodgers came in 1976, when he won 12 games, saved 18 contests, and posted a 2.21 ERA in 77 games.

In July 1980, the Texas Rangers (AL) purchased Hough's contract from Los Angeles for $15,000. Hough replaced Jon Matlack* in the Rangers' rotation in 1981. From 1982 through 1988, Hough annually led Ranger pitchers in victories and averaged 16 wins and 252 innings pitched per season. No other major league hurler won in double figures every year from 1982 through 1990. Hough relied primarily on a knuckleball thrown at different speeds. One of the better AL fielding pitchers, he consistently held runners close to the bases. Few pitchers made more pickoff throws to first base per year than Hough. In June 1988, the 40-year-old Hough enjoyed perhaps the finest month of his career. In six starts, he won 4 of 5 decisions, compiled a 1.26 ERA, and hurled at least 9 innings in every start. His only loss came in a 1–0 heartbreaker against the California Angels (AL). In 1988, Nolan Ryan* joined Hough in giving Texas one of the oldest 1–2 starting duos in baseball history with 83 years combined. Hough spent part of the 1989 campaign on the disabled list with tendinitis in the arm and won 5 of 7 decisions after returning to action. Hough anchored the Ranger rotation with Ryan through the 1990 season. In December 1990 the Chicago White Sox (AL) signed Hough as a free agent. Hough in 1991 failed to win 10 games for the first time in a decade. Hough finished his major league career with the expansion Florida Marlins (NL) in 1993 and 1994. In 1998, the Los Angeles Dodgers appointed him pitching coach.

In 25 major league seasons, Hough compiled 216 wins, 216 losses, 61 saves, 2,362 strikeouts, and a 3.75 ERA in 3,801 innings and 858 games. He pitched in the 1974, 1977, and 1978 World Series for the Los Angeles Dodgers, making five relief appearances. He also pitched for the AL in the 1986 All-Star Game.

BIBLIOGRAPHY: Phil Rogers, *The Impossible Takes a Little Longer* (Dallas, TX, 1991); William F. McNeil, *The Dodgers Encyclopedia* (Champaign, IL, 1997); Charlie Hough file, National Baseball Library, Cooperstown, NY; Tommy Lasorda and David Fisher, *The Artful Dodger* (New York, 1985); "A. L. West: Texas Rangers," *TSN*, July 11, 1988, p. 21; John Dewan and Don Zminda, *The Scouting Report: 1990* (New York, 1990); Zander Hollander, ed., *The Complete Handbook of Baseball 1983* (New York, 1983); Zander Hollander, ed., *The Complete Handbook of Baseball 1991* (New York, 1991); Phil Rogers, "A. L. West: Texas Rangers," *TSN Baseball* Special Issue, April 11, 1988, p. 21.

Frank J. Olmsted

HOUK, Ralph George "Major" (b. August 9, 1919, Lawrence, KS), player, manager, coach, and executive, is the son of George Houk and the fourth of five children. Houk, who grew up on a farm near Lawrence, played baseball weekends as a youngster for the semiprofessional Belvoirs, managed by his uncle, Charlie Houk. After performing in the outfield his first year with the Lawrence, KS team, he switched to catching and played that position most of his career. "I liked catching," Houk recalled. "I had the whole game in front of me. I was in on every pitch. At fifteen I was as solid as a rock,

170 pounds of hard muscled flesh. I could block baserunners at home plate. In fact, blocking was easy for me."

Houk graduated from Lawrence High School, where he was selected All-State in football. New York Yankees (AL) scouts spotted Houk at a national tournament and signed him. Houk began his minor league career in 1939 as a $75-a-month rookie with Neosho, MO (AML), where he hit .286. After moving up the minor league ranks, he hit .271 in 1941 with Augusta, GA (SAL). His progress toward the major leagues was interrupted by army service in World War II, where he earned a Purple Heart and Silver and Bronze Stars and rose to the rank of major.

Upon returning to baseball in 1946, Houk played with Kansas City, MO (AA) and Beaumont, TX (TL). He was promoted to the New York Yankees as third-string catcher in 1947 and played for Kansas City during the 1948 and 1949 seasons. Houk returned to the Yankees and completed his major league career as a reserve catcher there from 1950 through 1954. During his major league career, the right-handed Houk played in 91 games with a .272 batting average. He married Bette Porter on June 3, 1948 and has three children, Donna (Mrs. Walter Sloboden), Dick, and Robert.

The Yankees, impressed with Houk's leadership and baseball knowledge, appointed him manager of their Denver, CO (AA) team in 1955. The Triple A club finished third that year and second in 1956 and won the Little World Series in 1957. This successful, short stint with Denver earned him a coaching position in 1958 with the New York Yankees, where he served until named New York club manager for the 1961 season. During his three years as coach, Houk refused several offers to manage other major league teams. He managed the Yankees to AL pennants and World Series titles in 1961 and 1962. Following his AL pennant-winning season in 1963, he was promoted to a front office position with the Yankees. He managed the Yankees again from 1966 through 1973, making a .539 winning percentage in 11 seasons with New York. He signed a contract to manage the Detroit Tigers (AL) in 1974 and piloted them through 1978 with a composite five-season .450 winning percentage. From 1981 through 1984, Houk piloted the Boston Red Sox (AL) to a .542 winning percentage. In 20 managerial seasons, he guided major league clubs to 1,619 wins, 1,531 losses (.514 winning percentage), and three first place finishes. He served as vice president of the Minnesota Twins (AL) from 1986 through 1988 and as consultant for the Minnesota Twins from 1989 through 1992. He resides in Winter Haven, FL, where he fishes and golfs.

BIBLIOGRAPHY: Ralph Houk and Robert W. Creamer, *Season of Glory* (New York, 1988); Chuck McAnulla, "Ralph Houk," *SCD* 22 (June 1995), pp. 100–101; Leonard Koppett, *The Man in the Dugout* (New York, 1993); Tony Kubek and Terry Pluto, *Sixty-one* (New York, 1987); Jack Lautier, *Fenway Voices* (Camden, ME, 1990); Robert Redmount, *The Red Sox Encyclopedia* (Champaign, IL, 1998); Dom Forker, *Sweet Seasons* (Dallas, TX, 1991); Dom Forker, *The Men of Autumn* (Dallas, TX, 1989);

Thomas Aylesworth and Benton Minks, *The Encyclopedia of Baseball Managers* (New York, 1990); Mark Gallagher, *The Yankee Encyclopedia*, vol. 3 (Champaign, IL, 1997); Ralph Houk file, National Baseball Library, Cooperstown, NY; New York *Herald Tribune*, October 21, 1960, p. 24; *NYT*, October 21, 1960, p. 38; *NYT Magazine* (July 2, 1961); *The Baseball Encyclopedia*, 10th ed. (New York, 1996); *Time* 78 (October 6, 1961), pp. 76–77.

Albert J. Figone

HOWARD, Elston Gene "Ellie" (b. February 23, 1929, St. Louis, MO; d. December 14, 1980, New York, NY), player and coach, was a 6-foot 2-inch, 196-pound catcher–outfielder who threw and batted right-handed. Since his parents were divorced, he grew up with his mother, Emmalene, and his stepfather, Wayman Hill. The graduate of Vashon High School in St. Louis aspired to be a doctor, but Howard's baseball skills led him to the New York Yankees (AL) chain. With Toronto, Canada (IL) in 1954, he batted .330 and was named the IL's MVP. Howard's lack of speed clouded his future as an outfielder so Bill Dickey* tutored him as a catcher. Howard strove to be at least "half as good" as the National Baseball Hall of Famer, but the New York Yankees roster still included no black players. General Manager George Weiss* stated, "When a Negro comes along good enough to make the Yankees, we'll be glad to have him."

The dedicated, hard-working, reliable, determined Howard was chosen as the "right man" and joined the Yankees in 1955. He quickly earned his teammates' respect, as manager Casey Stengel* called him a "real Yankee." He married Arlene Henley in 1954 and had three children. Since Yogi Berra* was the regular catcher, he played mostly at first base and in the outfield. From 1955 to 1967, Howard participated in nine World Series and was chosen on six AL All-Star squads. He had assumed most of the catching from Berra by 1959 and was the AL's MVP in 1963. Howard was traded to the Boston Red Sox (AL) in August 1967 and helped the Red Sox win the AL flag despite a .178 batting average and an arthritic elbow. Howard coached for the New York Yankees from 1969 to 1979.

Interestingly, Howard invented a new bat weight, the "doughnut," a circular, cast-iron object that easily slipped over the handle and added leverage for on-deck hitters. By 1968, it had become standard equipment. Howard compiled a career .274 batting average in 1,605 games with 1,471 hits, 167 HR, and 762 RBI. Thoroughly devoted to the game, he died the year following his retirement as coach.

BIBLIOGRAPHY: Elston Howard file, National Baseball Hall of Fame, Cooperstown, NY; *The Baseball Encyclopedia*, 10th ed. (New York, 1996); Paul Dickson, ed., *The Dickson Baseball Dictionary* (New York, 1989); Larry Moffi and Jonathan Kronstadt, *Crossing the Line* (Jefferson, NC, 1994); John Thorn et al., eds., *Total Baseball*, 5th ed. (New York, 1997); Joe Trimble, "The Yankees' New No. 1 Catcher," *Sport* 28 (April 1959), pp. 50, 75–77; Mark Gallagher, *The Yankee Encyclopedia*, vol. 3 (Champaign, IL, 1997); Dom Forker, *Sweet Seasons* (Dallas, TX, 1991); Ralph Houk and Robert Creamer, *Season of Glory* (New York, 1988); Tony Kubek and Terry Pluto, *Sixty-one* (New York, 1987); David Halberstam, *October 1964* (New York, 1994); Dave Anderson et al., *The Yankees* (New York, 1978); *TSN*, April 1, 1955, August 3, 1955, August 19, 1967, November 9, 1968; *TSN Baseball Register, 1979*.

William J. Miller

HOWARD, Frank Oliver "Hondo," "The Capital Punisher" (b. August 8, 1936, Columbus, OH), baseball and basketball player, manager, coach, and executive, graduated in 1954 from South High School in Columbus, where he played baseball and basketball. At Ohio State University, the 6-foot 7-inch, 255-pound Howard captained the basketball squad, was named to the All-BTC basketball team, and starred in baseball. The Los Angeles Dodgers (NL) signed Howard for an $108,000 bonus baseball contract in 1958. After enjoying impressive minor league seasons as an outfielder with Green Bay, WI (3IL) in 1958, Victoria, TX (TL), and Spokane, WA (PCL) in 1959 and 1960, he joined the Los Angeles Dodgers in 1960 and was named NL Rookie of the Year. His 23 HR established a record for Dodgers rookies. Howard batted a career-high .296 in both 1961 and 1962 and hit .300 in the victorious 1963 World Series against the New York Yankees. Used primarily as an outfielder, he played with the Dodgers through 1964 before being traded that December to the Washington Senators (AL).

Howard enjoyed his greatest seasons with the Senators and set several records in 1968. He batted .274, drove in 106 runs, and led the AL with 44 HR and a .552 slugging average in 1968. From May 3 through May 18, Howard belted an incredible 12 HR. This streak included setting major league records for most HR in six consecutive games (10) and five straight games (8) and tying AL marks for most HR in four consecutive games (7) and most straight games with HR (6). Howard's career-high 48 HR came in 1969, when he batted .296, recorded 111 RBI and compiled a .574 slugging percentage. Howard, who topped the AL in total bases with 330 in 1968 and 340 in 1969, won the AL HR title in 1970 with 44. He batted .283 with a .546 slugging average and led the junior circuit with a career-high 126 RBI and 132 walks. In August 1972, the Senators sold Howard to the Detroit Tigers (AL). During 1973, his final season as a player, he appeared mainly as a DH.

The right-handed slugger belted 382 career HR and batted .273 lifetime with 1,774 hits and 1,119 RBI. In 1,895 games, he hit 245 doubles, scored 864 runs, struck out 1,460 times, and had a .499 slugging percentage. Howard's tape-measure HR led Ted Williams* to remark that the mammoth slugger hit balls farther and harder than anybody else he ever saw. After playing baseball in Japan in 1974, Howard embarked on a managerial and coaching career. He piloted Spokane, WA (PCL) in 1976 and then coached with the Milwaukee Brewers (AL) from 1977 through 1980. The San Diego

Padres (NL) named Howard manager for the 1981 season, during which he recorded a 41–69 mark. From 1982 through 1984, Howard served as a coach for the New York Mets (NL) and piloted them to a 52–64 slate on an interim basis for the last four months of the 1983 season. He coached for the Milwaukee Brewers in 1985 and 1986, Seattle Mariners (AL) in 1987 and 1988, New York Yankees (AL) in 1989, 1991, and 1992, New York Mets from 1994 through 1996, and Tampa Bay Devil Rays (AL) in 1998 and 1999. Howard managed the Gulf Coast, FL Braves (GCL) in 1997. As a manager, he garnered a 93–133 record (.412) and two sixth place finishes. In November 1999, Tampa Bay named him senior advisor for baseball operations. Howard married Cecilia Ann Johanski on February 7, 1959 and has six children, Tim, Cathy, Dan, Mitchell, Mary, and Becky.

BIBLIOGRAPHY: Thomas Aylesworth and Benton Minks, *The Encyclopedia of Baseball Managers* (New York, 1990); Fred Smith, *995 Tigers* (Detroit, MI, 1981); Frank Howard file, National Baseball Library, Cooperstown, NY; Craig Carter, ed., *TSN Daguerreotypes* (St. Louis, MO, 1990); *The Baseball Encyclopedia*, 10th ed. (New York, 1996); Ted Williams, *The Science of Hitting* (New York, 1971); James R. Hartley, *Washington's Expansion Senators (1961–71)* (Germantown, MD, 1998); William F. McNeil, *The Dodgers Encyclopedia* (Champaign, IL, 1997); Peter C. Bjarkman, ed., *Encyclopedia of Major League Baseball Team Histories American League* (Westport, CT, 1991); *TSN Official Baseball Record Book, 1998.*

Robert J. Brown

HOWELL, Henry "Harry," "Handsome Harry" (b. November 14, 1876, Brooklyn, NY; d. May 22, 1956, Spokane, WA), player, umpire, and scout, had two sisters, Julie and Nellie, and led the St. Louis Browns (AL) pitching staff from 1904 to 1908. During his major league career, he also performed at every other position except catcher. The 5-foot 9-inch right-hander broke into the major leagues with the Brooklyn Bridegrooms (NL) in 1898, finishing 2–0 after being scouted on his native city's sandlots. He had worked as a plumber previously. In his first full major league season in 1899, Howell compiled a creditable 13–8 mark with a 3.91 ERA for the Baltimore Orioles (NL).

The crafty spitballer assumed a journeyman's role, pitching for the Brooklyn Superbas (NL) in 1900 and the Baltimore Orioles (now AL) in 1901 and 1902. For the New York Highlanders (AL) in 1903, he enjoyed his best season to date with a 9–6 mark and a 3.53 ERA. Howell joined the St. Louis Browns in 1904, averaging 304 innings and nearly 15 wins per year there through 1908. With mediocre to awful St. Louis Browns teams, he achieved impressive statistics. He finished 16–15 with a scintillating 1.93 ERA in 1907, and 18–18 with a 1.89 ERA in 1908. A broken arm in 1910 forced his retirement as a player. As a scout for the St. Louis Browns, Howell was involved in the Ty Cobb*-Nap Lajoie* batting championship scandal. In the closing days of the 1910 season, he allegedly slipped the official scorer at a

St. Louis Browns home game a note offering him a new suit if he changed an error to a hit for Lajoie. The scorer ignored the request, but Howell was fired for his impropriety. After spending the next five years as an umpire, Howell worked as a mining engineer in Washington state until the late 1930s. He then began a plumbing business in Spokane, WA, performed light hauling, and managed a bowling alley and hotel. Howell became a well-liked Spokane eccentric, often heard singing hymns to his cats while banging away on an old piano. His wife, Marie, died in 1942. In 13 major league seasons, Howell pitched in 340 games with 131 victories, 146 losses, and a 2.74 ERA. He struck out 986 batters while walking just 677 and threw 20 shutouts. As a utility player, Howell batted .217 with 11 HR and 131 RBI.

BIBLIOGRAPHY: Harry Howell file, National Baseball Library, Cooperstown, NY; "Harry Howell," *TSN*, May 30, 1956; *The Baseball Encyclopedia*, 10th ed. (New York, 1996); Mike Shatzkin, ed., *The Ballplayers* (New York, 1990); Bill Borst, ed., *Ables to Zoldak*, vol. 1 (St. Louis, MO, 1988); Bill Borst, *Still Last in the American League* (West Bloomfield, MI, 1992).

John H. Ziegler

HOWSER, Richard Dalton "Dick" (b. May 14, 1936, Miami, FL; d. June 17, 1987, Kansas City, MO), player, coach, scout, and manager, was of German descent. He graduated from Palm Beach, FL High School and earned a Bachelor of Science degree in education from Florida State University, garnering All-American honors at shortstop in 1957 and 1958. The 5-foot 9-inch, 155-pound Howser received a $21,000 bonus to sign with the Kansas City Athletics (AL) in 1958. He played shortstop at Winona, MN (3IL) in 1958 and Sioux City, IA (3IL) in 1959 and 1960 and batted .338 over the final half of the 1960 campaign for Shreveport, LA (SL).

The right-handed Howser played 157 games at shortstop for the Kansas City Athletics in 1961, batting .280, scoring 108 runs, stealing 37 bases, leading AL shortstops in putouts, playing in the All-Star Game, and being voted AL Rookie of the Year. Injuries shortened Howser's 1962 campaign to 83 games. Kansas City traded him with catcher Joe Azcue to the Cleveland Indians (AL) for catcher Elston Howard* and $100,000 in May 1963. In 1964, Howser tied the AL record for games played at shortstop in a season by starting all 162 games. He scored 101 runs and reached a career-high 52 RBI. He split shortstop duties with Larry Brown in 1965 and 1966 before the Cleveland Indians traded Howser to the New York Yankees (AL) in December 1966. He served as a utility infielder with the New York Yankees in 1967 and 1968. Howser's career included 789 games, 617 hits, 398 runs, 16 HR, 165 RBI, 105 stolen bases, and a .248 batting average.

The New York Yankees retained Howser as third base coach from 1969 to 1978. He served as head baseball coach at Florida State University in 1979, leading the Seminoles to 43 wins, 17 losses, and one tie. Owner George Steinbrenner* hired Howser to manage the New York Yankees in 1980. Howser led New York to an AL East title with 103 victories, but the

Yankees lost three straight in the best of five AL Championship Series to the Kansas City Royals. Steinbrenner ordered Howser to fire third base coach Mike Ferraro as a scapegoat for failing to win the AL pennant. Howser quietly refused, however, and was dismissed with Ferraro.

The Kansas City Royals (AL) hired Howser to replace Jim Frey* as manager in August 1981. The Kansas City Royals won 20 of 33 games under Howser to win the second-half title in the split season but then lost three consecutive contests to the Oakland Athletics in the AL West playoff. The Kansas City Royals finished second under Howser in 1982 and 1983. Howser directed the Royals to the AL West title in 1984, but Kansas City lost the AL pennant to the Detroit Tigers in three games in the AL Championship Series. The Kansas City Royals in 1985 fielded virtually the same team, which many considered mediocre. Howser, nonetheless, won the AL West, came back from a three-games-to-one deficit to defeat the Toronto Blue Jays for the AL pennant and again overcame a three-games-to-one disadvantage to win the World Series over the St. Louis Cardinals (NL).

In 1986, Howser managed the AL All-Star team, but forgot the names of several players and seemed detached from the game. A week later on July 22, surgeons operated on Howser to remove a cancerous brain tumor. Royals coach Mike Ferraro, who had recovered from cancer of the kidney, was named interim manager. On December 5, 1986, Howser underwent experimental brain surgery called immunotherapy. He and his wife, Nancy, who had two daughters, Jan and Jill, received over 10,000 cards and bouquets from well-wishers. Howser tried to resume managerial duties with Kansas City in the spring of 1987, but retired after two days because of physical weakness. His teams won 507 games and lost 424 for a .544 winning percentage.

Players, managers, and umpires respected Howser for his loyalty, integrity, and warm personality. For him, the players were family and the fans were extended family. Baseball writer Thomas Boswell paid tribute to Howser, "In another 20 years of managing he probably would have won more pennants. But he could not have proved anything new about himself. All the best was already on display." The Dick Howser Trophy is awarded through the *BW* coaches' poll to the nation's outstanding college player.

BIBLIOGRAPHY: Thomas Aylesworth and Benton Minks, *The Encyclopedia of Baseball Managers* (New York, 1990); Mark Gallagher, *The Yankee Encyclopedia*, vol. 3 (Champaign, IL, 1997); Steve Cameron and George Brett, *Last of a Breed* (Dallas, TX, 1993); Thomas Boswell, *The Heart of the Order* (New York, 1989); Ron Fimrite, "Facing the Sad Truth," *SI* 66 (March 9, 1987), p. 96; Richard Howser file, National Baseball Library, Cooperstown, NY; Kansas City Royals, "Blending Talent Is Howser's Recipe for Success," *Grandslam* (1982); Bob Nightengale, "Biggest Game for K.C.'s Howser," *TSN*, July 28, 1986, p. 20; Bob Nightengale, "Experimental Surgery for Royals' Howser," *TSN*, December 15, 1986, p. 51; Bob Nightengale, "Royals Stadium: Empty Chair," *TSN*, August 4, 1986, p. 24; *NYT*, June 18, 1987, p. A-1.

Frank J. Olmsted

HOY, William Ellsworth "Dummy" (b. May 23, 1862, Houcktown, OH; d. December 15, 1961, Cincinnati, OH), player, became a deaf mute at age 3 because of a meningitis attack and could not attend local schools. In 1874 his parents sent him to Columbus, OH, where he enrolled at the Ohio State School for the Deaf. He completed grade and high school in six years, graduating as valedictorian of his class. Hoy opened a small shoe shop in Houcktown and played for the town baseball team on weekends. In 1886 he joined Oshkosh, WI (NWL), where his speed and outfield defensive skills excited onlookers. After becoming a dependable hitter his second year with Oshkosh, he joined the major leagues.

The left-handed batting Hoy spent fourteen major league seasons with the Washington Statesmen in 1888–1889, Senators (NL) in 1892–1893, Buffalo Bisons (PL) in 1890, St. Louis Browns (AA) in 1891, Cincinnati Reds (NL) from 1894 through 1897 and 1902, Louisville Colonels (NL) in 1898–1899, and Chicago White Stockings (AL) in 1901. A constant base-stealing threat, he led the NL with 82 thefts in his rookie 1888 season. His center field play helped the Chicago White Stockings win an AL championship in 1901. Hoy ended his professional career in 1903 with Los Angeles, CA (PCL).

Although only 5-feet 4-inches, and 150 pounds, Hoy demonstrated all-around offensive and defensive skills. Never a power hitter, he usually batted at or near the top of the lineup and reached base and scored frequently. In 1,796 major league games, he amassed 2,044 hits, scored 1,426 runs, stole 594 bases, and batted .287. A defensive standout, he is considered the first center fielder to play the position shallow. The speedy Hoy ran down balls hit behind him and possessed a powerful, accurate throwing arm. He threw out three runners at home plate on June 19, 1888, the first of only three players to accomplish this feat.

Hoy married the deaf Anna Maria Lowery, who became a prominent teacher of the deaf in Ohio, on October 26, 1898. After his playing career, Hoy purchased a farm in Mt. Healthy, OH. Born there were his son, Carson, later a distinguished Cincinnati jurist, and his daughter, Clover. He lived 99 years, longer than any major leaguer at his death.

BIBLIOGRAPHY: William Hoy file, National Baseball Library, Cooperstown, NY; Joseph M. Overfield, "William Ellsworth Hoy, 1862–1961," *TNP* 2 (Fall 1982), pp. 70–72; *The Baseball Encyclopedia*, 10th ed. (New York, 1996); Robert L. Tiemann and Mark Rucker, eds., *Nineteenth Century Stars* (Kansas City, MO, 1989); Lee Allen, *The Cincinnati Reds* (New York, 1948); Philip Von Borries, *Legends of Louisville* (West Bloomfield, MI, 1993); Philip Von Borries, *Louisville Diamonds* (Paducah, KY, 1997).

Dennis T. "Tom" Chase

HOYT, Dewey LaMarr (b. January 1, 1955, Columbia, SC), player, is the son of Dewey LaMarr Hoyt, minor league baseball pitcher, and graduated in 1973 from Columbia High School. The New York Yankees (AL) selected the 6-foot 2-inch, 244-pound right-handed pitcher in the fifth round of the

June 1973 draft and traded him to the Chicago White Sox (AL) in April 1977. Hoyt spent over seven minor league seasons with Johnson City, TN (ApL) in 1973, Fort Lauderdale, FL (FSL) in 1974 and 1975, West Haven, CT (EL) in 1975 and 1976, Knoxville, TN (SA) in 1977 and 1979, Appleton, WI (ML) in 1978, and Iowa (AA) in 1977, 1979, and 1980, briefly appearing with the Chicago White Sox in 1979.

Hoyt pitched for the Chicago White Sox from 1980 through 1984. After twin 9–3 marks as a middle reliever in 1980 and 1981, he compiled a 19–15 record with a 3.53 ERA as a starter in 1982. The control pitcher set a club record with 14 consecutive victories in 1981 and 1982 and led the AL in triumphs in 1982. His best major league season came in 1983, when he garnered the AL Cy Young Award and again paced the AL in victories. Hoyt won 22 of his final 26 decisions to finish 24–10 with a 3.66 ERA, as Chicago captured the AL West. No White Sox hurler had won 20 games since Jim Kaat* in 1975 or recorded that many victories since Wilbur Wood* in 1973. He walked only 31 batters, just 3 more than Cy Young's* 1904 AL record.

Hoyt accounted for the White Sox only victory in the 1983 AL Championship Series, besting the Baltimore Orioles, 2–1. *TSN* named him its AL Pitcher of the Year and as right-handed pitcher on its AL All-Star team. Hoyt's fortunes reversed in 1984, when he led the AL in losses with a 13–18 mark. He fired a one-hitter against the New York Yankees on May 2, but surrendered the second most HR with 31.

In a seven-player December 1984 transaction, Chicago traded Hoyt to the San Diego Padres (NL). Hoyt finished with a 16–8 record and 3.47 ERA in 1985 and earned the victory as the NL All-Star game starter. His major league career abruptly ended with an 8–11 mark in 1986. Commissioner Peter Ueberroth (OS) suspended him for the 1987 season because of a lingering drug problem. The White Sox granted him a tryout in 1988 after his 45-day prison term, but Hoyt returned to prison after enforcement officials uncovered marijuana and cocaine in his apartment.

In 8 major league seasons, Hoyt compiled a 98–68 mark, 3.99 ERA, and 681 strikeouts in 1,311.1 innings. No major league pitcher won more games in 1982 and 1983. The Prosperity, SC resident married Sylvia Ward in September 1980.

BIBLIOGRAPHY: Dewey LaMarr Hoyt file, National Baseball Library, Cooperstown, NY; *TSN Baseball Register*, 1987; *WWA*, 44th ed. (1986–1987), p. 1348; Jim Kaplan, "A Heady LaMarr Has Sox Fans in Ecstasy," *SI* 56 (May 31, 1982), pp. 26–29; *San Diego Padres 1986 Media Guide*; Richard Lindberg, *Who's on Third?* (South Bend, IN, 1983); Peter C. Bjarkman, ed., *Encyclopedia of Major League Baseball Team Histories American League* (Westport, CT, 1991).

David L. Porter

HOYT, Waite Charles "Schoolboy" (b. September 9, 1899, Brooklyn, NY; d. August 25, 1984, Cincinnati, OH), player and sportscaster, signed a major league contract at age 15 and became only the second player to have signed at such an early age. His father, Addison, worked as a businessman and sometime actor. Hoyt graduated from Erasmus High School in Brooklyn and chose to pursue a career in baseball rather than attend college. He pitched mostly for the New York Yankees (1921–1930) of the AL during his 20-year major league career. Hoyt also hurled for the Boston Red Sox (1919–1920), Detroit Tigers (1930–1931), and Philadelphia Athletics (1931), all AL teams, and for the Brooklyn Dodgers (1932, 1937–1938), New York Giants (1918, 1932), and Pittsburgh Pirates (1933–1937), all of the NL. He compiled a lifetime record of 237 wins and 182 losses and a 3.59 ERA. He was named to the National Baseball Hall of Fame in 1969 and subsequently served for several years on its Veterans Committee. He married Ellen Burbank in May 1933 and had one son.

Hoyt played in the minor leagues with Mt. Carmel, PA (PSL) and Hartford, CT-Lynn, MA (EL) in 1916, Memphis TN (SA) and Montreal, Canada (IL) in 1917, and Nashville, TN (SA) and Newark, NJ (IL) in 1918. Hoyt appeared in one game with the New York Giants (NL) in 1918 and was acquired in 1919 by the Boston Red Sox (AL). Following two mediocre seasons there, he was traded on December 15, 1920 to the New York Yankees (AL). Hoyt helped New York capture its first AL pennant in 1921 with a 19–13 mark and won 19 games again in 1922. In the 1921 World Series against the Giants, he pitched three complete games without allowing an earned run. The hard-throwing right-hander's best seasons came in 1927 and 1928, when he compiled 22–7 and 23–7 records, respectively. His .759 percentage, 2.63 ERA, and 8 saves in 1927 led the AL. After being traded to the Detroit Tigers (AL) in May 1930, he was shuttled during the next two years to the Philadelphia Athletics, Brooklyn Dodgers, New York Giants, and Pittsburgh Pirates and remained in Pittsburgh until June 1937. His last major league season came in 1938 with the Brooklyn Dodgers.

Following his retirement in 1938, Hoyt became a radio sportscaster in New York and from 1942 to 1965 broadcast games for the Cincinnati Reds (NL). One of the first former ballplayers to become an announcer, he made notable "rain delay" narrations of interesting episodes in his baseball career. The handsome, popular Hoyt possessed a nimble wit and fine command of the English language. He made famous the phrase, "It's great to be young and a Yankee." Known as "the aristocrat of baseball," Hoyt proved a fiery, tough competitor with tremendous pride in the Yankee organization. He contended that the great New York teams of the 1920s developed a unique tradition, mystique, and winning style copied by later Yankees clubs.

BIBLIOGRAPHY: Waite Hoyt file, National Baseball Library, Cooperstown, NY; *SEAL*, vol. 1 (1981–1985), pp. 404–405; *BM* 38 (December 1926), pp. 297–298, 328–330; "The Best of Waite Hoyt in the Rain," Personality Records (WHLP-537); Mark Gallagher, *The Yankee Encyclopedia*, vol. 3 (Champaign, IL, 1997); Noel Hynd, *The Giants of the Polo Grounds* (New York, 1988); Tom Knight, "Waite Hoyt," *TNP* 15

(1995), pp. 100–101; *Liberty* (August 26, 1939), pp. 57–58; Craig Carter, ed., *TSN Daguerreotypes* (St. Louis, MO, 1990); John Mosedale, *The Greatest of All: The 1927 New York Yankees* (New York, 1974); Leo Trachtenberg, *The Wonder Team* (Bowling Green, OH, 1995); Dave Anderson et al., *The Yankees* (New York, 1979); Frank Graham, *The New York Yankees* (New York, 1943); Fred Smith, *995 Tigers* (Detroit, MI, 1981); Eugene C. Murdock, interview with Waite Hoyt, March 12, 1976; *NYT*, June 4, 1967, February 7, 1969, August 26, 1984; *TSN*, February 10, 1938, December 4, 1941, April 2, 1942, October 15, 1952; Cincinnati *Enquirer*, August 26, 1984.

Eugene Murdock

HRABOSKY, Alan Thomas "Al," "The Mad Hungarian" (b. July 21, 1949, Oakland, CA), player and sportscaster, earned All-City and All-Orange County honors in football and baseball at Savannah High School in Anaheim, CA and made all-conference in baseball twice while attending Fullerton, CA JC. The St. Louis Cardinals (NL) selected Hrabosky in the first round of the February 1969 baseball draft. From 1969 to 1971, the 5-foot 10-inch, 180-pound southpaw recorded 19 victories in 23 decisions while striking out 226 batters in 240 innings as a starting pitcher for St. Louis Cardinal farm teams at Modesto, CA (CaL), Arkansas (TL), and Tulsa, OK (AA). Hrabosky won seven and lost 12 at Arkansas in 1972 and finished only 3–6 at Tulsa in 1973, but continued to strike out a batter per inning.

The St. Louis Cardinals recalled Hrabosky in 1970, 1971, and 1972 as a reliever. He returned to the Cardinals early in the 1973 campaign and quickly became the most reliable reliever in manager Red Schoendienst's* bullpen. He was called on 44 times and posted a 2.09 ERA. With a blazing fastball, good breaking pitch, and excellent control, Hrabosky ranked as a top reliever over the next three seasons. In 1974, he won eight of nine decisions and saved nine contests in 65 appearances. In 1975, no reliever performed better. Hrabosky won 13, lost three, and led the NL with 22 saves while recording a 1.67 ERA. The next season, he won eight and saved 13 despite struggling with a leg injury. Besides growing a fu manchu moustache, Hrabosky maintained a menacing grimace on his face, walked to the back of the mound between batters to psyche himself, and ended the ritual by slamming the ball into his glove and stomping back to the pitching rubber. The ritual provided great theatre and intimidated some batters. Hrabosky said it enabled him to capture the force of the adrenalin generated by his body when he became angry. The ritual also whipped fans into a frenzy. Hrabosky unnerved hitters by taking a lot of time between pitches. The Cardinals' public relations director nicknamed Hrabosky "The Mad Hungarian." Hrabosky won six games and saved 10 in 1977, but his ERA ballooned to 4.38.

In December 1977, St. Louis traded him to the Kansas City Royals (AL) for reliever Mark Littell and catcher Buck Martinez. Hrabosky regained his form for Kansas City, winning 17 games in relief and saving 31 in two seasons. He made three appearances without a save or decision in the 1978 AL Championship Series, which the New York Yankees won. In November 1979, Hrabosky became a free agent and signed a five-year, multimillion dollar contract with the Atlanta Braves (NL). He became the forgotten man in the Atlanta bullpen in 1980, as manager Bobby Cox* summoned Rick Camp and Gene Garber* in the late innings. Hrabosky won four and lost two with three saves in just 42 appearances. He started the 1981 and 1982 campaigns on the disabled list, triumphing only three times and saving just four games in two seasons. The Braves released him in August 1982 with two years remaining on a guaranteed contract of $390,000 each year and with deferred compensation of $100,000 per year for 30 years. Hrabosky's major league record included 545 games, with all but one in relief, 64 victories, 35 losses, 97 saves, 548 strikeouts, and a 3.10 ERA.

Hrabosky returned to St. Louis, becoming a sportscaster for KPLR television and co-hosting a radio show on KMOX with former Cardinal catcher Ted Simmons.* He announces St. Louis Cardinal games on KPLR television, handles Cardinal promotional events, broadcasts for Fox-Sports, and lectures on baseball. Hrabosky, who married Delores White on January 24, 1970 and has a daughter, Lisa, served in the U.S. Army reserves.

BIBLIOGRAPHY: David Craft et al., *Redbirds Revisted* (Chicago, IL, 1990); Zander Hollander, ed., *The Complete Handbook of Baseball 1980* (New York, 1980); Bob Cairns, *Pen Men* (New York, 1993); Rob Rains, *The St. Louis Cardinals* (New York, 1992); Bob Broeg and Jerry Vickery, *St. Louis Cardinals Encyclopedia* (Grand Rapids, MI, 1998); Jerry Lovelace and Marty Hendin, *St. Louis Cardinals 1974 Official Guide and Record Book for Press, Radio and TV* (St. Louis, MO, 1974); Tim Tucker, "Hrabosky Sorry 'I Let Ted Down,' " *TSN*, September 13, 1982, p. 29.

Frank J. Olmsted

HRBEK, Kent Alan (b. May 21, 1960, Minneapolis, MN), player, is the older of two children born to Ed Hrbek and Justina Hrbek and played first base and pitched in baseball at Kennedy High School in Bloomington, MN. His baseball talents, however, escaped professional scouts, including those of the Cincinnati Reds (NL) and Los Angeles Dodgers (NL) observing him at tryout camps. His playing abilities caught the attention of the Minnesota Twins (AL) through discussions that started in the concessions department and worked their way up to owner Calvin Griffith.* Griffith sent Minnesota Twins scout Angelo Giuliani to see Hrbek play. The Minnesota Twins signed Hrbek in the summer of 1978 and sent him to Elizabethton, TN (ApL). The 1980 season found Hrbek at Wisconsin Rapids, WI (ML), where he was named to the ML All-Star team. In 1981, Kent was promoted to Visalia, CA (CaL) and was selected to the CaL's All-Star squad.

The 6-foot 4-inch, 252-pound Hrbek joined the Minnesota Twins in September 1981, the 15th Minnesotan to play there. In his first major league game, he belted a twelfth-inning, game-winning HR off New York Yankee reliever George Frazier. With the Minnesota Twins from 1981 to 1994, the left-handed-hitting, right-handed-throwing first baseman ranked among the best all-around AL players. In 14 major league seasons, Hrbek batted .282 with 1,749 hits, 293 HR, and 1,086 RBI. During this span, he made only 82 errors in 13,226 total chances for a .994 fielding percentage. Hrbek played in the 1982 All-Star Game, two AL Championship Series against the Detroit Tigers in 1987 and Toronto Blue Jays in 1991, and two World Series against the St. Louis Cardinals in 1987 and the Atlanta Braves in 1991. The Minnesota Twins won both 7-game World Series. In 24 postseason games, Hrbek batted .154, with three HR and 12 RBI.

Hrbek, who retired in August 1994, resides in Bloomington, MN with his wife, Jeanie (Burns) Hrbek, and one daughter, Heidi.

BIBLIOGRAPHY: Kent Hrbek file, National Baseball Library, Cooperstown, NY; *The Baseball Encyclopedia*, 10th ed. (New York, 1996); *Minnesota Twins Media Guide*, 1994; Steve Wulf, "Local Boy Makes Good, Local Team Makes Bad," *SI 57* (July 5, 1982), pp. 24–27; Peter J. Bjarkman, ed., *Encyclopedia of Major League Baseball Team Histories American League* (Westport, CT, 1991).

James E. Welch

HUBBELL, Carl Owen "King Carl," "The Meal Ticket" (b. June 22, 1903, Carthage, MO; d. November 21, 1988, Scottsdale, AZ), player, executive, and scout, was the son of George Hubbell, a pecan farmer, and Margaret Hubbell and grew up in Meeker, OK. He graduated from Meeker High School in 1922. Hubbell married Lucille Harrington in January 1930 and had two sons. Widowed in 1964, he wed Julia Stanfield. In 1947 he was elected to the National Baseball Hall of Fame. Nicknamed "King Carl" and "The Meal Ticket," the 6-foot, 175-pound left-hander utilized a slow, cartwheel-like delivery of the screwball to record five consecutive 20-win NL seasons from 1933–1937. With sluggers Bill Terry* and Mel Ott* and pitcher Hal Schumacher,* he helped the powerful New York Giants to the 1933, 1936, and 1937 World Series.

After beginning his career with Cushing, OK (OKSL) in 1923, Hubbell signed in 1924 with the Detroit Tigers (AL). He spent four mediocre seasons pitching in their minor league system and allegedly was instructed by Ty Cobb* to forsake the screwball. Hubbell was saved from obscurity by being traded to the New York Giants' organization and pitching in 1928 for Beaumont, TX (TL). Giants manager John McGraw* encouraged Hubbell to utilize his best pitch. Several months later, Hubbell in 1928 joined the New York Giants (NL) roster. During his 16 years (1928–1943) with the Giants, he won 253 games, lost 154 decisions, and posted only one losing record. Hubbell compiled a 2.98 ERA, struck out 1,677 batters, and led the NL in wins and ERA three times, winning percentage twice, and shutouts once.

Hubbell enjoyed his best seasons in 1933 and 1936, winning the NL MVP Award both years. A 1–0 victory over the St. Louis Cardinals on July 2, 1933 typified his 23-win performance that year. In 18 innings, he did not walk a batter and struck out 12 from the powerful Gashouse Gang. In the 1933 World Series against the Washington Senators, he won two games, allowed no earned runs in 20 innings, and hurled 15 strikeouts. After receiving his MVP plaque, Hubbell made headlines at the 1934 All-Star Game. He struck out National Baseball Hall of Famers Babe Ruth,* Lou Gehrig,* Jimmie Foxx,* Al Simmons,* and Joe Cronin* consecutively, starting this string with no outs and two men on base. On May 8, 1929, he tossed a no-run, no-hit victory over the Pittsburgh Pirates.

Hubbell's most striking feats occurred in 1936. After compiling 10 victories and six defeats, Hubbell won 16 consecutive decisions from July 17 through the end of the season. He surrendered the winning HR to Lou Gehrig in Game 4 of the 1936 World Series, but had defeated the Yankees in Game 1 without allowing a single outfield chance. In the 1937 World Series, he secured the Giants' only victory over the Yankees. He finished with a 4–2 World Series career record and a strong 1.79 ERA in 50.1 innings pitched. From 1943 to 1978, he served as director of player development for the Giants' minor league system. From 1978 until his death, he scouted for the Giants. He died two days after suffering head and chest injuries in an automobile accident near his home.

BIBLIOGRAPHY: Carl Hubbell file, National Baseball Library, Cooperstown, NY; George Bulkley, "Carl Hubbell's 24 Straight," *BRJ* 12 (1983), pp. 76–81; John Benson et al., *Baseball's Top 100* (Wilton, CT, 1997); Bob Broeg, *Super Stars of Baseball* (St. Louis, MO, 1971); Anthony J. Connor, *Baseball for the Love of It* (New York, 1982); Arnold Hano, *The Greatest Giants of Them All* (New York, 1967); Fred Stein, *Under Coogan's Bluff* (Glenshaw, PA, 1978); Peter Williams, *When the Giants Were Giants* (Chapel Hill, NC, 1994); William Curran, "Dodgers End Hubbell's Record Streak," *TNP* 14 (1994), pp. 61–65; Glenn Dickey, *The History of National League Baseball* (New York, 1979); Craig Carter, ed., *TSN Daguerreotypes* (St. Louis, MO, 1990); Noel Hynd, *The Giants of the Polo Grounds* (New York, 1988); Jack Kavanagh, "Dizzy Dean vs. Carl Hubbell," *BRJ* 21 (1992), pp. 33–35; William B. Mead, *The Worst Ten Years of Baseball* (New York, 1978); *NYT*, July 11, 1934; November 22, 1988, p. B–8; *The Baseball Encyclopedia*, 10th ed. (New York, 1996); Joseph Vecchione, *The New York Times Book of Sports Legends* (New York, 1991).

Alan R. Asnen

HUDLIN, George Willis "Ace" (b. May 23, 1906, Wagoner, OK), player, was known primarily by his middle name and eventually as "Ace." He excelled as an all-around athlete in track and field, football, and baseball in high school at Wagoner. At the University of Oklahoma, Hudlin won early recognition as a pitcher and shortstop. In 1926 he debuted professionally with Waco, TX (TL), winning 16 games for a last place team. He joined the Cleveland Indians (AL) by the end of that season, appearing in eight games.

Affectionate Tribe fans, who appreciated Hudlin's ability as a workhorse and frequent winner, nicknamed him "Ace." He won 158 games and lost 156 in 16 major league seasons, hurling a season high of 280.1 innings in 1929. Ironically, Hudlin was never the staff ace because he pitched behind some exceptional Cleveland Indian moundsmen. Between 1927 and 1940, Mel Harder,* Wes Ferrell,* John Allen,* and Bob Feller* joined the rotation.

As a young 6-foot, 190-pound right-hander, Hudlin was nurtured by Cleveland's established catcher, Luke Sewell.* Hudlin, a hard thrower, resisted accepting the wisdom of changing speeds or throwing a breaking pitch. Instead, he achieved early success by throwing a crossfire pitch to right-handed hitters and throwing overhand to lefties. His 4.41 career ERA average was inflated by relatively weak campaigns from 1936 to 1940. His 1940 season included stints with the Cleveland Indians, Washington Senators (AL), St. Louis Browns (AL), and New York Giants (NL). Luke Sewell, who managed the St. Louis Browns (AL) to a wartime championship in 1944, coaxed Hudlin out of a three-year retirement to pitch in one game that season.

Hudlin described the highlight of his career as a 5–4 12-inning victory over the 1927 New York Yankees. Midway through that May afternoon, the field announcer told the crowd that aviator Charles Lindbergh had landed his solo flight in Paris. Shortly after breaking into professional baseball, Hudlin settled in Arkansas and remains in relatively good health living in Little Rock. Hudlin also has been a successful ham radio operator, a golfer, and a living endorsement of the quality of mineral baths in Arkansas.

BIBLIOGRAPHY: Willis Hudlin file, National Baseball Library, Cooperstown, NY; Walter Langford, "Willis Hudlin," *BRJ* 16 (1987), pp. 80–82; *The Baseball Encyclopedia*, 10th ed. (New York, 1996); *Who's Who in Major League Baseball* (Chicago, IL, 1933); Franklin Lewis, *The Cleveland Indians* (New York, 1949).

Dave Fitzsimmons

HUGGINS, Miller James "Hug," "The Mighty Mite" (b. March 27, 1879, Cincinnati, OH; d. September 25, 1929, New York, NY), player and manager, was the third of four children born to grocer James Thomas Huggins and Sarah (Reid) Huggins. Huggins, whose father had emigrated from England, attended public grammar and secondary schools in Cincinnati. An excellent student, he received a law degree from the University of Cincinnati and passed the Ohio bar exam in 1902.

Huggins completed the law degree to please his father, but preferred to play baseball. His professional baseball career began in 1899 at Mansfield, OH (ISL), where he assumed the name Proctor because his father disapproved of Sunday baseball. From 1901 to 1903, the 5-foot 6½-inch, 140-pound Huggins batted .322, .328, and .308 at St. Paul, MN (AA).

After being purchased by the Cincinnati Reds (NL), Huggins played second base there from 1904 to 1909. Although excellent defensively, he hit with little power. Huggins drew many bases on balls, showed good speed, and batted .292 with the Reds in 1906. Traded to the St. Louis Cardinals (NL) in February 1910, he twice drew over 100 walks, scored over 100 runs between 1910 and 1914, and hit a career-high .304 in 1912. He averaged around 30 stolen bases per season, but was caught 36 times in 68 attempts in 1914.

In 1913 Huggins became player–manager of a weak last place St. Louis Cardinals team. From 1913 through 1917, St. Louis fielded only two winning teams under Huggins. He retired as a player in 1916, when Rogers Hornsby* replaced him at second base. After new Cardinals owners named Branch Rickey* manager, Huggins piloted the New York Yankees (AL) to fourth and third place finishes in 1918 and 1919. Huggins instructed the front office to acquire Boston Red Sox pitcher–outfielder Babe Ruth.* New York purchased Ruth for $125,000 in January 1920, changing baseball history forever. Ruth often criticized Huggins publicly and regularly broke club rules, but the slugger enabled Huggins to construct a dynasty that captured six AL pennants and three world championships from 1921 to 1928. Many authorities rank Huggins' 1927 Yankees as the greatest baseball team in history. With Ruth, Lou Gehrig,* Earle Combs,* Tony Lazzeri,* Herb Pennock,* Waite Hoyt,* and other stars, New York compiled a 110–44 record and four straight World Series wins over the Pittsburgh Pirates. In September 1929, Huggins began losing weight and energy and turned the team over to Art Fletcher* with 11 games remaining. Huggins, a lifelong bachelor, lived with his sister, who cared for him in his final weeks. He suffered from neuritis and died from a blood infection caused by a cut beneath his eye.

In 1,586 major league games, Huggins made 1,474 hits, accumulated 1,003 bases on balls, stole 324 bases, and batted .265. His 1,413 wins and 1,134 losses as a manager included a 1,067–719 slate as Yankees skipper. Huggins, acknowledged as one of the finest managers in baseball history, was elected to the National Baseball Hall of Fame in 1964.

BIBLIOGRAPHY: Miller Huggins file, National Baseball Library, Cooperstown, NY; Frank Graham, *The New York Yankees* (New York, 1943); Martin Appel and Burt Goldblatt, *Baseball's Best: The Hall of Fame Gallery* (New York, 1977); Bob Broeg, *Redbirds: A Century of Cardinals' Baseball* (St. Louis, MO, 1981); *DAB* 9 (1946), pp. 345–346; John Mosedale, *The Greatest of All: The 1927 New York Yankees* (New York, 1974); Leo Trachtenberg, *The Wonder Team* (Bowling Green, OH, 1995); Frederick G. Lieb, *The St. Louis Cardinals* (New York, 1945); Rob Rains, *The St. Louis Cardinals* (New York, 1992); Mark Gallagher, *The Yankee Encyclopedia*, vol. 3 (Champaign, IL, 1997); Leonard Koppett, *The Man in the Dugout* (New York, 1993); Edwin Pope, *Baseball's Greatest Managers* (New York, 1960); Lowell Reidenbaugh, *Baseball's Hall of Fame—Cooperstown* (New York, 1993); Thomas Aylesworth and Benton Minks, *The Encyclopedia of Baseball Managers* (New York, 1990).

Frank J. Olmsted

HUGHES, Samuel Thomas "Sammy" (b. October 20, 1910, Louisville, KY; d. August 9, 1981, Los Angeles, CA), player, ranked among the finest Negro

League second basemen of the 1930s and 1940s. Hughes, the son of Henry Hughes and Susan (Cowherd) Hughes, attended school in Louisville through the eighth grade. The graceful 6-foot 4-inch infielder began his professional career in 1929 with the Louisville White Sox. The Washington Pilots selected him in 1932 as a first baseman, where he joined stars Mule Suttles,* Chet Brewer,* and Frank Warfield.* When Warfield died of a hemorrhage, Hughes claimed the second base job. The Pilots' financial troubles caused Hughes to quit the team. He joined the Nashville Elite Giants (NNL) in 1933 and continued to play with the team when it transferred successively to Columbus, Washington, and Baltimore.

An excellent hitter and a smart base runner, Hughes hit .296 in his NNL career and batted .263 in five East-West All-Star games. In 1936, the Elite Giants won the Denver *Post* semipro tournament. The same year, Hughes played with Satchel Paige* and Josh Gibson* against Rogers Hornsby's* Major League All-Stars. Hughes posted a .353 batting average against major league players and batted .246 in Cuba in 1939–1940. He married Mildred Shannon in 1941 and had two children, Spencer and Barbara, before their divorce in the early 1950s. In 1956, he married Thelma Smith. Hughes jumped with Roy Campanella* to Mexico in 1941, but returned to the Baltimore Elite Giants (NNL) in 1942. A proposed tryout by the two ballplayers with the Washington Senators that year never materialized. Hughes entered the U.S. Army in 1943, participating in the New Guinea invasion with the 196th Support Battalion, and was discharged in 1946. Upon returning to the Baltimore Elite Giants in 1946, Hughes tutored future Brooklyn Dodgers infielder James "Junior" Gilliam.* Hughes retired at the end of the 1946 season and worked for the Pillsbury Company and Hughes Aircraft Company in Los Angeles. Hughes helped bridge the gap between the Negro and major leagues. He and other Negro Leaguers demonstrated the requisite skills to play in the major leagues.

BIBLIOGRAPHY: Terry A. Baxter, correspondence with Jorge Figueroda, 1984, Cuban League statistics, Terry A. Baxter Collection, Lee's Summit, MO; Terry A. Baxter, correspondence with Andrew Porter, 1984, Terry A. Baxter Collection, Lee's Summit, MO; Terry A. Baxter, correspondence with Donn Rogosin, 1984, Terry A. Baxter Collection, Cedar Rapids, IA; Terry A. Baxter, telephone interview with Monford Irvin, 1984; Roy Campanella, *It's Good to Be Alive* (Boston, MA, 1959); John B. Holway, monograph on Sammy T. Hughes, John B. Holway Collection, Alexandria, VA; John B. Holway, *Voices from the Great Black Baseball Leagues* (New York, 1975); Robert W. Peterson, *Only the Ball Was White* (Englewood Cliffs, NJ, 1970); James A. Riley, *The All-Time All-Stars of Black Baseball* (Cocoa, FL, 1983); James A. Riley, *The Biographical Encyclopedia of the Negro Baseball Leagues* (New York, 1994); Donn Rogosin, *Invisible Men: Life in Baseball's Negro Leagues* (New York, 1983).

Terry A. Baxter

HUGHSON, Cecil Carlton "Tex" (b. February 9, 1916, Kyle, TX; d. August 6, 1993, San Marcos, TX), player, attended the University of Texas and began his professional baseball career with Moultrie, GA (GFL) in 1937. The following season, Hughson led the Canton, OH Terriers (MAL) pitchers with 22 wins and just seven losses. He pitched for Scranton, PA (EL) in 1939 before joining Louisville, KY (AA) in 1940. With Louisville, Hughson's career received a great boost from Boston Red Sox (AL) pitcher "Broadway" Charlie Wagner. Wagner spent some time in Louisville in 1940 and saw Hughson pitch in the sweltering heat. When Boston Red Sox manager Joe Cronin* asked Wagner about Louisville's best pitchers, the latter recommended Hughson.

After compiling a 7–1 win–loss record in 1941 with Louisville, Hughson joined the Boston Red Sox and finished with a 5–3 mark. The 6-foot 3-inch, 198-pound right-hander, who usually wore high-heel boots and spurs that jingled and dangled, probably ranked as the AL's best pitcher in 1942, when he compiled a 22–6 mark and led the AL in wins, complete games (22), innings (281), and strikeouts (113). He was named to the AL All-Star team for the first of three straight times and pitched two innings during the Summer Classic. He set a record by defeating the New York Yankees six consecutive times from July 1942 to April 1943. Hughson enjoyed a tremendous season in 1944 with an 18–5 mark before entering military service. His .783 winning percentage led the AL hurlers.

The tall Texan spent the 1945 season pitching for military service teams and returned to the Boston Red Sox in 1946 with a 20–11 record, leading Boston to the AL pennant. In the 1946 World Series against the St. Louis Cardinals, Hughson triumphed in the opening game and lost Game 4. St. Louis Cardinal star Stan Musial* claimed that Hughson had shown him the best stuff for Boston during the classic, which St. Louis won on Enos Slaughter's* run from first base in the eighth inning of the seventh game.

Recurring arm problems plagued Hughson the remainder of his career. He won 12 of 23 decisions in 1947, including four 1–0 victories, and three of four decisions in 1948. The Boston Red Sox in June 1948 sent Hughson to the Austin, TX Pioneers (BSL), where he wore the number 13 on his uniform. Hughson returned to the major leagues with the Boston Red Sox in 1949, recording a 4–2 mark. The Boston Red Sox traded Hughson to the New York Giants (NL) in 1950, but he was released before the season started. During his eight-year major league career, Hughson compiled a 96–54 record with a 2.94 ERA and .640 winning percentage. Hughson, who married Roena Moore in May 1937, retired to his farm in Kyle, TX and later resided in San Marcos, TX. The Hughsons had one son, Stanley, and two daughters, Dixie and Jane.

BIBLIOGRAPHY: Cecil Hughson file, National Baseball Library, Cooperstown, NY; John Drohan, "Tex Won Spurs After Broadway Boosting," *TSN*, June 26, 1946, p. 9; Weldon Hart, "Hughson Story Makes Unique Baseball History," Austin (TX) *Statesman*, June 2, 1948; *NYT*, August 8, 1993, p. 47; Ed Rummil, " 'Hold That Locker, I'll Be Back,' Says Tex on Departure," *TSN*, May 29, 1948; Mike Shatzkin, ed., *The*

Ballplayers (New York, 1990); Frederick G. Lieb, *The Boston Red Sox* (New York, 1947); Robert Redmount, *The Red Sox Encyclopedia* (Champaign, IL, 1998); Howard Liss, *The Boston Red Sox* (New York, 1982); Peter Golenbock, *Fenway* (New York, 1992).

William A. Borst

HULBERT, William Ambrose "Bill" (b. October 23, 1832, Burlington Flats, NY; d. April 10, 1882, Chicago, IL), executive, moved to Chicago with his parents at age two. After attending Chicago public schools, he matriculated at Beloit College, entered the wholesale grocery business in Chicago, married Jennie Murray, and became a member of the Chicago Board of Trade. The big, energetic, robust Hulbert proved an optimistic civic booster and often said, "I would rather be a lamp post in Chicago than a millionaire in any other city."

In 1875 Hulbert entered baseball as president of the Chicago White Stockings (NA), hoping to build a winning team. He signed many premier players, starting with Albert G. Spalding* of the Boston Red Stockings. Spalding helped persuade Boston stars Cal McVey,* James "Deacon" White,* and Ross Barnes,* along with Philadelphia Athletics stars Adrian Anson* and Ezra Sutton,* to sign secret contracts with Chicago. When the contracts, which violated the NA rule against signing players still under contract, became public knowledge, Hulbert and his signees faced possible expulsion from the NA.

Hulbert took the initiative in organizing a new league. Widespread support for a change already existed because the NA suffered from rumors of corruption, shifting membership, makeshift schedules, weak management, and competitive imbalance. In the fall of 1875, Hulbert and Spalding drafted a proposal for a new league. The St. Louis, Louisville, and Cincinnati clubs quickly accepted Hulbert's plan. He then arranged a meeting on February 2, 1876 in New York, where representatives from New York, Philadelphia, Boston, and Hartford joined the midwestern clubs in adopting Hulbert's proposal for a new league and named it the National League of Professional Base Ball Clubs.

Hulbert's NL constitution shifted control of the professional game from the players to the owners, attempted to assure respectability for the sport, and sought profits for the clubs. To these ends, he established a regular schedule of games, required clubs to maintain order at games, prohibited Sunday games, attempted to abolish gambling and the sale of alcohol in league parks, and restricted NL membership to one club per city. Morgan G. Bulkeley* of Hartford, CT became the NL's first president in a drawing, but Hulbert assumed the helm after the first season.

Hulbert exercised strong leadership during the NL's first few years. He expelled clubs and players that he believed threatened the game's reputation. Besides being NL president, he continued to operate the Chicago club until his death of heart disease in 1882. In the overblown 19th century rhetoric, he was called the "saviour of the game" for organizing the NL, establishing club owners' control of the sport, and assuring the professional game's reputation for honesty. In 1995, the Veterans Committee elected him to the National Baseball Hall of Fame.

BIBLIOGRAPHY: William Hulbert file, National Baseball Library, Cooperstown, NY; Arthur R. Ahrens, "The Chicago National League Champions of 1876," *BRJ* 11 (1982), pp. 84–90; Lee Allen, *The National League Story* (New York, 1961); Glenn Dickey, *The History of National League Baseball Since 1876* (New York, 1979); Eddie Gold, "Hall Would Be Home for Hulbert," *BMR* (1981), pp. 89–90; Brad Herzog, *The Sports 100* (New York, 1995); "How We Got to Where We Are," *Sport* 81 (July 1990), p. 56; Noel Hynd, *The Giants of the Polo Grounds* (New York, 1988); Peter Levine, *A. G. Spalding and the Rise of Baseball* (New York, 1985); Harold Seymour, *Baseball: The Early Years* (New York, 1960); Albert G. Spalding, *America's National Game* (New York, 1911); Robert L. Tiemann and Mark Rucker, eds., *Nineteenth Century Stars* (Kansas City, MO, 1989); Eddie Gold and Art Ahrens, *The Golden Era Cubs, 1876–1940* (Chicago, IL, 1985); Warren Brown, *The Chicago Cubs* (New York, 1946); Jim Enright, *Chicago Cubs* (New York, 1975).

William E. Akin

HUNT, Ronald Kenneth "Ron," "Zeke" (b. February 23, 1941, St. Louis, MO), player, graduated from Ritenor High School in St. Louis, where he starred in baseball and football. The Milwaukee Braves (NL) signed Hunt in 1959 and paid off his parents' home mortgage as part of his bonus. Hunt played third base for McCook, NE (NeSL) in 1959, but moved to second base at Cedar Rapids, IA (3IL) in 1960 and 1961. At Austin, TX the right-hander led TL second basemen in fielding average in 1962, and batted .309. The New York Mets (NL), acquired him from the Milwaukee Braves' organization in the off season.

Hunt started at second base and batted .272 for manager Casey Stengel's * New York Mets in 1963. Sportswriter Maury Allen wrote, "He was a tough-talking, gritty kid who made up in fight what he lacked in finesse. He was to prove to be the first homegrown Mets star." In 1964, Hunt batted .303, became the first New York Met to start on the NL All-Star team, and was named second baseman on the *TSN* 1964 All-Star team. In 1965 he fractured his shoulder in a collision at second base with the St. Louis Cardinals' Phil Gagliano. The 6-foot, 175-pound Hunt hit .288 in 1966 and again made the NL All-Star team.

To his dismay, the New York Mets traded Hunt and outfielder Jim Hickman to the Los Angeles Dodgers (NL) for outfielder Tommy Davis* in November 1966. Hunt played only one season with the Dodgers before being sent in February 1968 to the San Francisco Giants (NL) for catcher Tom Haller.* From 1968 to 1970, Hunt anchored second base for the Giants.

The San Francisco Giants traded Hunt to the Montreal Expos (NL) in December 1970 for first baseman Dave McDonald. Hunt recorded career-highs in games (152) and runs (89) in 1971 and batting average (.309) in 1973 with the Expos. The Montreal Expos sold Hunt to the St. Louis Cardinals (NL) in September 1974. He played briefly with the Cardinals and retired.

An excellent contact hitter, Hunt walked often and was hit by pitches at a record pace. He crowded the plate, wore loose fitting uniforms, and leaned into the pitches. His 243 career hit by pitches remains the NL record, while his 50 hit by pitches in 1971 set the major league single season record. Hunt also holds the major league record for leading a league in hit batsmen the most consecutive seasons with seven from 1968 to 1974. His major league career featured 1,429 hits, 223 doubles, 39 HR, 745 runs, 370 RBI, and a .273 batting average in 1,483 games. He was voted into the Montreal Expos Hall of Fame in 1996.

Hunt and his wife, Jackie, operate a cattle ranch near Wentzville, MO and have three children, Traci, Ronald, Jr., and Rae. In 1985, Hunt, upset at the coaching his son was receiving in American Legion baseball, built a baseball complex at his ranch and started Independent Eagles baseball teams for 14–16-year-old and 16–18-year-old boys. Hunt has drawn players from the U.S., Canada, and France and helped them earn countless college baseball scholarships. Hunt's teams have played across North America and Europe.

BIBLIOGRAPHY: Ron Hunt file, National Baseball Library, Cooperstown, NY; Maury Allen, *The Incredible Mets* (New York, 1969); Jeff Bradley, "The Hunt Club," *SI* 74 (June 17, 1991), p. 22; Darryl Howerton, "Why All the Brawls: A Hunt for Answers," *Sport* 85 (September 1994), p. 21; Ian MacDonald, "Hunt Makes 'Hit' as Expos' MVP," *TSN*, October 16, 1971, p. 37; Frank J. Olmsted, interviews with Seth Stinnett and Patrick Stinnett, March 21, 28, 1997; John Thorn and John B. Holway, *The Pitchers* (New York, 1987); Donald Honig, *The New York Mets* (New York, 1986); Jack Lang and Peter Simon, *The New York Mets* (New York, 1986).

                                                                            Frank J. Olmsted

HUNTER, James Augustus "Catfish" (b. April 8, 1946, Hertford, NC; d. September 9, 1999, Hertford, NC), player, pitched for the Oakland Athletics (AL) and New York Yankees (AL). The fourth son of eight children born to Abbot Hunter and Millie Hunter, he was reared on a farm. Hunter frequently missed elementary school to hunt and fish. He loved sports and starred in football and baseball at Perguimans High School. Upon graduating from high school in 1964, Hunter signed with the Oakland Athletics (AL) for a $50,000 bonus. He spent the 1964 season pitching batting practice and serving in promotional stunts devised by Oakland owner Charles Finley.* In one of these stunts, Satchel Paige,* the colorful pitcher from the black baseball leagues, was pictured in a rocking chair with Hunter sitting on his lap. Finley nicknamed Hunter "Catfish."

On July 27, 1965, the 6-foot, 190-pound, right-handed Hunter pitched his first win in professional ball with the Oakland Athletics and finished his first full season with an 8–8 mark. He made the AL All-Star team in 1966 despite his 9–11 season record. In May 1968, he pitched a perfect game against the Minnesota Twins. After enjoying his first winning season with an 18–14 record in 1970, he reached the 20-game victory plateau in 1971 with a 21–11 mark. In 1974, he was named the Cy Young Award winner and *TSN* Pitcher of the Year with a 25–12 record. The same year, he sued Finley for breach of contract for not paying $50,000 of his $100,000 salary on a deferred basis. Hunter won his case and was declared a free agent, triggering a precedent-setting bidding war for his services. On January 1, 1975, he signed a five-year contract with the New York Yankees (AL) for an estimated $3.75 million.

Hunter pitched for the Yankees until retiring in 1979. His best year with them came in 1975, when he finished 23–14 for his fifth consecutive year with at least 20 victories. His career record with the Athletics and Yankees included 224 wins and 166 losses (.574 winning percentage) with 2,012 strikeouts in 3,449.1 innings pitched and a 3.26 ERA. Hunter compiled a 4–3 mark in six AL Championship Series and a 5–3 mark in six World Series (1972–1974, 1976–1978). He led the AL twice in victories (1974–1975), finished first in winning percentage twice (1972–1973), and led the AL once each in ERA (1974), games started (1970), complete games (1975), and innings pitched (1975).

Hunter's pitching style was controlled and intelligent, although not overpowering. That distinctiveness fostered his success but contributed to some of his pitching problems. His repetitive motion led to great control, but caused him to surrender numerous HR. Hunter was elected to the National Baseball Hall of Fame in January 1987. Married to his high school sweetheart, Helen, he had two children, Todd and Kimberly, and lived on his 230-acre North Carolina farm. He coached Little League and enjoyed hunting and fishing. Doctors diagnosed him with a rare muscle disease called amyotrophic lateral sclerosis in September 1998.

BIBLIOGRAPHY: Jim Hunter file, National Baseball Library, Cooperstown, NY; Roy Blount, Jr., "Opening of the Catfish Season," *SI* 42 (March 17, 1975), p. 56; Peter Bonventre, "Pride of the Yankees," *Newsweek* 84 (March 24, 1975), p. 62; *CB* 36 (1975), pp. 196–199; Murray Chass, "Yankees Sign Up Catfish Hunter in Estimated $3.75 Million Deal," *NYT*, January 1, 1975, p. 1; Gerald Eskenazi, "Millionaire Pitcher James Augustus Hunter," *NYT*, January 1, 1975, p. 12; "Farmer Knows the Market," *NYT Biographical Service* 18 (January 1987), pp. 40–41; Mark Gallagher, *The Yankee Encyclopedia*, vol. 3 (Champaign, IL, 1997); Roy Fimrite, "A City on Pinstripes and Needles," *SI* 42 (April 2, 1975), pp. 24–27; Catfish Hunter and Armen Keteyian, *Catfish; My Life in Baseball* (New York, 1988); J. Anthony Lukas, "The Catfish Enigma," *NYT Magazine* (September 7, 1975), pp. 19–40; Ronald A. Mayer, *Perfect!* (Jefferson, NC, 1991); Bruce Markusen, *Baseball's Last Dynasty* (New York,

1998); Dave Anderson et al., *The Yankees* (New York, 1979); Ted O'Leary, "Time for a Catfish Fry in KC," *SI* 38 (June 25, 1973), pp. 24–26.

                                                                                                    Tony Ladd

HURST, Bruce Vee (b. March 24, 1958, St. George, UT), player, is the son of John T. Hurst and Elizabeth (Bruhn) Hurst and attended Dixie JC, helping his basketball team win the National JC tournament. The Boston Red Sox (AL) selected the 6-foot 3-inch, 219-pound Mormon left-handed pitcher in the first round of the 1976 draft and assigned him to Elmira, NY (NYPL) in 1976, Winter Haven, FL (FSL) in 1977 and 1979, Bristol, CT (EL) in 1978 and 1979, and Pawtucket, RI (IL) in 1980 and 1981.

Hurst briefly pitched with the Boston Red Sox in 1980 and 1981 and started there from 1982 to 1988, compiling an 88–73 overall win–loss mark. He led the Boston Red Sox staff with 15 pickoffs in 1984 and 189 strikeouts the following season. In 1986 Hurst helped the Boston Red Sox capture the AL pennant with a 13–8 overall mark and 2.99 ERA, averaging nearly one strikeout per inning. He recorded a 1–0 mark in his two AL Championship Series starts against the California Angels and defeated the New York Mets twice in the World Series. Hurst won the opening game, 1–0, surrendering four hits and striking out eight batters. He went the distance in a 4–2 Boston Red Sox triumph in Game 5 and also started Game 7 on just three days' rest. In 1987 Hurst triumphed 15 times, was selected to the AL All-Star team, and established a career-best 190 strikeouts, the most ever by a Boston left-hander. His career-high 18 victories the next season helped the Boston Red Sox win the AL East title. He became the second-winningest southpaw in Fenway Park history and compiled 11 victories following Boston losses, but the Oakland A's defeated him twice in the AL Championship Series.

In December 1988, the San Diego Padres (NL) signed Hurst as a free agent. In 1989, Hurst enjoyed a 15–11 slate and career-best 2.69 ERA. He shared the NL lead in complete games (10) and recorded 179 strikeouts, among the best in San Diego Padre history. The Atlanta Braves made only one hit against him on April 10, as 13 batters struck out. The following season, Hurst shared the NL lead in shutouts (4) and hurled 27 straight scoreless innings. He posted at least 11 victories 10 consecutive seasons from 1983 to 1992. In July 1993, the San Diego Padres traded Hurst and Greg Harris to the Colorado Rockies (NL). His major league career ended with the Texas Rangers (AL) in 1994. In 15 major league seasons, Hurst boasted a 145–113 mark and 3.92 ERA with 1,689 strikeouts, 63 pickoffs, and 23 shutouts.

He and his wife, Holly, have two sons, Ryan and Kyle, and one daughter, Jordan, and reside in St. George, UT.

BIBLIOGRAPHY: Bruce Hurst file, National Baseball Library, Cooperstown, NY; *San Diego Padres 1993 Media Guide*; Mike Shatzkin, ed., *The Ballplayers* (New York, 1990); Dan Shaughnessy, *The Curse of the Bambino* (New York, 1990); *TSN Official Baseball*

Register, 1994; Dan Shaughnessy, *One Strike Away* (New York, 1987); Robert Red-mount, *The Red Sox Encyclopedia* (Champaign, IL, 1998).

                                                                    David L. Porter

HUTCHINSON, Frederick Charles "Fred," "Big Bear," "Hutch" (b. August 12, 1919, Seattle, WA; d. November 12, 1964, Bradenton, FL), player and manager, was the son of Dr. J. L. Hutchinson, a physician. Uncertainty about Hutchinson's fastball kept him from getting a contract with a major league baseball organization despite an impressive amateur pitching record. In 1938, he signed with Seattle, WA (PCL) and won 25 games. *TSN* named him Minor League Player of the Year. The Detroit Tigers (AL), who could have signed him right out of high school, purchased his contract for $50,000 and four players. Hutchinson did not enjoy immediate success, however, shuttling between the Detroit Tigers and affiliates in Buffalo, NY (IL) and Toledo, OH (AA) the next three seasons. He remained with the Detroit Tigers long enough to win three games in both 1939 and 1940 and pitched an inning against the Cincinnati Reds in the 1940 World Series. He appeared in just two games with the Detroit Tigers in 1941, both as a pinch hitter, but won 26 games for Buffalo. Hutchinson then enlisted in the U.S. Navy, where he directed athletics and instructed recruits in rifle marksmanship. Hutchinson, who was discharged with the rank of lieutenant commander, married Patricia Finley in April 1943 and had four children, including Rick, Jack, and Patty.

After World War II, Hutchinson, a 6-foot 2-inch, 210-pound right-hander, used his control and assortment of off-speed pitches to win 10 or more games with the Detroit Tigers six consecutive seasons. He peaked with 18 victories in 1947 and 17 in 1950 and pitched in the 1951 All-Star Game. Arm trouble plagued Hutchinson in 1952. He replaced "Red" Rolfe* in July 1952 as manager of the Detroit Tigers, then mired in last place. He ended his pitching career the following season with a 95–71 career win-loss record and 3.73 ERA. As manager, he made progress in rebuilding the Detroit Tigers by adding youngsters Harvey Kuenn* and Al Kaline* to the lineup. The Detroit Tigers, however, did not climb above fifth place. Hutchinson resigned as pilot after the 1954 campaign, when Detroit refused to give him more than a one-year contract. After managing Seattle, WA (PCL) in 1955, he took over the St. Louis Cardinals' (NL) helm. Hutchinson led the St. Louis Cardinals to first-division finishes in 1956 and 1957 and was named NL Manager of the Year in 1957. The St. Louis Cardinals fired him in September 1958 when the club slumped.

On July 9, 1959, Hutchinson was named manager of the seventh-place Cincinnati Reds (NL). By season's end, the Cincinnati Reds, led by slugger Frank Robinson,* had risen to fifth place. Hutchinson enjoyed great success with the Cincinnati Reds. An outstanding handler of pitchers, Hutchinson demanded that his players work hard and insisted that "sweat is a ballplayer's only salvation." A fiery temper led him to smash lightbulbs and clubhouse furniture on several occasions, but he exhibited patience in handling personnel. Players knew that he would treat them fairly. Hutchinson guided the Cincinnati Reds to an NL pennant with a 93–61 record in 1961, the club's first title since 1940. The New York Yankees, however, defeated the Cincinnati Reds in the World Series. The Cincinnati Reds improved with 98 wins the following year, yet trailed both the Los Angeles Dodgers and San Francisco Giants in the standings. Cincinnati slumped in 1963, but Hutchinson added Pete Rose* to the lineup at second base and developed Jim Maloney* into a top pitcher. The Cincinnati Reds contended in 1964 before lung cancer forced Hutchinson to take a leave of absence on August 13. He died three months later. Hutchinson compiled an 830–827 win–loss record in 12 years as a major league manager.

BIBLIOGRAPHY: Fred Hutchinson file, National Baseball Library, Cooperstown, NY; Fred Smith, *995 Tigers* (Detroit, MI, 1981); "Angry Boss of the Reds," *Look 27* (August 27, 1963), pp. 67–69; Cincinnati Reds Public Relations Department, Cincinnati, OH; Lloyd Graybar, phone interview with Gordon Coleman, February 1, 1993; *NYT*, November 13, 1964; William M. Anderson, *The Detroit Tigers* (South Bend, IN, 1996); Thomas Aylesworth and Benton Minks, *The Encyclopedia of Baseball Managers* (New York, 1990); Rob Rains, *The St. Louis Cardinals* (New York, 1992); Bob Broeg and Jerry Vickery, *St. Louis Cardinals Encyclopedia* (Grand Rapids, MI, 1998); Donald Honig, *Cincinnati Reds* (New York, 1992).

                                                                    Lloyd J. Graybar

HUTCHINSON, William Forrest "Wild Bill" (b. December 17, 1859, New Haven, CT; d. March 19, 1926, Kansas City, MO), player, starred for Yale University in baseball as a shortstop and batter, graduating in 1880. Hutchinson, whose father served as a Yale University professor, did postgraduate work before moving to Kansas City, MO to enter the railroad and lumber business. Spurning professional offers, he played amateur baseball until pitching briefly for the Kansas City, MO Unions (WA) in 1884 and hurling for Des Moines, IA (NWL, WA) in 1887 and 1888. Reportedly his $3,800 salary was the highest in the minor leagues. In 1889, the 29-year-old rookie was sold to the Chicago White Stockings (NL). Definitely one of the earliest major leaguers to be a college graduate, Hutchinson was possibly the first such in White Stockings history. Hutchinson won 16 games and lost 17 his 1889 rookie year while striking out 136 batters.

The following three years with the Chicago Colts, this workhorse led the NL in victories (42, 43, and 37), games (including a high of 75), and innings pitched. Hutchinson averaged over 60 complete games per year. His 627 innings pitched in 1892 remains a Chicago record. On May 30, 1890, he won both games of a doubleheader, giving up only three earned runs. His fastball proved his best pitch, as he led the NL with 312 strikeouts in 1892. He had trouble controlling the pitch, however, and averaged over 170 walks per season from 1890 through 1893. Hutchinson also relieved, winning seven games and saving one in 1891, his best season. A better-than-average hitter for a pitcher, he batted .309 in 1894 and recorded a lifetime .216 mark. He belted 12 career HR, one of which on May 8, 1890 hit a horse and carriage in center field, helping the Chicago Colts rally to win, 18–9.

In 1893, the pitching distance was increased to 60-feet 6-inches from 50 feet. Hutchinson, among other pitchers, found it difficult to adjust. He never again recorded a winning record and saw his control problems worsen, with his bases on balls total nearly doubling his strikeouts. Hutchinson, released after a 13–21 season in 1895, failed in a comeback two years later with the St. Louis Browns (NL). The lifelong bachelor worked for many years with the Kansas Southern Railroad. His nine-year career in the major leagues resulted in a 183–163 record with a 3.59 ERA and .529 winning percentage.

BIBLIOGRAPHY: William Hutchinson file, National Baseball Library, Cooperstown, NY; Art Ahrens and Eddie Gold, *Day by Day in Chicago Cubs History* (West Point, NY, 1982); Eddie Gold and Art Ahrens, *The Golden Era Cubs, 1876–1940* (Chicago, IL, 1985); Robert L. Tiemann and Mark Rucker, eds., *Nineteenth Century Stars* (Kansas City, MO, 1989); William Wilbert and William Hageman, *Chicago Cubs: Seasons at the Summit* (Champaign, IL, 1997); Warren Brown, *The Chicago Cubs* (New York, 1946); Jim Enright, *Chicago Cubs* (New York, 1975).

                                                          Duane A. Smith

I

IRVIN, Monford Merrill "Monte" (b. February 25, 1919, Columbia, AL), player, scout, and executive, is the seventh of ten children born to farmer Cupid Irvin and Mary Eliza (Henderson) Irvin. The Irvins moved in 1947 to Orange, NJ, where he earned sixteen varsity letters and won All-State in four sports for East Orange High School. He became perhaps the finest schoolboy athlete in NJ history. Irvin declined a football scholarship to the University of Michigan because his parents could not afford the train fare to Ann Arbor, MI and instead attended Lincoln University in Oxford, PA for two years, majoring in political science.

In 1937 the 6-foot 1-inch, 195-pound Irvin joined the Newark, NJ Eagles (NNL) under the assumed name of Jimmy Nelson. The Eagles, managed by Willie Wells,* included several great baseball players. Irvin began as a shortstop and was named in 1939 to the East All-Star team. Subsequently, he played in four other Negro League All-Star Games (1941, 1946–1948). Irvin performed in both the infield and outfield for Newark and proved an excellent fielder with a tremendous arm. He also displayed fine batting skills, hitting .403 in 1939, .377 in 1940 and .400 in 1941. In 1942, Irvin hit .398 in Mexico. He spent the next three years in the U.S. Army, partly preventing him from being the first or among the first to break the major league color barrier. Irvin was named MVP of the 1946 PRWL and then returned to Newark, where he made NNL MVP by hitting .389 and scored the winning run in the Negro World Series.

Since the breaking of the color barrier killed the Negro Leagues, the Newark Eagles disbanded in 1948. Irvin played winter baseball in Cuba before signing with the New York Giants (NL) in 1949. The 30-year-old Irvin hit .373 with 9 HR and 52 RBI for Jersey City, NJ (IL) in 1949. After faring poorly when called up by the Giants, he was among the first players cut in the spring of 1950. At Jersey City, however, he hit 10 HR, drove in 33 runs, and batted .510 in 18 games. In the second game after being recalled by the Giants, he slugged a grand slam HR. By June, he started in left field and then was moved to first base. For the 1950 season, he hit .299 with 15 HR in 110 games. In 1951, Irvin returned to the outfield and befriended rookie Willie Mays.* Irvin batted over .400 the last six weeks of that season, as the Giants caught the Brooklyn Dodgers to set the stage for Bobby Thomson's* playoff game HR. Although the New York Yankees won the World Series, Irvin hit .458 and stole home in Game 1. During 1951, Irvin batted .312 with 24 HR, led the NL with 121 RBI, and finished third in the MVP balloting.

In 1952, Irvin broke his ankle in spring training. He hit .310 after his return in August, but his speed had diminished. He hit .329 the next year, until reinjuring his ankle in August. Irvin delivered several key hits in the 1954 Giants pennant drive, but his batting average dropped to .262. Although the Giants swept the Cleveland Indians in the World Series, Irvin hit only .222. After batting .253 in 51 games in 1955, he was sent to Minneapolis, MN (AA) and hit .352 in 75 games there. In 1956 Irvin joined the Chicago Cubs (NL), slugging 15 HR and batting .271 in 111 games to finish his playing career. Negro League records suggest that Irvin ranked among the finest players of his era. With the Giants, he also displayed his superior talent at bat and in the field. In eight NL seasons, he batted .293, made 731 hits, 97 doubles, 31 triples, and 99 HR, and knocked in 443 tallies. Irvin also batted a sparkling .394 in two World Series.

Although primarily a baseball player, Irvin owned a business and an apartment building and ran unsuccessfully for the New Jersey State Assembly in 1951. After retiring, he worked for a major brewery in Orange, NJ and frequently spoke at banquets. Irvin scouted for the New York Mets (NL) in 1967 and 1968 and joined the Office of the Commissioner of Baseball in August 1968 as a public relations representative, a job he held for 15 years. He also served on the committee to select deserving Negro League players to the National Baseball Hall of Fame and was chosen for baseball's highest honor in 1973. The Irvins retired to Homosassa, FL.

BIBLIOGRAPHY: Monte Irvin file, National Baseball Library, Cooperstown, NY; Martin Appel, *Yesterday's Heroes* (New York, 1988); Noel Hynd, *The Giants of the Polo Grounds* (New York, 1988); Ray Robinson, *The Home Run Heard 'Round the World* (New York, 1991); Thomas Kiernan, *The Miracle of Coogan's Bluff* (New York, 1975); Eddie Gold and Art Ahrens, *The New Era Cubs, 1941–1985* (Chicago, IL, 1985); Martin Appel and Burt Goldblatt, *Baseball's Best: The Hall of Fame Gallery* (New York, 1977); Anthony J. Connor, *Voices from Cooperstown* (New York, 1982); John Holway, *Voices from the Great Black Baseball Leagues* (New York, 1975); Robert W. Peterson, *Only the Ball Was White* (Englewood Cliffs, NJ, 1970); Donald Honig, *Baseball Between the Lines* (New York, 1976); Monte Irvin and James A. Riley, *Nice Guys Finish First* (New York, 1996); Larry Moffi and Jonathan Kronstadt, *Crossing the Line* (Jefferson, NC, 1994); *The Baseball Encyclopedia*, 10th ed. (New York, 1996); James A.

Riley, *The Biographical Encyclopedia of the Negro Baseball Leagues* (New York, 1994); Donn Rogosin, *Invisible Men: Life in Baseball's Negro Leagues* (New York, 1983); Ken Smith, *Baseball's Hall of Fame* (New York, 1979); Chris Stern, *Where Have They Gone? Baseball Stars* (New York, 1979); Chuck Wills and Pat Wills, *Beyond Home Plate* (Ocala, FL, 1993).

Douglas D. Martin

J

JACKSON, John W. *See* John W. Fowler.

JACKSON, Joseph Jefferson "Joe," "Shoeless Joe" (b. July 16, 1889, Pickens County, SC; d. December 5, 1951, Greenville, SC), player, was the son of George Jackson and Martha Jackson. In the 1910–1920 era, Jackson joined Ty Cobb,* Tris Speaker,* and George Sisler* as the AL's outstanding hitters. He would have joined the others in the National Baseball Hall of Fame, but was one of the eight Chicago White Sox (AL) players who accepted money from gamblers to throw the 1919 World Series to the Cincinnati Reds.

Jackson's role in baseball's greatest scandal was partly related to his background and lack of sophistication. He came from a large, very poor, southern, white family. His parents worked hard picking cotton and at a mill. Jackson, who received no formal education, began mill work at age 13 and soon excelled on the mill's baseball team. Manager Connie Mack* liked Jackson's great natural ability and induced the reluctant Southerner to play for his Philadelphia Athletics (AL) in 1908. Lacking Cobb's fierce competitiveness, Jackson experienced great difficulty adjusting to the urbanized North. From the outset, he reacted awkwardly and defensively because players and fans reminded him about his humble origins. Mack sought to provide him with a teacher to make him literate, but the self-conscious Jackson declined. He quit the team more than once, forcing Mack to release him after the 1909 season. The ever unsettled Jackson relied heavily on his wife, Katherine Wynn. They had no children.

Jackson, a rare natural athlete, resembled Babe Ruth* in classic batting stance, size, strength, and throwing arm. From 1910 to 1915, he compiled several fine batting averages ranging from .327 to .408 for the Cleveland Indians (AL). Financial exigencies forced his sale in 1915 to the Chicago White Sox (AL), owned by miserly Charles A. Comiskey.* At Chicago, Jackson never fully adjusted to his teammates or the owner. He led the AL thrice in triples (1912, 1916, 1920), twice in hits (1912, 1913), and once each in doubles (1913), on-base percentage (1911), slugging percentage (1913), and total bases (1912). Although never winning a batting title, he finished several times among the first five. Despite Jackson's amazing .408 batting average in 1911, Cobb won the AL batting title. Cobb allegedly shook Jackson's confidence to ensure the championship, but Jackson's biographer showed convincingly that the Detroit star consistently led Jackson in the latter part of the season. Jackson's career .356 batting average trails only those of the fabled Cobb and Rogers Hornsby.* In 1,330 games, Jackson made 1,772 hits, 307 doubles, and 168 triples, knocked in 785 runs, and stole 202 bases.

For his role in the 1919 World Series, Commissioner Kenesaw Mountain Landis* barred Jackson from organized baseball for life. Jackson tried unavailingly to be reinstated, winning considerable public sympathy by claiming that he performed at his best in the World Series. He reluctantly accepted $5,000 of gamblers' money and had been promised $20,000. Jackson batted a resounding .375, but made a couple of questionable defensive gaffes. Since surroundings and companions easily influenced Jackson, he may have half-heartedly participated in the "fix." In admitting his involvement before a Chicago grand jury in 1920, he expressed both regret and relief.

When Jackson left the courtroom, a little boy supposedly told him, "Say it ain't so, Joe." Jackson always denied it. His involvement in the scandal resulted partly from his own passivity in bad company. Jackson also greatly resented Comiskey for paying him only $8,000 a year and for criticizing his shipyard job in World War I.

After his expulsion, Jackson lived in his native South Carolina and for several years played intermittent "outlaw" baseball. He invested his baseball earnings in moderately successful small businesses and received slight attention through occasional news items, old fans' sympathy, and rare visits from one-time fellow players. Numerous people regretted that Judge Landis found it necessary to terminate the career of such an outstanding performer.

BIBLIOGRAPHY: Joe Jackson file, National Baseball Library, Cooperstown, NY; Eliot Asinof, *Eight Men Out* (New York, 1963); John Benson et al., *Baseball's Top 100* (Wilton, CT, 1997); Harvey Frommer, *Shoeless Joe and Ragtime Baseball* (Dallas, TX, 1992); Donald Gropman, *Say It Ain't So, Joe!*, rev. ed. (Chicago, IL, 1992); Frederick G. Lieb, *Baseball as I Have Known It* (New York, 1977); Victor Luhrs, *The Great Baseball Mystery* (New York, 1966); *NYT*, December 6, 10, 1959; W. Plummer, "Shoeless Joe: His Legend Survives the Man and Scandal," *PW* 32 (August 7, 1989), pp. 99–101; Wilfred Sheed, "One Man Out . . . Too Long," *GQ* 60 (August 1990), pp. 214–215; John Thorn et al., eds., *Total Indians* (New York, 1996); Dan Gutman, *Baseball Babylon* (New York, 1992); Daniel E. Ginsburg, *The Fix Is In* (Jefferson, NC, 1995); John Phillips, *Who Was Who in Cleveland Baseball 1901–10* (Cabin John, MD, 1989); Franklin Lewis, *The Cleveland Indians* (New York, 1949); Warren Brown, *The*

Chicago White Sox (New York, 1952); Richard Lindberg, *Who's on Third?* (South Bend, IN, 1983); Michael Hoban, "Shoeless Joe in the Hall of Fame?" *BRJ* 27 (1998), pp. 98–100; Bill Veeck, *The Hustler's Handbook* (New York, 1965).

Lowell L. Blaisdell

JACKSON, Lawrence Curtis "Larry" (b. June 2, 1931, Nampa, ID; d. August 28, 1990, Boise, ID), player, was the son of Lawrence L. Jackson and Aldythe Jackson. The 6-foot 1½-inch, 200-pound right-handed pitcher was an all-around athlete at Boise High School and Boise JC. After pitching semiprofessional baseball at Weiser, ID (IOBL), Jackson was signed by the St. Louis Cardinals (NL) in 1951 for a $5,500 bonus. In 1952 at Fresno, CA (CaL), he won 28 of 32 decisions with 351 strikeouts. Although the St. Louis Cardinals were only a .500 team from 1955 to 1962, Jackson compiled a 101–86 record there and established himself as one of the NL's best pitchers. In 1960, he led the NL in games started (38) and innings pitched (282), and took 18 of 31 decisions with a 3.48 ERA.

Jackson was traded to the Chicago Cubs (NL) in October 1962 and pitched effectively there in 1963, compiling a 2.55 ERA. His record plunged to 14–18 that year, however, as Chicago scored only 29 runs in his 18 losses. In 1964 he finished best in the major leagues with a 24–11 mark, although the Cubs finished last in the NL. On June 30 of that year, he came within inches of a no-hitter that was broken up by the Cincinnati Reds' Pete Rose.* He enjoyed an errorless season, tying a major league record by accepting 109 chances flawlessly. Jackson performed his best pitching for the Cubs, which is not reflected in his 52–52 record there.

In April 1966, Chicago sent Jackson to the Philadelphia Phillies (NL) in the Ferguson Jenkins* trade. In the 1968 expansion draft, the Montreal Expos (NL) paid the Phillies $125,000 for his services. Jackson, however, had asked the Phillies to trade him to any western team. When Philadelphia refused to comply, Jackson retired only six wins short of 200 victories. He compiled a 194–183 career win–loss record with a 3.40 ERA and a strikeout-to-walk ratio of better than 2 to 1. The four-time All-Star won the 1963 classic for the NL.

Back in Boise, ID, Jackson entered state politics as executive director of the Idaho Republican Party. He served eight years in the Idaho legislature, made an unsuccessful bid for governor in 1978, and operated an insurance company. Jackson, who married Dinah Ketchen in December 1952, had four children and lived in Garden Valley, north of Boise, ID. He was participating on the Industrial Commission at the time of his death from cancer.

BIBLIOGRAPHY: Larry Jackson file, National Baseball Library, Cooperstown, NY; *The Baseball Encyclopedia*, 10th ed. (New York, 1996); Bob Broeg and Jerry Vickery, *St. Louis Cardinals Encyclopedia* (Grand Rapids, MI, 1998); Jim Enright, *Chicago Cubs* (New York, 1975); Rich Westcott and Frank Bilovsky, *The New Phillies Encyclopedia*

(Philadelphia, PA, 1993); Jerry Gilliland, "Ex-Pro Pitcher Warms to Government," Idaho *Statesman*, January 16, 1977, p. 3-B; Eddie Gold and Art Ahrens, *The New Era Cubs, 1941–1985* (Chicago, IL, 1985); Gene Karst and Martin J. Jones, Jr., eds., *Who's Who in Professional Baseball* (New Rochelle, NY, 1973); *NYT*, August 31, 1990, p. D-16; "Player of the Week," *SI* 21 (September 28, 1964), p. 100; Jim Poore, "Larry Jackson: Baseball's Been Very Very Good to Him," Idaho *Statesman*, May 9, 1982, pp. D-1, 2; John Thorn et al., eds., *Total Baseball*, 5th ed. (New York, 1997).

                                                                    Gaymon L. Bennett

JACKSON, Reginald Martinez "Reggie," "Mr. October" (b. May 18, 1946, Wyncote, PA), player, is the son of semipro baseball player and Philadelphia tailor Martinez Jackson and Clara Jackson. His grandmother on his father's side was of Spanish descent. Jackson grew up in suburban Philadelphia, graduating in 1964 from Cheltenham Township High School and playing four sports there. He received a football scholarship at Arizona State University, but quit after coach Frank Kush (FB) switched him from offense to cornerback. Jackson turned to the university baseball team, which already included Sal Bando* and Rick Monday.* Jackson, an outfielder, became the first collegian to hit a HR run out of Phoenix Stadium. In 1966 *TSN* named him College Player of the Year.

In the first round of the 1966 amateur draft, the New York Mets (NL) bypassed him to pick an obscure catcher. Kansas City Athletics (AL) owner Charles O. Finley* selected Jackson in the second turn of that first round and signed him for a reported $90,000. A 6-foot, 206-pound left-hander, Jackson played with Lewiston, ID (NWL) and Modesto, CA (CaL) in 1966 and Birmingham, AL (SL) in 1967 before joining Kansas City in 1967. He followed the franchise to Oakland, helping the A's win three consecutive World Series (1972–1974). In 1968 he married Hispanic college friend Jeannie Campos, but the marriage ended in divorce after five years. During early 1969, Jackson appeared likely to surpass the then Babe Ruth*-Roger Maris* mark for most HR in a season. Jackson, however, ended the season with 47 round trippers, but that still established an Oakland record. In the 1972 playoff against the Detroit Tigers, Jackson stole home. He was named 1973 AL MVP, having made 32 HR and 117 RBI. Although Jackson tied for the AL HR lead with 36 in 1975, Finley became disenchanted with him and traded the outfielder in April 1976 to the Baltimore Orioles (AL). Within a year of becoming a free agent, Jackson bided his time with the Orioles. The slugger was interested in playing in New York and previously had declared that the city would name a candy bar after him if he played there.

The New York Yankees (AL) selected Jackson in the first-ever free agent draft. He played five stormy years with New York, hitting 144 HR and arguing publicly with Yankee owner George Steinbrenner* and several managers. Yankees captain Thurman Munson* was miffed that Jackson declared himself the team leader. The Reggie Bar also appeared. After a poor performance in strike-torn 1981, Jackson joined the California Angels (AL) in January 1982. He led the AL with 39 HR in 1982. His major league career ended with the Oakland A's in 1987. In 21 major league seasons, Jackson compiled a .262 batting average with 2,584 hits in 2,820 games, hit 463 doubles and 563 HR (6th best lifetime), and drove in 1,702 runs. On the other hand, he struck out 2,597 times and was not considered a good fielder. He had a .490 slugging average and .358 on-base percentage. Jackson appeared in 11 All-Star games and on 10 divisional winners. He led the AL five times in strikeouts, four times in HR, three times in slugging average, twice in runs scored, and once in RBI.

In five World Series, Jackson became "Mr. October." His .755 slugging average in fall classics surpassed all players appearing in a significant number of games. Jackson belted 10 World Series HR, placing fifth on the all-time list. In the deciding game of the 1977 World Series, he hit three HR on three consecutive pitches by Los Angeles Dodgers hurlers Burt Hooton,* Elias Sosa, and Charlie Hough.* Only Babe Ruth* previously had hit three HR in a World Series game. Jackson occasionally works as a sportscaster. He served on a Special Advisory Group for the New York Yankees in 1997 and 1998. In 1993, he was elected to the National Baseball Hall of Fame.

BIBLIOGRAPHY: Reggie Jackson file, National Baseball Library, Cooperstown, NY; Maury Allen, *Mr. October* (New York, 1981); M. Angell, "The Gall of Fame," *SI* 79 (August 2, 1993), pp. 58–64; *CB* (1974), pp. 181–83; Dallas *Times-Herald*, August 27, 1978; Mark Gallagher, *The Yankee Encyclopedia*, vol. 3 (Champaign, IL, 1997); Donald Honig, *The Power Hitters* (St. Louis, MO, 1989); J. Krich, "Reggie Jackson," *Sport* 78 (December 1987), pp. 91ff; W. Leavy, "Reggie Jackson: More than Just a Baseball Superstar," *Ebony* 41 (July 1986), pp. 104ff; John Benson et al., *Baseball's Top 100* (Wilton, CT, 1997); Dave Anderson et al., *The Yankees* (New York, 1979); Bruce Markusen, *Baseball's Last Dynasty* (New York, 1998); Reggie Jackson, *Reggie*, 2d ed. (New York, 1984); David L. Porter, ed., *African-American Sports Greats* (Westport, CT, 1995); Dan Valenti, *Clout: The Top Home Run Hitters in Baseball History* (Lexington, MA, 1989); Robert G. Kelly, *Baseball's Best* (Jefferson, NC, 1988); Bill Madden, "October Then" *Sport* 88 (November 1997), p. 58; Leigh Montville, "The First to Be Free," *SI* 72 (April 16, 1990), pp. 98–108; Rick Reilly, "That's Not All, Folks," *SI* 64 (March 31, 1986), pp. 40–43; D. Remnick, "Reggie at Sunset," *Esquire* 107 (June 1987), pp. 128–130; Robert Ward, "Reggie Jackson in No-Man's Land," *Sport* 64 (June 1977), pp. 89–96.

John David Healy

JACKSON, Travis Calvin "Stonewall" (b. November 2, 1903, Waldo, AR; d. July 27, 1987, Waldo, AR), player, manager, and coach, was the son of William C. Jackson, a grocer, attended public schools in the Waldo area, and graduated in 1923 from Ouachita Baptist College. Of Scotch-English descent, Jackson married Mary Blackman in January 1928 and had one son and one daughter. Jackson began his professional baseball career with Little Rock, AR (SA) in 1921 and the next season became the club's regular short-stop. Little Rock manager Norman "Kid" Elberfield* arranged for New York Giants (NL) manger John McGraw* to see his talented player. Mc-Graw met Jackson in April 1922 and purchased his contract after the Little Rock season ended. Jackson joined the Giants (NL) in September 1922, going hitless in two plate appearances in his initial game. He became the Giants' regular shortstop in 1924 and played with no other major league team in a 15-year career, serving as the Giants' field captain the last five seasons. In 1,656 games, he batted .291 with 1,768 hits, 291 doubles, 135 HR, and 929 RBI.

The 5-foot 10-inch, 160-pound Jackson excelled at shortstop, possessing among the most powerful arms and greatest ranges at the position. He led NL shortstops in assists four times, total chances three times, and fielding average and double plays twice. He suffered recurrent knee ailments, forcing him to shift to third base for the 1935 and 1936 seasons. Jackson, who made the 1934 NL All-Star squad, batted right-handed, proved a great bunter, and demonstrated surprising power.

Writer Arnold Hano captured the essence of the popular, workmanlike Jackson in the following description:

All through his career, one picture remains vivid, and that is the lean, dark-haired young man gliding to his right and rifling out runners at first. But he also ripped his share of base hits into the left-field corner, and he had another trait that nearly equaled his arm. On a team always known for its ability to bunt and squeeze out runs one at a time, Jackson was a master. He could sacrifice with deadly skill; better, he was one of the finest drag-bunters, for base hits, the game ever saw.

Jackson managed the Giants AAA farm team in Jersey City, NJ (IL) in 1937 and 1938 and coached for the New York Giants from 1938–1940 and 1947–1948. Before retiring in 1961, he managed 11 other minor league clubs, mostly in the Milwaukee Braves (NL) farm system. His managerial assignments included Jackson, MS (SEL) in 1946, Tampa, FL (FSL) in 1949, Owensboro, KY (KL) in 1950, Bluefield, WV (ApL) and Hartford, CT (EL) in 1951, Appleton, WI (WSL) in 1952 and 1953, Lawton, OK (SSL) from 1954 to 1957, Midland, TX (SpL) in 1958, Eau Claire, WI (NoL) in 1959, and Quad-City (ML) in 1960. In 1983, Jackson was elected to the National Baseball Hall of Fame.

BIBLIOGRAPHY: Travis Jackson file, National Baseball Library, Cooperstown, NY; Frank Graham, *McGraw of the Giants* (New York, 1944); Arnold Hano, *Greatest Giants of Them All* (New York, 1967); *NYT*, July 29, 1987, p. D-22; Lowell Reiden-baugh, *Baseball's Hall of Fame—Cooperstown* (New York, 1993); Noel Hynd, *The Giants of the Polo Grounds* (New York, 1988); Peter Williams, *When the Giants Were Giants* (Chapel Hill, NC, 1994); Frank Graham, *The New York Giants* (New York,

1952); Charles C. Alexander, *John McGraw* (New York, 1988); Fred Stein, *Under Coogan's Bluff* (Glenshaw, PA, 1978).

Fred Stein

JACOBSON, William Chester "Baby Doll" (b. August 16, 1890, Cable, IL; d. January 16, 1977, Orion, IL), player, was the son of an Illinois farm family. After attending Geneseo High School for three years, the 6-foot 3-inch, 210 pounder began his professional baseball career as an outfielder with Rock Island, IL (SML) in 1909. He played with Mobile, AL (SAL) and Chattanooga, TN (SAL) from 1912 to 1914 and appeared in 71 games for the Detroit Tigers (AL) and St. Louis Browns (AL) in 1915. Female fans at Mobile nicknamed him "Baby Doll" because he was such a dream boat. After a stint at Little Rock, AR (SA) in 1916, he rejoined the St. Louis Browns (AL) in 1917. After U.S. Army service in 1918, Jacobson stayed permanently in the major leagues. From 1919 to 1923, he combined with Ken Williams* and Johnny Tobin* of the Browns to form one of the most prolific outfields in baseball history. For those five years, each member of the outfield trio hit at least .300. The streak ended when Tobin slipped to .299 in 1924. In 1921 they averaged .350, as Williams and Jacobson each hit .352.

In 1922, the outfield propelled the Browns into an AL pennant fight and helped the club finish just one game behind the New York Yankees. Jacobson continued to surpass the .300 mark until being traded in June 1926 to the Boston Red Sox (AL) as part of a three-cornered deal. He finished 1926 at .299 and saw service with the Cleveland Indians (AL) and Philadelphia Athletics (AL) the next year before being sent to Baltimore, MD (IL) in 1928. From 1928 to 1930, "Baby Doll" still hit over .300 in the minor leagues. He hit .304 with Quincy, IL (3IL) in 1930 before retiring to his Illinois farm.

His career statistics included 1,472 games, 1,714 hits, 787 runs scored, 328 doubles, 94 triples, 84 HR, 819 runs knocked in, and a .311 batting average. Jacobson, a superior center fielder, held 13 fielding records at one time and made the most putouts and chances accepted in 1924. The right-handed Jacobson enjoyed his best year at the plate in 1920, when he hit .355 and knocked in 122 runs to place second behind Babe Ruth's* 137. In 1924 his 19 HR put him third behind Ruth and Philadelphia's Joe Hauser.* Jacobson, who married Vurl Cruse on March 6, 1919 and later Ida Rankin on April 5, 1948, had three sons and one daughter.

BIBLIOGRAPHY: William Jacobson file, National Baseball Library, Cooperstown, NY; Bill Borst, *Last in the American League* (St. Louis, MO, 1976); Bill Borst, ed., *Ables to Zoldak*, vol. 2 (St. Louis, MO, 1989); Bill Borst, *Still Last in the American League* (West Bloomfield, MI, 1992); Roger A. Godin, *The 1922 Browns* (Jefferson, NC, 1991); St. Louis *Post Dispatch*, January 18, 1977; Gene Karst and Martin J. Jones, Jr., *Who's Who in Professional Baseball* (New Rochelle, NY, 1973).

William A. Borst

JAMIESON, Charles Devine "Charlie" (b. February 7, 1893, Paterson, NJ; d. October 27, 1969, Paterson, NJ), player, performed for 18 major league seasons. Noted for his speed and spectacular fielding, the left-handed Jamieson on May 23 and June 9, 1928 became the only major league outfielder ever to initiate two triple-plays in one season. He married Edith Van Kirk in November 1913 and had two daughters and one son. The 5-foot 8½-inch, 165-pound Jamieson played from 1912 to 1915 with Buffalo, NY (IL), being used principally as a pitcher and part-time outfielder. The Washington Senators (AL) purchased him on August 15, 1915 for $3,000 and two players. After experiencing two mediocre seasons with the Senators as a pitcher–outfielder, he was waived in July 1917 to the Philadelphia Athletics (AL). He performed poorly with the Athletics in 1917 and 1918 and was dealt in March 1919 with Larry Gardner* and Elmer Myers to the Cleveland Indians (AL) for Bobby Roth.

At age 27, Jamieson blossomed into a star outfielder with the Indians. Although sharing duties in left field in 1920, he played a central role in helping Cleveland win its first AL pennant and world championship. The regular left fielder for the next decade, he enjoyed his highest batting averages in 1922 (.323), 1923 (.345), and 1924 (.359). Jamieson led American Leaguers in hits in 1923 (222), averaged 206 hits for each of the three seasons, and compiled a lifetime .303 batting average. In 1,779 games, he made 1,990 hits and 322 doubles, scored 1,062 runs, and stole 131 bases. He also pitched in 13 major league games, winning two of three decisions.

Jamieson's speed was reflected in his stolen base figures. Between 1922 and 1925, he stole 68 bases. His speed and hustle enabled him to lead the AL in singles several years. He often tricked opponents by bunting the ball rather solidly down the first base line and shielding it between his feet while dashing down the line. Jamieson, a superb, speedy outfielder, often made incredible diving catches, turned two or three somersaults, and landed on his feet prepared to throw. Blessed with a strong arm, he led all AL outfielders in 1928 with 22 assists. Veteran baseball writer Henry P. Edwards considered Jamieson the second best fielding left fielder behind Hugh Duffy* in the AL's first 30 years. After Cleveland released him in 1932, Jamieson spent his final season as a utility player with Jersey City, NJ (IL) in 1933.

BIBLIOGRAPHY: Charles Jamieson file, National Baseball Library, Cooperstown, NY; Cleveland *News*, 1931–1932; Cleveland *Plain Dealer*, January 1931, March 16, 1932; S. Crosby, "Charles Jamieson of the World's Champions," *BM* 36 (May 1926), pp. 549–550; Franklin Lewis, *The Cleveland Indians* (New York, 1949); Craig Carter, ed., *TSN Daguerreotypes*, 8th ed. (St. Louis, MO, 1990); *TSN*, September 11, 1924, November 8, 1969; "Why It Pays to Hustle: Interview with Charles Jamieson," *BM* 36 (May 1926), pp. 549–550; Mike Sowell, *The Pitch That Killed* (New York, 1989).
                                                                      Eugene Murdock

JANSEN, Lawrence Joseph "Larry" (b. July 16, 1920, Verboort, OR), player and coach, is one of eight children of Albert Jansen, a farmer, and Dora

(Van Dyke) Jansen. Jansen, who grew up on a farm, usually played shortstop in high school and sandlot baseball, but impressed scouts as a natural pitcher. Jansen declined to sign with the San Francisco, CA Seals (PCL) in 1939, but inked a contract with the Boston Red Sox (AL). Commissioner Kenesaw Mountain Landis* invalidated his contract when the Boston Red Sox failed to assign Jansen to a minor league team as the 1940 season neared. Jansen signed with the San Francisco Seals and was sent to Salt Lake City, UT (PrL), where he won 20 games. He pitched for the San Francisco Seals the next two years, but remained out of organized baseball in 1943 and 1944 to work on the family farm during World War II. After returning to the Seals late in the 1945 campaign, he won 30 games in 1946.

The 6-foot 2-inch, 190-pound right-hander joined the New York Giants in 1947, winning 21 games and leading the NL with an .808 winning percentage. The New York Giants tied the major league HR record but proved weak on the mound. As the New York Giants rebuilt to feature speed and defense, Jansen remained a stellar pitcher. He relied on an outstanding curve and superb control that enabled him to spot the ball on the corners of the plate. The highlight of his major league career came in the 1950 All-Star Game, which the NL won in an extra-inning thriller. Jansen hurled five innings, yielding only one hit and striking out six batters. In 1951, he won the final game of the regular season to clinch a first-place tie and relieved in the third, deciding playoff game with the Brooklyn Dodgers. He pitched a scoreless ninth inning and was credited with the victory on Bobby Thomson's* dramatic HR. Jansen pitched well, but lost the second game of the World Series against the New York Yankees. The Yankees shelled him in a fifth-game start.

Jansen began to lose his effectiveness by 1952 and did not play a significant role when the New York Giants won the World Series in 1954. He served as a pitcher–coach for the Seattle, WA Rainiers (PCL) in 1955 and returned to the major leagues the following year, when he won two games for the Cincinnati Reds (NL). After four seasons in the PCL as a pitcher and coach for Seattle and Portland, OR, Jansen coached for the San Francisco Giants from 1961 through 1971 and tutored Juan Marichal* and Gaylord Perry* at the start of their splendid careers. He spent the 1972 and 1973 seasons as a pitching coach with the Chicago Cubs before retiring to spend more time with his family. He later coached baseball at Pacific University. Jansen, who married Eileen Vandehey in August 1939, has 10 children.

In nine major league seasons, Jansen won 122 games, lost 89 decisions, compiled a 3.58 ERA, and hurled 17 shutouts. His best years were 1951 when he tied teammate Sal Maglie* for the NL lead in wins and 1950 when he hurled 5 shutouts to lead the NL.

BIBLIOGRAPHY: Larry Jansen file, National Baseball Library, Cooperstown, NY; Brent P. Kelley, *Baseball Stars of the 1950s* (Jefferson, NC, 1992); Thomas Kiernan, *The Miracle at Coogan's Bluff* (New York, 1974); Frank Graham, *The New York Giants* (New York, 1952); Rich Marazzi, "The Giants Swept the Indians in a Classic World

Series," *SCD* 21 (October 28, 1994), pp. 150–151; Noel Hynd, *The Giants of the Polo Grounds* (New York, 1988); Ray Robinson, *The Home Run Heard 'Round the World* (New York, 1991); Tom Meany, *Baseball's Greatest Pitchers* (New York, 1951); Joe Reichler, ed., *Inside the Majors* (New York, 1952).

Lloyd J. Graybar

JEFFERIES, Gregory Scott "Gregg" (b. August 1, 1967, Burlingame, CA), player, is a 5-foot 10-inch, 185-pound infielder/outfielder who throws right-handed and switch hits. He graduated in 1985 from Serra High School in San Mateo, CA, where he made All-State in football and baseball. Jefferies married Melanie Kouns and has one son, Jacob.

The New York Mets (NL) selected Jefferies in the first round of the 1985 free-agent draft. He split his first professional baseball season with Kings-port, TN (ApL) and Columbia, SC (SAL), batting .343 at Kingsport and being named ApL Player of the Year. In 1986 Jefferies started for Columbia, Lynchburg, VA (CrL), and Jackson, MS (TL), earning *BA* Minor League Player of the Year honors. He led the CrL in batting (.354) and slugging percentage (.549), garnering league MVP accolades. The following season, Jefferies batted .367 at Jackson, was chosen TL MVP, and repeated as *BA* Minor League Player of the Year. After playing six games for the New York Mets in 1987, he joined Tidewater, VA (IL) in 1988 and was named *BA* Minor League Player of the Decade. Recalled by the New York Mets in August 1988, Jefferies batted .321 in 29 games. He played in the NL Championship Series against the Los Angeles Dodgers and collected nine hits, the most ever by a rookie. Jefferies played three full seasons (1989–1991) with the New York Mets as a second baseman and third baseman. His best year with the Mets came in 1990, when he batted .283, scored a career-high 96 runs, collected 171 hits, led the NL with 40 doubles, hit 15 HR, and drove in 68 runs.

In December 1991, the New York Mets traded Jefferies to the Kansas City Royals (AL). He spent one season there, posting a .285 batting average. The Royals sent him to the St. Louis Cardinals (NL) in February 1993. Upon being moved to first base, Jefferies in 1993 established career-highs in batting average (.342), hits (186), HR (16), RBI (83), walks (62), and stolen bases (46). The following season, he led the Cardinals with a .325 batting average and made the NL All-Star team for the second time. Granted free-agency in 1994, Jefferies signed with the Philadelphia Phillies (NL). He played there from 1995 to 1998 with the exception of a rehabilitation as-signment to Scranton/Wilkes-Barre, PA (IL). Used as a first baseman/out-fielder by the Philadelphia Phillies, Jefferies batted .306 in 1995, .292 in 1996, and .256 in 1997. After Jefferies batted .297 with Philadelphia in 1998, the Anaheim Angels (AL) acquired him in August 1998. He hit .347 in 19 games, but Anaheim missed the 1998 playoffs. In December 1998, he joined the Detroit Tigers (AL) as a free agent.

In 12 major league seasons through 1999, Jefferies has batted .289, scored 743 runs, and made 1,554 base hits in 1,424 games. He has made 292 doubles, 27 triples, and 124 HR, produced 649 RBI, and recorded 457 walks, 338 strikeouts, and 196 stolen bases.

BIBLIOGRAPHY: Gregg Jefferies file, National Baseball Library, Cooperstown, NY; John Garrity, "Sweet Swinger," *SI* 81 (July 18, 1994), pp. 50–53; Jill Lieber, "Waiting to Splash Down," *SI* 68 (March 21, 1988), pp. 42–45; *Philadelphia Phillies Media Guide*, 1998; *TSN Official Baseball Register*, 1998; Bob Broeg and Jerry Vickery, *St. Louis Cardinals Encyclopedia* (Grand Rapids, MI, 1998).

John L. Evers

JENKINS, Ferguson Arthur "Fergie" (b. December 13, 1943, Chatham, Canada), player and coach, rejected a professional hockey offer to enter professional baseball. He is the son of Ferguson Holmes Jenkins, a chef, and Delores Louise Jenkins. Jenkins sang in musical competitions as a youth and developed poise, which later aided his success on the mound. He played hockey for a Junior B affiliate of the Montreal Canadiens (NHL) and starred in high school basketball for Chatham, later barnstorming with the Harlem Globetrotters. The limited Ontario schedule restricted his baseball starts to seven or eight in each of three amateur seasons. Jenkins pitched in the Philadelphia Phillies (NL) minor league system at Miami, FL (FSL), Chattanooga, TN (SL), and Little Rock, AR (AA), before reaching the major leagues in 1965. After being traded to the Chicago Cubs (NL) in April 1966, Jenkins blossomed into a consistent winner. He led the NL in complete games (20) in 1967 and strikeouts (273) in 1969.

Jenkins enjoyed six consecutive 20-game seasons from 1967 to 1972, recording an NL-leading 24 victories in 1971. The 6-foot 5-inch, 205-pound right-hander proved to be a workhorse for the Cubs, averaging over 300 innings and 200 strikeouts per season. He won the NL Cy Young Award and was named *TSN* NL Pitcher of the Year in 1971, leading the NL in victories, games started and completed, and innings pitched. Such success did not always mark his career, as Jenkins in 1968 tied a major league record by losing five 1–0 games. No Cubs pitcher demonstrated more durability in the post–World War II era. He completed 11 straight starts in 1972 and averaged over 20 starts per year from 1967 to 1972.

After finishing with a 14–16 win–loss mark in 1973, Jenkins was dealt that October to the Texas Rangers (AL) for Bill Madlock* in a trade that benefited both clubs. The next year, he won a career-high 25 games, led the AL in victories and had 29 complete games, and won the Comeback Player of the Year Award. In November 1975, Texas traded him to the Boston Red Sox (AL). The Texas Rangers reacquired him in December 1977. Jenkins became one of only four pitchers to win 100 games in both leagues. After returning to the Chicago Cubs in December 1981, he concluded his major league career in 1983 with a 284–226 composite win–loss record and 3,192 strikeouts and just 997 walks in 4,500.2 innings. Jenkins was selected to the NL All-Star team three times. In 1985, he was defeated in an election to Ontario's provincial parliament. Four years later, he compiled a 7–6 record for the Winter Haven, FL Super Sox (SPBA).

No other pitcher in baseball history struck out over 3,000 hitters and walked under 1,000 batters. Besides enjoying a career 3.34 ERA, the good fielder and hitter belted 13 HR, knocked in 85 runs, and pinch-hit twice in the AL. He and his wife, Katherine, had three children before her death in January 1991 from injuries sustained in an automobile accident. In 1991, the National Baseball Hall of Fame inducted him into membership. He coached for the Chicago Cubs in 1995 and 1996 and trains horses on a ranch in Guthrie, OK.

BIBLIOGRAPHY: Ferguson Jenkins file, National Baseball Library, Cooperstown, NY; Art Ahrens and Eddie Gold, *Day by Day in Chicago Cubs History* (West Point, NY, 1982); Eddie Gold and Art Ahrens, *The New Era Cubs, 1941–1985* (Chicago, IL, 1985); E. L. Greenspan and G. Jonas, "The Case for the Defense," *MacLeans* 100 (October 19, 1987), pp. 48–50ff; *1984 Chicago Cubs Media Guide*; William Humbar, "Ferguson Jenkins, CM, Comes to Cooperstown," *BRJ* 20 (1991), pp. 12–13; *NYT Biographical Service* 24 (January 1993), pp. 14–17; Robert Redmount, *The Red Sox Encyclopedia* (Champaign, IL, 1998); Ken Young, *Cy Young Award Winners* (New York, 1994); David L. Porter, interview with Ferguson Jenkins, Des Moines, IA, October 26, 1991; David L. Porter, ed., *African-American Sports Greats* (Westport, CT, 1995); Paul Post, "Hall of Fame Hurler True-Blue to Beloved Cubs," *SCD* 24 (September 5, 1997), pp. 140–141; D. Whitford, "Glory Amid Grief," *SI* 75 (July 15, 1991), pp. 54–56; Jim Enright, *The Chicago Cubs* (New York, 1975); Phil Rogers, *The Impossible Takes a Little Longer* (Dallas, TX, 1991).

Duane A. Smith

JENNINGS, Hugh Ambrose "Hughie," "Ee-Yah" (b. April 2, 1869, Pittston, PA: d. February 1, 1928, Scranton, PA), player, coach, and manager, grew up in the eastern Pennsylvania coal mining region, where his Irish immigrant father struggled in the mines to support his family. At about age 12, Jennings left school and worked in the mines as a breaker boy on the coal chutes for 90 cents a day. He soon made $5 a game playing semiprofessional baseball on Sundays. In 1890, he entered professional baseball with Allentown, PA (EIL). His hitting, base stealing, and deft infield play attracted the attention of a scout for the major league Louisville, KY Colonels (AA) team. In 1891 Jennings joined Louisville for 90 games, hitting a promising .292 average. The next year, he slumped to .222 against stronger pitching in the newly reorganized twelve-team NL and was sold in 1893 to the Baltimore Orioles (NL).

Jennings excelled at Baltimore under manager and part-owner Ned Hanlon.* Featuring the talented, colorful third baseman John McGraw,* catcher Wilbert Robinson,* and outfielders Willie Keeler* and Joe Kelley,* the Orioles from 1894 to 1896 won three straight NL pennants. Jennings, captain and right-hand hitting shortstop, became one of that great team's mainstays, hitting .335, .386, and .401 in the three NL pennant-winning seasons and stealing an aggregate 160 bases. Although the Orioles finished second to Boston in 1897, Jennings hit an impressive .355 and stole 60 times. A typical Oriole, the 5-foot 8½-inch, 165-pound Jennings was hot-tempered and fiercely competitive. He crowded the plate and dared pitchers to throw at him, being hit 49 times in 1896. The next year, he missed the last part of the season with a skull fracture from an errant pitch.

Following the 1898 season, Hanlon became manager and part-owner of the Brooklyn Superbas (NL) and took Jennings, Keeler, and Kelley with him. Although he hurt his arm, Jennings still played regularly at first base on the Superbas 1899–1900 champions. After being sold to Philadelphia (NL) in February 1901, Jennings became a part-time infielder–outfielder for the Phillies. He returned to the Brooklyn Superbas (NL) briefly early in 1903 and then managed Baltimore, MD (EL). During his major league career, Jennings compiled a .311 batting average with 1,527 hits, 232 doubles, and 359 stolen bases. Jennings directed Baltimore to four successive first division finishes and played part-time in the infield. After the 1906 season, Detroit (AL) signed him as a player and manager.

From 1907 to 1920, Jennings ranked among baseball's most colorful managers. By stamping his feet, clawing handfuls of grass, and yelling his ear-splitting "Ee-yah" from the coaching box, he entertained AL fans. Sparked by the incomparable Ty Cobb,* sturdy Sam Crawford,* and strong pitching from the likes of Bill Donovan* and George Mullin,* Jennings' Tigers won three consecutive AL pennants and lost three World Series in his first three seasons (1907–1909). Otherwise, his Tigers finished second twice, third twice, fourth three times, sixth twice, and seventh twice. Jennings handled his players firmly except for the thin-skinned, volatile Cobb, whom he allowed considerable freedom. The often sarcastic, tempestuous Jennings became increasingly unpopular with Detroit's players. After a dreary seventh place finish in 1920, he yielded the managerial job to Cobb.

Jennings, who had earned a law degree from Cornell University more than a decade earlier, practiced law with his brother at Scranton, PA. In 1921 he joined the New York Giants (NL) as coach under his old Orioles teammate, the brilliantly successful John McGraw. From 1921 to 1924, Jennings picked up World Series shares with the Giants. He managed the ballclub in 1925, when McGraw was ill. After that grueling year, Jennings suffered both a nervous collapse and the onset of physical decline. At an Asheville, NC, sanitarium, physicians discovered that he had tuberculosis. He died of spinal meningitis at his Scranton home, leaving his wife, Nora (O'Boyle) Jennings, and one married daughter. In 1945 the Veterans Committee of the BWAA selected the outstanding player–manager to the National Baseball Hall of Fame.

BIBLIOGRAPHY: Hugh Jennings file, National Baseball Library, Cooperstown, NY; Thomas Aylesworth and Benton Minks, *The Encyclopedia of Baseball Managers* (New York, 1990); Charles C. Alexander, *Ty Cobb* (New York, 1984); "Hugh Jennings: Why His Team Wins," *Outing* 54 (August 1909), pp. 559–560; Frederick Ivor-Campbell et al., eds., *Baseball's First Stars* (Cleveland, OH, 1996); James H. Bready, *Baseball in Baltimore* (Baltimore, MD, 1998); Charles C. Alexander, *McGraw* (New York, 1988); William M. Anderson, *The Detroit Tigers* (South Bend, IN, 1996); Richard Bak, *A Place for Summer* (Detroit, MI, 1998); Richard Bak, *Ty Cobb: His Tumultuous Life and Times* (Dallas, TX, 1994); Frederick G. Lieb, *The Detroit Tigers* (New York, 1946); Craig Carter, ed., *TSN Daguerreotypes*, 8th ed. (St. Louis, MO, 1990); *TSN*, February 9, 1928.

Charles C. Alexander

JENSEN, Jack Eugene "Jackie," "Golden Boy" (b. March 9, 1927, San Francisco, CA; d. July 14, 1982, Charlottesville, VA), athlete and baseball manager, was nicknamed "Golden Boy." He was married on October 16, 1949, to former U.S. Olympic diving star, Zoe Ann Olsen, in Oakland, CA and had three children, Jan, Jon, and Jay, before their divorce. Jensen attended the University of California at Berkeley, where he was selected an All-America in both football and baseball.

By age 25, the 5-foot 11-inch, 195 pounder had tasted a sports smorgasbord that may never be repeated and remains the only athlete ever to appear in the Rose Bowl and East–West Shrine football games, the World Series, and the Major League All-Star baseball game. Besides having an outstanding college football career, Jensen starred as a freshman in the NCAA College Baseball World Series and pitched and batted California to the NCAA title in 1947 against Yale University. Jensen skipped his senior year in college to sign a professional baseball contract with the Oakland, CA Oaks (PCL) in 1949 for $75,000. In 1950, he made his major league debut with the New York Yankees (AL) on opening day against the Boston Red Sox by pinch-running for Johnny Mize.*

Jensen was billed as heir apparent to 37-year-old Joe DiMaggio,* but he was traded in May 1952 to the Washington Senators (AL) for Irv Noren. Manager Casey Stengel* often called the trade one of his biggest mistakes. In December 1953, Washington traded Jensen to the Boston Red Sox (AL) for Maurice McDermott and Tom Umphlett. He batted clean-up following National Baseball Hall of Famer Ted Williams* and played in the same outfield with Jimmy Piersall.* The trio formed one of the best hitting outfields in the major leagues in the 1950s. A right-handed batter and thrower, he possessed one of the strongest arms in the major leagues. Jensen, who led the AL three times in RBI (1955, 1958, 1959) and once in stolen bases (1954), knocked in 667 wins from 1954 through 1959 to pace the major leagues. His slugging percentage during that time sparkled at .491. A year after winning the AL MVP award in 1958 with a .286 batting average and

122 RBI, Jensen quit baseball at age 32 to help save his skidding marriage and because of his extraordinary fear of flying. After sitting out the 1960 season, he returned to the Boston Red Sox (AL) in 1961 and then retired permanently as a player. His eleven-year major league totals included a .279 batting average, 143 stolen bases, 259 doubles, 199 HR, 929 RBI, and .460 slugging percentage. He played in the All-Star games in 1953, 1955, and 1958 and made one unsuccessful plate appearance in the World Series with the New York Yankees against the Philadelphia Phillies in 1950.

Jensen coached baseball at the University of Nevada and at his Alma Mater and also managed one year in the Boston Red Sox organization at Jamestown, NY (NYPL). In 1968 he married Katherine Cortesi, former illustrator and assistant editor at *Harper's Bazaar* in New York. Following his coaching stint at California-Berkeley, he moved to Scottsville, VA and operated a Christmas tree farm. Jensen maintained his interest in baseball, helping coach at Fork Union Military Academy.

BIBLIOGRAPHY: Jackie Jensen file, National Baseball Library, Cooperstown, NY; *The Baseball Encyclopedia*, 10th ed. (New York, 1996); Al Hirshberg, *The Jackie Jensen Story* (New York, 1961); Al Hirshberg, "My Ambition Is to Quit," *SEP* 231 (April 4, 1959), pp. 31–44; Al Hirshberg, "Why Jackie Jensen Is Coming Back," *Sport* 31 (February 1961), pp. 20–21, 66–68; Robert Redmount, *The Red Sox Encyclopedia* (Champaign, IL, 1998), Howard Liss, *The Boston Red Sox* (New York, 1982); Peter Golenbock, *Fenway* (New York, 1992); *NYT*, November 21, 1958; *TSN*, September 18, 1957, p. 7; Rich Westcott, *Diamond Greats* (Westport, CT, 1988).

Albert J. Figone

JETHROE, Samuel "Sam," "Jet" (b. January 20, 1918, East St. Louis, IL), player, is the son of farmer Albert Jethroe and domestic worker Janie Jethroe. After graduating from Lincoln High School, Jethroe played semiprofessional ball with the East St. Louis Colts and St. Louis Giants. He joined the Cincinnati Buckeyes (NAL) in 1942 as an outfielder and achieved immediate success by leading the NAL in batting average, runs scored, doubles, triples, stolen bases, and base hits. He married Elsie Allen on October 5, 1942 and has one daughter, Gloria. After moving with the Buckeyes to Cleveland in 1943, he led the NAL in hitting in 1944 (.353) and 1945 (.393) and paced the Buckeyes to a World Series sweep of the Homestead Grays in 1945. Jethroe tried out with the Boston Red Sox (AL) on April 16, 1945, but was not signed. He played winter ball in Cuba in 1947–1948 and 1948–1949, leading the CUWL in stolen bases both years.

The 6-foot 1-inch, 178-pound Jethroe broke into organized baseball in midseason 1948, when the Buckeyes sold him to the Brooklyn Dodgers (NL). At Montreal, Canada (IL), the switch-hitting Jethroe batted .322 and stole 18 bases in 76 games. The next season, he batted .326, slugged 17 HR, scored an IL high 154 runs, and stole an IL record 89 bases. Reputedly among the fastest men ever to play organized baseball, Jethroe was sold to the Boston Braves (NL) for a reported $100,000 and became the team's first black player in 1950. He earned the BBWAA Rookie of the Year honors by hitting .273, slugging 18 HR, and leading the NL in stolen bases with 35. Nicknamed "Jet," he in 1951 hit 18 HR, batted .280, and again led the NL in stolen bases with 35. Poor eyesight contributed to his sub-par defensive skills and low .232 batting average in 1952, causing him to be relegated to the minor leagues. He appeared briefly with the Pittsburgh Pirates (NL) in 1954. During his major league career, Jethroe batted .261 with 460 hits, 49 HR, 181 RBI, and 98 stolen bases. He played with Toledo, OH (AA) in 1953 and with Toronto, Canada (IL) from 1954 to his retirement in 1958. Jethroe, who performed in Cuba in 1954–1955, later participated in amateur ball and operated a bar and restaurant in Erie, PA.

Among the pioneers integrating major league baseball, Jethroe helped reestablish the stolen base as an offensive weapon. A double threat with his power and speed, he bridged the gap between the one-dimensional HR hitters of the 1930s and 1940s and today's complete players.

In July 1994, Jethroe filed a lawsuit against the MLPA alleging that he had been denied a pension illegally. He claimed that his civil rights had been violated because of the pension requirement that a player spend four years in the major leagues. His suit maintained that the union policy treated unfairly players who began their baseball careers before integration and asked that players be credited with compensatory time in the Negro or minor leagues.

BIBLIOGRAPHY: Sam Jethroe file, National Baseball Library, Cooperstown, NY; Bob Ajemian, "$100,000 Jethroe May Be Flop in Outfield," TSN, March 29, 1950; Terry A. Baxter, correspondence with Jorge Figueroda, 1984, Cuban League statistics, Terry A. Baxter Collection, Cedar Rapids, IA; Terry A. Baxter, correspondence with David Rutledge, 1984, Terry A. Baxter Collection, Cedar Rapids, IA; Terry A. Baxter, telephone interview with Monte Irvin, 1984; Terry A. Baxter, telephone interview with Sam Jethroe, 1984; Cy Kritzer, "Bisons Walk Pitcher to Slow Up Royals' Base Rocket, Jethroe," TSN, July 27, 1949; Cy Kritzer and Lloyd McGowan, "Jethroe Ready for Jump to Stardom?" TSN, November 16, 1949; Rich Marazzi, "Sam Jethroe," SCD 21 (November 11, 1994), pp. 110–111; Lloyd McGowan, "Royals' Jet-Propelled Jethroe Sprints Toward New International League Theft Record," TSN, June 29, 1949; Larry Moffi and Jonathan Kronstadt, Crossing the Line (Jefferson, NC, 1994); Gerry Moore, "Jethroe Recalls '45 Tryout by Red Sox," TSN, November 23, 1949; Joseph M. Overfield, "Richards and Jethroe," BRJ 16 (1987), pp. 33–35; Robert W. Peterson, Only the Ball Was White (Englewood Cliffs, NJ, 1970); The Baseball Encyclopedia, 10th ed. (New York, 1996); James A. Riley, The All-Time All-Stars of Black Baseball (Cocoa, FL, 1983); James A. Riley, Biographical Encyclopedia of the Negro Baseball Leagues (New York, 1994); Donn Rogosin, Invisible Men: Life in Baseball's Negro Leagues (New York, 1983); TSN Official Baseball Guide, 1954; TSN Baseball Questionnaire, December 22, 1949; Jules Tygiel, Baseball's Great Experiment (New York, 1983); Larry Whiteside, "The First to Play, Jethroe Came to Braves, But Sox Had First Crack," Boston Sunday Globe, July 22, 1979.

                                                                            Terry A. Baxter

JOCHUM, Betsy "Sockum" (b. February 8, 1921, Cincinnati, OH), player, is the daughter of Hungarian-German parents. Her father worked as a carpenter and cabinetmaker. Jochum began playing sandlot baseball at age eight and organized softball at age 12. After graduating from high school, Jochum was employed in a meat packing house and played softball on the company team in the Cincinnati League. The team participated in several national softball tournaments, including Chicago, IL. The 5-foot 7-inch, 140-pound Jochum competed in National AAU throwing contests, winning a championship medal in 1941. She also attended Cincinnati Business School.

Philip K. Wrigley* scouts invited Jochum to try out in Cincinnati when the AAGPBL was forming. Dottie Kamenshek* and Jochum were the only two of six selected in Cincinnati and travelled to Wrigley Field in Chicago for the final selection process. Jochum played six AAGPBL seasons from 1943 through 1948 as an outfielder, first baseman and pitcher, with the South Bend, IN Blue Sox. In her rookie season, she hit .273 and led the AAGPBL in at-bats (439), hits (120), singles (100), and doubles (12). Her defensive skills nearly equalled her offensive prowess. Her best season came in 1944, when she led the AAGPBL with a .296 batting average, stole 127 bases, and scored 72 runs in 112 games. Jochum also led the AAGPBL with 128 hits and 120 singles. Jochum recorded the fewest strikeouts in 1946, fanning only 10 times in nearly 450 plate appearances. That year, she also attained personal highs in total bases (316) and RBI (63). Her batting average steadily declined thereafter. For her career, Jochum batted .246, produced 232 RBI, stole 358 bases, and scored 307 runs in 645 games. She struck out only 104 times in over 2,600 plate appearances.

In her final season, Jochum tried pitching and finished 14–13 in 215 innings with a sparkling 1.51 ERA. South Bend boasted stars Lois Florreich,* Dottie Schroeder,* and Rose Gacioch and fielded some strong winning teams during her years there, but never won a regular season or playoff title. She quit the AAGPBL after the 1948 season, when Peoria, IL acquired her in a trade. She did not want to leave South Bend.

Jochum earned a Bachelor's degree in physical education and a Master's degree from Indiana University. She taught physical education in South Bend for 25 years and participated in golf, bowling, and the Run Jane Run Exhibition Games. The South Bend resident assisted in gathering and sorting memorabilia for the Northern Indiana Historical Society.

BIBLIOGRAPHY: Barbara Gregorich, *Women at Play* (San Diego, CA, 1993); W. C. Madden, *The Women of the All-American Girls Professional Baseball League* (Jefferson, NC, 1997); AAGPBL files, Northern Indiana Historical Society, South Bend, IN.

Dennis S. Clark

JOHN, Thomas Edward "Tommy" (b. May 22, 1943, Terre Haute, IN), player, is the son of utility employee Thomas John and Ruth John. He played basketball and baseball at Terre Haute Gerstmeyer High School and was offered numerous college basketball scholarships. In 1961, the pitcher signed as a free agent with the Cleveland Indians (AL) for a reported $40,000 bonus. After beginning his professional baseball career in 1961 at Dubuque, IA (ML), he pitched for Charleston, WV (EL), Jacksonville, FL (IL), and Portland, OR (PCL). After joining Cleveland in 1963, John in January 1965 was traded to the Chicago White Sox (AL). He won 82 games and lost 80 decisions there through the 1971 season and led the AL twice in shutouts. Between seasons, he attended Indiana State University. He married Sally Simmons in July 1970 and has four children, Tommy, Travis, Tami, and Taylor.

On December 2, 1971, John was traded to the Los Angeles Dodgers (NL). The talented 6-foot 3-inch, 190-pound southpaw enjoyed outstanding success there, winning 87 games and losing 42 contests through the 1978 campaign. He pitched in three World Series games in 1977–1978 for the Dodgers, winning one and losing one. Midway through the 1974 season, he suffered torn ligaments in his pitching arm and underwent the first ligament transplant surgery. Upon returning to the pitching mound in 1976, John won 10 of 20 decisions, received the Fred Hutchinson Award for his courageous effort, and was voted Comeback Player of the Year. After being granted free agency in November 1978, he signed with the New York Yankees (AL). He won 62 games and lost 36 decisions through August 1982, and was credited with one victory in the 1981 World Series. John was traded in August 1982 to the California Angels (AL) and won 22 of 50 decisions through June 1985. John pitched briefly for Modesto, CA (CaL) and Madison, WI (ML) in the Oakland A's (AL) organization in 1985 and joined the New York Yankees as a free agent in May 1986. He compiled a 29–24 record for the Yankees over the next four seasons, retiring after the 1989 campaign.

In 26 major league seasons, John pitched in 760 games, won 288 contests, lost 231 decisions, and hurled 46 shutouts. The three-time 20-game winner had a 3.34 ERA and recorded 2,245 strikeouts in 4,710 innings pitched. A member of the 1968 and 1978–1980 All-Star squads, he suffered the AL loss in 1980. In 1980 he led the AL in shutouts with six and was named the left-handed pitcher on *TSN* AL All-Star team. John, a strong, fierce looking, confident, and self-assured competitor, has a strong desire to succeed and a determination to fight back when down. Off the field, he is a gentle, caring, thoughtful man and places his family first. He has strong religious convictions and a deep faith that nothing is impossible with God. He and his wife are co-authors of *The Sally and Tommy John Story*, describing their life and the tragic accident of their son Travis. At age 2, Travis had fallen from an upper-level window and was in a coma 15 days. John handled color television commentary for the Minnesota Twins (AL) in 1994–1995 and resides in Charlotte, NC.

BIBLIOGRAPHY: Mark Gallagher, *The Yankee Encyclopedia*, vol. 3 (Champaign, IL, 1997); Tommy John file, National Baseball Library, Cooperstown, NY; William F. McNeil, *The Dodgers Encyclopedia* (Champaign, IL, 1997); Sally John and Tommy

John, *The Sally and Tommy John Story* (New York, 1983); Tommy John and Dan Valenti, *TJ: My Twenty-Six Years in Baseball* (New York, 1991); Gene Karst and Martin J. Jones, Jr., *Who's Who in Professional Baseball* (New Rochelle, NY, 1973); Robert E. Kelly, *Baseball's Best* (Jefferson, NC, 1988); Randy Schultz, "Tommy John: The Right-handed Left-hander," *SCD* 22 (October 6, 1995), pp. 170–171; *TSN Official Baseball Register*, 1990.

John L. Evers

JOHNSON, Alexander "Alex" (b. December 7, 1942, Helena, AR), player, performed 13 major league seasons as an outfielder and DH for eight different teams and grew up in Detroit, MI. His father, Arthur Johnson, worked in an auto plant and founded Johnson Trucking Company, renting dump trucks to construction companies. Johnson married Julia Augusta on February 2, 1963 and has one adopted child. His younger brother, Ron, played football at the University of Michigan and professionally with the New York Giants (NFL).

Johnson's three minor league seasons as a Philadelphia Phillies (NL) farmhand promised great things for him as a major league outfielder. In 1962 with Miami, FL the 6-foot, 205 pounder led the FSL in batting (.313), total bases (188), and outfield assists (19) and made the All-Star team. With Magic Valley, ID (PrL) in 1963, he paced the PrL in HR (35), RBI (128), and total bases (294), made the All-Star team, and was selected the PrL's MVP. He made the PCL All-Star team with Arkansas in 1964 and was called up to the Philadelphia Phillies in August.

With the Phillies as a part-time player, Johnson batted .303 in 1964 and .294 in 1965. In October 1965, the Philadelphia Phillies traded him to the St. Louis Cardinals (NL). He hit only .186 and .223 in parts of the next two seasons there and spent much of the 1966 campaign with Tulsa, OK (PCL), hitting .355. Johnson was traded to the Cincinnati Reds (NL) in January 1968 and enjoyed two outstanding seasons there, hitting .312 in 1968 and .315 in 1969 as a regular. In November 1969, the Cincinnati Reds traded him to the California Angels (AL). Johnson enjoyed his best major league season in 1970, batting .329 with 202 hits, making the All-Star team, and winning the batting championship on the last day.

Johnson's major league managers constantly worried about him, with Gene Mauch* calling him an enigma. Johnson spoke darkly of racial injustices. With the California Angels in 1970, he was accused of a lack of hustle. When he slumped in 1971, the charges became so insistent that the Angels put him on the suspended list for the rest of the season. Johnson appealed through the MLPA to an independent arbiter, who ruled that Johnson should have been placed on the disabled list. Psychiatrists for the MLPA and Major League Baseball agreed that his disability was mental. Marvin Miller* considered this a watershed moment for the MLPA both because major league baseball admitted the possibility of mental disability and because the MLPA had defended an African-American player. Johnson played for the Cleveland Indians (AL) in 1972, Texas Rangers (AL) in 1973 and 1974, and New York Yankees (AL) in 1974 and 1975, finishing his career with his hometown Detroit Tigers (AL) in 1976. During 13 major league seasons, he batted .288 with 1,331 hits, 78 HR, and 525 RBI. He has worked for his father's trucking company, running it since his father's death in 1985.

BIBLIOGRAPHY: Ron Fimrite, "For Failure to Give His Best . . ." *SI* 35 (July 5, 1971), pp. 12–17; Arnold Hano, "The Lonely War of Alex Johnson," *Sport* 50 (October 1970), pp. 38–40, 84–85; Alexander Johnson file, National Baseball Library, Cooperstown, NY; Marvin Miller, *A Whole New Ball Game* (New York, 1991); J. Pearlman, "Catching Upward," *SI* 88 (March 9, 1998), p. 30; Rich Westcott and Frank Bilovsky, *The New Phillies Encyclopedia* (Philadelphia, PA, 1993); John Thom, *Champion Batsman of the 20th Century* (Los Angeles, CA, 1992); Fred Smith, *995 Tigers* (Detroit, MI, 1981); Donald Honig, *The Cincinnati Reds* (New York, 1992).

Leverett T. Smith, Jr.

JOHNSON, Byron Bancroft "Ban" (b. January 6, 1863, Cincinnati, OH; d. March 28, 1931, St. Louis, MO), sportswriter and baseball executive, was founder and first president of the AL. His parents were Albert B. Johnson, a prominent school administrator in Cincinnati for almost 50 years, and Eunice (Fox) Johnson. Johnson attended Marietta College for one year and the University of Cincinnati Law School for over a year before joining the staff of the Cincinnati *Commercial-Gazette*. From 1887 to 1894, he served as sporting editor of the *Commercial-Gazette*, met many baseball figures, and developed a deep knowledge of the game. He disliked rowdy behavior on the field and umpire abuse and sought to correct those two problems. In 1891, he married Sara Jane Laymon of Spencer, IN; they had no children.

His familiarity with baseball prompted owners of the revived WL to invite Johnson in November 1893 to lead their organization. Although intending to remain only one year, he continued as WL president through the 1899 season. During those six years, Johnson apprenticed in baseball administration and made the WL the most successful minor league. Johnson aspired to head a major league and in the winter of 1899–1900 saw his opportunity. The NL had dropped the bottom four teams from its 12-club membership, which opened up important free territory. The WL agreement simultaneously expired and a major league players' group (Players' Protective Association) was formed. These developments inspired Johnson and his WL colleagues to move toward major league status. The WL became the AL before the 1900 season, but the circuit was bound by the National Agreement and remained a minor league.

In 1901, however, Johnson unsuccessfully pressed the NL to accept the AL as an equal. A two-year war broke out, during which time the NL hoped to crush the AL and the latter sought recognition as a second major league. During the "Great Baseball War," 87 National Leaguers jumped to the AL and established the credibility of the new major loop. After the AL won the attendance battle in 1902, the NL sought peace. The "peace conference," held in Cincinnati, OH in January 1903, created the basic structure governing organized baseball over half a century.

Under the new National Agreement, a three-man ruling body, the National Commission, was established. Cincinnati owner Garry Herrmann chaired the commission, but Johnson proved its most influential figure. Although not having unlimited authority, he was called the "Czar of Baseball." During Johnson's era, from 1903 to 1920, baseball prospered as never before and became known as the national pastime. His creation of a second major league, along with his efforts to upgrade umpires, crack down on rowdy players and fans, and make baseball "respectable family entertainment," contributed largely to the game's success.

Between 1916 and 1919, Johnson became involved in four controversial player dispute decisions and antagonized a number of owners in both leagues. In the most critical case, he overruled the sale in July 1919 of Carl Mays* by the Boston Red Sox to the New York Yankees. The New York State Supreme Court, however, later overruled Johnson, causing the latter's influence to decline. The National Commission also fell into disfavor because of Johnson's power over it and in 1920 was replaced by a single commissioner. With the election of Kenesaw Mountain Landis* to that post, Johnson's former influence vanished.

Thereafter, AL president Johnson clashed frequently with Landis. The final dispute, precipitated when Landis published the correspondence in the Ty Cobb*–Tris Speaker* scandal in the winter of 1926–1927, led to Johnson's forced resignation as the junior circuit's chief executive in July 1927. He refused to accept remuneration for the eight remaining years on his contract, a $320,000 sum. Johnson's already failing health worsened steadily after he left office. In 1937, he was elected to the National Baseball Hall of Fame.

BIBLIOGRAPHY: Ban Johnson file, National Baseball Library, Cooperstown, NY; John B. Foster, "Ban Johnson's Twenty-five Years in the American League," Chicago Daily News, January 2, February 10, 1928; Brad Herzog, The Sports 100 (New York, 1995); Ban Johnson, "Ban Johnson's Own Story," as told to John E. Wray and J. Roy Stockton, St. Louis Post-Dispatch, February 10, March 3, 1929; Ban Johnson, "My Thirty-four Years in Baseball," as told to Irving Vaughan, Chicago Tribune, February 24, March 3, 10, 1929; Eugene C. Murdock, Ban Johnson: Czar of Baseball (Westport, CT, 1982); Earl Obenshain, "Life of Ban Johnson," Baseball World Inc. (December 3, 1928–February 3, 1929); Branch Rickey (with Robert Riger), The American Diamond (New York, 1965).

Eugene Murdock

JOHNSON, David Allen "Davey" (b. January 30, 1943, Orlando, FL), player, instructor, and manager, tied Rogers Hornsby's* major league record for most single-season HR (42) by a second baseman as the 1973 NL Comeback

Player of the Year. With the Atlanta Braves (NL) that year, Johnson, Henry Aaron,* and Darrell Evans* became the first trio of major league teammates to hit at least 40 HR each in one season.

"Johnson is an intelligent, multi-dimensional man," wrote Bill Lyon. "Johnson has logged more than 1,000 hours as a pilot and has done some acrobatic flying. He gives water skiing lessons, teaches scuba diving, has a degree in math, and maneuvers his way around the golf course with a handicap that [like that of his late father] is very close to scratch." An All-SWC baseball shortstop and a basketball player at Texas A&M University, Johnson also attended Johns Hopkins University and graduated with a bachelor's degree in mathematics from Trinity University in San Antonio, TX. Johnson's penchant for using computers in managing undoubtedly stemmed from his mathematical background.

A slick fielding second baseman adept at turning the double play, Johnson won three Gold Gloves and led the NL with a .990 fielding percentage in 1972. He batted .261 lifetime with 136 HR (including a record-tying two pinch-hit grand-slam HR in 1978) and 609 RBI during 13 major league seasons with the Baltimore Orioles (AL, 1965–1972), Atlanta Braves (NL, 1973–1975), Philadelphia Phillies (NL, 1977–1978), and Chicago Cubs (NL, 1978). Back problems bothered him during a professional career that began with Stockton, CA (CaL) in 1962, but he nevertheless earned four major league All-Star team berths and played in four AL Championship Series and four World Series. Johnson, the first non-Oriental baseball All-Star in Japan, teamed with Japanese homer king Sadaharu Oh on the Yomiuri Giants in 1975 and 1976.

After managing and serving as a roving instructor in the New York Mets (NL) farm system, Johnson succeeded New York Mets manager Frank Howard* in 1984 and became the first NL pilot to win 90 games in each of his first five seasons from 1984 to 1988. Under Johnson, the Mets defeated the Boston Red Sox (AL) to win their first World Series in 17 years and captured an additional NL East title in 1988. Johnson, who also managed the 1987 NL All-Star team, was fired from his post as Mets pilot in May 1990. As the winningest Mets manager, he compiled a 595–417 record.

Johnson served as a consultant for the Cincinnati Reds (NL) from December 1992 to May 1993, when he became manager. He piloted the 66–48 Cincinnati Reds to first place in the NL Central Division in the strike-shortened 1994 season. In 1995, he guided the Cincinnati Reds to another first place finish in the NL Central Division with a 85–59 record. The Cincinnati Reds swept the Los Angeles Dodgers in the NL Division Series, but the Atlanta Braves bested them, 4–1, in the NL Championship Series. Following the 1995 season, the Baltimore Orioles named him manager. The Baltimore Orioles finished second in the AL East Division with a 88–74 mark in 1996 and defeated the Cleveland Indians in the AL Division Series, but lost to the New York Yankees in the AL Championship Series. In 1997,

Johnson guided the 98–64 Baltimore Orioles to first place in the AL East Division race. Baltimore defeated the Seattle Mariners in the AL Division Series, but lost to the Cleveland Indians in the AL Championship Series. Johnson resigned after the 1997 season due to differences with owner Peter Angelo. In October 1998, he replaced Glenn Hoffman as manager of the Los Angeles Dodgers (NL). The Dodgers finished 77–85 in 1999. In 13 major league seasons as manager, Johnson compiled a 1,062–812 record and .567 winning percentage.

BIBLIOGRAPHY: Davey Johnson file, National Baseball Library, Cooperstown, NY; Joseph Durso, "As the Mets Get Better, Dave Johnson Gets Bolder," *NYT Biographical Service* 17 (June 1986), pp. 786–787; Thomas Aylesworth and Benton Minks, *The Encyclopedia of Baseball Managers* (New York, 1990); Ted Patterson, *The Baltimore Orioles* (Dallas, TX, 1995); Gary Caruso, *The Braves Encyclopedia* (Philadelphia, PA, 1995); Donald Honig, *Baseball's 10 Greatest Teams* (New York, 1982); Davey Johnson and Peter Golenbock, *Bats* (New York, 1986); J. Klein, "Sports," *NY* 19 (September 15, 1986), pp. 786–787; Mike Lupica, "The Hardest Job Out of Baseball," *Esquire* 115 (April 1991), pp. 52ff; Bill Lyon, "Oh Would Hit 700 HRs in U.S., Says Johnson," *TSN*, January 7, 1978, p. 37; Bill Madden, "Manager for Hire," *Sport* 84 (June 1993), pp. 63–65; M. Martinez, "Disciplined Teams that Dave Johnson Manages Master the Tiniest Details," *NYT Biographical Service* 17 (October 1986), pp. 1222–1223; *The Baseball Encyclopedia*, 10th ed. (New York, 1996); Mike Shatzkin, ed., *The Ballplayers* (New York, 1990); *TSN Official Baseball Register, 1997*; Tom Verducci, "Who's the Boss," *SI* 83 (September 18, 1995), pp. 46–48; Tom Verducci, "Out in the Cold Again," *SI* 88 (February 23, 1998), pp. 78–81.

                                                                Thomas D. Jozwik

JOHNSON, Deron Roger (b. July 17, 1938, San Diego, CA; d. April 23, 1992, Poway, CA), player, coach, and manager, attended San Diego High School, where he was selected an All-American football player. The 6-foot 2-inch, 209-pound Johnson started in the New York Yankees (AL) farm system as an outfielder at Kearney, NE (NeSL) in 1956. In June 1961, the New York Yankees traded him to the Kansas City Athletics (AL).

After hitting just .209 in 1961 and .105 in 1962, Johnson signed with the Cincinnati Reds (NL) in late 1962. A solid 1963 season with San Diego, CA (PCL) led to a major league contract in 1964. With the Reds, Johnson enjoyed three impressive seasons from 1964–1966 primarily as a first baseman and averaged 26 HR. In 1965, he led the NL in RBI with 130 and shared the lead with 10 sacrifice flies. After he batted just .224 with only 13 HR in 1967, Cincinnati traded Johnson that October to the Atlanta Braves (NL) for outfielder Mack Jones and two other players. Johnson struggled in his only year with the Atlanta Braves, hitting only .208.

The Philadelphia Phillies (NL) acquired Johnson in December 1968, reviving the slugger's career. Between 1969 and 1971, Johnson hit 78 HR and averaged 89 RBI. His last productive year came in 1971, when he hit 34 HR with 95 RBI while batting .265. Johnson slugged four consecutive HR against the Montreal Expos, three coming in one game. He hit 22 HR at home, breaking Del Ennis'* 1950 Philadelphia record.

An injured calf in 1972 limited Johnson's playing time. After being traded in May 1973 to the Oakland Athletics (AL), he hit 19 regular season HR and batted .333 in Oakland's victory over the New York Mets in the 1973 World Series. Johnson then moved to the Milwaukee Brewers (AL) and Boston Red Sox (AL) in 1974 and Chicago White Sox (AL) in 1975 before finishing his playing career with the Boston Red Sox in 1975 and 1976.

In 1,765 games spanning 16 major league seasons, Johnson produced 245 HR with 1,447 hits, 923 RBI, and a .244 batting average. He coached with the New York Mets (NL) in 1981 and Philadelphia Phillies from 1982 through 1984 and also managed Salt Lake City, UT (PCL) one year.

Johnson married Lucille De Maria in October 1962 and had two sons, Deron Jr. and Dominick. He resided in Poway, CA, owning a construction company in San Diego and operating a 40 acre cattle farm. He died in 1992 after a long battle with cancer.

BIBLIOGRAPHY: Deron Johnson file, National Baseball Library, Cooperstown, NY; *NYT*, April 25, 1992, p. 12; Donald Honig, *The Cincinnati Reds* (New York, 1992); Allen Lewis, *The Philadelphia Phillies: A Pictorial History* (Virginia Beach, VA, 1981); Robert Redmount, *The Red Sox Encyclopedia* (Champaign, IL, 1998); *TSN Baseball Register*, 1976; Rich Westcott and Frank Bilovsky, *The New Phillies Encyclopedia* (Philadelphia, PA, 1993).

John P. Rossi

JOHNSON, George "Chappie," "Junior" (b. 1876, Bellaire, OH; d. August 17, 1949, Clemson, SC), player, coach, manager, and executive, was involved in professional baseball for over 25 years. He received a high school education in Bellaire and launched his baseball career in 1896 as an outfielder with the outstanding Adrian, MI Page Fence Giants all black team. The 5-foot 10-inch, 160-pound right-hander also played first base and soon became an excellent catcher.

Johnson remained with Adrian through 1898 and then caught for the Chicago Columbia Giants in 1899 and 1900 and Chicago Union Giants in 1901 and 1902. His fame as a receiver led to frequent switches of teams. He performed for the 1903 Cuban X-Giants, 1903 and 1904 Algona, IA Brownies, 1904 and 1906 Philadelphia Giants, and 1905 state champion Renville, MN club. From 1907 through 1909, Johnson played for the St. Paul, MN Gophers. His other clubs included the 1909 Chicago Leland Giants, 1910 Chicago Giants, 1911 and 1912 St. Louis Giants, 1912 Brooklyn Royal Giants, 1913 and 1914 Mohawk Giants, and 1914 Chicago American Giants. His playing career ended in 1921. Johnson's championship battery mates included Andrew "Rube" Foster* with the 1904 Philadelphia Giants and talented portsider George Wilson with 1905 Renville. He posted a .352

batting average, helping Philadelphia defeat the Cuban X-Giants for the 1904 crown.

Johnson's greatest renown, however, came as a coach and a manager. His instruction of young catchers even reached into organized (white) baseball. The Boston Beaneaters (NL) utilized Johnson in 1906 as a "trainer" in the spring, while class AAA St. Paul, MN (AA) hired him as a spring training coach from 1907 through 1912. Johnson's initial managerial experience probably came with the 1907 black St. Paul Gophers. He co-owned and managed the 1917 Dayton, OH Chappies and promoted his own team.

Johnson was affiliated with Custer's Baseball Club of Columbus, OH, the Philadelphia Royal Stars, and the Pennsylvania Red Caps of New York, the Atlantic City, NJ Bacharach Giants in 1919, and the Norfolk, VA Stars from 1919 to 1921. By 1925, he conducted his own baseball club in Montreal, Canada. The team operated into the 1930s as the Chappie Johnson All-Stars.

Johnson was respected and even revered by his players. He demonstrated strong character, insisted upon being addressed as Mr. Johnson, and dressed impeccably. Johnson, a popular and effective coach and manager, inspired his players to perform at their full potential. Although never playing in the Negro Baseball Leagues, he managed the Norfolk Stars through 1939. He also played winter baseball in Cuba in 1907 and for the Royal Ponciana Hotel Florida club in 1913.

BIBLIOGRAPHY: Dick Clark and Larry Lester, *The Negro Leagues Book* (Cleveland, OH, 1994); John B. Holway, *Voices From the Great Black Baseball Leagues* (New York, 1975); *Frank Leland's Chicago Giants Base Ball Club* (Chicago, IL, 1910); Robert Peterson, *Only the Ball Was White* (Englewood Cliffs, NJ, 1970); James A. Riley, *The Biographical Encyclopedia of the Negro Leagues* (New York, 1994).

Merl F. Kleinknecht

JOHNSON, Grant "Home Run" (b. 1874, Findlay, OH; d. 1964, Buffalo, NY), player and manager, attended Public School No. 9 in Findlay OH, and in 1894 played shortstop for the strong semipro Findlay Sluggers. The following year, he began his professional career that saw him play with the era's greatest black teams. A star for the Page Fence Giants of Adrian, MI, the Columbus Giants of Chicago, and the Cuban X-Giants, Johnson was the most famous shortstop in black baseball before John Henry Lloyd.* During baseball's dead ball era, the right-handed slugger earned the lifetime sobriquet "Home Run." On Sol White's* championship Philadelphia Giants of 1906, he teamed with greats Rube Foster,* J. Preston "Pete" Hill,* and Bill Monroe.* When Foster assembled the Leland Giants team in Chicago, he recruited Johnson to play second base and Hill to handle the outfield. The trio joined Lloyd, Bruce Petway,* Frank Wickware,* and Pat Dougherty* to form what was perhaps the greatest aggregation of talent in black baseball history. In 1910, the Giants compiled an incredible 123–6 record.

Johnson and Lloyd joined Louis Santop,* Joe Williams,* Dick Redding,* and Spot Poles* in 1911 on the great Lincoln Giants team. As at Chicago, Johnson played second base in deference to Lloyd's outstanding ability. After the team won the 1912 and 1913 championships and outclassed Foster's Chicago American Giants in the 1913 playoff, the Lincoln owner claimed that his club could defeat any major league team. Johnson subsequently excelled with the Lincoln Stars and Brooklyn Royal Giants, serving as player–manager with the latter team. In this same capacity, he guided the Lincoln Giants to a championship.

Johnson also captained the Havana, Cuba Reds to the CNL championship and became the first American to win a batting title there. The superior slugger hit .319 during five winters there and batted a sparkling .412 one season. After the 1910 season, the World Series champion Philadelphia Athletics (AL) played Johnson's Havana Reds in Cuba. Manager Connie Mack* pitched great moundsmen Eddie Plank,* Chief Bender,* and Jack Coombs,* but Havana captured the series. That same year, the line drive hitter batted .412 in exhibition games against the Detroit Tigers (AL) and outhit National Baseball Hall of Fame outfielders Ty Cobb* and Sam Crawford.* In 19 exhibition games against major leaguers, Johnson batted .293.

During his later years, he played with the Pittsburgh and Buffalo Colored Giants. The sturdy infielder kept in good physical condition and played 38 years before retiring in 1932 at age 58. He resided in Buffalo, where he worked with the New York Central Railroad Company.

BIBLIOGRAPHY: Dick Clark and Larry Lester, *The Negro Leagues Book* (Cleveland, OH, 1994); Robert W. Peterson, *Only the Ball Was White* (Englewood Cliffs, NJ, 1970); James A. Riley, *The Biographical Encyclopedia of the Negro Baseball Leagues* (New York, 1994); James A. Riley, interviews with former Negro League players, James A. Riley Collection, Cocoa, FL.

James A. Riley

JOHNSON, Howard Michael "Hojo" (b. November 29, 1960, Clearwater, FL), player and scout, attended St. Petersburg JC in St. Petersburg, FL. A selection in the 23rd round of the 1978 free agent draft, he started his professional baseball career with Lakeland, FL (FSL) in 1979. He joined the Detroit Tigers (AL) in 1982 after ascending through the parent chain with Birmingham, AL (SL) in 1980 and 1981 and Evansville, IN (AA) in 1982. He hit .316 in 54 games for the Detroit Tigers, but started the 1983 season with Evansville. Injuries sidelined him most of the 1983 season, as he appeared in only 27 games for Detroit.

Johnson's first full major league season came in 1984, when the 5-foot 11-inch, 195-pound switch-hitter hit 12 HR and knocked in 50 runs for the Detroit Tigers. His lack of aggressiveness at the plate caused manager Sparky Anderson* to trade him to the New York Mets (NL) in December 1984 for pitcher Walt Terrell. In New York his situation did not improve, as he shared duties with Ray Knight at third base. The Detroit Tigers had defeated the San Diego Padres in the 1984 World Series, while the New York Mets triumphed over the Boston Red Sox in the 1986 World Series. Johnson became just the 27th major leaguer to play for a World Series champion in both leagues.

The New York Mets traded Knight after the 1986 World Series, enabling Johnson to play regularly. Johnson came into his own in 1987, when he and Darryl Strawberry* became the first teammates to join the exclusive 30–30 HR, stolen base club. Johnson's season included 36 HR, a record for NL switch-hitters, 32 stolen bases, and 99 RBI. Whitey Herzog* and other NL managers checked his bats for cork, but New York Mets manager Davey Johnson* suggested they check his arms.

Although the New York Mets won an NL East Division title in 1988, Johnson produced just 24 HR to rank fifth in the NL in an injury-marred season. The following season, he enjoyed the best year of his career with 101 RBI (tied for fourth in the NL), 41 steals (tied for third), a .287 batting average, and 36 HR (second best in the NL). He became only the third player to produce two 30–30 seasons. Johnson was selected to the *TSN* All-Star team and his first All-Star Game. His 41 doubles marked a New York Mets record, while his 41 stolen bases tied for fourth in the NL. Johnson's .559 slugging average was ranked second in the NL. Although having an injury-plagued 1990 season, he hit at least 1 HR in the first seven positions in the batting order. After having off-season arthroscopic shoulder surgery, Johnson in 1991 enjoyed career highs, New York Mets records, and NL highs with 117 RBI, 38 HR, and a career-high 108 runs scored.

Johnson, nicknamed "Hojo," demonstrated his versatility in the field and willingness to help the team in 1992, when New York Mets manager Jeff Torborg made him opening day center fielder after finishing 1991 in right field. The experiment led to disastrous results for both Johnson and the New York Mets. Several nagging injuries, including a broken wrist that effectively ended his season in August, limited him to just seven HR, the lowest output of his career. In November 1993, the Colorado Rockies (NL) signed Johnson as a free agent. He played with the Rockies during the 1994 season. His major league career ended with the Chicago Cubs (NL) in 1995.

Johnson, a quiet, nearly shy individual, used to get free ice cream at Howard Johnson Restaurants as a youngster. A dead fastball hitter, Johnson always experienced trouble with the off-speed deliveries. He engaged reliever Todd Worrell in several duels over the years, with Johnson homering on several occasions. Johnson, who failed to hit in six World Series at bats, and his wife, Kim, have two daughters, Shannon Leigh and Kayla Mae, and one son, Glen. His 14-year career included a .249 batting average, 228 HR, 760 RBI, and 231 stolen bases. He has scouted for the Mets since 1999.

BIBLIOGRAPHY: Howard Johnson file, National Baseball Library, Cooperstown, NY; Duncan Bock and John Jordan, *The Complete Year-by-Year N.Y. Mets Fan's Almanac* (New York, 1992); Franz Lidz, "Three Men on a Roll," *SI* 67 (August 4, 1987), pp. 40–42; Barry Nightengale, "Hojo Risin'," *Sport* 83 (March 1992), pp. 34–38; Steve Rushin, "Looking for His Pitch," *SI* 76 (April 6, 1992), pp. 76–78; Mike Shatzkin, ed., *The Ballplayers* (New York, 1990); Davey Johnson and Peter Golenbock, *Bats* (New York, 1986).

William A. Borst

JOHNSON, Kenneth Lance "One Dog" (b. July 6, 1963, Cincinnati, OH), player, graduated from Princeton High School, north of Cincinnati, and attended Triton College in River Grove, IL and the University of South Alabama in Mobile, AL in 1983–1984. In June 1984, the St. Louis Cardinals (NL) selected him in the sixth round of the free agent draft. Johnson, who teamed with Kirby Puckett* at Triton and competed against him in the 1987 World Series, is married to Sharon Brown.

Johnson enjoyed a distinguished minor league career, hitting .301 with 235 stolen bases in six years. With Louisville, KY (AA) in 1987, he was voted AA MVP. Johnson was named team MVP with Vancouver, Canada (PCL) in 1988 and 1989. In February 1988, the St. Louis Cardinals traded Johnson and Ricky Horton to the Chicago White Sox (AL) for pitcher Jose DeLeon. Johnson established himself in 1990 as regular center fielder for Chicago. In 1991, he began a streak of leading the AL four straight seasons in triples. No player had ever paced either league in triples more than three consecutive years. A durable athlete, Johnson led the White Sox in games played from 1990 to 1994. He also seldom whiffed and fanned less than anyone else in 1994, averaging one strikeout for every 19.3 at-bats. His consecutive game hit streak of 25 in 1992 marked the then third longest in White Sox history. On September 23, 1995 in Minnesota's Metrodome, he tied the AL record for triples in a single game with three. White Sox announcer Ken Harrelson honored Johnson's consistent contributions by calling him "One Dog."

After leading the AL with 186 hits in 1995, Johnson signed a free agent contract with the New York Mets (NL). His 227 base hits led the NL in 1996, making him the first to pace both circuits in consecutive seasons. He also paced the NL with 21 triples in 1996. An August 1997 five-player trade sent Johnson to the Chicago Cubs (NL). His left-handed hitting and speed have made him one of major league baseball's most feared leadoff men. The Cubs released him in October 1999. In 13 major league seasons, he has batted .291 with 1,556 hits, 174 doubles, 117 triples, 484 RBI, and 325 stolen bases.

BIBLIOGRAPHY: Lance Johnson file, National Baseball Library, Cooperstown, NY; *Baseball America's 1998 Almanac*; *TSN Baseball Register*, 1998; *Chicago White Sox Media Guide*, 1995, 1996.

David Fitzsimmons

JOHNSON, Oscar "Heavy" (b. 1896, Atchison, KS; d. 1966, Cleveland, OH), player, carried 250 pounds on a 6-foot frame during a 14 year Negro League baseball career. He served in the U.S. Army before entering professional baseball, catching for the 25th Infantry team posted at Ft. Huachuca, AZ. John McGraw* and Casey Stengel* recommended him to Kansas City Monarchs (NNL) owner James L. Wilkinson.* Johnson and 25th Infantry teammates Bob Fagin, Lemuel Hawkins, Dobie Moore,* and Wilbur Rogan* joined the Kansas City Monarchs in 1920. Johnson became the starting right fielder for Kansas City.

Johnson's powerful bat kept him in the Negro Leagues through 1933. He starred with the Kansas City Monarchs through 1924, attaining batting averages of .389, .380, and .411 his final three seasons there. Johnson moved to the Baltimore Black Sox (ECL) in 1925, hitting .345 and .337 in two campaigns there. His batting average slipped to .316 with the 1927 Harrisburg, PA Giants (ECL) and to .279 with the 1928 Cleveland Tigers (NNL). Johnson finished 1928 with the Memphis, TN Red Sox (NNL), lifting his batting average to .315. He remained with the Memphis Red Sox through 1933, batting .353 in 1930 primarily as a pinch hitter. Johnson, a defensive liability, dropped from the top black baseball leagues as his hitting skills diminished. Johnson batted .337 in 12 Negro League seasons. He also possessed enormous power, belting a career high and NNL leading 18 HR in 46 games in 1923. Johnson led the NNL in batting in 1922 and stole 12 bases in the 28 game ECL schedule in 1926. His .602 career Negro League slugging average was accomplished with 489 hits, including 91 doubles, 42 triples, and 49 HR.

Johnson helped the Monarchs capture the 1923 and 1924 NNL titles and defeat the Hilldale Daisies, five games to four in the first Negro League World Series, in 1924. He batted .296 in the World Series conquest.

Johnson's reported 1966 death in Cleveland remains unconfirmed. His overweight condition probably reduced his longevity.

BIBLIOGRAPHY: Janet Bruce, *The Kansas City Monarchs* (Lawrence, KS, 1985); Chicago *Defender*, 1924; Dick Clark and Larry Lester, *The Negro Leagues Book* (Cleveland, OH, 1994); *The Baseball Encyclopedia*, 10th ed. (New York, 1996); Philadelphia *Tribune*, 1924; James A. Riley, *The Biographical Encyclopedia of the Negro Leagues* (New York, 1994).

Merl F. Kleinknecht

JOHNSON, Randall David "Randy," "The Big Unit" (b. September 10, 1963, Walnut Creek, CA), player, is the son of Bud Johnson, a policeman, and Carol Johnson. The unexpected death of his father from an aortic aneurysm on Christmas Day in 1992 inspired Johnson's determination and intensity. At 6-feet 10-inches, he joined former New York Mets (NL) pitcher Eric Hillman as the tallest players in major league history. His height, menacing "game face," and strikeout fastball, clocked at 95 mph or higher, make him one of the game's most dominating left-handers and earned Johnson his nickname from former Montreal Expos teammate Tim Raines.* Johnson and his wife, Lisa, who have a daughter, Samantha, and a son, Tanner, live in

Bellevue, WA. An avid photographer, Johnson has exhibited work at Art Expo '90 in Los Angeles, CA and photographed for Pinnacle baseball cards while out with an injury in 1996. He pitched in the film *Little Big League*.

Johnson ended his scholastic baseball career in 1982 by pitching a perfect game for Livermore High School. The Atlanta Braves (NL) originally drafted him in 1982, but he attended the University of Southern California on a baseball/basketball scholarship and concentrated solely on baseball his junior year. He was selected by the Montreal Expos (NL) in the second round of the 1985 free-agent draft. In his first three minor league seasons, Johnson was named a top prospect by *BA* (#3 in 1986, #2 in 1987, and #3 in 1988). After more than four seasons with the Montreal Expos organization and 11 major league appearances, he was traded with Gene Harris and Brian Holman to the Seattle Mariners (AL) in May 1989 for Mark Langston* and Mike Campbell.

Johnson ranks among the most feared power pitchers in the 1990s. He set a major league record by posting five straight seasons from 1991 to 1995 with a ratio of strikeouts per nine innings greater than 10 (10.2, 10.3, 10.9, 10.7, 12.4). In 1995 Johnson became only the fourth major league pitcher to lead both leagues in strikeouts four years in succession, joining Rube Waddell* (1903–1907), Dizzy Dean* (1932–1935), and Bob Feller* (1938–1941). Known for power and stamina on the mound, he led the Mariners to the 1995 AL West Division title by pitching a dramatic three-hit complete game effort against the California Angels in the one-game playoff.

Johnson won the 1995 AL Cy Young Award. He led the AL in ERA (2.48), winning percentage (.900), strikeouts (294), strikeouts per nine innings pitched (12.35), and batting average against (.201), finishing second in wins (18). His 12.35 strikeouts per nine innings set a new major league record, besting the 11.48 set by Nolan Ryan* in 1987 with the Houston Astros. He joined the 300 strikeout club in 1993 with 308 strikeouts, becoming the first pitcher in that decade to achieve the feat. His 1996 season was shortened by a back injury, requiring off-season surgery for an extruded disc herniation. In 1997, Johnson helped the Mariners win the AL West with a 20–4 record, 2.28 ERA, and 291 strikeouts in 213 innings. He struck out 19 batters against the Oakland A's on June 24 and 19 against the Chicago White Sox on August 8, but lost twice in the AL Championship Series against the Baltimore Orioles. Johnson compiled a lackluster 9–10 record with Seattle in 1998 before the Houston Astros (NL) acquired him in a July trade. He posted a brilliant 10–1 record and a 1.28 ERA with four shutouts, helping the Astros win the NL Central Division. Although pitching well in the NL Division Series, he lost both starts to the San Diego Padres. In November 1998, the Arizona Diamondbacks (NL) signed him to a $52.4 million, four-year contract. In 1999, he won the NL Cy Young Award with a 17–9 record and a 2.48 ERA. He led the NL in ERA and complete games (12) and the major leagues in strikeouts (364). Johnson lost his only start in the NL Division Series. Through 1999, Johnson compiled a career 160–88 win–loss record with a 3.26 ERA and 2,693 strikeouts in 2,250 innings.

Johnson made the AL All-Star team five times (1990, 1993–1995, 1997) and pitched two perfect innings in the 1993 game, including a memorable strikeout of Philadelphia's John Kruk.* The first pitch sailed over Kruk's head, so startling the batter that he bailed out on every subsequent pitch. Johnson was selected the AL All-Star starting pitcher in 1995 and 1997, again pitching two hitless innings both times. Johnson, the *Seattle Post-Intelligencer's* Sports Star of the Year for 1993, was named to the 1995 AP and *TSN* All-Star Teams and won *TSN* AL Pitcher of the Year honors for his AL Cy Young season. He was chosen as pitcher with the best fastball and best slider in *BA*'s annual Tools of the Trade in 1995. He made the NL and AP All-Star Teams in 1999. He ranked fourth in victories (150) in the 1990s.

Johnson, formerly involved with the Seattle Chapter of Cystic Fibrosis Foundation, co-chaired the Foundation's annual Celebrity Golf Tournament fund-raiser.

BIBLIOGRAPHY: Randy Johnson file, National Baseball Library, Cooperstown, NY; *Seattle Mariners Information Guide*, 1997; Hank Hersch, "Not Just a Tall Tale," *SI* 70 (March 20, 1989), pp. 42–44; Richard Hoffer, "Picture Perfect Pitcher," *SI* 76 (May 4, 1992), pp. 46–47; Terry Melia, "King of the Hill," *MM* 6 (1995), pp. 21–24; Tom Verducci, "The Intimidator," *SI* 82 (June 26, 1995), pp. 58–62; Rick Weinberg, "King of K," *Sport* 85 (June 1994), pp. 42–44; Gordon Wittenmyer, "Johnson Comes Back . . . In the Name of the Father," *BBW* 7 (July 3–9, 1997), pp. 34–36.

Sarah L. Ulerick

JOHNSON, Robert Lee "Bob," "Indian Bob" (b. November 26, 1906, Pryor, OK; d. July 6, 1982, Tacoma, WA), player and manager, was the son of Robert Johnson and Anna Blanche (Downing) Johnson and brother of outfielder Roy Johnson. He married Caroline Stout in December 1924 and had two daughters. He later wed Elizabeth Pastore in September 1950. Nicknamed "Indian Bob" because of his part-Cherokee Indian ancestry, Johnson became the mainstay of the Depression era Philadelphia Athletics (AL). From 1935 through 1941, he drove in at least 100 runs per season for Philadelphia manager Connie Mack.* In his first nine seasons, he never hit under 21 HR. During his 13 major league seasons, he slugged 288 HR. Johnson, who never batted under .265 and averaged over 150 hits per season, batted .296 lifetime, made 396 doubles, recorded 2,051 hits, and knocked in 1,283 career runs. In his second major league season (1934), he hit safely in 26 consecutive games and went six for six in an eleven-inning game on June 16. He set the AL record for the most RBI in one inning (6) and in one game for a player driving in all of his team's runs (8). Johnson made seven All-Star teams.

Johnson, who left school in the fifth grade when his family moved to Washington, began his professional baseball career with Wichita, KS-Pueblo, CO (WL) in 1929 and played from 1929 through 1932 with Portland, OR (PCL). He joined the Athletics in 1933 and played there until traded in March 1943 to the Washington Senators (AL). At Washington in 1943, Johnson experienced his worst season by batting .265 with only seven

HR. The 6 foot, 200 pound outfielder enjoyed fine seasons with the Boston Red Sox (AL) in 1944 and 1945, but then spent the remainder of his career in the minor leagues with Milwaukee, WI (AA) in 1946, Seattle, WA (PCL) in 1948, and Tacoma, WA (WIL) in 1949. Johnson, who injured his knee in 1948, managed the Tacoma club in 1949 and attempted a comeback as a player with Tijuana, Mexico (IL) in 1951. He worked for a brewing company and as an engineer in the Glendale, CA Fire Department before retiring to Tacoma, WA.

BIBLIOGRAPHY: Alan R. Asnen, interview with Jeff Kernan, August 21, 1984; Robert Johnson file, National Baseball Library, Cooperstown, NY; Gene Karst and Martin J. Jones, Jr., *Who's Who in Professional Baseball* (New Rochelle, NY, 1973); Craig Carter, ed., *TSN Daguerreotypes*, 8th ed. (St. Louis, MO, 1990); *The Baseball Encyclopedia*, 10th ed. (New York, 1996); Frederick G. Lieb, *Connie Mack* (New York, 1945); Connie Mack, *My 66 Years in the Big Leagues* (Philadelphia, PA, 1950); Robert Redmount, *The Red Sox Encyclopedia* (Champaign, IL, 1998); Frederick G. Lieb, *The Boston Red Sox* (New York, 1947).

Alan R. Asnen

JOHNSON, Roy Cleveland (b. February 23, 1903, Pryor, OK; d. September 10, 1973, Tacoma, WA), player and manager, was one of eight children of Robert Johnson and Anna Blanche (Downing) Johnson and the older brother of outfielder Robert Lee Johnson.* The Johnsons moved to Tacoma, WA when Roy was about 10 years old. After little formal schooling, the part Cherokee Indian blossomed into a semiprofessional star pitcher and outfielder with Everett, WA of the independent SWL in late 1922 and Ellensburg, WA in 1923 and 1924. Seattle, WA (PCL) acquired him in late 1924 for two games. In 1925 he played winter ball full-time in Los Angeles, CA and the San Francisco Bay district as an outfielder. He signed with the San Francisco, CA Seals (PCL) for the 1926 season and was shipped to Idaho Falls, ID (UIL). Johnson batted .306 for San Francisco in 1927 and scored 142 runs, stole 29 bases, hit 22 HR and batted .360 in 1928. The Detroit Tigers (AL) purchased the 5-foot 9-inch, 175-pound outfielder for $75,000.

In his first season with the Detroit Tigers in 1929, Johnson batted .314, scored 128 runs, stole 20 bases, led the AL in at-bats (640), and shared with two others for most doubles (45). Although his batting average dipped to .275 in 1930 and .279 in 1931, the graceful, speedy outfielder scored 107 runs, paced the AL in triples (19), and stole 33 bases in 1931. In June 1932, the Detroit Tigers traded Johnson and Dale Alexander* to the Boston Red Sox (AL) for Earl Webb. The left-hand hitting outfielder finished 1932 with 103 runs scored and a .281 batting average. He followed with batting averages of .313 in 1933, .320 in 1934, and .315 in 1935 and also recorded a career-high 119 RBI in 1934. The Boston Red Sox traded Johnson and Carl Reynolds* to the Washington Senators (AL) in December 1935 for Heinie Manush.* The New York Yankees (AL) acquired Johnson and Bump Hadley a month later for Jimmie DeShong and Jesse Hill. Johnson became a utility outfielder with the 1936 World Series champion New York Yankees, hitting .265. In 1937, the Yankees planned to start him as left fielder, but used 21-year-old future star Tommy Henrich* instead. Johnson was sent to the Boston Bees (NL) for $7,500 in May, batting .277. Johnson ended his major league career in 1938 with the Boston Bees. Milwaukee, WI (AA) acquired Johnson, and played him the remainder of the 1938 and 1939 seasons. Buffalo NY (IL) purchased Johnson and traded him to Syracuse, NY (IL) for John Kroner in 1940. He was sold to Baltimore, MD (IL) in 1941, and completed his professional baseball career with Seattle, WA (PCL) in 1944 and 1945.

Several clubs thought that Johnson never reached his full potential as a player. Although possessing an excellent arm, he compiled only an overall .938 fielding average. Johnson twice led the AL in assists, but also paced it in errors, and still holds the AL record with 31 outfield errors in 1929. The 10-year major leaguer compiled a .296 lifetime batting average, with 556 RBI, 717 runs, 1,292 hits, 58 HR, and 135 stolen bases. Johnson retired to Tacoma, WA and worked as a laborer. He married Helen Lucille Fraser on October 25, 1929, but they later divorced. They had one daughter, Marilyn. Johnson died of chronic alcoholism.

BIBLIOGRAPHY: *The Baseball Encyclopedia*, 10th ed. (New York, 1996); Roy C. Johnson file, National Baseball Library, Cooperstown, NY; John Thorn et al., eds., *Total Baseball*, 5th ed. (New York, 1997); Fred Smith, *995 Tigers* (Detroit, MI, 1981); Frederick G. Lieb, *The Detroit Tigers* (New York, 1946); Frederick G. Lieb, *The Boston Red Sox* (New York, 1947); Robert Redmount, *The Red Sox Encyclopedia* (Champaign, IL, 1998).

Jack C. Braun

JOHNSON, Walter Perry "The Big Train," "Barney" (b. November 6, 1887, Humboldt, KS; d. December 10, 1946, Washington, DC), player, manager, and sportscaster, was the son of farmer Frank Edwin Johnson and Minnie Johnson. In 1901 the Johnsons moved to Olinda, CA, where Walter attended Fullerton Union High School. In 1906, he entered professional baseball and tried out with Tacoma, WA (NWL). Since the NWL was too fast for the 16-year-old, he was sent to Weiser, ID (IdSL). Johnson pitched 75 scoreless innings there and averaged 15 strikeouts per game.

Johnson signed with the Washington Senators (AL) and lost his debut on August 2, 1907 against the Detroit Tigers, 3–2. In his second start, Johnson defeated Cleveland, 7–2, to win the first of 417 decisions spanning 21 seasons (1907–1927) at Washington. He lost 279 games for a mostly second division club. Twelve times Johnson won at least 20 games during one season. He captured 33 victories in 1912 and a career-high 36 triumphs the following year. Besides pitching 110 career shutouts, he lost 65 games when the Senators were shut out. He fanned 3,509 batters, pitched in the most games in

AL history (802), and hurled more complete games in modern times than any other major leaguer (531). Along with making 666 starts, he allowed only 1,902 runs in 5,914 innings and boasted a 2.17 career ERA. His lowest ERAs included 1.14 in 1913, 1.27 in 1918, and 1.49 in 1919. Twelve times Johnson led AL pitchers in strikeouts, with 313 in 1910, his one-season maximum. Johnson tied the AL mark for consecutive victories with 16 in 1912 and pitched three shutouts against the New York Yankees (then High-landers) in four days in 1908. After striking out four Boston Red Sox hitters in one inning in 1911, he established an AL record by hurling 56 consecutive scoreless innings in 1913. Johnson, who pitched a no-hitter against Boston in 1920 and compiled numerous one-hitters, received the AL MVP Award in 1913 and 1924.

Johnson pitched the opening game of the 1910 season with President William Howard Taft in attendance. This event marked the first of the "presidential openers" that became traditional in Washington. Johnson pitched 14 opening-day games, recording 7 shutouts. For the Senators, John-son also pitched in the 1924 and 1925 World Series. Although losing his first two starts for the World Series champion Senators against the New York Giants in 1924, he pitched four innings in the seventh and deciding game to earn the win. In 1925 he triumphed in his first two starts, but lost the crucial seventh game, 9–7, to the Pittsburgh Pirates. In Washington, fans quickly accepted Johnson as everybody's country cousin. A big, modest hick with a behind-the-plow gait, he did not fit into the city ways and was amazed that people thought he was so wonderful. The country bumpkin neither smoked nor drank and lived a social life of movie-going, hunting, and talking baseball with his longtime roommate Clyde Milan.* The shy Johnson lived in constant fear of hitting an opposing batter with one of his fast pitches.

Johnson married Hazel Lee Roberts, daughter of a Nevada congressman, in 1914 and had three sons, Walter, Jr., Edwin, and Robert, and two daugh-ters, Caroline and Barbara. In 1930 death came to his 36-year-old wife, a tragedy that thereafter left its mark on Johnson. Although a fabulous pitcher, he enjoyed somewhat less success as a manager. He piloted the Washington Senators (1929–1932) after managing Newark, NJ (IL) in 1928. His highest finish with Washington was second place in 1930. Johnson became manager of the Cleveland Indians (AL) in June 1933 and guided the 1934 Indians to a third place finish, but was replaced as manager in August 1935. His overall managerial record comprised 529 victories and 432 losses for a .550 winning percentage. After spending one season as a play-by-play radio announcer in Washington, he raised cattle on his farm and campaigned unsuccessfully for election to the U.S. Congress from Maryland. In 1936, Johnson, probably the fastest pitcher who ever lived, was elected one of the five charter mem-bers of the National Baseball Hall of Fame. He made Major League Base-ball's All-Century Team. He died of a brain tumor.

BIBLIOGRAPHY: Bob Broeg, *Super Stars of Baseball* (St. Louis, MO, 1971); Jim Kaplan, "The Best Pitcher Ever," *BRJ* 27 (1998), pp. 62–65; Morris Bealle, *The Washington Senators* (Washington, DC, 1947); Shirley Povich, *The Washington Senators* (New York, 1954); Jack Kavanagh, *Walter Johnson: A Life* (South Bend, IN, 1995); Gene Karst and Martin J. Jones, Jr., *Who's Who in Professional Baseball* (New Rochelle, NY, 1973); John P. McCarthy, *Baseball's All-Time Dream Team* (Cincinnati, OH, 1994); Tom Murray, *Sport Magazine All-Time All-Stars* (New York, 1948); Walter Johnson file, National Baseball Library, Cooperstown, NY; Shirley Povich, *The Baseball Hall of Fame 50th Anniversary Book* (New York, 1988); Henry W. Thomas, *Walter Johnson* (Washington, D.C., 1995); Joseph J. Vecchione, ed., *The New York Times Book of Sports Legends* (New York, 1991).

John L. Evers

JOHNSON, William Julius "Judy," "Jing" (b. October 26, 1899, Snow Hill, MD; d. June 14, 1989, Wilmington, DE), player, manager, scout, and coach, starred as a third baseman on the great Negro League Pittsburgh Crawfords during the 1930s. The son of William H. and Annie Johnson, he played childhood baseball in the Wilmington, DE area and attended Howard High School for one year. His father, a seaman, became athletic director of the Negro Settlement House in Wilmington. Johnson's first paid baseball job came with the semipro Chester Stars in Wilmington. He worked on a loading dock in Deepwater Point, NJ in 1918 and then joined the Atlantic City, NJ Bacharach Giants, a fine eastern barnstorming team. After a tryout with the Darby, PA Hilldale club, Johnson played with the Madison Stars. Hilldale purchased his contract in 1920 and made him regular third baseman the next year.

A superb defensive third baseman, Johnson played nine seasons with the Hilldales and starred on the pennant-winning ECL teams from 1923 through 1925 with batting marks of .391, .369, and .392. He married Anita T. Irons in 1923 and had one daughter, Loretta L., who married major league outfielder Bill Bruton.* In 1924 the Hilldales met the NNL's Kansas City Monarchs in the first Negro World Series. Johnson batted .341 and made six doubles, a triple, and a HR in a losing cause. The Hilldales secured revenge in 1925. With Monarchs star pitcher Wilbur "Bullet" Rogan* injured, the Hilldales defeated the Monarchs four games to one. Johnson hit .300 and contributed solid defensive play. He remained with Hilldale until 1929, batting .327 in 1926, .243 in 1927, .231 in 1928, and .390 with 22 stolen bases in 1929. The Hilldales did not win any more ECL pennants during this period, but Johnson sharpened his skills in Cuban winter ball. In the 1926–1927, 1927–1928, and 1928–1929 winter league seasons, he hit .374, .331, and .341, respectively. His composite CUWL average over four years (including 1930–1931) was .334.

With the collapse of the ECL, Johnson in 1930 joined the independent Homestead, PA Grays as player–manager. This team fielded Oscar Charleston,* "Smoky" Joe Williams,* and Josh Gibson,* whom Johnson lured from semipro ball. After a one year stint with the Darby, PA Daisies, Johnson in 1932 returned to Homestead (EWL). In midseason, Johnson and most of the Grays jumped to Gus Greenlee's* Pittsburgh Crawfords (NNL). As field captain of the Crawfords, Johnson played with stars Walter "Buck" Leonard,* Gibson, Leroy "Satchel" Paige,* John Henry Lloyd,* and Charleston. That fall the Crawfords defeated Casey Stengel's* major league All Stars in five of seven games. Nicknamed "Jing" in Pittsburgh, Johnson batted .333 in 1934 and that fall helped the Crawfords defeat Dizzy Dean* in three games. An excellent shortstop and an outstanding fielding third baseman, Johnson batted .367 and helped the Crawfords win the 1935 NNL pennant and defeat the New York Cubans in the NNL playoffs. Johnson hit .306 in 1936, played against Rogers Hornsby* and Jimmie Foxx* that fall in Mexico, and then retired in 1937 with .309 lifetime batting average. Johnson later worked as a supervisor for Continental Can Company in Wilmington and operated a general store with his brother in the 1940s.

Johnson, well respected for his intelligence and playing skills, later scouted and served as spring training instructor for the Philadelphia Athletics (AL), Milwaukee Braves (NL), and Philadelphia Phillies (NL). The pinnacle of his baseball career came in 1975 with his induction into the National Baseball Hall of Fame. A gentleman in an era of rough ballplayers, Johnson excelled as a fine all-around player. As field captain of the Crawfords, he exerted a steadying influence on his teammates and helped them establish the excellence of Negro League play. As a scout, he participated in the early days of major league integration and coached young black players in organized baseball.

BIBLIOGRAPHY: Judy Johnson file, National Baseball Library, Cooperstown, NY; Terry A. Baxter, correspondence with Jorge Figueroda, 1984, Cuban League statistics, Terry A. Baxter Collection, Cedar Rapids, IA; Terry A. Baxter, correspondence with Judy Johnson, 1984, Terry A. Baxter Collection, Cedar Rapids, IA; Terry A. Baxter, telephone interview with Judy Johnson, 1984; John Holway, "The Man Called Judy," John Holway Collection, Alexandria, VA; John Holway, TSN, July 5, 1982; John B. Holway, Blackball Stars (Westport, CT, 1988); John B. Holway, "Judy Johnson," BRJ 15 (1986), pp. 62–64; James Bankes, The Pittsburgh Crawfords (Dubuque IA, 1991); Kevin Kerrane and Rod Beaton, "Judy Johnson, Reminiscences by the Great Baseball Player," DT (May 1977); Gordon 'Red' Marston, "A Mission Arranged by Judy Johnson," TSN, March 1954; NYT, June 17, 1989, p. 29; Robert W. Peterson, Only the Ball Was White (Englewood Cliffs, NJ, 1970); Lowell Reidenbaugh, Baseball's Hall of Fame—Cooperstown (New York, 1993); James A. Riley, The All-Time All-Stars of Black Baseball (Cocoa, FL, 1983); James A. Riley, The Biographical Encyclopedia of the Negro Baseball Leagues (New York, 1990); Ellen Rendle, Judy Johnson: Delaware's Invisible Hero (Wilmington, DE, 1995); Donn Rogosin, Invisible Men: Life in Baseball's Negro Leagues (New York, 1983); Jules Tygiel, Baseball's Great Experiment (New York, 1983).

Terry A. Baxter

JONES, Charles Wesley "Baby," "Big Charley," "Knight of the Limitless Linen" (b. Benjamin Wesley Rippy, April 30, 1850, Alamance County, NC; d. unknown), player and umpire, was the third of six children of Abel Rippy, a yeoman farmer, and Delilah Rippy and moved to Princeton, IN following the death of his parents. His adolescent years were spent with Reuben Jones, an Indiana relative. Rippy, who adopted a new first name and Jones's surname, first played professional baseball as an outfielder with Evansville, IN and entered the major leagues with the weak Keokuk, IA Westerners (NA) in 1875. The inaugural 1876 NL season saw Jones perform as a center fielder for the Cincinnati Reds. After moving to left field, he batted .313 in 1877 and .310 in 1878 for the Reds. He also appeared in two games for the Chicago White Stockings (NL) while Cincinnati disbanded and reorganized during the 1877 campaign.

In 1879 Cincinnati traded Jones to the Boston Red Stockings (NL), where he batted .315, compiled a .510 slugging average, led the NL in runs scored (85), HR (9), and walks (29), shared the RBI lead (62), and paced NL outfielders defensively (.933). Jones played left field for Boston until September 1880, when autocratic club owner Arthur Soden suspended him for unsatisfactory play and aggravating conduct. Jones had protested that the Boston club owed him $506 in back salary. Although winning his salary in a court ruling, Jones was blacklisted by the NL and remained in limbo for two years. He operated a laundry and played minor league baseball in 1882. After readmittance to the major leagues in 1883, Jones patrolled center field and left field for the Cincinnati Red Stockings (AA) through July 1887. Jones made a strong comeback in the infant AA, batting .314 in 1884 and .322 in 1885. Cincinnati sold him to the New York Metropolitans (AA) in July 1887. Jones concluded his major league playing career at age 38 with the Kansas City Blues (AA) the next season. Jones's skills allegedly deteriorated rapidly after his wife discovered him with another woman and threw red pepper into his eyes. The incident supposedly damaged his batting eye permanently.

The popular, fancy dressing, hard-drinking, 6-foot, 200-pound righthander probably was baseball's first slugger. He ranked among his league's top five seven times in HR, five times in slugging average and triples, four times in runs scored, three times in hits and walks, twice in on-base average (leading the AA in 1884), and once in batting average. He batted .300 or higher in six seasons and on June 10, 1880 became the first NL player to hit two HR in one inning. His 12-year major league career resulted in a .299 batting average, 170 doubles, 98 triples, and 56 HR in 881 games. Despite losing two full seasons at the height of his career, Jones ranks 13th in productivity among regular 19th-century players.

Jones umpired in the AA in 1891 and later in the minor AtL. After moving to New York City he worked for the inspector of elections and resided in Staten Island. Baseball researchers have not yet ascertained where and when he died. His son, Charles, Jr., played minor league baseball and later became an Indiana physician.

BIBLIOGRAPHY: *The Baseball Encyclopedia*, 10th ed. (New York, 1996); Charles W. Jones file, National Baseball Library, Cooperstown, NY; David Nemec, *The Beer and Whisky League* (New York, 1994); Preston D. Orem, *Baseball (1845–1881) from the Newspaper Accounts* (Altadena, CA, 1961); Harold Seymour, *Baseball: The Early Years* (New York, 1960); Lee Allen, *The Cincinnati Reds* (New York, 1948); Gary Caruso, *The Braves Encyclopedia* (Philadelphia, PA, 1995); Robert Smith, *Baseball* (New York, 1947); Robert L. Tiemann and Mark Rucker, eds., *Nineteenth Century Stars* (Kansas City, MO, 1989); John Thorn et al., eds., *Total Baseball*, 5th ed. (New York, 1997).
                                        Frederick Ivor-Campbell and Frank P. Bowles

JONES, Douglas Reid "Doug" (b. June 24, 1957, Covina, CA), player, is the son of Rex Jones, an industrial sheet metal worker, and Hazel Jones, and grew up in Lebanon, IN. Jones attended Butler University and Central Arizona College, where he was selected a second team JC All-American as a 6-foot 2-inch, 195-pound right-handed pitcher. After being signed by Milwaukee Brewers (AL) scout Ray Pointenet in January 1978, he started the next seven seasons in the minor leagues. The Milwaukee Brewers released him in October 1984 following his mediocre 48–48 record. The Cleveland Indians (AL) signed him as a free agent in April 1985 on the condition that he become a relief pitcher.

After developing a circle changeup pitch, Jones gained his first major league victory and save in 1986 as a 30-year-old rookie for the Cleveland Indians. He credited pitching coach Mark Wiley with helping him become a successful closer. Jones made the AL All-Star team from 1988 through 1990, set a then team record of 43 saves in 1990, and twice was named Cleveland's Man of the Year by area sportswriters. His three-year ERA from 1988 through 1990 stood below 2.50.

After struggling in 1991, Jones was optioned to Colorado Springs, CO (PCL) and released in December. A non-roster invitee to spring training by the Houston Astros (NL) in 1992, he posted a career-high 11 wins with 36 saves and a 1.85 ERA, made the NL All-Star team, and was named Astros MVP. Lee Smith* edged him out by one point for the Rolaids Relief Man Award.

In December 1993, the Astros traded Jones to the Philadelphia Phillies (NL) for closer Mitch Williams. Jones again made the NL All-Star team, which led to his personal career highlight. He did not expect to get into the 1994 game, but the contest went into extra innings. Jones pitched the top of the tenth inning, striking out Cal Ripken, Jr.* and Chuck Knoblauch,* and earned the win when the NL won the contest in the last of the tenth inning.

A free agent, Jones signed with the Baltimore Orioles (AL) in March 1995. He signed with the Chicago Cubs (NL) as a free agent in December 1995 and split four decisions until being released in June 1996. After joining the Milwaukee Brewers later that month, Jones compiled a 5–0 record in 1996 and a 6–6 mark with 36 saves in 1997. He struggled in the bullpen after the Brewers switched to the NL in 1998. The Cleveland Indians acquired Jones in August 1998. He hurled 2.2 innings with a 6.75 ERA in the 1998 AL Division Series against the Boston Red Sox before being released in October 1998. In January 1999, the Oakland A's (AL) signed him as a free agent. Through 1999, he appeared in 792 games with 65 wins, 77 losses, and a 3.26 ERA. His 301 saves rank among the top 10 on the all-time list.

Unlike most closers who rely on 90-plus fastballs, Jones uses changeups, varies his speed, and throws what hitters disdainfully call "slop." He feels no pressure whatever the situation, causing scouts to say he has the guts of a burglar.

Jones married Debbie Maffai October 23, 1981. They have three sons, Dustin, Dylan, and Dawson, and live in Tucson, AZ. His off-season activities center around auto racing, which he would have pursued in some capacity if he had not made the switch to the role of reliever in 1985.

BIBLIOGRAPHY: Doug Jones file, National Baseball Library, Cooperstown, NY; *Baltimore Orioles 1995 Media Guide*; M. A. Jaffe, "A Change for the Better," *SI* 73 (July 30, 1990), p. 55; Mike Shatzkin, ed., *The Ballplayers* (New York, 1990); Norman L. Macht, personal interview with Douglas Jones, 1995; Jack Torry, *Endless Summers* (South Bend, IN, 1995); Terry Pluto, *The Curse of Rocky Colavito* (New York, 1994).

Norman L. Macht

JONES, Fielder Allison (b. August 13, 1871, Shinglehouse, PA; d. March 13, 1934, Portland, OR), player and manager, enjoyed a major league career that spanned two centuries. His playing career started in 1893 in the old OL as a catcher–outfielder. He also played for minor league teams in Corning, NY and Springfield, MA before reaching the major leagues, where the left-handed–hitting Jones performed for the Brooklyn Bridegrooms-Superbas (NL, 1896–1900) and Chicago White Sox (AL, 1901–1908).

With the exception of two games at shortstop in 1898, the aptly named Jones played in the outfield throughout his major league career and fielded flawlessly. In his first major league season, the 5-foot 11-inch, 180-pound Jones batted .354 in 104 games in 1896. Although never sporting such a lofty batting average again, Jones consistently starred for the Bridegrooms-Superbas and hit at least .300 in four of his five years with Brooklyn. When the current AL was organized in 1901, Jones joined Charles Comiskey's* Chicago White Sox and batted .311 and .321 in 1901 and 1902, respectively. Jones, then a player–manager, started as center fielder for the White Sox from 1904 to 1908. He retired following the 1908 season to "earn some money for a change" in a lumber business in Seattle, WA.

The highlight of Jones's baseball career came in 1906 season, when his White Sox compiled a pitiful .230 team batting average. Jones, a canny manager, emphasized running and pitching, as his team stole 214 bases that year. A typical White Sox rally included "a base on balls, a sacrifice, a passed ball, and a long fly." Nevertheless, the White Sox, the legendary "Hitless Wonders," squeaked by the New York Highlanders to win the AL pennant. The 1906 World Series pitted the White Sox against the favored crosstown Chicago Cubs (NL), marking the first World Series played between two teams from the same city. Jones's White Sox surprised the Cubs, four games to two. The upset victory helped to establish the AL as a legitimate competitor with the NL.

Toward the end of the 1914 season, the St. Louis Terriers (FL) enticed Jones out of retirement to replace manager Mordecai Brown.* Clearly, Jones provided a "big name" that St. Louis hoped would bring success to both the team and the fledgling FL. Jones also managed St. Louis for the entire 1915 season. With the demise of the FL, Jones remained in St. Louis to pilot the St. Louis Browns (AL) through 1918 and then returned to the lumber business. Jones compiled a career .285 batting average with 21 HR and 631 RBI and recorded a 683–582 win–loss mark in 10 managerial seasons. Jones baited umpires continuously and was outdone perhaps only by Ty Cobb* in this regard. He often ran in from center field to the infield to argue umpires' decisions and was frequently thrown out of games for kicking. Jones died of a heart inflammation.

BIBLIOGRAPHY: Fielder Jones file, National Baseball Library, Cooperstown, NY; Thomas Aylesworth and Benton Minks, *The Encyclopedia of Baseball Managers* (New York, 1990); AP, "Fielder Jones, Hitless Wonder Leader, Is Dead," March 14, 1934; Richard Goldstein, *Superstars and Screwballs* (New York, 1991); William F. McNeil, *The Dodgers Encyclopedia* (Champaign, IL, 1997); Bill Borst, ed., *Ables to Zoldak*, vol. 2 (St. Louis, MO, 1989); Richard Lindberg, *Who's on Third?* (South Bend, IN, 1983); Warren Brown, *The Chicago White Sox* (New York, 1952); *The Baseball Encyclopedia*, 10th ed. (New York, 1996); Eugene C. Murdock, *Ban Johnson: Czar of Baseball* (Westport, CT, 1982); Marc Okkonen, *The Federal League of 1914–1915* (Garrett Park, MD, 1989).

Jack P. Lipton and Susan M. Lipton

JONES, Randall Leo "Randy" (b. January 12, 1950, Fullerton, CA), player, is the son of James W. Jones and Helen (Parker) Jones and grew up in Brae, CA. Jones earned a B.A. degree in business in 1972 from Chapman College, where he played baseball. The San Diego Padres (NL) selected the 6-foot, 180-pound pitcher, who batted right and threw left-handed, in the fifth round of the June 1972 draft. Jones spent under two minor league seasons with Tri-City, WA (NWL) in 1972 and Alexandria, LA (TL) in 1972 and 1973.

Jones joined the San Diego Padres in 1973, winning seven of 13 decisions. After sharing the NL lead for most losses with 22 in 1974, he earned *TSN* Comeback Player of the Year accolades in 1975 with a 20–12 record and became the club's first 20 game winner. Jones led the senior circuit with a career-best 2.24 ERA and finished second in the NL Cy Young Award balloting. Besides tossing two one-hitters, he recorded a save in the 1975 All-Star Game. The first Padre developed superstar gave respectability to a struggling franchise. A sinker ball specialist with superb control, he induced batters to hit ground balls and hurled very short games. The crowd favorite boosted attendance at games by several thousand.

His banner 1976 season earned him the NL Cy Young Award. Jones finished with a 22–14 mark, recording senior circuit highs and season club records for wins, starts (40), complete games (25), and innings pitched (315.1). He captured 16 of 19 decisions before the All-Star break and tied Christy Mathewson's* NL record of 68 consecutive innings without allowing a walk. Half of his losses, including three shutouts, were by one run. Jones also set a major league record for most chances accepted by a pitcher (112) without making an error and won the 1976 All-Star Game.

Arm surgery for a snapped nerve limited Jones' effectiveness thereafter; he compiled a 13–14 mark and 2.88 ERA in 1978 and hurled three consecutive shutouts in May 1980. In December 1980, the Padres traded him to the New York Mets (NL). His final two major league seasons came with the New York Mets.

During his major league career, Jones compiled a 100–123 record with a 3.42 ERA and struck out 735 batters in 1,933 innings. The finesse pitcher still holds Padre career records for most starts (253), innings pitched (1,766), complete games (71), and shutouts (18) and ranks second in victories (92), fourth in ERA (3.30) and appearances (264), and fifth in strikeouts.

After arranging commissaries on military bases, Jones handled commentary on Padre games for KFMB-Radio and operates a barbecue business at Qualcomm Stadium. The Poway, CA resident married Marie Stassi and has two children.

BIBLIOGRAPHY: Randy Jones file, National Baseball Library, Cooperstown, NY; Peter C. Bjarkman, ed., *Encyclopedia of Major League Baseball Team Histories National League* (Westport, CT, 1991); Ron Fimrite, "Uncommon Success for a Common Man," *SI* 45 (July 12, 1976), pp. 20–22; Ross Forman, "Ex-Cy Young Winner Jones Is Barbecuing with Gas," *SCD* 24 (December 19, 1997), pp. 138–139; Ron Reid, "He Stoops to Low Tricks," *SI* 44 (May 17, 1976), pp. 56, 59; *TSN Official Baseball Register*, 1982.

David L. Porter

JONES, Samuel "Emperor," "Red," "Sad Sam," "Toothpick Sam" (b. December 14, 1925, Stewartsville, OH; d. November 5, 1971, Morgantown, WV), player, coach, and scout, grew up in impoverished rural West Virginia and began pitching while in the U.S. Army Air Corps. Jones pitched in 1946 for the Homestead Grays (NNL) and next two seasons for the Cleveland Buckeyes (NAL). The Cleveland Indians (AL), impressed by the exceptional curveball Jones had learned from Satchel Paige,* assigned him to Wilkes-Barre, PA (EL). The 6-foot 4-inch, 192-pound right-hander fanned an EL-high 169 batters in 219 innings and finished with a 17–8 record. For San Diego, CA (PCL) in 1951, he compiled a 16–13 mark and 2.76 ERA while leading the PCL in innings pitched (267), walks (175), and strikeouts (246). Jones made his major-league debut with the Indians in September 1951, posting a 0–1 record in two games. He pitched that winter for San Juan, PR (PRWL), recording a 13–5 mark in 118 innings.

Jones saw only limited action in 1952, finishing 2–3 for the Cleveland Indians and 4–0 for Indianapolis, IN (AA). He posted a 10–12 mark in 1953 and a 15–8 record in 1954 for Indianapolis. The following winter, he pitched for Santurce, PR (PRWL) and led the PRWL with 14 wins. In November 1954, the Cleveland Indians traded him to the Chicago Cubs (NL). In 1955, Jones finished 14–20 with a 4.10 ERA and led the NL in losses, walks (185), and strikeouts (198). His 185 bases on balls remain the NL single season record. The next year, he closed at 9–14 with a 3.91 ERA and again paced the NL in walks (115) and strikeouts (176).

In December 1956, the Chicago Cubs swapped Jones to the St. Louis Cardinals (NL). He finished with a 12–9 record and 3.60 ERA in 1957 and a 14–13 mark and 2.88 ERA in 1958, pacing the NL in walks (107) and strikeouts (225). His strikeouts comprised the most by an NL hurler in 22 years. In March 1959, the St. Louis Cardinals traded Jones to the San Francisco Giants (NL). In 1959, he led the NL in victories (21), shutouts (4), ERA (2.83), and walks (109) and captured *TSN* NL Pitcher of the Year award. The next season, he again ranked as the Giants' winningest pitcher with an 18–14 record and 3.19 ERA.

The San Francisco Giants traded Jones to the Houston Colt 45s (NL) in December 1961. He relieved for the Detroit Tigers (AL) in 1962 and pitched briefly for the St. Louis Cardinals in 1963 and the Baltimore Orioles (AL) in 1964. Jones hurled from 1964 through 1967 for Columbus, OH (IL), averaging 50 appearances per season and also serving as a coach. He later scouted briefly for the St. Louis Cardinals.

Known for his forlorn facial expression and the ever-present toothpick in his mouth, the taciturn Jones compiled a 102–101 major league career record and 3.59 ERA with 1,376 strikeouts and 822 walks in 1,643.1 innings. From 1955 through 1960, he averaged 32 starts, 15 wins, and 12 complete games per season. Jones appeared in the 1955 and 1959 All-Star Games. On May 12, 1955 against the Pittsburgh Pirates at Wrigley Field in Chicago, he became the first African-American to pitch a major league no-hitter. Jones pitched another no-hit gem against the San Francisco Giants at Busch Stadium in St. Louis, in a 1959 game halted by rain after seven innings. In 1981, he was voted into the West Virginia Sports Hall of Fame.

Jones worked for the American Laundry Company and the United Mine

Workers Association. He was survived by his widow Mary (Beans) Jones, whom he had married in February 1950, and sons, Mike and Nick.

BIBLIOGRAPHY: Samuel Jones file, National Baseball Library, Cooperstown, NY; Dick Clark and Larry Lester, eds., *The Negro Leagues Book* (Cleveland, OH, 1994); Eddie Gold and Art Ahrens, *The New Era Cubs, 1941–1985* (Chicago, IL, 1985); Ray Robinson, ed., *Baseball Stars of 1960* (New York, 1960); Jack Herman, "Sam Jones: The Toothpick Doesn't Grow Wild Any More," *BD* 17 (June 1958), pp. 45–49; *Jet* 41 (November 25, 1971), pp. 52–53; Larry Moffi and Jonathan Kronstadt, *Crossing the Line* (Jefferson, NC, 1994); Rob Rains, *The St. Louis Cardinals* (New York, 1992); Bob Broeg and Jerry Vickery, *St. Louis Cardinals Encyclopedia* (Grand Rapids, MI, 1998); John Thorn et al., eds., *Total Baseball*, 5th ed. (New York, 1997); *TSN*, November 20, 1971.

Raymond D. Kush

JONES, Samuel Pond "Sad Sam" (b. July 26, 1892, Woodsfield, OH; d. July 6, 1966, Barnesville, OH), player and coach, attended Woodsfield public schools. On his twenty-fourth birthday, he married Edith Mae Kerr. A 6-foot, 170-pound right-handed pitcher, Jones began his professional baseball career in 1913. After playing for minor league teams in Zanesville, OH (TSL), Portsmouth, OH (OSL), and Cleveland, OH (AA) in 1914, he relieved in one game for the Cleveland Indians (AL). Jones spent 1915 with the Indians, leading relievers in games and innings pitched. In April 1916, he was traded to the Boston Red Sox (AL) with infielder Fred Thomas and $50,000 for Tris Speaker.* Jones hurled sparingly the next two years for the pitching-rich Red Sox, but started regularly in 1918, winning 16 games and losing only 5 contests for an AL leading .762 winning percentage. In Game 5 of the 1918 World Series, he lost, 3–0, to Hippo Vaughn* of the Chicago Cubs.

Jones' 23 victories and AL-leading 5 shutouts in 1921 established him as one of baseball's top pitchers. The dynasty-building New York Yankees (AL) acquired Jones' contract in December 1921 and won three pennants during his five years with the club. Manager Miller Huggins* used him as both a starter and a reliever. In his best major league season (1923), Jones started 27 games, relieved in 12, and compiled a 21–8 won–lost record. He pitched a no-hit game against the Philadelphia Athletics on September 4 and started the first World Series game ever played at Yankee Stadium on October 12. He was defeated by the New York Giants' Art Nehf,* surrendering only Casey Stengel's* seventh inning HR. Three days later, he pitched two scoreless relief innings to save the deciding sixth game for the Yankees. Subsequently, Jones pitched for the St. Louis Browns (1927), Washington Senators (1928–1931), and Chicago White Sox (1932–1935), all of the AL. His career totals included 229 wins, 217 losses, 36 shutouts, and a 3.84 ERA. In 1940, he served as a pitcher–coach for Toronto, Canada (IL).

Jones set an AL longevity record by pitching 22 consecutive seasons. He attributed his longevity to his disinclination to throw to first base to hold enemy base runners close, preferring to conserve his energy for the batter. Although nicknamed "Sad Sam," he did not possess a lugubrious personality. The sobriquet was bestowed by a rookie sportswriter who had never met Jones and was impressed by his serious demeanor on the field.

BIBLIOGRAPHY: Samuel P. Jones file, National Baseball Library, Cooperstown, NY; Mark Gallagher, *The Yankee Encyclopedia*, vol. 3 (Champaign, IL, 1997); Frederick G. Lieb, *The Boston Red Sox* (New York, 1947); Robert Redmount, *The Red Sox Encyclopedia* (Champaign, IL, 1998); Frank Graham, *The New York Yankees* (New York, 1945); *The Baseball Encyclopedia*, 10th ed. (New York, 1996); Dave Anderson et al., *The Yankees* (New York, 1979); Bill Borst, ed., *Ables to Zoldak*, vol. 2 (New York, 1989); Shirley Povich, *The Washington Senators* (New York, 1954); Warren Brown, *The Chicago White Sox* (New York, 1952); Lawrence S. Ritter, *The Glory of Their Times* (New York, 1966).

Dennis T. "Tom" Chase

JONES, Stuart "Slim" (b. May 6, 1913, Baltimore, MD; d. December 1938, Baltimore, MD), player, ranks among the hardest-throwing pitchers ever to play baseball. During the mid-1930s, the 6-foot 6-inch, 185-pound left-hander dominated black baseball with his overpowering speed. National Baseball Hall-of-Famer Buck Leonard,* who faced both pitchers, asserts that Jones threw harder than Lefty Grove.* Catchers found Jones's low fastball almost as hard to handle as batters found it to hit. With a good curveball to complement his "running" fastball, Jones always was finished among the leaders in strikeouts. In 1933, he struck out 210 batters in the PRWL.

The following year, Jones earned an enviable 32–4 win–loss record to almost single-handedly lead the Philadelphia Stars to the NNL championship. His 2–0 shutout of the Chicago American Giants in the deciding seventh game capped the Stars' championship drive. Jones's last victory in the 1934 season came in a postseason exhibition against Dizzy Dean,* who had won 30 games for the World Champion St. Louis Cardinals. That season also marked the first of Jones's two consecutive selections (1934–1935) as the starting pitcher for the East squad in the East–West All-Star game. His two All-Star appearances produced six scoreless innings against the West's best hitters.

Duels between Jones and Satchel Paige* in Yankee Stadium in New York remained a featured attraction during the heart of the depression years. A 1–1 deadlock between these two great hurlers in 1934 is considered by many authorities on the Negro League to be the greatest game ever played in the history of black baseball. Jones pitched a perfect game for six innings. The game was halted by darkness after nine innings, with Jones achieving a three-hitter and nine strikeouts. Paige also fashioned a masterpiece, fanning a dozen batters while yielding only six hits. Jones's career was cut short after six superlative seasons in the Negro Leagues in 1938 when he encountered drinking problems and died of pneumonia.

BIBLIOGRAPHY: Robert W. Peterson, *Only the Ball Was White* (Englewood Cliffs, NJ, 1970); James A. Riley, *The All-Time All-Stars of Black Baseball* (Cocoa, FL, 1983); James A. Riley, *The Biographical Encyclopedia of the Negro Baseball Leagues* (New York, 1994); James A. Riley, interviews with former Negro League players, James A. Riley Collection, Cocoa, FL.

James A. Riley

JONES, Willie Edward "Puddinhead" (b. August 16, 1925, Dillon, SC; d. October 18, 1983, Cincinnati, OH), player, attended Laurel High School and served three years in the U.S. Navy from 1944 to 1946. Jones began playing semiprofessional baseball in the Carolinas and impressed Philadelphia Phillies scout (NL) Johnny Nec. He signed a $16,500 bonus and spent two years in the minor leagues before becoming the Philadelphia Phillies regular third baseman in 1949. He remained an integral part of the Whiz Kid aggregate for 11 seasons.

The 6-foot, 198-pound, right-handed Jones enjoyed his greatest major league season in 1950, when the Philadelphia Phillies won the NL pennant. He batted .267 with 25 HR, 88 RBI, and 100 runs scored. In the 1950 World Series, Jones hit .286 with one double against the New York Yankees. He clouted 22 HR in 1951 when most of his teammates slumped badly. Jones made the NL All-Star team both years, starting the 1950 contest. He led the NL in sacrifice hits in 1951 and tied a major league record by hitting four doubles on April 20, 1949 against the Boston Braves.

The superb fielder, deceptively agile for his size, led NL third basemen in fielding percentage from 1953 through 1956 and again in 1958. Legendary Pie Traynor,* who saw Jones play third base, remarked "he's better than I was" defensively. Jones paced NL third basemen in double plays in 1951 and 1952 and tied the major league mark for most seasons leading in putouts.

After averaging 14 HR and 61 RBI for 11 major league seasons, Jones was traded to the Cleveland Indians (AL) in June 1959. Cleveland the next month shipped him to the Cincinnati Reds (NL), where he completed his major league career in 1960.

In 15 major league campaigns, Jones batted .258 with 1,502 hits, 252 doubles, 190 HR and 812 RBI. He ranks second to Del Ennis* in career HR at Connie Mack* Stadium with 90. Jones also ranks among the top ten Philadelphia players in games played (1,520), total bases (2,236), RBI, sacrifice flies (32), HR (180) and walks (693).

Jones experienced difficulty adjusting to life after baseball, including a messy divorce. He married Carolyn Goodson on November 24, 1946. They had three children, Willie Jr., Brad, and Kathie.

BIBLIOGRAPHY: Willie Jones file, National Baseball Library, Cooperstown, NY; Robin Roberts and C. Paul Rogers III, *The Whiz Kids and the 1950 Pennant* (Philadelphia, PA, 1996); Frederick G. Lieb and Stan Baumgartner, *The Philadelphia Phillies* (New York, 1953); Allen Lewis, *The Philadelphia Phillies: A Pictorial History* (Virginia Beach, VA, 1981); Harry Paxton, *The Whiz Kids* (New York, 1950); Rich Westcott and Frank Bilovsky, *The New Phillies Encyclopedia* (Philadelphia, PA, 1993).

John P. Rossi

JOOST, Edwin David "Eddie" (b. June 5, 1916, San Francisco, CA), player and manager, was of German-Dutch descent and began his professional baseball career with the Mission, CA Reds (PCL) as a 16-year-old in 1933. Joost initially reached the major leagues with the Cincinnati Reds (NL) in September 1936, but spent most of the next two years in the minor leagues. After being a utility infielder with the Cincinnati Reds in 1939 and 1940, the 6-foot, 170-pound right-hander started at second base in the 1940 World Series against the Detroit Tigers and became the regular shortstop in 1941. He married Alice Bernard in October 1937, and, after losing their two-year-old son, Edwin, Jr., to illness, asked to be traded. The Reds in December 1942 sent Joost, who eventually had four other sons, David, Dennis, Donald, and Dean, to the Boston Braves (NL), where he batted a major league-low .185 in 1943.

Joost expected a call from the U.S. Army, which never came, and voluntarily retired in 1944. He returned to the Boston Braves in 1945, but broke an ankle and fractured a wrist. He mistakenly believed he had permission to return home after the second injury. The Braves, however, suspended him indefinitely for jumping the team. Philadelphia Athletics' (AL) manager Connie Mack,* impressed by Joost's strong season at Rochester, NY (IL) in 1946, brought him back to the major leagues. Joost played for the Philadelphia Athletics from 1947 to 1954, making the AL All-Star team in 1949 and 1952. Joost, who started wearing glasses in 1948, drew more than 100 walks and reached double figures in HR for six consecutive seasons from 1947 to 1952. He set a since-broken AL record for errorless games by a shortstop and participated in an infield that set numerous double play records.

Joost succeeded Jimmy Dykes* as Philadelphia Athletics manager in 1954, but was fired after the team finished last with a 51–103 record. He played with the Boston Red Sox (AL) in 1955 and managed the San Francisco, CA Seals (PCL) in 1956. Joost, who batted .239 with 134 HR, 601 RBI, and 1,043 walks in 17 major league seasons, lives in Santa Rosa, CA.

BIBLIOGRAPHY: Eddie Joost file, National Baseball Library, Cooperstown, NY; Dwight Chapin, "Joost's Numbers Rank with Current Elite," San Francisco *Examiner*, February 24, 1991, p. C-7; Len Fiorito, "Where Are They Now?" *OBN* 4 (1992), p. 3; Stan Grosshandler, "Eddie Joost: He Was an Ideal Leadoff Hitter," *BD* 51 (February 1992), pp. 39–41; Al Hirshberg, *The Braves, The Pick, and The Shovel* (Boston, MA, 1948); Harold Kaese, *The Boston Braves* (New York, 1948); Art Morrow,

"Joost Rules A. L. Roost at Short, Philly Claims," *TSN*, June 22, 1949, p. 5; Rich Westcott, *Masters of the Diamond* (Jefferson, NC, 1994); Lee Allen, *The Cincinnati Reds* (New York, 1948); Connie Mack, *My 66 Years in the Big Leagues* (Philadelphia, PA, 1950); Thomas Aylesworth and Benton Minks, *The Encyclopedia of Baseball Managers* (New York, 1990); Robert Redmount, *The Red Sox Encyclopedia* (Champaign, IL, 1998).

Lyle Spatz

JOSS, Adrian "Addie" (b. April 12, 1880, Woodland, WI; d. April 14, 1911, Toledo, OH), player, was the son of farmers Jacob Joss and Theresa (Staudenmeyer) Joss. After attending schools in Juneau, WI and Portage, WI, he entered St. Mary's College and played on the baseball team there. He started his professional career with the Toledo, OH Mud Hens (ISL) in 1900. He married Lillian Shinivar on October 11, 1902 and had one son and one daughter.

Joss became a major-league pitcher with Cleveland (AL) in 1902 and spent nine years with the Blues and Naps. He never experienced a losing season, winning 160 games while losing only 97. He pitched 234 complete games, hurled 45 shutouts, and compiled the second best lifetime ERA (1.89) in baseball history. In his major league debut on April 26, 1902, he pitched a one-hitter. He hurled six one-hitters in his major league career, but his greatest performance was the perfect game he pitched against the Chicago White Sox on October 2, 1908. Joss needed perfection to win, 1–0, because his mound opponent, Ed Walsh,* struck out 15 batters. He recorded a second no-hitter on April 20, 1910, against Chicago. The 6-foot 3-inch, 185-pound Joss possessed long arms and proved extremely graceful in fielding. AL president Ban Johnson* said of him, "He was one of the greatest pitchers the game has ever seen." In the off-season, Joss worked as a sportswriter for the Toledo *News Bee* and Cleveland *Press* and covered the 1907–1909 World Series for the *Press*.

Despite his stellar record, Joss experienced frequent illness. High fever cost him the last month of the 1903 season. He suffered a bout with malaria in April 1904 and missed several starts in 1905 because of a bad back. On July 25, 1910, he left a game in the fifth inning because of a sore arm and never pitched again. He went to spring training in 1911, but became ill on April 3 and died of tubercular meningitis 11 days later at age 31. On July 24, 1911, Cleveland played an All-Star team in a benefit game to raise over $13,000 toward defraying some debts that Joss had incurred from his illness. The Veterans Committee voted Joss into the National Baseball Hall of Fame in 1978.

BIBLIOGRAPHY: Adrian Joss file, National Baseball Library, Cooperstown, NY; Martin Appel and Burt Goldblatt, *Baseball's Best: The Hall of Fame Gallery* (New York, 1977); Jordan Deutsch et al., *The Scrapbook History of Baseball* (New York, 1975); Franklin A. Lewis, *The Cleveland Indians* (New York, 1949); Scott Longert, *King of the Pitchers: The Short Life of Addie Joss* (Cleveland, OH, 1998); Paul MacFarlane, ed.,

TSN Hall of Fame Fact Book (St. Louis, MO, 1983); Ronald A. Mayer, *Perfect!* (Jefferson, NC, 1991); *NYT Book of Baseball History* (New York, 1975); John Thorn et al., eds., *Total Indians* (New York, 1996); John Phillips, *Who Was Who in Cleveland Baseball 1901–10* (Cabin John, MD, 1989).

Emil H. Rothe

JOYCE, William Michael "Scrappy Bill" (b. September 21, 1865, St. Louis, MO; d. May 8, 1941, St. Louis, MO), player, manager, and scout, began his diamond career with Leavenworth, KS (WL). After several more minor league stops, he joined the Brooklyn Wonders (PL) for the 1890 season as a third baseman. Although batting only .252, Joyce showed real power with 18 triples, scored 121 runs, and led the PL with 123 walks. The 1891 campaign saw him play for the Boston Reds (AA), but he broke his leg after 65 games. Joyce struggled with the Brooklyn Bridegrooms (NL) in 1892. He was traded to the Washington Senators (NL) and sat out the whole 1893 season in a salary dispute.

Joyce rejoined Washington for the 1894 season and experienced probably his best year. In just 99 games, he scored 103 runs, hit 17 HR, batted .355, and compiled a .648 slugging percentage, fifth best in the 19th century. He also surpassed the .300 batting mark in 1895 and 1896 and in 1896 was traded to the New York Giants (NL). Joyce became playing manager in 1896 and paced the NL in HR with 13. In 1897 he led the Giants to a strong third-place finish behind the Boston Red Stockings and Baltimore Orioles, batting .304 and scoring 109 runs in 109 games. On May 18, 1897, Joyce hit 4 triples to tie a record that has not been equaled since. He moved to first base for the 1898 season and then retired.

The 5-foot 11-inch, 185-pound Joyce batted from the left side and threw right-handed. His eight-year major league career .294 batting average was augmented with considerable power, including 152 doubles, 106 triples, and 70 HR, the 7th highest number of HR during the 1890s decade. Besides scoring 820 runs, he walked 718 times and stole 264 bases in just 904 games. He was considered a better than average infielder and an unusually aggressive competitor. His managerial record from 1896 to 1898 with the New York Giants came to 179 wins and 122 losses for a .595 winning percentage. Joyce scouted many years for the St. Louis Browns (AL).

BIBLIOGRAPHY: William Joyce file, National Baseball Library, Cooperstown, NY; *The Baseball Encyclopedia*, 10th ed. (New York, 1996); Shirley Povich, *The Washington Senators* (New York, 1954); Morris Bealle, *The Washington Senators* (Washington, DC, 1947); Noel Hynd, *The Giants of the Polo Grounds* (New York, 1988); James D. Hardy, Jr., *The New York Giants Baseball Club* (Jefferson, NC, 1996); John Thorn et al., eds., *Total Baseball*, 5th ed. (New York, 1997); Robert L. Tiemann and Mark Rucker, eds., *Nineteenth Century Stars* (Kansas City, MO, 1989).

Frank P. Bowles

JOYNER, Wallace Keith "Wally" (b. June 16, 1962, Atlanta, GA), player, is the youngest of five children and graduated from Redan High School in Stone Mountain, GA, where he was named GA High School Player of the Year in 1980. The devout Mormon majored in business administration at Brigham Young University, where he made Second Team All-America in baseball in 1983. The California Angels (AL) selected the 6-foot 2-inch, 200-pound left-handed first baseman in the third round of the June 1983 draft. He spent three minor league seasons with Peoria, IL (ML) in 1983, Waterbury, CT (EL) in 1984, and Edmonton, Canada (PCL) in 1985.

Joyner played first base for the California Angels (AL) from 1986 through 1991 and initially displayed considerable power. His rookie season featured a .290 batting average, career-best 172 hits, 100 RBI, AL-best 12 sacrifice flies, and All-Star appearance. Joyner finished second in the AL Rookie of the Year balloting. He batted .455 with two doubles, one HR, and two RBI in the AL Championship Series loss to the Boston Red Sox. In 1987, Joyner hit .285, attained career highs with 100 runs, 34 HR, and 117 RBI, and clouted three HR on October 3 against the Texas Rangers. He became the only Angel to make 160 hits four consecutive seasons. A .301 batter in 1991, he led AL first basemen in chances in 1988 and 1991, putouts in 1988, 1989, and 1991, assists and double plays in 1988, and fielding percentage in 1989.

In December 1991, the Kansas City Royals (AL) signed Joyner as a free agent. Joyner remained there through 1995, belting a career-best 36 doubles in 1992 and 1993 and leading the club with a .311 batting average in 1994. His peak season there came in 1995, when he paced the club in batting (.310) and doubles (28), knocked in 83 runs, and led AL first basemen with a .998 fielding percentage. The Royals sent him to the San Diego Padres (NL) in December 1995. Joyner started sensationally in 1996 until breaking his thumb in early June. He led NL first basemen with a .997 fielding percentage and helped the Padres win the NL West, but struggled in the NL Division Series loss to the St. Louis Cardinals. In 1997, he batted a career-best .327 with 83 RBI. His .298 batting average, 30 doubles, 12 HR, and 80 RBI helped the Padres capture the NL West in 1998. Joyner clouted a two-run HR to help the Padres clinch the NL Division Series against the Houston Astros. After Joyner batted .313 with two RBI in the NL Championship Series against the Atlanta Braves, New York Yankee pitchers held him hitless in the World Series. In December 1999, the Braves acquired him.

Through the 1999 season, Joyner has batted .290 with 1,961 hits, 392 doubles, 196 HR, 1,060 RBI, and a .994 fielding percentage. The line drive spray hitter shows most of his power against right-handers. Although never winning a Gold Glove, he ranks among the leading first basemen defensively. He and his wife, Lesley, a former gymnast, have four children, Jessica, McKenzie, Crosby, and Chase.

BIBLIOGRAPHY: Wally Joyner file, National Baseball Library, Cooperstown, NY; Craig Neff, "The Wonderful World of Wally," *SI* 64 (May 26, 1986), pp. 26–28, 31; "The Wonders of Wally," *NYT Biographical Service* 17 (May 1986), pp. 667–668; *TSN Baseball Register*, 1998; *San Diego Padres Media Guide*, 1998.

David L. Porter

JUDGE, Joseph Ignatius "Joe" (b. May 25, 1894, Brooklyn, NY; d. March 11, 1963, Washington, DC), player and coach, was the son of Joseph Judge and Catherine Judge and attended New York City public schools. He married Alma Gauvreau in 1914 and had four children, Joseph, Jr., Catherine, Alma, and Dorothy. After playing minor league baseball in Lewiston, ME (NEL) in 1914 and Buffalo, NY (IL) in 1915, he joined the Washington Senators (AL) in 1915. Judge, a left-handed hitting and fielding first baseman, played with Washington from 1915 to 1932, the Brooklyn Dodgers (NL) in 1933, and the Boston Red Sox (AL) in 1933 and 1934. Although a small first baseman, the 5-foot 8½-inch, 160 pounder sparkled at his position and was rivaled only by George Sisler.* Judge, chosen on Walter Johnson's* all-time Washington team, led AL first basemen in fielding five times. During his career, he made 19,278 putouts, 1,301 assists, and only 142 errors for a .993 fielding percentage. In 1920, he saved the only no-hitter Walter Johnson ever pitched by robbing the last Boston Red Sox batter, Harry Hooper,* of a base hit.

Although not a great slugger and never leading the AL in any batting category, Judge hit very consistently and compiled a .298 lifetime batting average in 2,171 major league games. During his career, he reached the .300 mark 11 times. His 2,352 hits included 433 doubles, 159 triples, and 71 HR. He scored 1,184 runs, drove in 1,034 runs, and pilfered 213 bases. In the 1924 and 1925 World Series, he batted .286 in 14 games with one HR against the New York Giants and Pittsburgh Pirates. Judge, one of the most popular players ever to play in Washington, was honored in 1930 with $10,500 of the gate receipts and numerous other gifts. He managed Baltimore, MD (IL) in 1934 and coached for the Washington Senators from 1945 to 1946. He also served as coach of the Georgetown College baseball team.

BIBLIOGRAPHY: Joe Judge file, National Baseball Library, Cooperstown, NY; Morris Bealle, *The Washington Senators* (Washington, DC, 1947); Allison Danzig and Joseph L. Reichler, *The History of Baseball* (Englewood Cliffs, NJ, 1959); Ralph Hickok, *Who's Who in American Sports* (New York, 1971); "Joe Judge Dies, Former Nat's Star," Washington *Post*, March 11, 1963, pp. A23–24; *The Baseball Encyclopedia*, 10th ed. (New York, 1996); Shirley Povich, *The Washington Senators* (New York, 1954); Henry W. Thomas, *Walter Johnson* (Washington, DC, 1995); Robert Redmount, *The Red Sox Encyclopedia* (Champaign, IL, 1998); Washington *Post*, June 28, 1930, pp. 11–13; *Who's Who in American Sports* (Washington, DC, 1928).

James K. Skipper, Jr.

JURGES, William Frederick "Billy" (b. May 9, 1908, Bronx, NY; d. March 3, 1997, Clearwater, FL), player, coach, manager, and scout, was the son of Frederick Jurges, a shipping clerk, and Anna (Horstman) Jurges and grew up in Brooklyn, NY, where he attended Richmond High School. In 1927, he entered professional baseball with Manchester, NH (NEL). The good fielding, wide-ranging shortstop attracted the attention of the Chicago Cubs (NL), who signed him after he batted .322 in 1928. Jurges spent two years with Reading, PA (IL) before the Chicago Cubs brought him to the major leagues in 1931. Despite being shot by a spurned showgirl during the 1932 season, Jurges returned to bat .364 against the New York Yankees in the World Series. The scrappy 5-foot 11-inch, 175-pound Jurges teamed with second baseman Billy Herman* to become one of the famous Chicago Cubs' double play duos. For the next six seasons, the right-handed Jurges anchored the Chicago Cubs infield. Few NL infields were better in that era. He led NL shortstops in double plays in 1935 and four times paced NL shortstops in fielding percentage.

The Chicago Cubs finished no lower than third during this span, winning the NL pennant twice. His best major league season came in 1937, when Jurges batted .298 with 18 doubles and 10 triples. His .258 career batting average included 1,613 hits. Never a power hitter, Jurges hit only 43 HR during his 17-year major league career and knocked in 656 runs.

The Chicago Cubs offered Jurges the manager position in 1938, but he suggested Gabby Hartnett* instead. Hartnett led the Chicago Cubs to the NL pennant, only again to lose the World Series to the New York Yankees. In December 1938, the Chicago Cubs traded Jurges to the New York Giants (NL). Chicago later regretted the trade. Jurges had given them stability at shortstop, if not an outstanding bat. His best year with the New York Giants came in 1941, when he batted .293. After the 1943 season, his last as a regular, Jurges played third base and some shortstop. He later returned to the Chicago Cubs in 1946 as a utility player, staying two more seasons before retiring. Jurges then became a scout and minor league manager with Cedar Rapids, IA (3IL) in 1950 and Hagerstown, MD (PiL) in 1953. He returned to the major leagues as a coach with the Washington Senators (AL) from 1956 through July 1959. He landed a managerial job with the Boston Red Sox (AL) in July 1959 and was fired a year later with a 78–83 composite record. Under Jurges, infielder Pumpsie Green ended the Boston Red Sox status as the only major league team without an African-American player. Jurges, who married Mary Huyette in June 1933 and had one daughter, Suzanne, scouted for the Chicago Cubs from 1979 through 1982 and resided in Largo, FL.

BIBLIOGRAPHY: Billy Jurges file, National Baseball Library, Cooperstown, NY; Art Ahrens and Eddie Gold, *Day by Day in Chicago Cubs History* (West Point, NY, 1982); *The Baseball Encyclopedia*, 10th ed. (New York, 1996); Eddie Gold and Art Ahrens,

The Golden Era Cubs, 1876–1940 (Chicago, IL, 1985); Rich Westcott, *Diamond Greats* (Westport, CT, 1988); Thomas Aylesworth and Benton Minks, *The Encyclopedia of Baseball Managers* (New York, 1990); Jim Enright, *Chicago Cubs* (New York, 1975); Warren Brown, *The Chicago Cubs* (New York, 1946); Fred Stein, *Under Coogan's Bluff* (Glenshaw, PA, 1978); Peter Williams, *When the Giants Were Giants* (Chapel Hill, NC, 1994).

Duane A. Smith

JUSTICE, David Christopher "Dave" (b. April 14, 1966, Cincinnati, OH), player, overcame his father's abandonment as a child. His mother, Nettie, by enormous self-sacrifice, gave her only child unconditional love and most of his material needs. She sent him to Covington, KY Latin School, a high-powered Roman Catholic institution that required students to skip the seventh and eighth grades. As a 15-year-old senior, Justice averaged 25.9 points a game in basketball and excelled in other sports. Major college recruiters shied away because of his age. He attended Thomas More College, an NAIA institution in Kentucky, on a basketball scholarship. When Justice switched to baseball as a college sophomore, his play attracted considerable attention. As an 18-year-old senior, he signed a professional baseball contract with the Atlanta Braves (NL).

Justice labored as a first baseman in the minor leagues for six years, beginning with Pulaski, VA (ApL). He never hit more than 12 HR in a season as a minor leaguer, but belted 28 in 1990 in his first full campaign with the Braves. By August, he had moved from first base to right field following Dale Murphy's* departure. In the final two months, Justice clouted 20 HR, drove in 50 runs, and exhibited a rifle arm. Overall, he batted .282 with 78 RBI in only 127 games, earning NL Rookie of the Year honors. During the next two seasons, Justice faced difficult times and declining popularity largely because of a back injury and brashness. His marriage to actress Halle Berry momentarily turned his personal life around, but they were divorced in 1997. His most productive season came in 1993, when he clouted 40 HR, drove in 140 runs, and placed third in the MVP balloting. Various injuries have restricted his play in recent years. In the strike-shortened 1994 season, Justice batted .313 and belted 19 HR in 352 appearances. His batting average slipped to .253 in limited 1995 action, even though he hit 24 HR and drove in 78 runs. A dislocated shoulder sidelined him for virtually the entire 1996 season.

In NL postseason play through 1996, Justice hit .223 with seven HR. His best effort came against the Pittsburgh Pirates in the 1993 NL Championship Series, when he batted .280. In the sixth game of the 1995 World Series against the Cleveland Indians, his dramatic HR enabled the Braves to win 1–0 and clinch a World Series championship. Justice has also played in the 1993, 1994, and 1997 All Star games.

In March 1997, he and Marquis Grissom* were traded to the Cleveland

Indians (AL) for Kenny Lofton* and Allen Embree. Although suffering a hyperextended elbow, Justice blistered AL pitching for a .329 batting average, 33 HR, and 101 RBI as a DH and left fielder. He batted .300 with one HR and two RBI in the 1997 AL Division Series and Championship Series against the New York Yankees and the Baltimore Orioles, respectively. In the 1997 World Series against the Florida Marlins, he slumped to .185 with no extra base hits. The Indians were defeated in seven games. His .280 batting average, 21 HR, and 88 RBI helped the Indians capture the NL Central Division in 1998. He batted .313 with one HR and six RBI in the AL Division Series against the Boston Red Sox, but New York Yankees pitchers limited him to three hits in the World Series. The Indians won another AL Central Division title in 1999 as Justice batted .287 with 21 HR and 88 RBI. He also played in the AL Division Series. His career marks include a .283 batting average, 235 HR, and 799 RBI.

BIBLIOGRAPHY: *Atlanta Braves Media Guide*, 1997; Gary Caruso, *The Braves Encyclopedia* (Philadelphia, PA, 1995); D. Howerton, "David Justice," *Sport* 87 (June 1996), pp. 22ff; Jeff Schultz, "Lone Justice," *Sport* 83 (April 1992), pp. 63–64; John Ed Bradley, "Justice Prevails," *SI* 80 (June 6, 1994), pp. 67–70; Vincent Coppola, "Beauty and the Brave," *Redbook* 183 (July 1994), pp. 46, 48–50; I. J. Rosenberg, "David Justice," *Sport* 85 (June 1994), pp. 26, 28; Akron (OH) *Beacon Journal*, March 26, 1997; John Thorn et al., eds., *Total Braves* (New York, 1996).

James N. Giglio

Lou Gehrig
Unless otherwise credited, all photographs appearing in this volume are courtesy of
the National Baseball Hall of Fame Library, Cooperstown, NY.

Charlie Gehringer

Bob Gibson

Josh Gibson

Hank Greenberg

KEN GRIFFEY JR.

Ken Griffey, Jr.

Lefty Grove

Tony Gwynn

William Hamilton

Rickey Henderson

Rogers Hornsby

Joe Jackson

REGGIE JACKSON
Rightfielder
1981

Reggie Jackson

Ban Johnson

Walter Johnson

Al Kaline

Dorothy Kamenshek

Tim Keefe

Harmon Killebrew

Ralph Kiner

Judge Kenesaw Mountain Landis

Tony Lazzeri

Buck Leonard

John Henry "Pop" Lloyd

Joe McCarthy

Willie McCovey

John McGraw

Mark McGwire
(Photo credit: National Baseball Hall of Fame Library, Cooperstown, NY; courtesy
of Rich Pilling Photo)

Connie Mack

Greg Maddux

Mickey Mantle

Christy Mathewson

Willie Mays

Paul Molitor

Joe Morgan

Eddie Murray

Stan Musial

Kid Nichols

Mel Ott

Satchel Paige

K

KAAT, James Lee "Jim" (b. November 7, 1938, Zeeland, MI), player, coach, and sportscaster, became one of few major leaguers appearing in four decades by pitching from 1959 through 1983. After attending Hope College in Holland, MI, he began his baseball career with Superior, NE (NeSL) in 1957. He pitched for Missoula, MT (PrL) in 1958 and led hurlers in games started (30) and shutouts (5). Kaat performed for Chattanooga, TN (SA) in 1959 and Charleston, WV (AA) in 1960 and compiled a 1–7 record in brief appearances with the Washington Senators (AL) those seasons. The 6-foot 5-inch, 195-pound left-hander played for the AL Minnesota Twins (1961–1973), AL Chicago White Sox (1973–1975), NL Philadelphia Phillies (1976–1979), AL New York Yankees (1979–1980), and NL St. Louis Cardinals (1980–1983). In July 1983, the Cardinals released Kaat.

In 898 major league games, Kaat compiled a 283–237 won–lost record (237–191 in the AL; 46–43 in the NL), recorded a 3.45 ERA in 4,530.1 innings, and struck out 2,461 batters. The slick-fielding Kaat won 16 consecutive Gold Glove awards from 1962 through 1977, made three AL All-Star teams (1962, 1966, 1975) and two *TSN* All-Star teams (1966, 1975), and was named *TSN* AL Pitcher of the Year in 1966. His 16 career HR paced active major league pitchers at the time of his retirement.

Kaat made major league history in the Cardinals' opening game on April 6, 1982, when he surpassed Early Wynn* to become the first pitcher to appear in 24 major league seasons. Besides establishing a major league record for most career sacrifice flies allowed (134), he set AL marks for most games lost by a left-handed pitcher (191) and most career sacrifice flies allowed (108). During his major league career, Kaat won at least 20 games three times (1966, 1974, 1975) and reached a career-high 25–13 mark with the 1966 Twins. He recorded at least 10 victories for 15 consecutive seasons (1962–1976) and participated on the 1965 AL champion Minnesota Twins and 1982 World Series champion St. Louis Cardinals. Kaat also helped Minnesota and Philadelphia win division titles in 1970 and 1976, respectively. A resident of Stuart, FL, the very durable Kaat married Julie Anne Moore in October 1959 and later wed Linda Jankowski. He has two children, Jim, Jr., and Jill. Kaat served as pitching coach for the Cincinnati Reds (NL) in 1984 and 1985 and announced for the New York Yankees (AL) in 1986, Atlanta Braves (NL) in 1987, Minnesota Twins (AL) from 1988 through 1993, ESPN in 1994, and the New York Yankees since 1995. Kaat has been a leading participant in the Baseball Chapel Movement.

BIBLIOGRAPHY: Jim Kaat file, National Baseball Library, Cooperstown, NY; Peter C. Bjarkman, ed., *Encyclopedia of Major League Baseball Team Histories American League* (Westport, CT, 1991); *St. Louis Cardinals Media Guide* (1983); *TSN Official Baseball Register*, 1984; Rich Marazzi, "Jim Kaat," *SCD* 22 (November 3, 1995), pp. 170–171; Rich Marazzi, "Jim Kaat," *SCD* 22 (November 10, 1995), pp. 100–111; Bob Broeg and Jerry Vickery, *St. Louis Cardinals Encyclopedia* (Grand Rapids, MI, 1998); Rich Lindberg, *Who's on Third?* (South Bend, IN, 1983); Rich Westcott and Frank Bilovsky, *The New Phillies Encyclopedia* (Philadelphia, PA, 1993).

                                                                    Brian R. Kelleher

KALINE, Albert William "Al" (b. December 19, 1934, Baltimore, MD), player and sportscaster, is the youngest of the three children of broommaker Nicholas Kaline and housekeeper Naomi Kaline and has two older sisters, Margaret and Caroline. Nicholas, his two brothers, and his father played semiprofessional baseball on the Maryland Eastern Shore and encouraged him to play sandlot ball in Baltimore. At age 8 Kaline suffered from osteomyelitis, a bone disease that forced surgeons to remove two inches of bone from his left foot. This condition caused Kaline problems throughout his career. As a star at Southern High School in Baltimore, he made the All-Maryland team four seasons and hit .488 his senior year. In 1953, the Detroit Tigers (AL) paid the 6-foot 2-inch, 184-pound, right-handed Kaline a $30,000 bonus to sign. Kaline gave the money to his parents so that they could pay off their mortgage and finance an operation needed to save his mother's eyesight. Joining the Tigers after his graduation, Kaline hit only .250 in 30 games his initial season. In 1954, he raised his batting average to .276 and played a solid right field. Determined to become a consistent hitter, he improved his batting eye, swing, and arm and wrist strength. His remarkable 1955 season included leading both leagues with a .340 batting average (making him the youngest player ever to win a major league batting title), garnering an AL-leading 200 hits, driving in 102 runs, hitting 27 HR, and producing 321 total bases. This phenomenal season at age 20 put tremendous pressure on Kaline, who was compared to Ty Cobb* and Joe DiMaggio.* Although never winning another batting championship or again reaching the 200-hit level, he proved a consistent hitter and a spectacular outfielder noted for his speed, rifle arm, and smart defensive play. His second best season came in 1959, when he hit .327 and led the AL with a .530 slugging average. In the 1968 World Series against the St. Louis Cardinals, he batted .379 with 11 hits and eight RBI. During his 22 years with the Tigers through 1974, Kaline hit over .300 nine times, amassed 3,007 hits, knocked in 1,583 runs, slugged 399 HR, and compiled a .297 lifetime batting average. Like Mickey Mantle,* Kaline suffered numerous serious injuries and overcame them to return to the lineup with renewed dedication. The winner of 11 Gold Glove fielding awards, he became the first Tiger player to be paid over $100,000 a year. He married Louise Hamilton on October 16, 1954 and has two sons, Mark and Michael. The greatest Tigers player of the post–World War II era, Kaline was elected to the National Baseball Hall of Fame in 1980 in his first year of eligibility. Kaline's records speak for themselves, but his remarkable character, discipline, dedication, intensity of effort, and gentlemanly sportsmanship have enhanced his legend. Since retirement as an active player, he has served as an executive for a Detroit automotive engineering firm, a sportscaster of Tigers games with George Kell* for WDIV-TV, and a spring training coach for the Tigers. One of the most respected and honored players in Tigers baseball history, he was named by the fans in 1969 to the All-Time Tigers team. He has served as vice-president of the BBPAA since 1992.

BIBLIOGRAPHY: Al Kaline file, National Baseball Library, Cooperstown, NY; William Anderson, *The Detroit Tigers* (South Bend, IN, 1996); "Al Kaline: Better Than Most," *IS* 6 (October 1984), pp. 54, 56, 58; Hal Butler, *Al Kaline and the Detroit Tigers* (Chicago, IL 1973); *CB* (1970), pp. 211–214; Joe Falls, *Detroit Tigers* (New York, 1975); Gene Karst and Martin J. Jones, Jr., *Who's Who in Professional Baseball* (New Rochelle, NY, 1973); Joe LaPointe, "Detroit's Real Home Tome," Detroit *Free Press Sunday Magazine* (September 23, 1984); Fred Smith, *995 Tigers* (Detroit, MI, 1981); John Thom, *Champion Batsman of the 20th Century* (Los Angeles, CA, 1992).

Douglas A. Noverr

KAMENSHEK, Dorothy Mary "Dottie," "Kammie" (b. December 21, 1925, Cincinnati, OH), player, is the daughter of Nicolas Kamenshek, a barber, and Johanna (Bandenburg) Kamenshek and grew up in an impoverished family. Her father died when she was only nine years old. She started playing organized softball at age 12 and helped H. H. Meyers Packing Company to the National Championships two years later. She graduated from St. Bernard High School in 1943 and studied physical education at the University of Cincinnati from 1949 to 1951.

After competing in an industrial softball league, Kamenshek became the best AAGPBL player. She survived tryouts for the AAGPBL in Cincinnati and at Wrigley Field in Chicago. The 5-foot 6-inch, 136 pounder, who batted and threw left-handed, joined the Rockford Peaches as a 17-year-old outfielder for the inaugural 1943 AAGPBL season, batting .271 with a season-high 39 RBI and 42 stolen bases in 110 games. Manager Eddie Stumpf switched her to first base after just 12 games.

Kamenshek played first base for Rockford from 1943 to 1951 and in 1953, compiling a career .292 batting average with 1,090 hits, 304 RBI, and 657 stolen bases in 1,012 games. No long-time AAGPBL player compiled a higher career batting average. She struck out only 81 times in 3,736 plate appearances. She ranks as the AAGPBL career leader in hits, putouts (10,440), and defensive double plays (360) and remains second in runs scored (667). The AAGPBL selected her to its All-Star team in 1943 and six consecutive seasons from 1946 to 1951.

Kamenshek consistently ranked among the AAGPBL's top 10 batters and best base stealers. In 1944, she paced the AAGPBL with fewest strikeouts (6) and most at bats (447). The following year, Kamenshek scored the most runs (80) and recorded the most at bats (419). She led the AAGPBL twice in batting in the dead ball era, hitting .316 in 1946 and .306 in 1947. She attained season highs of 129 hits and 109 stolen bases in 1946 and six HR in 1947. Her batting average improved to .334 in 1950 and a season-high .345 in 1951 when the AAGPBL ball became smaller and livelier. Betty Foss,* however, won the batting crown those seasons.

Kamenshek formed the AAGPBL's best double play combination with second baseman Snooky Harrell* and pioneered the idea of first basemen stretching for throws from infielders. New York Yankees first baseman Wally Pipp* called Kamenshek "the fanciest fielding first baseman I've ever seen, man or woman." Pipp believed that she could have been the first woman to play in men's major league baseball. In 1947, Kamenshek declined an organized baseball contract from Fort Lauderdale, FL (FIL). "I was happy where I was," she recalled, "and I didn't want to be a guinea pig."

Rockford won AAGPBL regular season championships in 1945, 1949, and 1950 and the World Series in 1945, 1948, 1949, and 1950. In the 1945 semifinals against the Grand Rapids Chicks, Kamenshek made two singles and one triple in one game. She underwent physical therapy after suffering a back injury in 1949 and quit the AAGPBL in 1952 to study physical therapy at Marquette University. In 1953, Kamenshek returned to play home games for the financially ailing Peaches. She earned a B.S. degree from Marquette University in 1958 and was employed three years as a physical therapist in Michigan. After moving to California in 1961, Kamenshek worked as chief of the Los Angeles Crippled Children's Service Department until 1984. The Cathedral City, CA resident, who is single, is part of the character Dottie Hinson in the 1992 movie *A League of Their Own.*

BIBLIOGRAPHY: Lois Browne, *Girls of Summer* (New York, 1993); Barbara Gregorich, *Women at Play* (San Diego, CA, 1993); Dorothy Kamenshek, letter to David L. Porter, March 7, 1996, David L. Porter Collection, Oskaloosa, IA; W. C. Madden, *The Women of the All-American Girls Professional Baseball League* (Jefferson, NC, 1997);

Rich Marazzi, "Could Kammie Kamenshek Have Been the First Woman to Play in the Major Leagues?" *SCD* 22 (July 21, 1995), pp. 130–132.

David L. Porter

KAMM, William Edward "Willie" (b. February 2, 1900, San Francisco, CA; d. December 21, 1988, Belmont, CA), player, scout, and manager, was the son of baker Edward Kamm and Frieda Kamm, both of whom were German-born. He played baseball at Emerson Primary School, Hamilton Intermediate School, and in a semiprofessional league at age 15. At midseason of 1918, he joined Sacramento, CA (PCL) for two games as an infielder. The 5-foot 10½-inch, 170-pound Kamm, who batted and threw right-handed, performed for the San Francisco, CA Seals (PCL) from 1919 through 1922. Kamm's final season in 1922 proved his best, with 222 hits, 173 runs, 20 HR, and a .342 batting average.

Following the 1922 campaign, Charles A. Comiskey,* owner of the Chicago White Sox (AL), purchased Kamm's contract for $100,000. The amount then marked the highest sum ever paid for a minor leaguer. Kamm remained with the White Sox from 1923 to May 1931, when he was traded to the Cleveland Indians (AL) for Lou Fonseca.* An excellent third baseman and a consistent hitter, Kamm enjoyed his best season in 1928 with a .308 batting average. The expert on the hidden ball trick led AL third basemen in fielding percentage for six straight seasons from 1924 to 1929 and in 1933 and 1934 and was voted in 1954 to the All-Time White Sox team. He established two AL fielding records, compiling a .978 percentage in 1926 and 1929 and 243 putouts in 1928. His glove is displayed at the National Baseball Hall of Fame.

A disagreement with Cleveland manager Walter Johnson* during the 1935 season caused Kamm to become a scout for the Indians. He managed the San Francisco, CA Missions (PCL) for the next two seasons prior to his retirement. The .281 career hitter played in 1,693 games, made 1,643 hits, including 348 doubles, 85 triples, and 29 HR, scored 802 runs, drove in 826 runs, and stole 126 bases. Kamm, a bachelor until marrying Frances Mary Kotowicz in 1955, died of Parkinson's disease.

BIBLIOGRAPHY: Willie Kamm file, National Baseball Library, Cooperstown, NY; *The Baseball Encyclopedia*, 10th ed. (New York, 1996); Gene Karst and Martin J. Jones, Jr., *Who's Who in Professional Baseball* (New Rochelle, NY, 1973); *NYT*, December 24, 1988, p. 32; *TSN*, August 17, 1933, December 28, 1936, November 13, 1965, pp. 7, 12, January 9, 1989, p. 43; Lawrence S. Ritter, *The Glory of Their Times* (New York, 1966); Warren Brown, *The Chicago White Sox* (New York, 1952); Richard Lindberg, *Who's on Third?* (South Bend, IN, 1983); Franklin Lewis, *The Cleveland Indians* (New York, 1949).

John L. Evers

KAUFF, Benjamin Michael "Benny" (b. January 5, 1890, Pomeroy, OH; d. November 17, 1961, Columbus, OH), player, led the FL in batting and stolen bases in both years of its operation. Only one other major league baseball player, Honus Wagner,* won consecutive batting and stolen base titles. Later, baseball commissioner Kenesaw Mountain Landis* banned Kauff from professional baseball in a highly autocratic, arbitrary decision.

The son of a Slavic coal miner, William Kauff, he dropped out of school at age 11 to work as a breaker boy at the coal mines around Middletown, OH. Although only 5-feet 8-inches and 157 pounds, he developed thick, powerful legs and a barrel chest from the mine work. Foot speed, self-confidence, and a drive to escape the mines helped the left-handed hitter star on local teams, the amateur Keystone club in 1908 and the Middleport, OH semiprofessional team in 1909.

Kauff turned to baseball professionally in 1910 with Parkersburg, WV (VVL), where he led organized baseball with a .417 batting average and also stole 87 bases. In 1911 at Bridgeport, CT (CtL), he hit a solid .294. The New York Highlanders (AL) purchased him before the 1912 season, but shipped him to Rochester, NY (IL) after he hit .273 in only five games. Rochester sold him to Brockton, MA (NEL), where his poor .208 batting average led again to his sale to Hartford, CT (CtL). He regained his batting stroke with Hartford, hitting .321 for the remainder of 1912 and leading the EA in 1913 with a .345 batting average.

Kauff achieved his greatest fame as the outstanding player of the upstart FL. When the FL declared itself a major league, Kauff signed with the Indianapolis, IN Hoosiers. In 1914, he led the FL in batting (.370), on base percentage (.447), stolen bases (75), hits (211), doubles (44), and runs scored (120) and was lauded as "the Ty Cobb of the Federal League." Shifted to the Brooklyn Tip-Tops (FL) in 1915, Kauff again led the FL in batting (.342), on base percentage (.446), slugging percentage (.509), and stolen bases (55). New York Giants (NL) manager John McGraw* attempted to sign Kauff in 1915, but the deal was voided by the NL president. When the FL disbanded, McGraw's New York Giants purchased Kauff's contract from the Brooklyn Tip-Tops for $35,000. Kauff refused to report to the New York Giants until they agreed to pay him a $5,000 settlement.

Despite Kauff's foppish attire and rather disappointing playing statistics with the New York Giants, McGraw admired his hustle and aggressive playing style. To the fiery manager, Kauff was "a player of the old school. He thinks and lives baseball. . . . There aren't many players like that today." After hitting only .264 in 1916, Kauff raised his batting average to .308 in 1917 to help the New York Giants win the NL pennant. He batted a weak .160 in the New York Giants' World Series loss to the Chicago White Sox.

Kauff's fast living led to his banishment. He was rumored to have been involved in or at least to have known about the famous Chicago White Sox fix of the 1919 World Series. At the 1920 grand jury hearings in Chicago,

IL, Kauff testified that his 1919 teammates Hal Chase* and Heinie Zimmerman* had offered him bribes to throw games. As a result of Kauff's testimony, Zimmerman was suspended from baseball. In February 1920, Kauff was indicted in New York for auto theft. When his trial date was postponed, Kauff played in 1920. In July 1920, however, the New York Giants traded him to Toronto, Canada (IL) for Vernon Spencer. Commissioner Landis suspended Kauff from organized baseball before the 1921 season pending the outcome of his trial. The original charge of grand larceny was reduced to receiving stolen property. Character testimony from McGraw and former NL president John K. Tener* helped Kauff gain acquittal.

Despite the jury's verdict, Landis in August 1921 refused to lift Kauff's suspension. Kauff went to court to seek his return to baseball. At the trial, Landis labeled Kauff's earlier acquittal "one of the worst miscarriages of justice" and charged that Kauff's "mere presence in the line-up would inevitably burden patrons of the game with grave apprehensions as to its integrity." The New York Supreme Court ruled against Kauff. Kauff maintained, "I never did anything wrong." After 1921, he worked as a salesman in Columbus, OH for the John Lymann Company. In parts of eight major league seasons, he batted .311 with 49 HR, 454 RBI, and 234 stolen bases in 859 games. He died of a cerebral hemorrhage in Columbus, OH, still hoping a new commissioner would absolve him.

BIBLIOGRAPHY: Benny Kauff file, National Baseball Library, Cooperstown, NY; Charles C. Alexander, *John McGraw* (New York, 1988); Frank Graham, "There Was Only One Benny Kauff," *BD* 21 (February 1962), p. 81; Bob Lemke, "The Bleacher Bum: The Benny Kauff Story," *SCD* 20 (April 2–30, 1993); Marc Okkonen, *The Federal League of 1914–1915* (Garrett Park, MD, 1989); J. G. Taylor Spink, *Judge Landis and 25 Years of Baseball* (New York, 1947); Eliot Asinof, *Eight Men Out* (New York, 1963); Dan Gutman, *Baseball Babylon* (New York, 1992); Daniel E. Guinsburg, *The Fix Is In* (Jefferson, NC, 1995); Frank Graham, *The New York Giants* (New York, 1952); Noel Hynd, *The Giants of the Polo Grounds* (New York, 1988).

William E. Akin

KEAGLE, Merle Patricia "Pat" (b. March 21, 1923, Tolleson, AZ; d. November 12, 1960, Tolleson, AZ), player, was the daughter of Thomas Keagle, an automobile mechanic, and Marion Keagle. As a youngster with three older brothers, she participated in typical boyish activities from climbing trees to playing baseball. Keagle graduated from Tolleson's small high school in 1941 and excelled at all positions in several independent girls' softball leagues from age 15. In 1943, AAGPBL scout Bill Allington discovered Keagle in a summer league game and signed her for the Milwaukee Chicks franchise.

Upon arriving in Milwaukee for the 1944 season, Keagle did not look like a baseball player. The 5-foot 2-inch, 144-pound stylish blonde outfielder from the southwest desert dressed like a recent charm school graduate, but looks proved deceiving. In her first game with Milwaukee, she singled twice, doubled, and homered, and knocked in all four runs as the Chicks defeated the Kenosha Comets, 4–2. Defensively, the center fielder frequently took fly balls from her left field and right field teammates. Her skill and take-charge attitude pleased fans, who quickly dubbed her the "Blonde Bombshell."

The Chicks, paced by Keagle, won the 1944 AAGPBL championship. In 109 games, the aggressive power-hitter batted .264, led her team with 107 hits and 47 RBI, paced the AAGPBL with 145 total bases and shared the AAGPBL lead with 19 extra base hits. Her seven HR set an AAGPBL season record. Despite the title, attendance and fan support remained sparse. The Chicks, thus, moved from Milwaukee to Grand Rapids, MI for the 1945 season. Keagle left the Grand Rapids Chicks for Arizona to marry her fiancé, Charles, and give birth to their son.

The ever popular Keagle rejoined the Chicks in 1946 and continued her stellar outfield play, making the All-Star team. She also pitched six games, winning three while losing two. Offensively, she paced AAGPBL outfielders with a .284 batting average, shared the AAGPBL doubles title with 15, ranked third in RBI with 59, and made the All-Star team. Grand Rapids, however, finished a distant third in the AAGPBL standings. Keagle left the Chicks before the season ended due to fatigue and early signs of cancer.

Keagle, recuperating at her Arizona home, followed the Grand Rapids Chicks' 1947 season. As her health improved, she played several games with the independent Arizona Queens. In March 1948, Keagle reported to Opalacka, FL with a flashy wardrobe of sportswear and carrying an extra 10 pounds. But she remained as popular and mischievous as ever and quickly played herself into condition. Her offensive production declined, as she batted .251, with 23 extra base hits over 116 games. With just nine games remaining, she tore her left anklebone from its socket sliding into second base. The severity of her injury and recurrence of her illness forced Keagle to retire following the 1948 season. Her health remained a deterrent to the AAGPBL's demanding schedule. In three full seasons, Keagle batted .266, scored 216 runs, collected 63 extra base hits, clouted 12 HR, and stole 314 bases in 337 games. In 1951 she was diagnosed with cancer which ultimately ended her young, vibrant life.

BIBLIOGRAPHY: AAGPBL files, Joyce Sports Research Collection, Hesburgh Library, University of Notre Dame, South Bend, IN; Gai Berlage, *Women in Baseball* (Westport, CT, 1994); Lois Browne, *Girls of Summer* (New York, 1993); Susan M. Cahn, "No Freaks, No Amazons, No Boyish Bobs," *CH* 18 (Spring 1989), pp. 26–41; Harold T. Dailey, AAGPBL Records, Pattee Library, Pennsylvania State University, University Park, PA; Jay Feldman, "Glamour Ball," *SH* 1 (May/June 1987), pp. 59–69; Jack Fincher, "The Belles of the Ball Game Were a Hit with Their Fans," *Smithsonian* 20 (July 1989), pp. 88–97; Barbara Gregorich, *Women at Play* (San Diego, CA, 1993); Susan E. Johnson, *When Women Played Hardball* (Seattle, WA, 1994); Sue Macy, *A Whole New Ball Game* (New York, 1993); W. C. Madden, *The Women of the*

All-American Girls Professional Baseball League (Jefferson, NC, 1997); National Base-ball Hall of Fame Library, Cooperstown, NY; AAGPBL files, Northern Indiana Historical Society, South Bend, IN; Jack Stenbuck, "Glamour Girls of Big League Ball," *MD* (July 1946), pp. 70–73.

Jerry J. Wright

KEANE, John Joseph "Johnny" (b. November 3, 1911, St. Louis, MO; d. January 6, 1967, Houston, TX), player, coach, and manager, attended St. Louis Preparatory Seminary and Kenrick Seminary in St. Louis to study for the Roman Catholic priesthood. After Keane played the infield on the United Team in the local University City League, St. Louis Cardinals' (NL) scout Charley Barrett signed him. Keane, of Irish and French descent, began his professional baseball career at Waynesboro, VA (BRL). For a dozen sea-sons, he played shortstop and third base in Branch Rickey's* sprawling Cardinals' farm system. The good fielder and decent hitter might have made the major leagues as a player, but nearly died in 1935 after being hit in the head by a pitch from big right-hander Sig Jakucki. Keane married Lela Reid in November 1936 and had a daughter, Patricia.

Keane managed the St. Louis Cardinals' farm team at Albany, GA (GFL) in 1938 and piloted Redbird farm clubs for the next 21 years. From 1946 to 1958, Keane won five minor league pennants and five championship playoffs, managing at Houston, TX (TL), Rochester, NY (IL), Columbus, OH (IL) and Omaha, NE (AA). He won a Dixie Series title at Houston. When man-aging Houston, Keane made Houston his permanent residence. Keane's last minor league managing assignment came at Omaha, where he was instru-mental in developing pitcher Bob Gibson.*

In 1959, new St. Louis Cardinal skipper Solly Hemus* made Keane his third base coach. General manager Bing Devine fired Hemus in July 1961 and appointed Keane field boss. Keane made Gibson his top starting pitcher and made Curt Flood* and Stan Musial* part of the everyday lineup. The Cardinals won 47 of 80 games under Keane's leadership. He piloted St. Louis to an 84–78 record and sixth place finish in 1962. Shortstop Dick Groat (IS) was acquired from the Pittsburgh Pirates (NL). With Ken Boyer* at third base, Julian Javier at second base, and Bill White* at first base, Keane literally managed the 1963 NL All-Star game infield. St. Louis ended with 93 wins, its largest victory total since 1949, placing second to the Los An-geles Dodgers.

In 1964, Keane made two crucial personnel changes. The Cardinals dealt popular hurler Ernie Broglio to the Chicago Cubs in June for young out-fielder Lou Brock* and recalled 38-year-old knuckleballer Barney Schultz, acquired from the Cubs in 1963, from the minors. Brock hit .348 after join-ing the Cardinals in June, while Schultz saved 14 games down the stretch. The Cardinals trailed the Philadelphia Phillies by 6½ games with 12 games to play. Keane's club led a charge that included a three game sweep of the

Phillies to win the NL pennant by one game over Philadelphia and the Cincinnati Reds. Great hitting by Boyer, Brock, and Tim McCarver (IS) combined with the pitching of Gibson, and the leadership of Keane. The Cardinals won their first World Championship in 18 years by defeating the New York Yankees in seven games.

The day after the 1964 World Series, Keane startled St. Louis by abruptly resigning as manager. Four days later, the New York Yankees (AL) hired him as manager to replace Yogi Berra.* Keane was upset that the Cardinals had fired his friend, general manager Bing Devine, and with rumors that owner August A. Busch, Jr.* planned to hire Leo Durocher* unless the Cardinals won the NL pennant. Under Keane, the 1965 Yankees mustered only a 77–85 record for their first sub .500 season since 1925. When the shell-shocked Yankees lost 16 of their first 20 contests in 1966, Keane was fired. Eight months later, he died of a massive heart attack. As a major league manager, Keane won 398 games, lost 350, and tied once. Curt Flood* recalled, "Johnny Keane was a gentle person with competent grasp of the game but no special prowess." Keane spent 34 years in the St. Louis Cardinals' system as a player, coach, and manager.

BIBLIOGRAPHY: John Keane file, National Baseball Library, Cooperstown, NY; Thomas Aylesworth and Benton Minks, *The Encyclopedia of Baseball Managers* (New York, 1990); Mark Gallagher, *The Yankee Encyclopedia*, vol. 3 (New York, 1997); Bob Broeg, *Redbirds: A Century of Cardinals' Baseball* (St. Louis, MO, 1981); Curt Flood with Richard Carter, *The Way It Is* (New York, 1971); Bob Gibson with Phil Pepe, *From Ghetto to Glory* (New York, 1968); Rob Rains, *The St. Louis Cardinals* (New York, 1992); Bob Broeg and Jerry Vickery, *St. Louis Cardinals Encyclopedia* (Grand Rapids, MI, 1998); *St. Louis Cardinals 1961 Yearbook*; *St. Louis Cardinals 1962 Yearbook*; *1964 Official World Series Program*.

Frank J. Olmsted

KEATING, Edythe Perlick "Edie" (b. December 12, 1922, Chicago, IL), player, grew up in a German family in northwestern Chicago. Her father worked as an accountant. Keating, who has one sister, Jean, and a brother, Allan, played volleyball and softball, beginning at age 12, in the Chicago city leagues. She competed in softball after graduating from high school and attended teachers college for one year.

Ann Harnett, one of the AAGPBL organizers, knew of Keating's skills with the champion Chicago Rockolas. Keating became one of the first four players signed to an AAGPBL contract and spent her entire AAGPBL career from 1943 through 1950 as a left fielder with the Racine, WI Belles. Along with Joanne Winter,* Margaret Danhauser, Irene Hickson, Madeline English,* Eleanor Dapkus, and Sophie Kurys,* she played with Racine until the Belles disbanded after the 1950 season. In 1943, Keating batted .268 to help Racine win the AAGPBL's first championship. She also led the AAGPBL with 63 RBI and made the initial All-Star team. In 1946, she clouted four

HR as cleanup hitter. The Belles repeated in 1946, leading the AAGPBL during the regular season and winning the playoff series. Racine made the playoffs for the last time in 1947 as Keating batted .239 and made the All-Star team.

The 5-foot 3-inch, 128-pound, right-handed hitting outfielder batted .240 in 851 games, making 445 hits, driving in 392 runs, and clouting 18 HR. Her yearly statistics demonstrated consistent performance. She made the AAGPBL All-Star team in 1943, 1947, and 1948 and possessed great speed on the bases. Keating stole 88 bases in 1946, 83 in 1947, and 82 in 1948, compiling 481 in eight AAGPBL seasons. She was overshadowed, however, by Kurys, one of baseball's all-time great base stealers. Keating played the 1951 and 1952 campaigns in the Chicago NL.

Keating, selected one of the AAGPBL's top 20 all-time players, worked in Chicago for manufacturing firms A. B. Dick and Teletype Corporations. After moving to Ft. Lauderdale, FL, she worked another 25 years for Harris Corporation, a computer systems company. Keating, who married in 1953, retired to Pompano Beach, FL in 1993 and has a daughter, Susan.

BIBLIOGRAPHY: W. C. Madden, *The Women of the All-American Girls Professional Baseball League* (Jefferson, NC, 1997); AAGPBL files, Northern Indiana Historical Society, South Bend, IN.

Dennis S. Clark

KEEFE, Timothy John "Tim," "Sir Timothy" (b. January 1, 1857, Cambridge, MA; d. April 23, 1933, Cambridge, MA), player, umpire, and coach, was the son of Irish immigrants Patrick Keefe, a builder, and Mary (Leary) Keefe and grew up in Cambridge. A 5-foot 10½-inch, 185-pound, right-handed pitcher, Keefe began his baseball career with Utica, NY, New Bedford, MN, and Albany, NY (NA), in 1879 and 1880. Upon moving to the Troy, NY Haymakers (NL), Keefe won 41 games and lost 59 from 1880 to 1882. With the New York Metropolitans (AA) in 1883 and 1884, Keefe enjoyed his first big seasons. In 1883, he won 41 games for the Metropolitans and led the AA in innings pitched (619), strikeouts (359), and complete games (68). On July 4, 1883, Keefe allowed just one hit in the morning game against the Columbus Buckeyes, returned that afternoon to hurl a two-hitter, and won both games. The following season, Keefe added 37 victories, pacing New York to the AA flag.

Keefe joined the New York Giants (NL) in 1885 and the next season posted an NL-tying 42 victories and topped the NL in complete games and struck out 297 batters. He suffered a nervous breakdown in 1887 after one of his fastballs struck a batter in the temple. Keefe later teamed with Mickey Welch* to form one of the era's most potent mound duos. Over the next two seasons, Keefe won 63 games to lead the Giants to NL championships. Besides leading the NL in victories (35), strikeouts (335), and shutouts (8),

Keefe established a major league record in 1888 by winning 19 consecutive games and won 4 games in a post-season series to help the Giants defeat the St. Louis Browns (AA). After his performance, Keefe demanded $4,500 and became the highest paid Giant.

Keefe in 1890 joined many other National Leaguers in deserting to the newly formed PL. After winning 17 games and losing 11 for the New York Giants (PL), Keefe returned to the Giants (NL) in 1891 and was traded to the Philadelphia Phillies (NL) in August of that year. Upon completing his playing career with the Phillies in 1893, Keefe became an NL umpire in 1894 and 1895. Keefe then returned to Cambridge to enter the real estate business and also coached baseball at Harvard, Tufts, and Princeton universities. Keefe, who married Clara A. Gibson on August 19, 1889, ranks high on the all-time major league lists for pitchers in numerous departments. During 14 seasons, he compiled 342 victories (8th), 225 losses (22nd), started 594 games, completed 554 games (3rd), and pitched 5,047.2 innings (12th). He allowed 4,432 hits and 2,468 runs (6th), struck out 2,560 batters (18th), and issued 1,236 bases on balls (40th). Keefe posted at least 30 victories six times (2nd), 20 or more decisions seven times (5th), and 40 or more wins twice, and hurled 39 shutouts. In post-season play, he won 4 games and lost 3. The quiet, gentle Keefe avoided the spotlight and pioneered in the use of the change of pace to complement his fastball and curve. A master strategist, Keefe knew the weakness of every batter in the league. In 1964, he was elected to the National Baseball Hall of Fame.

BIBLIOGRAPHY: Timothy Keefe file, National Baseball Library, Cooperstown, NY; Noel Hynd, *The Giants of the Polo Grounds* (New York, 1988); Frederick Ivor-Campbell et al., eds., *Baseball's First Stars* (Cleveland, OH, 1996); Gene Karst and Martin J. Jones, Jr., *Who's Who in Professional Baseball* (New Rochelle, NY, 1973); Craig Carter, ed., *TSN Daguerreotypes*, 8th ed. (St. Louis, MO, 1990); Lowell Reidenbaugh, *Baseball's Hall of Fame—Cooperstown* (New York, 1993); James D. Hardy, Jr., *The New York Giants Baseball Club* (Jefferson, NC, 1996); Frank Graham, *The New York Giants* (New York, 1952); Rich Westcott and Frank Bilovsky, *The New Phillies Encyclopedia* (Philadelphia, PA, 1993).

John L. Evers

KEELER, William Henry "Willie," "Wee Willie" (b. William Henry O'Kelleher, March 3, 1872, Brooklyn, NY; d. January 1, 1923, Brooklyn, NY), player, was the son of a Brooklyn trolley car conductor and remained a bachelor throughout his life. He grew up in a blue-collar neighborhood and learned to play baseball at P.S. 26. He quit school at age 15 to play for the Acmes. From 1892 through 1910, he played with the Brooklyn Superbas (NL), Baltimore Orioles (NL), New York Giants (NL), and New York Highlanders (AL), and became one of few players to perform with all three traditional New York City teams. Although primarily a good defensive outfielder, the left-handed Keeler frequently played shortstop, second base, and third base. Contemporaries considered Keeler, whose slogan was "Keep your eye on the ball and hit 'em where they a'int," ranked among the best all-time bunters and place hitters. With the Orioles, he and John McGraw* perfected the hit-and-run play. Keeler originated the "Baltimore Chop," whereby he swung down, pounded the ball into the ground, and reached first base by the time the ball finally came down.

His 44-game hitting streak remains an NL record, although Pete Rose* tied it in 1978. Keeler's feat remained the major league record for 44 years, until Joe DiMaggio* hit safely in 56 games in 1941. His .424 batting average in 1897 ranks as the fourth highest in major league history behind Hugh Duffy's* .438 mark in 1894, Tip O'Neill's* .435 mark in 1887, and Nap Lajoie's* .426 in 1901, while his lifetime .341 mark is the 12th highest in baseball history. Keeler achieved the above averages despite being only 5-feet 4-inches tall and weighing 140 pounds. He made 2,932 hits during his 19-year career and undoubtedly would have easily surpassed the 3,000-hit milestone had the media stressed its significance then. Far fewer than the traditional 154 games per season were scheduled during some of his earlier seasons.

From 1894 to 1900, Keeler played on five NL pennant winners with the Baltimore Orioles (1894–1896) and Brooklyn Superbas (1899–1900). Due to common forms of ownership and the then-legal interlocking directorates between Baltimore and Brooklyn, he moved from the Orioles to the Super-bas with teammates Joe Kelley,* Hugh Jennings,* and manager Ned Hanlon.* Over a six-year period from 1894 to 1899, Keeler averaged 148 runs scored, 47 stolen bases, a .388 batting average, and 219 hits. He played briefly in the minor leagues at the beginning of his career with Binghamton, NY (EL) in 1892 and 1893 and at the end with Toronto, Canada (IL) in 1911. After retiring, he lived in Brooklyn and prospered in real estate. His oft-quoted cliché, "Hit 'em where they a'int," was first credited to Keeler by Brooklyn *Eagle* sportswriter Abe Yager. Keeler choked up on the bat so much that Sam Crawford* once remarked that "it seemed like he used only half of it." Although serious on the field and an excellent rightfielder, he was a practical joker off the field. In 1939, Keeler was among the first two dozen figures elected to the National Baseball Hall of Fame.

BIBLIOGRAPHY: Willie Keeler file, National Baseball Library, Cooperstown, NY; Charles C. Alexander, *John McGraw* (New York, 1988); James H. Bready, *Baseball in Baltimore* (Baltimore, MD, 1998); William F. McNeil, *The Dodgers Encyclopedia* (Champaign, IL, 1997); John Durant, *The Dodgers* (New York, 1947); Frank Graham, *The Brooklyn Dodgers* (New York, 1945); Tommy Holmes, *The Dodgers* (New York, 1972); Tot Holmes, *1979 Dodger Blue Book* (Gothenberg, NE, 1979); Donald Honig, *A Pictorial History of the Brooklyn Dodgers* (New York, 1982); Frederick Ivor-Campbell et al., eds., *Baseball's First Stars* (Cleveland, OH, 1996); Frank Graham, *The New York Yankees* (New York, 1943); Mark Gallagher, *The Yankee Encyclopedia*, vol. 3 (Champaign, IL, 1997); Daniel Okrent and Harris Lewine, eds., *The Ultimate Baseball Book*

(New York, 1981); David R. Phillips, ed., *That Old Ballgame* (New York, 1975); John Thorn, *A Century of Baseball Lore* (New York, 1974); Leo Trachtenberg, "Wee Willie Keeler: Fame and Failure," *TNP* 13 (1993), pp. 57–61.

Ronald L. Gabriel

KELL, George Clyde (b. August 23, 1922, Swifton, AR), player, scout, and sportscaster, is the oldest of three sons of Melvin Clyde Kell and Alma Kell. His father played semipro baseball, enabling him to grow up with the sport. After attending Arkansas State College at Jonesboro for one year, Kell played at Newport, AR (NEAL) in 1940 and 1941 and at Lancaster, PA (ISL) in 1942 and 1943. In 1943 he led the ISL in batting (.396 average), hits, runs, triples, putouts, assists, and fielding as a third baseman.

After playing one game with the Philadelphia Athletics (AL) in 1943, Kell hit .268 as regular third baseman the following season. Manager Connie Mack* guided Kell's development, continuing to play the youngster during batting slumps. Mack predicted that Kell would "never be a hitter." Accepting the challenge, Kell worked hard on his batting, changed his grip, used a lighter bat, and became a spray hitter. After hitting .272 in 1945, Kell was traded in May 1946 to the Detroit Tigers (AL) for Barney McCosky.* In 1946 he hit a sparkling .322 average, the first of nine seasons over .300.

In 1949, Kell dramatically captured the AL batting title. After trailing Ted Williams* by five percentage points, Kell surpassed the Boston star by two ten-thousandths of a point, .3429 to .3427. Although Kell could have won the title by not batting in the ninth inning in the season finale, he insisted on hitting since he did not want to be a "cheese champion." Kell, however, did not have to bat because his teammate hit into a double play to end the inning. In 1950, Kell batted .340, led the AL in hits (218) and doubles (56), and knocked in 101 runs. Billy Goodman* of the Boston Red Sox won the batting title by hitting .354 with 217 fewer times at bat. Kell said philosophically, "I won a close one and lost a close one."

In June 1952, Kell was traded to the Boston Red Sox (AL). He played for the Chicago White Sox (AL) from 1954 through May 1956, was traded to the Baltimore Orioles (AL), and retired after the 1957 season. During 15 major league seasons, Kell compiled a .306 lifetime batting average with 2,054 hits, 385 doubles, and 870 RBI. A fine fielder, he led AL third basemen in double plays in 1945 and 1946, in fielding percentage in 1946–1947, 1950–1951, 1953, 1955, and 1956, in putouts in 1945 and 1946, and in assists in 1945–1947 and 1951.

Kell, "an undemonstrative, no flare type both in and out of uniform," relied on "sheer merit" rather than showmanship. He worked hard at all facets of the game, relying on constant practice rather than natural talent. His unflamboyant style may have caused the BWAA to overlook him for the National Baseball Hall of Fame. In 1983 the Veterans Committee elected Kell to Hall of Fame membership. Brooks Robinson,* a player Kell had tutored at third base in 1957 at Baltimore, joined the Hall of Fame the same year. Kell scouted for the Detroit Tigers (AL) from 1971 through 1977 and annouced Detroit Tigers games on television for 38 years, teaming mostly with former baseball standout Al Kaline.*

BIBLIOGRAPHY: George Kell file, National Baseball Library, Cooperstown, NY; John Thom, *Champion Batsman of the 20th Century* (Los Angeles, CA, 1992); Robert Redmount, *The Red Sox Encyclopedia* (Champaign, IL, 1998); Richard Bak, *A Place for Summer* (Detroit, MI, 1998); William Anderson, *The Detroit Tigers* (South Bend, IN, 1996); Fred Smith, *995 Tigers* (Detroit, MI, 1981); Richard Bak, *Cobb Would Have Caught It* (Detroit, MI, 1991); Detroit *Free Press*, March 11, 1983; Detroit *News*, March 11, 1983; "Detroit's Impossible Kell," *AM* 151 (March 1951), pp. 106–111; Joe Falls, *Detroit Tigers* (New York, 1975); Gene Karst and Martin J. Jones, Jr., *Who's Who in Professional Baseball* (New Rochelle, NY, 1973); Lowell Reidenbaugh, *Baseball's Hall of Fame—Cooperstown* (New York, 1993); *The Baseball Encyclopedia*, 10th ed. (New York, 1996); George Kell with Dan Ewald, *Hello Everybody, I'm George Kell* (Champaign, IL, 1998); Rich Westcott, *Diamond Greats* (Westport, CT, 1988).

Lawrence E. Ziewacz

KELLER, Charles Ernest "Charlie," "King Kong," (b. September 12, 1916, Middletown, MD; d. May 23, 1990, Frederick, MD), player, was a hard-hitting outfielder for the New York Yankees (AL) and Detroit Tigers (AL) for 13 seasons. Born to German-American parents on a 140-acre dairy farm, Keller developed strong shoulders, arms, and wrists by doing farm chores as a youth. He attended public schools at Middletown prior to matriculating the University of Maryland, where he hit .500 for the Terrapins. The Maryland star was signed by the New York Yankees (AL) after batting .385 and .466 in the CPL during 1935 and 1936. For the Newark, NJ Bears (IL), he won consecutive batting titles in 1937 and 1938 with .353 and .365 marks. Keller earned the 1937 *TSN* MVP Award and led Newark to a victory in the Little World Series.

The Yankees promoted him in 1939 to the New York Yankees, where he batted .334. To adapt his swing to the Yankee Stadium dimensions, New York changed him into a pull hitter. The move resulted in increased HR production but lowered his batting average. His best year came in 1941, when he hit .298 with 33 HR and a .580 slugging percentage. Joe DiMaggio,* Tommy Henrich,* and Keller formed one of the greatest outfields in baseball history.

The 5-foot 10-inch, 185-pound left-handed slugger finished his major league career with a .286 batting average, 189 HR, and a .518 slugging percentage. His other career highlights included four World Series appearances (1939, 1941–1943) in which he batted .306, compiled a .611 slugging average, hit 5 HR, three All-Star games (1940, 1941, 1946), and AL-leading figures in walks (1940, 1943), strikeouts (1946), and pinch hits (1951).

Keller's lifetime statistics would have been even more impressive if he had not missed so much playing time because of U.S. Merchant Marine service during World War II (1944–1945) and injuries in 1947 (ruptured disc) and 1948 (broken hand). The back injury required surgery and adversely affected his playing skills. Keller, a perfectionist, believed he never fully realized his potential as a ballplayer, but had no regrets about playing professional baseball. He spent the 1950 and 1951 campaigns with the Detroit Tigers and returned briefly to the New York Yankees in 1952. His younger brother, Hal, played with the Washington Senators (AL) for three seasons. Keller married Martha Williamson on January 21, 1938. They retired to their Frederick, Maryland farm and became successful trotting horse breeders.

BIBLIOGRAPHY: Charlie Keller file, National Baseball Library, Cooperstown, NY; Frank Graham, *The New York Yankees* (New York, 1943); Dave Anderson et al., *The Yankees* (New York, 1979); Mark Gallagher, *The Yankee Encyclopedia*, vol. 3 (Champaign, IL, 1997); Dom Forker, *The Men of Autumn* (Dallas, TX, 1989); Fred Smith, *995 Tigers* (Detroit, MI, 1981); *The Baseball Encyclopedia*, 10th ed. (New York, 1996); David Halberstam, *Summer of '49* (New York, 1989); Ronald A. Mayer, *1937 Newark Bears—A Baseball Legend* (East Hanover, NJ, 1985); *NYT Biographical Service* 21 (May 1990), p. 498; *TSN Official Baseball Dope Book, 1972*.

James A. Riley

KELLEY, Joseph James "Joe" (b. December 9, 1871, Cambridge, MA; d. August 14, 1943, Baltimore, MD), player, manager, scout, and coach, was 5-feet 11-inches tall, weighed 190 pounds, and threw and batted right-handed. In 1891, he began his baseball career with Lowell, MA (NEL) and played 12 games with the Boston Beaneaters (NL) champions. While with the Pittsburgh Pirates (NL) in 1892, he attracted the attention of Baltimore (NL) manager Ned Hanlon.* Hanlon traded George Van Haltren* to Pittsburgh for Kelley and $2,000. Kelley joined "Wee Willie" Keeler,* John McGraw,* and Hugh Jennings* as part of the Baltimore "Big Four." As Baltimore's center and left fielder from 1892 through 1898, Kelley ranked among NL leaders in slugging and stolen bases and placed second in the NL in stolen bases in 1896.

From 1899 through early 1902, Kelley played under Hanlon with the Brooklyn Superbas (NL). Baltimore, which had joined the new AL, raided Brooklyn to get Kelley back. New York Giants owner John T. Brush* bought the Baltimore club in 1902, released its stars from their contracts, and urged those players to jump to the NL. Kelley left to manage the Cincinnati Reds (NL), taking "Cy" Seymour* and Mike Donlin* with him. As Cincinnati player–manager, Kelley released catcher Branch Rickey* in 1903 for refusing to play Sunday baseball. Kelley led the Reds to a third place finish in 1904, but was replaced by Hanlon after they dropped to fifth place in 1905. Kelley played for Cincinnati in 1906 and finished his major league career as player–manager for the 1908 Boston Doves (NL). Under Kelley's direction, his clubs won 338 games and lost 321.

During his 17-year major league career, Kelley batted .317 in 1,853 games, made 2,220 hits, including 358 doubles and 194 triples (9th best), stole 443 bases, scored 1,421 runs, knocked in 1,194 runs, and compiled a .451 slugging average. He played on championship teams at Boston (1891), Baltimore (1894–1896), and Brooklyn (1899–1900). In post-season play, he participated in four straight Temple Cups for Baltimore (1894–1897). He managed at Toronto, Canada (1907, 1909–1914), scouted for the AL New York Yankees (1915–1925), and coached for the NL Brooklyn Dodgers (1926). Kelley married Margaret Mahon, the daughter of prominent Maryland political figure John J. Mahon, and had two sons, Joseph J., Jr., and Ward. He served on the Maryland State Racing Commission. In 1971, the Veterans Committee elected him to the National Baseball Hall of Fame.

BIBLIOGRAPHY: Joseph Kelley file, National Baseball Library, Cooperstown, NY; Lee Allen, *The Cincinnati Reds* (New York, 1948); "Joe Kelley," *NYT*, August 15, 1943, p. 38; Frederick Ivor-Campbell et al., eds., *Baseball's First Stars* (Cleveland, OH, 1996); *TSN Official Baseball Guide, 1971*; John J. McGraw, *My Thirty Years in Baseball* (repr. New York, 1974); *The Baseball Encyclopedia*, 10th ed. (New York, 1996); James H. Bready, *Baseball in Baltimore* (Baltimore, MD, 1998); Richard Goldstein, *Superstars and Screwballs* (New York, 1991); Frank Graham, *The Brooklyn Dodgers* (New York, 1945); Lowell Reidenbaugh, *Baseball's Hall of Fame—Cooperstown* (New York, 1993); Noel Hynd, *The Giants of the Polo Grounds* (New York, 1988); Martin Appel and Burt Goldblatt, *Baseball's Best* (New York, 1980).

Steven P. Savage

KELLY, George Lange "High Pockets" (b. September 10, 1895, San Francisco, CA; d. October 13, 1984, Burlingame, CA), player, coach, and scout, was the seventh of nine children of police captain James Kelly and Mary (Lange) Kelly and came from a baseball family. He was a nephew of Bill Lange,* a Chicago Colts (NL) outfielder of the 1890s, and the elder brother of Reynolds "Ren" Kelly, who pitched seven innings for the Philadelphia Athletics (AL) in 1923. He married Helen O'Connor on November 3, 1927 and had three children. Kelly played sandlot baseball for an Owl Drug Company team while attending Polytechnic High School in San Francisco. He left during his senior year to begin his professional baseball career with Victoria, Canada (PNL) in 1914. Acquired by the New York Giants (NL) for $15,000 in 1915, the 6-foot 4-inch, 195-pound Kelly became a regular in 1920. He spent 16 years in the NL, mainly as first base anchor for great Giants infielders Frank Frisch,* Dave Bancroft,* and Heinie Groh.* Nicknamed "High Pockets," he missed the 1918 season serving in the U.S. Army Air Corps at Kelly Field, TX.

A long-ball hitter, Kelly led the NL in HR in 1921 with 23, twice hit three HR in one game (1923, 1924), and set an NL record in 1924 with seven HR in six games. He led the NL in RBI with 94 in 1920 and 136 in 1924, knocked in at least 100 runs in four consecutive seasons, and recorded 1,020 lifetime RBI. By accounting for all the Giants' eight runs, the three-HR splurge in 1924 set an NL record. Kelly hit over .300 for six straight seasons, compiled a career .297 batting average, made 1,778 hits, and belted 337 doubles and 148 round trippers. During the Giants' four World Series appearances in the 1920s, he struck out 23 times and batted only .248. Over the years, manager John McGraw* said, Kelly made "more important hits for me than any player I ever had."

As a first baseman, Kelly ranks fourth on the lifetime list for average per-game putouts (10.4) and third in chances (11.0). He has the second highest single-season mark for putouts (1,759) and the third highest for total chances (1,873), both set in 1920. In 1921, he made a brilliant throw to catch Yankee Aaron Ward sliding into third base and complete a game-ending, World Series winning double play. The right-handed Kelly, a placid, reserved, and adaptable performer, played 108 games at second base in 1925. McGraw wanted to keep his bat in the lineup after newcomer Bill Terry* took over at first base. Kelly even earned one pitching victory in five innings of relief against the Philadelphia Phillies and pitcher Joe Oeschger of longest game fame, in 1917.

Traded to the Cincinnati Reds (NL) in February 1927 for Edd Roush,* Kelly moved to the Chicago Cubs (NL) in 1930 and ended his active career with the Brooklyn Dodgers (NL) in 1932. He coached for the NL Cincinnati Reds (1935–1937, 1947–1948) and the NL Boston Braves (1938–1943) and then scouted and coached for Oakland, CA (PCL). Off-season, he worked for many years as a machinist for a San Francisco, CA engineering firm and as a ground transport dispatcher at San Francisco International Airport until retirement in 1960. Kelly helped incorporate Millbrae, CA, where he lived for 54 years, and served on its first city council in 1948. In 1973, he was named to the National Baseball Hall of Fame.

BIBLIOGRAPHY: *SEAL*, vol. 1 (1981–1985), pp. 445–447; George Kelly file, National Baseball Library, Cooperstown, NY; Eddie Gold and Art Ahrens, *The Golden Era Cubs, 1876–1940* (Chicago, IL, 1985); Noel Hynd, *The Giants of the Polo Grounds* (New York, 1988); Frank Graham, *The New York Giants* (New York, 1952); Lee Allen, *The Cincinnati Reds* (New York, 1948); Martin Appel and Burt Goldblatt, *Baseball's Best* (New York, 1980); Joseph Durso, *The Days of Mr. McGraw* (Englewood Cliffs, NJ, 1969); W. B. Hanna, "Long George Kelly, a True Star of the Diamond," *BM* 37 (August 1926), p. 411; Gene Karst and Martin J. Jones, Jr., *Who's Who in Professional Baseball* (New Rochelle, NY, 1973); *The Baseball Encyclopedia*, 10th ed. (New York, 1996); Lowell Reidenbaugh, *100 Years of National League Baseball* (St. Louis, MO, 1976); Harold Seymour, *Baseball: The Golden Age* (New York, 1971); A. D. Suehsdorf, telephone interviews with George Kelly, July 29, 1983, July 9, 1984; Oakland (CA) *Tribune*, October 15, 1984; *NYT*, October 16, 1984.

A. D. Suehsdorf

KELLY, Jay Thomas "Tom" (b. August 15, 1950, Graceville, MN), player, coach, and manager, graduated from St. Mary's High School in South Amboy, NJ and attended Mesa, AZ CC and Monmouth College in New Jersey. He was selected by the Seattle Pilots (AL) franchise, which moved to Milwaukee in 1970 as the Brewers, in the eighth round of the free agent draft in June 1968. Kelly played outfield with Newark, NJ (NYPL) in 1968, Clinton, IA (ML) in 1969, and Jacksonville, FL (SL) in 1970, but remained on the inactive list of most of that season. Jacksonville released him in April 1971, but he signed with Charlotte, FL (FSL) of the Minnesota Twins (AL) organization the same month. From 1972 through 1975, he alternated as an outfielder–first baseman for Tacoma, WA (PCL) and batted .181 in 49 games with the Minnesota Twins (AL). Tacoma loaned Kelly to Rochester, NY (IL) for the 1976 season. Kelly rounded out his minor league career with Tacoma, WA (PCL) in 1977, Toledo, OH (IL) in 1978, and Visalia, CA (CaL) in 1979.

Kelly began his managerial career as a player–manager with Tacoma in June 1972, piloting the PCL club for the remainder of the season. In 1978, he served as a player–coach at Toledo, OH (IL). After managing at Visalia in 1979 and 1980, he spent the next two seasons piloting Orlando, FL (SL). From 1983 until September 1986, Kelly coached with the Minnesota Twins (AL).

Kelly replaced Ray Miller as manager of the Minnesota Twins on September 12, 1986, with the club mired in seventh place with 59 wins and 80 losses. For the balance of the 1986 season under Kelly, the Minnesota Twins won 12 games and lost 11. In his first full season as Twins manager, Kelly piloted the 1987 Twins to first place in the AL West. The Minnesota Twins defeated the Detroit Tigers for the AL pennant and the St. Louis Cardinals, four games to three, in the World Series. Kelly guided the 1988 Twins to second place with 91 wins and 71 losses. Minnesota dropped to fifth place in 1989 with 80 wins and 82 losses and seventh place in 1990 with 74 wins and 88 losses.

With 95 victories and 67 defeats in 1991, the Minnesota Twins rose to first place in the AL West. Minnesota defeated the Toronto Blue Jays in the AL Championship Series and the Atlanta Braves in the World Series, four games to three. Under Kelly, Minnesota finished with a 90–72 mark in 1992, a 71–91 slate in 1993, and a 53–60 record in the strike-shortened 1994 season. The Twins continued to struggle, finishing 56–88 in 1995, 78–84 in 1996, 68–94 in 1997, 70–92 in 1998, and 63–97 in 1999.

In his first 14 years as a major league manager, all with the Minnesota Twins, his teams won 986 games while losing 1,074 for a .479 winning percentage. Kelly was named CaL Manager of the Year in 1980. His other honors included being named SL Manager of the Year in 1981 by both the *TSN* and the BBWAA and coaching the AL All-Star team in 1991.

BIBLIOGRAPHY: Tom Kelly file, National Baseball Library, Cooperstown, NY; Tom Kelly, letter to Stan W. Carlson, November 1993; Leonard Koppett, *The Man in the Dugout* (New York, 1993); Peter C. Bjarkman, ed., *Encyclopedia of Major League Baseball Team Histories American League* (Westport, CT, 1991); *Minnesota Twins Media Guide*, 1998; Steve Rushin, "Stress Management," *SI* 77 (August 3, 1992), pp. 70–74; "This is Kelly's Corner," *NYT Biographical Service* 18 (October 1987), pp. 1026–1027; *TSN Official Baseball Register*, 1998.

Stan W. Carlson

KELLY, Michael Joseph "King" (b. December 31, 1857, Troy, NY; d. November 8, 1894, Boston, MA), player and manager, began his baseball career with the Troy, NY Haymakers (1873–1875), Paterson, NJ Olympics (1876), and Columbus, OH Buckeyes (1877) and started his major league career with the Cincinnati, OH Red Stockings (NL) in 1878 and 1879. A versatile athlete who performed at every position including pitcher, Kelly principally played outfield and catcher. He was considered his era's greatest player and number one idol, resulting in the title "King of Baseball."

After joining the Chicago White Stockings (NL) in 1880, Kelly sparked Cap Anson's* NL club to five championships (1880–1882, 1885–1886). Kelly, ranked among baseball's great hitters, also became one of the most daring base stealers of his time. He stole at least 50 bases over five successive years, including a season-high 84 in 1887. His sensational base running and sliding led fans to cheer him on and to yell, "Slide, Kelly, Slide!" Kelly led the NL in doubles (1881–1882, 1889) and runs scored (1884–1886), and a .388 batting average (1886). After winning the batting crown, he was sold to the Boston Beaneaters (NL) for a record $10,000 in one of the biggest deals of baseball's early history. Chicago fans were so upset that they boycotted their own team except when Boston played there. Besides having a .322 batting average in 1887, Kelly scored six runs in a game against the Pittsburgh Pirates on August 27.

Kelly in 1890 joined many other NL performers in deserting to the newly formed PL. Named player–manager of the Boston Reds (PL) entry, Kelly stole six bases in one game and compiled a .326 batting average. His team captured the PL championship by posting a 81–48 record. In 1891, he was selected player–manager of the Cincinnati Kellys (AA). After his team finished fifth in the AA, Kelly returned to play for the Boston Reds and helped them win two NL titles (1891–1892). Kelly played a few games for the New York Giants (NL) in 1893 at age 35 and then drifted to the minor leagues. In 1894 he managed Allentown, PA (PSL) and later Yonkers, NY (EL).

Kelly performed on eight pennant winners in 16 major league seasons and compiled a .308 batting average. He played in 1,455 games, scored 1,357 runs, and collected 1,813 base hits, including 359 doubles, 102 triples, and 69 HR. Kelly, who recorded a .300 or better batting average eight times, was elected to the National Baseball Hall of Fame in 1945. The imaginative, quick-thinking Kelly was credited by Anson with devising the hit-and-run play. He studied the rules, took every advantage, found ways to get around them, and caused the league to make changes. Colorful both on and off the field, Kelly acted with flair and was admired and adored by fans. He wore the finest tailored clothes and the most current styles. American billboards featured this handsome, happy-go-lucky Irishman as the nation's best dressed man. Kelly supplemented his income with off-season stage appearances and authored *Play Ball*. Following his retirement from baseball, he opened a saloon in New York. At age 36, he died of pneumonia en route to Boston to appear in the Palace Theater.

BIBLIOGRAPHY: Peter Levine, *A. G. Spalding and the Rise of Baseball* (New York, 1985); Warren Wilbert and William Hageman, *Chicago Cubs: Seasons at the Summit* (Champaign, IL, 1997); Mike Kelly file, National Baseball Library, Cooperstown, NY; Martin Appel, *Slide, Kelly, Slide* (Lanham, MD, 1996); Frederick Ivor-Campbell et al., eds., *Baseball's First Stars* (Cleveland, OH, 1990); Warren Brown, *The Chicago Cubs* (New York, 1946); Gene Karst and Martin J. Jones, Jr., *Who's Who in Professional Baseball* (New Rochelle, NY, 1973); Noel Hynd, *The Giants of the Polo Grounds* (New York, 1988); Lee Allen, *The Cincinnati Reds* (New York, 1948); Eddie Gold and Art Ahrens, *The Golden Era Cubs, 1876–1940* (Chicago, IL, 1985); *National Baseball Hall of Fame and Museum Brochure* (Cooperstown, NY, 1974); Lowell Reidenbaugh, *Baseball's Hall of Fame—Cooperstown* (New York, 1993); Gary Caruso, *The Braves Encyclopedia* (Philadelphia, PA, 1995); Harold Kaese, *The Boston Braves* (New York, 1948); John Thorn et al., eds., *Total Braves* (New York, 1996).

John L. Evers

KELTNER, Kenneth Frederick "Ken," "Butch" (b. October 31, 1916, Milwaukee, WI; d. December 12, 1991, Greenfield, WI), player, was the youngest of three children of Fred Keltner, a railroad switchman and cemetery groundskeeper, and Alma (Zabel) Keltner, of English-German ancestry. On November 1, 1938, Keltner married Evelyn Goniu of Milwaukee, WI. They had two sons, Randy and Jeff, and resided in the Milwaukee area. During lunch breaks as a schoolboy, Keltner frequently played ice hockey in a neighborhood park. He did not participate in any sports at Boys Technical and Trade High School, but performed on amateur football and baseball teams. Al Schiefelbein, a local umpire, recommended Keltner to the Milwaukee Brewers (AA) in 1936. "They [the Brewers] took a look," Keltner recalled. "They liked what they saw and then signed me to a contract in Class D ball."

Keltner's professional baseball career began with Fieldale, VA (BSL) in 1936. He moved up to the Milwaukee Brewers (AA) in 1937 and began a 12-year tenure as the Cleveland Indians (AL) regular third baseman the following season. The 6-foot, 180-pound Keltner was best remembered for the two fine defensive plays that were primarily responsible for ending Joe DiMaggio's* 56-game hitting streak in 1941. Other career highlights included a three HR game against the Boston Red Sox on May 25, 1939, the game-winning HR in the 1948 sudden death AL playoff game against the Boston Red Sox, a key hit against Warren Spahn* of the Boston Braves in the decisive game of the 1948 World Series, and seven All-Star Game appearances.

His major league career ended with the Boston Red Sox in 1950. Keltner batted .276 lifetime, made 1,570 hits, belted 308 doubles and 163 HR, drove in 852 runs, and thrice led AL third sackers in fielding percentage. According to sportswriter Bob Dolgan, "Keltner was every bit as good . . . as [Brooks] Robinson"* defensively. Robinson has become the standard against which other third basemen are measured.

The popular Keltner, who threw and batted right-handed, was named by Cleveland fans to the all-time Indians team in 1969. More than 6,000 people signed petitions in an unsuccessful 1984–1985 Milwaukee-based effort to enshrine the hometown hero in the National Baseball Hall of Fame, but Keltner was selected to the Cleveland Indians, Ohio State Baseball, and Wisconsin Athletic Halls of Fame.

BIBLIOGRAPHY: Ken Keltner file, National Baseball Library, Cooperstown, NY; Franklin Lewis, *The Cleveland Indians* (New York, 1949); John Phillips, *Winners* (Cabin John, MD, 1987); Russell Schneider, *The Boys of Summer of '48* (Champaign, IL, 1998); *The Baseball Encyclopedia*, 10th ed. (New York, 1996); Bob Dolgan, "Keltner for Hall of Fame?" Cleveland (OH) *Plain Dealer*, December 24, 1984; Kenneth F. Keltner, interview with Thomas D. Jozwik, May 17, 1990; *NYT*, December 14, 1991, p. 11; Seymour Siwoff, ed., *The Book of Baseball Records* (New York, 1981); Bob Wolf, "Keltner in Hall of Fame? He Has a Shot," Milwaukee (WI) *Journal*, February 28, 1985, part 3, p. 3; Bob Feller with Bill Gilbert, *Now Pitching, Bob Feller* (New York, 1990).

Thomas D. Jozwik

KENNEDY, William P. "Brickyard," "Roaring Bill," "Peck" (b. October 7, 1867, Bellaire, OH; d. September 23, 1915, Bellaire, OH), player, was the son of Robert Crozier Kennedy and Elizabeth Kennedy and was nicknamed "Brickyard" because his Bellaire hometown was noted for its bricks. The 5-foot 11-inch, 160-pound right-hander threw so hard that he allegedly would split open his catchers' hands before the advent of gloves. The catcher soon stood far enough behind home plate to receive the ball after the first bounce.

Kennedy began his professional baseball career with Wheeling, WV (TSL) in 1889 and Denver, CO (WA) in 1890 and 1891. In 1892 he reportedly signed with the Spokane, WA Spokes (PNL), receiving a bonus of a train ticket and $100 in cash. Before Kennedy boarded the train, however, president Charles Byrne of the Brooklyn Bridegrooms (NL) showed up in Bellaire with a better offer. Spokane manager Ollie Beard protested the contract-jumping: "He sunk the gaff into me."

In 12 major league seasons, Kennedy compiled a respectable 187–159 record with a 3.96 ERA and struck out 797 batters in 3,021 innings. He recorded at least 20 victories in 1893, 1894, 1899, and 1900, helping Brooklyn win NL pennants the latter two seasons. Kennedy pitched for Brooklyn from 1892 through 1901, the New York Giants (NL) in 1902, and the Pittsburgh Pirates (NL) in 1903, winning at least 16 games four other times. His finest season came in 1899 with a 22–9 record, .710 winning percentage, and a 2.79 ERA. The Brooklyn Superbas finished 101–47 behind the managerial prowess of player–manager Ned Hanlon.*

Kennedy made his final major league pitching appearance with the Pittsburgh Pirates on his birthday in 1903 in Game 5 of the first World Series in major league history. He pitched against Cy Young* of the Boston Pilgrims. Although Kennedy doubled, four Pittsburgh errors led to their second loss in the series, 11–2. He pitched five minor league seasons with Wheeling, WV (CL) in 1904 and 1905 and Dayton, OH (CL) from 1906 to 1908. He returned to Bellaire and worked as a bartender. His wife, a Brooklynite, refused to move to Bellaire with him. The lovable, eccentric illiterate conversed at the top of his lungs and demonstrated a hot temper.

BIBLIOGRAPHY: Steve Calhoun, "Brickyard" Kennedy," *DB*, May 15, 1985; Peter Filichia, *Professional Baseball Franchises* (New York, 1993); Richard Goldstein, *Superstars and Screwballs* (New York, 1991); Frank Graham, *The Brooklyn Dodgers* (New York, 1945); William F. McNeil, *The Dodger Encyclopedia* (Champaign, IL, 1997); William P. Kennedy file, National Baseball Library, Cooperstown, NY; James K. Skipper, Jr., *Baseball Nicknames* (Jefferson, NC, 1992); John Thorn et al., eds., *Total Baseball*, 5th ed. (New York, 1997); Frederick Ivor-Campbell et al., eds., *Baseball's First Stars* (Cleveland, OH, 1996).

Scot E. Mondore

KESSINGER, Donald Eulon "Don," "Kess" (b. July 17, 1942, Forrest City, AK), player and manager, is the son of Howard M. Kessinger, a grocery store owner, and Ida (Bannister) Kessinger and was selected as an All-SEC baseball and basketball star at the University of Mississippi. He signed with the Chicago Cubs (NL) after his graduation in 1964. The lanky 6-foot 1-inch, 175-pound Kessinger made a token appearance with the Chicago Cubs at the end of the year, but was assigned to Dallas–Fort Worth, TX (TL) for more experience. The Chicago Cubs, desperate for a good fielding shortstop, rushed Kessinger back to the major leagues partway through the next season. He participated in three triple plays in 1965, but batted .201 and drove in only 14 runs.

The next season, Kessinger improved dramatically. His batting average soared to .274, as he joined with Ron Santo,* Glenn Beckert,* and Ernie Banks* to form one of the greatest infields in Chicago Cub history. Kessinger's fielding and defensive skills remained his strengths. The 1967 season amply displayed his talents, as he led the NL in assists, double plays, and most chances per game. For the first time in 22 years, the Chicago Cubs led the NL in fielding. In 1969, he led the NL in every defensive department and set a record of playing 54 consecutive errorless games. Kessinger won Gold Glove awards in 1969 and 1970 and was selected for the NL All-Star team five consecutive years from 1968 to 1972. The Chicago Cubs traded Kessinger, who established a Cub record of 1,618 games at shortstop, to the St. Louis Cardinals (NL) in October 1975.

Never a high percentage hitter, he compiled a .252 career batting average with 14 HR. Kessinger's best year came in 1972, when he hit .274. In 1971, he collected six hits on June 17, as the Chicago Cubs edged the St. Louis Cardinals, 7–6. When the Chicago Cubs defeated the Montreal Expos on August 31, he went five for six. He played one and one-half years with the St. Louis Cardinals before being traded in August 1977 to the Chicago White Sox (AL). Late in his career, he played some at second base and third base. In 1979 he served as player–manager for the Chicago White Sox, leading them to a 46–60 win–loss record before resigning. Simultaneously, he also retired as a player, ending a 16-year major league career. After a decade in the securities business, Kessinger has been baseball coach for the University of Mississippi since 1990. Kessinger, who married Carolyn Crawley and has two sons, R. Keith and Kevin M., lives in Oxford, MS. His son, R. Keith, played with the Cincinnati Reds (NL) in 1993.

BIBLIOGRAPHY: Don Kessinger file, National Baseball Library, Cooperstown, NY; *The Baseball Encyclopedia*, 10th ed. (New York, 1996); *Chicago Cubs Official Roster Book*, 1970, 1974, 1975; *Chicago Cubs Vineline* (February 1993); Jim Enright, *Chicago Cubs* (New York, 1975); Jim Langford, *The Game Is Never Over* (South Bend, IN, 1980); Bob Broeg and Jerry Vickery, *St. Louis Cardinals Encyclopedia* (Grand Rapids, MI, 1998); Eddie Gold and Art Ahrens, *The New Era Cubs, 1941–1985* (Chicago, IL, 1985).

Duane A. Smith

KEY, James Edward "Jimmy" (b. April 22, 1961, Huntsville, AL), player, is a 6-foot 1-inch, 185-pound left-handed pitcher who bats right-handed. He is the son of Cynthia K. Key and graduated in 1979 from Butler High School in Huntsville. Key attended Clemson University for three years, being named in 1982 the Tigers' MVP, first team ACC pitcher-DH, and All-Regional team member. He married Karin Kane and has a daughter, Jordan.

The Chicago White Sox (AL) selected Key in the 1979 free-agent draft, but did not sign him. He was chosen by the Toronto Blue Jays (AL) in the third round of the June 1982 free-agent draft, splitting his first professional assignment between Medicine Hat, Canada (PrL) and Florence, SC (SAL). Key spent the following season with Knoxville, TN (SL) and Syracuse, NY (IL), compiling a 10–13 record in 1983.

The Toronto Blue Jays used Key as a relief pitcher in 1984 before making him a starter from 1985 to 1992. He underwent rehabilitation assignments at Dunedin, FL (FSL) in 1988 and 1990. Key won between 12 and 17 games in each of his last eight seasons with Toronto, surpassing 200 innings pitched six times and compiling a 116–81 record. His 116 victories, 944 career strikeouts, and 3.42 career ERA rank among the Blue Jays all-time leaders. He posted 17 victories in 1987 and captured the AL ERA title at 2.76.

The Toronto Blue Jays granted Key free agency following the 1992 season. The New York Yankees (AL) signed him in December 1992. A Cy Young Award contender in 1993, the ace of the Yankee pitching staff finished the season with an 18–6 record, shared third in AL victories, ranked third with a 3.00 ERA, and led the AL with a .750 winning percentage. Key paced the major leagues with 17 victories in 1994, but the August 12 season-ending strike halted his run toward his first 20-win season. In May 1995, he suffered a season-ending injury to his shoulder. In four seasons with the Yankees he compiled a 48–23 record. In December 1996, the Baltimore Orioles (AL) signed him as a free agent. He and Scott Erickson led the Orioles with 16 victories in 1997.

Key's honors included appearing in the 1985, 1989, 1991–1992, and 1996–1997 AL Championship Series and the 1992 and 1996 World Series. His 2–0 record and 1.00 ERA led the Blue Jays past the Atlanta Braves in the 1992 World Series, while his victory clinched the 1996 World Series against the Atlanta Braves. The four-time All-Star game participant (1985, 1991, 1993–1994) was the winning pitcher in the 1991 classic. Key, a three-time member of *TSN* AL All-Star team (1987, 1993–1994), was named *TSN* AL Pitcher of the Year in 1987 and 1994 and received a Players Choice Award in 1994 as the outstanding AL pitcher in voting by his peers. Besides finishing second in the Cy Young Award voting in 1987 and 1994 and fourth in 1993, he was the only major league pitcher to record at least 12 victories each season from 1985 to 1994.

Key retired in January 1999. In 15 major league seasons through 1998, Key compiled 186 wins, 117 losses, and a 3.51 ERA. He appeared in 470 games, completing 34 of 389 starts and pitching 13 shutouts. Key surrendered 2,518 hits, 1,104 runs, and 668 walks in 2,591.2 innings pitched while striking out 1,538 batters.

BIBLIOGRAPHY: James Key file, National Baseball Library, Cooperstown, NY; *New York Yankees Media Guide*, 1996; *TSN Official Baseball Register*, 1998; Peter C. Bjarkman, ed., *Encyclopedia of Major League Baseball Team Histories American League* (Westport, CT, 1991).

John L. Evers

KILLEBREW, Harmon Clayton "Killer" (b. June 29, 1936, Payette, ID), player and sportscaster, is the youngest of four children of painter and sheriff H. C. Killebrew and Katherine Pearl (May) Killebrew. At Payette High School, he won letters in baseball, football, and basketball, and saw the school eventually retire his uniform number. He enrolled at the College of Idaho, declining an athletic scholarship from the University of Oregon. Senator Herman Welker of Idaho urged Clark Griffith,* owner of the Washington Senators (AL), to scout him. The 6-foot, 195-pound Killebrew was signed to a bonus contract on June 19, 1954 while hitting .847 in a semipro league. Under prevailing baseball rules, bonus players were kept on the major league roster for two seasons. This rule may have impeded young Killebrew's progress. In 1954–1955, he batted only 93 times, struck out 34 times, hit a combined .215 with 4 HR, and had defensive troubles.

After the bonus period expired, Killebrew was shuttled back and forth between Washington and the minor leagues until 1959. In 1959, Griffith decided that Killebrew was ready for the major leagues and traded third baseman Ed Yost.* Killebrew attracted attention early in the 1959 season when he belted 8 HR in 12 days. By midseason, he had slugged 28 HR and was chosen for the All-Star team. He finished with 42 HR to tie for the AL title. Used at third base, the outfield, first base, and eventually as DH, Killebrew played through the 1975 season. He moved in 1961 with Griffith's AL team to Minnesota, where he became the most famous and popular Twins player. He finished his career with the Kansas City Royals (AL) in 1975. Killebrew's HR remain legendary, many being hit high and deep. He remains the leading right-handed HR hitter in AL history with 573, and ranks fifth on the all-time list. He led the AL in HR six times (tied for the lead twice) and RBI three times and reached personal highs of 49 HR and 140 RBI in 1969, when he won the AL MVP Award. Killebrew's HR total exceeded 40 in eight seasons, while his RBI surpassed 100 nine times. He hit two round trippers in one game 46 times for eighth on the all-time list and connected for three in a game and four in one day in 1963. Eleven of his HR came with the bases full. He homered every 14.22 at bats, fourth on the all-time list behind Babe Ruth,* Mark McGwire,* and Ralph Kiner.*

Killebrew was selected for 13 All-Star games, hitting .308 and slugging HR in the 1961, 1965, and 1971 games. He appeared in two AL Championship Series with Minnesota (1969 and 1970), batting .211 with two HR. He played in the 1965 World Series for the Twins, hitting .286 with a HR against the Los Angeles Dodgers, after missing much of that season with an elbow injury. Although Killebrew's lifetime batting average is only .256, his enormous power made him one of the game's most feared hitters. In 2,435 games, he made 2,086 hits, 290 doubles, 1,283 runs scored, 1,584 RBI, 1,559 walks (12th), 1,699 strikeouts (10th), and a .509 slugging average. In 8,147 career at-bats, he was never asked to sacrifice bunt, a major league record. Killebrew, whose fielding improved after his first few seasons, once led AL first basemen in assists. Killebrew was inducted into the National Baseball Hall of Fame in 1984 and saw his uniform number (3) retired by the Minnesota Twins. The muscular, wide-shouldered Killebrew threw and batted right-handed. Although called "Killer," he is a modest, reserved, religious man. He married Elaine Roberts in October 1955 and has five children,

Cameron, Kenneth, Sharon, Kathryn, and Erin. He has worked as a baseball announcer for the Twins, Oakland A's (AL), and California Angels (AL). He resides in Scottsdale, AZ, enjoys hunting and fishing, and maintains an interest in a Boise, ID, insurance and securities firm.

BIBLIOGRAPHY: Wayne J. Anderson, *Harmon Killebrew, Baseball's Superstar* (Salt Lake City, UT, 1965); Peter C. Bjarkman, ed., *Encyclopedia of Major League Baseball Team Histories American League* (Westport, CT, 1991); Lowell Reidenbaugh, *Baseball's Hall of Fame—Cooperstown* (New York, 1993); *CB* (1966), pp. 218–220; Dave Mona and Dave Jarzyna, *Twenty-Five Seasons* (Minneapolis, MN, 1986); Harmon Killebrew file, National Baseball Library, Cooperstown, NY; John Benson et al., *Baseball's Top 100* (Wilton, CT, 1997); Donald Honig, *The Power Hitters* (St. Louis, MO, 1989); *Minnesota Twins Media Guide, 1984; The Oregonian*, October 26, 1983, January 11, 12, 1984; Shirley Povich, "Strong Boy of the Twins," *SEP* 235 (September 15, 1962), pp. 54–55; *SI* 10 (June 1, 1959), p. 18; Barbara Heilman, "Out of the Park on a Half Swing" (April 8, 1963), pp. 85–92; "The Nuclear Bomber," *Time* 84 (August 14, 1964), p. 44.

Phillip P. Erwin

KILLEN, Frank Bissell (b. November 30, 1870, Pittsburgh, PA; d. December 3, 1939, Pittsburgh, PA), player and umpire, twice led the NL in wins while pitching for his hometown Pittsburgh Pirates (NL). The 6-foot 1-inch, 200-pound left-hander drew notice in his youth as a baseball catcher before converting to pitching in his late teens. After turning professional at age 19, he compiled a 30–8 win–loss record for three minor league clubs in 1890. Killen recorded 21 wins and 15 losses by August 1891 for Minneapolis, MN (WA), when the club disbanded. The Milwaukee Brewers, another WA club, moved to the major league AA in August 1891 and signed Killen. Killen's 7–4 record for Milwaukee included a one-hitter against the pennant-bound Boston Reds.

When the AA folded after the 1891 season, Killen was assigned to the Washington Senators (NL). In 1892, he won 29 games while losing 26 for a tenth-place team in the 12-team NL. When Killen held out for more money in 1893, the Washington Senators traded him to the Pittsburgh Pirates. Some pitchers could not handle the lengthening of the pitching distance from 51 feet to 60 feet 6 inches that year. Killen, however, enjoyed his finest season, winning an NL-high 36 games while losing only 14 and leading the Pittsburgh Pirates to a strong second-place finish. A line drive broke his arm in July 1894, when his record stood at 14–11. Blood poisoning from an infected spike wound sidelined him in June 1895 with a 5–5 season record. He came back in 1896 to tie Kid Nichols* for the NL lead in victories, recording 30 wins against 18 losses and amassing NL and personal highs in complete games (44) shutouts (5), and innings pitched (432.1). He logged lackluster marks of 17–23 in 1897 and 10–11 through the following July when the Pittsburgh Pirates released him. The Washington Senators signed Killen, who finished 1898 winning just six of 15 decisions. The Washington Senators dropped Killen after he lost his first two starts the next April. The Boston Beaneaters (NL) signed him in May 1899, but released him two months later with a 7–5 record.

Killen's major league career ended in June 1900 with a 3–3 mark for the Chicago Orphans (NL). He lost one game for the Chicago White Stockings in the then-minor league AL in 1900 and finished his pitching career in the minor leagues at Wheeling, WV (WA) in 1901, Indianapolis, IN (AA) in 1902 and part of 1903, and Atlanta, GA (SL) the remainder of 1903.

During 10 major league seasons, Killen won 164 games and suffered 131 losses in 321 games. He completed 253 of 300 starts and compiled a 3.78 ERA, striking out 725 batters, yielding 2,730 hits, and issuing 822 walks. Following his playing career, Killen umpired a few seasons in the AA, CL, and SL and operated a bar in Pittsburgh, PA until his death.

BIBLIOGRAPHY: Frank Killen file, National Baseball Library, Cooperstown, NY; Shirley Povich, *The Washington Senators* (New York, 1954); Morris Bealle, *The Washington Senators* (Washington, DC, 1947); Frederick G. Lieb, *The Pittsburgh Pirates* (New York, 1948); John Thorn et al., eds., *Total Baseball*, 5th ed. (New York, 1997); Robert L. Tiemann and Mark Rucker, eds., *Nineteenth Century Stars* (Kansas City, MO, 1989).

Frederick Ivor-Campbell

KILROY, Matthew Aloysius "Matches," "Matt" (b. June 21, 1866, Philadelphia, PA; d. March 2, 1940, Philadelphia, PA), player, was the son of Irish immigrants and married Frances Denny in 1888. They had two daughters and two sons. The 5-foot 9-inch, 175-pound pitcher, who batted and threw left-handed, started his professional baseball career in 1885 with the Augusta, GA Browns (SL).

Kilroy reached the major leagues with the Baltimore Orioles (AA) in 1886, fanning at least 10 batters 21 times and setting an all-time record with 513 strikeouts. Although finishing 29–34 with a weak-hitting team, he led the AA with 68 appearances and 66 complete games. Besides hurling three one-hitters, Kilroy on October 6 authored a 6–0 no-hitter against the Pittsburgh Alleghenies. His best major league season came in 1887, when he paced the AA with 69 appearances, 66 complete games, 589.1 innings, 46 victories, and six shutouts. Kilroy struck out 217 batters, hurled doubleheader victories on July 26 and October 1, and set a major league record for most wins by a left-hander. The 75 triumphs in his first two major league seasons remain a major league record. He won 29 games in 1889, one-hitting Columbus on July 18 and no-hitting St. Louis in seven innings 11 days later.

During 10 major league seasons, Kilroy compiled 141 wins and 133 losses and completed 264 of his 292 starts. After hurling for Baltimore from 1886 through 1889, he performed for the Boston Reds (PL) in 1890, Cincinnati Kellys (AA) in 1891, Washington Senators (NL) in 1892, Louisville Colonels

(NL) in 1893 and 1894, and Chicago Orphans (NL) in 1898. Nagging shoulder injuries, which began developing in 1888, forced him gradually to shift from the mound to right field and miss the 1896 and 1897 campaigns altogether.

Kilroy drifted to the minor leagues with Syracuse, NY (EL) in 1894 and 1895 and Hartford, CT (EL) in 1899. As a fan of the game, the lifelong Philadelphia resident operated a restaurant not far from Shibe Park for many years. He supposedly never missed a game and relished coaching pitchers for manager Connie Mack's* Philadelphia Athletics (AL).

BIBLIOGRAPHY: Matthew Kilroy file, National Baseball Library, Cooperstown, NY; Peter Filichia, *Professional Baseball Franchises* (New York, 1993); Daniel Peterson, *Baseball in 1889* (Bowling Green, OH, 1993); David Nemec, *The Beer and Whisky League* (New York, 1994); John Thorn et al., eds., *Total Baseball*, 5th ed. (New York, 1997); Robert L. Tiemann and Mark Rucker, eds., *Nineteenth Century Baseball Stars* (Kansas City, MO, 1989); James H. Bready, *Baseball in Baltimore* (Baltimore, MD, 1998); Philip Van Borries, *Legends of Louisville* (West Bloomfield, MI, 1993); Philip Van Borries, *Louisville Diamonds* (Paducah, KY, 1997).

                                                                          Scot E. Mondore

KIMBRO, Henry Allen "Kimmie," "Jimbo," "Jumbo," "Scooter Motoneta" (b. February 19, 1912, Nashville, TN; d. July 11, 1999, Nashville, TN), player, was a six-time All-Star outfielder for the Baltimore Elite Giants (NNL) during the 1940s. He was the son of Will Kimbro, a farmer, and Sally Kimbro and completed the eighth grade before dropping out of school. He worked at a service station and played amateur baseball during summers. After honing his baseball skills in the Nashville sandlots, the 5-foot 8-inch, 175-pounder was signed by Tom Wilson and began his NNL career with the Elite Giants in 1937 when the franchise was still based in Washington, DC. With the exception of spending the 1941 season with the New York Black Yankees (NNL), he stayed with the Elite Giants through 1951.

An intense, all-around player with speed and power, Kimbro ranked as the best NNL center fielder in his prime. He possessed good range and proved especially adept at patrolling the outfield alleys. The left-handed batter, a dangerous line-drive hitter who hit for both batting average and power, loomed as a constant base stealing threat.

In 1944, Kimbro hit .329, paced the NNL in stolen bases, and finished only one HR behind NNL leaders Josh Gibson* and Buck Leonard.* The following season, he batted .291 and shared with "Cool Papa" Bell* the NNL lead in at-bats. The 1946 campaign saw him hit .371 and pace the NNL in runs scored. In 1947, Kimbro hit .353, topped the NNL in runs scored, and shared the lead in doubles. The next campaign, he batted .314. The Elite Giants won the first half title, but lost the playoff to the Homestead Grays. In 1949 Kimbro hit .352, helping the Elite Giants capture the NAL pennant in their first year in the league. His .370 batting average in 1950 ranked as the fourth highest NAL mark.

Kimbro also starred in the Latin American winter leagues and enjoyed his best season with Havana, Cuba (CUWL), leading the 1947–1948 CUWL with a .346 batting average. When the color bar was removed, he was considered too old by major league standards to make the transition to organized baseball. He retired in 1953 after spending his final two seasons with the Birmingham, AL Black Barons.

Kimbro, who batted around .320 during his Negro League career, bought and operated a service station and Bill's Cab Company in Nashville for 22 years. He and his wife, Erbia Coctade Mendoza, had two daughters and a son.

BIBLIOGRAPHY: *Afro-American*, 1937–1948; Chicago *Defender*, 1940–1948; New York *Age*, 1940–1943; Brent Kelley, "Henry Kimbro," *SCD* 24 (March 7, 1997), pp. 190–191; Robert W. Peterson, *Only the Ball Was White* (Englewood Cliffs, NJ, 1970); Pittsburgh *Courier*, 1937–1948; James A. Riley, *The All-Time All-Stars of Black Baseball* (Cocoa, FL, 1983); James A. Riley, *The Biographical Encyclopedia of the Negro Baseball Leagues* (New York, 1994); James A. Riley, interviews with former Negro League players, James A. Riley Collection, Cocoa, FL; *The Baseball Encyclopedia*, 10th ed. (New York, 1996).

James A. Riley

KINDER, Ellis Raymond "Old Folks" (b. July 24, 1914, Atkins, AR; d. October 16, 1968, Jackson, TN), player, quit a $175-a-month job driving a bulldozer to sign a professional baseball contract with Jackson, TN (KL) for $75 a month in 1938. The right-hander, who had only an eighth-grade education, attracted little attention until compiling a 21–9 win–loss record for Jackson in 1940, striking out 307 batters in just 276 innings. Kinder married Hazel McCabe on March 31, 1934. They had three children, Charles, Betty, and Jimmy. After their divorce, he married Ruth in 1951.

The New York Yankees (AL) purchased Kinder's contract conditionally in 1941 for $5,000, but returned him after he failed his short trial at Binghamton, NY (EL). Kinder pitched for Memphis, TN (SL) in 1942 and left baseball in 1943 for his off-season job as a pipefitter for the Illinois Railroad in Jackson.

The 6-foot, 215 pounder returned to the Memphis (SL) club in 1944, finishing 19–6 as a teammate of one-armed Pete Gray. The St. Louis Browns (AL) purchased his contract, but Kinder joined the Seabees before starting his major league career with the St. Louis Browns in 1946 at age 31. After having two mediocre seasons, Kinder was traded in December 1947 to the Boston Red Sox (AL). Kinder enjoyed the best season of his major league career in 1949, compiling a 23–6 win–loss record and leading the AL with a .793 winning percentage and six shutouts. His record stood at 4–4 in June. Kinder won 19 of his next 20 decisions before losing on the last day of the season to the New York Yankees with the AL pennant at stake. The defeat severely disturbed Kinder for the remainder of his life. With the Boston Red Sox losing 1–0, manager Joe McCarthy* lifted him for a pinch hitter in the eighth inning. The New York Yankees tagged successors Mel Parnell* and Tex Hughson* for four runs. The Boston Red Sox rallied, but lost the game and the AL pennant, 5–3. Kinder claimed, "The Yankees wouldn't have gotten any more runs off me."

Kinder developed into one of the premier AL relief pitchers after switching to the bullpen in 1950. Owner Tom Yawkey* suggested that manager Steve O'Neill* put Kinder in the bullpen, starting him on a new career. The 1951 campaign saw him lead the AL with 63 appearances and 14 saves. In 1953, the right-handed Kinder broke Ed Walsh's* AL record by appearing in 69 games for the Boston Red Sox with 27 saves. Kinder advised younger pitchers, "The main thing is to keep throwing each day, whether you pitched yesterday or not."

The Boston Red Sox in December 1955 sold Kinder to the St. Louis Cardinals (NL), who waived him in July 1956 to the Chicago White Sox (AL). The Chicago White Sox released him in May 1957, two months before his 43rd birthday. The wiry Tennesseean, who possessed a great curveball, pitched for San Diego, CA (PCL) before retiring. His major league career ended with a 102–71 mark and a 3.43 ERA in 484 games. Kinder, who gained notoriety for his late-night carousing, died of complications from open heart surgery.

BIBLIOGRAPHY: Bill Borst, ed., *Ables to Zoldak*, vol. 2 (St. Louis, MO, 1989); Bill Borst, *Still Last in the American League* (West Bloomfield, MI, 1992); Bob Cairns, *Pen Men* (New York, 1993); Robert Redmount, *The Red Sox Encyclopedia* (Champaign, IL, 1997); Howard Liss, *The Boston Red Sox* (New York, 1982); Peter Golenbock, *Fenway* (New York, 1992); Jack Lautier, *Fenway Voices* (Camden, ME, 1990); Dan Shaughnessy, *The Curse of the Bambino* (New York, 1990); David Halberstam, *Summer of '49* (New York, 1989); Gene Karst and Martin Jones, Jr., *Who's Who In Professional Baseball* (New Rochelle, NY, 1973); Steve O'Leary, "Wonder-Kid Kinder, 'Just Starting' at 35," *TSN*, September 28, 1949; *TSN*, March 16, 1955, p. 5, *TSN*, November 2, 1968, p. 44.

William A. Borst

KINER, Ralph McPherran (b. October 27, 1922, Santa Rita, NM), player, executive, and sportscaster, is the son of baker Ralph Macklin Kiner and Beatrice (Grayson) Kiner. He graduated from Alhambra, CA High School in 1940 and attended Pasadena JC from 1940 through 1942. Kiner married tennis star Nancy Chaffee in October 1951 and had three children, but their marriage ended in divorce in 1969. That same year, he married Barbara Batchelder. After divorce terminated that union, Kiner married Di Ann Shugart in December 1982.

Kiner spent the first two years of his professional baseball career (1941–

1942) as an outfielder with Albany, NY (EL). He moved to Toronto, Canada (IL) in 1943, but was inducted into the U.S. Navy Air Corps after only 43 games and spent the balance of 1943 and all of 1944 and 1945 in military service. He was discharged in time to start the 1946 season with the Pittsburgh Pirates (NL). During that year, he began establishing a HR record that neither Babe Ruth* nor any other slugger has ever equalled. For seven consecutive years, he led or shared the NL lead in HR. In 1949, he also paced the NL in RBI with 127. Kiner's second most productive HR output came in 1947, when he slugged 51 round trippers and a major league record eight HR in four consecutive September games. In two of those games, he made three consecutive HR. Kiner, who belted 369 major league HR, remains proudest of being the first National Leaguer to hit over 50 HR in two seasons (51 in 1947 and 54 in 1949). His 47 HR in 1950 established a then NL record of 102 HR over two consecutive seasons.

From 1946 through 1954, the durable Kiner appeared in 98 percent of his team's scheduled games and excelled as a "gamer." In the 1950 All-Star Game, his ninth inning HR tied the score and enabled his teammates to win the game eventually. At Chicago, a fever of 101° once prevented him from being in the lineup. Upon hearing that the Chicago Cubs had gone ahead, 10–8, in the seventh inning, Kiner thought he might be needed to pinch-hit and reported to the dugout. He told Pirates manager Billy Meyer, "I have one good swing in me." Kiner's swing produced a game-winning grand slam HR.

Besides being selected four times by *TSN* for its Major League All-Star team, Kiner in 1950 was named NL Player of the Year. In June 1953, Pittsburgh traded Kiner to the Chicago Cubs (NL) in a ten-player deal. He was traded to the Cleveland Indians (AL) in November 1954 and finished his playing career with 113 games there in 1955. In 10 major league seasons, Kiner batted .279 with 1,451 hits, 216 doubles, 971 runs scored, 1,015 RBI, and 1,011 walks. He led the NL three times in walks and slugging percentage and once in on-base percentage. From 1956 through 1960, he served as general manager of San Diego, CA (PCL). He became a radio announcer for the Chicago White Sox (AL) in 1961 and announced games over television for the New York Mets (NL) from 1962 through 1996. In 1975, he was elected to the National Baseball Hall of Fame.

BIBLIOGRAPHY: Martin Appel and Burt Goldblatt, *Baseball's Best: The Hall of Fame Gallery* (New York, 1977); Ralph Kiner file, National Baseball Library, Cooperstown, NY; John Benson et al., *Baseball's Top 100* (Wilton, CT, 1997); Richard L. Burtt, *The Pittsburgh Pirates, A Pictorial History* (Virginia Beach, VA, 1977); John F. Carmichael, *My Greatest Day in Baseball* (New York, 1963); Charles Einstein, ed., *Fireside Book of Baseball* (New York, 1961); Eddie Gold and Art Ahrens, *The New Era Cubs, 1941–1985* (Chicago, IL, 1985); Mark Goodwin, "Kiner's Style Corners the Market," *NYT Biographical Service* 19 (June 1986), pp. 81–82; Donald Honig, *The Power Hitters* (St. Louis, MO, 1989); Ralph Kiner and Joe Gergen, *Kiner's Korner* (New York,

1987); *The Baseball Encyclopedia*, 10th ed. (New York, 1996); Bob Smizik, *The Pittsburgh Pirates: An Illustrated History* (New York, 1990); Jim Enright, *Chicago Cubs* (New York, 1975).

Emil H. Rothe

KING, Charles Frederick "Silver" (b. Charles Frederick Koenig, January 11, 1868, St. Louis, MO; d. May 21, 1938, St. Louis, MO), player, was the third of seven children of bricklayer William Koenig and Dora Koenig. He married Stella (Adele, Della) Loring around 1900 and had four children. King turned professional as a pitcher in 1885 with Jacksonville, IL and pitched the following year for pennant-winning St. Joseph, MO (WL). A newspaperman there, struck by King's platinum-blond hair, nicknamed him "Silver." At season's end, he was given a trial by the Kansas City Cowboys (NL) and won one of four decisions. When that franchise folded in 1887, King joined his hometown St. Louis Browns (AA). The Browns won the AA pennant, as King contributed 32 victories for the first of four consecutive over–30 seasons. In 44 starts, he recorded 43 complete games. In a post-season "Travelling World Series" around the two circuits, the Browns were walloped 10 games to 5 by the NL's Detroit Wolverines. King took three losses and earned only one win.

When St. Louis captured its fourth consecutive AA pennant in 1888, King reached his zenith to lead the AA with 64 complete games in 65 starts, 45 wins, 21 losses, 585.2 innings pitched, 6 shutouts, and a 1.64 ERA. The Browns again fared poorly against the NL, losing 6 of a 10-game series with the New York Giants. Exhibitions and post-season games saw King pitch 121 innings, giving him 707 for the season. King compiled a 35–16 record in 1889, hurling 47 complete games in 53 starts. He then jumped to the PL, winning 30 and losing 22 in 56 starts for a fourth place the Chicago Pirates and pacing the PL with his 2.69 ERA. He also pitched an unusual losing no-hitter against the Brooklyn Wonders. Although Chicago was the home team, it elected to bat first. Since Brooklyn led, 1–0, in the bottom of the ninth inning and did not bat, King was credited only with an eight-inning no-hitter.

After the PBP collapsed, King returned to the NL in 1891 with the Pittsburgh Pirates. He was paid the highest salary of his career ($5,000), but slumped to an NL-leading 29 losses against 14 wins for the last place Pirates. King pitched his final iron-man season for the New York Giants (NL) in 1892, winning 22 and losing 24 complete games in 47 starts spanning 410.1 innings. He split 1893 between New York and the Cincinnati Reds (NL), finishing with a meager 8–10 record. The disgusted King sat out the next two seasons and worked instead at the bricklayer's trade. The Washington Senators (NL) coaxed him back, but his great skills had vanished. He won 10 and lost 7 in 1896 and finished with a 6–9 won–lost record in 1897.

His ten-year major league statistics included 203 victories, 153 defeats, and a 3.18 ERA. He pitched 328 complete games in 371 starts. King, a well-built 6-foot, 170-pound right-hander with big hands, relied chiefly on his fastball. He threw the occasional curve, but never mastered the spitter, fade-away, or other specialties of the next pitching generation. He continued in the contracting business in St. Louis until 1925 and built his own house. He lost all interest in baseball during his retirement and never saw another game.

BIBLIOGRAPHY: Daniel Peterson, *Baseball in 1889* (Bowling Green, KY, 1993); David Nemec, *The Beer and Whisky League* (New York, 1994); Stephen D. Boren, "Silver King Loses a No-Hitter," *BRJ* 20 (1991), p. 51; J. Thomas Hetrick, *Chris Von der Ahe and the St. Louis Browns* (Lanham, MD, 1999); Al Kermisch, "From a Researcher's Notebook," *BRJ* 9 (1980), p. 50; Craig Carter, ed., *TSN Daguerreotypes*, 8th ed. (St. Louis, MO, 1990); Noel Hynd, *The Giants of the Polo Grounds* (New York, 1988); Charles King file, National Baseball Library, Cooperstown, NY; *Reach's American Association Baseball Guide, 1888* (Philadelphia, PA, 1888); *The Baseball Encyclopedia*, 10th ed. (New York, 1996); Harold Seymour, *Baseball: The Early Years* (New York, 1960); *Spalding's Official Baseball Guide, 1888* (New York, 1888); St. Louis *Post-Dispatch*, June 20, 26, 1938; Robert L. Tiemann and Mark Rucker, eds., *Nineteenth Century Stars* (Kansas City, MO, 1989); David Quentin Voigt, *American Baseball*, vol. 1 (University Park, PA, 1983).

A. D. Suehsdorf

KINGMAN, David Arthur "King Kong," "Dave" (b. December 21, 1948, Pendleton, OR), player, is the son of Arthur Kingman, a United Airlines employee, and Captola Kingman. He attended Harper JC in Illinois and then the University of Southern California, where he switched from a pitcher to an outfielder. In 1970, Kingman led the Trojans to the NCAA College World Series championship. After signing with the San Francisco Giants (NL) organization, he played for Amarillo, TX (TL) in 1970 and Phoenix, AZ (PCL) in 1971 before joining the San Francisco Giants in July 1971. In 16 major league seasons, the 6-foot 6-inch, 210-pound Kingman played for seven different teams, hit prodigiously long HR, and struck out often. His .236 career batting average included 1,816 strikeouts, placing him fifth among all players. On the other hand, Kingman's 442 HR rank him 21st among all players. Kingman played for the NL in both the 1976 and 1980 All-Star games, but made no hits in his three times at bat. In the 1971 NL Championship Series, he batted .111 for the San Francisco Giants.

Kingman's low batting average, suspect defensive abilities, frequent contract difficulties, and surly disposition accounted for his inability to remain with one team for very long. His bad relationship with the press began in 1976 when he received much negative publicity for attempting to renegotiate his contract with the New York Mets (NL) after hitting 37 HR. Kingman shuffled among three teams (San Diego Padres, NL; California Angels, AL; and New York Yankees, AL) in 1977, and was signed as a free agent by the

Chicago Cubs (NL) in November 1977. He enjoyed the best year of his career in 1979 as a Cub, batting .288 and leading the NL with 48 HR and a .613 on base percentage.

After Kingman missed much of the 1980 season with a shoulder injury, the New York Mets held his services from 1981 through the 1983 season. He led the NL with 37 HR. He was signed by the Oakland A's (AL) prior to the 1984 season and blended well with that team. Despite hitting 35 HR in 1986, Kingman was not signed for the following season. His stormy major league career had ended. In 1989, he became a charter member of the West Palm Beach, FL Tropics (SPBA) and batted .271 with 8 HR and 40 RBI for the season.

BIBLIOGRAPHY: Dave Kingman file, National Baseball Library, Cooperstown, NY; *The Baseball Encyclopedia*, 10th ed. (New York, 1996); *CB* (1982), pp. 194–197; Eddie Gold and Art Ahrens, *The New Era Cubs, 1941–1985* (Chicago, IL, 1985); Warren Wilbert and William Hageman, *The Chicago Cubs: Seasons at the Summit* (Champaign, IL, 1997); Bruce Newman, "Kong," *SI* 51 (August 20, 1979), pp. 8–13; John Thorn et al., eds., *Total Baseball*, 5th ed. (New York, 1997); *TSN*, May 14, 1984; Steve Wulf, "Kong and Reggie: Remembrance of the Past," *SI* 60 (May 7, 1984), pp. 18–23; Donald Honig, *The New York Mets* (New York, 1986); Jack Lang and Peter Simon, *The New York Mets* (New York, 1986); Robert Obojski, "Former Mets Prove Popular Signers at NYC Area Shows," *SCD* 25 (December 18, 1998), pp. 126–127.

John E. Findling

KISON, Bruce Eugene (b. February 18, 1950, Pasco, WA), player and coach, is the son of Fred Kison, a building supply employee, and Bertha (Rogers) Kison. Kison graduated from Pasco High School, where he pitched two consecutive no-hitters, and attended Manatee JC and Central Washington State College. The Pittsburgh Pirates (NL) selected the quiet, baby-faced, 6-foot 4-inch, 173-pound right-hander in the sixth round of the June 1968 draft. He compiled a 30–9 record in less than four minor league seasons with Bradenton, FL (GCL) in 1968, Geneva, NY (NYPL) in 1969, Salem, VA (CrL) and Waterbury, CT (EL) in 1970, and Charleston, WV (IL) in 1971.

Kison joined the Pittsburgh Pirates in July 1971, hurling a two hit shutout in his second start and winning six of 11 decisions. He blanked the San Francisco Giants in 4.2 innings of relief to clinch the NL Championship Series. Kison relieved Luke Walker in the first inning of the fourth game of the 1971 World Series, the first night contest in fall classic history. The Baltimore Orioles made only one hit in 6.1 innings off his fastball and slider, losing, 4–3 for the turning point of the World Series.

The injury-prone Kison remained with the Pittsburgh Pirates through 1979, helping the Pirates win three more NL East Division titles with records of 9–7 in 1972, 9–8 in 1974, and 12–11 in 1975. He compiled 1–0 marks in both the 1972 NL Championship Series against the Cincinnati

Reds and in the 1974 NL Championship Series against the Los Angeles Dodgers. Kison became known for brush back pitches and quality stretch-run performances. His best seasons for Pittsburgh came in 1976 with a career-best 14–9 mark and 3.08 ERA and in 1979 with a 13–7 mark and 3.19 ERA. In June 1979, he hurled a one-hitter against the San Diego Padres.

In November 1979, the California Angels (AL) signed Kison as a free agent. Kison hurled five seasons with California, helping the Angels capture the AL West in 1982 with a 10–5 record and 3.17 ERA. He pitched brilliantly in the 1982 AL Championship Series against the Milwaukee Brewers, fanning 12 batters in 14 innings and winning his only decision. His major league career ended with the Boston Red Sox (AL) in 1985.

During 15 major league seasons, Kison compiled a 115–88 record and 3.66 ERA and struck out 1,073 batters in 1,809.2 innings. He tied a major league record for most victories in Championship Series play (4), yielding just 1.21 runs per game, and equaled a NL record for most triumphs (3) in three Championship Series. After serving as a minor league pitching instructor for the Pittsburgh Pirates, Kison served as pitching coach for the Kansas City Royals (AL) from 1992 through 1998 and for the Baltimore Orioles (AL) since 1999. The Bradenton, FL resident married Anna Marie Orlando on October 17, 1971 and has two children, Jennifer and Robert.

BIBLIOGRAPHY: Bruce Kison to David L. Porter, March 25, 1998, David L. Porter Collection, Oskaloosa, IA; Bruce Kison file, National Baseball Library, Cooperstown, NY; Pat Jordan, "An Old Hand with a Pro Prospect," *SI* 34 (June 14, 1971), pp. 72–76, 80, 82, 85–88, 90; Pat Jordan, "End of Innocence," *SI* 36 (April 10, 1972), pp. 86–90, 92, 94–96, 98–102, 104; *Boston Red Sox Media Guide*, 1985; *TSN Baseball Register*, 1986; Richard Burtt, *The Pittsburgh Pirates, A Pictorial History* (Virginia Beach, VA, 1977); Bob Smizik, *The Pittsburgh Pirates: An Illustrated History* (New York, 1990).

David L. Porter

KLEIN, Charles Herbert "Chuck" (b. October 7, 1904, Indianapolis, IN; d. March 28, 1958, Indianapolis, IN), player and coach, became one of the greatest left-handed sluggers in NL history. After attending Southport (IN) High School, he worked on a construction road gang and hurled around 200-pound ingots in a steel mill. The sturdy 6-foot, 195-pound Klein signed a minor league baseball contract with Evansville, IN (3IL) in 1927 and played less than one and a half seasons in the minor leagues. The Philadelphia Phillies (NL) bought his contract for $5,000 from Fort Wayne, IN (CL), outbidding the New York Yankees (AL). After only 100 games in the minor leagues, he joined the Phillies in July 1928, hit 14 doubles and 11 HR, and batted .360.

Between 1929 and 1933, Klein assembled the five greatest years of any left-handed power hitter in NL history. During that stretch, he averaged 36

HR, 139 RBI, 131 runs scored, 229 hits, a .635 slugging average, and a .359 batting average. He also established several NL records for a left-handed hitter for one season (1930), including 445 total bases, and 158 runs scored. His 107 extra-base hits (1930) remain a single-season NL record. Klein also knocked in 170 runs that year. The superb defensive right fielder holds the one-season mark with 44 assists in 1930. With the Phillies, Klein won one batting title and Triple Crown, captured four HR championships, and twice was named *TSN* NL MVP. Klein's records were downplayed by some baseball authorities because the marks were made in Baker Bowl, with its short 280-foot right-field fence. Although admitting that he benefited from the short dimensions, Klein remarked that he "also slammed a lot of drives off that tin that would have been home runs in bigger parks."

In November 1933, the financially destitute Phils traded Klein to the Chicago Cubs (NL) for shortstop Mark Koenig,* pitcher Ted Kleinhans, outfielder Harvey Hendrick, and $65,000. Klein's two and one-half seasons with the Cubs triggered his decline, although he hit .333 with one HR in the 1935 World Series. Upon returning to the Phillies in May 1936, he enjoyed one more good season and drove in over 100 runs for the sixth time. He slugged four HR in a July 1936 game against the Pittsburgh Pirates, the first National Leaguer to accomplish that feat in modern times.

Klein joined the Pittsburgh Pirates (NL) in June 1939, but returned to the Phillies in March 1940 and completed his playing career as a part-time outfielder and pinch hitter. From 1942 to 1945, he also coached for the Phillies. Klein's career totals included 2,076 hits, 398 doubles, 300 HR, 1,201 RBI, and a .320 batting average. He still holds several NL records, including most consecutive years with 200 or more hits (5, 1929–1933), most years with 400 or more total bases (3, 1929–1930, 1932) and most years with 150 or more runs in a season (2, 1930, 1932). After retiring as a player in 1944, he operated a bar until 1947 in the Kensington section of Philadelphia. Suffering from poor health due to heavy drinking, he moved back to Indianapolis in 1947 to live with his brother, Edward, and his wife. Klein, a semi-invalid the rest of his life, died of a cerebral hemorrhage brought on by heavy drinking. Married in May 1936 to Mary Torpey, he was divorced 20 years later and had no children. In 1980, Klein was elected to the National Baseball Hall of Fame.

BIBLIOGRAPHY: Chuck Klein file, National Baseball Library, Cooperstown, NY; Frederick G. Lieb and Stan Baumgarter, *New Philadelphia Phillies* (Philadelphia, PA, 1953); John Benson et al., *Baseball's Top 100* (Wilton, CT, 1997); Lowell Reidenbaugh, *Baseball's Hall of Fame—Cooperstown* (New York, 1993); Rich Westcott and Frank Bilovsky, *The New Phillies Encyclopedia* (Philadelphia, PA, 1993); Dave Nelson, "Chuck Klein's Five Great Years," *TNP* 15 (1995), pp. 118–119; Philadelphia *Evening Bulletin*, March 29, 1958; Ed Doyle, *The Forgotten Ones* (Philadelphia, PA, 1974); Eddie Gold and Art Ahrens, *The Golden Era Cubs, 1876–1940* (Chicago, IL, 1985); Jim Enright, *Chicago Cubs* (New York, 1975); Warren Brown, *The Chicago Cubs* (New

York, 1946); Allen Lewis, *The Philadelphia Phillies: A Pictorial History* (Virginia Beach, VA, 1981); Philadelphia *Inquirer*, March 29, 1958.

John P. Rossi

KLEM, William Joseph "Bill," "The Old Arbitrator," "Catfish" (b. William Joseph Klimm, February 22, 1874, Rochester, NY; d. September 1, 1951, Miami, FL), umpire, was nicknamed "The Old Arbitrator" and was of German descent. Before umpiring, he earned his living briefly as a baseball player, a bartender, and, with his brothers, a bridge-builder. Klem umpired in the CtSL (1902), NYSL (1903), and AA (1904). From 1905 to 1941, he umpired in the NL. He arbitrated in a record 18 different World Series. Klem absorbed the physical and mental punishment that homeplate umpires underwent daily on a full-season schedule for 16 consecutive years. From 1941 until his death, he served as the NL chief of umpires. He ranks as baseball's greatest umpire and was elected in 1953 to the National Baseball Hall of Fame, only one of seven umpires so honored.

In his difficult and unpopular pursuit, Klem resisted the constant abuse and the lonely life of early day umpires. In his reminiscences, Klem graphically recalled how rowdiness and loneliness gradually affected old-time umpires. John Gaffney became an alcoholic and Hank O'Day* a misanthrope, while Bob Emslie developed complete hirsutelessness. Klem repelled these dangers with his immense ego, which enabled him to reign supreme over any threatening players or fans. Klem assessed Judge Kenesaw Mountain Landis'* role in baseball as mere "window-dressing." He banished hotel room loneliness by having his childless wife, Marie Krans, whom he married in 1910, travel about with him during the regular season.

Klem's photos show him as average in size (5 feet 7½ inches) and weight (157 pounds), smaller than most umpires. Facially slightly piscine, he was nicknamed "Catfish." In vision, voice resonance, accuracy, and knowledge of the rules, Klem ranked with numerous other first-class umpires. In several vital areas, however, Klem made distinctive contributions. He helped all later umpires by asserting control over a game and "drawing the line" against obnoxious, charging players. At Klem's initiative, the dignity of umpires was upgraded via increasing salaries, using multiple arbiters, providing adequate quarters, and compelling managers to bring their lineups to home plate before a game. Klem gave verbal and visual definition to many functions of an umpire, including audible strike calls, handwaving on foul-line calls, and the sweeping gesture of the thumb on the close "out." Enhancing the integrity of umpires, Klem always asserted, "I never missed one in my life!" During his long career, the NL office actually reversed him two or three times. At a ceremony honoring him at the Polo Grounds on September 2, 1949, "The Old Arbitrator" declared, "Baseball to me is not a game; it is a religion."

BIBLIOGRAPHY: Bill Klem file, National Baseball Library, Cooperstown, NY; Jocko Conlan and Robert Creamer, *Jocko* (Philadelphia, PA, 1967); Noel Hynd, *The Giants of the Polo Grounds* (New York, 1988); William J. Klem, "I Never Missed One in My Heart," *Collier's* 127 (March 31, 1951), pp. 30–31ff; (April 7, 1951), pp. 30–31ff; (April 14, 1951), pp. 30–31ff; (April 21, 1951), pp. 30–31ff; *NYT*, September 17, 1951; *TSN*, October, 12, 1983.

Lowell L. Blaisdell

KLIMM, William Joseph. *See* William Joseph Klem.

KLINE, Maxine. *See* Maxine Kline Randall.

KLING, John Gradwohl "Johnny," "Noisy" (b. February 25, 1875, Kansas City, MO; d. January 31, 1947, Kansas City, MO), player, manager, and executive, ranked among the great catchers of the early 1900s. The 5-foot 9½-inch, 160-pound Kling, who threw and batted right-handed, began his career as a pitcher for the Kansas City Schmeltzers. Although only 18 years old, Kling served as team manager, pitcher, and first baseman. In 1895 he briefly joined the Rockford, IL (3IL) club, but returned to the Schmeltzers. After a short trial with Houston, TX (TL) he signed with St. Joseph, MO (WL) and was discovered there by the Chicago Cubs (NL). Kling remained with the Cubs from 1900 through part of 1911, except for holding out the entire 1909 season.

During this period, Kling performed most of the catching duties and helped lead Chicago to four NL flags (1906–1908, 1910) as a teammate of Joe Tinker,* Johnny Evers,* and Frank Chance.* The Cubs lost the 1906 World Series to the Chicago White Sox, but became world champions in 1907 and 1908. Chicago defeated Detroit both times, as the Tigers won only one game in the two World Series. The Cubs lost to the Philadelphia A's in the 1910 World Series, four games to one. Kling either holds or shares several World Series fielding records, including most chances accepted in a six-game World Series (56), most double plays in a six-game World Series (3), most players caught stealing in a five-game World Series (6), most assists in a nine-inning game (4), most passed balls in a nine-inning game (2), and most passed balls in World Series play (5). A fine catcher with a great arm, Kling led NL catchers in fielding average twice (1906–1907) and in putouts six years (1902–1907). Only Roy Campanella* and Gary Carter* equalled this mark. In 1,260 major league games, Kling compiled a .271 batting average and twice (1906, 1912) batted above .300.

In June 1911, Kling was traded to the Boston Braves (NL) and became player–manager in 1912. His club won 52 games, lost 101, and finished in eighth place. His final season in the major leagues came in 1913 with the Cincinnati Reds (NL). In 13 major league seasons, Kling collected 1,151 hits, slugging 181 doubles, 61 triples, and 20 HR, and compiled 513 RBI. In four World Series, he played in 21 games and batted only .185. Kling became a successful businessman, operating a billiard hall and owning two

Kansas City hotels and a dairy farm. He purchased Kansas City, MO (AA) in 1934 and sold the club in 1937 to the New York Yankees.

BIBLIOGRAPHY: John Kling file, National Baseball Library, Cooperstown, NY; Warren Brown, *The Chicago Cubs* (New York, 1952); Jim Enright, *Chicago Cubs* (New York, 1975); Warren Wilbert and William Hageman, *Chicago Cubs: Seasons at the Summit* (Champaign, IL, 1997); Eddie Gold and Art Ahrens, *The Golden Era Cubs, 1876–1940* (Chicago, IL, 1985); Gary Caruso, *The Braves Encyclopedia* (Philadelphia, PA, 1995); Richard M. Cohen et al., *The World Series* (New York, 1976); Gene Karst and Martin J. Jones, Jr., *Who's Who in Professional Baseball* (New Rochelle, NY, 1973); *The Baseball Encyclopedia*, 10th ed. (New York, 1996).

John L. Evers

KLUSZEWSKI, Theodore Bernard "Ted," "Klu" (b. September 10, 1924, Argo, IL; d. March 29, 1988, Cincinnati, OH), baseball and football player and coach, was the son of John Kluszewski and Josephine (Guntarski) Kluszewski. He played football, basketball, baseball, and softball at Argo Community High School. After graduation in 1942, he worked for the Corn Products Refining Company in Argo and played sandlot football on weekends. Offered a football scholarship by Indiana University, Kluszewski in 1945 won All-BTC and honorable mention All-American citations at end. Besides catching game-winning passes against the universities of Michigan and Illinois, he threw a touchdown pass to Pete Pihos (FB) on an end-around play to defeat Northwestern University, 6–0, and assure the Hoosiers an unbeaten season.

Kluszewski also played baseball at Indiana, where his hitting in the spring of 1945 impressed the Cincinnati Reds (NL), who were training at the Bloomington campus. Following the football season, he signed a professional baseball contract as a first baseman and celebrated by marrying Eleanor Rita Guckel on February 9, 1946. After winning batting titles for Columbia, SC (SAL) in 1946 and Memphis, TN (SA) in 1947 with .352 and .377 marks, Kluszewski became Cincinnati's first baseman in 1948. Kluszewski averaged .294 at the plate and 15 HR a season for his first five years with the Reds. To stress his intimidating 6-foot 2-inch, 240-pound physique, he discarded the undershirt of his sleeveless uniform to reveal massive shoulders and biceps. Since Kluszewski's normal batting stroke was through the middle, hurlers pitched him inside in sheer self-defense. After Kluszewski taught himself to pull the ball in 1953, he became an awesome offensive force. From 1953 to 1955, he batted .319, slugged 40, 49, and 47 HR, and led the NL in HR and RBI (141) in 1954 to become one of the most popular Reds ever. He led the NL in hits (192) in 1955. An inept fielder initially, he improved vastly and set a major league record for consecutive years leading the league in fielding at first base (1951–1955). On May 1, 1955, his six double plays in an extra-inning game tied a major league record.

In 1957, physical problems began plaguing Kluszewski. Hampered by a slipped disc, he spent most of the 1957 season on the Reds' bench. He was traded to the Pittsburgh Pirates (NL) for Dee Fondy in December 1957 and played there until the Chicago White Sox (AL) acquired him in August 1959. A regular down the stretch, Kluszewski in 1959 helped the White Sox win their first AL pennant in 40 years. He hit .391 and batted in a six-game record 10 runs in his only World Series opportunity. He finished his career with the expansion Los Angeles Angels (AL) in 1961. During his major league career, the left-handed Kluszewski slugged 290 doubles and 279 HR, batted .298, made 1,766 hits, and knocked in 1,028 runs. He struck out only once every 17 at bats, a remarkable ratio for a power hitter. Kluszewski, hired in 1970 as a coach by the Reds, became one of the baseball's best teachers of hitting. He coached with the Reds through 1978 and served as a minor league instructor for the Reds from 1979 until his death.

BIBLIOGRAPHY: Ritter Collet, *The Cincinnati Reds* (Virginia Beach, VA, 1976); Donald Honig, *The Cincinnati Reds* (New York, 1992); Ted Kluszewski file, National Baseball Library, Cooperstown, NY; *NYT Biographical Service* 19 (March 1988), p. 368; Bob Rathgeber, *Cincinnati Reds Scrapbook* (Virginia Beach, VA, 1982); Rich Lindberg, *Who's on Third?* (South Bend, IN, 1983); Donald Honig, *The October Heroes* (New York, 1979); Earl Lawson, "The Redlegs' One Man Gang," *SEP* 227 (March 19, 1955), pp. 32–33; Rich Westcott, *Diamond Greats* (Westport, CT, 1988).

Dennis T. "Tom" Chase

KNOBLAUCH, Edward Charles "Chuck" (b. July 7, 1968, Houston, TX), player, is a 5-foot 9-inch, 169-pound infielder who bats and throws right-handed. His father, Ray, pitched minor league baseball and coached him in high school baseball. A 1986 graduate of Bellaire High School in Houston, Knoblauch played semiprofessional baseball in 1987 and 1988 and studied agricultural economics at Texas A&M University. After making the freshman All-American baseball team, Knoblauch batted .364 as a junior in 1989 and earned second team *BA* All-America honors at shortstop. He married Lisa Johnson and has no children.

The Minnesota Twins (AL) signed Knoblauch as the 25th player selected in the 1989 free-agent draft. He split his first professional baseball season with Kenosha, WI (ML) and Visalia, CA (CaL). In 1990, Knoblauch was moved to second base and promoted to Orlando, FL (SL). Upon joining the Minnesota Twins for the 1991 season, he recorded a career-high 20-game hit streak, led the Twins in stolen bases, and paced the AL in stolen base percentage (.830). Knoblauch batted .281 and was named *TSN* and BBWAA AL Rookie of the Year. Knoblauch helped lead Minnesota to the Western Division Championship, an AL Championship Series triumph over the Toronto Blue Jays, and a World Series title over the Atlanta Braves. He set a record for most hits (7) by a rookie in a League Championship Series and hit safely in six of the seven World Series games. Knoblauch made 15 hits in postseason play, establishing the mark for most hits by a rookie. After batting .312 and leading the AL with a career-best 45 doubles in 1994,

Knoblauch the following season batted .333. In 1996, he established career-highs in batting (.341), runs scored (140), hits (197), triples (14), HR (13), RBI (72), and walks (98). He set club records for runs scored and being hit by a pitched ball (19) while leading the AL in triples and second basemen with a .988 fielding percentage, earning his first Gold Glove. In 1997, he ranked second in the AL with 62 stolen bases. Knoblauch's additional honors include being named to *TSN* AL All-Star Team in 1994 and 1997 and *TSN* AL Silver Slugger Team in 1995 and 1997. He won the Calvin R. Griffith Award as the Twins' MVP in 1995 and 1996 and made the 1992, 1994, 1996, and 1997 All-Star teams. In February 1998, Minnesota traded him to the New York Yankees (AL). Knoblauch batted a career-low .265 in 1998 and struggled in both the AL Division Series against the Texas Rangers and AL Championship Series against the Cleveland Indians. The Indians scored a run in the 12th inning of Game 2 when Knoblauch, covering first base on a bunt play, did not go after a ball that hit bunter Travis Fryman on the back. Knoblauch did not retrieve the ball in time because he thought Fryman ran out of the baseline. In the World Series triumph over the San Diego Padres, Knoblauch batted .455 with one HR and three RBI. His .292 batting average, 120 runs, and 28 stolen bases helped New York win another AL East title in 1999. He hit .333 in the AL Championship Series and .313 with one HR and RBI in the World Series, which New York won.

In nine major league seasons through 1999, Knoblauch has scored 950 runs and made 1,533 hits in 1,313 games. He has batted .298 with 271 doubles, 59 triples, and 78 HR, produced 523 RBI, and recorded 672 walks, 580 strikeouts, and 335 stolen bases.

BIBLIOGRAPHY: Chuck Knoblauch file, National Baseball Library, Cooperstown, NY; Tim Kurkjian, "Prime Chuck," *SI* 85 (August 5, 1996), pp. 127–129; Franz Lidz, "Second Wind," *SI* 88 (March 9, 1998), pp. 74–76; *Minnesota Twins Media Guide*, 1997; *TSN Official Baseball Register*, 1998.

John L. Evers

KOENIG, Charles Frederick. *See* Charles Frederick King.

KOENIG, Mark Anthony (b. July 19, 1904, San Francisco, CA; d. April 22, 1993, Willows, CA), player, joined the New York Yankees (AL) in 1925 and played shortstop there until traded to the Detroit Tigers (AL) in May 1930. He was acquired by the Chicago Cubs (NL) before the 1932 season and spent two years there. Koenig joined the Cincinnati Reds (NL) in December 1933 and finished his major league career with the New York Giants (NL) in 1935 and 1936. Although primarily a shortstop, he also played third base, second base, first base, and occasionally the outfield. He also pitched two games in 1930 and three games in 1931 for the Detroit Tigers, compiling an 0–1 record and an 8.44 ERA in 16 innings.

During his 12 year major league career, the 6-foot, 180-pound, switch-hitting Koenig batted .279, with 195 doubles, 443 RBI and just 28 HR in 1,162 games. He stole only 31 bases and fielded .927, leading the AL with 52 errors in 1926 and 47 errors in 1927. In the 1926–1928, 1932, and 1936 World Series, he batted .237, with three doubles, one triple, and five RBI.

Koenig's best year came in 1927, when he hit .285 as the New York Yankees' starting shortstop and led New York with a .500 batting average in its World Series victory over the Pittsburgh Pirates. Despite his frequent errors, he made an excellent double play combination with second baseman Tony Lazzeri.* In 1929, Leo Durocher* replaced him as the Yankees' starting shortstop. After two mediocre seasons with the Detroit Tigers, Koenig played with the San Francisco, CA Missions (PCL) until the Chicago Cubs bought him in August 1932. His .353 batting average in 33 games helped Chicago win the 1932 NL pennant, but the Cubs gave him only half a World Series share. Some historians allege that Chicago's frugality fired up Koenig's former team, the New York Yankees, who swept the Cubs in the 1932 World Series.

Koenig, who married Katherine Trumain and later Doris Bailey, resided in Orland, CA in retirement and was survived by a daughter, Gail Terry.

BIBLIOGRAPHY: Mark Koenig file, National Baseball Library, Cooperstown, NY; *NYT*, April 25, 1993, p. 52; Mike Shatzkin, ed., *The Ballplayers* (New York, 1990); Marshall Smelser, *The Life That Ruth Built* (Lincoln, NE, 1975); John Thorn et al., eds., *Total Baseball*, 5th ed. (New York, 1997); *The Baseball Encyclopedia*, 10th ed. (New York, 1996); Fred Smith, *995 Tigers* (Detroit, MI, 1981); Mark Gallagher, *The Yankee Encyclopedia*, vol. 3 (Champaign, IL, 1997); Frank Graham, *The New York Yankees* (New York, 1943); John Mosedale, *The Greatest of All: The 1927 New York Yankees* (New York, 1974); Leo Trachtenberg, *The Wonder Team* (Bowling Green, OH, 1995); Frederick G. Lieb, *The Detroit Tigers* (New York, 1946); Eddie Gold and Art Ahrens, *The Golden Era Cubs, 1876–1940* (Chicago, IL, 1985); Warren Brown, *The Chicago Cubs* (New York, 1946).

John E. Findling

KONETCHY, Edward Joseph "Ed," "Big Ed" (b. September 3, 1885, La Crosse, WI; d. May 27, 1947, Fort Worth, TX), player and manager, was the son of Bohemian parents who settled in La Crosse. Konetchy was educated at La Crosse public schools and then worked dipping chocolates in a local candy factory. An outstanding sandlot baseball player, he began his professional career at age 20 with La Crosse, WI (WSL). For La Crosse, he batted .222 his rookie season and .277 his second year. Konetchy's .358 batting average at the start of the 1907 season landed him a contract with the St. Louis Cardinals (NL). The 6-foot 2½-inch, 195-pound right-hander immediately became the starting Cardinals first baseman and stayed there through the 1913 season. He played with the Pittsburgh Pirates (NL) in 1914, Pittsburgh Rebels (FL) in 1915, Boston Braves (NL) from 1916 to 1918, and Brooklyn Robins (NL) in 1919, 1920, and 1921 and spent the last part of his final major league season with the Philadelphia Phillies (NL).

An outstanding fielder with excellent range and a powerful throwing arm, Konetchy led NL first basemen in percentage eight times and in putouts and assists several times. Konetchy compiled a .281 lifetime batting average, hit over .300 four times, and possessed above average power. He paced the NL in doubles (38) in 1911 and made 10 consecutive hits (1919), an NL record he shares with nine other players. In 2,085 career major league games, he made 2,150 hits, 344 doubles, 181 triples, 75 HR, 992 RBI, and 255 stolen bases. Often cited in box scores as "Koney," he performed at first base the entire major league record 26-inning game for Brooklyn against Boston in 1920. Following his baseball career, he pursued business in Fort Worth, TX. He managed Fort Worth, TX Cats (TL) from 1923 to 1939, playing with them from 1925 through 1927. He also piloted La Crosse, WI (WSL) from 1940 to 1942, but returned to Fort Worth as a foreman in the Convair plant during World War II.

BIBLIOGRAPHY: Ed Konetchy file, National Baseball Library, Cooperstown, NY; Gene Karst and Martin J. Jones, Jr., *Who's Who in Professional Baseball* (New Rochelle, NY, 1973); Frederick G. Lieb, *The St. Louis Cardinals* (New York, 1945); Ira L. Smith, *Baseball's Famous First Basemen* (New York, 1956); Bob Broeg and Jerry Vickery, *St. Louis Cardinals Encyclopedia* (Grand Rapids, MI, 1998); Harold Kaese, *The Boston Braves* (New York, 1948); Gary Caruso, *The Braves Encyclopedia* (Philadelphia, PA, 1995); Frank Graham, *The Brooklyn Dodgers* (New York, 1945); *NYT*, May 28, 1947; *The Baseball Encyclopedia*, 10th ed. (New York, 1996).

Robert E. Jones

KONSTANTY, James Casimir "Big Jim" (b. March 2, 1917, Strykersville, NY; d. June 11, 1976, Oneonta, NY), player and athletic administrator, became the first relief pitcher ever accorded special recognition when he was given the NL MVP award in 1950. With the NL titlist Philadelphia Phillies (NL) that year, the right-hander posted a 16–7 win–loss record. His NL-leading 74 relief appearances for the "Whiz Kids" featured 22 saves. Konstanty, a surprise starter in the first game of the 1950 World Series, pitched brilliantly in the 1–0 loss to Vic Raschi of the New York Yankees.

The son of Polish immigrants, John Konstanty and Apolonia Konstanty, he graduated from Syracuse University in 1939 with a bachelor's degree in physical education. A half-scholarship recipient, he became one of the Orangemen's few athletes to letter in four sports as a participant in baseball, basketball, football, and soccer. These accomplishments, combined with his 6-foot 1½-inch, 205-pound build, resulted in his nickname, "Big Jim." From 1940 to 1945, Konstanty taught physical education and coached several sports in high schools while pursuing a professional baseball career. He married Mary Burlingame in 1941 and had one son, James, and one daughter, Helen. After leading the EL with 19 losses at Springfield, MA in 1941, Konstanty pitched over two seasons with Syracuse, NY (IL) and recorded a 6–4 win–loss mark with the Cincinnati Reds (NL) in 1944. He served with the U.S. Navy toward the end of World War II in 1945 and was sent to the Boston Braves (NL) in April 1946. Most of that season and the 1947–1948 campaigns saw Konstanty hurling for Toronto, Canada (IL). Toronto manager Eddie Sawyer encouraged Konstanty to continue his baseball career despite his weak fastball and curveball.

Konstanty joined the Philadelphia Phillies (NL) in 1948 when Sawyer took over as manager of that club. Konstanty pitched for the Philadelphia Phillies from 1948 until he was traded to the New York Yankees (AL) in August 1954. He finished his major league career with the St. Louis Cardinals (NL) in 1956. Aside from his banner 1950 season, Konstanty's major league career remained relatively unimpressive. His 11-year major league career record included 66 wins, 48 losses, 74 saves, and a 3.46 ERA. Konstanty operated a sporting goods store in Oneonta, NY from 1948 to 1953 and served as Athletic Director at Hartwick College there from 1967 to 1972. In 1975, he bid unsuccessfully for the Republican nomination to represent the Sixth District in the New York State Legislature.

BIBLIOGRAPHY: Richie Ashburn, "Jim Konstanty, He Gave Relief Pitchers Dignity," *BD* 35 (September 1976), pp. 65–69; *The Baseball Encyclopedia*, 10th ed. (New York, 1996); Andy Duorcan, "Jim Konstanty, The All-Time Fireman," *Sport* 10 (May 1951), pp. 16–19; Gene Karst and Martin J. Jones, Jr., *Who's Who In Professional Baseball* (New Rochelle, NY, 1973); James Konstanty file, National Baseball Library, Cooperstown, NY; Milton Shapiro, *Heroes of the Bullpen* (New York, 1967); Frank Yeutter, *Jim Konstanty* (New York, 1951); Bob Cairns, *Pen Men* (New York, 1993); Allen Lewis, *The Philadelphia Phillies: A Pictorial History* (Virginia Beach, VA, 1981); Robin Roberts and C. Paul Rogers III, *The Whiz Kids and the 1950 Pennant* (Philadelphia, PA, 1996); Rich Westcott and Frank Bilovsky, *The New Phillies Encyclopedia* (Philadelphia, PA, 1993).

James K. Skipper, Jr.

KOOSMAN, Jerome Martin "Jerry" (b. December 23, 1942, Appleton, MN), player, is the son of farmer Martin William Koosman and Lydia (Graese) Koosman. He attended the University of Minnesota, Morris, MN (1960–1961), and the State School of Science, Wahpeton, ND (1961–1962). From 1962 to 1964, Koosman served in the U.S. Army. He married La Vonne Kathleen Sorum in February 1967 and has three children. The Bonita Springs, FL, resident's prowess as a pitcher on the Fort Bliss, TX Army baseball team impressed the New York Mets (NL), who signed him in 1964 to a professional contract and assigned him to Greenville, SC (WCL). The 6-foot 2-inch, 225-pound left-hander compiled a mediocre 27–30 won–lost record for several minor league teams, including Williamsport, PA (EL) in 1965, Auburn, NY (NYPL) in 1966, and Jacksonville, FL (IL) in 1967, and an unimpressive 0–2 mark for the New York Mets during his first three seasons (1965–1967). With the Mets in 1968, he won 19 games, posted a 2.08 ERA, captured *TSN* NL Rookie of the Year Award, and tied an NL rookie record for most shutout games won. Beginning in 1967, Koosman and teammate Tom Seaver* enjoyed several years as baseball's preeminent lefty–righty pitching duo.

In 12 seasons with the New York Mets (1967–1978), Koosman compiled a 3.09 ERA and a 140–137 record. Twenty-one of those victories came in 1976. After the Mets traded him to the Minnesota Twins (AL) in December 1978, Koosman in 1979 won 20 games for a second time. He garnered a cumulative 62–53 mark and 3.95 ERA during five AL campaigns with the Twins and Chicago White Sox (1979–1983). In 1984, he joined the Philadelphia Phillies (NL) and compiled a 14–15 mark. He retired following the 1985 season. In 19 major league seasons, he won 222 games, lost 209, struck out 2,556 batters in 3,839.1 innings, hurled 33 shutouts, and compiled a 3.36 ERA.

Koosman's 3–0 World Series record includes the "Miracle Mets' " decisive triumph over the Baltimore Orioles in 1969. Koosman pitched in two major league All-Star games (1968, 1969) and three Championship Series games (1969, 1973, 1983). During the 1968 season, Koosman set a dubious NL record for a pitcher by striking out 62 times. He led the NL in balks in 1970 and 1975 and surrendered Pete Rose's* 4,000th major league hit in 1984.

BIBLIOGRAPHY: Jerry Koosman file, National Baseball Library, Cooperstown, NY; Joseph Durso, *Amazing* (Boston, MA, 1970), Jack Lang and Peter Simon, *The New York Mets* (New York, 1986); Donald Honig, *The New York Mets* (New York, 1986); Richard M. Cohen et al., *The World Series* (New York, 1979); Stanley Cohen, *A Magic Summer* (San Diego, CA, 1988); Dave Mona and Dave Jarzyna, *Twenty-Five Seasons* (Minneapolis, MN, 1986); Zander Hollander, *The Complete Handbook of Baseball 1979* (New York, 1979); Milwaukee *Journal*, April 14, 1984; *The Baseball Encyclopedia*, 10th ed. (New York, 1996); *TSN Official Baseball Register, 1986; WWA*, 1984, 42nd ed. (1982–83), p. 1,859.

Thomas D. Jozwik

KOPPE, George Maceo. *See* George Joseph Cuppy.

KOUFAX, Sanford "Sandy" (b. Sanford Braun, December 30, 1935, Brooklyn, NY), player, instructor, and sportscaster, is the son of Jack Braun and Evelyn Braun and was an overpowering left-handed pitcher. After his parents divorced in 1938, his mother, an accountant, married attorney Irving Koufax. The young Koufax developed into a muscular athlete by playing baseball and basketball in the schoolyards and Jewish community clubs in Brooklyn and starred on his high school basketball team there. In 1953, the University of Cincinnati awarded him a basketball scholarship while he prepared for an architecture career.

Koufax, however, impressed major league baseball scouts as a pitcher when he struck out 51 batters in 32 innings for his college team. Despite his limited baseball background, the Brooklyn Dodgers (NL) in 1954 signed Koufax to a $20,000 contract containing a $14,000 bonus. Baseball's bonus rule required that the 19-year-old immediately join the major league squad and remain there two years. The Dodgers, contending for NL pennants in 1955 and 1956, assigned Koufax to the bench and gave him few opportunities to pitch. Koufax appeared in 28 games, winning four and losing six. Without minor league training, Koufax remained a raw talent. Although possessing blinding speed and a sharp curveball, he lacked control and pitching technique and finished 1957 with a mediocre 5–4 record in 104.1 innings.

Koufax began to pitch regularly for the Dodgers after the team moved to Los Angeles in 1958. Still plagued by control problems, he won 27 contests and lost 30 between 1958 and 1960, occasionally turning in brilliant performances. In 1959, Koufax struck out 18 Chicago Cubs hitters in nine innings and set a two-game major league strikeouts record with 31. Pitching delivery changes resulted in an impressive 1961 season, including an 18–13 record, an NL-leading 269 strikeouts in 255.2 innings, and only 96 walks. For the next five seasons, Koufax proved a dominating pitcher. In tandem with strong right-hander Don Drysdale,* he led the Dodgers to NL pennants in 1963, 1965, and 1966 and world championships in 1963 and 1965.

Koufax claimed his place among the great baseball pitchers with several stellar accomplishments between 1962 and 1966. He won 111 games and lost 34 decisions, led the NL in ERA each season (averaging under two earned runs per game during this period), paced the NL in strikeouts (1963, 1965, and 1966) and shutouts (3 seasons), and pitched four no-hitters, including a perfect game in 1965. Although winning the NL Cy Young Award in 1963, 1965, and 1966 and MVP Award in 1963, Koufax achieved these feats in pain. In 1963 a circulatory problem deadened the index finger on his pitching hand, causing wags to speak of the million-dollar arm with the ten-cent finger. Traumatic arthritis in his elbow the next year threatened permanent disability and hastened his retirement after the 1966 season. His 12-year major league career produced 165 wins and 87 losses, a 2.76 ERA in 397 games, 2,396 strikeouts and 817 walks in 2,324.1 innings, 40 shutouts, and a lowly .097 batting average.

In an unprecedented maneuver in 1966, Koufax united with Drysdale in a joint holdout for higher salary and hired an agent to bargain with the Dodgers. The strategy secured Koufax a $130,000 contract and encouraged the use of player agents. Koufax' introspective, bookish manner earned him a reputation as an anti-athlete athlete and disinterested sports hero, views which he rejected in his 1966 autobiography.

After retiring from the game, Koufax worked as a sportscaster for NBC from 1967 to 1972, dealt in real estate, served as pitching instructor for the Dodgers, and raised show horses. He married Anne Widmark, the daughter of actor Richard Widmark, in 1969 and resides in North Carolina. In 1971, at age 36, Koufax became the youngest inductee to the National Baseball Hall of Fame. He made Major League Baseball's All-Century Team.

BIBLIOGRAPHY: Sandy Koufax file, National Baseball Library, Cooperstown, NY; John Benson et al., *Baseball's Top 100* (Wilton, CT, 1997); Bob Broeg, *Super Stars of Baseball* (St. Louis, MO, 1971); Arnold Hano, *Sandy Koufax: Strikeout King* (New York, 1964); Sandy Koufax and Ed Linn, *Koufax* (New York, 1966); Ed Linn, "Sandy Koufax," *The Baseball Hall of Fame 50th Anniversary Book* (New York, 1988); Walter Alston and Si Burick, *Alston and the Dodgers* (New York, 1966); Erwin Lynn, *The Jewish Baseball Hall of Fame* (New York, 1987); Ronald A. Mayer, *Perfect!* (Jefferson, NC, 1991); Tom Murray, ed., *Sport Magazine's All-Time All-Stars* (New York, 1977); *NYT*, 1963–1966; J. Olsen, "The Very Best Act in Town," *SI* 80 (April 25, 1994), pp. 38–40; Mordecai Richler, "Koufax the Incomparable," *Commentary* 42 (November 1966), pp. 87–89; Ken Young, *Cy Young Award Winners* (New York, 1994); Jim Kaplan, "The Best Pitcher Ever," *BRJ* 27 (1998), pp. 62–65; Brent P. Kelley, *Baseball's Biggest Blunder* (Lanham, MD, 1996); Walter Alston with Jack Tobin, *A Day at a Time* (Waco, TX, 1976); William F. McNeil, *The Dodgers Encyclopedia* (Champaign, IL, 1997); Peter Golenbock, *Bums* (New York, 1984).

Joseph E. King

KOWALEWSKI, Harry Frank. *See* Harry Frank Coveleski.

KOWALEWSKI, Stanislaus. *See* Stanley Anthony Coveleski.

KREEVICH, Michael Andreas "Iron Mike" (b. June 10, 1908, Mt. Olive, IL; d. April 25, 1994, Pana, IL), player, was a right-hand hitting outfielder best known as the only .300 hitter on the 1944 St. Louis Browns' (AL) championship team. Of Austrian Croat extraction, he lost the middle finger off his left hand in a Southern Illinois coal mine accident.

The 5-foot 7½-inch, 170-pound Kreevich played five games for the Chicago Cubs (NL) in 1931 and spent the next four seasons in the minor leagues. The highlight of his minor league career came in 1935, when he batted .340 for Kansas City, MO (AA) and enjoyed a 38 game hitting streak from July 19 to August 10. This performance led to his late season promotion to the Chicago White Sox (AL), where he performed regularly for the next six seasons. Kreevich led the AL with 16 triples and AL outfielders with a .988 fielding percentage in 1937 and made the AL All-Star team in 1938. His best season with the White Sox came in 1939, when he hit .323. The following campaign, he paced the AL outfielders with 18 assists. In 1941, he paced AL outfielders with a .994 fielding percentage. Chicago traded Kreevich and pitcher Jack Hallet to the Philadelphia Athletics (AL) on December 9, 1941 for outfielder Wally Moses.* White Sox manager Jimmy Dykes* later recalled, "There's many a time when I wish I had him back."

The Philadelphia Athletics released Kreevich after the 1942 season, but St. Louis Browns' manager Luke Sewell* signed him as a free agent. After seeing limited service in 1943, Kreevich led the St. Louis Browns in hitting in 1944 with a .301 batting average. In the 1944 World Series loss to the St. Louis Cardinals, he hit only .231 in six games. St. Louis waived him to the Washington Senators (AL) in August 1945. Kreevich claimed the Browns' use of the one-armed outfielder Pete Gray caused him to quit. He retired after the 1945 season with a career .283 batting average, 1,321 hits, 45 HR, and 514 RBI. Boze Berger and Kreevich became the first AL players to hit consecutive HR to start a game, connecting on September 2, 1937 against Boston Red Sox pitcher Johnny Marcum.

Kreevich married Ann Gulick on January 2, 1933. They had two sons, Michael and Kenneth, and a daughter, Barbara. He later owned a bar and worked in the construction business.

BIBLIOGRAPHY: Mike Kreevich file, National Baseball Library, Cooperstown, NY; Warren Brown, *The Chicago White Sox* (New York, 1952); Rich Lindberg, *Who's on Third?* (South Bend, IN, 1983); Bill Borst, ed., *Ables to Zoldak*, vol. 2 (St. Louis, MO, 1989); Bill Borst, *Still Last in the American League* (West Bloomfield, MI, 1992); *The Baseball Encyclopedia*, 10th ed. (New York, 1996); Bill Carle, letter to Roger A. Godin, November 5, 1995; *TSN Complete Baseball Record Book* (St. Louis, MO, 1997); Roger A. Godin, telephone conversation with Barbara Kreevich Sarver, January 10, 1996; William B. Mead, *Even the Browns* (Chicago, IL, 1978); Chicago *Tribune*, April 27, 1995; Robert Obojski, *All Star Baseball* (Briarcliff, NY, 1980).

Roger A. Godin

KREMER, Remy Peter "Ray," "Wiz" (b. March 23, 1893, Oakland, CA; d. February 8, 1965, Pinole, CA), player, was of French descent. The right-handed pitcher signed with the San Francisco, CA Seals (PCL) in 1914 and was released at the end of the season. In 1915, he pitched for Salt Lake City, UT (PCL), Vancouver, WA (NWL), and briefly with the New York Giants (NL). He returned to Vancouver in 1916 and then pitched with great success for Oakland, CA (PCL) through 1923.

Kremer hurled for the Pittsburgh Pirates (NL) in 1924, winning 18 games and leading the NL with 41 appearances and four shutouts. The next six years saw the 6-foot 1-inch, 190-pound right-hander win at least 15 games annually. In 1925 he contributed 17 regular-season wins and two victories in three decisions, including his four-inning relief stint in the decisive seventh game against the Washington Senators in the World Series. Kremer's 20 wins, 2.61 ERA, and .769 winning percentage led the NL in 1926, while his 19 wins and NL-leading 2.47 ERA in 1927 helped the Pirates capture the NL pennant. However, Kremer lost one game in the 1927 World Series against the formidable New York Yankees. In 1930, his 20 wins and 276 innings pitched led the NL again, as did his 38 starts and 366 hits allowed. The two-fisted drinker and prankster pitched seven games with the Pirates in 1933 and finished his baseball career with Oakland, CA (PCL) in 1934. In his NL career, he won 143 games and lost 85 for a .627 winning percentage and 3.76 ERA.

Subsequently, he worked as a U.S. mail carrier until 1959. He and his wife, Beulah, had one daughter.

BIBLIOGRAPHY: Richard L. Burtt, *The Pittsburgh Pirates, A Pictorial History* (Virginia Beach, VA, 1977); Bob Smizik, *The Pittsburgh Pirates: An Illustrated History* (New York, 1990); *The Baseball Encyclopedia*, 10th ed. (New York, 1996); Remy Kremer file, National Baseball Library, Cooperstown, NY; Frederick G. Lieb, *The Pittsburgh Pirates* (New York, 1948); Richmond (CA) *Independent*, February 10, 1965; San Francisco, CA *Chronicle*, February 10, 1965.

Luther W. Spoehr

KRESS, Ralph "Red" (b. January 2, 1907, Columbia, CA; d. November 29, 1962, Los Angeles, CA), player, manager, and coach, spent his entire adult life in organized baseball. The youngest of nine children whose father died in a quarry accident, Kress overcame infantile paralysis as a youth to star in baseball and basketball at Berkeley, CA High School. The St. Louis Browns (AL) signed him in 1927 and optioned him to Tulsa, OK (WL), where he hit .329 at shortstop. After being called up by the Browns in September, Kress enjoyed three consecutive seasons of batting over .300 with 100 plus RBI from 1929 to 1931 and led AL shortstops with a .946 fielding percentage in 1929.

Kress's versatility may have hindered his playing career, but helped keep him in the game for decades. In 1930, St. Louis Browns manager Bill Killefer shifted him to third base from shortstop. After being traded to the Chicago White Sox (AL) in April 1932, Kress played outfield for manager Lew Fonseca.* In 1933, Kress filled in at first base in an emergency. Chicago traded Kress to the Washington Senators (AL) in May 1934, but a broken thumb sidelined him. After several sub-par seasons, he hit .298 in 1935 and .284 in 1936 while filling in at several positions and even pitching in three games. Following his release by the Senators, Kress in 1937 batted .334 with 27 HR for Minneapolis, MN (AA). He hit .302 in 150 games and led AL shortstops with a .965 fielding percentage for the St. Louis Browns in 1938. St. Louis traded Kress in May 1939 to the Detroit Tigers (AL), but he suffered a broken leg and in June 1940 was named a coach. He compiled a .286 batting average with 89 HR and 799 RBI in 1,391 major league games spanning 14 seasons.

Kress' managerial career began as a player–manager with St. Paul, MN (AA) in 1941. With Baltimore, MD (IL) on September 22, 1945, he pitched no-hit ball for 8.1 innings in a playoff game against the Montreal Royals. After four minor league seasons, Kress returned to the major leagues as a coach with the New York Giants (NL) in 1946 and even pitched in one game. He coached with the New York Giants from 1946 to 1949, Cleveland

Indians (AL) from 1953 to 1960, Los Angeles Angels (AL) in 1961, and New York Mets (NL) in 1962, managing in the minor leagues from 1950 to 1952.

Kress married Frances Lucille Baker on October 1, 1930 and had one daughter. Casey Stengel* considered him the hardest working coach in baseball. Kress, a master teacher of all aspects of the game, willingly provided extra instruction for players. A jovial optimist, he received a new automobile in July 1955 from Cleveland players in appreciation of his efforts.

BIBLIOGRAPHY: Ralph Kress file, National Baseball Library, Cooperstown, NY; Tommy Fitzgerald, "Red Kress—Everybody's Ball Player," *BD* 1 (November 1942), pp. 35–36; Harold (Speed) Johnson, *Who's Who in Major League Baseball* (Chicago, IL, 1933); *NYT*, November 30, 1962; Los Angeles *Times*, November 30, 1962; *TSN*, December 15, 1962; *The Baseball Encyclopedia*, 10th ed. (New York, 1996); John Thorn et al., eds., *Total Baseball*, 5th ed. (New York, 1997); Bill Borst, ed., *Ables to Zoldak*, vol. 2 (St. Louis, MO, 1989); Bill Borst, *Still Last in the American League* (West Bloomfield, MI, 1992); Shirley Povich, *The Washington Senators* (New York, 1954).

                                                              Edward J. Tassinari

KRUK, John Martin (b. February 9, 1961, Charleston, WV), player, was a 5-foot 10-inch, 220-pound, left-handed outfielder–first baseman. He is the son of Frank Kruk, a bottling company employee, and graduated in 1979 from Keyser, WV High School, where he played baseball and basketball. Kruk, who attended Allegheny, MD CC, married Jamie Miller on May 6, 1991 and has no children.

The Pittsburgh Pirates (NL) selected Kruk as a first baseman–outfielder in the 1981 free-agent draft, but did not sign him. He was chosen in the June 1981 amateur draft by the San Diego Padres (NL) and optioned to Walla Walla, WA (NWL). Kruk batted .311 with Reno, NV (CaL) in 1982 and .341 at Beaumont, TX (TL) in 1983. The following two seasons were spent with Las Vegas, NV (PCL), where he led all Class AAA players in 1985 with a .351 batting average.

Kruk played six games with Las Vegas in 1986 and played the remainder of the season with the San Diego Padres, batting .309. In 1987 he hit .313, fourth highest in the NL. After Kruk struggled the following season, San Diego in June 1989 traded infielder Randy Ready and him to the Philadelphia Phillies (NL) for outfielder Chris James. Kruk played for the Philadelphia Phillies from 1989 to 1994, spending rehabilitation assignments in 1994 at Reading, PA (EL) and Scranton/Wilkes Barre, PA (IL). In 1991 he set career-highs in games (152), total bases (260), HR (21), and RBI (92) while becoming the first Phillie since Greg Luzinski* in 1977 to lead the team in hitting (.294), HR, and RBI. Kruk batted .323 in 1992 and .316 in 1993, establishing career-bests in runs scored (100), hits (169), and doubles (33). His performances sparked the Philadelphia Phillies to the NL pennant. He batted .250 in the Phillies' triumph over the Atlanta Braves in the 1993 NL

Championship Series and recorded a .348 batting average in their loss to the Toronto Blue Jays in the 1993 World Series. Following cancer and knee surgery in 1994, Kruk was declared a free agent. He signed in May 1995 with the Chicago White Sox (AL), batting .308 in 45 games. Kruk retired from baseball following the 1995 season to his farm near Burlington, WV.

Kruk, who made the 1991–1993 NL All-Star teams, batted .300 or better for four straight seasons and seven times in his career. He owns the best on-base percentage in Philadelphia history (.400), with his .309 batting average ranking high on the Phillies' all-time list. In 10 major league seasons, Kruk scored 582 runs and made 1,170 hits in 1,200 games. He compiled a .300 batting average with 199 doubles, 34 triples, 100 HR, and 592 RBI, recording 649 walks, 701 strikeouts, and 58 stolen bases.

BIBLIOGRAPHY: John Kruk file, National Baseball Library, Cooperstown, NY; B. Anderson, "A Most Unlikely Slugger," *SI* 68 (May 23, 1988), p. 77; Rich Westcott and Frank Bilovsky, *The New Phillies Encyclopedia* (Philadelphia, PA, 1993); *Chicago White Sox Media Guide*, 1995; John Kruk and Paul Hagen, *"I Ain't an Athlete, Lady"* (New York, 1994); Franz Lidz, "What's a Kruk?" *SI* 76 (May 25, 1992), pp. 30–32, 37; *TSN Official Baseball Register*, 1996.

John L. Evers

KUENN, Harvey Edward, Jr. (b. December 4, 1930, Milwaukee, WI; d. February 28, 1988, Peoria, AZ), player and manager, was the son of shipping clerk Harvey Kuenn, Sr., and Dorothy (Wrensch) Kuenn. He graduated from Milwaukee Lutheran High School and attended Luther College. Kuenn transferred to the University of Wisconsin, where he played baseball and basketball. His father, an amateur baseball player–manager, exposed him to the sport at an early age. Kuenn married Dixie Sarchet in October 1955 and had two children, but that marriage ended in divorce. He married Audrey Cesar in 1974 and owned Cesar Inn in West Milwaukee. Kuenn's son, Harvey, gave up a promising baseball career to manage the family business.

Kuenn started his professional baseball career as a shortstop with Davenport, IA (3IL) in 1952 and joined the Detroit Tigers (AL) for 19 games late that season. As Detroit's regular shortstop in 1953, he led the AL in hits (209), demonstrated excellent fielding, and earned Rookie of the Year recognition from the BBWAA and *TSN*. After being shortstop his first three major league seasons, he played other infield positions and the outfield through 1966. In 1956, he was selected shortstop on *TSN* Major League All-Star team. He led the AL in 1959 with a .353 batting average, 198 hits, and 42 doubles and maintained a .303 career batting average. He led the AL in hits four times and doubles three times.

The day before the 1960 season opened, Kuenn was involved in a surprising trade. Detroit traded their 1959 batting champion to the Cleveland Indians (AL) for Rocky Colavito,* who won the 1959 HR crown. Kuenn was traded in December 1960 to the San Francisco Giants (NL) and in May

1965 to the Chicago Cubs (NL). The Cubs sold him in April 1966 to the Philadelphia Phillies (NL), where he finished his active career that season. In 1,833 career games, he made 2,092 hits, slugged 356 doubles, scored 951 runs, and knocked in 671 runs. In 1967 and 1968, he announced sports for WVTV in Milwaukee. After selling printing supplies for the next two years, he coached for the Milwaukee Brewers (AL) from 1971 to 1982 and managed them from June 2, 1982 through 1983. Kuenn regarded with pride winning the 1959 batting title, playing for San Francisco in the 1962 World Series, and managing his native Milwaukee to the AL championship in 1982. Kuenn, with Jim Smilgoff, authored *Big League Batting Secrets* (1958).

BIBLIOGRAPHY: Harvey Kuenn file, National Baseball Library, Cooperstown, NY; Charles Einstein, ed., *The Third Fireside Book of Baseball* (New York, 1968); Craig Carter, ed., *TSN Daguerreotypes*, 8th ed. (St. Louis, MO, 1990); Joe Falls, *Detroit Tigers* (New York, 1975); Fred Smith, *995 Tigers* (Detroit, MI, 1981); William M. Anderson, *The Detroit Tigers* (South Bend, IN, 1996); John Thorn, *Champion Batsman of the 20th Century* (Los Angeles, CA, 1992); Jack Torry, *Endless Summers* (South Bend, IN, 1995); David Plaut, *Chasing October* (South Bend, IN, 1994); *SI* 68 (March 7, 1988), p. 25; *The Baseball Encyclopedia*, 10th ed. (New York, 1996); *NYT*, February 29, 1988, p. D-15.

                                                                        Emil H. Rothe

KUHEL, Joseph Anthony "Joe" (b. June 25, 1906, Cleveland, OH; d. February 26, 1984, Kansas City, KS), player and manager, was the son of grocer Carl Kuhel and Agnes Kuhel. Kuhel, a first baseman, began his professional baseball career at Flint, MI (MOL) in 1924 and starred with Kansas City, MO (AA) from 1928 to 1930. He joined the Washington Senators (AL) at the end of the 1930 season. His unusual major league career was spent entirely with the Senators and Chicago White Sox (AL), between which he shifted on four occasions. The fast 6-foot, 180-pound Kuhel enjoyed his finest season in 1933, hitting .322 and leading first basemen with a .996 fielding percentage to help the Senators capture the AL pennant. On March 18, 1938, Kuhel was traded to the White Sox for Zeke Bonura,* a first baseman who represented Kuhel's antithesis. The left-handed Kuhel fielded adeptly and hit mainly singles, while the right-handed Bonura fielded poorly and demonstrated considerable power. The transaction produced years of debate in both cities.

After hitting .300 in 1939, Kuhel exhibited declining hitting skills. He returned to Washington at the waiver price on November 23, 1943 and enjoyed two excellent seasons, hitting .285 for the second place Senators team in 1945. After batting only .150 in the first 14 games of the 1946 season, Kuhel requested his release and signed again with the White Sox. In early 1947, he became manager of the White Sox' farm club in Hot Springs, AR (CSL). Although mainly known for his fielding, Kuhel compiled impressive batting statistics. He made 2,212 hits in 2,104 games, batted .277, hit 412 doubles, 111 triples, and 131 HR, knocked in 1,049 runs, and stole 178 bases. Kuhel managed the Washington Senators in 1948 and 1949, when Washington finished last and lost 104 games with particularly weak personnel. Upon being dropped as manager, Kuhel observed, "You can't make chicken salad out of chicken feathers." He managed the Kansas City, MO Blues (AA) in 1950 and thereafter engaged in sales work in the Kansas City area. He married Willette West on October 9, 1930 and had one child, Joseph, Jr.

BIBLIOGRAPHY: Joe Kuhel file, National Baseball Library, Cooperstown, NY; George W. Hilton, correspondence with Joseph A. Kuhel, Jr., George W. Hilton Collection, Columbia, MD; *The Baseball Encyclopedia*, 10th ed. (New York, 1996); Shirley Povich, *The Washington Senators* (New York, 1954); Morris Bealle, *The Washington Senators* (Washington, DC, 1947); Rich Lindberg, *Who's on Third?* (South Bend, IN, 1983); Warren Brown, *The Chicago White Sox* (New York, 1952); *TSN*, March 12, 1984; *WWIB, 1947*, 32nd ed.

George W. Hilton

KUHN, Bowie Kent (b. October 28, 1926, Takoma Park, MD), executive, is a descendant of frontiersman Jim Bowie and two Maryland governors. Kuhn, whose father worked in the retail oil business, grew up in Washington, DC and attended Theodore Roosevelt High School. Besides being president of his senior class, Kuhn substituted on the basketball team and played on the golf team. The basketball squad was coached by later renowned Boston Celtics mentor Arnold "Red" Auerbach (IS). During summer vacations, Kuhn worked the scoreboard at Washington Senators' (AL) baseball games in old Griffith Stadium.

Kuhn studied at Franklin and Marshall College and Princeton University, where he received a Bachelor of Arts degree in 1947. He earned his law degree from the University of Virginia in 1950 and joined the law firm of Willkie, Farr, and Gallagher of New York City. Kuhn began to receive baseball assignments at the firm and from the late 1950s through the 1960s served as legal counsel to several baseball teams. In 1968, he represented the NL club owners in negotiations with the MLPA, which was threatening to strike.

On December 6, 1968, Commissioner of Baseball William D. Eckert* was forced to resign. Michael Burke and Charles Feeney* were the leading candidates to replace Eckert, but the owners selected Kuhn as a compromise. On February 4, 1969, the owners elected Kuhn to a one-year team as Commissioner pro tempore. Kuhn, who faced baseball problems courageously and effectively, coaxed the owners back to the bargaining table and forced a settlement to the pension dispute. Kuhn also commanded certain owners with interests in Las Vegas gambling to sell those interests. On August 13, 1969, the owners signed him to a seven-year contract.

Kuhn's strong and inventive administration fit baseball's needs. He fought to improve and protect the game's integrity. In a few years, however, the situation began to change. The striking down of the old reserve clause by the MLPA, the shift of power from management to the players' union, and his battles with several owners turned the pendulum against Kuhn. Most observers considered Kuhn the best Commissioner possible under the restrictions imposed by the owners. The severest criticism leveled at Kuhn concerned his decision to keep Willie Mays* and Mickey Mantle* out of baseball after both took jobs with gambling casinos, his voiding in 1979 of Oakland Athletics (AL) executive Charlie Finley's* sale of three players for $3.5 million, and his failure to affect the 1981 player strike. Kuhn penalized several owners for violations, fining New York Yankees (AL) executive George Steinbrenner* $250,000. Kuhn also clashed in court with Steinbrenner, Finley, and Atlanta Braves' (NL) owner Ted Turner (OS). One-year suspensions of several players for drug involvement brought repercussions from the MLPA.

Kuhn survived a crisis the first time his contract came up for renewal in 1975 and received a second term. Although baseball enjoyed unparalleled attendance and lucrative TV contracts under Kuhn, the owners charged that he lacked the business expertise required to lead baseball and were opposed to his revenue-sharing plan. Kuhn's contract expired on August 12, 1983, but the owners could not find a replacement. He agreed to an interim appointment lasting until September 30, 1984. Peter Ueberroth (OS) was elected Commissioner of Baseball on March 3, 1984 and took office on October 1, 1984.

After 16 years as Commissioner, Kuhn returned to his New York City law firm. The 6-foot 5-inch, 240-pound Kuhn, an impressive person and an articulate speaker, lives with his wife, Luisa Hegeler, and four children in Ridgewood, NJ. Kuhn's recreations include golf, gardening, chess, reading, watching Princeton University football games, and attending baseball games.

BIBLIOGRAPHY: Bowie Kuhn file, National Baseball Library, Cooperstown, NY; *CB* (1970), pp. 236–237; M. Isikoff, "Bowie at the Bat," *NR* 196 (April 27, 1987); pp. 32–36; Bowie Kuhn, *Hardball* (New York, 1987); Jerome Holtzman, *The Commissioners* (New York, 1998); *TSN Official Baseball Guide, 1983, 1984, 1985*.

John L. Evers

KUROWSKI, George John "Whitey" (b. April 19, 1918, Reading, PA; d. December 8, 1999, Sinking Spring, PA), player and manager, was the son of Anthony F. Kurowski, a steel mill worker, and Victoria (Swiecicka) Kurowski and developed osteomyelitis at age eight, the result of an accident and blood infection. Two operations left the right-hander's throwing arm three inches shorter than the left arm. He played baseball two years at Wyomissing Poly High School. Caruthersville, MO (KOML) manager Harrison Wickel, a Reading, PA native, needed an infielder in 1937 and signed the 18-year-old

Kurowski for $70 per month. In 1938, the 5-foot 11-inch, 192-pound Kurowski led the MAL with a .386 batting average at Portsmouth, OH. Kurowski played in the St. Louis Cardinals (NL) farm system until he and Stan Musial* were promoted from Rochester, NY (IL) to the St. Louis Cardinals in September 1941. Amid his baseball success, Kurowski experienced personal tragedy. As he prepared for his first professional baseball assignment in 1937, his brother Frank was killed in a mining mishap. Kurowski's father collapsed from a fatal heart attack while the infielder tried to win a position on the St. Louis Cardinals during spring training in 1942.

From 1942 to 1947, Kurowski started at third base for the St. Louis Cardinals and remained a paradigm of consistency. He crowded home plate and used a 33-ounce, 34½-inch bat, hitting .323 in 1945, .301 in 1946, and .310 in 1947. Kurowski, who enjoyed a 22-game hitting streak in 1943, recorded career highs of 27 HR, 104 RBI, and 108 runs scored in 1947. Walker Cooper,* Kurowski, and Danny Litwhiler belted consecutive HR in a 1944 contest. Kurowski possessed decent speed despite a stocky build. Musial noted that it seemed that whenever a pitcher brushed back or knocked down Kurowski, he would hit the next pitch over the fence. Kurowski annihilated left-handed pitching.

Kurowski teamed with Musial, Red Schoendienst,* Marty Marion,* Enos Slaughter,* and Cooper to give the St. Louis Cardinals one of the most imposing batting orders of the 1940s. In 1942, the St. Louis Cardinals won a franchise-high 106 games and the NL pennant. Kurowski's greatest thrill came against the New York Yankees in the fifth game of the 1942 World Series, when his two-run HR off Red Ruffing* won the game and the World Championship. Kurowski's winner's share of $6,192 surpassed what he made the entire regular season. In the 1943 fall classic, Kurowski hit .222, as the New York Yankees dropped the St. Louis Cardinals in five games. He experienced his second World Championship in 1944, when the St. Louis Cardinals defeated the St. Louis Browns in six games. Kurowski played a central role in the St. Louis Cardinals' two-game sweep of the Brooklyn Dodgers in the first-ever major league playoff in 1946. He drove in the tying run and scored the winning run in the first game and plated two runs in the second game. Kurowski batted .296 with five RBI against the Boston Red Sox in the 1946 World Series, which the St. Louis Cardinals won, 4–3.

An increasingly painful right arm limited Kurowski to 77 games and a .214 batting average in 1948. Thirteen operations on his arm and elbow had taken a heavy toll, forcing Kurowski to retire after playing 10 games in 1949. Kurowski enjoyed his nine years with St. Louis because the Cardinals finished first four times and second five times. He made 925 hits in 916 games, scored 518 runs, hit 106 HR, tallied 529 RBI, and batted .286. He led NL third basemen three times in assists and twice in fielding percentage and putouts.

For the rest of the 1949 season, Kurowski managed the St. Louis Cardinals' farm club in Lynchburg, VA (PiL). He discovered talent and enjoyed managing, piloting St. Louis farm teams through the 1962 season in Allentown, PA (ISL), Peoria, IL (3IL), Billings, MT (PrL), Denver, CO (WL), Winnipeg, Canada (NoL), and Tulsa, OK (TL). Kurowski managed the New York Mets' (NL) top farm club at Buffalo, NY (IL) in 1964 and took the reins at Reading, PA (EL), a Cleveland Indian (AL) affiliate, in 1965. He later worked as an inspector of weights and measures for Berk County, PA. He married Joan Setley in November 1941 and lived near Reading in Shillington, PA, where he enjoyed visits with his four children, George, Jr., Joanne, James, and Georgeann, and played golf twice a week.

BIBLIOGRAPHY: Whitey Kurowski file, National Baseball Library, Cooperstown, NY; David Craft et al., *Redbirds Revisited* (Chicago, IL, 1990); Stan Musial: as told to Bob Broeg, *Stan Musial: "The Man's" Own Story* (Garden City, NY, 1964); Rob Rains, *The St. Louis Cardinals* (New York, 1992); Frederick G. Lieb, *The St. Louis Cardinals* (New York, 1945); Bob Broeg and Jerry Vickery, *St. Louis Cardinals Encyclopedia* (Grand Rapids, MI, 1998); Mike Shatzkin, ed., *The Ballplayers* (New York, 1990); Rich Westcott, *Diamond Greats* (Westport, CT, 1988).

Frank J. Olmsted

KURYS, Sophie "The Flint Flash" (b. May 14, 1925, Flint, MI), player, is the daughter of Anthony Kurys and Antonina Kurys. Her father was of Ukrainian ancestry, while her mother's family came from Poland. Kurys attended Flint Northern High School, playing in Flint softball leagues while in high school. She scored 4,563 points out of a possible 5,000 points in a pentathlon, which included the broad jump, high jump, 100-yard dash, baseball throw, and basketball free-throwing contest, and ran track events. In 1939 she played for the Michigan State Championship softball team. In 1942, a scout from Chicago, IL asked the 17-year old to try out for the new AAGPBL. Her father disliked the idea, but her mother granted her permission to join the league. The 5 foot 5 inch, 115 pound second baseman played for the Racine, WI Belles from 1943 through 1950. In 1943, she batted .271 and stole 44 bases in 106 games as a rookie earning $85 a week. In 1944, she led the AAGPBL with 166 stolen bases and 87 runs scored and pilfered seven bases on September 3.

For the next seven seasons, Kurys averaged more than a theft a game and stole 80 percent of the time she reached base. Altogether, she led the AAGPBL seven times in stolen bases and six times in runs scored. The speedster pilfered 1,114 bases in 914 games, causing sportswriters to dub her "The Flint Flash." The Racine Belles won the AAGPBL championship in 1943 and 1946, her finest season. She became the only major league competitor to steal over 200 bases in a single season in 1946, pilfering 201 bases in 203 attempts in 112 games. Kurys set the AAGPBL single season records in walks (93) and runs (117) and finished as the second leading hitter with a .286 batting average, earning the MVP Award in 1946.

Kurys, nicknamed "the Ty Cobb of the AAGPBL," made the AAGPBL All-Star team seven consecutive years from 1944 through 1950. In 1950, the pitching distance was extended to 55 feet and base paths lengthened to 85 feet. Kurys hit a career-high .307, led the AAGPBL with seven HR and 130 hits, and swiped 120 bases in 110 games in 1950. She played for the Battle Creek, MI Belles in 1952. Kurys stole 1,114 career bases and scored 688 runs, both career AAGPBL records. She ranks third in career hits (859) and walks (522). The All-Star second baseman played semiprofessional softball in Chicago for the Admiral Music Maids in 1953 and 1954 and and for the highly competitive Phoenix, AZ A-1 Queens in 1955, helping them capture the PCL championship.

Kurys moved back in 1956 to Racine, WI, where she served until 1972 as vice-president and secretary-treasurer for Apex Machine Products, Inc. She moved several years later to Scottsdale, AZ and still resides there. In 1988, Kurys and other noted AAGPBL luminaries were selected for the women's professional league section of the National Baseball Hall of Fame at Cooperstown, NY. Kurys demonstrated her outstanding base-stealing achievements and all-around play in the AAGPBL.

BIBLIOGRAPHY: Gai Ingham Berlage, *Women in Baseball* (Westport, CT, 1994); Debbi Dagavarian-Bonar, "The Runner Wore Skirts," *BRJ* 20 (1991), pp. 35–37; Barbara Gregorich, *Women at Play* (San Diego, CA, 1993); Sharon Roepke, *Diamond Gals* (Flint, MI, 1988); Susan Johnson, *When Women Played Hardball* (Seattle, WA, 1994); W. C. Madden, *The Women of the All-American Girls Professional Baseball League* (Jefferson, NC, 1997); James E. Odenkirk, personal interview with Sophie Kurys, Scottsdale, AZ, April 15, 1996.

James E. Odenkirk

L

LAJOIE, Napoleon "Nap," "Larry" (b. September 5, 1874, Woonsocket, RI; d. February 7, 1959, Daytona Beach, FL), player, manager, and executive, was the son of day laborer John Lajoie and Celina (Guertin) Lajoie, both of French-Canadian descent. He married Myrtle Everturk in 1906 and in 1937 became the sixth player selected to the National Baseball Hall of Fame. The happy, laughing, confident, decisive Lajoie excelled as baseball's most graceful infielder and led AL second basemen in fielding six times. Best remembered for his hitting prowess, Lajoie enjoyed his most productive year in 1901 by pacing the infant AL in hits, doubles, HR, runs scored, RBI, and slugging percentage and established the AL record batting average of .426. During his major league career, he batted .338, made 3,242 hits (tenth all-time), slugged 657 doubles (sixth all-time), scored 1,504 runs, knocked in 1,599 runs, and won four major league batting titles. His last batting title came with the Toronto, Canada Maple Leafs (IL) in 1917, when he compiled a .380 mark in 151 games at age 42.

After leaving Globe Public School following the eighth grade, Lajoie worked in south-central New England mills, became a taxi driver, and played semipro baseball in Rhode Island as a catcher and first baseman. In 1896, he began his professional career with Fall River, MA (NEL). After Lajoie batted .429 the first three months, the Philadelphia Phillies (NL) acquired him as a "throw in" in another deal. Lajoie, nicknamed "Larry" by pitcher Bill Taylor, helped solidify the Phillies' infield for over four seasons. Despite his talent and considerable charm, the rather reserved Lajoie seldom received any notoriety there.

In early 1901, Connie Mack* and Clark Griffith* attempted to sign the NL's best players to AL contracts. After losing Lajoie and two teammates, the Phillies owners filed an injunction to prohibit them from playing in Philadelphia. Lajoie's claim that the Phillies violated his constitutional rights and could not prevent him from signing or playing with another team comprised the first official court challenge to major league baseball's reserve clause. The court initially ruled for Lajoie in May 1901, but the Phillies appealed and the State Supreme Court reversed that decision in April 1902. After one season with the fledgling Philadelphia Athletics (AL), Lajoie, Elmer Flick,* and Bill Bernhard were "transferred" by edict of AL president Byron Johnson* to the Cleveland Broncos (AL). Within the first few months, that team was renamed the Naps in honor of Lajoie. Cleveland did not begin using the name Indians until 1915, when Lajoie was traded back to the Athletics.

The 6-foot 1-inch, 195-pound, right-handed Lajoie often used a special bat with two handles, one higher up for a solid grip on bunts and short-stroked, slashing line drives. This uncommon device worked well against the St. Louis Browns on October 9, 1910, when Lajoie bunted for seven infield hits and swung for a triple in eight at-bats. His batting average came within a few ten-thousandths of AL leader Ty Cobb* on that last day of the season. Byron Johnson awarded the batting title to Cobb, but the official Chalmers Award, an automobile, was presented to both players. Johnson, however, banned Browns manager Jack O'Connor for life from the AL for allegedly ordering a loose defense on Lajoie. In 1981 *TSN* discovered discrepancies in official records, indicating Lajoie as the true batting titlist. Commissioner Bowie Kuhn,* though, ruled that Johnson's decision should stand. Lajoie managed the Cleveland team to a 377–309 record (.550 winning percentage) from 1905 to 1909, but resigned to concentrate on playing. He later managed Toronto, Canada (IL) in 1917 and Indianapolis, IN (AA) in 1918 and served briefly as commissioner of the OPL. After working as a tire salesman, he retired to Florida in 1922.

BIBLIOGRAPHY: Nap Lajoie file, National Baseball Library, Cooperstown, NY; Alan R. Asnen, interview with Jeff Kernan, August 21, 1984, National Baseball Library, Cooperstown, NY; John Benson et al., *Baseball's Top 100* (Wilton, CT, 1997); Bob Broeg, *Super Stars of Baseball* (St. Louis, MO, 1971); Anthony J. Connor, *Baseball for the Love of It* (New York, 1982); Gene Karst and Martin J. Jones, Jr., *Who's Who in Professional Baseball* (New Rochelle, NY, 1973); Craig Carter, ed., *TSN Daguerreotypes*, 8th ed. (St. Louis, MO, 1990); John P. McCarthy, *Baseball's All-Time Dream Team* (Cincinnati, OH, 1994); J. M. Murphy, "Napoleon Lajoie: Modern Baseball's First Superstar," *TNP* 7 (Spring 1988), pp. 1–79; John Thorn et al., eds., *Total Indians* (New York, 1996); John Phillips, *Who Was Who in Cleveland Baseball, 1901–10* (Cabin John, MD, 1989); Franklin Lewis, *The Cleveland Indians* (New York, 1949); Martin Appel and Burt Goldblatt, *Baseball's Best: The Hall of Fame Gallery* (New York, 1977); Lowell Reidenbaugh, *Baseball's Hall of Fame—Cooperstown* (New York, 1993); Rich Westcott and Frank Bilovsky, *The New Phillies Encyclopedia* (Philadelphia, PA, 1993); Thomas Aylesworth and Benton Minks, *The Encyclopedia of Baseball Managers* (New York, 1990); Eugene C. Murdock, *Ban Johnson* (Westport, CT, 1982); *NYT*, February 8, 1959; *The Baseball Encyclopedia*, 10th ed. (New York, 1996); Lawrence S. Ritter,

The Glory of Their Times (New York, 1966); *TSN*, April 18, 1981; *TSN Baseball Record Book, 1998.*

Alan R. Asnen

LANDIS, Kenesaw Mountain (b. November 20, 1866, Millville, OH; d. November 25, 1944, Chicago, IL), executive, was the son of Army surgeon Abraham Landis and Mary (Kumler) Landis and was the first sole Commissioner of Baseball (1920–1944). Named Commissioner in 1920 amid the collapse of the old National Commission and the Chicago "Black Sox" scandal, he ruled baseball with an iron hand. Some argued that he restored the game to respectability. He was named for the June 1864 Civil War battle of Kenesaw Mountain, GA, where his father was wounded. Landis attended Logansport, IN High School, but never graduated. After enrolling at the YMCA Law School in Cincinnati, he received his law degree from the Union Law School of Chicago in 1891 and was admitted to the Illinois bar the same year. Landis practiced law in Chicago for the next 14 years except for a stint from 1893 to 1895 in Washington as private secretary to Secretary of State Walter Q. Gresham. He married Winifred Reed in 1895 and had one son and one daughter.

In 1905, President Theodore Roosevelt named Landis federal judge in the Northern District of Illinois. He attracted national attention in 1907 by fining the Standard Oil Company $29,240,000 for illegal rebating practices, but a higher court overturned the ruling. His hatred for radicals, socialists, and World War I pacifists was reflected in numerous harsh jail sentences. Landis won the sympathy of the baseball establishment in 1915, when the FL antitrust suit against organized baseball was argued in his court. By refusing to render a decision until the FL war was over and the suit was dropped, he preserved organized baseball's unique monopoly status. When the National Commission collapsed in 1920, baseball leaders turned to Landis to restore integrity to the game. He accepted the post of Commissioner on November 12, 1920, but retained his seat on the federal bench until February 1922. A move to impeach him for not immediately resigning his judgeship failed in the U.S. House of Representatives.

Upon assuming office, Landis demanded and received absolute power. No appeals of his rulings or public criticisms of his actions by owners were permitted. One writer commented, "No man in private life ever enjoyed such power as did Landis," while a federal judge called Landis "legally an absolute despot." Whenever owners challenged the judge's rule, he threatened to quit and the owners backed down. Although zealous in defense of players' rights, Landis in March 1921 barred Philadelphia Phillies pitcher Eugene Paulette for life for consorting with gamblers. In June 1921, he similarly blacklisted Cincinnati Reds pitcher Ray Fisher for negotiating with an "outlaw" team. He also disqualified New York Giants outfielder Benny

Kauff,* who had been indicted for and acquitted of auto theft. On August 3, 1921, the day after a jury acquitted the eight Chicago "Black Sox" of throwing the 1919 World Series, Landis banished the players permanently from organized baseball. In 1922 he blacklisted Giants pitcher "Shufflin' Phil" Douglas, who in a drunken state had hinted willingness to throw a game. In 1924, he permanently barred Jimmy O'Connell and "Cozy" Dolan for complicity in a bribe plot between the New York Giants and the Philadelphia Phillies. Phillies owner William D. Cox was expelled from the game in 1943 for betting on his own team.

In the last game of the 1934 World Series, Landis ordered from the field hard-hitting St. Louis leftfielder Joe Medwick,* who had been bombarded with fruit and garbage by Detroit Tiger fans. The Cardinals won the game and the series, defusing the controversy over removal of the St. Louis star. Landis could not break up baseball's farm system, which he strongly opposed. He proclaimed as free agents close to 200 players whom he believed parent clubs were "covering up." He also waged unceasing war against baseball personnel with race track connections. Due to dissatisfaction with Landis' autocratic rule, club owners have never granted subsequent commissioners comparable power. Although tough, profane, and opinionated, Landis displayed a warm personal side off the bench. The judge made the dedicatory address officially opening the National Baseball Hall of Fame at Cooperstown, NY on June 12, 1939 and was elected to the Hall of Fame within a month of his death.

BIBLIOGRAPHY: Kenesaw Mountain Landis file, National Baseball Library, Cooperstown, NY; Ron Fimrite, "His Own Biggest Fan," *SI* 79 (July 19, 1993), pp. 76–80; Brad Herzog, *The Sports 100* (New York, 1995); Jerome Holtzman, *The Commissioners* (New York, 1998); Gene Karst and Martin J. Jones, Jr., *Who's Who in Professional Baseball* (New Rochelle, NY, 1973); F. C. Lane, "Has Judge Landis Made Good?" *BM* 34 (February 1925), pp. 393–395, 428–430; Eugene C. Murdock, *Ban Johnson* (Westport, CT, 1982); David Pietrusza, *Judge and Jury* (South Bend, IN, 1998); Harold Seymour, *Baseball: The Golden Age* (New York, 1971); J. G. Taylor Spink, *Judge Landis and 25 Years of Baseball* (New York, 1947); *TSN*, December 6, 1923, November 30, 1944, July 2, 1947.

                                                                    Eugene Murdock

LANE, Ferdinand Cole "F.C." (b. October 25, 1885, near Moorehead, MN; d. April 20, 1984, Hyannis, MA), writer, was the fourth child of Alpheus Ferdinand Lane and the third (and youngest) child of Alpheus's second wife, Mary (Cole) Lane. Born on a wheat farm, Lane moved with his family to Minneapolis, MN, Akron, OH, Canton, OH, and Lowell, MA before settling at age seven in Truro, MA. Six years later, the Lanes moved to Marion, MA. Lane completed his secondary education at Tabor Academy and attended Boston University for seven years, receiving a B.A. degree in 1907.

Lane worked during graduate school as an assistant biologist for Boston University and the Massachusetts Commission of Fisheries and Game.

After spending half a year in a log cabin in Alberta to strengthen his weak lungs, Lane found employment writing for *BM* in Boston, MA and in New York. He soon was named *BM* editor. Under his leadership, *BM* became the game's premier monthly and devoted extensive and detailed analysis to baseball's personnel, events, and styles of play. Besides writing several hundred articles for *BM*, Lane performed ghostwriting and syndicate work. His 1925 instructional book, *Batting*, featured advice from the great hitters of the era.

After 27 years with *BM*, Lane tired of sportswriting and returned to Cape Cod in the later 1930s. Despite frequent absence, he regarded Cape Cod as home for the remainder of his life. From 1941 to 1943, he headed the Department of History at Piedmont College in Demorest, GA and established a journalism program there. Piedmont awarded him an honorary Doctor of Humanities degree in 1941.

A wanderlust first drew Lane to the Mediterranean during his college years. He and his wife, Emma, whom he had married in her Brooklyn, NY home in June 1914, made numerous overseas voyages and traveled around the world six times. In the 1940s and 1950s, Lane wrote several books on geography and nature for adults and youth. In 1958, he published *On Old Cape Cod*, a collection of his poems. The Lanes lived the final years of their nearly 70-year marriage in a Cape Cod nursing home, where Emma survived Ferdinand by 10 months.

BIBLIOGRAPHY: *BM*, 1910–1937; Jack Kavanagh, "F.C. Lane," *TNP* 16 (1996), pp. 58–59; Stanley J. Kunitz, ed., *Twentieth Century Authors*, 1st supp. (New York, 1955); F. C. Lane, *Batting* (New York, 1925); Ferdinand C. Lane file, National Baseball Library, Cooperstown, NY; Piedmont College Archives, Demorest, GA.

Frederick Ivor-Campbell

LANE, Frank Charles "Trader," "Frantic Frank" (b. February 1, 1896, Cincinnati, OH; d. March 19, 1981, Richardson, TX), executive and college official, was the son of Frank J. Lane, a druggist. He attended public high schools in Cincinnati, OH and studied law for two years at the University of Cincinnati. His first jobs involved officiating college sports, mostly BTC and SC football and basketball games. He married Selma Dent in 1931 and had one daughter, Nadi. During World War II, Lane served four years in the U.S. Navy as director of the Navy's physical fitness program.

Lane's baseball career began in Cincinnati in 1933, when Larry MacPhail* hired him as assistant general manager of the Cincinnati Reds (NL). He served as general manager of Cincinnati's farm team in Durham, NC (CrL), in 1937 and subsequently as farm director for the Reds organization. After his military service in World War II, Lane rejoined MacPhail, who was now with the New York Yankees (AL). He served for one year as general manager of the New York Yankees farm club at Kansas City, MO (AA) and two years (1947, 1948) as AA president. He joined the Chicago White Sox (AL) as general manager in 1948 and served there through 1955. Similar positions were held with the St. Louis Cardinals (NL) in 1956 and 1957, the Cleveland Indians (AL) from 1958 through 1960, and Kansas City Athletics (AL) in 1961. He served only eight months of an eight-year contract at Kansas City, a consequence of encountering a temperament as volatile as his own in Athletics owner Charles Finley.* Subsequently, he served the Baltimore Orioles (AL), Texas Rangers (AL), California Angels (AL), and San Diego Padres (NL) as consultant and scout. At age 75, he directed baseball operations for the Milwaukee Brewers (AL).

Although his teams captured no pennants, Lane achieved acclaim as "an immediate rebuilder." Nicknamed "Trader" Lane, he gained fame for his player deals and completed over 500 trades during his career. His best known team, the "Go-Go" Chicago White Sox of the early 1950s, featured Orestes Minoso,* Billy Pierce,* and Nelson Fox,* all acquired in shrewd deals. His later deals proved more notorious. He always insisted that he never contemplated trading Stan Musial* when he was with the St. Louis Cardinals. In April 1960, he traded 1959 HR champion Rocky Colavito* to the Detroit Tigers for 1959 batting champion Harvey Kuenn.* The deal backfired for the Cleveland Indians. In August 1960, he traded manager Joe Gordon* to Detroit for Jimmy Dykes.* Lane also was nicknamed "Frantic Frank" because of his "prodigious fund of energy." A nonstop talker, he intimidated even Casey Stengel.* The era of faceless New York Yankee (AL) domination saw Lane offer a heroic alternative.

BIBLIOGRAPHY: Rich Lindberg, *Who's on Third?* (South Bend, IN, 1983); Bob Vanderberg, *Sox: From Lane and Fain to Zisk and Fisk* (Chicago, IL, 1982); Jack Torry, *Endless Summers* (South Bend, IN, 1995); Terry Pluto, *The Curse of Rocky Colavito* (New York, 1994); Tim Cohane, "Frank Lane: Baseball's Noisiest Dynamo," *Look* 20 (June 12, 1956), pp. 123–126, 128, 130–131, 133; James Crusanberry, "Frank Lane—A Front Office Force," *BM* 86 (January 1951), pp. 259–260, 282; Mark Kram, "Would You Trade with This Man?" *SI* 29 (August 26, 1968), pp. 30, 32–35; Frank Lane file, National Baseball Library, Cooperstown, NY; Harry T. Paxton, "Baseball's Human Hurricane," *SEP* 225 (May 30, 1953), pp. 28–29, 106, 108; Roy Terrell, "Glad To Have You Aboard, But . . . ," *SI* 10 (March 30, 1959), pp. 50, 52.

Leverett T. Smith, Jr.

LANGE, William Alexander "Bill," "Little Eva" (b. June 6, 1871, San Francisco, CA; d. July 23, 1950, San Francisco, CA), player, coach, and scout, grew up in the Presidio section of San Francisco as the son of German-American parents. He quit the San Francisco public schools after the eighth grade and soon started his professional baseball career with Port Townsend, WA (1889–1890) and Seattle, WA (1891–1892). Lange performed from 1893 to 1899 for the Chicago Colts (NL), where he played center field and served as team captain. After his rookie season, he batted over .300 for six consecutive seasons and compiled a .330 career batting average. His .389 batting average in 1895 remains the season's standard for the franchise. During his seven-year major league career, he made 1,055 hits, 133 doubles, 80 triples, and 39 HR, scored 689 runs, and knocked in 578 runs. Although considered of gigantic size then, the 6-foot 1-inch, 180-pound Lange possessed great speed and still holds the team records for season (84 in 1896) and career (399) stolen bases. He led the NL with 73 stolen bases in 1892. His speed, strong arm, and almost reckless abandon made him one of the finest defensive outfielders before 1900.

Lange, with an ever present smile, ranked among the most colorful, popular players of the 1890s. When Lange retired, the Chicago *Tribune* described him as "the most popular man who ever wore a Chicago uniform." His reputation as one of Chicago's "Dawn Patrol Boys," who liked late hours, practical jokes, and women, delighted fans, but frustrated the team's puritanical manager, Adrian Anson.* Lange's unusual nickname, "Little Eva," probably derived from his peculiar strut.

Lange quit baseball at the peak of his career. In 1899 the 28-year-old Lange left the game to marry Californian Grace Geiselman, whose father forbade her to wed a pro baseball player. Despite numerous attractive offers, Lange refused to return as a player. He coached baseball at Stanford University, scouted for the Cincinnati Reds (NL), and owned a real estate and insurance business in San Francisco until his death. After his first marriage ironically ended in divorce, he married Sarah Griffith in 1925 and had one son, William, Jr. Contemporary sportswriters rated him the equal of National Baseball Hall of Fame outfielders. A. H. Spink, founder and editor of *TSN*, described Lange as "Ty Cobb* enlarged, fully as great in speed, batting skill and base running," while T. H. Murnane* of the Boston *Globe* listed the game's best outfielders up to 1914 as Cobb, Joe Jackson,* and Lange.

BIBLIOGRAPHY: Arthur R. Ahrens, "Lange's Classic Catch Reclassified," *BRJ* 9 (1980), pp. 87–90; Arthur R. Ahrens and Eddie Gold, *Day by Day in Chicago Cubs History* (West Point, NY, 1982); William E. Akin, "Bare Hands and Kid Gloves: The Best Fielders, 1880–1899," *BRJ* 10 (1981), pp. 60–65; Adrian C. Anson, *A Ball Player's Career* (Chicago, IL, 1900); James D. Smith III, "Bowing Out on Top," *TNP* 2 (Fall 1982), pp. 73–81; Alfred H. Spink, *The National Game* (St. Louis, MO, 1911); Robert L. Tiemann and Mark Rucker, eds., *Nineteenth Century Stars* (Kansas City, MO, 1989); Warren Brown, *The Chicago Cubs* (New York, 1946); Jim Enright, *Chicago Cubs* (New York, 1975); Eddie Gold and Art Ahrens, *The Golden Era Cubs, 1876–1940* (Chicago, IL, 1985).

William E. Akin

LANGSTON, Mark Edward (b. August 20, 1960, San Diego CA), player, graduated from Buchser High School in San Diego and attended San Jose State University. He married Michelle Garrett, an aspiring actress, and has two daughters, Katie and Gabriella. The Seattle Mariners (AL) selected the 6-foot 2-inch, 184-pound left-handed pitcher in the third round of the June 1981 draft and assigned him to Bellingham, WA (NWL).

Langston jumped from Class AA Chattanooga, TN (SL) to the Seattle Mariners in 1984 and became the first rookie since Herb Score* to lead the AL in strikeouts with 204. He finished 1984 with a 17–10 record and trailed only Alvin Davis* in the AL Rookie of the Year voting. His pitching repertoire includes a blazing fast ball, change up, hard slider, and curve ball.

Langston rebounded from an injury-plagued 1985 season to pace the AL with 245 strikeouts in 1986. He emerged as one of major league baseball's best hurlers in 1987, leading the AL with 262 strikeouts, notching 19 victories, making the AL All-Star team, and winning his first Gold Glove award. In 1988, Langston hurled a one-hitter against the Texas Rangers on September 24 and earned another Gold Glove. The Seattle Mariners traded Langston to the Montreal Expos (NL) in May 1989 for Gene Harris, Brian Holman, and Randy Johnson.*

The California Angels (AL) signed the highly coveted Langston as a free agent in December 1989. In his Angel debut on April 11, 1990, he combined with Mike Witt for a 1–0 no-hitter against Seattle. Langston, who led AL pitchers with 42 assists in 1990, finished 19–8 in 1991, won more Gold Gloves in 1991 and 1992, and made the AL All-Star teams in 1992 and 1993. In 1993, he fanned his 2,000th batter and shared the Angels MVP award with Tim Salmon. Langston lost a one game playoff against the Seattle Mariners to determine the 1995 AL Western Division crown after hurling seven superb innings. His 1995 season ended with a 15–7 record and 142 strikeouts. In February 1998, Langston joined the San Diego Padres (NL) as a free agent. He won only four of 10 decisions, as the Padres won the NL West and the NL Division Series against the Houston Astros. Langston appeared briefly in three NL Championship Series games against the Atlanta Braves and struggled in one World Series relief stint against the New York Yankees. Through the 1999 campaign, he has compiled 179 wins and 158 losses with a 3.97 ERA and 2,464 strikeouts in 2,962.2 innings. In 1999 he finished 1–2 for the Cleveland Indians (AL).

BIBLIOGRAPHY: "Mark Langston," *Microsoft Complete Baseball*, CD-ROM (Redmond, WA, 1994); Mark Langston file, National Baseball Library, Cooperstown, NY; Ron Fimrite, "A Wanted Man," *SI* 70 (April 24, 1989), pp. 34–36; *TSN Baseball Register*, 1998; *The Baseball Encyclopedia*, 10th ed. (New York, 1996).

Chad Israelson

LANIER, Hubert Max (b. August 18, 1915, Denton, NC), player, coach, scout, and manager, is the son of Stephen Ashley Lanier, a farmer and carpenter, and Remetta (Morris) Lanier, of Irish, English, and French descent, and graduated from Denton High School. He threw right-handed as a child, but a broken arm forced him to switch to left-handed. Although winning an athletic scholarship to Duke University, he signed a professional baseball contract with the St. Louis Cardinals (NL) in 1934 and joined Greensboro, NC (PiL). He left after a week to play semiprofessional baseball in North Carolina. Lanier accepted assignment to the St. Louis Cardinals' top farm club in Columbus, OH (IL) in 1937, winning 10 of 14 decisions. He compiled two victories and four defeats in trials with the St. Louis Cardinals in 1938 and 1939. From 1940 to 1942, St. Louis Cardinal skipper Billy Southworth* used Lanier as a spot starter and reliever with excellent results. Lanier posted a 20–14 record while starting and a 12–6 record from the bullpen. In 1943, he won 15 decisions and lost seven with a 1.90 ERA. In 1944, he followed with career-high 17 wins and 141 strikeouts. Lanier pitched for the St. Louis Cardinals in three straight World Series from 1942 to 1944, winning two of three decisions and recording a 1.71 ERA in 31.2 innings.

The 5-foot 11-inch, 180-pound southpaw entered the U.S. Army in 1945 at Ft. Bragg, NC and played on the army baseball team to entertain troops. By spring training 1946, Lanier returned to a St. Louis Cardinal uniform. After winning his first six starts, Lanier accepted a $125,000 contract from Jorge Pasquel and Bernardo Pasquel to play five years in their MEL. He had made only $11,000 the year before. Lanier, therefore, joined St. Louis Cardinal second baseman Lou Klein and reliever Fred Martin in jumping to Veracruz, Mexico (MEL). After the 1947 season, the Pasquels broke their contract with Lanier. The major leagues banned Lanier for five years, causing him to play semiprofessional ball in Canada in 1948. Lanier and Martin then brought a $2.5 million lawsuit against major league baseball. The case settled out of court, with Lanier, Martin, and Klein being reinstated by Commissioner Happy Chandler.* Lanier and Martin rejoined the St. Louis Cardinals in 1949. Lanier struggled to get back in shape, winning five and losing four in 15 starts and taking 11 of 20 decisions each of the next two seasons. The St. Louis Cardinals traded Lanier to the New York Giants (NL) in December 1951 for Eddie Stanky,* who was named St. Louis Cardinal manager. Released by the New York Giants following the 1952 season, Lanier pitched in 10 games and lost his only decision for the St. Louis Browns (AL) in 1953. His major league record included 327 games, 1,619.1 innings, 108 wins, 82 losses, a .568 winning percentage, 17 saves, and 821 strikeouts.

Lanier married Lillie Belle Daby in July 1934. She died in an automobile accident. Their son, Hal, played infield in the major leagues for 10 years, coached for the St. Louis Cardinals and Philadelphia Phillies (NL), and managed the Houston Astros (NL). Lanier and his second wife, Evelyn Jane, were married on August 29, 1948. Lanier worked as a representative of A. G. Edwards Investments and owned a restaurant in St. Petersburg, FL, for several years. He scouted for the San Francisco Giants (NL) in 1961 and 1962 and managed the Lexington, NC Giants (WCL) from 1963 to 1966 and the

Batavia, NY Trojans (NYPL) in 1967. Lanier, who suffered a heart attack in 1968, is retired and lives in Dunnellon, FL.

BIBLIOGRAPHY: Bob Broeg, *Redbirds: A Century of Cardinals' Baseball* (St. Louis, MO, 1981); Bob Broeg and Jerry Vickery, *St. Louis Cardinals Encyclopedia* (Grand Rapids, MI, 1998); Frederick G. Lieb, *The St. Louis Cardinals* (New York, 1945); David Craft et al., *Redbirds Revisited* (Chicago, IL, 1990); Donald Honig, *Baseball When the Grass Was Real* (New York, 1975); Max Lanier file, National Baseball Library, Cooperstown, NY; Stan Musial as told to Bob Broeg, *Stan Musial: "The Man's" Own Story* (Garden City, NY, 1964); Rob Rains, *The St. Louis Cardinals* (New York, 1992); Chuck Wills and Pat Wills, *Beyond Home Plate* (Ocala, FL, 1993).

Frank J. Olmsted

LANSFORD, Carney Ray (b. February 7, 1957, San Jose, CA), player, coach, and manager, is the son of Tony Ray Lansford and Bobbye (Wells) Lansford. Two brothers followed him into professional baseball. Phil was selected number one by the Cleveland Indians (AL) in 1978, while Joe was chosen first by the San Diego Padres (NL) the following year.

The California Angels (AL) drafted the 6-foot 2-inch, 195-pound third baseman out of Wilcox High School in San Jose, CA in the third round of the 1975 free agent draft. The California Angels assigned Lansford to Idaho Falls, ID (PrL) in 1975 and Quad Cities (ML) in 1976. For El Paso, TX (TL) in 1977, he batted .332 and led TL third basemen in every major defensive category.

Lansford, who batted and threw right-handed, began the 1978 season with the California Angels (AL) and was named Angels Rookie of the Year, finishing third in the AL balloting. After pacing the AL in putouts (135) and fielding average (.983) in 1979, he repeated in 1980 as putout leader (151) and led the AL in sacrifice flies (11). The California Angels traded Lansford to the Boston Red Sox (AL) in December 1980. He led the AL in hitting with a .336 batting average in 1981, the first right-hander to win the title in a decade. To make room for hitting star Wade Boggs,* the Boston Red Sox traded Lansford in December 1982 to the Oakland Athletics (AL).

Known for his bat control and clutch hitting, Lansford ranked among the leaders in most of the Oakland Athletics' offensive categories. He hit .300 or higher three times with Oakland, finishing second in the AL with a .336 batting average in 1989 and making his only All-Star Game appearance in 1988. Lansford played in five AL Championship Series, appearing with California in 1979 and with the Oakland Athletics from 1988 to 1990 and in 1992. In 1989, he paced all Oakland Athletics hitters in the AL Championship Series, batting .455 against the Toronto Blue Jays to help the Athletics prevail, 4–1. He made seven hits and batted .438, as the Oakland Athletics swept the San Francisco Giants in the earthquake-delayed World Series.

An injury in a 1991 snowmobile accident limited Lansford to only five games. He retired at the end of the 1992 season with a 15-year .290 major league batting average, a .411 slugging percentage, and 2,074 hits, including 332 doubles, 40 triples, and 151 HR. A sure-handed fielder, he led AL third basemen four times in fielding average and finished ninth all-time among third basemen with a career .966 fielding average.

Lansford coached for the Oakland Athletics in 1995 and for the St. Louis Cardinals (NL) in 1998 and managed Edmonton, CA in 1999. He resides in Baker City, OR, with his wife, Debbie, and their two sons and enjoys hunting and other outdoor sports with former teammate Joe Rudi.*

BIBLIOGRAPHY: Carney Lansford file, National Baseball Library, Cooperstown, NY; *The Baseball Encyclopedia*, 10th ed. (New York, 1996); Peter Gammons, "Carney Lansford: A Batting Champion without Fanfare," *BD* 41 (January 1982), pp. 42–45; Robert E. Kelly, *Baseball's Best* (Jefferson, NC, 1988); Carrie Seidman, "Carney Lansford: He'll Be One of the Stars of the '80s!" *BD* 39 (February 1980), pp. 63–65; Mike Shatzkin, ed., *The Ballplayers* (New York, 1990); John Thorn et al., eds., *Total Baseball*, 5th ed. (New York, 1997); *TSN Official Baseball Register*, 1986; Robert Redmount, *The Red Sox Encyclopedia* (Champaign, IL, 1998); John Thom, *Champion Batsman of the 20th Century* (Los Angeles, CA, 1992).

Gaymon L. Bennett

LARKIN, Barry Louis (b. April 28, 1964, Cincinnati, OH), player, is the son of Robert Larkin, a chemist for the federal government, and Shirley Larkin, a medical technician, and has three brothers, all athletes, and a sister. He graduated in 1982 from Cincinnati's Moeller High School, where he played baseball, football, and basketball. He batted .361 in baseball for three years at the University of Michigan. Larkin, the first baseball player ever named BTC MVP twice, made the 1984 U.S. Olympic team and twice earned All-America honors. He and his wife, Lisa (Davis) Larkin, have one daughter, Brielle, and one son, DeShane.

The Cincinnati Reds (NL) selected the 6-foot, 195-pound shortstop, who throws and bats right-handed, in the June 1985 free agent draft. He began his professional baseball career by helping Vermont win the EL crown. The following season, he was named AA MVP and Rookie of the Year with Denver, CO (AA). The Cincinnati Reds promoted him in August 1986 for 34 games. Larkin has played shortstop for Cincinnati since 1986, spending a rehabilitation assignment at Nashville, TN (AA) in 1989 and time on the disabled list in 1997. Larkin's career-highs include 32 doubles in 1988, 1992, and 1996, a .342 batting average in 1989, and 185 hits in 1990. He attained career pinnacles of 33 HR in 1996, six triples in 1992 and 1995, 89 RBI and 117 runs scored in 1996, and 51 stolen bases in 1995. Larkin batted .317 in an injury plagued 1997 season, .309 in 1998, and .293 in 1999.

In 1988, Larkin led all major league hitters by striking out only 24 times. He made the NL All-Star team 10 times (1988–1991, 1993–1997, 1999),

TSN All-Star team (1988–1992, 1995–1996, 1999), and *TSN* Silver Slugger team from 1988 to 1992, 1995–1996, and 1998. Larkin played in the 1990 NL Championship Series against the Pittsburgh Pirates, batting .261. In the 1990 World Series, he batted .353 to lead the Reds to a four game sweep of the Oakland A's. On June 27–28, 1991, Larkin became the first major league shortstop to hit five HR in two games. The Roberto Clemente Award was given him in 1993 as the player who best serves baseball on and off the field. A Gold Glove award winner 1994, 1995, and 1996, Larkin in 1995 ranked sixth in batting (.319), fifth in runs scored (98), and second in stolen bases (51), and was selected the BBWAA NL MVP. He led the Reds to the 1995 NL Central Division title and the NL Championship Series before losing to the Atlanta Braves. Larkin, the Reds' best post-season player, batted .385 with four stolen bases in the NL Division Series against the Los Angeles Dodgers and .389 with two doubles and one triple in the NL Championship Series.

In 11 major league seasons through 1999, Larkin has played in 1,707 games, scored 1,063 runs, and made 1,884 hits. He has batted .299 with 335 doubles, 65 triples, 168 HR, and 793 RBI, recording 764 walks, 633 strikeouts, and 345 stolen bases.

BIBLIOGRAPHY: Barry Larkin file, National Baseball Library, Cooperstown, NY; Donald Honig, *The Cincinnati Reds* (New York, 1992); B. Madden, "Safe at Home," *Sport* 87 (July 1996), pp. 76–78; Rich Marazzi, "Barry Larkin," *SCD* 21 (December 23, 1994), pp. 48–49; *Cincinnati Reds Media Guide*, 1998; Evansville (IN) *Courier*, November 16, 1995, p. 1C; W. Leavy, "Baseball's Two of a Kind," *Ebony* 51 (July 1996), pp. 100–102; Franz Lidz, "Right off the Bat," *SI* 82 (June 12, 1995), pp. 44–48; *TSN Official Baseball Register*, 1998; *USAT Baseball Weekly*, October 4–10, 1995, p. 43.

John L. Evers

LARKIN, Henry E. "Ted" (b. January 12, 1863, Reading, PA; d. January 31, 1942, Reading, PA), player and manager, began his professional baseball career in 1883 as an outfielder for Reading, PA (ISL) and made his major league debut in May 1884 with the Philadelphia Athletics (AA). With the Philadelphia Athletics, Larkin played the outfield from 1884 through 1887. The next season he moved to first base, the position he played for the rest of his career. In 1885 and 1886, Larkin led the AA in doubles, helping Philadelphia record two consecutive third-place finishes. Larkin, who batted and threw right-handed, enjoyed his best season in 1886, when he hit .319, collected 180 hits, scored 133 runs, and led the AA with a .390 on base percentage. In six years with the Philadelphia Athletics, he compiled an impressive .325 batting average and scored more than 100 runs on four occasions.

Unhappy in the AA, the 5-foot 10-inch, 175-pound Larkin jumped to the fledgling PL in 1890, joining well-known infielders Ed Delahanty* and Patsy Tebeau* on the Cleveland Infants. Larkin hit a personal-high .330 that season and piloted Cleveland to a 34–45 record as one of the three managers the Infants employed that year. In 1891 Larkin returned to the Philadelphia Athletics (AA), where he hit .279 and clouted a career-high 10 HR. The next year, Larkin signed with the Washington Senators of the newly expanded 12-team NL. The lowly Washington Senators finished in 10th place in 1892 and 12th place in 1893, as Larkin hit .295 and averaged 115 hits for those two seasons. During his 10-year major league career, Larkin batted a respectable .303 and collected 1,429 hits in 1,184 games. On June 7, 1892 against the Cincinnati Reds in the nation's capital, he collected six base hits to become only the 15th major league player to accomplish that feat.

BIBLIOGRAPHY: *The Baseball Encyclopedia*, 10th ed. (New York, 1996); Craig Carter, ed., *TSN Complete Baseball Record Book*, 1994 ed. (St. Louis, MO, 1994); Craig Carter, ed., *TSN Daguerreotypes*, 8th ed. (St. Louis, MO, 1990); Chicago (IL) *Tribune*, June 8, 1892; Henry Larkin file, National Baseball Library, Cooperstown, NY; David Nemec, *The Beer and Whisky League* (New York, 1994); John Thorn et al., eds., *Total Baseball*, 5th ed. (New York, 1997); Robert L. Tiemann and Mark Rucker, eds., *Nineteenth Century Stars* (Kansas City, MO, 1989).

Raymond D. Kush

LARSEN, Don James "Gooneybird" (b. August 7, 1929, Michigan City, IN), player, enjoyed a legendary major league baseball career. His 2–0 perfect game on October 8, 1956 against the Brooklyn Dodgers (NL) in the fifth game of the World Series at Yankee Stadium remains one of the greatest pitching feats in all of major league baseball history. Pitching without a windup, he struck out pinch hitter Loren Dale Mitchell* with umpire Babe Pinelli* behind the plate for his 27th straight out. The final out came on only his 97th pitch of the contest, played before 64,519 fans.

The 6-foot 4-inch, 230-pound-right-hander is the son of James Henry Larsen, a jeweler, and Charlotte Gimple (Brown) Larsen and broke into professional baseball with Aberdeen, SD (NoL) in 1947. Two seasons later, he pitched for Springfield, IL (3IL) and Globe-Miami, AZ (ArTL). He split the 1950 season with Wichita, KS (WL) and Wichita Falls, TX (BStL). The St. Louis Browns (AL) assigned him to San Antonio, TX (TL) for the 1951–1952 seasons, but Larsen spent those campaigns in military service. After an undistinguished minor league career in which his best season was his 17–11 record with Aberdeen in 1948, Larsen joined the St. Louis Browns in 1953 without ever pitching an inning for San Antonio.

Larsen compiled a 7–12 win–loss mark his first season with the St. Louis Browns. When the Browns moved to Baltimore in 1954, Larsen became the mainstay of the Orioles' pitching staff with a 3–21 mark. Two of his three wins came against the New York Yankees, who had won 103 games and still lost the AL pennant to the Cleveland Indians. The New York Yankees acquired Larsen in November 1954 in an 18-player deal, which included Larsen's soulmate "Bullet Bob" Turley.* New York Yankee general manager

George Weiss* believed that Larsen possessed more potential than Turley. Larsen had shown great promise with the St. Louis Browns, but had driven manager Marty Marion* to distraction with his curfew violations. Larsen married his first wife, Vivian, a telephone operator, in April 1955.

The New York Yankees optioned Larsen in 1955 to the Denver, CO Bears (AA), where he compiled a 9–1 mark for manager Ralph Houk.* The same season saw Larsen finish 9–2 with the New York Yankees. Although compiling an 11–5 record in 1956, Larsen had gotten off to a bad start during spring training. He wrapped his car around a telephone pole after falling asleep at the wheel at 5:00 A.M. in St. Petersburg, FL, prompting manager Casey Stengel* to quip, "He was probably out mailing a letter."

After Larsen slipped to 6–7 in 1959, the New York Yankees traded him to the Kansas City Athletics (AL). Larsen struggled with a 1–10 mark there in 1960. Called "Gooneybird," which is how he addressed everyone else, Larsen improved to a 7–2 mark for the Chicago White Sox (AL) in 1961. He pitched for the San Francisco Giants (NL) from 1962 to 1964 and Houston Colt-.45's-Astros (NL) in 1964 and 1965 before returning to the Baltimore Orioles for his last hurrah in 1965. The last active member of the St. Louis Browns, Larsen appeared in his final three major league games with the Chicago Cubs (NL) in 1967 and pitched in the minor leagues until he was nearly 40.

Larsen pitched 1,548 major league innings, compiling an 81–91 win–loss mark with a 3.78 ERA, 44 complete games, 11 shutouts, 725 walks, and 849 strikeouts. Larsen was credited with a World Series win for the San Francisco Giants over the New York Yankees, giving him a composite 4–2 mark and a 2.75 ERA in five classics. Larsen, who pinch-hit 66 times, batted .242 lifetime. Larsen set a major league record for pitchers with seven straight hits for the St. Louis Browns in 1953. Four of his 14 career HR came in 1958, when he hit .306 for New York. Larsen's .371 major league career slugging average ranks tenth highest among 20th-century pitchers. He married Corrine Audrey Bruess in December 1957 and worked as a salesman with the Blake, Moffet, and Thomas Paper Company in San Jose, CA. Larson retired in Hayden Lake, ID and has one son, Don Scott.

BIBLIOGRAPHY: Bill Borst, ed., *Ables to Zoldak*, vol. 2 (St. Louis, MO, 1989); Peter Golenbock, *Dynasty: The New York Yankees, 1949–1964* (New York, 1975); P. M. Hoose, "The Perfect Day," *RD* 138 (April 1991), pp. 59–62; Gene Karst and Martin Jones, Jr., *Who's Who in Professional Baseball* (New Rochelle, NY, 1973); Don Larsen with Mark Shaw, *The Perfect Yankee* (Champaign, IL, 1996); Ronald A. Mayer, *Perfect!* (Jefferson, NC, 1991); John Schulian, *TSN*, October 31, 1981, p. 16; Mike Shatzkin, ed., *The Ballplayers* (New York, 1990); Steve Smith, "Don Larsen Stunned the Dodgers (and the World) with Perfection," *SCD* 23 (September 27, 1996), pp. 128–129; Ted Patterson, *The Baltimore Orioles* (Dallas, TX, 1995); Mark Gallagher, *The Yankee Encyclopedia*, vol. 3 (Champaign, IL, 1997); Dom Forker, *Sweet Seasons* (Dallas, TX, 1991); Richard Lindberg, *Who's on Third?* (South Bend, IN, 1983); Art Spander,

"Fans Won't Let Larsen Forget His Perfecto," *TSN*, October 23, 1976, p. 11; Rich Westcott, *Diamond Greats* (Westport, CT, 1988).

William A. Borst

LaRUSSA, Anthony, Jr. "Tony" (b. October 6, 1944, Tampa, FL), player, coach, and manager, was born in the Latin section of Tampa, FL, to Anthony LaRussa, Sr., an Italian who worked as a milkman, and a Spanish mother, Oliva LaRussa. He developed fluent bilingual capabilities in Spanish and English which, in later years, facilitated in his dealing with Latin players. LaRussa began playing organized baseball in a Pee Wee Midget League at age six. His early heroes included National Baseball Hall of Fame manager Al Lopez,* also a Tampa native. LaRussa graduated in 1962 from Jefferson High School, where he captained the varsity baseball team while still a junior. All-Conference, All-City, and All-Florida recognition as a shortstop were earned as a senior. He also participated in Jefferson's football and basketball programs.

In 1962, Charles Gassaway of the Kansas City Athletics (AL) signed the 6-foot, 185-pound LaRussa to his first professional baseball contract. The following, he made his major league debut for the Kansas City Athletics and batted .250 in 34 games. LaRussa returned to the minor leagues in 1964 and led the PCL second basemen in fielding percentages (.976) at Vancouver, Canada, in 1968. He appeared briefly with the Oakland A's (AL) from 1968 through 1971, never appearing in over 52 games. The Atlanta Braves (NL) purchased his contract in August 1971 and sold it in October 1972 to the Chicago Cubs (NL). During his 16 professional seasons, LaRussa batted only .199 in 132 major league games. He coached in the St. Louis Cardinals organization in 1977 and for the Chicago White Sox (AL) in 1978.

LaRussa's greatest accomplishments came as a manager. In 1979, the Chicago White Sox hired the 35-year-old Tampa, FL native to manage their club. Four years later, LaRussa led the Chicago White Sox to the AL Western Division title for its first championship of any kind since 1959. LaRussa's triumph earned him BBWAA and *TSN* Manager of the Year awards. After the Chicago White Sox fired him, the Oakland Athletics (AL) hired LaRussa in 1986 to help their floundering ballclub. Two years later, he led the Oakland Athletics to 104 wins and the AL pennant. Although the Los Angeles Dodgers defeated the Athletics in that year's World Series, LaRussa received great praise from his peers and won the BBWAA Manager of the Year Award again. In 1989, his Athletics repeated as AL champions and won the World Series by sweeping the San Francisco Giants in four games. The 1990 Oakland Athletics captured a third consecutive AL pennant, but lost four straight contests to the Cincinnati Reds in the World Series. The Oakland Athletics struggled to a fourth place finish in 1991, but won the AL West Division with a 96–66 record in 1992. The Toronto Blue Jays defeated the Oakland Athletics in the AL Championship Series, but the BBWAA named him AL

Manager of the Year. The Oakland Athletics suffered through losing seasons in LaRussa's final three years there. In 1996, the St. Louis Cardinals hired him as manager. The St. Louis Cardinals finished first in the NL Central Division with a 88–74 record and swept the San Diego Padres in the NL Division Series. The Atlanta Braves, however, edged the St. Louis Cardinals in the NL Championship Series. LaRussa's club struggled in 1997 and 1999, but finished 83–79 in 1998 when Mark McGwire* broke the single-season record with 70 HR. In 21 major league seasons through 1999, LaRussa has guided his clubs to a 1,639–1,511 mark and .520 winning percentage.

LaRussa attended the University of Tampa and the University of Southern Florida, where he earned a bachelor's degree. He graduated from Florida State University with a law degree in 1978 and passed the bar exam one year later. During the off-season, he is engaged as a practicing attorney specializing in labor and corporate law. Only four other managers in baseball history have held law degrees. LaRussa lives in Tampa, FL with his wife, Elaine (Coker) LaRussa and two daughters, Bianca Tai and Devon.

BIBLIOGRAPHY: Tony LaRussa file, National Baseball Library, Cooperstown, NY; Leonard Koppett, *The Man in the Dugout* (New York, 1993); Kit Stier, "The Athletics," *TSN*, January 22, 1990, p. 43; Kit Stier, "How the A's Went from Zeros to Heroes: LaRussa," *TSN*, November 13, 1989, p. 53; John Thorn et al., eds., *Total Baseball*, 5th ed. (New York, 1997); George F. Will, "A Head for the Game," *SI* 72 (March 12, 1990), pp. 56–69; Richard Lindberg, *Who's on Third?* (South Bend, IN, 1983); Bob Logan, *Miracle on 35th Street* (South Bend, IN, 1983); Thomas Aylesworth and Benton Minks, *The Encyclopedia of Baseball Managers* (New York, 1990).

                                                            Samuel O. Regalado

LARY, Frank Strong "Mule," "Yankee Killer" (b. April 10, 1930, Northport, AL), player, is the son of J. Milton "Mitt" Lary, a farmer, and Margaret Lary. Lary, one of seven boys, grew up on a farm about five miles from Northport. "Mitt" Lary, a former semiprofessional pitcher, encouraged his sons to pitch after farm chores. Five Lary sons lettered in baseball for the University of Alabama. Frank, a 5-foot 11-inch, 180-pound right-hander and the smallest of the brothers, proved the most competitive and ultimately the most successful. Although the top punter in Alabama high school competition, Lary gave up football to concentrate on pitching for the University of Alabama team under manager Joe Sewell.* After his sophomore year at Alabama, Lary signed with the Detroit Tigers (AL) in 1950 for a modest bonus of about $15,000.

Lary split his first professional baseball season between Thomasville, GA (GFL) and Jamestown, NY (PoL) and then was drafted for military service. Discharged in time for the 1953 season, Lary won 17 games for Buffalo, NY (IL) and spent spring training with the Detroit Tigers in 1954. "He just couldn't get the ball over the plate," complained Tigers manager Fred

Hutchinson.* The Detroit Tigers optioned Lary to Buffalo, where he again pitched well. He finished the 1954 campaign with Detroit and made the Tigers rotation in 1955, winning 14 games. Mixing a fastball, curve, sinker, and occasional knuckler, Lary became a mainstay with the Detroit Tigers. "Once the fellow learned the knuckler," slugger Ted Williams* remarked, "he was able to keep you guessing. You never know what he's going to throw, and he's got the guts to fight you all the way." Lary started more than 30 games for seven consecutive seasons and led the AL in innings pitched and complete games three times. In 1962, arm problems caused him to struggle, relegating him to a spot starter role. The Detroit Tigers released him in 1964. Lary pitched briefly for the Milwaukee Braves (NL), New York Mets (NL), and Chicago White Sox (AL), retiring in the 1965 season.

Lary, who made the AL All-Star team in both 1960 and 1961, won 21 games in 1956 and a career-high 23 decisions in 1961. He closed his major league career with 128 victories, 116 losses, and a 3.49 ERA and struck out 1,099 batters in 2,162.1 innings. Lary married Emma Lou Barton in July 1951 and operates a carpet cleaning business with his brother, Al, in Northport, AL.

BIBLIOGRAPHY: Frank Lary file, National Baseball Library, Cooperstown, NY; Furman Bisher, "How Frank Lary Learned to Pitch," *Sport* 16 (August 1961), pp. 28–29, 58–59; Joe Falls, *Detroit Tigers* (New York, 1975); William M. Anderson, *The Detroit Tigers* (South Bend, IN, 1996); Richard Bak, *A Place for Summer* (Detroit, MI, 1998); Fred Smith, *995 Tigers* (Detroit, MI, 1981); Gene Karst and Martin J. Jones, *Who's Who in Professional Baseball* (New Rochelle, NY, 1973), p. 550.

Lloyd J. Graybar

LARY, Lynford Hobart "Lyn," "Broadway" (b. January 28, 1906, Armona, CA; d. January 9, 1973, Downey, CA), player, was the son of Clyde Lary. After graduating from Visalia High School in Long Beach, CA, he starred with the Oakland, CA Acorns (PCL). In January 1928, the New York Yankees (AL) paid $125,000 for the highly sought after shortstop and his double-play partner, Jimmy Reese.

Lary debuted with the New York Yankees in 1929, batting .309 in 80 games. In 1930, the 6-foot, 165-pound right-handed infielder hit .289. The following year saw him play full time, hitting .280, scoring 100 runs, and producing a career-high 107 RBI. Lary married Mary Lawlor, a musical comedy and motion picture actress, on July 14, 1931. He shared time at shortstop in 1932 with rookie Frankie Crosetti* and batted only .232. In the 1932 World Series Crosetti played all four games against the Chicago Cubs.

In May 1934, the New York Yankees traded Lary to the Boston Red Sox (AL) for Freddie Muller and $20,000. Lary led AL shortstops in fielding percentage (.965) that season. In October 1934, the Boston Red Sox traded Lary with $225,000 to the Washington Senators (AL) for Joe Cronin.* The Washington Senators sent him in June 1935 to the St. Louis Browns (AL).

Lary excelled for the Browns in 1936, hitting .289, walking 117 times, scoring 112 runs, and leading the major leagues with 37 stolen bases.

In January 1937, St. Louis traded Lary to the Cleveland Indians (AL) in a six player exchange. After hitting a composite .280 in two seasons with the Cleveland Indians, Lary was sent to the Brooklyn Dodgers (NL) in May 1939 and St. Louis Cardinals (NL) in August 1939. After retiring from professional baseball in 1942, he moved to Downey, CA and worked for North American Aviation as a purchasing agent.

Lary gained most notoriety for a baserunning mistake, which cost Lou Gehrig* sole possession of the 1931 HR title. Lary assumed that a Gehrig HR had been caught, veered to the dugout, and was passed on the basepaths by the Yankee first baseman. Gehrig was then called out. This infamous event unfortunately has overshadowed Lary's respectable career, in which he twice led AL shortstops in putouts, batted .269 with 1,239 hits, scored 805 runs, recorded 526 RBI, and stole 162 bases.

BIBLIOGRAPHY: Bob Broeg and Jerry Vickery, *St. Louis Cardinals Encyclopedia* (Grand Rapids, MI, 1998); Gene Karst and Martin J. Jones Jr., *Who's Who in Professional Baseball* (New Rochelle, NY, 1973); "Lyn Lary," *Microsoft Complete Baseball* CD-ROM (Redmond, WA, 1994); Franklin Lewis, *The Cleveland Indians* (New York, 1979); Mark Gallagher, *The Yankee Encyclopedia*, vol. 3 (Champaign, IL, 1997); Frank Graham, *The New York Yankees* (New York, 1943); Robert Redmount, *The Red Sox Encyclopedia* (Champaign, IL, 1998); Bill Borst, ed., *Ables to Zoldak*, vol. 2 (St. Louis, MO, 1989); Bill Borst, *Still Last in the American League* (West Bloomfield, MI, 1992); Lyn Lary file, National Baseball Library, Cooperstown, NY; "Mary Lawlor Is Wed to Lary, Shortstop," *NYT*, July 15, 1931, p. 21.

                                                                        Kent M. Krause

LASORDA, Thomas Charles "Tommy" (b. September 22, 1927, Norristown, PA), player, scout, manager, and executive, parlayed an undistinguished pitching career with the Brooklyn Dodgers (NL) and the Kansas City Athletics (AL) into an outstanding career as a manager. The second of five brothers, he is the son of working class immigrants Sabatino Lasorda and Carmella Lasorda and attended Holy Saviour School and Norristown High School.

Now known for both his boisterous temper and his bulging waistline, the 5-foot 10-inch, 185-pound Lasorda entered professional baseball with Concord, NC (NCSL) in 1945 and won only three of 15 decisions. Although having a great curveball, he exhibited control problems. Lasorda moved through the Philadelphia Phillies (NL) chain at Schenectady, NY (CAL) and Greenville, SC (SAL) before the Brooklyn Dodgers drafted him in 1948. He enjoyed several outstanding seasons with Montreal, Canada (IL), his best being a 17–8 win–loss mark in 1953.

The following season, Lasorda joined the famed "Boys of Summer" with Brooklyn Dodgers. Back with the Brooklyn Dodgers in 1955, Lasorda set a major league record of three wild pitches in the first inning of his May 5 start. The Brooklyn Dodgers sold him to the Kansas City Athletics (AL) in March 1956 for $35,000. With the Kansas City Athletics in 1956, he lost all his four major league decisions. Lasorda returned to the minor leagues and was traded to the New York Yankees (AL) organization in July 1956. The Brooklyn Dodgers organization reacquired him in May 1957. His outlook improved with Montreal (IL) in 1958. Lasorda's manager, Clay Bryant, was ejected for disputing an umpire's call. Lasorda became the Montreal Royals' acting pilot, delivered one of the club's few hits, and coached at third base. Bryant allowed him to coach at first base during the rest of the season, giving Lasorda the managing fever.

Lasorda became the "organization man" par excellence, progressing through virtually every stop on the Dodger chain. With the exception of his brief Kansas City and New York Yankee interludes, Lasorda has worked continuously for the Los Angeles Dodgers since 1948. He scouted for Los Angeles from 1961 to 1965, learning every facet of the organization from the inside out.

His first managerial job came with Ogden, UT (PrL) in 1969. He won three pennants there before piloting at Spokane, WA (PCL) and Albuquerque, NM (PCL). On September 30, 1976, he replaced Los Angeles Dodger mainstay Walter Alston.* Lasorda's teams won two World Series (1981, 1988), four NL pennants (1977, 1978, 1981, 1988), and eight Western Division titles (1977, 1978, 1981, 1983, 1985, 1988, 1994, 1995). The Los Angeles Dodgers in 1991 narrowly missed a 9th Western Division title, finishing one game behind the Atlanta Braves. The Los Angeles Dodgers struggled in 1992 and 1993, but regained first place in the NL West in the strike-shortened 1994 season. Los Angeles won the NL West again in 1995, but were swept by the Cincinnati Reds in the 1995 NL Division Series. Heart problems forced Lasorda, who had joined Connie Mack,* John McGraw,* and Walter Alston as the only managers to pilot the same club for at least two decades, to quit 76 games into the 1996 season. In 21 managerial seasons, he compiled 1,599 wins and 1,439 losses for a .526 winning percentage. Lasorda ranks 12th in career games managed and 13th in career victories as a pilot, developing nine NL Rookies of the Year. He has served as vice president of the Los Angeles Dodgers since 1997, temporarily assuming general manager duties in 1998. In 1997, the Veterans Committee elected him to the National Baseball Hall of Fame.

Lasorda married Joan Miller on April 14, 1950. Their union produced two children, Laura and Thomas Jr., now deceased. Lasorda possessed an emotional volatility that vacillated between a fondness for pasta and a stream of "blue" language, matching the color of his uniform. Much to his chagrin, Lasorda heard criticism for his ill-fated decision to pitch to St. Louis Cardinal slugger Jack Clark* in the 1985 NL Championship Series. Not known as a great field strategist in the mold of Whitey Herzog,* Lasorda compensated with enthusiam and an energetic affection for his players. Lasorda succeeded by psyching his players up to winning during a long season. He cajoled players, sometimes gently coaxing them into performing at their best. Lasorda's fluency in Spanish enabled him to communicate even more effectively with his players.

Lasorda remained an advertiser's delight. An indefatigable talker, he handled jokes about his girth with aplomb and style. On a bet with Los Angeles Dodgers stars Orel Hershiser* and Kirk Gibson* after their miraculous 1988 World Series victory against the Oakland Athletics, Lasorda agreed to lose 30 pounds or donate several thousand dollars to charity. Not only did the "artful Dodger" win the wager, he simultaneously promoted a diet formula and a string of restaurants.

Lasorda's bear hugs and constant talk of "bleeding Dodger blue" ingratiated him to a generation of Los Angeles Dodger fans and players alike. His stunt of having the Dodger schedule printed on his tombstone so mourners could visit him and find out when the Los Angeles Dodgers were playing exemplified his public relations panache.

BIBLIOGRAPHY: William F. McNeil, *The Dodger Encyclopedia* (Champaign, IL, 1997); Tommy Lasorda file, National Baseball Library, Cooperstown, NY; Bill Borst, *The Brooklyn Dodgers: A Fan's Memoir* (St. Louis, MO, 1982); Joe Curreri, "Lasorda Still Bleeds Dodger Blue," *SCD* 24 (August 13, 1997), pp. 90–91; B. Dumaine, "The Business Secrets of Tommy Lasorda," *Fortune* 120 (July 3, 1989), pp. 130–132; *CB Yearbook* (1989), pp. 321–324; Jay Johnstone, *Temporary Insanity* (New York, 1985); Thomas Aylesworth and Benton Minks, *The Encyclopedia of Baseball Managers* (New York, 1990); Leonard Koppett, *The Man in the Dugout* (New York, 1993); Tom Lasorda and David Fisher, *The Artful Dodger* (New York, 1985); M. Leahy, "Tommy Lasorda: Loud Foul or a Big Hit," *New Choices Retired Living* 32 (October 1992), pp. 54–56; *TSN*, June 18, 1958.

William A. Borst

LATHAM, Walter Arlington "Arlie," "The Freshest Man on Earth" (b. March 15, 1860, West Lebanon, NH; d. November 29, 1952, Garden City, NY), player, umpire, manager, coach, and executive, enjoyed a professional baseball career that spanned an incredible 76 years. The renowned free spirit earned his nickname from a song written for him as one of baseball's unique personalities. He led baseball in enthusiasm, alternating as a fierce competitor, cheerleader, clown, and merciless heckler.

A diminutive, 5-foot 8-inch 150 pounder, the stellar third baseman batted and threw right-handed and began his professional baseball career in 1875 at age 16. Latham played eight years in various cities before joining the St. Louis Browns (AA) and was the spark plug of Chris Von der Ahe's* highly successful teams, winners of four consecutive AA pennants. He led the AA with 152 runs in 1886 and 109 stolen bases in 1888. He played part of the 1890 season with the Chicago Pirates (PL), but moved to the Cincinnati

Reds (NL) later that year. After spending five seasons there, Latham found his playing days essentially over. He made several subsequent token appearances, the last coming at age 50. Latham stole a base in 1909, probably making him the oldest player to do so. He managed two games while still a player and then piloted in the minor leagues. He umpired in the NL in 1899, 1900, and 1902 and became baseball's first full-time, paid coach for the 1909 New York Giants (NL), teaching players the art of base stealing. The 1911 New York Giants stole a record 347 bases on their way to the NL pennant.

Latham's popularity carried over to the theater, where he performed during a short stage career. He began acting while still in baseball. After World War I, he lived 17 years in England and served as administrator (commissioner) of baseball. Latham mingled with British royalty, becoming a close friend of the Prince of Wales. Upon returning to the United States, he spent his last 16 years working for the New York clubs. Latham served as custodian of the New York Yankees (AL) press box when he died at age 92.

Latham batted over .300 three times in his 17 major league seasons and stole over 100 bases twice. He led his league in defensive statistics numerous times and possessed one of the strongest arms in the game. Latham remains in the record books as a career standout at his position, ranking high in assists, putouts, and total chances. In addition, he ranks high on the all-time list in runs scored per game. For his major league career, he played in 1,627 games, batted .269, stole 739 bases, and scored 1,478 runs.

Latham was married and the father of three daughters, Mrs. James Tait, Mrs. Frank Wakeman, and Mrs. Claude Sanford, and one son, Walter, Jr.

BIBLIOGRAPHY: Arlie Latham file, National Baseball Library, Cooperstown, NY; David Nemec, *The Beer and Whisky League* (New York, 1994); J. Thomas Hetrick, *Chris Von der Ahe and the St. Louis Browns* (Lanham, MD, 1999); Garden City (NY) *News*, December 4, 1952; John R. Husman, interview with Robert A. Latham, November 8, 1993, St. Petersburg, FL; Robert A. Latham, letter to John R. Husman, November 9, 1993; David Pearson, *Baseball in 1889* (Bowling Green, OH, 1993); Bill Borst, *Last in the American League* (St. Louis, MO, 1976); Frederick G. Lieb, *The St. Louis Cardinals* (New York, 1945); Lee Allen, *The Cincinnati Reds* (New York, 1948); John Thorn et al., eds., *Total Baseball*, 5th ed. (New York, 1997); Robert L. Tiemann and Mark Rucker, eds., *Nineteenth Century Stars* (Kansas City, MO, 1989); Toledo (OH) *Blade*, May 18, 1897.

John R. Husman

LAU, Charles Richard "Charlie" (b. April 2, 1933, Romulus, MI; d. March 18, 1984, Key Colony Beach, FL), player, manager, and coach, signed as a catcher with the Detroit Tigers (AL) in 1952 and enjoyed immediate success at Jamestown, NY (NYPL), batting .332 with 58 RBI. Lau spent two years in the U.S. Army but returned to professional baseball in 1955 at Durham, NC (CrL) and belted 18 HR with a .293 batting average. He married Barbara McCommins on September 16, 1955. From 1956 to 1959, the 6-foot, 185-pound, right-handed–throwing, left-handed–hitting catcher played for Charleston, WV (AA). The Tigers briefly called him up in 1956, 1958, and 1959 and in October 1959 traded him to the Milwaukee Braves (NL). After the Milwaukee Braves released Lau during the 1961 season, the Baltimore Orioles (AL) signed him. Lau batted .294 for the Orioles in 1962, hitting four doubles in a game on July 13. The Baltimore Orioles traded Lau to the Kansas City Athletics (AL) in July 1963 and then reacquired him from Kansas City in June 1964. On June 24, 1964, Lau made two pinch hits in one inning. He recorded a .295 batting average in 1965 with the Baltimore Orioles, but surgery on his right elbow in 1966 limited him to pinch hitting with Baltimore and the Atlanta Braves (NL) in 1967. Lau's major league career included 527 games, 298 hits, 105 runs, 16 HR, 140 RBI, and a .255 batting average.

Lau managed Shreveport, LA (TL) to a second-place finish in 1968 before returning to the Baltimore Orioles as hitting coach for the 1969 campaign. The Baltimore Orioles, however, did not renew his contract when he demanded $40,000 a year, double what most coaches then earned. He served as hitting coach for the Oakland Athletics (AL) in 1970, Kansas City Royals (AL) from 1971 to 1978, New York Yankees (AL) from 1979 to 1981, and Chicago White Sox (AL) from 1982 until his death.

Lau, regarded as one of the best hitting instructors in baseball, had carefully observed the mechanics of hitters as a catcher. He questioned age-old maxims of good hitting, spending countless hours analyzing videotapes of hitters until he could identify what he thought were the mechanics of the best hitters. He developed his "absolutes for hitting," the basis for his two highly acclaimed books, *The Art of Hitting .300* and *The Winning Hitter*.

Lau established four precepts of hitting: "Use the entire field, always keep your head down, rock back before moving forward in your swing, and hit through the ball." One of Lau's greatest pupils, the Kansas City Royals' George Brett,* reviewed the precepts every time he stood in the on-deck circle. Lau understood that most players lacked power, but could learn to knock line drives up the middle and poke hard ground balls into the gaps. Lau, recognized as an excellent teacher, said, "Knowing what I do about players, I almost think I'd rather err by praising them too much than by not doing it enough."

During the 1983 season, Lau voluntarily resigned his coaching position so that Chicago White Sox scout Loren Babe, who was suffering from lung cancer, could gain enough time to qualify for a 10-year major league pension. Babe died in February 1984, just one month before Lau succumbed to colon cancer.

BIBLIOGRAPHY: Charlie Lau file, National Baseball Library, Cooperstown, NY; Richie Ashburn, "Hitting According to the Gospel of Charlie Lau," *BD* 42 (June 1983), pp. 48–49; Del Black, "Royals Retain Herzog, Drop Lau as Coach," *TSN*,

November 4, 1978, p. 46; *TSN Official Baseball Register*, 1967; Brent P. Kelley, *The Case For: Those Overlooked by the Baseball Hall of Fame* (Jefferson, NC, 1992); Charlie Lau with Alfred Glossbrenner, *The Art of Hitting .300* (New York, 1980); Charlie Lau with Alfred Glossbrenner, *The Winning Hitter* (New York, 1984); Daniel Okrent, *Nine Innings* (New York, 1985); Mike Shatzkin, ed., *The Ballplayers* (New York, 1990).

Frank J. Olmsted

LAW, Vernon Sanders "Vern," "Deacon" (b. March 12, 1930, Meridian, ID), player and coach, is the father of former professional baseball player Vance Law. He is the second of three children of Jesse Law, a farmer, machinist, and mechanic of English descent, and Melva (Sanders) Law, of Swedish descent. He grew up in Meridian, winning 12 high school varsity letters and leading his baseball and football teams to state championships. He attended Boise JC and then signed a professional baseball contract with the Pittsburgh Pirates (NL) as a pitcher in 1948, partly through the efforts of Idaho Senator Herman Welker and singer Bing Crosby. Pittsburgh assigned him to Santa Rosa, CA (FWL) in 1948, Davenport, IA (3IL) in 1949, and New Orleans, LA (SA) in 1950 before calling him up to the Pittsburgh Pirates.

Law served in the U.S. Army during the 1952 and 1953 seasons and then joined Bob Friend* as one of the mainstays of the Pittsburgh Pirates' pitching staff, helping them rise to respectability. In 1955, he pitched 18 innings in a game and then hurled 13 more innings four days later. He finished with a 14–12 mark in 1958 and an 18–9 record in 1959. Law then produced a NL Cy Young Award-winning season in 1960, making the NL All-Star team and compiling a 20–9 slate with an NL-leading 18 complete games. That fall in the World Series he won two games against the New York Yankees and pitched well in the decisive seventh game, contributing significantly to the Pittsburgh Pirates' upset victory. An injured ankle led to a rotator cuff injury in 1961, as his record fell to 3–4. But by 1964 he resumed his work-horse status, pitching 192 innings and winning 12 games. His best overall season may have been 1965, when he won 17 of 26 decisions with a 2.15 ERA. He received the Lou Gehrig Memorial Award as Comeback Player of the Year. His performance then declined again. He retired after a 2–6 performance in 1967. In 16 major league seasons, the 6-foot, 2-inch, 195-pound right-hander won 162 games, lost 147 decisions, and hurled 2,672 innings with a 3.77 ERA.

Law coached for the Pittsburgh Pirates in 1968 and 1969, for 10 years at Brigham Young University, and for two years in Japan. After coaching at Denver, CO (AA) in 1982–1983, he left baseball to pursue business in Provo, UT. Law married his high school sweetheart, VaNita Cora McGuire, on March 3, 1950. They have six children, Veldon, Veryl, Vaughn, Varlin, VaLynda, and Vance. He is an ordained minister of the Church of Jesus Christ of Latter Day Saints. A rugged, durable performer, Law won acclaim mainly for his leadership of the 1960 World Champions.

BIBLIOGRAPHY: Richard L. Burtt, *The Pittsburgh Pirates, A Pictorial History* (Virginia Beach, VA, 1977); *CB* (1961), pp. 255–256; Dick Groat and Bill Surface, *The World Champion Pittsburgh Pirates* (New York, 1961); Vernon Law file, National Baseball Library, Cooperstown, NY; Bob Smizik, *The Pittsburgh Pirates: An Illustrated History* (New York, 1990); Luther Spoehr, interview with Vernon Law, July 8, 1993; John T. Bird, *Twin Killing: The Bill Mazeroski Story* (Birmingham, AL, 1995); Jim O'Brien, *Maz and the 1960 Bucs* (Pittsburgh, PA, 1994).

                                                                     Luther W. Spoehr

LAZZERI, Anthony Michael "Tony," "Poosh 'Em Up" (b. December 6, 1903, San Francisco, CA; d. August 6, 1946, Millbrae, CA), player and manager, was the son of boilermaker Augustin Lazzeri and Julia Lazzeri and grew up in San Francisco's Cow Hollow district. Upon leaving St. Theresa's Catholic School at age 15, the quiet youngster joined his father at the Maine Ironworks in San Francisco. He quickly developed into a lean, hard, 5-foot 11-inch, 170 pounder and planned a career as a boxer. While playing semipro baseball, Lazzeri was signed as an infielder by Salt Lake City, UT (PCL). He debuted professionally in 1922, batting an unimpressive .192 in 45 games. At Salt Lake City in 1925, however, he set PCL records with 60 HR, 202 runs scored, and 222 RBI, and compiled a .355 batting average. That winter, the New York Yankees (AL) purchased the powerful infielder for $75,000.

As the Yankees' regular second baseman from 1926 to 1937, the right-handed hitting Lazzeri helped the team capture six AL pennants and five World Series championships. He seven times drove in over 100 runs and five times surpassed the .300 batting mark. In 1929, he batted a career-high .354. Against the Chicago Cubs in the 1932 World Series, Lazzeri homered twice in one game. In the 1936 and 1937 World Series, he hit a grand slam HR and batted .400 against the New York Giants. He is best remembered, however, for the 1926 World Series, when Grover Cleveland Alexander* struck him out with the bases loaded in the seventh game to help preserve the St. Louis Cardinals' victory. On May 24, 1936, Lazzeri set the AL single-game record with 11 RBI by hitting a triple and three HR. Two of those HR came with the bases filled, a major league record since tied by six others. That same month, he set records for most HR in three consecutive (6) and four consecutive games (7).

After the 1937 season, he moved to the NL and played for the Chicago Cubs (1938), Brooklyn Dodgers (1939), and New York Giants (1939). From mid-1939 through 1943, he played and managed at Toronto, Canada (IL), San Francisco, CA (PCL), Portsmouth, VA (Pil), and Wilkes-Barre, PA (EL). Lazzeri married Maye Janes in April 1923 and had one son. After leaving baseball, he operated a tavern in San Francisco until his death. Lazzeri never led the AL in any offensive category except strikeouts (96 in 1926), but was considered an extremely valuable performer for his consistency, coolness under pressure, and quiet leadership. For his major league career, he batted .292 with 1,840 hits, 334 doubles, 178 HR, and 1,191 RBI. He played on the first AL All-Star team in 1933. Although an epileptic, he was never affected by the disease on the playing field. The popular Lazzeri attracted thousands of new fans to baseball from the nation's Italian-American population and became one of the most feared clutch hitters of his time. In 1991, he was elected to the National Baseball Hall of Fame.

BIBLIOGRAPHY: Tony Lazzeri file, National Baseball Library, Cooperstown, NY; Dick Beverage, "Tony Lazzeri: Baseball's First 60-Homer Man," *BRJ* 20 (1991), pp. 18–19; Mark Gallagher, *The Yankee Encyclopedia*, vol. 3 (Champaign, IL, 1997); Frank Graham, *The New York Yankees* (New York, 1943); Gene Karst and Martin J. Jones, Jr., *Who's Who in Professional Baseball* (New Rochelle, NY, 1973); *NYT*, 1926–1939, August 9, 1946; *TSN*, December 11, 1930; Dave Anderson et al., *The Yankees* (New York, 1979); John Mosedale, *The Greatest of All: The 1927 New York Yankees* (New York, 1974); Leo Trachtenberg, *The Wonder Team* (Bowling Green, OH, 1995); Marshall Smelser, *The Life that Ruth Built* (New York, 1975).

Joseph Lawler

LEACH, Frederick M. "Freddy" (b. November 23, 1897, Springfield, MO; d. December 10, 1981, Hagerman, ID), player, batted .307 and starred as a defensive outfielder in 13 NL seasons. Leach began his professional baseball career, hitting .383 with Waterloo, IA (MVL) in 1922. The Philadelphia Phillies (NL) purchased him before the 1923 season, when he batted .260 in 52 games. Philadelphia optioned Leach to Harrisburg, PA (NYPL) in 1924. After being recalled by Philadelphia that September, Leach batted .464 in eight games. He remained with Philadelphia until 1928, hitting over .300 each season. In October 1928, the Philadelphia Phillies traded Leach to the New York Giants (NL) for Lefty O'Doul* and $25,000.

Leach disliked playing for the New York Giants. The quiet player, who did not get along well with manager John McGraw,* remained constantly homesick for his family in Jerome, ID and became almost morose at times. Although Leach hit over .300 two of his three campaigns with New York, McGraw planned to trade him. During the 1931 season, McGraw refused the Boston Braves' (NL) $50,000 offer for Leach. In September 1931 against the Boston Braves, the score was tied with a Boston runner on third base. Leach made a spectacular catch against the left field fence of a ball at least 10 feet foul, allowing the winning run to score. McGraw, furious that Leach did not know he was in foul territory, sold him to the Braves for only $10,000 in March 1932. The Braves used him as a pinch hitter and part-time outfielder. Leach batted only .247 and retired following the 1932 season.

In 991 major league games spanning 10 major league seasons, Leach batted .307 and hit over .300 seven times. The 5-foot 11-inch, 183-pound Leach, who threw right-handed and batted left, lacked power, but connected for 196 doubles, 53 triples, and 72 HR. He made 1,147 hits, drew 163 walks, knocked in 509 runs, and scored 543 tallies.

Leach, who married Nettie Marie Clark on January 1, 1919 and had four children, worked as a railroad station agent and telegrapher during the off-season. After leaving baseball, he raised potatoes.

BIBLIOGRAPHY: Frank Graham, *The New York Giants* (New York, 1952); Harold Kaese, *The Boston Braves* (New York, 1948); Frederick G. Lieb and Stan Baumgartner, *The Philadelphia Phillies* (New York, 1953); *Baseball Encyclopedia*, 10th ed. (New York, 1996); *WWIB*, 1932, 17th ed.; Frederick Leach file, National Baseball Library, Cooperstown, NY; Rich Westcott and Frank Bilovsky, *The New Phillies Encyclopedia* (Philadelphia, PA, 1993); Charles C. Alexander, *John McGraw* (New York, 1988); Gary Caruso, *The Braves Encyclopedia* (Philadelphia, PA, 1995).

Ralph S. Graber

LEACH, Thomas William "Tommy" (b. November 4, 1877, French Creek, NY; d. September 29, 1969, Haines City, FL), player, manager, and scout, was the third of five children of Nelson Leach, a farmer, printer, and railroad worker, and Mary (Conway) Leach, both of English and Irish descent. His family moved to Cleveland, OH, when he was age five. He graduated from Immaculate Conception School and was apprenticed in bicycle repair, painting, and printing. Leach signed with Hanover, PA (CbL) in 1896 and then played third base with Petersburg, VA (VL). In 1897 he contracted with Youngstown, OH (ISL), but was released upon being injured and performed with Geneva, OH (independent). In 1898, he played with Auburn, NY (NYSL) and was sold to the Louisville Colonels (NL). After playing briefly with Worcester, MA (NEL), he played third base at Louisville. When the Louisville Colonels disbanded in 1900, Leach joined the Pittsburgh Pirates (NL). He played third base through 1908 and then moved to the outfield in 1909 because of an injured hip. Leach was traded in June 1912 to the Chicago Cubs (NL) and moved to the Cincinnati Reds (NL) after the 1914 season. He managed Rochester, NY (IL) in 1916 and then played with Kansas City, MO (AA) in 1917, and Chattanooga, TN (SA) in 1918. After rejoining Pittsburgh for the second half of the 1918 season, he performed for Shreveport, LA (TL) in 1919 and Tampa, FL (FSL) from 1920 through 1922.

At 5-feet 6-inches and 148 pounds, the speedy Leach numbered 266 doubles, 172 triples, and 63 HR among his 2,144 lifetime hits. His six HR and 22 triples topped the NL in 1902, while his 1,355 runs included an NL-leading 126 in 1909 and 99 in 1913. He batted .269 in 2,156 major league games, playing a prominent role on the 1901, 1902, 1903, and 1909 NL pennant-winning Pittsburgh clubs. In Pittsburgh's 1909 World Series victory over the Detroit Tigers (AL), he hit .320 and led with eight runs scored.

Leach retired to Haines City, FL to manage his citrus properties. He helped form the FSL and managed Tampa, FL from 1920 through 1923,

Lakeland, FL in 1924, and St. Petersburg, FL for part of 1928. From 1935 to 1941, he scouted for the Boston Braves (NL). He married Augusta Papcke and had one son. After her death, he married Sara Merron Darling in 1910 and had one daughter. Named to at least one All-Decade All-Star team for 1900–1910, he provided swift confirmation of the cliché about good things and small packages.

BIBLIOGRAPHY: Tommy Leach file, National Baseball Library, Cooperstown, NY; Richard L. Burtt, *The Pittsburgh Pirates, A Pictorial History* (Virginia Beach, VA, 1977); Bob Smizik, *The Pittsburgh Pirates: An Illustrated History* (New York, 1990); Warren Brown, *The Chicago Cubs* (New York, 1946); Eddie Gold and Art Ahrens, *The Golden Era Cubs, 1876–1940* (Chicago, IL, 1985); Frederick G. Lieb, *The Pittsburgh Pirates* (New York, 1948); Lawrence S. Ritter, *The Glory of Their Times* (New York, 1966).

Luther W. Spoehr

LEE, Thornton Starr "Lefty" (b. September 13, 1906, Sonoma, CA; d. June 9, 1997, Tucson, AZ), player and scout, was one of four children of Starr Lee, a railroad worker, and Celia (Steinhoff) Lee. The 6-foot 3-inch, 205-pound left-hander, an impressive figure on the mound, threw a deceptively sinking fastball. It took him a decade, however, to establish himself as a major league pitcher. He spent six seasons with seven minor league clubs and four disappointing campaigns with the Cleveland Indians (AL) before starring with Jimmy Dykes's* Chicago White Sox (AL) in 1937.

Lee graduated from high school and spent a year at California Polytechnic Institute before signing with the San Francisco, CA, Seals (PCL). San Francisco optioned him in 1928 to Salt Lake City, UT (UIL), where he shared pitching duties with rookie Curt Davis.* With fifth-place Toledo, OH (AA) in 1933, he compiled a 13–11 record and was purchased by the Cleveland Indians. Under managers Walter Johnson,* a notoriously poor handler of pitchers, and Steve O'Neill,* Lee struggled to a 12–17 mark between 1933 and 1936.

The Cleveland Indians traded Lee to the Chicago White Sox in a three-way exchange of pitchers that sent Chicago's Jack Salveson to the Washington Senators (AL) and Washington's Earl Whitehill* to Cleveland. Lee quickly became one of the AL's premier left-handers, largely due to the guidance of pitching coach Herold "Muddy" Ruel.* Lee attained his peak in 1941, when he pitched 300.1 innings while winning 22 and losing 11 decisions and making the AL All-Star team. His 2.37 ERA and 30 complete games led the AL, although the Chicago White Sox played only .500 percentage baseball in achieving third place. His opponents' .286 on-base percentage was the lowest allowed by any AL pitcher, while their combined .232 batting average was ranked the third lowest. As the first Chicago White Sox hurler to win more than 20 games since Ted Lyons's* 22 in 1930, Lee received a $2,500 bonus.

Bone chips and a fracture in Lee's throwing arm sidelined him for the next three seasons. He recovered to post a 15–12 record in 1945, but the Chicago White Sox released him after two more minimal seasons. His major league baseball career ended in 1948 with the New York Giants (NL) at age 42. In 16 major league seasons, he won 117 games and lost 124 with a 3.56 ERA. He worked as a cost analyst for an engineering firm and resided in Tucson, AZ. He scouted for the St. Louis Cardinals (NL) from 1973 through 1984 and for the San Francisco Giants (NL).

He married Esther Hill in December 1929 and had one son, Donald, a right-hander who compiled a 40–44 record with seven teams in a nine-year major league career from 1957 to 1966. Ted Williams* hit HR off both Thornton and Don, the only instance in baseball history of one hitter victimizing both father and son. Lee died of complications from Parkinson's disease.

BIBLIOGRAPHY: *The Baseball Encyclopedia*, 10th ed. (New York, 1996); Thornton Lee file, National Baseball Library, Cooperstown, NY; *NYT*, June 13, 1997, p. D21; A. D. Suehsdorf, telephone interviews with Don Lee, December 29, 1992, May 19, 1993; John Thorn et al., *Total Baseball*, 5th ed. (New York, 1997); Franklin Lewis, *The Cleveland Indians* (New York, 1949); Warren Brown, *The Chicago White Sox* (New York, 1952); Richard Lindberg, *Sox* (New York, 1984).

                                                                            A. D. Suehsdorf

LEE, William Crutcher "Big Bill" (b. October 21, 1909, Plaquemine, LA; d. June 15, 1977, Plaquemine, LA), player, was a prominent high school athlete in his hometown and attended Louisiana State University in 1928–1929. Branch Rickey* of the St. Louis Cardinals (NL) organization signed him to a minor league contract in 1929. Lee progressed through the St. Louis Cardinals farm system, pitching particularly well at Columbus, OH (AA) in 1932 and 1933. After the 1933 season, the Chicago Cubs (NL) purchased the 6-foot 3-inch, 210-pound right-hander for a reported $25,000 at the request of scout Clarence Rowland.* His 14-year major league career was spent mostly with the Chicago Cubs (1933–1943, 1947), but he also pitched for the Philadelphia Phillies (NL) from 1943 to 1945 and for the Boston Braves (NL) in 1945 and 1946. He compiled a major league career record of 169 wins and 157 losses and a 3.54 ERA with 182 complete games out of 379 starts. His best season came in 1938, when he led the Chicago Cubs to the NL pennant. Lee paced the NL in virtually every pitching category, finishing with a 22–9 win–loss record, a 2.66 ERA, 19 complete games, nine shutouts, and four successive shutouts. In 1938, he led the NL in victories, winning percentage (.710), shutouts and ERA. His other good seasons for Chicago were 1935, when he finished 20–6 with a 2.96 ERA and paced the NL with a .769 winning percentage and appeared in two World Series games against the Detroit Tigers, and 1936, when he compiled an 18–11 record with a 3.31 ERA and paced the NL with four shutouts. Lee hurled four

World Series games and lost two decisions, although boasting a 2.95 ERA and one save.

A quiet, good-natured player with a strong sense of attachment to the South, Lee relied on a curveball to retire opposing batters. Following his retirement from baseball in 1947, Lee returned to Plaquemine and engaged in private business until his death. He was married to Mary Amanda Fallon in October 1931 and had two children. The avid booster of Louisiana State University athletics was elected to the Louisiana Sports Hall of Fame in 1962.

BIBLIOGRAPHY: William C. Lee file, National Baseball Library, Cooperstown, NY; Warren Brown, *The Chicago Cubs* (New York, 1946); Warren Wilbert and William Hageman, *Chicago Cubs: Seasons at the Summit* (Champaign, IL, 1997); Eddie Gold and Art Ahrens, *The Golden Era Cubs, 1876–1940* (Chicago, IL, 1985); Eddie Gold and Art Ahrens, *The New Era Cubs, 1941–1985* (Chicago, IL, 1985); Jim Enright, *Chicago Cubs* (New York, 1975); Rich Westcott and Frank Bilovsky, *The New Phillies Encyclopedia* (Philadelphia, PA, 1993); *The Baseball Encyclopedia*, 10th ed. (New York, 1996); *NYT*, December 21, 1938, p. 31; John Thorn et al., eds., *Total Baseball*, 5th ed. (New York, 1997); *TSN*, September 29, 1938, July 2, 1977.

John E. Findling

LEE, William Francis, III "Bill," "Spaceman" (b. December 28, 1946, Burbank, CA), player, starred as a left-handed pitcher for the Boston Red Sox (AL) and Montreal Expos (NL) from 1969 to 1982. Lee grew up in southern California, where his father, William Francis Lee, Jr., worked for the telephone company. He received his bachelor's degree from USC in June 1968, and that summer married Mary Lou Helfrich. They had three children, Michael, Andy, and Caitlin, before their divorce. Lee in 1981 married his second wife, Pam.

Lee pitched at USC for legendary coach Rod Dedeaux,* helping the Trojans win the 1968 College World Series his senior year by contributing a win and a save. The Boston Red Sox signed him in June 1968 and assigned him to Waterloo, IA (ML). In 1969, he moved up to Winston-Salem, NC (CrL). Lee pitched for Boston from 1969 through 1978, winning more games (94) than any Red Sox left hander except Mel Parnell* and Lefty Grove.* He pitched from 1979 to 1982 with the Montreal Expos, finishing with a 119–90 won–lost record and a 3.62 ERA.

Although not overly fast, Lee relied on various breaking balls (55 he claimed), good control, fine fielding, and intense competitiveness. He made the 1973 All-Star team, but did not pitch in the game. His career may best be known for its low points. Lee started the seventh game of the 1975 World Series and gave up a monumental HR to Tony Perez* that turned the tide in the Cincinnati Reds' favor. The HR came off Lee's "moon ball" or "Leephus pitch." In 1976, he injured his shoulder severely in a brawl with the

New York Yankees. His form did not return fully until 1979, when he won 16 games in his first season with the Montreal Expos.

But Lee was better known for his statements off the field than his play on it, having grown up in California in the 1960s and playing in Boston with its immense population of college students in the 1970s. He articulated a counter-cultural, anti-corporate America point of view that made and kept him a folk hero. Lee played semiprofessional baseball after he left the major leagues in 1982 and traveled the college lecture circuit. He called himself a "baseball traditionalist" and wondered why he wasn't known as Earth man rather than Spaceman. Lee admitted "using" marijuana and spoke strongly against the abuses of alcohol and caffeine around him. The outspoken anti-authoritarian infuriated many of his managers and baseball executives, particularly Don Zimmer,* his last Boston manager. But even Zimmer called Lee "a great competitor." Teammate Carl Yastrzemski* recalled Lee was "between the lines, all business," while George "Boomer" Scott* aptly said "You know, Billy Lee jes' a whole bunch of fun."

BIBLIOGRAPHY: William F. Lee file, National Baseball Library, Cooperstown, NY; Tom Clark, *Fan Poems* (Plainfield, VT, 1976); J. Collins, "Still Spaceman After All These Years," *Yankee* 57 (August 1993), pp. 76–83; Peter Gammons, *After the Sixth Game* (Lexington, MA, 1985); Peter Golenbock, *Fenway* (New York, 1992); Curry Kirkpatrick, "In an Orbit All His Own," *SI* 49 (August 7, 1978), pp. 58–62, 65–68; Bill Lee, "Penthouse Interview," *Penthouse II* (October 1979), pp. 128–130, 182–184, 186; Bill Lee with Dick Lally, *The Wrong Stuff* (New York, 1985); George M. Plasketes, "The Rebel Hero in Baseball: Bill 'Spaceman' Lee in an Orbit All His Own," *JPC* 21 (Summer 1987), pp. 121–138; Alan Steinberg, "Bill Lee: Free Floating Above the Madding Crowd," *IS* 7 (February 1985), pp. 18–25; Howard Liss, *The Boston Red Sox* (New York, 1982); Robert Redmount, *The Red Sox Encyclopedia* (Champaign, IL, 1998); Dan Shaughnessy, *The Curse of the Bambino* (New York, 1990).

Leverett T. Smith, Jr.

LEEVER, Samuel "Deacon," "The Goshen Schoolmaster" (b. December 23, 1871, Goshen, OH; d. May 19, 1953, Goshen, OH), player and manager, was the fourth of eight children of farmer Edward C. Leever and Ameridith Ardelia (Watson) Leever. After attending the district elementary school and Goshen High School, he taught for seven years before entering professional baseball. He married Margaret Molloy on February 27, 1904; they had no children. Leever signed as a pitcher with Richmond, VA (AtL) in 1897 at the advanced age of 25 and posted a 20–15 record, thus earning a tryout with the Pittsburgh Pirates (NL) the following spring. He reported with a sore arm and was returned to Richmond, where he contributed 14 triumphs to the club's pennant-winning season. Recalled by Pittsburgh in late 1898, he won his only decision and began a 13-year career as a Pirates mainstay.

A sturdy 5-foot 10½-inch, 175-pound right-hander with a quiet, somber temperament and excellent curve, Leever often was overshadowed by Pittsburgh stalwarts Deacon Phillippe* and Jesse Tannehill.* Nevertheless, he compiled an impressive record with 21 wins in 1899, 25 in 1903, 20 in 1905, and 22 in 1906. His other outstanding marks included appearing in an NL-leading 51 games in 1899, surrendering a mere two HR in 232.2 innings of pitching in 1900, and recording the NL's best winning percentages of .781 in 1903 and .800 in 1905. In 1902 Pittsburgh won the second of three straight NL pennants by the largest margin in major league history (27½ games), while the Pirates staff achieved 130 complete games in 141 starts. Leever completed 23 of 26 starts, winning 15 games and losing only seven.

Overall, 1903 comprised "The Schoolmaster's" greatest year. He led the NL in winning percentage, ERA (2.06), and shutouts, completed 30 of 34 starts, pitched one of his three career no-hitters, and won two of a remarkable string of six consecutive Pirates shutouts, still a major league record. Leever, however, injured his right shoulder in a trapshooting contest and developed a sore arm for the first World Series ever held, losing twice to the Boston Pilgrims.

Although enjoying respectable seasons through 1908, Leever managed only 6 wins against 5 losses in 1910 and retired. His 194 career victories and 100 defeats gave him a .660 winning percentage, fifth only to Whitey Ford's* .690 among 20th-century major league pitchers and eighth on the all-time list. In 388 appearances, he completed 241 of 299 starts, struck out 847 batters, and compiled a 2.47 ERA. Leever pitched in 26 games for Minneapolis, MN (AA) in 1911 and two years later briefly managed the Covington, KY–Kansas City, MO franchise of the then independent FL. He retired to a 70 acre farm in Goshen, OH, acquired during his playing days, and maintained his local reputation as an expert trapshooter.

BIBLIOGRAPHY: Clermont (OH) *Sun*, May 28, 1953; Richard M. Cohen et al., *The World Series* (New York, 1979); Hugh Fullerton, "Sam Leever's Sad Plight," *Liberty* (July 28, 1928), pp. 71–72; Raymond Gonzalez, "Pitchers Giving Up Home Runs," *BRJ* 10 (1981), p. 26; Lawrence S. Katz, "Pittsburgh's Pitching Twins: Phillippe and Leever," *BRJ* 26 (1997), pp. 133–135; Dennis De Valeria and Jean De Valeria, *Honus Wagner: A Biography* (New York, 1996); Samuel Leever file, National Baseball Library, Cooperstown, NY; Frederick G. Lieb, *The Pittsburgh Pirates* (New York, 1948); Craig Carter, ed., *TSN Daguerreotypes*, 8th ed. (St. Louis, MO, 1990); *The Baseball Encyclopedia*, 10th ed. (New York, 1996); Lowell Reidenbaugh, *100 Years of National League Baseball* (St. Louis, MO, 1976); *SL*, December 1, 1906; Richard L. Burtt, *The Pittsburgh Pirates: A Pictorial History* (Virginia Beach, VA, 1977); William Hageman, *Honus: The Life and Times of a Baseball Hero* (Champaign, IL, 1996).

A. D. Suehsdorf

LEFLORE, Ronald "Ron," "Twinkle Toes Bosco" (b. July 16, 1948, Detroit, MI), player, is the son of John LeFlore, an auto factory worker, and Georgia (Kincaide) LeFlore. LeFlore, of African-American descent, grew up in the drug and crime infested east side of Detroit and completed five years at

Eastern Martin Luther King High School. He had three brothers, two of whom were killed. His youngest brother, Gerald, was killed in a drug related shooting, while his oldest brother, Harry, died of a head injury during a professional fight. In April 1970, LeFlore was arrested for armed robbery and sentenced from five to 15 years at the State Prison of Southern Michigan. Although LeFlore claimed to have been 17 years old, subsequent records pushed his birth date back from 1952 to 1948.

LeFlore's baseball skills in prison interested the Detroit Tigers (AL), who arranged a one day tryout. The Detroit Tigers signed LeFlore when he was paroled from prison in July 1973 and made the right-hand batter and thrower their starting center fielder in August 1974. The quick, 6-foot, 200-pound LeFlore spent from 1974 to 1979 with the Detroit Tigers, compiling a 30 game hit streak and making the All-Star team in 1976. He led the AL in stolen bases (68) and runs scored (126) in 1978 and batted .300 and stole 78 bases in 1979.

In December 1979, the Detroit Tigers traded LeFlore to the Montreal Expos (NL) for pitcher Dan Schatzeder. In 1980, his 97 stolen bases led the NL. Teammate Rodney Scott stole 63 bases, giving the pair a then major league record for combined stolen bases. LeFlore played for the Chicago White Sox (AL) the next two seasons and accumulated 64 more stolen bases, retiring following the 1982 season. During nine major league seasons, he hit over .300 three times. He had a daughter, LaRhonda, with Deborah Hutchins in May 1976. LeFlore worked as a baggage handler for Eastern Airlines in Sarasota, FL and later attended umpire school. He wrote an autobiography, *Breakout: From Prison to the Big Leagues*, which was later made into a motion picture.

BIBLIOGRAPHY: Ron LeFlore file, National Baseball Library, Cooperstown, NY; Ron LeFlore with Jim Hawkins, *Breakout: From Prison to the Big Leagues* (New York, 1978); "Ron LeFlore," *Microsoft Complete Baseball*, CD-ROM (Redmond, WA, 1994); Larry Keith, "A Tiger Burning Bright," *SI* 44 (June 7, 1976), pp. 58, 61; Nicholas Dawidoff, "A Former Base Thief Answers the Call," *SI* 68 (February 22, 1988) p. 12; Chuck Wills and Pat Wills, *Beyond Home Plate* (Ocala, FL, 1993); Joe Falls, *Detroit Tigers* (New York, 1975); Fred Smith, *995 Tigers* (Detroit, MI, 1981); William M. Anderson, *The Detroit Tigers* (South Bend, IN, 1996); Richard Lindberg, *Who's on Third?* (South Bend, IN, 1983).

Lowell D. Smith

LEIBRANDT, Charles Louis, Jr. "Charlie," "Rembrandt" (b. October 4, 1956, Chicago, IL), player, is the son of restauranteurs Charles Leibrandt and Anne Leibrandt. After graduating from Loyola Academy in Wilmette, IL, Leibrandt received a Bachelor's degree in business management from Miami University in Ohio.

The 6-foot 3-inch, 195-pound pitcher debuted in the major leagues with the Cincinnati Reds (NL) on September 17, 1979. Leibrandt started 27 games in 1980, finishing 10–9. He then shuttled between Cincinnati and Indianapolis, IN (AA) before the Reds traded him to the Kansas City Royals (AL) in June 1983 for Bob Tufts. Although not possessing one outstanding pitch, Leibrandt learned to paint the edge of the strike zone. In 1984, he compiled an 11–7 record with the Kansas City Royals and suffered a three-hit, 1 to 0, loss to the Detroit Tigers in the AL Championship Series.

Leibrandt enjoyed his best season in 1985, ending 17–9 with a 2.69 ERA. Although losing his two starts against the Toronto Blue Jays in the 1988 AL Championship Series, he relieved to win Game 7. In Game 2 of the 1985 World Series, Leibrandt tossed eight shutout innings before losing on a late St. Louis Cardinal rally. In his Game 6 start, he allowed only one run into the eighth inning in the Royals' victory.

The left-hander compiled a solid 43–34 record over the next three seasons before slumping to a 5–11 campaign in 1989. In December 1989, the Kansas City Royals traded Leibrandt and Rick Luecken to the Atlanta Braves (NL) for Gerald Perry and Jim LeMasters. Leibrandt pitched well the next three seasons for the Braves, compiling a 39–31 record. In the 1991 World Series against the Minnesota Twins, he lost his Game 1 start and surrendered an 11th-inning HR to Kirby Puckett* to end Game 6. The next year, Leibrandt served up a decisive two-run double to Dave Winfield* of the Toronto Blue Jays in the final game of the 1992 World Series. In December 1992, the Atlanta Braves traded him to the Texas Rangers (AL). He finished his major league career there with a 9–10 record in 1993.

Leibrandt married his wife, Corinne, in 1982 and has two children. Despite his post-season misfortunes, he formed an integral part of Kansas City's championship in 1985 and Atlanta's 1991 and 1992 NL pennants. During his 14 year major league career, the Alpharetta, GA resident posted a 140–119 record and 3.71 ERA.

BIBLIOGRAPHY: Gary Caruso, *The Braves Encyclopedia* (Philadelphia, PA, 1995); Alan Eskew, *A Royal Finish* (Chicago, IL, 1985); "Charlie Leibrandt," *Microsoft Complete Baseball*, CD-ROM (Redmond, WA, 1994); Charlie Leibrandt file, National Baseball Library, Cooperstown, NY; Mike Shatzkin, ed., *The Ballplayers* (New York, 1990); Bob Verdi, "Leibrandt Is a Work of Art," Chicago (IL) *Tribune*, October 21, 1985, Sec. 3, p. 1.

Kent M. Krause

LEIFIELD, Albert Peter "Lefty" (b. September 5, 1883, Trenton, IL; d. October 10, 1970, Alexandria, VA), player, coach, and manager, bolstered a pitching staff that transformed the perennial second division Pittsburgh Pirates (NL) into pennant contenders in the first decade of the 20th century. He began his professional baseball career with Joplin, MO (MVL) in 1903 and advanced to Des Moines, IA (WL), in 1904 and 1905. Leifield's 19–14 and 23–8 win–loss records then earned him promotion to the Pittsburgh Pirates in September 1905. The slender 6-foot 1-inch, 165-pound southpaw made his major league debut on September 3, 1905 and hurled for the Pittsburgh Pirates until traded to the Chicago Cubs (NL) in June 1912.

After leaving the Chicago Cubs during 1913, Leifield played for San Francisco, CA (PCL) and St. Paul, MN (AA) in the high minor leagues and returned to the major leagues with the St. Louis Browns (AL) from 1918 through 1920. His best major league seasons comprised 20 wins in 1907, 19 victories in 1909, and 18 triumphs in 1906 for the Pirates. Leifield compiled a career 124–97 win–loss major league record with a 2.47 ERA in 296 games and 33 shutouts. He hurled three one-hitters, losing one to the Chicago Cubs when he made the only Pirate hit. His last great game, a one-hit shutout, came over the Boston Red Sox in August 1919. A sore arm hampered his later career.

Leifield coached with the St. Louis Browns (AL) from 1921 to 1923, Boston Red Sox (AL) from 1924 to 1926, and Detroit Tigers (AL) from 1927 to 1928. Managerial assignments followed at Oklahoma City, OK (TL) in 1929 and at St. Paul, MN (AA) from 1930 to 1932.

BIBLIOGRAPHY: Albert Leifield file, National Baseball Library, Cooperstown, NY; *The Baseball Encyclopedia*, 10th ed. (New York, 1996); John Thorn et al., eds., *Total Baseball*, 5th ed. (New York, 1997); *TSN Baseball Register, 1940*; Frederick G. Lieb, *The Pittsburgh Pirates* (New York, 1948); Richard L. Burtt, *The Pittsburgh Pirates, A Pictorial History* (Virginia Beach, VA, 1977); Bill Borst, ed., *Ables to Zoldak*, vol. 2 (St. Louis, MO, 1989).

Robert B. Van Atta

LEMON, Chester Earl "Chet" (b. February 12, 1955, Jackson, MS), player, performed 16 seasons with the Chicago White Sox (AL) and Detroit Tigers (AL). He graduated from Fremont High School in Los Angeles, noted for the athletes it has produced in several sports. The 6-foot, 190-pound Lemon attended Cerritos College and Pepperdine University. A 1972 Oakland A's (AL) first-round draft selection, he played third base and shortstop for several minor league teams until traded in June 1975 to the Chicago White Sox. In September 1975, Lemon was brought up to the major leagues to stay. By 1976, the Chicago White Sox made him the regular center fielder. In 1977, Lemon set AL records for most putouts (512) and chances (524) by an outfielder. He eventually set the AL record for most years (5) with 400 or more outfield putouts. Lemon batted .300, .318, .292, and .302 for the Chicago White Sox between 1978 and 1981, led the AL with 44 doubles in 1979, and played in the 1978 and 1979 All-Star Games.

The Chicago White Sox traded Lemon to the Detroit Tigers in November 1981. He belted 24 HR in 1983. The right-hand–batting and –throwing Lemon, an important cog in the 1984 "wire-to-wire" World Series championship juggernaut, played outstanding defense while batting .287 with 20 HR and 11 game-winning hits. An AL All-Star again, he went hitless in the AL Championship Series against the Kansas City Royals and batted .294 in the World Series against the San Diego Padres. Lemon, an important part of the 1987 Detroit Tiger AL East champions, hit .277 with 20 HR in the regular season and batted .294 with two HR in the five-game AL Championship Series. The Tigers, however, lost the AL Championship Series to the Minnesota Twins.

By the close of his 16-year major league career in 1990, Lemon sported a .273 career batting average with 1,875 hits, 215 HR, and 884 RBI. His 2.60 career average for outfield putouts per game ranked him among the top 20 in major league history. With his crowd-the-plate batting stance, he was hit by 151 pitches to rank fifth on the all-time list. The speedy, hustling, but erratic base runner frequently slid headfirst into first base and stole 58 career bases.

Lemon married Valerie Jones and had four children, Geneva, Chester, Jr., David, and Marcus Devon. He founded Chet Lemon's School of Baseball in Orlando, FL and resides in Lakeland, FL.

BIBLIOGRAPHY: Chet Lemon file, National Baseball Library, Cooperstown, NY; *Detroit Tigers Yearbooks and Media Guides*, 1982–1990; *The Official Major League Baseball 1991 Statbook* (New York, 1991); Seymour Siwoff et al., *The 1991 Elias Baseball Analyst* (New York, 1991); *TSN Official Baseball Register*, 1991; Richard Lindberg, *Who's on Third?* (South Bend, IN, 1983); Bob Vanderberg, *Sox: From Lane and Fain to Zisk and Fisk* (Chicago, IL, 1982); William M. Anderson, *The Detroit Tigers* (South Bend, IN, 1996); Richard Bak, *A Place for Summer* (Detroit, MI, 1998).

Sheldon L. Appleton

LEMON, Robert Granville "Bob" (b. September 22 1920, San Bernardino, CA; d. January 11, 2000, Long Beach, CA), player, manager, scout, and coach, became possibly the most outstanding performer to shift from the infield or outfield to the mound. Lemon, the son of iceman Earl Lemon and Ruth Lemon, began playing baseball professionally as an outfielder and shortstop at Springfield, OH (MAL) in 1938, but minor league managers recognized his strong throwing arm and made him a third baseman. In 1941 and 1942, he played a single game at third base for the Cleveland Indians (AL), making one hit in nine times at bat. He played in 1942 at Baltimore, MD (IL) and entered military service that year. On January 14, 1944, he married Jane H. McGee; they had three sons, Jeff, Jim, and Jerry.

Although he had pitched only two innings in the minor leagues, the 6-foot, 180-pound right-handed Lemon became a pitcher on his return to the Indians out of doubt that he had major league batting ability. In 1946 he played 12 games in the outfield and pitched in 32 contests, winning four and losing five. In 1947, he spent only two games in the outfield and compiled an 11–5 record in 37 pitching appearances. Thereafter Lemon hurled full-time, rapidly establishing himself as one of the AL's premier right-handers. He won 20 or more games seven times, leading the AL in victories with 23 in 1950 and 1954 and with 18 in 1955. A strong, durable arm allowed him to pace the AL in innings pitched in 1948, 1950, 1952, and 1953, and in complete games in 1948, 1950, 1952, 1954, and 1956. Besides pitching a no-hit game against the Detroit Tigers on June 30, 1948, Lemon the same year won two of the Indians' four World Series victories over the Boston Braves. In 1954, he lost two World Series games to the New York Giants. Leg and elbow injuries made Lemon ineffective after 1956 and caused him to retire in 1958. Over his career, Lemon compiled a 207–128 record in 460 games with 188 complete games in 350 starts—a remarkable performance given his late conversion to pitching. In 2,850 innings pitched, he struck out 1,277 batters and compiled a 3.23 ERA.

Lemon recorded a lifetime .232 batting average, made 31 pinch hits for a .291 pinch-hitting average, and slugged 37 HR, one less than the major league record for a pitcher. In 1976, he was elected to the National Baseball Hall of Fame. Lemon managed the Kansas City Royals (AL) from 1970 to 1972 and the Chicago White Sox (AL) in 1977 and early 1978. He served as the New York Yankees (AL) manager twice, from July 1978 through June 1979 and from September 1981 to April 1982. Although winning AL pennants in 1978 and 1981, he was replaced on both occasions with his immediate predecessor, Billy Martin* and Gene Michael, respectively. In 1978, he became the first manager in AL history to win a pennant after shifting teams during the season. As a major league manager, he compiled 430 wins and 403 losses for a .516 winning percentage. The aplomb with which he accepted discharge as part of managership was noted widely by journalists. Lemon also scouted for Cleveland (1959), Kansas City (1973), and the New York Yankees (1982–1995); coached for Cleveland (1960), the NL Philadelphia Phillies (1961), the AL California Angels (1967–1970), and the AL New York Yankees (1976); and managed Honolulu, HI (PCL) in 1964, Seattle, WA (PCL) in 1965 and 1966, Sacramento, CA (PCL) in 1974, and Richmond, VA (IL) in 1975.

BIBLIOGRAPHY: Robert Lemon file, National Baseball Library, Cooperstown, NY; Franklin Lewis, *The Cleveland Indians* (New York, 1949); John Thorn et al., eds., *Total Indians* (New York, 1996); Russell Schneitder, *The Boys of Summer of '48* (Champaign, IL, 1998); John Phillips, *Winners* (Cabin John, MD, 1987); George W. Hilton, correspondence with Robert G. Lemon, 1984, George W. Hilton Collection, Columbia, MD; Thomas Aylesworth and Benton Minks, *The Encyclopedia of Baseball Managers* (New York, 1990); Mark Gallagher, *The Yankee Encyclopedia*, vol. 3 (Champaign, IL, 1997); *The Baseball Encyclopedia*, 10th ed. (New York, 1996); *TSN Official Baseball Guide, 1940–1983; WWIB*, 1952, 53rd ed.

George W. Hilton

LEONARD, Dennis Patrick (b. May 8, 1951, Brooklyn, NY), player, is the son of William M. Leonard. He graduated from high school in Island Park, NY and attended Iona College in New Rochelle, NY for three years, playing baseball there. The Kansas City Royals (AL) selected him in the second round of the June 1972 free agent draft. He divided the 1972 season between Kingsport, TN (ApL) and Waterloo, IA (ML), winning six of 10 decisions and striking out a batter per inning. On July 15, Leonard pitched a 3–0 no-hitter for Waterloo against Quincy, IL. At San Jose, CA (CaL) the next year, he won 15, lost nine, recorded 212 strikeouts, and posted a 2.58 ERA. On April 26, 1973, he held Visalia, CA hitless in a 2–0 masterpiece. With the Omaha, NE Royals (AA) in 1974, Leonard pitched better than his 12–13 record indicated. His 223 innings pitched led the AA, while he allowed only 178 hits and struck out 192 batters. He lost all four decisions with the Kansas City Royals in September.

After starting the 1975 season with Omaha, Leonard joined a solid Royals' rotation of Steve Busby, Al Fitzmorris, and Paul Splittorff.* He won 15 and lost 7, helping the Royals to their best record (91–71) to that date. The 6-foot 1-inch, 195-pound right-hander used a hard fastball, slider, and curveball to notch 17 victories in 1976. The fiercely competitive Leonard's motto was, "Win or lose, take something out of a game that will help me the next time." He recorded 20 or more victories in 1977, 1978, and 1980, becoming the first Royals pitcher to win 20 games three times. His 20 triumphs in 1977 led the AL, while his 244 strikeouts ranked second in the AL to Nolan Ryan.* In 1979, Leonard triumphed 14 times and paced the AL with five shutouts. He produced a career best 2.99 ERA in 1981 with 13 victories. From 1975 to 1982, Leonard won more games (130) than any other major league righthander. Ironically, he never appeared in an All Star game, perhaps because Royals' position players like George Brett,* Darrell Porter,* Frank White,* and Hal McRae* regularly made the AL All-Star team.

Leonard won 10 games in 1982, but missed half the season after breaking a finger trying to stop a line drive. After starting 6–3 in 1983, he severely ruptured the patellar tendon in his left leg on May 28 on a pitch to Cal Ripken, Jr.* of the Baltimore Orioles (AL). Doctors repaired the tendon surgically, but half the tendon dissolved three months later. Leonard underwent two tendon grafts, battled infections, and took rehabilitation therapy for over two years. After minor league rehabilitation assignments in August 1985, he made two successful relief appearances for the Royals in September. In 1986, Leonard honored the final year of his contract, finishing 8–13 with two shutouts.

Leonard's major league career featured 144 wins, 106 defeats, 23 shutouts, and 1,323 strikeouts in 2,187 innings and 103 complete games in 312 appearances. He appeared in the AL Championship Series with the Kansas City Royals in 1976, 1977, 1978, and 1980. Leonard lost the first game and won the fourth contest of the 1980 World Series, but the Philadelphia Phillies won in six games. He was named Royals' Pitcher of the Year in 1975, 1977, and 1979.

Leonard and wife, Audrey, met at Lincoln Oren Jr. High School in Island Park, NY and were married December 18, 1971. They have two sons, Dennis, Jr. and Ryan and make their home in Blue Springs, MO. Leonard has served on the Kansas City Home Medical Support Services Board and worked with the Blue Springs Little League.

BIBLIOGRAPHY: Dennis Leonard file, National Baseball Library, Cooperstown, NY; Monsie Cameron, "Dennis Leonard: 'My Goal Is the Hall of Fame,' " *BD* 38 (May 1979), pp. 22–26; J. Friedman, "From the Bigs to the Littles and Back Again," *PW* 25 (June 23, 1986), pp. 49–50; Kansas City Royals, *Grandslam*, 1982, p. 55; Jill Lieber, "A Fight Against Pain And Doubt," *SI* 68 (July 29, 1985), pp. 40–43, 46, 51–52; Craig Neff, "Back on the Mound, and in the Groove," *SI* 64 (April 21, 1986), p. 72; Sid Bordman, *Expansion to Excellence* (Marceline, MS, 1981); Mike Shatzkin, ed., *The Ballplayers* (New York, 1990).

Frank J. Olmsted

LEONARD, Emil John "Dutch" (b. March 25, 1909, Auburn, IL; d. April 17, 1983, Springfield, IL), player and coach, grew up in central Illinois with parents of Belgian descent and graduated from Auburn High School. The 6-foot, 175-pound Leonard married Rose Dolenc in May 1934 and had two sons and one daughter. Leonard, a right-handed hurler, switched clubs frequently because of depressed minor league baseball conditions and the vagaries of his "out" pitch, the knuckleball. His minor league stops included Canton, OH (CL) and Mobile, AL (SA), 1930; St. Joseph, MO (WL) and Springfield-Quincy-Decatur, IL (3IL), 1931; Decatur (3IL), 1932; York, PA (NYPL), 1933; and Atlanta, GA (SA), 1936 and 1937.

As a major league pitcher, Leonard frequently moved. The Brooklyn Dodgers (NL) employed him in 1934 and 1935 and for parts of 1933 and 1936. From 1938 to 1946, he pitched for the Washington Senators (AL). After the old knuckleballer hurled for the Philadelphia Phillies (NL) in 1947 and 1948, he toiled for the Chicago Cubs (NL) from December 1948 through 1953. Leonard pitched 18 full and two partial major league seasons. He showed great knuckleball skill and outstanding control, proving equally adept in starting and relieving roles. Leonard spent his Dodgers and Cubs years mostly as a reliever and his campaigns with the Senators and Phillies as a starter. He led relievers in saves with 8 (1935) and won 20 games (1939). Although he pitched for losing teams all but three seasons, he compiled a 191–181 career won–lost record, struck out 1,170 batters, appeared in 640 games, and had a 3.25 ERA. His winning percentage exceeded that of the teams he served by a remarkable 61 points.

Leonard's most memorable victory occurred on October 1, 1944, when he defeated the Detroit Tigers, 4–1, to enable the otherwise forlorn St. Louis Browns to win their only AL pennant. Before the game, he spurned a bribe to "throw" the game that far exceeded his annual $14,000 salary. The Illinois native served as a Chicago Cubs coach (1954–1956) and for many years conducted baseball clinics from his hometown of Auburn. Heart trouble caused his death.

BIBLIOGRAPHY: Emil Leonard file, National Baseball Library, Cooperstown, NY; John Thorn et al., eds., *Total Baseball*, 5th ed. (New York, 1997); Frank Graham, *The Brooklyn Dodgers* (New York, 1945); Morris Bealle, *The Washington Senators* (Washington, DC, 1947); Shirley Povich, *The Washington Senators* (New York, 1954); Rich Westcott and Frank Bilovsky, *The New Phillies Encyclopedia* (Philadelphia, PA, 1993); Jim Enright, *Chicago Cubs* (New York, 1975); Eddie Gold and Art Ahrens, *The New Era Cubs, 1941–1985* (Chicago, IL, 1985); *NYT*, April 19, 1983; *TSN*, March 12, 1966, May 2, 1983.

Lowell L. Blaisdell

LEONARD, Hubert Benjamin "Hub," "Dutch" (b. April 16, 1892, Birmingham, OH; d. July 11, 1952, Fresno, CA), player, enjoyed a very successful major league career as a pitcher from 1913 through 1925. The 5-foot 10-inch, 185 pounder threw and batted left-handed.

Leonard entered professional baseball off the Santa Clara, CA College campus in 1912 and spent only a year in the minor leagues at Denver, CO (WL), where he won 22 and lost nine. He pitched for the Boston Red Sox (AL) from 1913 through 1918 and the Detroit Tigers (AL) from 1919 to 1921 and in 1924 and 1925. A rara avis, Leonard starred as a left-handed spitball pitcher and likewise possessed an excellent fastball. Several indicators attest to his unusual ability. Leonard still holds the one-year major league ERA record at 0.96, set in 1914. In four different years, he ranked among the first five AL pitchers in winning percentage, strikeouts, shutouts, wins, complete games, ERA, and (retroactive) saves. Leonard pitched no-hit games on August 30, 1916 against the St. Louis Browns and on June 3, 1918 against the Detroit Tigers. He defeated the great Grover Cleveland Alexander* of the Philadelphia Phillies, 2–1, in the 1915 World Series and Rube Marquard* of the Brooklyn Robins, 6–2, in the 1916 World Series. Leonard's major league career featured 139 wins, 112 losses, a .554 winning percentage, a 2.76 ERA, 1,160 strikeouts in 2,192 innings, and 33 shutouts.

Leonard did not pitch many years or achieve career statistics of National Baseball Hall of Fame proportions because of his obstreperous, vain, suspicious, and defiant personality. He repeatedly disputed with baseball authorities, engaged in salary disputes, and more than once quit his team. In 1926, he accused superstars Tris Speaker* and Ty Cobb* of knowingly participating in the Cleveland Indians' alleged deliberate loss to the Detroit Tigers on September 25, 1919. A careful review of the circumstantial evidence indicates that Leonard and two other players bet on the game, but that Cleveland's loss was not prearranged. Cobb's and Speaker's exoneration by Commissioner Kenesaw Mountain Landis* was justified. Leonard probably sought revenge against Detroit Tiger manager Cobb for releasing him in 1925 after a successful but incomplete half season of service.

Leonard married actress Sybil Hitt in 1917 and was divorced in 1932. His second wife, Viola, survived him. Leonard enjoyed outstanding success in

California viniculture, leaving to his widow and brothers an estate worth more than $2 million.

BIBLIOGRAPHY: Hub Leonard file, National Baseball Library, Cooperstown, NY; *The Baseball Encyclopedia*, 10th ed. (New York, 1997); Tyrus R. Cobb, *My Life in Baseball, the True Record* (New York, 1961); Frederick G. Lieb, *The Boston Red Sox* (New York, 1947); Robert Redmount, *The Red Sox Encyclopedia* (Champaign, IL, 1998); Fred Smith, *995 Tigers* (Detroit, MI, 1981); Frederick G. Lieb, *The Detroit Tigers* (New York, 1946); Dan Gutman, *Baseball Babylon* (New York, 1992); Daniel E. Ginsburg, *The Fix Is In* (Jefferson, NC, 1995); *NYT*, December 21–31, 1926, January 6, 1927, January 10–15, 1927, January 24, 1927, January 25, 1927, January 28, 1927, January 29, 1927, July 12, 1952.

Lowell L. Blaisdell

LEONARD, Jeffrey N. "Hac Man," "Jeff" (b. September 22, 1955, Philadelphia, PA), player, coach, and manager, is the son of Wilson Leonard, a semiprofessional baseball player, and Johnee Mae (Artkins) Leonard and played football and basketball at Overbrook High School. Mike Bortnicker, Leonard's high school baseball coach, helped him secure a professional contract with the Los Angeles Dodgers (NL) organization. In June 1973, he began his career with Bellingham, WA (NWL). His June 7, 1976 marriage to Cynthia Scott produced a son, Jeffrey, Jr.

The 6-foot 2-inch, 200-pound right-handed outfielder spent six seasons in the minor leagues. After winning the PCL batting championship with Albuquerque, NM in 1978, Leonard was traded to the Houston Astros (NL) that September. In 1979, he hit .290 and was named *TSN* NL Rookie of the Year. But the 1980 campaign saw his batting average drop to .213 in 88 games. He batted only three times in the 1980 NL Championship Series against the Philadelphia Phillies.

The Houston Astros traded Leonard in April 1981 to the San Francisco Giants (NL), but he spent part of 1981 and 1982 with Phoenix, AZ (PCL). Leonard and his second wife, Yvonne, have a son, Marcus. From 1983 to 1987, he represented "the spirit and conscience" for the San Francisco Giants and became the team captain. Teammates named him "Hac-Man." Manager Roger Craig* declared "No doubt he's the MVP of this club." In the 1987 NL Championship Series against the St. Louis Cardinals, Leonard decided to "make [St. Louis] mad" by using a taunting 50-second HR trot in Game 3 with one arm up and one arm at his side. His four HR and .417 batting average enabled him to become only the third major league player to win a postseason MVP award while on the losing team.

The San Francisco Giants traded Leonard to the Milwaukee Brewers (AL) in June 1988. After being sent to the Seattle Mariners (AL) in December 1988, he taught Ken Griffey, Jr.* to play hard every day. Seattle released Leonard in October 1990. He joined the Kansas City Royals (AL) in 1991 and was optioned to Omaha, NE (AA), retiring after 68 games. During his

15 major league seasons, he batted .266 with 1,342 hits, 144 HR and 723 RBI. In 1997, Leonard managed Modesto, CA (CaL) in the Oakland A's organization. He joined the Montreal Expos (NL) as a roving hitting instructor in November 1998.

BIBLIOGRAPHY: Jeff Leonard file, National Baseball Library, Cooperstown, NY; Franz Lidz, "Three Men on a Roll," *SI* 67 (August 24, 1987), pp. 40–42; B. Shapiro, "Don't Call Him Jeff," *Sport* 78 (August 1987), pp. 82–84; *TSN*, January 26, 1980, March 30, 1987, October 19, 1987, June 20, 1988; San Francisco *Chronicle*, April 23, 1984, March 5, 1985; *USAT*, June 17, 1987, April 7, 1995.

Thomas H. Barthel

LEONARD, Walter Fenner "Buck" (b. September 8, 1907, Rocky Mount, NC; d. November 27, 1997, Rocky Mount, NC), player and executive, was a black baseball star never given the opportunity to play in the major leagues. He was elected to the National Baseball Hall of Fame in 1972. The son of John Leonard, a railroad fireman, and Emma Leonard, he left public school at age 14 and worked the next twelve years as a shoeshine boy, mill hand, and for the Atlantic Coast Line Railroad. During this time, he also played semipro baseball around Rocky Mount with the Elks and the Black Swans. After losing his job with the railroad in 1933, he found his only job opportunity in professional baseball. This idea initially did not seem too firm. According to Leonard, "I had almost given up baseball. . . . I had just about decided I wouldn't play any more because twenty-five is a pretty good age around here in the semipro lots." Leonard, who resided in Rocky Mount, eventually completed his high school education, graduating from the American School in Chicago on May 28, 1959 after taking a correspondence course. On December 31, 1937, he married Sarah Wroten. They remained married until her death on February 22, 1966, and had no children. His second wife, Eugenia, survived him.

In 1933, Leonard signed a professional contract with the Baltimore Stars under manager–first baseman Ben Taylor,* whom Leonard credited with teaching him how to play first base. When the Stars went bankrupt later that year, Leonard joined the Brooklyn Royal Giants. Smoky Joe Williams,* then tending bar in New York, persuaded him to sign with the Homestead, PA Grays (NNL) for 1934. Leonard remained with the Grays until 1950, when the NNL disbanded. There he teamed with Josh Gibson* to form a formidable offensive combination called the Babe Ruth* and Lou Gehrig* of black baseball. During these years, the Grays won NNL championships nine straight years from 1937 to 1945 and again in 1948. Leonard was selected to play in the Negro League All-Star Game 12 times. In 1953, he batted .333 in 10 games for Portsmouth, VA (PiL).

Leonard played baseball year round, participating in winter league baseball in Puerto Rico, Cuba, and Venezuela between 1935 and 1955. At age 48, he played his last game in 1955. In 1962, he helped organize the Rocky Mount, NC (CrL) club and served as its vice-president. During the winter of 1943, he played on Satchel Paige's* All-Star team against a major league All-Star team in California and batted .500 in eight games. The teams played eight games before Commissioner Kenesaw Mountain Landis* ordered them halted. At least twice during their long careers with the Grays, Leonard and Gibson were approached by major league owners about the possibility of playing major league baseball. Since the Grays played their home games first in Pittsburgh and then in Washington, Pittsburgh Pirates (NL) owner Bill Benswanger and Washington Senators (AL) owner Clark Griffith* naturally approached them first. White owners feared introducing black players into the major leagues, while black management was apprehensive about what it would do to the black baseball leagues. Consequently, no offer was ever made to Leonard and Gibson.

Although statistics from the NNL are sparse, Leonard was clearly a superior hitter and fielder. Many experts contend that Leonard fielded like George Sisler* and Hal Chase* and hit for a high average and with power. John Holway asserted that "Leonard hit over .400 four times, and over .390 six times, the last in 1948 when he hit a league-leading .391 and tied Luke Easter for the league home run crown." His lifetime batting average was .341 in Negro League play and .382 in exhibition games against major leaguers. Eddie Gottlieb (IS) stated: "Buck Leonard was as smooth a first baseman as I ever saw. In those days, the first baseman on a team in the Negro League often played the clown. They had a funny way of catching the ball so the fans would laugh, but Leonard was strictly baseball: a great glove, a hell of a hitter, and drove in runs." He died of complications from a stroke.

BIBLIOGRAPHY: Walter Leonard file, National Baseball Library, Cooperstown, NY; Martin Appel and Burt Goldblatt, *Baseball's Best: The Hall of Fame Gallery* (New York, 1977); William Brashler, *Josh Gibson* (New York, 1978); John B. Holway, *Voices from the Great Black Baseball Leagues* (New York, 1975); Brent Kelley, "Negro League Legend Buck Leonard Interviewed," *SCD* 22 (September 22, 1995), pp. 170–171; Brent Kelley, *Voices from the Negro Leagues* (Jefferson, NC, 1997); Buck Leonard with James A. Riley, *Buck Leonard: The Black Lou Gehrig* (New York, 1996); Robert W. Peterson, *Only the Ball Was White* (Englewood Cliffs, NJ, 1970); David L. Porter, ed., *African-American Sports Greats* (Westport, CT, 1995); Art Rust, Jr., *Get That Nigger off the Field!* (New York, 1976); James A. Riley, *The Biographical Encyclopedia of the Negro Baseball Leagues* (New York, 1994); Red Smith, "Fame on Sixty Cents a Day," *NYT*, February 9, 1972; Jules Tygiel, *Baseball's Great Experiment* (New York, 1983).

Leverett T. Smith, Jr.

LEWIS, George Edward "Duffy" (b. April 18, 1888, San Francisco, CA; d. June 17, 1979, Salem, NH), player, manager, and executive, joined Tris

Speaker* and Harry Hooper* in a Boston Red Sox (AL) outfield regarded by many as the finest defensive unit ever. Nicknamed "Duffy" after his mother's maiden name, Lewis played for his hometown Alameda (CA) High School baseball team, performed a year for St. Mary's College in Oakland, CA, and then professionally for Yuma, AZ (IVL) and Oakland (PCL). After signing with the Boston Red Sox for $2,400 in 1910, he married Eleanor Keane the following year. They had no children.

Lewis, Speaker, and Hooper performed together with Boston for six seasons, with the former contributing 1,544 putouts, 144 assists, and 25 double plays to the group's totals of 5,101 putouts, 455 assists, and 102 double plays. The uniquely difficult embankment at the base of Fenway Park's wall was Lewis's responsibility as left fielder. He met the challenge so adroitly that the embankment became known as "Duffy's cliff." He always found it harder to run down the slope than up.

His partners hit better, but the 5-foot 10½-inch, 165-pound right-hander compiled a respectable .284 batting average over 11 major league seasons in the dead ball era. His 1,518 hits included 289 doubles, 68 triples, and 38 HR. He played on the victorious Red Sox World Series squads of 1912, 1915, and 1916, excelling in the latter two. He led Boston with a .444 batting average against Grover Cleveland Alexander's* Philadelphia Phillies in 1915 and with .353 batting and .588 slugging averages against the Brooklyn Robins in 1916.

After missing the 1918 season because of U.S. Navy service, Lewis was traded that December to the New York Yankees (AL) with Ernie Shore and Hub Leonard* for four players and cash. It marked the first of the many deals made by owner Harry Frazee, wrecking the Boston Red Sox to the benefit of the New York Yankees. Lewis' last season (1921) saw him dealt in January to the Washington Senators (AL) with pitcher George Mogridge* for Braggo Roth.

Lewis managed in the minor leagues, lastly for Portland, ME (NEL) before becoming road secretary of the Boston Braves (NL) in 1935. This post was held by Lewis for 30 years in Boston and Milwaukee. Lewis fancied good clothes, with his wardrobe being stocked with well-cut suits and flamboyant vests. He ranked among the few who ever pinch-hit for Babe Ruth,* and saw "The Bambino" loft the first and last of his 714 HR. He was proud of having been thrown out of a game by an umpire only once in his major league career, and regretted that he never made it to the National Baseball Hall of Fame with Speaker and Hooper.

BIBLIOGRAPHY: Richard M. Cohen et al., *The World Series* (New York, 1979); George "Duffy" Lewis file, National Baseball Library, Cooperstown, NY; Frederick G. Lieb, *The Boston Red Sox* (New York, 1947); Philip J. Lowry, *Green Cathedrals* (Cooperstown, NY, 1986); Lawrence S. Ritter, *The Glory of Their Times* (New York, 1966); Harold Seymour, *Baseball: The Golden Age*, vol. 2 (New York, 1971); John

Thorn et al., eds., *Total Baseball*, 5th ed. (New York, 1997); Robert Redmount, *The Red Sox Encyclopedia* (Champaign, IL, 1998); Dan Shaughnessy, *The Curse of the Bambino* (New York, 1990); Frank Graham, *The New York Yankees* (New York, 1943).

A. D. Suehsdorf

LEWIS, John Kelly, Jr. "Buddy" (b. August 10, 1916, Gastonia, NC), player and coach, is a 6-foot 6-inch 175 pounder from a small-town environment. His parents were John Kelly Lewis, Sr., and Ada Mae Lewis. Lewis, talented in several sports, played football one year for Wake Forest College, but did not graduate. Junior Legion baseball, however, primarily attracted him. Although virtually ignored at a New York Giants (NL) tryout camp at age 18, Lewis persevered and played third base for Chattanooga, TN (SA) in 1934. After Lewis spent just two years in the minor leagues, the parent Washington Senators (AL) promoted him in September 1935. Lewis, however, hit only .107 in just eight games. Nonetheless, he played so impressively the following spring that Ossie Bluege,* veteran third-sacker for the club, admitted, "That skinny kid is my successor." Opening day presented Lewis a problem with President Franklin D. Roosevelt and a crowd of 34,000 in attendance. An obviously tense Lewis asked manager "Bucky" Harris* to delete him from the lineup, admitting, "I'm just plain scared." Harris commended Lewis for his honesty and saw him hit .291 for his rookie 1936 season. He led the AL in at-bats (668) in 1937 and triples (16) in 1939. Lewis was chosen for the AL All-Star team in 1939 and 1947. He began switching to the outfield around 1940, but surely had become an established performer.

Flying became Lewis's second interest. During spring training in 1940, he took flying lessons at an Orlando, FL airport without President Clark Griffith's* knowledge. He joined the U.S. Army Air Corps in 1942 during World War II and put a transport plane into a dive as a farewell over Griffith Stadium in Washington while his teammates waved from their dugout. Subsequently, he served 15 months overseas in the China-Burma-India Theater, flying some 369 missions in a C-47. For the Burma invasion in 1944, he flew a dual-glider tow over the "Hump." *Yank* commended his achievement, remarking that it was "done with the same . . . split-second timing" as on the ball field. The Distinguished Flying Cross was awarded him. When Lewis fought overseas, Clark Griffith kept his framed picture on his desk. Lewis named his plane *Old Fox* after his boss.

Lewis resumed his major league baseball career as an outfielder in 1945, but his crash into a fence severely injured his hip and forced his retirement by 1949. In 11 major league seasons, he batted .297 with 1,563 hits, 71 HR, and 607 RBI. He returned to Gastonia, operating his automobile business for the next 30 years and coaching American Legion teams. He married Frances Oates and had three children. His town named a street after him. He kept flying until 1990, when he sold his Cessna 182, but still retained his commercial license. "He's a real gentleman," one neighbor said, and the baseball world respected him highly as well.

BIBLIOGRAPHY: John Lewis file, National Baseball Library, Cooperstown, NY; Morris Bealle, *The Washington Senators* (Washington, DC, 1947); Shirley Povich, *The Washington Senators* (New York, 1954); *The Baseball Encyclopedia*, 10th ed. (New York, 1996); "Buddy Lewis of Senators Hangs Up Spikes at 33," *TSN*, March 8, 1950; "Buddy Lewis Would Pilot Team on Tour," *TSN*, July 26, 1945; Shirley Povich, "Can Buddy Lewis Come Back?" *BD* 8 (May 1949); Shirley Povich, "John 'Buddy' Lewis, a Boy Who Does a Man Size Job," *TSN*, July 23, 1936; Shirley Povich, "Lewis Spikes Capital Tale He'll Doff Spikes Again," *TSN*, November 9, 1949; Shirley Povich, "This Morning," Washington (DC) *Post*, February 17, 1944; Jack Smith, "Bud Lewis—Ace of Giant Discards," New York (NY) *Daily News*, August 14, 1938; John Thorn et al., eds., *Total Baseball*, 5th ed. (New York, 1997).

William J. Miller

LEYLAND, James Richard "Jim" (b. December 15, 1944, Toledo, OH), player, coach, manager, and scout, grew up in Perrysburg, OH as one of seven children of James Leyland, a Libbey-Owens-Ford glass factory foreman, and Veronica Leyland. He played football, basketball, and baseball at Perrysburg High School, graduating in 1963, and then signed as a catcher with the Detroit Tigers (AL). After playing six minor league seasons, he coached with Montgomery, AL (SL) in 1970 and managed Bristol, VA (ApL), Clinton, IA (ML), Montgomery, AL, Lakeland, FL (FSL), and Evansville, IN (AA), the Detroit Tigers' top farm team. He led his minor league teams to postseason play six times in 11 years, three times being named Manager of the Year. From 1982 through 1985, he coached at third base for the Chicago White Sox (AL) under manager Tony LaRussa.*

Before the 1986 season, Leyland became manager of the Pittsburgh Pirates (NL), a team that had lost 104 games the previous year. The Pittsburgh Pirates improved steadily under Leyland for three years, slumped in 1989, and then won three consecutive NL East titles. Pittsburgh lost in the NL Championship Series in 1990 to the Cincinnati Reds and in 1991 and 1992 to the Atlanta Braves. After the 1992 season, financial pressures forced the virtual dismantling of the team. Expensive stars, such as Barry Bonds,* Doug Drabek,* and Jose Lind, were lost to free agency or traded for less distinguished players. The Pittsburgh Pirates struggled to a 75–87 mark and a fifth-place East Division finish in 1993 and a 53–61 slate and a third place Central Division finish in the strike-shortened 1994 season. Pittsburgh continued to struggle in 1995 and 1996.

Leyland's 852 victories (against 864 losses) made him among the winningest managers in Pittsburgh Pirates history. He was named NL Manager of the Year by the BBWAA and the *TSN* managers' poll in 1990, finished runner-up for the BBWAA award in 1991, and shared the *TSN* award with Tommy Lasorda* in 1988. In 1990 he also won the Dapper Dan Man-of-the-Year Award.

In October 1996, the Florida Marlins (NL) named Leyland manager. He guided the star-studded Marlins to an NL East second place finish in 1997 with a 92–70 record. The Marlins swept the San Francisco Giants in the 1997 NL Division Series, upset the Atlanta Braves, 4–2, in the NL Championship Series, and defeated the favored Cleveland Indians, 4–3, in the World Series, with a dramatic extra inning comeback in the seventh game. The financially strapped Marlins dealt their high salaried players and finished only 54–108 in 1998. In October 1998, Leyland replaced Don Baylor* as manager of the Colorado Rockies (NL). He resigned after managing Colorado to a 72–90 record in 1999 and joined the St. Louis Cardinals as a major league scout that November. Through 1999, Leyland compiled a 1,069–1,134 record in 14 major league seasons.

Leyland, who resides in Pittsburgh with his second wife, Katie, and their son, Patrick, was active in the arthritis and epilepsy foundations and enjoys hunting in the off-season. Generally considered one of the best managers in contemporary baseball, Leyland helped to rebuild two franchises in disarray and then saw two teams taken apart by economic forces beyond their control.

BIBLIOGRAPHY: Jim Leyland file, National Baseball Library, Cooperstown, NY; Peter Pascarelli, *The Toughest Job in Baseball* (New York, 1993); C. Pierce, "The Last Pittsburgh Innocent," *GQ* 66 (May 1996), pp. 61–62; Thomas Aylesworth and Benton Minks, *The Encyclopedia of Baseball Managers* (New York, 1990); Bob Smizik, *The Pittsburgh Pirates: An Illustrated History* (New York, 1990); Dave Rosenbaum, *If They Don't Win It's a Shame* (Tampa, FL, 1998); Steve Rushin, "Glad to Be in the Game," *SI* 78 (January 25, 1993), pp. 42–46.

Luther W. Spoehr

LEZCANO, Sixto Joaquin (Curras) "The Sixto Kid" (b. November 28, 1953, Arecibo, PR), player and coach, is the son of Angel Lezcano and Maria (Curras) Lezcano and graduated from Fernando Callejo High School in Manati, PR, lettering in baseball, basketball, and track and field. He played American Legion baseball in 1969 and 1970. Scout Felix Delgado of the Milwaukee Brewers (AL) signed him to his first professional contract in October 1970.

Lezcano hit .289 with seven HR in 53 games for Newark, NY (NYPL) in 1971 and .270 with 10 HR in 114 games for Danville, IL (ML) in 1972. The 5-foot 11-inch, 175-pound Lezcano led the TL in doubles (35), triples (7), and assists for outfielders (17) in 1973, while batting .293 for Shreveport, LA. His last minor league season came in 1974, when he hit .325, slugged 34 HR, scored 100 runs, and knocked in 99 runs for Sacramento, CA (PCL).

The right-handed Lezcano played his entire professional baseball career as an outfielder, appearing occasionally as a DH. He performed for the Milwaukee Brewers (AL) from 1974 to 1980, St. Louis Cardinals (NL) in 1981, San Diego Padres (NL) in 1982 and 1983, Philadelphia Phillies (NL) in 1983 and 1984, and Pittsburgh Pirates (NL) in 1985. His first major league game came in September 1974. He played in at least 109 games for Milwaukee each season from 1974 to 1980. Lezcano belted 21 HR in 1977 despite missing 46 games with a broken hand. He provided career highs in runs scored (84), hits (152), doubles (29), HR (28), RBI (101), and batting average (.321) in 1979, batting 10 HR in August.

Lezcano played on three championship teams in winter ball in Puerto Rico, winning the batting title in 1977 with a .366 average. He paced AL outfielders in assists with 18 in 1978 and shared the NL lead with 16 in 1982. In 1982 Lezcano led NL outfielders in double plays with 8. Besides winning a Gold Glove in 1979, he was named Milwaukee Brewer MVP by local baseball writers. Lezcano tied a then major league record for most HR in an opening day game with two against the Boston Red Sox on April 10, 1980.

Lezcano appeared in four games as an outfielder and pinch-hitter in the 1983 NL Championship Series for the Philadelphia Phillies against the Los Angeles Dodgers, batting .308 with one HR. He batted only .125 for the Phillies against the Baltimore Orioles in the 1983 World Series. His 12 year major league career featured 148 HR, 591 RBI, and a .271 batting average. Lezcano and his wife, Maryanjelly, have one son, Michael. He coaches with Omaha, NE (AA) in the Kansas City Royals (AL) organization.

BIBLIOGRAPHY: Sixto Lezcano file, National Baseball Library, Cooperstown, NY; Lou Chapman, "Ex-midget Lezcano Packs a Big Wallop for Brewers," *TSN*, April 30, 1977, p. 18; Rick Hummel, "Money Talk Disturbs Lezcano," *TSN*, April 18, 1981, p. 31; Jeff Everson, *This Date in Milwaukee Brewers History* (Appleton, WI, 1987); Rich Westcott and Frank Bilovsky, *The New Phillies Encyclopedia* (Philadelphia, PA, 1993).

David A. Goss

LINDSTROM, Frederick Anthony. *See* Frederick Charles Lindstrom.

LINDSTROM, Frederick Charles "Freddie," "The Boy Wonder," "Lindy" (b. Frederick Anthony Lindstrom, November 21, 1905, Chicago, IL; d. October 4, 1981, Chicago, IL), player, sportscaster, manager, and coach, was the youngest of five children of plumbing contractor Frederick Lindstrom, Sr., and Mary (Sweeney) Lindstrom. Lindstrom married Irene Kiedaisch, whom he had known since childhood, on February 14, 1928 and had three sons. Charles, the youngest son, caught one game for the Chicago White Sox (AL) in 1958. Lindstrom pitched in the public parks and parochial schools of Chicago, but switched to the infield at Tilden High School there. He transferred to Loyola Academy, where he graduated in 1922 and where former major league pitcher Jake Weimer* coached him. After Weimer recommended Lindstrom to New York manager John McGraw,* the Giants (NL) signed him.

Although only 16 years old, Lindstrom hit .304 in 18 games at Toledo,

OH (AA) in 1922. After playing for Toledo in 1923, he joined the New York Giants in 1924. He played very infrequently in 1924 until replacing regular third baseman Heinie Groh,* who injured his knee severely. Lindstrom hit .253 in 52 games, as the Giants won the NL pennant. At 18 years, 2 months old, he became the youngest player to appear in a World Series game. Lindstrom batted .333 in the 1924 World Series against the Washington Senators, making 10 hits altogether and four hits against Walter Johnson* in one game. A ground ball, however, bounced crazily over his head to bring in the Senators' World Series-winning run in the seventh, deciding game.

The 5-foot 11-inch, 170-pound right-handed Lindstrom, one of his era's best fielding third basemen with a powerful arm and good range, excelled as an outfielder from 1931 through 1936. Hitting still remained his forte. Nicknamed "The Boy Wonder," he hit .358 in 1928 and .379 in 1930 and collected a remarkable 231 hits each season. His 231 hits led the NL in 1928. Lindstrom compiled a .311 batting average, 1,747 hits, 301 doubles, 895 runs scored, and 779 RBI over 13 major league seasons. He exhibited sharp wit and spirited independence and willingly spoke up to his bosses, including the fearsome McGraw. He suffered a major disappointment in June 1932, when the Giants named Bill Terry* as McGraw's replacement. Lindstrom, who believed he had been promised the job, remained very bitter and was traded to the Pittsburgh Pirates (NL) in December 1932. He played with the Pirates in 1933 and 1934, Chicago Cubs (NL) in 1935, and Brooklyn Dodgers (NL) in 1936 before retiring.

After conducting a radio sports program in Chicago in 1937 and 1938, Lindstrom managed Knoxville, TN (SA) in 1940–1941 and Fort Smith, AR (WA) in 1942. Lindstrom left organized baseball, but coached the sport at Northwestern University from 1951 to 1954. He was named U.S. Postmaster in Evanston, IL, where he remained until 1972. In 1976, Lindstrom was elected to the National Baseball Hall of Fame.

BIBLIOGRAPHY: Fred Lindstrom file, National Baseball Library, Cooperstown, NY; *SEAL*, vol. 1 (1981–1985), pp. 496–498; Arnold Hano, *The Greatest Giants of Them All* (New York, 1967); Fred Stein, *Under Coogan's Bluff* (Glenshaw, PA, 1978); Martin Appel and Burt Goldblatt, *Baseball's Best: The Hall of Fame Gallery* (New York, 1977); Frank Graham, *McGraw of the Giants* (New York, 1944); Noel Hynd, *The Giants of the Polo Grounds* (New York, 1988); Fred Stein and Nick Peters, *Day by Day in Giants History* (New York, 1984); *NYT*, August 26, 1954, January 9, 1961, January 31, 1975, October 6, 1981; *TSN*, January 1, 1966; Peter Williams, *When the Giants Were Giants* (Chapel Hill, NC, 1994).

Fred Stein

LLOYD, John Henry "Pop," "Cuchara" (b. April 25, 1884, Palatka, FL; d. March 19, 1965, Atlantic City, NJ), player and manager, was the son of Afro-American parents. Lloyd, whose father died when John was an infant, left grade school to work as a delivery boy. In 1905 Lloyd launched his professional baseball career as catcher for the Macon, GA, Acmes, a team that had no catcher's gear. After being hit by errant balls, he wore a wire basket over his face when catching. That winter, Lloyd waited on tables and played baseball in Florida. In 1906 he played second base for the Cuban X-Giants, a Philadelphia black team. The Cuban X-Giants lost to manager Connie Mack's* Philadelphia Athletics (AL) once, although Lloyd made four hits. Lloyd spent the next three seasons as shortstop with the Philadelphia Giants, managed by black baseball pioneer Sol White.*

Lloyd frequently played in the strong CUWL, often competing with white major leaguers. The Cuban fans adored Lloyd and nicknamed him "Cuchara" (a scoop or shovel), perhaps because of his prominent chin or big hands. His finest performance perhaps came there in November 1910 against Ty Cobb* of the Detroit Tigers. The Tigers sailed south for several games with the Havana, Cuba Reds. Although Detroit won the series, Cobb did not steal a base in five games and was outhit by three Reds black stars. Lloyd batted .500 (11 for 22), while Grant Johnson* hit .412 and catcher Bruce Petway* hit .388. Cobb finished as the fourth best hitter at .369 and vowed never to compete against blacks again. When the world champion Philadelphia Athletics came to Havana, Lloyd batted 3 for 10 against Chief Bender* and Eddie Plank* and averaged a composite .438 versus top AL pitching. Available figures indicate that he posted a .305 career average off major league competition. Twelve winter seasons in Cuba between 1908 and 1930 produced a .321 career batting average.

Lloyd first managed in 1911 and compiled his best record with the 1915 New York Lincoln Stars, who played the Chicago American Giants for the black championship. Each team won five times, as Lloyd paced hitters with a .390 batting average. In 1918 he worked at the U.S. Army Quartermaster Depot in Chicago. A left-handed batter, he played with several top black teams through 1932 and compiled a lifetime .368 Negro League batting average. His clubs included the Chicago Leland Giants, New York Lincoln Giants, Chicago American Giants (NNL), Brooklyn Royal Giants (ECL), Columbus, OH Buckeyes (NL), Atlantic City, NJ Bacharach Giants (ECL), Philadelphia Hilldale Daisies (ECL), and New York Harlem Stars. Lloyd helped open Yankee Stadium to black clubs when his Lincoln Giants and the Baltimore Black Sox played the first game there on July 10, 1930.

Following his baseball career, Lloyd became a janitor in Atlantic City, NJ at the post office and in the school system. Lloyd and his wife, Nan, had no children, but he loved youngsters and served as the city Little League commissioner. In 1949, the $150,000 John Henry Lloyd Baseball Park was dedicated in Atlantic City. The clean-living, gregarious Lloyd always had kind words for those around him.

Honus Wagner* commented of Lloyd, "They called him the Black Wagner and I was anxious to see him play. . . . after I saw him I felt honored that they would name such a great player after me." Connie Mack stated, "You could put Wagner and Lloyd in a bag together, and whichever one you pulled out you couldn't go wrong." In 1977, Lloyd was elected to the National Baseball Hall of Fame.

BIBLIOGRAPHY: John Henry Lloyd file, National Baseball Library, Cooperstown, NY; John B. Holway, "The Black Wagner: John Henry Lloyd," John B. Holway Collection, Springfield, VA; John B. Holway, *Blackball Stars* (Westport, CT, 1988); Robert W. Peterson, *Only the Ball Was White* (Englewood Cliffs, NJ, 1970); David L. Porter, ed., *African-American Sports Greats* (Westport, CT, 1995); James A. Riley, *The Biographical Encyclopedia of the Negro Baseball Leagues* (New York, 1994).

John B. Holway and Merl F. Kleinknecht

LOBERT, John Bernard "Hans," "Hans Number Two," "Honus" (b. October 18, 1881, Wilmington, DE; d. September 14, 1968, Philadelphia, PA), player, coach, manager, and scout, was the son of a cabinetmaker and brother of Frank Lobert, an infielder with the Baltimore Terrapins (FL) in 1915. Lobert grew up in Williamsport, PA and moved to Pittsburgh, PA as a teenager. In September 1903, Pittsburgh Pirates (NL) owner Barney Dreyfuss* discovered Lobert playing third base for the Pittsburgh AC and invited him to try out with the Pirates at Exposition Park. The 5-foot 9-inch, 170-pound right-handed youngster was welcomed by National Baseball Hall of Fame shortstop Honus Wagner,* whose facial features and German ancestry he shared. Lobert did not play during the 1903 World Series against the Boston Pilgrims and spent 1904 with Des Moines, IA (WL). The 1905 campaign found him in the Chicago Cubs' (NL) organization, hitting .337 and stealing 57 for Johnstown, PA (TSL).

In March 1906, Lobert was dealt to the Cincinnati Reds (NL) for Harry Steinfeldt.* He always regretted the trade since Steinfeldt joined the fabled Chicago Cub infield of Joe Tinker,* Johnny Evers,* and Frank Chance.* By 1906 Lobert established himself as a major league third baseman and mainly played there through 1917. His career included tenures with the Cincinnati Reds from 1906 to 1910, Philadelphia Phillies (NL) from 1911 to 1914, and New York Giants (NL) from 1915 to 1917. Lobert coached baseball at the United States Military Academy at West Point from 1918 to 1925 and with the New York Giants from 1926 to 1929. He subsequently managed in their minor league chain with Bridgeport, CT (EL) from 1929 to 1931 and Jersey City, NJ (IL) from 1932 to 1934. The 1935 to 1941 campaigns saw Lobert coach the Philadelphia Phillies (NL). In late September 1938, he served as interim manager for two games. Lobert managed the Phillies in 1942, but a 42–109 win–loss record led to his dismissal. From 1944 until his death, he scouted for the New York Giants mostly in the Philadelphia, PA area.

Known as a "speed king," Lobert once circled the bases in 13.8 seconds and often raced (and sometimes defeated) horses and motorcyclists. He stole over 40 bases in four seasons and batted over .300 four times. Lobert played in 1,317 games with 1,252 hits for a .274 batting average. In his 14-year major league career, Lobert made 159 doubles, 82 triples, and 32 HR. He scored 640 runs, produced 482 RBI, and stole 316 bases. The genial, well-liked sportsman, who married Rae Campbell, spent 65 years in baseball, ranking second only to Connie Mack.*

BIBLIOGRAPHY: Hans Lobert file, National Baseball Library, Cooperstown, NY; Thomas Aylesworth and Benton Minks, *The Encyclopedia of Baseball Managers* (New York, 1990); Lee Allen, *The Cincinnati Reds* (New York, 1948); Frank Graham, *The New York Giants* (New York, 1952); *NYT*, September 18, 1968; Gene Karst and Martin J. Jones, *Who's Who in Professional Baseball* (New Rochelle, NY, 1973); J. C. Kofoed, "The Star of the Phillies Infield," *BM* 13 (September 1914), pp. 41–44; Frederick G. Lieb and Stan Baumgartner, *The Philadelphia Phillies* (New York, 1953); *TSN*, September 28, 1968, p. 30; John B. Lobert, "Breaking into the Major Leagues," *BM* 9 (May 1912), pp. 27–31; Lawrence S. Ritter, *The Glory of Their Times* (New York, 1966); Mike Shatzkin, ed., *The Ballplayers* (New York, 1990); Fred Russell, "He Really Beat the Horses," *BD* 11 (May 1952), pp. 4–5, Rich Westcott and Frank Bilovsky, *The New Phillies Encyclopedia* (Philadelphia, PA, 1993).

John H. Ziegler

LOCKMAN, Carroll Walter "Whitey" (b. July 25, 1926, Lowell, NC), player, coach, manager, scout, and executive, is one of five children of Charles Ramsey Lockman, a textile factory overseer, and Eunice (Jenkins) Lockman. Lockman, who learned to play baseball for the Leaksville Woolen Mill Midget team in 1935, participated in baseball and basketball at Paw Creek High School and in American Legion baseball. He graduated from Paw Creek High School in 1943 at age 16. After signing with the New York Giants (NL) in 1943, he spent part of that season with Springfield, MA (EL) and from 1943 to 1945 with Jersey City, NJ (IL).

Lockman was promoted to the New York Giants in 1945 and homered in his first major-league at bat on July 5, 1945. He spent the 1946 season and most of the 1947 campaign in military service. Lockman started at first base for the New York Giants from 1948 until June 1956, when traded to the St. Louis Cardinals (NL). The New York Giants reacquired him in February 1957. He finished his major league baseball career with the Baltimore Orioles (AL) in 1959 and Cincinnati Reds (NL) in 1959 and 1960.

Lockman, a consistent hitter and solid fielder, batted .301 in 1949 and made the 1952 NL All-Star team. His double drove Don Newcombe* of the Brooklyn Dodgers out of the famous 1951 final NL playoff game, setting the stage for Bobby Thomson's* dramatic, NL pennant-winning HR. Lockman batted .240 in the 1951 World Series against the New York Yankees and only .111 in the 1954 World Series against the Cleveland Indians. He finished his major league career with a .279 batting average, 114 HR, 1,658 hits, and 563 RBI.

Lockman, a coach for the San Francisco Giants (NL) from 1961 to 1964 and the Chicago Cubs (NL) in 1966, managed Dallas-Fort Worth, TX (TL) in 1965 and Tacoma, WA (PCL) from 1967 to 1972. He won 1965 TL Manager of the Year honors and the 1969 PCL title. Lockman piloted the Chicago Cubs from July 1972 through July 1974, compiling a 157–162 win–loss record. After a brief stint as Cubs vice president, he scouted for the Montreal Expos (NL) from 1977 through 1991 and became senior adviser for player personnel for the Florida Marlins (NL) in 1992.

Lockman married Shirley Elizabeth Conner in July 1950 and has six children, Linda, Cheryl, Martha, Nancy, Robert, and James. Lockman belongs to the North Carolina Sports Hall of Fame.

BIBLIOGRAPHY: Eddie Gold and Art Ahrens, *The New Era Cubs, 1941–1985* (Chicago, IL, 1985); Brent Kelley, "Whitey Lockman," *SCD* 22 (June 16, 1995), pp. 150–152; Thomas Aylesworth and Benton Minks, *The Encyclopedia of Baseball Managers* (New York, 1990); Frank Graham, *The New York Giants* (New York, 1952); Noel Hynd, *The Giants of the Polo Grounds* (New York, 1988); Peter Williams, *When the Giants Were Giants* (Chapel Hill, NC, 1994); Fred Stein, *Under Coogan's Bluff* (Glenshaw, PA, 1978); Barry Kremenko, "Lockman, Unsung Hero of the Giants," *BD* 14 (September 1955), pp. 55–61; Rich Marazzi, "The Giants Swept the Indians in a Classic World Series," *SCD* 21 (October 28, 1994), pp. 150–151; Jack Orr, "Look at Lockman Now," *Sport* 12 (November 1952), pp. 36–37; Mike Royko, "The Boss of the Cubs," *Sport* 56 (September 1973), pp. 68–69.

Jim L. Sumner

LOFTIN, Louis. *See* Louis Loftin Santop.

LOFTON, Kenneth "Kenny" (b. May 31, 1967, East Chicago, IN), player, is a 6-foot, 180-pound outfielder who bats left and throws right-handed. Lofton's mother, Annie, a teenager at his birth, moved to Alabama. He was brought up by his blind grandmother, Rosie Person. Lofton attended Washington High School in East Chicago, where he played baseball and basketball. He led his basketball team to a 24–2 record and a berth in the state's final four. Lofton continued his basketball career at the University of Arizona (PTC), serving as the sixth man on the Wildcats' team that advanced to the 1988 Final Four. He started at guard the next season when Arizona finished 29–4 and was ranked first in the nation. Lofton completed his basketball career with a 4.8 points scoring average and ranked as the Wildcats' all-time leader in steals. As a junior, he walked on and made Arizona's baseball team. Although Lofton played little, the Houston Astros (NL) gambled by selecting him in the 17th round of the 1988 draft.

Lofton, who remains single, began his professional baseball career with Auburn, NY (NYPL) in 1988 and split the following season with Auburn and Asheville, NC (SAL). In 1990, he batted .333 with Osceola, FL (FSL) and led the FSL in hits. A year later, Lofton played for Tucson, AZ (PCL) and led the PCL in hits and triples before being promoted to the Houston Astros for 20 games. Houston traded him to the Cleveland Indians (AL) in December 1991.

Lofton paced the AL in stolen bases from 1992 to 1996 and in 1992 established the AL rookie-season record for most stolen bases (66), finishing second in the junior circuit Rookie of the Year voting. Besides being a Gold Glove Award winner four consecutive seasons from 1993 to 1996, Lofton also made the 1994, 1995, 1996, and 1998 All-Star teams. In 1994, he paced the AL with 160 hits and owned a career-high .349 batting average. Lofton topped the junior circuit in triples with 13 and stolen bases with 54 in 1995. The Cleveland Indians won the AL Championship series over the Seattle Mariners, as Lofton led both teams with 11 hits and a sparkling .458 batting average. In Cleveland's six game World Series loss to the Atlanta Braves, Lofton batted .200 with five hits and six runs scored. In the third game of the fall classic, Lofton reached base six consecutive times, tying the World Series record. In March 1997, Cleveland traded Lofton to the Atlanta Braves (NL) for David Justice* and Marquis Grissom.* He batted .333 in 1997 to help the Braves win the NL East but struggled in both the NL Division Series and NL Championship Series. Cleveland reacquired Lofton as a free agent in December 1997. His .282 batting average and 54 stolen bases helped Cleveland capture the 1998 AL Central Division. Lofton batted .375 with two HR and four RBI in the AL Division Series against the Boston Red Sox and clouted a double and HR with three RBI in the AL Championship Series against the New York Yankees. His best major league season came in 1996, when he established career highs in runs (132), hits (210), doubles (35), HR (14), RBI (67), and stolen bases (75). His .301 batting average and 25 stolen bases helped Cleveland win another AL Central title in 1999.

In nine major league seasons from 1991 to 1999, Lofton has played in 1,996 games, scored 852 runs, made 1,356 hits, including 212 doubles, 60 triples, and 63 HR, recorded 412 RBI, and compiled a .310 batting average. The Cortano, AZ resident has received 537 bases on balls, struck out 590 times, and stolen 433 bases. He ranked third in stolen bases (433) in the 1990s.

BIBLIOGRAPHY: Kenny Lofton file, National Baseball Library, Cooperstown, NY; Bob Klapisch, "The New Man of Steal," *TSN 1995 Baseball Yearbook*, pp. 46–48; Michael Silver, "Close to the Heart," *SI* 82 (May 1, 1995), pp. 96–98, 100–101; *TSN Official Baseball Register*, 1998; *USAT*, October 4, 1995, p. 7C; John Thorn et al., eds., *Total Indians* (New York, 1996); Jack Torry, *Endless Summers* (South Bend, IN, 1995); Russell Schneider, *The Glorious Summer of 1995* (Cleveland, OH, 1996).

John L. Evers

LOGAN, John Theodore, Jr. "Johnny," "Yachta" (b. March 23, 1927, Endicott, NY), player and scout, performed for the Milwaukee Braves (NL) as a key supporting player on their 1957 World Championship team and 1958 NL pennant winners. He is the son of John Logan, Sr., a Russian-born machinist in the Endicott forging works, and Helen Logan and made All-State in football, baseball, and basketball at Union-Endicott High School. Logan declined several college athletic scholarships and was drafted into the U.S. Army in 1945. He was signed by the Boston Braves (NL) and spent several seasons in the minor leagues as a shortstop. Logan attended Harpur College for one year. After beginning his major league career with the Boston Braves in 1951, the scrappy, 5-foot 11-inch, 175-pound shortstop moved with the Braves to Milwaukee in 1953 and remained there through the 1956–1959 "glory years." The Milwaukee Braves in June 1961 traded Logan to the Pittsburgh Pirates (NL), where he finished his 13-year major league career in 1963.

Logan batted a career-high .297 in 1955, when he led the NL in doubles (37). In 1956, the Milwaukee Braves lost the NL pennant to the Brooklyn Dodgers on the last day of the season. Milwaukee won the 1957 NL flag and defeated the New York Yankees in a seven-game World Series, featuring three wins by pitcher Lew Burdette.* Although Logan hit only .185 for the World Series, his solo HR in the second game contributed to Burdette's 4–2 victory. In 1958 the Milwaukee Braves topped the NL again, but this time lost the World Series to the New York Yankees in seven games. Logan batted only .120 in the 1958 fall classic. The following year, the Milwaukee Braves tied the Los Angeles Dodgers for first place during the regular season only to lose two straight contests in a playoff. Logan enjoyed one of his best years in 1959, hitting .291 with 13 HR.

With the Milwaukee Braves, the right-handed–batting and –throwing Logan was overshadowed by future National Baseball Hall of Famers Henry Aaron,* Eddie Mathews,* Warren Spahn,* and Red Schoendienst* and stars Burdette and Joe Adcock.* Usually batting in the second slot between Schoendienst or Billy Bruton* and Mathews, Logan combined steady hitting (.268 lifetime batting average) with outstanding defensive play at the key shortstop position. His play proved critical to the Milwaukee Braves' success and was recognized by knowledgeable observers. John Thorn and Pete Palmer rate him as the top major league defensive player at any position in 1953 and among the top five in the NL in 1954 and 1957. Logan led NL shortstops in fielding percentage from 1952 through 1954. He made the 1955 and 1958 All-Star teams and received MVP votes four of the five years from 1953 through 1957. In 1,503 games, Logan hit 93 HR and knocked in 547 runs. He married Dorothy Ahlmeyer in October 1953 and has a stepson, Bruce. They reside in Milwaukee, WI, where Logan sold advertising novelties. He has scouted for the Milwaukee Brewers (AL, NL) since 1993.

BIBLIOGRAPHY: John Logan file, National Baseball Library, Cooperstown, NY; Red Gleason, "Johnny Logan's a Fighter," *Sport* 21 (June 1956), pp. 42–44, 92–93; Rich Marazzi and Lew Fiorito, *Aaron to Zuverink* (New York, 1982); John Thorn et al., eds., *Total Baseball*, 5th ed. (New York, 1997); John Thorn et al., eds., *Total Braves* (New York, 1996); Bob Buege, *The Milwaukee Braves: A Baseball Eulogy* (Milwaukee, WI, 1988); Gary Caruso, *The Braves Encyclopedia* (Philadelphia, PA, 1995).

Sheldon L. Appleton

LOLICH, Michael Stephen "Mickey" (b. September 12, 1940, Portland, OR), player, began his association with organized baseball as the batboy for the Portland, OR Beavers (PCL). His father, Steve, worked for the Portland

Park Bureau, while his mother, Margaret, was a secretary for a lumber company. An only child, Lolich starred on his high school baseball team. The 6-foot 1-inch, 170-pound Lolich, who attended Clark JC of Vancouver, WA, is the first cousin of former baseball players Ron Lolich and Frank Lolich. Bob Scheffing, then manager of a California minor league team, saw the left-handed Lolich pitch batting practice and recommended him to the Detroit Tigers (AL), who signed the 18-year-old pitcher in 1958 to a three-year contract and a $30,000 bonus.

After working in the minor leagues from 1959 to 1963, he was promoted to the Detroit Tigers from Syracuse, NY (IL) in 1963 and compiled a 5–9 win–loss record in 33 appearances. Lolich quickly matured as a pitcher, winning 18 games and losing only 9 in 1964 and ranking among the best major league pitchers in ratio of strikeouts to bases on balls. From 1964 to 1974, Lolich won at least 14 games per season. In 1967, he led the AL with 6 shutouts. He went from the losingest AL pitcher (19) in 1970 to its winningest hurler (25) in 1971. His remarkable 1971 season included AL-leading figures in complete games (29), innings pitched (376), and strikeouts (308). His 376 innings pitched comprised the highest since Grover Cleveland Alexander's* 388 innings hurled in 1917.

His greatest accomplishments included the 1968 World Series against the St. Louis Cardinals, with his three complete-game victories, a masterful five-hitter in the seventh game, and an overall 1.67 ERA. In 1972 he compiled a 22–14 record and a 2.50 ERA, the second lowest of his 16-year major league career. After two losing seasons with Detroit in 1974 and 1975, Lolich played with the New York Mets (NL) in 1976 and San Diego Padres (NL) in 1978 and 1979. In 1974 Lolich's fastball was clocked at 90.9 miles per hour. During his major league career, he averaged seven strikeouts per nine-inning game, won 217 games, lost 191 contests, recorded 2,832 strikeouts, pitched 195 complete games, hurled 41 shutouts, and compiled a 3.44 ERA. Lolich entered private business and owns and operates a family doughnut shop in Lake Orion, MI. He married Joyce Fleenor in November 1964 and has three daughters, Kimberly, Stacy, and Jody Jo.

BIBLIOGRAPHY: Mickey Lolich file, National Baseball Library, Cooperstown, NY; J. Buckley, Jr., "World Series: Kings of the Hill," *SI* 75 (October 7, 1991), pp. 45ff; Ross Drake, "For Six Boys of Summer Grown Older, the Game Has Ended, but There Is Life after Baseball," *PW* 19 (April 11, 1983), pp. 78, 82; Joe Falls, *Detroit Tigers* (New York, 1975); Lloyd Graybar, "World Series Rarities—The Three-Game Winners," *BRJ* 11 (1982), pp. 18–25; Gene Karst and Martin J. Jones, Jr., *Who's Who in Professional Baseball* (New Rochelle, NY, 1973); Edward Kiersh, *Where Have You Gone, Vince DiMaggio?* (New York, 1983); Brent P. Kelley, *The Case For: Those Overlooked by the Baseball Hall of Fame* (Jefferson, NC, 1992); Fred Smith, *995 Tigers* (Detroit, MI, 1981); William M. Anderson, *The Detroit Tigers* (South Bend, IN, 1996); "Mickey Lolich: Just Working at a Job," *IS* 7 (October 1984), pp. 58–61.

Douglas A. Noverr

LOLLAR, John Sherman (b. August 23, 1924, Durham, AR; d. September 24, 1977, Springfield, MO), player, coach, and manager, attended Pittsburg State Teacher's College in Pittsburg, KS and began playing baseball professionally with Baltimore, MD (IL) in 1943. After winning the IL batting championship with a sparkling .364 mark in 1945, he advanced to the Cleveland Indians (AL) in 1946. In December 1946, Cleveland traded the 6 foot, 185 pound Lollar to the New York Yankees (AL). The Yankees sent him to the St. Louis Browns (AL) in December 1948. In an eight-player trade in November 1951, he was dealt to the Chicago White Sox (AL) for catcher Gus Niarhos. This trade appeared to be only an exchange of second-string catchers, but the White Sox had secured the player who anchored their formidable teams of the next decade and the 1959 AL pennant winner.

Lollar, an excellent receiver, and manager Paul Richards* developed Chicago's strong pitching staffs of the period. Lollar won Gold Glove Awards in 1957, 1958, and 1959 and led AL catchers in fielding percentage in 1951, 1953, 1956, 1960, and 1961. He developed into a strong pull hitter, belting 155 career HR. He ran with a long graceful stride, which was developed as a basketball player in his youth, and possessed the slow speed typical of catchers. He was thrown out at the plate to snuff out a rally in the second game of the 1959 World Series against the Los Angeles Dodgers when coach Tony Cuccinello* unaccountably waved him in.

Lollar retired as a player after the 1963 season, having batted .264 and knocked in 808 runs in 1,752 major league games. After coaching for the Baltimore Orioles (AL) from 1964 to 1967 and Oakland Athletics (AL) in 1968, he managed Iowa (AA) from 1970 to 1972 and Tucson, AZ (PCL) in 1973 and 1974. He returned to Springfield, MO, where he had lived since 1953 and where he owned a bowling alley. He married Constance Maggard in April 1949 and had two sons, John Sherman III and Kevin. The prime candidate for a major league managership lost a widely publicized bout with cancer in 1977.

BIBLIOGRAPHY: John Sherman Lollar file, National Baseball Library, Cooperstown, NY; Bill Borst, ed., *Ables to Zoldak*, vol. 2 (St. Louis, MO, 1989); Bill Borst, *Still Last in the American League* (West Bloomfield, MI, 1992); Richard Lindberg, *Sox* (New York, 1984); Richard Lindberg, *Who's on Third?* (South Bend, IN, 1983); *The Baseball Encyclopedia*, 10th ed. (New York, 1996); Chicago (IL) *Sun-Times*, September 27, 1977; Chicago (IL) *Tribune*, September 25, 1977; Brent P. Kelley, *The Case For: Those Overlooked by the Baseball Hall of Fame* (Jefferson, NC, 1992); Springfield (MO) *News and Leader*, September 25, 1977; *TSN Baseball Register, 1963*; *TSN Official Baseball Guide*, 1963; Bob Vanderberg, *Sox: From Lane and Fain to Zisk and Fisk* (Chicago, IL, 1982); *WWIB, 1963*, 48th ed.

George W. Hilton

LOMBARDI, Ernesto Natali "Ernie," "Schnoz," "Bocci" (b. April 6, 1908, Oakland, CA; d. September 26, 1977, Santa Cruz, CA), player, was a powerful 6-foot 3-inch, 230-pound right-handed batter who caught for 17 years in the NL for the Brooklyn Dodgers (1931), Cincinnati Reds (1932–1941), Boston Braves (1942), and New York Giants (1943–1947). Lombardi received a trial with hometown Oakland, CA (PCL) but was assigned to Ogden, UT (UIL) and batted .398 in 50 games in 1927. He pounded PCL pitching for .377, .366, and .370 batting averages for Oakland from 1928 through 1930 before joining Brooklyn. The Dodgers, for whom Lombardi batted .297 in 1931, traded him to Cincinnati in March 1932. He achieved his highest batting average with .343 in 1935, hit .333 and .334 the next two seasons, and led the NL with a .342 hitting mark in 1938. The NL MVP that year, Lombardi became only the second catcher to win a batting title. Although his batting average dropped to .287 in 1939, Lombardi slugged a career-high 20 HR and knocked in 85 runs to help lead the Reds to their first of two consecutive NL pennants. He batted .319 in 1940, when Cincinnati captured the World Series by defeating the Detroit Tigers in seven games.

In February 1942 Cincinnati sold Lombardi to Boston, where he won his second NL batting crown with a .330 mark to become the only catcher to win two batting titles. After being traded to the New York Giants in April 1943, he caught over 100 games during the 1943–1945 seasons while batting over .300 twice. Following the 1947 season, the Giants released Lombardi. He closed out his active playing career with Sacramento, CA (PCL) in 1948. Although grounding into the most double plays four different seasons, he compensated for his lack of speed with his power hitting. Lombardi batted over .300 10 times and compiled a .306 lifetime average. An excellent receiver, Lombardi caught over 100 games 14 consecutive seasons and in five All-Star games. He caught pitching greats Eppa Rixey,* Paul Derringer,* Bucky Walters,* and Johnny Vander Meer,* including the last's consecutive no-hit pitching performances.

In 1,853 career major league games, Lombardi scored 601 runs, knocked in 990 runs, and collected 1,792 hits, 277 doubles, 27 triples, and 190 HR. He caught 1,544 games and 11 times surpassed 100 hits in a season. Lombardi in 1935 equalled the major league record for most doubles in one game (4) and two years later tied an NL mark by making hits in six consecutive times at bat. On five occasions, Lombardi made five or more hits in one game. Lombardi, who married Bernice Marie Ayres in June 1944, experienced difficulties after his baseball career. He attempted suicide in 1953 and later was employed by the New York Giants. Embittered over his failure to be elected to the National Baseball Hall of Fame, Lombardi worked as a gas station attendant prior to his death. In 1986, the Veterans Committee elected him to the National Baseball Hall of Fame.

BIBLIOGRAPHY: Ernest Lombardi file, National Baseball Library, Cooperstown, NY; Gary Caruso, *The Braves Encyclopedia* (Philadelphia, PA, 1995); Frank Graham, *The New York Giants* (New York, 1952); Peter Williams, *When the Giants Were Giants*

(Chapel Hill, NC, 1994); Craig Carter, ed., *TSN Daguerreotypes*, 8th ed. (St. Louis, MO, 1990); Frank Stevens, *Baseball's Forgotten Heroes* (Netcong, NJ, 1984); *TSN*, October 15, 1977, p 51; Noel Hynd, *The Giants of the Polo Grounds* (New York, 1988); Lee Allen, *The Cincinnati Reds* (New York, 1948); John Thom, *Champion Batsman of the 20th Century* (Los Angeles, CA, 1992); Bob Rathgeber, *Cincinnati Reds Scrapbook* (Virginia Beach, VA, 1982); Ritter Collett, *The Cincinnati Reds* (Virginia Beach, VA, 1976); Harold Kaese, *The Boston Braves* (New York, 1948).

John L. Evers

LONBORG, James Reynold "Jim," "Gentleman Jim" (b. April 16, 1942, Santa Maria, CA), player, is the son of Reynold H. Lonborg, a college professor, and Ada (Ryan) Lonborg, and graduated in 1960 from San Luis Obispo, CA High School, where he lettered in baseball and basketball. A straight-A student, he earned an academic scholarship to Stanford University and graduated with a B.A. degree in biology.

The lanky, 6-foot 6-inch, 210-pound right-handed pitcher signed with the Boston Red Sox (AL) as a free agent. He pitched for Winston-Salem, NC (CrL) and Seattle, WA (PCL) in 1964, joining the Boston Red Sox in 1965. Lonborg in 1967 won the AL Cy Young Award and *TSN* Pitcher of the Year honors, leading the AL in wins (22), strikeouts (246), and games started (39), losing only nine contests, and posting a 3.16 ERA. He won a dramatic 5–3 AL pennant-clinching victory in the season's final game against the Minnesota Twins. In Game 2 of the World Series against the St. Louis Cardinals, Lonborg pitched a one-hit, 5–0 shutout. He also hurled a three-hit, 3–1 victory in Game 5, establishing a World Series record for fewest hits allowed in two consecutive complete games (4). After having only two days' rest, he lost the crucial seventh game against Bob Gibson.* Lonborg made the 1967 AL All-Star team, but did not play.

A serious leg injury, suffered in an off-season skiing accident, and arm problems, caused Lonborg to struggle over the next four seasons. The Boston Red Sox traded Lonborg to the Milwaukee Brewers (AL) in October 1971, where he recorded a 14–12 mark and career-best 2.83 ERA in 1972. Lonborg was sent to the Philadelphia Phillies (NL) in October 1972 and remained there through his final season in 1979. He compiled marks of 17–13 in 1974, 18–10 in 1976, and 11–4 in 1977, but finished 0–2 in the 1976 and 1977 NL Championship Series. For his 15-year major league career, Lonborg recorded 157 wins, 137 losses, a .534 winning percentage, 15 shutouts, 1,475 strikeouts, 823 walks, and a 3.86 ERA in 2,464.1 innings.

The intelligent, articulate, and charming Lonborg enjoys hunting, music, and reading. He earned a D.M.D. degree from Tufts University Dental School in Boston, MA in 1983 and has a thriving dental practice in Hanover, MA. Lonborg, who married Rosemary Feeny in 1970, has six children, Nicholas, Claire, Phoebe, Nora, John, and Jordan, and lives in Scituate, MA.

BIBLIOGRAPHY: Jim Lonborg file, National Baseball Library, Cooperstown, NY; Jack Lautier, *Fenway Voices* (Camden, ME, 1990); William Craig, "Don't Dig in on Gentleman Jim," *SEP* 240 (September 9, 1967), pp. 70–73; *TSN*, July 1, 1967, p. 3; Daphne Hurford, "A Gentler Style for a Gentleman," *SI* 44 (May 31, 1976), pp. 71–72; Jim Lonborg, letter to Edward J. Pavlick, January 1996; *TSN Baseball Register*, 1980; Rich Westcott and Frank Bilovsky, *The New Phillies Encyclopedia* (Philadelphia, PA, 1993); Allen Lewis, *The Philadelphia Phillies, A Pictorial History* (Virginia Beach, VA, 1981); Robert Redmount, *The Red Sox Encyclopedia* (Champaign, IL, 1998); Peter Golenbock, *Fenway* (New York, 1992); Dan Shaughnessy, *The Curse of the Bambino* (New York, 1990); Howard Liss, *The Boston Red Sox* (New York, 1982); Bill Mc-Sweeny, *The Impossible Dream* (New York, 1968); Carl Yastrzemski with Al Hirshberg, *Yaz* (New York, 1968); Ken Coleman and Dan Valenti, *The Impossible Dream Remembered* (Lexington, MA, 1987); Rich Westcott, *Diamond Greats* (Westport, CT, 1988).

Edward J. Pavlick

LONG, Herman C. "Germany" (b. April 13, 1866, Chicago, IL; d. September 17, 1909, Denver, CO), player and manager, was the son of German immigrants and married Anna Hillock. A contemporary rated Long, a shortstop through most of his 16-year career, as "one of the most brilliant infielders the game ever produced." He entered professional baseball in 1887 with Arkansas City, KS (KSL) and Emporia, KS (WL) and reached the major leagues two years later with the Kansas City Cowboys (AA). The Boston Beaneaters (NL) purchased his contract in 1890 for $6,500. Long anchored its infield through the 1902 season, including the championship 1891–1893 and 1897–1898 campaigns. The 5-foot 8½-inch, 160 pounder fielded brilliantly from the outset. In April 1890, a reporter, who questioned whether his ability was overrated, confessed, "His brilliant stops would not make him the star player that he is were it not for the fact that he seems to be a remarkably quick man on his feet." A master at handling thrown balls and covering a "vast amount of territory," he was lauded as "the fastest and best playing shortstop in the National League." He led NL shortstops in fielding in 1901 and 1902.

Long's fame also came from his batting. This left-handed hitter, who threw right-handed, batted over .300 for four consecutive years from 1894 to 1897 and compiled a career .277 batting average in 1,874 games. He showed both power and speed, slugging 91 career HR and leading the NL with 12 HR in 1900. Long stole 534 career bases and scored 1,455 runs, topping the NL with 149 in 1893. Long moved to the New York Highlanders (AL) in 1903, but enjoyed little success there and was soon traded to the Detroit Tigers (AL). After appearing in one game for the Philadelphia Phillies (NL) the next year, he played for and managed Toledo, OH (AA) in 1904, Des Moines, IA (WL) in 1905, and Omaha, NE (WL) in 1906. In 1905, he guided Des Moines to the WL championship. The intelligent, quick-witted Long ended his baseball career that season, allegedly because of his "love of drink and misdirected generosity." Since Long suffered from consumption, he traveled to Colorado in hopes that the clear, dry air would effect a cure. There he died, virtually penniless and friendless.

BIBLIOGRAPHY: Herman Long file, National Baseball Library, Cooperstown, NY; *The Baseball Encyclopedia*, 10th ed. (New York, 1996); *Spalding's Official Base Ball Guide*, 1894–1898, 1900 (New York, 1894–1898, 1900); Robert L. Tiemann and Mark Rucker, eds., *Nineteenth Century Stars* (Kansas City, MO, 1989); John Thorn et al., eds., *Total Braves* (New York, 1996); Harold Kaese, *The Boston Braves* (New York, 1948); Gary Caruso, *The Braves Encyclopedia* (Philadelphia, PA, 1995).

                                                                                                                      Duane A. Smith

LOPAT, Edmund Walter "Junk Man," "Ed," "Steady Eddie" (b. Edmund Walter Lopatynski, June 21, 1918, New York, NY; d. June 15, 1992, Darien, CT), player, manager, coach, and scout, was a left-handed 5-foot 10-inch, 185-pound pitcher for the Chicago White Sox (AL), New York Yankees (AL), and Baltimore Orioles (AL) and compiled a career 166–112 win–loss record and 3.21 ERA in 12 major league seasons from 1944 to 1955. He threw screwballs, knucklers, sliders, and curves, consequently being nicknamed "Junk Man." Batters claimed that he threw only "garbage." His excellent New York Yankees win–loss records from 1948 to 1954 were 17–11, 15–10, 18–8, 21–9, 10–5, 16–4, and 12–4, but his nickname of "Steady Eddie" hardly fit his nervous personality. Lopat won four of five decisions in seven World Series appearances, spanning five fall classics. In the 1951 World Series, he triumphed twice against the New York Giants and compiled a sparkling 0.50 ERA.

Born of Polish immigrant parents, Lopat completed high school in New York City. Lopat began his professional baseball career as a first baseman in 1937 with Greensburg, PA (PSA) and languished in the minor leagues for seven years with nine different clubs. Lopat's nervous disposition caused him to worry constantly about his performance and display tantrums when developments did not go his way. His wife, Mary Elizabeth (Howell), whom he married in December 1940, and physicians helped Lopat partially overcome his propensity to worry. Before being traded to the New York Yankees in February 1948, Lopat spent his first four major league seasons with the Chicago White Sox and posted a 50–49 win–loss record. His major league baseball career ended with the Baltimore Orioles in 1955.

As a player–manager at Richmond, VA (IL) in 1956, Lopat won 11 games while dropping 6 decisions. He piloted Richmond in 1957 and 1958 and coached for the New York Yankees in 1960, Minnesota Twins (AL) in 1961, and Kansas City Athletics (AL) in 1962. He managed the Kansas City Athletics to an eighth-place finish in 1963 and was fired 52 games into the 1964 season with an overall 90–124 record. He became a special assignment scout for the Montreal Expos (NL) in 1971 and managed Caugas, PR (PRWL). Lopat scouted for Montreal through 1985.

BIBLIOGRAPHY: *The Baseball Encyclopedia*, 10th ed. (New York, 1996); Thomas Ayles-worth and Benton Minks, *The Encyclopedia of Baseball Managers* (New York, 1990); Maury Allen, *Baseball: The Lives Behind the Seams* (New York, 1990); Dom Forker, *The Men of Autumn* (Dallas, TX, 1989); Mark Gallagher, *The Yankee Encyclopedia*, vol. 3 (Champaign, IL, 1997); Dave Anderson et al., *The Yankees* (New York, 1979); Warren Brown, *The Chicago White Sox* (New York, 1952); William Evans, "Nobody Wanted Lopat," *Sport* 12 (June 1952), pp. 42–43; Sol Gittleman, "Raschi, Lopat, and Reynolds," *BRJ* 22 (1973), pp. 78–79; David Halberstam, *Summer of '49* (New York, 1989); W. C. Heinz, "The Yankees' Crafty Ace," *SEP* 224 (May 10, 1952), p. 29; Gene Karst and Martin J. Jones, Jr., *Who's Who in Professional Baseball* (New Rochelle, NY, 1973); Edmund Lopat file, National Baseball Library, Cooperstown, NY; Ed Lopat, "How I Licked the Jitters," *AM* 158 (July 1953), pp. 26–27; Thomas Meany, "Lopat—The Junk Man," *BD* 11 (June 1952), pp. 94–97; *NYT*, June 16, 1992, p. B8; Harold Sheldon, "Speaking of Star Lefties: There's Lopat of the Yanks," *BD* 30 (February 1951), pp. 83–87; Rich Westcott, *Diamond Greats* (Westport, CT, 1988).

James K. Skipper, Jr.

LOPATYNSKI, Edmund Walter. *See* Edmund Walter Lopat.

LOPES, David Earl "Davey" (b. May 3, 1945, East Providence, RI), player, coach, and manager, is the son of James Lopes and Mary (Rose) Lopes. At Iowa Wesleyan College in Mt. Pleasant, IA, he was named an NAIA All-American in baseball. Lopes transferred to Washburn University in Topeka, KS, where he received his bachelor's degree in education in 1969.

Lopes refused a $5,000 bonus from the San Francisco Giants (NL) in 1967 and signed with the Los Angeles Dodgers (NL) in 1968, only one semester shy of graduation. The 5-foot 9-inch, 170-pound Lopes, who threw and batted right-handed, played two partial seasons at Class A Daytona, FL (FSL). He was promoted to Triple A Spokane, WA (PCL) by manager Tom Lasorda,* who converted him from an outfielder to second baseman.

In 1973 the speedy Lopes joined the major leagues' longest continuously intact infield, which included Steve Garvey,* Bill Russell,* and Ron Cey.* Lopes tied a 70-year-old NL record when he stole five bases in a game in 1974. He established a major league record for most consecutive stolen bases in a season (38) in 1975 and led the NL in steals with 77 in 1975 and 63 in 1976. He was selected to play in four All-Star Games, receiving the most fan votes for second basemen in 1980.

With the Dodgers, Lopes appeared in the NL West Division Series in 1981 and NL Championship and World Series in 1974, 1977, 1978, and 1981. He established records for total NL Championship Series stolen bases (9), including most steals in a five-game NL Championship Series (5) in 1981. His World Series records include most chances accepted (40) and most putouts (26) by a second baseman and most stolen bases in a six-game Series (4) in 1981. His record of 10 postseason steals that year stood until Rickey Henderson's* 11 stolen bases in 1989.

In February 1982, Los Angeles traded Lopes to the Oakland Athletics (AL). He returned to the NL with the Chicago Cubs in August 1984 and played parts of three seasons in Chicago before being dealt to the Houston Astros (NL) in July 1986. He appeared in the 1984 NL Championship Series with Chicago and the 1986 NL Championship Series with Houston to tie the NL record for appearances with the most clubs (3).

Houston released Lopes in 1987. He completed a 16-year major league career with 557 stolen bases, ranking 22nd on the all-time list. Lopes compiled a .263 batting average with 232 doubles, 155 HR, and 614 RBI. He coached for the Texas Rangers (AL) from 1988 through 1991 and the Baltimore Orioles (AL) from 1992 through 1994. From 1995 to 1999, he coached for the San Diego Padres (NL). The Milwaukee Brewers named him manager in November 1999. He and his wife, Linda, have one daughter, Vanessa.

BIBLIOGRAPHY: Davey Lopes file, National Baseball Library, Cooperstown, NY; *The Baseball Encyclopedia*, 10th ed. (New York, 1996); Eddie Gold and Art Ahrens, *The New Era Cubs, 1941–1985* (Chicago, IL, 1985); Davey Lopes, "The Game I'll Never Forget," *BD* 41 (April 1982), pp. 57–60; Joe McDonnell, "Davey Lopes: Captain of the Dodgers," *Sepia* 28 (September 1978), pp. 22–28; Lawrence S. Ritter and Donald Honig, *The Image of Their Greatness* (New York, 1979); Dick Schaap, "The Unlikely Key to the Dodgers—Davey Lopes," *Sport* 65 (August 1977), pp. 80–92; John Thorn, et al., eds., *Total Baseball*, 5th ed. (New York, 1997); *TSN Official Baseball Register, 1987*; *WWA*, 42nd ed., 1982–1983; William F. McNeil, *The Dodgers Encyclopedia* (Champaign, IL, 1997); Tommy Lasorda and David Fisher, *The Artful Dodgers* (New York, 1985).

Gaymon L. Bennett

LOPEZ, Alfonso Ramon "Señor" (b. August 20, 1908, Tampa, FL), player and manager, is the son of Modesto Lopez and Faustina Lopez, who emigrated from Madrid, Spain to work in the cigar trade. Lopez attended high school in Tampa and at age 16 became a schoolboy celebrity by being selected to catch Walter Johnson* in an exhibition game. Lopez began his professional baseball career with Tampa, FL (FSL) from 1925 to 1926, Jacksonville, FL (SEL) in 1927, and Macon, GA (SAL) in 1928. He joined the Brooklyn Dodgers (NL) for three games in 1928, but was sent to Atlanta, GA (SA) in 1929. For the next six years, the 5-foot 11½-inch, 165-pound, slightly built right-hander caught in at least 111 games for the Dodgers. Although not a power hitter, Lopez hit above .300 twice. He was traded to the Boston Braves (NL) in December 1935, Pittsburgh Pirates (NL) in June 1940, and Cleveland Indians (AL) in December 1946. In 19 major league seasons, Lopez played in 1,950 games and collected 1,547 hits, including 206 doubles, 42 triples, and 51 HR. He compiled a .261 lifetime batting average, with 613 runs scored and 652 RBI. Lopez held the major league record for most games caught during his career (1,918) and the NL record for most games caught (1,861). He tied the NL record for fewest passed balls in one season (none in 1941); shared the NL record of most years catching at least 100 games (12); and caught at least 100 games eight consecutive seasons.

Lopez began his managerial career with Indianapolis IN (AA) from 1948 to 1950, winning 278 of 460 games. Indianapolis fielded a pennant winner his first season and made two second place finishes. In 1951, Lopez moved to the Cleveland Indians as manager and produced an AL champion three years later. The 1954 Indians compiled 111 victories (AL record) and were rated heavy favorites in the World Series, but lost to the New York Giants in four games. After moving to Chicago (AL) in 1957, Lopez two years later led the White Sox to their first AL title since 1919. Chicago, however, lost the World Series to the Los Angeles Dodgers in six games. Lopez exhibited skill in handling teams with limited talent, as his clubs consistently wielded the best AL pitching. In 15 full seasons as manager, Lopez saw his team finish either first or second 12 times. Health problems forced Lopez to retire after the 1965 season, but he returned as White Sox manager for brief periods in 1968 and 1969. In 17 major league seasons, his teams won 1,410 games and lost only 1,004 contests. Lopez married Evelyn Kearney on October 7, 1939 and had one son, Alfonso Ramon, Jr. Lopez was elected to the National Baseball Hall of Fame in 1977 and remains the oldest living member.

BIBLIOGRAPHY: *CB* (1960), pp. 241–242; Bob Vanderberg, *Sox: From Lane and Fain to Zisk and Fisk* (Chicago, IL, 1982); Al Lopez file, National Baseball Library, Cooperstown, NY; Donald Honig, *The Man in the Dugout* (Lincoln, NE, 1995); Frank Graham, *The Brooklyn Dodgers* (New York, 1945); Richard Goldstein, *Superstars and Screwballs* (New York, 1991); Harold Kaese, *The Boston Braves* (New York, 1948); Gene Karst and Martin J. Jones, Jr., *Who's Who in Professional Baseball* (New Rochelle, NY, 1973); Leonard Koppett, *The Man in the Dugout* (New York, 1993); Lowell Reidenbaugh, *Baseball's Hall of Fame-Cooperstown* (New York, 1993); Frederick G. Lieb, *The Pittsburgh Pirates* (New York, 1948); John Thorn et al., eds., *Total Indians* (New York, 1996); Thomas Aylesworth and Benton Minks, *The Encyclopedia of Baseball Managers* (New York, 1990); Charles Wesley Singletary, "Senor: The Life of Al Lopez," M.A. Thesis, Florida State University, n.d.; Rich Westcott, *Diamond Greats* (Westport, CT, 1988); Jack Torry, *Endless Summers* (South Bend, IN, 1995); Bruce Dudley, *Bittersweet Season* (Annapolis, MD, 1995); David Condon, *The Go to Chicago White Sox* (New York, 1960); Richard Lindberg, *Who's on Third?* (South Bend, IN, 1983); John Phillips, *Winners* (Cabin John, MD, 1987).

John L. Evers

LOWE, Robert Lincoln "Bobby," "Link" (b. July 10, 1868, Pittsburgh, PA; d. December 8, 1951, Detroit, MI), player and manager, was a trained machinist and played weekend semiprofessional baseball until turning professional with Eau Claire, WI (NWL) in 1887. He moved up to Milwaukee, WI (WL) and was acquired by the Boston Beaneaters (NL) in 1890 for $700 at the urging of new manager Frank Selee.*

Lowe became the first major-leaguer to hit four HR in one game. At Boston in the second game of a twin bill on Memorial Day 1894, he cleared the left-field fence in four consecutive at-bats. The Beaneaters defeated Elton "Icebox" Chamberlain* of the Cincinnati Reds, 20–11. Lowe's feat so delighted the spectators that he was showered with $160 in coins as he circled the bases. A late-inning single gave him a fifth hit in six tries.

Nicknamed "Bobby" by the fans and "Link" by teammates, the 5-foot 10-inch 150-pound right-handed batter played all outfield and infield positions and even pitched an inning. He settled at second base in 1893, combining with Fred Tenney,* Herman Long,* and Jimmy Collins* from 1897 through 1900 in what many consider to be the 19th century's finest infield.

Although a leadoff man with only fair power, Lowe once made four singles, a double, and a HR in six at-bats. In his best year (1894), he made 212 hits and scored 158 runs. His 17 HR trailed NL-leading Hugh Duffy* of the Boston Beaneaters by only one. Over 18 major league seasons, Lowe hit a modest 71 HR and batted .273. His greatest defensive achievement was developing with Tenney the first base-to-second base-to-first base double play.

Lowe, Long, and Kid Nichols* played on all five of Selee's Boston NL pennant winners in the 1890s. When Selee moved to the Chicago Cubs (NL) as manager in 1902, Lowe accompanied him. He played one game for the Pittsburgh Pirates (NL) in April 1904 before being sold to the Detroit Tigers (AL). He served a utility role in Detroit and piloted the Tigers to a 30–44 mark for half the 1907 season. Lowe never made more than $3,000 a year. Subsequently, he spent many years with the Detroit Department of Public Works.

BIBLIOGRAPHY: *The Baseball Encyclopedia*, 10th ed. (New York, 1996); Harold Kaese, *The Boston Braves* (New York, 1948); Bobby Lowe file, National Baseball Library, Cooperstown, NY; Robert L. Tiemann and Mark Rucker, eds., *Nineteenth Century Stars* (Kansas City, MO, 1989); John Thorn et al., eds., *Total Braves* (New York, 1996); Gary Caruso, *The Braves Encyclopedia* (Philadelphia, PA, 1995); Eddie Gold and Art Ahrens, *The Golden Era Cubs, 1876–1940* (Chicago, IL, 1985).

A. D. Suehsdorf

LUCAS, Charles Fred "Red" (b. April 28, 1902, Columbia, TN; d. July 9, 1986, Englewood, TN), player, coach, and manager, was the son of farmers Washington Lucas and Ella (Dawson) Lucas. The Lucas family moved to Nashville, TN during World War I so that Washington could work in a gun powder factory. The young redheaded Lucas began his baseball career as a hurler in the low minor leagues in 1920 and moved up to Nashville, TN (SA) at the end of the 1921 season. He won 20 games there in 1922 and debuted with the New York Giants (NL) in 1923. The 5-foot 9-inch,

170-pounder threw right-handed, but batted left-handed. His productive hitting caused much indecision about his future role. He was sent to San Antonio, TX (TL) for most of the 1923 season and was then sold to the Boston Braves (NL), who used him as a relief hurler and reserve infielder in 1924. Seattle, WA (PCL) employed him in this capacity in 1925 and found him an able pinch hitter. On October 18, 1925, he played all nine positions without error and hit a HR and single in a 2–0 victory over Portland, OR.

Despite his versatility, Lucas insisted he was a pitcher. The Cincinnati Reds (NL) gave him that opportunity in 1926. The next year, he won 18 games for the seventh-place club. He became a reliable starter, pitching 27 consecutive complete games from August 13, 1931 to July 15, 1932. He performed well in extra-inning games, defeating the St. Louis Cardinals, 5–4, in 17 innings on April 25, 1928 and outdueling Roy Parmelee of the New York Giants, 1–0, in 15 innings on July 16, 1933. He led the NL for three seasons in complete games (1929, 1931–1932) and finished 68 percent of his 301 career starts. His complete games resulted largely from his precise control and hitting ability. In 1931, he walked only 39 batters in 238 innings. During his career, he averaged 1.61 walks per game to rank him among the all-time leaders. He enjoyed a lifetime .281 batting average and was used extensively as a pinch hitter. He led the NL in pinch hits for four seasons and concluded his career in 1938 with 114 pinch hits in 437 at-bats. This record, a remarkable achievement for a hurler, was not approached by any player for another generation.

His effective hitting nor pitching elevated his club very high in the standings, as the Reds finished seventh four times and last three times. Cincinnati dealt Lucas to the Pittsburgh Pirates (NL) in November 1933. Three years later, Lucas compiled a 15–4 mark with the fourth-place Pirates. His career resulted in a 157–135 win–loss mark, 79 points higher than his team's win–loss percentage. His career 3.72 ERA came in a heavy-hitting era.

From 1939 to 1949, he played, coached, or managed in the minor leagues. He kept up his remarkable pinch hitting at age 43, collecting 16 hits and 10 walks in 46 plate appearances for Nashville, TN (SA) in 1945. He worked from 1953 to 1977 in Nashville as a deputy sheriff and as a truck inspector. He and his wife, Ruth (Jackson) Lucas, who died in 1977, had two sons and one daughter, all college-educated.

BIBLIOGRAPHY: Frank Graham, "Red Lucas Arrives at Last," *BM* 52 (February 1934), pp. 403–404; Red Lucas file, National Baseball Library, Cooperstown, NY; Nashville (TN) *Banner*, July 10, 1986; Allen H. Quimby, "An Afternoon with Red Lucas," *BRJ* 10 (1980), pp. 28–33; Bob Rathgeber, *Cincinnati Reds Scrapbook* (Virginia Beach, VA, 1982); Lee Allen, *The Cincinnati Reds* (New York, 1948); Donald Honig, *The Cincinnati Reds* (New York, 1992); Frederick G. Lieb, *The Pittsburgh Pirates* (New York, 1948).

L. Robert Davids

LUCAS, Henry Van Noye (b. September 5, 1857, St. Louis, MO; d. November 15, 1910, St. Louis, MO), owner and executive, was a St. Louis businessman and avid baseball enthusiast. He used a million-dollar inheritance from his father, James H. Lucas, to buy his own team and essentially his own league. After being denied an NL franchise, he organized the UA. The UA competed on a major league level with the NL and the AA in 1884. Lucas was elected UA president because of his baseball and business knowledge and personal wealth, being the fledgling league's driving force and its principal source of enthusiasm, ideas, and capital. He once declared, "I am the Union Association." Many players jumped to the UA from the other leagues, as Lucas made public his disdain for the reserve rule. The UA promised a newer, more exciting, and high-scoring game because of a lively ball.

Lucas owned the St. Louis Maroons (UA) franchise, resplendent in their silk stockings and lamb's wool sweaters, and built for them a spectacular park on his suburban estate. The Palace Park of America seated 10,000 spectators and contained many features, including caged canaries. The St. Louis Maroons made a shambles of the UA pennant race with a 94–19 win–loss mark, the all-time best major league record. But his team's enormous success helped kill spectator interest in the UA, which folded after only one season. Lucas lost more than $250,000 in the venture.

In exchange for dropping the UA and reversing his stance on the reserve rule, Lucas was granted an NL franchise for the St. Louis Maroons in 1885. The St. Louis Maroons finished in last place in 1885, however, and improved only to sixth place in 1886. The St. Louis Maroons could not compete with the crosstown St. Louis Browns (AA), who sold beer, played on Sundays, halved ticket prices, and won AA pennants both years.

Lucas left baseball permanently after the 1886 season, his NL experience having cost him over $100,000 in losses. Soon he suffered more business failures and saw his entire fortune disappear. After separating from his wife, Louise (Espenscheid) Lucas, he worked as a railway clerk and later tried other unsuccessful ventures. Upon his death, he was earning only $75 a month as an employee of the St. Louis Street Department.

BIBLIOGRAPHY: Henry Lucas file, National Baseball Library, Cooperstown, NY; Charles C. Alexander, *Our Game* (New York, 1991); *The Baseball Encyclopedia*, 10th ed. (New York, 1996); Harvey Frommer, *Primitive Baseball* (New York, 1988); David Pietrusza, *Major Leagues* (Jefferson, NC, 1991); *SpL*, November 26, 1910; Robert L. Tiemann and Mark Rucker, eds., *Nineteenth Century Stars* (Kansas City, MO, 1989); David Quentin Voigt, *American Baseball*, vol. 1 (Norman, OK, 1966).

John R. Husman

LUCIANO, Ronald Michael "Ron" (b. June 28, 1937, Endicott, NY; d. January 18, 1995, Endicott, NY), umpire, was the son of Perry Luciano and Josephine Luciano, Italian immigrants. Luciano's father, who owned a bar and grill, died when his son was only 11 years old.

A 1954 graduate of Union-Endicott High School, Luciano received a Bachelor's degree in mathematics from Syracuse University and played tackle on the football team. Luciano, who played in the 1957 Cotton and 1959 Orange Bowls, was named All-America in 1958 and selected as an offensive tackle in the second round of the 1959 NFL draft by the Baltimore Colts. The Baltimore Colts immediately traded him to the Detroit Lions, (NFL) but a shoulder injury suffered in the college All-Star game that August prevented him from ever playing with them. He played two games in 1961 with the Buffalo Bills (AFL) before a knee injury ended his football career. Luciano, who became a junior high school math teacher after earning a Master's degree in education administration from Syracuse, attended the Al Somers Umpire School in 1964 and began his professional umpiring career in the Class A FSL. He advanced to the Class AA EL in 1965 and to the Class AAA IL in 1966.

After being promoted to the AL in September 1968, Luciano umpired 11 full AL seasons, handled 3 AL Championship Series (1971, 1975, 1978), and received one All-Star Game (1973) and World Series (1974) assignment. In contrast to the traditional conservative demeanor of umpires, the extroverted Luciano exhibited a flamboyant style. Some considered his style "colorful showmanship," while others considered it disgraceful clowning. His antics included signaling an "out" by forming a "gun" with his fingers and shooting the runner "dead" and gesturing repeatedly or "dancing" to emphasize a close call. Despite legendary verbal confrontations between the 6-foot 4-inch, 280-pound Luciano and the diminutive 5-foot 5-inch Baltimore Orioles manager Earl Weaver,* a notorious umpire-baiter, the controversial umpire's irrepressible good humor and engaging personality made him extremely popular with players, fans, and the press.

Luciano, who had been reelected to a second term as president of MLUA, resigned just prior to the 1980 season and served as a commentator for NBC baseball telecasts for two years. A popular speaker on the banquet circuit, he co-authored four best-selling autobiographical books that featured humorous anecdotes about players, managers, and umpires.

Luciano married Polly Dixon, a flight attendant, in 1975. They divorced two years later and had no children. Luciano became increasingly depressed when his mother, institutionalized in a nursing home with Alzheimer's disease in 1990, ceased to recognize him. He committed suicide by means of carbon monoxide poisoning.

BIBLIOGRAPHY: Ron Luciano file, National Baseball Library, Cooperstown, NY; "Interview: Ron Luciano," *Referee* 1 (September–October 1976), pp. 7–12; Ron Luciano and David Fisher, *The Umpire Strikes Back* (New York, 1982), *Strike Two* (New York, 1984), *The Fall of the Roman Umpire* (New York, 1986), and *Remembrance of Swings Past* (New York, 1988); *NYT*, February 25, 1979, January 20, 1995, p. B7; Binghamton (NY) *Press & Sun-Bulletin*, January 19–23, 1995.

                                                            Larry R. Gerlach

LUDERUS, Frederick William "Fred," "Ludy" (b. September 12, 1885, Milwaukee, WI; d. January 5, 1961, Three Lakes, WI), player and manager, was the youngest of five children of Peter Luderus, a laborer, and Johanna (Bliese) Luderus. Luderus, who batted left-handed but threw right-handed, played four years of minor league baseball. The Chicago Cubs (NL) bought him for $2,200 in 1909 after he led the WIL with a .321 batting average for cellar-dwelling Freeport, IL. Luderus replaced ailing first baseman Frank Chance* for a few games, but the Chicago Cubs traded him to the Philadelphia Phillies (NL) in July 1910 for Bill Foxen, a journeyman pitcher.

In 1911, Philadelphia Phillies manager Red Dooin replaced the elegant, aging Kitty Bransfield at first base with the burly 5-foot 11½-inch, 185-pound Luderus, who batted .301 with 16 HR, 99 RBI, and 260 total bases. Through 1919, Luderus proved a consistent, reliable, yet underrated performer. Teammate Gavvy Cravath* overshadowed him as a hitter, while pitchers believed Luderus could not hit curveballs. Luderus, slow afield and on the bases, never led the NL league statistically in anything. Yet his impressive HR production included 16 in 1911, the NL's second-best total, and 18 in 1913, trailing Cravath by one. His 56 HR between 1911 and 1914 marked the most ever in a four-year span to that time. Luderus, the first player to blast two HR over the Baker Bowl fence in one game, was never lifted for a pinch hitter in a 1,346-game career.

In 1915, Luderus was named team captain and enjoyed his best season at the plate, hitting a career-high .315 to help the Philadelphia Phillies win its first NL pennant and becoming the only Phillie able to solve Boston Red Sox pitching in the losing World Series. He pounded the ball for a .438 batting average and batted in six of Philadelphia's 10 runs. In 12 major league seasons, he batted .277, with 251 doubles, 84 HR, and 642 RBI. Although leading NL first basemen in errors four times, he compiled a respectable .986 lifetime fielding average and tied a major league record with seven assists in one game. Luderus, an "Iron Man," played 533 consecutive games between 1915 and 1919 to set a then-major league record.

After the Philadelphia Phillies released him in 1920, Luderus signed with Toledo, OH (AA) and began a successful eight-year career as a minor league playing manager. He and his wife, Emmy, had five children. He rebuilt his Three Lakes, WI home with the help of architect Fred "Cy" Williams,* the longtime NL outfielder, Philadelphia Phillie teammate, and neighbor.

BIBLIOGRAPHY: *The Baseball Encyclopedia*, 10th ed. (New York, 1996); J. C. Kofoed, "A Much Underrated Star," *BM* 11 (July 1915), pp. 33–36; Fred Luderus file, National Baseball Library, Cooperstown, NY; *NYT*, January 6, 1961; *Phillies Report*, August 16, 1990; *TSN*, n.d., 1947; Frederick G. Lieb and Stan Baumgartner, *The Philadelphia Phillies* (New York, 1953); Allen Lewis, *The Philadelphia Phillies: A Pictorial History* (Virginia Beach, VA, 1981); Rich Westcott and Frank Bilovsky, *The New Phillies Encyclopedia* (Philadelphia, PA, 1993).

                                                              A. D. Suehsdorf

LUNDGREN, Carl Leonard "Lundy" (b. February 16, 1880, Marengo, IL; d. August 21, 1934, Marengo, IL), player, coach, and executive, was the son of Pear Hjalmar Lundgren, a painter born in Sweden, and Dililah (Renwick) Lundgren. Lundgren spent most of his life associated with his native state. After growing up in Marengo, he starred in athletics for the University of Illinois and pitched his entire major league career from 1902 through 1909 with the Chicago Cubs (NL). Lundgren married Maud Cohoon in September 1904.

At the University of Illinois, Lundgren starred in football at halfback for three years. He also served as the baseball team's captain and leading pitcher, during the 1902 season. After graduating from the University of Illinois in 1902, he finished 9–9 with a 1.97 ERA for the Chicago Cubs and completed 17 of his 18 starts. During his eight-year major league career through 1909, Lundgren compiled a 91–55 overall record and 2.42 ERA. His best seasons came in 1906 and 1907, when he hurled 17–6 and 18–7 marks for the NL pennant winners. He slumped to a 6–9 record, however, during their third consecutive NL pennant-winning season in 1908. His 1.17 ERA in 1907 ranked second in the NL to teammate Jack Pfiester's* 1.15 ERA.

The 5-foot 11-inch, 175-pound Lundgren threw and batted right-handed. The *Reach Baseball Guide* once termed him "the best cold-weather pitcher in the profession," while another report called him "the cool Lundy." Despite his outstanding records in 1906 and 1907, he never pitched in a World Series game. Chicago manager Frank Chance* used only Mordecai Three Finger Brown,* Orval Overall,* Jack Pfiester, and Ed Reulbach* in Chicago's three World Series appearances. The 1908 *Guide* called Lundgren a star pitcher who was held back for an emergency which never came.

Lundgren pitched in only two games in 1909 before Chicago optioned him to Toronto, Canada (IL). He refused to go and played semiprofessional baseball in Chicago. Lundgren reported to Toronto in 1910, but was transferred to Hartford, CT (VaL). He moved in 1911 to Troy, NY (NYSL) which released him in 1912. Lundgren coached baseball at the University of Michigan (BTC) until 1921 and then returned to the University of Illinois, where he served as baseball coach and assistant athletic director until his death.

BIBLIOGRAPHY: Carl Lundgren file, National Baseball Library, Cooperstown, NY; Warren Brown, *The Chicago Cubs* (New York, 1946); Eddie Gold and Art Ahrens, *The Golden Era Cubs, 1876–1940* (Chicago, IL, 1985); Warren Wilbert and William Hageman, *The Chicago Cubs: Seasons at the Summit* (Champaign, IL, 1997); *Reach Baseball Guide*, 1908; *Spalding Official Base Ball Guide*, 1909.

Michael J. McBride

LUNDY, Richard "Dick," "King Richard" (b. July 10, 1898, Jacksonville, FL; d. January 5, 1965, Jacksonville, FL), player, coach, and manager, generally was acclaimed the outstanding Negro baseball league shortstop during the

1920s. He attended Florida Baptist Academy and played baseball at Cook-
man Institute. His baseball career began with his hometown Jacksonville
Duval Giants as a third baseman. He remained with them when they moved
north to become the Atlantic City, NJ Bacharach Giants in 1916. Lundy
then spent the following two seasons in Philadelphia with Ed Bolden's Hilldale Daisies and split 1919 between Atlantic City and the Hilldales. This
same year, the Bacharach Giants divided into two teams and based the second squad in New York City. In 1920 Lundy signed contracts with all three
teams, but a Philadelphia court eventually awarded him to the New York
Bacharachs.

In 1921 Lundy returned to the Atlantic City Bacharach Giants (ECL) and
remained there through 1928. He spent 1929 through 1932 with the Baltimore Black Sox (ANL), moved to the Philadelphia Stars (NNL) for 1933,
and performed with the Newark, NJ Dodgers (NNL) in 1934 and New York
Cubans (NNL) in 1935. He played in 1937 with the Newark, NJ Eagles
(NNL) and then coached and managed them through 1948. The switch-
hitting, 5-foot 10-inch, 180-pound Lundy exhibited a smooth, graceful style
of play that resulted in his sobriquet of "King Richard." Offensively, he
proved an excellent hitter and base runner with good power. Defensively,
he possessed sure hands, wide range, and a strong arm. Available statistics
place his Negro League career batting average around .330. He hit .289 in
Black World Series competition (.325 in 1926 and .250 in 1927) and produced a .341 mark in eight CUWL seasons. Against white major league
competition, he batted .344.

The soft-spoken Lundy, a natural leader, served as Atlantic City manager
from 1925 through 1928. He led the Bacharach Giants to ECL titles in 1926
and 1927, but lost both years to manager Dave Malarcher's* Chicago American Giants in the Black World Series. Lundy also piloted the Philadelphia
Stars, Newark Dodgers, Newark Eagles and New York Black Yankees. As
shortstop of the celebrated 1929 Baltimore infield featuring Jud Wilson* at
first, manager Frank Warfield* at second, and Oliver Marcelle* at third, he
helped the Black Sox capture the ANL crown. In 1933 and 1934, Lundy
was selected starting East shortstop for the first two East-West (Negro
Leagues) All-Star Games and went hitless in seven at-bats.

Although only his father's surname is known, he was the son of Millie
Ann (La Gere) Lundy. He died from a lingering illness and was survived by
his wife, Elese, five daughters, Linda, Sandra, Millie, Barbara, and Elaine,
and five sons, Richard Jr., Arnold, Ronald, Maurice, and Frank. He also
spent several years as a red cap at the Jacksonville, FL Terminal Station.

BIBLIOGRAPHY: Atlantic City (NJ) *Press*, October 1–2, 5–7, 9, 11–12, 14–15, 1926;
Baltimore (MD) *Sun*, August 28, 1977; Chicago (IL) *Defender*, October 9, 16, 23,
1926, October 8, 15, 22, 1927; Florida *Times Union*, January 7, 1962; John Holway,
"Baltimore's Great Black Team," Baltimore (MD) *Sun*, 1977; John B. Holway, *Blackball Stars* (Westport, CT, 1988); Robert W. Peterson, *Only the Ball Was White* (En-

glewood Cliffs, NJ, 1970); Pittsburgh (PA) *Courier*, October 8, 15, 1927; James A. Riley, *The All-Time All-Stars of Black Baseball* (Cocoa, FL, 1983); James A. Riley, *The Biographical Encyclopedia of the Negro Baseball Leagues* (New York, 1994); James Overmyer, *Effa Manley and the Newark Eagles* (Metuchen, NJ, 1993).

Merl F. Kleinknecht

LUQUE, Adolfo "Dolf" "The Pride of Havana" (b. August 4, 1890, Havana, Cuba; d. July 3, 1957, Havana, Cuba), player and coach, was the first Latin American–born ballplayer to appear in a World Series game. He hurled five scoreless relief innings for the Cincinnati Reds (NL) against the Chicago White Sox in the scandal-ridden 1919 World Series. Luque spoke only hesitant English and kept largely to himself during most of his career, causing the public to perceive him as a hot-tempered, moody foreigner. Luque once tired of taking verbal abuse from the opposing New York Giants (NL) bench during a 1922 outing at Cincinnati's Redlands Field. Suddenly he placed both glove and ball on the mound, charged directly to the New York dugout, and slugged the apparent perpetrator, Casey Stengel,* squarely in the mouth.

One of the first in a long line of successful Cuban major league athletes, Luque debuted in organized baseball in the United States in 1912 with Long Branch, NJ (NYNJL) and compiled a superlative 22–5 mark there in 1913. After making four brief winless appearances with the Boston Braves (NL) the next two seasons, the diminutive Cuban right-hander joined the Cincinnati Reds permanently in 1918 (6–3, 3.80 ERA) and compiled a 154–152 mark during the next dozen summers there. Luque's one truly spectacular season came in the 1923 campaign, with a 27–8 mark for the second place Reds. Luque led the Senior Circuit in games won (27), winning percentage (.771), shutouts (6), and ERA (1.93), and finished second to Burleigh Grimes* of the Brooklyn Robins (NL) in total innings pitched. This marked his only 20-game victory season, ironically coming after he had paced the NL the previous year in losses (23). The fiery Cuban boasted ten consecutive summers with 10 wins or more and enjoyed an additional double-figure victory campaign with the Brooklyn Robins (NL) in 1930. He led the NL in shutouts (3) in 1921 and in ERA (2.63) in 1925 and triumphed in the final game of the 1933 World Series for the Giants in relief over the Washington Senators. Luque completed his 20-year career in a short stint as a New York Giants' (NL) reliever from 1932 to 1935. He ranks high on the all-time victory list among Latin American hurlers with a 194–179 mark, trailing Dennis Martinez,* Juan Marichal,* and Luis Tiant* among others. He remains one of only four Caribbean-born pitchers to hurl 3,000 major league innings (3,220.1) and lost more major league games than any other pitcher of Latin American birthright except Martinez. Luque, who compiled a lifetime 3.24 ERA and hurled 26 shutouts, coached for the New York Giants from 1936 to 1938 and from 1941 to 1945. He also served regularly as a winter league manager in Mexico and his native Cuba for three decades from the 1930s to the 1950s, developing such future major league stars as New York Giants and Brooklyn Dodgers (NL) pitching ace Sal Maglie* and Cleveland Indians (AL) infielder Bobby Avila.* (In 1945 Avila became the first Latin American to win a major league batting title.) Luque remained an active pitcher in Cuba, recording his final CUWL game at the remarkable age of 56 in 1946.

BIBLIOGRAPHY: Dolf Luque file, National Baseball Library, Cooperstown, NY; Peter Williams, *When the Giants Were Giants* (Chapel Hill, NC, 1994); Fred Stein, *Under Coogan's Bluff* (Glenshaw, PA, 1978); Peter C. Bjarkman, *Baseball with a Latin Beat* (Jefferson, NC, 1994); Peter C. Bjarkman, "Dolf Luque: Latin America's Quiet Baseball Hero," *BRJ* 19 (1990), pp. 28–32; Peter C. Bjarkman, "Dodgers with a Latin Beat," *DM* 34 (July 1990); Ira L. Smith, *Baseball's Famous Pitchers* (New York, 1954); Bob Rathgeber, *Cincinnati Reds Scrapbook* (Virginia Beach, VA, 1982); Lee Allen, *The Cincinnati Reds* (New York, 1948); Donald Honig, *The Cincinnati Reds* (New York, 1992); Frank Graham, *The New York Giants* (New York, 1952); Noel Hynd, *The Giants of the Polo Grounds* (New York, 1988).

Peter C. Bjarkman

LUZINSKI, Gregory Michael "The Bull" (b. November 22, 1950, Chicago, IL), player and coach, excelled as a right-handed, power-hitting outfielder for the Philadelphia Phillies (NL) from 1971 to 1980 and DH for the Chicago White Sox (AL) from 1981 to 1984. His brothers, Richard and William, also played professional baseball. The highly sought after athlete from Notre Dame High School in Niles, IL was signed as the Philadelphia Phillies' first selection in the June 1968 draft. In four minor league seasons with Huron, MI (NoL), Raleigh-Durham, NC (CrL), Reading, PA (EL), and Eugene, OR (PCL), he hit 113 HR and belted at least 30 HR in three straight years. After a brief major league trial in September 1971, Luzinski became the Philadelphia Phillies' regular left fielder in 1972 and held that position until being traded to the Chicago White Sox in March 1981.

Luzinski enjoyed his best years with the Philadelphia Phillies and drove in 100 runs four times. He produced an NL-leading 120 RBI in 1977, a year in which he finished second to George Foster* for the MVP award. Luzinski hit 30 or more HR four times, three times with the Phillies. His career high 39 HR came in 1977. Luzinski, who also hit over .300 for three consecutive years from 1975 to 1977, achieved fame for his mammoth HR and his clutch hitting. His HR off the Liberty Bell ornament on the third level of Veterans Stadium in Philadelphia remains one of the longest HR in Phillie history. In 16 NL Championship Series games for the Phillies, Luzinski hit .310 and slugged 5 HR. During the late 1970s, leg problems began troubling the 6-foot 1-inch, 240 pounder. His power productivity for the Phillies declined in 1979, while his mediocre fielding became a liability.

With the Chicago White Sox from 1981 through 1984, Luzinski's career revived as a DH. His best seasons in Chicago came in 1982 and 1983, when he drove in a total of 197 runs and clouted 50 HR. He finished his major league career in 1984 with a lifetime .276 batting average, 1,795 hits, 1,128 RBI, and 307 HR.

From 1986 through 1992, Luzinski coached freshman baseball at Holy Cross High School in Delran, NJ, and coached varsity baseball and football there in 1994. He coached for the Oakland A's (AL) in 1993 and Kansas City Royals (AL) from 1995 through 1997. He and his wife, Jean, live in Medford, NJ, and have two children, Kimberley Ann and Ryan. Following in his father's footsteps, Ryan is regarded highly as a baseball prospect.

BIBLIOGRAPHY: Greg Luzinski file, National Baseball Library, Cooperstown, NY; *The Baseball Encyclopedia*, 10th ed. (New York, 1996); Rich Westcott and Frank Bilovsky, *The New Phillies Encyclopedia* (Philadelphia, PA, 1993); Rich Marazzi, "Shooting the Bull with the Bull," *SCD* 23 (June 28, 1996), pp. 90–91; Allen Lewis, *The Philadelphia Phillies: A Pictorial History* (Virginia Beach, VA, 1981); Richard Lindberg, *Who's on Third?* (South Bend, IN, 1983); Bob Logan, *Miracle on 35th Street* (South Bend, IN, 1983); John Thorn et al., eds. *Total Baseball*, 5th ed. (New York, 1997).

John P. Rossi

LYLE, Albert Walker "Sparky" (b. July 22, 1944, DuBois, PA), player and manager, ranked among modern baseball's premier relief pitchers and is the son of building contractor Albert Lyle and Margaret Lyle. Nicknamed "Sparky" by his father, Lyle grew up in Reynoldsville, PA and played high school football and basketball there. Lyle played sandlot baseball, pitched for an American Legion team, and worked as a manual laborer after graduating from high school. The left-hander signed with the Baltimore Orioles (AL) in 1964 and pitched for Bluefield, WV (ApL) and Fox Cities, WI (ML) before the Boston Red Sox (AL) drafted him the next year. Lyle pitched for Red Sox farm clubs in Winston-Salem, NC (CrL), Pittsfield, MA (EL), and Toronto, Canada (IL) until joining the parent club during the 1967 AL pennant drive. In his rookie season, he appeared in 27 games with a 2.28 ERA. An arm injury, however, kept him out of the 1967 World Series.

Lyle, famous for his slider and sense of humor, developed the former upon the advice of Ted Williams* and the latter at the expense of his teammates. The slider allowed Lyle to become an effective reliever without having an overpowering fastball. Although the 6-foot 1-inch, 182-pound Lyle experienced modest success in his four and one-half seasons with the Red Sox, he enjoyed his best years following a trade to the New York Yankees (AL) in March 1972. In 1972, he set an AL record with 35 saves and won the Fireman of the Year Award. He also exhibited a zest for clubhouse pranks. Lyle's best years came in 1974, 1976, and 1977. In 1974, he made 66 appearances, compiled a 9–3 mark, saved 15 games, and compiled a 1.66 ERA. Lyle slumped in 1975, but the following year led the AL with 23 saves. In 1977, he made 72 appearances, won 13 and lost five, saved 26 games, and paced the AL with a 2.17 ERA in becoming the first AL relief pitcher to win a Cy

Young Award. Lyle appeared in three AL Championship Series and three World Series with the Yankees from 1976 through 1978.

Lyle played his last season with the Yankees in 1978. After a feud with owner George Steinbrenner* over a lack of playing time, he was traded to the Texas Rangers (AL) in November 1978. Lyle pitched for the Rangers until September 1980, when the Philadelphia Phillies (NL) acquired him. Lyle remained with Philadelphia until sold in August 1982 to the Chicago White Sox (AL). The White Sox released him in October 1982. Lyle married Mary Massey in April 1977 and has three children, Dane (by an earlier marriage), Shane, and Scott. Lyle set records for the most innings pitched by a relief pitcher lifetime (1,390.2), most consecutive relief appearances lifetime (899), and most games by a relief pitcher without a start (899). He concluded his career with 99 wins, 76 losses, 238 saves, and a 2.88 ERA. Lyle manages the New Jersey–based team in the Independent League and works for the MLBAA, making appearances for corporate and business clients whenever he can.

BIBLIOGRAPHY: Rich Westcott and Frank Bilovsky, *The New Phillies Encyclopedia* (Philadelphia, PA, 1993); Dave Anderson et al., *The Yankees* (New York, 1979); Bob Cairns, *Pen Men* (New York, 1993); Robert Redmount, *The Red Sox Encyclopedia* (Champaign, IL, 1997); Ken Coleman and Dan Valenti, *The Impossible Dream Remembered* (Lexington, MA, 1987); Martin Appel, *Yesterday's Heroes* (New York, 1988); Arnold C. Bailey, "Cy Young Winner Lyle Spelled Relief for Yankees," *SCD* 25 (April 3, 1998), pp. 150–151; Sparky Lyle file, National Baseball Library, Cooperstown, NY; *CB* (1978), pp. 261–263; Mark Gallagher, *The Yankee Encyclopedia*, vol. 3 (Champaign, IL, 1997); Peter Golenbock, *Fenway* (New York, 1992); Jack Lautier, *Fenway Voices* (Camden, ME, 1990); Sparky Lyle and Peter Golenbock, *The Bronx Zoo* (New York, 1979); *Philadelphia Phillies Press Guide, 1982; TSN Baseball Register, 1983.*

Eric C. Schneider

LYNCH, Thomas J. "Tom," "King of the Umpires" (b. 1859, New Britain, CT; d. February 27, 1924, New Britain, CT), umpire and executive, was the son of Patrick Lynch, attended local schools, and starred as a catcher in local amateur leagues. He married Minnie Holmes in 1890 and had no children. Lynch umpired in the NL from 1888 to 1899 and officiated the first New York Giants game in 1897. Nicknamed "King of the Umpires" in the 1890s, he often left games when threatened by fans or players and did not appear when dissatisfied with the pay. Above all, he contributed materially to the emergence of professionalism in the umpiring corps.

Lynch then managed the Lyceum Theatre, which he had helped found in New Britain, CT in 1893. He became NL president as a compromise candidate in 1909, when the owners disagreed over John Heydler* as temporary president. A dapper man with bushy mustache, Lynch possessed a brusque manner and a strong personality and provided firm leadership at this critical

juncture of NL history. His personal traits caused difficulties with the owners, especially when he backed umpires in disputes with managers and players. Owners, dissatisfied by four consecutive losses in the World Series by
NL teams, removed him in 1913. Lynch again managed the Lyceum Theatre
and served as a prominent leader in the New Britain arts community until
his death.

BIBLIOGRAPHY: Thomas Lynch file, National Baseball Library, Cooperstown NY;
Gene Karst and Martin J. Jones, Jr., *Who's Who in Professional Baseball* (New Rochelle,
NY, 1973); New Britain (CT) *Herald*, February 27, 1924; *NYT*, December 19, 1909,
November 19, 20, 1913, February 28, 1924; Harold Seymour, *Baseball: The Early
Years* (New York, 1960); Robert Smith, *Baseball* (New York, 1970); Hy Turkin and
S. C. Thompson, *The Official Encyclopedia of Baseball*, 5th rev. ed. (New York, 1970).
                                                                Charles R. Middleton

LYNN, Fredric Michael "Fred" (b. February 3, 1952, Chicago, IL), player, is
the only child of Fredric Lynn and Marie Lynn. He grew up in El Monte,
CA and starred in baseball, basketball, and football at El Monte High School.
Although drafted upon graduation by the New York Yankees (AL) in 1970,
he chose instead an athletic scholarship (football initially, but switched to
baseball) from the University of Southern California. A baseball All-America
selection in 1972 and 1973, the outfielder helped USC to three consecutive
College World Series titles and led the nation's collegians in HR in 1972.

Lynn signed after his junior year with the Boston Red Sox (AL), who
drafted him in the second round in 1973. He played at Bristol, CT (EL) in
1973 and Pawtucket, RI (IL) and for a few games at Boston in 1974. In 1975
Lynn enjoyed perhaps the most extraordinary rookie season in recent baseball history, becoming the only player to win both the AL Rookie of the
Year and MVP Awards the same season. The center fielder in 1975 received
many awards, including a Gold Glove, AP and UPI Athlete of the Year, and
TSN Player of the Year. Besides batting .331, Lynn led the AL in doubles
(47, a record for rookies), slugging (.566, the only time a rookie has accomplished that feat), and runs (103), hit 21 HR, and drove in 105 runs to help
Boston capture the AL pennant.

The 6-foot 1-inch, 185-pound left-hander continued with Boston through
the 1980 season, enjoying probably his best all-around campaign in 1979.
He won the AL batting title (.333), led the AL in slugging percentage (.637),
and achieved personal highs in runs scored (116), hits (177), HR (39), and
RBI (122). Lynn was traded to the California Angels (AL) in January 1981
and played there through 1984. In December 1984, he entered the free agent
draft and signed with the Baltimore Orioles (AL). In August 1988, the Orioles traded him to the Detroit Tigers (AL). His major league career ended
in 1990 with the San Diego Padres (NL).

In 17 major league seasons, Lynn batted .283 in 1,969 games with 1,960
hits, 388 doubles, 306 HR, 1,063 runs scored, and 1,111 RBI. Lynn was

selected for nine All-Star games from 1975 through 1983, batting .300 with four HR and ten RBI. His grand slam HR in the 1983 game, the first ever in All-Star competition, earned him the game MVP Award. Lynn's four HR rank him second to Stan Musial* and tie him with Ted Williams* in All-Star Game history. In 1975 post-season play with the Red Sox, Lynn hit .364 against Oakland in the AL Championship Series and batted .280 with a HR in the 1975 World Series against the Cincinnati Reds. His .611 slugging percentage for California against Milwaukee in the 1982 AL Championship Series stands as the AL playoff record and earned him MVP honors for that series. He hit safely in all eight of his AL Championship Series games.

One of the game's best outfielders, Lynn won four Gold Glove awards and succeeded in 76 percent of his base stealing attempts. His best hitting game of his career perhaps came against the Detroit Tigers on June 18, 1975 when he hit 3 HR, a triple, and a single for 16 total bases and 10 RBI. Lynn married Diane May Minkle in 1974 and has one son, Jason, and one daughter, Jennifer. They reside in Carlsbad, CA. Lynn serves as a color analyst for ESPN.

BIBLIOGRAPHY: *Baltimore Orioles Media Guide, 1985*; John Benson et al., *Baseball's Top 100* (Wilton, CT, 1997); Fred Lynn file, National Baseball Library, Cooperstown, NY; Howard Liss, *The Boston Red Sox* (New York, 1982); Robert Redmount, *The Red Sox Encyclopedia* (Champaign, IL, 1997); Peter Golenbock, *Fenway* (New York, 1992); Peter Gammons, *Beyond the Sixth Game* (Boston, MA, 1985); Dan Shaughnessy, *The Curse of the Bambino* (New York, 1990); Ted Patterson, *The Baltimore Orioles* (Dallas, TX, 1995); Terry Pluto and Jeffrey Newman, *A Baseball Winter* (New York, 1986); Peter Bonventre and Sylvester Monroe, "Classic Rookie," *Newsweek* 86 (July 7, 1975), p. 63; *California Angels Media Guide, 1984*; Peter Gammons, "New Big Socker for the Sox," *SI* 50 (May 7, 1979), pp. 47–48; Vin Gilligan, "The Best Is Yet to Come," *Sport* 68 (November 1979), pp. 91–93ff; Jim Kaplan, "Lynn Had a Grand Time," *SI* 59 (July 18, 1983), pp. 52, 54; Robert E. Kelly, *Baseball's Best* (Jefferson, NC, 1988); Jack Lautier, *Fenway Voices* (Camden, ME, 1990).

Phillip P. Erwin

LYONS, Dennis Patrick Aloysius "Denny" (b. March 12, 1866, Cincinnati, OH; d. January 2, 1929, West Covington, KY), player, ranks third in career batting (.310) among major league third basemen behind Wade Boggs* and Pie Traynor,* and second at his position behind Jerry Denny with 1.56 putouts per game. After spending a season at Columbus, GA (SL) in 1885, the 5-foot 10-inch, 185-pound right-handed Lyons played four games for the Providence Grays (NL). He joined Atlanta, GA (SL) for part of the 1886 campaign before the major league Philadelphia Athletics (AA) purchased his contract.

In his first full major league season, Lyons in 1887 ranked among the AA's top five hitters in most offensive categories and finished third with a career-high .367 batting average. Defensively, his 255 putouts remain a major league record for third basemen. His batting average slipped to .296 in 1888, but rebounded to .329 the next season. Although missing the latter part of the 1890 season with a suspension for drunkenness in late August, Lyons enjoyed his most productive year. He topped the AA in slugging percentage (.531) and on-base average (.461), finished second in batting average (.354), and tied for second in doubles (29) and for third in HR (7). His .909 fielding average led AA third basemen.

The St. Louis Browns (AA) signed him for the 1891 campaign. Lyons batted over .300 for the fourth time with a .315 mark and hit a career-high 11 HR to share second place. However, his drinking continued to be a disruptive influence. The 1892 season found him with the New York Giants (NL), for whom he batted only .257. For the Pittsburgh Pirates (NL) the next season, he raised his batting average to .306 and drove in 105 runs. He batted .323 in a partial season with Pittsburgh in 1894 and missed much of the 1895 campaign with the St. Louis Browns (NL) because of an injured knee. After Pittsburgh signed him in 1896, Lyons batted .307 in 118 games. He batted just .206 in only 37 games the next year, ending his major league career. In 1,121 major league games, Lyons batted .310 and made 1,333 hits, including 244 doubles, 69 triples, and 62 HR.

Lyons concluded his playing career in the minor leagues at Omaha, NE (WL) and St. Joseph, MO (WL) in 1898, Wheeling, WV (ISL) in 1889 and 1900, and Beaumont, TX (STL) in 1903.

BIBLIOGRAPHY: *The Baseball Encyclopedia*, 10th ed. (New York, 1996); Dennis Lyons file, National Baseball Library, Cooperstown, NY; Craig Carter, ed., *TSN Daguerreotypes*, 8th ed. (St. Louis, MO, 1990); John Thorn et al., eds., *Total Baseball*, 5th ed. (New York, 1997); Robert L. Tiemann and Mark Rucker, eds., *Nineteenth Century Stars* (Kansas City, MO, 1989); David Q. Voigt, "Denny Lyons' 52-Game Hitting Streak," *TNP* 13 (1993), pp. 45–49; David Nemec, *The Beer and Whisky League* (New York, 1994); J. Thomas Hetrick, *Chris Von der Ahe and the St. Louis Browns* (Lanham, MD, 1999); Frederick G. Lieb, *The Pittsburgh Pirates* (New York, 1948).

Frederick Ivor-Campbell

LYONS, James "Jimmie" (b. Chicago, IL), player and manager, exhibited incredible speed and proved an all-around baseball performer typifying Rube Foster's* style of play. A good hitter and an expert drag bunter, he utilized his speed at the plate, in the field, and on the bases. He played baseball in Chicago's Church League as a youngster and began his professional career in 1910 with the St. Louis Giants. Lyons in 1911 joined the great New York Lincoln Giants, hitting .452 in limited action as a left fielder for manager John Henry Lloyd's* squad. With Spotswood Poles,* Lyons formed the fastest outfield duo in black baseball history. In an exhibition game against a white all-star team featuring Hall of Fame shortstop Honus Wagner,* the rookie leadoff batter collected two hits against Walter Johnson.* During the

1912 winter season in Cuba, Lyons hit .288. He returned to the St. Louis Giants in 1912 and hit .375 for the eastern champion Brooklyn Royal Giants in 1914. Lyons spent 1916 and early 1917 as center fielder for the St. Louis Giants, but the team dissolved in May. His next tenure came with Charles I. Taylor's* champion Indianapolis ABC's in 1917 and 1918.

During World War I, he performed military duty in France with teammate Dave Malarcher* and played baseball in the Allied Expeditionary Force League in LeMans, France. Ty Cobb's* brother, a teammate, claimed that Lyons played better than Ty. In 1920, Lyons was assigned by Foster to the Detroit Stars to provide better balance for the newly formed NNL. In 1920, Lyons hit .386 and led the NNL with 22 stolen bases in 414 games. Following the 1920 season, Lyons rejoined Malarcher on the Chicago American Giants (NNL) and helped make them the dominant black baseball team of the early 1920s. Lyons' all-around ability and .289 and .249 batting averages contributed to successive American Giants pennants in 1921 and 1922. The American Giants released Lyons at spring training in 1925. Lyons closed out his career in 1932 as manager of the Louisville, KY Black Caps (NSL).

BIBLIOGRAPHY: Robert W. Peterson, *Only the Ball Was White* (Englewood Cliffs, NJ, 1970); James A. Riley, *The All-Time All-Stars of Black Baseball* (Cocoa, FL, 1983); James A. Riley, *Biographical Encyclopedia of the Negro Baseball Leagues* (New York, 1994); Paul Debono, *The Indianapolis ABCs* (Jefferson, NC, 1997); James A. Riley, interviews with former Negro League players, James A. Riley Collection, Cocoa, FL.

                                                                                    James A. Riley

LYONS, Theodore Amar "Ted" (b. December 28, 1900, Lake Charles, LA; d. July 25, 1986, Sulphur, LA), player, manager, coach, and scout, was the son of rancher A. F. Lyons. He grew up in Vinton, LA with two brothers and a sister and played infield for Vinton High School. With plans for law school, he attended Baylor University, made good grades, was elected president of his class, and played on the basketball team. After his baseball coach converted him to a pitcher, Lyons enjoyed exceptional success and abandoned his law plans. On his graduation in 1923, he declined an offer from the Philadelphia Athletics (AL) and signed with Charles Comiskey* (whose AL Chicago White Sox trained in Waco, TX) for $300 a month and a $1,000 bonus. Lyons, who never pitched in the minor leagues, joined the Chicago White Sox in St. Louis, MO and relieved against the St. Louis Browns in the first major league game he ever saw. From 1924 through 1942, he started for the White Sox.

Lyons pitched well for the White Sox, who scarcely contended for the AL pennant and always finished at least eight games out of first place. In his second full year, he in 1925 tied for the AL lead with 21 wins for a fifth place team and lost a no-hitter to the Washington Senators by yielding a ninth-inning, two-out single. In 1926, he accomplished a no-run, no-hit game against the Boston Red Sox. Lyons' greatest season perhaps came in

1927, when he compiled a 22–14 record, completed 30 of 34 starts, led the AL in innings pitched (307.2), and shared first in wins for a fifth place club. His career record included 260 wins, 230 losses, and a 3.67 ERA. Although not famed for strikeouts, he walked only 1,121 men in 4,161 innings. Consequently, he pitched very fast games, one taking only one hour and 18 minutes.

After injuring his arm during spring training in 1931, Lyons lost his fastball and fashioned a second career by perfecting the knuckleball. In 1939, Lyons became a Sunday pitcher for manager Jimmy Dykes* to save his arm and draw crowds. Lyons followed this pattern each year through the 1942 season and curiously compiled his best marks. During his last four full years, Lyons won 52 and lost 30 for a .634 percentage and completed 72 games out of 85 starts. In 1942 at age 41, the right-hander completed every game started (20), won 14, maintained an AL-leading 2.10 ERA and walked only 26 men in 180.1 innings for the sixth place White Sox. After defeating the Chicago Cubs in the City Series, he enlisted in the U.S. Marines and served part of his three years in combat duty in the South Pacific. He won only one of five decisions in 1946 before retiring. The 5 foot 11 inch, 200 pound, switch-hitting Lyons often pinch-hit and ranked among the best fielding pitchers of his era. He made the AL All-Star team in 1939 and was elected to the National Baseball Hall of Fame in 1955. In 1940 Chicago honored him with thousands of dollars in gifts, although the White Sox asked people to give only dimes because of Lyons' popularity with children. Lyons, who never married, managed the Chicago White Sox to a 185–245 mark for three years (1946–1948), coached for the AL Detroit Tigers (1949–1953) and NL Brooklyn Dodgers (1954), and scouted for the White Sox (1955–1966). He retired to manage a Louisiana rice plantation with his sister.

BIBLIOGRAPHY: Richard Lindberg, *Sox* (New York, 1984); Art Berke and Paul Schmitt, *This Date in Chicago White Sox History* (New York, 1982); Ted Lyons file, National Baseball Library, Cooperstown, NY; Lee Allen, *The American League Story* (New York, 1952); Martin Appel and Burt Goldblatt, *Baseball's Best: The Hall of Fame Gallery* (New York, 1977); Warren Brown, *The Chicago White Sox* (New York, 1952); Donald Honig, *Baseball When the Grass Was Real* (New York, 1975); Thomas L. Karnes, "The Sunday Saga of Ted Lyons," *BRJ* 10 (1981), pp. 159–165; Thomas L. Karnes, interviews and correspondence with Dr. Edward Compere, John B. Conlan, Lew Fonseca, Charles J. Grimm, Yosh Kawana, Robert Kennedy, Thornton Lee, and Edward Prell, 1983–1984, Thomas L. Karnes Collection, Round Rock, TX; Richard Lindberg, *Who's On Third?* (South Bend, IN, 1983); *NYT*, July 26, 1986, p. 8; Lowell Reidenbaugh, *Baseball's Hall of Fame—Cooperstown* (New York, 1993); Lyle Spatz, "Ted Lyons, 1942," *TNP* 15 (1995), pp. 129–130.

                                                                    Thomas L. Karnes

M

McAULIFFE, Richard John "Dick," "Mac," "Muggs" (b. November 29, 1939, Hartford, CT), player and manager, is the youngest of five children of William L. McAuliffe, a machinist, and Mary (Rose) McAuliffe. A three-sport star at Farmington, CT High School, McAuliffe signed for a $500 bonus with the Detroit Tigers (AL) and began his professional baseball career with a .206 batting average for Erie, PA (NYPL) in 1957. In 1958, he played for Augusta, GA (SAL) and the Valdosta, GA (GFL) pennant winners. McAuliffe split 1959 with Knoxville, TN (SAL) and Durham, NC (CrL), ending the season with the SAL championship Knoxville club. He remained with Knoxville until the Detroit Tigers promoted him in September 1960. McAuliffe was sent to Denver, CO (AA) in 1961, leading the AA in triples, doubles, hits, runs, and batting average (.353) after 64 games. He finished the season with the Detroit Tigers, hitting .256 in 80 games.

McAuliffe became an infield fixture with the Detroit Tigers in 1962 for the next 12 seasons, alternating at second base, shortstop, and third base. The 5-foot 11-inch, 175-pound McAuliffe, known for his wide-open batting stance and Mel Ott* style kick, developed into an All-Star at shortstop in 1965 and 1966 and again at second base in 1967. He recorded a 16-year major league career .977 fielding average. McAuliffe never hit over .274 in his major league career and batted .247 overall. Nevertheless, the left-handed hitter set the HR record for Tiger shortstops with 24 in 1964, led the AL at that position with 23 HR in 1966, and clouted 22 HR in 1967. In a major league career spanning 1,763 games, McAuliffe hit 197 HR, scored 888 runs, and recorded 697 RBI. A spark plug for the 1968 AL pennant and World Series winning Tigers, he tied a major league record that year for those playing in at least 150 games by not grounding into a double play all season and led the AL in runs scored with 95. In the World Series against the St. Louis Cardinals, he fielded perfectly, batted .222 and walked four times. In

Game 6, he tied two World Series records by scoring twice in one inning and walking twice in another. After missing half the 1969 season with a knee injury, McAuliffe in 1970 tied the AL single game record for second baseman with 11 assists and established a .987 club fielding mark for the position in 1971.

McAuliffe hit only .240 as the Detroit Tigers won the AL Eastern Division in 1972, but tied his single season high with a .274 batting average in 1973. In October 1973, Detroit traded him to the Boston Red Sox (AL) for outfielder Ben Oglivie.* After one season with the Boston Red Sox in 1974, he managed their AA Bristol, CT (EL) club in 1975. Although reactivated for seven games with Boston, he guided the farm club to the 1975 EL championship. From 1976 to 1985, McAuliffe worked as a franchise owner of coin-operated laundry machines in apartment complexes and colleges in Connecticut and Massachusetts. McAuliffe, a gold key recipient, was elected to the Connecticut Sports Hall of Fame in 1984 and to the Michigan Sports Hall of Fame in 1986. The Avon, CT resident married Jo Anne Lee Cromack on March 3, 1962. They have two children, Mary Elizabeth and Michael John.

BIBLIOGRAPHY: *Boston Red Sox Press-TV-Radio Guide*, 1974, 1975; *The Baseball Encyclopedia*, 10th ed. (New York, 1996); *Detroit Tigers Press-TV-Radio Guide*, 1961–1973; Lloyd Johnson and Brenda Ward, *Who's Who in Baseball History* (Greenwich, CT, 1994); Richard McAuliffe file, National Baseball Library, Cooperstown, NY; Richard McAuliffe, telephone interview with Jack C. Braun, January 19, 1997; Jerry Green, *Year of the Tiger* (New York, 1969); Rich Marazzi, "Dick McAuliffe Was a Vital Cog in Tigers' Glory Seasons," *SCD* 25 (October 2, 1998), pp. 80–81; Fred Smith, *995 Tigers* (Detroit, MI, 1981); Joe Falls, *Detroit Tigers* (New York, 1995); William M. Anderson, *The Detroit Tigers* (South Bend, IN, 1996); John Thorn et al., eds., *Total Baseball*, 5th ed. (New York, 1997).

Jack C. Braun

McBRIDE, Arnold Ray "Bake," "Fulton Flash" (b. February 3, 1949, Fulton, MO), player, is the son of Arnold McBride and Wanna (Robinson) McBride and made All-State in football, played forward and center on the basketball team, and starred in track and field at Fulton, MO High School. McBride received a Bachelor of Arts degree in physical education from Westminster College in Fulton, where he played the outfield and pitched for the baseball team and ran the 100, 220, and 440 yard dashes on the track and field team. The St. Louis Cardinals (NL) selected him in the 37th round of the June 1970 free agent draft, the first player the club ever chose without anyone in the organization having seen him play.

McBride, who batted from the left side and threw right-handed, played at Sarasota, FL (GCL), Modesto, CA (CaL), Little Rock–based Arkansas (TL), and Tulsa, OK (AA) between 1970 and 1973, hitting .314 with 119 stolen bases. After batting .302 in 40 games for the St. Louis Cardinals in

1973, he was named 1974 NL Rookie of the Year for his .309 batting average, 173 hits, and 30 thefts. He ran the 100 yard dash in 9.8 seconds, making him difficult to double up. On September 11, 1974, McBride dashed home all the way from first base after a wild throw on a pick-off attempt in the 25th inning to give the Cardinals a 4–3 victory over the New York Mets in the second longest major league game. He batted .300 the next season and .335 in 1976 despite spending 10 weeks on the disabled list. The St. Louis Cardinals traded him to the Philadelphia Phillies (NL) for southpaw Tom Underwood in June 1977. The 6-foot 2-inch, 185-pound McBride recorded career bests with 15 HR and 36 stolen bases.

McBride patrolled right field and frequently led off for the Philadelphia Phillies from 1978 to 1980, batting .309 with a career-high 87 RBI in 1980. Philadelphia won the 1977, 1978, and 1980 NL Eastern Division titles, as he batted .229 in three NL Championship Series. He batted .304 with five RBI in Philadelphia's 1980 World Series Championship over the Kansas City Royals.

McBride missed over half the 1981 season with injuries and was traded to the Cleveland Indians (AL) in February 1982. He batted a composite .312 in two seasons with the Cleveland Indians, but spent five months on the disabled list and retired after the 1983 season. McBride's recorded 1,153 hits with 167 doubles, 55 triples, 63 HR, 548 runs, 430 RBI, and a .299 batting average in 1,071 major league games. He married Celeste Woodley on December 11, 1970 and has a daughter, Tabitha.

BIBLIOGRAPHY: Bob Broeg, *Redbirds: A Century of Cardinals' Baseball* (St. Louis, MO, 1981); Jerry Lovelace and Marty Hendin, *St. Louis Cardinals' 1974 Official Guide and Record Book for Press, Radio & TV* (St. Louis, MO, 1974); Arnold McBride file, National Baseball Library, Cooperstown, NY; Rob Rains, *The St. Louis Cardinals* (New York, 1992); Bob Broeg and Jerry Vickery, *St. Louis Cardinals Encyclopedia* (Grand Rapids, MI, 1998); Rich Westcott and Frank Bilovsky, *The New Phillies Encyclopedia* (Philadelphia, PA, 1993); Allen Lewis, *The Philadelphia Phillies: A Pictorial History* (Virginia Beach, VA, 1981); Mike Shatzkin, ed., *The Ballplayers* (New York, 1990).

Frank J. Olmsted

McBRIDE, James Dickson "Dick" (b. 1845, Philadelphia, PA; d. October 10, 1916, Philadelphia, PA), player and manager, enjoyed a 16-year major league baseball career with the Philadelphia Athletics (NL). He joined the club at its inception in 1860 as an outfielder, but served also as catcher and shortstop and emerged as one of the great pitchers of the decade before the NL's formation.

The 5-foot 9-inch, 150-pound right-hander was noted for a hot temper, a sharp tongue, and an inclination to argue with umpires. By 1864, a year after his pitching debut, he was the Philadelphia Athletics' premier hurler. Throwing underhand from a level pitcher's box 50 feet from the plate, he was described by the sporting newspaper New York *Clipper* as "an . . . effective player . . . possessing command of the ball, great speed, considerable powers of endurance, and plenty of pluck withal."

In 1871, when the NA structured itself as a professional league, the Philadelphia Athletics were its first champions and McBride was its leading pitcher with a .783 winning percentage. To the A's 21–7 record, he contributed 25 complete games, 18 wins, and five losses. He served as team captain or on-field manager and was elected to its board of directors.

McBride finished 30–14 in 1872, pitching the Philadelphia A's entire schedule for a fourth-place club. In 1873, as the team slipped to fifth, his 24–19 record included a two-hit shutout, the first "whitewash" ever for the powerful Boston Red Stockings. He led the NA with three shutouts. The New York *Clipper* awarded him "the palm of [pitching] supremacy" for the season, picking him even over the great Albert Spalding.* In 1874 McBride again provided all of Philadelphia's 33 wins and 22 losses, all complete games, and compiled a NA best 1.64 ERA.

In midseason, the Philadelphia Athletics and Boston Red Stockings sailed to England for a series of exhibition baseball games and occasional cricket matches against British sides. The Philadelphia A's won eight of 13 games, including a McBride triumph over Spalding. The two pitchers also combined as bowlers to win a cricket match.

Home again, the Philadelphia A's finished third. The New York *Clipper* saw signs of dissension: "Blundering" directors did not permit Captain McBride to "place his men as he wanted them," while the team suffered from "jealousies and weaknesses."

In 1875, McBride achieved his peak performance with 44 wins, 14 losses, 59 complete games, and a 2.33 ERA. The Philadelphia Athletics once more trailed Boston. But McBride's final game for Philadelphia was a humiliating one. After being hit hard, he was removed by the board of directors and deposed as captain in favor of first baseman Adrian Anson.*

A nucleus of the Athletics stayed with the Philadelphia entry in the new NL in 1876, but McBride joined the Boston Red Caps (NL) and compiled a 0–4 record that ended his career. Overall, in his six seasons of organized baseball, he recorded 149 wins and 74 losses. Of his 233 starts, 224 were complete games and 10 were shutouts. In 2,049 innings, his ERA was 2.70.

BIBLIOGRAPHY: Dick McBride file, National Baseball Library, Cooperstown, NY; *Baseball Encyclopedia*, 10th ed. (New York, 1996); New York (NY) *Clipper*, 1864–1873; Frederick Ivor-Campbell et al., eds., *Baseball's First Stars* (Cleveland, OH, 1996); Preston Orem, *Baseball (1845–1881) from the Newspaper Accounts* (Altadena, CA, 1961); Philadelphia (PA) *Record*, 1871–1876; Philadelphia, PA *Times*, 1871–1876; William J. Ryczek, *Blackguards and Redstockings* (Jefferson, NC, 1992), John Thorn et al., eds., *Total Baseball*, 5th ed. (New York, 1997).

                                                                                    A. D. Suehsdorf

McCARTHY, Joseph Vincent "Joe," "Marse Joe" (b. April 21, 1887, Philadelphia, PA; d. January 13, 1978, Buffalo, NY), player and manager, grew
up in the Germantown section of Philadelphia of Irish descent. McCarthy,
his era's most successful baseball manager, suffered a broken kneecap as a
boy, thwarting a possible major league career. After attending Niagara University, he joined Wilmington, DE (TSL) in 1907 as a shortstop and third
baseman. He played with numerous minor league teams through 1921.

After finishing 1907 at Franklin, PA (TSL), McCarthy performed with the
Toledo, OH Mud Hens (AA) from 1908 to 1911 and briefly in 1911 with
Indianapolis, IN (AA). He was sold to Wilkes-Barre, PA (NYSL) in 1912
and the next year was appointed manager and achieved a career-high .325
batting average. From 1914 through 1915, he participated with Buffalo, NY
(IL). In 1916 he signed with the FL, which collapsed before the season
opened. McCarthy instead joined the Louisville, KY Colonels (AA) and in
July 1919 became manager there. He closed his playing career in 1921 and
managed the Colonels to their first AA pennant. McCarthy, who became
known nationally as perhaps the best minor league manager, piloted Louisville in 1925 to another AA pennant.

In 1926 William Wrigley, Jr., chewing-gum millionaire and Chicago Cubs
(NL) owner, hired McCarthy as manager of his last place club. McCarthy
sold Grover Cleveland Alexander,* whom he considered uncooperative. Under McCarthy's firm leadership, the Cubs finished fourth in 1926 and 1927
and third in 1928. In 1929, Chicago won the NL pennant and lost the World
Series to Connie Mack's* Philadelphia Athletics. Bitter fan disappointment
over that World Series loss caused McCarthy to resign in September 1930.
Rogers Hornsby,* whom McCarthy had purchased for the Cubs in 1928,
became manager.

McCarthy replaced Bob Shawkey as New York Yankees (AL) manager in
1931. After finishing second in the AL in McCarthy's initial season, the
Yankees in 1932 won the AL pennant and defeated the Chicago Cubs in the
World Series. From 1933 through 1935, the Yankees remained in second
place. In 1935 Babe Ruth* left the Yankees to join the Boston Braves, giving
McCarthy complete control of the club. From 1936 through 1945, McCarthy enjoyed one of the greatest managerial tenures in major league history.
Joe DiMaggio* joined the Yankees in 1936 and helped the club clinch the
AL pennant on September 9, 1936, the earliest in the league's history to
that time. The Yankees overpowered rivals for four AL pennants and World
Series titles from 1936 through 1939, drawing heavily upon farm club talent
from the Newark, NJ Bears (IL) and the Kansas City, MO Blues (AA). The
new talent included Phil Rizzuto,* Red Rolfe,* and Joe Gordon.* The Yankees won 102 games in both 1936 and 1937, 99 games in 1938, and 106
games in 1939. The Yankees also captured the 1941 through 1943 AL pennants, clinching the 1941 AL title on September 4. In the 1943 World Series,

the Yankees defeated the St. Louis Cardinals in five games and provided McCarthy with his sixth world title in eight seasons. World War II, however, depleted McCarthy's talent following the 1943 season.

McCarthy, beset by a stomach ailment and a personality clash with new Yankees president Larry MacPhail, Sr.,* resigned in 1946. He did not manage in 1947, but the next two seasons piloted the Boston Red Sox (AL). After the Red Sox lost photo-finish AL pennants to the Cleveland Indians in 1948 and the Yankees in 1949, McCarthy permanently retired in June 1950.

McCarthy's Yankees teams demonstrated impressive teamwork. Although the Yankees comprised great stars, McCarthy instilled cooperation masterfully in his players. McCarthy, a strict disciplinarian, always reprimanded his players in private and thus earned the utmost respect in return. He remained very close to his players and was disliked by only a few. His .627 winning percentage as a Yankees manager ranked as the best in major league history. In his 24-year major league managerial career, his clubs won 2,125 games and lost 1,333 (.615), the highest winning percentage in major league history.

Nicknamed "Marse Joe" by Harry Neily of the Chicago *Evening American*, the 5-foot 8-inch, 190-pound McCarthy was married in February 1921 to Elizabeth "Babe" McCave and lived for many years on a 61-acre farm near Buffalo, NY. McCarthy, whose wife died on October 18, 1971, managed seven AL All-Star teams and was elected in 1957 to the National Baseball Hall of Fame. He spent his retirement quietly in his colonial house far from the tumultuous scenes of his Yankees heyday and died from pneumonia.

BIBLIOGRAPHY: Joe McCarthy file, National Baseball Library, Cooperstown, NY; Mark Gallagher, *The Yankee Encyclopedia*, vol. 3 (Champaign, IL, 1997); Donald Honig, *The Man in the Dugout* (Lincoln, NE, 1995); Peter Golenbock, *Fenway* (New York, 1992); Thomas Aylesworth and Benton Minks, *The Encyclopedia of Baseball Managers* (New York, 1990); Warren Brown, *The Chicago Cubs* (New York, 1946); Eddie Gold and Art Ahrens, *The Golden Era Cubs, 1876–1940* (Chicago, IL, 1985); Jim Enright, *Chicago Cubs* (New York, 1975); Dave Anderson et al., *The Yankees* (New York, 1979); Frank Graham, *The New York Yankees* (New York, 1943); Richard Goldstein, *Spartan Seasons* (New York, 1980); David Halberstam, *Summer of '49* (New York, 1989); Robert Redmount, *The Red Sox Encyclopedia* (Champaign, IL, 1998); Gene Karst and Martin J. Jones, Jr., *Who's Who in Professional Baseball* (New Rochelle, NY, 1973); Leonard Koppett, *The Man in the Dugout* (New York, 1993); *NYT*, January 15, 1978; Joe McCarthy, "An Old Yankee Manager Recalls the Joy of His Job," *NYT*, September 25, 1977; Red Smith, "Joe McCarthy," *NYT*, January 22, 1978.

Arthur F. McClure

McCARTHY, Thomas Francis Michael "Tommy," "Pudge," "The Kid," "Little Mac" (b. July 24, 1863, South Boston, MA; d. August 5, 1922, Boston, MA), player, manager, scout, and coach, was the son of liquor dealer Daniel McCarthy and Sarah (Healy) McCarthy. Of Irish descent, he graduated from

Andrew Grammar School in 1877 and worked in the clothing business. On the Boston sandlots, he starred with the bundle boys, the Actives and Chickering Piano baseball teams. In 1884, manager Tim Murnane* of the Boston Reds in the ill-fated UA discovered the speedy outfielder playing for Emerson Piano (CmA). Not yet age 21, McCarthy was held hitless in his July 10 major league debut by Chicago Browns' Hugh "One Arm" Daily. For 1884, McCarthy lost all seven decisions as a pitcher and batted .215 in 53 games.

In the NL with the Boston Beaneaters (1885) and Philadelphia Quakers (1886–1887), McCarthy batted .184 in 66 contests. McCarthy finished the 1885 season in Haverhill, MA (NEL) and spent most of 1886 at Providence, RI (EL) and Brockton, MA (NEL), where he batted an improved .327 in 76 games. After starring on a pennant-winning Oshkosh, WI (NWL) team in 1887, McCarthy enjoyed a superb spring series with the St. Louis Whites in 1888. Charles Comiskey* promoted him to the St. Louis Browns (AA). McCarthy helped the Browns to their fourth straight AA pennant by batting .274, stealing 93 bases, scoring 107 runs, and leading outfielders with 44 assists and 12 double plays. On July 17, he batted five for five, stole six bases, and scored three runs.

During four seasons with the St. Louis Browns (1888–1891), McCarthy batted .307 and averaged 127 runs scored, 68 stolen bases, and 31 outfield assists. In 1890, he batted .350 and led the AA with 83 stolen bases. A widely respected, "smart" ballplayer, he perfected the outfield trap play by juggling fly balls to catch base runners. McCarthy's tactics inspired the "infield fly" and "tag up" rules. He also popularized the fake bunt, the hit-and-run play, and sign stealing. At 5-feet 7-inches and ranging from 145 to 200 pounds, he was nicknamed "Pudge," "The Kid," and "Little Mac."

McCarthy enjoyed his greatest fame with the hometown Boston Beaneaters, whom he helped win NL championships in 1892 and 1893. Joining Hugh Duffy* in the "Heavenly Twins" outfield, McCarthy from 1892 through 1895 averaged .304, 109 runs scored, and 40 stolen bases for Boston. After being sold to the Brooklyn Bridegrooms (NL), he retired following the 1896 campaign. The right-handed batting and throwing McCarthy compiled a .292 lifetime batting average and was elected in 1946 to the National Baseball Hall of Fame. In 1,275 games, he made 1,496 hits and 192 doubles, scored 1,069 runs, knocked in 735 runs, walked 537 times, and stole 468 bases.

Subsequently he operated a Boston bowling alley and saloon, "Duffy and McCarthy." He scouted for the NL Cincinnati Reds (1909–1912), NL Boston Braves (1914, 1917), and AL Boston Red Sox (1920). After managing the St. Louis Browns briefly in 1890 to 13 losses, he piloted Newark NJ (IL) in 1918 and coached baseball at Dartmouth, Holy Cross, and Boston colleges. McCarthy married Margaret McCluskey, who died in 1897. They had three daughters, Sadie, Edith, and Margaret ("Reta").

BIBLIOGRAPHY: Gary Caruso, *The Braves Encyclopedia* (Philadelphia, PA, 1995); Thomas McCarthy file, National Baseball Library, Cooperstown, NY; J. Thomas Hetrick, *Chris Von der Ahe and the St. Louis Browns* (Lanham, MD, 1999); Martin Appel and Burt Goldblatt, *Baseball's Best: The Hall of Fame Gallery* (New York, 1977); John Gruber, "Tom McCarthy," *TSN*, February 12, 1914, p. 8; "Hundreds Mourn for Tom McCarthy, One of Greatest Outfielders of All Time," Boston *Herald*, August 6, 1922, p. B–2; Frederick Ivor-Campbell et al., eds., *Baseball's First Stars* (Cleveland, OH, 1996); Frederick G. Lieb, *The St. Louis Cardinals* (New York, 1945); John Thorn et al., eds., *Total Braves* (New York, 1996); Harold Kaese, *The Boston Braves* (New York, 1948); Ken Smith, *Baseball's Hall of Fame* (New York, 1947); "Tom McCarthy, Noted Old Ball Player, Dead," Boston *Evening Globe*, August 5, 1922, p. 8.

James D. Smith III

McCLELLAN, Dan "Danny" (b. unknown; d. 1931, unknown), player and manager, ranked among the pioneering figures of early African-American professional baseball. From 1902 until 1931, he played on and managed several professional and semiprofessional nines. The left-handed McClellan pitched for and played right field for the Philadelphia Giants in 1902 and 1903 and the Cuban X Giants in 1903 and 1904. He returned to the Philadelphia Giants in 1904 and remained there as a pitcher and first baseman through 1910. McClellan finished his playing career in the upper echelons of African-American professional baseball by pitching for the New York Lincoln Giants in 1911. For the next two decades, he served as a player-manager and as manager for mostly semiprofessional teams. McClellan piloted the Philadelphia Giants in 1923 and 1924 and the Wilmington, DE Potomacs in 1925. He managed the Wilmington Quaker Giants in 1930 and 1931 and also the Smart Set, Washington Potomacs, and the Brooklyn Royal Giants.

Besides being a clever, off-speed left-handed pitcher, the relatively small McClellan proved a good left-handed hitter and fine fielder. His best professional seasons came with the Philadelphia Giants from 1904 to 1910. The outstanding Philadelphia Giants featured legendary second baseman Charley Grant, pitcher Rube Foster,* and Sol White,* and won three consecutive championships from 1904 to 1906. McClellan, one of the decade's best pitchers, hurled a perfect game for the Cuban X Giants in 1903 against York, PA (TSL). No pitcher had hurled a perfect game in the Negro Leagues previously. In 1911, the African-American newspaper, the Indianapolis *Freeman*, selected him for the first Negro League All-Star team with John Henry Lloyd,* Bruce Petway,* and other outstanding players.

As a manager, McClellan earned considerable respect from players and followers of African-American baseball. McClellan's players acknowledged his generosity and toughness. He developed many young ballplayers, who reached the highest levels of African-American professional baseball.

BIBLIOGRAPHY: Arthur Ashe, Jr., *A Hard Road to Glory* (New York, 1988); Dick Clark and Larry Lester, eds. *The Negro Leagues Book* (Cleveland, OH, 1994); John Holway, *Life in the Negro Leagues from the Men Who Lived It* (New York, 1991); James A. Riley, *The Biographical Encyclopedia of the Negro Baseball League* (New York, 1994).

Joel S. Franks

McCORMICK, Frank Andrew "Buck" (b. June 9, 1911, New York, NY; d. November 21, 1982, Manhasset, NY), player, manager, coach, and scout, was the son of railroad worker Andrew McCormick and Ann McCormick. The 6-foot 4-inch, 210-pound McCormick's physique was well suited for first base, the position he played in the major leagues except for very brief appearances in 1937 at second base and in the outfield. McCormick also excelled at high school and church league basketball in New York City. After finishing high school in the Yorkville section of New York and packing antiques for the American Art Association, he was invited to major league tryouts with the Philadelphia Athletics (AL), Washington Senators (AL), and New York Giants (NL). McCormick, however, failed to impress scouts enough to sign him to a professional contract. The determined McCormick borrowed $50 from his uncle and took a bus to the Cincinnati Reds' (NL) tryout camp in Beckley, WV. Roderick Wallace,* former major league short-stop and scout, recommended that the Reds sign him. He played first base for Beckley (MAL) in 1934 in his initial pro baseball season. McCormick batted .347 in 120 games for Beckley and .315 for the Cincinnati Reds at the end of the campaign. After playing in the minor leagues in 1935, 1936, and part of the 1937 season, he started with Cincinnati from 1938 through 1945. On October 8, 1938, he married Vera Preedy in Hamilton, OH. They had two daughters, Judith and Nancy.

McCormick hit above .300 in five of his eight full seasons with Cincinnati and led NL batters in hits in 1938, 1939, and (tied) 1940, RBI in 1939, doubles in 1940, and fewest strikeouts (150 games or more) in 1938, 1939, and 1941. He played major roles in Cincinnati's 1939 and 1940 NL pennants and 1940 World Series title over the Detroit Tigers, earning the NL's MVP Award in 1940. He was sold to the Philadelphia Phillies (NL) in December 1945 and played the 1946 season and part of the 1947 season there before being released. He joined the Boston Braves (NL) and batted .354 for the remainder of the 1947 campaign. In 1948, he played part-time and assisted the Braves in their NL pennant triumph. From September 26, 1945 through September 23, 1946, he played 138 consecutive games at first base without committing an error. In 13 major league campaigns, McCormick batted .299, made 1,711 hits, 334 doubles, and 128 HR, knocked in 951 runs, and struck out only 189 times.

Following the 1948 season, McCormick retired as a player and remained in baseball in other capacities. Besides managing in the minor leagues, he coached, scouted, and conducted tryout camps for Cincinnati and handled television broadcasts of Reds games. Prior to his death, he served as director of group and season ticket sales for the New York Yankees (AL).

BIBLIOGRAPHY: *SEAL*, vol. 1 (1981–1985), pp. 524–526; Frank McCormick file, National Baseball Library, Cooperstown, NY; Lee Allen, *The Cincinnati Reds* (New York, 1948); Bob Rathgeber, *Cincinnati Reds Scrapbook* (Virginia Beach, VA, 1982); Ritter Collett, *The Cincinnati Reds* (Virginia Beach, VA, 1976); Rich Westcott and Frank Bilovsky, *The New Phillies Encyclopedia* (Philadelphia, PA, 1993); Gary Caruso, *The Braves Encyclopedia* (Philadelphia, PA, 1995); Richard Goldstein, *Spartan Seasons* (New York, 1980); Donald Honig, *Baseball When the Grass Was Real* (New York, 1975); *The Baseball Encyclopedia*, 10th ed. (New York, 1996); Ira L. Smith, *Baseball's Famous First Basemen* (New York, 1956); *NYT*, November 24, 1982.

Albert J. Figone

McCORMICK, James "Jim" (b. November 3, 1856, Glasgow, Scotland; d. March 10, 1918, Paterson, NJ), player and manager, became one of baseball's most durable pitchers and ranks tenth in major league complete games with 466. The son of James McCormick and Rose (Lowrey) McCormick, he came to the United States at an early age and grew up in Paterson, NJ. In 1873, he and boyhood friend Mike Kelly* helped form a baseball club there. McCormick became the club's pitcher in 1876, and the next year pitched for the Buckeye Club of Columbus, OH. He entered the NL in 1878, pitching 14 games for the Indianapolis Hoosiers (NL). The following year, he joined the Cleveland Blues (NL) as pitcher and manager.

In his two years as manager, McCormick pitched in over 81 percent of Cleveland's games. In 1879, he won 20 games and lost 40 for his 27–55 sixth place club. The next year, McCormick lowered his ERA .57 points to 1.85. Cleveland rose to third place with a 47–37 won–lost record. McCormick led NL pitchers with 72 complete games and 45 wins (against 28 losses) and finished second in strikeouts and shutouts.

Although replaced as manager after 1880, McCormick remained Cleveland's leading pitcher until mid-1884. In 1881 and 1882, he again paced the NL in complete games with 57 and 65. His won–lost record slipped to 26–30 in 1881, but he rebounded in 1882 to lead the NL a second time in wins with his 36–30 record. In 1883, McCormick and Cleveland appeared headed for their finest season. McCormick already had won 28 games (losing only 12) when an injured arm sidelined him for the rest of the season. His 1.84 ERA and .675 winning percentage led the NL, but Cleveland slipped from first place to fourth after his injury.

In the midst of a disappointing 19–22 season in 1884, McCormick and two teammates deserted Cleveland for the Cincinnati Outlaw Reds (UA). At Cincinnati his fortunes improved, as he led the UA in ERA (estimated 1.54), shutouts (7), and winning percentage (.875) and won 21 of 24 decisions. McCormick returned to the NL with the Providence Grays in 1885, but saw little action (1 win, 3 losses) before joining the Chicago White Stockings (NL) in midseason. He helped Chicago win NL pennants in 1885 (20 wins, 4 losses) and 1886 (31–11), but broke club regulations against drinking and was sold to the Pittsburgh Alleghenys. In 492 career games, he compiled a 265–214 record (.553 winning percentage), struck out 1,704 batters in 4,275.2 innings, hurled 33 shutouts, and made a 2.43 ERA.

Following an ineffective 1887 season (13 wins, 23 losses) at Pittsburgh (NL), McCormick left baseball because he could not gain his release from the club. He operated a cafe for many years in Paterson, retiring a few years before his death from cirrhosis of the liver. McCormick married about 1883 and was survived by a son, James, and a daughter, Mrs. Francis Dunkerly.

BIBLIOGRAPHY: Henry Chadwick Scrapbooks, Albert Spalding Collection, New York Public Library; Franklin Lewis, *The Cleveland Indians* (New York, 1949); John Phillips, *The Spiders—Who Was Who* (Cabin John, MD, 1991); Warren Wilbert and William Hageman, *Chicago Cubs: Seasons at the Summit* (Champaign, IL, 1997); Peter Levine, *A. G. Spalding and the Rise of Baseball* (New York, 1985); Mike Kelly, *Play Ball* (Boston, MA, 1888); Craig Carter, ed., *TSN Daguerreotypes*, 8th ed. (St. Louis, MO, 1990); James McCormick file, National Baseball Library, Cooperstown, NY; Paterson (NJ) *Evening News*, March 11, 1918; *The Baseball Encyclopedia*, 10th ed. (New York, 1996); John C. Tattersall Scrapbooks, National Baseball Library, Cooperstown, NY; Robert L. Tiemann and Mark Rucker, eds., *Nineteenth Century Stars* (Kansas City, MO, 1989); Warren Brown, *The Chicago Cubs* (New York, 1946); Eddie Gold and Art Ahrens, *The Golden Era Cubs, 1876–1940* (Chicago, IL, 1985).

Frederick Ivor-Campbell

McCOVEY, Willie Lee "Stretch," "Big Mac" (b. January 10, 1938, Mobile, AL), player and executive, was nicknamed "Stretch" and later "Big Mac," and quietly shared the limelight alongside Willie Mays* as the best power hitters in San Francisco Giants (NL) history. The shy first baseman exhibited considerable power during a 22-year NL career spanning over three decades from 1959 to 1980. He is tied with Ted Williams* in 10th place on the all-time HR list and led all NL left-handed batters with 521 round trippers. He ranked 13th all-time in HR percentage (6.4) and struck out 1,550 times. In 2,588 career games, he compiled 2,211 hits, 353 doubles, 1,229 runs, 1,555 RBI, a .270 batting average, and a .515 slugging percentage. Additionally, he holds the NL records for HR by a first baseman (439), grand slam HR (18), pinch hit grand slams (3, tied for the major league record), and intentional walks in a single season (45 in 1969). McCovey led the NL in HR and slugging percentage three times, RBI twice, and walks once. He paced the NL in HR percentage five times, including an incredible four consecutive seasons from 1967 to 1970. In 1969, he earned NL MVP honors with 45 HR (9.2 percent of his at-bats for the highest major league percentage that season), 126 RBI, a .458 on base percentage, and a remarkable .656 slugging percentage. In his third of six All-Star games, he led the NL in 1969 to a 9–3 victory with two HR and three RBI.

A dead pull hitter, McCovey consistently slashed line drives to right field, proved a constant threat to reach the fence, and made numerous marks with his long balls. In 1970, the 6-foot 4-inch, 198-pound left-hander homered in all 12 NL parks. He slugged three consecutive HR twice in his career and belted two HR in the same inning twice. In June 1977, he hit grand slam and solo HR in the same inning against the defending NL champion Cincinnati Reds. McCovey debuted in the major leagues with four hits in four at-bats, including two triples, against Robin Roberts* and earned NL Rookie of the Year honors.

McCovey's path to the major leagues included stops at Sandersville, GA (GSL) in 1955, Danville, VA (CrL) in 1956, Dallas, TX, (TL) in 1957, and Phoenix, AZ (PCL) in 1958. After beginning the 1959 season at Phoenix, he was called up to the parent Giants' club. Except for briefly returning to the minor leagues with Tacoma, WA (PCL) in 1960, McCovey remained with the Giants through 1973. The San Francisco management rankled fans, however, by trading Mays to the New York Mets (NL) in May 1972 and McCovey to the fledgling San Diego Padres (NL) in October 1973. Attendance at Candlestick Park in San Francisco declined dramatically following McCovey's departure. McCovey had mediocre performances with the Padres for three seasons before being traded in August 1976 to the Oakland Athletics (AL), for whom he never played. After being invited to spring training by new management, McCovey made the San Francisco Giants roster in 1977, brought back the fans, and helped lead the club back into contention. He retired midway through the 1980 season, serving the Giants' public and community relations staff through 1986 and as special assistant to the general manager from 1987 through 1992.

McCovey appeared in only one NL Championship Series, batting .429 with two HR and six RBI against the Pittsburgh Pirates in 1971. In the 1962 World Series, he played a key role against the New York Yankees. Facing Ralph Terry in the second game, he belted a two-run HR to give the Giants a 2–0 victory. McCovey confronted Terry again in the seventh game with two men out, a runner in scoring position, and the club one run behind in the ninth inning. McCovey lined a drive toward right field, but Yankees second baseman Bobby Richardson* timed a perfect leap and dramatically ended the World Series. McCovey's at-bat was discussed repeatedly and even became the subject of a series of "Peanuts" cartoon strips. In 1986, he was elected to the National Baseball Hall of Fame.

BIBLIOGRAPHY: Willie McCovey file, National Baseball Library, Cooperstown, NY; John Benson et al., *Baseball's Top 100* (Wilton, CT, 1997); Donald Honig, *The Power Hitters* (St. Louis, MO, 1989); Charles Einstein, *Willie Mays* (New York, 1963); Charles Einstein, *Willie's Time* (New York, 1979); Craig Carter, ed., *TSN Daguerreotypes*, 8th ed. (St. Louis, MO, 1990); Larry Moffi and Jonathan Kronstadt, *Crossing the Line* (Jefferson, NC, 1994); Nick Peters, *Giants Diary* (Berkeley, CA, 1988); *NYT,*

November 21, 1969; David L. Porter, ed., *African-American Sports Greats* (Westport, CT, 1995); *The Baseball Encyclopedia*, 10th ed. (New York, 1996).

Alan R. Asnen

McDANIEL, Lyndall Dale "Lindy" (b. December 13, 1935, Hollis, OK), player, is the son of farmer Newell McDaniel and was salutatorian of his senior class at Arnett High School. After attending Oklahoma University and Abilene Christian College for two years, McDaniel signed as a pitcher with the St. Louis Cardinals (NL) for a $50,000 bonus in 1955. Brothers Kerry and Von also signed with St. Louis. Named after aviator Charles Lindbergh, McDaniel pitched in four games for the Cardinals in 1955 without any minor league experience. He hurled an impressive 15–9 season in 1957, but slumped badly the next year and was sent to Omaha, NE (AA). McDaniel switched to the bullpen after having started his first four seasons and rebounded to become one of the best relief pitchers in baseball history. A sidearm pitcher, he also changed his motion to three-quarters.

The St. Louis Cardinals traded him to the Chicago Cubs (NL) in a multiplayer deal in October 1962. McDaniel pitched with the San Francisco Giants (NL) from 1966 to July 1968 and found a successful niche with the New York Yankees (AL) in July 1968. He had developed a highly effective forkball by this time and enjoyed some of his most successful years as a Yankee. That year, he retired 32 consecutive batters in one period. In 1970 he recorded a career-high 29 saves, but did not lead the AL. In 1973, he hurled a complete game in his first start since 1960. McDaniel finished his 21-year career with the Kansas City Royals (AL) in 1974 and 1975.

In 987 career games, he compiled a 141–119 record, a 3.45 ERA, and 119 relief wins, second behind Hoyt Wilhelm.* He played in 225 NL games without committing an error, an NL record. He was voted *TSN* Fireman of the Year in 1960 and 1963, when he led the NL in saves with 26 and 22, respectively. He also paced the NL in saves with 15 in 1959 and tied an NL mark by allowing three grand slams in 1963. The father of two boys and a girl, McDaniel married Audrey Kahn on January 24, 1957 and resides in Hollis, OK. A devout Christian, McDaniel manages a Bible Book Store in Kansas City and lectures and publishes on the values of religion, family, and the Bible.

BIBLIOGRAPHY: Lindy McDaniel file, National Baseball Library, Cooperstown, NY; Bob Broeg, *Redbirds: A Century of Cardinal Baseball* (St. Louis, MO, 1981); Eddie Gold and Art Ahrens, *The New Era Cubs, 1941–1985* (Chicago, IL, 1985); Brent P. Kelley, *They Too Wore Pinstripes* (Jefferson, NC, 1998); Gene Karst and Martin J. Jones, Jr., *Who's Who in Professional Baseball* (New Rochelle, NY, 1973); Richard Marazzi and Len Fiorito, *Aaron to Zuverink* (New York, 1982); Bob Broeg and Jerry Vickery, *St. Louis Cardinals Encyclopedia* (Grand Rapids, MI, 1998); Jim Enright, *Chi-*

cago Cubs (New York, 1975); Mark Gallagher, *The Yankee Encyclopedia*, vol. 3 (Champaign, IL, 1997).

William A. Borst

McDONALD, Webster "Mac," "56 Varieties" (b. January 1, 1900, Wilmington, DE; d. June 12, 1982, Philadelphia, PA), player and manager, pitched underhand and boasted many pitches. He hurled for three NNL Championship teams and managed one titlist.

Before joining the Chicago American Giants in 1925, the 6-foot, 190 pounder, who initially played baseball on the south Philadelphia playgrounds, pitched mostly with less distinguished teams. He also spent short stints with the Detroit Stars (NNL) in 1920 and New York Lincoln Giants (ECL) in 1922. McDonald posted marks of 14–9 in 1926 and 10–5 in 1927 to help the American Giants to NNL pennants and victories over the ECL champion Atlantic City, NJ Bacharach Giants in both Negro World Series. He won his only decision, recording a 2.07 ERA in the 1927 World Series. After hurling three years with Chicago, he joined the Homestead, PA Grays (ANL) in 1928 and pitched four seasons for an independent white semipro team in Little Falls, MN.

McDonald pitched for the Hilldale Daisies (EWL) in 1930 and 1931, Baltimore Black Sox (EWL) in 1930, and Washington Pilots (EWL), where he managed part of the 1932 season. In 1933, he and Ed Bolden organized the Philadelphia Stars (NNL). McDonald managed the Philadelphia Stars to a pennant in 1934 in their first NNL season. He contributed an 8–2 record and a crucial win in the playoffs over Chicago American Giants' ace Willie Foster.* McDonald managed two more seasons and remained with the Philadelphia Stars through 1940, except for a brief stint with the Washington Black Senators (NNL) in 1938.

The submariner enjoyed success against major leaguers in exhibition games, winning four games over Dizzy Dean.* McDonald, a quiet, dignified, widely respected gentleman, worked in Philadelphia at the U.S. Mint and with the U.S. Postal Service. He later lived in a north Philadelphia housing project.

BIBLIOGRAPHY: *Afro-American*, 1928–1940; Chicago (IL) *Defender*, 1920–1934; Kansas City (MO) *Call*, 1921–1934; Robert W. Peterson, *Only the Ball Was White* (Englewood Cliffs, NJ, 1970); Philadelphia (PA) *Tribune*, 1922–1940; Pittsburgh (PA) *Courier*, 1928–1940; James A. Riley, *The All-Time All-Stars of Black Baseball* (Cocoa, FL, 1983); James A. Riley, *The Biographical Encyclopedia of the Negro Baseball Leagues* (New York, 1994); James A. Riley, interviews with former Negro League players, James A. Riley Collection, Cocoa, FL; *The Baseball Encyclopedia*, 10th ed. (New York, 1996).

James A. Riley

McDOUGALD, Gilbert James "Gil," "Smash" (b. May 19, 1928, San Francisco, CA), player, is the son of William J. McDougald, a U.S. Post Office supervisor, and Ella (McGuire) McDougald and attended Stanford University one year. He began his professional baseball career in the New York Yankees (AL) organization in 1948 at Twin Falls, ID (PrL), where he hit .340. The next year at Victoria, Canada (WeIL), he batted .344 with 13 HR and 116 RBI. In 1950 as a second baseman under manager Rogers Hornsby,* he enjoyed another tremendous year at Beaumont, TX (TL) with 13 HR, 115 RBI, and a .336 batting average. His honors included being named the All-Star second baseman and the TL MVP.

McDougald, a 6-footer weighing 180 pounds who threw and batted right-handed, joined the New York Yankees (AL) in 1951. His ability and attitude impressed manager Casey Stengel.* A month before McDougald's 23rd birthday, the New York Yankees made him the regular third baseman. In July 1951, regular second baseman Jerry Coleman was benched and McDougald was switched there. Altogether, he played 82 games at third base and 55 games at second base. His .306 batting average led the New York Yankees, helping him become the AL Rookie of the Year. A versatile infielder, McDougald remains the only player in New York Yankee history to excel at third base (1952, 1953, 1960), second base (1954, 1955, 1958), and shortstop (1956, 1957).

The confident, gutsy McDougald ranked among the most versatile infielders in major league baseball history. This was shown especially in 1959, when he played 53 games at second base, 52 at shortstop, and 25 at third base and consistently performed the best at any infield position he played. Three times, he led the AL in making double plays at three different positions. He led AL second basemen with a .985 fielding percentage in 1955.

McDougald hit for both average and power, twice batting higher than .300. Only seven right-handed New York Yankee batters surpassed his 112 HR. On May 3, 1951, he knocked in six runs in the ninth inning against the St. Louis Browns to tie the AL record for most RBI in one inning. The 1950's Yankee "Murderers Row" included McDougald, Mickey Mantle,* Yogi Berra,* and Bill Skowron,* among others.

On May 7, 1957, McDougald hit a wicked liner up the middle that struck Cleveland Indians pitcher Herb Score* near the right eye. Three bones were broken in Score's face. Score recovered, but never regained his outstanding form.

During 10 New York Yankee seasons, McDougald proved a vital cog in eight AL titles and five World Series victories. In 1956, he finished second in the AL MVP voting and hit .311. McDougald made the AL All-Star team five seasons (1952, 1956–1959) and was an All-Star starter at third base, second base, and shortstop. He retired in 1960, but the Los Angeles Angels (AL) selected him in the expansion draft of that year. Despite a large contract offer, he decided to remain retired while on top.

McDougald, who married Lucille Tochlin on April 8, 1948, batted .276 lifetime with 1,291 hits, 112 HR, and 576 RBI. The McDougalds have four

children, Christina, Gilbert, Jr., Todd, and Denise. He owns Yankee Maintenance Company in Spring Lake, NJ and coached baseball at Fordham
University for several years.

BIBLIOGRAPHY: Don Albaugh, "Indians' Herb Score and Yankees' Gil McDougald,"
SCD 24 (November 21, 1997), pp. 150–151; Gil McDougald file, National Baseball
Library, Cooperstown, NY; Mark Gallagher, *The Yankee Encyclopedia*, vol. 3 (Cham-
paign, IL, 1997); *The Baseball Encyclopedia*, 10th ed. (New York, 1996); Peter Golen-
bock, *Dynasty* (Englewood, Cliffs, NJ, 1975); Dave Anderson et al., *The Yankees* (New
York, 1979); Robert W. Creamer, *Stengel: His Life and Times* (New York, 1984);
Dom Forker, *Men of Autumn* (Dallas, TX, 1989); Dom Forker, *Sweet Seasons* (Dallas,
TX, 1991); Gil McDougald, letter to Stan Carlson, December 1992; *New York Yankees Media Guide, 1994*; John Thorn et al., eds., *Total Baseball*, 5th ed. (New York,
1997).

Stan W. Carlson

McDOWELL, Jack Burns (b. January 16, 1966, Van Nuys, CA), player, is a
6-foot 5-inch, 188-pound, right-handed pitcher who graduated from Notre
Dame High School in Van Nuys. McDowell led Stanford University to the
College World Series Championship in 1987, when the Cardinals defeated
the University of Oklahoma in the title game. His three year 35–13 win–
loss record at Stanford included two trips to the NCAA College World
Series and a school record 337 strikeouts in 392.2 innings pitched. McDowell married Meredith Peters in 1993 and has a son, Lucas Jackson. During
the off-season, the Van Nuys resident works as the lead singer, songwriter,
and guitar player for the progressive rock group V.I.E.W.

The Boston Red Sox (AL) selected McDowell in the 1984 draft, but the
hurler did not sign. McDowell joined the Chicago White Sox (AL) in 1987
after appearing in just six games for Sarasota, FL (GCL) and Birmingham,
AL (SL). In his first full season with the Chicago White Sox in 1988, he
won 5 games while losing 10 times. Due to a hip injury, he split the following
season with Vancouver, Canada (PCL) and Sarasota. After returning to the
Chicago White Sox in 1990, he won 83 games while losing only 48 times
over the next five seasons. McDowell ranked third in the AL with 20 wins
and 260.2 innings pitched in 1992, finishing second in the AL Cy Young
Award voting to Oakland A's Dennis Eckersley.* The following season, he
compiled a 22–10 record with a 3.37 ERA. McDowell became the third
Chicago White Sox pitcher to win the AL Cy Young Award, joining Early
Wynn* and LaMarr Hoyt.* The same season, he was named *TSN* AL Pitcher
of the Year and led the AL in victories and shutouts. McDowell hurled the
Chicago White Sox into the AL Championship Series, where he lost two
games to the Toronto Blue Jays.

McDowell recorded AL leading performances in complete games in 1991
(15), 1992 (13), and 1995 (8), and finished second in games started in 1991
(35). He shared the AL lead in games started in 1994 (25) and made the AL

All-Star team (1991–1993), being the losing pitcher in the 1993 game. After a 10–9 record in 1994, McDowell was traded to the New York Yankees (AL) for pitcher Keith Heberling. He compiled a 15–10 mark in 1995 to help the Yankees reach the AL Division Series, where they lost to the Seattle Mariners. McDowell in December 1995 signed a two year contract with the Cleveland Indians (AL). He compiled a 13–9 record in 1991 and started one game without decision in the AL Division Series against the Baltimore Orioles. After missing nearly all of the 1997 season because of an elbow injury, he joined the Anaheim Angels (AL) in February 1998.

In 12 major league seasons through 1999, McDowell has compiled a 127–87 record and a 3.85 ERA. He has appeared in 277 games, completing 62 of 275 starts and pitching 13 shutouts. McDowell has surrendered 1,854 hits, 870 runs, and 606 walks and has struck out 1,311 batters in 1,889 innings pitched. From 1990 to 1995, he ranked among the top 10 major league pitchers in victories (98) and strikeouts (976). He made the USA Baseball All-Time Team for his 1985 US National Team performance.

BIBLIOGRAPHY: Jack McDowell file, National Baseball Library, Cooperstown, NY; Richard Hoffer, "The Band Leader," *SI* 79 (August 2, 1993), pp. 30–32; Tom Keegan, "One on One: Jack McDowell," *Sport* 83 (August 1992), pp. 16, 18–19; Franz Lidz, "Jack of Two Traders," *SI* 75 (July 29, 1991), p. 75; *New York Yankees Media Guide*, 1995; *TSN Official Baseball Register*, 1998; *USAT*, October 4, 1995, p. 7C.

John L. Evers

McDOWELL, Samuel Edward Thomas "Sudden Sam" (b. September 21, 1942, Pittsburgh, PA), player, is the son of Thomas McDowell and Mary-irene (Donald) McDowell. His father, a former University of Pittsburgh football back, profoundly influenced his athletic career and constantly pressured him to improve. As McDowell recalled, "He never complimented me," but did impart sound baseball fundamentals. McDowell married Carol Ann Beisgen on February 19, 1962.

McDowell's major league career as a left-handed pitcher came principally with the Cleveland Indians (AL) and spanned from 1961 to 1975. As an Indian, he led the AL in strikeouts five times (1965, 1966, 1968, 1969, 1970) and once each in ERA (2.18, 1965), shutouts (5, 1966) and innings pitched (305, 1970) and appeared in four All-Star Games. His best season (1970) saw him produce 20 wins and 12 losses. McDowell, whose nickname came from his great fastball, followed his own inclinations. Manager "Birdie" Tebbetts* questioned both McDowell's reluctance to use his hard stuff in critical situations and his outspokenness. McDowell, who possessed a 6-foot 5-inch, 220-pound frame, always held outstanding promise. Sportswriters called him "the American League's Sandy Koufax."* The Minnesota Twins (AL) termed him faster than the Los Angeles Dodger great after the 1965 World Series. McDowell emulated Bob Feller,* the Indians' pitching star of the previous generation.

Following McDowell's successful 20-victory season in 1970, his baseball career unfortunately declined. McDowell's 13–17 win–loss season the following year resulted in his November 1971 trade to the San Francisco Giants (NL) for pitcher Gaylord Perry* and infielder Frank Duffy. The deal seemingly gave the Giants the age advantage because 29-year-old McDowell was four years younger than Perry, but the former compiled only a 10–8 record during his first NL season in 1972. Following his June 1973 sale to the New York Yankees (AL) for $150,000, he finished just 5–8 the next year. McDowell spent his last season with his hometown Pittsburgh Pirates (NL) in 1975 at age 33. His final major league totals included 141 games won, 134 contests lost, a .513 winning percentage, a 3.17 ERA, and 2,453 strikeouts in 2,492.2 innings pitched.

In December 1983 at the owners' winter meetings in Honolulu, HI, McDowell appealed for a players' drug rehabilitation program. McDowell described candidly the detrimental effects of alcoholism on his career.

BIBLIOGRAPHY: Sam McDowell file, National Baseball Library, Cooperstown, NY; *The Baseball Encyclopedia*, 10th ed. (New York, 1996); Craig Carter, ed., *TSN Daguerreotypes*, 8th ed. (St. Louis, MO, 1990); Pat Jordan, "Sam of a 1,000 Ways," *SI* 33 (August 17, 1970), pp. 36–40; Jack Mann, "Sam, You Make the Ball Too Small," *SI* 24 (May 23, 1966), pp. 40–42, 45–46; Roy McHugh, "Sam McDowell: Problems of a Power Pitcher," *Sport* 43 (September 1966), pp. 79–83; Bob Sudyk, "Why McDowell Stars When He's Scared," *Sport* 40 (October 1965), pp. 65, 99–100; *TSN*, November 14, 1964, April 16, 1966, September 2, 1967, December 11, 1971, March 7, 1983; John Phillips, *Winners* (Cabin John, MD, 1987); Terry Pluto, *The Curse of Rocky Colavito* (New York, 1994); Jack Torry, *Endless Summers* (South Bend, IN, 1995); John Thorn et al., eds., *Total Indians* (New York, 1996).

William J. Miller

McDUFFIE, Terris "Speed," "Elmer the Great," "Terris the Terrible" (b. July 22, 1910, Mobile, AL; d. New York, NY), player, was a flamboyant, strong-armed right-handed pitcher for two decades. The 6-foot 1-inch, 200 pounder played for the Newark, NJ Eagles (NNL) and many other teams.

McDuffie started his baseball career as an outfielder with the Birmingham, AL Black Barons (NNL) in 1930 and 1931, but soon switched to the mound and developed a wide variety of pitches. In 1934, he hurled the Pennsylvania Red Caps of New York to an 18-inning, 3–1 victory over the Jacksonville Red Caps. The following season, McDuffie pitched a no-hitter for the Brooklyn Eagles (NNL) against the House of David. In his first campaign with the Newark Eagles in 1936, he hurled two victories over Satchel Paige* in three matchups.

The cocky, colorful McDuffie pleased crowds. He wore a jacket with the words "The Great McDuffie" emblazoned on the back in large letters. Upon striking out a batter, McDuffie sometimes "boogied" on the mound. The flashy dresser and ladies man was involved in a romantic relationship with Effa Manley, the wife of the Newark Eagles' owner. Abe Manley, upon becoming aware of the relationship, traded McDuffie in 1938 to the New York Black Yankees (NNL).

For the next decade, McDuffie split his time between the Negro Leagues and the MEL. He jumped to the MEL from the Philadelphia Stars (NNL) in 1940, but the Homestead, PA Grays (NNL) signed him the next spring. The Homestead Grays won the 1941 NNL pennant, with McDuffie winning the All-Star game.

After returning to the Philadelphia Stars in 1942, McDuffie again jumped to the MEL the following season. He rejoined the Newark Eagles in 1944 because of his draft status and started his second All-Star game. Although past his prime, McDuffie joined Showboat Thomas in a highly publicized tryout with the Brooklyn Dodgers (NL) in the spring of 1945. General Manager Branch Rickey,* however, was not impressed with the pair.

McDuffie spent the 1945 and 1946 seasons in the MEL, but illnesses restricted his productivity. He remained a favorite in Cuba, spending eight winter seasons there with five different teams. Other winters saw him play in Puerto Rico, Venezuela, and the Dominican Republic. In 1954, McDuffie closed out his baseball career with Dallas, TX (TL).

BIBLIOGRAPHY: *Afro-American*, 1936–1948; Chicago (IL) *Defender*, 1930–1948; James Overmyer, *Effa Manley and the Newark Eagles* (Metuchen, NJ, 1993); Robert W. Peterson, *Only the Ball Was White* (Englewood Cliffs, NJ, 1970); Pittsburgh (PA) *Courier*, 1930–1948; James A. Riley, *The All-Time All-Stars of Black Baseball* (Cocoa, FL, 1983); James A. Riley, *The Biographical Encyclopedia of the Negro Baseball Leagues* (New York, 1994); James A. Riley, interviews with former Negro League players, James A. Riley Collection, Cocoa, FL; Art Rust, *Get That Nigger Off the Field* (New York, 1976); Mike Shatzkin, ed., *The Ballplayers* (New York, 1990); *The Baseball Encyclopedia*, 10th ed. (New York, 1996).

James A. Riley

McGANN, Dennis Lawrence "Dan," "Cap," "Old Ky" (b. July 15, 1871, Shelbyville, KY; d. December 13, 1910, Louisville, KY), player, starred as a first baseman with eight major league teams. The switch-hitting, 6-foot, 190-pound McGann batted .284 lifetime.

McGann grew up in Shelbyville, KY and played semiprofessional and minor league baseball for Shelbyville, KY, Harrodsburg, KY, Lexington, KY, and Maysville, KY from 1891 to 1894 and Lynchburg, VA (VL) in 1895 and 1896. He hit .345 during 1896 and joined the Boston Beaneaters (NL) in August, batting .322 in 43 games. Defensively, however, McGann fielded only .905 at second base.

McGann hit well for Toronto, Canada (EL) in 1897 and was switched to first base, where he excelled defensively. He played for the Baltimore Orioles (NL) in 1898 and the Brooklyn Superbas (NL) and the Washington Senators (NL) in 1899. Although batting .300 and leading NL first basemen with a .988 fielding percentage, he was sent to the St. Louis Cardinals (NL) in

January 1900 and played there in 1900 and 1901. He again paced NL first basemen with a .990 fielding percentage in 1900.

McGann started the 1902 season with the Baltimore Orioles (AL), but jumped with three other players and manager John McGraw* to the New York Giants (NL) in midseason. He played with the New York Giants through 1907, leading the NL in fielding from 1903 through 1906 and knocking in four runs during the 1905 World Series against the Philadelphia Athletics.

McGann, swift afoot, stole 282 bases during his major league career. In 1904, he stole five bases in one game, a feat not surpassed until Otis Nixon stole six in 1991. He also was involved in numerous fights on and off the field and especially clashed with manager McGraw. When McGann's batting average slipped to .237 in 1906, McGraw platooned him in 1907. New York traded McGann to the Boston Doves (NL) in December 1907. McGann tussled with McGraw in a Boston hotel lobby in 1908 after the latter insulted him during a game.

McGann hit only .240 for the Boston Doves in 1908, his last major league campaign. During 13 major league seasons, he batted .284 with 1,482 hits, 842 runs scored, and 727 RBI. McGann tried to resurrect his career in the minor leagues, but hit poorly for Milwaukee, WI (AA) in 1909 and 1910. In December 1910, McGann committed suicide at Bosler's Hotel in Louisville, KY.

McGann's death shocked many because he enjoyed good health, had made several wise financial investments, and was the principal figure in an impending trade to Louisville, KY (AA) that would have pleased him. Rumors of foul play abounded, heightened by stories of an alleged missing diamond ring. His surviving relatives listed his cause of death as murder. McGann's death, however, was ruled a suicide, with $1,000 being found on his body. Tragedy and mental instability had fated his family. A sister and brother had committed suicide, while another brother died from infection after an accidental gunshot. McGann, a secretive man who assumed an older brother's name, never married.

BIBLIOGRAPHY: "Dan McGann," *Microsoft Complete Baseball*, CD-ROM (Redmond, WA, 1994); Robert Creamer, *Stengel: His Life and Times* (New York, 1984); Frank Graham, *The New York Giants* (New York, 1952); Charles C. Alexander, *John McGraw* (New York, 1988); Ray Robinson, *Matty: An American Hero* (New York, 1993); Noel Hynd, *The Giants of the Polo Grounds* (New York, 1988); Louisville (KY) *Times*, December 14, 1910; Dan McGann file, National Baseball Library; Cooperstown, NY; *The Baseball Encyclopedia*, 10th ed. (New York, 1996); Harold Seymour, *Baseball: The Golden Age* (New York, 1971).

                                                                         Robert E. Weir

McGEE, Willie Dean (b. November 2, 1958, San Francisco, CA), player, is the son of Hurdice McGee, a machinist in the Oakland, CA Naval Yards, and Jessie Mae (Jennings) McGee. He graduated from Harry Ellis High School in Richmond, CA and completed one year at Diablo Valley CC in Pleasant Hill, CA. The New York Yankees (AL) drafted him in January 1977. After McGee spent five seasons in the farm system, the New York Yankees traded him to the St. Louis Cardinals (NL) for pitcher Bob Sykes in October 1981.

McGee, an instant success and fan favorite with St. Louis, was installed by Cardinals manager Whitey Herzog* in center field. He batted .296, utilizing his great speed to swipe 24 bases and cover the spacious reaches of Busch Stadium as a rookie. The 6-foot 1-inch, 176-pound McGee said, "The best way to judge whether a player is doing his job is if his team gets into the World Series." By that criterion, McGee performed his job very well. The St. Louis Cardinals appeared in the World Series three of McGee's first six years, making the 1982, 1985, and 1987 fall classics. On June 23, 1984, McGee hit for the cycle and drove in six runs against the Chicago Cubs. McGee was named NL MVP for 1985, when he led the NL in hits (216), triples (18), and batting average (.353) and established the NL record for highest season batting average for a switch-hitter. Two years later, McGee reached personal highs in doubles (37), HR (11), and RBI (105).

In 1990 McGee became the only player in major league history to win a batting title while finishing the season in the other league. He batted .335 for the St. Louis Cardinals before being dealt to the AL pennant-bound Oakland Athletics for outfielder Felix Jose and third baseman Stan Royer in August. The San Francisco Giants (NL) signed McGee as a free agent following the 1990 season. He batted .312 in 1991, .297 in 1992, .301 in 1993, and .282 in the strike-shortened 1994 season for the San Francisco Giants.

In June 1995, the Boston Red Sox (AL) acquired McGee. He batted .285 in limited action with Boston in 1995 and rejoined the St. Louis Cardinals (NL) as a free agent in December 1995. After batting .307 in 1996 to help the St. Louis Cardinals win the NL Central Division, he hit .333 in the NL Championship Series against the Atlanta Braves. A .310 batting mark followed in 1997, marking the sixth time he has surpassed .300.

McGee, notorious for swinging at pitches high and inside and breaking balls in the dirt, struck out at least 80 times eight seasons and never drew more than 38 bases on balls in a season. He hit pitches thrown just about anywhere, owning a .295 career batting average through 1999. McGee, who won a 1985 *TSN* Silver Slugger Award and *TSN* Gold Gloves in 1983, 1985, and 1986, played on four NL All-Star teams. He played in 2,201 major league games, had 2,254 hits and 1,010 runs scored, and pilfered 352 bases.

McGee, a quiet, hardworking, deeply religious player who does not complain, remains very modest about his many accomplishments. McGee's father, a deacon in the Pentecostal church, anoints his hands and feet with holy oil each season that they may be spared from injury. McGee and his wife, Vivian (Manyweather) McGee, have two children and reside in Hercules, CA.

BIBLIOGRAPHY: Willie McGee file, National Baseball Library, Cooperstown, NY; Peter Alfano, "Willie McGee: The Cardinals' Man of Many Talents," *BD* 45 (January 1986), pp. 26–28; John Dewan, ed., *The Scouting Report: 1990* (New York, 1990); Jeff Gordon, "St. Louis Will Ever Remember a Cardinal Named Willie," *BD* 50 (January 1991), pp. 37–41; Zander Hollander, ed., *The 1991 Complete Handbook of Baseball* (New York, 1991); Kip Ingle and Jim Toomey, *St. Louis Cardinals 1986 Media Guide* (St. Louis, MO, 1986); Willie McGee and George Vass, "The Game I'll Never Forget," *BD* 46 (April 1988), pp. 79–81; Rob Rains, *The St. Louis Cardinals* (New York, 1992); Bob Broeg and Jerry Vickery, *St. Louis Cardinals Encyclopedia* (Grand Rapids, MI, 1998); Mark Whicker, "Willie McGee: The Cardinals' Self-Made Star," *BD* 44 (December 1985), pp. 29–32.

                                                                              Frank J. Olmsted

McGILLICUDDY, Cornelius. *See* Connie Mack.

McGINNIS, George Washington "Jumbo" (b. February 22, 1864, Alton, IL; d. May 18, 1934, St. Louis, MO), player and umpire, hurled 77 victories for the St. Louis Brown Stockings (AA) in three major league seasons before reaching age 21. After declining production over three seasons, he concluded his playing career at age 23. Nicknamed "Jumbo" because of his girth, the 5-foot 10-inch right hander was officially listed at 197 pounds but saw his weight vacillate. He began pitching for the semipro St. Louis Brown Stockings in 1879 at age 15. When the St. Louis Browns joined the new major league AA in 1882, McGinnis and three other players remained with the upgraded team.

In 1882, McGinnis' 25–18 win–lost record accounted for 68 percent of the fifth-place St. Louis Browns' victories. He enjoyed his best season in 1883, sharing pitching duties with 35 game winner Tony Mullane.* His six shutouts shared the AA lead, while his 28–16 record helped the St. Louis Browns finish a close second to the Philadelphia Athletics. *Total Baseball* ranks McGinnis as the AA's fourth best player for 1883.

When Mullane left for the Toledo Blue Stockings (AA) in 1884, McGinnis again became the St. Louis ace and fared 24–16 for the fourth place Browns. His five shutouts included consecutive one-hitters against the Brooklyn Trolley-Dodgers. Second-year hurlers Bob Caruthers* and Dave Foutz* led St. Louis to an AA pennant in 1885, while McGinnis finished 6–6. After compiling a 5–5 record in 1886, he was sold in July to the Baltimore Orioles (AA). McGinnis fared 11–13, defeating his AA pennant-bound former teammates four times.

A shoulder injury ended McGinnis' major league career after a 3–5 record with the Cincinnati Red Stockings (AA) in 1887. He pitched two games for Milwaukee, WI (NWL) and then resumed his off-season job as a glass blower in St. Louis. McGinnis served the AA as a substitute umpire in 1888 and 1889. He gradually lost his eyesight, but surgery—paid for with money raised by a St. Louis newspaper—restored it.

In 187 games spanning six major league seasons, McGinnis won 102 and lost 79 with a .564 winning percentage. He compiled a 2.95 ERA in 1,603.2 innings with 18 shutouts and 562 strikeouts.

BIBLIOGRAPHY: Jumbo McGinnis file, National Baseball Library, Cooperstown, NY; David Nemec, *The Beer and Whisky League* (New York, 1994); John Thorn et al., eds., *Total Baseball*, 5th ed. (New York, 1997); Robert L. Tiemann and Mark Rucker, eds., *Nineteenth Century Stars* (Kansas City, MO, 1989); J. Thomas Hetrick, *Chris Von der Ahe and the St. Louis Browns* (Lanham, MD, 1999); Frederick G. Lieb, *The St. Louis Cardinals* (New York, 1945).

Frederick Ivor-Campbell

McGINNITY, Joseph Jerome "Joe," "Iron Man," "The Blond Giant" (b. March 19, 1871, Rock Island, IL; d. November 14, 1929, Brooklyn, NY), player, coach, manager, and scout, was selected in 1946 to the National Baseball Hall of Fame. The 5-foot 11-inch, 206-pound, right-handed pitcher, who never experienced a losing major league season, was nicknamed "Iron Man" for his staying power and for his off-season work in an iron foundry. Known as the "Blacksmith from Indian Territory" and the "Blond Giant," McGinnity joined Christy Mathewson* and Jack Chesbro* among the era's highest paid players and earned over $5,000 in 1904 at the height of his career. He led the NL in wins five times between 1899 and 1906. In 1904, he recorded a career-high 35 victories and paced the NL with an .814 winning percentage, a 1.61 ERA, nine shutouts, and five saves. The previous season, he had established a major league record by pitching both games on the same day five times and an NL record for pitching most innings in one season (434). He led the NL in appearances six times between 1900 and 1907, including 55 games in 1903, and in innings pitched four times between 1899 and 1904. In his only World Series performance, McGinnity allowed no earned runs in 17 innings, but was the victim of poor fielding and emerged with a 1–1 record in the famous "Pitchers' Series" of 1905 against the Philadelphia Athletics.

McGinnity's 36-year professional career began with Montgomery, AL (SA) in 1893 and continued at Kansas City, MO (WL) the next year. After marrying in the midst of a nationwide financial depression, he left pro baseball for three years. McGinnity pitched in a semipro league in Decatur, IL and worked at his father-in-law's iron foundry. A solid 10–3 season at Peoria, IL (WL) in 1898 led the NL's Baltimore Orioles to sign him in 1899. In several financial maneuvers engineered by co-player John McGraw,* McGinnity and 15 other Orioles were released. Several players, including McGinnity and McGraw, ended up with former Baltimore manager Wilbert Robinson,* pilot of the Brooklyn Superbas (NL). These actions quickly brought the demise of the Baltimore franchise, rumored to be part of a plan by McGraw, Ban Johnson* (then trying to form the AL), and others. McGinnity and McGraw enjoyed a successful season in Brooklyn and played for the Baltimore Orioles' newly formed AL franchise in 1901. McGinnity, who became involved in the developing feud between McGraw and Johnson, experienced mediocre seasons in 1901 and 1902. In July 1902, he joined McGraw and others in jumping to the New York Giants (NL). McGinnity began a string of six remarkable seasons (1903–1908), rarely equalled in over-all domination of the competition. His 10-year major league career ended in 1908 with 246 wins, 142 losses, and a sterling 2.66 ERA. McGinnity completed 314 of 381 starts, struck out 1,068 batters in 3,441.1 innings pitched, and hurled 32 shutouts.

McGinnity joined Newark, NJ (EL), as the team owner and manager in 1909, and led the EL in games (55), innings pitched (422), and wins (29). He journeyed through the minor leagues as a player–manager for 16 years with Tacoma, WA (NWL), Venice, CA (PCL), Butte, MT (NWL), Van-couver, Canada (PCL), and Danville, IL–Dubuque, IA (MVL), amassing over 200 additional wins. In 1923, he incredibly garnered 15 victories as pitcher–manager at Dubuque, IA at age 52. In 1926 manager Wilbert Rob-inson hired McGinnity as a pitching instructor and first base coach for the Brooklyn Robins (NL). Robinson, who later regretted his choice, remarked, "Every time I give Joe a sign, it's like ringing a fire alarm. I don't know if the players are gettin' the sign, but I know everybody in the park is, including the peanut vendor." After conducting laboratory work for several Brooklyn physicians in 1927, McGinnity scouted for the Dodgers from 1928 until succumbing to cancer the next year. He also coached baseball at Williams College.

McGinnity utilized a sidearm (nearly underhanded) delivery of a most effective rising curveball he nicknamed "Old Sal." In 1908, he was involved in the famous Fred Merkle* play that ultimately caused the Giants to lose the NL championship. After Giant Fred Merkle failed to touch second base on what appeared to be the game-winning hit, the Chicago Cubs appealed the play and the game officially was declared a tie. McGinnity claimed to have thrown the actual game ball into the stands. Some observers contended that McGinnity acted too exuberantly, while others commented that McGinnity shrewdly noticed his teammate's error and that the Cubs had used a spare ball supplied from their dugout. This contest became one of the most controversial baseball games ever played.

BIBLIOGRAPHY: John McGinnity file, National Baseball Library, Cooperstown, NY; G. H. Fleming, *The Unforgettable Season* (New York, 1981); Craig Carter, ed., *TSN Daguerreotypes*, 8th ed. (St. Louis, MO, 1990); Noel Hynd, *The Giants of the Polo Grounds* (New York, 1988); Eugene C. Murdock, *Ban Johnson* (Westport, CT, 1982); *NYT*, October 22, November 15–19, 1929; *The Baseball Encyclopedia*, 10th ed. (New York, 1996); Lowell Reidenbaugh, *Baseball's Hall of Fame—Cooperstown* (New York, 1993); Steven A. Reiss, *Touching Base* (Westport, CT, 1980); Lawrence S. Ritter, *The*

Glory of Their Times (New York, 1966); John Thorn, *The Relief Pitcher* (New York, 1979); Richard Goldstein, *Superstars and Screwballs* (New York, 1991); Frank Graham, *The New York Giants* (New York, 1952); Charles C. Alexander, *John McGraw* (New York, 1988); Ray Robinson, *Matty: An American Hero* (New York, 1993); Frank Graham, *McGraw of the Giants* (New York, 1944).

Alan R. Asnen

McGOWAN, William Aloysius "Bill," "Willie," "Big Shot," "No. 1" (b. January 18, 1896, Wilmington, DE; d. December 9, 1954, Silver Springs, MD), umpire, was one of three children of John A. McGowan and Catherine (McCarthy) McGowan. After spending the 1912 season as a semiprofessional second baseman, McGowan began umpiring. He began professional baseball at age 19 in the Class C VL in 1915 and rapidly advanced to the Class B NYSL and Class AA IL in 1916. The IL demoted him to the Class D BRL in 1917. McGowan, who spent the 1918 campaign as a shipyard worker, donned the mask again in the IL from 1919 to 1922 and Class A SA in 1923 and 1924 before joining the AL in 1925.

During the next three decades, the 5-foot 9-inch, 178-pound McGowan became the premier AL umpire and arguably the best arbiter in baseball history. He introduced a new umpiring style with his vigorous, aggressive, demonstrative gestures. Players and managers alike ranked him as the best AL plate umpire and as peerless in conducting a game. A *TSN* poll of players cited him as the AL's Outstanding Umpire of 1935. His selection to umpire the first All-Star game in 1933 and to serve as umpire-in-chief in 1948 for the first play-offs in AL history testified to his status as the circuit's top arbiter. Nicknamed "Big Shot" early in his career, he later respectfully was named "No. 1" by fellow umpires and sportswriters.

McGowan umpired with arrogance, fierce pride, a sharp tongue, and consummate professionalism, being tough-minded but fair. It was universally said of McGowan, "He never ran away, but knew when to walk." Although rarely ejecting anyone from a game, he displayed a temper and irascibility. No other umpire has been suspended twice. His suspensions were 10 days in 1948 for verbally assaulting and throwing his ball-strike indicator at a Washington Senators player and four days in 1952 for "insulting" the press in St. Louis, MO.

McGowan umpired four All-Star games (1933, 1937, 1942, 1950) and 43 contests in eight World Series (1928, 1931, 1935, 1939, 1941, 1944, 1947, 1949). He ranks fifth among major league umpires in length of service and shares third place in World Series assignments. The popular belief is that he umpired 2,541 consecutive games during his first 17 AL seasons, but actually he missed two games on June 25–26, 1931. When diabetes forced McGowan's retirement in 1954, AL owners acknowledged his greatness by doubling his pension payment.

In 1939 McGowan opened the nation's second professional baseball umpire school at the University of Maryland. McGowan taught AL umpiring techniques, in contrast to George Barr's* "NL school." McGowan's school moved in 1940 to Jackson, MS, suspended operations during World War II, and subsequently relocated to Cocoa, FL. His school, the larger and more successful of the two umpire training programs, taught a generation of arbiters and professionalized umpiring.

McGowan married Magdalien "Madge" Ferry in February 1919. They had one son, William A., Jr., and one foster son, William A., who changed his last name from Ferry to McGowan at age 21. In 1977, the Delaware Sports Hall of Fame inducted McGowan posthumously. In 1992, McGowan belatedly was elected to the National Baseball Hall of Fame.

BIBLIOGRAPHY: Bob Addie, "Willie-on-the-Spot McGowan," *BD* 12 (January 1953), pp. 30–32; Clifford Bloodgood, "The Dean of Active Major League Umpires," *BM* 22 (January 1944), pp. 259–260; Dan Daniel, "McGowan's School for Umpires . . .," *BM* 26 (May 1946), pp. 63, 74–75; William A. McGowan file, National Baseball Library, Cooperstown, NY; William A. McGowan file, *TSN* Archives, St. Louis, MO; William A. McGowan, Jr., letter to Larry R. Gerlach; [William] Bill McGowan, "Umpiring under Difficulties," *TSN*, November 4, 1926; *NYT*, December 10, 1954; *TSN*, December 15, 1954; *TSN Baseball Register*, 1943–1954.

Larry R. Gerlach

McGRAW, Frank Edwin, Jr. "Tug" (b. August 30, 1944, Martinez, CA), player, starred as a relief pitcher with the New York Mets (NL) from 1975 to 1984. After the Mets signed the 19-year-old, McGraw spent just four years in the minor leagues. He made the major leagues permanently in 1969, the same year that the Mets miraculously rose from ninth place to win both the NL pennant and World Series. With a superb screwball and the perfect temperament for a reliever, the 6-foot, 180-pound McGraw won nine contests and saved 12 games in 1969. His outgoing, friendly personality also made him a fan favorite first in New York and then with the Philadelphia Phillies (NL), where he was traded in December 1974 for John Stearns, Mac Scarce, and Del Unser. McGraw's best year with the Mets came in 1973, when he saved 25 games. Many of the saves occurred in September, as he helped lead New York to the World Series behind his slogan, "You Gotta Believe." He won one game in the 1973 World Series against the Oakland A's, but the Mets were defeated, four games to three. McGraw also was the NL winning pitcher in the 1972 All-Star Game.

After being traded to the Philadelphia Phillies, McGraw anchored a strong bull pen there from 1975 to 1981. McGraw's stellar performances helped the Phillies continually during their 1980 World Championship season. McGraw was sidelined from late June to mid-July with tendonitis in his shoulder. After coming off the disabled list in July 1980, McGraw proved virtually unhittable and surrendered just three earned runs in 52 innings. He seemed equally overpowering in the NL Championship Series and the World Series, winning one game and saving four others. McGraw's arm never recovered after the 1980 season. He pitched four more years, but was relegated to a backup role in the bull pen. He retired after the 1984 season, having won 96 games and lost 92 decisions with a 3.14 ERA. His record of 180 saves ranked high among left-handed pitchers.

McGraw entered broadcasting for WPVI-TV, an ABC affiliate, in Philadelphia, PA. McGraw and his wife, Phyllis, had two children, one daughter and one son, before their divorce. McGraw, who currently lives in San Marino, CA, owns a sports marketing consulting company in Longwood, FL, and chairs the Major League Baseball Players Marketing Division.

BIBLIOGRAPHY: Tug McGraw file, National Baseball Library, Cooperstown, NY; *The Baseball Encyclopedia*, 10th ed. (New York, 1996); Rich Westcott and Frank Bilovsky, *The New Phillies Encyclopedia* (Philadelphia, PA, 1993); Tom Hultman, "Pressure Never 'Tugged' at McGraw," *SCD* 21 (September 16, 1994), pp. 130–132; Stanley Cohen, *A Magic Summer* (San Diego, CA, 1988); Joseph Durso, *Amazing* (Boston, MA, 1970); Donald Honig, *New York Mets* (New York, 1986); Jack Lang and Peter Simon, *The New York Mets* (New York, 1986); Robert Obojski, "Former Mets Prove Popular Signers at NYC Area Shows," *SCD* 25 (December 18, 1998), pp. 126–127; John Thorn et al., eds., *Total Baseball*, 5th ed. (New York, 1997).

John P. Rossi

McGRAW, John Joseph "Mugsy," "Little Napoleon" (b. April 7, 1873, Truxton, NY; d. February 25, 1934, New Rochelle, NY), player and manager, was the son of Irish-born Civil War veteran John McGraw, who settled in Truxton in 1871. The elder McGraw married Ellen Comerfort and had eight children, four of whom died in infancy. McGraw attended a local grade school and worked as a farmhand and candy butcher on the Elmira, Cortland, and Northern Railroad. He married Blanche Sindall in January 1902 and had no children.

McGraw pitched for the Truxton town team and began his professional baseball career with Olean, NY (NYPL) in 1890. Although an unsuccessful pitcher with Olean, McGraw played well at shortstop and joined Cedar Rapids, IA (3IL) in 1891. In August 1891, he signed with the Baltimore Orioles (AA) and hit .270 in 33 games. In 1892 the Baltimore club merged into an expanded twelve-team NL. McGraw performed brilliantly for the famous rough-and-ready Orioles through the 1899 season. The scrappy 5 foot 7 inch, 155 pound McGraw played third base for the Orioles and hit over .320 seven straight seasons, leading the NL twice in both runs, walks, and on base percentage. McGraw and teammate "Wee Willie" Keeler* developed the hit-and-run play, one of the Orioles' major innovations. McGraw, who hit .334 in his 16-year major league career, managed Baltimore in 1899. After moving to the St. Louis Cardinals (NL) as a player in 1900, he jumped to the new AL and accepted Ban Johnson's* offer to manage the

Baltimore Orioles club in 1901. In 1,099 games, he made 1,309 hits, scored 1,024 runs, walked 836 times, stole 436 bases, and knocked in 462 runs.

McGraw feuded with AL founder and president Johnson when the latter consistently backed his umpires in battles with the fiery McGraw. McGraw consequently accepted the offer of owner Andrew Freedman* to manage the New York Giants (NL) in July 1902. Nicknamed "Little Napoleon," Mc-Graw guided the ineffectual Giants to second place in 1903 and an NL pennant in 1904. The Giants became the most successful NL team for the next thirty years under McGraw's leadership. McGraw engendered high excitement and emotions as manager. Famed sportswriter Grantland Rice* (OS) wrote of McGraw: "His very walk across the field in a hostile town is a challenge to the multitude." Most fans either loved or disliked him intensely, but he helped bolster attendance at baseball games. McGraw stimulated the growth of baseball from the early 1900s until the 1920s, when the lively ball era further elevated the sport's popularity and commercial importance.

Most experts consider McGraw the greatest manager ever. He ranks second only to Connie Mack* in major league games managed (4,769) and in games won (2,763). He captured 10 NL pennants and three world championships over 30 seasons with the Giants and guided New York to only two second division finishes. McGraw's managerial genius produced strategic and tactical innovations and attracted and developed superb players. He had continuing impact on the game through the leadership exerted by his players. McGraw's career evoked continuous arguments, fistfights, and controversies with NL presidents, owners, umpires, opposing managers and players, and off-the-field acquaintances. The bon vivant, raconteur, and man of varied non-baseball interests helped downtrodden players.

McGraw demanded unquestioning obedience from his players and strict compliance with curfew rules. His iron-fisted approach succeeded admirably until the mid–1920s, when several players rebelled openly against his long clubhouse diatribes, vicious tongue-lashings, and fines. Not surprisingly, Mc-Graw failed to win another NL pennant from 1925 through June 3, 1932, when he relinquished managerial duties to first baseman Bill Terry.* In 1937, McGraw was elected to the National Baseball Hall of Fame.

BIBLIOGRAPHY: Charles C. Alexander, *John McGraw* (New York, 1988); Ray Robinson, *Matty: An American Hero* (New York, 1993); Joseph Durso, *Casey and Mr. McGraw* (St. Louis, MO, 1989); Frank Graham, *The New York Giants* (New York, 1952); James H. Bready, *Baseball in Baltimore* (Baltimore, MD, 1998); John McGraw file, National Baseball Library, Cooperstown, NY; Martin Appel and Burt Goldblatt, *Baseball's Best: The Hall of Fame Gallery* (New York, 1977); Frank Graham, *McGraw of the Giants* (New York, 1944); Noel Hynd, *The Giants of the Polo Grounds* (New York, 1988); Joe King, *The San Francisco Giants* (Englewood Cliffs, NJ, 1958); Leonard Koppett, *The Man in the Dugout* (New York, 1993); Tom Knight, "26 Straight for McGraw," *TNP* 11 (1992), pp. 28–30; Daniel Okrent and Harris Lewine, eds., *The Ultimate Baseball Book* (Boston, MA, 1979); Lawrence Ritter, *The Glory of Their Times* (New York, 1966); Fred Stein and Nick Peters, *Day by Day in Giants History* (New York, 1984); Joseph J. Vecchione, ed., *The New York Times Book of Sports Legends* (New York, 1991).

Fred Stein

McGREGOR, Scott Houston (b. January 18, 1954, Inglewood, CA), player, is the son of John McGregor, a tax consultant, and Frances McGregor, a secretary. As a left-handed pitcher for El Segundo High School, McGregor compiled a 51–4 win–loss record and 0.39 ERA in four seasons. During his senior year, he hit better than teammate George Brett.* His El Segundo team won the 1969 Babe Ruth world championship.

The New York Yankees (AL) selected the 6-foot 1-inch, 192-pound McGregor in the first round of the 1972 draft. He won 7 and lost 3 with Ft. Lauderdale, FL (FSL) that year. In June 1976, while pitching for Syracuse, NY (IL), McGregor was involved in a 10-player trade between the New York Yankees and the Baltimore Orioles (AL). He completed the 1976 season with Rochester, NY (IL). His overall 12–6 record and IL-leading six shutouts earned him a promotion to the Baltimore Orioles in September. His first major league start on September 29 resulted in a loss to the Milwaukee Brewers.

McGregor grew up as a fan of the Los Angeles Dodgers' southpaw Sandy Koufax,* but could not match the latter's fastball. He relied on changing speeds and control, frustrating fastball-crushing sluggers. McGregor averaged 2.18 walks per nine innings, leading the AL with 1.16 in 1979. He also developed a deceptive pickoff move that limited base stealers to a 59 percent success rate. In 1987, he picked off a career-high 10 base runners.

McGregor was plagued by arm and shoulder problems and other injuries throughout his career. In 1984, a broken finger on his pitching hand sidelined him for the final month. Still, he won at least 13 games in eight of his 13 years with the Orioles from 1978 to 1985, being the only major league pitcher during that period to compile a .500 or better record each year. On the Baltimore Orioles' all-time pitching list, he ranks fourth in innings (2,124), fifth in wins (138), games (352), shutouts (23), and complete games (83), and seventh in strikeouts (894).

McGregor's only 20-victory season came in 1980, when he finished with 20 wins and eight losses and earned a place on the 1981 All-Star team. He retired in 1988 with a 138–108 record for a .561 winning percentage and 3.99 ERA.

McGregor fared 1–1 in AL Championship Series action and 2–2 in the 1979 World Series against the Pittsburgh Pirates and the 1983 fall classic against the Philadelphia Phillies. His personal career highlights included his

8–0 win over the California Angels to clinch the 1979 AL pennant and his 5–0 five-hit victory over the Philadelphia Phillies to give the Baltimore Orioles the 1983 world championship.

McGregor began working with youth groups in 1980 serving as youth pastor at The Rock Church in Baltimore. In 1987, he founded an anti-drug program and traveled to Korea on behalf of the Christian Youth Athletic program. He is now an ordained minister in Dover, DE.

On September 27, 1976, McGregor married Cara Bell. They have three children, Eric, Katherine, and Michael.

BIBLIOGRAPHY: Ted Patterson, *The Baltimore Orioles* (Dallas, TX, 1995); Earl Weaver and Berry Stainback, *It's What You Learn After You Know It All That Counts* (Garden City, NY, 1982); *Baltimore Orioles 1988 Media Guide*; Rex Barney, *Rex Barney's Orioles Memories* (Woodbury, CT, 1994); Baltimore (MD) *Evening Sun*, June 15, 1990.

                                                                        Norman L. Macht

McGRIFF, Frederick Stanley "Fred" (b. October 31, 1963, Tampa, FL), player, is the youngest of five children of Earl McGriff, a television repair shop owner–operator, and Eliza McGriff, an elementary school teacher, and starred in baseball as a junior and senior at Jefferson High School in Tampa, FL. The New York Yankees (AL) drafted McGriff in the ninth round in June 1981 and assigned him to Bradenton, FL (GCL).

In December 1982, the New York Yankees traded the patient, easygoing, 6-foot 3-inch, 215-pound left-hander to the Toronto Blue Jays (AL). His minor league stops from 1983 through 1986 included Florence, SC (SAL), Kinston, NC (CrL), Knoxville, TN (SL), and Syracuse, NY (IL). The Toronto Blue Jays promoted McGriff briefly in 1986 and named him DH in 1987, when he broke Jesse Barfield's* rookie club record for HR (20). Although striking out frequently, McGriff walked often, recorded high on-base and slugging percentages, and belted tape measure HR. No major leaguer matched his 106 HR from 1988 to 1990. In 1988, he led AL first basemen in fielding (.997) and finished second in HR (34), slugging percentage (.552), and extra base hits (73). McGriff, who belted the Skydome's first HR, paced the AL with 36 HR, knocked in 92 runs, and established a club record with 119 walks in 1989, helping the Toronto Blue Jays take the AL East title. McGriff's honors included making the *TSN* Silver Slugger and All-Star teams. In 1990, he batted .300, clouted 35 HR, and ranked second in on-base percentage (.400).

In a blockbuster December 1990 trade, the Toronto Blue Jays sent McGriff and Tony Fernandez* to the San Diego Padres (NL) for Roberto Alomar* and Joe Carter.* McGriff knocked in 106 runs and led the NL in intentional walks (26) in 1991. He tied a major league record in August, belting grand-slam HR in consecutive games against the Houston Astros. In June 1992, the NL suspended McGriff four games for charging the mound and fighting San Francisco Giants pitcher Trevor Wilson. He still plated 104 runs and became the first San Diego Padre to pace the NL in HR (35). No other player previously had led both major leagues in HR. McGriff made two hits in his first All-Star Game and received *TSN* NL All-Star and Silver Slugger team honors. McGriff also helped newly acquired third baseman Gary Sheffield* enjoy a superlative season.

In July 1993, the San Diego Padres traded McGriff to the Atlanta Braves (NL) for three minor leaguers. The Atlanta Braves possessed the NL's best pitching staff, but floundered at the plate until McGriff arrived. Subsequently, the Atlanta Braves averaged nearly six runs a game, compiled a 54–19 record the second half of the season to overtake the San Francisco Giants for the NL West crown, and set a then franchise record with 104 victories. McGriff finished the 1993 season with a .291 batting average, a career-high 37 HR (including 19 with the Atlanta Braves), and 101 RBI. The Philadelphia Phillies upset the Atlanta Braves in the NL Championship Series, as McGriff batted .435 with one HR and four RBI. During the strike-shortened 1994 season, he batted a career-best .318 with 34 HR and 94 RBI. His dramatic game-tying HR for the 1994 NL All-Stars in the ninth inning earned him MVP honors, enabling the NL ultimately to end a six-game losing streak to the AL All-Stars. In 1994, he became only the ninth player in major league history to belt at least 30 HR seven consecutive seasons.

McGriff batted .280 with 27 HR and 93 RBI in 1995, helping the Atlanta Braves capture the NL East. He hit .333 and clouted two HR with six RBI in the NL Division Series against the Colorado Rockies. He set single game NL Division Series records by knocking in five runs and belting two HR on October 7. His .438 batting average and four doubles sparked Atlanta in the NL Championship Series against the Cincinnati Reds. He clouted a HR in his first World Series at-bat and finished with a .261 batting average, two HR, and three RBI to help defeat the Cleveland Indians. In 1996, McGriff's .295 batting average, 28 HR, and 107 RBI aided Atlanta in taking the NL East title. He hit .333 with one HR and three RBI in the NL Division Series against the Los Angeles Dodgers and recorded two HR and seven RBI against the St. Louis Cardinals in the NL Championship Series. McGriff batted .300 with two HR and six RBI against the triumphant New York Yankees in the World Series and made the NL All-Star team in both 1995 and 1996. After knocking in 97 runs in 1997, he plated four runs in the NL Championship Series loss to the Florida Marlins. He shares the NL Championship Series record for most doubles with nine. In November 1997, the expansion Tampa Bay Devil Rays (AL) drafted him. McGriff batted .310 with 32 HR and 104 RBI in 1999.

In 14 major league seasons, the Tampa, FL resident has batted .287 with 354 doubles, 380 HR, and 1,192 RBI. Thirty-nine percent of his 1,946 hits have been for extra bases. He and his wife, Veronica, married in October 1988 and have two children, Erick and Ericka.

BIBLIOGRAPHY: Fred McGriff file, National Baseball Library, Cooperstown, NY; "The Quiet Man," *TSN 1994 Baseball Yearbook*, pp. 138–139; *San Diego Padres 1991 Media Guide*; B. Keidan and W. Ladson, "Compadres," *Sport* 84 (March 1993), pp. 58–61; Mike Shatzkin, ed., *The Ballplayers* (New York, 1990); *TSN Official Baseball Register*, 1998; John Thorn et al., eds., *Total Braves* (New York, 1996); Ralph Wiley, "Hit It a Mile," *SI* 70 (May 8, 1989), pp. 34–36.

David L. Porter

McGUIRE, James Thomas "Deacon," "Jim" (b. November 18, 1863, Youngstown, OH; d. October 31, 1936, Duck Lake, MI), player, manager, coach, and scout, began his professional baseball career as a bare-handed catcher. The 6-foot 1-inch, 185-pound, right-handed–batting, left-handed–throwing McGuire attracted major league attention in 1881 as battery mate of Charles "Lady" Baldwin* in Hastings, MI. McGuire, whose nickname "Deacon" reflected his fair play, began his record 26-year major league career with the Toledo, OH Blue Stockings (AA) in 1884. He played in the minor leagues with Indianapolis, IN (WL) for part of the 1885 season until the Detroit Wolverines (NL) signed him.

The Detroit Wolverines traded McGuire in 1886 to the Philadelphia Phillies (NL), where he played two and a half seasons. The 1888 campaign saw him appear with Philadelphia, Detroit, and the Cleveland Blues (AA) while the 1889 season saw him with minor league Toronto, Canada (IA). After spending 1890 with the Rochester, NY Broncos (AA) and 1891 with the Washington, D.C. Statesmen (AA), McGuire returned to the NL with the Washington Senators from 1892 to 1899 and performed his best baseball there. In 1895, he established a record for catchers by appearing in 132 games for Washington. He led NL catchers in putouts (408) and assists (181) that year and in putouts (351) and double plays (14) in 1896. In 1897, the Senators benefited from McGuire's career best .343 batting average. Washington compiled a 21–47 win–loss mark under manager McGuire in 1898.

In 1899 Washington traded McGuire at mid-season to the first-place Brooklyn Superbas (NL), thus helping the Superbas capture the NL pennant with McGuire's .318 batting average. McGuire caught for NL pennant–winning Brooklyn in 1900 and moved permanently in 1902 to the new AL, performing for the Detroit Tigers in 1902 and 1903 and the New York Highlanders from 1904 to 1907. In 1904, he ranked first among AL catchers in double plays (11) and second in putouts (536). Managerial stints followed with the Boston Red Sox (AL) in 1907 and 1908 and the Cleveland Naps (AL) from 1909 to 1911, with McGuire attaining a 189–240 record. Altogether, McGuire compiled a 210–287 mark as a major league manager. McGuire finished his major league career as coach (1911–1916) and scout (1917–1924) with the Detroit Tigers (AL). In his final game as a player, he made one hit and scored one run for Detroit in 1912. Albion (MI) College hired him as a baseball coach in 1926.

McGuire compiled a .278 lifetime major league batting average with 300 doubles, 79 triples, 45 HR, and 117 stolen bases. The career catching records list McGuire first in assists (1,859) and high in double plays (142). He broke every finger of both hands during his career, but these injuries never sidelined him for long. He retired with his wife, May, on his Duck Lake farm near Albion, MI.

BIBLIOGRAPHY: Thomas Aylesworth and Benton Minks, *The Encyclopedia of Baseball Managers* (New York, 1990); Robert Redmount, *The Red Sox Encyclopedia* (Champaign, IL, 1998); *The Baseball Encyclopedia*, 10th ed. (New York, 1996); Frank Graham, *The New York Yankees* (New York, 1943); Frederick C. Lieb, *The Detroit Tigers* (New York, 1946); Fred Smith, *995 Tigers* (Detroit, MI, 1981); Morris Bealle, *The Washington Senators* (Washington, DC, 1947); Shirley Povich, *The Washington Senators* (Washington, DC, 1954); David Nemec, *The Beer and Whisky League* (New York, 1994); Bill James, *The Bill James Historical Baseball Abstract* (New York, 1986); James McGuire file, National Baseball Library, Cooperstown, NY; Robert Miller Smith, *Heroes of Baseball* (New York, 1952); John Thorn et al., eds., *Total Baseball*, 5th ed. (New York, 1997); Robert L. Tiemann and Mark Rucker, eds., *Nineteenth Century Stars* (Kansas City, MO, 1989).

                                                                 Gaymon L. Bennett

McGUNNIGLE, William Henry "Billy," "Mac," "Cap," "Gunner" (b. January 1, 1855, Boston, MA; d. March 9, 1899, Brockton, MA), player and manager, ranked among the most competent, beloved baseball figures of the 19th century. The son of Captain James McGunnigle, a Civil War veteran, McGunnigle attended East Houghton (now Avon), MA schools and married Mary McCullough in 1874. They had seven children.

The 5-foot 9-inch, 155-pound right-hander broke into professional baseball with the Howard Juniors of Brockton, MA (MasL) in 1875 and spent the 1876 and 1877 seasons with Fall River, MA (NEL). He invented the catcher's mitt, in reality a padded mason's glove with the fingertips cut out. The 1878 through 1880 campaigns found McGunnigle with the Buffalo, NY Bisons (NL) and Worcester, MA Ruby Legs (NL), where he excelled defensively as a right fielder. In 1879, his rifle arm cut down 28 batters who had "singled" to right field, thus earning him the New York *Clipper*'s medal as the year's best right fielder. After a brief hiatus, McGunnigle returned to baseball with Saginaw, MI (NWL) in 1883 as a right fielder, pitcher, and captain. McGunnigle moved to Bay City, MI (NWL) in 1884 and caught John Clarkson.* In 1885 McGunnigle managed Brockton to a first place NEL finish. After spending another year in Brockton, McGunnigle piloted Lowell, MA (NEL) to an NEL pennant in 1887. McGunnigle managed the Brooklyn Trolley-Dodgers (AA) to second place in 1888 and the Bridegrooms to first place with a 94–43 record in 1889. Brooklyn moved to the NL in 1890, finishing first with a 86–43 mark. After a disagreement with Brooklyn's president C. H. Byrne in 1891, McGunnigle signed at mid-season

to manage the woeful Pittsburgh Pirates (NL) to a 24–33 record. Mc-
Gunnigle in 1892 took Brockton from the cellar to an NEL pennant. In
1894 and 1895, he organized polo teams in Providence, RI and Pawtucket,
RI. McGunnigle managed the Louisville Colonels (NL) to a 36–76 mark in
1896, but left because of the incessant infighting there.

McGunnigle also enjoyed success as a cigar and shoe salesman. His baseball shoe, "The McGunnigle," proved very popular in New England. He
owned and managed a Rollo-Polo rink for hockey on roller skates and a bar
in Brockton. In 1897, he suffered a severe injury to his hip in a trolley car–
wagon collision in Brockton, MA. His health gradually declined prior to his
death from pneumonia. McGunnigle's three year major league playing career
as an outfielder and pitcher included a .173 batting average and an 11–8
mark with a 2.81 ERA. He won 328 games while losing 247 for a .570
winning percentage in five major league seasons as a manager.

BIBLIOGRAPHY: Bill McGunnigle file, National Baseball Library, Cooperstown, NY;
The Baseball Encyclopedia, 10th ed. (New York, 1996); Richard Goldstein, *Superstars
and Screwballs* (New York, 1991); Frank Graham, *The Brooklyn Dodgers* (New York,
1945); David Pearson, *Baseball in 1889* (Bowling Green, OH, 1993); David Nemec,
The Beer and Whisky League (New York, 1994).

John H. Ziegler

McGWIRE, Mark David (b. October 1, 1963, Pomona, CA), player, is the
son of John McGwire, a dentist, and Ginger McGwire and attended Damien
High School in Claremont, CA. McGwire played three years of college baseball at the University of Southern California, setting the PTC record for
HR in a season with 32. His brother, Dan, quarterbacked for the Seattle
Seahawks (NFL) from 1991 through 1994. The 6-foot 5-inch, 225-pound
first baseman, who throws and bats right-handed, was selected by the Montreal Expos (NL) in the eighth round of the free agent draft in June 1981.

McGwire enrolled at Southern California as a promising pitcher, rated by
coach Rod Dedeaux* as having major league ability on the mound. His future
changed when, after his freshman season, he led the ASL in hitting. As a
freshman pitcher, he won four decisions and lost four games with a 3.04
ERA. He was switched to first base as a sophomore, hitting .319 with 19
HR. His junior year saw him bat .387 with 32 HR.

McGwire played on the Pan-American and U.S. Olympic teams in 1984.
Selected by the Oakland Athletics (AL) in the first round of the June 1984
free agent draft (tenth overall pick), he played briefly with Modesto, CA
(CaL) in 1984. He spent a full season there in 1985, hitting 24 HR, pro-
ducing 106 RBI and batting .274. In 1986, he played 55 games at Huntsville,
AL (SL), 78 games at Tacoma, WA (PCL), and 18 games with the Oakland
Athletics (AL) at third base. He made 41 errors in 1986, trying to master
third base.

Fourteen games into the 1987 season, McGwire became the regular Oakland Athletics first baseman. In 1987, he established a major league record for most HR by a rookie with 49 and also set a mark for extra bases on long hits (183). His honors included being named *TSN* and BBWAA AL Rookie of the Year. From 1987 through 1994, McGwire's major league production included 238 HR and 657 RBI. McGwire shares the major league record for most HR in two consecutive games (5), hitting three on June 27 and two more on June 28, 1987. He holds the AL rookie season record for highest slugging percentage, attaining .618 in 1987.

In four AL Championship Series (1988–1990, 1992), McGwire batted .258 with three HR and 11 RBI. In three World Series (1988–1990), he batted an anemic .188 with a single HR. He was selected on the AL All-Star team six consecutive times from 1987 to 1992 and from 1995 through 1997. In 1984, McGwire was named *TSN* College Player of the Year and first base-man on the *TSN* College All-America team. Besides being AL Gold Glove first baseman, he in 1992 was named first baseman on the *TSN* AL All-Star and Silver Slugger teams. McGwire paced AL first basemen in 1990 with 1,429 total chances. Injuries sidelined him for much of the 1993–1995 sea-sons, but he clouted 39 HR with 90 RBI in 104 games in 1995. McGwire hit three HR on June 11, 1995 against the Boston Red Sox. His HR pro-duction soared dramatically the next three seasons. In 1996, he led the AL with 52 HR and a .730 slugging percentage, batted .312, and knocked in 113 runs, the most since his rookie season. The following season, he clouted 34 HR with 81 RBI in 105 games for Oakland. In July 1997, the Oakland Athletics traded him to the St. Louis Cardinals (NL). McGwire went on a HR binge, clouting 24 in just 59 games for St. Louis. His 58 HR marked the most in the major leagues since Roger Maris* belted 61 in 1961. He reached his 400th career major league HR faster than any player in history and made the NL All-Star team in 1998 and 1999.

The AP Player of the Year in 1998, McGwire clouted 70 HR to shatter the 37-year-old single season HR record of 61 set by Roger Maris of the New York Yankees (AL) in 1961. His historic HR chase captivated a nation and reinvigorated the sport, which had slumped since the 1994 player strike. McGwire led the major leagues in slugging percentage (.752) and on base percentage (.470), helped by tying the NL-single-season record 162 walks. In 1998, he batted .299 with 130 runs scored and 147 RBI in 155 games and homered every 7.3 at-bats. McGwire began his season record onslaught with a grand slam HR against the Los Angeles Dodgers on opening day at Busch Stadium in St. Louis and broke Maris's record at 8:18 P.M. on September 8 at Busch Stadium. Steve Trachsel of the Chicago Cubs surrendered the record-breaking 62nd HR, ironically McGwire's shortest HR (only 341 feet) of the season, in the fourth inning. McGwire homered five times in his last 11 at-bats of the season against the Montreal Expos and clouted two HR on September 27 in the season finale at Busch Stadium. His historic 377 foot 70th HR came in the seventh inning off Carl Pavano on his final swing of the season. Television cameras captured McGwire celebrating the record by giving his 10-year-old son, Matt, heart-tugging hugs. He set the record with remarkable humility, paying respect throughout the pursuit to the Maris family and Sammy Sosa* of the Chicago Cubs, who had challenged McGwire with 66 HR. McGwire, who led the HR race with Sosa for all but 103 minutes, enjoyed 10 multi-HR games and clouted one HR 550 feet, finishing second in the NL MVP balloting. In 1999, he led the NL with 65 HR and 147 RBI and ranked second in slugging percentage (.697) and walks (133). He and Sosa became the first major leaguers to clout at least 60 HR in two consecutive seasons. On August 5, he became the 16th player with 500 HR.

From 1987 through 1999, McGwire's major league production included 1,498 hits, 522 HR, 1,277 RBI, and a .265 batting average. He holds major league records for most HR by a right-hander in two consecutive seasons with 128 in 1997 and 1998, three consecutive seasons with 180 in 1996, 1997, and 1998, and four consecutive seasons with 245 from 1996 to 1999 and most HR by a right-handed batter (70) and by a first baseman (70). He also shares the major league record for most HR in one inning (2) in the fifth inning on September 22, 1996 and holds the Oakland A's all-time records for most HR (363) and RBI (941). He earned *TSN* AL All-Star team and AL Silver Slugger awards in 1996, *TSN* NL All-Star team and NL Silver Slugger awards in 1998, and *TSN* Sportsman of the Year in 1997. In 1999, he was named to the USA Baseball All-Time Team. He led the major leagues with 405 HR in the 1990s and made Major League Baseball's All-Century Team. He resides in Pomona, CA, plays golf for a hobby, is divorced from Kathy Williamson, and has one son, Matthew.

BIBLIOGRAPHY: Mark McGwire file, National Baseball Library, Cooperstown, NY; Dennis Bracken, "Mr. Nice Guy," Minneapolis (MN) *Star Tribune*, July 31, 1987, pp. 1, 70; Stan Carlson, Clipping file 1987–1990, Minneapolis, MN; Ron Fimrite, "The Bay Area Bombers," *SI* 68 (April 4, 1988), pp. 44–49; R. Kroichick, "Double Damage!" *Sport* 81 (October 1990), pp. 106–107; "Mark McGwire," *A&E Biography*, September 26, 1998; A. Murphy, "In Sight," *SI* 85 (August 26, 1996), pp. 32–34; Hank Hersch, "Mark McGwire," *SI* 67 (July 13, 1987), pp. 42ff; Jonathan Hall, *Mark McGwire: A Biography* (New York, 1998); Tom Verducci, "Stroke of Genius," *SI* 89 (December 21, 1998), pp. 44–53; Daniel Okrent, "A Mac for All Seasons," *Time* 152 (December 28, 1998–January 4, 1999), pp. 138–142; *Oakland Media Guide*, 1994; *TSN Official Baseball Register*, 1998; *USAT*, September 9, 27, 1998; Tom Verducci, "Man on a Mission," *SI* 88 (March 23, 1998), pp. 76–84; Steve Wulf, "Most Happy Fella," *SI* 76 (June 1, 1992), pp. 42–45; Dan Valenti, *Clout: The Top Home Runs in Baseball History* (Lexington, MA, 1989); George Vecsey et al., *McGwire and Sosa* (New York, 1998); Leif Schreiber, *Race for the Record* (New York, 1998).

Stan W. Carlson

McHALE, John Joseph (b. September 21, 1921, Detroit, MI), player and executive, is the son of John and Catherine (Kelly) McHale and graduated in 1947 from the University of Notre Dame, where he played football two years. The 6-foot, 200-pound McHale joined the Detroit Tigers (AL) organization as a first baseman. Between 1943 and 1948, he performed at first base for Muskegon, MI (MISL), Beaumont, TX (TL), Winston-Salem, NC (CrL), and Buffalo, NY (IL). He played several games with the Detroit Tigers in 1945 and 1947 and made brief appearances in 1943, 1944, and 1948. McHale, who served in the U.S. Navy from 1943 to 1944, threw right-handed and batted left-handed. In 64 major league games, he collected 22 hits, 1 double, 3 HR, and 12 RBI, and compiled a .193 batting average. McHale made three pinch-hitting appearances for Detroit against the Chicago Cubs in the 1945 World Series.

After failing to win the regular first base position, McHale moved to the Tigers' front office. Under general managers "Red" Rolfe,* Charles Gehringer,* Muddy Ruel,* and Spike Briggs,* McHale served as assistant director of minor league clubs (1948), assistant farm director (1948–1953), director of minor league clubs (1954–1955), and director of player personnel (1956–1957) before becoming general manager on April 30, 1957. The Milwaukee Braves (NL) made him their vice-president and general manager in early 1959 and named him club president two years later. McHale remained in that position until becoming administrative assistant to the Commissioner of Baseball for the 1967 and 1968 seasons.

In 1968, McHale was appointed president and chief executive officer of the Montreal Expos (NL) when the Canadian team entered the NL. He held the presidency through 1986 and was chief executive officer through 1987. McHale also participated on the board of directors, being deputy chair in 1988 and 1989. He served as NL vice-president from 1970 through 1986. Several months after accepting the Montreal job, McHale was seriously considered for the Commissioner of Baseball position when General William Eckert* was dismissed. McHale, however, later withdrew his application to remain with the Expos. He spent 1993 and 1994 as executive of baseball operations of the expansion Colorado Rockies (NL) and as president and chief executive officer of the Detroit Tigers (AL) since 1995. He chairs the Major League Baseball Promotion Corporation and belongs to both baseball's executive council and the board of directors of the Perini Corporation, which formerly owned the Boston Braves (NL) and Milwaukee Braves (NL). He also presides over the Association of Professional Baseball Players of America. McHale married Patricia Ann Cameron on February 15, 1947 and has six children, Patricia, John, Kevin, Anne, Brian, and Mary.

BIBLIOGRAPHY: John McHale file, National Baseball Library, Cooperstown, NY; Gene Karst and Martin J. Jones, Jr., *Who's Who in Professional Baseball* (New Rochelle, NY, 1973); *The Baseball Encyclopedia*, 10th ed. (New York, 1996); *WWA*, 39th ed. (1976–1977), p. 2112; Joe Falls, *Detroit Tigers* (New York, 1975); Bob Buege, *The Milwaukee Braves: A Baseball Eulogy* (Milwaukee WI, 1988); Gary Caruso, *The Braves Encyclopedia* (Philadelphia, PA, 1995).

John L. Evers

McINNIS, John Phalen "Stuffy" (b. September 19, 1890, Gloucester, MA; d. February 16, 1960, Ipswich, MA), player, manager, and coach, batted .307 lifetime and set numerous fielding records for first basemen during a 19-year major league career. McInnis was the son of Stephen McInnis and

Udavilla (Grady) McInnis of Gloucester. His father worked as a caretaker, chauffeur, and assistant chief of the town's fire department. After attending Babson Elementary School, McInnis graduated from Gloucester High School, where he played on the baseball team. In 1908, the teenager jumped from semi-pro baseball to the minor leagues with Haverhill, MA (NEL). He joined the Philadelphia Athletics (AL) in 1909 and stayed there through 1917.

After two seasons as a substitute shortstop, McInnis became the regular Philadelphia first baseman in 1911 and joined Eddie Collins,* Jack Barry,* and "Home Run" Baker* to form the famed "$100,000 Infield," still considered among the best of all time. During nine years with the Athletics, McInnis batted below .300 as a regular only one season (.295 in 1916). The Athletics won four AL pennants and captured three world championships, defeating the Chicago Cubs in 1910 and the New York Giants in 1911 and 1913. In the 1914 World Series, McInnis's club was swept in four games by the underdog Boston Braves.

McInnis was traded to the Boston Red Sox (AL) in January 1918 and helped them capture the AL pennant and world championship that year. Another trade sent McInnis to the Cleveland Indians (AL) in December 1921. The 1923 season found him back in Boston, where the Braves (NL) had claimed him on waivers. After being released by the Braves in April 1925, he signed with the Pittsburgh Pirates (NL) and sparked them to a pennant and World Series victory by batting .368 in 59 games.

As manager of the 1927 Philadelphia Phillies (NL), McInnis completed his major league playing career by appearing in one game and led the team to a last place finish with a 51–103 record. He returned to the NEL in 1928, closing out his player–manager days with the Salem, MA club. From 1929 through 1954, McInnis coached baseball at Norwich University, The Brooks School, and Harvard University. McInnis married Elsie Sherman Dow in 1918 and had one daughter.

Although just 5-feet 9½-inches tall and 162 pounds, the right-hander became a superb first baseman. A league leader in fielding average six times, putouts three times, and assists twice; he compiled a .993 career average. His records included the major league season marks for highest average (.999), fewest errors (1), and most chances accepted without error (1,300) by a first baseman, all in 1921. That same season, he played in an AL-record 119 consecutive errorless games. Over a two-year span (1921–1922), he played 163 straight games without an error to set another major league record. In 20 World Series games, he committed just one error in over 200 chances.

McInnis, although renowned for his glovework, proved a dangerous contact hitter, seldom struck out, and consistently batted at or near the .300 mark throughout his long career. In 2,128 major league games, he made 2,405 hits, drove in 1,062 runs, and compiled 312 doubles, 101 triples, 20

HR, 872 runs scored, and 172 stolen bases. His best year came in 1912, when he batted .327, drove in 101 runs, and led the AL in putouts, assists, and double plays.

BIBLIOGRAPHY: Thomas Aylesworth and Benton Minks, *The Encyclopedia of Baseball Managers* (New York, 1990); Frederick G. Lieb, *Connie Mack* (Philadelphia, PA, 1945); Connie Mack, *My 66 Years in the Big Leagues* (Philadelphia, PA, 1950); Ira L. Smith, *Baseball's Famous First Basemen* (New York, 1956); Frederick G. Lieb, *The Pittsburgh Pirates* (New York, 1948); Gloucester (MA) *Daily Times*, March 4, 1972; Gene Karst and Martin J. Jones, Jr., *Who's Who in Professional Baseball* (New Rochelle, NY, 1973); John McInnis file, National Baseball Library, Cooperstown, NY; *NYT*, February 17, 1960; Providence (RI) *Journal*, February 17, 1960; Jerome C. Romanowski, *The Mackmen* (Upper Darby, PA, 1979); Frederick G. Lieb, *The Boston Red Sox* (New York, 1947); Robert Redmount, *The Red Sox Encyclopedia* (Champaign, IL, 1998).

Joseph Lawler

MACK, Connie "The Tall Tactician" (b. Cornelius Alexander McGillicuddy, December 22, 1862, East Brookfield, MA; d. February 8, 1956, Germantown, PA), player, manager, and executive, was the son of Irish immigrants Michael McGillicuddy and Mary McGillicuddy. His father fought in the Civil War and worked in the cotton mills and shoe factories around Brookfield. Mack left school as a teenager for a job in the shoe factory to help support his family after his father's death. The tall, lanky 6-foot 1-inch, 150-pound Mack began an undistinguished baseball playing career in 1884 by catching for Meriden, CT (CtL) and for Hartford, CT (NECSL) in 1885 and (EL) in 1886. Between 1886 and 1889, he played for the Washington Statesmen (NL). Although known more for his defensive than hitting skills, he jumped to the Buffalo Bisons (PL) in 1890 and enjoyed his most active year as a player (123 games) there. Mack performed with the Pittsburgh Pirates (NL) from 1891 to 1896 and became playing manager in 1894 partly because of his reputation as a tricky catcher who distracted hitters by talking and tipping their bats. From 1894 to 1896, Mack managed Pittsburgh to a 149–134 win–loss record. He compiled a lifetime .245 batting average with 659 hits, 391 runs, and 265 RBI spanning 11 major league seasons. Mack was married twice: in 1887 to Margaret Hogan, who died in 1892 and had three children, Roy, Earle, and Margaret; and in 1910 to Katherine A. Hallahan, who had five children, Mary, Connie, Jr., Ruth, Rita, and Elizabeth.

A friendship with Byron Johnson* won Mack the managing job at Milwaukee, WI (WL) from 1897 to 1900, when the former granted Ben Shibe* and Mack the Philadelphia Athletics franchise in the new AL. The part-owner of the Athletics and manager for a record 50 years, Mack symbolized the game's striving for respectability and a public image of gentlemanly conduct on and off the field. He provided that model through his abstemious habits, mild manners, devotion to family, and conservative managing style.

Mack always remained a shrewd businessman who enticed members from the crosstown Phillies to build his team and kept a tight rein on player salaries. Mack played collegian Eddie Collins* in the major leagues under a false name, costing the latter his amateur standing at Columbia University.

Known as "The Tall Tactician," Mack built and dismantled great Athletics teams. Mack's clubs won four AL pennants and three World Series between 1910 and 1914 by combining good pitching and the "$100,000 infield," led by Collins and "Home Run" Baker.* Refusing to meet higher salaries offered to team members by the upstart FL, Mack sold his stars in 1915. The Athletics consequently dropped into last place from 1915 through 1921. The AL pennant returned to Philadelphia between 1929 and 1931 and world championships came in 1929 and 1930, due to Mack's impressive blend of power pitcher Lefty Grove* and sluggers Al Simmons,* Jimmie Foxx,* and Mickey Cochrane.* Once again, however, he broke up a winning combination, claiming operating losses from the Great Depression. Mack reportedly commented that good teams with high-paid stars proved less profitable than his poor ones. He retired from managing after the 1950 season, leaving a record of nine AL pennants, five World Series championships, 17 cellar finishes, and first place among managers in total games (7,755), wins (3,731), and losses (3,948) for a .486 winning percentage.

Remembered for wearing street clothes on the bench and waving his scorecard to give directions, Mack appeared aloof and taciturn. He earned the respect of players with his gentle and patient manner, a style often contrasted earlier with the pugnacious ways of New York Giants manager John J. McGraw.* He proved a keen judge of playing talent and a skillful handler of diverse personalities, ranging from college stars Collins, Eddie Plank,* and Chief Bender* to the man-child Rube Waddell,* who won 131 games for the Athletics between 1902 and 1907. Mack adjusted to the changing style of the game, building great teams in both the dead and live ball eras. Philadelphia honored Mack for his service to the city with the prestigious Bok Award in 1930. In 1937, Mack was named to the National Baseball Hall of Fame.

BIBLIOGRAPHY: Bob Considine, "Mister Mack," *Life* 25 (August 9, 1948), pp. 92–98; Frederick Ivor-Campbell et al., eds., *Baseball's First Stars* (Cleveland, OH, 1996); Leonard Koppett, *The Man in the Dugout* (New York, 1993); Thomas Aylesworth and Benton Minks, *The Encyclopedia of Baseball Managers* (New York, 1990); Frederick G. Lieb, *Connie Mack* (New York, 1945); Connie Mack, *My 66 Years in the Big Leagues* (Philadelphia, PA, 1950); Jerome C. Romanowski, *The Mackmen* (Upper Darby, PA, 1979); Daniel Okrent and Harris Lewine, eds., *The Ultimate Baseball Book* (Boston, MA, 1979); John R. Tunis, "Connie Mack: First Citizen of Philadelphia," *AM* 166 (August 1940), pp. 212–216; Joseph J. Vecchione, ed., *The New York Times Book of Sports Legends* (New York, 1991).

Joseph E. King

McKEAN, Edward John "Ed," "Mack" (b. June 6, 1864, Grafton, OH; d. August 16, 1919, Cleveland, OH), player and manager, captained and played shortstop for the Cleveland Spiders (NL) in the 1890s. He grew up in Cleveland, OH, where he and his wife, Belle, had three sons and one daughter. He started his professional baseball career with Youngstown, OH (IOL) in 1884 and played for Providence, RI (EL) and Rochester, NY (IL) in 1886 before making the major leagues.

In 1887, McKean joined his hometown Cleveland Blues, an AA team until shifting to the NL as the Spiders two years later. The 5-foot 9-inch, 160-pound right-handed McKean was known for hustle, aggressive play, and umpire baiting, leading him to be named team captain in 1891. The following year, Cleveland joined the Boston Beaneaters and Baltimore Orioles as the dominant teams when Denton "Cy" Young* and Jesse Burkett* came to the Spiders. In 1892, Cleveland captured the second half championship of the NL's only scheduled split season after Boston had easily won the first half. When Boston swept the Spiders in the post-season playoffs, the NL abolished the split season format and instituted the Temple Cup series between first and second place finishers. In the 1895 Temple Cup series, second place Cleveland upset the Baltimore Orioles, four games to one. Burkett and McKean, who hit .300, gave Cleveland a strong one-two combination to back Young's three pitching victories. The two clubs again played for the Temple Cup in 1896, but the Orioles swept the series.

McKean enjoyed his best major league seasons between 1893 and 1896, batting over .300 (.357 in 1894, .342 in 1895, and .338 in 1896), scoring over 100 runs, driving in at least 100 runs for four straight seasons, and fielding well. The performance of McKean and Cleveland declined after 1896. McKean finished his 13-year major league career with the St. Louis Perfectos (NL) in 1899 and compiled a .302 lifetime batting average. In 1,654 major league games, he made 2,083 hits, 272 doubles, 158 triples, 635 walks, and 323 stolen bases, scored 1,227 runs, and knocked in 1,124 runs. Following his major league career, McKean managed minor league teams at Rochester, NY (IL), Springfield, OH (CL) and Dayton, OH (CL).

BIBLIOGRAPHY: Ed McKean file, National Baseball Library, Cooperstown, NY; Lee Allen, *The National League Story* (New York, 1961); Joseph Durso, *The Days of Mr. McGraw* (Englewood Cliffs, NJ, 1969); Franklin Lewis, *The Cleveland Indians* (New York, 1949); Robert L. Tiemann and Mark Rucker, eds., *Nineteenth Century Stars* (Kansas City, MO, 1989); John Phillips, *The Spiders—Who Was Who* (Cabin John, MD, 1991); J. Thomas Hetrick, *The Misfits* (Jefferson, NC, 1991).

William E. Akin

McKECHNIE, William Boyd "Bill," "Deacon" (b. August 7, 1886, Wilkinsburg, PA; d. October 29, 1965, Bradenton, FL), player, manager, and coach, was the son of Scottish immigrants and grew up in a devout Methodist-

Episcopal home. After attending high school in Wilkinsburg, McKechnie signed professionally with Washington, PA and from 1906 to 1909 played third base for Washington, PA (POML), Canton, OH (OPL), and Wheeling, WV (CL). He received a brief trial with the Pittsburgh Pirates (NL) in 1907. After marrying Beryl Bien on June 15, 1911, he had four children, William, Jr., president of the PCL from 1968 to 1973, Beatrice, James, and Carol.

McKechnie spent from 1910 to 1912 as a utility infielder with the Pittsburgh Pirates. After starting the 1913 season with St. Paul, MN (AA), he played briefly for the Boston Braves (NL) and New York Yankees (AL). In 1914 he jumped to the FL and hit .304 with the Indianapolis Hoosiers. After the franchise shifted to Newark, NJ, the 27-year-old third baseman was named player–manager in June 1915 and led the Peppers to a 54–45 record. The New York Giants (NL) signed the 5-foot 10-inch, 180-pound switch-hitter in 1916, but traded him in July to the Cincinnati Reds (NL). In 1918 Cincinnati sold McKechnie to the Pittsburgh Pirates (NL), where he hit .255. Although temporarily retiring in 1919, he returned as a utility infielder with the Pirates in 1920 and played for Minneapolis, MN (AA) in 1921. His major league statistics included 713 hits, 319 runs scored, 240 RBI, 127 stolen bases, and a .251 batting average in 846 games.

McKechnie, named manager of the Pirates in July 1922, led Pittsburgh to a 53–36 mark. After making strong third place finishes in 1923 and 1924, he steered the 1925 Pirates, which had few stars, to a world championship over the Washington Senators and Walter Johnson.* He finished third in 1926 and joined the St. Louis Cardinals (NL) coaching staff the next year. McKechnie was appointed Cardinals pilot in 1928 and led St. Louis to an NL pennant by two games over John McGraw's* Giants. After dropping four straight contests to the New York Yankees in the World Series, he was demoted to manage the Rochester, NY farm club (IL). When St. Louis faltered in 1929, however, McKechnie returned to manage the Cardinals.

McKechnie became manager of the cellar-dwelling Boston Braves (NL) in 1930 and guided them for eight seasons. In 1937, he was named Manager of the Year for leading the hapless Braves to a 79–73 finish. In 1938, McKechnie was hired to manage the Cincinnati Reds (NL) for $25,000. From 1938 through 1946, he led the Reds to two NL pennants (1939, 1940), a world championship (1940), and seven upper division finishes. McKechnie's 25-year managerial career record of 1,896 wins and 1,723 losses places him in the top ten for total games, wins, and losses as a pilot. He coached with the AL Cleveland Indians (1947–1949) and Boston Red Sox (1952–1953) before retiring to Bradenton, FL in 1953.

McKechnie sang in a Methodist church choir for 25 years and impressed others as generous, honest, and pleasant. He owned several oil wells and considerable real estate in Pittsburgh, PA and Florida. McKechnie, recognized as one of the finest managers in baseball history for his expertise on pitching and defense, was elected to the National Baseball Hall of Fame in 1962.

BIBLIOGRAPHY: Robert S. Fuchs and Wayne Soini, *Judge Fuchs and the Boston Braves, 1923–1935* (Jefferson NC, 1998); Ritter Collett, *The Cincinnati Reds* (Virginia Beach, VA, 1976); Bob Rathgeber, *Cincinnati Reds Scrapbook* (Virginia Beach, VA, 1982); Lee Allen, *The Cincinnati Reds* (New York, 1948); Bill McKechnie file, National Baseball Library, Cooperstown, NY; Martin Appel and Burt Goldblatt, *Baseball's Best: The Hall of Fame Gallery* (New York, 1977); Bill Borst, *The Pride of St. Louis* (St. Louis, MO, 1984); Bob Broeg, *Redbirds: A Century of Cardinals' Baseball* (St. Louis, MO, 1981); *DAB*, Supp. 7, (1961–1965), pp. 501–502; Leonard Koppett, *The Man in the Dugout* (New York, 1993); *NYT*, October 30, 1965; Gary Caruso, *The Braves Encyclopedia* (Philadelphia, PA, 1995); Harold Kaese, *The Boston Braves* (New York, 1948); Frederick G. Lieb, *The Pittsburgh Pirates* (New York, 1948); Lowell Reidenbaugh, *Baseball's Hall of Fame-Cooperstown* (New York, 1993); Ken Smith, *Baseball's Hall of Fame*, rev. ed. (New York, 1970); John Thorn et al., eds., *Total Braves* (New York, 1996); Rob Rains, *The St. Louis Cardinals* (New York, 1992); Bob Broeg and Jerry Vickery, *St. Louis Cardinals Encyclopedia* (Grand Rapids, MI, 1998).

Frank J. Olmsted

MACKEY, Raleigh "Biz" (b. July 27, 1897, Eagle Pass, TX; d. 1959, Los Angeles, CA), player and manager, excelled in the Negro Leagues. After moving to Luling, TX as an infant, he grew up and learned to play baseball there. At age 18 he joined the good local Prairie League baseball team, which also included his brothers, Ray and Ernest. Mackey, who threw right-handed and learned to be a switch-hitter, played two years for the Luling Oilers and then began his professional career in 1918 as a catcher with the San Antonio, TX Black Aces. Mackey played with San Antonio until being sold with several other players to the Indianapolis, IN ABCs (NNL) in 1920. Indianapolis, under manager C. I. Taylor,* fielded one of the era's strongest clubs and featured Oscar Charleston* in the outfield and Ben Taylor* at first base. After the 1922 season, Mackey jumped to the Philadelphia Hilldale Daisies team. The versatile Mackey remained with Hilldale for six years and supposedly played every position. In 1923 Hilldale won the first ECL pennant, as Mackey led the ECL with a .423 batting average. Hilldale repeated as ECL champions in 1924, but lost the Negro World Series to the Kansas City Monarchs five games to four. In 1925 Hilldale again won the ECL pennant and defeated Kansas City five games to one in the Negro World Series, as Mackey batted .350. He also batted .337 in 1924 and 1929, .400 in 1930, and .376 in 1931.

Mackey joined the Philadelphia Stars, an NNL club based on the Hilldale team, from 1933 through 1935. After playing with the Washington Elite Giants (NNL) in 1936 and 1937, he became player–manager of the Baltimore Elite Giants (NNL) the following year and signed catcher Roy Campanella.* In 1939 Baltimore owner Tom Wilson, confident that the Mackey–

trained Campanella could handle the catching responsibilities, traded Mackey to the Newark Eagles (NNL). Mackey remained with Newark from 1939 through 1941, 1945 through 1947, and in 1950. He initially was used as a catcher and managed the club from 1946 through 1950. Mackey's Eagles won both halves of the 1946 NNL season and then defeated the Kansas City Monarchs in the Negro League World Series. In 1947, Newark won the first half of the season and finished second overall. As Eagles manager, Mackey handled interference by owner Effa Manley in team operations fairly well. Mackey's players at Newark included future major leaguers Larry Doby,* Monte Irvin,* and Don Newcombe.* After the major league color barrier was broken, the Negro Leagues experienced hard times. The Eagles disbanded following the 1950 season, ending Mackey's managerial career.

Mackey, one of his era's great players, still caught regularly and batted .307 in 1945 at age 48. The fiercely competitive Mackey handled pitchers very well and may have been the best all-around catcher produced by the Negro Leagues. Josh Gibson* possessed better offensive skills and a stronger arm, but Mackey had few peers as a defensive catcher. Mackey batted .335 in Negro League play and .326 against major league competition in exhibition games. He played in five East–West All-Star games (1933, 1935–1936, 1938, and 1947), the last at age 50. In a 1954 Pittsburgh *Courier* poll, Mackey edged Gibson as the greatest Negro League catcher. As a manager, he also enjoyed success with the Baltimore Elite Giants and Newark Eagles and helped develop several future major league players. He later resided in Los Angeles, CA and ran a forklift.

BIBLIOGRAPHY: William Brashler, *Josh Gibson* (New York, 1978); Roy Campanella, *It's Good to Be Alive* (New York, 1959); Anthony J. Connor, *Voices from Cooperstown* (New York, 1982); John B. Holway, *Voices from the Great Black Baseball Leagues* (New York, 1975); John B. Holway, *Blackball Stars* (Westport CT, 1988); Raleigh Mackey file, National Baseball Library, Cooperstown, NY; Robert W. Peterson, *Only the Ball Was White* (Englewood Cliffs, NJ, 1970); James A. Riley, *The Biographical Encyclopedia of the Negro Baseball Leagues* (New York, 1994); Donn Rogosin, *Invisible Men: Life in Baseball's Negro Leagues* (New York, 1983).

Douglas D. Martin

McLAIN, Dennis Dale "Denny," "Big Mouth" (b. March 29, 1944, Chicago, IL), player, is the son of Thomas McLain and Betty (Koss) McLain and grew up on the Chicago Southside of Irish-Catholic parentage. He graduated in 1962 from Mount Carmel High School, where he starred as a pitcher. When he was 15 years old, McLain lost his 36-year-old father to a heart attack. The trauma of losing someone whom he idolized, along with his mother's quick remarriage, turned McLain into a confrontational, rebellious, cocky personality, who sought pleasure and excitement prior to his own anticipated premature death. "I like to travel fast—and always first class," he bluntly remarked. He graduated from high school in 1962 and married Sharyn Alice Boudreau, the daughter of a National Baseball Hall of Famer

Lou Boudreau* in October 1963. They have four children. After a brief minor league stint, McLain was promoted to the Detroit Tigers (AL) in September 1963 and compiled a 2–1 record.

The 6-foot 1-inch, 185-pound McLain matured as a pitcher, winning 16 games in 1965 and 20 contests in 1966. He reached the pinnacle of success in 1968, when he became the first major leaguer since Dizzy Dean* in 1934 to win 30 games. He won 31 of 37 decisions with a 1.96 ERA and led the AL in innings pitched (336), complete games (28), and winning percentage (.838). The Detroit Tigers defeated the St. Louis Cardinals to capture the 1968 World Series. The key to McLain's 1968 success included an over-powering overhand and sidearm fastball, a wicked slider, a devastating slow curve-ball, and uncanny control, as he struck out 280 batters and walked only 63 batters. His honors that season were the AL MVP and AL Cy Young Awards. In 1969, he shared the AL Cy Young Award in posting a 24–9 record and hurled an AL-leading 9 shutouts and 325 innings pitched.

Never has a ballplayer risen so fast and fallen so quickly, for the now–225-pound McLain plunged to a 3–5 mark in 1970 and failed to have another winning season. He lost 22 games in 1971 for the Washington Senators (AL) and split the 1972 campaign with the Oakland Athletics (AL) and Atlanta Braves (NL). After the 1972 season, he left baseball with a 131–91 win–loss record and a 3.39 ERA. Two drawbacks plagued McLain: A nagging shoulder problem required increasing amounts of cortisone, and his rakish lifestyle featured frequent evening jaunts to gambling casinos and night clubs, where he performed as a professional organist. His nocturnal behavior nearly cost him his marriage, his life (he suffered a mild heart attack while ballooning to nearly 300 pounds), and his freedom. In the 1980s, he spent 29 months in prison for racketeering, drug dealing, and extortion. After his 1987 release, McLain was involved in assorted businesses in Fort Wayne, IN and hosted a radio talk show. He served another prison term in the 1990s.

BIBLIOGRAPHY: Martin Appel, *Yesterday's Heroes* (New York, 1988); Larry Amman, "Denny McLain in 1968," *BRJ* 17 (1988), pp. 38–40; John Benson et al., *Baseball's Top 100* (Wilton, CT, 1997); Denny McLain with Dave Diles, *Nobody's Perfect* (New York, 1975); Fred Smith, *995 Tigers* (Detroit MI, 1981); W. Ladson, "Can We Talk?" *Sport* 84 (October 1993), pp. 63–65; Dennis McLain file, National Baseball Library, Cooperstown, NY; Denny McLain, *Strikeout* (St. Louis, MO, 1988); Mark Mulvoy, "Dizzy Dream for Jet-Set Denny," *SI* 29 (July 29, 1968), pp. 42–45; William Nack, "Starting Over," *SI* 67 (December 14, 1987), pp. 92–102; *NYT Biographical Service* 19 (August 1988), pp. 910–911; Steve Rushin, "The Season of High Heat (1968)," *SI* 79 (July 19, 1993), pp. 30–37; Joe Falls, *Detroit Tigers* (New York, 1975); Joe Falls, *The Detroit Tigers* (New York, 1989); Jerry Green, *Year of the Tiger* (New York, 1969); John Thorn et al., eds., *Total Baseball*, 5th ed. (New York, 1997); Ken Young, *Cy Young Award Winners* (New York, 1994).

                                                              James N. Giglio

McMAHON, Donald John "Don" (b. January 4, 1930, Brooklyn, NY; d. July 22, 1987, Los Angeles, CA), player and coach, was the son of Charles Mc-

Mahon, a public transportation worker. McMahon, who graduated from Boys High School in 1948, played basketball and starred as third baseman on the school's city championship baseball team his senior year. McMahon signed a minor league contract with Owensboro, KY (KL), in 1949, but struggled as a hitter. He was converted to a pitcher because of his strong, accurate arm. After having only moderate success at his new position, McMahon spent the 1951–1952 seasons with the U.S. Army in Korea. He struggled over four more minor league seasons as a starter with Evansville, IN (3IL), Atlanta, GA (SL), Toledo, OH (AA), and Wichita, KS (AA) before joining the Milwaukee Braves (NL) as a 27-year-old reliever in June 1957.

The Milwaukee Braves were involved in a tight NL pennant race. The 6-foot 2-inch, 225-pound McMahon performed like a veteran. In his first six outings, he blanked opponents on five hits, one walk, and nine strikeouts. The fastball specialist won two games, lost three, and collected nine saves with a 1.54 ERA, contributing significantly to the Milwaukee Braves' NL pennant. In the World Series against the New York Yankees, McMahon hurled five scoreless innings and closed out three games for the champion Braves. In 1958, McMahon made the NL All-Star team and helped the Braves notch another NL pennant. He appeared in Game 6 of the World Series against the New York Yankees with no decision. In 1959, McMahon recorded five wins and three losses in 60 games and shared the NL lead with 15 saves. Following a horrible 1960 season, the right-handed fastballer won six of 10 decisions with eight saves in 1961. After one early season 1962 loss, Braves manager Birdie Tebbetts* lost confidence in his closer and sold him to the Houston Colt '45s (NL) that May. McMahon quickly refuted Tebbetts' judgment with five wins, 8 saves, and a 1.53 ERA in 76.2 innings.

The nomadic McMahon pitched for the Houston Colt '45s in 1962 and 1963, the Cleveland Indians (AL) from 1964 to 1966, Boston Red Sox (AL) in 1966 and 1967, Chicago White Sox (AL) in 1967 and 1968, Detroit Tigers (AL) in 1968 and 1969, and San Francisco Giants (NL) from 1970 to 1974. With the Detroit Tigers in 1969, he won three games and saved 11 contests. McMahon, who married Darlene Sater in February 1955 and had four children, moved to Garden Grove, CA in 1970. After winning nine games with 19 saves and a 2.96 ERA in 1970, he at age 41 won 10 games and saved four to lead the San Francisco Giants to the 1971 NL West title. McMahon appeared in only nine contests with no decisions in his final 1974 season.

His major league career spanned 18 seasons and seven clubs, featuring 90 victories, 68 losses, a .570 winning percentage, a 2.96 ERA, and 153 saves. McMahon, an accomplished amateur photographer, was rarely without a camera in the bullpen or the dugout. He worked as a pitching coach in the Los Angeles Dodger (NL) organization until being diagnosed with a fatal cancer in 1983.

BIBLIOGRAPHY: Bob Buege, *Eddie Mathews and the National Pastime* (Milwaukee, WI, 1994); Bob Buege, *The Milwaukee Braves: A Baseball Eulogy* (Milwaukee, WI, 1988); Bob Buege, "Milwaukee Madness," *OTBN* 6 (1994), pp. 12–14; Gary Caruso, *The*

Braves Encyclopedia (Philadelphia, PA, 1995); Patrick Harrigan, *The Detroit Tigers* (Toronto, Canada, 1997); Donald McMahon file, National Baseball Library, Cooperstown, NY; William F. McNeil, *The Dodgers Encyclopedia* (Champaign, IL, 1997); *NYT Biographical Service* 18 (August 1987), p. 755; *Milwaukee Braves Yearbook*, 1957–1961; John Thorn et al., eds., *Total Baseball*, 5th ed. (New York, 1997).

Jerry J. Wright

McMAHON, John Joseph "Sadie" (b. September 19, 1867, Wilmington, DE; d. February 20, 1954, Wilmington, DE), player, grew up in the Wilmington, DE area and finished high school at age 17. The 5-foot 9-inch, 185-pound McMahon worked as a carpenter for a few years and played amateur baseball in Wilmington with the Blue Rose Club in 1886 and the Americas Club. After signing professionally with Norristown, PA in 1889, he joined the Philadelphia Athletics (AA) and won 14 of 26 decisions in 1884. In late 1890, manager Bill Barnie convinced right-handed McMahon and battery mate Wilbert Robinson* to move to his Baltimore Orioles team (AA). He pitched seven seasons for Baltimore, two in the AA (1890–1891) and five in the NL (1892–1896). McMahon helped the fabulous Orioles to NL pennants in 1894, 1895, and 1896, playing with Robinson, "Wee Willie" Keeler,* Hughie Jennings,* and John McGraw.* His heroic work in the stretch drive of 1895 proved crucial. After returning from a pulled shoulder tendon, McMahon pitched 15 games in the season's last six weeks, won 10 and lost four, and hurled three late victories over the Cleveland Spiders to wrest the NL championship from them. He also pitched several wins in the Temple Cup competition.

In 1890, McMahon led the AA in games appeared in (60), games started (57), complete games (55), innings pitched (509), strikeouts (291), and wins (36). The following year, he paced again in games started (58), complete games (53), innings pitched (503), and wins (35). He hurled the most shutouts in 1891 (5) and 1895 (4). In compiling a 173–127 lifetime major league record and 3.51 ERA, he won 36 games in 1890, 35 in 1891, 19 in 1892, 23 in 1893, and 25 in 1894. In 1892, his drinking led to his suspension for the final month. When the Brooklyn Superbas (NL) hired Baltimore manager Ned Hanlon* in 1897, McMahon joined him and played his last major league season there. He played sporadically around Wilmington for a few years and in 1903 was coaxed out of retirement by manager Jennings of the Baltimore, MD (EL) Orioles. He won the second game of a doubleheader with Newark, NJ on August 15, driving in the winning run. McMahon scouted for the New York Giants (NL) from 1911 to 1925, but claimed that the game took too much out of him.

BIBLIOGRAPHY: Al Kermisch, "From a Researcher's Notebook," *BRJ* 10 (1981), pp. 69–70; John McMahon file, National Baseball Library, Cooperstown, NY; *The Baseball Encyclopedia*, 10th ed. (New York, 1996); Robert L. Tiemann and Mark Rucker, eds., *Nineteenth Century Stars* (Kansas City, MO, 1989); David Nemec, *The Beer and Whisky League* (New York, 1994); James M. Bready, *Baseball in Baltimore*

(Baltimore, MD, 1998); Wilmington (DE) *Star*, December 23, 1951, February 21, 1954.

Mark D. Rucker

McMANUS, Martin Joseph "Marty" (b. March 14, 1900, Chicago, IL; d. February 18, 1966, St. Louis, MO), player and manager, attended the 12th and Morgan School in the slum section of Chicago and worked as a bookkeeper when World War I began. Although playing semiprofessional baseball with the famous Gunthers in Chicago, McManus did not flourish as a baseball player until his U.S. Army days at Camp Gaillard in the Canal Zone. A St. Louis Browns (AL) scout sent him to Tulsa, OK (TL), where Spencer Abbott managed him.

McManus's big opportunity came when the St. Louis Browns' incumbent second baseman Joe Gedeon was expelled from baseball along with eight Chicago White Sox (AL) players for his knowledge of the World Series fix in 1919. McManus played seven seasons for the Browns, appearing with the best players in the franchise's checkered history. He hit over .300 in three of his first four full seasons in St. Louis, including .312 in 1922 and a career-high .333 in 1924. In 1922 he ranked third in the AL with an incredible 109 RBI, four more than teammate George Sisler.* McManus was a fierce competitor in the same mold as Ty Cobb.* The Browns traded him to the Detroit Tigers (AL) in a seven-player deal in January 1927. As a Tiger, McManus frequently clashed with manager George Moriarty and once engaged in a celebrated fight with Cobb.

In August 1931, the Tigers sent McManus to the Boston Red Sox (AL). The following season, McManus replaced Shano Collins* as manager to become the youngest AL pilot at the time. Boston fired him after the 1933 campaign, the Red Sox having compiled a composite record of 95–153 (.383 winning percentage) with eighth- and seventh-place finishes in 1932 and 1933, respectively. McManus finished his active career in the majors by hitting .276 for the Boston Braves (NL) in 1934.

McManus, who played mostly second and third base, led the AL in doubles with 44 in 1925 and stolen bases with 23 and fielding percentage with .966 in 1930. The 5 foot 10 inch McManus, who played at 160 pounds, appeared in 1,831 career games and batted a laudable .289. His 1,926 career hits included 401 doubles, 88 triples, and 120 HR. McManus scored 1,008 runs, drove in 996 teammates, and registered 675 walks, 558 strikeouts, and 126 stolen bases. He batted .320 for the Tigers in 1930 and slugged a career-high 18 HR in 1929.

McManus managed in the minor leagues at St. Paul, MN (AA) in 1935, Tulsa, OK (TL) in 1936, and Albany, NY (EL) in 1937, his last year as an active player. He split the next four seasons piloting Williamsport, PA (EL) and San Antonio, TX (TL). In 1947, McManus managed at Denver, CO (WL). Several of his players, including Vern Stephens,* Bob Muncrief, and Monty Stratton, subsequently appeared in the major leagues.

In June 1951, McManus testified before the American Federation of Labor Executive Council that if the major leagues began unionizing in the minor leagues, they would take care of themselves in six or seven years. He married Norma Wahl of St. Louis, MO in 1925 and had one son and two daughters. He died of cancer.

BIBLIOGRAPHY: Marty McManus file, National Baseball Library, Cooperstown, NY; *The Baseball Encyclopedia*, 10th ed. (New York, 1996); Bill Borst, ed., *Ables to Zoldak*, vol. 2 (St. Louis, MO, 1989); Ellery Clark, Jr., *Boston Red Sox: 75th Anniversary History* (Hicksville, NY, 1975); Bill Borst, *Still Last in the American League* (West Bloomfield, MI, 1992); Frederick G. Lieb, *The Detroit Tigers* (New York, 1945); Fred Smith, *995 Tigers* (Detroit, MI, 1981); Frederick G. Lieb, *The Boston Red Sox* (New York, 1947); Robert Redmount, *The Red Sox Encyclopedia* (Champaign, IL, 1997); Thomas Aylesworth and Benton Minks, *The Encyclopedia of Baseball Managers* (New York, 1990).

William A. Borst

McMILLAN, Roy David "Mac" (b. July 17, 1930, Bonham, TX; d. November 2, 1997, Bonham, TX), player, scout, coach, and manager, was the son of Robert McMillan, a barber, and Hazel (Curtis) McMillan and participated in varsity football, basketball, tennis, and track and field at Bonham High School. Neither the school nor the town fielded a baseball team, but McMillan played third base on a local softball team. After spending one semester at Texas A&M University, he attended a Cincinnati Reds (NL) tryout camp in McKinney, TX in 1947. Although lacking baseball experience, McMillan impressed Cincinnati Reds scout Hack Miller with his fielding and signed a professional contract. From 1947 to 1950, he moved up through the Reds minor league system.

With the Cincinnati Reds from 1951 to 1960, the wiry, 5-foot 11-inch, 164-pound right-hander ranked as the best major league shortstop. McMillan won *TSN* Gold Glove Award from 1957 to 1959 in its initial three years. He played more consecutive games (584) at shortstop than any NL player from 1951 to 1955, set the NL record for most double plays (129) at shortstop in 1954, and started at shortstop in the 1956 and 1957 All-Star games. In desperate need for pitching, the Reds traded McMillan to the Milwaukee Braves (NL) for Joey Jay and Juan Pizarro* in December 1960. After spending three seasons with the Milwaukee Braves, he completed his major league career with the New York Mets (NL) from 1964 to 1966. He started a triple play in a 23-inning marathon game against the San Francisco Giants (NL) in 1964.

After serving as player–coach for Jacksonville, FL (IL) in 1967, McMillan managed Visalia, CA (CaL) in 1968 and piloted Memphis, TN (TL) to a division championship in 1969. He returned to the major leagues as a coach with the Milwaukee Brewers (AL) from 1970 to 1972 and New York Mets (NL) from 1973 to 1976. In brief stints as interim manger with the Milwaukee Brewers in 1972 and New York Mets in 1975, McMillan compiled a 27–28 win–loss record. He piloted teams in the Minnesota Twins (AL) minor league system from 1977 to 1980 and scouted the Texas area for the Montreal Expos (NL) from 1982 to 1997.

Although never a power hitter, McMillan proved a good "clutch" batter. In a 16-year major league career, he batted .243 with 356 extra base hits, 68 HR, and 594 RBI. He married Joan Lawrence in October 1952 and had two sons and a daughter.

BIBLIOGRAPHY: Robert Creamer, "Wreck of the Redlegs," *SI* 7 (September 9, 1957), pp. 44–46; "Former All-Star Roy McMillan," *SCD* 24 (November 28, 1997), p. 10; Murray Olderman, "Roy McMillan, The New Mr. Shortstop?" *Sport* 14 (May 1953), pp. 22, 64–65; Tom Meany, "The Best Infielder in the Majors," *Collier's* 135 (May 27, 1955), pp. 98–101; Ritter Collett, *The Cincinnati Reds* (Virginia Beach, VA, 1976); Floyd Conner and John Snyder, *Day-by-Day in Cincinnati Reds History* (West Point, NY, 1984); Bob Rathgeber, *Cincinnati Reds Scrapbook* (Virginia Beach, VA, 1982); Bob Buege, *The Milwaukee Braves: A Baseball Eulogy* (Milwaukee, WI, 1994); Gary Caruso, *The Braves Encyclopedia* (Philadelphia, PA, 1995); Jack Lang and Peter Simon, *The New York Mets* (New York, 1986).

Richard D. Miller

McNALLY, David Arthur "Dave" (b. October 31, 1942, Billings, MT), player, is the son of oil salesman James McNally and social case worker Beth McNally. His father served in World War II and was killed in action in Okinawa in July 1945. McNally attended Billings Central Catholic High School, which fielded no baseball team. In 1960, he led Post No. 4 to the American Legion World Series with an 18–1 pitching mark and five no-hitters. Later that year, the Baltimore Orioles (AL) signed him for a reported $80,000. McNally married Jean Marie Hoefer in December 1961 and has five children, Jeff, Pamela, Susan, Annie, and Michael. After minor league seasons with Victoria, TX (TL) and Fox Cities, WI (3IL) in 1961 and Elmira, NY (EL) in 1962, McNally joined the Baltimore Orioles in late 1962. In his major league debut at age 19, he hurled a two-hit shutout over the Kansas City Royals. Following two uneventful years, he pitched well in 1965 and 1966 and shut out the Los Angeles Dodgers in the 1966 World Series. An arm ailment lessened his effectiveness in 1967.

From 1968 through 1971, the 5-foot 11-inch, 190-pound left-hander became the most successful hurler in baseball by winning 87 of 118 decisions (plus six in post-season play). Only one other hurler, Ferguson Jenkins,* won as many contests, while McNally's .737 winning percentage was .078 above that of his nearest competitor. In 1968, McNally finished 22–10 with a 1.95 ERA and 202 strikeouts and allowed only 5.8 hits per nine innings. His 24 victories led the AL in 1970. In 1971, he compiled a 21–5 mark despite missing five weeks with an elbow injury and led the AL with a .808 winning percentage. From September 22, 1968 through July 30, 1969, McNally won 17 straight decisions to tie AL records for consecutive victories and wins at the beginning of a season (15). He was named to All-Star teams in 1969,

1970, and 1972, and made *TSN* All-Star team in 1968. In post-season play, he pitched for the Orioles in the 1969, 1970, 1971, 1973, and 1974 AL Championship Series and in the 1966, 1969, 1970, and 1971 World Series. McNally compiled a 3–2 mark and 2.68 ERA in playoffs and a 4–2 slate with a 2.34 ERA in World Series.

A right-handed batter, McNally slugged nine regular season HR, remains the only pitcher to belt a grand slam HR in the World Series, and is one of the only two pitchers to hit two World Series homers. The good fielding southpaw made only one error in each of the seasons from 1967 through 1971.

In December 1974, McNally was traded to the Montreal Expos (NL). He then held lifetime Orioles records for games pitched, innings, wins, complete games, shutouts, strikeouts, and walks, plus several single-season records. He retired at age 32 after pitching 12 games for the Expos. In 14 major league seasons, he compiled a 184–119 (.607 winning percentage) mark, 3.24 ERA, struck out 1,512 batters in 2,730 innings, and hurled 33 shutouts. In 1975, McNally and Andy Messersmith* challenged the reserve clause, which had bound players to their teams for as long as the team wished. An arbitrator ruled that, by playing for a year without contracts, the players had fulfilled their legal obligations and were free agents. This decision led to other cases, permanently altering labor relations in baseball. McNally personally never benefitted from the free agency decision, as he never pitched another major league game. He and his brother operate a Ford automobile dealership in Billings, MT.

BIBLIOGRAPHY: Dave McNally file, National Baseball Library, Cooperstown, NY; *Baltimore Orioles Press Guide, 1974*, pp. 74–75; Billings (MT) *Gazette*, July 28, 1945; Roy Blount, Jr., "Three Birds Who Mainly Stay," *SI* 33 (October 12, 1970), pp. 30–32; Peter Bonventre, "Off the Reservation," *Newsweek* 87 (January 5, 1976), p. 51; "Flying High," *Time* 94 (July 11, 1969), pp. 45–46; "Highlight," *SI* 30 (June 16, 1969), p. 80; Gene Karst and Martin J. Jones, Jr., *Who's Who in Professional Baseball* (New Rochelle, NY, 1973); Rich Marazzi, "Dave McNally Had an Impact on Baseball On and Off the Field," *SCD* 24 (June 20, 1997), pp. 110–111; Ted Patterson, *The Baltimore Orioles* (Dallas, TX, 1995); Earl Weaver and Berry Stainback, *It's What You Learn After You Know It All That Counts* (Garden City, NY, 1982); *Montreal Expos Press Guide, 1975*, p. 66; *NYT*, June 10, 1975, p. 50; *The Baseball Encyclopedia*, 10th ed. (New York, 1996); *TSN Official Baseball Guide, 1968–1975*; *TSN Official Baseball Register, 1962–1976*; James H. Bready, *Baseball in Baltimore* (Baltimore, MD, 1998).
Bruce Erricson

McNAMARA, John Francis "Mac" (b. June 4, 1932, Sacramento, CA), player, manager, coach, and scout, is the son of an Irish immigrant railroad worker, who died when McNamara was only 12. He and five siblings were brought up by their mother. Upon graduation from Sacramento High School in 1951, the 5-foot 10-inch, 175-pound McNamara, a catcher who batted and threw right-handed, signed with the St. Louis Cardinals (NL). After breaking into professional baseball with Fresno, CA (CaL) in 1952, he spent 1953 and 1954 in the U.S. Army and attended Sacramento State College. Although released by the St. Louis Cardinals in 1955, the smooth-fielding, light-hitting catcher played minor league baseball with Houston, TX (TL), Lynchburg, VA (PiL), Lewiston, ID (NWL), Sacramento, CA (PCL), Tulsa, OK (TL), Binghamton, NY (EL), Dallas, TX (PCL), Mobile, AL (SL), and Birmingham, AL (SL). He compiled a lifetime .239 batting average over a 14-year minor league career.

McNamara became player–manager at Lewiston in 1959 and piloted his team to the 1961 NWL title. He advanced in the Kansas City Athletics (AL) farm system to pilot Binghamton in 1963, Dallas in 1964, Mobile in 1966, and Birmingham in 1965 and 1967. At Mobile in 1966 and Birmingham in 1967, McNamara won SL titles with future National Baseball Hall of Famers Reggie Jackson* and Rollie Fingers.* His decision to remove his team from an Alabama restaurant that refused to serve blacks prompted Jackson's praise.

When the Kansas City Athletics moved to Oakland (AL) in 1968, McNamara became their third base coach. A year later, owner Charles O. Finley* promoted him to manager. After McNamara guided the Oakland A's to second-place in 1970, Finley replaced him with the more colorful, accomplished Dick Williams.* After serving as the third base coach with the San Francisco Giants (NL) from 1971 to 1973, McNamara managed the fledgling San Diego Padres (NL) from 1974 to 1977. Although never finishing above .500 under McNamara, the San Diego Padres improved their record each year.

McNamara coached for the California Angels (AL) in 1978 and succeeded Sparky Anderson* as manager of the powerful Cincinnati Reds (NL) in 1979. Led by Johnny Bench,* Joe Morgan,* and Tom Seaver,* the Cincinnati Reds won the NL West title in 1979 with a 90–71 mark but lost the NL Championship Series to the Pittsburgh Pirates in three games. The steady loss of key players to free agency caused the Cincinnati Reds to fall into the NL West cellar by 1982 and prompted McNamara's dismissal. He spurned an offer to replace managing legend Earl Weaver* of the Baltimore Orioles (AL) in 1983 and took the helm with the California Angels instead. McNamara skippered the California Angels to fifth and second-place finishes before the Boston Red Sox (AL) hired him to replace retiring Ralph Houk* in 1985. The Boston Red Sox finished in fifth place in McNamara's first year, but Roger Clemens,* Wade Boggs,* and Jim Rice* helped Boston win the AL pennant with a 95–66 record in 1986. When the Boston Red Sox lost the World Series to the New York Mets in seven games, critics largely blamed McNamara for the devastating sixth game loss. He was second-guessed for lifting ace Clemens prematurely for a pinch hitter and for not using a defensive replacement for injured first baseman Bill Buckner,* whose error brought in the winning run. The Boston Red Sox dropped to fifth place in the AL East in 1987. McNamara was fired at mid-season in 1988 and scouted for the Seattle Mariners (AL) before becoming manager of the Cleveland Indians (AL) in 1990. The Cleveland Indians hired him primarily to teach coach Mike Hargrove* the finer points of major league managing and dismissed McNamara in favor of his pupil in 1991. He returned to the California Angels as a catching instructor for the next five years and was appointed interim Angels manager for 44 games upon the firing of Marcel Lachemann in August 1996.

An excellent handler of pitchers and teacher of baseball fundamentals, the low-key McNamara has managed six different major league teams. In 19 seasons, his major league clubs had won 1,167 games and lost 1,242 contests for a .484 winning percentage. McNamara, the BBWAA and *TSN* AL Manager of the Year in 1986, had four children with his first wife, Kathleen. He later married Ellen Goode and lives in Brentwood, TN.

BIBLIOGRAPHY: John McNamara file, National Baseball Library, Cooperstown, NY; *The Baseball Encyclopedia*, 10th ed. (New York, 1996); *Boston Red Sox 1988 Media Guide*; Dan Shaughnessy, *One Strike Away* (New York, 1987); Peter Golenbock, *Fenway* (New York, 1992); Leonard Koppett, *The Man in the Dugout* (New York, 1993); Terry Pluto, *The Curse of Rocky Colavito* (New York, 1994); Robert Redmount, *The Red Sox Encyclopedia* (Champaign, IL, 1998); Thomas Aylesworth and Benton Minks, *The Encyclopedia of Baseball Managers* (New York, 1990); Bruce Markusen, *Baseball's Last Dynasty* (New York, 1998); Peter C. Bjarkman, ed., *Encyclopedia of Major League Baseball Team Histories National League* (Westport, CT, 1991); Robert H. Walker, *Cincinnati and the Big Red Machine* (Bloomington, IN, 1988); Jack Torry, *Endless Summers* (South Bend, IN, 1995).

Richard H. Gentile

McNAUGHTON, Alice Marie Hohlmayer "Lefty" (b. January 19, 1925, Springfield, OH), player and manager, starred in the AAGPBL. The daughter of Carl Hohlmayer, milkman and laundromat owner, and Marguerite (Waggaman) Hohlmayer, she graduated from Springfield High School in 1942. McNaughton played softball at age five with her brothers and later served as a bat girl and player for the Finke and Herne team, which toured across Ohio. In the 1937 State Women's Tournament, she was selected all-star first baseman. Officials, however, banned her innovative "trappers" mitt. Nicknamed "Lefty" from school days, she also played basketball, volleyball, and tennis.

In 1943, McNaughton entered Ohio State University. During a 1945 softball tournament, she was scouted by the AAGPBL and contacted by president Max Carey.* Following a tryout in Pascagoula, MS, she signed for $80 a week with the Kenosha, WI Comets (AAGPBL) for 1946. As a rookie, the 5-foot 6-inch, 160-pound first baseman batted .223 with 21 stolen bases in 110 games. McNaughton began pitching in 1949, finishing 7–6 with a 1.88 ERA. After graduating in 1949 from Ohio State with Bachelors degrees in physical education and health, she was traded to the Muskegon, MI Lassies (AAGPBL) for three players. When the Lassies moved to Kalamazoo, MI in 1950, McNaughton was traded to the Peoria, IL Redwings (AAGPBL). For the Peoria Redwings in 1951, she batted .267 and produced an outstanding 15–11 mark with a 2.02 ERA. The versatile, established star once made 21 putouts at first base in a game and fielded .979 lifetime. McNaughton compiled a lifetime 33–32 win–loss mark with a 2.58 ERA and hurled 42 straight scoreless innings. She batted .203 with 128 RBI in 486 games. In an exhibition game, she made a base hit off Satchel Paige.*

In 1952, however, McNaughton left the AAGPBL to help save the family business and married William McNaughton of the US Air Force. When widowed in 1960, she brought up her two children, Michele and Sean. She worked 17 years for the City of Fairfield, CA finance department and coached Little League baseball. After retiring in 1979, McNaughton played on a "men's 55+" team and advanced to the World Slo-Pitch Tournament. After managing five years, she moved to San Diego, CA.

On November 5, 1988, McNaughton was enshrined among AAGPBL standouts at the National Baseball Hall of Fame. When the 1992 movie *A League of Their Own* brought public recognition, she helped organize the four "Legendary Ladies of Baseball." She has appeared at educational and charity events and at sports memorabilia shows.

BIBLIOGRAPHY: Jeff Archer, "Baseball for Women Only," *DSM* 1 (March–April 1992), pp. 14–17; Lois Browne, *Girls of Summer* (New York, 1992); Barbara Gregorich, *Women at Play* (San Diego, CA, 1993); W. C. Madden, *The Women of the All-American Girls Professional Baseball League* (Jefferson, NC, 1997); Susan Johnson, *When Women Played Hardball* (Seattle, WA, 1994).

James D. Smith III

MacPHAIL, Leland Stanford, Sr. "Larry" (b. February 3, 1890, Cass City, MI; d. October 1, 1975, Miami, FL), executive, was the son of William Curtis MacPhail, a Scottish immigrant storekeeper and banker. MacPhail attended various Michigan schools and Staunton Military Academy in Virginia. He passed the entrance exam for the U.S. Naval Academy at Annapolis, MD at age 16 but instead enrolled at Beloit College. MacPhail subsequently attended the University of Michigan Law School and George Washington University and passed the bar exams of Michigan, Illinois, and Washington, DC. After practicing law in Chicago, he became chief of a Nashville, TN department store. During World War I, MacPhail enlisted in the U.S. Army as a private, rose to captain, served in France, and was wounded. After the armistice, he and others tried unsuccessfully to capture Kaiser Wilhelm, who was in exile in Holland. MacPhail, though, claimed that he took the Kaiser's ashtray as a souvenir.

MacPhail tried several unsuccessful business ventures in Ohio and refereed BTC football games on weekends. He obtained an option on the impoverished Columbus, OH baseball club (AA) and sold it to the St. Louis Cardinals (NL) to become a farm club. St. Louis made MacPhail president of the Columbus team, although he had no previous experience administering a baseball club. The Cardinals built a new ballpark and installed lights at Columbus. MacPhail implemented innovative, successful promotions, but was fired by the Cardinals in June 1933 for his personal actions in and out of baseball.

A bank that had reluctantly taken over the financially struggling Cincinnati Reds (NL) hired MacPhail before the 1934 season. He contacted Powel Crosley, Jr.,* owner of radio stations and factories that produced electrical appliances and radio receivers. Crosley knew nothing about baseball, but was persuaded to take an option on the baseball club partly as a civic duty. With Crosley's financial backing, MacPhail immediately instituted several changes in the stadium, obtained new players, and persuaded club owners to permit night baseball for the first time in major league history. MacPhail persuaded President Franklin D. Roosevelt in May 1935 to touch the signal in the White House turning on the lights for the historic first night game. Night baseball, along with MacPhail's mammoth fireworks displays, attracted almost capacity crowds. In June 1936, Crosley exercised his option to buy the ball club from the bank.

Although attendance improved greatly at Cincinnati ball games, MacPhail and Crosley parted at the end of the 1936 season. MacPhail spent 1937 in Michigan in the banking business. In 1938 a bank called on MacPhail to rescue the Brooklyn Dodgers (NL) from severe financial problems. Breaking with tradition again, MacPhail persuaded the bank to put up the cash to install lights in Ebbets Field. He also ended the agreement with the New York Yankees (AL) and New York Giants (NL) barring play-by-play broadcasts of baseball games in the New York area, and brought Red Barber* (OS) from Cincinnati to announce the Dodgers games. MacPhail talked the bank into advancing cash to buy prominent players Dolf Camilli,* Mickey Owen, Pee Wee Reese,* Whitlow Wyatt,* Fred "Dixie" Walker,* Billy Herman,* Joe Medwick,* and Kirby Higbe. He hired Leo Durocher* as manager and made the Dodgers into a contender for the top NL spot. During the MacPhail regime, Brooklyn finished seventh, third, and second from 1938 through 1940 and placed first in the NL in 1941. The Dodgers finished second in 1942, when the United States again was at war. MacPhail returned to the army as a colonel, serving as a special assistant to the Secretary of War.

After VJ Day, MacPhail promoted a partnership backed by Dan Topping* and Del Webb to buy the New York Yankees (AL) from the heirs of the late Colonel Jacob Ruppert* for $2.8 million. The bargain deal included Yankee Stadium, the team's minor league farm system, and considerable real estate. MacPhail received one-third interest in the partnership and a 10-year contract to administer the ball club. Once more MacPhail instituted many innovations, including installing lights in Yankee Stadium for the first time in history. The Yankees finished in third place in 1946 and captured the 1947 AL pennant and World Series. During a victory celebration on the day the Yankees won the world championship, MacPhail engaged in a loud public brawl. The next day, Topping and Webb terminated MacPhail's contract for a $1.5 million payoff.

MacPhail retired to a Maryland farm, where he raised Black Angus cattle, and briefly became president of Bowie Race Track. In 1978, he was elected to the National Baseball Hall of Fame. MacPhail married Inez Thompson of Oak Park, IL and had three children, Leland S. Jr. (Lee),* William, and Marian McDermott. Lee became AL president, while William served as a television executive and Marian headed research at *Time* magazine. After being divorced, MacPhail married Jean Bennett Wanamaker in 1945 and had one daughter, Jennie.

BIBLIOGRAPHY: William F. McNeil, *The Dodgers Encyclopedia* (Champaign, IL, 1997); Lee Allen, *The Cincinnati Reds* (New York, 1948); Frank Graham, *The Brooklyn Dodgers* (New York, 1945); Peter Golenbock, *Bums* (New York, 1984); Al Figone, "Larry MacPhail and Dolph Camilli," *TNP* 14 (1994), pp. 106–109; Mark Gallagher, *The Yankee Encyclopedia*, vol. 3 (Champaign, IL, 1997); Noel Hynd, *The Giants of the Polo Grounds* (New York, 1988); Larry MacPhail, Sr. file, National Baseball Library, Cooperstown, NY; Don Warfield, *The Roaring Redhead: Larry MacPhail* (South Bend, IN, 1987); Gene Karst and Martin J. Jones, Jr., *Who's Who in Professional Baseball* (New Rochelle, NY, 1973); *NYT*, October 2, 1975.

Gene Karst

MacPHAIL, Leland Stanford, Jr. "Lee" (b. October 25, 1917, Nashville, TN), executive, is the son of Leland Stanford MacPhail, Sr.,* and Inez (Thompson) MacPhail. In 1939, he received the Bachelor of Arts degree from Swarthmore College and married Jane M. Hamilton. They have four children, Leland Stanford III, Allen, Bruce, and Andrew. After a year in corporate management, MacPhail launched a career in baseball administration. Assistance and encouragement came from his father, a prominent major league executive.

MacPhail's initial assignments included being business manager of Reading, PA (ISL) in 1941, and general manager of Toronto, Canada (IL) in 1942–1943. Following a tour of duty as a U.S. Navy lieutenant (j.g.) during World War II (1944–1945), he served as general manager of the New York Yankees farm team at Kansas City, MO (AA) from 1946 to 1948. (His father was co-owner and executive vice-president–general manager of the Yankees from 1945 to 1947.)

As director of player personnel for the Yankees from 1948 to 1958, MacPhail helped to assemble the talent that produced nine AL pennants and seven World Series championships in 10 years. He then joined the lowly Baltimore Orioles (AL) as president and general manager (1958–1965) and supervised the building of a team that won the 1966 World Series. When William D. Eckert* was named Commissioner of Baseball in November 1965, MacPhail became his chief administrative assistant and the real baseball authority in the office. For his achievements, *TSN* named him Major League Executive of the Year for 1966. MacPhail returned to the Yankees in October 1966 as executive vice-president and general manager. He was chosen AL president in October 1973 and took office on January 1, 1974. He resigned that office at the end of 1983. Since January 1, 1984, he has served as president of the Major League Player Relations Committee, the agency representing the owners in negotiations with the MLPA.

As a baseball executive, MacPhail's quiet, soft-spoken, introverted personality sharply contrasted with that of his explosive, outspoken, extroverted father. But like his father, he emphasized the farm system as the best way to build strong teams. When AL president, he preserved the controversial DH rule. As AL president and head of the Major League Player Relations Committee, he defended the financial interests of club owners in an era of arbitration, free agency, and collective bargaining by the MLPA. In 1998, the Veterans Committee elected him to the National Baseball Hall of Fame.

BIBLIOGRAPHY: Lee MacPhail file, National Baseball Library, Cooperstown, NY; Gene Karst and Martin J. Jones, Jr., *Who's Who in Professional Baseball* (New Rochelle, NY, 1973); Lee MacPhail, *My Nine Innings* (Westport, CT, 1989); Mark Gallagher, *The Yankee Encyclopedia*, vol. 3 (Champaign, IL, 1997); Ted Patterson, *The Baltimore Orioles* (Dallas, TX, 1995); James H. Bready, *Baseball in Baltimore* (Baltimore, MD, 1998); *NYT*, November 6, 1958, December 12, 1959, November 18, 1965, October 14, 1966, October 24, 1973, December 5, 1983; *TSN*, December 3, 1966, September 12, 1981, June 27, 1983; *WWA*, 42nd ed. (1982–1983), p. 2,101.

Larry R. Gerlach

McPHEE, John Alexander "Biddy," "Bid" (b. November 1, 1859, Massena, NY; d. January 3, 1943, San Diego, CA), player, manager, and scout, was the fourth of five children of saddler John McPhee and Maria (Button) McPhee. In 1866 the McPhees moved to Keithsburg, IL, where he learned to play baseball. He entered professional baseball with Davenport, IA (NWL) in 1877, first as a catcher and then as a second baseman and outfielder. In 1879, he worked as a clerk at a Davenport commission house. After returning to baseball a year later as a second baseman with a semipro team in Akron, OH, he signed in 1882 with the Cincinnati Red Stockings in the newly formed AA. Thereafter, he owned second base in Cincinnati, playing eight fine seasons with the Red Stockings (AA) and ten with the Reds (NL).

A capable leadoff hitter, McPhee compiled a .271 career batting average with 2,250 hits in 2,135 major league games. His specialty was hitting triples, ranking eleventh on the all-time list (188). A right-handed batter, he led the AA with 19 triples in 1887, hit 22 for the Reds in 1890, and made three in one game against the New York Giants in 1890. He also tallied over 100 runs in ten different seasons, placing twenty-first lifetime. He stole 568 bases, mostly between 1887 and 1897, when bases advanced on a teammate's hit or out were scored as thefts. McPhee also made 303 doubles, scored 1,678 runs, knocked in 1,067 runs, and walked 981 times.

Although his career .944 fielding average frequently has been exceeded in the modern era, McPhee ranked among the premier nineteenth century second basemen. He led his league in fielding average eight seasons, finished second six times, and never placed below fourth. McPhee also paced his league for eleven years in double plays, eight in putouts, and six in assists. For second basemen, McPhee's .978 fielding average in 1896 comprised the best in the major leagues during his 18-year career, and his 529 putouts in 1886 remain a single-season record. Overall, McPhee ranks first for putouts (6,545), fourth in assists (6,905), second in average chances per game (6.3), and high in total double plays (1,145). McPhee's records are the more remarkable because he was one of the last barehanded players. Although gloves were in general use by 1886, he disdained them until 1897 when his career was nearly ended.

In 1882, he participated in the first post-season Championship Series against the Chicago White Stockings (NL). The teams split two games before an interleague dispute ended the competition.

In 1899, McPhee played in 111 games and batted .279. To the city's dismay, McPhee, nearly 40 years old, retired before the 1900 season, proud of never having been fined or ejected from a game. Although exciting to watch in an era that appreciated fine fielding, McPhee personally lacked color. The trim 5-foot 8-inch, 152 pounder wore the typical center part and curly mustache of his time, conducted himself soberly, and always remained in shape. He managed the Reds to an eighth place finish in 1901 and to seventh in 1902, resigning part way through the season with a 79–124 composite record. On August 7, 1902, he married Julia Caroline Broerman; they had no children. From 1903 through 1909, McPhee served as a Reds scout. He retired to Southern California in 1917.

BIBLIOGRAPHY: William E. Akin, "The Great Fielders of 1880–1899," *BRJ* 10 (1981), pp. 62–65; Lee Allen, *The Cincinnati Reds* (New York, 1948); Lee Allen, "The Cincinnati Reds: The Oldest Club in Baseball," *Sport* 11 (May 1951), p. 52: Cincinnati *Enquirer*, April 12, 1890; Cincinnati *Times-Star*, January 4, 1943; John Alexander McPhee file, National Baseball Library, Cooperstown, NY; Robert L. Tiemann and Mark Rucker, eds., *Nineteenth Century Stars* (Kansas City, MO, 1989); Ralph C. Moses, "Bid McPhee," *TNP* 14 (1994), pp. 48–50; David Nemec, *The Beer and Whisky League* (New York, 1994); Bob Rathgeber, *Cincinnati Reds Scrapbook* (Virginia Beach, VA, 1982); *The Baseball Encyclopedia*, 10th ed. (New York, 1996); Harold Seymour, *Baseball: The Early Years* (New York, 1960); *SL* April 7, 1900, p. 3; *TSN*, June 5, 1897; David Quentin Voigt, *American Baseball*, vol. 1 (University Park, PA, 1983).

                                                                          A. D. Suehsdorf

McQUINN, George Hartley "The Patient Scot" (b. May 29, 1910, Arlington, VA; d. December 24, 1978, Little Rock, AR), player, manager, and scout, grew up in the Ballston, VA area. McQuinn pitched and played first base for Arlington High School and performed for Lem Owens's baseball team in northern Virginia. Owens had sat out the 1931 season over a salary dispute with George Weiss's* New Haven, CT (EL) club. When Owens finally secured his deal, he took McQuinn with him. Scout Gene McCann then signed him to a contract with Wheeling, WV (MAL).

McQuinn's minor league advancement was stymied by the continuing career of the New York Yankees' (AL) stalwart Lou Gehrig,* a 15-year fixture at first base. Over the next eight seasons in the Yankees chain, "The Patient Scot" slowly progressed through the farm system. He played for Scranton, PA (NYPL) in 1931, Albany, NY (EL) in 1932, Binghamton, NY (NYPL) in 1932–1933, Toronto, Canada (IL) in 1933–1934, and Newark, NJ (IL) in 1935. He married Kathleen Baxter of Belfast, Ireland in October 1937. They had two children.

The New York Yankees sold McQuinn to the Cincinnati Reds (NL) in 1936, but he hit only .201 in 38 games that year and was returned to the Newark Bears. McQuinn rejoined Toronto in 1937 and then returned to Newark. In 1938, the Yankees let the St. Louis Browns (AL) draft him from the Newark Bears' roster. The Browns surprisingly chose McQuinn instead of pitcher Joe Beggs,* who had won 21 of 25 decisions for the Bears. A defensive stylist at first base, McQuinn was often compared to George Sisler* and patterned himself after Joe Judge* of the Washington Senators (AL). He hit .324 in 1938 and .316 in 1939 and proved a steady, reliable hitter for the rest of his 12-year major league career.

McQuinn's best seasons came from 1938 to 1945 with the St. Louis Browns as a premier first baseman. Despite a back ailment that kept him out of military service, McQuinn helped St. Louis in 1944 to its only AL pennant in its 52-year history. In the World Series against the rival St. Louis Cardinals, McQuinn won the first game, 2–1, with a dramatic two-run HR off Mort Cooper.* McQuinn led all regulars with a sparkling .438 batting mark in the 1944 classic.

McQuinn, a 5-foot 11-inch 170 pounder, compiled a 34-game hitting streak with the St. Louis Browns in 1938, then one of the longest in baseball history. He led first basemen in fielding percentage in 1940, 1941, and 1944 and paced first basemen virtually every year in most fielding departments. He proved especially adept at turning the first base–shortstop–first base double play. McQuinn hit for the cycle on July 19, 1941 and played in the 1944 All-Star game.

St. Louis traded McQuinn to the Philadelphia Athletics (AL) in October 1945 for Dick Siebert,* who refused to report over a salary conflict. Philadelphia manager Connie Mack* released McQuinn after he hit a paltry .225 in 1946. Larry MacPhail,* the volatile owner of the New York Yankees, who

had always liked McQuinn, signed him as a free agent. McQuinn helped the
Yankees win another AL pennant in 1947 by hitting .304 in 144 games. In
the 1947 World Series against the Brooklyn Dodgers, he slumped to a .130
batting mark. Altogether, he hit .256 in World Series play. In 1,550 career
major league games, he made 1,588 hits, batted .276, scored 832 runs and
knocked in 794 runs on 315 doubles, 64 triples, and 135 HR.

After being released by the New York Yankees in 1948, McQuinn spent
the next 24 years in baseball as the player–manager for Quebec, Canada
(ProL), Atlanta, GA (SL), and Boise, ID (PrL). He later scouted for the
Montreal Expos (NL) before suffering a fatal stroke.

BIBLIOGRAPHY: George McQuinn file, National Baseball Library, Cooperstown,
NY; William B. Mead, *Even the Browns* (Chicago, IL, 1978); Mark Gallagher, *The
Yankee Encyclopedia*, vol. 3 (Champaign, IL, 1997); Bill Borst, ed., *Ables to Zoldak*, vol.
2 (St. Louis, MO, 1989); Bill Borst, *Last in the American League* (St. Louis, MO,
1979); Bill Borst, *Still Last in the American League* (West Bloomfield, MI, 1992); Gene
Karst and Martin J. Jones, Jr., *Who's Who in Professional Baseball* (New Rochelle, NY,
1973).

William A. Borst

McRAE, Harold Abraham "Hal," "Mr. Ribbie" (b. July 10, 1945, Avon Park,
FL), player, coach, and manager, is one of ten children of custodian–gardener–citrus worker Willie McRae and Virginia (Foster) McRae. McRae
graduated from Douglas High School in Sebring, FL, where he lettered in
baseball, basketball, and football. McRae, who played baseball at Florida
A&M University, married Johncyna Williams on April 21, 1966 and has
three children. His son, Brian, plays outfield for the New York Mets (NL).
He entered professional baseball with Tampa, FL (FSL) in 1965 and played
second base with Peninsula, VA (CrL) in 1966 and Knoxville, TN (SA) and
Buffalo, NY (IL) in 1967. McRae switched to the outfield with Indianapolis,
IN (AA) in 1968 and 1969. A part-time player with the Cincinnati Reds
(NL) for four years, McRae excelled in the 1972 World Series by batting
.444 against the winning Oakland A's. As a National Leaguer, he compiled
a .257 batting average.

McRae's stardom, however, was achieved in the AL after being traded in
November 1972 to the Kansas City Royals. With the Royals chiefly as a
DH, McRae hit the ball to all fields and enjoyed six seasons of hitting at
least .303. He averaged .293 at the plate for the Royals and was named the
AL's top DH five times. A student of the renowned Charlie Lau* and Rocky
Colavito,* McRae kept his strikeouts to a minimum and still hit with power.
In 1976, teammate George Brett* hit an inside-the-park HR on what ap-
peared to be a catchable fly ball to win a controversial batting crown over
McRae. McRae won only three hitting categories in his career, leading the
AL in on base percentage with .412 in 1976 and doubles with a club record
54 in 1977, and tying for the lead in doubles with 46 in 1982. In 1982 he

won the RBI title with 133, a Royals record and among the highest ever for an AL DH. Nicknamed "Mr. Ribbie" by teammates for his clutch hitting, he set Royals records for total bases (330) and extra-base hits (86) in 1977.

Besides his hitting, McRae exhibited a hard-sliding, aggressive, running style of play and consequently suffered several injuries. He missed an entire season (1969) on the disabled list, breaking a leg in four places by sliding into home plate during a Puerto Rican game in winter ball. The fiery, outspoken leader played brilliantly in three World Series, hitting 18 for 44, batting .409, and slugging six doubles with six RBI. McRae batted consistently, very rarely played two or three straight games without a hit, and generally made hits in three of every four games. When the Royals captured the Western Division title in 1985, McRae knocked in 70 runs in 320 at-bats and made nine game-winning hits as a DH. He batted .261 and knocked in three runs in the Royals' successful AL Championship Series against the Toronto Blue Jays. Since the DH was not used in the 1985 World Series triumph over the St. Louis Cardinals, McRae made only one official at-bat. McRae retired following the 1987 season with 2,081 hits, 484 doubles, 66 triples, 191 HR, 1,097 RBI, and a .290 batting average. McRae, twice named Kansas City Player of the Year (1974, 1982), participated in two All-Star games (1975, 1982) and was named to *TSN* All-League team four times (1976, 1977, 1982, 1983).

McRae managed the Kansas City Royals from 1991 to 1994, compiling a 286–277 overall win–loss record. He also coached the Kansas City Royals in 1987, the Montreal Expos (NL) in 1990 and 1991, the Cincinnati Reds in 1995 and 1996, and the Philadelphia Phillies (NL) since 1997.

BIBLIOGRAPHY: Hal McRae file, National Baseball Library, Cooperstown, NY; John E. DiMeglio, correspondence with Johncyna McRae, John E. DiMeglio Collection, Mankato, MN; Ron Fimrite, "The Dean of the DHs," *SI* 57 (July 19, 1982), pp. 26–27ff; Sid Bordman, *Expansion to Excellence* (Marcelline, MS, 1981); Robert H. Walker, *Cincinnati and the Big Red Machine* (Bloomington, IN, 1988); W. Leavy, "Baseball's Minority Managers: Taking Charge on the Field," *Ebony* 48 (May 1993), pp. 110–112; D. C. Lyons, "Like Father, Like Son," *Ebony* 46 (October 1991), pp. 126ff; Leigh Montville, "Every Day Is Father's Day," *SI* 74 (June 17, 1991), pp. 54–56; Jim Selman, "Hal McRae; A Premier DH in Twilight of His Career," *BD* 43 (August 1984), pp. 69–70.

John E. DiMeglio

McREYNOLDS, Walter Kevin (b. October 16, 1959, Little Rock, AR), player, graduated from Sylvian Hills High School in North Little Rock, AR and attended the University of Arkansas, where he set a Razorback record for most HR and made *TSN* College All-America baseball team in 1981. The San Diego Padres (NL) selected the 6-foot 1-inch, 225-pound outfielder, who batted and threw right-handed, in the first round as the sixth pick overall in the June 1981 draft. He spent under two minor league seasons with Reno, NV (CaL) and Amarillo, TX (TL) in 1982 and Las Vegas, NV (PCL) in 1983, being named CaL MVP in 1982 and *TSN* Minor League Player of the Year and PCL Player of the Year in 1983.

McReynolds joined the San Diego Padres in 1983 and played there three full seasons. After batting .278 with 75 RBI and sharing the team lead in HR (20) as regular center fielder in 1984, he hit .300 with a three-run HR in Game 3 of the NL Championship Series against the Chicago Cubs. A broken wrist, however, sidelined him from the World Series. McReynolds, who led NL outfielders in putouts in both 1984 and 1985, enjoyed his best San Diego Padre season in 1986 with 26 HR, 96 RBI, and a .287 batting average.

In December 1986, the San Diego Padres traded McReynolds to the New York Mets (NL). He played there through 1991, clouting career-high 32 doubles and 29 HR with 95 RBI in 1987 and leading NL outfielders in assists in 1988 and 1990. His best season with New York came in 1988, when he batted a career-high .288 with 30 doubles, 27 HR, and a career-best 99 RBI. No major leaguer had ever recorded between 95 and 99 RBI three consecutive years. McReynolds batted .250 with two doubles, two HR, and four RBI in the NL Championship Series against the Los Angeles Dodgers, tying a single game record with four hits. He set a major league record by stealing 34 consecutive bases in 1988 and 1989 and hit for the cycle on August 1, 1989 against the St. Louis Cardinals.

The Kansas City Royals (AL) acquired McReynolds in a blockbuster December 1991 trade. After struggling two seasons there, he ended his major league career with the New York Mets in 1994.

In 12 major league seasons, McReynolds batted .265 with 1,439 hits, 284 doubles, 211 HR, and 807 RBI in 1,502 games. He and his wife, Jackie, have one child, Amanda, and reside in Sherwood, AR.

BIBLIOGRAPHY: Peter C. Bjarkman, ed., *Encyclopedia of Major League Baseball Team Histories National League* (Westport, CT, 1991); Kevin McReynolds file, National Baseball Library, Cooperstown, NY; *San Diego Padres 1986 Media Guide; TSN Baseball Register*, 1994.

David L. Porter

McVEY, Calvin Alexander "Cal" (b. August 30, 1850, Montrose, IA; d. August 20, 1926, San Francisco, CA), player and manager, excelled as a hitter in the early years of professional baseball. He played every position, including pitcher, during his career and starred as a catcher and right fielder. After moving with his family at age 11 to Indianapolis, IN, McVey in his mid-teens played amateur ball for several Indianapolis clubs. In 1869 manager Harry Wright* hired him to play for the Cincinnati Red Stockings, baseball's first openly professional club. In 1871, McVey accompanied Wright to the Boston Red Stockings of the newly formed NA, baseball's first professional league. Following two years as Boston's catcher, McVey played in 1873 for the Baltimore Marylands (also managing the club part of the season to a 20–13 won–lost record) and returned to Boston for two more years. McVey led the NA twice in hits (1871, 1874) and once in runs scored (1874). His five-year .362 batting average ranked second in the NA to Ross Barnes'* .390. In three of his four years with Boston, he helped the Red Stockings win the NA championship.

When the NA gave way to the NL, McVey became one of the notorious "big four" (which included Barnes, Al Spalding, * and Deacon White*) who deserted Boston for the Chicago White Stockings and led them to the NL's first championship in 1876. McVey batted .347 in 1876, fifth highest in the NL. In 1877 he raised his batting average to .368, third best in the NL, and ranked second in hits, runs, and total bases. Chicago, however, fell to fifth place in the six-club league. McVey concluded his NL career as an infielder and manager at Cincinnati. In 1878 he managed the Reds to second place with a 37–23 won–lost record, but his 34–28 1879 record in a partial season as manager produced only a fifth place finish. During his four NL seasons, McVey batted .328 to give him a nine-year .346 major league batting average.

McVey remained active in baseball for another decade in California. He organized and managed clubs in Oakland, Hanford, and San Diego, working as an irrigation company superintendent and owner of a stock farm. In 1906, he lost his home and possessions in the San Francisco earthquake and—with his aged father, William, and his invalid wife—was reduced to living in a shack. In 1913, he was injured severely in a 30-foot fall in a Nevada mine. With encouragement and financial assistance from baseball friends, McVey recovered from each adversity. One former teammate found him at age 73 in good health and employed as night watchman for a lumber company. In 1968, McVey was elected to the Iowa Sports Hall of Fame.

BIBLIOGRAPHY: Bill Bryson, "Cal McVey Joins 'Hall,' " Des Moines Sunday Register, April 14, 1968; Seymour R. Church, Base Ball (San Francisco CA, 1902; repr. Princeton, NJ, 1974); Jerry E. Clark, Anson to Zuber: Iowa's Boys in the Major Leagues (Omaha, NE, 1992); Cal McVey file, National Baseball Library, Cooperstown, NY; The Baseball Encyclopedia, 10th ed. (New York, 1996); Robert L. Tiemann and Mark Rucker, eds., Nineteenth Century Stars (Kansas City, MO, 1989); Lee Allen, The Cincinnati Reds (New York, 1948); Greg Rhodes and John Erardi, The First Boys of Summer (Cincinnati, OH, 1994); William J. Ryczek, Blackguards and Red Stockings (Jefferson, NC, 1994).

Frederick Ivor-Campbell

MADDOX, Garry Lee (b. September 1, 1949, Cincinnati, OH), player and sportscaster, was called "the Secretary of Defense" of the great Philadelphia Phillies (NL) teams of the 1975–1983 era and enjoyed a distinguished 15-year major league career. After growing up in California, Maddox attended

Harbor College in Wilmington, CA and spent two years in Vietnam from 1968 to 1970.

The 6-foot 3-inch, 205-pound right-hander came up to the San Francisco Giants (NL) in 1972 after only two years in the minor leagues as the center field successor to Willie Mays.* Maddox played three seasons with the San Francisco Giants before being traded to the Philadelphia Phillies (NL) in May 1975 for first baseman Willie Montanez.* Maddox achieved stardom with the Philadelphia Phillies as the premier center fielder of his era. He won eight Gold Gloves, averaging over 400 putouts for five straight years from 1976 to 1980.

Maddox's career .285 batting average included two .300 seasons. His stellar .330 batting mark in 1976 ranked him third in the NL. He also tied for third in doubles with 37 that season. During his major league career, he recorded 1,802 hits, 337 doubles, 117 HR, and 754 RBI. He stole 248 bases, establishing a season high of 33 in 1978.

Maddox, essentially a gap and line drive hitter, proved a vital cog, as the Philadelphia Phillies won five NL East Division titles, two NL pennants, and one World Series crown during his tenure there. The high point of his major league career came in Game 5 of the dramatic 1980 NL Championship Series with the Houston Astros, when he doubled to score Del Unser and give the Philadelphia Phillies their first NL pennant in 30 years. Back injuries forced him to retire in May 1986.

Maddox and his wife, Sondra, have two sons and reside in the Philadelphia, PA area. He works in the Philadelphia Phillies' Community Relations Department and serves as a color commentator for the Phillies' cable TV games. He also remains active in charitable organizations, including the Philadelphia Child Guidance Center.

BIBLIOGRAPHY: Garry Maddox file, National Baseball Library, Cooperstown, NY; Rich Westcott and Frank Bilovsky, *The New Phillies Encyclopedia* (Philadelphia PA, 1993); Jill Lieber, "And One Who Prospered: With Agents' Help, Ex-Outfielder Garry Maddox Made a Fortune," *SI* 67 (October 19, 1987), p. 96; Allen Lewis, *The Philadelphia Phillies: A Pictorial History* (Virginia Beach, VA, 1981); Hal Bodley, *The Team That Wouldn't Die* (Wilmington, DE, 1981); Frank Dolson, *The Philadelphia Story* (South Bend, IN, 1981); *Philadelphia Phillies Media Guide*, 1976–1986.

John P. Rossi

MADDUX, Gregory Alan "Greg" (b. April 24, 1966, San Angelo, TX), player, is the son of David Maddux, a retired US Air Force officer, and Linda (Martin) Maddux and has a brother, Mike, who also pitches in the major leagues. Maddux graduated in 1984 from Valley High School in Las Vegas, NV, where he made All-State in baseball his junior and senior seasons. He and his wife, Kathy, have one daughter, Amanda.

The Chicago Cubs (NL) selected the 6-foot, 175-pound pitcher, who throws and bats right-handed, in the June 1984 free agent draft and assigned him to Pikeville, KY (ApL). He pitched in 1985 for Peoria, IL (ML) and in

1986 for Pittsfield, MA (EL) and Des Moines–based Iowa (AA) before appearing in six games for the Chicago Cubs. Maddux defeated his brother, Mike, of the Philadelphia Phillies, on September 29, 1986 in the first match-up of rookie brothers in major league history. In 1987, he won all three games at Iowa before joining the Chicago Cubs starting rotation. Maddux pitched for the Chicago Cubs from 1986 to 1992, compiling a 95–75 record. He finished 18–8 in 1988 and posted a 19–12 mark and a 2.95 ERA while leading the 1989 Cubs to the NL Eastern Division title. Maddux started twice in the NL Championship Series against the San Francisco Giants, losing one contest. In 1992, he led NL hurlers in victories with a 20–11 record and 2.18 ERA and with 268 innings pitched.

Maddux, granted free agency by the Chicago Cubs in October 1992, signed with the Atlanta Braves (NL) in December 1992. In his first season with the Atlanta Braves, he won 20 games and registered his first post-season victory in the NL Championship Series against the Philadelphia Phillies. Maddux in 1994 won 16 games and compiled a career-best 1.56 ERA, the third best in the major leagues since 1919. Bob Gibson* had recorded a 1.12 ERA in 1968 and Dwight Gooden* a 1.53 ERA in 1985. Maddux allowed the fewest earned runs (35) in franchise history based on 180 innings pitched. He won 19 of 21 decisions in 1995 for a .905 winning percentage, a major league record for pitchers with at least 20 decisions. His two season record of 35 victories and eight losses with a 1.60 ERA made him the first hurler since Walter Johnson* in 1918–1919 to boast an ERA less than 1.80 in consecutive campaigns. His 1.63 ERA in 1995 fell an extraordinary 2.55 below the NL average of 4.18. Maddux registered one victory each in the NL Division Series against the Colorado Rockies, the NL Championship Series against the Cincinnati Reds and split two decisions against the Cleveland Indians in the triumphant six-game 1995 World Series. In 1996, Maddux compiled a 15–11 mark with a 2.86 ERA and blanked the Los Angeles Dodgers in the NL Division Series. He split two decisions with a 2.51 ERA in the NL Championship Series against the St. Louis Cardinals. Maddux held the New York Yankees scoreless in Game 2 of the 1996 World Series, but lost the final Game 6, 3–2. His 19–4 record and 2.20 ERA helped the Braves capture another NL East title in 1997. He pitched a brilliant 2–1 victory over the Houston Astros in the NL Division Series, but dropped two hard luck decisions to the Florida Marlins in the NL Championship Series. Maddux compiled an 18–9 mark in 1998, defeating the Chicago Cubs with a 2.57 ERA in his only NL Division Series start. After losing Game 3 of the NL Championship Series to the San Diego Padres, he picked up the first save of his major league career in Game 5 of the NL Championship Series. Maddux finished 19–9 with a 3.57 ERA in 1999, helping Atlanta repeat as NL East titlists. He lost his only decision in the NL Division Series, fared 1–0 with a 1.93 ERA in the NL Championship Series, and was 0–1 with a 2.57 ERA in the World Series.

Numerous achievements recorded by Maddux include leading the NL in victories (1992, 1994–1995), ERA (1993–1995, 1998), games started (1990–1993), games completed (1993–1995), shut outs (1994–1995, 1998), innings pitched (1991–1995), and winning percentage (1995, 1997). His honors include NL All-Star team member (1988, 1992, 1994–1998), Gold Glove Award (1991–1999), *AP* Major League Player of the Year and *USAT Baseball Weekly* NL MVP (1995), *TSN* NL Pitcher of the Year (1990–1995), and the NL Cy Young Award (1992–1995). Maddux extended his unprecedented string of Cy Young Awards by winning his fourth consecutive in 1995, marking his second consecutive year with unanimous selection by the BBWAA. Sandy Koufax* remains the only other pitcher unanimously selected for two consecutive years, while Steve Carlton* the only other four-time winner. Roger Clemens* has won five Cy Young Awards.

Maddux in 14 major league seasons has compiled a 221–126 record and 2.81 ERA. He has appeared in 436 games, completing 93 of 432 starts and pitching 28 shutouts. Maddux has hurled 3,068.2 innings, surrendered 2,761 hits, 1,104 runs, 959 earned runs, and 671 walks, and struck out 2,160 batters. He ranked first in victories (176) in the 1990s.

BIBLIOGRAPHY: Greg Maddux file, National Baseball Library, Cooperstown, NY; *Atlanta Braves Media Guide*, 1998; John Benson et al., *Baseball's Top 100* (Wilton, CT, 1997); G. Castle, "Greg Maddux," *Sport* 84 (May 1993), pp. 19–20; *CB* 57 (February 1996), pp. 22–26; D. Dieffenbach, "Sport Lifestyle: Off the Mound with Greg Maddux," *Sport* 86 (January 1995), pp. 34–35; Evansville (IN) *Courier*, November 14, 1995, p. 1C; *TSN Official Baseball Register*, 1998; John Thorn et al., eds., *Total Braves* (New York, 1996); Gary Caruso, *The Braves Encyclopedia* (Philadelphia, PA, 1995); *USAT Baseball Weekly*, October 4–10, 1995, pp. 33, 43; Tom Verducci, "Drive for Show, Pitch for Dough," *SI* 82 (May 1, 1995), pp. 110–119; Tom Verducci, "Once in a Lifetime," *SI* 83 (August 14, 1995), pp. 22–28.

John L. Evers

MADLOCK, Bill, Jr. "Mad Dog" (b. January 12, 1951, Memphis, TN), player and coach, grew up in difficult family circumstances without his father, Bill, Sr. Before he was one month old, he was sent to live with his grandmother, Annie Polk. At age two, Madlock moved with his grandmother to Decatur, IL. His aunt and uncle, Sarah and Wardie Sain, assisted in his upbringing there. Madlock attended Dwight D. Eisenhower High School in Decatur, where he earned nine letters in various sports and made All-State halfback in football. He married Cynthia Johnson in 1969 and had four children, Sarah, Stephen, William, and Jeremy, before their divorce. In 1969, Madlock rejected over 100 football scholarships to play baseball for Southeastern CC in Keokuk, IA.

In January 1970 Madlock signed a professional baseball contract with the Washington Senators (AL), who had selected him in the secondary phase of the draft. The 1970 season saw him play for Geneva, NY (NYPL) where he toiled at shortstop, batted .269, and slugged 6 HR. During the next two years, he played for Pittsfield, MA (EL) under manager Joe Klein. Klein helped Madlock develop a more disciplined swing, which contributed to a .328 batting average in 1972. During a banner 1973 season with the Spokane, WA Indians (PCL), Madlock batted .338, belted 22 HR, contributed 90 RBI, and led the PCL in runs scored with 119. In September 1973, Madlock was promoted to the Texas Rangers (AL) and batted .351 in their final 21 games. In October 1973, Texas traded him to the Chicago Cubs (NL).

From 1974 to 1976, the right-handed Madlock played second base for the Chicago Cubs (NL) and led the NL in batting average with .354 (1975) and .339 (1976) percentages. In February 1977 Madlock was dealt to the San Francisco Giants (NL), where he batted over .300 twice. Madlock remained with the Giants until traded on June 28, 1979 to the Pittsburgh Pirates (NL). In the 85 remaining games, Madlock batted .328 and played outstanding third base to help the Pirates win the Eastern Division and NL pennant. Madlock provided instrumental help in the Pirates' World Series victory over the Baltimore Orioles by batting .375.

In the strike-shortened 1981 season, Madlock won his third batting title with a healthy .341 mark to become only the sixth major league player to win batting titles with two different clubs. Madlock won his fourth batting title with a .323 average in 1983, becoming one of only eleven major league players to have captured that many batting titles. In August 1985, he was traded to the Los Angeles Dodgers (NL) for three players and helped them capture the 1985 Western Division title. Madlock batted .333 in the NL Championship Series against the St. Louis Cardinals with 3 HR, 1 double, and 7 RBI. His major league career ended with the Detroit Tigers (AL) in 1987. In 15 major league seasons, he batted .305 with 2,008 hits, 348 doubles, 163 HR, 860 RBI, and 174 stolen bases.

Although not known for his power, the 5-foot 11-inch, 190-pound Madlock in 1982 belted 19 HR and drove in 95 runs. His career was somewhat tarnished in 1980 when he hit umpire Jerry Crawford in the face with a glove during an argument. Madlock, nicknamed "Mad Dog" because of the incident, was assessed the largest fine ever levied for an on-the-field incident ($5,000) and the second longest suspension in major league history (15 days).

Following the incident, Madlock's temperament rebounded admirably and his leadership qualities blossomed. In September 1982, he was named captain of the Pirates. Off the field, he operates Hitter's Challenge, a promotional company arranging sports speakers. Madlock also collects clocks, is a partner in the restaurant business, and advises the President's Council on Physical Fitness and Sports. In 1999, he served as a hitting coach for Buffalo, NY (IL) and for the Detroit Tigers in 2000.

BIBLIOGRAPHY: Eddie Gold and Art Ahrens, *The New Era Cubs, 1941–1985* (Chicago, IL, 1985); Bill Madlock file, National Baseball Library, Cooperstown NY; Zander Hollander, ed., *The Complete Handbook of Baseball, 1983* (New York, 1983); Robert E. Kelly, *Baseball's Best* (Jefferson, NC, 1988); W. Ladson, "Riches to Rags," *Sport*

85 (January 1994), pp. 34–37; Harris Lewine and Daniel Okrent, eds., *The Ultimate Baseball Book* (New York, 1983); William C. Matney, ed., *Who's Who Among Black Americans* (Northbrook, IL, 1977); Robert Obojski, *Bush League: A History of Minor League Baseball* (New York, 1975); Rich Westcott, "Bill Madlock: Four Time Batting Champ Is in Tune with the Hobby," *SCD* 21 (September 16, 1994), pp. 140–142; D. Whitford, "Glad Dog," *Sport* 77 (May 1986), pp. 70–72; John Thom, *Champion Batsman of the 20th Century* (Los Angeles, CA, 1992); Bob Smizik, *The Pittsburgh Pirates: An Illustrated History* (New York, 1990); Steve Wulf, "Glad Times for Mad Dog," *SI* 58 (May 9, 1983), pp. 48–57.

Samuel O. Regalado

MAGEE, Sherwood Robert "Sherry" (b. August 6, 1884, Clarendon, PA; d. March 13, 1929, Philadelphia, PA), player and umpire, was a son of oilfield worker James S. Magee and Drusilla (Hall) Magee. He entered professional baseball in 1903 at Allentown, PA and began the 1904 season at Carlisle, PA, where Philadelphia Phillies (NL) scout Jim Randall signed him. The burly 5-foot 11-inch, 179-pound right-hander reported to Philadelphia in June 1904 and played left field for the Phillies through 1914, serving as field captain in 1914. After disappointment at not being named manager, he was traded at his own request to the Boston Braves (NL) in December 1914. Magee was waived to the Cincinnati Reds (NL) in August 1917 and finished his NL career there in 1919. Subsequently he played for Columbus, OH (AA) in 1920, Minneapolis, MN (AA) in 1921 and 1922, St. Joseph, MO (WL) in 1923, Milwaukee, WI (AA) in 1923, 1924, and 1925, and Baltimore, MD (IL) in 1925 and 1926.

Although playing during the dead ball era, Magee batted .291 in 2,087 NL games, with 2,169 hits, 1,112 runs, 1,176 RBI, 441 stolen bases, and a .427 slugging percentage. During his 11 seasons with Philadelphia, he hit .299, usually as the fourth batter in the lineup, and slugged .447 (35 percent above the NL average). In 1910, Magee hit .331 to win the NL batting championship and led the NL in runs scored (110), RBI (123), on base percentage (.445) and slugging average (.507). In 1914, he paced the NL in hits (171), doubles (39), RBI (103), and slugging average (.509). He also topped the NL in RBI in 1907 (85) and 1918 (76).

The smart, aggressive Magee, a fast, excellent fielder with a strong, accurate throwing arm, proved a superior base runner and hit sharp line drives to all fields. He always played hard to win, constantly scolded teammates and himself for mistakes and lapses, and experienced difficulties because of his hot temper. On July 10, 1911, he knocked out umpire Bill Finneran with one punch after the latter ejected him for exhibiting displeasure over a called third strike. Although originally suspended for the season, he subsequently was reinstated on August 16. Off the field, however, he was a gentle, warm person, exhibited much wit and humor, abstained from hard liquor, and remained extremely popular.

Magee began umpiring in 1927 in the NYPL and received such favorable notice that NL president John Heydler* appointed him to the NL staff. Contrary to some expectations, Magee worked efficiently and got along well with players during his rookie 1928 season. Before the next season, however, he contracted pneumonia and died. Magee was survived by his widow, Edna May (Cary) Magee, whom he had married in 1905, and three children, Erwin, Robert, and Charlotte.

BIBLIOGRAPHY: Philadelphia (PA) *Evening Bulletin*, March 14, 1929; Craig Carter, ed., *TSN Daguerreotypes*, 8th ed. (St. Louis, MO, 1990); Frederick G. Lieb and Stan Baumgartner, *The Philadelphia Phillies* (New York, 1953); Sherwood Magee file, National Baseball Library, Cooperstown, NY; *The North American* (Philadelphia), July 11, 16, 1911; Frank V. Phelps, correspondence with Derek B. McKown, Curator, Warren County (PA) Historical Society, October 23, 1985, Frank V. Phelps Collection, King of Prussia, PA; Philadelphia (PA) *Inquirer*, March 14, 17, 1929; Philadelphia (PA) *Public Ledger*, March 14, 15, 1929; *The Baseball Encyclopedia*, 10th ed. (New York, 1996); Allen Lewis, *The Philadelphia Phillies: A Pictorial History* (Virginia Beach, VA, 1981); Rich Westcott and Frank Bilovsky, *The New Phillies Encyclopedia* (Philadelphia, PA, 1993).

Frank V. Phelps

MAGLIE, Salvatore Anthony "Sal," "The Barber" (b. April 26, 1917, Niagara Falls, NY; d. December 28, 1992, Niagara Falls, NY), player, coach, and scout, began his professional baseball career after high school graduation as a pitcher for Elmira, NY (EL) and Jersey City, NJ (IL) from 1938 to 1942. After quitting organized baseball in 1943, he rejoined Jersey City in 1945 and made his major league debut with the New York Giants (NL) in August 1945. Maglie quit the Giants in 1946 for the "outlaw" MEL and pitched there for two years.

Organized baseball banned Maglie through 1949 because he had jumped to Mexico. The 6-foot 2-inch, 180-pound Maglie returned to the New York Giants in 1950 as a tough, well-seasoned pitcher. Possessing pinpoint control, he had developed a biting curveball and a purposeful approach to the pitching art in Mexico. The right-hander's persistent inside pitches earned him the nickname "The Barber," a reflection of the "close shave" he gave hitters. Maglie himself did not shave on the days he pitched. Many hitters admitted to being intimidated by his swarthy, unshaven countenance and vicious inside pitches.

Maglie spent the first half of the 1950 season in the bullpen and then triumphed in 11 consecutive games as a starter to finish with an 18–4 record. Between July 1950 and May 1952, Maglie won 45 decisions while losing only seven contests. He led the NL with 23 victories as the New York Giants won a "miracle" NL pennant in 1951. Despite back problems, he won 18 games in 1952 and 14 contests for the 1954 World Champion Giants. He was waived to the Cleveland Indians (AL) in July 1955 and pitched for the

Brooklyn Dodgers (NL) in 1956, hurling a no-hitter on September 25, 1956 against the Philadelphia Phillies. He joined the New York Yankees (AL) in September 1957 and completed his career with the St. Louis Cardinals (NL) in 1958. His major league career record included 119 wins, 62 losses, a .657 winning percentage, and a 3.15 ERA.

Maglie scouted for the St. Louis Cardinals and coached for the Boston Red Sox (AL) from 1960 through 1962 and 1966 to 1967 and the Seattle Pilots (AL) in 1969. He later worked with the Niagara Falls Convention Bureau. Maglie married Kathleen Pileggi on May 31, 1941 and had two adopted children. In 1982 Hyde Park Stadium in Niagara Falls, NY was named in his honor.

BIBLIOGRAPHY: Sal Maglie file, National Baseball Library, Cooperstown, NY; *The Baseball Encyclopedia*, 10th ed. (New York, 1996); Herman Kaufman, "Sal Maglie: A Study in Frustration," *TNP* 2 (fall 1982), pp. 34–38; Rich Marazzi, "The Giants Swept the Indians in a Classic World Series," *SCD* 21 (October 28, 1994), pp. 150–151; *NYT*, December 29, 1992, pp. A–12, B–6; Noel Hynd, *The Giants of the Polo Grounds* (New York, 1988); Thomas Kiernan, *The Miracle at Coogan's Bluff* (New York, 1975); Leo Durocher, *Nice Guys Finish Last* (New York, 1975); John Thorn et al., eds., *Total Baseball*, 5th ed. (New York, 1997); Fred Stein and Nick Peters, *Giants Diary* (Berkeley, CA, 1987); Bobby Thomson et al., *The Giants Win the Pennant!* (New York, 1991); Roy Robinson, *The Home Run Heard 'Round the World* (New York, 1991); Frank Graham, *The New York Giants* (New York, 1952); John Phillips, *Winners* (Cabin John, MD, 1987); William F. McNeil, *The Dodgers Encyclopedia* (Champaign, IL, 1997); Bob Broeg and Jerry Vickery, *St. Louis Cardinals Encyclopedia* (Grand Rapids, MI, 1998); Rich Westcott, *Diamond Greats* (Westport, CT, 1988).

Fred Stein

MAHON, Elizabeth B. "Lib" (b. November 18, 1919, Greenville, SC), player, starred as an AAGPBL outfielder–second baseman and is the daughter of Scotch-Irish textile plant workers. She began playing baseball with Greenville boys at age six. After being selected "Best Athlete," she graduated from Parker High School in Greenville in 1937. Mahon, who graduated from Winthrop College, with an education degree, taught school, worked in a post office during World War II, and also played with the Springfield Spinners softball team. In 1944, an AAGPBL scout signed her to a contract for $60 a week with Minneapolis, MN. Kenosha, WI manager Marty McManus acquired her in a 1944 trade.

The 5-foot 7-inch, 135-pound right-handed Mahon, who never married, played with the Kenosha, WI Comets (AAGPBL) in 1944 and spent the last eight seasons from 1945 through 1952 with the South Bend, IN Blue Sox (AAGPBL). She batted .281 in 837 career games, recording 721 hits, 400 RBI, and 364 stolen bases. Her RBI marked the third highest in team history. Mahon tied an AAGPBL record in 1944 by hitting safely in 13 consecutive games from July 27 to August 9. Mahon, a clutch hitter, made the All-Star team in 1946 and 1949 and led the AAGPBL in RBI with 72 in 1946 and 60 in 1949. In 1946, she also stole 114 bases and led the AAGPBL in total bases with 326 and runs scored with 90. In 1950, she paced AAGPBL outfielders with just one error. South Bend won the AAGPBL championship in 1951 and 1952, when the Blue Sox compiled the best regular season won–lost record. Her AAGPBL career ended in 1952, when she and five other Blue Sox players walked out after manager Karl Winsch suspended Shorty Pryor.

Mahon taught for 36 years until 1981 in South Bend, and enjoyed playing all sports, including basketball, volleyball, bowling, and golf.

BIBLIOGRAPHY: W. C. Madden, *The Women of the All-American Girls Professional Baseball League* (Jefferson, NC, 1997); AAGPBL files, Northern Indiana Historical Society, South Bend, IN.

Dennis S. Clark

MALARCHER, David Julius "Gentleman Dave" (b. October 18, 1894, Whitehall, LA; d. May 11, 1982, Chicago, IL), player and manager, excelled for the black Chicago American Giants (NNL-NSL) as a player and manager from 1920 through 1928 and 1933 through 1934. The youngest of ten children born to plantation laborer Henry Louis Malarcher and former slave Martha Malarcher, he attended Dillard University and Xavier University and served with the U.S. Army in France during World War I. His wife, Mabel Eupora (Sylvester) Malarcher, died in 1946. Malarcher had no children, but many of his nieces and nephews were aided by a scholarship fund he established in his mother's name.

The switch-hitting 5-foot 7-inch, 147 pounder entered organized black baseball with C. I. Taylor's* Indianapolis ABCs (NNL) from 1916 to 1918 and soon was acclaimed the game's best third baseman. He spent the 1919 season with the Detroit Stars (NNL) prior to joining Rube Foster's* Chicago American Giants, where he spent most of his career. Malarcher possessed great speed and played the game skillfully and intelligently. He often influenced a contest's outcome. The clutch performer often scored or drove in decisive runs. Although batting .333 in five games against white major leaguers, he hit around .250 in 20 Black World Series Games in 1926 and 1927. Nevertheless, he scored 17 runs and produced five RBI, seven stolen bases, and eight sacrifice hits in Black World Series competition. Chicago won Black World Series Championships against the Atlantic City, NJ Bacharach Giants in 1926 and 1927, with Malarcher serving as Chicago's player–manager. He also performed at third base for Foster's three NNL titlists from 1920 to 1922, batting .344 in 1920.

Malarcher succeeded Foster as the Chicago American Giants' pilot in 1926, serving six seasons from 1926 to 1928 and 1932 to 1934. He also led the Chicago American Giants to three pennants (NNL, 1926–1927; NSL,

1932) and won the NNL crown in 1933. Partial figures show that his clubs compiled a 172–66 regular season log. Chicago won three of five NNL-NSL championship series under his tutelage, taking 20 of 36 decisions, and finished with 10 wins, seven losses, and three ties in its two Black World Series triumphs.

Malarcher established a real estate business in south Chicago and also became an accomplished poet. His "Sunset Before Dawn" appeared in John Holway's *Voices from the Great Black Baseball Leagues*. His sobriquet, "Gentleman Dave," reflected his personal conduct on and off the field. Malarcher never drank or smoked and served as a trustee in Chicago's Woodlawn African Methodist Episcopal Church for over 30 years. He never argued with an umpire and helped secure the introduction of black umpires into the NNL.

BIBLIOGRAPHY: *Alumni News of Dillard University*, 1973; Atlantic City (NJ) *Press*, 1926; Baltimore (MD) *Afro-American*, 1926; Chicago (IL) *Defender*, 1924–1928, 1932, 1934; John B. Holway, *Blackball Stars* (Westport, CT, 1988); John B. Holway, *Voices from the Great Black Baseball Leagues* (New York, NY, 1975); Nashville (TN) *Tennessean*, 1932; Robert W. Peterson, *Only the Ball Was White* (Englewood Cliffs, NJ, 1970); Philadelphia (PA) *Record*, 1926; Philadelphia (PA) *Tribune*, 1924, 1943; Pittsburgh (PA) *Courier*, 1924, 1927–1928, 1934; James A. Riley, *The Biographical Encyclopedia of the Negro Baseball Leagues* (New York, 1994); Paul Debono, *The Indianapolis ABCs* (Jefferson, NC, 1997); *Tuesday Magazine* (1976).

Merl F. Kleinknecht

MALONE, Perce Leigh "Pat" (b. September 25, 1902, Altoona, PA; d. May 13, 1943, Altoona, PA), player, was a colorful, hard-throwing, right-handed pitcher and the son of Christian Malone, a railroad worker, and Anna (Murphy) Malone. The well-built Malone played on a semiprofessional baseball team at age 15 and fibbed about his age to work as a fireman on the Pennsylvania Railroad at 16. He joined the U.S. Army at 17, serving with the U.S. Cavalry in Arizona. He also boxed professionally as Kid Williams and attended Juniata College in Huntington, PA in 1920, playing baseball and football.

The 6-foot, 200-pound Malone toiled for seven years as a minor league pitcher, beginning with Knoxville, TN (ApL) in 1921. After Malone won 20 games for Minneapolis, MN (AA) in 1927, the Chicago Cubs (NL) acquired him. He lost his first seven decisions with Chicago in 1928, but finished with an 18–13 record and 2.84 ERA. In 1929, Malone led the Cubs to the NL pennant with a 22–10 mark, pacing the NL in wins, strikeouts (166), and shutouts (5). He again led the NL in victories (20) and complete games (22) in 1930, posting a 20–9 mark.

After Malone won 115 games in seven seasons, the Chicago Cubs traded him to the St. Louis Cardinals (NL) in October 1934. The New York Yankees (AL) acquired him in March 1935 and used him mainly in relief. In

1936, he won 12, lost four, and led the AL in relief victories (8) and saves (9). For 10 major league seasons from 1928 to 1937, Malone appeared in 357 games, pitched 1,915 innings, won 134 games and lost 92 decisions for a .593 winning percentage, struck out 1,024 batters, walked 705 batters, and compiled a 3.74 ERA. In the 1929, 1932, and 1936 World Series, he posted a 0–3 record with 17 strikeouts in 21 innings and a 3.00 ERA.

The tough, mean, mound competitor was well liked by teammates as a fun-loving prankster and enjoyed the night-life carousing. He married Marion Seeley of Milan, OH in 1921 and had a daughter, Patricia. Malone operated a cafe-bar in downtown Altoona until his death of acute pancreatitis.

BIBLIOGRAPHY: *The Baseball Encyclopedia*, 10th ed. (New York, 1996); Pat Malone file, National Baseball Library, Cooperstown, NY; Eddie Gold and Art Ahrens, *The Golden Era Cubs, 1876–1940* (Chicago, IL, 1988); Warren Brown, *The Chicago Cubs* (New York, 1946); Warren Wilbert and William Hageman, *Chicago Cubs: Seasons at the Summit* (Champaign, IL, 1997); Jim Enright, *Chicago Cubs* (New York, 1975); Mark Gallagher, *The Yankees Encyclopedia*, vol. 3 (Champaign, IL, 1997); Ira Smith, *Baseball's Famous Pitchers* (New York, 1954); *TSN Daguerreotypes*, 4th ed. (St. Louis, MO, 1961); Altoona (PA) *Mirror*, April 13, 1987.

Edward J. Pavlick

MALONEY, James William "Ace" (b. June 2, 1940, Fresno, CA), player, coach, and manager, is the son of Earl "Hands" Maloney, a popular local athlete, and Marjorie Maloney. After participating in Little League, he played shortstop for Fresno High School and led his team to three Northern Yosemite League titles from 1956 to 1958. He remains the only Fresno High School athlete to earn eight varsity letters playing baseball, basketball, and football. As an American Legion performer for Fresno Post Four, he won the Outstanding Player Award at the 1957 Junior Legion tournament. Maloney briefly attended the University of California at Berkeley before transferring to Fresno City College in 1959. At Fresno City College, he once pitched 19 consecutive no-hit, no-run innings.

Cincinnati Reds (NL) scout Bobby Mattick signed the 6-foot 2-inch, 190-pound Maloney to his first professional baseball contract in 1959. Maloney spent most of the next two seasons as a minor league pitcher. For Nashville, TN (SA) in 1960, Maloney led all SA pitchers in winning percentage (.737) with a 14–5 record. He was promoted later that year to the Cincinnati Reds and remained with them for 1961. During the 1961 World Series against the New York Yankees (AL), Maloney appeared briefly in relief. After a short minor league stint to fine-tune his control the following year, he rejoined the Cincinnati Reds from June 1962 until 1971.

With the Cincinnati Reds, Maloney twice won 20 or more games (1963, 1965) and recorded 15 or more victories in four other seasons (1964, 1966–1968). He also compiled 200 or more strikeouts per season between 1963 and 1966, led the NL in strikeouts per game (9.5) in 1963, and shared the NL lead in shutouts (5) in 1966. He struck out eight consecutive Milwaukee Braves in one 1963 contest and made a relief appearance in the 1965 All-Star Game. Maloney's most impressive achievements, however, remain his three no-hit games, including a 10-inning affair against the Chicago Cubs (NL) on August 19, 1965. The right-hander also hurled a no-hitter until the 11th inning against the New York Mets (NL) on June 14, 1965 before allowing two hits in a 1–0 loss. A baseball committee on statistical accuracy in 1991 dropped Maloney's second game from the list of no-hitters, defining a no-hitter as a game of nine innings or more ending with no hits. His final no-hitter came in a 10–0 conquest over the Houston Astros (NL) on April 30, 1969. Upon his retirement, Maloney shared the NL record for most 1-hit pitched games in a lifetime (5). In December 1970, he signed as a free agent with the California Angels (AL). The St. Louis Cardinals (NL) enlisted him one year later, but injuries sidelined the veteran and forced his retirement. Maloney's career statistics included 134 wins, 84 losses, a 3.19 ERA, and 1,605 strikeouts. Maloney served as a pitching coach for the Fresno, CA Giants (CaL) in 1981 and managed Fresno to a 25–45 mark in 1982.

Maloney married Carolyn Ruth Daugherty in October 1961 and has three children, Jamie, Shannon, and Jason. Maloney, whose hobbies include hunting and fishing, directs Fresno's Alcoholism and Drug Abuse Council.

BIBLIOGRAPHY: Jim Maloney file, National Baseball Library, Cooperstown, NY; Lonnie Wheeler and John Baskin, *The Cincinnati Game* (Wilmington, OH, 1988); Cincinnati Reds Press Release, November 1959, *TSN* Archives, St. Louis, MO; John Donovan, "Memories of Maloney," Fresno (CA) *Bee*, June 17, 1990; Earl Lawson, "Maloney Masters Bender, Rates as Red Ace," *TSN*, June 8, 1963; Jim Maloney, interview with Samuel O. Regaldo, June 21, 1990; John Thorn et al., eds., *Total Baseball*, 5th ed. (New York, 1997); Robert H. Walker, *Cincinnati and the Big Red Machine* (Bloomington, IN, 1988); Ritter Collett, *The Cincinnati Reds* (Virginia Beach, VA, 1976); Floyd Conner and John Snyder, *Day-by-Day in Cincinnati Reds History* (West Point, NY, 1984); Bob Rathgeber, *Cincinnati Reds Scrapbook* (Virginia Beach, VA, 1982).

Samuel O. Regalado

MALZONE, Frank James (b. February 28, 1930, Bronx, NY), player, coach, and scout, is the son of Frank Malzone, a New York City Sanitation Department worker, and Pauline (Dezago) Malzone, of Italian-American descent and planned to become an electrician. After graduating from the Bronx's Samuel Gompers High School in 1948, Malzone signed a professional baseball contract with scout Cy Phillips of the Boston Red Sox (AL) organization.

Malzone spent parts of the 1948–1951 and 1954–1956 seasons in the Boston Red Sox farm system with Milford, DE (ESL), Oneonta, NY (CAL), Scranton, PA (EL), Louisville, KY (AA), and San Francisco, CA (PCL). A serious ankle fracture, service in the United States Army in 1952 and 1953, and depression over the death of an infant daughter delayed the third baseman's advancement. Malzone appeared in six games in 1955 and 27 contests in 1956 for the Boston Red Sox.

In his first complete major league season, Malzone batted .292 with a career-best 103 RBI for the Boston Red Sox in 1957. The 5-foot 10-inch, 180-pound third baseman became the first modern major leaguer to lead his position in games played, putouts, assists, double plays, fielding percentage (.954), and, ironically, errors. In 1958, he paced the AL in games played and at-bats. Malzone remained the Boston Red Sox starting third baseman through the 1965 season. Malzone played for the California Angels (AL) in 1966 before retiring from active play.

An excellent fielder, Malzone led AL third-basemen in putouts and fielding average once (1957), assists thrice (1957–1959), and double plays five times (1957–1961). Due to his large number of chances accepted, he also paced AL third basemen in errors five times (1957–1961). The three time Gold Glove recipient (1957–1959) made six AL All-Star teams (1957–1960, 1963–1964).

A good batter with solid power, Malzone averaged more than 16 HR and 87 RBI per season from 1957 through 1963 and hit .280 or better five times during that period. From 1955 to 1966, he compiled a career .274 batting average. In 1,441 games, he made 1,486 hits, including 239 doubles and 133 HR, scored 647 runs, and accumulated 728 RBI.

On August 25, 1951, Malzone married Amy Gennarino. They had two daughters and four sons. A son, John, played several years in the Boston Red Sox farm system. The Needham, MA resident has served the Boston Red Sox organization as an instructional coach and advance scout for many years. Malzone, among the best all-around infielders in Red Sox history, was inducted into the New England Sports Hall of Fame in 1995.

BIBLIOGRAPHY: Larry Claflin, "Crisp Clouting Backs Malzone Claim to Job," *TSN*, June 15, 1963, p. 3; Peter Golenbock, *Fenway* (New York, 1992); Hy Hurwitz, "Rugged Road Led Malzone to Boston Stardom," *TSN*, September 11, 1957, pp. 5–6; Brent P. Kelley, *Baseball Stars of the 1950s* (Jefferson, NC, 1992); Brent P. Kelley, "Frank Malzone Was Mr. Consistency," *SCD* 17 (November 16, 1990), pp. 240–242; Jack Lautier, *Fenway Voices* (Camden, ME, 1990); Frank Malzone file, National Baseball Library, Cooperstown, NY; Kevin Mannix, "Malzone Again Heads RA-A-Red Sox Caravan," Boston *Record American*, June 23, 1971, p. 52; Rich Marazzi, "Baseball First Glover at Third Base," *SCD* 21 (October 14, 1994), pp. 180–182; Howard Liss, *The Boston Red Sox* (New York, 1982); Robert Redmount, *The Red Sox Encyclopedia* (Champaign, IL, 1998); Dan Shaughnessy, *The Curse of the Bambino* (New York, 1990).

William M. Simons

MANNING, Maxwell Cornelius "Max," "Emillio," "Dr. Cyclops" (b. November 18, 1918, Rome, GA), player, was a tall, bespectacled, sidearm power pitcher for the Newark, NJ Eagles (NNL) during the 1940s and is the son of Robert Manning, a teacher, and Helen Manning. Manning graduated from Pleasantville, NJ High School in 1937, where he starred as a hurler on the school's integrated baseball team. Had he been white, Manning would have signed with the Detroit Tigers (AL). He instead pitched with the semi-pro Camden, NJ Giants and attended Lincoln University before Eagles' owner Abe Manley signed Monte Irvin* and him in 1938. In his initial game as an Eagle, he fanned the first five batters.

Manning's baseball career was interrupted in 1942 by military service during World War II. He served in Europe as a truck driver on the Red Ball Express, supplying General George Patton's Third Army. After his discharge, he rejoined the Newark Eagles in 1946 and helped them win the 1946 NNL Championship. The six-foot, four-inch, 185 pounder finished the regular NNL season with an 11–1 record and compiled the NNL's second highest strikeout total. Manning hurled three games in the 1946 World Series against the Kansas City Monarchs, splitting two decisions. He then pitched for Satchel Paige's* All-Stars against Bob Feller's* All-Stars in a post-season barnstorming tour.

The following year, Manning posted a 15–6 record for Newark and pitched in the East–West All-Star game. In 1948, the New York Giants (NL) scouted but did not sign him. After missing most of spring training, Manning suffered a shoulder separation and never completely recovered. Despite losing speed and pitching in pain, he still compiled records of 10–4 in 1948 and 8–4 in 1949.

During his career, Manning also played winters in Puerto Rico, the Dominican Republic, Mexico, Cuba, and Venezuela. His final season in 1951 saw him play both with Torreon, Mexico (MEL) and with Sherbrooke and Brantford, Canada (ProL).

Manning earned his B.S. degree from Glassboro College and taught until 1983. He married Dorothy Janet Winder on February 1, 1947 and has four children.

BIBLIOGRAPHY: *Afro-American*, 1938–1948; Chicago (IL) *Defender*, 1938–1948; John Holway, *Black Diamonds* (Westport, CT, 1989); Brent P. Kelley, *Voices from the Negro Leagues* (Jefferson, NC, 1997); James Overmyer, *Effa Manley and the Newark Eagles* (Metuchen, NJ, 1993); Newark (NJ) *Herald*, 1946; Robert W. Peterson, *Only the Ball Was White* (Englewood Cliffs, NJ, 1970); Pittsburgh (PA) *Courier*, 1938–1948; James A. Riley, *The All-Time All-Stars of Black Baseball* (Cocoa, FL, 1983); James A. Riley, *The Biographical Encyclopedia of the Negro Baseball Leagues* (New York, 1994); James A. Riley, interviews with former Negro League players, James A. Riley Collection, Cocoa, FL; *The Baseball Encyclopedia*, 10th ed. (New York, 1996).

James A. Riley

MANTLE, Mickey Charles "The Commerce Comet" (b. October 20, 1931, Spavinaw, OK; d. August 13, 1995, Dallas, TX), player and coach, was the oldest of five children of Elvin "Mutt" Mantle and Lovell (Richardson) Mantle. The elder Mantle, a former semipro player and zinc miner, vowed that his son would never have to be a miner and taught Mickey, named after Detroit Tiger catcher Mickey Cochrane,* baseball's fine points. With Mickey's grandfather, "Mutt" made Mantle into a switch-hitter by age seven. Mantle, a star football player for Commerce (OK) High School, was kicked in the shins in a freak accident in 1946 and developed a chronic bone infection that plagued him throughout his career.

Mantle played baseball for a local team called the Whiz Kids and impressed a scout for the New York Yankees (AL). Three weeks after his high school graduation, Mantle signed a contract for a $1,000 bonus with Tom Greenwade of the New York Yankees. He joined Independence, MO (KOML) in 1949 as a shortstop in Class D at $140 a month. In 1950, Mantle hit .383, made 199 hits, and slugged 26 HR for Joplin, MO (WA). Mantle led the WA in hitting, but made 55 errors at shortstop. He joked later that he played 1.000 percent, hitting .250 and fielding .750.

In 1951, the Yankees signed Mantle to the parent club for $5,400. Playing alongside Joe DiMaggio* in right field, Mantle experienced some difficulty adjusting to the major leagues. His first HR, a gargantuan shot, went over 450 feet to the deepest part of Chicago's Comiskey Park. On July 15, the Yankees optioned him to Kansas City, MO (AA) to regain his confidence. Mantle, however, suffered a batting slump and considered quitting baseball. Mantle's father, terminally ill with Hodgkins disease, visited Kansas City and talked him out of it. Mantle returned to Yankee Stadium and appeared in the World Series against the "Miracle" New York Giants. In the second game, Willie Mays* hit a fly to right center that DiMaggio caught. Mantle tripped over an uncapped drain, severely spraining his knee. The muscular 5-foot 11½-inch, 195-pound Mantle suffered several serious injuries in his 18-year major league career. He did not follow a strict exercise regimen and preferred instead to have fun because no male in the Mantle family had lived to age 40. Carousing with drinking buddies Whitey Ford* and Billy Martin* attracted him more than staying in perfect shape, probably shortening his career by at least three years.

Despite his physical ailments, Mantle achieved incredible diamond accomplishments. Mantle, who hit HR from both sides of the plate in the same game 10 times, scored 1,677 runs and made 2,415 hits in only 2,401 games. He knocked in 1,509 runs, slugged 344 doubles and 536 HR, and compiled a .298 career batting average. Three times (1956, 1957, 1962), he won the AL's MVP Award. In 1956, he won the coveted Triple Crown with a .353 batting average, 52 HR, and 130 RBI.

Mantle compiled outstanding World Series statistics, setting major league marks with 18 HR, 42 runs scored, 40 RBI, 123 total bases, 26 extra-base hits, 43 walks, and 54 strikeouts. Only his .257 World Series batting average seemed ordinary. In Game 5 of the 1953 World Series, Mantle hit a grand slam HR off Brooklyn Dodger pitcher Russ Meyer. In 1974, Mantle was elected to the National Baseball Hall of Fame.

After his retirement in 1968, Mantle served as a batting instructor with the Yankees in 1970 and did promotional work for gambling casinos in Atlantic City, NJ and for other corporations. Mantle's casino connections caused Commissioner Bowie Kuhn* to exclude him from active involvement with baseball. In 1985, Commissioner Peter Ueberroth (OS) lifted the ban. Mantle pursued his business interests with the Robert J. True firm in Dallas, TX and played golf on two very sore knees. Mantle suffered from a drinking problem and cirrhosis of the liver and received treatment at the Betty Ford Clinic in 1994. He died of aggressive cancer following a liver transplant in June 1995. Mantle had married Merlyn Johnson on December 23, 1951 and had four sons, including David, Mickey, Jr., and Daniel. Mantle and his wife were separated at the time of his death. He had co-authored five books and operated a restaurant in New York City. Mantle made Major League Baseball's All-Century Team and and ranked 37th among ESPN's top century athletes

BIBLIOGRAPHY: Jim Bouton, *Ball Four* (New York, 1970); *Colliers* 127 (June 2, 1951), p. 24; *CB* (1953), pp. 411–413; David Falkner, *The Last Hero* (New York, 1995); Whitey Ford, Mickey Mantle, and Joseph Durso, *Whitey and Mickey* (New York, 1977); Mark Gallagher, *The Yankees Encyclopedia*, vol. 3 (Champaign, IL, 1997); Gene Karst and Martin J. Jones, Jr., *Who's Who in Professional Baseball* (New Rochelle, NY, 1973); *Life* 33 (April 30, 1951), p. 71; *Look* 16 (August 12, 1952), p. 61; John P. McCarthy, *Baseball's All-Time Dream Team* (Cincinnati, OH, 1994); Mickey Mantle, "Time in a Bottle," *SI* 80 (April 18, 1994), pp. 66–72; Mickey Mantle, *The Education of a Baseball Player* (New York, 1967); Dom Forker, *Sweet Seasons* (Dallas, TX, 1991); Dom Forker, *The Men of Autumn* (Dallas, TX, 1989); Ralph Houk and Robert Creamer, *Season of Glory* (New York, 1988); Mickey Mantle file, National Baseball Library, Cooperstown, NY; Stephen J. Gould, "Mickey Mantle," *Sport* 77 (December 1986), pp. 74–75ff; Stephen J. Gould, "Mickey Mantle, Myth and Man," *Sport* 82 (October 1991), pp. 65–66; Mickey Mantle and Lewis Early, *Mickey Mantle* (Champaign, IL, 1993); Mickey Mantle with Mickey Herskowitz, *A Hero All His Life* (New York, 1996); Mickey Mantle and Phil Pepe, *My Favorite Summer, 1956* (New York, 1991); R. Wetzsteon, "The Mick Hits 60," *NY* 24 (September 30, 1991), pp. 40–47; Mickey Mantle and Herb Gluck, *The Mick* (New York, 1985); *NYT*, April 8, 1951; *NYT Biographical Service* 26 (August 1995), pp. 1182–1186; *NYT Magazine*, June 3, 1951, p. 23; Mark Gallagher, *Explosion! Mickey Mantle's Legendary Home Runs* (New York, 1987); Donald Honig, *Mays, Mantle, Snider, a Celebration* (New York, 1987); Tony Kubek and Terry Pluto, *Sixty-One* (New York, 1987); Rich Marazzi, "Passing of Mantle Was a Loss to Millions of Fans," *SCD* 22 (October 20, 1995), pp. 126–127; Robert Obojski, "Reese, Mantle, and Rizzuto," *SCD* 22 (April 28, 1995), pp. 42–43; Donald Honig, *The Power Hitters* (St. Louis, MO, 1989); Robert Lipsyte, *The Baseball Hall of Fame 50th Anniversary Book* (New York, 1988); Dan Valenti, *Clout! The Top Home Run in Baseball History* (Lexington, MA, 1989); *SEP* 225 (April 18, 1953), p. 31; *SI* 83 (August 21, 1995), pp. 18–28; *Time* 61 (June 15, 1953), p. 64; *WWA*, 41st ed. (1980–1981), p. 2,140.

William A. Borst

MANUSH, Henry Emmett "Heinie" (b. July 20, 1901, Tuscumbia, AL; d. May 12, 1971, Sarasota, FL), player, manager, scout, and coach, was one of seven sons, six of whom played professional baseball. As a 17-year-old student at Massey Military Academy in Pulaski, TN, Manush struck out on his own. He worked in his brother's plumbing business in Burlington, IA and then drifted westward. Manush made his baseball debut in 1921 with the Edmonton, Canada (WCaL) club. After playing at Omaha, NE (WL) in 1922, 21-year-old Manush joined the Detroit Tigers (AL) in 1923 to begin a 17-year major league career.

The 6-foot 1-inch, 200-pound, left-handed Manush played outfield for the Tigers from 1923 to 1927. Manush won the AL batting title with a .378 average in 1926, edging Babe Ruth* with six hits in nine at-bats in the closing day's doubleheader. After slumping to a .298 mark in 1927, Manush was traded to the St. Louis Browns (AL) that December and hit .378 again in 1928. Manush lost the crown by one point to Goose Goslin,* for whom he was exchanged two years later. In 1928, he paced the AL in base hits (241) and tied for the lead in doubles (47). The Browns traded Manush on June 30, 1930 to the Washington Senators (AL), where he performed through 1935. Besides finishing runner-up to Jimmie Foxx* with a .336 batting average, Manush in 1933 led the AL with 221 hits and 17 triples and helped the Senators win the AL pennant. Washington lost the World Series in five games to the New York Giants, as Manush became the first player in the history of the classic to be ejected from a game. In an argument with umpire Charley Moran (FB), Manush was banished from the game. Commissioner Kenesaw Mountain Landis* backed Moran's action, but ruled that henceforth only the commissioner could eject a player in a World Series. A .349 batting mark in 1934 earned Manush his only All-Star game selection. After being traded to the Boston Red Sox (AL) in December 1935, Manush closed out his major league career with the Brooklyn Dodgers (NL) in 1937 and 1938 and Pittsburgh Pirates (NL) in 1938 and 1939.

In 2,008 major league games, Manush scored 1,287 runs, collected 2,524 hits, 491 doubles, 160 triples, 110 HR, 1,183 RBI, and compiled a .330 batting average. He batted over .300 11 seasons, including seven consecutive campaigns, and made over 200 hits four seasons. Only 10 players have topped his .334 batting average as a rookie. Manush made at least five hits on seven different occasions and batted safely in 33 consecutive games in 1933. His 241 base hits in the 1928 season placed him tenth on the all-time list.

Manush played for Toronto, Canada (IL) in 1938 and 1939 and served as player–manager for Rocky Mount, NC (PiL), Greensboro, NC (PiL), and Roanoke, VA (PiL) from 1940 to 1943. He piloted Scranton, PA (EL) in 1944 and Martinsville, VA (CrL) in 1945 and scouted for the Boston Braves (NL) and Pittsburgh Pirates (NL) from 1946 to 1948. Manush coached

(1953–1954) and scouted (1961–1962) for the Washington Senators before leaving baseball. Married to Betty Lloyd in 1928, Manush was enshrined in the National Baseball Hall of Fame in 1964.

BIBLIOGRAPHY: Heinie Manush file, National Baseball Library, Cooperstown, NY; Craig Carter, ed., *TSN Daguerreotypes*, 8th ed. (St. Louis, MO, 1990); *National Baseball Hall of Fame and Museum Brochure* (Cooperstown, NY, 1974); Morris Bealle, *The Washington Senators* (Washington, DC, 1947); Shirley Povich, *The Washington Senators* (New York, 1954); Bill Borst, *Still Last in the American League* (West Bloomfield, MI, 1992); Bill Borst, ed., *Ables to Zoldak*, vol. 2 (St. Louis, MO, 1989); John Thom, *Champion Batsman of the 20th Century* (Los Angeles, CA, 1992); Frederick G. Lieb, *The Detroit Tigers* (New York, 1946); Joe Falls, *Detroit Tigers* (New York, 1975); Lowell Reidenbaugh, *Baseball's Hall of Fame—Cooperstown* (New York, 1993).

John L. Evers

MARANVILLE, Walter James Vincent "Rabbit" (b. November 11, 1891, Springfield, MA; d. January 5, 1954, New York, NY), player and manager, attended Springfield High School for one year and played semipro baseball several years. Maranville, who began his career in 1911 with New Bedford, MA (NEL) for $125 per month, joined the Boston Braves (NL) at the end of the 1912 season for $3,000 and became regular shortstop the next year. After helping the 1914 "Miracle Braves" win the NL pennant, he batted .308 in the World Series sweep of the Philadelphia Athletics. During his 23-year major league career, he played in the NL with the Boston Braves (1912–1920, 1929–1935), Pittsburgh Pirates (1921–1924), Chicago Cubs (1925), Brooklyn Dodgers (1926), and St. Louis Cardinals (1927–1928). He made 2,605 hits, 380 doubles, 177 triples, 884 RBI, 1,255 runs scored, and 291 stolen bases. His .258 lifetime batting average included a single-season high of .295 in 1922. Noted for his fielding, Maranville led the NL in putouts and assists several times at both shortstop and second base. He paced NL shortstops five times in fielding percentage.

Known for his off- and on-field escapades, Maranville once swam the Charles River in Boston rather than walk to a bridge, crawled between the legs of umpire Hank O'Day,* and often sat on opposing players after tagging them out at second base. After being demoted to Rochester, NY (IL) by Brooklyn in 1927, Maranville stopped drinking and launched a comeback at age 35. He became the regular shortstop for the St. Louis Cardinals in 1928 and batted .308 in the World Series loss to the New York Yankees. Maranville, who served in the U.S. Navy in 1918, married Elizabeth Shea on November 11, 1914. He later wed Helene Bertrand on February 20, 1921. As manager of the Chicago Cubs (NL) in 1925, he piloted the club to a 23–30 record. Maranville also managed Elmira, NY (NYPL) in 1936, Montreal, Canada (IL) in 1937–1938, Albany, NY (EL) in 1939, and Springfield, MA (EL) in 1941. He later ran baseball clinics for the Hearst newspapers. He set the NL record (since broken) for years as a player with 23 and was enshrined by the National Baseball Hall of Fame in 1954.

BIBLIOGRAPHY: Bob Carroll, *Who Was "Rabbit" Maranville?* (Cleveland, OH, 1991); Harold Kaese, *The Boston Braves* (New York, 1948); Gary Caruso, *The Braves Encyclopedia* (Philadelphia, PA, 1995); Frederick G. Lieb, *The Pittsburgh Pirates* (New York, 1948); Richard L. Burtt, *The Pittsburgh Pirates: A Pictorial History* (Virginia Beach, VA, 1977); Robert J. Fuchs and Wayne Soini, *Judge Fuchs and the Boston Braves, 1923–1935* (Jefferson, NC, 1998); Gene Karst and Martin J. Jones, Jr., *Who's Who in Professional Baseball* (New Rochelle, NY, 1973); Walter Maranville file, National Baseball Library, Cooperstown, NY; *The Baseball Encyclopedia*, 10th ed. (New York, 1996); John Thorn et al., eds., *Total Braves* (New York, 1996).

Horace R. Givens

MARAS, Roger Eugene. *See* Roger Eugene Maris.

MARBERRY, Fredrick "Firpo" (b. November 30, 1899, Streetman, TX; d. June 30, 1976, Mexia, TX), player and umpire, was major league baseball's first great relief pitcher. He attended high school for three and a half years and married Mattie Louise Womack on March 11, 1923. Marberry, a 6-foot 1-inch, 195-pound right-hander, began pitching professionally in 1922 for Mexia, TX (TOL), Jackson, MS (CSL), and Little Rock, AR (SA). The next year saw him at Little Rock again until being promoted in September to the Washington Senators (AL). Marberry starred for Washington through 1932. Marberry was traded to the Detroit Tigers (AL) in December 1932 and pitched there through April 1935. He served most of 1935 as an AL umpire, but spent 1936 pitching for the New York Giants (NL), Washington Senators, and Dallas, TX (TL). Subsequent stops included Dallas in 1937, Toledo, OH (AA) in 1937 and 1938, and Fort Worth, TX (TL) from 1938 through early 1941.

Marberry, who was converted to a relief pitcher early in his major league service, appeared in 50 or more games five seasons, led the AL in games pitched six times and in (retroactive) saves five times, and finished second in winning percentage twice, third once, and fifth once. Besides winning 148 major league games and losing 88 contests, he enjoyed an excellent .627 winning percentage and compiled a 3.63 ERA. He appeared in the 1924, 1925, and 1934 World Series, recording three saves. His greatest feat comprised stopping the Pittsburgh Pirates in the ninth inning of the third game of the 1925 World Series in a bases-loaded and one-out situation. Marberry secured a fly ball for the last out after falling behind on the count of three balls and no strikes.

Washington Senators manager Bucky Harris* made Marberry into the first high-volume relief specialist. With the exception of the short-term New York Yankees (AL) phenomenon Wilcy Moore,* Harris' innovation did not lead to the immediate emergence of the relief star as a type. Not until a decade or more after Marberry's heyday did the relief ace fully blossom. Marberry enjoyed success in the wholesale gas distribution business, but a severely disabling injury in an automobile accident in 1949 limited Marberry's activity. Subsequently, he owned and operated a recreation center.

BIBLIOGRAPHY: *The Baseball Encyclopedia*, 10th ed. (New York, 1996); Fredrick Marberry file, National Baseball Library, Cooperstown, NY; Fredrick Marberry file, *TSN* Archives, St. Louis, MO; J. C. Taylor Spink, comp., *TSN Daguerreotypes of Great Stars of Baseball* (St. Louis, MO, 1961); Bob Cairns, *Pen Men* (New York, 1993); Shirley Povich, *The Washington Senators* (New York, 1954); Morris Bealle, *The Washington Senators* (Washington, DC, 1947); Henry W. Thomas, *Walter Johnson* (Washington, DC, 1995); Frederick G. Lieb, *The Detroit Tigers* (New York, 1946); Fred Smith, *995 Tigers* (Detroit, MI, 1981).

Lowell L. Blaisdell

MARCEL, Oliver H. *See* Oliver H. Marcelle.

MARCELL, Oliver H. *See* Oliver H. Marcelle.

MARCELLE (MARCELL or MARCEL), Oliver H. **"Ghost"** (b. June 24, 1897, Thibodaux, LA; d. June 12, 1949, Denver, CO), player, completed eighth grade at Tomey Lafon Elementary School and attended high school at New Orleans University. The 5-foot 9-inch, 160-pound infielder began his Negro League baseball career in 1914 and four years later joined the Brooklyn Royal Giants (ECL). A superior defensive third baseman, he outperformed all other black players at his position in the 1920s. Whether making spectacular plays to his left or right or fielding bunts like a master, he delighted the fans who idolized him. For the Atlantic City, NJ Bacharach Giants (ECL) from 1920 to 1922 and 1925 to 1928, he teamed with Dick Lundy* to form an almost impregnable left side of the infield and helped his club win the 1926–1927 ECL pennants. In the 1926 Negro World Series against the Chicago American Giants, he hit a solid .293 in a losing effort.

After the ECL dissolved, Marcelle moved with Lundy to the Baltimore Black Sox (ANL) in 1929 and batted a respectable .288 that season. A good hitter and a dangerous clutch performer, he batted .305 lifetime in Negro League competition. During eight winter seasons in Cuba, "Ghost" compiled a .305 average and led the CUWL with .371 in 1923–1924 and hit .333 in exhibitions against major leaguers. The competitive Creole also played for the Lincoln Giants (ANL) from 1923 to 1925 and Detroit Stars (NNL) in 1919. Marcelle's quick and fiery temper frequently antagonized umpires, opponents, and teammates and indirectly led to his withdrawal from league play.

Married to Hazel Taylor, Marcelle had two sons, Oliver, Jr., and Everett "Ziggy." Ziggy played baseball for 10 years in the NNL and two years in organized baseball at Quebec and also played professional basketball for the

Harlem Globetrotters. After retiring from baseball in 1934, Marcelle worked as a painter in Denver, and died there of arteriosclerosis. Marcelle was selected as the greatest third baseman in black baseball history in a 1952 Pittsburgh *Courier* poll.

BIBLIOGRAPHY: John B. Holway, *Blackball Stars* (Westport, CT, 1988); Oliver Marcelle file, National Baseball Library, Cooperstown, NY; Robert W. Peterson, *Only the Ball Was White* (Englewood Cliffs, NJ, 1970); James A. Riley, *The All-Time All-Stars of Black Baseball* (Cocoa, FL, 1983); James A. Riley, *Biographical Encyclopedia of the Negro Baseball Leagues* (New York, 1994); James A. Riley, interviews with former Negro League players, James A. Riley Collection, Cocoa, FL.

James A. Riley

MARICHAL, Juan Antonio Sanchez "Manito," "The Dominican Dandy," "Laughing Boy" (b. October 20, 1937, Laguna Verde, DR), player, scout, and executive, grew up in a palm bark shack. His father, an impoverished farmer, died when Juan was only three years old, after which his mother and older brother, Gonzalo, brought him up. Gonzalo and Prospero Villona, Juan's brother-in-law, stimulated his interest in baseball. Marichal quit high school after the eleventh grade and played amateur baseball as a shortstop and pitcher for Monte Cristi, the United Fruit Company, and the Dominican Air Force and professionally with the Escogido Leones. He married 16-year-old Alma Rosa Carrajal on March 28, 1962 and has three children.

In 1958, San Francisco Giants (NL) scouts Horacio Martinez and Alex Pompez signed Marichal for a $500 bonus. Marichal pitched for Michigan City, IN (ML) in 1958, Springfield, MA (EL) in 1959, and Tacoma, WA (PCL) in 1960 until joining the San Francisco Giants (NL) at midseason. The ML and EL leader in several pitching categories, the 6-foot, 185-pound, high-kicking right-hander varied his deliveries of the fastball, curve, and slider. His incredible control led to 575 strikeouts and only 131 walks in 655 minor league innings pitched. Marichal's chubby face, impish grin, agility, and grace masked his fierce determination. In his major league debut on July 19, 1960, he shut out the Philadelphia Phillies, 2–0, and surrendered only an eighth-inning single by Clay Dalrymple. A 6–2 mark and 2.66 ERA highlighted his rookie season. In 1962, he compiled an 18–11 slate to help the Giants capture the NL pennant, but pitched only four innings in the World Series loss to the New York Yankees because of an injured finger.

From 1963 to 1969, Marichal compiled six 20-game victory seasons as the period's winningest hurler. During that span, Marichal enjoyed four consecutive 20-game victory seasons (1963–1966) and led the NL twice in victories (1963, 1968), complete games (1964, 1968), innings pitched (1963, 1968), and shutouts (1965, 1969) and once in best pitching percentage (1966) and ERA (1969). His 20-game victory seasons included 25–8 in 1963, 21–8 in 1964, 22–13 in 1965, 25–6 in 1966, 26–9 in 1968, and 21–11 in 1969. He compiled ERAs below 3.00 nine times, struck out over 200 batters six seasons, pitched over 300 innings three times, won at least 25 games three times, and walked at least 60 batters only twice. In 1971, he recorded an 18–11 slate to help the Giants win the Western Division title. The Giants lost the NL Championship Series to the Pittsburgh Pirates, as Marichal dropped his only decision. Marichal, who did not experience a losing season until 1972, was sold by the Giants in December 1973. He posted a 5–1 mark with the Boston Red Sox (AL) in 1974 and pitched briefly for the Los Angeles Dodgers (NL) in 1975 before retiring to his 1,000 acre mechanized farm in Santo Domingo.

During his 16-year major league career, the injury-prone Marichal won 243 games, lost 142 decisions, and recorded a 2.89 ERA in 471 contests. Only Dennis Martinez* won more games among Latin American pitchers. Marichal completed 244 of 457 starts, struck out 2,303 batters and walked only 709 in 3,507.1 innings, and hurled 52 shutouts. San Francisco manager Alvin Dark* once commented, "Put your club a run ahead in the later innings, and Marichal is the greatest pitcher I ever saw." An eight-time NL All-Star, Marichal surrendered only two runs in 18 innings. He won the first 1962 All-Star Game and the 1964 All-Star Game and was named the MVP of the 1965 contest. *TSN* named Marichal to its NL All-Star team in 1963, 1965–1966, and 1968. He hurled a no-hit game on June 15, 1963 against the Houston Colt 45s and a one-hit shutout on August 2, 1966 against the Dodgers. In June 1963, he outdueled Warren Spahn* of the Milwaukee Braves, 1–0, in 16 innings. Marichal's six opening season games (1962, 1964, 1966, 1971–1973) set another NL record.

At Candlestick Park on August 22, 1965, the normally easygoing, good-natured Marichal struck Los Angeles catcher John Roseboro on the head with his bat in the third inning. Dodgers pitcher Sandy Koufax* had just pitched inside, and Roseboro had fired the ball hard back to the pitcher just past Marichal's ear. Marichal was ejected from the game, suspended for nine days, and fined $1,750, then the stiffest penalty in NL history. In 1983, he became the first Latin American player chosen to the National Baseball Hall of Fame through the regular selection process. He served as director of minor league scouting for the Oakland A's (AL) from 1992 to 1995 and heads sports information in the DR.

BIBLIOGRAPHY: John Benson et al., *Baseball's Top 100* (Wilton, CT, 1997); Peter Bjarkman, *Baseball with a Latin Beat* (Jefferson, NC, 1994); Peter C. Bjarkman and Jose De Jesus, Jr., "Marichal the Magnificent," *TNP* 11 (1992), pp. 83–85; Juan Marichal file, National Baseball Library, Cooperstown, NY; Fred Stein and Nick Peters, *Giants Diary* (Berkeley, CA, 1987); David Plaut, *Chasing October* (South Bend, IN, 1994); "The Dandy Dominican," *Time* 87 (June 10, 1966), pp. 88–92; David L. Porter, ed., *African-American Sports Greats* (Westport, CT, 1995); Charles Einstein, "Juan Marichal at the Crossroads," *Sport* 45 (April 1968), pp. 58–60, 88; Charles Einstein, "The Juan Marichal Mystery," *Sport* 35 (June 1963), pp. 49–51, 72; "Juan Marichal," *The Lincoln Library of Sports Champions*, vol. 8 (Columbus, 1974); *The Baseball Ency-*

clopedia, 10th ed. (New York, 1996); Lowell Reidenbaugh, *Baseball's Hall of Fame—Cooperstown* (New York, 1993); Al Stump, "Always They Want More, More, More," *SEP* 240 (July 29, 1967), pp. 68–71; *TSN Baseball Register, 1967, 1975.*

David L. Porter

MARION, Martin Whiteford "Marty," "Slats," "The Octopus" (b. December 1, 1917, Richburg, SC), player, manager, and executive, was the mainstay of the St. Louis Cardinals (NL) infield from 1940 to 1950 and one of the greatest fielding shortstops in baseball history. A descendant of Francis Marion ("The Swamp Fox" of Revolutionary War fame), he was one of the four sons of John Marion and Virginia Marion and younger brother of Washington Senators (AL) outfielder John Marion. The 6-foot 2-inch, 170-pound Marion grew up in the Atlanta, GA area and attended Georgia Institute of Technology for one year. After the St. Louis Cardinals signed him in 1936 to a four-year contract averaging about $3,000 annually, he played with Huntington, WV (MAL) in 1936 and Rochester, NY (IL) from 1937 through 1939. Joining the parent Cardinals in 1940, he batted .278 in 125 games and rapidly became one of the decade's dominant infielders. Never a high average or power hitter, he batted .263 and belted 36 HR in a 13-year major league career. In 1,572 games, he made 1,448 hits and 272 doubles and knocked in 624 runs. Marion developed into a clutch hitter, leading the NL in doubles (38) in 1942 and adeptly hitting to the opposite field.

Marion is best remembered as a fielder. Nicknamed "The Octopus," the tall, lanky Marion possessed sure hands, vast range, and a strong, accurate arm. Equally adept at charging balls and going behind second base, he made easy, precise throws. In the last (fifth) game of the 1942 World Series, Marion and catcher Walker Cooper* collaborated on a dramatic pickoff play of Joe Gordon* to climax the Cardinals' rout of the New York Yankees. In 1944, Marion batted .267 and was voted both the NL's MVP and baseball's Player of the Year. A member of four NL pennant winners (1942–1944, 1946), he helped the Cardinals capture three World Series championships.

A childhood leg injury kept Marion from World War II military service and combined with recurrent back trouble to shorten his career. After the Cardinals' first second division finish in over a decade, he replaced Eddie Dyer* in 1951 as manager and guided St. Louis to a respectable 81–73 mark and a third place finish. In 1952, he joined the crosstown AL St. Louis Browns and piloted them to two losing seasons. He managed the Chicago White Sox (AL) in 1955 (91–63) and 1956 (85–69) to third place finishes. In six years as manager, Marion compiled 356 wins, 372 losses, and a .489 winning percentage.

After retiring from playing and managing, Marion owned the Houston, TX (TL) franchise in 1960 and managed the St. Louis Stadium Club (a center for area sportsdom) for 18 years. The suburban St. Louis, MO resident married Mary Dallas in December 1937, has four daughters, farms near

St. Louis, and duck hunts. His biggest baseball thrill came in 1942, when the Cardinals upset the Yankees. Marion played a considerable role in bringing the Cardinals from nine and one-half games behind the Brooklyn Dodgers in mid-August to capture the NL pennant. Like many right-handed batters of his era, he considered Ewell Blackwell* of the Cincinnati Reds as the toughest pitcher. Marion regarded Frank Crespi, maimed in World War II, as the greatest single-season (1941) second base teammate.

BIBLIOGRAPHY: Bob Broeg, and Jerry Vickery, *St. Louis Cardinals Encyclopedia* (Grand Rapids, MI, 1998); Frederick G. Lieb, *The St. Louis Cardinals* (New York, 1945); Marty Marion file, National Baseball Library, Cooperstown, NY; Bob Broeg, *Redbirds: A Century of Cardinals' Baseball* (St. Louis, MO, 1981); Richard Lindberg, *Sox* (New York, 1984); Richard Lindberg, *Who's on Third?* (South Bend, IN, 1983); Bill Borst, *Still Last in the American League* (West Bloomfield, MI, 1992); Bill Borst, ed., *Ables to Zoldak*, vol. 2 (St. Louis, MO, 1989); Thomas Aylesworth and Benton Minks, *The Encyclopedia of Baseball Managers* (New York 1990); David Craft et al., *Redbirds Revisited* (Chicago, IL, 1990); William B. Mead and Harold Rosenthal, *The Ten Worst Years of Baseball* (New York, 1978); Larry Moffi, *This Side of Cooperstown* (Iowa City, IA, 1996); Stan Musial as told to Bob Broeg, *Stan Musial: The Man's Own Story* (New York, 1964); Rob Rains, *The St. Louis Cardinals* (New York, 1992); *The Baseball Encyclopedia*, 10th ed. (New York, 1996); Lawrence Ritter and Donald Honig, *The Image of Their Greatness* (New York, 1979); Rich Westcott, *Masters of the Diamond* (Jefferson, NC, 1994).

Leonard H. Frey

MARIS, Roger Eugene (b. Roger Eugene Maras, September 10, 1934, Hibbing, MN; d. December 14, 1985, Houston, TX), player, was the son of Rudolph Maras and Connie Maras, whose family name was legally changed to Maris. His father worked as a railroad supervisor and played town and semipro baseball. Maris moved at age 12 with his parents to Fargo, ND and completed his education at Shanley High School, where he excelled in football, basketball, and track and field. He played Little League baseball, but his high school had no organized team. Maris instead performed for the Fargo American Legion baseball team and was named its MVP in 1950. The Cleveland Indians (AL) signed Maris for $15,000 in 1953 and assigned the outfielder to hometown Fargo-Moorehead, MN (NoL), where he hit .325 and belted 9 HR. At Keokuk, IA (3IL) the following year, he blossomed into a long-ball hitter with 32 HR, 111 RBI, a .315 batting average, and 25 stolen bases. Brief stints followed at Tulsa, OK (TL), Reading, PA (EL), and Indianapolis, IN (AA) before Maris joined the Cleveland Indians in 1957.

Maris batted .235 his rookie year with 14 HR and 51 RBI for Cleveland. In June 1958, he was traded in a multi-player deal to the Kansas City Athletics (AL), where he batted .240, slugged 28 HR, and drove in 80 runs. Although stricken with appendicitis the following year, he still compiled a

.273 batting average and 16 HR. On December 11, 1959, the New York Yankees (AL) traded established players Hank Bauer,* Norm Siebern,* Marv Throneberry, and Don Larsen* to Kansas City for the hard-hitting, solid-fielding Maris and infielders Joe DeMaestri and Kent Hadley. With the Yankees, the 6-foot, 200-pound, pull-hitting right fielder reached his potential as a player and left an indelible mark on baseball history. In 1960, Maris helped the Yankees win the AL pennant by batting .283 with 39 HR and 112 RBI. His RBI figure and .581 slugging percentage paced the AL. This outstanding effort earned Maris both the AL MVP and Gold Glove (.985 fielding average) Awards and an AL All-Star team selection.

Maris made 1961 an exciting, memorable baseball year by dueling teammate Mickey Mantle* for the HR title. After homering just once in April, he belted 11 in May, 15 in June, 13 in July, 11 in August, and 9 in September. His then record-setting 61st round tripper came on October 1 against Boston Red Sox right-hander Tracy Stallard. This HR, hit on the last day of the regular season, enabled the mentally and physically exhausted Maris to surpass the legendary Babe Ruth* as the then major league player with the most HR in a single season. The record lasted 37 years until Mark McGwire* shattered it with 70 HR in 1998. Maris also won the RBI (142) and runs scored (132) titles, led the AL in total bases (366), tied Lou Gehrig's* record for most HR (30) in a single season at Yankee Stadium, belted 7 HR in 6 consecutive games (August 11–16), and tied an AL standard for most HR in a doubleheader (4) on July 25, hitting two in each game. Maris also had to endure the intense media and psychological pressure associated with his feat. Baseball Commissioner Ford Frick* ruled that the new HR record would have an asterisk attached because it was accomplished in 162 games rather than within the 154 game schedule of the Ruth era. The many accolades and awards for that exceptional season included Maris being named AL MVP again and recipient of the Hickok Belt as the world's top pro athlete.

In 1962, Maris hit 33 HR, drove in 100 runs, and batted .256, but his HR and RBI production thereafter gradually declined due to several nagging injuries. He was traded to St. Louis (NL) in December 1966 and helped the Cardinals win NL pennants in 1967 and 1968. After retiring from baseball following the 1968 campaign, he operated an Anheuser-Busch distributorship (Maris Distributing Company) in Gainesville, FL. In 12 major league seasons, Maris batted .260 with 1,325 hits, 195 doubles, 275 HR, 851 RBI, and a .476 slugging average. The outstanding right fielder compiled a .982 lifetime fielding average. He played in five World Series with the New York Yankees (1960–1964) and two with the Cardinals (1967–1968), making 33 hits, 6 HR, 18 RBI, and a .217 batting average. From 1959 through 1962, he made the AL All-Star team. Maris, who died of cancer, married Patricia Ann Carvell on October 13, 1956 and had six children, Susan, Roger, Jr., Kevin, Richard, Sandra, and Randy.

BIBLIOGRAPHY: *SEAL*, vol. 1 (1981–1985), pp. 545–547; Maury Allen, *The Record Breakers* (Englewood Cliffs, NJ, 1968); Maury Allen, *Roger Maris* (New York, 1986); John Benson et al., *Baseball's Top 100* (Wilton, CT, 1997); Mike Bryan, "Baseball Lives," *SI* 70 (April 24, 1989), pp. 85ff; N. Cohen, "Who Framed Roger Maris?" *Sport* 82 (August 1991), pp. 78–82; Arthur Daley, *Kings of the Home Run* (New York, 1962); Mark Gallagher, *Fifty Years of Yankee All Stars* (New York, 1984); Mark Gallagher, *The Yankees Encyclopedia*, vol. 3 (Champaign, IL, 1997); Tony Kubek and Terry Pluto, *Sixty-one* (New York, 1987); Ralph Houk and Robert W. Creamer, *Season of Glory* (New York, 1988); David Halberstam, *October 1964* (New York, 1994); Dom Forker, *Sweet Seasons* (Dallas, TX, 1991); Dave Anderson et al., *The Yankees* (New York, 1979); Zander Hollander and Larry Fox, *The Home Run Story* (New York, 1966); Craig Carter, ed., *TSN Daguerreotypes* (St. Louis, MO, 1990); Roger Maris file, National Baseball Library, Cooperstown, NY; Roger Maris and Jim Ogle, *Roger Maris at Bat* (New York, 1962); Richard Rainbolt, *Baseball's Home Run Hitters* (Minneapolis, MN, 1975); *The Baseball Encyclopedia*, 10th ed. (New York, 1996); Ray Robinson, *The Greatest Yankees of Them All* (New York, 1969); Harvey Rosenfeld, *Roger Maris* (Fargo, ND, 1992); Milton J. Shapiro, *Champions of the Bat* (New York, 1970); Milton J. Shapiro, *The Day They Made the Record Book* (New York, 1968); Leonard Shecter, *Roger Maris: Home Run Hero* (New York, 1961); Dan Valenti, *Clout! The Top Home Runs in Baseball History* (Lexington, MA, 1989); Rich Westcott, *Diamond Greats* (Westport, CT, 1988); *NYT*, December 15, 1985; *TSN*, May 1, 1957; January 14, 1967; Roger Kahn, "Pursuit of #60: The Ordeal of Roger Maris," *SI* (October 2, 1961); Rick Telander, "The Record Broke Him," *SI* (June 20, 1977); Don Nelson, "A Tale of Two Sluggers: Roger Maris and Hack Wilson," *TNP* 1 (Fall 1982), pp. 32–33.

                                                              Louis J. Andolino

MARQUARD, Richard William "Rube" (b. October 9, 1889, Cleveland, OH; d. June 1, 1980, Baltimore, MD), player, manager, scout, and coach, was the son of Frederick Marquard, Cleveland's chief engineer. He married three times and did not have any children. He wed actress Blossom Seeley in 1913 and appeared with her in a vaudeville dance routine during the off-season. After the couple divorced in 1920, Marquard in 1921 married Naomi Wrigley of Baltimore, MD. Following her death in 1954, he wed Jane Ottenheimer of Baltimore in 1954. Although nicknamed "Rube" because of his resemblance to Philadelphia Athletics left-hander Rube Waddell,* the far more sophisticated Marquard never smoked, drank, or missed curfew.

Marquard at age 17 pitched (and won) one game for Waterloo, IA (IoSL), but quit the club when not offered a contract. When the 1907 baseball season opened, Marquard worked for a Cleveland ice cream plant and pitched for the company baseball team. Later that season, he signed with Indianapolis, IN (AA) and was optioned to Canton, OH (CL), where he led the CL in victories with a 23–13 record. In 1908 he pitched superbly for Indianapolis, pacing the AA with 28 wins. The New York Giants (NL) outbid several other major league clubs and purchased Marquard's contract for $11,000, then a record price for a minor league player. The 6-foot 3-inch,

180-pound, 18-year-old left-hander was initially labeled "the $11,000 beauty," but was called the "$11,000 lemon" after losing 13 of 18 decisions. Following another mediocre season in 1910, Marquard in 1911 mastered control of his curveball and blossomed into a 24–7 pitcher. He led the NL with a .774 winning percentage and 237 strikeouts. That year, he and his roommate Christy Mathewson* led the Giants to the first of three consecutive pennants.

Marquard enjoyed his most notable season in 1912, compiling a 26–11 record. He won his first 19 decisions, a major league one-season consecutive game-winning record shared with old-time Giants right-hander Timothy Keefe.* Due to then-existing rules, Marquard was denied one win he would have been awarded now and yet paced the NL in victories. In 1913, he won 23 games and lost only 10. Marquard's fortunes reversed in 1914, when he lost 12 straight games and dropped to a 12–22 record. Although winning a remarkable 21-inning triumph over the Pittsburgh Pirates, Marquard helped cause the Giants to drop to second place. The Boston Braves moved from last place on July 4 to a "miracle" NL pennant win. In 1915 Marquard pitched a no-hitter against the Brooklyn Robins on April 15, but pitched inconsistently thereafter. When permitted by disenchanted manager John McGraw* to arrange a deal, Marquard was sold to the Brooklyn Robins (NL) for $7,500 that August. He remained with Brooklyn through its NL pennant-winning season in 1920 and played the 1921 season for the Cincinnati Reds (NL). The Reds traded Marquard in February 1922 to the Boston Braves (NL), for whom he pitched the last four years of his major league career. Marquard compiled a 201–177 record over 18 major league seasons, winning over 20 games three consecutive seasons. He appeared in 536 games, struck out 1,593 batters, and compiled a 3.08 ERA.

Subsequently Marquard managed and pitched part-time for Providence, RI (EL) in 1926, Baltimore, MD (IL) and Birmingham, AL (SA) in 1927, and Jacksonville, FL (SEL) in 1929–1930. After umpiring in the EL and being assistant baseball coach at Assumption College, he coached and scouted for Atlanta, GA (SA) in 1932 and completed his baseball career at age 43 by managing Wichita, KS in 1933. Marquard settled in Baltimore in 1930 and remained there, working in mutuel windows at various race tracks for many years. In 1971 he was elected to the National Baseball Hall of Fame.

BIBLIOGRAPHY: Rube Marquard file, National Baseball Library, Cooperstown, NY; *DAB*, Supp. 10 (1976–80), pp. 508–509; Charles C. Alexander, *John McGraw* (New York, 1988); Martin Appel and Burt Goldblatt, *Baseball's Best: The Hall of Fame Gallery* (New York, 1977); Frank Graham, *McGraw of the Giants* (New York, 1944); Robert J. Fuchs and Wayne Soini, *Judge Fuchs and the Boston Braves, 1923–1935* (Jefferson, NC, 1998); W. F. McNeil, *The Dodgers Encyclopedia* (Champaign, IL, 1997); Gary Caruso, *The Braves Encyclopedia* (Philadelphia, PA, 1995); Harold Kaese, *The Boston Braves* (New York, 1948); Frank Graham, *The Brooklyn Dodgers* (New York, 1945);

Frank Graham, *The New York Giants* (New York, 1952); Noel Hynd, *Marquard & Seeley* (New York, 1996); Noel Hynd, *The Giants of the Polo Grounds* (New York, 1988); Gene Karst and Martin J. Jones, Jr., *Who's Who in Professional Baseball* (New Rochelle, NY, 1973); Larry D. Mansch, *Rube Marquard* (Jefferson, NC, 1998); Lawrence Ritter, *The Glory of Their Times* (New York, 1966).

Fred Stein

MARSHALL, Michael Grant "Mike" (b. January 15, 1943, Adrian, MI), player and coach, in 1974 became the first relief pitcher to win the NL Cy Young Award and holds both the AL (90) and NL (106) records for most games pitched in a season. According to sportswriter Jonathan Maslow, "Mike Marshall probably knows more about pitching than anyone who ever lived." Marshall used his knowledge of pitching and exercise physiology to condition himself into the record books.

Marshall's professional career began in September 1960 as a shortstop in the Philadelphia Phillies (NL) organization and ended 21 years later as a pitcher in 1981. After six minor league seasons, Marshall spent 15 major league campaigns with nine different teams: the Detroit Tigers (AL, 1966–1968), Seattle Pilots (AL, 1969), Houston Astros (NL, 1970), Montreal Expos (NL, 1970–1973), Los Angeles Dodgers (NL, 1974–1976), Atlanta Braves (NL, 1976–1977), Texas Rangers (AL, 1977), Minnesota Twins (AL, 1978–1980), and New York Mets (NL, 1981).

Marshall established major league records for the most seasons pacing the major leagues in games finished (4), most seasons leading his league in saves (3), most games by a pitcher in a season (106, 1974), most innings pitched by a reliever in a season (208, 1974), most consecutive seasons topping the major leagues in games finished (3), most contests finished in a season (84, 1979), and most consecutive games pitched (13, June 18–July 3, 1974). Marshall led the NL in saves with 31 in 1973 and 21 in 1974 and the AL in saves with 32 in 1979. *TSN* named him NL Fireman of the Year in 1973 and 1974 and Pitcher of the Year in 1974. During his career, the right-handed Marshall compiled a 97–112 win–loss record with 188 saves and a 3.14 ERA in 723 total games. Marshall, who stood 5-feet 10-inches, enjoyed a career-high 32 saves in 1974. After undergoing weight training in 1974, Marshall increased his playing weight from 180 to 210 pounds.

His record-breaking accomplishments become truly more amazing because he only played five complete seasons with the same team: 1972–1973 with the Montreal Expos, managed by Gene Mauch;* 1974 with the Los Angeles Dodgers, piloted by Walter Alston;* and 1978–1979 with the Minnesota Twins, managed by Mauch. Marshall believes that he was traded so many times partly because of his union activities, including service on the executive board of the MLPA. Throughout his career, he was voted team representative. After being released by Minnesota in June 1980 in the middle of his contract, Marshall filed a legal action with the National Labor Relations Board alleging that the Twins had released him because of his union activities. Since Marshall prevailed in this suit, the Twins were forced to pay him for the remainder of his contract. In *Ball Four*, Jim Bouton explained Marshall's frequent trades: "I'm afraid Mike's problem is that he's too intelligent and has too much education. It's like the army. When a sergeant found out that a private had been to college, he immediately assumed he couldn't be a good soldier."

Marshall's accomplishments demonstrate the knowledge he acquired through extensive study and the partnership he found in Mauch and Alston. Marshall reflected, "I will never play for you, I will only play with you." Alston gave him the freedom to be his own man and the results were record breaking. Marshall patterned his own coaching style after Alston, although the latter relied on him to be the expert. Marshall, as the expert and coach, has since imparted his vast knowledge to his students.

Marshall received his Bachelor of Arts (1965), Master of Arts (1967), and Ph.D. (1978) degrees from Michigan State University. His doctoral dissertation was entitled "Comparison of an Estimate of Skeletal Age with Chronological Age When Classifying Adolescent Males for Motor Proficiency Norms." Since 1981, Marshall has concentrated full-time on teaching and research. His teaching experience ranges from graduate courses in human movement to sixth grade physical education. Marshall has addressed numerous academic and professional organizations.

Marshall's futuristic college teams have set incredible records. Marshall served as a professor of physical education and coached baseball at Henderson State University in Arkadelphia, AR from 1989 through 1991. His 1989 team set the NAIA record for most stolen bases in a season with 279. At St. Leo (FL) College, his team established the NCAA Division II stolen base record with 291 in 51 games. He coached West Texas A&M University to a dismal 8–48 mark in 1994.

Marshall married Nancy Matthes on January 16, 1963 in East Lansing, MI and divorced her in 1983. Marshall has three daughters, Debra, Rebecca, and Kerry, and resides in Zephyrhills, FL.

BIBLIOGRAPHY: Walter Alston, *A Year at a Time* (Waco, TX, 1976); Bob Cairns, *Pen Men* (New York, 1993); Mike Marshall file, National Baseball Library, Cooperstown, NY; William F. McNeil, *The Dodgers Encyclopedia* (Champaign, IL, 1997); Joe Falls, *Detroit Tigers* (New York, 1975); *The Baseball Encyclopedia*, 10th ed. (New York, 1996); Ira Berkow, "Marshall, 38, Still on Mission," *NYT*, August 27, 1981, p. B–13; Jim Bouton, *Ball Four Plus Ball Five* (New York, 1981); Ross Forman, "For Doc Marshall, Pitching Has Always Been a Science," *SCD* 22 (February 24, 1995), pp. 130–132; Carson Van Lindt, *The Seattle Pilots Story* (New York, 1993); Neil Labar, NCBWA statistician, correspondence with Jack Lipton, February 1990; Michael Marshall, interviews with Susan Lipton, December 1989–February 1990; "Marshall, Twins Settle Grievance," *NYT*, January 7, 1981, p. B–8; Jonathan E. Maslow, "Mike Marshall's Strange Spring," *SR* 6 (April 28, 1979), pp. 48–49; *NAIA Baseball Media*

Guide (Kansas City, MO, 1989); T. Nolan, "The Marshall Plan for Pitching," *CAD* 67 (November 1997), pp. 44–53; *TSN Baseball Register, 1982.*

Susan M. Lipton and Jack P. Lipton

MARTIN, Alfred Manuel "Billy" (b. May 16, 1928, Berkeley, CA; d. December 25, 1989, Johnson City, NY), player, scout, coach, manager, and sportscaster, was the son of itinerant Portuguese musician Alfred Manuel Martin, who deserted his mother, Joan (Salvini) Downey. Martin's feisty, outspoken mother became the major influence on her son. Martin grew up in the tough region of West Berkeley, where, as he remembered, "From the time I was twelve years old until I was maybe fifteen, I awoke every morning knowing that there was a good chance I was going to have to get in a fight with somebody." He attended public schools, but showed classroom ability only in history and other subjects that he liked. Sports, especially baseball, kept him out of serious conflicts with the law. As a high school ballplayer, he impressed Casey Stengel,* the Oakland, CA Oaks' (PCL) manager. Martin's professional baseball career started as a second and third baseman with Idaho Falls, ID (PrL) in 1946 and at Phoenix, AZ (ArTL) in 1947. In 1948, he played under Stengel at Oakland. Stengel, who became the New York Yankees' (AL) manager in 1949, remembered his brash pupil. In 1950, Martin joined the Bronx Bombers after spending the first 29 games with the Yankees farm club at Kansas City, MO (AA).

As a major leaguer, the 5-foot 11-inch, 170-pound Martin compensated for a lack of size and skills with intelligence and drive. Martin's mediocre .257 career batting average belied his skills in the clutch. After saving the 1952 World Series with a desperation catch, he won the 1953 classic MVP Award by hitting .500 with a record 12 hits in a six-game series. As a New York Yankee from 1950 to 1957, he became Stengel's favorite and absorbed many of the "Old Professor's" insights into managing. Martin's off-the-field conduct, however, displeased the team ownership, which viewed him as a harmful influence on his drinking buddy, team star Mickey Mantle.* After a brawl at the Copacabana night club, Martin was traded in January 1957 to the Kansas City Athletics (AL). His nondescript post-Yankees career saw him play with Kansas City in late 1957, the Detroit Tigers (AL) in 1958, Cleveland Indians (AL) in 1959, Cincinnati Reds (NL) in 1960, and Milwaukee Braves (NL) and Minnesota Twins (AL) in 1961. In 1,021 games, he amassed 877 hits, 137 doubles, 28 triples, and 64 HR, scored 425 runs, and knocked in 333 runs.

Martin's off-the-field life was troubled. His first marriage to Lois Berndt on August 4, 1950, produced a daughter, Kelly Ann, but ended in divorce in 1953. Martin married Gretchen Winkler in October 1959 and had a son, Billy Joe. Martin's reputation for fighting and drink led to several incidents that overshadowed a generosity and attachment to friends that seldom received publicity.

After serving as a scout and coach with the Minnesota Twins from 1962 through 1967, Martin began managing with the Denver, CO Bears (AA) in 1968. He started major league managing the next year by leading the Twins to the division championship. His managerial career fell into a predictable, if exciting, pattern. He produced winners on the field, but off-the-field troubles with owners and incidents resulted in his being fired or resigning. He managed Minnesota in 1969, the Detroit Tigers from 1971 to September 1, 1973, the Texas Rangers (AL) from September 8, 1973 to July 1975, the Oakland A's (AL) from 1980 to 1982, and the New York Yankees on five different occasions from 1975 to 1988. In each place except Texas, he produced at least one division winner. With the lowly Rangers, he secured the then highest finish in the history of the franchise. Martin's success resulted from his intense study of the game and ability to motivate players. An active manager, Martin sought to control most aspects of play, from calling pitches to approving attempted steals. He seemed best at propelling average players to good performances, but sometimes encountered difficulties with superstars and young players.

The most publicized and longest running of Martin's managerial efforts involved the New York Yankees. Hired by owner George Steinbrenner* to rekindle Yankees greatness in late 1975, Martin delivered the first Yankees AL pennant in 11 years in 1976. The Cincinnati Reds, however, defeated the Yankees in four straight games in the World Series. In 1977 Steinbrenner added slugger Reggie Jackson,* initiating several highly publicized feuds between manager and superstar. Highlights included a near fight in a nationally televised game, the benching of Jackson in the AL Championship Series, and the star's record-shattering performance leading the Yankees to victory in the 1977 World Series. The next year, Steinbrenner first fired Martin in midseason and then promised to rehire him. Martin returned as manager in 1979, only to be dismissed after an off-the-field incident. Between Yankees firings, Martin managed Oakland and won a divisional flag there in 1981 before being relieved in 1982. He again managed the Yankees in 1983, was relieved, and returned as the club's manager in 1985. Martin piloted the Yankees to a 91–54 mark for the remainder of 1985, but then was replaced by Lou Piniella.* He guided the Yankees to a 40–28 record in his final stint in 1988. His career managerial record included 1,253 wins and 1,013 losses, a .553 winning percentage, five divisional championships, two AL titles, and one World Series championship. He participated in the New York Yankees' announcing team in 1986 and 1987. Martin died of injuries suffered in a pickup-truck crash in Binghamton, NY.

BIBLIOGRAPHY: Billy Martin file, National Baseball Library, Cooperstown, NY; Robert W. Creamer, *Stengel* (New York, 1984); Frank Deford, "Love, Hate and Billy Martin," *SI* 42 (June 2, 1975), p. 70; David Falkner, *The Last Yankee: The Turbulent Life of Billy Martin* (New York, 1992); Dom Forker, *The Men of Autumn* (Dallas, TX, 1989); Mark Gallagher, *The Yankees Encyclopedia*, vol. 3. (Champaign, IL, 1997); Dom

Forker, *Sweet Seasons* (Dallas, TX, 1991); Thomas Aylesworth and Benton Minks, *The Encyclopedia of Baseball Managers* (New York, 1990); Dan Anderson et al., *The Yankees* (New York, 1979); Peter Golenbock, *Dynasty: The New York Yankees, 1949–1964* (New York, 1975); Peter Golenbock, *Wild, High, and Tight* (New York, 1994); Reggie Jackson with Mike Lupica, *Reggie* (New York, 1984); Larry Keith, "Billy Boy Is Back," *SI* 51 (July 2, 1979), pp. 14–18; Leonard Koppett, *The Man in the Dugout* (New York, 1993); Ed Linn, *Steinbrenner's Yankees* (New York, 1982); Sparky Lyle and Peter Golenbock, *The Bronx Zoo* (New York, 1979); Billy Martin and Peter Golenbock, *Number 1* (New York, 1980); Billy Martin and Phil Pepe, *Billyball* (New York, 1987); Craig Nettles, *Balls* (New York, 1984); *NYT*, December 26, 1989, p. A-1; B. J. Phillip and P. A. Witteman, "Happy Playing Billy Ball," *Time* 117 (June 4, 1981), p. 88; Richard Scheinin, *Field of Screams* (New York, 1994); *TSN Baseball Register, 1978*, pp. 449–450; *WWA*, 43rd ed. (1984–1985), p. 2,116.

James W. Harper

MARTIN, Johnny Leonard Roosevelt "Pepper," "The Wild Hoss of the Osage" (b. February 29, 1904, Temple, OK; d. March 5, 1965, McAlester, OK), player, coach, and manager, was the son of Oklahoma prairie farmer George Washington Martin and Celia Martin. Nicknamed "Pepper," Martin attended high school for two years at Classen, OK and served in the Reserve Officer Training Corps. Friends called Martin "Johnny" because he disliked the nickname "Pepper." A Rochester, NY reporter later called him "The Wild Hoss of the Osage" because of his gridiron exploits at age 19 for Guthrie in Osage County, OK. Martin began his professional baseball career with Greenville, TX (ETL) in the St. Louis Cardinals farm system in 1924 and played at Fort Smith, AR (WA) in 1925, Syracuse, NY (IL), and Rochester, NY (IL), in 1926 and 1930, and Houston, TX (TL) in 1927. Although a pinch runner with the St. Louis Cardinals (NL) in 1928, he did not win a permanent place on the roster as an outfielder until 1931.

Martin's aggressive spirit and desire to play the game abounded in the 1931 World Series, in which he virtually defeated the Philadelphia Athletics single-handedly by making a record of 12 hits, batting .500, and stealing 5 bases. In 1932, the 5-foot 8-inch, 170-pound Martin slumped to a .238 batting average. He had spent a night sleeping in tall, wet grass on a hunting trip, causing a persistent skin infection that severely hampered his play. He also suffered a broken hand, compounding his misfortunes. In 1933, he switched to third base and raised his batting average to .316. Although a steady outfielder, Martin played the infield adventurously. He discouraged bunting by aiming throws at the runner going down the line.

Martin learned his head-first sliding style, characteristic of the "Gashouse Gang," from manager Frankie Frisch.* The fiery Martin, who never wore sanitary hose or underwear, led the NL in runs scored (122) and stolen bases (26) in 1933. Twice more (1934, 1936), he led the NL in stolen bases with 23. Martin also organized a highly publicized band, The Mudcats. He returned to the minor leagues after the 1940 season, although he had hit .316

that year. An itinerant minor league manager, he made stops at Sacramento, CA (PCL), Miami, FL (FIL), and Fort Lauderdale, FL (FIL). During 1944, he returned briefly to the Cardinals and hit .279. In 1,189 career games, he made 1,227 hits and 270 doubles, scored 754 runs, knocked in 501 runs, and batted .298. In three World Series, he hit a superlative .418. Martin was planning to coach for the Tulsa, OK Oilers (TL) when he was stricken with a fatal heart attack. His last major league appearance came as a Chicago Cubs' (NL) coach in 1965. He left his widow, Ruby, whom he had married on November 9, 1927, and three married daughters.

BIBLIOGRAPHY: Pepper Martin file, National Baseball Library, Cooperstown, NY; G. F. Fleming, *The Dizziest Season* (New York, 1984); Bob Broeg and Jerry Vickery, *St. Louis Cardinals Encyclopedia* (Grand Rapids, MI, 1998); Robert Gregory, *Diz* (New York, 1992); Bill Borst, *Baseball Through a Knothole* (St. Louis, MO, 1978); Bob Broeg, *Redbirds: A Century of Cardinals' Baseball* (St. Louis, MO, 1981); Robert Hood, *The Gashouse Gang* (New York, 1976); Gene Karst and Martin J. Jones, Jr., *Who's Who in Professional Baseball* (New Rochelle, NY, 1973); Frederick G. Lieb, *The St. Louis Cardinals* (New York, 1945); Frederick G. Lieb, *The Story of the World Series* (New York, 1965); Craig Carter, ed., *TSN Daguerreotypes*, 8th ed. (St. Louis, MO, 1990); *NYT*, March 6, 1965; Rob Rains, *The St. Louis Cardinals* (New York, 1992).

William A. Borst

MARTINEZ, Constantino "Tino" (b. December 7, 1967, Tampa, FL), player, is the son of Rene Martinez, Sr. and Sylvia Martinez, a school teacher. He grew up in Tampa and learned the value of hard work from his father, general manager of the family-owned Villazon Cigar Company. He and his wife, Marie, have three children, Olivia, Victoria, and T. J., and live in New York City.

Martinez made the state champion varsity baseball team as a freshman at Tampa Catholic High School and transferred the next year to Jefferson High School. The Boston Red Sox (AL) selected Martinez in the third round 1985 free agent draft, but he enrolled instead at the University of Tampa. He became Tampa's all-time leader in batting average (.398), HR (54), and RBI (222), earning three-time Division II All-America and Academic All-America honors. Martinez played for the US team in the 1987 Pan-American Games and led the 1988 US Olympic team to a gold medal in Seoul, South Korea, being named first baseman on *TSN* College All-American team that year. The Seattle Mariners (AL) made him their number-one draft pick in 1988.

The 6-foot 2-inch, 210-pound first baseman began his professional base-ball career in 1989 at Williamsport, PA (EL). He spent the next season with Calgary, Canada (PCL), where his .320 batting average, 17 HR, 93 RBI, and PCL-leading .991 fielding percentage earned him *USAT* Minor League Player of the Year honors. After a brief September promotion to the Seattle Mariners, Martinez returned to Calgary in 1991 and was selected the PCL MVP and All-Star first baseman. He received another late-season promotion and became the Mariners' starting first baseman in 1992.

Martinez sparkled with the Seattle Mariners in 1994, hitting 20 HR and compiling a .997 fielding percentage, ranking second behind New York Yankee legend Don Mattingly.* In 1995, Martinez came into his own as a powerful line-drive hitter, setting then career highs with 31 HR, a .293 batting average, and 111 RBI. He made the AL All-Star team and helped lead the Seattle Mariners to their dramatic Division Series victory over the New York Yankees, hitting .409 with five RBI in the five-game series.

The Seattle Mariners traded Martinez to the New York Yankees (AL) on his birthday in 1995 to face the unenviable task of replacing Mattingly. Although starting slowly, Martinez finished the 1996 season first in fielding among AL first baseman (.996) and batted .292 with 25 HR and a team high of 117 RBI. No New York Yankee first baseman had produced so many runs since Mattingly's 1985 season. In 1997, Martinez ensured his place in Yankee lore by setting a major league record for RBI in April (35), including seven RBI on three HR one night against the Seattle Mariners in the Kingdome. He finished 1997 with a .296 batting average and trailed only MVP Mariner Ken Griffey Jr.* in HR (44) and RBI (141). His 1997 HR total ranked second behind Lou Gehrig's* among New York Yankee first basemen. In the 1997 AL Division Series against the Baltimore Orioles, Martinez batted .222 with four RBI. His 28 HR and 123 RBI helped New York capture the AL East with an AL record 114 victories in 1998. He batted .273 with two doubles in the AL Division Series against the Texas Rangers. Cleveland Indian pitchers limited him to one hit in the AL Championship Series, but he batted .364 and clouted a grand slam HR in the World Series triumph over the San Diego Padres. His 28 HR and 105 RBI helped New York repeat as AL East titlists in 1999. He batted .263 with one HR and three RBI in the AL Championship Series and .267 with one HR and five RBI in the World Series. Through the 1999 season, Martinez batted .275 with 225 doubles, 213 HR, and 798 RBI.

BIBLIOGRAPHY: Tino Martinez file, National Baseball Library, Cooperstown, NY; Scott Gorman, "It's Tino Time," *MM* 6 (1995), pp. 27–30; "On Deck," *Sport* 79 (July 1988), p. 82; Jeff Redd, "Born to Play Baseball," *MM* 4 (1993), pp. 56–59; Tom Verducci, "Teeing Off," *SI* 86 (June 9, 1997), pp. 56–63; New York Yankees website, URL: www.yankees.com/web/home/main.html.

Sarah L. Ulerick

MARTINEZ, Edgar (b. January 2, 1963, New York, NY), player, moved with his parents, Jose Martinez and Christina Salgado, back to their native Puerto Rico when he was two. He grew up in PR with his hardworking grandparents, who shaped his work ethic. He graduated from Jose S. Alegria High School in Dorado, PR and attended American College in PR before signing with the Seattle Mariners (AL) as a free agent in 1982. The Kirkland, WA resident has spent his entire professional career in the Seattle Mariners organization. He met his wife, Holli, a Seattle, WA native, in 1991 and has a son, Alexander. They own and manage an embroidery business in Redmond, WA.

Martinez, a cousin to former major league first baseman Carmelo Martinez, began his professional baseball career as a third baseman with Bellingham, WA (NWL) in 1983 and progressed through the Mariners farm system at Wausau, WI (ML), Chattanooga, TN (SL), and Calgary, Canada (PCL). Martinez shuttled between the Calgary Cannons and Seattle Mariners from 1987 to 1989. The Cannons MVP in 1987 and Player of the Year in 1988, he won the PCL 1988 batting title with a .363 average. The 5-foot 11-inch, 200-pound right-hander landed the opening-day start at third base with the Seattle Mariners in 1990, his first full major league season. He shifted to the DH position in 1995 after injury-plagued 1993 and 1994 seasons.

Martinez, a hitting machine and the epitome of a professional hitter, ranks among the best pure hitters today, with AL batting championships in 1992 (.343) and in 1995 (.356). Despite battling a sore right shoulder in 1992, Martinez still won the batting title, led the AL with 44 doubles, and finished second with a .544 slugging percentage.

Injuries limited Martinez to only 42 games in 1993 and 89 contests in 1994. In 1995, his first healthy season in three years, his .356 batting average marked the highest by an AL right-handed hitter since Joe DiMaggio's* .381 in 1939. He led the AL in on-base percentage (.482), shared the lead in runs (121) and doubles (52), and clouted a career high 29 HR. Martinez played in every game and never went more than two games without a hit.

Prior to a rib injury in the 1996 season, Martinez was headed to destroy Earl Webb's long-standing record of 67 doubles in 1931. He ended the season with 52 doubles in 139 games, becoming only the fifth major league player and the first since Joe Medwick* in 1936 and 1937 to have consecutive 50-plus double seasons. His .330 batting average, 28 HR, and 108 RBI helped Seattle win the AL West in 1997. He hit .322 with 29 HR and 102 RBI in 1998 and .337 with 24 HR and 86 RBI, leading the AL with a .447 on-base percentage. He ranked third in batting average (.322) in the 1990s.

Martinez remained little known outside the Seattle market until the 1995 post-season when the Mariners dramatically won the AL West Division and defeated the New York Yankees in an historic five-game Division Series, the first post-season division playoffs involving a wild-card team. He hit .571 in that series and became the first player to drive in seven runs in a single post-season game in Seattle's come-from-behind win in Game 4, hitting a three-run HR in the third inning and a grand slam HR in the eighth frame to put the Mariners ahead, 10–6. Martinez continued his clutch hitting in Game 5, doubling home the tying and winning runs and sending the Mariners to the AL Championship Series for the first time in franchise history. In the 1997 AL Division Series, he clouted two HR with three RBI against the Baltimore Orioles.

In 13 major league seasons through 1999, Martinez has batted .320 with

880 runs, 1,558 hits, 372 doubles, 198 HR, and 780 RBI. Martinez, who possesses a quiet manner and diligence, appeared in the 1992, 1995, 1996, and 1997 All-Star games and started at DH in 1995 and 1997. He was voted the Seattle *Post-Intelligencer*'s Sports Star of the Year for 1992, making *TSN* AL All-Star team in 1992 and 1995 and the AP All-Star squad in 1995. Martinez also was named 1995 Outstanding DH of the Year by the AL and *Latino Sports* 1995 Latino MVP. In 1995, Martinez finished third in AL MVP voting and also was selected "best hitter" in *BA*'s annual Tools of the Trade. The PUL dedicated their 1996 All-Star Game to Martinez, in recognition for his offensive achievements in 1995 and his ongoing contributions to Puerto Rican youth baseball.

BIBLIOGRAPHY: Edgar Martinez file, National Baseball Library, Cooperstown, NY; Tol Broome, "Edgar Martinez: Seattle's Unassuming Superstar," *SCD* 22 (September 29, 1995), p. 132; *Seattle Mariners Information Guide*, 1997; Steve Marantz, "This Is Edgar Martinez," *TSN*, August 1995, p. 16; Tom Moore, "Edgar Es Senor Double," *MM* 7 (1996), pp. 29–31; Tom Verducci, "5 Days of Hardball," *SI* 83 (October 16, 1995), pp. 22–35.

                                                                        Sarah L. Ulerick

MARTINEZ, Jose Dennis (Emilia) (b. May 14, 1955, Grenada, Nicaragua), player, studied engineering at a Nicaraguan college and signed with the Baltimore Orioles (AL) in December 1973. His impressive arm enabled him to reach the major leagues by 1976. The 6-foot 1-inch, 185-pound right-handed pitcher possessed an especially effective overhand sinker. His first full season with the Baltimore Orioles in 1977 produced a 14–7 mark with 107 strikeouts. He also proved "tough and gritty," teammate Ken Singleton* affirmed. Martinez's 14 wins led the AL in a strike-shortened 1981 season, but a severe alcoholism problem emerged. He admitted, "to me happiness was drinking. . . . I lived in a fantasy." Struggling years followed with a 7–16 mark in 1983 and a 6–9 record in 1984. He attended Alcoholics Anonymous meetings on the road and also followed a hospital program in Baltimore. The Baltimore Orioles traded Martinez in June 1986 to the Montreal Expos (NL). He had considered the Orioles "like my family." Mike Flanagan* and Eddie Murray* were almost like "brothers." His fortunes reached the nadir when no major league club signed him for 1987.

Luckily, Martinez regained control of his life and signed with Miami, FL (FSL), a Montreal Expo farm club. He returned to the Montreal Expos, posting a capable 11–4 mark and leading the NL with a .733 winning percentage for 1987. He declared, "I thank God He made me humble. I didn't quit." His 2.39 ERA and five shutouts topped the NL in 1991. A dramatic climax came on July 28, 1991, when he hurled a perfect 2–0 game against the Los Angeles Dodgers. The contest was televised directly to his native Nicaragua. Nicaraguans had followed his career closely and loved "El Presidente!" Martinez contributed regularly to charities at home and visited schools and hospitals. He pitched for the Cleveland Indians (AL) from 1994 to 1996 and the Seattle Mariners (AL) in 1997. In January 1998, the Atlanta Braves (NL) signed him as a reliever. His four victories in 1998 enabled him to surpass Juan Marichal* for most triumphs by a Latin American pitcher. He hurled 3.1 shutout innings in the NL Championship Series against the San Diego Padres and then retired in February 1999. Over 23 major league seasons, he won 245 games and lost 193 decisions with a 3.70 ERA. He made the NL All-Star team from 1990 to 1992 and the AL All-Star squad in 1995. Martinez loved his baseball career, commenting "after my family, I view my career in baseball as the greatest blessing of all." The Miami, FL resident and his wife, Luz, have four children, Dennis, Erica, Gilberto, and Ricardo.

BIBLIOGRAPHY: Dennis Martinez file, National Baseball Library, Cooperstown, NY; Ken Nigro, "Dennis Martinez Is O's New Ace," *TSN*, June 27, 1981; Jim Henneman, "Martinez Blames Woes on Alcohol," *TSN*, March 5, 1984; Jim Henneman, "An Emotional Goodbye for D. Martinez," *TSN*, June 30, 1986; Kent Baker, "Expos Give Martinez New Life, but He's Still an Oriole at Heart," Baltimore (MD) *Sun*, August 5, 1987; Jeff Gordon, "New Life: Martinez Rejects Bottle, Bitterness," St. Louis *Post-Dispatch*, September 6, 1989; "El Perfecto for 'El Presidente,' " *TSN*, August 5, 1991; Bruce Newman, "Return of the Native," *SI 75* (December 30, 1991– January 6, 1992), pp. 102–108; Ted Patterson, *The Baltimore Orioles* (Dallas, TX, 1995); Mike Phillips, "A Blessed Life Playing Game of Baseball," St. Louis *Post-Dispatch*, June 21, 1997; Tom Van Hyning, "Dennis Martinez in Puerto Rico," *TNP* 16 (1996), pp. 51–53; John Thorn et al., eds., *Total Indians* (New York, 1998); Russell Schneider, *The Glorious Summer of 1995* (Cleveland, OH, 1996); David Srinivasan and Doug Myers, eds., *The Scouting Report, 1997* (New York, 1997); Zander Hollander, ed., *1997 The Complete Handbook of Baseball* (New York, 1997); *WWIB, 1998*, 83rd ed.; *TSN Official Baseball Register*, 1998.

William J. Miller

MARTINEZ, Pedro Jaime (b. July 25, 1971, Manoquayabo, DR), player, is the son of civil servants and attended Ohio Dominican College. His parents divorced when he was eight years old, but kept the six children close. His brother Ramon* pitches for the Boston Red Sox (AL), while another brother, Jesus, hurls in the Cincinnati Reds (NL) organization. Pedro, a 5-foot 11-inch, 175-pound pitcher who bats and throws right-handed, signed as a free agent with the Los Angeles Dodgers (NL) in June 1988. He spent five minor league seasons with Santo Domingo, DR (DSL) in 1988 and 1989, Great Falls, MT (PrL) in 1990, Bakersfield, CA (CaL) and San Antonio, TX (TL) in 1991, and Albuquerque, NM (TL) for parts of the 1991 through 1993 seasons. *TSN* named him Minor League Player of the Year in 1991, when he finished 8–0 with a 2.05 ERA for Bakersfield, 7–5 with a 1.76 ERA for San Antonio, and 3–3 with a 3.66 ERA for Albuquerque.

After joining Los Angeles briefly in 1992, Martinez compiled a 10–5 record, 2.61 ERA and 119 strikeouts in 107 innings as a reliever with the Dodgers in 1993. In November 1993, the Los Angeles Dodgers traded him to the Montreal Expos (NL). Montreal made Martinez a starter in the strike-shortened 1994 campaign, as he compiled an 11–5 record, 3.42 ERA, and 142 strikeouts in 144.2 innings. Although leading the NL with 11 hit batsmen in 1995, he won 14 of 24 decisions with a 3.51 ERA and 174 strikeouts in 194.2 innings. His best major league game came on June 3, 1995, when he pitched nine perfect innings against the San Diego Padres. Martinez was relieved after surrendering a leadoff double in the top of the tenth inning. He fanned 222 batters in 216.2 innings in 1996, recording a 13–10 mark with a 3.70 ERA.

In 1997, Martinez garnered the NL Cy Young Award and made the NL All-Star team. Atlanta Braves pitchers had won the award four consecutive years. Besides finishing 17–8, Martinez led the major leagues with a career-best 1.90 ERA and became the first ERA leader with 300 strikeouts since Steve Carlton* in 1972. Opponents batted a major league low .184 against him. His 13 complete games led both leagues, while his career-best 305 strikeouts ranked second. No right-hander since Walter Johnson* in 1912 had registered an ERA under 2.00 and over 300 strikeouts in a season. The Montreal Expos did not want to pay him a large salary in arbitration. In December 1997, Martinez signed a record $75 million, six year contract with the Boston Red Sox (AL). Martinez compiled a 19–7 record in 1998 and ranked second in ERA (2.89) and strikeouts (251), helping the Red Sox gain the wild card berth and finishing a distant second in the AL Cy Young Award balloting. He captured the only victory for Boston in the AL Division Series against the Cleveland Indians. He won the AL Cy Young Award in 1999 with a 23–4 record, leading the AL in victories, ERA (2.07), and strikeouts (313). He struck out 5 batters in 2 innings to win the All-Star Game and helped his club earn another Wild Card berth. He hurled 6 hitless relief innings to win decisive Game 5 of the AL Division Series and pitched 7 scoreless innings with 12 strikeouts to win Game 3 of the AL Championship Series. He earned *TSN* AL Pitcher of the Year and AP AL All-Star Team honors.

The Manoquayabo, DR resident, who remains single, has compiled a 107–50 record with a 2.83 ERA, completed 110 of 247 starts, and struck out 1,534 batters in 1,359.1 innings through 1999.

BIBLIOGRAPHY: Pedro Martinez file, National Baseball Library, Cooperstown, NY; *TSN Baseball Register*, 1999; Mark Starr, "Passion in Every Pitch," *Newsweek* 131 (April 6, 1998), p. 57.

David L. Porter

MARTINEZ, Ramon Jaime (b. March 22, 1968, Santo Domingo, DR), player, is the son of civil servants. His parents divorced when he was 11 years old, but kept the six children close. He is the oldest of three pitching brothers, all of whom made the 40-man rosters of major league teams before turning 21 years of age. His younger brother, Pedro,* became major league baseball's highest paid player when the Boston Red Sox (AL) signed him to a multiyear contract in December 1997. Brother Jesus pitches in the Cincinnati Reds (NL) organization. All three brothers began their professional careers as members of the Los Angeles Dodgers (NL) organization. Fifteen cousins also have joined the three Martinez brothers as either professionals or Olympic team members.

The 6-foot 4-inch Ramon, the tallest of the Martinez brothers, is a right-handed thrower who switch hits. In his nine full seasons as a Dodger, he lost considerable time to injury; his game appearances ranged from 15 in 1998 to 33 in 1990, his first full season. When healthy, Martinez started regularly in the Los Angeles rotation from 1990 to 1998. In 1990, he led the NL with 12 complete games and recorded three shutouts. He also struck out 18 Atlanta Braves on June 4, 1990 and threw a 7–0 no-hit victory against the Florida Marlins on July 14, 1995. His annual ratio of walks to strikeouts indicated a gradual loss of command. In 1990, Martinez fanned 223 batters or nearly four times as many hitters as he walked. His ratio nearly dropped to even in 1993, when he led the NL in walks.

His first full time season as a 22 year old in 1990 proved spectacular with a 20–6 record and 2.92 ERA, as he finished second in the NL Cy Young Award balloting. He followed that with 17 wins and a 3.27 ERA in 1991 and was the youngest opening day major league starter in 1992. His control problems involved a failure to throw a high fast ball for strikes. Between 1990 and 1992, Martinez finished 33–15 with a 2.82 ERA when he recorded more fly outs than groundouts, and only 8–12 with a 4.39 ERA when his ground ball outs exceeded his fly outs.

Martinez, who is single, compiled a 125–78 record and 3.44 ERA with 1,329 strikeouts in 1,752.1 innings in his first 12 major league seasons. He lost his only decision in the 1995 NL Division Series against the Cincinnati Reds and allowed only one run in his lone start in the 1996 NL Division Series against the Atlanta Braves. Most significantly, he followed Juan Marichal* and Jose Rijo* out of desperate poverty in the DR and paved the way for prosperity for himself and other family members. The Los Angeles Dodgers released him in October 1998. In March 1999, he signed with the Boston Red Sox (AL). After recovering from shoulder surgery, Martinez finished 2–1 with a 3.05 ERA. He hurled 5.2 innings without decision in a Game 3 victory in the AL Division Series and pitched 6.2 innings in a Game 2 loss in the AL Championship Series.

BIBLIOGRAPHY: Ramon Martinez file, National Baseball Library, Cooperstown, NY; Hank Hersch, "Leveraged to the Max," SI 73 (August 20, 1990), p. 58; William F. McNeil, *The Dodgers Encyclopedia* (Champaign, IL, 1997); *TSN Baseball Register, 1998*; Seymour Siwoff and Steve Hirdt, *The 1993 Elias Baseball Analyst* (New York, 1993).
David Fitzsimmons

MATHEWS, Edwin Lee, Jr. "Eddie" (b. October 13, 1931, Texarkana, TX), player, coach, manager, and scout, is the son of Western Union telegraph operator Edwin Mathews, Sr. and spent fifteen of 17 major league seasons with the Boston, Milwaukee, and Atlanta Braves (NL). He signed with the Boston Braves for a $6,000 bonus on graduation from Santa Barbara High School. Mathews played third base with High Point–Thomasville, NC (NCSL) in 1949, Atlanta, GA (SA) in 1950 and 1951, and Milwaukee, WI (AA) in 1951. After joining the Boston Braves in 1952, he performed with the Braves in Milwaukee (1953–1965) and Atlanta (1966). His final two seasons were spent with the Houston Astros (NL) and the Detroit Tigers (AL). The 6-foot 1-inch, 190-pound Mathews performed primarily as a third baseman, but played first base his final two seasons. Mathews, an above average third baseman, exhibited hitting prowess that attracted widespread attention. In his first season, he broke Ralph Kiner's* record for HR by a rookie with 25. That season, he hit a rookie record three HR in one game. He learned quickly in the batter's box, leading the NL with 115 strikeouts and drawing only 59 walks his rookie season. Two years later, he struck out only 61 times and walked on 113 occasions. He never again led the NL in strikeouts, but paced in walks four times.

A left-handed batter who threw right-handed, Mathews led the major leagues in HR in 1953 and 1959 by hitting 47 and 46, respectively. He slugged 512 HR in his major league career, averaging over 30 per season. Contemporary sluggers Mickey Mantle* and Willie Mays* averaged fewer HR per season. Blessed with good health and good luck, Mathews played in 134 or more games in each of his first 11 seasons and batted at least 436 times per season over that span. Since Hank Aaron* played on the Braves, opposing catchers could not pitch around Mathews. Mathews and Aaron combined for 1,267 HR, exceeding Babe Ruth* and Lou Gehrig* by 60 career round trippers. In 2,391 games, he made 2,315 hits, slammed 354 doubles, knocked in 1,453 runs, walked 1,444 times, struck out 1,487 times, and batted .271. Mathews participated in the 1957 and 1958 World Series with Milwaukee and in the 1968 fall classic with Detroit. His 1957 and 1968 teams won World Series championships. Mathews coached, managed, and scouted for the Atlanta Braves from 1972 through 1974. He served as a minor league instructor–scout for the Milwaukee Brewers (AL) from 1975 through 1978 and scouted for the Oakland A's (AL) from 1982 to 1984. His squads compiled losing records (149–161), with his best team finish being fourth place. In 1978 he was elected to the National Baseball Hall of Fame in his first year of eligibility. The Del Mar, CA resident suffered a serious accident while boarding a cruise ship from the Cayman Islands in November 1996.

BIBLIOGRAPHY: John Benson et al., *Baseball's Top 100* (Wilton, CT, 1997); Donald Honig, *The Power Hitters* (St. Louis, MO, 1989); Eddie Mathews and Bob Buege, *Eddie Mathews and the National Pastime* (Milwaukee, WI, 1994); Gary Caruso, *The Braves Encyclopedia* (Philadelphia, PA, 1995); Bob Buege, *The Milwaukee Braves: A Baseball Eulogy* (Milwaukee, WI, 1988); Thomas Aylesworth and Benton Minks, *The Encyclopedia of Baseball Managers* (New York, 1990); *The Baseball Encyclopedia*, 10th ed. (New York, 1996); Lowell Reidenbaugh, *Baseball's Hall of Fame—Cooperstown* (New

York, 1993); Eddie Mathews file, National Baseball Library, Cooperstown, NY; John Thorn et al., eds., *Total Braves* (New York, 1996).

Stephen D. Bodayla

MATHEWS, Robert T. "Bobby," "Little Bobby" (b. November 21, 1851, Baltimore, MD; d. April 17, 1898, Baltimore, MD), player, performed for 10 baseball teams from 1868 through 1887. His clubs included the Fort Wayne Kekiongas (1871), Lord Baltimores (1872), and New York Mutuals (1873–1875) of the NA; New York Mutuals (1876), Cincinnati Red Stockings (1877), Providence Grays (1879–1881), and Boston Red Caps (1881–1882) of the NL; and Philadelphia Athletics (1883–1887) of the AA. From 1871 through 1887, the masterly 5-foot 5½-inch, 145-pound right-hander compiled a 297–248 win–loss record. After winning 131 and losing 112 decisions in the NA from 1871 to 1875, he won 166 and lost 136, struck out 1,199 batters, and compiled a 3.00 ERA in the NL from 1876 to 1887. A star pitcher for the famed New York Mutuals, he reached a career high 42 wins and 22 losses in 1874. A *NYT* sportswriter lauded his 2–0, three-hit victory on May 30, "undoubtedly the best ever played in this vicinity and with one exception—Kekionga and Forest City, the best ever played in the United States." Coincidentally, Mathews also hurled that earlier game, helping Fort Wayne defeat Cleveland's Forest City on May 4, 1871. In a day characterized by much higher scores, Mathews' five-hit shutout was considered a remarkable feat and comprised the "smallest score made in a regular match during the season." During 1875 and 1876, he won 29 and 21 victories, respectively, and yet experienced losing seasons because his teams sagged. In 1875, he led the NA with 38 losses.

In 1877, Mathews encountered his worst season by winning only three of 15 decisions. Surviving changing pitching rules and techniques, he quickly regained his pitching ability. From 1883 to 1885, he compiled three superb 30-game victory seasons for the Philadelphia Athletics (AA) and in 1883 led them to the championship. Mathews, a control expert, threw within a hair's breadth of a mark. Relying on mastery of pitches rather than overpowering speed, he "generally outguessed the batter." He struck out 16 batters in one game in 1884 and averaged over six strikeouts per game the next year. During his three 30-game seasons, Mathews walked only 137 batters and struck out 775. Several contemporary reporters credited him with developing the curveball, but this claim has since been challenged. To keep hitters off balance, he threw a variety of pitches ("hardly ever using the same delivery twice"). He was hailed as "without doubt the most versatile boxman of his day." Hank O'Day,* later manager of the Chicago Cubs, claimed that Mathews threw an early-day spitball and controlled the pitch with remarkable skill.

Mathews' inept hitting, however, pleased opposing teams. From 1871 through 1875, he batted .216. He averaged only .192 from 1876 to 1887 and occasionally played the outfield and infield. The slightly built Mathews did not need to rely on his hitting because he was a scientific pitcher who "occupied the spotlight of the baseball stage for fourteen years." Physical ailments limited him to seven games in 1887 and forced Mathews to retire from baseball. The Baltimore *Sun* on April 18, 1898, recounted his sad post-baseball career: "From that time until his mind failed he tried a number of occupations, and was in rather straitened circumstances, having saved little in his prosperous days." He spent time at Maryland University Hospital and Spring Grove Asylum before dying at his parents' home. He never married.

BIBLIOGRAPHY: *Base Ball Player*, 1872–1876; *De Witt's Base Ball Guide*, 1876–1881; Robert Mathews file, National Baseball Library, Cooperstown, NY; *NYT*, 1873–1874; David Nemec, *The Beer and Whisky League* (New York, 1994); *The Baseball Encyclopedia*, 10th ed. (New York, 1996); *Spalding's Base Ball Guide, 1880–1888* (New York, 1880–1888); Baltimore (MD) *Sun*, April 18, 1898; Robert L. Tiemann and Mark Rucker, eds., *Nineteenth Century Stars* (Kansas City, MO, 1989); William J. Ryczek, *Blackguards and Red Stockings* (Jefferson, NC, 1992).

Duane A. Smith

MATHEWSON, Christopher "Christy," "Big Six" (b. August 12, 1880, Factoryville, PA; d October 7, 1925, Saranac Lake, NY), player, coach, manager, and executive, was the son of gentleman farmer Gilbert B. Mathewson and Minerva J. (Capwell) Mathewson. After prepping at Keystone Academy in Factoryville, he entered Bucknell College in 1898 on a scholarship. He played football, basketball, and baseball there, but did not graduate. He married Jan Stoughton and had one child, Christopher, Jr. His brother, Henry, briefly pitched with the New York Giants (NL). An outstanding college pitcher, Mathewson began his professional baseball career in 1899 with Taunton, MA (NEL) and started the 1900 season with Norfolk, VA (VL). Norfolk sold the 20–2 Mathewson in midsummer to the New York Giants (NL), where he pitched for 17 years and became one of the NL's greatest pitchers.

The 6-foot 1½-inch, 195-pound right-handed Mathewson specialized in his "fadeaway," described by journalist John Kieran (OS) as "a ball that dropped deceptively and on the 'inside' for a right-handed batter." He won 373 games, third highest in major league history, and compiled a .665 winning percentage, the seventh best all-time mark. Mathewson lost only 188 games, completed 434 of 551 starts, pitched 4,780.2 innings, struck out 2,502 batters, and walked only 844. A 37-game winner in 1908, the consistent Mathewson triumphed in at least 22 games per season from 1903 through 1914. Five times he led the NL in ERA, including a sparkling 1.14 in 1909. His 2.13 career ERA stands as baseball's fifth best. Seldom pitching under 300 innings, he hurled 390.2 innings to lead the NL in 1908 and completed 34 games. An overpowering pitcher, he five times led the NL in strikeouts and exhibited great control. Only two pitchers have surpassed his 79 career shutouts. Mathewson's World Series record augmented his fame. Although winning only 5 of 10 decisions in four World Series, he in 1905 incredibly hurled three shutouts against the Philadelphia Athletics. Besides holding the record for most World Series shutouts (4) and complete games (10), he failed to complete only one World Series game that he started and compiled a composite 1.15 ERA.

In early 1916, Mathewson became manager of the Cincinnati Reds (NL) and won in his only mound appearance there. From 1916 to 1918, he piloted the Reds to 164 wins, 176 losses, and two fourth place finishes. On August 20, 1917, he and Giants manager John McGraw* were arrested because their teams had violated a New York law prohibiting games on Sunday. The episode publicized the movement to secure Sunday baseball in New York, particularly because Mathewson had promised his mother never to play on the Sabbath. In 1918, Mathewson enlisted in the U.S. Army as a captain and served overseas in the Gas and Flame Division of the American Expeditionary Force in France. A poisonous gas victim, he suffered pulmonary tuberculosis thereafter. Mathewson rejoined the New York Giants as a coach after World War I and remained with the club until 1920. During that span, Mathewson spent much time at Saranac Lake, NY recuperating from tuberculosis. In 1923, the lowly Boston Braves (NL) made him president as a public relations ploy because Mathewson could work only part-time.

Mathewson, a public hero, substantially elevated the professional baseball player's image. The college man epitomized the Christian athlete, did not smoke or drink, and acted as a gentleman and scholar. Lester Chadwick's "Baseball Joe," a series of juvenile sports books, used Mathewson as a model. John Wheeler ghostwrote juvenile books under Mathewson's name, among them *Pitching in a Pinch* and *Pitcher Pollock*. After Mathewson's death, newspapers and periodicals throughout the United States eulogized him. *Commonweal* wrote,

No other pitcher ever loomed so majestically in young minds, quite overshadowing George Washington and his cherry tree or even that transcendant model of boyhood, Frank Merriwell. Such men have a very real value about and beyond the achievements of brawn and sporting skill. They realize and typify in a fashion the ideal of sport— clean power in the hands of a clean and vigorous personality.

In 1936 Mathewson was elected to the National Baseball Hall of Fame in the very first year of balloting. He made Major League Baseball's All-Century Team.

BIBLIOGRAPHY: Charles Alexander, *John McGraw* (New York, 1988); John Benson et al., *Baseball's Top 100* (Wilton, CT, 1997); J. Buckley, Jr., "World Series Kings of the Hill," *SI* 75 (October 7, 1991), pp. 45ff; Chicago *Daily News*, July 5, 7, 1913; *Commonweal* 2 (October 21, 1925), p. 579; *DAB* 12 (1933), pp. 407–408; John McCormick Harris; " 'Pinhead' Mathewson," *TNP* 10 (1990), pp . 17–20; Noel Hynd, *The Giants of the Polo Grounds* (New York, 1988); A. W. Laird, *Ranking Baseball's Elite* (Jefferson, NC, 1990); John McGraw, *My Thirty Years in Baseball* (New York, 1923); Ronald A. Mayer, *Christy Mathewson* (Jefferson, NC, 1993); E. A. Sterling, "Matty as Man and Boy," *TNP* 16 (1996), pp. 36–41; *NYT*, 1900–1916, August 21, 22, 1917, October 8, 1925; *The Baseball Encyclopedia*, 10th ed. (New York, 1996); Steven A.

Riess, *Touching Base* (Westport, CT, 1980); Lawrence S. Ritter, *The Glory of Their Times* (New York, 1966); Harold Seymour, *Baseball: The Golden Age* (New York, 1971); Christopher Mathewson file, National Baseball Library, Cooperstown, NY; Ray Robinson, *Matty: An American Hero* (New York, 1993); Frank Graham, *The New York Giants* (New York, 1952); Lee Allen, *The Cincinnati Reds* (New York, 1948); Thomas Aylesworth and Benton Minks, *The Encyclopedia of Baseball Managers* (New York, 1990); David Quentin Voigt, *American Baseball*, vol. 2 (Norman, OK, 1970); Douglas Wallop, *Baseball: An Informal History* (New York, 1969).

Steven A. Riess

MATHIS, Verdell Lester "Lefty" (b. November 18, 1914, Crawfordsville, AR; d. October 30, 1998, Memphis, TN), player, made the All-Star team six times for the Memphis Red Sox (NAL) and was considered the best NAL left-hander. The son of Jackson Mathis, a Missouri Pacific Railroad Line worker, and Sarah Mathis, he attended Booker Washington High School in Memphis, TN until eleventh grade.

Mathis possessed only one year of semipro experience upon joining the Memphis Red Sox in 1940 as an outfielder and pitcher. He preferred to play center field so he could appear every day, but soon became the ace of the staff. His boyhood hero, Satchel Paige,* and Mathis remain the only pitchers to win two East-West games. Although pitching for a losing team, he won consecutive All-Star games in 1944 and 1945 and held the East scoreless each time. After joining the NAL, he faced Paige several times and defeated him on three occasions. His victories included 1–0, in 11 innings in New Orleans, LA, 2–1 in Kansas City, MO, and 2–1 again in Chicago, IL on "Satchel Paige Day" in front of 30,000 fans.

The slender 5-foot 11-inch, 150-pound competitor possessed a terrific curve, good fastball, screwball and change-of-pace and learned a great pick-off move from Luis Tiant, Sr. Following the 1945 season, he needed surgery to remove bone chips from his left elbow. Mathis never regained his previous form, as the injury cut short his career. He spent almost his entire 10-year baseball career in Memphis and, like many outstanding southern players, never received the publicity accorded to players elsewhere.

Besides his East-West appearances, Mathis pitched in two North-South All-Star games. He also played winter ball with Vargas, Mexico (MEL) in 1947–1948 and with Tampico, Mexico (MEL), where he once defeated Mexico City in a doubleheader. Mathis also toured with Satchel Paige's* All-Stars against Bob Feller's* All-Star team in 1946.

After retiring from baseball in 1950, Mathis moved to Queens, NY and stayed there 18 years. He worked as a plasterer except for six years when Jackie Robinson* gave him a job in the commissary at Chock-Full-of-Nuts. Mathis then returned to Memphis, where he was employed 15 years at the Colonial GC as the manager of the men's lockers until 1984.

Mathis married Helen Dunn on June 3, 1936 and had four children during their 56 years together.

BIBLIOGRAPHY: *Afro-American*, 1940–1948; Chicago (IL) *Defender*, 1940–1948; John Holway, *Black Diamonds* (Westport, CT, 1989); Kansas City (MO) *Call*, 1940–1946; Robert W. Peterson, *Only the Ball Was White* (Englewood Cliffs, NJ, 1970); Pittsburgh (PA) *Courier*, 1940–1948; James A. Riley, *The All-Time All-Stars of Black Baseball* (Cocoa, FL, 1983); James A. Riley, *The Biographical Encyclopedia of the Negro Baseball Leagues* (New York, 1994); James A. Riley, interviews with former Negro League players, James A. Riley Collection, Cocoa, FL; *The Baseball Encyclopedia*, 10th ed. (New York, 1996).

James A. Riley

MATLACK, Jonathan Trumpbour "Jon" (b. January 19, 1950, West Chester, PA), player and coach, graduated from Henderson High School in 1967 and attended the University of Pittsburgh for one year before transferring to West Chester State College.

The New York Mets (NL) selected Matlack as the number four pick in the 1967 amateur draft. He started his professional baseball career in 1967 as a pitcher with Williamsport, PA (EL) and spent the next season with Raleigh-Durham, NC (CrL). The 6-foot 3-inch, 200-pound lefthander pitched the 1969–1971 seasons with Tidewater, VA (IL) before debuting with the New York Mets on July 11, 1971. He lost all three decisions his rookie season with New York.

In 1972, Matlack improved to a 15–10 mark and received NL Rookie of the Year honors from both *TSN* and the BWAA. The New York Mets won the NL pennant in 1973, as he recorded one victory in the NL Championship Series. He pitched three games in the 1973 World Series against the Oakland A's, winning one and losing two. Matlack remained with the New York Mets through the 1977 season and made the NL All-Star squad from 1974 to 1976, winning the game's MVP award in 1975.

The Texas Rangers (AL) obtained Matlack and John Milner for Willie Montanez,* Tom Grieve, and Ken Henderson in December 1977. Matlack placed second on the Texas Rangers staff with 15 victories the following season. Elbow problems limited Matlack's effectiveness thereafter. He retired as an active player after the 1983 season with 125 wins, 126 losses, 1,516 strikeouts in 2,363 innings, and a 3.18 ERA.

Matlack stayed out of baseball until joining the San Diego Padres (NL) organization as a coach in 1988 and served stints in Scottsdale, AZ (InL), Riverside, CA (CaL), Wichita, KS (AA), and Las Vegas, NV (PCL) through 1992. He coached for the Chicago White Sox (AL) in 1993 and 1994, Las Vegas Stars (PCL) in 1995, and Detroit Tigers (AL) in 1996. Matlack lives in Sugar Grove, OH, with his wife, Dee, and three children, Kristen, Jennifer, and Daniel.

BIBLIOGRAPHY: Jon Matlack file, National Baseball Library, Cooperstown, NY; Donald Honig, *The New York Mets* (New York, 1986); Jack Lang and Peter Simon, *The New York Mets* (New York, 1986); *TSN Baseball Register*, 1983.

John Hillman

MATTHEWS, Gary Nathaniel "Sarge" (b. July 5, 1950, San Fernando, CA), player, coach, and sportscaster, performed well on the 1984 Chicago Cubs (NL) Eastern Division winning team. Matthews started playing baseball in Little League and spent several minor league seasons at Decatur, IL (ML), Fresno, CA (CaL), Amarillo, TX (TL), and Phoenix, AZ (PCL). He came to the major leagues in September 1972 with the San Francisco Giants (NL). The 1973 NL Rookie of the Year, Matthews enjoyed three more productive years with the San Francisco Giants. In November 1976, he signed as a free agent with the Atlanta Braves (NL). In 1979 Matthews compiled his best statistical season, hitting .304, slugging 27 HR, recording 90 RBI, and having 12- and 13-game hitting streaks. The Atlanta Braves traded him to the Philadelphia Phillies (NL) in March 1981. Matthews spent two impressive seasons there, but his batting average dropped the year the Phillies won the 1983 NL pennant. In March 1984, Matthews and Bobby Dernier were traded to the Chicago Cubs (NL). The trade put the Cubs on the road to the Eastern Division title.

The 6-foot 2-inch, 185-pound, right-handed Matthews became a team leader for the Cubs in 1984. As general manager Dallas Green* stated, "He talks when it's time to talk, and he produces when it's time to produce." Matthews produced on the field in 1984, pacing the NL with 19 game-winning hits, 103 walks, and a .417 on-base percentage. He hit two HR and drove in five runs as the Cubs lost the 1984 NL Championship Series to the San Diego Padres. Matthews's production declined at bat and in the field the next two seasons because injuries mounted. In July 1987, Chicago traded him to the Seattle Mariners (AL). Matthews ended his major league career there primarily as a DH. In 16 major league seasons, he batted .281, made 2,011 hits, slugged 319 doubles and 234 HR, and knocked in 978 runs. He served as a hitting coordinator for the Chicago Cubs from 1995 through 1997 and coached for the Toronto Blue Jays (AL) in 1998 and 1999 and became a radio broadcaster for Toronto in November 1999. His son, Gary, Jr., plays outfield in the San Diego Padres organization.

BIBLIOGRAPHY: Gary Matthews file, National Baseball Library, Cooperstown, NY; *Chicago Cubs Media Guide*, 1986, 1987; Eddie Gold and Art Ahrens, *The New Era Cubs, 1941–1985* (Chicago, IL, 1985); Mike Shatzkin, ed., *The Ballplayers* (New York, 1990); Fred Stein and Nick Peters, *Giants Diary* (Berkeley, CA, 1987); Rich Westcott and Frank Bilovsky, *The New Phillies Encyclopedia* (Philadelphia, PA, 1993).

                                                                          Duane A. Smith

MATTINGLY, Donald Arthur "Don" (b. April 20, 1961, Evansville, IN), player, was the New York Yankees' (AL) finest first baseman since Lou Gehrig* and the greatest Yankee never to play in a World Series. He is the youngest of five children born to Bill Mattingly, a postman, and Mary Mattingly. A brother, Jerry, was killed in a highway construction accident at age

23. Don, who was only seven at the time, wore the number 23 in Jerry's memory.

At Evansville Memorial High School, Mattingly played basketball, football, and baseball. Most teams expected Mattingly to attend Indiana State University. As a result, he was not selected until the 19th round of the 1979 draft. The New York Yankees signed him for a $25,000 bonus. Mattingly, who played in the minor leagues from 1979 to 1983, became the New York Yankees' regular first baseman in June 1983.

In 1984, his first full major league season, Mattingly hit .343 and became the New York Yankees' first AL batting champion since Mickey Mantle* in 1956. He also led the AL with 207 hits and 44 doubles. Early in 1985, Mattingly underwent arthroscopic knee surgery. He enjoyed a great year, leading the AL in six offensive categories, winning MVP honors, and becoming the New York Yankees' first AL RBI league leader (145) since Roger Maris* in 1961.

In a 1986 poll of major leaguers, Mattingly was selected as baseball's best player. He hit a career-high .352 and finished second in the AL MVP balloting. Mattingly topped Gehrig's team record for doubles (53) and broke a New York Yankee record for hits (238), set by Earle Combs.* His batting average made him the eighth Yankee to crack the .350 mark. In 1987, a disc problem in his back ended his 335 consecutive game-playing streak. Nevertheless, his six grand slam HR set a major league mark. During a hot streak in July, Mattingly homered in eight straight games to tie a major league record.

Mattingly batted .311 in 1988 and .303 in 1989, becoming the sixth player in New York Yankee history and the first since Joe DiMaggio* to hit .300 or better for six consecutive years. In 1990, disabled by back problems from late July through mid-September, he slipped to .256. Mattingly, named team captain for 1991, rebounded to hit .288, although his HR total dropped to nine. In mid-August, he was benched in a dispute over the length of his hair. Mattingly proved the New York Yankees' most productive hitter in 1992, batting .287 with 86 RBI. In 1993, Mattingly was involved in his first real AL pennant race and helped keep the Yankees in contention. He finished with a .291 batting average, 17 HR, and 86 RBI. In the strike-shortened 1994 season, he hit .304 with 51 RBI to help the Yankees win the AL East. His major league career ended in 1995. In 14 major league seasons, he batted .307 with 442 doubles, 222 HR, and 1,099 RBI. He did not play in a postseason game until the 1995 AL Division Series, when he batted .417 with six RBI against the Seattle Mariners. The six-time AL All-Star (1984–1989) also won eight career Gold Glove awards, the most by any New York Yankee, one ahead of George Scott* for most among AL first basemen. He led AL first basemen seven times in fielding percentage and holds the major league record for the highest fielding percentage (.996) for a first baseman.

Mattingly married Kim Sexton on September 8, 1979 and has three children, Taylor Patrick, Preston Michael, and Jordon William.

BIBLIOGRAPHY: Don Mattingly file, National Baseball Library, Cooperstown, NY; Don Burke, "The Missing Link," *YM* 14 (June 8, 1993), pp. 12–16; Peter Cava, telephone interview with Thelma Halvorson, general manager, Mattingly's 23 Restaurant, Evansville, IN, October 26, 1993; *CB Yearbook* (1988), pp. 359–363; Jack Curry "Different Mattingly Still Gains Respect," Indianapolis (IN) *News*, April 14, 1993, p. B4; Joe Mancano, "Does Mattingly Rate with the Greats?" *BRJ* 16 (1987), pp. 7–8; Peter Gammons, "The Man Hits Back," *SI* 70 (February 6, 1989), pp. 54–58; Moss Klein, "At Last, Mattingly May Find a Happy Ending," Newark (NJ) *Star-Ledger*, August 6, 1993, p. 73; Mike Lupica, "The Last Great Yankee," *Esquire* 124 (July 1995), pp. 29–31; Sean McAdam, "Mattingly the Most Disappointed of All Yankees After Late Swoon," Indianapolis (IN) *Star*, September 29, 1993, p. C6; Mark Gallagher, *The Yankee Encyclopedia*, vol. 3 (Champaign, IL, 1997); *1992 New York Yankees Team Media Guide*, pp. 172–180; *NYT Biographical Service* 19 (April 1988), pp. 390–393; Murray Chess, "Every Pitcher's Nightmare," *NYT Magazine* (April 3, 1988), pp. 22–24; E. M. Swift, "The Banger in the Bronx," *SI* 64 (April 14, 1986), pp. 54–56; G. Wolff, "Who Is Baseball's Best? Players Say Mattingly," *NYT Biographical Service* 17 (July 1986), pp. 857–858; Steve Rushin, "First-Rate," *SI* 79 (August 30, 1993), pp. 14–17; Allan Simpson, *The Baseball Draft* (Durham, NC, 1990), p. 180; *TSN Official Baseball Register*, 1996; Tom Weir, "Mattingly Finally Gets Satisfaction," *USAT*, September 30, 1993, p. C3.

Peter J. Cava

MAUCH, Gene William "Skip," "The Little General" (b. November 18, 1925, Salina, KS), player, manager, and coach, experienced a contradictory career as a major league manager. Although widely respected for his managerial skills and leadership abilities, Mauch piloted for 26 (1960–1982, 1985–1987) major league seasons without ever winning a pennant. Mauch managed the 1964 Philadelphia Phillies (NL) and 1986 California Angels (AL), which almost won pennants.

After the Depression ruined the family bakery business in Salina, KS, the Mauchs moved to California so that young Gene could concentrate on athletics during the entire year. A star high school infielder in Los Angeles, CA, he quit high school to join the Brooklyn Dodgers (NL) organization. Mauch began his professional playing career at Durham, NC (Pil) in 1943 and joined the Brooklyn Dodgers in 1944 at age 19. Mauch's playing career was interrupted for military service in 1945, and he married Nina Lee Taylor in December 1945. After World War II, the 5-foot 10-inch, 173-pound Mauch continued his playing career in the organizations of the Brooklyn Dodgers (1946, 1948), Pittsburgh Pirates (NL, 1947), Chicago Cubs (NL, 1948–1949, 1954–1956), Boston-Milwaukee Braves (NL, 1950–1953), St. Louis Cardinals (NL, 1952), and Boston Red Sox (AL, 1956–1957).

Mauch, a utility infielder, appeared in only 304 major league games spanning 10 seasons and hit only 5 HR. Mauch enjoyed his best offensive year in 1956, batting .348, belting 20 HR, and driving in 84 runs for the Los Angeles Angels (PCL). Mauch, who was frequently sold or traded, shuttled to and from the minor leagues. The exposure to so many different organizations and managers may have contributed to Mauch's later success as a major league manager. The Milwaukee Braves gave Mauch his first managerial experience, installing him as player–manager of the Atlanta, GA Crackers (SL) in 1953. Mauch piloted the Minneapolis, MN Millers in 1958 and 1959, being named AA Manager of the Year both years.

In 1960, Mauch began an 8½-year stretch as pilot of the Philadelphia Phillies (NL). In 1964, the Phillies stood 6½ games ahead with two weeks left and then lost 10 straight contests in the stretch drive to finish in a second-place tie. Many critics blamed Mauch for the Phillies' dramatic collapse, although he was named the 1964 AP NL Manager of the Year and also won that honor in 1962 and 1967. After a widely publicized dispute with Richie Allen,* Mauch was fired by the Phillies in June 1968. The Montreal Expos joined the NL in 1969 and hired Mauch as their first manager. Mauch piloted there until 1975, being named 1973 *TSN* and AP NL Manager of the Year. Mauch subsequently managed the Minnesota Twins (AL, 1976–1980) and California Angels (AL, 1981–1982, 1985–1987). The closest Mauch got to winning an AL pennant came in 1982 and in 1986. His Angels won the AL Western Division title both years, but twice lost the AL Championship Series by one game. Mauch compiled a major league managerial career record of 1,902 wins and 2,037 losses for a .483 winning percentage. He coached for the Kansas City Royals (AL) in 1995.

An avid golfer, Mauch resides in Rancho Mirage, CA and is related through marriage to former major leaguers Roy Smalley, Jr. (1948–1958) and Roy Smalley, III (1975–1987). The Mauchs have one daughter, Leanne.

BIBLIOGRAPHY: Dan Turner, *The Expos Inside Out* (Toronto, Canada, 1983); Frank Dolson, *The Philadelphia Story* (South Bend, IN, 1981); David Halberstam, *October 1964* (New York, 1994); Rich Westcott and Frank Bilovsky, *The New Phillies Encyclopedia* (Philadelphia, PA, 1993); Thomas Aylesworth and Benton Minks, *The Encyclopedia of Baseball Managers* (New York, 1990); Gene Mauch file, National Baseball Library, Cooperstown, NY; Ed Richter, *View from the Dugout* (Philadelphia, PA, 1964); Dave Anderson, "Not Even Mauch Understood It," *NYT*, October 9, 1986, p. 13; Myron Cope, "The Whip Who Put Snap in the Phillies," *SEP* 236 (August 8, 1964), pp. 74, 79; *CB* (1974), pp. 261–263; Leonard Koppett, *The Man in the Dugout* (New York, 1993); William Leggett, "The Rise and Fall of the Phillies," *SI* 22 (March 1, 1965), pp. 52, 57–63; John R. McDermott, "Mauch of the Calamity Phils Says 'Wait Till This Year,' " *Life* 58 (March 26, 1965), pp. 75–76, 78A; *TSN Baseball Register, 1988*.

Jack P. Lipton and Susan M. Lipton

MAY, Lee Andrew (b. March 23, 1943, Birmingham, AL), player and coach, is the brother of outfielder–first baseman Carlos May and starred for the

Cincinnati Reds (NL), Houston Astros (NL), and Baltimore Orioles (AL). May's father strung together mattresses, while his mother plucked chickens. After his parents divorced, he lived with his grandmother. He married childhood sweetheart Terrye Perdue in January 1962, and has three children. Upon graduating from high school, May attended Miles College in Birmingham, AL and signed with the Cincinnati Reds (NL) for $12,000. He played with Tampa, FL (FSL) in 1961 and 1962, Rocky Mount, NC (CrL) in 1963, Macon, GA (SL) in 1964, San Diego, CA (PCL) in 1965, Buffalo, NY (IL) in 1966, and the Reds from 1965 through 1971. In a July 15, 1969 doubleheader, May slugged four HR and knocked in 10 runs. In 1970, May set a Reds' record by hitting three grand slam HR and striking out 142 times. A star of the 1970 NL championship team, he hit .389 in the World Series against the Baltimore Orioles. In November 1971, however, May was sent to the Houston Astros (NL) in an eight-player trade. In the sixth inning of an April 29, 1974 game against the San Diego Padres, May became the 20th major leaguer to belt two HR in one inning. He was traded to the Baltimore Orioles (AL) in December 1974 and led the AL in 1976 in RBI (109). His major league career ended in 1981 and 1982 with the Kansas City Royals (AL). During his major league career, May appeared in 2,071 games, made 2,031 hits, slugged 340 doubles and 354 HR, batted .267 lifetime, knocked in 1,244 runs, and compiled a .459 slugging average. His 1,570 strikeouts ranked him among the 15 highest on the all-time list. A 6-foot 3-inch, 200-pound right-hander, May hit with power to all fields by "going with the pitch." Critics noted that the slow May stole only 39 career bases and played only adequately on defense. He coached for the Kansas City Royals from 1984 through 1986 and 1992 through 1994, the Cincinnati Reds from 1988 to 1989, and the Baltimore Orioles (AL) from 1995 to 1996.

BIBLIOGRAPHY: Lee May file, National Baseball Library, Cooperstown, NY; Robert H. Walker, *Cincinnati and the Big Red Machine* (Bloomington, IN, 1988); Bob Rathgeber, *Cincinnati Reds Scrapbook* (Virginia Beach, VA, 1982); Ted Patterson, *The Baltimore Orioles* (Dallas, TX, 1995); Cincinnati *Enquirer*, July 16, 1969; Houston *Post*, April 30, 1974; Mark Ribowsky, "May Gives Orioles Edge in AL East," *BS* (August 1975), pp. 48–51; *TSN*, February 20, 1984.

John David Healy

MAYBERRY, John Claiborn "Big John" (b. February 18, 1949, Detroit, MI), player and coach, graduated from Northwestern High School in Detroit, the same school that produced major leaguers Willie Horton* and Alex Johnson.* Mayberry later attended the University of Michigan and was drafted in the first round by the Houston Astros (NL) in 1967, receiving a $40,000 bonus. After a modest start at Covington, KY (ApL) in 1967, Mayberry blossomed the next season with a combined .320 batting average at Cocoa, FL (FSL), Greensboro, NC (CrL), and Oklahoma City, OK (PCL) and was called up that September to the Houston Astros. Mayberry hit well at

Oklahoma City from 1969 to 1971, but faltered at the plate each year after being recalled by Houston. In December 1971, the Astros dealt him to the Kansas City Royals (AL).

Mayberry became a fan favorite in Kansas City, as the 6-foot 3-inch, 222-pound left-hander drove a towering HR over the right-field wall and played nearly flawlessly at first base. Opposing teams employed an exaggerated shift to right field against him. In his first campaign with the Royals in 1972, he batted .298 with 25 HR and 100 RBI and led AL first basemen with a .995 fielding average. The 1973 season proved a virtual carbon copy of the 1972 campaign. In 1975, Mayberry reached career pinnacles in doubles (38), HR (34), runs scored (95), and RBI (106). On July 1, 1975, he hit three HR against Texas Ranger Ferguson Jenkins.* Mayberry was chosen AL Player of the Month in July 1975 for batting .365 with 12 HR. One eight-game stretch in 1975 saw him connect for eight round-trippers. Mayberry finished second in the 1975 AL MVP balloting to Thurman Munson* and was selected an AL All-Star in 1973 and 1974.

Mayberry slumped badly in 1976 and 1977, hitting only .232 and .230. In the fourth game of the 1977 AL Championship Series, Mayberry broke Royals' manager Whitey Herzog's* cardinal rule: "Show up on time; be ready to play." Mayberry arrived very late at Royals Stadium for a day game after a late night party. He played poorly defensively and struggled offensively. Herzog, who had "always loved the way John played," told the front office that Mayberry must leave. Kansas City sold Mayberry to the Toronto Blue Jays (AL) in April 1978. Mayberry hit 90 HR from 1978 to 1981, including 30 HR in 1980, but never recaptured his 1975 form. Toronto traded him to the New York Yankees (AL) in May 1982. His major league career record included 1,379 hits, 733 runs, 255 HR, 879 RBI, and a .253 batting average in 1,620 games. He retired with the 12th best major league career fielding average for first basemen. After five years as a minor league instructor with the Toronto Blue Jays, Mayberry coached for the Kansas City Royals in 1989 and 1990. The Kansas City, MO resident works for the Kansas City Royals Community Affairs Department and was inducted into the Kansas City Royals Hall of Fame in 1996.

BIBLIOGRAPHY: John Mayberry file, National Baseball Library, Cooperstown, NY; Ross Forman, " 'Big John' Mayberry," SCD 24 (June 13, 1997), pp. 150–151; Sid Bordman, *Expansion to Excellence* (Marceline, MS, 1981); John Garrity, *The George Brett Story* (New York, 1981); Peter C. Bjarkman, *The Toronto Blue Jays* (New York, 1990); Whitey Herzog and Kevin Horrigan, *White Rat* (New York, 1988); Zander Hollander, ed., *The Complete Handbook of Baseball*, 7th ed. (New York, 1977); Kansas City Royals, *Grandslam, 1976*; Bob Nightengale, "Not Just a Peacemaker," TSN, March 6, 1989, p. 28.

Frank J. Olmsted

MAYS, Carl William "Sub" (b. November 12, 1891, Liberty, KY; d. April 4, 1971, El Cajon, CA), player and scout, excelled as a right-handed "submarine pitcher" in both the AL and NL from 1915 to 1929. Mays, one of eight children born to William Henry Mays, a Methodist minister and farmer, and Louisa (Callie) Mays, was forced to leave school when his father died in 1904. The 5-foot 11½-inch, 195-pound Mays began his professional baseball career with Boise, ID (WTL) in 1912. He pitched with Portland, OR (NWL) in 1913 and compiled a 24–8 mark with Providence, RI (IL) in 1914. He joined the Boston Red Sox (AL) and became one of their mound mainstays from 1915 to July 1919.

On July 13, 1919, Mays quit the Boston Red Sox in the middle of a game, claiming that he "could not win" for the team. Two weeks later, he was traded to the New York Yankees (AL). Ban Johnson,* AL president, tried to block the deal, but the New York State Supreme Court overruled him. Mays enjoyed very good seasons with New York in 1920 and 1921, but feuded with Yankees manager Miller Huggins* and was sold to the Cincinnati Reds (NL) in December 1923. He appeared in the 1916 and 1918 World Series with Boston and in the 1921 and 1922 fall classics with New York, winning 3 of 7 decisions with a 2.20 ERA. On August 16, 1920, Mays struck Cleveland Indian shortstop Ray Chapman* on the left temple with a pitch in the strike zone. Chapman died that night, the only major league fatality in history. Mays was absolved of all blame in the tragedy when a move to bar him from the game failed.

Mays spent five years with the Cincinnati Reds (NL) from 1924 to 1929, experiencing two good seasons there, and finished his major league career with the New York Giants (NL) in 1929. He hurled for Portland, OR (PCL) and in 1930 and for Toledo, OH-Louisville, KY (AA) in 1930–1931, retiring following the latter season. Mays won at least 20 games five times in the major leagues, compiled a lifetime record of 208 wins and 126 losses (.623), completed 231 of 325 starts, struck out 862 batters, hurled 29 shutouts, and boasted a 2.92 ERA. In his best year (1921), Mays finished 27–9 and led the AL in games won, best winning percentage (.750), games (49), and innings pitched (336.1). Mays scouted for the AL Cleveland Indians (1958–1961), AL Kansas City Athletics (1962), and NL Milwaukee Braves (1963) in the northwest and operated a boys' baseball school.

BIBLIOGRAPHY: Carl Mays file, National Baseball Library, Cooperstown, NY; Frederick G. Lieb, *The Boston Red Sox* (New York, 1947); Robert Redmount, *The Red Sox Encyclopedia* (Champaign, IL, 1998); Frank Graham, *The New York Yankees* (New York 1943); Gene Karst and Martin J. Jones, Jr., *Who's Who in Professional Baseball* (New Rochelle, NY, 1973); F. C. Lane, "Carl Mays' Cynical Definition of Pitching Efficiency," *BM* 37 (August 1928), pp. 391–392; Craig Carter, ed., *TSN Daguerreotypes*, 8th ed. (St. Louis, MO, 1990); Brent P. Kelley, *The Case For: Those Overlooked by the Baseball Hall of Fame* (Jefferson, NC, 1992); Bob McGarigle, *Baseball's Greatest Tragedy* (Hicksville, NY, 1972); Carl Mays, "Is Hornsby Baseball's Greatest Hitter?" *BM* 34 (February 1925), pp. 391–392; Carl Mays, "My Attitude Towards the Unfortunate Chapman," *BM* 25 (November 1920), pp. 575–577, 607; Eugene C. Murdock, *Ban*

Johnson (Westport, CT, 1982); Eugene C. Murdock, taped interview with Waite Hoyt, March 12, 1976; Richard Scheinin, *Field of Screams* (New York, 1994); Mike Sowell, *The Pitch That Killed* (New York, 1989); Mark Gallagher, *The Yankee Encyclopedia*, vol. 3 (Champaign, IL, 1997); Lee Allen, *The Cincinnati Reds* (New York, 1948); *TSN*, February 14, 1944, August 10, 1963, April 17, 1971.

Eugene Murdock

MAYS, Willie Howard "Say Hey" (b. May 6, 1931, Westfield, AL), player, coach, and executive, is the son of steel mill worker William Mays and Ann Mays, both excellent athletes. Since Mays' parents were divorced soon after his birth, he grew up with his Aunt Sarah in Fairfield, AL. Mays attended Fairfield Industrial High School, where he starred in basketball, football, and especially baseball. A semi-pro baseball player early, Mays joined the Birmingham, AL Barons (NNL) at age 17. In 1950, the New York Giants (NL) purchased the 5-foot 10½-inch, 170-pound right-handed outfielder and assigned him to Trenton, NJ (ISL). After 35 games with Minneapolis, MN (AA) in 1951, Mays joined the New York Giants. Under manager Leo Durocher,* Mays became the regular center fielder and helped the Giants win the NL pennant after being 13½ games behind the Brooklyn Dodgers. He was named NL Rookie of the Year.

After serving in 1952 and 1953 in the U.S. Army, Mays in 1954 returned to the Giants and captured the NL batting title with a .345 average. He led the NL with 13 triples, sparked the Giants to the NL pennant and world championship in four games over the Cleveland Indians, and made an unbelievable catch of a towering drive by the Indians' Vic Wertz.* No player ever made a more publicized catch, which many considered to be the greatest ever made on any baseball diamond. This feat epitomized Mays' career. His defensive play, ranging from his famous basket-catch to nailing a runner at home plate with a perfect throw, was accomplished with a unique flair.

With the Giants in New York (1951, 1954–1957) and San Francisco (1958–1971), Mays continually amazed baseball crowds and batted above .300 10 times. He led the NL in HR four times, slugging 51 in 1955 and 52 ten years later, hit at least 30 HR 11 different seasons, and scored over 100 runs 12 consecutive seasons. Besides winning the NL's MVP Award (1954, 1965), he was named *TSN* Outstanding NL Player (1954, 1965), outfielder on All-Star major league teams (1954, 1957–1960) and on NL All-Star fielding teams (1958–1968), and baseball's Player of the Decade (1960–1969). Mays slugged four HR in one game once and three in one game twice and set the NL record by hitting two or more round trippers in one game 63 times. The first major league player to hit at least 50 HR and steal at least 20 bases in a season (1955), he remains one of the few players in major league history to slug 30 HR and steal 30 bases in the same season (1956–1957).

Between 1954 and 1973, Mays played in every All-Star game with a composite .315 batting average. He participated in 20 World Series games (1951,

1954, 1962, and 1973) and batted .239. An excellent base runner, Mays stole 40 bases in 1957 and 338 career bases. He also set NL standards for most putouts (7,095) and chances (7,431) accepted by an outfielder. In May 1972, Mays was traded to the New York Mets (NL). The Mets ownership assumed his playing contract and signed him to 10-year pact (as a goodwill ambassador and part-time coach), taking effect after his retirement. Mays helped the Mets win the NL flag in 1973, but New York lost the World Series to the Oakland A's.

Mays retired at the end of the 1973 season. In his 22-year career, he played in 2,992 games with 2,062 runs scored, 3,283 hits, 523 doubles, 140 triples, 660 HR, 1,903 RBI, a .981 fielding average, and a .302 batting average. His 660 HR rank third on the all-time list behind Henry Aaron* and Babe Ruth.* Within three months after his induction into the National Baseball Hall of Fame (1979), Mays was ordered by Commissioner Bowie Kuhn* to choose between employment by the Mets and a company owning a hotel gambling casino. On October 29, 1979, Mays signed a 10-year contract with the Bally Manufacturing Corporation and ended his participation in baseball. In 1985, Commissioner Peter Ueberroth (OS) lifted the ban on Mays' involvement in baseball. Mays served as special assistant to the general manager of the San Francisco Giants in 1994. He made Major League Baseball's All-Century Team and ranked eighth among ESPN's top century athletes. Mays married Marghuerite Wendell Kennedy Chapman in February 1956 and adopted a son, Michael. After the marriage ended in divorce in 1961, Mays wed social worker Mae Allen in 1971.

BIBLIOGRAPHY: Willie Mays file, National Baseball Library, Cooperstown, NY; Barbara Carlisle Bigelow, ed., *Contemporary Black Biography*, vol. 3 (Detroit, MI, 1993), pp. 152–155; Mitchell Burkhardt, *Willie Mays* (Cupertino, CA, 1992); John Benson et al., *Baseball's Top 100* (Wilton, NC, 1997); Charles Einstein, *Willie Mays* (Greenwich, CT, 1972); Charles Einstein, *Willie's Time* (New York, 1992); John P. McCarthy, *Baseball's All-Time Dream Team* (Cincinnati, OH, 1994); Larry Moffi and Jonathan Kronstadt, *Crossing the Line* (Jefferson, NC, 1994); Ron Fimrite, *The Baseball Hall of Fame 50th Anniversary Book* (New York, 1988); Donald Honig, *Mays, Mantle, Snider* (New York, 1987); Donald Honig, *The Power Hitters* (St. Louis, MO, 1989); Noel Hynd, *The Giants of the Polo Grounds* (New York, 1988); J. Klein, "Willie Mays," *Sport* 77 (December 1986), pp. 61ff; G. Richard McKelvey, *Fisk's Homer, Willie's Catch and the Shot Heard 'Round the World* (Jefferson, NC, 1998); Willie Mays and Lou Sahidi, *Say Hey* (New York, 1988); Arnold Hano, *Willie Mays* (New York, 1966); Fred Stein and Nick Peters, *Giants Diary* (Berkeley, CA, 1987); Tom Murray, *Sport Magazine's All-Time All Stars* (New York, 1977); David L. Porter, ed., *African-American Sports Greats* (Westport, CT, 1995); *TSN Official Baseball Register, 1974*.
                                                                      John L. Evers

MAZEROSKI, William Stanley "Bill," "Maz" (b. September 5, 1936, Wheeling, WV), player and coach, set several major league fielding records as Pittsburgh Pirates (NL) second baseman from mid-1956 through 1972. A graduate of Warren Consolidated High of Tiltonsville, OH, he played basketball and pitched baseball there. He began his professional baseball career as a 17-year-old shortstop with Williamsport, PA (EL) in 1954. Midway through the following season, he joined the Hollywood, CA Stars (PCL) as a second baseman. After 80 games there in 1956, he came to the Pittsburgh Pirates as the NL team's second baseman. Although chosen for the first of seven years of All-Star appearances in 1958, Mazeroski did not attract national fame until he hit a HR in the 1960 World Series. In the deciding seventh game on October 13, Mazeroski slugged a dramatic HR in the last half of the ninth inning in a tie game to give the Pirates the championship over the New York Yankees.

During his major league career with Pittsburgh, he played 2,163 games, made 2,016 hits, including 294 doubles, 62 triples, and 138 HR, drove in 853 runs, and compiled a .260 batting average. A superior fielder, he led the NL's second basemen five times in putouts, nine times in assists, and three times in fielding percentage. He also played in three NL Championship Series and in two World Series, hitting .308. Mazeroski established major league records among second basemen for most double plays and games played in a season, most years leading the NL in assists and double plays, most consecutive years pacing in double plays, and most lifetime double plays. His NL records for second basemen included most years leading the NL in chances accepted, most career games, chances accepted, putouts, and assists.

Mazeroski, named *TSN* Major League Player of the Year in 1960, was selected as second baseman on NL All-Star fielding teams seven years and on several all-NL and all-major league teams by other publications and news services. Mazeroski served as a coach for the Pittsburgh Pirates in 1973 and Seattle Mariners (AL) in 1979–1980 and as a minor league batting instructor. The right-handed batter and thrower stood 5-feet 11-inches and weighed from 180 to 195 pounds during his playing career. Mazeroski married Milene Ruth Nicholson on October 11, 1958, has two sons, Darren and Daun, and lives near Greensburg, PA. A hunting and fishing enthusiast, he owns and operates a golf course at Rayland, OH and a nearby restaurant and bar at Yorkville, OH. As a major league player-participant, Mazeroski won several Astrojet golf tournaments conducted for professional athletes by an airline. Besides being inducted into several local sports halls of fame, he was named to the Pennsylvania Sports Hall of Fame in 1985. The Pirates retired his uniform number 9 in 1987.

BIBLIOGRAPHY: Bill Mazeroski file, National Baseball Library, Cooperstown, NY; John T. Bird, *Twin Killing: The Bill Mazeroski Story* (Birmingham, AL, 1995); Greensburg (PA) *Tribune-Review*, 1956–1972; Ron Fimrite, "The Valley Boys," *SI* 68 (May 23, 1988), p. 78–84; Jim Kaplan, "Bill Mazeroski,"*BRJ* 17 (1988), pp. 21–22; Brent P. Kelley, *The Case For: Those Overlooked by the Baseball Hall of Fame* (Jefferson, NC, 1992); Jim O'Brien, *Maz and the 1960 Bucs* (Pittsburgh, PA, 1994); Dick Groat and

Bill Surface, *The World Champion Pittsburgh Pirates* (New York, 1961); *Pittsburgh Pirates News Media Guides*, 1956–1972; Pittsburgh *Post-Gazette*, 1956–1972; Pittsburgh *Press*, 1956–1972; Chet Smith and Marty Wolfson, *Greater Pittsburgh Illustrated History of Sports* (Pittsburgh, PA, 1969); Dan Valenti, *Clout! The Top Home Runs in Baseball History* (Lexington, MA, 1989); Robert B. Van Atta, interview with Bill Mazeroski, n.d.; Bob Smizik, *The Pittsburgh Pirates* (New York, 1990); Richard L. Burtt, *The Pittsburgh Pirates, A Pictorial History* (Virginia Beach, VA, 1977); Rich Westcott, *Diamond Greats* (Westport, CT, 1988).

Robert B. Van Atta

MEADOWS, Henry Lee "Specs" (b. July 12, 1894, Oxford, NC; d. January 29, 1963, Daytona Beach, FL), player, was the first 20th-century major leaguer to wear glasses, leading to his distinctive nickname. Meadows grew up near Oxford, where his father produced tobacco, and attended nearby Horner Military Academy. He began wearing glasses at age six and was ridiculed frequently by opposing players during his youth. Meadows signed with the Durham, NC Bulls (NCSL) in 1913. He won 21 games 1913 and 19 the following season for Durham. His contract was sold to the St. Louis Cardinals (NL), where he played until being traded in July 1919 to the Philadelphia Phillies (NL). The Philadelphia Phillies shipped Meadows to the Pittsburgh Pirates (NL) in May 1923. He finished his career with Pittsburgh in 1929. During his major league career, Meadows won 188 games with 180 losses and a 3.37 ERA. He pitched 490 games and 3,160.2 innings. Meadows led the NL with 20 wins in 1926 and in losses with 23 in 1916 and 20 in 1919. His best seasons came with the Pittsburgh Pirates, where he compiled successive marks of 19–10, 20–9, and 19–10 from 1925 through 1927. Meadows pitched in the 1925 and 1927 World Series against the Washington Senators and New York Yankees, losing one game each time. The compact 5 foot 9 inch, 190 pound right-hander, who batted left, specialized as a spitballer early in his career and gave up that pitch when it was outlawed. He developed a career-ending sore arm in 1928.

Meadows made several unsuccessful minor league comeback attempts during the middle 1930s and managed Leesburg, VA (VL) in 1937 and Deland, FL (FSL) in 1938. He worked with the Internal Revenue Service in Daytona Beach, FL until his retirement in 1951. Meadows, who married Carrie Woodworth Meadows and has two children, is a member of the North Carolina Sports Hall of Fame.

BIBLIOGRAPHY: Lee Meadows file, National Baseball Library, Cooperstown, NY; *TSN*, February 9, 1963; Frederick G. Lieb, *The St. Louis Cardinals* (New York, 1945); Frederick G. Lieb and Stan Baumgartner, *The Philadelphia Phillies* (New York, 1953); Frederick G. Lieb, *The Pittsburgh Pirates* (New York, 1948); Richard L. Burtt, *The Pittsburgh Pirates, A Pictorial History* (Virginia Beach, VA, 1977); Bob Smizik, *The Pittsburgh Pirates: An Illustrated History* (New York, 1990).

Jim L. Sumner

MEDWICK, Joseph Michael "Joe," "Ducky," "Muscles" (b. November 24, 1911, Carteret, NJ; d. March 21, 1975, St. Petersburg, FL), player, manager, and coach, was the son of factory worker John Medwick and Elizabeth Medwick. A star athlete at Carteret High School, Medwick rejected an offer to play football at Notre Dame University to sign as an outfielder in 1929 with the St. Louis Cardinals (NL). In 1930, he hit .419 his first season at Scottdale, PA to lead the MAL. After batting .354 at Houston, TX (TL) in 1932, he joined the Cardinals and hit .349 that same season. During the next decade, Medwick hit at least .300 in the major leagues. In 1937, he won the coveted Triple Crown with a .374 batting mark, 31 HR, and 154 RBI.

In June 1940, the Cardinals traded Medwick to the Brooklyn Dodgers (NL) with pitcher Curt Davis* for four players and $125,000. Cardinals pitcher Bob Bowman beaned the 5-foot 10-inch, 187-pound, right-handed hitting slugger, putting him in the hospital with a severe concussion. Medwick survived the incident, which was investigated by Commissioner Kenesaw Mountain Landis* and a New York district attorney, but thereafter lacked his fierce edge at the plate. Although retaining his philosophy of "base hits and bucks," he lost his competitive determination. Medwick hit .337 for the New York Giants (NL) in 1944, but was traded to the Boston Braves (NL) in June of the next season. He returned to the Brooklyn Dodgers (NL) in 1946 and spent 1947 and part of 1948 with the St. Louis Cardinals (NL). Subsequently, he served as minor league player–manager at Houston, TX (TL) in 1948, Miami Beach, FL (FSL) in 1949, Raleigh, NC (CrL) in 1951 and Tampa, FL (FIL) in 1952. Medwick also was assistant baseball coach at St. Louis University from 1961 to 1965 and farm system hitting instructor for the St. Louis Cardinals (NL) from 1966 to 1975.

Medwick's National Baseball Hall of Fame (1968) career produced 2,471 hits in 1,984 games, 540 doubles, 113 triples, 205 HR, 1,383 RBI, a .324 batting average, and .505 slugging average. Medwick hit .326 in two World Series, but became the only player ever removed from a game for safety reasons. Angry Detroit Tigers fans bombarded him with fruit and garbage following his scuffle with Tigers third baseman Marv Owen in the final 1934 Series game. In July 1936, Medwick equalled the NL mark by making 10 consecutive hits. Besides setting the NL mark with 64 doubles the same season, he tied the major league mark by leading the NL in RBI from 1936 through 1938. On June 29, 1935, Medwick made a single, double, triple, and HR. He hit 40 or more doubles seven consecutive years from 1933 through 1939, made *TSN* All-Star team from 1935 through 1939, and won the NL's MVP Award in 1937.

Known as "Muscles" to his friends, Medwick received the nickname "Ducky" from a woman fan in Houston during the 1931 season. A manufacturer named a candy bar "The Ducky-Wucky," a name he truly despised. He married Isabelle Heutel of St. Louis on August 24, 1936 and had one son and one daughter.

BIBLIOGRAPHY: John Thom, *Champion Batsman of the 20th Century* (Los Angeles, CA, 1992); William F. McNeil, *The Dodgers Encyclopedia* (Champaign, IL, 1997); Richard Goldstein, *Superstars and Screwballs* (New York, 1991); Ducky Medwick file, National Baseball Library, Cooperstown, NY; Bob Broeg and Jerry Vickery, *St. Louis Cardinals Encyclopedia* (Grand Rapids, MI, 1998); Bill Borst, *Baseball Through a Knothole* (St. Louis, MO, 1977); Bob Broeg, *The Redbirds: A Century of Cardinals' Baseball* (St. Louis, MO, 1981); Robert Hood, *The Gashouse Gang* (New York, 1976); Peter Golenbock, *Bums* (New York, 1984); Gene Karst and Martin J. Jones, Jr., *Who's Who in Professional Baseball* (New Rochelle, NY, 1973); Frederick G. Lieb, *The St. Louis Cardinals* (New York, 1945); *Newsweek* 85 (March 31, 1975), p. 53; *NYT*, March 24, 1975, p. 34; Rob Rains, *The St. Louis Cardinals* (New York, 1992); Joseph Skrec, "Fame Forgotten: Joe Medwick," *TNP* 14 (1994), pp. 94–96; *Time* 105 (March 31, 1975), p. 83.

William A. Borst

MEEKIN, George Jouett (b. February 21, 1867, New Albany, IN; d. December 14, 1944, New Albany, IN), player, enjoyed a spectacular 1894 season that may have ruined his pitching career. He was the son of James H. Meekin, who once ran for mayor of New Albany, and Jennie (Russell) Meekin, and had one brother, Charles. His professional baseball career began in 1887. In 1891, the 6-foot, 180-pound right-hander entered the major leagues with the Louisville, KY Colonels (AA). Louisville joined the NL in 1892 and sent Meekin that season to the Washington Senators (NL). The New York Giants (NL) acquired him after the 1893 campaign.

In 1894, Meekin joined Indiana native Amos Rusie* in the New York Giants' pitching rotation. Nicknamed "The Iron Twins," Rusie won 36 games and Meekin compiled 33 victories against nine losses. Meekin's .786 winning percentage led the NL. The New York Giants finished second, but defeated the pennant-winning Baltimore Orioles in four straight games to take the Temple Cup Series. A fastball pitcher, Meekin also hit capably and belted three triples against the Cleveland Spiders (NL) on July 4, 1894.

After his one superb 1894 season, Meekin developed chronic arm problems. From 1895 to 1897, he posted records of 16–11, 26–14, and 20–11. The arm soreness caused Meekin to struggle with a 16–18 mark in 1898. In August 1899, the New York Giants sold him to the Boston Beaneaters (NL). Meekin's final major league season resulted in an 0–2 record with the Pittsburgh Pirates (NL) in 1900.

Meekin's major league career featured 153 wins, 133 losses, and a 4.07 ERA. He struck out 900 batters and walked 1,058 in 2,603.1 innings. Meekin, who also batted .243 lifetime, spent over 25 years with the New Albany Fire Department. He remained single and died of complications resulting from injuries sustained in a fall.

BIBLIOGRAPHY: *The Baseball Encyclopedia*, 10th ed. (New York, 1996); Peter J. Cava, Indiana-born major league player files, Peter J. Cava Collection, Indianapolis, IN;

Peter J. Cava, conversation with Betty Mengus, New Albany, IN Public Library, November 27, 1995; Jouett Meekin file, National Baseball Library, Cooperstown, NY; John Phillips, *CPC Baseball Almanac* (Cabin John, MD, 1993); Robert L. Tiemann and Mark Rucker, eds., *Nineteenth Century Baseball Stars* (Kansas City, MO, 1989); Bill Madden, *The Hoosiers of Summer* (Indianapolis, IN, 1994); Noel Hynd, *The Giants of the Polo Grounds* (New York, 1988); James D. Hardy, Jr., *The New York Giants Baseball Club* (Jefferson, NC, 1996); Frank Graham, *The New York Giants* (New York, 1952).

Peter J. Cava

MELE, Sabath Anthony "Sam" (b. January 21, 1923, Astoria, NY), player, scout, coach, and manager, spent 10 major league seasons as a player with six different teams including five AL clubs and one NL team. Despite his many trades and moves, Mele remained a remarkably consistent player both defensively and offensively. Mele attended NYU, where he starred in basketball for the Violets in 1943. One of his best games came when NYU defeated Temple University for their 11th consecutive victory. Mele tallied 17 points to lead both teams in scoring. Mele then served in the U.S. Marines and was stationed at Pearl Harbor.

Mele's professional baseball career began in 1946 with Louisville, KY (AA) and Scranton, PA (EL), where he hit a career-high .342. He opened the 1947 season in right field for the Boston Red Sox (AL) and hit .302, his best major league season. Over the next two seasons, Mele's batting average dropped to the .230s. The Boston Red Sox traded Mele to the Washington Senators (AL) in June 1949. During his four years with the Washington Senators, Mele batted in the .270 range and ranked second in 1950 and first in 1951 in the clutch-hitting index. In 1951, he shared the AL lead in doubles at 36 with George Kell* and teammate Eddie Yost* and netted a career-high 94 RBI.

Mele bounced around over the next four years with the Chicago White Sox (AL) from May 1952 to February 1954, Baltimore Orioles (AL) until July 1954, Boston Red Sox (AL) through June 1955, and Cincinnati Reds (NL) until January 1956, ending his major league playing career with the Cleveland Indians (AL). In the fourth inning on June 10, 1952, Mele tied a major league record for most RBI (6) and long hits (2) in an inning with a three-run HR and bases loaded triple against the Philadelphia Athletics. He played two more minor league seasons with Indianapolis, IN (AA) and Buffalo, NY (IL), retiring after the 1958 campaign. Mele fielded well, never making more than five errors in any of his 10-year major league seasons and finishing with a .985 career fielding average. In 1,046 games, he batted .267 with 80 HR and 544 RBI.

The Washington Senators (AL) hired Mele as a scout in 1959 and coach from July 1959 through 1960. After the Washington Senators became the Minnesota Twins in 1961, Mele replaced Cookie Lavagetto as Twins manager on June 23. He managed the Minnesota Twins through 1967, guiding them to second-place finishes in 1962 and 1966 and an AL pennant in 1965. In seven managerial seasons, Mele piloted the Minnesota Twins to a 524–436 win–loss mark. The Twins featured slugger Harmon Killebrew,* outfielder Tony Oliva,* and pitchers Jim Kaat* and Camilo Pascual.* The Minnesota Twins lost the 1965 World Series in seven games to the Los Angeles Dodgers. *TSN* named Mele Major League Manager of the Year in 1965. Mele, who married Constance Mary Clemens in January 1949, scouted for the Boston Red Sox from 1967 through 1994. During off-seasons, he wrote a sports column for the Quincy (MA) *Ledger*.

BIBLIOGRAPHY: Sam Mele file, National Baseball Library, Cooperstown, NY; Thomas Aylesworth and Benton Minks, *The Encyclopedia of Baseball Managers* (New York, 1990); Dave Moina and Dave Jarzyna, *Twenty-five Seasons* (Minneapolis, MN, 1986); Shirley Povich, *The Washington Senators* (New York, 1954); Robert Redmount, *The Red Sox Encyclopedia* (Champaign, IL, 1998); Jack Lautier, *Fenway Voices* (Camden, ME, 1990); *NYT*, 1943; Mike Shatzkin, ed., *The Ballplayers* (New York, 1990); John Thorn et al., eds., *Total Baseball*, 5th ed. (New York, 1997); *TSN Baseball Register*, 1967.

Lee E. Scanlon

MELTON, William Edwin "Bill" (b. July 7, 1945, Gulfport, MS), player, grew up in Southern California and graduated in 1963 from Duarte, CA High School, where he played football and basketball. The 6-foot 1-inch, 190-pound Melton did not play baseball until entering Citrus JC in Azuza, CA. The Chicago White Sox (AL) signed Melton in 1964. He played for Sarasota, FL (FSL) in 1965, Appleton, WI (ML) in 1966, and Evansville, IN (SL) in 1967 and split 1968 between Hawaii (PCL), Syracuse, NY (IL), and the Chicago White Sox.

Melton became the Chicago White Sox starting third baseman in 1969, batting .255, clouting 23 HR, including three on June 24 against the Seattle Pilots, and knocking in 87 runs. In 1970, he batted .263, set a then club record with 33 HR, and knocked in a career-high 96 RBI. The following season, Melton again hit 33 HR to become the first Chicago White Sox player to lead the AL in that category. He compiled 86 RBI and a .269 batting average in 1971 and made the AL All-Star team.

Melton missed two-thirds of the 1972 season due to a herniated disk in his back. The injury dealt a serious blow to the Chicago White Sox, but newly acquired slugger Dick Allen* became AL MVP that campaign. Melton returned in 1973 to belt 20 HR, drive in 87 runs, and produce a career-high .277 average. His offensive production declined thereafter. The Chicago White Sox traded him in December 1976 to the California Angels (AL). Melton finished his major league career with the Cleveland Indians (AL) in 1977.

The power hitting Melton in July 1970 established or tied several major league and AL strikeout records, including most consecutive strikeouts in official at-bats (11), in a doubleheader (7), in three consecutive games (10), and in four consecutive games (12). Defensively, Melton encountered problems. He led AL third basemen in errors in 1974 (24) and 1975 (26) and compiled a lifetime .949 fielding average. In 10 major league seasons, Melton played in 1,114 games, garnered 1,004 hits, 162 doubles, 160 HR, 496 runs scored, 591 RBI, and a .253 batting average. Melton, whose wife is Rybak, sold office buildings in Southern California. The Chicago, IL resident works for the Chicago White Sox community relations department.

BIBLIOGRAPHY: Larry Keith, "Secret Weapon of the Sox," *SI* 35 (August 9, 1971), pp. 40–41; Bill Melton file, National Baseball Library, Cooperstown, NY; *Chicago White Sox Media Guide, 1972*; Ross Forman, "Former Chisox Slugger Bill Melton Interviewed," *SCD* 20 (July 30, 1993), pp. 240–242; Ross Forman, "Melton Changes Mind, Won't Sign at National," *SCD* 20 (July 30, 1993), pp. 250–251; *TSN Baseball Register*, 1978; Richard Lindberg, *Sox* (New York, 1984); Richard Lindberg, *Who's on Third?* (South Bend, IN, 1983); Bob Vanderberg, *Sox: From Lane and Fain to Fisk and Zisk* (Chicago, IL, 1982).

Edward J. Pavlick

MENDEZ, Jose de la Caridad (b. March 19, 1887, Cardenas, Cuba; d. October 31, 1928, Havana, Cuba), player and manager, was a lean, rangy, right-handed pitcher with a smooth delivery and tremendous deceptive speed. A smart hurler with changing speeds, a rising fastball, and sharp-breaking curveball, the small, 5-foot 8-inch, 160-pound Mendez developed into one of the greatest black pitchers of all time. Mendez possessed long arms and exceptionally long fingers, enabling him to put great spin on the ball. He threw with such graceful ease that batters found it difficult to time his pitches. The velocity of his fastball was considered by some to exceed that of Smoky Joe Williams.* Superstar John Henry Lloyd* claimed that he never saw a pitcher superior to Mendez.

During his prime, the Cuban hurler outpitched National Baseball Hall-of-Famers Christy Mathewson* and Eddie Plank* in exhibition games in his native nation. His CUWL record for the 1908–1909 season came to 15–6. In 1910, he posted a 7–0 record in the CUSL and 11–2 in the CUWL. Mendez finished his Cuban career with a 74–25 ledger, with 40 percent of his losses coming after 1913.

Mendez came to the United States in 1908 to pitch for the Brooklyn Royal Giants and is credited with a superb 44–2 record for the Cuban Stars in 1909. For the Cuban Stars in 1910, he engaged with Rube Foster* in a classic 11-inning duel that was ended by darkness with a 4–4 deadlock. Mendez joined J. L. Wilkinson's* multiracial All-Nations club in 1912 and remained there until developing arm trouble in 1917. The versatile Mendez continued his career as a shortstop and outfielder for the Chicago American Giants in 1918 and Detroit Stars in 1919.

Mendez reunited with Wilkinson in 1920 as player–manager of the Kansas City Monarchs (NNL), where he performed at shortstop and still pitched occasionally. Under his leadership, the Monarchs won NNL pennants in 1923, 1924, and 1925. In the victorious 1924 World Series against the Philadelphia Hilldale club, Mendez pitched in four games, hurled a shutout in his only start, won two decisions without a loss, and recorded an impressive 1.42 ERA. In his last season in the Negro Leagues, the Monarchs lost to the Chicago American Giants in the hard-fought 1926 NNL Championship Series. Mendez, who died of bronchopneumonia, was elected to the Cuban Hall of Fame in 1939.

BIBLIOGRAPHY: Janet Bruce, *The Kansas City Monarchs* (Lawrence, KS, 1985); John B. Holway, *Blackball Stars* (Westport, CT, 1988); John B. Holway, "Cuba's Black Diamond," *BRJ* 10 (1981), pp. 139–144; Robert W. Peterson, *Only the Ball Was White* (Englewood Cliffs, NJ, 1970); James A. Riley, *The All-Time All-Stars of Black Baseball* (Cocoa, FL, 1983); James A. Riley, *The Biographical Encyclopedia of the Negro Baseball Leagues* (New York, 1994); James A. Riley, interviews with former Negro League players, James A. Riley Collection, Cocoa, FL.

James A. Riley

MENKE, Denis John (b. July 21, 1940, Algona, IA), player, manager, and coach, is the son of Walt Menke, a minor league baseball player and farmer, and Mary Menke and grew up in the rural northwestern Iowa. Authorities rated him the best baseball player to come out of the Hawkeye state since Bob Feller.* As a St. John's High School pitcher, Menke finished 34–0 and exhibited good hitting potential. His excellent fielding skills and strong throwing arm made him one of the most sought-after prospects in baseball history. Following Menke's high school graduation in 1958, scout Eddie Dancisak signed the 17-year-old to a $125,000 bonus contract with the Milwaukee Braves (NL).

The 6-foot, 180-pound Menke spent five minor league seasons with Cedar Rapids, IA (3IL) and Midland, TX (SpL) in 1958, Cedar Rapids, IA (3IL) in 1959, Yakima, WA (NWL) in 1960, and Vancouver, Canada (PCL) in 1961. During this span, Menke batted .299 with 70 HR, and 307 RBI in 524 games. These impressive statistics earned Menke a promotion to the major leagues in 1962. As a rookie with the Milwaukee Braves, Menke played every position except pitcher and catcher. His offensive production suffered, as he batted just .192 with two HR and 16 RBI in 50 games. By the All-Star break, Milwaukee returned Menke to the minor leagues with Toronto, Canada (IL).

In 1963, Menke returned to the major leagues permanently with Milwaukee. Although playing 82 of his 146 games at shortstop, the utility man also performed at four other positions. He batted .234 with 11 HR and 50 RBI and credited his success to teammates Eddie Mathews* and Roy McMillan.* Menke became the Milwaukee Braves starting shortstop in 1964, batting .283

with a career high 20 HR and 65 RBI. Menke seemed on the verge of fulfilling his high school expectations. Several setbacks, including a dislocated shoulder and recurring back spasms limited him to 71 games and a .243 batting average in 1965. Menke's injury affected his play at shortstop and at the plate. Following the Braves' move to Atlanta, he batted .251 with 15 HR in 1966. After a horrible spring training and weak 1967 season, Menke was traded to the Houston Astros (NL) that October.

With the Houston Astros from 1968 to 1971, Menke blossomed. After replacing injured Joe Morgan* at second base, he hit .249 with six HR and 56 RBI and garnered team MVP honors. Menke tied major league records by twice taking part in five double plays in a single game, twice clouting grand slam HR to win games in the bottom of the ninth inning, and belting two grand slam HR in one game. He made the NL All-Star teams in both 1969 and 1970. His best season came in 1970, when he posted a .304 batting average with 92 RBI and 13 HR. Menke became the Houston Astros' full-time first baseman in 1971, but his batting average dipped to .246. In November 1971, he and Morgan were involved in a deal that helped establish Cincinnati's "Big Red Machine." With the Cincinnati Reds, Menke finally started at his favorite position, third base. He batted .233 with nine HR and homered off Catfish Hunter* of the Oakland A's in Game 5 of the 1972 World Series. Menke batted only .191 in 1973 and returned to the Houston Astros in February 1974 for his final major league season.

In 13 major league seasons, Menke batted .250 with 101 HR and 606 RBI. The ultimate utility player appeared in 841 games at shortstop, 420 at third base, 233 at second base, 162 at first base, and five in the outfield. Menke entered the insurance and real estate business in Houston and managed Burlington, IA (ML) in 1977 and Dunedin, FL (FSL) in 1978 and 1979. He later coached for the Toronto Blue Jays (AL) in 1980 and 1981, Houston Astros from 1983 to 1988, Philadelphia Phillies (NL) from 1989 to 1996, and Cincinnati Reds since 1997. He married Jean Gitzinger in October 1963 and has three children.

BIBLIOGRAPHY: Bill Ballew, "Denis Menke," *SCD* 21 (July 8, 1994), pp. 170–171; Gary Caruso, *The Braves Encyclopedia* (Philadelphia, PA, 1995); Robert H. Walker, *Cincinnati and the Big Red Machine* (Bloomington, IN, 1988); Bill Ballew, "Honor Roll," *Tomahawk* 6 (June 1994), p. 27; Bob Buege, *The Milwaukee Braves: A Baseball Eulogy* (Milwaukee, WI, 1988); Bob Buege, "Milwaukee Madness," *OTBN* 6 (1994), pp. 12–14; Bob Buege, *Eddie Mathews and the National Pastime* (Milwaukee, WI, 1994); Denis Menke file, National Baseball Library, Cooperstown, NY; *Milwaukee Braves Yearbook*, 1963–1964; Mike Shatzkin, ed., *The Ballplayers* (New York, 1990); John Thorn et al., eds., *Total Baseball*, 5th ed. (New York, 1997); Don Wade, "Bonus Baby Denis Menke Is Still in the Game," *Tomahawk* 7 (September 1997), p. 28.

Jerry J. Wright

MERKLE, Frederick Charles "Fred" (b. December 20, 1888, Watertown, WI; d. March 2, 1956, Daytona Beach, FL), player, was born of German parentage and grew up in Toledo, OH. The 6-foot 1-inch, 190-pound first baseman played semiprofessional baseball in Toledo in 1905 and 1906 before signing his first professional contract with Tecumseh, MI (SML). His success with Tecumseh in 1907 motivated manager John McGraw* of the New York Giants (NL) to purchase him for $2,500. Merkle made 47 plate appearances that year with the New York Giants, hitting .255.

The following year, the 19-year-old rookie was involved in one of the most controversial plays in baseball history. On September 23, the New York Giants met the Chicago Cubs at the Polo Grounds in New York. Both teams, along with the Pittsburgh Pirates, were involved in a tight race for the NL championship. Fred Tenney,* the New York Giants' regular first baseman, was out of the lineup with an injury, thus thrusting Merkle into his first start of the season. The game entered the bottom of the ninth inning tied, 1–1. With two men out, Harry "Moose" McCormick singled. Merkle followed with a single, sending McCormick to third base. Shortstop Al Bridwell then lined a shot to center field, scoring McCormick with the putative winning run. Merkle, assuming that the game had ended, sprinted to the locker room without touching second base. After some confusion, Chicago Cubs second baseman Johnny Evers* got the ball and tagged second base.

A heated argument arose, with umpires Hank O'Day* and Bob Emslie finally agreeing with the Chicago Cubs that Merkle was the third out, that McCormick's run did not count, and that the game was still tied. Since the spectators had swarmed onto the field, extra innings were an impossibility. Ultimately, the NL office backed the umpires and declared that the game would have to be replayed at season's end, if necessary. The Chicago Cubs and the New York Giants finished the regular season with identical records of 98 wins, 55 losses, as the Cubs captured the playoff.

Sportswriters and fans endlessly excoriated Merkle for his rookie mistake. The *NYT*, for example, began its account of the game with the words "censurable stupidity by player Merkle." Merkle's teammates and McGraw stood by him, however. Within a few years, he had become the New York Giants' regular first baseman.

Merkle enjoyed a solid 16-year major league career with the New York Giants, Brooklyn Robins (NL), New York Yankees (AL), and ironically, the Chicago Cubs, compiling a .273 lifetime batting average. He made 1,580 hits, including 290 doubles and 733 RBI, and also stole 272 bases. He appeared in 27 World Series games (1911–1913, 1916, 1918), hitting .239. But baseball authorities forever remembered him for one "bonehead" play on September 23, 1908. He was survived by three daughters, Mrs. L. J. Robinson, Mrs. John Kasbaum, and Jeannette.

BIBLIOGRAPHY: *The Baseball Encyclopedia*, 10th ed. (New York, 1996); G. H. Fleming, *The Unforgettable Season* (New York, 1982); Frederick Merkle file, National Baseball Library, Cooperstown, NY; Warren Brown, *The Chicago Cubs* (New York, 1946); Frank Graham, *The Brooklyn Dodgers* (New York, 1945); Charles C. Alexander, *John*

McGraw (New York, 1988); Ray Robinson, *Matty: An American Hero* (New York, 1993); Frank Graham, *The New York Giants* (New York, 1952); Noel Hynd, *The Giants of the Polo Grounds* (New York, 1988); G. H. Fleming, "The Merkle Blunder; A Kaleidoscopic View," *TNP* 1 (Fall 1982), pp. 26–31; Lawrence Ritter, *The Glory of Their Times* (New York, 1966).

David S. Matz

MESSERSMITH, John Alexander "Andy" (b. August 6, 1945, Toms River, NJ), player, was a 6-foot 1-inch, 200-pound right-handed pitcher who grew up in Southern California. After winning second-team All-American baseball honors at the University of California, Berkeley, he signed with the California Angels (AL) for $30,000 in 1966. In July 1968, California promoted Messersmith from Seattle, WA (PCL) and inserted him in the starting rotation. Messersmith's first full season saw him compile a 16–11 win–loss record on a 1969 Angels team that triumphed only 71 times. During Messersmith's five seasons with the Angels from 1968 to 1972, his .557 winning percentage far surpassed California's .467 mark.

California traded Messersmith in November 1972 to the Los Angeles Dodgers (NL), where he enjoyed three successful seasons. In 1974, he led the NL in winning percentage (.769), shared the honor for most victories (20 against only 6 losses), and placed second in strikeouts (221) and innings pitched (292.1). He enjoyed an MVP-quality season in 1975, leading the NL in games started (40) and completed (19), innings pitched (321.2), shutouts (7), and fewest hits per nine innings (6.8), and ranking second with a 2.29 ERA. Managers named him to four All-Star teams (1971, 1974–1976), but he appeared only in the 1974 classic. He helped the Dodgers take the 1974 NL Championship Series but both lost decisions in the World Series to the victorious Oakland A's. In March 1976, he received free agency in a much publicized challenge to the "reserve clause." The reserve clause was a clause in the contract of a professional athlete that bound the player to that particular team. The Atlanta Braves (NL) in April 1976 signed Messersmith, who struggled to produce winning records on a losing team. His final seasons came with the New York Yankees (AL) in 1978 and Los Angeles Dodgers in 1979.

A right-handed batter, Messersmith tied a major league record for pitchers by doubling three times on April 25, 1975. He bunted and executed the hit and run effectively, ran the bases well, and often slid recklessly. His 12-year major league career featured a 130–99 win–loss record and 2.86 ERA. Opponents compiled the third lowest batting average (.212) against Messersmith, behind only Sandy Koufax* and Nolan Ryan.* Messersmith allowed the fourth fewest hits per game (6.94). Over the last four decades, Messersmith's ERA remains third lowest behind Koufax and Greg Maddux.*

BIBLIOGRAPHY: Andy Messersmith file, National Baseball Library, Cooperstown, NY; *The Baseball Encyclopedia*, 10th ed. (New York, 1996); Roy Blount, Jr., "Lots of

Stuff and No Nonsense," *SI 32* (March 1972), pp. 22–29; Gene Brown, ed., *The New York Times Encyclopedia of Sports* 2 (New York, 1979); Gene Karst and Martin J. Jones, Jr., *Who's Who in Professional Baseball* (New Rochelle, NY, 1973); Dave Masterson and Timm Boyle, *Baseball's Best: The MVP's* (Chicago, IL, 1985); Ross Newhan, *The California Angels* (New York, 1982); William F. McNeil, *The Dodgers Encyclopedia* (Champaign, IL, 1997); Walter Alston, *A Year at a Time* (Waco, TX, 1976); John Thorn et al., eds., *Total Baseball*, 5th ed. (New York, 1997); *TSN Official Baseball Register, 1980*.

Gaymon L. Bennett

MEUSEL, Emil Frederick "Irish" (b. June 9, 1893, Oakland, CA; d. March 1, 1963, Long Beach, CA), and **Robert William "Long Bob" MEUSEL** (b. July 19, 1896, San Jose, CA; d. November 28, 1977, Downey, CA), players and coach, were the last of six children of teamster Charles F. Meusel and Mary (Smith) Meusel. They were educated in Los Angeles schools, with Emil completing three years at Manual Arts High School and Robert graduating from Los Angeles High School. Emil married Evangeline R. Proctor on May 17, 1917 and Estella R. Dansereau on October 1, 1945, having an adopted son in the first marriage. Robert wed Edith Cowan on December 14, 1921 and had one daughter.

For six years, the Meusel brothers were outfield rivals on the two New York teams. Emil played for the New York Giants (NL) and Robert for the New York Yankees (AL). From 1921 to 1923, they opposed each other in the World Series. The Meusels reached the major leagues rather late. Emil, nicknamed "Irish" because of a ruddy complexion and presumably Irish appearance, spent five seasons in the minor leagues before being drafted by the Philadelphia Phillies (NL) in 1918 at age 25. Robert joined the New York Yankees in 1920 at age 24 after three seasons with Vernon, CA (PCL) and a U.S. Navy hitch.

The 5-foot 11½-inch, 178-pound Irish was traded to the New York Giants (NL) in July 1921, when he achieved a career-high .343 batting average. Released after the 1926 season, he played briefly for the Brooklyn Robins (NL) and Toledo OH (AA) in 1927, returned to the PCL with Oakland, CA in 1928 and Sacramento, CA in 1929, and in 1930 rejoined the New York Giants (NL) as coach. After a few games with Omaha, NE (WL) in 1931, he retired from baseball. For 15 years until his death, he served as a gate guard at the Santa Anita and Hollywood Park Race Tracks in California. A solid, nonspectacular left fielder, the right-handed Irish compiled a .310 career average over 11 seasons (he had a one-game tryout with the Washington Senators [AL] in 1914), but was hampered by a weak throwing arm. He made 1,521 hits, 250 doubles, and 106 HR, scored 701 runs, and knocked in 819 runs. In 1923, he led the NL with 125 RBI. He averaged .276 in four World Series, outhit Robert in the 1921–1923 contests, and was regarded as a hard out with men on base.

Robert batted one point less than his brother (.309) in 11 years with the AL New York Yankees (1920–1929) and NL Cincinnati Reds (1930). His batting average in six World Series was only .225 and included 24 strikeouts. In 1,407 major league games, he made 1,693 hits, 368 doubles, and 156 HR and struck out 619 times. Nevertheless, Robert proved the superior player. Batting right-handed, the 6-foot 3-inch, 190 pounder exceeded .300 in seven of his first eight seasons with the New York Yankees. In 1925, his one off-year for batting average (.290), he led the AL in HR (33) and RBI (138). Only two other players have equalled his mark of hitting for the cycle (single, double, triple, and HR in one game) three times. Although many have exceeded his career 1,067 RBI, he ranks 14th all-time for productivity with a remarkable .76 runs driven in per game. He became a legitimate member of the Yankees' famed "Murderers' Row."

Robert patrolled left field (the Yankee sun field) and compensated for his sometimes casual pursuit of fly balls with one of baseball's strongest, most accurate throwing arms. Since his throwing motion imparted a spin to the ball that made it bounce eccentrically, he threw on the fly like an infielder. Even Ty Cobb* held third base on sacrifice flies to Meusel. Robert tied for the AL lead in outfield assists in 1921 with 28 and led the following year with 24. After being released by Cincinnati in 1930, he played two years in the minor leagues. In his last 15 years, he served as a security guard at a U.S. Navy installation. In contrast to the ebullient Irish, handsome Bob was taciturn and self-contained. Reputedly, he said "Hello" to his teammates at the beginning of the season, "Good-bye" at the end, and little else in between.

BIBLIOGRAPHY: Joseph G. Donner, "Hitting for the Cycle," *BRJ* 10 (1981), pp. 75–81; Joseph Durso, *Casey* (Englewood Cliffs, NJ, 1967); Frank Graham, *The New York Yankees* (New York, 1943); Mark Gallagher, *The Yankee Encyclopedia*, vol. 3 (Champaign, IL, 1997); Leo Trachtenberg, *The Wonder Team* (Bowling Green, OH, 1995); Dave Anderson et al., *The Yankees* (New York, 1979); Noel Hynd, *The Giants of the Polo Grounds* (New York, 1988); Frank Graham, *The New York Giants* (New York, 1952); Donald Honig, *Baseball When the Grass Was Real* (New York, 1977); Donald Honig, *October Heroes* (New York, 1979); Los Angeles *Times*, March 16, 1963; Emil Meusel and Robert Meusel files, National Baseball Library, Cooperstown, NY; John Mosedale, *The Greatest of All: The 1927 New York Yankees* (New York, 1975); *NYT*, November 30, 1977; Lawrence S. Ritter, *The Glory of Their Times* (New York, 1966); George Herman Ruth, *Babe Ruth's Own Book of Baseball* (New York, 1928); A. D. Suehsdorf, interviews with Mark Koenig, July 12, 22, 1983.

A. D. Suehsdorf

MEUSEL, Robert William "Long Bob." *See* Emil Frederick "Irish" Meusel.

MEYERLE, Levi Samuel "Long Levi" (b. July 16, 1845, Philadelphia, PA; d. November 4, 1921, Philadelphia, PA), player, was the son of laborer–shoe-cutter Jacob Meyerle and Margaret Meyerle, of German descent. Meyerle was educated in the Philadelphia schools and learned the building trades, but preferred sharpening his athletic skills on the city's fields during the post-Civil War baseball boom. As a pitcher, he played for the Geary Base Ball Club of Philadelphia, PA in 1867. By 1869 he became "first substitute" for the Philadelphia Athletics, appearing as catcher, pitcher, third baseman, and right fielder in 34 of the team's 49 games. Teamed with Alfred Reach* and other notables, he developed into an excellent batter. The following season, Meyerle joined the original professional Chicago White Stockings for $1,500 annually. Meyerle concentrated on third base, the position he played most frequently through 1884.

In 1871, Meyerle returned to the Philadelphia Athletics of the newly formed NA and led them to the championship with a superlative .492 batting average, .500 on-base percentage and .700 slugging average. By a decisive margin, he won pro baseball's first batting crown. Meyerle remained with the Athletics in 1872, but performed for the rival Philadelphia Whites (NA) in 1873 and 1875. In 1874, he starred for the Chicago White Stockings (NA). During these five NA seasons, the right-handed batting and throwing Meyerle compiled a .365 batting average, made 390 hits, and scored 249 runs in 222 games. The 6-foot 1-inch, 177-pound Meyerle earned the nick-name "Long Levi" in an era of much smaller players. Defensively, he lacked quickness and agility and was described by the press as "good hit, no field." Alfred H. Spink stated, "Meyerle was a very fair fielder, but his best asset was his ability to hit the ball hard."

On April 21, 1876, Meyerle played for the Philadelphia Athletics in the first NL game. For a weak team, he batted .340 and fielded only .791. In December, the NL expelled the Athletics and New York Mutuals for failing to play out the schedule. This move virtually ended the major league career of Meyerle, a Philadelphia favorite. He batted .327 in 27 games for the woeful Cincinnati Red Stockings (NL) of 1877 and briefly returned to the major leagues in 1884 for three games with the Philadelphia Keystones (UA). From 1877 to 1883, Meyerle made minor league stops in Philadelphia, PA, Springfield, MA, Washington, DC, and Rochester, NY. In 85 NL games, he batted .329 with 123 hits, 57 runs scored, and 49 RBI. He and his Irish bride, Anna, had no children. After 1884 they remained in Philadelphia, where he worked as a lather, plasterer, painter, and carpenter.

BIBLIOGRAPHY: Levi Meyerle file, National Baseball Library, Cooperstown, NY; Lee Allen, "Cooperstown Corner: Pro Ball's First Batting Champ," TSN (August 31, 1968), p. 6; Weston Fisler Notebook, National Baseball Library, Cooperstown, NY; "Levi Meyerle," New York Clipper 27 (June 21, 1879), p. 101; Alfred E. Spink, The National Game (St. Louis, MO, 1911); Robert L. Tiemann and Mark Rucker, eds., Nineteenth Century Stars (Kansas City, MO, 1989); William J. Ryczek, Blackguards and Red Stockings (Jefferson, NC, 1992).

James D. Smith III

MEYERS, John Tortes "Chief" (b. July 29, 1880, Riverside, CA; d. July 25, 1971, San Bernardino, CA), player, caught in the major leagues for nine seasons, including the first six with the New York Giants (NL). He played on four NL pennant winners, the 1911–1913 New York Giants and the 1916 Brooklyn Robins. Meyers came from the Cahuilla tribe, usually called the Mission Indians of Southern California. His father, a Union army veteran, died in 1887. Meyers, who was brought up by his mother, Felicite, married Anna B. Brower in 1910. They had no known children. His Riverside, CA *Press* obituary denies that he ever married.

Meyers attended Riverside High School and played semiprofessional baseball in southern California, Arizona, and New Mexico. In the summer of 1905, the 25-year-old, 5-foot 1-inch, 194 pounder caught for the Clifton, AZ team in an Albuquerque, NM tournament. Dartmouth College student Ralph Glaze, who also played in the tournament, liked Meyers' athletic ability and recruited him. Meyers spent most of the 1905–1906 academic year at Dartmouth, but never played on the college baseball team.

In 1906, Meyers left with Dartmouth College baseball coach Billy Hamilton* to join the Harrisburg, PA club (TSL). At almost 26 years old, he played his first season in organized baseball in 1906. After minor league stops at Butte, MT, and St. Paul, MN, Meyers joined the New York Giants in September 1908 and witnessed the bizarre finish of that NL pennant race. The New York Giants sent catcher Roger Bresnahan* to the St. Louis Cardinals as player–manager in December 1908, giving Meyers some catching duties. Between 1910 and 1915, Meyers caught regularly for the New York Giants. He batted particularly well during the NL pennant-winning seasons from 1911 to 1913, hitting .332, .358, and .312. He batted .300 in the 1911 World Series against the Philadelphia Athletics and .357 with 15 hits in the 1912 World Series against the Boston Red Sox. In the 1913 fall classic against the Philadelphia Athletics, he played in just one game and went hitless. Meyers spent the 1916 season with the NL champion Brooklyn Robins and divided the next campaign between Brooklyn and the Boston Braves (NL). In the 1916 World Series against the Boston Red Sox, he batted .200 and caught three of the five games. Two years followed in the minor leagues before his retirement from organized baseball. In nine major league seasons, he batted .291 with 826 hits and 363 RBI in 992 games.

Meyers served in the U.S. Marine Corps during World War I and returned to his native California to work as a police chief for the Mission Indian agency. He remembered fondly his association with the New York Giants of John McGraw* and with anger his minority status as a Native American.

BIBLIOGRAPHY: Chief Meyers file, National Baseball Library, Cooperstown, NY; Lawrence Ritter, *The Glory of Their Times* (New York, 1966); Noel Hynd, *The Giants of the Polo Grounds* (New York, 1988); Charles C. Alexander, *John McGraw* (New York, 1988); Ray Robinson, *Matty: An American Hero* (New York, 1993); Frank Graham, *The New York Giants* (New York, 1952); Frank Graham, *McGraw of the Giants* (New York, 1944).

Leverett T. Smith, Jr.

MILAN, Jesse Clyde "Deerfoot" (b. March 25, 1887, Linden, TN; d. March 3, 1953, Orlando FL), player, manager, coach, and scout, began his professional baseball career in 1906 with Wichita, KS (WA) and joined the Washington Senators (AL) in 1907. Cliff Blankenship, a convalescent catcher, was sent to Wichita to sign Milan. Before returning to Washington, Blankenship scouted and signed Walter Johnson* in Weiser, ID. Milan and Johnson both came from rural areas and became roommates and inseparable friends. The more competitive 5-foot 9-inch, 185-pound Milan, who batted left and threw right-handed, often drove Johnson when he became lackadaisical. During the winter months, they invariably hunted together in either Texas or Tennessee. Considered faster than Ty Cobb,* Milan made an excellent center-fielder with Washington and played shallow like Tris Speaker.* Although an average player for manager Joe Cantillon (1907–1909), he starred under Jimmy McAleer (1910–1911). After a lengthy hold-out with Johnson in 1911, he hit .315. Besides achieving a lifetime .285 batting average, he made 2,100 hits, 240 doubles, and 105 triples, scored 1,004 runs, stole 495 bases, and knocked in 617 runs.

During Milan's first four years, the Washington Senators finished last three times and seventh once. Clark Griffith,* who became manager in 1912, improved the team partially by fully utilizing Milan's speed. Milan dethroned Cobb as base-stealing champion by pilfering 88 bases in 1912 and retained the title the following year with 75 thefts. The Senators reached second place those years, but Milan never played in a World Series. In 1922, he managed the Senators and led a relatively talented team to a 69–85 sixth place finish. Griffith fired Milan, who was bothered by ulcers, at the end of the season, but kept him in the Washington organization. Milan managed Minneapolis, MN (AA) in 1923, New Haven, CT (EL) in 1924, Memphis, TN (SA) in 1925–1926, Birmingham, AL (SA), from 1930 to June 1935, and Chattanooga, TN (SA) from June 1935 to 1937. He also coached for the Senators in 1928 and 1929 and from 1938 through 1952, and scouted for them in 1937. In 1953, Milan died at spring training while hitting fungoes. Milan married Margaret Bowers in November 1913 and had two daughters.

BIBLIOGRAPHY: Jesse Milan file, National Baseball Library, Cooperstown, NY; Shirley Povich, "Necrology," *TSN*, March 11, 1953; Shirley Povich, *The Washington Senators* (New York, 1954); Lawrence S. Ritter, *The Glory of Their Times* (New York, 1966); Henry W. Thomas, *Walter Johnson* (Washington, DC, 1995); Morris Bealle, *The Washington Senators* (Washington, DC, 1947); Lowell Reidenbaugh, *Baseball's Hall of Fame-Cooperstown* (New York, 1993); Roger Treat, *Walter Johnson—King of Pitchers* (New York, 1948).

Anthony J. Papalas

MILLER, Edmund John "Bing" (b. August 30, 1894, Cheney, IA; d. May 7, 1966, Philadelphia, PA), player and coach, was the son of farmer Norman Eugene Miller and Philomena Miller. His father, along with two brothers, played organized baseball. Nicknamed after the comic strip character George Washington Bing, he attended Polk No. 7 rural grammar school in Benton County, IA. Miller starred as a 16-year-old pitcher for the Vinton, IA Cinders and signed in 1914 as a pitcher–outfielder for $80 a month with Clinton, IA (CA). As a minor leaguer, he played outfield with Clinton from 1914 to 1917, with Peoria, IL (CA) in 1917, and with Atlanta, GA (SA) in 1919. After Miller hit .322 with Little Rock, AR (SA) in 1920, the Washington Senators (AL) and Pittsburgh Pirates (NL) both claimed him. Commissioner Kenesaw Mountain Landis,* in his first major decision, ruled that Washington owned Miller's contract. Miller married Helen Fetrow of Philadelphia, PA in March 1930 and had no children.

Miller played outfield 16 AL seasons with the Washington Senators (1921), Philadelphia Athletics (1922–1926, 1928–1934), St. Louis Browns (1926–1927), and Boston Red Sox (1935–1936). In 1,820 major league games, the 6 foot, 185 pound Miller made 1,934 hits and compiled a .311 career batting average. Miller, who played with Hall of Famers Jimmie Foxx,* Al Simmons,* Mickey Cochrane,* and Lefty Grove,* batted over .300 nine times. A powerful hitter, he slugged 116 HR, 95 triples, and 389 doubles, scored 946 runs, and knocked in 990 runs. Defensively, he handled right field with finesse and compiled a lifetime .971 fielding percentage. In a 1930 World Series contest against the St. Louis Cardinals, he made a record seven putouts.

The humorous, flamboyant Miller reached peak performance with Connie Mack's* Athletics. A line drive hitter, he batted .335 in 1922 and a career pinnacle .342 in 1924. Miller helped the Athletics capture AL pennants from 1929 through 1931 as well as the 1929 World Series championship. In 1929 he batted .331 during the regular season and .368 in the World Series against the Chicago Cubs. Miller participated in Philadelphia's dramatic, come from behind, ten-run seventh inning to erase a 7–0 Chicago lead in Game 4. In the ninth inning of the final game, Miller drove in the winning run with a towering double. He led the AL in pinch hits in 1934 and 1935. After retiring as an active player in 1936, he coached in the AL for the Boston Red Sox (1937–1938), Detroit Tigers (1939–1941), Chicago White Sox (1942–1949), and Philadelphia Athletics (1950–1953), the latter two stints at the request of his very close friend Jimmy Dykes.* In May 1966, he died of a heart attack following an automobile accident.

BIBLIOGRAPHY: Bing Miller file, National Baseball Library, Cooperstown, NY; Jerry E. Clark, *Anson to Zuber: Iowa Boys in the Big Leagues* (Omaha, NE, 1992); Des Moines *Register*, March 26, 1961, May 8, 1966; Ed Fitzgerald, ed., *The American League* (New York, 1963); Frederick G. Lieb, *Connie Mack* (New York, 1945); George S. May, "Major League Baseball Players from Iowa," *The Palimpsest* 36 (April 1955), pp. 133–

165; Tom Meany, *Baseball's Greatest Teams* (New York, 1949); *NYT*, May 8, 1966; David L. Porter, correspondence with Mrs. Eddie Dyson, April 27, 1984, David L. Porter Collection, Oskaloosa, IA; David L. Porter, correspondence with Mrs. Ida Grubbs, May 6, 1984, David L. Porter Collection, Oskaloosa, IA; Shirley Povich, *The Washington Senators* (New York, 1954); Connie Mack, *My 66 Years in the Big Leagues* (Philadelphia, PA, 1950), Bill Borst, ed., *Ables to Zoldak*, vol. 2 (St. Louis, MO, 1989); Frederick G. Lieb, *The Boston Red Sox* (New York, 1947); Bill Borst, *Still Last in the American League* (West Bloomfield, MI, 1992); Robert Redmount, *The Red Sox Encyclopedia* (Champaign, IL, 1998); *The Baseball Encyclopedia*, 10th ed. (New York, 1996).

David L. Porter

MILLER, Edward Robert "Eddie" (b. November 26, 1916, Pittsburgh, PA; d. July 31, 1997, Lake Worth, FL), player and coach, was a 5-foot 10-inch, 185-pound shortstop who batted and threw right-handed. The son of Charles Miller and Amelia (Wagner) Miller, he married Swan Anna Ott on November 30, 1936 and had four children. His high school coach considered him too small, but that made the determined, spirited young player more resolute.

The Pittsburgh Pirates (NL) signed the 17-year-old hometown shortstop, but he was sold to the Cincinnati Reds (NL) and New York Yankees (AL) organizations. The Boston Bees (NL) club acquired him in August 1938. Boston teammates included great second baseman Tony Cuccinello,* Miller's "best teacher," and catcher, Al Lopez.* Miller learned that shortstops and second basemen must collaborate on double plays. After suffering a broken leg in 1939, he started in 1940 at shortstop. Miller masterfully handled hard ground balls and perfected Rabbit Maranville's* "basket catch." Blessed with great hands and an acute mind, Miller achieved a phenomenal .983 fielding mark in 1942 and made only 13 errors in 142 games. He led NL shortstops in fielding percentage from 1940 through 1943 and in 1945.

The Boston Braves (NL) needed pitching and returned Miller in December 1942 to the Cincinnati Reds. Miller hit his stride there, hitting several HR on opening days and making the NL All-Star teams from 1940 through 1947. He regarded the 1947 season as his best, leading the NL in doubles (38), belting 19 HR, and recording 87 RBI. His 1947 campaign proved truly remarkable because he suffered persistent pain with a fractured right throwing arm. After spending the 1948 and 1949 seasons with the Philadelphia Phillies (NL), Miller signed with the St. Louis Cardinals (NL) in April 1950. He replaced injured shortstop Marty Marion* for the first 14 games, performing errorless baseball. Marion and Miller often played opposite ends of a doubleheader, using very different styles masterfully remaining in complete command at shortstop. The year 1950 marked Miller's final season, even though his fielding skills remained admirably consistent. Miller, who compiled a .972 career fielding percentage, batted .238 with 1,270 hits and 640

RBI. He acted as infield instructor in the St. Louis Cardinals' farm system and at baseball schools at Koko, FL, Springfield, IL, and Del Rio, TX. Phillies' President Bob Carpenter* best summarized Miller's career and contributions to baseball, remarking, "We like your spirit!"

BIBLIOGRAPHY: Eddie Miller file, National Baseball Library, Cooperstown, NY; John Thorn et al., eds., *Total Baseball*, 5th ed. (New York, 1997); *The Baseball Encyclopedia*, 10th ed. (New York, 1996); David S. Neft et al., eds., *The Sports Encyclopedia: Baseball, 1996*, 16th ed. (New York, 1996); Mike Shatzkin, ed., *The Ballplayers* (New York, 1990); "Former All-Star Infielder Eddie Miller," *SCD* 24 (September 12, 1997), p. 10; Harold Kaese, *The Boston Braves* (New York, 1948); Gary Caruso, *The Braves Encyclopedia* (Philadelphia, PA, 1995); Lee Allen, *The Cincinnati Reds* (New York, 1948); Bob Rathgeber, *Cincinnati Reds Scrapbook* (Virginia Beach, VA, 1982); Rich Westcott and Frank Bilovsky, *The New Phillies Encyclopedia* (Philadelphia, PA, 1993); Frederick G. Lieb and Stan Baumgartner, *The Philadelphia Phillies* (New York, 1953); *TSN*, June 8, 1939, December 17, 1942, June 22, 1944, p. 5, February 22, 1945, p. 5, December 27, 1945, February 18, 1948, p. 3, April 7, 1948, May 24, 1950, April 6, 1955; *TSN Baseball Register*, 1950; Frank Yeutter, "Eddie Miller Switches to Second," *BM* (August 1949).

William J. Miller

MILLER, Marvin Julian (b. April 14, 1917, New York, NY), executive, served as executive director of the MLPA from 1966 to 1983 and is the son of clothing salesman Alexander Miller and Gertrude (Wald) Miller. A gifted student, Miller graduated from high school at age 15, worked his way through New York University, and graduated from there with a Bachelor's degree in economics in 1938. In 1939, he married psychology professor Theresa Morgenstern; they have two children. As an economist for the U.S. government, Miller trained labor mediators during World War II. In 1950, he became research director of the United Steel Workers of America. The frequently promoted Miller served as assistant to USW presidents David McDonald and I. W. Abel.

At the suggestion of Wharton School professor George Taylor, a search committee of the MLPA asked Miller in 1966 to become their paid executive director because the foundering organization needed strong leadership. Founded in 1953, the MLPA comprised the fifth attempt by major league players to organize in quest of bargaining rights with club owners. The four previous efforts had failed. Miller's appointment was approved, 489–136, by the major league players, but was opposed by club owners and league officials.

Opponents' fears of Miller were not misplaced. He transformed the MLPA into a strong bargaining agency within two years and became one of the most powerful figures in major league baseball. By rallying players behind his goals and methods, Miller helped MLPA membership swell to 600 by 1968. Using National Labor Relations Board procedures, Miller forced owners to bargain collectively with the MLPA and promulgate formal contracts.

During Miller's tenure, five labor contracts (Basic Agreements) were concluded. The first increased owner contributions to the pension fund, raised the minimum salary of players, and exacted a promise from owners to review the reserve clause. Ratified in 1970, the second agreement recognized the MLPA as the players' official bargaining agency in all matters except salary disputes, allowed players to be represented by agents in salary negotiations, and permitted arbitration of disputes between players and owners. This pact expired in 1971 without any successor. In 1972, Miller led the players in a brief strike yielding a new contract. This third agreement extended the arbitration principle to salary disputes, a concession sending salary levels sharply upward.

In 1975, an arbitration panel headed by Peter Seitz circumvented the reserve clause by ruling that players Andy Messersmith* and Dave McNally* had played out the option year of their contracts and could negotiate contracts with other clubs. When sustained by a federal court, this judgment precipitated a lockout by angry owners in 1976. A fourth agreement compromised on this issue by limiting free agency to six-year veterans, who could participate in newly established re-entry drafts.

Such drafts augmented soaring salaries and prompted angry owners to demand as compensation established major league players for any players lost to re-entry drafts. This impasse precipitated the 1981 player strike, which lasted 50 days and ended in a compromise. The fifth agreement compensated owners losing players in re-entry drafts by allowing them to pick established players from a general pool, but the MLPA emerged from the strike stronger than ever.

Miller was the catalyst forging the MLPA into a powerful force. By masterly use of labor laws and charismatic leadership, Miller scored successes at bargaining tables empowering players, improving working conditions, and raising salaries and pension rights to the highest level in pro sports. At his retirement in 1984, MLPA members hailed Miller as "the players' Commissioner." In 1994, *SI* selected the New York City resident as the seventh most significant sports luminary of the era since 1954.

BIBLIOGRAPHY: Marvin Miller file, National Baseball Library, Cooperstown, NY; "Baseball's Misbegotten Season," *Time* 118 (October 19, 1981), pp. 83, 86; R. H. Boyle, "This Miller Admits He's a Grind," *SI* 40 (March 11, 1974), pp. 22–23, 25–26; W. F. Buckley, "Marvin Miller," *Sport* 77 (December 1986), pp. 36–37; Curt Flood and Richard Carter, *The Way It Is* (New York, 1971); Brad Herzog, *The Sports 100* (New York, 1995); Lee Lowenfish and Tony Lupien, *The Imperfect Diamond* (New York, 1980); Marvin Miller, *A Whole Different Ball Game: The Sport and Business of Baseball* (New York, 1991); J. Nocera, "The Union Rep Who Changed Baseball," *Newsweek* 113 (April 10, 1989), p. 46; Lance Morrow, "Summer of Our Discontent," *Time* 117 (June 29, 1981), pp. 12–13; Harold Parrott, *The Lords of Baseball* (New York,

1975); B. J. Phillips, "Baseball Heads for the Showers," *Time* 117 (June 22, 1981), p. 55; Del Reddy and Allan Hayes, "Marvin Miller," *SCD* 22 (June 23, 1995), pp. 182–183; David Quentin Voigt, *American Baseball*, vol. 3 (University Park, PA, 1983).

David Q. Voigt

MILLER, Stuart Leonard "Stu" (b. December 26, 1927, Northampton, MA), player, pitched in the major leagues for 16 seasons between 1952 and 1968. Before starting his professional baseball career, he served in the U.S. Navy in 1946 and 1947 and attended Davidson College for one semester in 1947–1948. On October 18, 1952, he married Jayne Munro. They have three sons, Marc, Gary, and Matthew, and reside in Cameron Park, CA. Since 1968, he has owned and operated a liquor store in San Carlos, CA.

The 5-foot 11½-inch, 165-pound Miller began his major league career with the St. Louis Cardinals (NL) and enjoyed moderate success as a starting pitcher. He finished with a 6–3 win–loss record and a 2.05 ERA in 11 starts, but manager Eddie Stanky* found him "more like an office worker" than a major league pitcher. Miller lasted another full season and part of a third campaign with the Cardinals before being first sent in 1954 to the minor leagues and traded in May 1956 to the Philadelphia Phillies (NL). In October 1956, Philadelphia traded him to the New York Giants (NL). During the next 11 seasons, including five with the New York Giants and six with the Baltimore Orioles (AL), he became one of the era's premier relief pitchers. During his major league career, Miller won 105 games, saved 154 contests, and lost 103 decisions. He pitched two games for the Atlanta Braves (NL) in 1968, his final season in professional baseball.

His major league career featured many highlights. In 1958, Miller led the NL with a 2.47 ERA. The 1958 campaign marked the only season that his total innings pitched qualified him for the title. He was named NL Fireman of the Year in 1961, when he won 14 games and saved a NL-leading 17 contests with a 2.66 ERA. In 1963 he was selected AL Fireman of the Year, as he triumphed five times and saved an AL-leading 27 contests with a 2.24 ERA for the Baltimore Orioles.

Miller's success resulted from a tricky method of delivering the ball. His numerous head and shoulder moves frequently bewildered batters, who expected the ball to arrive more quickly than it actually did. Miller's change-of-pace prompted one sportswriter to call him "the only softball pitcher on a major league roster." During the first 1961 All-Star game played in Candlestick Park in San Francisco, he committed a balk in the ninth inning because a strong wind blew him off the pitching rubber. Although this story points out the limitations of Candlestick Park as a baseball facility, Miller reminds people that he stayed in the game and eventually was the winning pitcher.

BIBLIOGRAPHY: Stu Miller file, National Baseball Library, Cooperstown, NY; Stu Miller file, SABR Biography Committee; Mike Shatzkin, ed., *The Ballplayers* (New

York, 1990); Bob Cairns, *Pen Men* (New York, 1993); Steve Bitker, *The Original San Francisco Giants* (Champaign, IL, 1998); David Plaut, *Chasing October* (South Bend, IN, 1994); Nick Peters, *Giants Almanac* (Berkeley, CA, 1988); Ted Patterson, *The Baltimore Orioles* (Dallas, TX, 1995); James H. Bready, *Baseball in Baltimore* (Baltimore, MD, 1998).

Leverett T. Smith, Jr.

MILLIGAN, John "Jocko" (b. August 8, 1861, Philadelphia, PA; d. August 29, 1923, Philadelphia, PA), player and manager, was the son of Pennsylvania natives William Milligan and Margaret (Dunbar) Milligan. He ranks among his era's most productive players even though playing full time in only one of 10 major league seasons. The 6-foot, 192-pound right-handed catcher–first baseman entered professional baseball with Pottstown, PA in 1881. In 1884, he joined the Philadelphia Athletics (AA) and accepted 8.83 chances per game, third best all-time for a major league catcher. The next year, he handled 8.25 chances per game for eighth all-time. When rookie catcher Wilbert Robinson* arrived in 1887, Milligan divided his time between catcher and first base for two seasons.

After being traded to the St. Louis Browns (AA) for 1888, Milligan backed up catcher Jack Boyle for two years. He caught eight of the 10 1888 World Series games, batting .400. Although playing too little in 1889 for his averages to be ranked, Milligan enjoyed one of his finest seasons. He batted .366 in 72 games with a .623 slugging percentage, 98 points above the official AA leader. His career-high 12 HR ranked fourth.

Milligan jumped to the Philadelphia Quakers (PL) in 1890 and remained with the club when it replaced the old Athletics in the AA for 1891. His only full-time season came in 1891, when he led the AA in doubles (35), finished second with a .505 slugging percentage, shared second with 11 HR, and ranked fourth with a career-best 106 RBI in 118 games. The Philadelphia Athletics disbanded after 1891, when the NL and AA merged. Milligan joined the Washington Senators (NL) in 1892 and concluded his major league career with the Baltimore Orioles (NL) and New York Giants (NL) in 1893. Milligan played minor league baseball from 1894 to 1896, managing Allentown/Reading, PA (PSL) the second half of 1895.

In 772 major league games as a catcher and first baseman, Milligan batted .286 with a .433 slugging percentage. His 848 hits included 189 doubles, 50 triples, and 49 HR. In *Total Baseball's* position player ratings, Milligan ranks 20th in his era and shares 237th all-time. Milligan died at age 62 of chronic heart disease and was survived by his wife, Isabella.

BIBLIOGRAPHY: Frederick Ivor-Campbell et al., eds., *Baseball's First Stars* (Cleveland, OH, 1996); John Milligan file, National Baseball Library, Cooperstown, NY; David Nemec, *The Beer and Whisky League* (New York, 1994); Joan M. Thomas, correspondence with Frederick Ivor-Campbell, 1996; John Thorn et al., eds., *Total Baseball*, 5th ed. (New York, 1997); Frederick G. Lieb, *The St. Louis Cardinals* (New York,

1945); J. Thomas Hetrick, *Chris Von der Ahe and the St. Louis Browns* (Lanham, MD, 1999); Daniel Peterson, *Baseball in 1889* (Bowling Green, OH, 1993).

Frederick Ivor-Campbell

MILLS, Abraham Gilbert "The Bismarck of Baseball" (b. March 12, 1844, New York, NY; d. August 26, 1929, Falmouth, MA), counsel and executive, maintained a lifelong interest in sports and baseball in particular. After growing up in New York City, Mills enlisted with the 5th New York Volunteers in 1862 and served in the Civil War. He was commissioned a second lieutenant in 1864 and later held the honorary rank of colonel. As a soldier, he always carried a bat and baseball in his field gear and spread the gospel of baseball.

Mills graduated from Columbian (now George Washington University) Law School in 1869, but never practiced. His first involvement in baseball came in 1876, when he published an article attacking baseball clubs for breaking up opposing teams by hiring away their players. That same year, he became associated with William Hulbert* as counsel to the future NL president. After Hulbert's death, Mills was elected NL president. Mills staunchly supported the reserve rule as "The Father of the National Agreement." The Tripartite National Agreement constituted a milestone pact between the NL, AA, and NWL, in which Mills awarded major league status to the AA and high minor league status to the NWL. The parties agreed to pay players at least $1,000 per season and, most important, to respect each others' reserve lists. Players were prohibited from dealing with other teams between April 1 and October 20. Exclusive territorial rights were also defined.

Mills's termination as NL president oddly resulted from the failure of the competing UA in 1884. Players who had jumped to the rival UA were allowed to return to the NL by the NL owners, while former UA president Henry Lucas* was given a franchise. Due to his opposition to these moves, Mills was removed from office in November 1884. He returned to the baseball scene in 1905 with a six-man group, the Mills Commission, charged to determine the origins of baseball. The Mills Commission, influenced by Albert Spalding,* who wanted a purely American basis for the National Pastime, adopted the grossly inaccurate immaculate conception theory that the game was the brainchild of Abner Doubleday.

Mills worked with the Otis Elevator Company for over 50 years, serving as its senior vice president of sales from 1898 until his death. He married Mary Chester Steele in 1872 and had three daughters. He continued his involvement in sports, organizing the AOA, participating in the AAU, and serving as president of the New York AC.

BIBLIOGRAPHY: Charles C. Alexander, *Our Game* (New York, 1991); Harvey Frommer, *Primitive Baseball* (New York, 1988); John R. Husman, interview with James

Mallinson, Floral Park, NY, December 8, 1993; *NYT*, August 28, 1929, p. 25; Frederick Ivor-Campbell et al., eds., *Baseball's First Stars* (Cleveland, OH, 1996); Abraham Mills file, National Baseball Library, Cooperstown, NY; *Otis Bulletin* (April–May 1949); David Pietrusza, *Major Leagues* (Jefferson, NC, 1991); David Quentin Voigt, *American Baseball*, vol. 1 (Norman, OK, 1966).

John R. Husman

MINOSO, Saturnino Orestes Armas Arrieta "Minnie" (b. November 29, 1922, Havana, Cuba), player, coach and executive, earned lasting fame as one of the most flamboyant, colorful players during the 1950s and pioneered as one of the first great Latin American black baseball stars of the modern era. Although past his 75th birthday, Minoso remains in trim playing shape and is a regular fixture at old-timers All-Star games throughout Latin America and the United States. Minoso, one of the inaugural class of 12 inductees honored by the World Baseball Hall of Fame during 1990, enjoys special status among the most colorful baseball ambassadors within his native Caribbean homeland.

The Cuban star became one of the earliest black players to appear in AL action with the 1949 Cleveland Indians (AL). As the earliest true Latin American black superstar, the flamboyant Minoso paved the way for hundreds of dark-skinned Caribbean and Latin ballplayers to become major leaguers in the four decades after Jackie Robinson.* Nearly 30 years old at the time of his first full major league season, Minoso was still technically a rookie when he was traded to the Chicago White Sox (AL) in April 1951. He finished the 1951 season with a career-high .326 batting average and was named *TSN* AL Rookie of the Year. As a flashy outfielder, daring baserunner, and solid hitter, Minoso starred with the White Sox and Indians during the next decade, leading the Junior Circuit once in hits (184, 1960) and doubles (36, 1957) and three times in both triples (1951, 1954, 1956) and stolen bases (1951, 1952, 1953). He was traded to the Cleveland Indians in December 1957 and returned to the Chicago White Sox in December 1959. He joined the St. Louis Cardinals (NL) in November 1961 and the Washington Senators (AL) in April 1963. He compiled an impressive 17 year .298 lifetime major league batting average, stroked 1,963 base hits, belted 336 doubles, 83 triples, and 186 HR, knocked in 1,023 runs, and stole 205 bases. In his 16 AL seasons, he also established an AL record of being hit by enemy pitches 189 times. Although his active playing career ended in 1964, Minoso returned to major league action for token appearances with the Chicago White Sox in 1976 and 1980 (age 58). He thus achieved the rare distinction of playing in five different decades and also becoming the oldest player (nine months past his 53rd birthday in 1976) to record a major league base hit. The colorful Minoso has faithfully served the Chicago White Sox front office in a public relations and goodwill ambassador capacity. He also coached for the Chicago White Sox each season from 1976 through 1981 except for

1979. AL president Bobby Brown* denied Minoso's request in 1990 to join the White Sox roster for an unprecedented appearance as an active major league player in each of six decades. In April 1991, Baseball Commissioner Fay Vincent's* office rejected Minoso's contract with Miami, FL (FSL). Minoso married Edelia Del Gado on February 26, 1961.

BIBLIOGRAPHY: Bob Vanderberg, *Sox: From Lane and Fain to Zisk and Fisk* (Chicago, IL, 1982); John Phillips, *Winners* (Cabin John, MD, 1987); Jack Torry, *Endless Summers* (South Bend, IN, 1995); Minnie Minoso file, National Baseball Library, Cooperstown, NY; Richard C. Lindberg, "Minoso By Any Other Name," *TNP* 12 (1992), pp. 55–57; Peter C. Bjarkman, *Baseball with a Latin Beat* (Jefferson, NC, 1994); Des Moines (IA) *Register*, April 10, 1991; Tim Hufford, "Minoso One of the Oldest," *BRJ* 6 (1977), pp. 30–36; Richard Lindberg, *Sox* (New York, 1984); Richard Lindberg, *Who's on Third?* (South Bend, IN, 1983); Brent P. Kelley, *The Case For: Those Overlooked by the Baseball Hall of Fame* (Jefferson, NC, 1992); Rich Marazzi and Len Fiorito, *Aaron to Zuverink* (New York, 1982); Orestes "Minnie" Minoso with Herb Fagen, *Just Call Me Minnie* (Champaign, IL, 1994); Orestes "Minnie" Minoso with Fernando Fernandez and Robert Kleinfelder, *Extra Innings* (Chicago, IL, 1983); Larry Moffi and Jonathan Kronstadt, *Crossing the Line* (Jefferson, NC, 1994); Ira L. Smith, *Baseball's Famous Outfielders* (New York, 1954); Rich Westcott, *Diamond Greats* (Westport, CT, 1988); Andrew S. N. Young, *Great Negro Baseball Stars and How They Made the Major Leagues* (New York, 1953).

                                                                        Peter C. Bjarkman

MITCHELL, Kevin Darrell (b. January 13, 1962, San Diego, CA), player, grew up in San Diego. His parents separated when he was two years old. He was brought up primarily by his paternal grandmother, Josie Whitfield, and lived in a very tough neighborhood, being shot three times as a teenager. Participation in sports, including baseball, was encouraged by his grandmother. After graduation from Claremont High School, Mitchell played in a baseball league in San Diego and was signed by the New York Mets (NL) as an undrafted free agent in 1980. Mitchell began his minor league baseball career at Kingsport, TN (ApL) in 1981 and performed stints at Lynchburg, VA (CrL) in 1982, Jackson, TX (TL) in 1983, and Tidewater, VA (IL) in 1984 and 1985. The right-handed hitter compiled minor league batting averages of .335, .318, .299, .243, and .290. During most of his stay in the minor leagues, he played third base and the outfield. Tidewater, however, also used him at first base.

In his rookie season with the New York Mets in 1986, Mitchell hit .277 with 43 RBI and 12 HR. Mitchell played six different positions including first base, third base, shortstop, left field, center field, and right field and finished third in the balloting for the NL Rookie of the Year. In December 1986, the New York Mets traded Mitchell to the San Diego Padres (NL). Subsequent trades sent him to the San Francisco Giants (NL) in July 1987, Seattle Mariners (AL) in December 1991, and Cincinnati Reds (NL) in November 1992. The 5-foot 11-inch, 210-pound muscular Mitchell emerged as one of the game's most feared sluggers in 1989. Besides hitting .291, he led the NL in HR (47), RBI (125), total bases (345), slugging percentage (.635), and extra base hits (87). He set a major league record for a right-handed hitter by receiving 32 intentional walks. His honors for the 1989 season included the NL MVP Award, *TSN* Major League Player of the Year Award, and selection to *TSN* All-Star and Silver Slugger teams. Mitchell batted a career-high .341 in 1993 and .326 with 30 HR and 77 RBI in the strike-shortened 1994 season. Cincinnati finished first in the NL Central division with a 66–48 mark in 1994. After playing with the Daiei, Japan Hawks (JPL) in 1995, he split 1996 between the Boston Red Sox (AL) and Cincinnati Reds (NL), spent 1997 with the Cleveland Indians (AL), and Oakland A's (AL) in 1998. Mitchell, a member of the 1989 and 1990 NL All-Star teams, batted .291 in three NL Championship Series (1986, 1987, 1989) and .280 in two World Series against the 1986 Boston Red Sox and the 1989 Oakland A's. Through the 1998 season, his career totals included a .284 batting average, a .520 slugging average, 234 HR, and 760 RBI. He is single and lives in San Diego, CA.

BIBLIOGRAPHY: Barry M. Bloom, "Hope Dies by Degrees," *USAT Baseball Weekly*, May 19–25, 1993, p. 23; Kevin Mitchell file, National Baseball Library, Cooperstown, NY; *1993 Cincinnati Reds Media Guide*; Franz Lidz, "Granny and the Giant," *SI* 70 (June 26, 1989), pp. 36–38; Nick Peters, "A New Image for Giants Mitchell," *TSN*, May 8, 1989, p. 16; Mark Purdy, "Earth to Mitchell," *TSN 1990 Baseball Yearbook*, pp. 4–8, 10, 12; Rob Rains, "Mitchell Suffering Guilt by Association," *USAT Baseball Weekly*, May 19–25, 1993, pp. 22–23; S. K. Reed, "Putting the Mean Streets Behind Him, Slugger Kevin Mitchell Now Does His Hitting on the Field," *PW* 31 (June 19, 1989), pp. 93ff; *TSN Official Baseball Register*, 1998; John Thorn et al., eds., *Total Baseball*, 5th ed. (New York, 1997); Tom Verducci, "Livin' Large," *SI* 86 (June 16, 1997), pp. 76–81; Rick Weinberg, "Kevin Mitchell," *Sport* 83 (July 1992), pp. 48–53.

Robert J. Brown

MITCHELL, Loren Dale (b. August 23, 1921, Colony, OK; d. January 5, 1987, Tulsa, OK), player, was involved in one of major league baseball's most dramatic moments. The tall, slender left-hander strode forward and then held back his swing as umpire Babe Pinelli* raised his arm in the classic strike pose. The called strike three marked the third and final out of Don Larsen's* historic no-hit gem for the New York Yankees against the Brooklyn Dodgers in Game 5 of the 1956 World Series. To his dying day, Mitchell of the Brooklyn Dodgers (NL) thought the pitch was off the plate for a ball. The memory remained unfair to Mitchell, who played 11 major league seasons and never saw his career batting average dip below its final .312 mark. He ranks 67th on the all-time batting average list ahead of stars Willie Mays,* Harvey Kuenn,* Pete Rose,* Mel Ott,* Hank Aaron,* and George Brett.*

The 6-foot 1-inch, 195-pound Mitchell began his professional baseball career in 1946 with Oklahoma City, OK (TL), leading the TL with a sparkling .337 batting average. He made his major league debut with the Cleveland Indians (AL) in September 1946, hitting .432 in 11 games. The performance impressed player–manager Lou Boudreau,* who named Mitchell his starting center fielder in spring training the following year. Mitchell played for the Cleveland Indians until sold to the Brooklyn Dodgers in July 1956. In Cleveland's championship 1948 season, he hit .336 to rank third in the AL behind Boudreau (.355) and batting champion Ted Williams* (.369). Mitchell also finished second in the AL in hits with 204 and fourth in stolen bases with 13. In 1949, Mitchell led the AL in hits (203) and triples (23) and ranked fourth in batting (.317) and total bases (274). He finished second in the AL batting race in 1952 with .323, four points behind Ferris Fain's* .327.

Mitchell played in the 1948, 1954, and 1956 World Series, making four hits in 29 at-bats and batting only .139. All four of his World Series hits came in the 1948 fall classic, when the Indians defeated the Boston Braves in six games. The New York Giants swept the favored Cleveland Indians in the 1954 World Series. Mitchell appeared in the 1949 and 1952 All-Star Games and was selected for the 1951 contest, knocking in one run with a double as a late-inning substitute for Ted Williams in 1949. During 11 major league seasons, he struck out only 119 times in 3,984 at-bats. An outstanding defensive outfielder, he led outfielders in fielding percentage in 1948 (.991) and 1949 (.994). Mitchell married Margaret Emerson on May 26, 1942 and worked as a manager for an oil company in Tulsa, OK.

BIBLIOGRAPHY: Dale Mitchell file, National Baseball Library, Cooperstown, NY; *NYT*, January 7, 1987, p. A-20; Franklin Lewis, *The Cleveland Indians* (New York, 1949); John Phillips, *Winners* (Cabin John, MD, 1987); Russell Schneider, *The Boys of Summer of '48* (Champaign, IL, 1998); David Kaiser, *Epic Season* (Amherst, MA, 1998); John Thorn et al., eds., *Total Indians* (New York, 1996); Bruce Dudley, *Bittersweet Season* (Annapolis, MD, 1995); Ronald A. Mayer, *Perfect* (Jefferson, NC, 1991); Mike Shatzkin, ed., *The Ballplayers* (New York, 1990); John Thorn et al., eds., *Total Baseball*, 5th ed. (New York, 1997); *TSN Daguerreotypes of Great Stars of Baseball* (St. Louis, MO, 1968).

Lee E. Scanlon

MIZE, John Robert "Johnny," "Big Cat" (b. January 7, 1913, Demorest, GA; d. June 2, 1993, Demorest, GA), player, scout, and coach, excelled in baseball and tennis at Tipton (GA) High School and attended Piedmont College for two years. Mize became one of the foremost baseball performers in the history of the St. Louis Cardinals (NL), New York Giants (NL), and New York Yankees (AL). After playing for Greensboro, NC (PiL), Elmira, NY (NYPL), and Rochester, NY (IL) between 1930 and 1935, Mize debuted with the St. Louis Cardinals in 1936, and was named NL Rookie of the

Year. The 6-foot 2-inch, 215-pound left-handed first baseman followed right-handed slugger Joe Medwick* in the lineup to make one of baseball's finest one–two combinations. Mize, who batted .329, .364, and .337 from 1936 through 1938 as Medwick's counterpart, led the NL in 1939 with a .349 mark. Besides his outstanding hitting achievements, Mize proved an excellent fielder.

In December 1941, the St. Louis Cardinals traded Mize to the New York Giants (NL). Mize spent three years in the U.S. Navy and in 1947 became the only NL left-handed batter to hit 50 or more HR in one season, tying Ralph Kiner* for the NL lead with 51. New York made plans for a running team and consequently sold Mize in August 1949 to the New York Yankees (AL). Under manager Casey Stengel,* the Yankees drove to their first of five consecutive world championships and used Mize as an excellent part-time player in pinch-hitting and reserve situations. Mize played on five world championship teams (1949–1953), slugging three HR and batting .400 to lead the Yankees past the Brooklyn Dodgers in seven games in 1952. He became only the second player in World Series history to make a pinch hit HR. In 1953, he established an AL record by getting five consecutive pinch hits and finished the season with 19 pinch hits, just one short of the league record. Mize's 53 career pinch hits included eight HR.

In his major league career, Mize paced the NL or tied for the lead in HR four times and won four slugging titles, three RBI crowns, and one batting championship. Mize shared the NL lead in doubles in 1941 and in 1938 paced the circuit with 16 triples. He slugged three HR in one game six times (a record unequalled) and two HR in one game 30 times, collected over 100 RBI eight times, made over 100 hits 11 times, and batted over .300 nine consecutive times. Mize hit for the cycle in a 1940 contest, held the St. Louis club record for most HR in a season (43), and belted HR in all 15 ballparks in use during his career.

In 1,884 major league games, Mize scored 1,118 runs, collected 2,011 hits, 367 doubles, 83 triples, 359 HR and 1,337 RBI, and compiled a .312 lifetime batting average. His .577 NL slugging average ranks second only to Rogers Hornsby's* .578 mark. After retiring as an active player following the 1953 season, Mize scouted for the New York Giants in 1955 and coached in 1961 for the Kansas City A's (AL). He married Jane Adams in August 1937. Mize and his second wife, Marjorie, owned and operated orange groves in Florida for several years. In 1981, Mize was enshrined in the National Baseball Hall of Fame.

BIBLIOGRAPHY: Craig Carter, ed., *TSN Daguerreotypes*, 8th ed. (St. Louis, MO, 1990); Dave Anderson et al., *The Yankees* (New York, 1979); Robert Creamer, *Stengel: His Life and Times* (New York, 1984); Frank Graham, *The New York Giants* (New York, 1952); John Mize file, National Baseball Library, Cooperstown, NY; Dom Forker, *The Men of Autumn* (Dallas, TX, 1989); Donald Honig, *Baseball When the Grass Was Real* (New York, 1975); *NYT*, June 3, 1993, p. D24; Noel Hynd, *The Giants of the Polo Grounds* (New York, 1988); Fred Stein, *Under Coogan's Bluff* (Glenshaw, PA, 1978); Peter Williams, *When the Giants Were Giants* (Chapel Hill, NC, 1994); Joseph L. Reichler, *The Great All-Time Baseball Record Book* (New York, 1981); Rob Rains, *The St. Louis Cardinals* (St. Louis, MO, 1992); Frederick G. Lieb, *The St. Louis Cardinals* (New York, 1945); Bob Broeg and Jerry Vickery, *St. Louis Cardinals Encyclopedia* (Grand Rapids, MI, 1998); Lowell Reidenbaugh, *Baseball's Hall of Fame-Cooperstown* (New York, 1993); Rich Westcott, *Diamond Greats* (Westport, CT, 1988).

John L. Evers

MOGRIDGE, George Anthony "Mug" (b. February 18, 1889, Rochester, NY; d. March 4, 1962, Rochester, NY), player, was the son of Charlie Mogridge and Theresa (Nobles) Mogridge and attended the University of Rochester from 1909 to 1910, where he played baseball. His professional baseball career began at Galesburg, IL (CA), where the 6-foot 2-inch, 172-pound left-handed pitcher won 20 games in 1911. Mogridge, who married Clara Hart, began the next season with the Chicago White Sox (AL). After being optioned to Lincoln, NE (WL), he returned to Chicago for the last month of the season and compiled a 3–4 mark. He spent from 1913 through August 1915 in the WL with the Minneapolis, MN Millers and Des Moines, IA Boosters. The New York Yankees (AL) purchased Mogridge's contract on June 28, 1915 for $5,500, with arrival in September. Mogridge appeared in six games for New York, winning two.

From 1915 though 1919, his ERA never exceeded 2.98. Mogridge on April 24, 1917 pitched a no-hitter against the Boston Red Sox, a regular season feat not repeated by a New York Yankee for 34 years. He finished 16–13 in 1918, ranking seventh in the AL in ERA, sixth in wins, first in appearances, and first in saves with seven. Upon receiving a low contract offer, he threatened to retire and "learn a trade" with Bethlehem Steel.

The New York Yankees traded Mogridge in January 1921 to the Washington Nationals (AL). He won 18 games in 1921 and 1922, but declined to 13–13 in 1923. The 1924 season saw the 35 year old win 16 contests. Mogridge started and won Game 4 of the 1924 World Series against the New York Giants. In a surprise move in the seventh game, manager Bucky Harris* brought him in with two out in the first inning and used him through the fifth frame. Mogridge was traded to the St. Louis Browns (AL) in June 1925 and finished his major league career in 1926 and 1927 with the Boston Braves (NL). During 15 major league seasons, Mogridge pitched 2,265.2 innings and averaged a walk every four innings and strikeout every three frames. Since his career ERA is only 3.23, his 132–131 record does not reflect the quality of his pitching.

BIBLIOGRAPHY: George Mogridge file, National Baseball Library, Cooperstown, NY; Mark Gallagher, *The Yankee Encyclopedia*, vol. 3 (Champaign, IL, 1997); Frank Graham, *The Yankees* (New York, 1943); Morris Bealle, *The Washington Senators* (Washington, DC, 1947); Henry W. Thomas, *Walter Johnson* (Washington, DC,

1995); Bill Borst, ed., *Ables to Zoldak*, vol. 2 (St. Louis, MO, 1989); Robert S. Fuchs and Wayne Soini, *Judge Fuchs and the Boston Braves, 1923–1935* (Jefferson, NC, 1998); Rochester (NY) *Times-Union*, March 28, 1936; Shirley Povich, *The Washington Senators* (New York, 1954); *TSN*, March 14, 1962.

Thomas H. Barthel

MOLITOR, Paul Leo (b. August 22, 1956, St. Paul, MN), player, sportscaster, and coach, began his diamond career at Cretin High School in St. Paul and performed at the University of Minnesota for Dick Siebert.* The Milwaukee Brewers (AL) signed Molitor in 1978. He joined them immediately and never played in the minor leagues. A versatile player, he batted .273 his first season and performed mainly at second base with stints at shortstop, third base, and as a DH. In his second season, Molitor made 188 hits and compiled an impressive .322 batting average. Molitor's .469 slugging average and 33 stolen bases also highlighted his 1979 campaign. In 1980, he batted .304 and stole 34 bases.

Molitor enjoyed an excellent season in 1982, making 201 hits for a .302 batting average. His .450 slugging average included 19 HR. He batted .297 in 140 games in 1985. In 1987, Molitor tallied 164 hits for a career-high .353 batting average. His .566 slugging average featured 16 HR and AL-best 41 doubles. He stole 45 bases, marking a career high. During the 1987 season, Molitor hit safely in 39 consecutive games from July 16 to August 25. The 6-foot, 185-pound right-hander batted .312 in 1988 and .315 in 1989. Molitor enjoyed another banner season in 1991, leading the AL in runs scored (133) and hits (216), sharing first in triples (13), and ranking fourth in total bases (325) and fifth in batting average (325). Besides driving in 75 runs as a leadoff batter, he hit 32 doubles and 17 HR. In 1991 he was named to the AL All-Star team for the third time.

The Milwaukee Brewers appeared in the NL Eastern Division Series in 1981, as Molitor batted .250. The Brewers won the 1982 AL Championship Series, with Molitor garnering six hits, belting two HR, batting .316, and compiling a .684 slugging average. In the 1982 World Series against the St. Louis Cardinals, Molitor made 11 hits and batted .355 in a losing cause.

Molitor, who batted .320 for Milwaukee in 1992, holds the Brewers all-time records for highest batting average (.303) and most stolen bases (412). In December 1992, the Toronto Blue Jays (AL) signed him as a free agent. He batted .332 with 111 RBI in 1993 and led the AL with 211 hits, helping the Blue Jays capture the AL East. Molitor hit .391 with five RBI to earn Series MVP honors as the Toronto Blue Jays defeated the Chicago White Sox in the AL Championship Series. His two doubles, two triples, two HR, eight RBI, and .500 batting average helped the Toronto Blue Jays defeat the Philadelphia Phillies in the World Series. He batted .341 in 1994 for the Toronto Blue Jays and signed with the Minnesota Twins (AL) as a free agent in December 1995. His batting average soared again to .341 with the Minnesota Twins in 1996, as he produced a career-high 113 RBI and led the AL with a career-best 225 hits. On September 16, 1996, he became the 21st player in major league history to collect 3,000 hits, tripling in the fifth inning against Jose Rosado of the Kansas City Royals. No other major league player had tripled for his 3,000th hit.

Through the 1998 season, Molitor has recorded 3,319 hits with 605 doubles, 114 triples, and 234 HR in 2,683 games. His .306 batting average, .455 slugging percentage, and 504 stolen bases highlight his major league career. He was named DH on the *TSN* AL All-Star team in 1987 and from 1993 through 1996 and AL Silver Slugger team in 1987, 1988, 1993, and 1996. He served as broadcaster for the Minnesota Twins in 1999 and as coach in 2000.

BIBLIOGRAPHY: Peter C. Bjarkman, ed., *Encyclopedia of Major League Baseball Team Histories American League* (Westport, CT, 1991); Jeff Everson, *This Date in Milwaukee Brewers History* (Appleton, WI, 1987); *Milwaukee Brewers' 1989 Official Yearbook*; Danny Knobler, "Baseball's Best Leadoff Hitters," *Sport* 81 (July 1990), pp. 40–42; Paul Molitor file, National Baseball Library, Cooperstown, NY; *The Baseball Encyclopedia*, 10th ed. (New York, 1996); M. Bishop, "More than Halfway There," *SI* 67 (August 24, 1987), pp. 26–27; S. Buckley, "Paul Molitor," *Sport* 85 (April 1994), pp. 22ff; Rick Hoffer, "Career Move," *SI* 78 (March 29, 1993), pp. 44–46; *Milwaukee Brewers Media Guide 1992*; Stuart Broomer, *Paul Molitor* (Toronto, Canada, 1994); Paul Molitor, letter to Stan W. Carlson, April 1990; Tom Verducci, "The Complete Player," *SI* 79 (November 1, 1993), pp. 28ff.

Stan W. Carlson

MONDAY, Robert James "Rick" (b. November 20, 1945, Batesville, AR), player and sportscaster, was the initial player selected in major league baseball's first free-agent draft in June 1965 after leading Arizona State University to the NCAA College World Series championship. Monday, named the College Player of the Year in 1965, never hit full stride with the Kansas City/Oakland A's (AL) although becoming a regular outfielder in 1967. In November 1971, Oakland traded Monday to the Chicago Cubs (NL). With the Cubs, Monday enjoyed five productive seasons and belted a career-high 32 HR in 1976. He furnished the top of their lineup with both power and speed. On April 25, 1976, the centennial of the Cubs' first game, he received national publicity. Monday rescued an American flag from two men who tried to set it afire in the outfield in the fourth inning at Dodger Stadium in Los Angeles, CA. The 6-foot 3-inch, 193-pound left-hander was considered the best defensive center fielder for the Cubs since Andy Pafko.*

After a lengthy dispute over a multiyear contract and a significant pay increase, Monday was traded to the Los Angeles Dodgers (NL) in January 1977 for Bill Buckner* and Ivan DeJesus. Chicago owner Philip K. Wrigley* resisted the salary demands of Monday and Bill Madlock,* stating, "No ball player is worth more than $100,000 and I'm not sure they're worth that much." The trade, however, benefited both teams. Injuries slowed Monday frequently, but his HR on October 19, 1981 gave the Dodgers a 2–1 victory over the Montreal Expos in the deciding game of the NL Championship Series. His other World Series appearances with the Dodgers came in 1977 and 1978. Monday played 19 major league seasons, retiring in midseason 1984. He batted .264 lifetime with 1,619 hits, 248 doubles, 241 HR, and 775 RBI and announced over radio for the San Diego Padres (NL) from 1989 through 1992. He had previously served as sports anchor for KTTV in Los Angeles and handled Dodger games on cable. Monday has announced for the Los Angeles Dodgers since 1994. He and his wife, Karen, have two children, Michael and Heather.

BIBLIOGRAPHY: *Chicago Cubs 1876/1976* (Chicago, IL, 1976); Eddie Gold and Art Ahrens, *The New Era Cubs*, 1941–1985 (Chicago, IL, 1985); Jim Langford, *The Game Is Never Over* (South Bend, IN, 1980); *San Diego Padres 1992 Media Guide*; Bruce Markusen, *Baseball's Last Dynasty* (New York, 1998); Jim Enright, *Chicago Cubs* (New York, 1975); Tommy Lasorda and David Fisher, *The Artful Dodger* (New York, 1985).

Duane A. Smith

MONEY, Donald Wayne "Don" (b. July 6, 1947, Washington, DC), player and manager, is the son of Robert J. Money, Jr., a carpenter, and Frances (Greenfield) Money and performed 16 years in the major leagues with the Philadelphia Phillies (NL) from 1968 to 1972 and Milwaukee Brewers (AL) from 1973 to 1983. The highly touted infielder was signed by Syd Thrift and Joe Consoli and began his career at Salem, VA (ApL) in the Pittsburgh Pirates (NL) organization in 1965. Along with Woodie Fryman, Bill Laxton, and Harold Clem, Money was traded to the Philadelphia Phillies in December 1967 for pitcher Jim Bunning.* Money's brief trial with the Philadelphia Phillies in 1968 was followed by his joining the team full-time in 1969. On opening day of 1969, he hit two HR against the Chicago Cubs. Money started as a shortstop, but was moved to third base when the Philadelphia Phillies brought up Larry Bowa* in 1970.

The 6-foot 1-inch, 190-pound right-hander enjoyed his best of four seasons with the Philadelphia Phillies in 1970. He batted over .300 most of the season and fielded his position brilliantly. He hit .295, committed just 15 errors, and fielded .961, placing him second in the NL behind Doug Rader* of the Houston Astros. After Money hit in the .220s the next two seasons, the Philadelphia Phillies traded Money and two others to the Milwaukee Brewers (AL) in October 1972 for Ken Brett, Jim Lonborg,* and two other pitchers.

At age 25, Money came into his own with the Milwaukee Brewers and developed into a solid all-around player. The third baseman, nicknamed "Brooks" for his defensive skills, began serving as a DH in 1977 when the Milwaukee Brewers got Sal Bando* from the Oakland A's to play third base. Money experienced his best years between 1973 and 1978, averaging around

.280 at the plate for that span. Money was selected to the AL All-Star teams in 1974 and from 1976 through 1978.

In 1977, Money hit 25 HR and drove in 83 runs, both career highs. The next season, he scored a career-high 88 runs. Money's major league career featured a .261 batting average with 1,623 hits, 302 doubles, 176 HR, and 729 RBI. Among Brewers, he ranks among the top five or six in every career offensive category. The high point of Money's career came in 1982, when he served as DH for the Brewers in the AL Championship Series against the California Angels and in the World Series against the St. Louis Cardinals. He hit .231 in that World Series.

Money retired from major league baseball after the 1983 season. He played briefly in Japan in 1984 and returned to his Vinland, NJ home after that season. He coached high school baseball in the Vinland area for five years and managed Beloit, WI (ML) since 1998. He and his wife, Sharon Ann, live in Vinland and have two sons.

BIBLIOGRAPHY: Don Money file, National Baseball Library, Cooperstown, NY; Rich Westcott and Frank Bilovsky, *The New Phillies Encyclopedia* (Philadelphia, PA, 1993); Allen Lewis, *The Philadelphia Phillies: A Pictorial History* (Virginia Beach, VA, 1981); Frank Dolson, *The Philadelphia Story* (South Bend, IN, 1980); Jeff Everson, *This Date in Milwaukee Brewers History* (Appleton, WI, 1987); *Milwaukee Brewers' 1989 Official Yearbook*; John P. Rossi, interview with Donald Money, January 1993; Bert Sugar, *Baseballistics* (New York, 1990).

John P. Rossi

MONROE, William "Bill" (b. circa 1876; d. March 16, 1915, Chicago, IL), player, starred in early-20th-century Negro League baseball. Although playing all infield positions, he excelled as a second baseman. Monroe began his baseball career in 1896 and played shortstop and second base with the Chicago Unions in 1899 and 1900. He joined the Philadelphia Giants in 1903 and played an integral role on their 1906 Black Championship team. Throughout his career, Monroe remained a crowd favorite and entertained the spectators with his showmanship and baseball skills. The keystone performer's public acceptance extended to Cuba, where he played CUWL ball and compiled a .333 batting average during the 1907–1908 season. After leaving Philadelphia, Monroe played with the Quaker Giants of New York in 1908 and the Brooklyn Royal Giants in 1907, 1909, and 1910 and then joined Rube Foster's* Chicago American Giants in 1911. Monroe's next three seasons were spent with Foster, although he performed part of the 1913 season with the Chicago Giants.

By 1914, Foster had assembled what many consider to be one of the greatest teams of all time. Joe Williams,* John Henry Lloyd,* Pete Hill,* Bruce Petway,* Pat Dougherty,* Frank Wickware,* Ben Taylor, and Monroe starred on that illustrious squad. Monroe compiled a .348 batting average for the 1914 season, hitting fifth in the lineup. The Giants swept the Eastern champion Brooklyn Royal Giants in four straight games. Monroe's best offensive production came in the third game victory, in which he made four hits. Monroe's untimely death in 1915 brought a productive 19-year career to an abrupt end. Former managers Sol White* and Foster both praised the veteran infielder, while New York Giants (NL) pilot John McGraw* predicted that Monroe would have excelled in the major leagues had he been given the opportunity to play there.

BIBLIOGRAPHY: Robert W. Peterson, *Only the Ball Was White* (Englewood Cliffs, NJ, 1970); James A. Riley, *The All-Time All-Stars of Black Baseball* (Cocoa, FL, 1983); James A. Riley, *Biographical Encyclopedia of the Negro Baseball Leagues* (New York, 1994); James A. Riley, interviews with former Negro League players, James A. Riley Collection, Cocoa, FL.

James A. Riley

MONTANEZ, Guillermo (Naranjo) "Willie" (b. April 1, 1948, Catano, PR) player and scout, graduated from Catano High School. The 6-foot 190-pound left-handed outfielder was signed by the St. Louis Cardinals (NL) in 1965. In November 1965, the California Angels (AL) drafted him. With Rock Hill, SC (WCL) in 1966, Montanez hit .281 with 11 HR and earned a brief September trial with the California Angels. The Angels returned him to the St. Louis Cardinal organization in May 1966.

In April 1970, the St. Louis Cardinals sent Montanez to the Philadelphia Phillies (NL) as compensation for Curt Flood,* who refused to report to the Philadelphia Phillies. Montanez played one season for the Phillies top farm club at Eugene, OR (PCL), hitting .276 with 16 HR and 80 RBI. After briefly appearing with the Philadelphia Phillies in September 1970, Montanez became their starting center fielder the following season.

Montanez played four full seasons with the Philadelphia Phillies. His 1971 season saw him hit 30 HR, which remains a club rookie record. He also drove in 99 runs while batting .255. Montanez and Caesar Cedeno* of the Houston Astros shared the NL lead in doubles with 39 in 1972. In 1973, Montanez moved to first base and trailed only Mike Jorgenson of the Montreal Expos for a Gold Glove. Montanez hit .304 with 79 RBI the next season to give the Philadelphia Phillies among the best major league offensive infields, including third baseman Mike Schmidt,* shortstop Larry Bowa,* and second baseman Dave Cash.*

The Philadelphia Phillies in May 1975 traded the popular Montanez, nicknamed "Willie the Phillie" because of his showmanship and outgoing personality, to the San Francisco Giants (NL) for outfielder Garry Maddox.* Montanez enjoyed his best all-around season with Philadelphia and the San Francisco Giants in 1975, batting .302 while driving in 101 runs on 182 hits. He also led all NL first baseman in assists (81) and double plays (114). The Giants shipped him to the Atlanta Braves (NL) in June 1976. Montanez hit a career-best .317 with 84 RBI and 206 hits. After slumping in 1977, he was traded to the Texas Rangers (AL) in December 1977. The Texas Rangers sent him to the New York Mets (NL) on the same day.

Montanez in 1978 drove in 96 runs for the New York Mets, hitting 17 HR and batting .256. The New York Mets returned him to the Texas Rangers in August 1979. In February 1980, Texas traded Montanez to the San Diego Padres (NL) for pitcher Gaylord Perry.* The 1980 campaign marked Montanez' last full time season. In August 1980, he moved to the Montreal Expos (NL). Montanez finished his major league career as a pinch-hitter with the Montreal Expos, Pittsburgh Pirates (NL) in 1981 and 1982, and Philadelphia Phillies in 1982.

During 14 major league seasons, Montanez batted .275 with 1,604 hits, 279 doubles, 139 HR, and 802 RBI. Montanez resides in Caguas, PR with his wife, Maria, and their three children, Miriam, Zoraida, and Guillermo Jr. Since 1992, he has scouted Puerto Rico for the Philadelphia Phillies.

BIBLIOGRAPHY: Willie Montanez file, National Baseball Library, Cooperstown, NY; Allen Lewis, *The Philadelphia Phillies: A Pictorial History* (Virginia Beach, VA, 1981); Frank Dolson, *The Philadelphia Story* (South Bend, IN, 1980); Nick Peters, *Giants Almanac* (Berkeley, CA, 1988); Rich Westcott and Frank Bilovsky, *The New Phillies Encyclopedia* (Philadelphia, PA, 1993).

John P. Rossi

MONTERO, Samuel Peralta. *See* Samuel Peralta Sosa.

MONTGOMERY, Jeffrey Thomas "Jeff" (b. January 7, 1962, Wellston, OH), player, is the son of Tom Montgomery, a construction company partner, and Mary Montgomery, who is semi-retired from Pillsbury Company. At Wellston High School, he made the First Team All-Ohio squads in both baseball and football. Montgomery's pitching success continued at Marshall University, where he was selected the SC's Freshman of the Year in 1981. He earned a bachelor's degree in computer science. In June 1983, the Cincinnati Reds (NL) selected him in the ninth round of the free agent draft.

Montgomery spent four years in the minor leagues before his August 1987 major league debut with Cincinnati. In February 1988, the Cincinnati Reds traded him to the Kansas City Royals (AL) for Van Snider. The Kansas City Royals used Montgomery as their right-handed setup reliever, as he finished 7–2 with a 3.45 ERA. *BD* named him to its All-Rookie team for 1988. Montgomery began 1989 as a middle reliever, but became the Kansas City Royals' closer in July. He finished the season with a 7–3 record, 18 saves, and a career-best 1.37 ERA.

Despite Montgomery's impressive numbers, the Kansas City Royals signed free agent Mark Davis for their closer in 1990. After Davis proved ineffective, Kansas City again used Montgomery as the stopper. He compiled 24 saves and a 2.39 ERA for the season. In 1991, his first full campaign as closer, Montgomery recorded 33 saves with a 2.90 ERA. He steadily improved, saving 39 games in 46 opportunities with a 2.18 ERA in 1992. He led the AL with 45 saves in 1993, winning his first Rolaids Relief Man Award. In July 1993, Montgomery pitched in his second consecutive All-Star Game. After saving 27 games in 32 opportunities in the strike-shortened 1994 season, he recorded 31 saves in 1995, 24 saves in 1996, and 36 saves in 1998.

The 5-foot 11-inch, 180-pound Montgomery ranked among the AL's most reliable closers through most of the 1990s. Through 1999 he has compiled a 46–52 record with a 3.27 ERA. His 304 saves surpassed Dan Quisenberry* for the Kansas City Royals' club record. Montgomery resides in Leawood, KS, with his wife, Tina, and three children.

BIBLIOGRAPHY: Jeff Montgomery file, National Baseball Library, Cooperstown, NY; *Kansas City Royals 1998 Media Guide;* "Jeff Montgomery," *Microsoft Complete Baseball,* CD-ROM (Redmond, WA, 1994); "Reliever Signs for $11 Million," *NYT,* February 16, 1993, p. B15.

Kent M. Krause

MOON, Wallace Wade "Wally" (b. April 3, 1930, Bay, AR), player and coach, is the son of Henry A. Moon, a farmer–laborer, and Margie (Vernon) Moon, is of Scotch and Irish heritage, and graduated from Bay High School. He earned a Bachelor of Science degree in physical education and a Master of Education degree in administrative education from Texas A&M University. The 6-foot, 175-pound, right-handed, athletically built Moon received a $6,000 signing bonus from the St. Louis Cardinals (NL) in 1950. From 1950 to 1952, the St. Louis Cardinals allowed Moon to report late to Omaha, NE (WL) after his college semesters were completed. Moon, who batted .307 in 131 games at Rochester, NY (IL) in 1953, was booed in St. Louis at his first major league game in April 1954. To make room for him, the Cardinals had traded popular outfielder Enos Slaughter* to the New York Yankees (AL) the day before. The jeers turned quickly to cheers, as Moon clouted a HR in his first major league at-bat. He compiled a .304 batting average with 12 HR, 106 runs, and 76 RBI, edging out Henry Aaron* to become the first St. Louis Cardinal to win the NL Rookie of the Year Award. From 1954 to 1957, Moon remained a paradigm of consistency in the St. Louis lineup, never batting below .295. In 1957, he belted a career-high 24 HR and enjoyed a 24-game hitting streak. Moon played first base 51 games in 1955 and 52 games in 1956 on days when regular first baseman Stan Musial* moved to the outfield.

St. Louis Cardinals general manager Bing Devine, however, wanted to improve the outfield defensively after the 1958 season. Moon did not have a strong arm and just had completed an injury-marred season, batting only .238. In December 1958 the St. Louis Cardinals traded him to the Los Angeles Dodgers (NL) for outfielder Gino Cimoli.

In the Los Angeles Coliseum, the left field wall stood only 251 feet away from home plate and was topped with a 40-foot screen. Moon developed an inside-out swing to loft opposite field HR. In 1959, he belted 14 of his 19 HR, or "Moon shots," over the left field screen, batting third in the Los Angeles Dodger lineup ahead of Duke Snider.* Moon, who also led the NL in triples with 11 and batted .302, hit .261 in the 1959 World Series, helping the Los Angeles Dodgers defeat the Chicago White Sox in six games. Moon batted .299 and won a Gold Glove in 1960 while compiling a career-high .328 batting average and leading the NL with a .438 on-base percentage the following season. In the early 1960s, the Los Angeles Dodgers developed young outfielders Tommy Davis,* Willie Davis,* and Frank Howard.* They gradually pushed Moon into a utility, pinch-hitting role from 1962 until his retirement after the 1965 season. His major league record included 1,457 games, 737 runs, 1,399 hits, 212 doubles, 142 HR, 661 RBI, and a .289 batting average.

Moon married Bettye Lewis Knowles on December 21, 1951 and has five children, Wallace Joseph, Zola, Elizabeth, Mary, and Larhesa. He served as athletic director at John Brown University from 1967 to 1977 and coached baseball until the program was discontinued. Moon presides over Triangle Financial Corporation in Bryan, TX and lives in College Station, TX.

BIBLIOGRAPHY: Bob Broeg, *Redbirds: A Century of Cardinals' Baseball* (St. Louis, MO, 1981); Bob Broeg and Jerry Vickery, *St. Louis Cardinals Encyclopedia* (Grand Rapids, MI, 1998); William F. McNeil, *The Dodgers Encyclopedia* (Champaign, IL, 1997); Henry L. Freund, Jr., "Change of Allegiance Inspired by a New Hero," *BRJ* 14 (1985), pp. 33–34; Gene Karst and Martin J. Jones, Jr., *Who's Who in Professional Baseball* (New Rochelle, NY, 1973); Wallace Moon file, National Baseball Library, Cooperstown, NY; Stan Musial as told to Bob Broeg, *Stan Musial: "The Man's" Own Story* (Garden City, NY, 1964).

Frank J. Olmsted

MOORE, Earl Alonzo "Crossfire" (b. July 29, 1879, Pickerington, OH; d. November 28, 1961, Columbus, OH), player, was born on a farm to parents of English descent and was the 12th of 14 children. Moore, a 6-foot, 195-pound right-hander who had eight years of schooling, began his professional baseball career with Dayton, OH (ISL) in 1899 at $50 a month. In 1901, he joined the Cleveland Blues (AL) at a $3,000 salary for the season. On May 9, 1901, Moore pitched the AL's first no-hitter by holding the Chicago White Sox hitless through nine innings. In the tenth inning, however, Chicago's Sam Mertes singled to help the White Sox win, 4–2.

After a 16–14 rookie season and 17–17 mark in 1902, Moore won 19 games and led the AL with a 1.74 ERA in 1903. A crossfire delivery and an outstanding curve ball made him one of the AL's top pitchers in his first five seasons. In 1906, he was hit on the instep by a batted ball against the New York Highlanders (AL) and pitched just five games that season. The

Cleveland Naps (AL) traded him to the New York Highlanders for Walter Clarkson in May 1907. Moore struggled at 2–6 before New York optioned him to Jersey City, NJ (EL).

The Philadelphia Phillies (NL) purchased Moore's contract in 1908. He rewarded them with several big seasons. Moore's best campaign came in 1910, when he won 22 games and led the NL in shutouts (6) and strikeouts (185). His performance declined thereafter due to a recurrence of his old foot problems and his reluctance to stay in good playing condition. The Philadelphia Phillies sold him to the Chicago Cubs (NL) in July 1913. Moore finished his professional career with the Buffalo Feds (FL) in 1914. In 14 major league seasons, he pitched in 388 games with 162 wins, 154 losses, and a 2.78 ERA.

Moore, who married Blanche Patneau in February 1903, served in the US Army during World War I and sold real estate in Ohio.

BIBLIOGRAPHY: Franklin Lewis, *The Cleveland Indians* (New York, 1949); Earl Moore file, National Baseball Library, Cooperstown, NY; *TSN*, January 10, 1962; John Phillips, *Who Was Who in Cleveland Baseball 1901–10* (Cabin John, MD, 1989); Frederick G. Lieb and Stan Baumgartner, *The Philadelphia Phillies* (New York, 1953); Rich Westcott and Frank Bilovsky, *The New Phillies Encyclopedia* (Philadelphia, PA, 1993).
                                                                                         Lyle Spatz

MOORE, Joseph Gregg "Joe," "Jo-Jo," "The Gause Ghost" (b. December 25, 1908, Gause, TX), player, is the son of Charles Moore and Rowena Moore and graduated in 1927 from Crystal City High School. He attended Texas A&M University briefly before signing as an outfielder with Coleman, TX (WTxL) in 1928.

Moore remained in Coleman for the 1929 campaign and played for San Antonio, TX (TL) in 1930. San Antonio sold him to the New York Giants (NL) at season's end. He debuted with the New York Giants on September 17, 1930. New York optioned Moore to Newark, NJ (IL) in 1931. He opened the 1932 season with Jersey City, NJ (IL). Bill Terry* replaced John McGraw* as New York Giants manager and recalled Moore in June 1932.

The 5-foot 10-inch, 157 pounder patrolled left field for the New York Giants through the 1941 campaign, leading the NL in at-bats in 1935 with 681. Moore batted .298 with 1,615 career hits, 79 HR, and 513 RBI, making the NL All-Star squad six times. He appeared in the 1933, 1936, and 1937 World Series, batting .274 in 16 post-season contests against the Washington Senators and New York Yankees.

Following his major league tenure, Moore spent two seasons with Indianapolis, IN (AA) and then ranched on 1,500 acres near Gause. He married Jewell Ely on January 29, 1931. They had one son, Joseph, Jr.

BIBLIOGRAPHY: *The Baseball Encyclopedia*, 10th ed. (New York, 1996); John Hillman, telephone interview with Joseph Moore, August 20, 1997; Brent P. Kelley, *The Early*

Stars (Jefferson, NC, 1997); Joseph Moore file, National Baseball Library, Cooperstown, NY; Noel Hynd, *The Giants of the Polo Grounds* (New York, 1998); Peter Williams, *When the Giants Were Giants* (Chapel Hill, NC, 1994); Fred Stein, *Under Coogan's Bluff* (Glenshaw, PA, 1978); *Who's Who in the Major Leagues* (Chicago, IL, 1935).

John Hillman

MOORE, Terry Bluford (b. May 27, 1912, Vernon, AL; d. March 29, 1995, Collinsville, IL), player, manager, and coach, ranked among the greatest defensive center fielders in NL history. The 5-foot 11-inch, 195-pound right-hander possessed large hands and exceptional mobility. As with Tris Speaker,* he played a shallow center field and easily moved both laterally and backward. The fiery competitor and clutch hitter captained and led the St. Louis Cardinals (NL) for several seasons and combined well with outstanding outfielders Joe Medwick,* Enos Slaughter,* and Stan Musial* during some of the Cardinals' best seasons in the 1930s and 1940s.

Moore spent his entire baseball playing career with the St. Louis Cardinals organization, posting a .325 batting average at Elmira, NY (NYPL) and Columbus, OH (AA) in 1934 and 1935. He started for the St. Louis Cardinals from 1935 through 1942, averaging .284 at the plate with 1,067 hits, 221 doubles, and 423 RBI. In 1939 and 1940, he hit a career-high 17 HR. His baseball career was interrupted by three years of World War II military service, including work in Panama as an Army physical training instructor in 1943. He returned to the St. Louis Cardinals in 1946 and matched his prewar work the following year with a .283 batting average.

In 1,298 major league games lifetime, he batted .280, made 1,318 hits, and scored 719 runs. He appeared in the victorious 1942 and 1946 World Series against the New York Yankees and Boston Red Sox, respectively, and was selected to the NL All-Star teams from 1939 through 1942. Moore tied a major league record by making six hits in six at-bats on September 5, 1935, made four extra-base hits in one game on August 25, 1935, and led NL outfielders in fielding average (1939) and in putouts (1936, 1940). After finishing his playing career in 1948, Moore coached for the St. Louis Cardinals from 1949 to 1952 and 1956 to 1958 and managed the 1954 Philadelphia Phillies (NL) to a 35–42 mark. A hunting enthusiast, Moore resided in Collinsville, IL.

BIBLIOGRAPHY: Terry Moore file, National Baseball Library, Cooperstown, NY; Frederick G. Lieb, *The St. Louis Cardinals* (New York, 1945); Rob Rains, *The St. Louis Cardinals* (New York, 1992); Mike Shatzkin, ed., *The Ballplayers* (New York, 1990); *TSN Baseball Register*, 1936–1949; Rich Westcott, *Masters of the Diamond* (Jefferson, NC, 1994); Bob Broeg and Jerry Vickery, *St. Louis Cardinals Encyclopedia* (Grand Rapids, MI, 1998); Thomas Aylesworth and Benton Minks, *The Encyclopedia of Baseball Managers* (New York, 1990).

Leonard H. Frey

MOORE, Walter "Dobie" (b. 1893, Fayetteville, GA; d. circa 1938 to 1942, Detroit, MI), player, starred for the Kansas City Monarchs (NNL) from 1920 through 1926. Moore lived in Georgia with his grandparents by 1900. He joined the U.S. Army as a young adult and helped the powerful Philippines-based 25th Infantry black team gain acclaim as the armed forces' top baseball club in 1911. In 1915, Moore starred as the Hawaii baseball 25th Infantry squad gained their post's championship. His final military assignment came at Fort Huachuca, AZ, where he still played baseball for the 25th Infantry. In 1919, the Monarchs signed Moore and teammates Wilbur Rogan,* Lemuel Hawkins, and Oscar Johnson.

During his seven-year NNL stint, Moore became recognized as the circuit's outstanding shortstop. The stout right-handed batter with power stood 5-feet 11-inches and weighed over 200 pounds. He batted .385 in 1922 and .365 in 1923. Moore attained a .365 career batting average as a Kansas City Monarch, including an NNL-leading .453 in 1924. Moore also led the NNL in 1924 with 139 hits and 26 doubles while posting 10 HR and a .694 slugging average. A loop leading 12 triples followed in 1925.

Moore continued to pound the ball, with a .381 batting average, when tragedy struck in May 1926. The married Moore suffered multiple leg fractures from gun shots fired by a local female acquaintance, Elsie Brown, with whom he had a questionable relationship. Moore vowed annually to make a comeback even into the 1930s, but the wounds ended his baseball career.

During Moore's brief, illustrious sojourn in professional baseball, he also proved an outstanding base runner and defensive shortstop. His play drew raves from major leaguers John McGraw* and Casey Stengel* as well as teammates and opponents in the U.S. Army and the NNL.

The Kansas City Monarchs claimed consecutive NNL pennants from 1923 through 1925 and won the 1924 Black World Series with Moore at shortstop. Moore hit .323 in 16 World Series contests during the 1924 and 1925 classics and .356 in the CUWL.

Moore, who married Frances Davis, probably spent his final years in Detroit, MI.

BIBLIOGRAPHY: *The Baseball Encyclopedia*, 10th ed. (New York, 1996); Chicago (IL) *Defender*, 1924–1925; Phil Dixon, *The Negro Baseball Leagues* (Mattituck, NY, 1992); John B. Holway, *Blackball Stars* (Westport, CT, 1988); John B. Holway, "Dobie Moore," *BRJ* 11 (1982), pp. 168–172; Larry Lester, Negro Leagues Baseball Museum, Kansas City, MO, letter to Merl F. Kleinknecht, December 12, 1992; Robert W. Peterson, *Only the Ball Was White* (Englewood Cliffs, NJ, 1970); Philadelphia (PA) *Tribune*, 1924–1925; Pittsburgh (PA) *Courier*, 1924–1925; James A. Riley, *The Biographical Encyclopedia of the Negro Baseball Leagues* (New York, 1994).

Merl F. Kleinknecht

MOORE, William Wilcy "Cy" (b. May 20, 1897, Bonita, TX; d. March 29, 1963, Hollis, OK), player and manager, worked on his family's cotton farm in rural Oklahoma and attended Hollis, OK High School. After playing semiprofessional baseball locally in 1920, he in July 1921 signed a contract with Fort Worth, TX (TL) and was sent to Paris, TX (ETL). The 6-foot, 195-pound right-hander helped pitch Paris to the ETL title in 1922 and played briefly with Fort Worth in 1923. He was shipped to Ardmore, OK (OKSL) and suffered a subpar season due to illness. Ardmore traded Moore in 1924 to Okmulgee, OK (OKSL), where he severely cut two fingers of his throwing hand on a water bottle. The injury delayed his rise to the major leagues by a year. The resulting scars, combined with a broken wrist incurred in 1925 when he was hit by a batted ball, gave him an unusual sinking curve ball that ultimately made him a successful major league pitcher.

After spending the 1925 season with Greenville, SC (SAL), Moore won 30 games and lost only four in 1926 there. Moore's 17 game winning streak interested the New York Yankees (AL), who bought him following the 1926 season for $3,500. He pitched three years for the New York Yankees, but suffered a bad season in 1929. New York sent Moore to St. Paul, MN (AA), where he won 22 games in 1930. After returning to the major leagues with the Boston Red Sox (AL) in 1931, he was traded to the New York Yankees in May 1932 and finished his major league career there in 1933. His major league career record included 51 wins and 44 losses with a 3.70 ERA. As a reliever, he finished 39–26 with 49 saves and a 3.52 ERA.

Moore's best season came in 1927, when he became the New York Yankees' premier reliever. He posted a 19–7 record and an AL-leading 2.28 ERA. As a reliever, he won 13 and lost three with 13 saves. Baseball writers named him the sport's top pitcher in 1927. During the offseason, Moore fell off a barn and injured his arm. The injury limited him to 60 innings in 1928. Although leading the AL with 10 saves in 1931, he never again achieved his 1927 success.

After his major league career ended in 1933, Moore pitched for the Kansas City, MO Royals (AA) and Oakland, CA Oaks (PCL) from 1934 to 1937, Oklahoma City, OK (TL) in 1938 and 1939, and St. Paul, MN (AA) in 1939. His baseball career ended as manager of Borger, TX (WTNML) in 1940. Moore lived on his Hollis, OK farm with his wife, Grace. They had three sons and a daughter.

BIBLIOGRAPHY: Cy Moore file, National Baseball Library, Cooperstown, NY; *NYT*, April 1, 1963; Mike Shatzkin, ed., *The Ballplayers* (New York, 1990); Marshall Smelser, *The Life that Ruth Built* (New York, 1975); TSN, March 16, 1933, April 13, 1963; John Thorn et al., eds., *Total Baseball*, 5th ed. (New York, 1997); *The Baseball Encyclopedia*, 10th ed. (New York, 1996); Dave Anderson et al., *The Yankees* (New York, 1979); Mark Gallagher, *The Yankee Encyclopedia*, vol. 3 (Champaign, IL, 1997); Frank Graham, *The New York Yankees* (New York, 1943); John Mosedale, *The Greatest of All: The 1927 New York Yankees* (New York, 1974); Leo Trachtenberg, *The Wonder Team* (Bowling Green, OH, 1995); Bob Cairns, *Pen Men* (New York, 1993).

John E. Findling

MORAN, Patrick Joseph (b. February 7, 1876, Fitchburg, MA; d. March 7, 1924, Orlando, FL), player and manager, spent 14 years as a mediocre major league catcher before becoming a highly successful major league manager with the Philadelphia Phillies (1915–1918) and the Cincinnati Reds (1919–1923). Although compiling a .235 lifetime batting average with the Boston Beaneaters (NL, 1901-1905), Chicago Cubs (NL, 1906-1909), and Philadelphia Phillies (NL, 1910–1914), the 5-foot 10-inch, 180-pound Moran was considered a keen student of baseball in general and pitching in particular. He was named manager of the Philadelphia Phillies following the 1914 season, inheriting a talented, erratic team that included outfielder Gavvy Cravath,* first baseman Fred Luderus,* pitcher Grover Cleveland Alexander,* and catcher Bill Killefer. Moran, a stern disciplinarian, developed the Phillies into a tough playing unit behind the outstanding pitching of Alexander and long ball hitting of Cravath. Alexander won 31 games, hurled 12 shutouts, and boasted a 1.22 ERA, while Cravath led the NL with 24 HR and 115 RBI. The Phillies started quickly in 1915, and won the NL pennant with a 90–72 record, 7 games ahead of the Boston Braves. In the 1915 World Series against the Boston Red Sox, Alexander won the first game. The Phillies lost three straight 2–1 games before dropping the last contest, 5–1. Under Moran's direction, the Phillies finished second for the next two seasons. Since the hitters, however, were aging, Alexander's solid pitching alone kept the Phillies in contention.

After the 1917 season, financially pressed Phillies owner William Baker began selling his stars. The Chicago Cubs acquired Alexander and catcher Killefer for $60,000. The Phillies faded quickly to sixth place in 1918, resulting in the firing of Moran. The Cincinnati Reds immediately hired Moran, who duplicated his earlier success by winning an NL pennant in his first year as pilot. The Reds won the the 1919 World Series against the scandal-ridden Chicago White Sox. Moran kept the Reds in contention for the next three seasons, but died on the eve of the 1924 season. His Bright's disease and pneumonia had been brought on by a lifetime of hard drinking. The 48-year-old Moran left a wife and two children. Moran, a talented manager, compiled a career record of 748 wins versus 586 losses and ranks high with a .561 winning percentage among those managing at least 1,000 major league games.

BIBLIOGRAPHY: Ritter Collett, *The Cincinnati Reds* (Virginia Beach, VA, 1976); Floyd Connor and John Snyder, *Day-by-Day in Cincinnati Reds History* (West Point, NY, 1984); Tom Meany, *Baseball's Greatest Teams* (New York, 1949); Philadelphia (PA) *Public Ledger*, March 8, 1924; Edwin Pope, *Baseball's Greatest Managers* (Garden City, NY, 1960); Rich Wescott and Frank Bilovsky, *The New Phillies Encyclopedia* (Philadelphia, PA 1993); Thomas Aylesworth and Benton Minks, *The Encyclopedia of Baseball Managers* (New York, 1990); Harold Kaese, *The Boston Braves* (New York, 1948); Warren Brown, *The Chicago Cubs* (New York, 1946); Frederick G. Lieb and Stan Baumgartner, *The Philadelphia Phillies* (New York, 1953); Allen Lewis, *The Philadel-*

phia Phillies: A Pictorial History (Virginia Beach, VA, 1981); Lee Allen, *The Cincinnati Reds* (New York, 1948).

John P. Rossi

MORELAND, Bobby Keith (b. May 2, 1954, Dallas, TX), player, coach, and sportscaster, is the son of Bobby Charles Moreland and Barbara (Henderson) Moreland and graduated in 1972 from R. L. Turner High School in Carrollton, TX, where he excelled in baseball and football. He also played on the Connie Mack* world championship baseball team. In 1972, Moreland entered the University of Texas on a football–baseball scholarship. He led the freshman football team with seven interceptions and lettered as a reserve defensive back on the 1973 SWC championship team.

As a third baseman for the Longhorns baseball team, Moreland received All-America honors three straight years. He was named SWC Player of the Year as a freshman in 1973 and batted .410 for the 1975 NCAA championship squad. He remains the second-leading career hitter in school history with a .388 batting average, having made 274 hits. He married Cindy Scott on August 30, 1975 and has a daughter, Courtney, and son, Cole.

The Philadelphia Phillies (NL) selected Moreland in the seventh round of the 1975 free agent draft. He spent four seasons in the minor leagues before appearing briefly with the Philadelphia Phillies in 1978. The Phillies converted the good hitter, average fielder, and slow runner into a catcher, but most of his major league playing time came as an outfielder, third baseman, and first baseman.

At Oklahoma City, OK (AA) in 1979, Moreland batted .302 with 20 HR and 107 RBI. He joined the Philadelphia Phillies as a reserve in 1980 and 1981 before being traded to the Chicago Cubs (NL) in December 1981. Moreland, who had batted .333 in the 1980 World Series against the Kansas City Royals, started with the Cubs for six seasons and reached his potential as a hitter. His highlights included a .302 batting average in 1983, a .307 batting average and career-high 106 RBI in 1985, and a career-best 27 HR in 1987. Chicago traded him to the San Diego Padres (NL) in February 1988. Moreland ended his major league career with the Detroit Tigers (AL) and Baltimore Orioles (AL) in 1989. In 1,306 career major league games, he batted .279 with 121 HR and 674 RBI.

After completing his Bachelor's degree requirements at the University of Texas in 1991, Moreland coached baseball part-time for the Texas Longhorns and Southwest Texas State University. He founded the Baseball Academy of Texas in 1994, owns a candy distributorship, and serves as a color commentator for an Austin, TX television station, which carries Longhorns games.

BIBLIOGRAPHY: Eddie Gold and Art Ahrens, *The New Era Cubs, 1941–1985* (Chicago, IL, 1985); Robert E. Kelly, *Baseball's Best* (Jefferson, NC, 1988); Rich Westcott and Frank Bilovsky, *The New Phillies Encyclopedia* (Philadelphia, PA, 1993); Frank

Dolson, *The Philadelphia Story* (South Bend, IN, 1981); *TSN Baseball Register*, 1990; *University of Texas 1996 Baseball Media Guide*; Keith Moreland, letter to Jay Langhammer, February 1996; Keith Moreland file, National Baseball Library, Cooperstown, NY.

Jay Langhammer

MORGAN, Joe Leonard (b. September 19, 1943, Bonham, TX), player and sportscaster, grew up in Oakland, CA and developed as an athlete there. Morgan attended Castlemount High School, where he excelled in baseball as a second baseman. After graduation, he in April 1967 married high school sweetheart Gloria Stewart with whom he has two daughters, Lisa and Angela. After attending Merritt JC and earning all-conference honors on the baseball team there, he enrolled at California State University, Hayward. In 1963, he began his professional baseball career with the Houston Colt 45s (NL) organization at Modesto, CA (CaL) and spent two years in the minor leagues. After batting .332 at Durham, NC (CrL) in 1963, he batted .323 the following year, collected 160 hits, and belted 12 HR for San Antonio, TX (TL) and won the TL MVP Award.

As a rookie with the Houston, TX (NL) club in 1965, the left-handed batting Morgan collected 163 hits, contributed 14 HR, and led the NL with 97 bases on balls. Those achievements earned him *TSN* NL Rookie of the Year Award. Morgan continued performing for Houston until November 1971, when he was traded to the Cincinnati Reds (NL). The 5-foot 7-inch, 164-pound second baseman enjoyed his finest years with the Reds and had banner seasons in 1975 and 1976. In 1975, he batted .327, made 163 hits, and 17 HR and knocked in 94 runs. In addition, he stole 67 bases and led the NL with 132 walks. In 1976, the talented Morgan hit .320, belted 27 HR, drove in 111 runs, and stole 60 bases. Both years, he served as the chief catalyst in the Reds' championship drives and earned two consecutive NL MVP awards. Morgan's fielding proved equally impressive during his stay at Cincinnati, as the right-handed second baseman set a major league record with 91 straight errorless games in 1977–1978.

In January 1980, Cincinnati returned Morgan to the Houston Astros (NL). After one season there, he joined the San Francisco Giants (NL) as a free agent in February 1981 and spent the 1981 and 1982 seasons with them. Morgan's second season with the Giants saw him belt 14 HR, drive in 61 runs, and contribute a .289 batting average. His achievements that year earned him the NL Comeback Player of the Year Award. In December 1982, Morgan was dealt to the Philadelphia Phillies (NL) and helped lead the Phillies to the 1983 NL crown. Morgan's last year in the major leagues was spent with the Oakland Athletics (AL) in 1984. In 1984, he replaced Rogers Hornsby* as the most prolific HR-hitting second baseman of all time. After that season, he retired and became an announcer for the Cincinnati Reds. Morgan finished his career with a .271 batting average, 2,517 hits, 449 doubles, 96 triples, 268 HR, 689 stolen bases, 1,133 RBI, and 1,865 walks—the latter being an NL record. Besides these accomplishments, Morgan made the NL All-Star team nine times and won five Gold Glove Awards.

He announced for the San Francisco Giants from 1986 through 1993 and served as NBC Game of the Week announcer. Since 1994, he has announced for ESPN. Off the field, Morgan enjoys playing golf, tennis, billiards, and dominos. Although using his activities for exercise, Morgan claimed that they also strengthened his concentration and coordination. In 1990, he was elected to the National Baseball Hall of Fame.

BIBLIOGRAPHY: Nathan Aaseng, *Little Giants of Pro Sports* (New York, 1980); J. Armstrong, "Little Joe," *Sport* 88 (November 1997), pp. 60ff; Joe Morgan and David Falkner, *Joe Morgan* (New York, 1993); John Benson et al., *Baseball's Top 100* (Wilton, CT, 1997); Floyd Conner and John Snyder, *Day-by-Day in Cincinnati Reds History* (West Point, NY, 1984); Bob Hertzel, *The Big Red Machine* (Englewood Cliffs, NJ, 1976); Bob Rathgeber, *Cincinnati Reds Scrapbook* (Virginia Beach, VA, 1982); Robert H. Walker, *Cincinnati and the Big Red Machine* (Bloomington, IN, 1988); Mark Mulvoy, "The Little Big Man," *SI* 44 (April 12, 1976), pp. 52–60; Robert Obojski, *Bush League* (New York, 1975); Joe Morgan file, National Baseball Library, Cooperstown, NY; David L. Porter, ed., *African-American Sports Greats* (Westport, CT, 1995); Tom Seaver, *Tom Seaver's All-Time Baseball Greats* (New York, 1984); "The Hot New Rich," *Time* 109 (June 13, 1977), p. 76; *WWA*, 41st ed. (1980–1981), p. 2366.

Samuel O. Regalado

MORRILL, John Francis "Honest John" (b. February 19, 1855, Boston, MA; d. April 2, 1932, Boston, MA), player, manager, umpire, and sporting goods executive, was one of Boston's most respected and beloved sportsmen. He played mostly at first base in 13 years with the Boston Red Caps (NL) and Boston Beaneaters (NL), but also performed at every other position including pitcher. The son of Jeremiah Morrill and Bridget (Moylan) Morrill, he organized the Stars as a teenager. The baseball club became Massachusetts junior champions. In 1875 he played for Boston's Lowells, which won the state's senior amateur title. His performance in a preseason game against Boston (NL) led the Red Stockings to sign him to a multi-year contract.

When shortstop George Wright* left Boston to manage the Providence Grays (NL) in 1879, Morrill replaced him as team captain. Boston manager Harry Wright* was fired after a sixth-place finish in 1881. Morrill took his place and led Boston to a third-place tie in 1882. He yielded the captaincy to second-baseman Jack Burdock in 1883, but reassumed it in midseason and brought the club from fourth place to the NL pennant.

The 5-foot 10½-inch, 155-pound right-hander rarely hit for power and batted .260 in 1,265 major league games. His 1,275 hits included 239 doubles, 80 triples, and 43 HR for a .367 slugging average. He ranked among NL offensive leaders in 1883, finishing fifth in HR, fourth in RBI, and second to Dan Brouthers* of the Buffalo Bisons in slugging average (.525), total bases (212), and triples (16). Morrill also led NL first basemen for the only time with a .974 fielding average, posted his only win as a pitcher, and recorded a career-high .319 batting average.

Morrill co-authored with New York Metropolitans (AA) pitcher Tim Keefe* the first baseball instructional manual in 1884. The Boston Red Stockings finished second to Providence that year and in fifth place the next two seasons. Morrill remained manager in 1887, but was replaced as captain by Michael "King" Kelly.* Morrill's captaincy was restored in September, with the club again finishing fifth. After Boston rose to fourth in 1888, Morrill engaged in a preseason dispute with the club owners in 1889 and was sold to the Washington Statesmen (NL). He played first base and managed the Washington Statesmen until his release in July. He had broken his finger playing for the last place club. In 696 games under his field leadership, Morrill's teams compiled a 348–334 record for a .510 winning percentage.

In March 1890, Morrill opened a sporting goods store in Boston. He also served as assistant treasurer of the Boston Reds (PL), playing in two games, and substituted as NL umpire in 1891 and 1896.

Around 1892, Morrill accepted a management position at Boston's Wright & Ditson sporting goods company. During the 1895–1897 baseball seasons, he wrote a column for the Boston *Sunday Journal*. Subsequently, he became an avid golfer.

Morrill suffered a stroke in the 1920s, but recovered. He retired as Wright & Ditson's general manager in 1931, five months before his death from double pneumonia. He was survived by Georgene M. (Hogsett) Morrill, his wife of 54 years, and by four of their seven children.

BIBLIOGRAPHY: Thomas Aylesworth and Benton Minks, *The Encyclopedia of Baseball Managers* (New York, 1990); Gary Caruso, *The Braves Encyclopedia* (Philadelphia, PA, 1995); Boston (MA) *Sunday Globe*, April 3, 1932, p. 20; Boston (MA) *Sunday Post*, April 3, 1932, p. 18; James Charlton, ed., *The Baseball Chronology* (New York, 1991); Harold Kaese, *The Boston Braves* (New York, 1948); John Morrill file, National Baseball Library, Cooperstown, NY; Bob Richardson, correspondence with Frederick Ivor-Campbell, 1997; Robert L. Tiemann and Mark Rucker, eds., *Nineteenth Century Stars* (Kansas City, MO, 1989); John Thorn et al., eds., *Total Baseball*, 5th ed. (New York, 1997).

Frederick Ivor-Campbell

MORRIS, Edward "Cannonball" (b. September 29, 1862, Brooklyn, NY; d. April 12, 1937, Pittsburgh, PA), player, ranked among the best major league pitchers for four seasons in the 1880s before injuries and strong drink prematurely ended his playing career. Morris grew up in San Francisco, CA, playing for the National and Mystic clubs from 1880 to 1882 and then caught for Philadelphia, PA (ECA). With Reading, PA (ISL) in 1883, the 165-pound, switch-hitting left-hander became a pitcher and compiled a 16–6 win–loss record.

For the major league Columbus, OH Buckeyes (AA) in 1884, Morris won

34 games, lost only 13 decisions, hurled a no-hitter in May against the Pittsburgh Alleghenys, and compiled an AA-high .723 winning percentage. His pitching helped propel the Columbus Buckeyes to a second-place finish from sixth the previous year. The AA dropped Columbus when the league shrank from 12 clubs to eight, sending Morris and nine of his teammates to revive the struggling Pittsburgh Alleghenys. The Alleghenys improved from tenth place in 1884 to third in 1885, as Morris won 39 games, one less than the AA leader. He led the AA with 63 complete games, 581 innings pitched, 298 strikeouts, and seven shutouts. In 1886, the Pittsburgh Alleghenys rose to second place. Morris tied Dave Foutz* of the St. Louis Browns for the AA lead with 41 wins, again pacing the AA with 12 shutouts. Both figures remain Pittsburgh Alleghenys records. Morris incredibly completed all his 126 games started in 1885 and 1886. Ralph Horton's Relative Performance System rates Morris the top pitcher in the AA for both seasons.

The Pittsburgh Alleghenys moved from the AA to the NL in 1887, finishing sixth. Morris, plagued by a sore arm, a new pitching rule that curbed his leaping delivery, a suspension for refusing to pitch in a game, and fines for drunkenness, appeared in only 38 games and compiled a 14–22 win–loss record. In the off-season, Morris mastered the pitching restriction. Although the Pittsburgh Alleghenys again finished sixth in 1888, Morris regained much of his former effectiveness. He led the NL with 54 complete games, winning 29 and losing 23. A sore arm and stomach muscle injury limited Morris to 21 games and a subpar 6–13 record in 1889. He jumped to the Pittsburgh Burghers (PL) for 1890, his final major league year. Morris missed part of the season under expulsion for heavy drinking and pitched in only 18 games, compiling an 8–7 record. In seven major league seasons, Morris won 171 games and lost 122. He struck out 1,217 batters, yielded 2,468 hits in 2,678 innings, and compiled a 2.82 ERA. He completed 297 of his 307 starts and hurled 29 shutouts.

Morris lived in Pittsburgh after his playing career, building and operating a hotel near the ball park. He four years later opened another nearby hotel, which he operated until 1902. He also helped operate a pool hall and earned extra money providing legal assistance "as an attorney in fact." From 1907 to 1912, he formed a wholesale liquor business. In 1912, he was appointed as night captain at Rockview Penitentiary. Morris was hired in 1916 by former major league pitcher Ad Gumbert, who had been elected an Allegheny County commissioner, as a highway department foreman and worked for the county until complications of a toe infection brought on his final illness.

BIBLIOGRAPHY: Ralph L. Horton, *Baseball's Best Pitchers 1876–1992* (St. Louis, MO, 1993); David Nemec, *The Beer and Whisky League* (New York, 1994); Frederick G. Lieb, *The Pittsburgh Pirates* (New York, 1948); Ed Morris file, National Baseball Library, Cooperstown, NY; John Thorn et al., eds., *Total Baseball*, 5th ed. (New York, 1997); Robert L. Tiemann and Mark Rucker, eds., *Nineteenth Century Stars* (Kansas City, MO, 1989).

Frederick Ivor-Campbell

MORRIS, John Scott "Jack" (b. May 16, 1955, St. Paul, MN), player, is the son of Arvid Morris, an electric technician, and Donna Morris and was a 6-foot 2-inch, 195-pound right-handed pitcher. The Morris family believed strongly in sports, with Jack participating in all the youth athletic programs. Since his father regarded winning as the only criteria of success, Morris developed an explosive temperament that later slowed his professional development.

After pitching in high school and for Brigham Young University, Morris was selected fifth by the Detroit Tigers (AL) in the 1976 baseball draft. He spent the 1976 season with Montgomery, AL (SL), winning two and losing three. He began the 1977 season with Evansville, IN (AA), but made his major league debut with the Detroit Tigers on July 26 against the Chicago White Sox. He developed a sore right shoulder, thus shortening his 1977 and 1978 campaigns. In 1979 he started the season with Evansville, but won 17 games and lost seven contests after being recalled by the Detroit Tigers.

In 1980, he fired a one-hitter against the Minnesota Twins and won 16 decisions. The following season, he triumphed an AL-best 14 times while losing 7 to share the AL lead in pitching. He finished third in the 1981 AL Cy Young Award voting and pitched two scoreless innings in the All-Star game. The 1981 season saw Morris enjoy an eight-game winning streak. Morris ranked among the AL leaders in several categories in 1982, taking 17 of 33 contests. He won 20 games and lost 13 decisions in 1983, leading the AL in innings pitched and strikeouts. After recording 19 victories in 1984 and 16 in 1985, he recorded 21 triumphs against only 8 losses and led the AL with 6 shutouts in 1986. Morris sought arbitration in February 1987 and won a $1,850,000 salary, the largest such award up until that time. The next two seasons resulted in 18–11 and 15–13 marks for Morris. In February 1991, Morris joined the Minnesota Twins as a free agent. Morris compiled an 18–12 record and 3.43 ERA, helping the Twins become the first AL team to rise from last to first place in a single season. He struck out 163 batters in 246.2 innings, ranking third in innings pitched. Morris, Scott Erickson, and Kevin Tapani tied the club record for most victories by a starting trio (54), set by Dave Boswell, Jim Perry,* and Jim Kaat* in 1969. Detroit selected him as opening-day pitcher for nine consecutive years. Morris achieved more victories in the 1980s (162) than any other major league pitcher. In 1988 he hurled a one-hit game against the Baltimore Orioles.

The Toronto Blue Jays (AL) signed Morris as a free agent in December 1991. In 1992, Morris led the AL with 21 victories and compiled a 21–6 record to help Toronto win the AL East. His major league career ended with the Cleveland Indians (AL) in 1994.

Morris was named to five AL All-Star teams and pitched in the AL Championship Series in 1984, 1987, 1991, and 1992. In the 1984 World Series against the San Diego Padres, he won two games, lost none, hurled two complete games, and compiled an impressive 2.00 ERA. In the 1991 AL

Championship Series, Morris defeated the Toronto Blue Jays twice to help the Twins win the AL pennant. In Game 1 of the 1991 World Series, Morris surrendered only two runs in seven innings to help Minnesota defeat the Atlanta Braves, 5–2. He also started Game 4 and allowed one run in six innings, but was not involved in the decision. Morris shut out the Braves, 1–0, on seven hits in 10 innings in the decisive seventh game at the Metrodome, giving the Twins the hard-earned 1991 World Series title. He won the World Series MVP award, being the first pitcher since Tom Seaver* of the New York Mets in 1969 to hurl ten consecutive innings in a World Series game. He lost once in the 1992 AL Championship Series to the Oakland A's and twice in the 1992 World Series to the Atlanta Braves. Morris enjoyed a 4–3 record in World Series competition and a 7–4 overall mark in post-season games.

In 18 major league seasons, Morris boasted a 254–186 win–loss record and a 3.90 ERA. He appeared in 549 major league games and hurled 175 complete games in 527 starts with 28 shutouts. He later pitched for the St. Paul, MN Saints (NWL).

BIBLIOGRAPHY: Jack Morris file, National Baseball Library, Cooperstown, NY; Sparky Anderson and Dan Ewald, *Bless You Boys* (Chicago, IL, 1984); Joe Falls, *The Detroit Tigers: An Illustrated History* (New York, 1989); *The Baseball Encyclopedia*, 10th ed. (New York, 1996); *Detroit Tigers Media Guide, 1988*; Richard Hoffer, "Change Up," *SI* 77 (October 5, 1992), pp. 54–57; Fred T. Smith, *Tiger Tales and Trivia* (Lathrup Village, MI, 1988); Minneapolis (MN) *Star and Tribune*, February 14, 1987; Jack Morris, letter to Stan W. Carlson, 1990.

Stan W. Carlson

MOSEBY, Lloyd Anthony "Shaker" (b. November 5, 1959, Portland, AR), player and coach, is the son of Terry Moseby, a farmer, and married Adrienne Brown. They have two children, Alicia and Lloyd II. Moseby, an All-American basketball and baseball player at Oakland, CA High School, was considered by many to be the nation's premier high school hitting prospect. The Toronto Blue Jays (AL) signed him as the second player chosen in the 1978 draft. Seventy-five colleges offered the 6-foot, 205-pound basketball guard scholarships. He was named an All-Star his first two minor league seasons at Medicine Hat, Canada (PrL) in 1978 and Dunedin, FL (FSL) in 1979, making the 1979 Topps Class A All-Star team.

The Toronto Blue Jays promoted the center fielder in 1980. His batting average jumped from .236 in 1982 to .315 in 1983, setting a major-league record improvement from one full season to the next. He no longer tried to pull everything, but used the whole field to capitalize on his strength and speed. He shared the AL lead in triples with 15 in 1984. Moseby, a smart and aggressive base runner, stole 24 or more bases in seven consecutive seasons from 1983 to 1989 and remained dangerous on the base paths throughout his career. He earned a *TSN* Silver Slugger Award and *TSN* AL

All-Star team honors in 1983 and played in the 1986 AL All-Star game. In 1987, Moseby combined a .282 batting average with personal highs of 26 HR, 96 RBI, and 106 runs. He, George Bell,* and Jesse Barfield* ranked among the best major league outfields in the mid-1980s. A bad back and loss of arm strength eventually diminished his fielding skills.

Moseby joined the Detroit Tigers (AL) for the 1990 and 1991 seasons and concluded his playing career with the Yomiuri, Japan Giants (JCL) in 1992 and 1993. His major league career included a .257 batting average, 737 RBI, 280 stolen bases, and 169 HR. He hit .255 in 12 1985 and 1989 AL Championship Series games with Toronto. In 1997, he coached St. Catherines, Canada (NYPL) in the Toronto organization and for the Blue Jays in 1999.

BIBLIOGRAPHY: Lloyd Moseby file, National Baseball Library, Cooperstown, NY; Peter C. Bjarkman, *The Toronto Blue Jays* (New York, 1990); Jim Brosnan, "Lloyd Moseby: Red Hot Blue Jay," *BL* 74 (September 1984), pp. 24–33; *Detroit Tigers Yearbook*, 1990, 1991; Bob Hertzel, "Lloyd Moseby: He's Racing Toward Big League Stardom," *BD* 42 (December 1983), pp. 59–60; *The Scouting Report*, 1984, 1986 (New York, 1984, 1986); *Toronto Blue Jays Media Guide*, 1982.

John T. English

MOSES, Wallace, Jr. "Wally," "Peep Sight" (b. October 8, 1910, Uvalda, GA; d. October 10, 1990, Vidalia, GA), player, coach, and scout, was the son of Wallace Moses, Sr. and the archetype of the small, speedy, hustling outfielder. A non–power hitter, he made 2,138 hits, batted .291, and hit 89 HR in 17 AL seasons with the Philadelphia Athletics (1935–1941, 1949–1951), Chicago White Sox (1942–1946), and Boston Red Sox (1946–1948). Moses came to the AL at age 25 after playing outfield with Augusta, GA (PlmL) and Elmira, NY (PoL) in 1931, Monroe, LA (CSL) and Tyler, TX (TL) in 1932, and Galveston, TX (TL) in 1933 and 1934. Moses hit over .300 for the Philadelphia Athletics each year from 1935 to 1941. His best year on the basepaths came with the White Sox in 1943, when he pilfered 56 bases. He led the AL with 12 triples in 1943 and 35 doubles in 1945.

A career marked by holdouts and toiling for second division clubs culminated in July 1946, when the Boston Red Sox (AL) purchased the veteran as pennant insurance. The left-handed, 5-foot 10-inch, 160-pound Moses hit .239 during the season and batted 5 for 12 in his only World Series for a .417 mark against the St. Louis Cardinals. In 2,012 major league career games, he made 435 doubles, 110 triples, 821 walks, and 174 stolen bases, scored 1,124 runs, and knocked in 679 runs. Moses retired as a player in 1951 and enjoyed a distinguished career as one of the game's best batting coaches for the Philadelphia Athletics (1952–1954), NL Philadelphia Phillies (1955–1958), NL Cincinnati Reds (1959–1960), AL New York Yankees (1961–1963, 1966), and AL Detroit Tigers (1967–1970). From 1964 through 1966, he scouted for the New York Yankees. Nicknamed "Peep Sight" with the White Sox for his fine batting eye, he taught his skills of placing the ball, running down the first base line fast, and catching flaws in a batting stroke. He tutored batting champions Ferris Fain* and Richie Ashburn,* both of whom hit in Moses' basic style. On December 2, 1936, Moses married Billie Mae Haines.

BIBLIOGRAPHY: Warren Brown, *The Chicago White Sox* (New York, 1952); Frederick G. Lieb, *Connie Mack* (New York, 1945); Wally Moses file, National Baseball Library, Cooperstown, NY; Rich Westcott, *Masters of the Diamond* (Jefferson, NC, 1994); Connie Mack, *My 66 Years in the Big Leagues* (Philadelphia, PA, 1950); Richard Lindberg, *Sox* (New York, 1984); Frederick G. Lieb, *The Boston Red Sox* (New York, 1947); Robert Redmount, *The Red Sox Encyclopedia* (Champaign, IL, 1998).

Eric Solomon

MOSTIL, John Anthony "Johnny," "Bananas" (b. June 1, 1896, Chicago, IL; d. December 10, 1970, Midlothian, IL), player, manager, and scout, was a fast and wide-ranging outfielder for the Chicago White Sox (AL) who might have been ranked among the greats of the 1920s except for a bizarre suicide attempt that ruined his career. A lifelong Chicagoan, Mostil was the son of Casper Mostil of suburban Whiting, IN. The Chicago White Sox signed him as a second baseman off the sandlots in 1918. He played 10 major league games before the end of the 1918 season but was optioned to Milwaukee, WI (AA) for two years. Having Eddie Collins* at second base, the Chicago White Sox encouraged Mostil's conversion to the outfield. After returning in 1921, Mostil peaked in the middle of the decade. He scored an NL-leading 135 runs in 1925—a team record that still stands—and batted a career-high .328 in 1926. He led the AL in stolen bases in both years, but was considered shy, withdrawn, and neurasthenic. He also paced AL outfielders with a .985 fielding percentage in 1925.

The 5-foot 8-inch, 169-pound right-hander joined the Chicago White Sox for spring training for 1927 in the Youree Hotel in Shreveport, LA. On March 8, after a reportedly amicable conversation with pitcher Red Faber* and Irene Walsh Faber, Mostil rushed impulsively to the room of Pat Prouty, a fan who had accompanied the White Sox. Mostil gashed himself with a razor blade and pocketknife 13 places on his neck, torso, legs, and left arm. Mostil hemorrhaged so severely that he was given the last rites of the Roman Catholic Church. The press reported that the suicide attempt stemmed from despondency at the spread of neuralgia. Rumors quickly arose that the meeting with Faber and his wife, Irene, had actually been a violent confrontation in which Faber accused Mostil of an adulterous affair with Irene Faber. The episode broke Mostil's engagement to Margaret Carroll of Hammond, IN.

Mostil survived the ordeal, but never married and was not expected to resume baseball because of damage to ligaments in his left wrist. He recovered enough to rejoin the Chicago White Sox for 13 games at the end of the season, but his ability was clearly diminished. He batted .270 in 1928, but appeared in only 12 games in 1929 because of a broken ankle. The Chicago White Sox released him to Toledo, OH (AA) in January 1930. He participated in spring training with the New York Giants (NL) in 1930, but failed to make the team. He played for Toledo in 1930 and 1931 and Little Rock, AR (SA) in 1932 and then became a successful minor league manager, mainly in the NoL.

Mostil became a Chicago White Sox career employee, serving as scout, instructor, and manager in their farm system until two years before his death. In 972 major league games, he batted .301 with 1,054 hits, 376 RBI, and 176 stolen bases.

BIBLIOGRAPHY: Mike Shatzkin, ed., *The Ballplayers* (New York, 1990); John Mostil file, National Baseball Library, Cooperstown, NY; Obituaries, Chicago (IL) *Tribune* and Chicago (IL) *Sun-Times*, December 11, 1970, and *TSN*, December 26, 1970; *TSN Baseball Register*, 1952; Larry Woltz, "Mostil, Sox Star, Cuts Throat," Chicago (IL) *Herald & Examiner*, March 9, 1927, p. 1; Warren Brown, *The Chicago White Sox* (New York, 1952); Richard Lindberg, *Sox* (New York, 1984); Richard Lindberg, *Who's on Third?* (South Bend, IN, 1983).

George W. Hilton

MUELLER, Donald Frederick "Don," "Mandrake the Magician" (b. May 14, 1927, St. Louis, MO), player, performed as an outfielder for the New York Giants (NL) from 1948 to 1957 and Chicago White Sox (AL) in 1958 and 1959. He is the son of Walter Mueller, an outfielder for the Pittsburgh Pirates (NL) between 1922 and 1926 and truck business operator in St. Louis, and Caroline (Heinrichs) Mueller. Mueller married Genevieve C. Babor on May 23, 1949, has two sons, and resides in Maryland Heights, MO. During and after World War II, he served in the U.S. Merchant Marine.

Mueller played baseball for Christian Brothers High School and the American Legion in St. Louis until 1944, when the New York Giants signed him to a professional contract with their Jersey City, NJ (IL) farm club. From 1944 to 1946, he served mostly in the U.S. Merchant Marine and appeared occasionally for the Jersey City Giants. He batted .348 with Jacksonville, FL (SAL) in 1947 and shuttled the next two seasons between the New York Giants and their top farm teams. From 1950 to 1957, the 6-foot, 180 pounder started in right field for the New York Giants and appeared in at least 122 games each season. He spent one full season and part of another with the Chicago White Sox before a bad groin pull and arthritis forced him to retire in 1959.

Although a sub-par fielder with less than average speed, Mueller remained a major leaguer because he hit very well. His lifetime .296 batting average included sparkling .333, .342, and .306 marks from 1953 to 1955. In 1954, he lost the NL batting championship on the final day to teammate Willie Mays* and led the major leagues in hits with 212. His biggest offensive display, though, came in a two-game sweep of the Brooklyn Dodgers on

September 1–2, 1951. Mueller hit five HR in those two games, tying a record then shared by Adrian Anson,* Ty Cobb,* Tony Lazzeri,* and Ralph Kiner.* He hit for the cycle on July 11, 1954 against the Pittsburgh Pirates. He utilized Cobb's omit style of hitting in the mid-1950s, choking up on the bat and placing his hits. Ken Smith, who called him a "modern Willie Keeler,"* wrote that "his hits seemed to be led by an invisible seeing eye dog into clear spaces, even as the boatmen of his native Mississippi River Country used to pilot craft through the shoals with amazing helm handling."

Mueller contributed a single to the New York Giants' ninth-inning comeback on October 3, 1951 against the Brooklyn Dodgers to take the NL pennant. Some claimed that Mueller would have been out if Brooklyn first baseman Gil Hodges* had been in proper defensive position, but he replied, "if he had been playing back, I wouldn't have hit it where I did. I probably would have gone through the middle." In 12 major league seasons, he hit 65 HR and knocked in 520 runs. Mueller, who participated in the 1954 and 1955 All-Star games, sprained his left ankle sliding into third base in the ninth inning of the third playoff game with Brooklyn in 1951, and missed the World Series that year. In the 1954 World Series, he batted .389 against the Cleveland Indians. He inspected buildings for St. Louis Underwriters, scouted for the San Francisco Giants (NL), farmed, raised cattle, and operated a fish hatchery.

BIBLIOGRAPHY: Frank Graham, "The Singles Hitter of the Giants," *Sport* 20 (August 1955), pp. 40–41, 75–76; Walter Langford, "Don Mueller: He Was a Magician with the Bat," *BD* 47 (March 1988), pp. 86–92; Leo Durocher, *Nice Guys Finish Last* (New York, 1975); Rich Marazzi, "The Giants Swept the Indians in a Classic World Series," *SCD* 21 (October 28, 1994), pp. 150–151; Frank Graham, *New York Giants* (New York, 1952); Thomas Kiernan, *The Miracle at Coogan's Bluff* (New York, 1975); Fred Stein and Nick Peters, *Giants Diary* (Berkeley, CA, 1987); Ray Robinson, *The Shot Heard 'Round the World* (New York, 1991); Noel Hynd, *The Giants of the Polo Grounds* (New York, 1988); Don Mueller file, National Baseball Library, Cooperstown, NY; Harold Sheldon, "Don Mueller—Star by Birth," *BD* 10 (November 1951), pp. 67–70; Ken Smith, "He's Called Mandrake Mueller," *BD* 14 (May 1955), pp. 15–24; Fluffy Saccucci, "Mueller Was a Standout for '54 World Champion Giants," *SCD* 23 (May 3, 1996), pp. 164–165.

Leverett T. Smith, Jr.

MULLANE, Anthony John "Tony," "Count," "The Apollo of the Box" (b. January 20, 1859, Cork, Ireland; d. April 25, 1944, Chicago, IL), player, emigrated from Ireland with his parents as a child. The gifted athlete proved a fine skater and boxer and pursued baseball when the sport was becoming the "national pastime" of post–Civil War America. Mullane began his professional baseball career in 1880 as a right-handed pitcher with an independent team in Akron, OH. During the 1881 season, he joined the Detroit Wolverines (NL) and began pitching with his left arm following an injury to his right arm. The recovery of Mullane's right arm enabled him to pitch with either arm, but he rarely hurled left-handed. His ambidexterity allowed the barehanded pitcher to field and throw with either hand and gave him a devastating pickoff move.

In 1882, Mullane joined the Louisville Eclipse in the new AA and won 30 of 54 decisions for the first of five consecutive 30-victory seasons. He moved in 1883 to the St. Louis Browns (AA), where he enjoyed another fine season with a career high 35 wins. Before the 1884 season, Mullane jumped his contract with the Browns and temporarily signed with the St. Louis Maroons of the upstart UA. Before joining the UA, however, he switched to the Toledo Blue Stockings (AA) when that franchise agreed to meet his salary request for 1884. At Toledo he formed a popular battery with Moses Fleetwood Walker,* the first black major league baseball player. Since the Toledo Blue Stockings collapsed after the 1884 season, Mullane was sold back to the Browns (AA). Refusing to report to the Browns, he instead signed with the Cincinnati Red Stockings (AA) for 1885. Protests from Browns owner Chris Von der Ahe* culminated in Mullane's suspension for the entire 1885 season. He nevertheless remained with Cincinnati from 1886 to June 1893 (in 1890 the franchise shifted to the NL), except for a brief stint with Butte, MT (MtL) because of an 1892 salary dispute. He was traded to the Baltimore Orioles (NL) in 1893 and split his last major campaign (1894) between the Orioles and the Cleveland Spiders (NL). After pitching for St. Paul, MN (WL) from 1895 to 1897, he ended his playing career with Toronto, Canada (EL) in 1899.

Mullane's major league pitching career included 555 games, 4,531.1 innings pitched, 1,803 strikeouts, 284 wins, 220 losses, and a 3.05 ERA. His 30 career shutouts included a no-hit victory against Cincinnati on September 11, 1882, the first AA no-hitter. Mullane led the AA twice in shutouts (1884, 1887) and once each in winning percentage (1883), games started, and strikeouts (1882). Besides pitching, he played all positions except catcher. The hard-hitting Mullane compiled a .243 lifetime batting average and swung mostly right-handed. The 5-foot 10½-inch, 165-pound Mullane ranked among the era's most colorful, popular players. Sporting a handlebar mustache, he was nicknamed "Count" for his elegant attire. After his baseball career, he became a police officer in Chicago, IL and worked as a detective from 1904 until 1924. He spent his retirement years in a predominantly Irish neighborhood on the south side of Chicago, married several times, and was survived by one daughter.

Although one of the leading players of the 1880s, Mullane remains largely forgotten today because he never played on a championship team, enjoyed his great years in the neglected AA, and (though exonerated) was once charged with throwing games. Mullane's showmanship, independence, and all-around athletic ability made him the embodiment of the 19th century baseball hero.

BIBLIOGRAPHY: Tony Mullane file, National Baseball Library, Cooperstown, NY; Chicago (IL) *Daily Tribune*, April 27, 1944; Craig Carter, ed., *TSN Daguerreotypes*, 8th ed. (St. Louis, MO, 1990); Lee Allen, *The Cincinnati Reds* (New York, 1948); J. Thomas Hetrick, *Chris Von der Ahe and the St. Louis Browns* (Lanham, MD, 1999); David Nemec, *The Beer and Whisky League* (New York, 1994); Richard Scheinin, *The Field of Screams* (New York, 1994); Harold Seymour, *Baseball: The Early Years* (New York, 1960); Robert L. Tiemann and Mark Rucker, eds., *Nineteenth Century Stars* (Kansas City, MO, 1989).

Clark Nardinelli

MULLIN, George Joseph "Wabash George" (b. July 4, 1880, Toledo, OH; d. January 7, 1944, Wabash, IN), player, started his baseball career in 1898 with a semipro team in Fort Wayne, IN. He shared pitching duties with rookie Addie Joss,* who later starred with the Cleveland Indians. In 1901, Mullin began his professional career with Fort Wayne, IN (WA) and then broke a contract with the Brooklyn Superbas (NL) to accept a more lucrative offer from the Detroit Tigers (AL). Although his 1902 rookie record of 13 wins, 16 losses, and 3.67 ERA proved unimpressive, he debuted with three doubles. Mullin, an excellent hitter with a .262 lifetime batting average, became one of only three pinch hitters for Ty Cobb.* In 1911, Cleveland left-hander Eugene Krapp entered the ninth inning with a big lead. Mullin batted for Cobb, who had taken an early shower, not expecting to bat again.

In 1903, the right-hander became a star by winning 19 games, losing 15, and lowering his ERA to 2.25 for a fifth place club. Mullin won the respect of New York Highlander manager Clark Griffith,* who considered him one of baseball's premier pitchers. Mullin's duels with New York ace Jack Chesbro* became classics, appreciated by fans of the fledgling AL. Griffith arranged with Detroit general manager Ed Barrow* to add Mullin to his New York Highlanders staff, but Detroit's new owner, William Yawkey, cancelled the deal.

Mullin led the Detroit pitching staff with 66 wins during the AL pennant seasons of 1907–1909. In 1909, he paced major league pitchers by winning 29 out of 37 decisions, led the AL in victories and winning percentage, and posted a 2.22 ERA and two World Series victories against the Pittsburgh Pirates. Mullin, who relied on an excellent fastball, a good curve, and exceptional control, used psychological ploys such as talking to batters and stalling at critical times to counter incipient rallies. On several occasions, he intentionally threw the ball over the catcher's head and off the wooden grandstands at Bennett Park. The ball bounced back to the catcher, who tagged out runners trying to score from third base. Despite his skill and cunning, Mullin believed that his success largely came from luck. During the 1908 and 1909 seasons, he attributed his victories partly to a black orphan and Detroit mascot, Lil Rastus.

Mullin, among the most sociable Detroit players, maintained close relations with Ty Cobb and often visited him at his Augusta, GA home. For a time, his best friend was Christy Mathewson.* In 1911, he won a friendly wager with Mathewson by backing the Philadelphia Athletics against the New York Giants in the World Series. Mullin won 21 and lost 12 in 1910 and posted an 18–10 record the following year. He began the 1912 season well and peaked with a July 4 no-run, no-hit game against the St. Louis Browns. Slumping the rest of the season, he finished with 12 victories against 17 defeats. After 1 win and 6 losses in 1913, he was sold that May to the Washington Senators (AL). Manager Clark Griffith, however, failed to restore Mullin to his former greatness. The 5-foot 11-inch, 188-pound Mullin, overweight for most of his career, liked the bright lights and fast life and did not keep in good condition.

After completing the 1913 season with Washington, he jumped to the Indianapolis Hoosiers (FL) in 1914 and ended his major league career with the Newark Peppers (FL) in 1915. He won 16 and lost 12 in his two-year FL stint. After playing semipro ball the next five years in Indiana and Ohio, he settled with his wife, Grace, and daughter in Toledo in 1920 and became a police officer. Mullin won 228 games and lost 196 (.538 winning percentage) in a 14-year major league career. He compiled a 2.82 ERA in 487 games, completed 353 of 428 starts, hurled 35 shutouts, and struck out 1,482 batters in 3,686.2 innings pitched. Besides being a clutch pitcher, he was considered nearly unbeatable in big games in his peak years. Mullin achieved near National Baseball Hall of Fame statistics and probably fell only one good season short of being elected to that august institution.

BIBLIOGRAPHY: George Mullin file, National Baseball Library, Cooperstown, NY; Fred Smith, *995 Tigers* (Detroit, MI, 1981); Detroit Baseball Club Letterbooks, 12 vols. (1900–1912), Ernie Harwell Collection, Detroit Public Library; Detroit *News*, 1905–1912, January 8, 1944; Brent P. Kelley, *The Case For: Those Overlooked by the Baseball Hall of Fame* (Jefferson, NC, 1992); Joe Falls, *Detroit Tigers* (New York, 1975); Charles C. Alexander, *Ty Cobb* (New York, 1984); Richard Bak, *Ty Cobb* (Dallas, TX, 1994); William M. Anderson, *The Detroit Tigers* (South Bend, IN, 1996); Frederick G. Lieb, *The Detroit Tigers* (New York, 1946).

Anthony J. Papalas

MUMPHREY, Jerry Wayne (b. September 9, 1952, Tyler, TX), player, is the son of Roscoe Mumphrey and Evelyn (Wynn) Mumphrey and graduated from Chapel Hill High School in 1971. The St. Louis Cardinals (NL) selected him in the fourth round of the 1971 amateur draft and assigned him to Sarasota, FL (GCL). Mumphrey progressed rapidly through the Cardinals' minor league system with Cedar Rapids, IA (ML) in 1972, St. Petersburg, FL (FSL) in 1972 and 1973, Arkansas (TL) in 1974, and Tulsa, OK (AA) in 1975 and 1976.

The 6-foot 2-inch, 200-pound switch-hitting outfielder debuted with the St. Louis Cardinals in September 1974 and broke into the starting lineup in

1976. In December 1979, the St. Louis Cardinals traded him to the Cleveland Indians (AL). Two months later, however, Cleveland shipped Mumphrey to the San Diego Padres (NL). The right-handed outfielder spent just one season with the San Diego Padres before the New York Yankees (AL) acquired him in April 1981.

Mumphrey played two and one-half campaigns with the New York Yankees, making his only postseason appearances in 1981 against the Milwaukee Brewers in the AL Division Series, Oakland Athletics in the AL Championship Series, and Los Angeles Dodgers in the World Series. He batted .500 in the AL Championship Series. In August 1983, the New York Yankees dealt him to the Houston Astros (NL). Mumphrey played two seasons with Houston and represented the Astros in the 1984 All-Star game.

The Chicago Cubs (NL) acquired him in December 1985. In 1987, Mumphrey enjoyed career highs with a .333 batting average and 13 HR. Chicago used him strictly as a pinch hitter in 1988, when his batting average plummeted to .136. The Tyler, TX resident retired from professional baseball following the 1988 campaign with a .289 lifetime batting average, 1,442 hits, 70 HR, 575 RBI, and 174 stolen bases. He married Gloria Stine and has one daughter, Tamara.

BIBLIOGRAPHY: Bob Broeg and Jerry Vickery, *St. Louis Cardinals Encyclopedia* (Grand Rapids, MI, 1998); Mark Gallagher, *The Yankee Encyclopedia*, vol. 3 (Champaign, IL, 1997); *The Baseball Encyclopedia*, 10th ed. (New York, 1996); Jerry Mumphrey file, National Baseball Library, Cooperstown, NY.

John Hillman

MUNGO, Van Lingle (b. June 8, 1911, Pageland, SC; d. February 12, 1985, Pageland, SC), player and manager, was a colorful right-handed pitcher with a fastball said to be as swift as Bob Feller's.* His lilting name, deriving from his Dutch ancestry (Lingle was his mother's maiden name) became the title of a popular song by Dave Frishberg in 1970.

Mungo signed in 1929 as an outfielder with Charlotte, NC (PiL). Mungo, who possessed a powerful arm, was switched to pitching and spent most of the year at Fayetteville, NC (ECaL). He spent 1930 with Winston-Salem, NC (PiL) and 1931 with Hartford, CT (EL). His 15–5 win–loss record there led to his being acquired in September 1931 by the Brooklyn Dodgers (NL).

One of the top NL pitchers, Mungo remained with the Brooklyn Dodgers until spring 1941. The Brooklyn Dodgers demoted Mungo to Montreal, Canada (IL) because of arm problems and his off-field behavior. During spring training with the Brooklyn Dodgers in Havana, Cuba, in 1941, he was hastily sent back to the United States when he became involved, according to one account, with a former bullfighter and his girlfriend and, to another, in a fight with a Cuban dance team. By his own admission, Mungo paid $15,000 in fines during his career and was suspended by managers several times.

Mungo's pitching and pinch hitting helped Montreal win the IL playoffs in 1941. After a fracas with top Montreal officials, however, he was traded to Minneapolis, MN (AA). His record there in 1942 led to his being acquired by the New York Giants (NL) late that year. He left the New York Giants to enter the U.S. Army in February 1944. After his discharge, he rejoined the New York Giants in 1945. He retired as a player in spring 1946 and finished the year as manager of Clinton, NC (TSL). He later coached the Pageland American Legion team, operated a movie theater, a dry-goods store, and a trucking business in Pageland.

In his 14-year major league career, Mungo appeared in 364 games, pitched 2,113 innings, and won 120 and lost 115 with 1,242 strikeouts, 868 walks, and a 3.47 ERA. He led the NL in 1934 in innings pitched (315.1), in 1935 in shutouts (4), and in 1936 in strikeouts (238) and was selected to the NL All-Star team in 1934 and 1937. He recorded career-high 18 victories in both 1934 and 1936. After injuring his arm in the 1937 All-Star game, he developed an illegal slippery elm pitch to compensate for the loss of his great fastball and sharp curve. A good hitter for a pitcher, he batted .345 in 1939.

Mungo married Eloise Camp on December 10, 1932 and had two sons, Van Lingle, Jr., and Ernest. A 2.5 mile boulevard in Pageland was named for him in 1983. In addition to the popular "Van Lingle Mungo" song, a tempera painting by Richard Merkin, "Van Lingle Mungo's Havana" (1973), and a poem, "Van Lingle Mungo" (1985), by Paul Parker kept his name alive.

BIBLIOGRAPHY: Van Lingle Mungo file, National Baseball Library, Cooperstown, NY; Frank Graham, *The Brooklyn Dodgers* (New York, 1945); Paul Green, "An Interview with Van Lingle Mungo," *SCD* 11 (December 7, 1984), pp. 142–144; Kirby Higbe and Martin Quigley, *The High Hard One* (New York, 1967); Gene Karst and Martin J. Jones, Jr., *Who's Who in Professional Baseball* (New Rochelle, NY, 1973); *NYT*, February 14, 1985, Sec. II, p. 12; Paul Parker, "Van Lingle Mungo," *TNP* 4 (Winter 1985), p. 64; Richard Goldstein, *Superstars and Screwballs* (New York, 1991); William F. McNeil, *The Dodgers Encyclopedia* (Champaign, IL, 1997); Tommy Holmes, *The Dodgers* (New York, 1975); Robert L. Tiemann, *Dodger Classics* (St. Louis, MO, 1983).

Ralph S. Graber

MUNSON, Thurman Lee (b. June 7, 1947, Akron, OH; d. August 2, 1979, Canton, OH), player, died tragically in the flaming wreckage of his Cessna Citation, a twin engine jet, while attempting to land his plane at Akron-Canton, OH Airport. The whole baseball world mourned the loss of the taciturn New York Yankee (AL) captain. His premature death was reminiscent of that of another Yankee captain, Lou Gehrig,* who had died some 38 years earlier. The son of Darrel Munson and Ruth Munson, he starred in football and baseball at Kent State University in Ohio. He played halfback and linebacker in football and made the NCAA College All-America squad in baseball. Scout Gene Woodling* signed him to a New York Yankee contract for a $75,000 bonus in 1968.

After Munson had played just 99 games for Binghamton, NY (EL) and Syracuse, NY (IL), the New York Yankees promoted him for 26 games in September 1969. In 1970 he was voted the AL's Rookie of the Year, batting .302. He was named the AL's 1976 MVP, hitting .302 and driving in 105 runs. His bat demolished Cincinnati Reds pitching in the 1976 World Series to the tune of a robust .529 batting average. The "Big Red Machine's" sweep of the Yankees, however, took some of the luster off his great season.

Munson, a loner, kept most of his thoughts to himself and often feuded with the fans, the press, management, and Reggie Jackson.* He frequently played in pain, being troubled by arm and knee problems. The dedicated family man spent as much time as he could with his wife, Diana Lynn, and their three small children. Since their young son was hyperactive, Munson wanted to fly home more often on off days. He flew his plane in order to reach home more quickly. (On the day of his death, he was practicing plane landings.) Much of his trouble with the New York front office revolved around his desire to be traded to the Cleveland Indians (AL) so that he could be closer to his family.

A compact, sturdy, 5-foot 11-inch, 190-pound right-hander, Munson assumed the quiet leadership of a resurgent Yankee franchise until disturbed by Jackson's intrusion in 1977. Their celebrated argument revolved around team leadership and salaries. The Yankees previously had agreed that Munson would be the highest-paid player. The signing of free-agent Jackson, along with his boastful comments about being "the straw that stirred the Yankees' drink," always upset Munson.

In 1,423 major league games, Munson hit 113 HR and compiled a career .292 batting average and 701 RBI. He performed in three World Series from 1976 to 1978, tying or breaking several records. In 16 World Series games, he batted .373 with 25 hits and recorded one of the best batting marks in history. He drove in 100 or more runs three times and surpassed a .300 batting average five times. During his 10 full seasons with the Yankees, he was named an AL All-Star six times. In the AL Championship Series, Munson hit .339 with 2 HR. The potent line-drive hitter was batting a characteristic .288 at the time of his death.

BIBLIOGRAPHY: Thurman Munson file, National Baseball Library, Cooperstown, NY; Reggie Jackson and Mike Lupica, *Reggie* (New York, 1984); Dick Lally, *Pinstriped Summers* (New York, 1985); Sparky Lyle and Peter Golenbock, *The Bronx Zoo* (New York, 1979); *The Baseball Encyclopedia*, 10th ed. (New York, 1996); Mark Gallagher, *The Yankee Encyclopedia*, vol. 3 (Champaign, IL, 1997); Dave Anderson et al., *The Yankees* (New York, 1979); Gene Karst and Martin J. Jones, Jr., *Who's Who in*

Professional Baseball (New Rochelle, NY, 1973); John Thorn et al., eds., *Total Baseball*, 5th ed. (New York, 1997).

William A. Borst

MURCER, Bobby Ray (b. May 20, 1946, Oklahoma City, OK), player, sportscaster, and executive, is the son of Robert Harland Murcer and Maybelle (Ferguson) Murcer and graduated from Southeast High School in Oklahoma City, where he starred in football, basketball, and baseball. He signed his first professional baseball contract with the New York Yankees (AL) in 1964 and started his career with Johnson City, TN (ApL), where he was chosen the ApL's All-Star shortstop. The next season, he batted .322 for Greensboro, NC (CrL) and was selected the CrL's MVP.

Murcer, a 5-foot 11-inch, 180 pounder, made his major league debut with the New York Yankees in September 1965, hitting .243 in 11 games. In 1966, he batted .266 in 133 games for Toledo, OH (IL) and hit .174 in 21 games for the New York Yankees in September. After a two-year stint in the U.S. Army, he joined the Yankees in 1969 in center field as the successor to Mickey Mantle.* Murcer's six seasons with New York from 1969 to 1974 saw the left-handed hitter bat .285 and average 23 HR and 89 RBI per season. He paced the AL in on base percentage (.429), finished second in the AL in batting average (.331) and slugging percentage (.543) in 1971, and led the AL in runs scored (102) and total bases (314) in 1972. A strong and accurate right-handed thrower, he shared the AL lead in outfield assists in 1970 (15) and 1973 (14). New York gave Murcer a $120,000 contract for the 1974 season, making him at that time the highest-paid Yankee ever.

The 1974 season saw Murcer lead AL outfielders with 21 assists, but hit only 10 HR. In October 1974, New York traded Murcer to the San Francisco Giants (NL) for outfielder Bobby Bonds.* In two seasons with the Giants, he averaged .279, 17 HR, and 90 RBI. In February 1977 San Francisco dealt Murcer to the Chicago Cubs (NL), who gave him a well-publicized five-year contract. For the Cubs, Murcer hit .265 with 27 HR and 89 RBI that season and batted .281 with nine HR and 64 RBI the following year. Chicago swapped him in June 1979 to the New York Yankees, who employed him as a part-time outfielder through 1980 and a DH from 1981 through 1983. He appeared in one game in both the 1980 and 1981 AL Championship Series and made four pinch-hitting appearances in the 1981 World Series against the Los Angeles Dodgers. Following his retirement in 1983, Murcer joined Phil Rizzuto* and Bill White* on the New York Yankees broadcasting team. In October 1989, Murcer was named president of the Oklahoma City 89ers (AA), a Texas Rangers (AL) affiliate. He has announced for the New York Yankees since 1992.

In his 15-year major league career, Murcer hit .277 with 252 HR and 1,043 RBI. His honors included being chosen an AL All-Star in 1971, 1972, 1973, and 1974 and an NL All-Star in 1975. Murcer hit four consecutive

HR in a doubleheader against the Cleveland Indians on June 24, 1970 and hit for the cycle against the Texas Rangers on August 29, 1972. He also clouted three HR against the Kansas City Royals on July 13, 1973. Murcer married Diane K. Rhodes on October 14, 1966 and resides in Oklahoma City with their two children, Todd and Tory.

BIBLIOGRAPHY: Dave Anderson et al., *The Yankees* (New York, 1979); Dick Lally, *Pinstriped Summers* (New York, 1985); Craig Carter, ed., *TSN Daguerreotypes*, 8th ed. (St. Louis, MO, 1990); *Chicago Cubs Official Press, Radio, and TV Roster Book, 1979*; Eddie Gold and Art Ahrens, *The New Era Cubs, 1941–1985* (Chicago, IL, 1985); Bobby Murcer file, National Baseball Library, Cooperstown, NY; John Thorn et al., eds., *Total Baseball*, 5th ed. (New York, 1997); Ed Lucas and Paul Post, "Murcer Regrets Not Saving His Cards, Memorabilia," *SCD* 25 (December 18, 1998), p. 90; Mark Gallagher, *The Yankee Encyclopedia*, vol. 3 (Champaign, IL, 1997).

Raymond D. Kush

MURNANE, Timothy Hayes "The Silver King" (b. June 4, 1852, Naugatuck, CT; d. February 7, 1917, Boston, MA), player, manager, executive, and writer, married Emma Manning on April 23, 1878 and had two daughters. He later married Mary Agnes Dowling on February 22, 1898 and had three sons and a daughter.

Murnane attended Holy Cross Prep School from 1868 to 1870 and began his baseball career as a catcher for Stratford, CT in 1869 and Savannah, GA in 1870 and 1871. His major league career included stints as a first baseman–outfielder with the Mansfields of Middletown, CT (NA) in 1872, Philadelphia Athletics (NA) in 1873 and 1874, Philadelphias (NA) in 1875, Boston Red Caps (NL) in 1876 and 1877, and Providence, RI Grays (NL) in 1878. The 5-foot 9½-inch 172 pounder, who batted left-handed and threw right-handed, enjoyed his best year with Middletown in 1872, when he hit .359. His .261 major league batting average spanned 384 games.

In 1879 Murnane played center field for the Capital City team of Albany, NY (NA), which transferred to Rochester, NY. After playing briefly with Albany in 1880, he retired to pursue business. Murnane returned to baseball in 1884 to organize the Boston Reds (UA), serving as player–manager. His club compiled a 58–51 record, finishing fifth. Rookie Tommy McCarthy* of Boston became the UA's only National Baseball Hall of Fame member. Murnane's playing career ended in 1885 with Jersey City, NJ (EL). He organized the Boston Blues (NEL) in 1886, but soon sold them.

Murnane's journalism career began in the 1880s with the publication of the periodicals *BR* and *ST*. He began covering baseball for the Boston *Globe* around 1887 and later served as baseball and sports editor until his death. Murnane also edited the *Minor League Guide*. From 1893 to 1915, he presided over the NEL. The NEL merged with the EA to form the EL in 1916, with Murnane as president the first year. He participated on the board of the NA, being elected vice-president in 1915.

Murnane, perhaps the era's most respected baseball writer, was noted as a raconteur and remained much in demand as an after-dinner speaker. He stayed very popular because of his warmth and honesty. Murnane defended players' rights as an executive, but opposed high salaries. Since he died without a sizable estate, a benefit game raised an estimated $14,000 for his family. In the game, Babe Ruth* pitched a shutout for the Boston Red Sox against AL All-Stars.

BIBLIOGRAPHY: Frederick Ivor-Campbell et al., eds., *Baseball's First Stars* (Cleveland, OH, 1996); Mike Shatzkin, ed., *The Ballplayers* (New York, 1990); *TSN* 62 (February 15, 1917), pp. 4, 6; Tim Murnane file, National Baseball Library, Cooperstown, NY; William J. Ryczek, *Blackguards and Red Stockings* (Jefferson, NC, 1992); Gary Caruso, *The Braves Encyclopedia* (Philadelphia, PA, 1995).

William E. McMahon

MURPHY, Dale Bryan (b. March 12, 1956, Portland, OR), player, is the son of Charles Murphy and Betty M. Murphy. He planned to attend Arizona State University on a baseball scholarship after graduation from Woodrow Wilson High School in Portland, but instead signed with the Atlanta Braves (NL) after being selected in the first round of the June 1974 free agent draft. Murphy, who attended Portland CC and Brigham Young University, married Nancy Thomas in 1979 and has three children, Chad, Travis, and Shawn.

Touted as "the next Johnny Bench,*" Murphy began his career as a catcher with Kingsport, TN (ApL) and moved quickly through Greenwood, SC (WCL), Savannah, GA (SL), and Richmond, VA (IL), to the major leagues in 1976. A mental block that produced erratic throws to second base led to experiments with him playing first base and the outfield. The Braves moved the 6-foot 4-inch, 220-pound Murphy to the outfield permanently in 1982 to utilize his strong throwing arm and excellent speed.

After moving to center field, the right-handed Murphy emerged as a superstar with unusually consistent performances. From 1982 through 1984, he played in all 162 games each season, hit 36 HR each year, and averaged 174 hits, 110 RBI, 24 stolen bases, and a .290 batting average. For each of those three years, *TSN* named him to the NL All-Star Fielding (Gold Glove) and Silver Slugger teams. The seven-time All-Star team selection (1980, 1982–1987) was named in 1982 and 1983 the NL MVP by the BBWAA and Player of the Year by *TSN*, making Murphy the youngest player ever to win those honors in consecutive years. In 1985, he again played in 162 games, led the NL in HR (37), runs scored (118), and walks (90), and finished second in RBI (111), third in slugging percentage (.539), and fifth in hits (185) and on-base percentage (.388). Murphy's consecutive game streak ended at 740 in July 1986. In August 1990, the Braves traded Murphy to the Philadelphia Phillies (NL). His major league career ended with the expansion Colorado Rockies (NL) in 1993. In 18 major league seasons, he batted .265 with 2,111 hits, 350 doubles, 398 HR, and 1,266 RBI. He led or tied in games played (1982–1985), RBI (1982–1983), slugging average (1983–1984), and total bases (1984). Murphy won Gold Glove Awards in 1985 and 1986.

Excelling in every phase of the game on the field, Murphy off the field remained a model of decorum, a soft-spoken, unassuming athlete who did not use alcohol, tobacco, or profanity and objected strenuously to the presence of female sportswriters in the locker area after games. According to former manager Joe Torre*: "Murphy is the closest thing there is to the all-American boy. He's a complete ballplayer. All he does is play baseball better than anyone else."

BIBLIOGRAPHY: Michele Bartmess, "Dale Murphy: Nice Guys Don't Always Finish Last," *TP* 4 (April/May 1983), pp. 42–46; Joseph Dalton, "Too Good for His Own Good," *Sport* 75 (June 1984), pp. 24–30; Peter Gammons, "A Man Who Can't Say No," *SI* 67 (December 21, 1987), pp. 16–17; Val Hale, "Dale Murphy," *TP* 5 (February 1984), pp. 60–61; J. Hayes, "Dale Murphy: Baseball's Mr. Nice Guy," *SEP* 258 (October 1986), pp. 48–49; Robert E. Kelly, *Baseball's Best* (Jefferson, NC, 1988); *The Baseball Encyclopedia*, 10th ed. (New York, 1996); Dale Murphy and Curtis Patton, *Ask Dale Murphy* (Chapel Hill, NC, 1987); Dale Murphy et al., *Murph* (Salt Lake City, UT, 1986); Robert Grayson, "The Class of '99," *SCD* 25 (December 25, 1998), pp. 80–81; Rick Reilly, "So Good, He's Scary," *SI* 62 (June 3, 1985), pp. 74–88; Dale Murphy file, National Baseball Library, Cooperstown, NY; John Thorn et al., eds., *Total Braves* (New York, 1996); Gary Caruso, *The Braves Encyclopedia* (Philadelphia, PA, 1995); *TSN Official Baseball Register, 1985*; Wayne Stewart, "Dale Murphy: Will He Win a Third Straight MVP Award?" *BD* 43 (March 1984), pp. 18–22; *TSN*, September 20, 1982, November 21, 28, 1983; Tim Tucker, "Is Dale Murphy for Real?" *IS* 5 (November 1983), pp. 36–40; *WWA*, 43rd ed., (1984–1985), p. 2361; Steve Wulf, "Murphy's Law Is Nice Guys Finish First," *SI* 59 (July 4, 1983), pp. 24–31.

Larry R. Gerlach

MURPHY, Daniel Francis "Danny," "Old Reliable" (b. August 11, 1876, Philadelphia, PA; d. November 22, 1955, Jersey City, NJ), player, manager, scout, and coach, began his professional baseball career as a second baseman with Worcester, MA (NEL) in 1894. He remained with Worcester until 1899, when an independent North Attleboro, MA team secured his services. In 1900, he joined Norwich, CT (CtL). His performance impressed the New York Giants (NL), who purchased him that September. Murphy debuted with the Giants on September 17 and stayed there the first part of the 1901 season, but then was returned to Norwich. His sensational play with Norwich in 1902 featured a .462 batting average in 49 games. Manager Connie Mack's* Philadelphia Athletics (AL), who had failed to retain star Nap Lajoie,* purchased Murphy in July 1902.

Murphy's 1902 debut as the Philadelphia Athletics' second baseman remains surely one of the most auspicious in major league history. Arriving late in Boston on July 8, he did not enter the game with the Boston Pilgrims until the second inning. Murphy then made six hits, including a grand-slam HR, in six times at bat. Defensively, he handled 14 chances for five putouts, seven assists, and two errors as the Philadelphia Athletics defeated the Boston Pilgrims, 22–9. The 5-foot 9-inch, 175-pound right-handed–hitting infielder finished the season with a .313 batting average, helping Mack win his first AL pennant. The Philadelphia Athletics captured four more AL crowns during Murphy's tenure there.

Murphy played with the Philadelphia Athletics the next 11 seasons, batting .319 in his last four years with the Mackmen. He performed at second base until the middle of the 1908 season, when Mack switched him to right field to make room for future National Baseball Hall of Famer Eddie Collins.* Murphy appeared in the 1905, 1910, and 1911 World Series with the Philadelphia Athletics. His timely hitting against the Chicago Cubs in 1910 and New York Giants in 1911 accounted for 10 runs and keyed Philadelphia championships. Murphy batted .350 in the 1910 and .304 in the 1911 fall classics. The excellent sign stealer was well liked by his teammates, Mack, and the Quaker City fans. The quiet, retiring, but quick-thinking Murphy captained the Philadelphia Athletics in 1911. A knee injury sidelined him for much of the 1912 and 1913 seasons.

The Philadelphia Athletics released Murphy to the Baltimore, MD Orioles (IL) before the 1914 season. Murphy, however, jumped to the Brooklyn Tip Tops of the newly formed FL. Advancing age and injuries limited his play the following two seasons, but management designated him as an unofficial adviser, coach, and scout. His major league career ended with the demise of the Brooklyn Tip Tops and the FL following the 1915 season. In his 16-year major league career spanning 1,496 games in the "dead ball" era, Murphy scored 705 runs, recorded 702 RBI, and compiled a .289 batting average. His .977 fielding average led AL outfielders in 1909. He finished with a .953 career fielding average.

Murphy managed two EL clubs, New Haven, CT from 1916 to 1918 and Hartford, CT in 1919, and scouted and coached with Mack's Philadelphia Athletics from 1921 to 1924. Murphy concluded his professional baseball career in 1927, when former A's teammate and newly appointed manager Stuffy McInnis* appointed him as a coach with the Philadelphia Phillies (NL).

Subsequently, Murphy became a hardware dealer in Jersey City, NJ and was employed by Hudson County, NJ at the County Institutions in Laurel Hill. He married Catherine Moriarity in 1902 and had no children.

BIBLIOGRAPHY: *The Baseball Encyclopedia*, 10th ed. (New York, 1996); Connie Mack, *My 66 Years in the Big Leagues* (Philadelphia, PA, 1950); Frederick G. Lieb, *Connie Mack* (New York, 1945); Danny Murphy file, National Baseball Library, Cooperstown, NY; Daniel Okrent and Harris Lewine, eds., *The Ultimate Baseball Book* (Boston, MA, 1979); Jerome C. Romanowski, *The Mackmen* (Upper Darby, PA, 1979); John Thorn et al., eds., *Total Baseball*, 5th ed. (New York, 1997).

Jack C. Braun

MURPHY, John Joseph "Grandma" (b. July 14, 1908, New York, NY; d. January 14, 1970, New York, NY), player, scout, and executive, was the son of a New York City waterworks employee and became an outstanding right-handed relief pitcher. He received a bachelor's degree from Fordham University in 1929 and married Elizabeth Haveland on December 31, 1931. They had two sons, John, Jr., and Thomas.

Murphy spent his entire adult life in professional baseball. At 6-feet 2-inches and 190 pounds, he possessed a pitcher's build and began hurling in his Fordham University days. He pitched for Scottdale, PA (MAL) in 1928, Albany, NY (EL) in 1929, St. Paul, MN (AA) in 1930 and 1931, and Newark, NJ (IL) in 1932 and 1933. After a brief appearance with the New York Yankees (AL) in 1932, he rejoined the Yankees in 1934 and developed into one of the early star relief pitchers. He stayed with the New York Yankees through 1946 except for World War II military service in 1944 and 1945. His last major league season came with the Boston Red Sox (AL) in 1947. In a dozen major league seasons, Murphy won 93 games, lost 53 contests, recorded 107 saves, and compiled a 3.50 ERA. He led the AL in saves four times (1938, 1939, 1941, 1942) and in victories among relief pitchers six times. Postseason play saw him win two World Series games, appear in eight contests spread over six series, and record four saves. His most famous save occurred in the last game of the 1936 World Series against the New York Giants.

Murphy, among others, helped to organize the MLPA. The rather staid, fastidious "Grandma" scouted for the Boston Red Sox in 1948 and for the New York Mets (NL) in 1961 and 1962 and directed the Boston Red Sox farm system from late 1948 into 1960. He became vice-president of the New York Mets in 1964 and general manager in 1967, negotiating for Gil Hodges'* release from the Washington Senators (AL) to become the Mets' field manager. Murphy contributed substantially to the development of the "Miracle Mets," which became the NL and World Champions in 1969. Soon after this exhilarating success, the accumulation of overwork triggered a fatal heart attack.

BIBLIOGRAPHY: *The Baseball Encyclopedia*, 10th ed. (New York, 1996); John Murphy file, National Baseball Library, Cooperstown, NY; John Murphy file, *TSN* Archives, St. Louis, MO; *NYT*, January 15, 1970, January 16, 1970; Bob Cairns, *Pen Men* (New York, 1993); Mark Gallagher, *The Yankee Encyclopedia*, vol. 3 (Champaign, IL, 1997); Dave Anderson et al., *The Yankees* (New York, 1979); Frank Graham, *The New York Yankees* (New York, 1943); J. C. Taylor Spink, comp., *TSN Daguerreotypes of Great Stars of Baseball* (St. Louis, MO, 1961).

Lowell L. Blaisdell

MURRAY, Eddie Clarence (b. February 24, 1956, Los Angeles, CA), player, is the eighth of 12 children born to hourly worker Charles Murray and Carrie Murray. All five Murray boys played professional baseball, Richard having performed with the San Francisco Giants (NL) and in the Cleveland Indians (AL) farm system. Murray learned to bat by hitting tennis balls with a stick and played Little League, Babe Ruth,* and Connie Mack* League baseball. He also participated in baseball at Locke High School with future major leaguers Ozzie Smith* and Darrell Jackson. The Baltimore Orioles (AL) selected Murray in the third round of the June 1973 amateur draft and signed him for a $25,000 bonus. Murray spent four seasons in the minor leagues. At Bluefield, WV (ApL), in 1973, he hit .287 with 11 HR. In 1974, he belted 12 HR and batted .289 for Miami, FL (FSL) and played two games for Asheville, NC (SL). For Asheville in 1975, Murray played both first base and third base, hit .264, and slugged 17 HR. Murray hit .298 and made 12 HR in 88 games at Charlotte, NC (SL), in 1976 before joining Rochester, NY (IL). At Rochester, he played first base, third base, and outfield and batted .274 with 11 HR and 40 RBI in 54 games. In each minor league season, Murray contended for the league lead in HR and made the league All-Star team. With Asheville, the 6-foot 2-inch, 190-pound right-hander began switch-hitting.

Murray played with the Baltimore Orioles from 1977 through 1988. In 1977 he performed at first base and in the outfield, but was used mostly as a DH. He batted .283 with 27 HR and 88 RBI to win AL Rookie of the Year honors. He became the regular first baseman in 1978 and steadily improved his fielding, earning three consecutive Gold Gloves from 1982 through 1984. Despite his excellent fielding, however, Murray made the most impact with his bat. He led the AL in HR (22) and RBI (78) in strike-shortened 1981 and walks (107) and games (162) in 1984 and finished second in RBI (124) in 1985. Defensively, he led AL first basemen in putouts in 1978 and 1984, assists in 1981 and 1984, and fielding average in 1981 and 1982. In December 1988, the Orioles traded him to the Los Angeles Dodgers (NL). In 1990, he batted a career-high .330 with 95 RBI, and made *TSN* NL All-Star and Silver Slugger teams. The New York Mets (NL) acquired him as a free agent in November 1991. He reached 100 RBI for the sixth time in his major league career in 1993. In December 1993, the Cleveland Indians (AL) signed him as a free agent. He batted .385 with 3 RBI in the 1995 Division Series against the Baltimore Orioles and clouted a three-run HR in the 1995 World Series against the Atlanta Braves. In July 1996, the Baltimore Orioles reacquired him in a trade. He batted .400 in the AL Division Series against the Cleveland Indians and .267 in the AL Championship Series against the New York Yankees. His final major league season came in 1997 with the Anaheim Angels (AL) and Los Angeles Dodgers.

In 21 major league seasons, Murray batted .287 with 3,255 hits, 560 doubles, 504 HR, and 1,917 RBI. He attained his 3,000th hit against the Minnesota Twins on June 30, 1995 and clouted his 500th HR against the Detroit Tigers on September 6, 1996. Only two other major leagues combined 3,000 hits and 500 HR. He ranks second in career grand slam HR (19) and holds major league records for most games with switch-hit HR (11), most sacrifice flies (128), most games by a first baseman (2,413), and most assists by a first baseman (1,865).

The premier offensive player was named to eight All-Star teams (1978, 1981–1986, 1991) and appeared in three World Series (1979, 1983, 1995). The AL Player of the Month several times, he was mentioned in the MVP balloting frequently and finished second to Robin Yount* in 1982 and team-mate Cal Ripken* in 1983. Murray was chosen Most Valuable Oriole four times (1978, 1981–1982, 1984) and ranked among the highest-paid major league players. Active in charity and community work, he resides in Luth-erville, MD and has coached for the Baltimore Orioles since 1998.

BIBLIOGRAPHY: Eddie Murray file, National Baseball Library, Cooperstown, NY; Ted Patterson, *The Baltimore Orioles* (Dallas, TX, 1995); James H. Bready, *Baseball in Baltimore* (Baltimore, MD, 1998); William F. McNeil, *The Dodgers Encyclopedia* (Champaign, IL, 1997); John Thorn et al., eds., *The Cleveland Indians* (New York, 1996); Russell Schneider, *The Glorious Summer of 1995* (Cleveland, OH, 1996); *American League Red Book, 1977–1985* (New York, 1977–1985); *Baltimore Orioles Media Guide, 1977–1985*; James H. Bready, *The Home Team* (Baltimore, MD, 1979); Skip Dorer and Wayne Kaiser, *In the O-Zone* (Cherry Hill, NJ, 1980); David Falkner, "Murray's Quiet, Inner Drive," *NYT Biographical Service* 17 (June 1986), pp. 731–733; Peter Gammons, "It's Twilight Time," *SI* 68 (March 14, 1988), pp. 30–32; David L. Porter, ed., *African-American Sports Greats* (Westport, CT, 1995); Dan Schlossberg, *Baseball Stars 1985* (New York, 1985); *TSN Baseball Register, 1998*; Tom Verducci, "At Arms Length," *SI* 82 (May 22, 1995), pp. 56–58; Robert E. Kelly, *Baseball's Best* (Jefferson, NC, 1988).

Douglas D. Martin

MURRAY, John Joseph "Red" (b. March 4, 1884, Arnot, PA; d. December 4, 1958, Sayre, PA), player, was the son of William Maurice Murray, a coal miner from Edinboro, Scotland, and Hanna (Sheehan) Murray and married Beatrice Riley on August 5, 1919. After attending Arnot, PA public schools, Murray played semiprofessional baseball in Elmira, NY for the Father Mathew team. He spent two years at Lock Haven College, playing football, baseball, and basketball, and transferred to the University of Notre Dame in 1905–1906, catching for the baseball team.

The St. Louis Cardinals (NL) signed the 5-foot 10½-inch Murray in 1906 and made him the regular left fielder the next season. In December 1908, the St. Louis Cardinals traded Murray and Bugs Raymond to the New York Giants (NL) for Roger Bresnahan.* Murray compiled impressive batting, base running, and fielding statistics for the next seven seasons, ranking among the top NL right fielders. Manager John McGraw's* juggernaut from

1911 to 1913 featured a very balanced, speedy lineup, winning three consecutive NL pennants. Murray shared with Fred Merkle* and Fred Snodgrass the team stolen base lead (121) for that period. Only Bob Bescher* stole more bases than Murray during that span.

Murray produced runs, batting in the clean-up slot. From 1909–1912, he ranked third in the NL in total RBI and trailed only Honus Wagner* and Sherry Magee.* Although playing during the dead ball era, Murray and Wagner belted the most major league HR (21) from 1907 to 1909. He achieved the NL HR title in 1909 with only seven, hitting nearly 5 percent of the NL's 151 HR. On May 27, 1907, Murray hit a 471 foot HR for the then longest clout in St. Louis history.

Murray possessed possibly the most powerful NL throwing arm, leading the NL in assists in 1909 (30) and 1910 (26). From 1907 through 1910, no other major league outfielder accumulated more than 100 assists. On August 16, 1909, Murray made the greatest catch in Forbes Field history to save the game. McGraw called Murray's leaping fingertip catch the "greatest and most dramatic" he ever saw.

Murray often led his competing NL outfielders in RBI, HR, assists, and stolen bases. J. C. Kofoed wrote, "His throwing arm was the best ever, his ground covering ability and sureness of eye were classic." Murray went hitless against the Philadelphia Athletics in the 1911 World Series, but rebounded to hit .323 against the Boston Red Sox in the 1912 World Series. In 1,264 career major league games, he batted .270 with 37 HR, 579 RBI, and 321 stolen bases.

Murray owned and operated a battery and tire store for two decades and served as the recreation director for Elmira, NY. In 1950, he was voted Elmira's greatest baseball player of the half century. Murray, who ranks with Mel Ott* among great New York Giant right fielders, died of leukemia after a short illness.

BIBLIOGRAPHY: Ray Robinson, *Matty: An American Hero* (New York, 1993); Frank Graham, *The New York Giants* (New York, 1952); Frank Graham, *McGraw of the Giants* (New York, 1944); Joseph Durso, *The Days of Mr. McGraw* (Englewood Cliffs, NJ, 1969); Lee Allen, *The National League Story* (New York, 1965); Christy Mathewson, *Pitching in a Pinch* (New York, 1912); Noel Hynd, *The Giants of the Polo Grounds* (New York, 1988); John Murray file, National Baseball Library, Cooperstown, NY.

Cappy Gagnon

MURTAUGH, Daniel Edward "Danny" (b. October 8, 1917, Chester, PA; d. December 2, 1976, Chester, PA), player, coach, and manager, was the third child and only son among five children of Daniel J. Murtaugh, a shipyard worker, and Ellen (McCarey) Murtaugh, both of Irish descent. He played semiprofessional baseball and graduated from Chester High School in 1935.

A 1937 tryout with the St. Louis Cardinals (NL) led to professional baseball contracts in 1937 and 1938 with Cambridge, MD (ESL). He played infield with Rochester, NY (IL) and Columbus, OH (AA) in 1939 and Houston, TX (TL) in 1940 and 1941. He performed for the Philadelphia Phillies (NL) in 1941, stealing an NL-leading 18 bases in only 85 games. After remaining with the Philadelphia Phillies in 1942 and 1943, he served in the U.S. Infantry in 1944 and 1945 and saw World War II combat in Czechoslovakia. In 1946, he hit .322 with Rochester and appeared with the Philadelphia Phillies briefly. The right-handed Murtaugh was drafted by the Boston Braves (NL) in November 1946 and assigned for 1947 to Milwaukee, WI (AA), where he hit .302 and fielded .989. The Pittsburgh Pirates (NL) acquired him from the Boston Braves in November 1947 and usually used him as their regular second baseman from 1948 through 1951. Murtaugh's major league career included a .254 batting average, 661 hits, 219 RBI, and 49 stolen bases.

Murtaugh managed New Orleans, LA (SA) from 1952 through 1954, Charleston, WV (AA) in 1955, and Williamsport, PA (EL) in 1956 before Pittsburgh Pirates General Manager Joe L. Brown promoted him to coach there. In August 1957, the Pittsburgh Pirates named him field manager. He led the surprising Pirates to second place in 1958 and a title over the New York Yankees in the 1960 World Series, winning Manager of the Year honors both times. The 5-foot 9-inch, 170-pound, stocky, swarthy Murtaugh was understated and wry. With reporters, he held forth from his rocking chair and punctuated his comments with streams of tobacco juice.

Retirement initially came after the 1964 season, but Murtaugh returned for half a season in 1967 before health problems sidelined him again. He resurfaced in 1970, guiding the Pirates to the NL Eastern Division title and earning NL Manager of the Year honors. After Murtaugh's club won the 1971 World Series over the Baltimore Orioles, he became Pittsburgh's director of player acquisition and development. Murtaugh managed Pittsburgh yet again for part of the 1973 season, won NL Eastern Division crowns in 1974 and 1975, and retired permanently after the 1976 campaign. His .540 managerial winning percentage over 15 years included 1,115 victories and 950 losses. His teams fared 4–10 in NL Championship Series and won 8 of 14 World Series games. He married Kathleen Patricia Clark on November 29, 1941 and had three children.

BIBLIOGRAPHY: Danny Murtaugh file, National Baseball Library, Cooperstown, NY; Jim O'Brien, *Maz and the 1960 Bucs* (Pittsburgh, PA 1994); *The Baseball Encyclopedia*, 10th ed. (New York, 1996); *CB* (1961), pp. 333–334; Dick Groat and Bill Surface, *The World Champion Pittsburgh Pirates* (New York, 1961); Leonard Koppett, *The Man in the Dugout* (New York, 1993); Kathleen Clark Murtaugh, letter to Luther W. Spoehr, January 30, 1990; *NYT*, December 3, 1976, p. D–17; Thomas Aylesworth and Benton Minks, *The Encyclopedia of Baseball Managers* (New York, 1990); Bob

Smizik, *The Pittsburgh Pirates: An Illustrated History* (New York, 1990); Richard L. Burtt, *The Pittsburgh Pirates: A Pictorial History* (Virginia Beach, VA, 1977); John T. Bird, *Twin Killing: The Bill Mazeroski Story* (Birmingham, AL, 1995).

Luther W. Spoehr

MUSIAL, Stanley Frank "Stan," "Stan the Man," "The Donora Greyhound" (b. November 21, 1920, Donora, PA), player and executive, is the son of mill worker Lukasz Musial and Mary (Lancos) Musial. After graduating from Donora High School in 1938, he rejected a University of Pittsburgh basketball scholarship to sign a professional baseball contract as a pitcher with the St. Louis Cardinals (NL). In November 1939, on his 19th birthday, he married Lillian Labash of Donora and has four children. Musial began his professional career in 1938 with Williamson, WV (MtnSL). During his third minor league season (1940), the left-handed Musial compiled an impressive 18–5 record with Daytona Beach, FL (FSL). The hard-throwing 6-foot, 175-pound Musial, however, damaged his shoulder trying to make a tumbling catch in the outfield. Musial, an accomplished gymnast, had made many outstanding tumbling catches, but the ironic injury permanently weakened his throwing arm. Dickie Kerr, his manager, converted Musial to a full-time outfielder and refused to change his unique peek-a-boo batting stance.

In 1941, Musial enjoyed a meteoric rise from Class C Springfield, MO (WA), where he hit .379 and compiled a .738 slugging average, to Class AA Rochester, NY (IL), where he batted .326. At the end of the 1941 season, he played 12 games with the parent St. Louis (NL) club and hit a phenomenal .426. From 1941 through 1963, Musial performed at all three outfield positions and first base for the Cardinals. During 1945, he served in the U.S. Navy. Musial, dubbed "The Man" by Brooklyn fans for his devastating hitting in Ebbets Field, hustled constantly and played all out. Nicknamed "The Donora Greyhound," he displayed considerable speed. During Musial's first four full major league seasons, the Cardinals captured four NL pennants and three world championships. Although the Cardinals won no other NL titles during his career, Musial won seven batting championships (1943, 1946, 1948, 1950–1952, 1957) and in 1948 hit a career-high .376 mark.

Musial led the NL in doubles eight times, in base hits, total bases, and slugging average six times, in triples and runs scored five times, and RBI twice. Until Henry Aaron* broke them, Musial held NL career records for games played (3,026), at-bats (10,972), runs scored (1,949), and RBI (1,951). Although Musial still holds the NL record for doubles with 725, Pete Rose* passed his NL mark for hits (3,630). Aaron also broke Musial's major league career records for most total bases (6,134) and extra-base hits (1,377). Musial batted .340 through the 1958 season, but his lifetime average subsequently dropped to .331. The aging, injury-plagued Musial averaged only .283 over his final five seasons. Although his 3,630 hits were equally divided home and away, Musial compiled a .336 batting average in home games and .326 in road contests. He hit an impressive .340 in daylight, much higher than his .320 in night games. In 24 All-Star Game appearances, he averaged .317, made 20 hits, and slugged 6 HR.

In 1969, his first year of eligibility, Musial was named to the National Baseball Hall of Fame. Besides being named the NL's MVP three times (1943, 1946, and 1948), he was selected as *TSN* NL Player of the Year in 1943, 1948, 1951, and 1957, *TSN* Major League Player of the Year in 1946 and 1951, and its first Player of the Decade in 1956. Twelve times Musial made *TSN* All-Star Major League team. Alongside his records, Musial exhibited gentlemanly behavior, friendliness, openness, and cheerfulness.

In active retirement, Musial continued as a popular restauranteur, served in the Cardinals front office, owned hotels and other real estate, and participated in numerous civic and charity affairs. Musial's extensive travels included an audience with the Pope, visits to Poland, and big game hunting in Kenya and Tanzania. In 1964 President Lyndon Johnson named him head of the national physical fitness program. Musial, who serves on the Veterans Selection Committee for the National Baseball Hall of Fame, battled cancer in the early 1990s. He made Major League Baseball's All-Century Team.

BIBLIOGRAPHY: Stan Musial file, National Baseball Library, Cooperstown, NY; John Benson et al., *Baseball's Top 100* (Wilton, CT, 1997); Furman Bisher, "Get Any Hits, Stan?" *SEP* 236 (May 25, 1963), pp. 30ff; T. Bohnen, "The Man," *AH* 43 (October 1992), pp. 35–36; Bob Broeg, *The Man Stan* (St. Louis, MO, 1977); Roger Kahn, *A Season in the Sun* (New York, 1978); Jerry Lansche, *Stan "The Man" Musial, Born to Be a Ballplayer* (Dallas, TX, 1994); Stan Musial as told to Bob Broeg, *Stan Musial* (Garden City, NY, 1964); Frederick G. Lieb, *The St. Louis Cardinals* (New York, 1945); Bob Broeg, *Redbirds: A Century of Cardinals' Baseball* (St. Louis, MO, 1981); Rob Rains, *The St. Louis Cardinals* (New York, 1992); Bob Broeg and Jerry Vickery, *St. Louis Cardinals Encyclopedia* (Grand Rapids, MI, 1998); John Thom, *Champion Batsman of the 20th Century* (Los Angeles, CA, 1992); Theodore M. O'Leary, "Last Time Around with Stan," *SI* 19 (October 7, 1963), pp. 20–25; Harry T. Paxton, "A Visit with Stan Musial," *SEP* 230 (April 19, 1958), pp. 32–33ff; John Reddy, "Stan, the Incredibly Durable Man," *RD* 82 (April 1963), pp. 175–180.

John E. DiMeglio

MUSSINA, Michael Cole "Mike" (b. December 8, 1968, Williamsport, PA), player, is the son of Malcolm Mussina, an attorney, and Eleanor (Cole) Mussina, a registered nurse. At Montoursville, PA High School, he was selected 1986 and 1987 PA Baseball Player of the Year as a pitcher and made all-conference football defensive back, kicker, and punter. He also played basketball point guard, scoring 1,382 career points. The Baltimore Orioles (AL) drafted him in 1987, but he attended Stanford University and compiled a 9–4 record for the 1988 NCAA College World Series championship team. He only pitched 45.2 innings in 1989 due to a strained tendon in his elbow.

As a Stanford junior in 1990, Mussina compiled a 14–5 record, 3.35 ERA, and 111 strikeouts and was selected by the Baltimore Orioles in the first round of the June free agent draft. He pitched in the minor leagues for Hagerstown, MD (EL) and Rochester, NY (IL) before returning to Stanford to receive a Bachelor's degree in economics in December 1990.

After winning 10 games for Rochester in 1991, Mussina joined the Baltimore Orioles in July and proved the team's most effective starter over the last two months. He finished fourth in the AL Cy Young Award voting in 1992, posting an 18–5 record, an AL best .783 winning percentage, and a third-best 2.54 ERA.

Despite missing six weeks of the 1993 season with a sore shoulder and lower back pains, Mussina finished with a 14–6 record and 4.46 ERA. During the strike-shortened 1994 season, he led Orioles starters with a 16–5 record and 3.06 ERA and made the AL All-Star squad for the third straight year. The 1995 season saw him lead the AL with 19 victories and four shutouts while placing fifth in the AL Cy Young Award balloting. His 19–11 record helped Baltimore win the Wild Card in 1996, but he struggled in both the AL Division Series and Championship Series. In 1997, Mussina paced the Oriole staff with a 15–8 record and 3.20 ERA. He bested Randy Johnson* of the Seattle Mariners twice with a 1.93 ERA in the AL Division Series and pitched brilliantly without decision in the AL Championship Series against the Cleveland Indians. He set AL Championship Series records by striking out 15 batters in Game 3 and 25 batters in the entire series. Altogether, his post-season 41 strikeouts established another mark. In 1998, he overcame being hit by a line drive in the face to post a 13–10 record and 3.49 ERA. He finished 18–7 in 1999, ranking third in victories and ERA (3.50) and making the AL All-Star Team for the fifth time. Mussina has won four consecutive *TSN* Gold Glove Awards from 1996 through 1999. Through the 1999 season, he has compiled a 136–66 career record and 3.50 ERA with 1,325 strikeouts in 1,772 innings. Mussina, who is single, enjoys reading Stephen King novels and has worked as a volunteer basketball coach at Montoursville High School.

BIBLIOGRAPHY: Mike Mussina file, National Baseball Library, Cooperstown, NY; *Baltimore Orioles 1997 Media Guide*; Mike Mussina, letter to Jay Langhammer, January 1996; Tol Broome, "Mike Mussina," *SCD* 22 (April 7, 1995), p. 60; Ted Patterson, *The Baltimore Orioles* (Dallas, TX, 1995); James H. Bready, *Baseball in Baltimore* (Baltimore, MD, 1998); *Stanford 1990 Baseball Media Guide*; Tom Verducci, "The M&M Boys: Plain and Peanut," *SI* 81 (July 18, 1994), pp. 16–22.

Jay Langhammer

MUTRIE, James "Smilin' Jeems" (b. June 13, 1851, Chelsea, MA; d. January 24, 1938, New York, NY), player and manager, played cricket after completing grade school and played several years for his hometown baseball club, the Chelsea Drednaughts. He played shortstop for the Androscoggin Club of Lewiston, ME in 1875 and for Fall River, MA in 1876 and 1877. The enterprising Mutrie arrived in New York City in 1880 and convinced factory owner John B. Day* to finance a professional baseball team, the Metropolitans. New York joined the AA in 1883.

The flamboyant, 5-foot 11-inch, 165-pound Mutrie also formed the New York Gothams in 1883 to replace the Troy, NY Haymakers as an NL member franchise. The Gothams, later the New York Giants, included such National Baseball Hall-of-Famers as catcher Buck Ewing,* pitcher Mickey Welch,* and first baseman Roger Connor.* Mutrie, who handled the New York Gothams' off-field dealings from 1883 to 1885 while serving as sometime field manager of the New York Mets, arranged the Gothams' acquisition of future National Baseball Hall of Famers infielder John Montgomery Ward* from the Providence Grays (NL) and pitcher Timothy Keefe* from the New York Mets (AA).

At this time, the NL set attendance prices at 50 cents per admission compared with the AA's 25 cent charge. Accordingly, Mutrie took over as full-time manager of the potentially more profitable New York Gothams in 1885. His improving club vaulted into second place, just two games behind the Chicago White Stockings (NL). Mutrie's jubilant postgame victory shouts, "My big fellows! My Giants! We are the people!" as his relatively good-sized players won led to the club's adoption of the famous name "Giants" in 1886.

The slender Mutrie, with his trademark tall hat and handlebar mustache, led the New York Giants to their first two NL pennants in 1888 and 1889. Mutrie and his players reigned as the toast of New York, but the club's fortunes plummeted in 1890. The first baseball "war" between the BPBP and the NL caused the decimated Giants to tumble into sixth place. The NL reorganized in 1892, but a syndicate took control of the Giants and removed Mutrie and Day. Mutrie compiled a splendid 658–419 (.611 winning percentage) career managerial record.

Mutrie entered the hotel business in Elmira, NY and then operated a newsstand in Staten Island. He encountered financial and health problems in the 1920s and subsequently supported his wife, Catherine, and daughter, Grace, with a pension provided by the New York Giants.

BIBLIOGRAPHY: Noel Hynd, *The Giants of the Polo Grounds* (New York, 1988); *NYT*, January 25, 1938; John J. O'Malley, "Mutrie's Mets of 1884," *TNP* 4 (Spring 1985), pp. 39–41; Fred Stein and Nick Peters, *Giants Diary* (Berkeley, CA, 1987); Robert L. Tiemann and Mark Rucker, eds., *Nineteenth Century Stars* (Kansas City, MO, 1989); Thomas Aylesworth and Benton Minks, *The Encyclopedia of Baseball Managers* (New York, 1990); Frank Graham, *The New York Giants* (New York, 1952).

Fred Stein

MYER, Charles Solomon "Buddy" (b. March 16, 1904, Ellisville, MI; d. October 31, 1974, Baton Rouge, LA), player, was the son of Charles Myer and Maud Myer. His father, a merchant and cotton buyer, had German Jewish antecedents, while his mother noted an English lineage. After attending public schools in the Ellisville area, Myer matriculated in 1921 at Mississippi Agricultural and Mechanical College and excelled at basketball and baseball. On February 10, 1927, he married Minnie Lee Williams; they had two sons. In 1925, Myer left Mississippi A&M before graduation to join the spring training camp of the Cleveland Indians (AL). After the Indians failed to retain him, Myer joined New Orleans, LA (SA) and hit .336. In September 1925, the Washington Nationals (AL) purchased Myer's contract. Washington traded shortstop Myer to the Boston Red Sox (AL) in May 1927, but reacquired him in December 1928. From 1929 until his 1941 release, Myer remained with Washington mainly at second base and captained the team for several years.

Although not a superstar, Myer played 17 major league seasons as one of the era's better infielders defensively and offensively. Primarily a second baseman, the 5-foot 10½-inch, 163-pound Myer also played shortstop, third base, and the outfield. With a lifetime .974 fielding average, he led AL second basemen in fielding once (1938) and tied for the AL leadership on another occasion (1931). Meyer exceeded the .300 mark nine times and compiled a .303 lifetime batting average. During his major league career, he made 2,131 hits, drove in 850 runs, scored 1,174 runs, stole 156 bases, accumulated 130 triples, and registered 353 doubles. Myer won the 1935 AL batting title with a .349 average and led the AL with 30 stolen bases in 1928.

The underrated player lacked recognition because post–1920 baseball tended to overvalue HR hitters. The left-handed hitting, right-handed throwing Myer slugged just 38 HR during his career. He played for only two AL pennant winners (1925, 1933) and frequently labored on second division teams. Myer's reserve was leavened by pride and determination. Several times he fought anti-Semitic opponents. Despite offers to manage, Myer retired from baseball after his playing days to Baton Rouge and became a successful mortgage banker.

BIBLIOGRAPHY: Buddy Myer file, National Baseball Library, Cooperstown, NY; Morris Bealle, *The Washington Senators* (Washington, DC, 1947); Bob Broeg, "Myer Uncrowned Super Star," *TSN*, November 16, 1974, p. 52; "Charles Solomon (Buddy) Myer," *TSN*, November 16, 1974, p. 74; Shirley Povich, *The Washington Senators* (New York, 1954); Harold Ribalow, *The Jews in American Sports*, rev. ed. (New York, 1954); John Thom, *Champion Batsman of the 20th Century* (Los Angeles, CA, 1992).

                                                                    William M. Simons

MYERS, Randall Kirk "Randy" (b. September 19, 1962, Vancouver, WA), player, graduated from Evergreen, WA High School and attended Clark (WA) CC, where he played on the basketball team and helped coach the women's basketball squad. The Cincinnati Reds (NL) selected him in the third round of the January 1982 draft, but he did not sign. The New York Mets (NL) selected Myers in the secondary phase of the June 1982 draft and signed him.

The 6-foot 1-inch, 225-pound left-handed pitcher started during his first four minor league seasons with Kingsport, TN (ApL), Columbia, SC (SAL), Lynchburg, VA (CrL), Jackson, TX (TL), and Tidewater, VA (IL), earning CrL Pitcher of the Year honors in 1984. In 1986, he switched to a reliever and recorded 12 saves for Tidewater. The New York Mets called him up briefly from 1984 to 1986 before he made the major league roster permanently in 1987. Myers quickly emerged as the team's stopper with 26 saves in 1988 and 24 saves in 1989 and won two games in the 1988 NL Championship Series against the Los Angeles Dodgers.

After being traded to the Cincinnati Reds (NL) in December 1989, Myers enjoyed a spectacular 1990 season. He ranked second in the NL with 31 saves, made the All-Star team, and recorded four saves in postseason games, including the final game of the World Series sweep of the Oakland A's. Myers, who remains single, was used both as a reliever and starter in 1991, struggling with a 6–13 mark. In December 1991, the Cincinnati Reds traded him to the San Diego Padres (NL).

Although saving 38 games for the San Diego Padres in 1992, Myers compiled a 4.29 ERA and signed with the Chicago Cubs (NL) as a free agent in December 1992. The next two years proved strong ones for Myers, who in 1993 led the major leagues with a NL record 53 saves and won the Rolaids Relief Man Award. After leading the NL with 38 saves in an injury-plagued 1995 season, he signed as a free agent with the Baltimore Orioles (AL). His 4–4 record and 31 saves helped the Orioles win the Wild Card in 1996. Myers saved two games in the AL Division Series against the Cleveland Indians, but lost his only decision in the AL Championship Series against the New York Yankees. In 1997, he led the AL with 45 saves and recorded a 1.51 ERA to spark Baltimore to the AL East title. Myers struck out five of the six batters he faced with one save in the AL Division Series against the Seattle Mariners, but dropped his only decision with a 5.06 ERA in the AL Championship Series against the Cleveland Indians. In November 1997, the Toronto Blue Jays (AL) signed him as a free agent. He compiled a 3–4 record with 28 saves for Toronto until being traded in August 1998 to the San Diego Padres. Myers won only one of four decisions as San Diego won the NL-West Division. He struggled in both the NL Championship Series against the Atlanta Braves and World Series against the New York Yankees. He missed the 1999 season with an injured shoulder. Myers' career record through 1999 included 44 wins, 63 losses, a 3.18 ERA and 347 saves.

BIBLIOGRAPHY: Randy Myers file, National Baseball Library, Cooperstown, NY; *Chicago Cubs 1994 Information Guide* (Chicago, IL, 1994); *1995 Chicago Cubs Organizational Record Book* (Chicago, IL, 1995); *TSN Official Baseball Register, 1997*; Donald Honig, *The Cincinnati Reds* (New York, 1992); James H. Bready, *Baseball in Baltimore* (Baltimore, MD, 1998).

Duane A. Smith

N

NASH, William Mitchell "Billy" (b. June 24, 1865, Richmond, VA; d. November 15, 1929, East Orange, NJ), player and manager, entered the major leagues in 1884 with the Richmond Virginians of the expanded, 12-team AA. The 19-year-old rookie batted only .199 in 45 games, but his promising third base play prompted the Boston Beaneaters (NL) to sign him in 1885. Nash was used sparingly as a utility infielder that season, hitting .255. A 5-foot 8½-inch, 167-pound right-hander, Nash won the third base job in 1886 and performed the next nine seasons as a solid hitter with power. His .275 career batting average included 1,606 hits, 266 doubles, 87 triples, 60 HR, and 977 RBI.

A member of the BPBP, Nash joined the Boston Reds of the rebel PL in 1890. His .266 batting average and stellar third base play sparked Boston to the PL pennant. Nash's teams won four consecutive pennants. Upon rejoining the Boston Beaneaters (NL) in 1891, Nash anchored an infield that won acclaim for its "head work and private signals." "They work together as one man," commented John Ward.* Ward added that "team work at the bat is the latest wrinkle and the Boston have it down fine." Under Frank Selee,* who compiled the fourth best all time win–loss percentages among managers, the Beaneaters won three consecutive NL pennants from 1891 to 1893. The Beaneaters thus retired the Dauvray Cup, which was permanently awarded to the first NL club to win three pennants.

In 1892, Boston named Nash team captain. Although replaced by King Kelly* in the second half of that split season, Nash captained the Beaneaters until 1896. Boston traded Nash to the Philadelphia Phillies (NL) for outfielder Billy Hamilton* in a blockbuster deal. Boston followers regarded the popular, handsome Nash as the Beaneaters' spark plug. Nash served as player–manager of the 1896 Phillies but was dismissed as manager when 62–68 Philadelphia finished 8th in the 12-club NL. Nash ended his major league career with the Phillies in 1898, batting .243 in 20 games. His best hitting effort of .291 came in 1893, the year that the pitching distance was lengthened to 60 feet 6 inches.

BIBLIOGRAPHY: Frederick Ivor-Campbell et al., eds., *Baseball's First Stars* (Cleveland, OH, 1996); Harold Kaese, *The Boston Braves* (New York, 1948); Gary Caruso, *The Braves Encyclopedia* (Philadelphia, PA, 1995); Rich Westcott and Frank Bilovsky, *The New Phillies Encyclopedia* (Philadelphia, PA, 1993); Frederick G. Lieb and Stan Baumgartner, *The Philadelphia Phillies* (New York, 1953); *Spalding Guide, 1896*; A. D. Suehsdorf, "Frank Selee, Dynasty Builder," *TNP* 4 (Winter 1985), pp. 35–41; David Quentin Voigt, *American Baseball*, vol. 1 (University Park, PA, 1983).

David Q. Voigt

NAVIN, Frank "Lucky Frank," "The Jap" (b. March 7, 1871, Adrian MI; d. November 13, 1935, Detroit, MI), executive, was the son of Irish-born parents. His father, a railroad worker, sent Navin to study business and law at the Detroit College of Law. Navin's brother Tom, a prominent Republican politician in Michigan, influenced him to seek the office of justice of the peace. Navin's subsequent defeat and his brother's imprisonment for embezzling a large sum of money convinced Navin to quit politics. Although a good student of jurisprudence, he never practiced law. Navin instead worked as an accountant for Sam Angus, insurance company owner and chief Detroit Tigers (AL) stockholder. Navin kept accounts for the ballclub and toiled in a gambling establishment, acquiring a shady reputation. He avoided payment of a gambling debt to Frank Croul, later police commissioner. A vindictive Croul made it difficult for Navin to have Sunday baseball in Detroit.

With Angus' finances in disarray, Navin persuaded William Yawkey, the scion of a wealthy Michigan family, to purchase the Tigers. Navin bought a small share of the Detroit Tigers with a packet won in a card game. Navin, who believed that receipts should balance with expenditures, clashed with the club's general manager Ed Barrow.* Barrow wished to make liberal use of Yawkey's money to build a winning team. Navin, however, gained Yawkey's confidence and forced Barrow to resign. Although not having a professional grasp of baseball, he became Tigers general manager and learned much from manager William Armour. Armour persuaded Navin to purchase a pugnacious teenager, Ty Cobb.* Navin resisted pressure to trade the Georgia troublemaker and made several other astute acquisitions to build the 1907–1909 AL championship teams. In gratitude, Yawkey gave Navin half ownership of the club. Nicknamed "Lucky Frank," he became a solid Detroit citizen and contributed to many charities. He managed to have the ballpark named in his honor and conducted widely publicized annual contract negotiations with Cobb.

Walter Briggs* purchased a substantial share of the Tigers when Yawkey died in 1920. Although attendance skyrocketed and Navin became wealthy,

Detroit did not win an AL championship that decade. Critics blamed Navin's parsimonious policies and Cobb's inept managing. In 1931, Navin was nearly ruined by the Depression and horse racing gambling losses and did not have enough money to take the Tigers to spring training. Briggs bought most of the Tiger stock and pumped funds into the operation, building the 1934 and 1935 AL championship teams. Nicknamed "The Jap" because of his inscrutable features, Navin was an emotional man who often used pithy, colloquial language in intimate and business letters. Navin's intimates appreciated his fine sense of humor and generosity, particularly to old ballplayers. When Navin died, the city of Detroit mourned "Mr. Baseball."

BIBLIOGRAPHY: Frank Navin file, National Baseball Library, Cooperstown, NY; Richard Bak, *A Place for Summer* (Detroit, MI, 1998); William M. Anderson, *The Detroit Tigers* (South Bend, IN, 1996); W. Malcolm Bingay, *Detroit Is My Home Town* (New York, 1951); W. Malcolm Bingay, *Of Me I Sing* (New York, 1949); Detroit Baseball Club Letterbooks, vols. 1–12, Ernie Harwell Collection, Detroit Public Library, Detroit, MI; Detroit (MI) *News*, November 13, 1935; Joe Falls, *Detroit Tigers* (New York, 1975); Charles C. Alexander, *Ty Cobb* (New York, 1984); Richard Bak, *Ty Cobb: His Tumultuous Life and Times* (Dallas, TX, 1994); Frederick G. Lieb, *The Detroit Tigers* (New York, 1946); John L. Lodge, *I Remember Detroit* (Detroit, MI, 1949).

Anthony J. Papalas

NEHF, Arthur Neukom "Art," "The Terre Haute Terror" (b. July 31, 1892, Terre Haute, IN; d. December 18, 1960, Phoenix, AZ), player, was a slightly built, 5-foot 9-inch, 170-pound, southpaw pitcher. After attending a Terre Haute high school, he played baseball at Rose Polytechnic Institute (IN) and earned a Bachelor of Science degree there in 1913. Since engineers received low salaries in that era, Nehf pursued a professional baseball career. Chicago Cubs (NL) president Charles Webb Murphy offered Nehf a tryout, but field manager John Evers* considered him too small. Nehf pitched for Kansas City, MO (AA) and Sioux City, IA (WL) in 1913 and won 30 games and lost only 17 for Terre Haute, IN (CL) the next two seasons. In 1915, he led the CL with 218 strikeouts and a sparkling 1.38 ERA.

After joining the Boston Braves (NL) for a reported $3,500 in 1915, Nehf compiled a 52–41 record there until traded on August 17, 1919 to John McGraw's* New York Giants (NL) for four players and $40,000. Nehf hurled for the Giants until developing arm problems and was sold in May 1926 to the Cincinnati Reds (NL). Nicknamed "The Terre Haute Terror," Nehf won 87 games between 1920 and 1924, compiled a 107–60 overall win–loss mark with the Giants, and led them to four consecutive NL pennants from 1921 to 1924. From 1921 to 1924, he finished with 20–10, 19–13, 13–10, and 14–4 marks. Nehf lost his first two World Series starts against the New York Yankees in 1921, but shut them out on four hits in the seventh, deciding game to win the world championship for the Giants. He pitched three complete games, allowing a record low 13 base hits. In the 1922 World Series, Nehf defeated the Yankees, 5–3, in the fifth game to wrap up another world championship. He pitched a shutout victory over New York in the third game of the 1923 World Series, but the Yankees won their first title, four games to two. Nehf bested Walter Johnson* of the Washington Senators in the first game of the 1924 World Series, but lost the sixth game as the Senators won the title in seven games. In 12 World Series games, he pitched 79 innings, won four, lost four, and had a 2.16 ERA. After pitching for the Reds in 1926 and 1927, Nehf signed with the Chicago Cubs (NL) in August 1927. He won 8 games in his final major league season (1929) and appeared in one more World Series, but did not figure in any decisions.

During his 15 major league seasons, Nehf pitched in 451 games, recorded 184 victories and 120 losses, and compiled a 3.20 ERA. He hurled 2,707.2 innings and completed 182 games, including 28 shutouts. On August 1, 1918, Nehf pitched a 21-inning, 2–0, loss against the Pittsburgh Pirates. He participated in 12 double plays in 1920, equalling the NL record for a pitcher. In 1918 he completed 28 games and surrendered 274 base hits and 107 runs, leading the NL in each category. After retiring from baseball, the arthritic Nehf was employed by Cubs owner William Wrigley in hotel management and entered the real estate business in Arizona. Nehf married Elizabeth Bird May on November 1, 1916 and was honored when Rose Polytechnic Institute named its baseball field after him.

BIBLIOGRAPHY: Warren Brown, *The Chicago Cubs* (New York, 1946); Eddie Gold and Art Ahrens, *The Golden Era Cubs, 1876–1940* (Chicago, IL, 1985); Arthur Nehf file, National Baseball Library, Cooperstown, NY; Harold Kaese, *The Boston Braves* (New York, 1948); Gary Caruso, *The Braves Encyclopedia* (Philadelphia, PA, 1995); Gene Karst and Martin J. Jones, Jr., *Who's Who in Professional Baseball* (New Rochelle, NY, 1973); Noel Hynd, *The Giants of the Polo Grounds* (New York, 1988); Frank Graham, *McGraw of the Giants* (New York, 1944); Frank Graham, *The New York Giants* (New York, 1952); Joseph Durso, *The Days of Mr. McGraw* (Englewood Cliffs, NJ, 1969); Lee Allen, *The Cincinnati Reds* (New York, 1948); Paul MacFarlane, ed., *TSN Daguerreotypes of Great Stars of Baseball* (St. Louis, MO, 1971); *The Baseball Encyclopedia*, 10th ed. (New York, 1996); *TSN*, October 10, 1915, December 4, 1965.

David S. Matz and John L. Evers

NESBITT, Mary. *See* Mary Nesbitt Wisham.

NETTLES, Graig "Puff" (b. August 20, 1944, San Diego, CA), player and coach, followed Lou Gehrig* and Thurman Munson* as a New York Yankee (AL) captain. Nettles's unusual first name was his mother's idea. His father, Wayne, a policeman–teacher, encouraged Nettles to play baseball from an early age. Graig's brother, Jim, followed him into the major leagues.

Nettles participated in baseball at San Diego High School, but the 6-foot, 180 pounder attended San Diego State University on a basketball scholarship. As a summer semiprofessional baseball player in Alaska, Nettles drew the attention of a Minnesota Twins (AL) scout. In 1965 the Minnesota Twins drafted Nettles, who had completed three years of college, and signed him to a $15,000 contract. In his first professional baseball season with Wisconsin Rapids, WI (ML), second baseman–third baseman Nettles in 1966 hammered a ML-leading 28 HR. He shared the SL title with 19 HR for Charlotte, NC in 1967 and paced the AL with 32 HR in 1976. The slugger's best professional season for HR (37) and RBI (107) came in 1977 with the New York Yankees (AL). His 319 career HR as a third baseman remain an AL record.

Nettles began his major league career with the Minnesota Twins, appearing in 121 games from 1967 to 1969. After playing three years as a Cleveland Indians (AL) regular, Nettles was traded to the New York Yankees in November 1972. He spent 11 years in New York and commented, "I'll always be a Yankee" after the New York pinstripe uniform phase of his career had ended. As a New York Yankee, Nettles participated in five All-Star Games, six AL Championship Series (including being the 1978 MVP), and four World Series. He ended his major league tenure in the NL with the San Diego Padres (1984–1986), Atlanta Braves (1987), and Montreal Expos (1988). With the Padres, he performed in another All-Star Game and the 1984 NL Championship Series and World Series. In 1989, Nettles joined the Bradenton, FL Explorers of the new SPBA and batted .301 with 34 RBI.

The lifetime .248 major league batter made 2,225 hits, 328 doubles, and 1,314 RBI. An accomplished fielder who admired the third base play of rival Brooks Robinson,* Nettles won two Gold Gloves, made two All-Star fielding teams, and led the AL once in fielding average and at least twice in each of several other fielding categories. His third base work helped the Yankees prevail in the 1978 World Series over the Los Angeles Dodgers. In November 1965, Nettles married Virginia Meckling, a college classmate, and has four children. He coached for the New York Yankees (AL) in 1991 and San Diego Padres in 1995.

BIBLIOGRAPHY: *CB* (1984), pp. 298–302; Dick Lally, *Pinstriped Summers* (New York, 1985); Sparky Lyle and Peter Golenbock, *The Bronx Zoo* (New York, 1979); *San Diego Padres 1986 Media Guide*; Graig Nettles file, National Baseball Library, Cooperstown, NY; Mark Gallagher, *The Yankee Encyclopedia*, vol. 3 (Champaign, IL, 1997); Robert E. Kelly, *Baseball's Best* (Jefferson, NC, 1988); Terry Pluto, *The Curse of Rocky Colavito* (New York, 1994); Jack Torry, *Endless Summers* (South Bend, IN, 1995); Dave Anderson et al., *The Yankees* (New York, 1979); Maury Allen, *Damn Yankee* (New York, 1980); Graig Nettles and Peter Golenbock, *Balls* (New York, 1984); Mike Shatzkin, ed., *The Ballplayers* (New York, 1990); *TSN Official Baseball Register, 1987*; Steve Wulf,

"The Best Team in Baseball," *SI* 60 (April 16, 1984), p. 22; *Yankees Magazine 1984 Yankees Information Guide*, pp. 88–90.

Thomas D. Jozwik

NEWCOMBE, Donald "Don," "Newk" (b. June 14, 1926, Madison, NJ), player, became one of the first successful black pitchers in modern major league baseball. The 6-foot 4-inch, 230-pound Newcombe pitched for the Brooklyn Dodgers (NL) from 1949 to 1957 and moved with the club to Los Angeles at the start of the 1958 season. After only 11 games on the West Coast, Newcombe was traded to the Cincinnati Reds (NL) in June 1958 and pitched there until July 1960. He completed his major league career that season with the Cleveland Indians (AL). Prior to entering the major leagues, Newcombe pitched for the Newark, NJ Eagles (NNL) and Nashua, NH Dodgers (NEL) in 1946 and 1947, and Montreal, Canada Royals (IL) in 1948 and 1949.

Newcombe's 10 major league baseball seasons included 344 appearances and 294 starts. Newcombe struck out 1,129 batters and walked only 490 in 2,154.2 innings pitched and compiled a 3.56 ERA. His career .623 winning percentage (149 wins, 90 losses) ranks him high among all major league pitchers with at least 100 career victories. Newcombe won 20 games in 1951 and 1955 and led the NL in 1956 with 27 victories and a .794 winning percentage. His other NL leading performances included winning percentage (.800) in 1955, strikeouts (164) in 1951, and shutouts (5, tied with three others) in 1949. Newcombe was selected NL Rookie of the Year in 1949, NL MVP in 1956, and initial recipient of the Cy Young Award in 1956. He pitched for the Dodgers in the 1949, 1955, and 1956 World Series, compiling a 0–4 record. An NL All-Star performer in 1949 and 1951, he was the losing pitcher in the former contest.

Newcombe, an exceptionally able batter, often pinch-hit for the Dodgers. He posted a .271 career batting average, .367 slugging average, 15 lifetime HR, and 108 RBI. In 1955, he batted .359 with a .632 slugging percentage in 117 at-bats, the latter still a modern major league record for pitchers. Newcombe, who married Freddie Cross, has two children and lives in Los Angeles. He has operated Don Newcombe Enterprises, a personal services company, since 1976 and has served as director of community relations for the Los Angeles Dodgers since 1970. A recovering alcoholic, he created the Dodger Drug and Alcoholic Awareness Program in 1980 and is a consultant for the National Institute on Alcohol Abuse and Alcoholism. He serves as director for special projects for the New Beginning Alcohol and Drug Treatment Program.

BIBLIOGRAPHY: *CB* (1957), pp. 399–401; Don Newcombe file, National Baseball Library, Cooperstown, NY; Ross Forman, "Newcombe Makes Pitch for HOF," *SCD* 21 (June 3, 1994), pp. 136–138; David Halberstam, *Summer of '49* (New York, 1989); Roger Kahn, *The Boys of Summer* (New York, 1972); Tommy Holmes, *The Dodgers*

(New York, 1975); Edwin B. Henderson et al., *The Black Athlete: Emergence and Arrival* (Cornwall Heights, NJ, 1979); Gene Karst and Martin J. Jones, Jr., *Who's Who in Professional Baseball* (New Rochelle, NY, 1973); Larry Moffi and Jonathan Kronstadt, *Crossing the Line* (Jefferson, NC, 1994); Randy Schultz, "Don Newcombe," *SCD* 24 (March 7, 1997), pp. 140–141; Guy Waterman, "Don Newcombe: Grace Under Pressure," *BRJ* 23 (1994), pp. 27–31; William F. McNeil, *The Dodgers Encyclopedia* (Champaign, IL, 1997); Richard Goldstein, *Superstars and Screwballs* (New York, 1991); Peter Golenbock, *Bums* (New York, 1984).

William J. Serow

NEWHOUSER, Harold "Hal," "Prince Hal" (b. May 20, 1921, Detroit MI; d. November 10, 1998, Detroit, MI), player and scout, was the son of pattern-maker Theodore Newhouser and homemaker Emilie Newhouser. He grew up in Detroit, where he became an outstanding Sandlot Class E Pitcher and starred for the American Legion Post 286 team. Detroit Tigers (AL) scout Wish Egan encouraged the high school youth to practice pitching at Briggs Stadium in Detroit outside the foul lines. After graduation from Wilbur Wright High School, 17-year-old Newhouser accepted a $400 bonus and $150 a month salary to sign with the Detroit Tigers.

After spending 1939 with Alexandria, LA (EvL) and Beaumont, TX (TL), the 6-foot 2-inch, 180-pound left-hander pitched from late 1939 to July 1953 with the Detroit Tigers and finished his career in 1954 with the Cleveland Indians (AL). During 1944, 1945, and 1946, he stood at the forefront of major league pitchers. In 1945, he compiled a 25–9 record and 1.81 ERA and led the AL in victories, winning percentage (.735), complete games (29), shutouts (8), innings pitched (313), strikeouts (212), and ERA (1.81). He holds the Detroit Tigers record for the lowest single-season ERA (1945) and most season victories by a left-hander (29, 1944). *BD* ranked his 1944 win–loss record the best achievement by an AL pitcher in the 1940s.

Although prone to surrendering walks and hits, Newhouser frequently pitched out of difficult situations and usually made timely outs. He averaged over 21 victories in a season from 1944 to 1950, and made the AL All-Star team six times. After hurting his arm in the 1948 finale, Newhouser experienced declining effectiveness. A loyal hometown boy, Newhouser could have jumped his bonus contract with the Tigers and signed with the Cleveland Indians for $15,000 and a new car. Newhouser wanted to serve in the U.S. Army during World War II, but was rejected because of a heart problem. He married Beryl Margaret Steele on December 20, 1941 and had two daughters.

Newhouser, who compiled 207 career wins and 150 losses (.580 winning percentage), also hurled 26 victories in 1946 and 21 in 1948. In 1945, he pitched the AL pennant-clinching win and two key victories in the World Series against the Chicago Cubs. In 1944 and 1945, he became the first of few players to win consecutive AL MVP awards. In 488 appearances, he completed 212 of 374 starts, pitched 2,993 innings, struck out 1,796 batters, and hurled 33 shutouts. After retirement as a player in 1955, Newhouser scouted for the AL Baltimore Orioles (1956–1961), Cleveland Indians (1961–1964), and NL Houston Astros (1985–1993) and became a bank executive in Pontiac, MI. He is active in community affairs, including the YWCA, Boy Scouts, and fund-raising efforts. In 1992, the Veterans Committee elected him to the National Baseball Hall of Fame.

BIBLIOGRAPHY: Hal Newhouser file, National Baseball Library, Cooperstown, NY; Larry Amman, "Newhouser and Trout in 1944," *BRJ* 12 (1983), pp. 18–21; John Benson et al., *Baseball's Top 100* (Wilton, CT, 1997); Frederick G. Lieb, *The Detroit Tigers* (New York, 1946); William M. Anderson, *The Detroit Tigers* (South Bend, IN, 1996); Richard Bak, *A Place for Summer* (Detroit, MI, 1998); Fred Smith, *995 Tigers* (Detroit, MI, 1981); Glenn Dickey, *The History of the American League Since 1901* (New York, 1980); Joe Falls, *Detroit Tigers* (New York, 1975); Richard Goldstein, *Spartan Seasons* (New York, 1980); David M. Jordan, *A Tiger in His Time* (South Bend, IN, 1990); Brent P. Kelley, *The Case For: Those Overlooked by the Baseball Hall of Fame* (Jefferson, NC, 1992); Gene Karst and Martin J. Jones, Jr., *Who's Who in Professional Baseball* (New Rochelle, NY, 1973); George Voss, "Top Player Achievements of the Last Four Decades!" *BD* 41 (August 1982), p. 61; Rich Westcott, *Diamond Greats* (Westport, CT, 1988).

Douglas A. Noverr

NEWSOM, Louis Norman "Buck," "Bobo" (b. August 11, 1907, Hartsville, AL; d. December 7, 1962, Orlando, FL), player and sportscaster, was the son of Henry Newsom and Lillian (Hicks) Newsom. He married Bessie Lucille Arant on February 19, 1927. Following the couple's divorce, he on December 31, 1943 wed Ruth Griffiths. They had one son and one daughter. The colorful, loquacious, much-traveled pitcher entered organized baseball in 1928 with Raleigh, NC (PrL) and Greenville, SC (ECaL). During the next five years, he hurled for six minor league teams, appeared in a few games for the Brooklyn Dodgers (NL) in 1929 and 1930, and pitched in one game for the Chicago Cubs (NL) in 1932. The St. Louis Browns (AL) acquired Newsom in 1934. He remained there until being sold in May 1935 to the Washington Senators (AL). He pitched for the Senators until June 1937, when he was traded to the Boston Red Sox (AL). Boston sent him to the St. Louis Browns in December 1937. In May 1939, he was dealt to the Detroit Tigers (AL). Detroit sold him in March 1942 to the Washington Senators (AL), with whom he remained until being acquired by the Brooklyn Dodgers (NL) in August 1942. In July 1943, he was waived to the St. Louis Browns. The next month, the Washington Senators (AL) bought him from the St. Louis Browns. In December 1943, the Washington Senators traded him to the Philadelphia Athletics (AL). In June 1946 the Philadelphia Athletics released Newsom at his own request so that he could sign with the Washington Senators (AL). In July 1947, the New York Yankees (AL) claimed him on waivers. He was released in 1948 and signed with the New York Giants (NL). The New York Giants waived him that year. Newsom did not appear again in the major leagues until 1952, when he pitched for both the Washington Senators (AL) and Philadelphia Athletics (AL). Newsom was released after a few games with the Philadelphia Athletics in 1953 and became a sportscaster.

Newsom, who pitched mainly for weak teams, compiled a 3.98 ERA, struck out 2,082 batters in 3,759.1 innings, won 211 games, and lost 222 decisions. He recorded 20 or more victories three times (1938–1940) and paced the AL with 31 complete games and 329.2 innings pitched in 1938, and with 24 complete games in 1939. He also led the AL hurlers in losses four times (20 in 1934, 1941, and 1945; 18 in 1935), games started four times (1936–1939), hits surrendered once (1938), walks twice (1934, 1937), and strikeouts once (1942). The 1940 campaign saw Newsom achieve a 21–5 win–loss record and tie a World Series record by pitching three complete games against the Cincinnati Reds. In 1938, he hurled 9.2 hitless innings for the St. Louis Browns against the Boston Red Sox in a 2–1 loss.

The courageous Newsom was hit on the knee by a devastating line drive, but still pitched six more innings for the St. Louis Browns. Subsequent X-rays revealed that his kneecap had been shattered. One day after Newsom had won the opener of the 1940 World Series, his father died of a heart attack. Newsom's father had attended the initial game. The undaunted Newsom shut out the Cincinnati Reds in the fifth game, but lost the deciding seventh game, 2–1, on only one full day of rest. In 1943, Newsom fought his suspension by Brooklyn Dodgers manager Leo Durocher* and was supported by his teammates. Newsom's reinstatement averted a strike.

BIBLIOGRAPHY: Frank Graham, *The Brooklyn Dodgers* (New York, 1945); Donald Honig, *Baseball Between the Lines* (New York, 1976); Donald Honig, *Baseball When the Grass Was Real* (New York, 1975); Brent P. Kelley, "Baseball's Hard-Luck Losers," *SCD* 16 (October 13, 1989), pp. 220–221; Bobo Newsom file, National Baseball Library, Cooperstown, NY; Brent P. Kelley, *The Case For: Those Overlooked by the Baseball Hall of Fame* (Jefferson, NC, 1992); Joe Falls, *Detroit Tigers* (New York, 1975); Frederick G. Lieb, *The Detroit Tigers* (New York, 1946); Frederick G. Lieb, *The Story of the World Series* (New York, 1965); William B. Mead, *Even the Browns* (Chicago, IL, 1978); *NYT*, December 8, 1962; Shirley Povich, *The Washington Senators* (New York, 1943); Jimmy Powers, *Baseball Personalities* (New York, 1949); Joe Reichler and Ben Olan, *Baseball's Unforgettable Games* (New York, 1960); *TSN*, December 22, 1962; Fred Smith, *995 Tigers* (Detroit, MI, 1981); Bill Borst, *Still Last in the American League* (West Bloomfield, MI, 1992); Bill Borst, ed., *Ables to Zoldak*, vol. 2 (St. Louis, MO, 1989); Morris Bealle, *The Washington Senators* (Washington, DC, 1947); Mike Ross, "Bobo Newsom," *TNP* 10 (1990), pp. 75–78.

Ralph S. Graber

NICHOLS, Charles Augustus "Kid" (b. September 14, 1869, Madison, WI; d. April 11, 1953, Kansas City, MO), player, manager, and coach, starred as a pitcher between 1890 and 1905 and ranked among the steadiest all-time winners. The 5-foot 10½-inch, 175-pound right-hander hurled for Kansas City, MO (WA), Omaha, NE (WA), and Memphis, TN (SL) between 1887 and 1889. After joining the Boston Beaneaters (NL) in 1890, Nichols topped the 25-victory mark nine consecutive seasons. An overhand pitcher with a smooth delivery, Nichols depended on speed, good control, and a durable arm. In his first five major league seasons, he compiled impressive innings-pitched totals of 424, 425, 453, 425, and 407. He toiled over 300 innings in seven of the next eight years. As a 20-year-old rookie, Nichols led Boston pitchers with 27 victories (including 7 shutouts) and then achieved four consecutive seasons with 30 or more triumphs. In his first nine seasons, Nichols sparked Boston to five championships and led his team in victories. He recorded his most victories (35) in 1892 and paced the NL in wins three years in succession from 1896 to 1898.

Following the 1901 season, Nichols bought a part-interest in the Kansas City, MO (WA) club and pitched 47 victories (1902–1903) as their player–manager. As pitcher–manager for the St. Louis Cardinals (NL) in 1904 and part of 1905, Nichols guided the Cardinals to 80 wins in 169 games. In 1904, he won 21 games and on August 11 struck out 15 Brooklyn Superbas batters in a 17-inning game. After being released as Cardinals manager in mid-June, Nichols joined the Philadelphia Phillies (NL) and completed the season with an 11–11 record. In early 1906, he retired from baseball at age 36.

Nichols won 361 games in his major league career and, at nine months and 23 days past his 30th birthday, became the youngest pitcher ever to win 300 games. Only five moundsmen, Cy Young,* Walter Johnson,* Christy Mathewson,* Grover Alexander,* and Warren Spahn,* have registered more victories, while only three pitchers have hurled more complete games. Although Nichols did not attain the win standards achieved by Young and Johnson, he, nevertheless, remains one of the five premier 19th century baseball pitchers with Tim Keefe,* John Clarkson,* Charles Radbourne,* and Young.

Nichols, who ranks high on the all-time major league lists for pitchers in numerous statistical categories, participated in 620 contests, started 561 games, completed 531 games (4th), pitched 5,056 innings (10th), struck out 1,873 batters, walked 1,268 batters, and hurled 48 shutouts. In 15 seasons, Nichols compiled 208 losses and won 20 or more contests 11 years (5th) and at least 30 games seven years (1st).

Subsequently, Nichols entered the motion picture business and real estate and also managed one of the largest bowling alleys in Missouri, gaining recognition as one of the finest bowlers in Kansas City. At age 64, Nichols won the Class A Championship. Nichols also coached the Missouri Valley College baseball team in Marshall, MO and in 1949 was enshrined in the National Baseball Hall of Fame.

BIBLIOGRAPHY: Charles Nichols file, National Baseball Library, Cooperstown, NY; John Thorn et al., eds., *Total Braves* (New York, 1996); Gary Caruso, *The Braves Encyclopedia* (Philadelphia, PA, 1995); Craig Carter, ed., *TSN Daguerreotypes*, 8th ed. (St. Louis, MO, 1990); Bob Broeg and Jerry Vickery, *St. Louis Cardinals Encyclopedia* (Grand Rapids, MI, 1998); Frederick Ivor-Campbell et al., eds., *Baseball's First Stars* (Cleveland, OH, 1996); Harold Kaese, *The Boston Braves* (New York, 1948); Frederick G. Lieb, *The St. Louis Cardinals* (New York, 1945); *National Baseball Hall of Fame and Museum Brochure* (Cooperstown, NY, 1974); Lowell Reidenbaugh, *Baseball's Hall of Fame-Cooperstown* (New York, 1993).

John L. Evers

NICHOLSON, William Beck "Swish" (b. December 11, 1914, Chestertown, MD; d. March 8, 1996, Chestertown, MD), player, was the son of Albert Nicholson and Alverta Nicholson and went from Washington College to the Philadelphia Athletics (AL) in 1936 as an outfielder. Minor league stops followed at Oklahoma City, OK (TL) and Williamsport, PA (NYPL). The Chicago Cubs (NL) purchased Nicholson in June 1939 after his outstanding season at Chattanooga, TN (SL). Nicholson homered in his first game on August 1, 1939. He hit 235 career HR, including eight with the bases loaded, over the next 10 years and became a favorite of the Windy City crowd. He led the NL in HR and RBI in 1943 and 1944, tying a record shared by Babe Ruth* and Jimmie Foxx.* The pinnacle of his major league career came in a weekend series with the New York Giants in 1944, when he hit a major league record six HR in 40 hours. Despite a swollen hand, he helped the NL win the 1944 All-Star Game with his hitting.

Nicholson's batting production declined after the 1944 season, but he played an important role on the 1945 NL pennant–winning Cubs. His eight RBI in the 1945 World Series against the Detroit Tigers tied a fall classic record. Nicholson's color blindness caused the Cubs to block off a section of the center field seats to give him a better hitting background.

The skillfully fielding Nicholson possessed a strong throwing arm that kept runners from seeking an extra base. With a tremendous swing, the 6-foot, 205-pound Nicholson often struck out and also hit some monumental homers in Wrigley Field. In October 1948, the Philadelphia Phillies (NL) acquired him to serve as a pinch hitter. It was disclosed in 1950 that he suffered from diabetes, an illness that kept him from playing in the World Series against the New York Yankees that year. Nicholson retired in 1953 with a career major league .268 batting average, 1,484 hits, 235 HR, and 948 RBI. He married Nancy Kane in December 1937 and had two sons before their divorce. After retiring from baseball, he farmed, operated a bowling alley, and conducted a private hunting preserve. His second wife, Diana, survived him.

BIBLIOGRAPHY: Bill Nicholson file, National Baseball Library, Cooperstown, NY; Frank Dolson, *The Philadelphia Story* (South Bend, IN, 1981); Harry Paxton, *The*

Whiz Kids (New York, 1950); Robin Roberts and C. Paul Rogers III, *The Whiz Kids and the 1950 Pennant* (Philadelphia, PA, 1996); Art Ahrens and Eddie Gold, *Day by Day in Chicago Cubs History* (West Point, NY, 1982); *The Baseball Encyclopedia*, 10th ed. (New York, 1996); Eddie Gold and Art Ahrens, *The New Era Cubs, 1941–1985* (Chicago, IL, 1985); Jim Langford, *The Game Is Never Over* (South Bend, IN, 1980); Bob Mayer, "Swish Nicholson," *TNP* 15 (1995), pp. 149–150; *NYT*, March 12, 1996, p. B6; Rich Westcott, *Diamond Greats* (Westport, CT, 1988); Jim Enright, *Chicago Cubs* (New York, 1975); Richard Goldstein, *Spartan Seasons* (New York, 1980); Frederick G. Lieb and Stan Baumgartner, *The Philadelphia Phillies* (New York, 1953); Rich Westcott and Frank Bilovsky, *The New Phillies Encyclopedia* (Philadelphia, PA, 1993); Allen Lewis, *The Philadelphia Phillies: A Pictorial History* (Virginia Beach, VA, 1981).

Duane A. Smith

NICOL, Helen. *See* Helen Nicol Fox.

NIEKRO, Joseph Franklin "Joe" (b. November 7, 1944, Martins Ferry, OH), player and coach, is the son of coal miner Philip Niekro and Henrietta (Klinkoski) Niekro, both of Polish descent. The younger brother of major league pitcher Phil Niekro,* he followed Phil's footsteps by excelling in baseball and basketball at Bridgeport (OH) High School. After attending West Liberty State College in West Virginia, the 6-foot 1-inch, 190-pound right-hander pitcher signed in 1966 with the Chicago Cubs (NL).

Niekro pitched with Treasure Valley, ID (PrL), Quincy, IL (ML), and Dallas-Fort Worth, TX (TL) before making the Chicago Cubs roster in 1967. He recorded 24 victories with Chicago until traded to the San Diego Padres (NL) in April 1969. Niekro hurled against brother, Phil, of the Atlanta Braves on July 4, 1967 and lost 8–3, marking the first time that brothers opposed each other on the mound in the NL. They met again in eight other encounters, with Joe winning five and Phil three. His only major league HR came off Phil in May 1976. After being traded to the Detroit Tigers (AL) in December 1969, Niekro hurled for the Tigers and Toledo, OH (IL) until sold on waivers to the Atlanta Braves (NL) in August 1973. Niekro captured 21 composite decisions for the Tigers and pitched a seven-inning, 2–0, perfect game for Toledo against Tidewater, VA (IL) on July 16, 1972. At Atlanta and Richmond, VA (IL) Niekro collected 13 victories in 1973 and 1974 before being sold to the Houston Astros (NL) in April 1975.

Following seven appearances for Des Moines–based Iowa (AA) in 1975, Niekro became one of the leading Houston Astros pitchers. On July 2, 1985, Niekro collected his 200th career major league victory with a 3–2 win over the San Diego Padres. Niekro, a knuckleball artist, recorded 144 victories with Houston from 1975 to 1985 and boasted 21 wins in 1979, both club records. Besides topping the NL in wins and tying for the lead with 5 shutouts (1979), Niekro paced the NL in games started with 38 (1983–1984).

Named *TSN* NL Pitcher of the Year and to the NL All-Star team (1979), Niekro pitched in two post-season playoff games (1980–1981). Although failing to gain a decision, Niekro did not allow a single run in 18 innings. In September 1985, he was sent to the New York Yankees (AL) and joined his brother Phil there. The Yankees traded him to the Minnesota Twins (AL) in June 1987. His only World Series appearance came in 1987 against the St. Louis Cardinals. His major league career ended with Minnesota in 1988. In 22 major league seasons, he pitched 3,584.2 innings in 702 games with 221 wins, 204 losses, 1,747 strikeouts, 29 shutouts, and a 3.59 ERA. He served as a pitching coach with Portland, OR (PCL) and Bend, OR (NWL) in 1993, and Colorado Silver Bullets in 1995 and 1996.

BIBLIOGRAPHY: Joe Niekro file, National Baseball Library, Cooperstown, NY; Ron Fimrite, "The Valley Boys," *SI* 68 (May 23, 1988), pp. 78–84; Chuck Greenwood, "Niekro Keeps Love of Baseball in Family," *SCD* 23 (August 30, 1996), pp. 160–161; Gene Karst and Martin J. Jones, Jr., *Who's Who in Professional Baseball* (New Rochelle, NY, 1973); Robert E. Kelly, *Baseball's Best* (Jefferson, NC, 1988); Phil Niekro et al., *The Niekro Files* (Chicago, IL, 1988); Phil Niekro and Tom Bird, *Knuckle Balls* (New York, 1986); Fred Smith, *995 Tigers* (Detroit, MI, 1981); Jim Enright, *Chicago Cubs* (New York, 1975), Eddie Gold and Art Ahrens, *The New Era Cubs, 1941–1985* (Chicago, IL, 1985); Paul Burke, "Houston Astros," *TM* (December 1980), pp. 156–161, 264–271; Peter C. Bjarkman, *Encyclopedia of Major League Baseball Team Histories National League* (Westport, CT, 1991); Nolan Ryan and Harvey Frommer, *Throwing Heat* (New York, 1988); Lyle Spatz, "The Opening Day Woes of the Niekro Brothers," *BRJ* 27 (1998), pp. 8–10; *TSN Baseball Register, 1989*; Steve Wulf, "Knucksie Hasn't Lost His Grip," *SI* 60 (June 4, 1984), pp. 91–94ff.

John L. Evers

NIEKRO, Philip Henry "Phil" (b. April 1, 1939, Blaine, OH), player and manager, is the son of Philip Niekro and Henrietta (Klinkoski) Niekro, and brother of major league pitcher Joe Niekro.* His parents, both of Polish descent, settled in eastern Ohio near Wheeling, WV. His father, a coal miner and sandlot baseball player, taught the sport to Phil and Joe. Niekro attended grade school in Lansing and high school in Bridgeport, OH, where he excelled in athletics. Although offered a college baseball scholarship, he instead signed a professional baseball contract with the Milwaukee Braves (NL). From 1959 to 1966 (except for military service in 1963), Niekro pitched for minor league clubs in Wellsville, NY (NYPL), McCook, NE (NeSL), Jacksonville, FL (SAL), Louisville, KY (AA), Austin, TX (TL), Denver, CO (AA), and Richmond, VA (IL). He utilized the knuckleball, taught to him by his father. Niekro's minor league progress proved slow primarily because catchers encountered difficulty catching his knuckleball.

The 6-foot 1-inch, 180-pound right-hander pitched his first major league game for the Milwaukee Braves (NL) in 1964 and was farmed out each season until 1967, by which time the franchise had been shifted to Atlanta. In his first full season, he led the NL with a 1.87 ERA in 1967. In 1969 he won 23 games and led the Braves to the Western Division title, the first year that the expansion system was used. Although pitching good ball, including a no-hit game over the San Diego Padres in 1973, Niekro did not win many more games than he lost because Atlanta fielded average teams.

In 1974 Niekro led the NL in innings pitched and complete games and again won 20 games. Despite advancing years, Niekro became the NL workhorse. From 1977 through 1979, he led the NL in games started, games completed, and innings pitched. He also paced the NL with 262 strikeouts in 1977 and, at age 40 in 1979, tied his brother, Joe, of the Houston Astros for the NL lead in games won with 21. During their long major league careers, the Niekro brothers faced each other nine times. Joe won five of these games, including a 1–0 thriller on July 13, 1969, while Phil took four. On May 29, 1976, Joe hit his only major league HR off his brother Phil in a 4–3 victory. These fraternal confrontations posed a dilemma for their parents in this close-knit family.

Niekro ended his long association with the Braves after winning 11 of 21 decisions in 1983. In January 1984, the New York Yankees (AL) signed him to a two-year contract. Niekro compiled an impressive 16–8 mark and 3.09 ERA in 1984 and a 16–12 record and 4.09 ERA in 1985. On October 8, 1985, Niekro recorded his 300th victory in an 8–0 four-hitter over the Toronto Blue Jays and became the oldest major league pitcher ever to hurl a shutout. Niekro signed with the Cleveland Indians (AL) in March 1986. In August 1987, the Indians traded him to the Toronto Blue Jays (AL). His final major league appearance came with the Atlanta Braves in September 1987. In 24 major league seasons, Niekro appeared in 864 games with 318 wins, 274 losses, 45 shutouts, 3,342 strikeouts in 5,403.2 innings pitched, and a 3.35 ERA. The knuckleball, although slowing his progress to the major leagues in the 1960s, prolonged his career beyond age 40. An excellent fielding pitcher, he won Gold Gloves at that position four years.

The fierce, competitive Niekro was loquacious, friendly, and trusting off the field. During the off-season, he participated extensively in community service activities. This volunteer work brought him humanitarian and service awards named for the late Lou Gehrig,* Roberto Clemente,* and Brian Piccolo. He managed the Colorado Silver Bullets from 1994 through 1997. In 1997, he was elected to the National Baseball Hall of Fame. Niekro married Nancy Ferrand, a former airline stewardess, in Richmond, VA in August 1966 and has three sons, Michael, John, and Philip.

BIBLIOGRAPHY: L. Robert Davids, ed., *Insider's Baseball* (New York, 1983); Furman Bisher, "Niekro, a Real Phil for the Game," *Atlanta Braves Yearbook, 1979*; Jim Bouton, "Baseball's Working Class Hero," *IS* 4 (May 1982); Ron Fimrite, "The Valley Boys," *SI* 68 (May 23, 1988), pp. 78–84; Chuck Greenwood, "Niekro Keep Love of Baseball in Family," *SCD* 23 (August 30, 1996), pp. 160–161; Lyle Spatz, "The Opening Day Woes of the Niekro Brothers," *BRJ* 27 (1998), pp. 8–10; Pat Jordan, "Undaunted by Skeptics, Graybeard Phil Niekro Knuckles toward a New Season and Social Security," *PW* 25 (April 28, 1986), pp. 109–110; Phil Niekro and Tom Bird,

Knuckle Balls (New York, 1986); Phil Niekro et al., *The Niekro Files* (Chicago, IL, 1988); John Thorn et al., eds., *Total Braves* (New York, 1996); Gary Caruso, *The Braves Encyclopedia* (Philadelphia, PA, 1995); Mark Onigman, *This Date in Braves History* (New York, 1982); Gene Karst and Martin J. Jones, Jr., *Who's Who in Professional Baseball* (New Rochelle, NY, 1973); Robert E. Kelly, *Baseball's Best* (Jefferson, NC, 1988); Phil Niekro file, National Baseball Library, Cooperstown, NY; Dan Schlossberg, "Headed for the Hall," *SCD* 22 (August 25, 1995), p. 131.

L. Robert Davids

NOLAN, Gary Lynn (b. May 27, 1948, Herlong, CA), player, pitched for the Cincinnati Reds (NL) during their Big Red Machine glory years with at least 15 wins every year. His records of 18–7 in 1970, 15–5 in 1972, 15–9 in 1975, and 15–9 in 1976 helped the Cincinnati Reds reach the World Series.

Nolan, the Reds' first selection in the June 1966 free agent draft, was optioned to Sioux Falls, SD (NoL), where he compiled a 7–3 mark and a 1.82 ERA. The Cincinnati Reds in 1967 made the 18-year old rookie a starting pitcher. Nolan posted a 14–8 record with five shutouts, 206 strikeouts, and a 2.58 ERA, striking out Willie Mays* of the San Francisco Giants four times in one game. In 1968, Nolan strained his shoulder at spring training and began the season with Tampa, FL (FSL). After rejoining the Reds, he finished the season 9–4 with a team-leading 2.40 ERA. Throughout his career, Nolan suffered arm trouble because of a herky-jerky delivery and spent extended periods on the disabled list. He appeared only twice for the Cincinnati Reds in 1973 and missed the entire 1974 season after the surgical removal of a bone spur from his shoulder.

When healthy, the 6-foot 3-inch, 190-pound right-hander won consistently and possessed consummate control. At the 1972 All-Star break, he held a 13–2 record with a 1.81 ERA. He made the All-Star team, but developed a sore arm and started only six games. His season ended with a 15–5 mark, 1.99 ERA, and an NL-leading .750 winning percentage.

In both 1975 and 1976, Nolan posted 15–9 records. He led the NL both years in fewest walks per nine innings, averaging only 1.24 in 1975 and 1.02 in 1976. The 1975 season saw him earn the Fred Hutchinson Comeback Player of the Year Award.

Nolan pitched in the 1970, 1972, 1975, and 1976 NL Championship Series and World Series. He won Game 1 of the 1970 NL Championship Series against the Pittsburgh Pirates and Game 4 of the 1976 World Series against the New York Yankees to complete the Reds' four-game sweep. Nolan's arm troubles surfaced again in 1977. The Cincinnati Reds traded him in June 1977 to the California Angels (AL), where he compiled an 0–3 record. The California Angels released him in January 1978.

In a major league career that ended before he reached 30 years old, Nolan compiled a 110–67 win–loss record with a 3.08 ERA, 1,039 strikeouts, and 413 walks in 674.2 innings. He was elected to the Cincinnati Reds Hall of

Fame in 1984. Nolan married Carol Widener in February 1965 and became a father at age 17. They have three sons, Gary, Jr., Tim, and Mark, and a daughter, Kathy. Nolan in 1978 moved to Las Vegas, NV to work as a blackjack dealer at the Golden Nugget and became executive casino host at the Mirage in 1989.

BIBLIOGRAPHY: Gary Nolan file, National Baseball Library, Cooperstown, NY; Bill Bryson, "Was Own Boss at Ten," *BD* 26 (August 1967), pp. 72–75; Floyd Connor and John Snyder, *Day-by-Day in Cincinnati Reds History* (West Point, NY, 1984); Jeanne McClow, ed., *A Baseball Century* (New York, 1976); Bob Hertzel, *The Big Red Machine* (Englewood Cliffs, NJ, 1976); Bob Rathgeber, *Cincinnati Reds Scrapbook* (Virginia Beach, VA, 1982); Robert M. Walker, *Cincinnati and the Big Red Machine* (Bloomington, IN, 1988); Henry Hecht, "The Ordeal of Gary Nolan," *BD* 35 (February 1976), pp. 80–83; Bob Hertzel, "Gary Nolan Sheds No Tears for Lost Glory," *BD* 40 (January 1981), pp. 74–82.

Richard D. Miller

NORTHRUP, James Thomas "Jim," "The Gray Fox" (b. November 24, 1939, Breckenridge, MI), player, was a clutch left-handed hitter for the Detroit Tigers (AL). During the Tigers' championship 1968 season, Northrup delivered several key hits and tied a major league record with three grand slam HR in a month.

A sought-after football quarterback, Northrup attended Alma College and married Jean Anne Trieschmann on September 10, 1960. The Detroit Tigers signed him as an outfielder in 1960. Northrup spent four seasons in the minor leagues, winning Rookie of the Year honors with Syracuse, NY (IL) in 1964. He appeared briefly for the Detroit Tigers in 1964 and in 80 contests in 1965 before becoming the club's regular center fielder in 1966. Between 1966 and 1973, Northrup's batting average never dipped below .261. His .307 batting percentage in 1973 marked a career best. Northrup patrolled the Detroit outfield with talented teammates Al Kaline,* Mickey Stanley, and Willie Horton.* The capable defensive player never made more than nine errors in a season and compiled a .981 lifetime fielding percentage.

Northrup enjoyed an extraordinary 1968 season. By the end of May, he had broken up three no-hit bids by opponents. On four occasions, Northrup belted grand slam HR. Two came in consecutive at-bats on June 24 against the Cleveland Indians. He added a third on June 29 to establish a major-league mark of three grand slam HR in a week. In the hard-fought 1968 World Series against the St. Louis Cardinals, Northrup hit another grand slam HR off Larry Jaster in Game 6. He belted a key two-run triple off St. Louis ace Bob Gibson* in Game 7, as the Tigers rallied from a 3–1 game deficit to win the World Series. Northrup made hits in all six at-bats in a 13-inning victory over the Oakland A's on August 28, 1969. The game ended on a Northrup HR which sailed completely out of Tiger Stadium.

After spending his entire career with the Detroit Tigers, Northrup was traded twice in 1974. He played 21 games for the Montreal Expos (NL) and eight contests for the Baltimore Orioles (AL). Northrup retired after the 1975 season, having played in 1,392 big-league games with a .267 batting average, 153 HR, and 610 RBI. In his lone World Series appearance, Northrup batted .250 with two HR and 8 RBI. He batted .357 in the 1972 AL Championship Series against the Oakland A's.

BIBLIOGRAPHY: Joe Falls, *Detroit Tigers* (New York, 1975); Fred Smith, *995 Tigers* (Detroit, MI, 1981); Bill Freehan, *Behind the Mask* (New York, 1970); Jerry Green, *Year of the Tiger* (New York, 1969); Fred T. Smith, *Tiger Factor* (Lathrup Village, MI, 1986); William M. Anderson, *The Detroit Tigers* (South Bend, IN, 1996); Mike Shatzkin, ed., *The Ballplayers* (New York, 1990); Seymour Siwoff, ed., *The Book of Baseball Records* (New York, 1986); *The Baseball Encyclopedia*, 10th ed. (New York, 1996).

John G. Robertson

NUXHALL, Joseph Henry "Joe" (b. July 30, 1928, Hamilton, OH), player and sportscaster, is the son of Orville Nuxhall and Naomi Nuxhall. His father, a stationary engineer for Fisher Body, played semiprofessional baseball and helped develop his four sons' athletic talents. On October 4, 1947, Nuxhall married Donzetta Houston. They have two sons, Philip and Kim, and reside in Fairfield, OH.

Nuxhall, a fine major league left-handed pitcher, good fielder, and above-average hitter with 15 career HR, remains the youngest modern player to appear in a major league game. After receiving a $500 signing bonus from the Cincinnati Reds (NL), the 6-foot 3-inch, 195-pound youngster entered his first game on June 10, 1944, less than two months before his 16th birthday. In a mop-up role against the St. Louis Cardinals at Cincinnati's Crosley Field, he retired two of the first three batters. Nuxhall did not finish the inning, however, surrendering two hits, five walks, and five runs. The move, brought on by the manpower shortage of World War II, was something Nuxhall later regretted. "I was mature physically," he said, "but mentally I was still a kid."

After pitching some minor league baseball and skipping two years of scholastic sports, Nuxhall regained amateur status for his senior year and starred in basketball and football for Hamilton High School. The hard-throwing Nuxhall overcame both control problems and a fiery temper to reach the major leagues in 1952, improving from 145 walks in 102 innings in 1947 to just 59 walks in 166.2 innings in 1954. Better control and the addition of a slider pitch made him one of the NL's top lefthanders. He finished 12–5 in 1954 and 17–12 in 1955, leading the NL with five shutouts, ranking third with a .586 winning percentage, and appearing in the All-Star Game. After spending the 1961 season with the Kansas City Athletics (AL) and the first part of 1962 with the Los Angeles Angels (AL), Nuxhall returned to the Cincinnati Reds and won another 46 games. His win–loss records included

5–0 in 1962, 15–8 in 1963, and 11–4 in 1965. He retired after the 1966 season with a 135–117 career record and a 3.90 ERA. His sole regret involved missing Cincinnati's 1961 NL pennant season.

For many years, Nuxhall announced basketball games on radio for Miami University. Since 1967, he has been a popular announcer with the Cincinnati Reds.

BIBLIOGRAPHY: Floyd Connor and John Snyder, *Day-by-Day in Cincinnati Reds History* (West Point, NY, 1984); Jeanne McGlow, ed., *Baseball Century* (New York, 1986); Bob Rathgeber, *Cincinnati Reds Scrapbook* (Virginia Beach, VA, 1982); Donald Honig, *The Cincinnati Reds* (New York, 1992); Joe Nuxhall file, National Baseball Library, Cooperstown, NY; Earl Lawson, "New Nuxhall Nixed His Old 'Wild Man' Rap," *TSN*, January 26, 1955, pp. 5–6; Earl Lawson, "Nuxhall Nixed Temper and Improved Control," *TSN*, February 29, 1956, p. 5.

Allen E. Hye

O

OBERKFELL, Kenneth Ray "Ken," "Obie" (b. May 4, 1956, Highland, IL), player, is the son of Kenneth M. Oberkfell and Racine (Harrison) Oberkfell and graduated from Collinsville, IL High School, where he twice earned MVP honors in baseball as a shortstop. He was named 1975 JC Baseball All-America as a second baseman at Belleville Area CC in Belleville, IL. In May 1975, St. Louis Cardinals' (NL) scout Fred McAllister signed Oberkfell. The 6-foot 1-inch, 185-pound second baseman batted .351 in 1975, dividing the season between Johnson City, TN (ApL) and St. Petersburg, FL (FSL). Oberkfell advanced through St. Louis Cardinal farm system at Little Rock, AR (TL), New Orleans, LA (AA), and Springfield, IL (AA), developing into a good line drive hitter and sure-handed infielder. He threw right-handed, but batted from the left side.

After late season trials in 1977 and 1978, Oberkfell won the St. Louis Cardinals' second base job from veteran Mike Tyson in 1979. He batted .301 and led NL second sackers with a .985 fielding average in 1979. Oberkfell recovered from knee surgery in May 1980 to bat .303. From 1979 to 1984 with St. Louis, he batted .297, walked often, and rarely struck out. In 1981, the St. Louis Cardinals moved him to third base to make room for rookie Tom Herr at second base. In 1982 and 1983, he led NL third basemen in fielding average. Oberkfell batted .200 in the St. Louis Cardinals' three-game sweep of the Atlanta Braves in the 1982 NL Championship Series and hit .292 in the Cardinals' 1982 World Series conquest of the Milwaukee Brewers in seven games.

After being displaced by rookie Terry Pendleton,* Oberkfell was traded to the Atlanta Braves (NL) in June 1984 for relief pitcher Ken Dayley and first basemen Mike Jorgensen. Elbow and knee injuries in 1985 hampered his defensive play, but his good bat and high on base percentage kept him at third base for the Braves until an August 1988 trade to the Pittsburgh

Pirates (NL). The Pittsburgh Pirates sent him to the San Francisco Giants (NL) in May 1989. In 1989, his 18 pinch hits led the NL and set a Giants' team record. Oberkfell finished his major league career in utility roles with the Houston Astros (NL) in 1990 and 1991 and California Angels (AL) in 1992.

In 16 major league campaigns, Oberkfell made 1,354 hits, clouted 29 HR, scored 558 runs, drove in 446 runs and batted .278 in 1,602 games. After leaving baseball for two years, he managed the Sullivan Mountain Lions (NeL) in 1995, the Elmira, NY Pioneers (NeL) in 1996, and the Piedmont, NC Boll Weevils (SAL) since 1997. Oberkfell lives in Highland, IL with his wife, Bonnie (Rittgers) Oberkfell, and their three children.

BIBLIOGRAPHY: Kenneth Oberkfell file, National Baseball Library, Cooperstown, NY; Bill Ballew, "Former NL Second Sacker Oberkfell Now Manages the Boll Weevils," *SCD* 25 (May 1, 1998), pp. 138–139; Bob Broeg and Jerry Vickery, *St. Louis Cardinals Encyclopedia* (Grand Rapids, MI, 1998); Gary Caruso, *The Braves Encyclopedia* (Philadelphia, PA, 1995); Bob Broeg, *Redbirds: A Century of Cardinals' Baseball* (St. Louis, MO, 1981); John Dewan, ed., *The Scouting Report: 1990* (New York, 1990); Rob Rains, *The St. Louis Cardinals* (New York, 1992); Mary Beth Sullivan, ed., *The Scouting Report: 1986* (New York, 1986); *TSN Official Baseball Register 1993*; *St. Louis Cardinals 1984 Media Guide* (St. Louis, MO, 1984).

Frank J. Olmsted

O'CONNOR, John Joseph "Rowdy Jack," "Peach Pie" (b. June 2, 1869, St. Louis, MO; d. November 14, 1937, St. Louis, MO), player, coach, and manager, played 21 major league seasons primarily as a catcher. He is best remembered for the final day of his major league career on October 9, 1910. As St. Louis Browns (AL) manager, he permitted (some say ordered) his third baseman to play deep and enabled opponent Larry Lajoie* of the Cleveland Naps to garner six bunt hits in an effort to overtake the hated Ty Cobb* of the Detroit Tigers for the 1910 AL batting title.

The son of Irish immigrants Patrick O'Connor and Johanna (Connors) O'Connor, he grew up in the Goose Hill section of St. Louis. He played baseball for the local semipro Peach Pies, Jacksonville, IL, and St. Joseph, MO (WL) prior to his major league debut at age 17 with the Cincinnati Red Stockings (AA) in 1887. After being suspended in 1888 for a "big fight" with his manager, O'Connor finished the season with an "outlaw" Denver, CO club and rejoined the AA in 1889 with the Columbus, OH Buckeyes. In 1890, his one outstanding season, the 5-foot 10-inch, 170-pound right hander achieved career highs in batting average (.324), hits (148), and runs (89) and led AA catchers in fielding average for the second straight year.

When the Columbus Buckeyes released him for drunkenness in July 1891, O'Connor finished the season at Denver (WA). He returned to the major leagues in 1892 with the Cleveland Spiders (NL), managed by childhood friend Oliver Wendell "Patsy" Tebeau,* and remained there seven years. In a massive 1899 player exchange, O'Connor, Tebeau, and 17 other Cleveland Spiders were sent to the St. Louis Cardinals (NL). The Pittsburgh Pirates (NL) bought O'Connor in May 1900, but suspended him in 1902 for recruiting Pirate players for the rival AL. In 1903, O'Connor joined the New York Highlanders (AL). New York traded him in October 1903 to the St. Louis Browns (AL), where he remained through 1908 as player and coach. He captained Little Rock, AR (SA) in 1909 until returning to the St. Louis Browns in July. St. Louis named him manager for 1910 with a two-year contract. The Browns finished last in 1910 with a 47–107 record and .305 winning percentage.

AL president Ban Johnson* ordered O'Connor fired for his role in the October 9 Lajoie incident, but O'Connor sued successfully for $5,000 of his 1911 salary. He managed the St. Louis Terriers (FL) in their 1913 minor league season and scored their games in 1914. After leaving baseball, he promoted boxing in St. Louis.

In 1,451 major league games, O'Connor batted .263 with 1,417 hits, 713 runs, and 738 RBI. In 12 World Series games in 1892, 1896 (Temple Cup), and 1900 (Chronicle-Telegraph Cup), he batted .200 and drove in two runs.

BIBLIOGRAPHY: Bill Borst, *Still Last in the American League* (West Bloomfield, MI, 1992); Frederick G. Lieb, *The Pittsburgh Pirates* (New York, 1948); Bill Borst, ed., *Ables to Zoldak*, vol. 2 (St. Louis, MO, 1989); Thomas Aylesworth and Benton Minks, *The Encyclopedia of Baseball Managers* (New York, 1990); David Nemec, *The Beer and Whisky League* (New York, 1994); J. Thomas Hetrick, *Misfits!* (Jefferson, NC, 1991); James Charlton, ed., *The Baseball Chronology* (New York, 1991); Frederick Ivor-Campbell et al., eds., *Baseball's First Stars* (Cleveland, OH, 1996); John O'Connor file, National Baseball Library, Cooperstown, NY; John Phillips, *The Spiders: Who Was Who* (Cabin John, MD, 1991); John Thorn et al., eds., *Total Baseball*, 5th ed. (New York, 1997).

Frederick Ivor-Campbell

O'DAY, Henry Francis "Hank" (b. July 8, 1862, Chicago, IL; d. July 2, 1935, Chicago, IL), player, manager, and umpire, was one of six children born to James O'Day and Mary O'Day and served as an apprentice plumber with his father before pursuing a professional baseball career. The right-handed O'Day, who reportedly possessed one of the game's fastest, sharpest-breaking curve balls, pitched for the Toledo, OH Blue Stockings (AA) in 1884, Pittsburgh Alleghenys (AA) in 1885, Washington Statesmen (NL) from 1886 to 1889, and New York Giants (NL) in 1889. A multitalented athlete, he occasionally played several outfield and infield positions in the 1880s. Washington traded O'Day to the Giants at midseason in 1889. O'Day earned nine wins in 10 decisions and added two victories in the World Series against the Brooklyn Bridegrooms. In 1890 he hurled for the New York Giants (PL), posting a career best 22–13 win–loss record. The major leagues blacklisted O'Day for jumping to the short-lived PL, forcing him to spend the next three seasons in the minor leagues. O'Day compiled a 77–110 record and 3.74 ERA in seven major league seasons. He umpired in the NWL in 1894 and NL for 31 years. He twice quit umpiring, managing the 1912 Cincinnati Reds (NL) to a fourth-place finish with a 75–78 mark and the 1914 Chicago Cubs (NL) to an identical place with a 78–76 record. The NL welcomed him back as an umpire both times because of his integrity and talent.

O'Day, one of the greatest major league umpires in history, was chosen as the NL umpire in the first modern World Series of 1903 and served from 1928 to 1931 as the NL's first umpire supervisor and scout. If one counts the times he substituted for absent umpires (1888–1890) and a brief NL appearance in 1893, O'Day's major league umpiring career spanned 35 years and ranks second only to Bill Klem's* 36 years. O'Day worked 59 games in 10 World Series (1903, 1905, 1907–1908, 1910, 1916, 1918, 1920, 1923, 1926), second to Klem's 18 World Series assignments. The ex-pitcher called only two no-hitters in his long career and umpired at second base when Bill Wambsganss of the Cleveland Indians in 1920 executed the only unassisted triple play in World Series history against the Brooklyn Robins. O'Day's most memorable call came when he called out Fred Merkle* of the New York Giants for failing to touch second base after an apparent game-winning hit in the bottom of the ninth inning against the Chicago Cubs on September 23, 1908.

O'Day earned recognition as a great ball-and-strike umpire and a stickler on the rules, who enforced decisions with an iron hand and caustic tongue. Off the field, the reticent recluse and lifelong bachelor lived in Chicago hotels and remained secretive about his personal life and minor league career. Aside from horse racing, he literally devoted his adult life to umpiring.

BIBLIOGRAPHY: *The Baseball Encyclopedia*, 10th ed. (New York, 1996); Frederick Ivor-Campbell et al., *Baseball's First Stars* (Cleveland, OH, 1996); Noel Hynd, *The Giants of the Polo Grounds* (New York, 1988); G. H. Fleming, *The Unforgettable Season* (New York, 1981); Henry O'Day file, National Baseball Library, Cooperstown, NY; Henry O'Day file, TSN Archives, St. Louis, MO; Henry O'Day, "A Big League Umpire's View," *BM* 1 (June 1908), pp. 30–32; John Thorn et al., eds., *Total Baseball*, 5th ed. (New York, 1997).

Larry R. Gerlach

O'DOUL, Frank Joseph "Lefty" (b. March 4, 1897, San Francisco, CA; d. December 7, 1969, San Francisco, CA), player, manager, and executive, attended Bayview School in San Francisco, CA. The San Francisco Seals (PCL) originally signed him as a pitcher, but O'Doul developed into one of the most outstanding batters in baseball history. The 6-foot, 180-pound left-hander led the NL in batting twice, hitting .398 in 1929 with the Philadelphia Phillies (NL) and .368 in 1932 with the Brooklyn Dodgers (NL). O'Doul also hit .383 with Philadelphia in 1930 and .336 with Brooklyn in

1931. His .349 lifetime batting average, spanning 11 major league seasons including as a pitcher, featured 1,140 hits, 113 HR, and 542 RBI. O'Doul made five hits in a game on eight separate occasions and hit safely for eight consecutive turns at bat in 1933.

O'Doul began his baseball career as a pitcher with Des Moines, IA (WL) in 1917. He posted a 13–9 win–loss record with the San Francisco, CA Seals in 1918 and was drafted by the New York Yankees (AL). Arm trouble limited his appearances with the New York Yankees in 1919 and 1920. The New York Yankees in 1921 returned him to San Francisco, where he led the PCL's pitchers with a 25–9 record. Although returning to New York in 1922, he pitched little for the Yankees and was traded to the Boston Red Sox (AL) that July. Boston sold O'Doul to Salt Lake City, UT (PCL) in 1924. O'Doul switched to the outfield and batted .392 that year. After three more minor league seasons, he returned to the major leagues with the New York Giants (NL) in 1928. In October 1928, New York sold O'Doul to the Philadelphia Phillies. In 1929, O'Doul set the NL record for hits (254), led the NL with a .465 on base percentage, and belted 32 HR. O'Doul was traded to the Brooklyn Dodgers in October 1930 and to the New York Giants (NL) in June 1933. His major league career ended in 1934, whereupon he managed the San Francisco Seals through 1951. His other managerial assignments came with San Diego, CA (PCL), 1952–1954; Oakland, CA (PCL), 1955; Vancouver, Canada (PCL), 1956; and Seattle, WA (PCL), 1957. O'Doul also coached college teams and made numerous trips with baseball teams to Japan, helping to organize the professional leagues in that nation. The Japanese named their Tokyo team the Giants in honor of the very popular O'Doul's former major league association. O'Doul married Abigail Lacey in April 1924. After their divorce, he married Jean Goodman in 1954.

BIBLIOGRAPHY: *The Baseball Encyclopedia*, 10th ed. (New York, 1996); Richard Leutzinger, *Lefty O'Doul* (Carmel Bay, CA, 1997); John Thom, *Champion Batsman of the 20th Century* (Los Angeles, CA, 1992); Rich Westcott and Frank Bilovsky, *The New Phillies Encyclopedia* (Philadelphia, PA, 1993); Frederick G. Lieb and Stan Baumgartner, *The Philadelphia Phillies* (New York, 1953); Allen Lewis, *The Philadelphia Phillies: A Pictorial History* (Virginia Beach, VA, 1981); William F. McNeil, *The Dodgers Encyclopedia* (Champaign, IL, 1997); Frank Graham, *The Brooklyn Dodgers* (New York, 1945); Richard Goldstein, *Superstars and Screwballs* (New York, 1991); Robert Obojski, *Bush League* (New York, 1975); Francis O'Doul file, National Baseball Library, Cooperstown, NY; Joseph L. Reichler, *The Great All-Time Baseball Record Book* (New York, 1981); Lawrence Ritter, *The Glory of Their Times* (New York, 1966); Ira L. Smith, *Baseball's Famous Outfielders* (New York, 1954).

Horace R. Givens

O'FARRELL, Robert Arthur "Bob" (b. October 19, 1896, Waukegan, IL; d. February 20, 1988, Waukegan, IL), player and manager, was of Irish and

English descent and graduated from Waukegan High School. O'Farrell was scouted playing sandlot baseball by future National Baseball Hall of Fame catcher Roger Bresnahan,* who later taught him receiving skills. The Chicago Cubs (NL) signed O'Farrell in 1915. From 1915 to 1917, he caught for Milwaukee, WI (AA) and Peoria, IL (3IL) and briefly appeared with Chicago. O'Farrell, a reserve catcher for the Chicago Cubs in 1918 and 1919, became starting receiver in 1920. His best offensive seasons came in 1922, when he produced a career-high .324 batting average, and 1923, when he batted .319 and belted a career best 12 HR. In 1924, he sustained a fractured skull when a foul tip smashed through his catcher's mask. O'Farrell considered catching dangerous work because "there were so many offbeat pitches like the spitball, the emery ball and the shine ball." The emergence of catcher Gabby Hartnett* caused the Chicago Cubs to trade O'Farrell to the St. Louis Cardinals (NL) in June 1925.

In 1926, O'Farrell caught 146 games, batted .293, and produced career highs in doubles (30) and triples (9) to help the St. Louis Cardinals win their first NL pennant. For his outstanding defense and ability to throw out potential base stealers, O'Farrell was voted 1926 NL MVP. He batted .304 in the World Series, but claimed his greatest thrill came in the ninth inning of the seventh game. With the Cardinals leading the New York Yankees, 3–2 with two outs, Babe Ruth* unexpectedly attempted to steal second base. O'Farrell's perfect throw to Rogers Hornsby* nailed Ruth and gave the St. Louis Cardinals the World Championship. Owner Sam Breadon* made O'Farrell player-manager in 1927. The St. Louis Cardinals won three more games that season with a 92–61 record, but finished second, 1½ games behind the Pittsburgh Pirates. O'Farrell played in just 61 games due to a sore arm and broken thumb and literally grabbed former major leaguer Johnny Schulte out of the stands to help with the catching. Despite the fine season, Breadon was not satisfied with O'Farrell's managerial skills and returned him to player status exclusively with a $5,000 raise.

In May 1928, the St. Louis Cardinals traded O'Farrell to the New York Giants (NL) for outfielder George Harper. He backed up Shanty Hogan through the 1932 season, batting .306 in 1929 and .301 in 1930. O'Farrell returned to the St. Louis Cardinals in a five player October 1932 trade to catch behind Jimmie Wilson.* He was named player–manager of the Cincinnati Reds (NL) in January 1934, but was fired in July after winning only 30 of 90 games. O'Farrell finished the 1934 campaign as a reserve behind Gabby Hartnett with the Chicago Cubs. He completed his major league career in 1935 with the St. Louis Cardinals.

O'Farrell's 21 major league seasons included 1,120 hits, 517 runs, 51 HR, 549 RBI, and a .273 batting average in 1,492 games. As a major league manager, he won 122 games, lost 121, and tied once. He married Arolene Edwards on February 15, 1928 and owned and operated a bowling alley in Waukegan for many years.

BIBLIOGRAPHY: Bob Broeg, *Redbirds: A Century of Cardinals' Baseball* (St. Louis, MO, 1981); David Falkner, *Baseball's Great Glove Men on the Fine Art of Defense* (New York, 1990); Gene Karst and Martin Jones, Jr., *Who's Who in Professional Baseball* (New Rochelle, NY, 1973); *NYT*, February 25, 1988, p. A–32; Robert O'Farrell file, National Baseball Library, Cooperstown, NY; Rob Rains, *The St. Louis Cardinals* (New York, 1992); Lawrence S. Ritter, *The Glory of Their Times* (New York, 1966); Warren Brown, *The Chicago Cubs* (New York, 1946); Eddie Gold and Art Ahrens, *The Golden Era Cubs, 1876–1940* (Chicago, IL, 1985); Frederick G. Lieb, *The St. Louis Cardinals* (New York, 1945); Bob Broeg and Jerry Vickery, *St. Louis Cardinals Encyclopedia* (Grand Rapids, MI, 1998).

Frank J. Olmsted

OGLIVIE, Benjamin Ambrosio (Palmer) "Ben" (b. February 11, 1949, Colon, Panama), player and coach, is the son of a ship oiler and moved to New York City at age 17. After starring in soccer and baseball at Roosevelt High School, he attended Bronx CC, Northeastern University, and Wayne State University. The 6-foot 2-inch, 170-pound first baseman–outfielder, who batted and threw left-handed, was selected by the Boston Red Sox (AL) in the seventh round of the June 1968 draft and spent minor league seasons with Jamestown, NY (NYPL) in 1968, Greenville, SC (WCrL) and Winter Haven, FL (FSL) in 1969, Pawtucket, RI (EL) in 1970, and Louisville, KY (IL) in 1971.

After joining the Boston Red Sox in September 1971, Oglivie spent the next two seasons as a reserve outfielder there. The Boston Red Sox considered him a weak fielder, who lacked speed and struggled against left-handed pitchers. In October 1973, Boston traded him to the Detroit Tigers (AL). Oglivie saw increased playing time, batting .286 in 1975 and .285 in 1976 and clouting 21 HR with 61 RBI in 1977. In December 1977, the Detroit Tigers traded Oglivie to the Milwaukee Brewers (AL).

Oglivie reached his major league pinnacle with the Milwaukee Brewers, batting .303 in 1978 and clouting 29 HR in 1979. His best major league season came in 1980, when he shared the AL lead with a career-best 41 HR. Mel Ott* remains the only major leaguer that light to belt more HR in a season. Oglivie also produced career highs in batting average (.304), hits (180), RBI (118), and slugging percentage (.563) with 12 game-winning RBI. *TSN* named him to its AL All-Star and Silver Slugger teams. He made the AL All-Star teams in 1980, 1982, and 1983. Although Oglivie slumped the next two seasons, his 34 HR and 102 RBI helped Milwaukee win the AL pennant in 1982. He homered in both the 1982 AL Championship Series against the California Angels and 1982 World Series against the St. Louis Cardinals. In Game 6, he tied World Series records by making four consecutive outfield putouts and all three putouts in the seventh inning. He played in Japan in 1987 and 1988.

In 16 major league seasons through 1986, Oglivie batted .273 with 1,615 hits, 235 HR, and 901 RBI. He clouted three-HR on July 8, 1979 and June 20, 1982 against the Detroit Tigers and on May 14, 1983 against the Boston Red Sox. Only Lou Gehrig* recorded more AL three-HR games. Oglivie struck out 80 times in a season only twice. He coached for Hickory, NC (SAL) in 1999 and joined the San Diego Padres as minor league hitting coordinator in November 1999. The Tempe, AZ resident, an avid philosophy reader, married Tammy Hunsinger in 1978 and has two children, Trianna and Benji, Jr.

BIBLIOGRAPHY: Ben Oglivie file, National Baseball Library, Cooperstown, NY; Steve Wulf, "Swingo, Ergo Sum," *SI* 54 (June 8, 1981), pp. 42, 47–48, 50; *TSN Baseball Register*, 1987; Fred Smith, *995 Tigers* (Detroit, MI, 1981); Jeff Everson, *This Date in Milwaukee Brewers History* (Appleton, WI, 1987); *Milwaukee Brewers 1983 Official Yearbook*; *Milwaukee Brewers 1989 Official Yearbook*.

David L. Porter

OJEDA, Robert Michael "Bob" (b. December 17, 1957, Los Angeles, CA), player, is the son of Robert C. Ojeda and Dora (Bowman) Ojeda and is of Spanish descent and attended the College of the Sequoias in Visalia, CA. The 6-foot 1-inch, 185-pound Ojeda married Tammy Ann Gann on January 2, 1977 and has two children, Janna Lee and Robert Michael. The left-handed pitcher suffered a numerous injuries and accidents, spraining his right shoulder in 1982, undergoing surgery on his elbow in May 1987 and nearly severing his left middle finger while using electric hedge clippers in September 1988. On March 22, 1993, Ojeda was involved in a boating accident that claimed the lives of teammates Tim Crews and Steve Olin. Ojeda never fully returned to baseball.

In June 1978, Ojeda started professional baseball with Elmira, NY (NYPL) and pitched the last inning of the longest game in professional history. The 33 inning game lasted eight hours, 25 minutes. He entered the major leagues briefly in July 1980 with the Boston Red Sox (AL). His 1981 rookie season saw him rank third in AL Rookie of the Year voting with a 6–2 record and 3.12 ERA in 12 starts. After having a disappointing 1982 season, Ojeda ended the 1983 season with a spectacular 7–1 streak and finished the campaign with a 12–7 mark and 4.04 ERA. In 1984 he pitched five shutouts, tying Geoff Zahn for the AL high. The Boston Red Sox traded him to the New York Mets (NL) in November 1985. With the New York Mets in 1986, Ojeda compiled a 18–5 record, led the NL with a .783 winning percentage, and boasted the second best ERA with 2.57. His pitching helped the New York Mets garner a World Series Championship over the Boston Red Sox that year. After being injured most of 1987, he played in the major leagues until 1994. The Los Angeles Dodgers (NL) acquired him in a December 1990 trade. As a Los Angeles Dodger in 1991, Ojeda struck out 120 batters and performed errorless in 46 chances. The 1991 season brought his 100th win, 1,000th strikeout, and first HR. Through 1992, he boasted a .203 batting average against lefthanders. The March 1993 boating accident after joining the Cleveland Indians (AL) sidelined him for most of that season. He pitched two poor games for the New York Yankees (AL) in 1994 and was released. His career record featured 115 wins, 98 losses, a .540 winning percentage, and a 3.65 ERA.

BIBLIOGRAPHY: M. Huzinec, "A Victim of Careless Gardening," *PW* 31 (March 27, 1989), pp. 107–108; "Bob Ojeda," *Microsoft Complete Baseball*, CD-ROM (Redmond, WA, 1994); Bob Ojeda file, National Baseball Library, Cooperstown, NY; W. Plummer, "A Darkened Spring," *PW* 39 (April 5, 1993), pp. 45–46; Peter Golenbock, *Fenway* (New York, 1992); Dan Shaughnessy, *The Curse of the Bambino* (New York, 1990); Robert Redmount, *Red Sox Encyclopedia* (Champaign, IL, 1997); Davey Johnson and Peter Golenbock, *Bats* (New York, 1986); Mike Shatzkin, ed., *The Ballplayers* (New York, 1990).

Lowell D. Smith

O'KELLEHER, William Henry. *See* William Henry Keeler.

OLIVA, Pedro Lopez "Tony" (b. July 20, 1940, Pinar del Rio, Cuba), player and coach, ranked among the dominating AL hitters of the 1960s and was a perennial crowd favorite throughout his illustrious 15-year All-Star career with the Minnesota Twins (AL). An AL Rookie of the Year in 1964, an AL All-Star team fixture between his rookie season and 1971, a three-time AL batting champion (1964–1965, 1971), and a Gold Glove selection in 1966, Oliva remains high on the all-time list of Latin American major league hitters with a .304 career batting average. Only seven other Latin-born players have garnered more career hits than Oliva, who amassed 1,917 safeties. Orlando Cepeda* (379), Tony Perez* (379), and Roberto Clemente* (240) were the only Latin players to have bettered Oliva's career mark (220) for HR as of his retirement. He ranks high on the all-time Latin American RBI list with 947. His flair, grace, intensity, and dramatic debut remain unmatched. No other player won league batting titles in both his first two full-time major league seasons, as he became one of the most graceful, proficient natural hitters of all time. A nagging knee injury prevented this Cuban-born legend from reaching the pinnacle as the greatest Latin American major league slugger.

Washington Senators superscout Joe Cambria signed Oliva, who debuted in organized baseball in 1960 with a .410 batting average for Wytheville, VA (ApL), and earned the Silver Louisville Slugger Award as the top hitter in professional baseball. Oliva's spectacular 1964 AL rookie season brought AL titles in hits (217), runs scored (109), and doubles (43), plus his first AL batting crown with a .323 average. Oliva's 217 hits established an AL rookie mark as he also led the entire major leagues that season with a team-record 374 total bases, 71 multihit games, and 84 extra-base hits. A sophomore-season batting title (.321) and second consecutive AL standard for base hits (185) gave Oliva the best two-year start ever enjoyed by a major league slugger. In his third season, Oliva again paced the Junior Circuit in safeties (191), but dropped to second (.307) in the AL batting race. Oliva eventually paced the AL in hits five times (including 1969–1970) and in doubles on four occasions (1964, 1967, 1969–1970). He was named *TSN* AL Player of the Year during the Twins' AL pennant–winning 1965 season. In 1969, he tied Joe DiMaggio's* record for having been named to the AL All-Star Game roster in each of his first six seasons. Despite capturing a third AL batting title with a career-high .337 average in 1971, Oliva suffered a severe knee injury that summer while diving for an errant flyball in Oakland. The nagging injury eventually sidelined the Cuban star for virtually all the 1972 campaign and relegated him to a DH role for much of the remainder of his career. Oliva stroked the first HR ever by a DH in April 1973 in Oakland. Since he used his brother's passport to enter the United States for the first time as a minor leaguer in 1961, his sibling's name (Antonio) remained with him thereafter. Oliva served from 1976 to 1978 and 1985 through 1991 as a coach and hitting instructor for the Minnesota Twins. The Twins defeated the St. Louis Cardinals in the 1987 World Series and the Atlanta Braves for the 1991 World Series.

BIBLIOGRAPHY: Tony Oliva file, National Baseball Library, Cooperstown, NY; Peter C. Bjarkman, *Baseball with a Latin Beat* (Westport, CT, 1991); Pat Jordan, "Clemente and Oliva: Same Ends, Different Means," *Sport* 50 (November 1970), pp. 40–43; Brent P. Kelley, *The Case For: Those Overlooked by the Baseball Hall of Fame* (Jefferson, NC, 1992); Tony Oliva, with Bob Fowler, *Tony O!* (New York, 1973); Dave Mona and Dave Jarzyna, *Twenty-five Seasons* (Minneapolis, MN, 1986); Mike Shatzkin, ed., *The Ballplayers* (New York, 1990); Rich Westcott, *Diamond Greats* (Westport, CT, 1988).

                                                        Peter C. Bjarkman

OLIVER, Albert, Jr. "Al," "Mr. Scoop" (b. October 14, 1946, Portsmouth, OH), player, is the son of bricklayer Albert Oliver, Sr. and attended Kent State University. His mother died when he was age 11, while his father died the day he was called up to the major leagues. A left-handed baseball catcher in high school, he rejected a basketball scholarship at Kent State to sign with the Pittsburgh Pirates (NL) in 1964 for $5,000. Oliver began his professional baseball career with Salem, VA (ApL), but did not play. As a left-handed hitting first baseman with Gastonia, NC (WCL) in 1965, he led the WCL with 159 hits. He performed with Raleigh, NC (CrL) in 1966, Macon, GA (SL) and Raleigh (CrL) in 1967, and Columbus, OH (IL) in 1968.

The 6-foot 1-inch, 200-pound Oliver joined the Pittsburgh Pirates as a part-time first baseman in 1969 and spent nine seasons there in the outfield and at first base, batting above .300 four times and usually finishing among NL leaders in batting average, total bases, and doubles. He played in five NL Championship Series between 1970 and 1975 and batted .211 in the Pirates' 1971 World Series triumph over the Baltimore Orioles. In December 1977, Oliver was traded to the Texas Rangers (AL). He hit well above .300 each season there and seldom struck out. In March 1982, Oliver was traded to the Montreal Expos (NL) and enjoyed the finest season of his career. Besides hitting at a .331 NL-leading clip, he paced the NL with 204 hits and 43 doubles for 317 total bases and tied for the NL lead with 109 RBI. An average defensive player, he led NL first basemen with 19 errors in 1982. Montreal traded Oliver in February 1984 to the San Francisco Giants (NL), where he played half a season before being sent in August to the Philadelphia Phillies (NL). He split 1985 between the Los Angeles Dodgers (NL) and Toronto Blue Jays (AL). In the 1985 AL Championship Series against the Kansas City Royals, Oliver batted .375, knocked in three runs, doubled once, and delivered two game-winning hits. He retired as a player in November 1985.

Oliver appeared in seven All-Star Games between 1972 and 1983, but started only in the last contest. If not underrated, he remained under-recognized. In contrast with well-known Reggie Jackson,* Oliver in two fewer major league seasons produced 233 more hits and a .303 batting average, 40 points higher than Jackson's. Oliver's 2,743 hits and 529 doubles placed him high on the lifetime list. Oliver's .303 batting average, 1,189 runs scored, and 1,326 RBI also ranked high among active players. The Portsmouth, OH resident hit 77 triples and 219 HR, and stole 84 bases. He coached baseball at Shawnee State University and serves as a motivational public speaker.

BIBLIOGRAPHY: Al Oliver file, National Baseball Library, Cooperstown, NY; Ross Forman, "Former Baseball Players Reminisce at Fan Fest," *SCD* 21 (August 12, 1994), pp. 60–61; Chuck Greenwood, "Scoops," *SCD* 23 (August 23, 1996), pp. 158–159; Al Oliver with Andrew O'Toole, *Baseball's Best Kept Secret* (Pittsburgh, PA, 1997); Jim Laise, "Al Oliver: The Solution or Part of the Problem?" *Sport* 73 (October 1982), p. 44; *The Baseball Encyclopedia*, 10th ed. (New York, 1996); W. C. Rhoden, "Oliver: Quiet Brilliance," *NYT Biographical Service* (August 1983), pp. 977–978; *TSN Official Baseball Register, 1985*; Steve Wulf, "You Don't Know Me, Says Al," *SI* 52 (April 21, 1980), pp. 58–63; *WWA*, 43rd ed. (1984–1985), p. 2,519; Richard L. Burtt, *The Pittsburgh Pirates, A Pictorial History* (Virginia Beach, VA, 1977); Bob Smizik, *The Pittsburgh Pirates: An Illustrated History* (New York, 1990).

Gaymon L. Bennett

O'LOUGHLIN, Francis "Frank," "Silk" (b. August 15, 1872, Rochester, NY; d. December 20, 1918, Boston, MA), umpire, was the son of John O'Loughlin and Mary O'Loughlin and was educated in the Rochester public and parochial schools. O'Loughlin, nicknamed "Silk" as a youngster because of the length and texture of his curly hair, played amateur baseball and worked as an inspector for the city water department and then in the family's tavern. He began umpiring amateur and semiprofessional baseball games in Rochester in 1894 at the urging of his brother-in-law, Stump Weidman, a former major league pitcher, and was soon in great demand for games in western NY. He launched his professional umpiring career in 1897 with the AtL, moved later that season to the NYSL, and advanced in 1900 to the EL.

The recently formed AL in 1902 hired O'Loughlin, a key acquisition in President Ban Johnson's* plan to use strong umpires to make the AL a more disciplined league than the NL. O'Loughlin, a fair and fearless autocrat schooled in single-umpire system that existed until the early 20th century, tolerated no challenge to his decisions. Fellow AL umpire Billy Evans* called him "the czar of the diamond." O'Loughlin issued the famous dictum, "The umpire is always right" and frequently told players who questioned a decision: "I have never missed one in my life and it's too late to start now. The Pope for religion, O'Loughlin for baseball. Both infallible."

O'Loughlin used emphatic gestures when making calls, saying "t-u-h!" instead of "two" when calling strikes, and urged players to speed up the game. Besides calling three no-hit games, he umpired five World Series (1906, 1909, 1912, 1915, 1917) and served on the first four-man World Series crew in 1909.

O'Loughlin married Agnes Swift in 1905 and had no children. His 17-year major league umpiring career was cut short when he died of double pneumonia following an attack of influenza while in Boston on assignment in Army intelligence for the U.S. Justice Department. Clark Griffith,* player–manager of the Washington Senators (AL), lauded him: "No squarer or more honest official ever made decisions in a ball park. He had the courage of his convictions always, and was admired and respected by players and fans alike."

BIBLIOGRAPHY: Silk O'Loughlin file, National Baseball Library, Cooperstown, NY; William J. Burke, "Why Umpire O'Loughlin Is 'Silk,' " *BM* 1 (July 1908), pp. 9–11; Rochester (NY) *Democrat and Chronicle*, December 20–24, 1918; *TSN*, December 26, 1918, January 2, 9, 1919.

Larry R. Gerlach

O'MALLEY, Walter Francis (b. October 9, 1903, New York, NY; d. August 9, 1979, Rochester, MN), executive, was the most influential club owner of baseball's early expansion era. The son of wealthy New York City Commissioner of Public Markets Edwin J. O'Malley and Alma (Feltner) O'Malley, he attended Jamaica High School in Queens and Culver Military Academy in Indiana. He graduated from the University of Pennsylvania in 1926 and earned a law degree from Fordham Law School. O'Malley practiced law for 20 years before concentrating on operating the Brooklyn Dodgers (NL) baseball team. He married Kay Hanson in 1931 and had two children, including eventual club president, Peter.

In 1941, O'Malley became the Dodgers' attorney and began investing in the team. He gained control in 1950 by driving his rival, Branch Rickey,* whose flamboyant leadership O'Malley resented, from the presidency and forcing him to sell his quarter interest for $1.05 million. O'Malley purchased the remaining 50 percent of the stock from the Ebbets estate for $1 million, cheaply acquiring the NL's most prominent franchise. From 1950 through 1956, the Dodgers won four NL pennants and a world championship and led the NL in attendance. Although Rickey built the farm system and signed star African-American players, O'Malley saw that the team maintained its formidable player development program.

Dodgers owner O'Malley concentrated on baseball interests and soon became a power in the baseball establishment. Although keeping a low profile, he served on key committees and became the most powerful voice in league councils. In 1950, he led a successful movement to oust assertive Commissioner Albert B. "Happy" Chandler* and proved instrumental in choosing more compliant successor Commissioners Ford Frick,* William Eckert,* and Bowie Kuhn.*

Despite the strength and profitability of his Brooklyn Dodgers, O'Malley fretted over the inadequacy of Ebbets Field. Determined to expand his profit base, he pressured New York State politicians for land for a new park. When disputes over location and cost reached an impasse, O'Malley moved his team west to lucrative Los Angeles, CA. O'Malley persuaded New York Giants owner Horace Stoneham* to join him in 1959 in the westward move, ushering in major league baseball's expansion era.

The move triggered a storm of protest and made O'Malley's name anathema to New Yorkers. O'Malley testified before Congressional investigators that he had permission from his colleagues and had acquired the territorial rights to the Los Angeles area. Los Angeles politicians allowed him to purchase cheaply 300 acres of public land and also financed access roads for the new stadium, which O'Malley agreed to pay for. As his team played four seasons in the Los Angeles Coliseum, O'Malley supervised construction of $16 million Dodger Stadium. The Dodgers occupied the new facility in 1962. With its 56,000 seating capacity, the stadium annually attracted 2 million paid fans and in 1979 set a major league record by passing the 3 million paid mark. A promotional genius, O'Malley kept ticket prices low and profited from concession sales and a shrewd local television policy. In 1977 O'Malley's Dodgers enterprise was worth an estimated $50 million, twice the value of the average major league franchise.

In 1970 O'Malley turned the presidency over to his son, Peter, but remained chairman of the board until his death. As unofficial adviser to commissioners, O'Malley continued to be a formidable power. Above all, he was the catalyst to the game's continental expansion. His westward move triggered the rival CntL movement of 1959. O'Malley helped defuse this movement by persuading major league owners to add two teams to each existing major league in 1961–1962, preempting key cities eyed by CntL promoters. In 1969, a second round of expansion swelled major league membership to

24 teams. Eight years later, the AL's unilateral expansion raised membership to 26. Such dynamic growth was credited to O'Malley's initial decision to move westward.

BIBLIOGRAPHY: Walter O'Malley file, National Baseball Library, Cooperstown, NY; Neil J. Sullivan, *The Dodgers Move West* (New York, 1987); Cary S. Henderson, "Los Angeles and the Dodger War, 1957–1962," *SCQ* 62 (Fall 1980), pp. 264–276; Brad Herzog, *The Sports 100* (New York, 1995); Roger Kahn, *The Boys of Summer* (New York, 1973); Richard Kowet, *The Rich Who Own Sports* (New York, 1977); Lee Lowenfish, "A Tale of Many Cities: The Westward Expansion of National Baseball in the 1950s," *JW* 17 (July 1978); Harold Parrott, *The Lords of Baseball* (New York, 1975); Al Stump, "On Deck for the Dodgers—O'Malley the Younger," *Signature* (August 1971); Bill Veeck, "The Baseball Establishment," *Esquire* 62 (August 1964), pp. 45–47ff; William F. McNeil, *The Dodgers Encyclopedia* (Champaign, IL, 1997); Peter Golenbock, *Bums* (New York, 1984); Tommy Holmes, *The Dodgers* (New York, 1975); Richard Goldstein, *Superstars and Screwballs* (New York, 1991).

David Q. Voigt

O'NEIL, John Jordan, Jr. "Buck" (b. November 13, 1911, Carabelle, FL), player, manager, and scout, is the son of John O'Neil, Sr., a sawmiller, and Luella (Taswell) O'Neil, a restaurant cook and part-time teacher. He married Ira Lee Owen from Memphis, TN, in 1946 and had no children.

O'Neil's initial baseball preparation came from hard-nosed coach "Ox" Clemons at Edward G. Waters College in Jacksonville, FL. O'Neil played with several semiprofessional teams, including the Tampa, FL Smokers in 1931, Miami, FL Giants from 1932 to 1934, and Shreveport, LA Acme Giants in 1935 and 1936. His first professional team was the Memphis, TN Red Sox (NAL) in 1937. The following season, O'Neil, a first baseman, joined the Kansas City, MO Monarchs (NAL). A two-year tour with the U.S. Navy in 1944 and 1945 interrupted his baseball career.

The 6-foot 2-inch, 190-pound right-hander played in three East–West All-Star Games (1942, 1943, 1949) and demonstrated his leadership abilities as manager of the West squad from 1951 through 1955. In 1942, O'Neil batted a World Series high .353 in the Kansas City Monarchs' four-game sweep of the powerful Homestead, PA Grays. In 1946, he won the NAL batting crown with a .350 average. That season, the Kansas City Monarchs met the Newark, NJ Eagles for the Black World Series championship. He hit .333 against the Newark Eagles with two HR (including one grand slam), but the Kansas City Monarchs lost in seven games. O'Neil's lifetime batting average came to exactly .300. He batted .345 in 1940, .358 in 1947 and .330 in 1949.

O'Neil became manager of the Kansas City Monarchs in 1948 and sent more than three dozen players into major league organizations. His noteworthy players included George Altman, Gene Baker, Willard Brown,* Elston Howard,* Connie Johnson, Lou Johnson, Satchel Paige,* Hank

Thompson,* and Bob Thurman. In 1955, the Chicago Cubs (NL) signed O'Neil as a scout. His notable finds included star players Ernie Banks,* Lou Brock,* and Joe Carter.* Perhaps O'Neil's greatest personal accomplishment came in 1962, when the Chicago Cubs named him as the first African-American coach in major league baseball. O'Neil scouted for the Kansas City Royals (AL) from 1988 through 1993. He also serves on the Veterans Committee for the National Baseball Hall of Fame and is chairman of the board for the Negro Leagues Baseball Museum in Kansas City, MO. O'Neil provided commentary on the Negro Leagues for the 1994 documentary film *Baseball* by Ken Burns.

BIBLIOGRAPHY: M. S. Goodman, "A League of His Own," *PW* 42 (September 26, 1994), pp. 105–106; John B. Holway, *Black Diamonds* (Westport, CT, 1989); Janet Bruce, *The Kansas City Monarchs* (Lawrence, KS, 1985); Larry Lester Collection, Kansas City, MO; Larry Lester interviews with John O'Neil, December 1991, January 1992; Buck O'Neil file, National Baseball Library, Cooperstown, NY; Buck O'Neil et al., *I Was Right on Time* (New York, 1996); James A. Riley, *The Biographical Encyclopedia of the Negro Baseball Leagues* (New York, 1994); Steve Wulf, "The Guiding Light," *SI* 81 (September 19, 1994), pp. 148–150.

Larry Lester

O'NEILL, James Edward "Tip" (b. May 25, 1858, Woodstock, Canada; d. December 31, 1915, Montreal, Canada), player and executive, perhaps ranks as the greatest Canadian-born hitter. O'Neill, among his era's most popular players, starred on the St. Louis Brown Stockings (AA) dynasty of the 1880s.

O'Neill grew up in an Irish-Canadian family in Woodstock, Ontario. His father, who owned and operated O'Neill House, the town's hotel, brought up four sons and three daughters. Young O'Neill grew to 6 feet, 167 pounds and began pitching for the local amateur clubs, including the Harriston Browns and the Young Canadians of Woodstock, the Canadian amateur champions in 1880. He left home in 1881 to play for the barnstorming Hiawatha Grays, a Detroit, MI-based professional team. The following year, he signed with the original New York Metropolitans, the top U.S. independent professional team. In 1883, the New York owner, John B. Day,* gained an AA franchise for the Metropolitans and an NL club, the Gothams. Day shifted O'Neill to the New York Gothams, where the young right-hander won only five of 17 games and batted an anemic .179.

In 1884, O'Neill joined the St. Louis Browns, the AA's best and most colorful team. Day attempted to return O'Neill to the New York Mets, but Canadian-born St. Louis sportswriters Alfred Spink and Billy Spink convinced O'Neill to sign with the St. Louis Browns. O'Neill posted a good (11–4, 2.68 ERA) pitching record, but experienced arm trouble. Before the 1884 season ended, he became the Browns left fielder.

With O'Neill established as their leading hitter as third batter in the order, the St. Louis Browns from 1885 through 1888 became the only 19th-century team to capture four straight pennants. During that span, O'Neill batted .350 in 1885, .328 in 1886, a monster .435 in 1887, and an AA-leading .335 in 1888. In the era's loosely organized World Series, the Browns tied the Chicago White Stockings (NL) in the disputed 1885 fall classic. St. Louis won in 1886 against Chicago, as O'Neill batted .400. The St. Louis Browns lost badly to the Detroit Wolverines in 1887 and dropped a heartbreaking 11-game series, 6–5, to the New York Giants in 1888. In the 1886 fall classic, he became the first player to hit two HR in a World Series game.

O'Neill became a crowd favorite, especially with Irish-Americans. Clean shaven in an era of facial hair, he cut a handsome figure. Browns' center fielder Curt Welsh nicknamed O'Neill "Tip," short for Tipperary, an obvious reference to his Irish heritage.

O'Neill enjoyed a phenomenal season in 1887, when he dominated his league as no player before or since. He swept all offensive categories, leading or sharing the AA lead in base hits (225), doubles (52), triples (19), HR (14), RBI (123), total bases (357), batting average (.435), on base percentage (.490), slugging average (.691), and runs scored (167). He set new major league records for hits, batting average, doubles, runs, total bases, and slugging average, a record that stood until broken by Babe Ruth.* His .435 batting average marks the highest achieved prior to the 60-feet pitching distance.

O'Neill's statistics slipped in 1888, but he still led the AA in batting (.335) and in base hits (177). Both O'Neill and the Browns slipped a notch in 1889, although his .335 batting average and the Browns ranked second best. O'Neill followed with two more .300 seasons, batting .302 with the Chicago Pirates (PL) in 1890 and .321 with the St. Louis Browns (AA) in 1891. His final season came in 1892 with the Cincinnati Reds (NL). In 10 major league seasons, the lifetime bachelor batted .326 with 222 doubles, 92 triples, 52 HR, and 757 RBI.

When his father died, O'Neill, his mother, three brothers, and a sister moved to Montreal and acquired Hoffman Cafe on Notre Dame Street. He served as president of Montreal's EL club when the city acquired a franchise in 1897. After his brother George died in 1909, O'Neill operated the saloon and restaurant until his death.

BIBLIOGRAPHY: James O'Neill file, National Baseball Library, Cooperstown, NY; David Nemec, *The Beer and Whisky League* (New York, 1994); J. Thomas Hetrick, *Chris Von der Ahe and the St. Louis Browns* (Lanham, MD, 1999); Daniel Peterson, *Baseball in 1889* (Bowling Green, OH, 1993); Harvey Frommer, *Primitive Baseball* (New York, 1988); William Humber, *Cheering for the Home Team* (Erin, Canada, 1983); Jerry Lansche, *Glory Fades Away* (Dallas, TX, 1991); Robert L. Tiemann and Mark Rucker, eds., *Nineteenth Century Stars* (Kansas City, MO, 1989).

William E. Akin

O'NEILL, Paul Andrew (b. February 25, 1963, Columbus, OH), player, is the youngest of seven children and grew up in a blue-collar family. His father, Charles, pitched in the minor leagues from 1945 to 1948. O'Neill graduated from Brookhaven High School in Columbus, OH, where he attained All-State honors in basketball and baseball, and attended Oberlin College. He primarily pitched, although his boyhood idol was Willie Mays.* Gene Bennett scouted O'Neill, who was chosen by the Cincinnati Reds (NL) in the fourth round of the June 1981 free-agent draft. The left-handed O'Neill played mainly outfield and some first base for Billings, MT (PrL) in 1981. By 1984 with the Burlington-based Vermont Reds (EL), the 6-foot 4-inch, 205-pound O'Neill was labeled a prime prospect.

In 1985, O'Neill hit .305 for Denver, CO (AA) and led the AA in hits, doubles, games played, and at-bats. He also demonstrated a strong arm, leading all outfielders in assists and double plays. O'Neill appeared in five games for the Cincinnati Reds at the end of the 1985 season, but an injury sidelined him and affected his performance in 1986. He began the 1987 campaign with Nashville, TN (AA), but batted .256 after returning to the Cincinnati Reds. The next season, O'Neill started in right field for the Cincinnati Reds and batted .252 with 16 HR, and 73 RBI.

O'Neill hit .276 with comparable power statistics in 1989, although spending time on the disabled list. In 1991, he demonstrated more slugging power by clouting 28 HR and driving in 91 runs. He led NL outfielders with a .997 fielding percentage in 1992. His offensive production diminished in 1992, causing the Cincinnati Reds to trade him that November to the New York Yankees (AL) for Roberto Kelly.

O'Neill blossomed instantly with the New York Yankees. In 1993, he batted .311, belted 34 doubles and 20 HR, and drove in 75 runs. The following season, O'Neill led the AL with a .359 batting average. No New York Yankee had accomplished that feat since Don Mattingly* in 1984 or had compiled a higher team average since Mickey Mantle's* .365 in 1957. He hit over .400 until June 17, was chosen for the AL All-Star squad, and ranked among the strongest-armed AL outfielders. He led the Yankees to the best record in major league baseball in the strike-shortened season.

O'Neill batted .300 and paced the Yankees with 22 HR and 96 RBI in 1995 despite missing three weeks due to a sprained wrist. On June 15, he collected his 1,000th career major league hit. His leadership helped the New York Yankees capture the AL Wild Card and make their first post-season appearance since 1981. In the AL Championship Series against the Seattle Mariners, O'Neill batted .471 with 17 hits. In 1996, he led AL outfielders defensively with a 1.000 fielding average and hit .302 with 91 RBI. His best full season came in 1997, when he batted .324 and established career highs with 179 hits, 42 doubles, and 117 RBI. In the AL Division Series, he ravaged Cleveland Indians pitchers with a .421 batting average, two doubles, two HR (including a grand slam), and seven RBI. His .317 batting average, 24 HR, and 116 HR helped the Yankees secure the AL East with a franchise record 114 victories in 1998. O'Neill batted .364 with two doubles and one HR in the AL Division Series against the Texas Rangers and .300 with two doubles, one HR, and three RBI to help New York win the AL Championship Series against the Cleveland Indians. San Diego Padres pitchers held him to two hits in the World Series. His .285 batting average, 19 HR, and 110 RBI helped New York win the AL East again in 1999. Despite a shoulder injury, he batted .250 in the AL Division Series, .286 with one RBI in the AL Championship Series, and .250 with four RBI in the World Series.

Through the 1999 season, O'Neill has batted .242 with 223 HR and 1,096 RBI. He and his wife, Nevalee, have two sons, Andrew and Aaron.

BIBLIOGRAPHY: Franz Lidz, "Paul O'Neill," *SI* 79 (July 26, 1993), pp. 42–43; Donald Honig, *The Cincinnati Reds* (New York, 1992); *New York Daily News*, August 26, 1993; *NYT*, September 15, 1994; *NYT Biographical Service* 21 (October 1990), pp. 957–960; "Paul O'Neill," *Microsoft Complete Baseball*, CD-ROM (Redmond, WA, 1994); The New York Yankees "Home Plate" Website, 1995; Paul O'Neill file, National Baseball Library, Cooperstown, NY.

Robert E. Weir

O'NEILL, Stephen Francis "Steve" (b. July 6, 1891, Minooka, PA; d. January 26, 1962, Cleveland, OH), player, scout, coach, and manager, was the best known representative of baseball's most numerous family. The son of Irish immigrants Michael O'Neill and Mary O'Neill, he had five brothers and seven sisters. His brothers, Jack, Mike, and Jim, spent brief careers in the major leagues. He married Mary Boland on August 20, 1914 and had four daughters. His son-in-law, James "Skeeter" Webb, played infield in the AL during the 1940s.

O'Neill worked as a coal breaker in the Pennsylvania mines, but his baseball ability enabled him to move into that far more congenial occupation. At 5-feet 10-inches and 215 pounds, the right-hander possessed a catcher's archetypal build. He caught at Elmira, NY (NYSL) in 1910 and 1911 and moved up to the Cleveland Indians (AL) in September 1911. He caught for the Cleveland Indians for 12 full seasons through 1923 and for the Boston Red Sox (AL) in 1924. His 1925 campaign was split between the New York Yankees (AL) and Reading, PA (IL). The 1927 and 1928 seasons found O'Neill back in the major leagues with the St. Louis Browns (AL). On a limited scale, he caught for Toronto, Canada (IL) from 1929 to 1931, Toledo, OH (AA) from 1932 to 1934 and Beaumont, TX (TL) for one game in 1942. For his major league career, O'Neill batted .263 and garnered 248 doubles, 34 triples, and 13 HR. He fielded .972 and led the AL twice each in assists and errors and once in fielding percentage. O'Neill still holds the record for double plays by a catcher in a season (36) and ranks high in that category lifetime. On July 11, 1917, he completed an unassisted double play. In the 1920 World Series, O'Neill batted .333 for the victorious Cleveland Indians over the Brooklyn Robins.

The genial O'Neill also succeeded in nonplaying capacities. In the minor leagues, he managed Toronto, Canada (IL) from 1929 to 1931, caught, coached, and managed for Toledo, OH (AA) in 1933 and 1934, piloted

Buffalo, NY (IL) from 1938 to 1940, and managed Beaumont, TX (TL) in 1942. In the major leagues, he coached for the Cleveland Indians in 1935 and 1949, managed there from 1935 to 1937, and scouted there from 1955 to 1958. He coached for the Detroit Tigers (AL) in 1941 and piloted them from 1943 to 1948, coached and managed for the Boston Red Sox in 1950 and 1951, and piloted the Philadelphia Phillies (NL) from mid-1952 through 1954. Under his tutelage, O'Neill's major league teams won 1,040 games and lost 821 contests for an impressive .559 winning percentage. His greatest managerial accomplishment came with the Detroit Tigers' seven game triumph over the Chicago Cubs in the 1945 World Series. His career resembles that of National Baseball Hall of Fame catcher–managers Raymond Schalk* and Alfonso Lopez.* Subsequently, O'Neill worked for the Cleveland Recreation Department.

BIBLIOGRAPHY: *The Baseball Encyclopedia*, 10th ed. (New York, 1996); Peter Golenbock, *Fenway* (New York, 1992); Dan Shaughnessy, *The Curse of the Bambino* (New York, 1990); Robert Redmount, *The Red Sox Encyclopedia* (Champaign, IL, 1998); Howard Liss, *The Boston Red Sox* (New York, 1982); Stephen O'Neill file, National Baseball Library, Cooperstown, NY; J. G. Taylor Spink, comp., *TSN Daguerreotypes of Great Stars of Baseball* (St. Louis, MO, 1961); Thomas Aylesworth and Benton Minks, *The Encyclopedia of Baseball Managers* (New York, 1990); Franklin Lewis, *The Cleveland Indians* (New York, 1949); Bill Borst, ed., *Ables to Zoldak*, vol. 2 (St. Louis, MO, 1988); Bill Borst, *Still Last in the American League* (West Bloomfield, MI, 1992).

Lowell L. Blaisdell

O'ROURKE, James Henry "Jim," "Orator Jim" (b. September 1, 1850, Bridgeport, CT; d. January 8, 1919, Bridgeport, CT), player, manager, umpire, and executive, ranks as perhaps the most versatile performer in major league history. The only player to perform in at least 100 games at six fielding positions, he covered all three outfield spots, catcher, first base, and third base. O'Rourke fielded adequately, lacked a strong arm, and possessed about average speed. The muscular 5-foot 8-inch, 185 pounder remained a powerful right-handed hitter throughout his career. Born into an Irish family and the brother of major leaguer John O'Rourke, he began his career with the Osceola Club of Bridgeport, CT in 1871. The next year, he entered professional baseball with the Middletown, OH Mansfields (NA).

From 1873 to 1880, he played with the powerful Boston Red Stockings (NA through 1875, NL thereafter) except for spending the 1879 season with the Providence Grays (NL). Starting in 1881, he played four seasons with the Buffalo Bisons (NL). From 1885 to 1892, he starred for the New York Giants (NL) except for one season (1890) with the New York Giants (PL). He concluded his career with the Washington Senators (NL) in 1893, but returned for a single game with the New York Giants (NL) in 1904 at age 52. A consistent hitter, O'Rourke batted at least .300 14 times in his 23-year career. He compiled a four-year .317 batting average in the NA and a .310 mark in the NL and PL. One of the era's power hitters, he produced 414 doubles, 132 triples, and 50 HR in the NL and PL. O'Rourke also made 2,304 hits, scored 1,446 runs, knocked in 1,010 runs, and stole 191 bases.

O'Rourke, unlike most ball players, successfully shifted from the playing field to the front office. As player–manager in Buffalo from 1881 to 1884, O'Rourke piloted four teams to a composite 206–169 winning record. He served as player–manager of the 1893 Washington Senators (NL) team and as a major league umpire the next year. His managerial record in the major leagues comprised 246 wins and 258 losses (.488 winning percentage). After spending two years (1895–1896) as manager of the independent Victors of Bridgeport, he returned to professional baseball as pilot of Bridgeport, CT (CtL) from 1897 to 1908 and played there from 1904 to 1907. From 1907 through 1913, he served as CtL President. O'Rourke, EL president in 1914, was elected to the National Baseball Hall of Fame in 1945.

BIBLIOGRAPHY: Frederick Ivor-Campbell et al., eds., *Baseball's First Stars* (Cleveland, OH, 1996); William J. Ryczek, *Blackguards and Red Stockings* (Jefferson, NC, 1992); Gary Caruso, *The Braves Encyclopedia* (Philadelphia, PA, 1995); Harold Kaese, *The Boston Braves* (New York, 1948); John Thorn et al., eds., *Total Braves* (New York, 1996); Frank Graham, *The New York Giants* (New York, 1952); James O'Rourke file, National Baseball Library, Cooperstown, NY; Noel Hynd, *The Giants of the Polo Grounds* (New York, 1988); Paul MacFarlane, ed., *Hall of Fame Fact Book* (St. Louis, MO, 1982); *The Baseball Encyclopedia*, 10th ed. (New York, 1996); *Spalding's Official Base Ball Guide 1887* (New York, 1887).

Gordon B. McKinney

ORR, David L. "Dave," "Big Dave" (b. September 29, 1859, New York, NY; d. June 3, 1915, Brooklyn, NY), player and manager, was the son of laborer James Orr and Rachel Orr, of Scotch-Irish descent. Orr attended New York elementary school, but did not excel. He worked odd jobs and began his baseball career on the city's independent teams, including the Alaskas of Brooklyn, NY. A right-handed batter and thrower, Orr in 1883 played for the Metropolitan Reserves of Newark, NJ (later Hartford, CT). In 1883, colorful manager Jim Mutrie* recruited Orr to play 13 games for the original New York Metropolitans (AA). Orr also replaced Roger Connor* for a single game with the New York Giants (NL). During an eight-season major league career ended prematurely by a crippling disability in 1890, Orr hit .342 lifetime and never batted below .300. Besides playing with the New York Metropolitans (AA) from 1884 to 1887, he performed for the Brooklyn Dodgers (AA) in 1888, Columbus, OH Buckeyes (AA) in 1889, and Brooklyn Wonders (PL) in 1890.

Teamed with Timothy Keefe,* Orr in 1884 placed second in the AA in batting (.354) and hits (162). He powered the New York Metropolitans to a championship and the first "World Series" title. In December 1884, he heroically saved a child's life in a railroad accident. During the following two seasons, his slugging fame blossomed. Orr led the AA in triples each season, with his 31 in 1886 the second highest mark ever. He also paced the AA with 7 HR and became the first player to surpass 300 total bases in a single season. The immensely strong Orr stood just under 6 feet and eventually weighed nearly 250 pounds. His size regularly cost him extra bases and often aggravated injuries. Although plagued by leg problems, Orr in 1887 batted .368 and stole 17 bases. He also served as interim manager (3 wins, 5 losses) of the now-decimated Metropolitans in their second year as "Indians" on Staten Island. At season's end, Charles Byrne and Charles Ebbets* of the Brooklyn Dodgers (AA) purchased the team. After a single season with the Dodgers, Orr was sold to the new Columbus Buckeyes (AA) team. In 1889, he led AA first basemen in assists, one of several times he led in fielding categories.

With John M. Ward's* Brooklyn Wonders (PL), Orr in 1890 batted .371 and knocked in 124 runs. After sustaining two broken ribs from being hit by a pitch in July, he suffered a stroke at season's end that paralyzed his left side and terminated his career. A powerful HR hitter (37 lifetime), Orr was one of only four 19th century players to compile a lifetime .500 slugging mark. In 791 games, he made 1,125 hits, 198 doubles, 108 triples, and 536 runs scored, and batted .342. Subsequently, he resided in Brooklyn and Manhattan and worked as a stonecutter and stagehand. When Ebbets Field was built, he was named caretaker. When the Brooklyn Feds (FL) opened at Washington Park in 1914, Ward made Orr responsible for the press box. Orr, whose wife, Emily Ann, died in 1906, had no children.

BIBLIOGRAPHY: David Orr file, National Baseball Library, Cooperstown, NY; David Nemec, *The Beer and Whisky League* (New York, 1994); " 'Dave' Orr, Famous Ball Player, Dies," Brooklyn *Daily Eagle*, June 3, 1915, p. 20; Preston Orem, *Baseball 1845–1881* (Altadena, CA, 1961); "Orr, Mighty Hitter of the Eighties, Dead," *TSN*, June 10, 1915, p. 3; Robert L. Tiemann and Mark Rucker, eds., *Nineteenth Century Stars* (Kansas City, MO, 1989).

James D. Smith III

ORTA, Jorge Nuñez "Charolito" (b. November 26, 1950, Mazatlan, Mexico), player and coach, is the son of Pedro Orta and Juana (Nuñez) Orta. His father, a standout baseball player known as the Babe Ruth* of Cuba during the 1940s, later played in Mexico. The younger Orta began playing professional baseball in Mexico in 1968, and was signed by the Chicago White Sox (AL) organization in 1971. After joining the Chicago White Sox in 1972, he was initially mentored by Dick Allen.* He also played for the Cleveland Indians (AL) in 1980 and 1981, Los Angeles Dodgers (NL) in 1982, Toronto Blue Jays (AL) in 1983, and Kansas City Royals (AL) from 1984 to 1987.

Orta's .978 fielding average ranked third among regular AL second basemen in 1975, causing some to regard his reputation as a defensive liability to be exaggerated. He also performed at third base, left field, and right field, finishing his career as a DH. With a lifetime .278 batting average, Orta hit over .300 in 1974 and 1975. His .316 batting average in 1974 placed him second to Rod Carew.* An All-Star in 1975 and 1980, he played in the 1984 and 1985 AL Championship Series, hitting .100 with one triple and one RBI against the Detroit Tigers in 1984 and going hitless against the Toronto Blue Jays in 1985. Orta batted .333 as a pinch-hitter in the 1985 World Series against the St. Louis Cardinals. The 5-foot 10-inch 170-pound left-handed hitter and right-handed thrower made six hits on June 15, 1980 against the Minnesota Twins and was inducted into the Mexican Baseball Hall of Fame in 1976.

The quiet, modest Orta, unlike his loquacious parents, termed himself "an average player" and added, "I've never been a real popular player, or super-star, or anything like that. I think God already gave me more than I deserve. I've been around a long time." Often perceived as painfully shy before he learned English, Orta enjoyed speaking engagements for the Chicago White Sox. He especially enjoyed talking with children and learned to speak English well, asking a reporter to recommend good writers so he could improve his command of the language. Orta has coached for New Orleans, LA (PCL) since 1999. He and his wife, Geraldine, whom he married in 1970, have two sons, Jorge, Jr. and Craig, and live in Torreon, Mexico.

BIBLIOGRAPHY: Jorge Orta file, National Baseball Library, Cooperstown, NY; Jim Kaplan, "By Jorge, He's Got It Now!" *SI* 53 (July 7, 1980), pp. 37–38; Mike Shatzkin, ed., *The Ballplayers* (New York, 1990); John Thorn et al., eds., *Total Baseball*, 5th ed. (New York, 1997); *WWIB*, 1987, 72nd ed.; Richard Lindberg, *Sox* (New York, 1984); Richard Lindberg, *Who's on Third?* (South Bend, IN, 1983).

                                                                                                        Victor Rosenberg

ORTH, Albert Lewis "Al," "Smiling Al," "The Curveless Wonder" (b. September 5, 1872, Tipton, IN; d. October 8, 1948, Lynchburg, VA), player, coach, and umpire, was the son of the Lewis Orth. After being educated in the Danville, IN public schools and at DePauw University, he married Jimmie Allen and had two sons. Orth, a pitcher nicknamed "The Curveless Wonder," broke into the major leagues in 1895 after an outstanding season at Lynchburg, VA (VL), where he won 28 games by August 8. This feat impressed the Philadelphia Phillies (NL), which purchased his contract for $1,000. Orth continued his winning ways there with a 8–1 record. In 1899, he compiled a 14–3 mark and led the NL with a 2.49 ERA. *Spalding's Base Ball Guide* praised him for "being especially effective against the five first division clubs." The right-handed Orth jumped to the Washington Nationals (AL) in 1902 and finished his career with the New York Highlanders (AL). In 15 seasons, the 6-foot, 200 pounder won 204 games, lost 189, and triumphed in at least 20 games twice. Besides completing 324 of 394 starts, he struck out 948 batters in 3,354.2 innings and recorded a 3.37 ERA.

A "wily boxman" who knew the batters well, Orth became famous for his spitball. According to Manager Clark Griffith,* "He mastered his delivery, which was rapidly falling into disuse, more completely than any other pitcher in the American League. He pitches easily, but he has excellent control of the wet ball." The skillful Orth still ranks among major league leaders in fewest walks per game (1.77) during his career. During his banner 27–17 1906 season, he walked only 66 batters in 338.2 innings and completed 36 of 39 games started. Orth's .273 career batting average, including 12 HR, ranks him among best hitting pitchers in major league history. The left-handed hitting Orth batted over .300 five seasons and also played in the outfield and infield occasionally. Following his retirement as a player, he briefly managed the Lynchburg, VA (VL) squad in 1909 and umpired in the NL (1913–1916) and VL (1912, 1920–1923) until a knee injury ended his career. Orth later coached baseball at Washington and Lee University and Virginia Military Institute. The Lynchburg (VA) *News* eulogized him: "Baseball today could use a young Al Orth who could win games on either side of the plate. That was Al Orth's almost unique versatility."

BIBLIOGRAPHY: Lynchburg (VA) *News*, October 9, 1948; Bill Madden, *The Hoosiers of Summer* (Indianapolis, IN, 1994); Frederick G. Lieb and Stan Baumgartner, *The Philadelphia Phillies* (New York, 1953); Rich Westcott and Frank Bilovsky, *The New Phillies Encyclopedia* (Philadelphia, PA, 1993); Shirley Povich, *The Washington Senators* (New York, 1954); Frank Graham, *The New York Yankees* (New York, 1943); Mark Gallagher, *The Yankee Encyclopedia*, vol. 3 (Champaign, IL, 1997); Albert Orth file, National Baseball Library, Cooperstown, NY; *The Baseball Encyclopedia*, 10th ed. (New York, 1996); *Spalding's Base Ball Guide, 1895–1900* (New York, 1895–1900).

Duane A. Smith

ORZECHOWSKI, Daniel Leonard. *See* Daniel Leonard Ozark.

OSTEEN, Claude Wilson "Wimpy," "Gomer" (b. August 9, 1939, Caney Spring, TN), player and coach, is the son of Claude L. Osteen and Pauline Osteen and was signed out of Reading (OH) High School by the Cincinnati Reds (NL) in 1957. The 18-year-old southpaw debuted for the Cincinnati Reds after hurling only 13 innings at Nashville, TN (SL). In 1958, Osteen won 19 games, lost eight contests, and struck out 214 batters at Wenatchee, WA (NWL) and Seattle, WA (PCL). After spending another season at Seattle, the 6-foot, 170-pound Osteen relieved for the Cincinnati Reds in 1960. He married Georgie Crosby in July 1962 and had five children, David, Brian, Erick, Gavin, and Jennifer, before their divorce. David and Gavin pitched in the minor leagues.

In September 1961, the Cincinnati Reds traded Osteen to the Washington Senators (AL). The first-year expansion team let the youthful hurler start regularly. From 1962 to 1964, Osteen compiled a 32–40 win–loss record, led Senators pitchers in victories in 1963 and 1964, improved his control, and lowered his ERA each season.

After being traded to the Los Angeles Dodgers (NL) for slugger Frank

Howard* in December 1964, Osteen embarked on an extremely productive nine-year stint in the starting rotation with Sandy Koufax,* Don Drysdale,* and Don Sutton.* From 1965 through 1973, Osteen averaged over 16 wins and 266 innings pitched per season. He won 20 games in 1969 and 1972 and led Dodger pitchers in victories in 1967, 1969, 1970, and 1972. His five hit shutout of the Minnesota Twins in the third game of the 1965 World Series and his three shutout innings and victory for the NL in the 1970 All-Star game comprised his greatest achievements.

Osteen was sent to the Houston Astros (NL) in December 1973 and the St. Louis Cardinals (NL) in August 1974. Osteen once commented that he "wasn't sure which is more insulting, being offered in a trade or having it turned down." On September 11, 1974 with the Cardinals, he entered a game in the 14th inning and hurled 9.1 scoreless relief innings. St. Louis defeated the New York Mets, 4–3, in 25 innings. Osteen finished his major league career with the Chicago White Sox (AL) in 1975. His major league career totals included 196 wins, 195 losses, 40 shutouts, 1,612 strikeouts, and a 3.30 ERA in 541 games.

Osteen served as pitching coach with the Philadelphia Phillies (NL) organization in 1976, St. Louis Cardinals (NL) from 1977 to 1980, and Philadelphia Phillies from 1982 to 1988. After instructing pitchers in the Los Angeles Dodgers system, he coached for the Texas Rangers (AL) in 1993 and 1994 and the Albuquerque, NM Dukes (PCL) in 1997. His baseball thrills included coaching Steve Carlton,* John Denny,* and Steve Bedrosian* in their NL Cy Young Award seasons.

BIBLIOGRAPHY: Walter Alston with Jack Tobin, *A Year at a Time* (Waco, TX, 1976); Rich Marazzi and Len Fiorito, *Aaron to Zuverink* (New York, 1982); James R. Hartley, *Washington's Expansion Senators* (Germantown, MD, 1998); William F. McNeil, *The Dodgers Encyclopedia* (Champaign, IL, 1997); Tommy Holmes, *The Dodgers* (New York, 1975); Kevin Nelson, *Baseball's Greatest Quotes* (New York, 1982); Claude Osteen file, National Baseball Library, Cooperstown, NY; Claude Osteen, letter to Frank Olmsted, January 23, 1990; John Scher, "Bill Bene's 92 mph Weapon Strays a Long Way Off Course," *BA*, December 10–24, 1989, p. 3; *TSN Baseball Register*, 1976.

Frank J. Olmsted

OTIS, Amos Joseph (b. April 26, 1947, Mobile, AL), player, graduated in 1965 from Williamson High School in Mobile, AL, where he starred in football and played basketball and baseball. Otis married Alice Bowick on October 10, 1964 and has three children. The 5-foot 11½-inch, 165-pound, right-handed Otis was signed out of high school by the Boston Red Sox (AL) and assigned to Harlan, KY (ApL), where he played third base and batted .329. After a modest season at Oneonta, NY (NYPL), he was drafted by the New York Mets (NL) in November 1966. He played the 1967 season with Jacksonville, FL (IL), and appeared in 19 games with the Mets in Sep-

OTT, MELVIN THOMAS 1155

tember. Although connecting for a .327 batting average for Tidewater, VA (IL) in 1969, Otis batted only .151 in 48 games for the Mets and was traded with pitcher Bob Johnson that December to the Kansas City Royals (AL) for third baseman Joe Foy.*

For 14 major league seasons, Otis played regular center fielder for the Kansas City Royals. Besides hitting .301 in 1971 and .300 in 1973, he led the AL in stolen bases with 52 in 1971 and slugged a career-high 26 HR in 1973. In 1970 and 1971, Otis led AL outfielders in total chances and putouts. Otis won Gold Glove Awards for his fielding excellence in 1971, 1973, and 1974 and was voted Kansas City Royals Player of the Year in 1971, 1973, and 1978 by the BBWA local chapter. Otis starred for the Royals in 1978 and 1979, hitting .298 and .295 and leading AL outfielders in fielding average.

In his only World Series, Otis belted three HR and batted .478 in 1980 against the Philadelphia Phillies. Otis signed a $1.27 million contract with the Royals for 1982–1983, but Kansas City did not take a third-year option on his contract. He joined the Pittsburgh Pirates (NL) on December 19, 1983, but injuries and a .165 batting average led to his release on August 5, 1984. Although a slick fielder, he often was criticized for his easy style and one-handed catches. Otis, who smoked four packs of cigarettes a day until 1976, was selected to the AL All-Star team five times. He finished his major league career with 2,020 hits, 374 doubles, 193 HR, 341 stolen bases, 1,092 runs scored, 1,007 RBI, and a .277 batting average. He served as a roving instructor for the San Diego Padres (NL) in 1986, 1987, and 1992 and coached for the San Diego Padres from 1988 through 1990, Colorado Rockies (NL) in 1993, and the Colorado Springs, CO Sky Sox (PCL) in 1994 and 1995.

BIBLIOGRAPHY: Del Black, " 'I'm Your Centerfielder,' Otis Tells Royals," *TSN*, March 24, 1979; Charley Feeney, "Otis Becomes a Tanner Fan," *TSN*, April 16, 1984; Gary Herron, "Another Famous Amos (Otis) Offers Some Pretty Startling Revelations . . . for the Record," *SCD* 23 (February 9, 1996), pp. 140–142; Sid Bordman, *Expansion to Excellence* (Marcelline, MS, 1981); Zander Hollander, *The Complete Handbook of Baseball, 1977* (New York, 1977); Zander Hollander, *The Complete Handbook of Baseball, 1982* (New York, 1982); Joe McGuff, "One-Handed Grabs Are Trademark of Royals' Otis," *TSN*, July 10, 1971, p. 9; Amos Otis file, National Baseball Library, Cooperstown, NY.

Frank J. Olmsted

OTT, Melvin Thomas "Mel," "Master Melvin" (b. March 2, 1909, Gretna, LA; d. November 21, 1958, New Orleans, LA), player, manager, and sportscaster, was the son of oil refinery worker Charles Ott and played baseball, football, and basketball at Gretna High School. Ott, who married Mildred Mattigny in October 1930 and had two daughters, was elected to the National Baseball Hall of Fame in 1951. One of few major league players to spend his entire career with one franchise, he starred with the New York Giants (NL) from 1926 to 1947. Ott became the first National Leaguer to slug over 500 HR and ranked third in lifetime HR (511) behind Babe Ruth* and Jimmie Foxx* when he retired. He led the NL in HR six times, slugging a career high 42 in 1929. Ott, nicknamed "Master Melvin," proved a consistent performer whose steady production paced a powerful lineup and helped the Giants capture three NL championships in the 1930s. Defensively, he led NL outfielders in double play assists twice and played third base when needed in the late 1930s. Twice, Ott scored six runs in one game. Ott's patience at the plate netted him the NL record for most walks (1,708), a mark Joe Morgan* surpassed in 1982. Ott also holds the NL mark for the most seasons with over 100 bases on balls (10).

Ott, perhaps best remembered for his personality and unique batting stance, played semipro ball in 1926 for the Paterson, NJ Grays, whose owner Harry Williams knew Giants manager John McGraw* very well. At age 16, Ott received a penny postcard from the Giants' front office, stating, "Report to McGraw, Polo Grounds," and immediately dismissed the message as a prank by one of his teammates. Williams physically put Ott on a train to New York, where he quickly became McGraw's personal development project. McGraw decided that Ott lacked major league catching skills, being too small (5-feet 9-inches and 170 pounds), too quiet, and too much of a "southern gentleman." After witnessing Ott's classic "foot in the bucket" batting style, McGraw kept the teenager at his side on the Giants bench rather than entrust him to any minor league manager. Casey Stengel* offered to assist young Ott at Toledo, OH (AA), but McGraw insisted, "Ott stays with me!" Nurturing the soft-spoken Louisiana native slowly, McGraw did not use Ott regularly until three seasons later.

Ott's unusual natural swing would have been altered by any minor league manager or coach. By stepping high and into each pitch with his bat slung low and nearly parallel to his upper arm, Ott produced a smooth, rhythmic swing resulting in a .304 lifetime batting average and 2,876 base hits. In 2,730 games, he made 488 doubles, 1,859 runs (9th best), 1,860 RBI (10th best), 1,708 walks (6th best), and a .533 slugging percentage. No other player duplicated Ott's motion with any great success, however, and Ott never tried to teach anyone his swing. Ott proved too easygoing to insist on anyone doing anything in particular and compiled a 464–530 (.467 winning percentage) record as Giants manager from 1942 to 1948. In 1947 Ott's soft-spoken managerial style prompted Leo Durocher* to comment, "Nice guys finish last." The next season, Ott was fired by owner Charles Stoneham* and replaced by Durocher. The trials of major league managing may have caused Ott to lose much of his famed good humor. Nevertheless, he was one of only five baseball personalities selected to tour European battlefields with the USO during 1944–1945.

After three seasons with the New York Giants' farm system, Ott piloted the Oakland, CA Oaks (PCL) in 1951 and 1952. He retired in 1953 and moved into the front office of a local Louisiana construction firm. During the late 1950s, he broadcast Detroit Tigers (AL) games. On November 14, 1958, he and his wife were seriously injured in a head-on automobile collision. Ott died from complications due to the accident at a New Orleans, LA hospital.

BIBLIOGRAPHY: Mel Ott file, National Baseball Library, Cooperstown, NY; Charles C. Alexander, *John McGraw* (New York, 1988); John Benson et al., *Baseball's Top 100* (Wilton, CT, 1997); Bob Broeg, *Super Stars of Baseball* (St. Louis, MO, 1971); Richard Goldstein, *Spartan Seasons* (New York, 1980); Craig Carter, ed., *TSN Daguerreotypes*, 8th ed. (St. Louis, MO, 1990); Donald Honig, *The Power Hitters* (St. Louis, MO, 1989); Noel Hynd, *The Giants of the Polo Grounds* (New York, 1988); William B. Mead, *The Worst Ten Years of Baseball* (New York, 1978); *NYT*, November 22, 1950; *The Baseball Encyclopedia*, 10th ed. (New York, 1996); Lowell Reidenbaugh, *Baseball's Hall of Fame-Cooperstown* (New York, 1993); Fred Stein, *Mel Ott* (Jefferson, NC, 1999); Fred Stein, "No Cheap Home Runs for Ott," *BRJ* 20 (1991), pp. 70–72; Fred Stein, *Under Coogan's Bluff* (Glenshaw, PA, 1978); Frank Graham, *The New York Giants* (New York, 1952); Frank Graham, *McGraw of the Giants* (New York, 1944); Peter Williams, *When the Giants Were Giants* (Chapel Hill, NC, 1994).

Alan R. Asnen

OVERALL, Orval "Orvie" (b. February 2, 1881, Farmersville, CA; d. July 14, 1947, Fresno, CA), player, excelled as one of the nonpareil right-handed pitchers during the Chicago Cubs' (NL) glory years from 1907 to 1910. "Three-Finger" Brown* and Ed Reulbach* endured longer, but on his best days Overall more than matched them.

He was the son of Daniel G. Overall and Cynthia (Haws) Overall. His father owned a Visalia, CA hotel and served as Tulare County sheriff. At the University of California, Berkeley, Overall majored in agriculture and captained the baseball and football teams as a pitcher–first baseman and fullback–guard. Physically the biggest football squad member, he plunged for short yardage between the tackles, bolstered the defensive line, and made 60-yard punts and unerring place kicks.

Upon graduation in 1904, Overall signed with Tacoma, WA (PCL) for an above-average, well-earned $300 a month and won 32 of 57 decisions there. In 1905 Tacoma sold Overall to the Cincinnati Reds (NL), making him the first California-Berkeley graduate to make the major leagues. For the fifth-place Reds, the workhorse pitcher won 18 games and lost 23 decisions while hurling 318 innings. In a shrewd June 1906 trade, the Chicago Cubs secured Overall for right-hander Bob Wicker and $2,000. The 6-foot 2-inch, 214-pound Overall improved his 4–5 win–loss record in Cincinnati with a handsome 12–3 mark in Chicago. In the surprise 1906 World Series loss to the Chicago White Sox, he pitched 12 innings of no-decision relief spanning two successive days.

In 1907, Overall enjoyed his finest season with 23 victories and 7 defeats. His .767 winning percentage was exceeded only by Brown and Reulbach, while his ERA was an impressive 1.68. Overall's 8 shutouts tied Christy Mathewson* and Eddie Plank.* In the 1907 World Series against the Detroit Tigers, he bested "Wild Bill" Donovan* in Game 4. After recording a 15–11 season in 1908, he whipped Donovan twice more in the 1908 World Series. Overall won 20 games against 11 losses in 1909 and led the NL in strikeouts (205) and shutouts (9), but his record dropped to 12–6 in 1910 because of intermittent arm trouble. He lost the 1910 World Series opener to "Chief" Bender* of the Philadelphia Athletics.

Treatment by "Bonesetter" Reese, an early specialist in sore arms, did not bring about Overall's recovery. Overall's disability and an argument with Cubs owner Charles Murphy over salary prompted him to "retire" for two campaigns. He then joined his father in a gold-mining venture and pitched weekends and holidays for Stockton, CA in the "outlaw" CaSL. Overall returned to the Chicago Cubs in 1913, but clearly did not regain his old form. Manager Johnny Evers* released the 4–5 Overall to San Francisco, CA (PCL), where he finished the season at 8–9 and retired permanently. Lifetime, Overall won 108 victories, suffered 71 defeats, and compiled a 2.23 ERA, the eighth lowest in major league history. He pitched 133 complete games with 935 strikeouts and 30 shutouts.

Subsequently, Overall worked in a brewery whose owner also backed the Vernon, CA (PCL) club. He then became a citrus-fruit farmer and entered banking in 1922. Originally an appraiser, he progressed through several institutions and was vice-president of the Fresno, CA branch of the Security First National of Los Angeles at the time of his death. He married Ethelyn M. Hinson on February 27, 1908, but had no children.

BIBLIOGRAPHY: Lee Allen, *The Cincinnati Reds* (New York, 1948); *The Baseball Encyclopedia*, 10th ed. (New York, 1996); Warren Brown, *The Chicago Cubs* (New York, 1946); Richard M. Cohen et al., eds., *The World Series* (New York, 1979); Jim Enright, *Chicago Cubs* (New York, 1975); G. H. Fleming, *The Unforgettable Season* (New York, 1981); Eddie Gold and Art Ahrens, *The Golden Era Cubs, 1876–1940* (Chicago, IL, 1985); Warren Wilbert and William Hageman, *Chicago Cubs: Seasons at the Summit* (Champaign, IL, 1997); Orval Overall file, National Baseball Library, Cooperstown, NY; John Thorn et al., eds., *Total Baseball*, 5th ed. (New York, 1997).

A. D. Suehsdorf

OZARK, Daniel Leonard "Danny" (b. Daniel Leonard Orzechowski, November 24, 1923, Buffalo, NY), player, coach, and manager, is the son of Leo Ozark and Margaret (Cieslewicz) Ozark and graduated from East High School in 1942. Scout Heinie Groh* of the Brooklyn Dodgers (NL) signed Ozark in December 1941 as a second baseman, but he switched to first base after one minor league season. After three years in the military, Ozark returned to the Brooklyn Dodgers' minor league system in 1946 and spent the next 16 years there as a player and manager. Despite some good seasons, he never rose above the Triple A level as a player.

In 1956, Ozark started managing in the Brooklyn Dodgers minor league system. He piloted Spokane, WA, their top Pacific Coast League affiliate, to the PCL pennant in 1963 and was named PCL Manager of the Year. In 1965, Ozark was named third base coach with the Los Angeles Dodgers (NL).

Ozark's career peaked when he signed as manager of the Philadelphia Phillies (NL) in November 1972. Ozark inherited a poor team that had finished in the cellar for two straight seasons. He stressed Dodger style fundamentals and, aided by several shrewd trades, sparked the Philadelphia Phillies' improvement. By the mid-1970s, Philadelphia became one of the best major league baseball teams. After finishing a close second to the Pittsburgh Pirates in 1975, the Philadelphia Phillies captured the NL Eastern Division with 101 wins and 61 losses in 1976 and 1977. The Philadelphia Phillies won a third straight NL Eastern Division title in 1978.

Ozark never attained an NL pennant, as the Philadelphia Phillies were eliminated by the Cincinnati Reds in the 1976 NL Championship Series and Los Angeles Dodgers in 1977 and 1978 NL Championship Series. The media criticized his handling of the pitching staff and his lack of control over the team. His club won only two of nine post-season games. In August 1979, the struggling Philadelphia Phillies replaced him with Dallas Green.*

Under Ozark, the Phillies won 594 games and lost only 510 contests for the third highest victory total in team history. Ozark coached for the Los Angeles Dodgers in 1980 and then moved in 1983 to the San Francisco Giants (NL). He replaced Frank Robinson* as manager in August 1984, compiling a 24–32 record.

Ozark retired after the 1984 season with a 618–542 managerial mark and .533 winning percentage in eight major league seasons. He lives in Vero Beach, FL with his wife, Virginia (Zdinski) Ozark, whom he married in February 1946. They have two children, Dwain and Darlene.

BIBLIOGRAPHY: Daniel Ozark file, National Baseball Library, Cooperstown, NY; Rich Westcott and Frank Bilovsky, *The New Phillies Encyclopedia* (Philadelphia, PA, 1993); *Philadelphia Phillies Media Guides, 1973–1979*; Thomas Aylesworth and Benton Minks, *The Encyclopedia of Baseball Managers* (New York, 1990); Allen Lewis, *The Philadelphia Phillies: A Pictorial History* (Virginia Beach, VA, 1981); Frank Dolson, *The Philadelphia Story* (South Bend, IN, 1981); Allen Lewis and Larry Shenk, *This Date in Philadelphia Phillies History* (New York, 1979).

John P. Rossi

P

PAFKO, Andrew "Pruschka," "Handy Andy" (b. February 25, 1921, Boyce-
ville, WI), player, is the son of Michael Pafko and Susie Pafko. He joined
the Chicago Cubs (NL) as an outfielder in September 1943, hitting .379
after an inconsistent minor league career at Eau Claire, WI (NoL), Green
Bay, WI (WSL), Macon, GA (SAL), and Los Angeles, CA (PCL). Only 312
faithful followers saw his splendid Chicago debut of two hits in three at-bats
on a miserably cold September 24, 1943. In 1944 the 6-foot, 190-pound
Pafko became the Chicago Cubs' regular center fielder, leading the NL in
assists and emerging as a star. Gifted with a strong, accurate arm, he patrolled center field in a style seldom equaled in Wrigley Field in the post–
World War II years. Pafko's unusual batting stance did not hinder his career
HR production (213), .285 batting average, 1,796 hits, or 976 RBI.

Pafko starred on the 1945 NL pennant winners, hitting .298 and driving
in 110 runs. An injury-plagued 1946 was followed by a strong 1947 season
that saw Pafko selected to the NL All-Star team. After switching to third
base in 1948, he enjoyed another banner year. Pafko returned to the outfield
and hit 36 HR in 1950, combining with Hank Sauer* for 68 HR to provide
major league baseball's most potent duo that season. Chicago traded the
popular Pafko to the Brooklyn Dodgers (NL) in an eight-player exchange
in June 1951, a deal Chicago Cubs fans never forgave or forgot. One sports
reporter called it "the deal that defies the laws of sanity."

Pafko played on the formidable 1951 Brooklyn team, which lost the NL
pennant on Bobby Thomson's* dramatic ninth-inning HR for the New York
Giants. Brooklyn's outfield of Pafko, Duke Snider,* and Carl Furillo* fur-
nished one of the era's best. The Dodgers traded him to the Milwaukee
Braves (NL) in January 1953. A regular until yielding his position to Hank
Aaron* in 1955, he finished his major league career with Milwaukee in 1959.
Pafko, who married Ellen Kapusta in February 1947, managed in the Braves'

farm system and scouted for the Montreal Expos (NL) before retiring from baseball. He also worked at a golf course and resides in Mount Prospect, IL.

BIBLIOGRAPHY: Andy Pafko file, National Baseball Library, Cooperstown, NY; Peter Golenbock, *Bums* (New York, 1984); Richard Goldstein, *Superstars and Screwballs* (New York, 1991); Tommy Holmes, *The Dodgers*, (New York, 1975); Bob Buege, *The Milwaukee Braves: A Baseball Eulogy* (Milwaukee, WI, 1988); Gary Caruso, *The Braves Encyclopedia* (Philadelphia, PA, 1995); Art Ahrens and Eddie Gold, *Day by Day in Chicago Cubs History* (West Point, NY, 1982); *The Baseball Encyclopedia*, 10th ed. (New York, 1996); Eddie Gold and Art Ahrens, *The New Era Cubs, 1941–1985* (Chicago, IL, 1985); Brent P. Kelley, *The Early All-Stars* (Jefferson, NC, 1997); Jim Langford, *The Game Is Never Over* (South Bend, IN, 1980); Rich Westcott, *Diamond Greats* (Westport, CT, 1988); Warren Brown, *The Chicago Cubs* (New York, 1946); Jim Enright, *Chicago Cubs* (New York, 1975); William F. McNeil, *The Dodgers Encyclopedia* (Champaign, IL, 1997); Roger Kahn, *The Boys of Summer* (New York, 1972).

Duane A. Smith

PAGE, Joseph Francis "Joe," "Fireman" (b. October 28, 1917, Cherry Valley, PA; d. April 21, 1980, Latrobe, PA), player, was the finest relief pitcher of the late 1940s. He grew up in the hard-scrabble coal camps of western Pennsylvania, the eldest of seven children born to Joseph Page, a miner, and Laurena (Couch) Page. A rebellious youth, he quit high school and baseball after an argument with his father and worked in the mines. An automobile accident hospitalized Page for nearly a year and later provided him with a 4F draft exemption. After rehabilitation, he signed a professional baseball contract with McKeesport, PA (PSA) in 1938. McKeesport released him believing that his future was in the mines.

In 1940, Page signed with the New York Yankee (AL) farm team in Butler, PA (PSA). The muscular 6-foot 3-inch, 215-pound left-handed pitcher overpowered batters with a blazing fastball. After recording an 11–3 record at Butler, he moved up to Augusta, GA (SAL) in 1941, and Newark, NJ (IL) in 1942. After posting a 14–5 mark in 1943, he reached the major leagues.

In his first three major league seasons with the New York Yankees from 1944 to 1946, Page acquired the reputation of "baseball's bad boy" with a poor work ethic and a fondness for nightlife. He showed flashes of brilliance, starting with a 5–1 record as a rookie and making the AL All-Star team. A shoulder injury and six straight losses prompted his return to Newark. In 1945 and 1946, New York Yankee manager Joe McCarthy* suspended Page on several occasions.

Page's fortunes improved in 1947. He agreed to contract incentives for adhering to team rules and roomed with the staid Joe DiMaggio.* Bucky Harris* took over as manager and converted Page to a relief pitcher. Page became the best relief specialist in baseball and among the most popular New York Yankees. He appeared in 56 games and led the AL with 17 saves while recording 14 wins, eight losses, and a 2.48 ERA. In the 1947 World Series, Page pitched in four games and blanked the Brooklyn Dodgers the last five innings of the deciding seventh game to pick up the win. *Sport Magazine* selected Page as its Athlete of the Year for 1947.

The New York Yankees and Page slipped in 1948, although the latter led the AL with 55 appearances. Both came back in 1949. Page again paced the AL with 60 appearances and 27 saves to accompany 13 wins and a 2.59 ERA. He pitched in three of the five World Series games against the Brooklyn Dodgers, winning one, saving another, and garnering MVP honors.

Injuries and ineffectiveness plagued Page's career after his great 1949 season. Following a 3–7 performance with the New York Yankees in 1950, he was optioned to the minor leagues. After stops at Kansas City, MO (AA), San Francisco, CA (PCL) and Syracuse, NY (IL), the Pittsburgh Pirates (NL) gave him a 7 game trial in 1954.

Page operated two taverns, "The Bull Pen" in Irwin, PA and "Page's Rocky Lodge" in Laughlintown, PA. He married Catherine Carrigan in 1941, but they divorced 14 years later. Page then married Mildred Brown and had three children. In the 1970s, he suffered from heart problems, throat cancer, and protracted law suits stemming from an imposter posing as Page. He died of a heart attack.

BIBLIOGRAPHY: Joe Page file, National Baseball Library, Cooperstown, NY; Dave Anderson et al., *The Yankees* (New York, 1979); Dom Forker, *The Men of Autumn* (Dallas, TX, 1989); Mark Gallagher, *The Yankee Encyclopedia*, vol. 3 (Champaign, IL, 1997); Robert W. Creamer, *Stengel: His Life and Times* (New York, 1984); Peter Golenbock, *Dynasty* (Englewood Cliffs, NJ, 1975); Milton Gross, *Yankee Doodles* (Boston, MA, 1948); David Halberstam, *Summer of '49* (New York, 1989); William C. Heinz, *Once They Heard the Cheers* (New York, 1979); Joe Page with Joe Trimble, "I Was Baseball's Bad Boy," *SEP* 220 (May 22, 1948), pp. 28, 145–49; Milton J. Shapiro, *Heroes of the Bullpen* (New York, 1967); *DAB*, Supp. 10, pp. 613–615; Leo Trachtenberg, "When Joe Page Came Striding In," *YM* 47 (February 7, 1983).

William E. Akin

PAGE, Theodore Roosevelt "Ted" (b. April 22, 1903, Glasgow, KY; d. December 1, 1984, Pittsburgh, PA), player, was a 5-foot 11-inch, 175-pound Negro League center fielder–first baseman from 1923 through 1936. Page's major fortes included speed and aggressive playing style.

The Page family moved in 1911 to the "Monkeys Nest" neighborhood in Youngstown, OH, where the father worked in the local steel mill. In the Booker T. Washington Settlement recreation center, Page excelled at baseball, basketball, and football. Ohio State University sought Page about a football scholarship, but he pursued a baseball career after high school. In 1923 he signed a contract with Rube Foster's* Toledo, OH (NAL) club, but did not make the team and began barnstorming with a central Ohio team for $10–$15 per game. He in 1924 joined the Buffalo, NY Giants, managed by Grant "Home Run" Johnson.* Johnson also arranged for Page to play winter baseball for the Breakers Hotel in Florida, where rival hotels employed black baseball players at $30 per month plus room and board to wait tables and play baseball. Page's success in Buffalo and Florida through 1925 prompted an offer the following season from the Newark, NJ Stars (ECL), managed by Sol White.* After the Newark Stars folded at midseason in 1926, Page barnstormed with the Mohawk, NY Giants until Chappie Johnson* signed him for his Montreal, Canada club in 1928. Johnson honed Page's skills as a tough, aggressive base runner, who utilized his speed with the bunt and intimidation with his spikes on the base paths. Page played in 1929 and 1930 for the Brooklyn Royal Giants (ECL), managed by Negro League All-Star pitcher Dick Redding.* Following the 1929 and 1930 seasons, Page joined the Baltimore Black Sox (ECL) against major league all-star teams. Page performed well in his 16 Negro League–major league exhibition games from 1930 through 1935, reportedly batting .429.

Cum Posey's* Homestead, PA Grays (ANL) enlisted Page in 1931. Page batted .315 to help Homestead post 136 wins against only 17 losses. He began the next year with the New York Black Yankees (NNL) but jumped at mid-season to the Pittsburgh Crawfords (NNL). Owner Gus Greenlee* sought to assemble "blackball's" greatest team, including National Baseball Hall of Famers Oscar Charleston,* Satchel Paige,* "Cool Papa" Bell,* Judy Johnson,* and Josh Gibson.* His three seasons with the Crawfords highlighted his career, as he batted .352 in 1932, .362 in 1933, and .275 in 1934 mostly as a leadoff batter. He earned $200 per month during the season and $60 per month during the off season as a lookout for Greenlee's Pittsburgh gambling operations. In 1934, Page sustained a serious knee injury while sliding into first base in Jackson, MS. The injury severely hampered his speed, shortening his career. Page began the 1935 season with the Newark, NJ Eagles (NNL), but was released in mid-May. He ended his baseball career with a .351 batting average in 1937.

Page married Juanita Bass of Pittsburgh, PA and had no children. After working as a public relations consultant for the Gulf Oil Corporation, he in 1946 became co-owner of the Meadow Lanes Bowling Alley. He enjoyed a prominent career in national bowling circles through the AmBC and WIBC, campaigning to integrate bowling activities. Page, who wrote a sports column for the Pittsburgh (PA) *Courier*, was inducted into the Negro Baseball Hall of Fame, Pennsylvania Sports Hall of Fame, and Western Pennsylvania Hall of Fame. He was beaten to death with a baseball bat in a robbery attempt by a young man whom Page had befriended and hired to do work around his house.

BIBLIOGRAPHY: James Bankes, *The Pittsburgh Crawfords* (Dubuque, IA, 1991); John B. Holway, *Blackball Stars* (Westport, CT, 1988); John B. Holway, *Voices of the Great Black Baseball Leagues* (New York, 1975); Pittsburgh (PA) *Courier*, December 15,

1984; James A. Riley, *The Biographical Encyclopedia of the Negro Baseball Leagues* (New York, 1994).

David Bernstein

PAIGE, Leroy Robert "Satchel" (b. July 7, 1906, Mobile, AL; d. June 8, 1982, Kansas City, MO), player and coach, excelled as the Negro Leagues' main star attraction. His athletic prowess, phenomenal durability, and incredible showmanship guaranteed large crowds wherever he pitched for over three decades. From his birth in a shotgun house in black Mobile, AL to gardener John Paige and washerwoman Lula Paige until his belated selection to the National Baseball Hall of Fame in 1971, Paige embodied Negro League life.

Although probably making more money than any other Negro Leaguer, Paige was banned from the white major leagues until the color barrier ended in 1947. The following year, 42-year-old Paige became the oldest rookie in major league history and the first black pitcher in the AL. Bill Veeck* of the Cleveland Indians (AL) signed him for the 1948 AL pennant drive. His major league statistics, including 28 wins and 31 losses, 476 innings pitched, and a 3.29 ERA, represent the tip of an iceberg hidden beneath the nation's racial blindness.

In 1961, Paige concluded that he had pitched in about 2,500 games and won over 2,000 contests. His varied opponents included sandlot, semipro, Negro League, Caribbean, and barnstorming white major league teams. Opponents almost unanimously judged Paige about the best pitcher they had ever faced. On at least 55 occasions, he blanked the opposition without a hit or run. In other instances, he called his outfielders in and struck out the side. As teammate Jimmie Crutchfield* noted, "When Satchel got to that ball park it was like the sun just came out."

From his first season with the black semi-pro Mobile, AL Tigers in 1924 until his last summer riding the bus with the Indianapolis, IN Clowns in 1967, Paige pitched before an estimated 10 million fans. Between 1929 and 1958, he annually played both summer and winter ball and may have been the most widely seen player ever. His "have arm—will pitch" style carried him through Canada, the United States, the Dominican Republic, Cuba, and Mexico. Baseball aficionados throughout the Western Hemisphere carry vivid memories of the gangly 6-foot 3-inch, 180-pound Paige with his "bee ball," hesitation pitch, and pinpoint control.

Paige acquired his nickname as a 7-year-old by carrying satchels from the Mobile train station. At age 12, he was sent to the Mt. Meigs, AL reform school for black youths after stealing several toy rings from a store. Although he had played for his W. C. Council school team, Paige blossomed as a pitcher during his five years at reform school. Paige pitched for the Mobile, AL Tigers in 1924 and 1925 and joined the Chattanooga, TN Black Lookouts (NSL) in 1926. Two years later, he was sold to the Birmingham, AL

Black Barons (NNL). In 1931, the Nashville, TN Elite Giants (NSL) bought the hard-throwing right-hander. The franchise moved to Cleveland, OH during the season, but faced fiscal problems and disbanded.

Gus Greenlee,* the Pittsburgh, PA numbers mogul who had recently assumed control of the Pittsburgh Crawfords (NNL), quickly persuaded Paige to join his team. Through the 1933 season, Paige pitched for the barnstorming Crawfords and several semipro clubs that hired him on a per game basis. He jumped in 1934 to a white semipro club in Bismarck, ND, but returned to the Pittsburgh Crawfords (NNL) for the 1936 season. During spring training in 1937, Paige traveled to the Dominican Republic to pitch for dictator Rafael Trujillo's team and resumed barnstorming for the Trujillo All-Stars upon returning to the United States. When Greenlee sold him to the Newark, NJ Eagles (NNL), Paige headed to Mexico. He developed arm trouble during the summer of 1938 and, with his future in doubt, returned to the United States.

After most Negro League clubs bypassed him, Paige signed with the Kansas City, MO Monarchs' (NAL) second team, which toured the Northwest and Canada. Appearing a few innings each day, the once formidable athlete seemed finished. When his arm revived that summer, however, Paige never looked back again. Between 1939 and 1947, Paige anchored the Monarchs' pitching staff. In the 1942 Negro League World Series (the first played since 1927), Paige won three of his team's four victories over the Homestead, PA Grays.

In 1948, Paige joined the white major leagues and helped the Cleveland Indians (AL) win the AL pennant with his 6–1 record. His first three starts drew over 200,000 fans and helped set night game attendance records in Cleveland, OH and Chicago, IL. Paige was released after the 1949 season and barnstormed until 1951, when Veeck, now owner of the St. Louis Browns (AL), signed him. In 1952, Paige won 12 games and was selected to the AL All-Star team. He remained with the Browns until 1953 and then barnstormed except for stints with Miami, FL (IL) from 1956 to 1958 and Portland, OR (PCL) in 1961. In 1965, Paige made his last major league appearance in a three-inning outing with the Kansas City Athletics (AL). Paige played with the barnstorming Indianapolis, IN Clowns in 1967 and coached for the Atlanta Braves (NL) in 1968. In his autobiography, *Maybe I'll Pitch Forever* (1962), Paige advised his readers to "keep the juices flowing by jangling around gently as you move." He succumbed in June 1982 after a long siege of heart trouble and emphysema.

BIBLIOGRAPHY: Bill Borst, *Still Last in the American League* (West Bloomfield, MI, 1992); Bill Borst, ed., *Ables to Zoldak*, vol. 2 (St. Louis, MO, 1989); John Thorn et al., eds., *Total Indians* (New York, 1996); David Kaiser, *Epic Season* (Amherst, MA, 1998); Russell Schneider, *The Boys of Summer of '48* (Champaign, IL, 1998); John Phillips, *Winners* (Cabin John, MD, 1987); Franklin Lewis, *The Cleveland Indians* (New York, 1949); Satchel Paige file, National Baseball Library, Cooperstown, NY;

SEAL, vol. 1 (1981–1985), pp. 623–625; Barbara Carlisle Bigelow, ed., *Contemporary Black Biography*, vol. 7 (Detroit, MI, 1994); Janet Bruce, *The Kansas City Monarchs* (Lawrence, KS, 1985); Brad Herzog, *The Sports 100* (New York, 1995); John B. Holway, *Josh and Satch* (Westport, CT, 1991); Larry Moffi and Jonathan Kronstadt, *Crossing the Line* (Jefferson, NC, 1994); Leroy Satchel Paige and David Lipman, *Maybe I'll Pitch Forever* (Garden City, NY, 1962); Leroy Satchel Paige, *Pitchin' Man* (Westport, CT, 1992); Robert W. Peterson, *Only the Ball Was White* (Englewood Cliffs, NJ, 1970); David L. Porter, ed., *African-American Sports Greats* (Westport, CT, 1995); Mark Ribowsky, *Don't Look Back* (New York, 1994); James A. Riley, *The Biographical Encyclopedia of the Negro Baseball Leagues* (New York, 1994); Donn Rogosin, *Invisible Men: Life in Baseball's Negro Leagues* (New York 1983); *NYT*, June 9, 1982.

Robert L. Ruck

PAIRE, LaVonne. *See* LaVonne Paire Davis.

PALERMO, Stephen Michael "Stevie," "Steve" (b. October 9, 1949, Worcester, MA), umpire, sportscaster, and executive, is the son of Vincent Palermo, a school principal, and Angela (Gentile) Palermo. Palermo began umpiring Little League games at age 13 in Oxford, MA and attended Leicester JC and Worcester State College. He left Norwich University in Northfield, VT to attend the BUDS in 1972. Upon graduating, he skipped the normal rookie league assignment and signed with the Class A NYPL. He began 1973 with the Class A CrL, but advanced to the Class AA EL by season's end. In the off-season, he umpired in the FlnL, DRWL, and PRWL and from 1973 to 1976 was a BUDS instructor. He reached Class AAA in 1975 and was promoted to the AL in September 1976.

As suggested by his rapid rise to the major leagues in only five years, Palermo proved to be a gifted arbiter with natural umpiring instincts and confidence that bordered on cockiness. He quickly established himself as one of the premier AL ball-strike arbiters without employing the ball-strike indicator used by all other umpires. After the strike-induced split season of 1981, Palermo umpired the AL West Division playoffs between the Oakland Athletics and Kansas City Royals. He also umpired three AL Championship Series (1980, 1982, and 1989), the 1983 World Series, and the 1986 All-Star Game. Palermo, who recovered from a serious case of mononucleosis that sidelined him for most of 1988, easily topped a 1990 poll of general managers as the AL's best umpire.

His career was suddenly interrupted on July 7, 1991, when he was shot while attempting to apprehend muggers who had assaulted two waitresses outside a Dallas, TX restaurant. Palermo, paralyzed from the waist down by a bullet that hit his spinal column, challenged the medical prognosis that he probably would never walk again by undertaking torturous therapy. With the aid of crutches and full leg braces, he threw out the first ball of the 1991 World Series. Over the next two years, he increased his mobility to a point where he needed only canes to walk. In November 1993, he risked permanent, total paralysis by undergoing high-risk surgery. The successful surgery permitted further rehabilitation and thus kept alive his dream of returning to umpiring.

His 1975 marriage ended in divorce seven years later. He married Debbie Aaron in February 1991, five months before being shot, and has no children. In recognition of his heroism, Palermo was inducted in 1992 as an honorary member of the Texas Baseball Hall of Fame. He worked as a part-time sportscaster for the New York Yankees in 1995 and in 1996 as a speaker for the baseball commissioner's office.

BIBLIOGRAPHY: "Interview: Steve Palermo," *Referee* 14 (October 1989), pp. 20–23; Kansas City (MO) *Star*, November 14, 1993; Rich Marazzi, "The Heroic Story of Disabled AL Umpire Steve Palermo," *SCD* 23 (October 11, 1996), pp. 90–91; Rich Marazzi, "Steve Palermo's Incredible Comeback from Tragedies," *SCD* 23 (October 18, 1996), pp. 80–81; Bruce Newman, "Pain and Progress," *SI* 76 (July 6, 1992), pp. 28–33; Steve Palermo file, National Baseball Library, Cooperstown, NY; *TSN*, October 28, 1991, December 23, 1991; "The Umpire Won't Call Himself Out," *PW* 37 (April 27, 1992), pp. 105–106; *USAT Baseball Weekly*, November 11, 1993.

Larry R. Gerlach

PALMEIRO, Rafael (Corrales) (b. September 24, 1964, Havana, Cuba), player, is the son of Jose Palmeiro and Maria Palmeiro and married Lynne Walden. The Cuban refugee graduated from Jackson High School in Miami, FL and earned a B.A. degree from Mississippi State University, where he starred in baseball and won the SEC Triple Crown in 1984. After being signed by the Chicago Cubs (NL) in 1985, the 6-foot, 188-pound outfielder was chosen the 1986 EL MVP after hitting .306 with 95 RBI for Pittsfield, MA.

Palmeiro appeared briefly for the Chicago Cubs in 1986, but was optioned to Des Moines–based Iowa (AA) in April 1987. The Chicago Cubs recalled him in 1987 for 84 games. The 1988 campaign marked his first full major league season, as the outfielder–first baseman hit .307. In December 1988, the Chicago Cubs sent Palmeiro as part of a nine-player trade to the Texas Rangers (AL). Palmeiro enjoyed five outstanding years with the Texas Rangers, hitting over .300 twice. He also developed into a power hitter, belting 37 HR in 1993. Granted free agency after the 1993 season, he signed with the Baltimore Orioles (AL) that December.

Palmeiro, who bats and throws left-handed, experienced an outstanding strike-shortened 1994 campaign, batting .319 with 23 HR and 76 RBI. In 1995, he batted .310 with 39 HR and 104 RBI. His 39 HR and career-high 142 RBI helped Baltimore win a wild card berth in 1996. Palmeiro belted a HR with two RBI in the AL Division Series against the Cleveland Indians and two HR with four RBI in the AL Championship Series against the New York Yankees. His 38 HR and 110 RBI helped Baltimore capture the AL East in 1997. After batting .286 in the AL Division Series against the Seattle Mariners, he hit .280 with two doubles, one HR, and two RBI in the AL Championship Series against the Cleveland Indians. Palmeiro batted .296

with 43 HR and 121 RBI in 1998. In December 1998, the Texas Rangers (AL) signed him to a $45 million, five-year contract. The smooth fielding first baseman has led the AL in assists five times and paced the AL in 1993 and 1996 in putouts and total chances. *TSN* Player of the Year in 1999, he batted .324 with a career-high 47 HR and 148 RBI to help Texas win the AL Central Division. He ranked second in HR, RBI, total bases (356), and slugging percentage (.630). He hit .273 in the AL Division Series. Palmeiro's career statistics through 1999 include a .296 batting average, 361 HR, and 1,227 RBI. He made the 1988 NL All-Star team and the 1991, 1998, and 1999 AL All-Star teams and earned *TSN* AL Gold Glove Awards in 1997, 1998, and 1999 and *TSN* AL Silver Slugger Award in 1998 and 1999. He ranked first in games (1,526), second in hits (1,747), and fourth in RBI (1,068) in the 1990s.

BIBLIOGRAPHY: Rafael Palmeiro file, National Baseball Library, Cooperstown, NY; *TSN Baseball Register*, 1998; *1987 and 1988 Chicago Cubs Media Guides*; Rick Weinberg, "Texas Terror," *Sport* 83 (May 1992), pp. 38–40.

Duane A. Smith

PALMER, James Alvin "Jim" (b. October 15, 1945, New York, NY), player and sportscaster, was adopted two days after birth by Moe Wiesen, a Jewish dress manufacturer, and Polly (Kiger) Wiesen, a Catholic boutique owner. His early years were spent in the luxury of a Park Avenue apartment and Westchester County estates. When his father died in 1954, the family moved to California. His mother married Max Palmer, a television character actor. The family lived briefly in Beverly Hills, CA before her arthritis prompted a move to Scottsdale, AZ. At Scottsdale High School, Palmer made All-State in football, basketball, and baseball. After graduating from high school, he signed a baseball contract with the Baltimore Orioles (AL) for a $60,000 bonus in August 1963. Six months later, he married his high school sweetheart, Susan Ryan. Palmer, who has two daughters, Jamie and Kelly, briefly attended Arizona State University and Towson (MD) State College.

In a brilliant rookie year in the minor leagues in 1964, he compiled an 11–3 record and a no-hitter for Aberdeen, SD (NoL). Palmer was promoted to the major leagues in 1965. He became a starting pitcher in 1966 and threw a shutout in the World Series that year against the Los Angeles Dodgers. At age 20, he became the youngest hurler ever to pitch a shutout in a World Series and the youngest in a half-century to pitch a complete World Series game. Arm and back problems forced his return to the minor leagues in 1967–1968, but he made a brilliant comeback in 1969 and pitched a no-hitter against the Oakland Athletics on August 13. Except for 1974, which he spent on the disabled list, Palmer won at least 20 games eight of the next nine years between 1970 and 1978 to become the first AL pitcher to record eight 20-game seasons since Lefty Grove.* The only AL pitcher to win the Cy Young Award three times (1973, 1975–1976), Palmer was named to the

All-Star team six times (1970–1972, 1975, 1977–1978) and received four Gold Gloves for fielding excellence (1976–1979).

Despite recurring physical ailments, the 6-foot 3-inch, 190-pound right-handed fastballer ranked among the most consistent pitchers in major league history. In 19 years with Baltimore, he compiled 268 wins and 152 losses for a .638 winning percentage. Appearing in 558 games, 521 as a starter, he pitched 3,948 innings, struck out 2,212 batters, and posted a 2.86 ERA. He led the AL four times in innings pitched (1970, 1976–1978), three times in wins (1975–1977), twice in ERA (1973, 1975), winning percentage (1969, 1982), and shutouts (1970, 1975), and once in complete games (1977). At his best in important games, Palmer enjoyed a 4–1 record in six AL Championship Series and a 4–2 record in six World Series.

The intelligent, articulate, and opinionated Palmer engaged in legendary feuds with manager Earl Weaver.* Teammates jokingly called him "Reginald" because of his wealthy background and "Cakes" because of his Jockey underwear commercials. After his retirement from baseball in May 1984, Palmer began a career in broadcasting as a sports commentator for ABC television and an analyst for local Baltimore baseball telecasts. In 1990, he was elected to the National Baseball Hall of Fame.

BIBLIOGRAPHY: Jim Palmer file, National Baseball Library, Cooperstown, NY; *CB* (1980), pp. 301–303; Joel H. Cohen, *Jim Palmer* (New York, 1978); Frank Deford, "In a Strike Zone of His Own," *SI* 45 (July 26, 1976), pp. 28–34; Ron Fimrite, "Kings of the Hill Again," *SI* 43 (July 21, 1975), pp. 14–17; Jackie Lapin, "Jim Palmer of the Orioles," *Sport* 60 (March 1975), pp. 66, 71–77; Jim Palmer and Jim Dale, *Together We Were Eleven Foot Nine* (Kansas City, MO, 1996); Ted Patterson, *The Baltimore Orioles* (Dallas, TX, 1995); James H. Bready, *Baseball in Baltimore* (Baltimore, MD, 1998); Jim Palmer with Joel H. Cohen, *Pitching* (New York, 1975); W. Plummer, "Refusing to Go Gentle into Life's Dugout, Jim Palmer Plots a Comeback," *PW* 35 (February 25, 1991), pp. 53–54; *The Baseball Encyclopedia*, 10th ed. (New York, 1996); Mark Ribowsky, "Jim Palmer," *Sport* 68 (May 1979), pp. 69–75; *TSN Official Baseball Register, 1985*; Robert Ward, "Jim Palmer," *Sport* 74 (April 1983), pp. 21–26; Steve Wulf, "The Biggest Bird in the Bushes," *SI* 59 (August 15, 1983), pp. 44–45; Ken Young, *Cy Young Award Winners* (New York, 1994); Earl Weaver with Barry Stainback, *It's What You Learn After You Know It All that Counts* (Garden City, NY, 1982).

Larry R. Gerlach

PAOLINELLI, Rinaldo Angelo. *See* Ralph A. Pinelli.

PAPASTEGIOS, Miltiades Stergios. *See* Milton Stephen Pappas.

PAPPAS, Milton Stephen "Milt," "Gimpy" (b. Miltiades Stergios Papastegios, May 11, 1939, Detroit, MI), player, pitched for Cooley High School in Detroit and starred in Junior Legion baseball. In 1957, former pitcher Hal Newhouser* scouted Pappas and signed him with the Baltimore Orioles (AL) for $4,000. The same year, Pappas pitched three games for Knoxville, TN (SAL), made his major league debut with Baltimore on August 10 in relief against the New York Yankees, and performed four other relief stints. In 1958, Pappas started 21 games and garnered a 10–10 record for the sixth place Orioles. Since Pappas was the youngest AL starter, manager Paul Richards* invariably pulled him after 70 pitches to protect his arm. Pappas continued to hurl for Baltimore through 1965 and won 16 games in 1963 and 1964. For Baltimore, he never experienced a losing season and amassed 110 wins despite injuries. Pappas, who married Carole Tragge in February 1960 and had two children, pitched in three All-Star games (in both 1962 games and in 1965). In December 1965, the Orioles traded Pappas and two other players to the Cincinnati Reds (NL) for Frank Robinson.*

Pappas spent the rest of his career in the NL, finishing at 12–11 in 1966 and 16–13 in 1967 with Cincinnati. He compiled a 2–5 slate in 1968 until traded in June to the Atlanta Braves (NL). After recording a 10–8 mark for the remainder of the 1968 season, he fell to a 6–10 record the following year. He relieved in Game 2 of the 1969 NL Championship Series against the New York Mets. In 1970, he compiled a 2–2 slate until being sold to the Chicago Cubs in June. At Chicago, he finished with a 10–8 standard and 3.34 ERA. Pappas enjoyed 17–14 and 17–7 records in 1971 and 1972 and the latter year made his best ERA (2.77) since 1965. In 1972, Pappas hurled for a fifth place team in the NL East and recorded an 8–0 no-hitter against the San Diego Padres on September 2. The Cubs dropped to last place in the NL East in 1973, as Pappas won only seven of 19 decisions. Overall, Pappas recorded 99 victories for three NL teams.

During his 17-year major league career, Pappas compiled a 209–164 record and 3.40 ERA, pitched 43 shutouts, struck out 1,728 batters and walked only 858 in 3,186 innings. Pappas remains one of only two major league pitchers having at least 200 wins without a 20-victory season. His 99 NL victories left him only one triumph short of joining Cy Young* and Jim Bunning* as the only hurlers to have gained 100 wins in each major league. In 1985, Pappas was selected to the Baltimore Orioles Hall of Fame. His wife disappeared in September 1982 and neither she nor her car has ever been found. Pappas remarried in 1984, has another daughter, lives in Beecher, IL, and works for Metropolitan Supply Company. His son is a computer programmer.

BIBLIOGRAPHY: Milt Pappas file, National Baseball Library, Cooperstown, NY; Ted Patterson, *The Baltimore Orioles* (Dallas, TX, 1995); James H. Bready, *Baseball in Baltimore* (Baltimore, MD, 1998); Jim Enright, *Chicago Cubs* (New York, 1995); Gary Caruso, *The Braves Encyclopedia* (Philadelphia, PA, 1993); *Baltimore Orioles Official Yearbook, 1958–1965*; Baltimore (MD) *Orioles Scorebook 1985*; Baltimore (MD) *Sun*, September 17, 1982, June 2, 1985; James H. Bready, *The Home Team* (Baltimore, MD, 1979); *NYT*, September 17, 1982; *The Baseball Encyclopedia*, 10th ed. (New York,

1996); Eddie Gold and Art Ahrens, *The New Era Cubs, 1941–1985* (Chicago, IL, 1985); Rich Westcott, *Diamond Greats* (Westport, CT, 1988).

Douglas D. Martin

PARKER, David Gene "Dave," "The Cobra" (b. June 9, 1951, Calhoun, MS), player and coach, is the son of foundry worker Richard Parker and Dannie (Fox) Parker. His father moved the family of six children to Cincinnati when Dave was three years old. A knee injury Parker's senior year at Cincinnati Courter Tech High School kept him out of football, limited his baseball activity, and caused the strong prospect to be drafted late. After being selected in 1970 by the Pittsburgh Pirates (NL) in the 14th round of the free agent draft, the 6-foot 5-inch, 230-pound outfielder played for Bradenton, FL (GCL) in 1970, Waterbury, CT (EL) and Monroe, NC (WCL) in 1971, and climaxed his minor league career in 1972 at Salem, VA (CrL) by winning the CrL MVP Award. He joined the Pittsburgh Pirates from Charleston, WV (IL), the next year and became a regular in 1975.

Parker, who threw right-handed and batted left-handed, played 11 seasons for Pittsburgh primarily in right field and helped lead the Pirates to NL pennants in 1974, 1975, and 1979. Parker became the Pirates' "franchise player" and constantly hit above .300 from 1975 to 1979. In 1977, he topped the NL in hits (215), doubles (44), and batting average (.338). Supporting his claim as "the complete player," Parker also led the NL in putouts (389) and assists (26). Many of Parker's 15 errors that season came from his all-out play. He led NL outfielders in chances accepted (430) and double plays (9) and received the first of his three Gold Glove awards.

In 1978 Parker, nicknamed "The Cobra" for his quick-striking swing, again won the NL batting championship with a .334 average. He paced the NL with 340 total bases for a .585 slugging percentage and won the NL MVP Award. The next year, he batted .345 and made 10 hits to lead the Pirates to the World Series championship over the Baltimore Orioles. Although popular with his teammates for giving 100 percent and often playing with injuries, he became unpopular with some Pittsburgh journalists and fans. After his five-year, $5 million contract in 1979 made him the highest paid player in baseball, Parker began to receive negative press coverage and fan abuse. The criticism worsened in 1981 and 1982, when injuries lowered his batting average to .258 and .270.

Granted free agency after an improved 1983 season, Parker signed with his hometown Cincinnati Reds (NL). In 1984, he batted .285, made 173 hits (44 for extra bases), scored 73 runs, and produced 94 RBI for a fifth place team. Inspired by the return of Pete Rose* as player–manager, Parker regained his 1970s form in 1985. Parker's 1985 season included a .312 batting average, 198 hits, 42 doubles, a .551 slugging percentage, and a career-high 34 HR and 125 RBI. Besides finishing second in the NL MVP balloting, he led the NL in doubles and RBI, placed second in hits, HR, and slugging percentage, and tied for second in game-winning hits (18). In 1986, Parker finished second in the NL in RBI (116) and tied for second in HR (31). In December 1987, the Reds traded Parker to the Oakland A's (AL). He helped the A's win AL pennants in both 1988 and 1989, batting .200 in the 1988 World Series against the Los Angeles Dodgers and clouting a HR in the 1989 World Series against the San Francisco Giants. The Milwaukee Brewers (AL) signed him as a free agent in December 1989. In 1990, he batted .289 with 92 RBI, making *TSN* AL All-Star and Silver Slugger teams. His final major league season came with the California Angels (AL) and Toronto Blue Jays (AL) in 1991.

In 19 major league seasons, Parker batted .290 with 2,712 hits, 526 doubles, 339 HR and 1,493 RBI. A participant in six All-Star games (four as a Pirate), he established the record for most assists in a game by an outfielder with two. Parker and his wife, Kellye, have two children and live in Cincinnati, where Parker was involved in commercial real estate. His hobbies include archery, photography, fishing, and bicycling. Commissioner Peter Ueberroth (OS) in February 1986, suspended Parker for one year for his involvement in drugs. Parker avoided the suspension by donating 10 percent of his salary to a drug rehabilitation program, contributing 100 hours of community service, and agreeing to periodic testing. He joined the St. Louis Cardinals (NL) as a coach in 1998.

BIBLIOGRAPHY: Joseph Dalton, "For Sale: Dave Parker," *Sport* 74 (October 1983), pp. 41–48; Jim O'Brien, "The Cobra Strikes Back," *Sport* 72 (June 1981), pp. 13–18; "Plutocrat from Pittsburgh," *Time* 113 (April 16, 1979), p. 88; *The Baseball Encyclopedia*, 10th ed. (New York, 1996); Derek A. Reveron, "Dave Parker: Big Man, Big Bat, and Baseball's Biggest Salary," *Ebony* 34 (October 1979), pp. 84–92; *TSN Official Baseball Register, 1992*; Dave Parker file, National Baseball Library, Cooperstown, NY; Robert E. Kelly, *Baseball's Best* (Jefferson, NC, 1988); B. Shapiro, "Sport Interview," *Sport* 77 (June 1986), pp. 15–18; Rick Weinberg, "One on One: Dave Parker," *Sport* 82 (August 1991), pp. 27–28; John Thom, *Champion Batsman of the 20th Century* (Los Angeles, CA, 1992); Richard L. Burtt, *The Pittsburgh Pirates: A Pictorial History* (Virginia Beach, VA, 1977); Bob Smizik, *The Pittsburgh Pirates An Illustrated History* (New York, 1990); Lou Sahidi, *The Pirates* (New York, 1980); *WWA*, 43rd ed. (1984–1985), p. 2,465.

Gaymon L. Bennett

PARNELL, Melvin Lloyd "Mel," "Dusty" (b. June 13, 1922, New Orleans, LA), player, scout, manager, executive, and sportscaster, is the second of two children of Patrick Louis Parnell, a machinist with the Illinois Central Railroad, and Anna Mae (Trauth) Parnell and is of Irish and German descent. Parnell, who played four years of varsity and American Legion baseball before graduating from Samuel J. Peters High School in New Orleans in 1941, began playing professional baseball with Owensboro, KY (KL) and Centreville, MD (ESL). After appearing in several games as an outfielder with

Canton, OH (MAL) in 1942, he made his mark as a pitcher. From 1942 to 1946, he served in the U.S. Army Air Corps and pitched Blytheville, AR to the regional military service championship. He compiled a 1.30 ERA in 21 games for Scranton, PA (EL) in 1946 and was promoted to the Boston Red Sox (AL) for the 1947 season, but finished the campaign with Louisville, KY (AA).

The stylish left-hander excelled as a starter for the Boston Red Sox in 1948, helping the Red Sox stay in the race until the season's last day. Although Parnell was ready to pitch the AL playoff game against the Cleveland Indians, manager Joe McCarthy* started Denny Galehouse instead. In 1949, his 25 wins, 27 complete games, and 295.1 innings pitched led the AL and again kept the Red Sox alive until the season's last game. Parnell also compiled a career-best 2.77 ERA. He recorded 18 victories in both 1950 and 1951 and 21 triumphs in 1953 despite pitching home contests in Fenway Park, which supposedly remains a graveyard for left-handers because of its short left field. The 6-foot, 180 pounder did not possess blazing speed, but jammed right-handed batters with inside sliders. He appeared in the 1949 and 1951 All-Star games.

Although hampered by an injury suffered in 1954, Parnell pitched a no-hitter against the Chicago White Sox (AL) on July 14, 1956. Offseason elbow surgery forced his retirement in 1957. He won 123 major league decisions to rank first among Red Sox left-handers, lost 75 contests, and compiled a career 3.50 ERA. In 1958, Parnell coached baseball at Tulane University. He served as general manager and manager of the New Orleans, LA Pelicans (SA) in 1959 and piloted Boston Red Sox farm teams at Alpine, TX (SpL) in 1961, York, PA (EL) in 1962, and Seattle, WA (PCL) in 1963. He scouted for the Boston Red Sox in 1960 and broadcast Red Sox games from 1965 through 1968. After handling Chicago White Sox broadcasts in 1969, he returned to New Orleans and operated a pest control business there. He married Velma Agnes Buras on October 25, 1947 and has four children.

BIBLIOGRAPHY: *The Baseball Encyclopedia*, 10th ed. (New York, 1996); David Halberstam, *Summer of '49* (New York, 1989); Lee Heiman, et al., *When the Cheering Stops* (New York, 1990); Brent P. Kelley, *The Early All-Stars* (Jefferson, NC, 1997); Dan Shaughnessy, *The Curse of the Bambino* (New York, 1990); Robert Redmount, *The Red Sox Encyclopedia* (Champaign, IL, 1998); Mel Parnell file, National Baseball Library, Cooperstown, NY; Mel Parnell, interview with Luther W. Spoehr, December 26, 1989; Rich Westcott, *Diamond Greats* (Westport, CT, 1988); Howard Liss, *The Boston Red Sox* (New York, 1982); Peter Golenbock, *Fenway* (New York, 1992).
                                                                Luther W. Spoehr

PARRISH, Lance Michael (b. June 15, 1956, Clairton, PA), player and coach, starred as the outstanding major league catcher in the mid-1980s. A football All-America and star baseball third baseman at Walnut High School in California, the right-handed-batting and -throwing Parrish declined a UCLA football scholarship. The Detroit Tigers (AL) selected him in the first round of the June 1974 draft and signed Parrish. After spending a season as a third baseman with Bristol, VA (ApL), he switched to catching with Lakeland, FL (FSL) in 1975 and led the SL in 1976 and AA in 1977 in fielding average. An All-Star with Evansville, IN (AA) in 1977, he was promoted to the Detroit Tigers in September.

The 6-foot 3-inch, 210-pound Parrish remained with the Detroit Tigers through 1986, winning three Gold Gloves (1983–1985) and six AL All-Star selections (1980, 1982–1986). From 1982 through 1985, he averaged 30 HR and 99 RBI per year. Parrish, one of the keys to the Detroit Tigers' 1984 world championship, blasted HR in the first game of their AL Championship Series sweep of the Kansas City Royals and in the decisive fifth game of their World Series triumph against the San Diego Padres. During these years, his on-the-field performance and bulging biceps made him a special favorite of female Tiger fans.

Parrish, however, in 1986 suffered a back injury, which dogged him for the rest of his major league career. Since the Detroit Tigers were unwilling to assume the risk of the long-term contract that free agent Parrish wanted, he signed with the Philadelphia Phillies (NL) in March 1987. He endured two subpar seasons with Philadelphia and was traded to the California Angels (AL) in October 1988. Parrish regained his earlier form in 1990, when he batted .268 with 24 HR and led AL catchers in percentage of runners caught stealing. He finished the 1992 season with the Seattle Mariners (AL) and split the 1993 campaign between Albuquerque, NM (PCL) and the Cleveland Indians (AL). In February 1994, the Detroit Tigers signed Parrish to a minor league contract. Parrish finished the strike-shortened 1994 season with the Pittsburgh Pirates (NL). His major league career ended with the Toronto Blue Jays (AL) in 1995. His 18-year major league career featured a .252 batting average, 324 HR, 1,070 RBI, a .991 fielding average, and eight All-Star selections (1980, 1982–1986, 1988, 1990).

Parrish coached for the Detroit Tigers in 1999. The Yorba Linda, CA, resident, who married Arlyne Nolan, has three children, David, Matthew, and Ashley Lyne.

BIBLIOGRAPHY: Lance Parrish file, National Baseball Library, Cooperstown, NY; *Detroit Tiger Media Guides*, 1978–1986; Robert E. Kelley, *Baseball's Best* (Jefferson, NC, 1988); John Thorn et al., eds., *Total Baseball*, 5th ed. (New York, 1997); *TSN Official Baseball Register*, 1996; Fred Smith, *995 Tigers* (Detroit, MI, 1981); William M. Anderson, *The Detroit Tigers* (South Bend, IN, 1996); Sparky Anderson and Dan Ewald, *Bless You Boys* (Chicago, IL, 1984); Sparky Anderson and Dan Ewald, *Sparky* (New York, 1990); Richard Bak, *A Place for Summer* (Detroit, MI, 1998); Rich Westcott and Frank Bilovsky, *The New Phillies Encyclopedia* (Philadelphia, PA, 1993).

Sheldon L. Appleton

PARRISH, Larry Alton "Gov" (b. November 10, 1953, Winter Haven, FL), player, coach, and manager, is the son of Alton Parrish and Sara (Ennis)

Parrish. His father, a construction worker, helped design the Boston Red Sox (AL) spring-training complex in Winter Haven, FL. Parrish began his professional baseball career with West Palm Beach, FL (FSL) in 1972, joining the Montreal Expos (NL) in 1974. The 6-foot 3-inch, 190–200–pound Parrish batted .274 as the Montreal Expos' starting third baseman in 1975, but slumped to .232 and .246 the following two seasons. Montreal fans so thoroughly booed him that he wanted to be traded. After being coached that winter in Venezuela by Ozzie Virgil, he improved to .277 in 1977 and .307 with 30 HR in 1978.

The Montreal Expos traded Parrish and Dave Hostetler to the Texas Rangers (AL) in March 1982 for Al Oliver.* Parrish clouted over 20 HR four times and drove in 100 runs twice with the Rangers, recording season highs of 32 HR in 1987 and 101 RBI in 1984. Parrish belted three HR in a game four times, a mark matched or exceeded by only five other players. Slugger Lou Gehrig* also enjoyed three three-HR games and one four-HR game. Parrish finished his major league career with the Boston Red Sox (AL) in 1988. His lifetime record comprised 256 HR, 360 doubles (including 42 in 1984 and 39 in both 1978 and 1979), 992 RBI, and a .263 batting average. He also performed as an outfielder and, especially after a 1985 knee injury, as a DH. An All-Star in 1979 and 1987, Parrish batted .150 in the 1981 Division playoff series against the Philadelphia Phillies with one double and one RBI and .263 in the NL Championship Series against the Los Angeles Dodgers with two doubles and two RBI. He went hitless for the Boston Red Sox in the 1988 AL Championship Series against the Oakland A's.

Parrish married Jessica Wensink, on May 15, 1980. They have one child, Jessica, and reside in Niagara Falls, NY. He coached in the Detroit Tigers (AL) organization from 1992 to 1996 and was promoted to the major league club in 1997. He replaced Buddy Bell* as manager in September 1998, guiding the Detroit Tigers to a 13–12 win–loss record. Parrish managed the Tigers to a 69–92 record in 1999 and was fired that October.

BIBLIOGRAPHY: Larry Parrish file, National Baseball Library, Cooperstown, NY; Mark Whicker, "How Expos' Larry Parrish Silenced His Critics," *BD* 39 (February 1980), pp. 70–73; Mike Shatzkin, ed., *The Ballplayers* (New York, 1990); John Thorn et al., eds., *Total Baseball*, 5th ed. (New York, 1997); *WWIB*, 1988, 73rd ed.; Jeanne McClow, ed., *A Baseball Century* (New York, 1976); Dan Turner, *The Expos Inside Out* (Toronto, Canada, 1983); Phil Rogers, *The Impossible Takes a Little Longer* (Dallas, TX, 1991).

                                                                                          Victor Rosenberg

PASCUAL, Camilo Alberto y Lus "Little Potato" (b. January 20, 1934, Havana, Cuba), player and scout, is one of three children born to Camilo Pascual and Maria Pascual and started playing organized baseball at age 12 as a shortstop and pitcher. In 1951, the Washington Senators (AL) signed him to a professional baseball contract as a pitcher. In his first season, Pascual divided his time between Geneva, NY (BL), Big Springs, TX (LL), and

Chickasha, OK (SSL) and compiled five wins and four losses. The 1952 campaign found the right-hander beginning the year in Havana, Cuba (FIL), but a midseason trade sent him to Tampa, FL (FIL). He finished the 1952 season with eight wins and six losses. Pascual returned in 1953 to Havana, Cuba (FIL), where he recorded 10 wins and six losses.

The 5-foot 11-inch, 175-pound curveballer joined the Washington Senators (AL) in 1954, the first of 18 consecutive major league seasons. From 1954 to 1960, Pascual compiled a 57–84 win–loss record with 10 saves in 248 games. He pitched 1,180.2 innings during that span, striking out 891 batters, completing 47 games, and hurling 13 shutouts. He led the AL in complete games (17) and shutouts (6) in 1959.

In 1961, the Washington Senators became the Minnesota Twins (AL). For the next six seasons, Pascual anchored the Minnesota Twins' starting rotation. Over this period, he took the mound in 184 games, pitched in 1,284.2 innings, completed 72 contests, hurled 18 shutouts, struck out 994 batters, and walked only 431. Pascual led the AL in strikeouts in 1961 (221), 1962 (206), and 1963 (202), shutouts in 1961 (8) and 1962 (5), and complete games in 1962 (18) and 1963 (18). His best season came in 1963, when he finished 21–9 with a 2.46 ERA. In 248.1 innings that season, he struck out 202 batters while walking only 81, completed 18 of 31 starts, and shut out opponents three times. In the 1965 World Series against the Los Angeles Dodgers (NL), Pascual lost his only start. He made four All-Star teams (1961, 1962 twice, 1964), losing the first 1962 contest at Washington.

His last five major league seasons were spent with four different clubs, including the Washington Senators (AL) from 1967 to 1969, Cincinnati Reds (NL) in 1969, Los Angeles Dodgers (NL) in 1970, and Cleveland Indians (AL) in 1971. During 18 major league seasons, Pascual won 174 games, lost 170, and produced 36 shutouts with a career 3.63 ERA. In 2,930.2 innings, he struck out 2,167 batters while walking 1,069. At the plate, Pascual batted .205 in 967 plate appearances with five HR. Although considered one of the best fielding pitchers, he was overshadowed by Gold Glove teammate Jim Kaat.*

Pascual scouts in Latin America for the Los Angeles Dodgers and lives in Miami, FL with his wife, Rachel. They have two sons and two daughters.

BIBLIOGRAPHY: Camilo Pascual file, National Baseball Library, Cooperstown, NY; *The Baseball Encyclopedia*, 10th ed. (New York, 1996); *Minnesota Twins Yearbooks*, 1961–1966; James E. Welch, phone conversation with Camilo Pascual, January 1993; Rich Westcott, *Diamond Greats* (Westport, CT, 1988); Dave Moina and Dave Jarzyna, *Twenty-five Seasons* (Minneapolis, MN, 1986); Ed Fitzgerald, ed. *The American League*, rev. ed. (New York, 1966).

James E. Welch

PASKERT, George Henry "Dode" (b. August 28, 1881, Cleveland, OH; d. February 12, 1959, Cleveland, OH), player, was the son of Bernard Paskert, an iron molder and German immigrant, and Annie Paskert, of Dutch parentage, and attended St. Stephen's School in Cleveland for 12 years. Paskert, who played baseball on local sandlots and worked as a laborer, married Emily Belle DeKalb in September 1902 and had one son, Arthur.

Paskert entered organized baseball in 1904 with the Dayton, OH Triangles (CL). After playing regularly in the Dayton outfield for three seasons, he batted .289 for the Atlanta, GA Crackers (SL) in 1907. The Cincinnati Reds (NL) purchased him following the SL season. He hit .280 in 16 contests for the Cincinnati Reds in 1907 and played three more seasons there. In a February 1911 eight-player transaction, the Cincinnati Reds traded him to the Philadelphia Phillies (NL). An extraordinary defensive player, the 5-foot 11-inch, 167-pound Paskert patrolled center field for seven seasons there.

In December 1917, the Philadelphia Phillies traded Paskert to the Chicago Cubs (NL) for outfielder Fred "Cy" Williams.* The trade benefited the Phillies, as Williams starred for a decade with Philadelphia. After Paskert spent 1918 through 1920 with Chicago, the Cubs waived Paskert to the Cincinnati Reds in February 1921. The Cincinnati Reds released him three months later. He remained a capable regular outfielder in his forties with the Kansas City, MO Blues (AA) in 1921, Columbus, OH Senators (AA) in 1922 and 1923, and Nashville, TN Volunteers (SL) and Atlanta, GA Crackers (SL) in 1924. Subsequently, he worked many years as a machine operator in Cleveland, OH.

The speedy, durable Paskert, who batted and threw right-handed, hit .268 with 1,613 hits, 868 runs, and 293 stolen bases during 15 major league seasons. He led NL outfielders in fielding percentage (.984) in 1917 and played in the 1915 and 1918 World Series against the Boston Red Sox. Although a good hitter and base runner, he made outstanding defensive accomplishments with sure hands, a strong arm, and exceptional range. Authorities observed, "He excels (Amos) Strunk* in going back after the long ones over his head, he is better than (Tris) Speaker* in going to his left, and he can go further than (Ty) Cobb* in any direction."

BIBLIOGRAPHY: Lee Allen, *The Cincinnati Reds* (New York, 1948); Eddie Gold and Art Ahrens, *The Golden Era Cubs, 1876–1940* (Chicago, IL, 1985); Frederick G. Lieb and Stan Baumgartner, *The Philadelphia Phillies* (New York, 1953); Rich Westcott and Frank Bilovsky, *The New Phillies Encyclopedia* (Philadelphia, PA, 1993); Warren Brown, *The Chicago Cubs* (New York, 1996); "Dode Paskert Dies at 77," *TSN*, February 25, 1959; George Paskert file, National Baseball Library, Cooperstown, NY; Cleveland (OH) *Plain Dealer*, February 13, 1959; John Thorn et al., eds., *Total Baseball*, 5th ed. (New York, 1997); "Time Does Not Dim Him," *TSN*, January 17, 1918.
                                                                            Frank V. Phelps

PASSEAU, Claude William (b. April 9, 1909, Waynesboro, MS), player, graduated with a bachelor's degree from Millsaps College in 1932, pitched four seasons in the minor leagues with eight teams altogether, and joined the Pittsburgh Pirates (NL) in 1935 for one game. The Pirates traded him in November 1935 to the Philadelphia Phillies (NL), where he enjoyed several good seasons with 38 wins for a losing club. In May 1939, the 6-foot 3-inch, 198-pound Passeau joined the Chicago Cubs (NL) and emerged as a star. A power pitcher early in his career, he led the NL in strikeouts with 137 in 1939 and won a career-high 20 games in 1940.

He finished with a 17–9 win–loss record for the 1945 champion Chicago Cubs and pitched a memorable World Series contest against the Detroit Tigers. His one-hitter on October 5 saw him face only 28 Tiger batters, as the Cubs won 3–0. The often-injured Passeau was hurt in his next appearance, and the Cubs eventually lost the World Series. He endured pain on numerous occasions, hurling for the entire 1945 season with bone chips in his elbow. Nevertheless, he still won 124 games for the Cubs before being released following the 1947 season.

Passeau, a remarkable fielder, handled 273 chances without an error from September 1941 to May 1946. He also demonstrated some offensive power, belting 15 career HR and batting .282 in 1936. Flouting superstition, he wore uniform number 13 throughout his career and believed it to be "my lucky number." He was involved in two memorable brawls with Leo Durocher*–managed Brooklyn Dodger teams, including a July 19, 1940 free-for-all at Wrigley Field in Chicago. Passeau finished 188 of his 331 starts and enjoyed pitching in his home stadium, something many pitchers would not claim. His career 162–150 win–loss record included a 3.32 ERA in 444 games. Passeau married Agnes B. Spofford on November 1, 1938 and resides in Lucedale, MS.

BIBLIOGRAPHY: Claude Passeau file, National Baseball Library, Cooperstown, NY; Warren Brown, *The Chicago Cubs* (New York, 1946); Jim Enright, *Chicago Cubs* (New York, 1975); Warren Wilbert and William Hageman, *Chicago Cubs: Seasons at the Summit* (Champaign, IL, 1997); Art Ahrens and Eddie Gold, *Day by Day in Chicago Cubs History* (West Point, NY, 1982); *The Baseball Encyclopedia*, 10th ed. (New York, 1996); Eddie Gold and Art Ahrens, *The New Era Cubs, 1941–1985* (Chicago, IL; 1985).

Duane A. Smith

PATTERSON, Andrew Lawrence "Pat" (b. December 19, 1911, Chicago, IL; d. May 1984, Houston, TX), player, graduated from Wiley College in Marshall, TX, where he starred in both football and baseball. He chose Wiley over NYU because he wanted to play baseball more than any other sport. Patterson performed for nearly 16 Negro League seasons from 1934 to 1949. The versatile Patterson played shortstop, second base, third base, and the outfield in an era when Negro League clubs fielded as few as 14 players.

Patterson appeared in four East-West All Star games, achieving a .300 batting average. His baseball career began in 1934 with the Pennsylvania

Red Caps of New York, Cleveland Red Sox (NNL), and Homestead, PA Grays (NNL). Patterson batted .346 to help the Pittsburgh Crawfords win the 1935 NNL championship. He also starred for the Kansas City, MO Monarchs (NAL) in 1936 and 1941, and the Philadelphia Stars (NNL) in 1938, 1939, 1941, and 1942. After serving a three-year military stint during World War II, Patterson played for the champion Newark, NJ Eagles (NNL) in 1946 and 1947. His playing career ended with the Houston, TX Eagles (NNL) in 1949. He also played numerous winters throughout Latin America, marrying his wife, Gladys, while in Mexico.

Patterson later resided in Houston, where he taught, coached, and served as an athletic director and superintendent of schools. He became the first black coach selected for the Texas Coaches Hall of Fame, honoring his work with black schools in Houston. Patterson's teammates and opponents described him as a good contact hitter with a little power, good speed, and better than average fielding.

BIBLIOGRAPHY: James A. Riley, *The Biographical Encyclopedia of the Negro Leagues* (New York, 1994); Donn Rogosin, *Invisible Men* (New York, 1983); James Bankes, *The Pittsburgh Crawfords* (Dubuque, IA, 1991); Janet Bruce, *The Kansas City Monarchs* (Lawrence, KS, 1985).

Leslie Heaphy

PAUL, Gabriel Howard, Sr. "Gabe" (b. January 4, 1910, Rochester, NY; d. April 26, 1998, Tampa, FL), baseball executive and sportswriter, was one of ten children born to tailor Morris Paul and Cecelia (Snyder) Paul and played sandlot baseball. In 1924, he became batboy for the Rochester, NY Red Wings (IL), St. Louis Cardinals farm club. Two years later, Paul began reporting local sports for the Rochester (NY) *Democrat & Chronicle*. Warren Giles* hired Paul as Rochester Red Wings publicity director in 1928 and promoted him to road secretary in 1934. Paul married Mary Frances Copps on April 17, 1935 and had four sons and one daughter. His eldest son, Gabe, Jr., serves as vice president of stadium operations for the Milwaukee Brewers (NL).

In 1937, Giles joined the Cincinnati Reds (NL) and designated Paul publicity director. Paul then served as traveling secretary (1938–1948) except for a stint in the U.S. Army in World War II, assistant to the president (1948–1949) and vice-president (1949). When Giles became NL president in 1950, Paul was named Cincinnati club president. Paul presided over the Cincinnati organization for a decade, making 86 separate trades in a continuing effort to improve a mediocre team. Cincinnati's best year came in 1956 with a third place finish, when Paul was selected Major League Executive of the Year, Birdie Tebbetts* was named Manager of the Year, and Frank Robinson* became Rookie of the Year. After 1956, however, Cincinnati slipped back into the second division. Paul opposed an attempt by owner Powel

Crosley, Jr.,* to move the club and resigned in October 1960. He became the first general manager of the Houston Colt .45s (NL) franchise, but was replaced by Paul Richards* in April 1961.

Paul joined the Cleveland Indians (AL) as general manager (1961–1963) and then served as president (1963–1972). Despite making 110 trades, however, the Indians remained mired in the second division. At Cleveland, Paul met local businessman George Steinbrenner.* After Cleveland owner Vernon Stouffer sold the Indians in 1972, Paul helped forge the group that bought the New York Yankees (AL) from CBS in 1973. After the ouster of a major partner in the new Yankee ownership, Paul became New York club president. Paul's years with the Yankees proved both turbulent and fruitful. The turbulence stemmed from primary owner George Steinbrenner's personal involvement in the daily operation of the organization even though he knew little about baseball and his desire to improve the team by seeking high-priced talent to remain competitive with the New York Mets for both media attention and the fans' dollars.

During these fruitful years, New York bought top quality players. Paul, however, could not make any deal without Steinbrenner's approval, which he did not always receive. Nevertheless, Paul acquired several excellent players, including Chris Chambliss,* Willie Randolph,* Oscar Gamble,* Bucky Dent, and Mickey Rivers* through trades and also signed Reggie Jackson,* Jim Hunter,* and others through free agency. Paul was named Major League Executive of the Year in 1974 and received other honors in 1975 and 1976. Paul's reconstructed team won AL pennants from 1976 through 1978 and the World Series the latter two years. By December 1977, however, Paul resigned in a dispute over Steinbrenner's handling of volatile Billy Martin.*

Paul immediately was hired as president of the Cleveland Indians (AL), where he completed his major league career. Again he turned to trades to construct a contender, but was hampered by the organization's relative poverty. Paul made 68 trades between 1978 and 1984, with 21 of the club's 40-man 1982 roster being through trade or acquisition. Only two players in Cleveland's 1984 opening day lineup had belonged to the 1982 squad. By Paul's retirement in 1984, the Indians had acquired a core of good, young players and provided a base upon which others would build. Paul, the traditional baseball executive, spent his adult career with four major league franchises. He made over 500 trades and also changed with the times. He showed at New York and Cleveland that he would seek talent through free agency, but undoubtedly preferred the wheeling and dealing of the preferred agency era. He served on the Cleveland Indians Board of Directors through 1986 and resided with his wife in Tampa, FL.

BIBLIOGRAPHY: Gabe Paul file, National Baseball Library, Cooperstown, NY; *Cleveland Indians Press-Radio TV Guide*, 1978–1984; *Cleveland Indians Yearbook*, 1979; Alvin Dark and John Underwood, *When in Doubt, Fire the Manager* (New York, 1980); Mark Gallagher, *The Yankee Encyclopedia*, vol. 3 (Champaign, IL, 1997); Jack Torry,

Endless Summers (South Bend, IN, 1995); Terry Pluto, *The Curse of Rocky Colavito* (New York, 1994); Sparky Lyle and Peter Golenbock, *The Bronx Zoo* (New York, 1979); Billy Martin and Peter Golenbock, *Number One* (New York, 1980); Douglas D. Martin, telephone interview with Gabriel Paul, Jr., June 1985; Graig Nettles and Peter Golenbock, *Balls* (New York, 1984); *NYT*, April 28, 1998, p. B7; Joseph L. Reichler, ed., *The Baseball Trade Register* (New York, 1984); Dick Schaap, *Steinbrenner!* (New York, 1982).

Douglas D. Martin

PAVESKOVICH, John Michael. *See* John Michael Pesky.

PAYKOS, John Quinn. *See* John Picus Quinn.

PEARCE, Richard J. "Dickey" (b. February 29, 1836, Brooklyn, NY; d. October 12, 1908, Wareham, MA), player, manager, and umpire, was the son of William Pearce and Louisa Pearce and began playing in Brooklyn. Although only 5-feet 3½-inches and 161 pounds, Pearce ranked among his era's greatest professional baseball players. From the 1850s through the mid–1870s, Pearce played shortstop primarily for the Brooklyn Atlantics (1856–1870, 1873–1874), New York Mutuals (1871–1872), and St. Louis Brown Stockings (1875–1877). Pearce averaged .254 and made 308 hits in 258 games for the 1871–1875 NA seasons. In the NA, he managed New York to a 10–6 record in 1872 and St. Louis to a 39–29 mark in 1875. Although playing as early as 1856 for the Brooklyn Atlantics, he first gained attention in the 1858 series between the Brooklyn and New York "match" nines. A participant in two of the three games at shortstop, he scored seven runs for Brooklyn and was credited with playing "remarkably well." Throughout the next decade, he generally batted first and played various positions. Pearce caught, played shortstop and right field, and even pitched occasionally for the powerhouse Brooklyn team. A reporter noted that he showed "pluck in facing hot balls." The veteran had appeared in over 200 games by 1870 and scored 907 runs for the Atlantics.

Even in losing efforts, Pearce was recognized for his distinguished play. The *NYT* (July 20, 1860) credited him "for some good play as catcher and at short," although his team lost, 23–4. A decade later, he played an instrumental part in ending the long two-season 78-game winning streak of the Cincinnati Red Stockings. When the Atlantics beat the Red Stockings, 8–7, in 11 innings, Pearce earned praise for his "work" and his adept base running in scoring the tying run. In five NA seasons, he batted .257 with 308 hits and 123 RBI. Pearce, who married, ended his long playing career with St. Louis (NL) in 1876 and 1877, hitting only .198 for 33 games. Pearce invented the "fair-foul" hit by artfully striking the ball down and "blocking it in front of the home base, from which point it bounded off into foul ground." This type of hit was abolished in 1876, probably helping to end his career. Following his retirement, Pearce umpired until at least the late 1880s.

BIBLIOGRAPHY: Richard Pearce file, National Baseball Library, Cooperstown, NY; Henry Chadwick Scrapbooks, Albert Spalding Collection, New York Public Library, New York, NY; *Base Ball Player*, 1861–1877; *NYT*, 1858–1877; Preston Orem, *Baseball, 1845–1881* (Altadena, CA, 1961); Harry C. Palmer et al., *Athletic Sports in America, England and Australia* (Philadelphia, PA, 1889); Duane A. Smith, "Dickey Pearce," *TNP* 10 (1990), pp. 38–42; Robert L. Tiemann and Mark Rucker, eds., *Nineteenth Century Stars* (Kansas City, MO, 1989); William Ryczek, *Blackguards and Red Stockings* (Jefferson, NC, 1992); William J. Ryczek, *When Johnny Came Sliding Home* (Jefferson, NC, 1998); David Quentin Voigt, *American Baseball*, vol. 1 (Norman, OK, 1966).

Duane A. Smith

PEARSON, Montgomery Marcellus "Monte" (b. September 2, 1909, Oakland, CA; d. January 27, 1978, Fresno, CA), player, began his baseball career as a catcher and third baseman at Fresno High School. The four-sport letterman, who possessed a strong arm, soon became a pitcher. Following scholastic baseball, Pearson spent 1929 with Bakersfield, CA (CaSL). He signed a contract with the Oakland, CA Oaks (PCL) and was optioned to Phoenix, AZ (ArSL) in 1930. By 1931, he joined Oakland's regular rotation with 17 wins and 16 losses. The Cleveland Indians (AL) soon purchased the contract of the 6-foot, 170-pound right-hander with the sharp-breaking curve ball. After performing poorly for the Cleveland Indians in early 1932, Pearson was shipped to Toledo, OH (AA) and struggled through a 3–9 season. In 1933, he rebounded with 11 wins and five losses for the Toledo Mud Hens. He performed even more impressively after the Cleveland Indians recalled him in early July, finishing 10–5 and leading the AL with a 2.33 ERA. Pearson improved to 18–13 despite a 4.52 ERA in 1934 before collapsing to 8–13 in 1935. The Cleveland Indian management, concluding that Pearson would probably never fulfill his considerable potential, traded him with pitcher Steve Sundra in December 1935 to the New York Yankees (AL) for the fiery righthander Johnny Allen.*

Pearson regained his form with the World Champion New York Yankees, leading the AL in winning percentage in 1936 with a 19–7 record and recording 9–3, 16–7, and 12–5 marks for the 1937–1939 seasons. In a July 15, 1940 contest against the Cleveland Indians' Bob Feller,* he suffered a career-shortening torn shoulder ligament. The Cincinnati Reds (NL) obtained Pearson on waivers that December. Pearson retired after a disappointing 1–3 effort in 1941. In 10 major league seasons, he compiled a 100–61 record with a .621 winning percentage, 94 complete games in 191 starts, and a 4.00 ERA.

Pearson hurled a 13–0 no-hitter against the Cleveland Indians on August 27, 1938 and won World Series games four consecutive years from 1936 to

1939. His 1936 World Series victory over left-handed great Carl Hubbell* of the New York Giants in Game 4 stopped the latter's consecutive win streak at 17. In those four seasons, Pearson pitched as effectively as New York Yankee Hall of Fame aces Charles "Red" Ruffing* and Vernon "Lefty" Gomez.*

Pearson married Cleo Wimer of Fresno, CA in January 1931. They had two children, Wesley and Anita May. His second wife, Nellie, provided him with a son, Larry. Pearson's life after baseball brought difficulty. In 1962, as chief sanitation engineer for Madera, CA, he was convicted for accepting a bribe. He then faced a lengthy fatal battle with cancer.

BIBLIOGRAPHY: Cleveland (OH) *Plain Dealer*, March 30, 1935, October 5, 1939, December 30, 1940, November 10, 1962, January 28, 1978; Fresno (CA) *Bee*, January 28, 1939; *SL* clipping file, courtesy of archivist Steve Gietschier, *TSN*, St. Louis, MO; Monte Pearson file, National Baseball Library, Cooperstown, NY; Franklin Lewis, *The Cleveland Indians* (New York, 1949); Frank Graham, *The New York Yankees* (New York, 1943); Dave Anderson et al., *The Yankees* (New York, 1979); Mark Gallagher, *The Yankee Encyclopedia*, vol. 3 (New York, 1997); John Thorn et al., eds., *Total Baseball*, 5th ed. (New York, 1997).

James N. Giglio

PECKINPAUGH, Roger Thorpe (b. February 5, 1891, Wooster, OH; d. November 17, 1977, Cleveland, OH), player, manager, and executive, batted and threw right-handed. The 5-foot 10½-inch, 165-pound Peckinpaugh originally signed with the Cleveland Naps (AL) in 1910 and played shortstop for New Haven, CT (EL) that year and Portland, OR (NWL) in 1911. He performed for the Cleveland Naps in 1912 and the New York Highlanders (AL) from 1913 through 1921. In December 1921 New York traded him to the Boston Red Sox (AL), who sent him three weeks later to the Washington Senators (AL). Peckinpaugh enjoyed his most productive years from 1922 through 1926 with the Washington Senators and ended his playing career with the Chicago White Sox (AL) in 1927.

An outstanding fielder, Peckinpaugh batted .259 lifetime with 1,876 hits and 739 RBI. He compiled a 10–10 win–loss mark as New York Highlander manager in September 1914 after Frank Chance* was fired, making the 23-year-old Peckinpaugh the youngest pilot of a major league team. Peckinpaugh's shortstop skills helped Washington win AL pennants in 1924 and 1925. The Senators captured their only World Series in 1924, defeating the New York Giants in seven games. Peckinpaugh's .417 batting average paced Washington. Peckinpaugh experienced a disastrous World Series, however, in 1925 against the Pittsburgh Pirates. The AL announced Peckinpaugh as its MVP before the fall classic started, but he made eight errors defensively. His errors in the second and seventh games contributed directly to Washington losses. Although his HR in the seventh game gave the Senators a temporary lead, he emerged as the goat of the World Series. Thereafter, MVP awards always were announced after completion of the World Series.

From 1928 through 1933, Peckinpaugh managed the Cleveland Indians (AL) to a 415–402 win–loss mark. He held several minor league managerial and front office positions and worked for the AL front office. In 1941, he returned to the Cleveland Indians as manager and compiled a 75–79 mark. Peckinpaugh's clubs finished 500–491 in his eight seasons as a major league manager. In 1942, he joined the Indians' front office as vice-president and general manager. His baseball career ended with Buffalo, NY (IL) as general manager in 1947. Peckinpaugh married Mildred Stidger on February 22, 1911 and had four sons Roger, Jr., Walter, Ralph, and John.

BIBLIOGRAPHY: Thomas Aylesworth and Benton Minks, *The Encyclopedia of Baseball Managers* (New York, 1990); Frank Graham, *The New York Yankees* (New York, 1943); Mark Gallagher, *The Yankee Encyclopedia*, vol. 3 (Champaign, IL, 1997); Morris Bealle, *The Washington Senators* (Washington, DC, 1947); Shirley Povich, *The Washington Senators* (New York, 1954); Henry W. Thomas, *Walter Johnson* (Washington, DC, 1995); Franklin Lewis, *The Cleveland Indians* (New York, 1949); *The Baseball Encyclopedia*, 10th ed. (New York, 1996); Donald Honig, *The Man in the Dugout* (Lincoln, NE, 1995); Gene Karst and Martin J. Jones, Jr., *Who's Who in Professional Baseball* (New Rochelle, NY, 1973); Roger Peckinpaugh file, National Baseball Library, Cooperstown, NY; Joseph L. Reichler, ed., *The Great All-Time Baseball Record Book* (New York, 1981).

Horace R. Givens

PEÑA, Antonio Francisco Padilla "Tony" (b. June 4, 1957, Monte Christi, DR), player and manager, is the son of Octaviano Peña and Rosalio Padilla. His brother Arturo played in the Pittsburgh Pirates (NL) farm system, while Ramon, another brother, pitched for the Detroit Tigers (AL) in 1989. Peña attended Liceo-Marti High School in Monte Christi and learned baseball from his mother, an outstanding softball player. As a child, Peña idolized major league catchers Manny Sanguillen* and Johnny Bench.* The Pittsburgh Pirates (NL) signed Peña as a free agent and used him as a catcher in their minor league system from 1976 to 1978, but he struggled at the plate. Peña, however, slugged 34 HR and batted .313 at Buffalo, NY (EL) in 1979 and followed with a .327 batting average at Portland, OR (PCL) the next season.

Peña shared catching chores with Pittsburgh Pirate Steve Nicosia in 1981, but his .300 batting average and strong defense won him full-time duties behind the plate. From 1982 to 1986, Peña batted .285, hit at least 10 HR each year, and demonstrated good speed on the bases. His catching position of almost sitting with one leg thrust out enabled him to block the plate very effectively. Despite the unusual receiving stance, Peña threw out even the best base stealers with his quick release and rifle arm.

St. Louis Cardinals (NL) manager Whitey Herzog* believed he could win an NL pennant in 1987 if he could acquire a solid catcher. In April 1987, the Cardinals traded center fielder Andy Van Slyke,* catcher Mike La-Valliere, and pitcher Mike Dunne to the Pittsburgh Pirates for Peña. A few games into the 1987 season, Peña broke his thumb and spent six weeks on the disabled list. Although hitting only .214 for the campaign, he started wearing glasses late in the season and batted .381 in the NL Championship Series against the San Francisco Giants and .409 in the World Series versus the Minnesota Twins. Peña led the NL in fielding average in 1988 and 1989. The Cardinals did not resign the five-time NL All-Star in 1990 because youthful catchers Todd Zeile and Tom Pagnozzi were ready for the major leagues.

Peña signed a $6.4 million, three-year contract with the Boston Red Sox (AL). After a productive offensive 1990 season, he batted only .231 in 1991 and .241 in 1992. He won a fourth Gold Glove in 1991, however, and remained a good handler of pitchers. Peña signed a one-year, $2.5 million contract to stay in Boston for 1993, but batted only .181 that year. The Boston Red Sox released him following the 1993 season. In February 1994, the Cleveland Indians (AL) signed Peña, who batted .295 in 40 games. Pena clouted a HR in the 1995 AL Division Series against the Boston Red Sox and batted .333 in the AL Championship Series against the Seattle Mariners, but made only one hit against the Atlanta Braves in the World Series. His final season with the Cleveland Indians came in 1996. He retired after splitting the 1997 season between the Chicago White Sox (AL) and Houston Astros (NL).

In 18 major league seasons, Pena batted .260 with 107 HR and 708 RBI. He managed the New Orleans Zephyrs (PCL) in 1999. Peña married Amaris Garcia on January 7, 1976. They have two children, Tony, Jr., and Jennifer, and reside in Santiago, DR, where his family has a farm.

BIBLIOGRAPHY: John Dewan, ed., *The Scouting Report: 1990* (New York, 1990); Zander Hollander, ed., *The Complete Book of Baseball 1994* (New York, 1994); Kip Ingle and Brian Bartow, *The St. Louis Cardinals Media Guide 1988* (St. Louis, MO, 1988); Larry Moffi and Jonathan Kronstadt, *Crossing the Line* (Jefferson, NC, 1994); Antonio Peña file, National Baseball Library, Cooperstown, NY; Bob Smizik, *The Pittsburgh Pirates: An Illustrated History* (New York, 1990); Rob Rains, *The St. Louis Cardinals* (New York, 1992); Bob Broeg and Jerry Vickery, *St. Louis Cardinals Encyclopedia* (Grand Rapids, MI, 1998); Robert Redmount, *The Red Sox Encyclopedia* (Champaign, IL, 1998); Russell Schneider, *The Glorious Indian Summer of 1995* (Cleveland, OH, 1996); George Vass, "Major Leagues Facing a Crisis in Catching," *BD* 49 (July 1990), pp. 20–24.

Frank J. Olmsted

PENDLETON, Terry Lee (b. July 16, 1960, Los Angeles, CA), player, graduated from Channel Island High School in Oxnard, CA, where he lettered in baseball, football, and basketball. He majored in physical education at Oxnard College and Fresno State College. As a senior at Fresno State, Pendleton played the outfield, batted .397, and collected 65 RBI. The St. Louis Cardinals (NL) selected Pendleton in the seventh round of the June 1982 draft. The 5-foot 9-inch, 193-pound, right-handed Pendleton played second base at Johnson City, TN (ApL) and St. Petersburg, FL (FSL) in 1982. In 1983, a fractured wrist limited him at Little Rock–based Arkansas (TL). The switch-hitting Pendleton moved to third base at Louisville, KY (AA) in 1984 and batted .297 in 91 games before the St. Louis Cardinals purchased his contract. Pendleton made 65 consecutive starts at third base for the St. Louis Cardinals, enjoying 24 multiple hit games and batting .324. In 1985, Pendleton hit just .240 with only 24 extra base hits. He batted .208 in the triumphant NL Championship Series against the Los Angeles Dodgers and .261 in the World Series, which the St. Louis Cardinals lost in seven games to the Kansas City Royals.

Pendleton's 1986 season proved a carbon copy of the 1985 campaign. Pitchers knew Pendleton swung freely and pitched him out of the strike zone. His .239 batting average included only one HR. Despite a short, stocky physique, Pendleton showed tremendous range at third base and worked hard to improve his glove work. In 1985 and 1986, Pendleton came to the ball park every afternoon to field 100 extra ground balls. From 1986 to 1992, Pendleton led NL third basemen five times in assists, twice in putouts, and once in fielding percentage and earned three Gold Gloves. His over-the-shoulder catches while running away from home plate were remarkable.

Pendleton's best season with the St. Louis Cardinals came in 1987, when he batted .286 with 12 HR and 96 RBI. He collected four hits against the San Francisco Giants in the NL Championship Series, but a pulled ribcage muscle limited him to three games as a pinch hitter and DH in the World Series. The St. Louis Cardinals lost the fall classic in seven games to the Minnesota Twins. Hamstring and knee injuries limited Pendleton's 1988 campaign to 110 games and a .253 batting average. He rebounded in 1989 to play 162 games and hit .264. Pendleton never got on track in 1990, as the St. Louis Cardinals tried catcher Todd Zeile at third base. Pendleton rode the bench in September, finishing with a .230 batting average.

The Atlanta Braves (NL) signed Pendleton in December 1990 to a four-year deal worth $10.2 million. Few players have made more dramatic turn-arounds. In 1991, Pendleton led the NL with 187 hits and a .319 batting average, solidifying the Atlanta Braves infield and being named NL MVP and Comeback Player of the Year. Although Pendleton batted only .167 in the NL Championship Series against the Pittsburgh Pirates, he hit .367 with two HR in the World Series. The Atlanta Braves, however, lost the fall classic in seven games to the Minnesota Twins. In 1992, Pendleton reached personal highs of 98 runs scored, 105 RBI, and 199 hits, batted .311, and played in his first All-Star Game. The Atlanta Braves won the NL West, again defeating the Pittsburgh Pirates for the NL pennant. Pendleton batted only .240 in the World Series, which the Toronto Blue Jays garnered in six games.

In 1993, Pendleton, who general manager John Schuerholz called "the cornerstone of the club," joined teammates in coming alive at midseason. Pendleton finished 1993 with a .272 batting average, 17 HR, and 84 RBI, helping Atlanta win a third consecutive NL West title. Pendleton was denied a fifth World Series appearance, though, when the Philadelphia Phillies overcame the Atlanta Braves in the NL Championship Series.

In April 1995, the Florida Marlins (NL) signed Pendleton as a free agent. He spent 1995 and 1996 with the Marlins until the Atlanta Braves (NL) reacquired him in August 1996. Pendleton appeared as a pinch hitter in the 1996 NL Division Series against the Los Angeles Dodgers and NL Championship Series against the St. Louis Cardinals and batted .222 in the World Series against the New York Yankees. After spending 1997 with the Cincinnati Reds (NL), he played in 1998 with the Kansas City Royals (AL). In December 1998, he retired from professional baseball.

In 15 major league seasons, Pendleton batted .270 with 851 runs, 1,897 hits, 140 HR, 946 RBI, and 127 stolen bases in 1,893 games. He married Catherine Grindulo Marguez in October 1984 and lives in Oxnard, CA.

BIBLIOGRAPHY: Terry Pendleton file, National Baseball Library, Cooperstown, NY; John Dewan, ed., *The Scouting Report: 1990* (New York, 1990); David Falkner, *Nine Sides of the Diamond* (New York, 1990); Zander Hollander, ed., *The Complete Handbook of Baseball, 1994* (New York, 1994); Larry Moffi and Jonathan Kronstadt, *Crossing the Line* (Jefferson, NC, 1994); Rob Rains, "Pendleton's Attitude Keeps Braves Sharp," *USAT Baseball Weekly*, September 16–22, 1993, p. 8; Rob Rains, *The St. Louis Cardinals* (New York, 1992); Bob Broeg and Jerry Vickery, *St. Louis Cardinals Encyclopedia* (Grand Rapids, MI, 1998); Gary Caruso, *The Braves Encyclopedia* (Philadelphia, PA, 1995); *St. Louis Cardinals 1990 Media Guide*; John Sonderegger, "Cardinals' Terry Pendleton Comes of Age as a Hitter," *BD* 46 (October 1987), pp. 42–45.

Frank J. Olmsted

PENNOCK, Herbert Jeffries "Herb," "The Knight of Kennett Square" (b. February 10, 1894, Kennett Square, PA; d. January 30, 1948, New York, NY), player, coach, and executive, attended a Friends' School in West Town, PA, Cedar Croft School, and Wenonah Military Academy. Pennock, who married Esther Freck of Kennett Square on October 28, 1915 and had two children, was an avid fox hunter and raised silver foxes on his farm. After Pennock pitched a no-hitter in 1911 with the Atlantic City, NJ Collegians, catcher Earle Mack persuaded his father, Philadelphia Athletics' manager Connie Mack,* to sign him. In 1912 the tall, slender 6-foot, 165-pound southpaw joined the Philadelphia Athletics (AL). Pennock was claimed on waivers by the Boston Red Sox (AL) in June 1915 and was traded to the New York Yankees (AL) in January 1923. He pitched with the Yankees through the 1933 season and spent his final campaign in 1934 with the

Boston Red Sox (AL). Nicknamed "The Knight of Kennett Square," Pennock exhibited a stylish, smooth, effortless delivery during his 22-year major league career. Besides his excellent curveball, he possessed masterful control and a baffling change of pace. In many games, he did not throw over one dozen fastballs.

Pennock compiled a 241–162 lifetime win–loss record in 617 major league games and toiled 3,571.2 innings. Elected to the National Baseball Hall of Fame in 1948, Pennock also recorded 35 shutouts, walked only 916 batters, and had a 3.60 ERA. From 1919 to 1923, the workhorse hurler appeared in over 30 games per season with the Red Sox. Although New York manager Miller Huggins* thought Pennock's best years were behind him, the Yankees acquired him in 1923 as a stopgap measure. The veteran southpaw became the ace of the Yankees staff, winning 115 games the next six seasons. Pennock compiled a 19–6 record for the best AL winning percentage (.760) in 1923 and made *TSN* Major League All-Star team in 1926. Manager Huggins called Pennock the greatest left-handed pitcher of all time. On July 5, 1925, he bested Lefty Grove* of the Athletics, 1–0, in 15 innings. Pennock faced the minimum 18 batters the first six innings and only 21 batters in the final seven frames.

Unbeatable in World Series competition, Pennock won two games each in the 1923 and 1926 fall classics and one contest in 1927 and posted an impressive 1.95 ERA in 10 games. In the 1927 World Series, Pennock no-hit the Pittsburgh Pirates for 7⅓ innings and eventually defeated the club, noted for hitting southpaws, by an 8–1 margin. Pennock later served as coach (1936–1940) and farm system supervisor (1941–1943) for the Boston Red Sox (AL) and as general manager of the Philadelphia Phillies (NL) from 1944 until his death.

BIBLIOGRAPHY: Herb Pennock file, National Baseball Library, Cooperstown, NY; Mark Gallagher, *The Yankee Encyclopedia*, vol. 3 (Champaign, IL, 1997); Frank Graham, *The New York Yankees* (New York, 1943); Harold (Speed) Johnson, *Who's Who in Major League Baseball* (Chicago, IL, 1933); Craig Carter, ed., *TSN Daguerreotypes*, 8th ed. (St. Louis, MO, 1990); Frederick G. Lieb, *Connie Mack* (New York, 1945); Dave Anderson et al., *The Yankees* (New York, 1979); Leo Trachtenberg, *The Wonder Team* (Bowling Green, OH, 1995); Robert Redmount, *The Red Sox Encyclopedia* (Champaign, IL, 1998); John Mosedale, *The Greatest of All: The 1927 New York Yankees* (New York, 1974); Nathan Salant, *This Date in New York Yankee History* (New York, 1979).

B. Randolph Linthurst

PEPITONE, Joseph Anthony "Joe," "Pepi" (b. October 9, 1940, Brooklyn, NY), player and excutive, performed on the last of the New York Yankees' (AL) dynasty teams in the early 1960s, but underachieved during his 12-year major league career. His private life remained turbulent almost from the beginning. He grew up in urban Brooklyn, the first son of William Pepitone, a domineering construction worker, and Angelina Pepitone, and suffered violence both on the streets and within the family. At age 17, he was shot accidentally by a schoolmate, the same week that his father died of a stroke. Pepitone married three times and has four children. He first wed Barbara Kogerman in December 1959 and had two children, Eileen and Joseph, Jr. Following their divorce, he married Diana Sandre in February 1966, and had one child, Lisa Ann. He later wed Stephanie Deeker and had one child, Billy Joe.

Pepitone, who attracted publicity as a Brooklyn youngster playing semi-professional baseball for Nathan's Hot Dogs, was considered by many a "flake" for his odd or eccentric behavior. The 6-foot 2-inch, 200 pounder played first base and outfield for the New York Yankees (AL) from 1962 to 1969. He brought a 1960s image to a New York Yankee team which embodied the colorless, efficient 1950s. Hard-nosed working men at heart, the New York Yankees of the 1950s were considered men in gray flannel suits and the darlings of successful suburbanite businessmen. The flamboyant Pepitone, however, was interested in the latest dress styles and styling his hair. He did not care if people knew he wore a wig and clashed with authority. His autobiography indicates he spent far too much time drinking and entertaining women. Pepitone's devotion to nightlife led to marital discord. He did not budget his money well and remained continually deeply in debt. With all these distractions, it is remarkable he achieved what he did on the diamond.

Pepitone performed adequately as an offensive player and outstanding as a defensive one both at first base and in the outfield. In 12 major league seasons, he batted .258 in an age of pitching dominance and demonstrated legitimate power with 219 lifetime HR and 721 RBI. In 1966, Pepitone belted a career-high 31 HR. He led first basemen in fielding percentage three times, winning Gold Gloves in 1965, 1966, and 1969. Pepitone made the AL All-Star team in 1963, 1964, and 1965 and batted .154 in both the 1963 World Series against the Los Angeles Dodgers and the 1964 World Series against the St. Louis Cardinals. He completed his major league career with the Houston Astros (NL) in 1970, Chicago Cubs (NL) from 1970 to 1973, and Atlanta Braves (NL) in 1973. Pepitone played briefly with the Yakuruto, Japan Atoms in 1973 and played and managed in a professional softball league in the late 1970s. In the mid-1980s, he was charged with possession of narcotics and a loaded handgun and served time in jail. An entrepreneur since the 1960s, he operated a clothing store and restaurant and worked with R&P Capital Resources, Inc. He rejoined the Yankees as special assistant in 1999.

BIBLIOGRAPHY: Eddie Gold and Art Ahrens, *The New Era Cubs, 1941–1985* (Chicago, IL, 1985); Jim Enright, *Chicago Cubs* (New York, 1975); Milton Gross, "Pep Tune from Pepitone?" *BD* 25 (May 1966), pp. 85–86; Jack Mann, *The Decline and Fall of the New York Yankees* (New York, 1967); Dick Lally, *Pinstriped Summers* (New York, 1985); Dave Anderson et al., *The Yankees* (New York, 1979); Peter Golenbock,

Dynasty (Englewood Cliffs, NJ, 1975); Robert Obojski, "Pepitone, Kranepool Had the Big Apple in Their Eye," *SCD* 25 (October 16, 1998), pp. 130–131; Joe Pepitone file, National Baseball Library, Cooperstown, NY; Dom Forker, *Sweet Seasons* (Dallas, TX, 1991); "Joe Pepitone," *CB* (1973); Joe Pepitone, "It Was Fun While It Lasted," *BD* 50 (February 1991), pp. 61–64; Joe Pepitone with Berry Stainback, *Joe, You Coulda Made Us Proud* (Chicago, IL, 1975); Berry Stainback, "The Freshest Rookie I Ever Saw," *Sport* 28 (December 1963), pp. 40–41, 58–61; George Vecsey, "Peace, Joe Pep," *Sport* 35 (April 1970), pp. 42–45, 65–66.

Leverett T. Smith, Jr.

PEREZ, Atanasio Rigal "Tony," "Mr. Clutch" (b. May 14, 1942, Ciego de Avila, Camaguey, Cuba), player, coach, manager, and executive, was one of baseball's most likeable and underrated players over a 23-year major league career. His greatest fame came as a vital member of Cincinnati's (NL) powerful "Big Red Machine" during the middle 1970s. Perez grew up near a sugar plantation, where he and his family toiled. In 1959, Cincinnati Reds scouts spotted Perez playing on the factory baseball team and signed the 17-year-old to a professional baseball contract. As a rookie at Geneva, NY (NYPL), the young Cuban hit 27 HR, drove home 128 tallies, and batted .328. Perez's development continued as he progressed through the Reds' minor league chain. With the San Diego, CA Padres (PCL) in 1964, he slugged 34 HR, drove in 107 runs, and batted .309. These credentials earned him the 1964 PCL MVP award and a promotion to the Cincinnati Reds. The 6-foot 2-inch, 175-pound Perez played a reserve role in 1965 and 1966, but became the regular third baseman for the Reds in 1967 and was named for the first of seven times to the NL All-Star team. In the 1967 All-Star contest, his 15th inning HR won the game for the NL.

Perez's major league career included employment on four different clubs (Cincinnati Reds, NL, 1964–1976, 1984–1986; Montreal Expos, NL, 1977–1979; Boston Red Sox, AL, 1980–1982; Philadelphia Phillies, NL, 1983), as the Cuban slugger established some impressive marks. He drove in 90 or more runs in a season 12 times and accomplished that feat 11 consecutive seasons, earning him the title "Mr. Clutch." In May 1970 he slammed 18 HR, tying the NL record for HR that month. In 1975, he also tied an NL mark for most at-bats in one game (7). Defensively, Perez proved equally effective. In 1968, Perez tied the NL record for most double plays started by a third baseman (33). After being converted to a first baseman, he led the NL in double plays (131) in 1970. For his efforts, *TSN* named him to its All-Star team as a third baseman in 1970. The same year, he was chosen the NL first baseman in the All-Star game. Perez hit 379 major league career HR and drove in 1,652 runs for 18th overall. Perez batted .279 lifetime with 2,732 hits, 505 doubles, and 1,867 strikeouts.

Perez saw vast postseason action in six NL Championship Series (1970, 1972–1973, 1975–1976, 1983) and four World Series (1970, 1972, 1975–1976) with the Cincinnati Reds and in 1983 with the Philadelphia Phillies.

He also holds the NL record for most RBI for a total series (13). Following the 1986 season, Perez retired as a player. He coached with the Cincinnati Reds from 1987 through 1992 and managed Cincinnati to a 20–24 mark in 1993. The Reds swept the 1990 World Series against the Oakland Athletics. He served with the Florida Marlins (NL) as director of international relations from 1994 through 1997 and as special assistant to the general manager since 1998. The National Baseball Hall of Fame enshrined him in 2000. Perez and his wife, Juana, who became U.S. citizens in 1971, have two sons, Victor and Eduardo.

BIBLIOGRAPHY: Tony Perez file, National Baseball Library, Cooperstown, NY; Art Burke, *Unsung Heroes of the Major Leagues* (New York, 1976); Robert E. Kelly, *Baseball's Best* (Jefferson, NC, 1988); Floyd Connor and John Snyder, *Day-by-Day in Cincinnati Reds History* (West Point, NY, 1984); Bob Hertzel, *The Big Red Machine* (Englewood Cliffs, NJ, 1976); Bob Rathgeber, *Cincinnati Reds Scrapbook* (Virginia Beach, VA, 1982); Robert H. Walker, *Cincinnati and the Big Red Machine* (Bloomington, IN, 1988); Earl Lawson, "Perez . . . A Perfect Temperament," *TSN*, March 16, 1968; W. Leavy, "Baseball's Minority Managers: Taking Charge on the Field," *Ebony* 48 (May 1993), pp. 110–112; Bill Libby, *Heroes of the Hot Corner* (New York, 1972); John Thorn et al., eds., *Total Baseball*, 5th ed. (New York, 1997); A. Verschoth, "Tony Perez," *SI* 64 (June 30, 1986), pp. 62–63; *Who's Who Among American Blacks, 1980–1981*, 3rd ed. (Northbrook, IL, 1981).

                                                          Samuel O. Regalado

PERLICK, Edythe. *See* Edythe Perlick Keating.

PERRANOSKI, Ronald Peter "Ron" (b. Ronald Peter Perzanowski, April 1, 1936, Paterson, NJ), player and coach, is the son of Peter Perzanowski. Stan Perzanowski, his cousin, pitched in the major leagues from 1971 to 1978. The skinny left-hander catapulted his Fair Lawn (NJ) High School baseball team to the state championship in 1954 and pitched for Michigan State University, where he grew to 6-feet, 180 pounds and roomed with pitcher Dick Radatz.* He won the Spartans' top pitcher award in 1957 and 1958, earning BTC first team honors with Radatz in 1958.

Perranoski signed in 1958 with the Chicago Cubs (NL) for $21,000 and pitched two years in their farm system. In 1960, Chicago traded Perranoski and two other players to the Los Angeles Dodgers (NL) for infielder Don Zimmer.* After splitting the 1960 season with Montreal, Canada (IL) and St. Paul, MN (AA), Perranoski appeared regularly in the 1961 Dodger bullpen relieving Johnny Podres,* Don Drysdale,* Sandy Koufax,* and other starters.

The 1962 campaign featured the even-tempered reliever leading the NL in games pitched (70). The following season, Perranoski paced the NL in winning percentage (.842), relief wins (16), and games pitched (69), and recorded 21 saves. His 1.67 ERA bettered Koufax's official NL-leading 1.88 ERA. He proved instrumental in securing the 1963 and 1965 NL pennants for the Dodgers, but did not figure in any of the 1963, 1965, and 1966 World Series decisions.

Los Angeles traded Perranoski in November 1967 to the Minnesota Twins (AL), where he led the AL in saves in 1969 (31) and 1970 (34) and garnered AL Fireman of the Year honors both seasons. He moved to the Detroit Tigers (AL) on waivers in July 1971, but was released in August 1972. He rejoined the Los Angeles Dodgers in August 1972, winning two decisions in nine games. His major league career ended with the California Angels (AL) in 1973, but he appeared in only eight games.

In 13 major league seasons, Perranoski compiled a 79–74 win–loss record and 2.79 ERA as a reliever. As of 1999, he ranks fourth in relief wins for a season (16, 1963), with 736 career relief appearances, 179 saves, 258 relief wins plus saves, and 79 relief wins. He started only one major league game and did not pitch a complete game. The Tarazana, CA resident served as the Los Angeles Dodgers' pitching coach from 1981 through 1994. Los Angeles won the 1981 and 1988 World Series against the New York Yankees and Oakland Athletics, respectively, and appeared in the 1983 and 1985 NL Championship Series. He has coached for the San Francisco Giants (NL) since 1997.

BIBLIOGRAPHY: Ron Perranoski file, National Baseball Library, Cooperstown, NY; *The Baseball Encyclopedia*, 10th ed. (New York, 1996); Bob Cairns, *Pen Men* (New York, 1993); William F. McNeil, *The Dodgers Encyclopedia* (Champaign, IL, 1997); Walter Alston with Jack Tobin, *One Year at a Time* (Waco, TX, 1976); Tommy Holmes, *The Dodgers* (New York, 1975); Dave Mona and Dave Jarzyna, *Twenty-five Seasons* (Minneapolis, MN, 1986); Gene Karst and Martin J. Jones, Jr., *Who's Who in Professional Baseball* (New Rochelle, NY, 1973); Ron Perranoski, "The Game I'll Never Forget," *BD* 41 (December 1982), pp. 78–81; Milton J. Shapiro, *Heroes of the Bullpen: Baseball's Great Relief Pitchers* (New York, 1967); John Thorn, *The Relief Pitcher* (New York, 1979); John Thorn et al., eds., *Total Baseball*, 5th ed. (New York, 1997).

Gaymon L. Bennett

PERRY, Gaylord Jackson *See* James Evans Perry.

PERRY, James Evans "Jim" (b. October 30, 1936, Williamston, NC) and **PERRY, Gaylord Jackson** (b. September 15, 1938, Williamston, NC), players, grew up in Farm Life, ten miles from Williamston. The children of tenant farmers Evan Perry and Ruby Perry, the right-handers won 529 games and lost 439 decisions between them in the major leagues and compiled more victories than any other brother combination. Both brothers attended Williamston High School in the 1950s. Jim headed the pitching staff as Williamston won the 1955 state tournament, while Gaylord played third base and also pitched. In *Me and the Spitter* Gaylord commented that "baseball was everything when Jim and I were growing up. It was work the fields, go to worship on Sunday and play ball."

Six-foot 4-inch, 190-pound Jim graduated from Campbell JC (now Campbell University) in Buies Creek, NC and received a $4,000 bonus for signing a professional contract with the Cleveland Indians (AL) in 1956. He began his career that same year with North Platte, NE (NeSL) and joined the Cleveland Indians (AL) in 1959. Six-foot 4-inch, 205-pound Gaylord finished his senior year at Williamston High School and then attended Campbell JC. He signed his first professional contract with the San Francisco Giants (NL) in 1958 and received a $60,000 bonus. He pitched with St. Cloud, MN (NoL) that year and first joined the San Francisco Giants in 1962. Both Perrys are characterized as strong family men. Jim married Daphne Kay Snell in December 1960 and has three children, Chris, Pam, and Michelle. Gaylord wed Blanche Hodges Manning in December 1959 and has four children, Amy, Beth, Allison, and Jack.

Jim spent his entire 17-year career (1959–1975) in the AL, winning 215 games and losing 174 (.553 winning percentage) for the Cleveland Indians (1959–1963, 1974–1975), Minnesota Twins (1963–1972), Detroit Tigers (1973), and Oakland Athletics (1975). In 630 games, he struck out 1,576 batters in 3,285.2 innings, hurled 32 shutouts, and compiled a 3.45 ERA. With Cleveland in 1960, he led the AL in games won (18). He repeated in 1970 with Minnesota (24), winning the Cy Young Award as the AL's best pitcher. Both Perrys played together the 1974 season, combining for 38 wins, and for part of the 1975 season at Cleveland. They pitched against each other just twice, once in a regular season game and once at the 1970 All-Star Game. No brothers previously had pitched against one another at an All-Star game.

Gaylord pitched in both major leagues for 22 years, winning the Cy Young Award in the AL in 1972 with Cleveland and in the NL in 1978 with the San Diego Padres. No other pitcher had won the award in both leagues. During his major league career, he won 314 games and lost 265. In 777 games, he struck out 3,534 batters in 5,350.1 innings and compiled a 3.11 ERA. The majority of the victories came in the NL, where he finished 175–135 for the San Francisco Giants (1962–1971), the San Diego Padres (1978–1979), and the Atlanta Braves (1981). He compiled a 139–130 mark for five AL clubs: the Cleveland Indians (1972–1975), New York Yankees (1980), Texas Rangers (1980), Seattle Mariners (1982–1983), and Kansas City Royals (1983). Gaylord led the NL in victories (23) in 1970 with San Francisco and in 1978 (21) with San Diego. His 24 victories for Cleveland paced the AL in 1972. He also topped the NL in innings pitched in 1969 (325) and 1970 (329). On September 17, 1968, he pitched a no-hit, no-run game against the St. Louis Cardinals and bested Bob Gibson,* 1–0, on a first-inning home run by Ron Hunt.

The extraordinary tenacity of the Perry brothers may be attributed to their rural upbringing: "work that instills great doggedness and tensile strength, if not 100% fluidity; a desire for some sociable and celebrated outlet for persistence than just hard work; an attunement to long, hot, ordered periods of time, compared to which six-run innings are brisk; and an urge to get away to the city." Of the two brothers, Gaylord earned more notoriety. Called "the most infamous spitball pitcher of modern times," he mastered and used variants of the spitball between 1966 and 1973. Perry's notoriety led to considerable rule changes regarding the spitball after the 1973 season. Although Gaylord claimed that he developed a new pitch in 1973 to substitute for the spitter, many opposing managers and players disagreed. Perry consequently achieved the status of a trickster hero, one who dominates through craft and intensity. Gaylord, who was elected to the National Baseball Hall of Fame in 1991, lives on a Kill Devil Hills, NC ranch and enjoys fishing.

BIBLIOGRAPHY: Pete Axthelm, "The Conquering Con Man," *Newsweek* 99 (May 17, 1982), pp. 89–90; Gaylord Perry and James Perry files, National Baseball Library, Cooperstown, NY; Peter C. Bjarkman, ed., *Encyclopedia of Major League Baseball Team Histories American League* (Westport, CT, 1991); Peter C. Bjarkman, ed., *Encyclopedia of Major League Baseball Team Histories National League* (Westport, CT, 1991); Nick Peters, *Giants Almanac* (Berkeley CA, 1988); John Benson et al., *Baseball's Top 100* (Wilton, CT, 1997); Terry Pluto, *The Curse of Rocky Colavito* (New York, 1994); Jack Torry, *Endless Summers* (South Bend, IN, 1995); Ray Blount, Jr., "Return of the Natives," *SI* 34 (March 29, 1971), pp. 58–75; A. J. Carr, "Pitching Perrys Share Family Fame," Raleigh (NC) *News & Observer*, April 29, 1984, p. 28; *CB* (1982), pp. 315–318; Glenn Dickey, *The Great No-Hitters* (Radnor, PA, 1976); Ron Fimrite, "Bound for Glory," *SI* 55 (August 24, 1981), pp. 92–106; Gaylord Perry with Bob Sudyk, *Me and the Spitter* (New York, 1974); Dave Mona and Dave Jarzyna, *Twenty-five Seasons* (Minneapolis, MN, 1986); Paul Post, "Hall of Fame, but No World Series," *SCD* 24 (March 7, 1997), pp. 184–185; Rich Westcott, *Diamond Greats* (Westport, CT, 1988); Ken Young, *Cy Young Award Winners* (New York, 1994); John Thorn et al., eds., *Total Indians* (New York, 1996).

Leverett T. Smith, Jr.

PERZANOWSKI, Ronald P. *See* Ronald P. Perranoski.

PESKY, John Michael "Johnny" (b. John Michael Paveskovich, September 27, 1919, Portland, OR), player, manager, coach, and sportscaster, is the son of mill worker Jacob Paveskovich and Maria (Bejama) Paveskovich. He had his name legally changed to Pesky in 1947. He married Ruth Hickey on January 10, 1945 and has one son. Pesky entered professional baseball as a shortstop with Rocky Mount, NC (PIL) in 1940 and played with Louisville, KY (AA) in 1941. The 5-foot 9-inch, 168 pound Pesky debuted with the Boston Red Sox (AL) in 1942 and replaced longstanding All-Star shortstop and manager Joe Cronin.* Pesky, who batted left and threw right-handed, led the major leagues in hits (205), batted .331, scored 105 runs, and was named AL Rookie of the Year in 1942.

After spending the next three years in the military, Pesky in 1946 led the AL in hits (208), batted .335, pounded 43 doubles, scored 115 runs, and helped the Red Sox win their first pennant since 1918. Pesky again led the AL in hits (207) in 1947, tying the major league record for consecutive years leading a league in hits. He batted .324 and struck out only 22 times in 638 at-bats. In 1948 new Red Sox manager Joe McCarthy* moved Pesky to third base, where the latter led both leagues in double plays by a third baseman (48). His batting average, however, dropped to .281. Pesky rebounded by batting .306, .312, and .313 the next three seasons, but then injuries removed him from regular starting status. After being traded to the Detroit Tigers (AL) in an eight-player June 1952 deal, he ended his playing career with the Washington Senators (AL) in 1954. Pesky compiled 1,455 hits and struck out only 218 times in 4,745 at bats, hitting .307 in his 10-year major league career. Pesky made 226 doubles, 50 triples, 867 runs scored, 662 walks, and 404 RBI.

After batting .343 as a player–coach at Denver, CO (AA) in 1955, Pesky managed at Durham, NC (CrL); Birmingham, AL (SA); Lancaster, PA (EL); Knoxville, TN (SAL); and Victoria, TX (TL) in the Detroit organization from 1956 through 1960. After managing the Red Sox' Seattle, WA (PCL) farm team in 1961 and 1962, he piloted the Boston Red Sox (AL) in 1963 and 1964 to a 146–175 record before being fired. Pesky coached for the Pittsburgh Pirates (NL) from 1965 to 1967, managed Columbus, OH (IL) in 1968, and served as Red Sox broadcaster from 1969 to 1974. Pesky coached for the Red Sox from 1975 to 1984, compiling a 1–3 record as an interim manager with Boston in 1980. He served as special assistant to the general manager from 1988 through 1992 and as special assistant for player development from 1993 through 1999.

BIBLIOGRAPHY: John Pesky file, National Baseball Library, Cooperstown, NY; Ellery H. Clark, Jr., *Boston Red Sox: 75th Anniversary History* (Hicksville, NY, 1975); John E. DiMeglio, correspondence with Johnny Pesky, 1984, John E. DiMeglio Collection, Mankato, MN; John E. DiMeglio interview, Johnny Pesky, 1984; Jack Lautier, *Fenway Voices* (Camden, ME, 1990); Frederick G. Lieb, *The Boston Red Sox* (New York, 1947); Howard Liss, *The Boston Red Sox* (New York, 1982); David Halberstam, *Summer of '49* (New York, 1982); Peter Golenbock, *Fenway* (New York, 1992); Dan Shaughnessy, *The Curse of the Bambino* (New York, 1990); Robert Redmount, *The Red Sox Encyclopedia* (Champaign, IL, 1998); Harvey Frommer, *Baseball's Greatest Rivalry*, rev. ed. (New York, 1984); Al Hirshberg, *What's the Matter with the Red Sox?* (New York, 1973).

                                                                    John E. DiMeglio

PETERS, Gary Charles (b. April 21, 1937, Grove City, PA), player, grew up in Mercer, PA and is the son of Thomas Peters, a gas heater plant foreman, and Elizabeth (Rowe) Peters. An All-State interscholastic basketball player, Peters starred as a hoopster at Grove City College. Neither his high school nor college fielded a baseball team, but Peters played sandlot and American Legion baseball, winning recognition as a hard-hitting first baseman–outfielder. The Chicago White Sox (AL) signed Peters in 1952 and converted him to a pitcher on the recommendation of coach Ray Berres. His first season of professional baseball at Holdredge, NE (NeSL) saw Peters lead the NeSL in strikeouts and innings pitched. He married Jean A. Jackal on January 31, 1958 and has two daughters.

Although never winning more than 13 games in a minor league season, Peters impressed Chicago management and won steady promotions. Peters pitched briefly for the Chicago White Sox from 1959 through 1962, but inconsistency plagued him. The Chicago White Sox, who had used up Peters' options, finally kept him on their roster in 1963. Manager Al Lopez* needed an additional starter in May and turned to Peters, who soon settled into the rotation and became AL Rookie of the Year. A 6-foot 2-inch, 200-pound southpaw, Peters batted left-handed and was used frequently as a pinch hitter in most of his major league campaigns. With the exception of 1968, when he won only four games for a ninth-place team, Peters recorded 10 or more victories for the Chicago White Sox each season from 1963 through 1969. His best years saw him rely on a slider and especially on a sinking fastball that he had first learned to throw properly in PRWL ball. No longer a dominant pitcher, Peters was traded to the Boston Red Sox (AL) in a four-player deal in December 1969. Peters pitched for Boston three years and retired in the spring 1973 after failing to win a spot with the Kansas City Royals (AL).

During his major league career, Peters won 124 games and lost 103 decisions with a 3.25 ERA and 23 shutouts. He led the AL in ERA with 2.33 in 1963 and 1.98 in 1966 and in victories with 20 in 1964. He triumphed 19 times in 1963 and recorded 16 victories for the Chicago White Sox in 1967 and Boston Red Sox in 1970. In 1959, he pitched a no-hitter against the Minneapolis, MN Millers (AA). Peters resides in Sarasota, FL and works as a construction company foreman.

BIBLIOGRAPHY: Gary Peters file, National Baseball Library, Cooperstown, NY; Martin Appel, *Yesterday's Heroes* (New York, 1988); David Condon, *The Go-Go Chicago White Sox* (New York, 1960); Richard Lindberg, *Sox* (New York, 1984); Richard Lindberg, *Who's on Third?* (South Bend, IN, 1983); Bob Vanderberg, *Sox: From Lane and Fain to Zisk and Fisk* (Chicago, IL, 1982); Robert Redmount, *The Red Sox Encyclopedia* (Champaign, IL, 1998); Howard Liss, *The Boston Red Sox* (New York, 1982); Peter Golenbock, *Fenway* (New York, 1992); "For Peters' Sake," *SS* (April 10, 1964), p. 84; Lee Heiman et al., *When the Cheering Stops* (New York, 1991); Jerome Holtzman, "Prize Rookie Pitcher Polishes Hill Weapons," *TSN*, December 28, 1963, p. 7; Gene Karst and Martin J. Jones, *Who's Who in Professional Baseball* (New Rochelle, NY, 1973).

Lloyd J. Graybar

PETROCELLI, Americo Peter "Rico" (b. June 27, 1943, Brooklyn, NY), player, manager, and coach, is the youngest of seven children of Attilio Petrocelli, a foundry worker, and Louise Petrocelli, both Italian immigrants, and graduated from high school in Brooklyn. The Boston Red Sox (AL) signed him in 1961 to a bonus contract eventually worth $60,000. Petrocelli, a 6-foot, 188-pound, right-handed shortstop, gained minor league experience with Winston-Salem, NC (CrL) in 1962, Reading, PA (EL) in 1963, and Seattle, WA (PCL) in 1964. The moody, sensitive Petrocelli often clashed with managers, but gradually matured.

Petrocelli played shortstop with the Boston Red Sox from 1965 through 1970. The resurgent Red Sox captured the 1967 AL pennant, as Petrocelli, an AL All-Star team selection, batted .259 with 17 HR and 66 RBI. Petrocelli caught Rich Rollins's short fly to clinch the AL pennant against the Minnesota Twins. The Boston Red Sox lost a seven-game World Series to the St. Louis Cardinals, but Petrocelli belted two HR in Game 6 at Fenway Park. In the fourth inning, Carl Yastrzemski,* Reggie Smith,* and Petrocelli set a World Series record by slugging HR in the same stanza.

Petrocelli's best season came in 1969, when he batted a career-best .297 with 97 RBI and made the AL All-Star team for the second time. He established an AL mark for most HR by a shortstop (40), led AL shortstops defensively for the second consecutive year, and tied an AL standard for fewest single-season errors (14) at his position. The Boston Red Sox shifted Petrocelli to third base in 1971 upon acquiring shortstop Luis Aparicio.* Petrocelli adjusted well, pacing third basemen in fielding that year. The powerful Petrocelli belted 29 HR with a career-high 103 RBI in 1970 and 28 HR with 89 RBI in 1971. Injuries diminished his offensive production thereafter. The Boston Red Sox won the AL pennant in 1975, but Petrocelli slumped offensively. The Cincinnati Reds defeated the Boston Red Sox in a seven-game World Series, as Petrocelli batted .308 with eight hits and four RBI. During 13 major league seasons through 1976, Petrocelli batted .251 with 1,352 hits, 237 doubles, 210 HR, and 773 RBI.

The Lynfield, MA resident, who managed Pawtucket, RI (IL) in 1992 and served as hitting and infield instructor for New Britain, CT (EL) in 1994, married Elsie Jensen in March 1965 and has four children.

BIBLIOGRAPHY: Rico Petrocelli file, National Baseball Library, Cooperstown, NY; Ross Forman, " '67 Red Sox Rehash the Impossible Dream," *SCD* 19 (November 6, 1992), pp. 140–142; Peter Golenbock, *Fenway* (New York, 1992); Al Hirshberg, "How Rico Put 'Pop' in His Game," *Sport* 44 (September 1967), pp. 26–27, 29, 83–84; Barry McDermott, "Petrocelli Pulls Up His Sox," *SI* 36 (April 3, 1972), pp. 67,

70; Mike Shatzkin, ed., *The Ballplayers* (New York, 1990); *TSN Baseball Register*, 1976; Dan Shaughnessy, *The Curse of the Bambino* (New York, 1990); Robert Redmount, *The Red Sox Encyclopedia* (Champaign, IL, 1998); Howard Liss, *The Boston Red Sox* (New York, 1982); Ken Coleman and Dan Valenti, *The Impossible Dream Remembered* (Lexington, MA, 1987); Al Hirshberg, *What's the Matter with the Red Sox?* (New York, 1973); Bill McSweeney, *The Impossible Dream* (New York, 1968).

David L. Porter

PETRY, Daniel Joseph "Dan," "Peaches" (b. November 13, 1958, Palo Alto, CA), player, is the son of Ronald Petry and graduated from El Dorado High School in Placentia, CA. He married Christina Cairns and has two sons, Matthew and Jeffrey. The Detroit Tigers (AL) signed Petry as their fourth pick in the June 1976 draft. Pitchers Jack Morris* and Petry provided the best one-two combination in the AL during the mid-1980s. Morris compiled a 72–51 mark from 1982 to 1985, while Petry finished with 67–41. His best records included 19–11 in 1983, when he led the AL with 38 starts, and 18–8 in 1984, when he and Morris led the Detroit Tigers to the AL pennant.

The 6-foot 4-inch, 215-pound right-hander threw 90 mph fastballs, using a no-windup delivery. He also threw a curve ball, a change-up, and what Frank Robinson* called "the best slider in the league." He led AL pitchers in fielding in 1982 and 1985 and started 10 double plays in 1983.

Petry, who played in the 1985 All-Star game, accumulated 93 wins through that season, and seemed to have a bright future at only 27 years old. Elbow surgery in 1986, however, diminished his effectiveness. The Detroit Tigers traded him to the California Angels (AL) in December 1987 for outfielder Gary Pettis. Petry returned to the Detroit Tigers as a free agent for the 1990 season and began strongly. He compiled a 10–9 record, marking the first time since 1985 that he had won in double digits. Arm troubles returned in 1991, when Petry split his final season between the Detroit Tigers, Atlanta Braves (NL), and Boston Red Sox (AL).

Petry's major league career included 125 wins, 104 losses, and a 3.95 ERA. He pitched in the 1984 and 1987 AL Championship Series for Detroit with no decisions and a 1.74 ERA. He compiled an 0–1 record in eight innings in two 1984 World Series games against the San Diego Padres, starting the clinching Game 5.

BIBLIOGRAPHY: Daniel Petry file, National Baseball Library, Cooperstown, NY; *Detroit Tigers Yearbook*, 1980, 1983, 1985, 1990, 1991; *Detroit Tigers Press/TV/Radio Guide*, 1986; *The Scouting Report, 1985, 1986, 1991* (New York, 1985, 1986, 1991); John Thorn et al., eds., *Total Baseball*, 5th ed. (New York, 1997); William M. Anderson, *The Detroit Tigers* (South Bend, IN, 1996); Sparky Anderson and Dan Ewald, *Sparky* (New York, 1990); Richard Bak, *A Place for Summer* (Detroit, MI, 1998); Sparky Anderson and Dan Ewald, *Bless You Boys* (Chicago, IL, 1984); Fred T. Smith, *Tiger Tales and Trivia* (Lathrup Village, MI, 1988).

John T. English

PETWAY, Bruce "Buddy" (b. 1883, Nashville, TN; d. July 4, 1941, Chicago IL), player and manager, starred as the premier catcher of his era and the first great receiver in black baseball history. His strong and accurate arm, still regarded as one of the best ever, intimidated base runners and made Petway always in demand by the top teams. His prime years (1906–1918) mainly were spent with Rube Foster's* superb Chicago Leland Giants and Chicago American Giants, when they dominated black baseball and virtually were perennial champions.

Petway first caught for the Chicago Leland Giants in 1906 after leaving Nashville's Meharry Medical College. Following his rookie season, he caught for the Brooklyn Royal Giants and Philadelphia Giants before rejoining the Chicago Leland Giants for the 1910 season. There he teamed with John Henry Lloyd,* Pete Hill,* Frank Wickware,* Grant "Home Run" Johnson,* and Foster to form an aggregation of talent that Foster regarded as the greatest club, black or white, in baseball.

Petway contributed a .397 batting average to the team's 135–6 record, but gained his greatest notoriety when he threw out Detroit Tiger (AL) immortal Ty Cobb* three times on three attempted steals in CUWL exhibition games. Petway, a left-handed batter, also hit .390 in that series and batted .333 for the CUWL in 1916 on his last trip to the island.

Although referred to as "Home Run Petway" early in his career, the speedy 170 pounder lacked genuine power and posed a greater threat in base stealing than as a slugger. His prowess on the bases was demonstrated when he led the 1912 CUWL with 20 stolen bases. An excellent bunter, he welcomed Foster's racehorse style of baseball and often batted in the leadoff position.

The scrappy backstop was disabled twice by strained ligaments in his throwing arm and once by a leg injury, losing substantial playing time from the 1914 through 1916 seasons. Petway, a student of the game, spent the last seven years of his baseball career as player–manager for the Detroit Stars (NNL), where he hit .313, .268, .337, and .334 during the 1921–1924 seasons before retiring in 1925.

BIBLIOGRAPHY: Bruce Petway file, National Baseball Library, Cooperstown, NY; Chicago (IL) *Defender*, 1910–1916; Robert W. Peterson, *Only the Ball Was White* (Englewood Cliffs, NJ, 1970); James A. Riley, *The All-Time All-Stars of Black Baseball* (Cocoa, FL, 1983); James A. Riley, *Biographical Encyclopedia of the Negro Baseball Leagues* (New York, 1994); James A. Riley, interviews with former Negro League players, James A. Riley Collection, Cocoa, FL.

James A. Riley

PFEFFER, Edward Joseph "Jeff," "Hassen" (b. March 4, 1888, Seymour, IL; d. August 15, 1972, Chicago, IL), player, pitched in major league baseball between 1911 and 1924, compiling a lifetime 158–112 win–loss mark and a 2.77 ERA. The 6-foot 3-inch, 220-pound right-handed hurler, the younger brother of pitcher Francis Xavier "Big Jeff" Pfeffer, began his professional baseball career in 1909 with LaCrosse, WI (MWL), winning 18 games. In the fall of 1909, his contract was purchased by Fort Wayne, IN (CL). Pfeffer pitched for Fort Wayne in 1910 and 1911, triumphing in 29 games over the two seasons. His work in Fort Wayne attracted the attention of the St. Louis Browns (AL), who gave him a brief, undistinguished trial in September 1911.

After pitching for Grand Rapids, MI (CL) the next two seasons and winning 25 games in 1913, Pfeffer returned to the major leagues in September 1913 with the Brooklyn Dodgers (NL). He pitched for the Brooklyn Robins (NL) from 1914 until June 1921, serving in the U.S. Navy Reserves in 1918 and attaining 67 victories from 1914 to 1916. In June 1921, the Brooklyn Robins traded Pfeffer to the St. Louis Cardinals (NL) for pitcher Ferdie Schupp and utility infielder Hal Janvrin. He won 19 games in 1922 for the St. Louis Cardinals and closed out his major league career in 1924 with the Pittsburgh Pirates (NL). Pfeffer later hurled for San Francisco, CA (PCL) in 1925 and Toledo, OH (AA) in 1926 and 1927. Pfeffer also pitched in two World Series with Brooklyn, appearing in 1916 against the Boston Red Sox and 1920 against the Cleveland Indians. His only World Series decision, a 4–1 setback, came in the fifth and decisive game of the 1916 fall classic.

An amusing story about a card game involving Pfeffer occurred during one of the St. Louis Cardinals' railroad trips. Left-handed pitcher Bill Bailey criticized a play Pfeffer made in the game, whereupon Pfeffer commented in an uncomplimentary fashion about the intelligence of southpaws. Bailey retorted, "Well, you never saw one of them digging a ditch, did you?" "No," replied Pfeffer, "but that's because they want the ditches straight."

BIBLIOGRAPHY: Frank Graham, *The Brooklyn Dodgers* (New York, 1943); Richard Goldstein, *Superstars and Screwballs* (New York, 1991); William F. McNeil, *The Dodgers Encyclopedia* (Champaign, IL, 1997); Tommy Holmes, *The Dodgers* (New York, 1975); Frederick G. Lieb, *The St. Louis Cardinals* (New York, 1945); Bob Broeg, *Redbirds: A Century of Cardinals' Baseball* (St. Louis, MO, 1981); Bob Broeg and Jerry Vickery, *St. Louis Cardinals Encyclopedia* (Grand Rapids, MI, 1998); *The Baseball Encyclopedia*, 10th ed. (New York, 1996); Jeff Pfeffer file, National Baseball Library, Cooperstown, NY.

David S. Matz

PFEFFER, Nathaniel Frederick (b. March 17, 1860, Louisville, KY; d. April 10, 1932, Chicago, IL), player, coach, and manager, performed in 16 major league seasons between 1882 and 1897. Perhaps the premier second baseman of his time, Pfeffer participated in the Chicago White Stockings' (NL) "Stonewall Infield" of the 1880s. Pfeffer's parents may have been immigrants because he spoke German as an adult. Pfeffer and his wife, Ida, had no children.

The 5-foot 10½-inch, 168-pound Pfeffer began his baseball career in 1879 with the semiprofessional Louisville, KY Eclipses. He joined the Troy, NY

Haymakers (NL) in 1882 and played with Adrian Anson's* Chicago White Stockings (NL) from 1883 through 1889. An enthusiastic member of the BPBP, Pfeffer helped organize the Chicago Pirates (PL) and played for them in 1890. After returning to the Chicago White Stockings in 1891, he spent the 1892 through 1895 seasons with the Louisville Colonels (NL) and managed them for part of the 1892 campaign. A brief stint with the New York Giants (NL) in 1896 was followed by his rejoining the Chicago White Stockings through June 1897. Pfeffer remained in baseball for several years thereafter, managing Decatur, IL (3IL) in 1902 and coaching in the minor leagues. He coached baseball at the University of Wisconsin. He kept a saloon in Chicago, IL until Prohibition started and subsequently worked as a press box guard at several Chicago race tracks.

Pfeffer, known for his excellent fielding, played bare-handed and accepted an unusually large number of chances. Between 1884 and 1891, he led second basemen in putouts every season, in double plays six times, and in assists four times. According to Anson, "as a thrower, fielder, and base runner [Pfeffer] was in the first class."

Pfeffer authored one of the first baseball books, publishing *Scientific Ball* in 1889. The 82-page book begins with a "Biography of the Author" by sportswriter DeWitt Ray and ends with Ray's poem, "I'm Going to Be an Empire." Pfeffer's part of the book concentrates on instructions for defensive play and on base-running strategy. Pfeffer either printed statements by other players about how to play a particular position or related how they told him it should be played. The book argues "that there is more winning play in brainy play than in hand or leg work."

Anson considered Pfeffer "only fair" as a batter, but the latter made the best of his talents. Pfeffer batted only .255 lifetime, but he scored and drove in runs frequently. He made 1,671 career hits, scored 1,094 runs, knocked in 1,019 runs, and struck out only 498 times in 6,555 at-bats. In 1884, he hit each of his 25 HR at friendly Lake Front Park in Chicago.

BIBLIOGRAPHY: Arthur Ahrens, "Fred Pfeffer, Stonewall Second Baseman," *BRJ* 8 (1979), pp. 46–52; Eddie Gold and Art Ahrens, *The Golden Era Cubs, 1876–1940* (Chicago, IL, 1985); Warren Brown, *The Chicago Cubs* (New York, 1946); Warren Wilbert and William Hageman, *Chicago Cubs: Seasons at the Summit* (Champaign, IL, 1997); Jim Enright, *Chicago Cubs* (New York, 1975); Philip Van Borries, *Legends of Louisville* (West Bloomfield, MI, 1993); Fred Pfeffer file, National Baseball Library, Cooperstown, NY; N. Fred Pfeffer, *Scientific Ball* (Chicago, IL, 1889); Robert L. Tiemann and Mark Rucker, eds., *Nineteenth Century Stars* (Kansas City, MO, 1989).

Leverett T. Smith, Jr.

PFIESTER, John Albert "Jack" (b. John Albert Hagenbush, May 24, 1878, Cincinnati, OH; d. September 3, 1953, Loveland, OH), player, enjoyed his best seasons as a pitcher with the Chicago Cubs (NL) from 1906 through 1910. His professional baseball career started with Spokane, WA (NWL) and San Francisco, CA (PCL) in 1902–1903. The Pittsburgh Pirates (NL) gave him brief trials in 1903 and 1904, as he won one of four decisions. He returned to the minor leagues with Omaha, NE (WL), triumphing in 24 games in 1904 and 22 games in 1905.

The Chicago Cubs signed Pfiester for the 1906 season, in which he compiled a 20–8 record and 1.51 ERA. His 153 strikeouts ranked fourth in the NL. The fast ball and curve ball proved his best pitches. He fanned 17 St. Louis Cardinal batters in a 15-inning game on May 30, 1906, but lost, 4–2. After pitching a three hit, 19–0 victory against the New York Giants that season, the 5 foot 11 inch, 180 pound Pfiester gained the nickname "Jack the Giant Killer." On October 4, 1906, he shut out the Pittsburgh Pirates, 4–0, to give the Chicago Cubs 116 victories, still a major league record.

Pfiester's performance remained solid, but less spectacular from 1907 to 1910. He finished 14–9 with a league-leading 1.15 ERA in 1907, 12–10 in 1908, 17–6 in 1909, and 6–3 in 1910. He won one World Series game against the Detroit Tigers in 1907, but lost two to the Chicago White Sox in 1906 and one to the Detroit Tigers in 1908. The Chicago Cubs released him after a 1–4 mark in mid-1911. Pfiester, who married Laul Hoffman, played in the minor leagues for several more seasons before retiring. His major league record included 71 wins, 44 losses, a .617 winning percentage, and a 2.04 ERA.

BIBLIOGRAPHY: John Pfiester file, National Baseball Library, Cooperstown, NY; Art Ahrens and Eddie Gold, *Day-by-Day in Chicago Cubs History* (West Point, NY, 1982); Eddie Gold and Art Ahrens, *The Golden Era Cubs, 1876–1940* (Chicago, IL, 1985); *The Baseball Encyclopedia*, 10th ed. (New York, 1996); A. D. Suehsdorf, "Jack the Giant Killer," *BRJ* 18 (1989), p. 46; Warren Brown, *The Chicago Cubs* (New York, 1946); Jim Enright, *Chicago Cubs* (New York, 1975); Warren Wilbert and William Hageman, *Chicago Cubs: Seasons at the Summit* (Champaign, IL, 1997).

Duane A. Smith

PHELPS, Ernest Gordon "Babe," "Blimp" (b. April 19, 1908, Odenton, MD; d. December 10, 1992, Odenton, MD), player, was the son of Arthur F. Phelps, a block operator for the Pennsylvania Railroad, and Maggie L. (Hood) Phelps. Familiarly called "Gordon," he attended grade school in Odenton and became a deliveryman for a general store. Phelps played baseball for the Odenton town team until his left-handed slugging deeply impressed Joe Cambria, a Washington Senators (AL) scout. After Washington signed him for $250 per month, he played outfield for Hagerstown, MD (BRL) and led the BRL with a .376 batting average. In 1931, Phelps performed briefly with Chattanooga, TN (SA) and led the MAL with a .408 batting mark while catching for Youngstown, OH. He ended the 1931 season by pinch hitting three times for the Washington Senators. The following year, the 6-foot 2-inch, 225 pounder played first base for Youngstown, OH (CL) and hit .373 to win his third consecutive minor league batting championship.

When Phelps refused to report to Atlanta, GA (SA) for 1933, the Washington Senators sold him outright to Albany, NY (IL). As a first baseman, he batted .293. The Chicago Cubs (NL) bought him as backup to catcher Gabby Hartnett* and inserted him in three games in 1933 and 44 contests in 1934. In December 1934, the Chicago Cubs sold him on waivers to the Brooklyn Dodgers (NL). From 1935 through 1940, the powerful, line-drive hitting Phelps batted .315 cumulatively in 581 games. Frequent finger injuries sidelined him because of a bad habit of catching pitches without clenching his right hand in a fist. His best season's batting average of .367 came in 1935.

In June 1941, the Brooklyn Dodgers suspended Phelps for the balance of the season because he failed to accompany the team on a western trip. His reason for the refusal, unrevealed at the time, was a fear of flying. The Brooklyn Dodgers traded him that December to the Pittsburgh Pirates (NL), for whom he batted .289 in 1942.

The Odenton resident refused to play any major league baseball thereafter, working instead for the Pennsylvania Railroad and later as a machine operator for a plastics manufacturer.

Phelps married Mable Fedoria Hood in February 1930 and had one daughter, Janet. During his 11-year major league career, he batted .310 in 726 games, mostly as a catcher. He hit .365 in 493 minor league games, giving him a career .336 batting mark in 1,219 games.

BIBLIOGRAPHY: Ernest Phelps file, National Baseball Library, Cooperstown, NY; Tommy Holmes, "Another Bench Ride Thumbed by Phelps," *TSN*, July 7, 1938; Paul MacFarlane, ed., *TSN Daguerreotypes of Great Stars of Baseball* (St. Louis, MO, 1981); "Ernest 'Babe' Phelps, Major League Catcher," Obituaries, Baltimore (MD) *Sun*, December 11, 1992; John Thorn et al., eds., *Total Baseball*, 5th ed. (New York, 1997); Frank Graham, *The Brooklyn Dodgers* (New York, 1945); Richard Goldstein, *Superstars and Screwballs* (New York, 1991); Tommy Holmes, *The Dodgers* (New York, 1995).

Frank V. Phelps

PHILLEY, David Earl "Dave" (b. May 16, 1920, Paris, TX), player, scout, and manager, is the son of M. O. Philley and Leila Philley and graduated in 1938 from Chicota High School, where he participated in basketball, baseball, and track and field and won the Eastern Texas Golden Gloves middleweight boxing championship. The 6-foot, 195-pound catcher attended East Texas State University two years before signing a professional baseball contract. Philley played for Marshall, TX (ETL) in 1940 and Monroe, LA (CSL) in 1941, soon switching to the outfield. In 1941, he also appeared briefly with Shreveport, LA (TL) and the Chicago White Sox (AL). The Chicago White Sox assigned him to St. Paul, MN (AA) in 1942. After spending 40 months in military service, Philley batted .329 for Milwaukee, WI (AA) in 1946.

The Chicago White Sox installed Philley as a starting outfielder in 1947. He remained with the Chicago White Sox until April 1951, when a complex three-way, seven player trade sent him to the Philadelphia Athletics (AL). The Philadelphia Athletics used him as their right fielder through the 1953 season. The switch hitter batted .303 in 1953, marking his career high as a full-time player. In February 1954, the Philadelphia Athletics traded Philley to the Cleveland Indians (AL). He batted just .125 in his only post-season appearance against the New York Giants in the 1954 World Series.

Philley played for many teams the next eight campaigns. The Baltimore Orioles (AL) acquired him on waivers in July 1955 and traded him to the Chicago White Sox in May 1956. The Detroit Tigers (AL) obtained Philley in June 1957, but sold him to the Philadelphia Phillies (NL) that December. Philley set a major league record by collecting eight consecutive pinch hits to finish the 1958 campaign and hitting safely in his first attempt the next season. The Philadelphia Phillies sold him to the San Francisco Giants (NL) in May 1960. The Baltimore Orioles reacquired Philley in September 1960 and released him in October 1961. He signed with the expansion Houston Colt .45s (NL), but was traded to the Boston Red Sox (AL) during spring training.

Philley finished his 18 year major league tenure with a .270 batting average. His .299 career pinch hitting average ranks ninth highest all time, while his 24 pinch hits in 1961 mark the third highest in one season. Philley managed in the Houston Astros (NL) and Boston Red Sox minor league systems and scouted for Boston and the Atlanta Braves (NL). In 1975, he retired to his ranch outside Paris, TX.

Philley married Nell Bratcher in June 1942. They have two sons, Billy and Paul.

BIBLIOGRAPHY: *TSN Official Baseball Register*, 1961; *The Baseball Encyclopedia*, 10th ed. (New York, 1996); Dave Philley file, National Baseball Library, Cooperstown, NY; Warren Brown, *The Chicago White Sox* (New York, 1952); Richard Lindberg, *Sox* (New York, 1984); Richard Lindberg, *Who's on Third?* (South Bend, IN, 1983); John Phillips, *Winners* (Cabin John, MD, 1987); Bruce Dudley, *Bittersweet Season* (Annapolis, MD, 1995); Rich Westcott and Frank Bilovsky, *The New Phillies Encyclopedia* (Philadelphia, PA, 1993).

John Hillman

PHILLIPPE, Charles Louis "Deacon" (b. May 23, 1872, Rural Retreat, VA; d. March 30, 1952, Avalon, PA), player, married Belle M. Phillippe and had one daughter. The 6-foot, 180-pound right-hander ranked among the best pitchers at the turn of the century. He first played baseball on the South Dakota prairies until Minneapolis, MN (WL) signed him in 1897. The Louisville Colonels (NL) drafted Phillippe in 1898. The next year, he finished with a 21–17 mark for Louisville and hurled a no-hitter against the New York Giants.

After joining the Pittsburgh Pirates (NL) in 1900, Phillippe became a mound mainstay for the next 11 years and helped them capture NL pennants in the 1901–1903 and 1909 seasons. His most outstanding campaigns came in the first three pennant-winning seasons, when he compiled 22–12, 20–9, and 25–9 marks. Thereafter, he enjoyed only one more 20-victory season (1905). In his last successful year (1910), he finished with a 14–2 mark and boasted a 7–1 record as a relief pitcher. Although appearing in relief as early as 1899, he never repeated his 1910 performance. Phillippe was never considered an overpowering pitcher, but exhibited outstanding control. He walked only 363 batters while striking out 929 during his career.

Perhaps his finest moment in baseball came in the first World Series in 1903. Although Pittsburgh lost the World Series to the Boston Pilgrims, Phillippe paced the Pirates' injured and decimated pitching staff. A local paper crowed, "Deacon Phillippe has the American League Champions at his mercy." Since Phillippe completed five games and won three, appreciative fans presented him with a diamond stickpin. Having no other choice, manager Fred Clarke* asked him to pitch the last two games. As the paper said, the worn out Phillippe "went to the rubber too often." He lost both games, the last one 3–0. Weak team hitting crippled Pittsburgh's chances more than their pitching.

The quiet pitcher avoided the limelight throughout his career. His 189–109 career record (.634 winning percentage) included a 2.59 ERA over 372 games and 2,607 innings. Phillippe completed 242 of his 289 starts and pitched 27 shutouts during his 13 major league years. Phillippe batted only .189 lifetime with a personal high of .244 in 1906. Following his retirement from baseball, he worked in a Pittsburgh steel mill and then as a bailiff in a local court. In 1969, Pirate fans voted him Pittsburgh's all-time right-hander.

BIBLIOGRAPHY: Lawrence S. Katz, "Pittsburgh's Pitching Twins: Phillippe and Leever," *BRJ* 26 (1997), pp. 133–135; Frederick G. Lieb, *The Pittsburgh Pirates*, (New York, 1948); Richard L. Burtt, *The Pittsburgh Pirates, A Pictorial History* (Virginia Beach, VA, 1977); Dennis De Valeria and Jeanne Burke De Valeria, *Honus Wagner: A Biography* (New York, 1996); William Hageman, *Honus: The Life and Times of a Baseball Hero* (Champaign, IL, 1996); Charles Phillippe file, National Baseball Library, Cooperstown, NY; *The Baseball Encyclopedia*, 10th ed. (New York, 1996); *Spalding Base Ball Guide, 1900* (New York, 1900).

                                                                                                       Duane A. Smith

PIAZZA, Michael Joseph "Mike" (b. September 4, 1968, Norristown, PA), player, is the son of Vincent Piazza, an automobile dealer, and Veronica Piazza and graduated from Phoenixville, PA Area High School. The 6-foot 3-inch, 215-pound right-handed hitting Piazza won high school league MVP and American Legion MVP honors in baseball and played baseball one year at Miami-Dade North CC. At the urging of close family friend manager Tommy Lasorda,* the Los Angeles Dodgers (NL) signed him as a catcher in the 62nd round of the June 1988 free agent draft.

The Dodgers optioned Piazza to Salem, OR (NWL), where he hit .268 and made the NWL All-Star team in 1989. At Vero Beach, FL (FSL) in 1990, he batted .250 with six HR and 45 RBI in 88 games. His 1991 season at Bakersfield, CA (CAL) resulted in a .277 batting average, 80 RBI, and a CAL leading .540 slugging percentage. Piazza's 29 HR ranked fourth among all minor leaguers. He opened the 1992 season at San Antonio, TX (TL), hitting .377 with seven HR and 20 RBI in 31 games. With Albuquerque, NM (PCL), Piazza batted .341 with 16 HR and 69 RBI and was named to the PCL All-Star team. The Los Angeles Dodgers summoned him in September 1992, when he hit .232 and started 16 games.

Piazza, who became the regular Los Angeles Dodger catcher in 1993, hit .318 with a .561 slugging percentage and drove in 112 runs in 149 games. His 35 HR established a major league record for rookie catchers. Defensively, he ranked first in the NL with 98 assists and shared the lead with 11 errors. He became just the ninth player selected unanimously as NL Rookie of the Year and was named *TSN* and *BA* Rookie of the Year. He also was chosen for the UPI and AP All-Star teams. During the strike-shortened 1994 season, Piazza hit .319 with 92 RBI, 24 HR, and a .541 slugging average in 107 games to repeat as an NL All-Star. Despite being on the disabled list from May 11 to June 4, 1995, he batted .346 with 32 HR, 93 RBI, and a .606 slugging average in 112 games. His 866 total chances and 12 passed balls led NL catchers. He and Dodger teammate Hideo Nomo started the 1995 All-Star game for the NL. Piazza clouted a HR and double in the 1995 All-Star game. He batted .362 with 40 HR, 124 RBI, and a .638 slugging percentage in 1997, becoming the first major league catcher to make 201 hits in a season. The Los Angeles Dodgers traded him to the Florida Marlins (NL) in May 1998. The New York Mets (NL) acquired him one week later. In 1998, he batted .328 with 32 HR and 111 RBI. The Mets in October signed Piazza to a record $91 million, seven-year contract. His .303 batting average, 40 HR, and 124 RBI helped the Mets win a Wild Card berth. He batted .222 in the NL Division Series and .182 with one HR and four RBI in the NL Championship Series. From 1993 to 1999, *TSN* named him catcher on its NL All-Star and Silver Slugger teams. Through the 1999 season, he has batted .328 with 240 HR and 768 RBI. His 239 HR mark the most ever by a catcher in his first seven full seasons. He ranked second in batting average (.329) in the 1990s. Piazza, who is single, lives in Manhattan Beach, CA.

BIBLIOGRAPHY: Mike Piazza file, National Baseball Library, Cooperstown, NY; Richard Hoffer, "Catching a Rising Star," *SI* 84 (May 13, 1996), pp. 74–77; "Can Piazza Win Batting Title as Catcher?" *BA* 16 (August 5–18, 1996), p. 11; *Los Angeles Dodgers 1997 Media Guide*; *WWIB*, 1996; William P. McNeil, *The Dodgers Encyclopedia* (Champaign, IL, 1997); Tomas Rubalcava, "Mike Piazza: Best-Hitting Catcher Ever?" *BRJ* 25 (1996), pp. 100–102; T. Singer, "Mike Piazza," *Sport* 85 (May 1994), pp. 26ff; K. Whiteside, "A Piazza with Everything!" *SI* 79 (July 5, 1993), pp. 12–17; *TSN Official Baseball Register*, 1998.

Robert J. Brown

PIERCE, Walter William "Billy" (b. April 2, 1927, Detroit, MI), player and scout, ranked among baseball's leading left-handed pitchers and is the son of pharmacist Walter Pierce and Julia Pierce. An outstanding high school pitcher in Detroit, Pierce signed with the Detroit Tigers (AL) and spent the 1945–1947 seasons with the Buffalo, NY (IL) farm club. Pierce pitched briefly with the Tigers at the end of 1945 and compiled a 3–0 record there in 1948, but the management questioned his control and in November 1948 traded him to the Chicago White Sox (AL) for catcher Aaron Robinson. The transaction proved one of the most favorable in White Sox history because the 5-foot 10-inch, 160-pound Pierce helped make Chicago a contender beginning in 1951 and the 1959 AL pennant winner.

After two losing seasons, Pierce in 1951 compiled a 15–14 record. He quickly became one of major league baseball's best left-handers, peaking in 1956 and 1957 with 20–9 and 20–12 records. He led the AL in every positive category: victories in 1957, ERA (1.97) in 1955, strikeouts (186) in 1953, and complete games (21, 16, and 19) from 1956 through 1958. He started in the All-Star games of 1953, 1955, and 1956, losing the 1956 contest. An excellent base runner, Pierce was used frequently as a pinchrunner. He never pitched a no-hit game, but came within a single out of a perfect game on June 27, 1958, when Ed FitzGerald batted for the Washington Senators' pitcher and doubled with two out in the ninth inning. In 1959, Pierce won 14 games and made 3 relief appearances in the World Series against the Los Angeles Dodgers.

In November 1961, Pierce was traded to the San Francisco Giants (NL). Pierce enjoyed one of his finest seasons (16–6), never lost at home, and retired the Los Angeles Dodgers in the ninth inning of a playoff to clinch the 1962 NL pennant. He started two games in the World Series, winning one and losing one. Pierce retired at the end of the 1964 season, during which his 3–0 record ironically matched his first record in Detroit. In 585 games, Pierce won 211 and lost 169, pitched 38 shutouts, struck out 1,999 batters, and compiled a 3.27 ERA. His 186 victories established the White Sox record for left-handed pitchers. Pierce married Gloria McCreadie on October 22, 1949 and has three children, William, Patti, and Robert. Following his baseball career, he engaged in sales work and developed an excellent reputation as a White Sox scout. The Evergreen Park, IL resident serves as director of social services for an envelope company.

BIBLIOGRAPHY: Billy Pierce file, National Baseball Library, Cooperstown, NY; George W. Hilton, correspondence with Billy Pierce, George W. Hilton Collection, Columbia, MD; Richard Lindberg, *Sox* (New York, 1984); Richard Lindberg, *Who's on Third?* (South Bend, IN, 1983); Bob Vanderberg, *Sox: From Lane and Fain to Fisk and Zisk* (Chicago, IL, 1982); Nick Peters, *Giants Diary* (Berkeley, CA, 1988); David Plaut, *Chasing October* (South Bend, IN, 1994); Craig Carter, ed., *TSN Daguerreotypes*, 8th ed. (St. Louis, MO, 1990); *TSN Baseball Register, 1950–1964*; *TSN Official Baseball Guide, 1946–1965*; *WWIB, 1949–1964*, 34th–49th eds.

George W. Hilton

PIERSALL, James Anthony "Jimmy" (b. November 14, 1929, Waterbury, CT), player, manager, coach, and sportscaster, starred in basketball at Waterbury High School before attracting the attention of baseball scouts. Piersall broke into professional baseball as an outfielder with Scranton, PA (EL) in 1948 and played for Louisville, KY (AA) in 1949 and 1950. In 1950, the Boston Red Sox (AL) promoted the 6-foot, 175-pound outfielder to the parent club. He spent the 1951 season shuffling between Louisville and Birmingham, AL (SL), finishing with a .346 batting mark for Birmingham. The following season, he was hospitalized for a nervous breakdown. His breakdown was poignantly recounted in a book and then a baseball film, aptly entitled *Fear Strikes Out*.

On June 10, 1953, in the first game of a doubleheader against the St. Louis Browns (AL), Piersall made six hits in six trips to the plate for the Boston Red Sox, tying an AL record. The performance marked his comeback and his new philosophy for dealing with the taunts of unruly fans who rode him unmercifully. Piersall replaced Dom DiMaggio* as the regular Boston Red Sox center fielder the following season and was named an AL All-Star in 1954 and 1956. Piersall's career was characterized by numerous bizarre and zany antics, including a celebrated fight with New York Yankee ruffian Billy Martin.*

In December 1958, the Boston Red Sox traded Piersall to the Cleveland Indians (AL) for Vic Wertz* and Gary Geiger. The right-handed Piersall played a very shallow center field, but won Gold Gloves in 1958 and 1961. He led AL outfielders in fielding percentage in 1956, 1961, and 1962. His best offensive production included his AL-leading 40 doubles in 1956, 19 HR and 103 runs scored in 1957, and a career-high 18 steals for the Cleveland Indians in 1960, fifth best in the AL. The best batting average of his major league career, a .322 mark for the 1961 Cleveland Indians, placed him fourth in the AL. Manager Casey Stengel* once said of him, "He's great, but you got to play him in a cage."

Piersall in 1961 earned $45,000, his highest salary. He was traded to the expansion Washington Senators (AL) in October 1961 and New York Mets (NL) in May 1963 for first baseman Gil Hodges,* who became the Washington Senators manager. Piersall's running the bases backwards after hitting his 100th major league HR epitomized his zany approach to the game. The HR came on July 26, 1963 off Dallas Green* of the Philadelphia Phillies at the Polo Grounds.

Manager Casey Stengel released him the next day, saying, "There's room for just one clown on this team!" Piersall trekked down from the Polo Grounds to Yankee Stadium, where the Los Angeles Angels (AL) were playing the New York Yankees and asked old friend and manager Bill Rigney* for a job. He hit .314 for the Los Angeles Angels in 1964 as a part-timer, being voted the Comeback Player of the Year.

After retiring as a player in 1967, Piersall spent two years as the general manager of the Roanoke, VA Buckskins (ACFL). In 1973, he managed the Orangeburg, SC Cardinals (WCL). The high-strung, volatile Piersall carried his combative nature to the broadcast booth, where he announced for the Chicago White Sox (AL) before being fired for criticizing management. From 1995 to 1999, he served as roving minor league outfield instructor for the Chicago Cubs (NL).

During his 17-year major league career, Piersall compiled a lifetime .272 batting average in 1,734 games. He made 1,604 hits with 256 doubles, 52 triples, 104 HR, and 591 RBI. Piersall married Mary Teevan on October 22, 1949 and had nine children, including Eileen, Doreen, Claire, and Jimmy. Since their divorce, he has married two other times.

BIBLIOGRAPHY: Dan Shaughnessy, *The Curse of the Bambino* (New York, 1990); Robert Redmount, *The Red Sox Encyclopedia* (Champaign, IL, 1998); Howard Liss, *The Boston Red Sox* (New York, 1982); Peter Golenbock, *Fenway* (New York, 1992); Jimmy Piersall file, National Baseball Library, Cooperstown, NY; Gene Karst and Martin Jones, Jr., *Who's Who in Professional Baseball* (New Rochelle, NY, 1973); Jimmy Piersall and Al Hirshberg, *Fear Strikes Out* (New York, 1956); Jimmy Piersall with Richard Whittingham, *The Truth Hurts* (Chicago, IL, 1984); Mike Shatzkin, ed., *The Ballplayers* (New York, 1990); George Sullivan, *Baseball's Wacky Players* (New York, 1984); Al Hirshberg, *What's the Matter with the Red Sox?* (New York, 1973).

William A. Borst

PINELLI, Ralph Arthur "Babe," "The Soft Thumb" (b. Rinaldo Angelo Paolinelli, October 18, 1895, San Francisco, CA; d. October 22, 1984, Daly City, CA), player and umpire, was the son of Italian immigrants Rafael Paolinelli, a grocer, and Ermida (Silvestri) Paolinelli. He left school at age 10 to help support the family after his father died in the San Francisco, CA earthquake of 1906. A tough street kid, he gained local prominence as an amateur boxer and a scrappy infielder in semiprofessional baseball leagues. He signed with Portland, OR (PCL) in 1917 and adopted an Anglicized version of his name at the request of a sportswriter. Pinelli joined the Chicago White Sox (AL) as a wartime replacement at the end of the 1918 season, but returned to Sacramento, CA (PCL) for 1919. After a trial with the Detroit Tigers (AL) in 1920 and an outstanding year with Oakland, CA (PCL) in 1921, Pinelli took over as the regular third baseman of the Cincinnati Reds (NL) in 1922. He proved a solid contact hitter with little power in six years with the Cincinnati Reds. Besides hitting over .300 in two of his first three seasons, he posted a career .276 batting average with only five HR. A "smart" player and master of the "hidden-ball trick," he performed sparingly the last two years because of defensive shortcomings. Pinelli, released during the 1927 season, returned to the PCL, where he averaged over .300 at the plate in five seasons with San Francisco and Oakland and once hit two grand-slam HR in a single game.

Pinelli started as a PCL umpire in 1933, using personal contacts to overcome his lack of experience, and joined the NL two years later. His understanding of the game and affable personality made him a popular, highly respected arbiter. Although a fiery umpire-baiter during his playing days, Pinelli earned the nickname "The Soft Thumb" for his reluctance to eject players and managers. He worked four All-Star Games (1937, 1941, 1950, and 1956) and six World Series (1939, 1941, 1947, 1948, 1952, and 1956). He also umpired the first night game in major league history on May 24, 1935, at Cincinnati, OH between the Philadelphia Phillies and the Cincinnati Reds. Pinelli's finest hour occurred at the end of his career. The plate umpire for the fifth game of the 1956 World Series between the New York Yankees (AL) and the Brooklyn Dodgers (NL), he called a game-ending third strike on Brooklyn Dodger pinch-hitter Dale Mitchell* to preserve the first perfect game in World Series by Don Larsen* of the New York Yankees. Some claimed that the pitch was low and outside by a few inches, but the veteran Pinelli never hesitated in calling a strike and thereby enforced baseball's unwritten code requiring a batter to swing at a close pitch in that situation.

Pinelli, who claimed never to have missed a game during 22 major league seasons, retired after the 1956 campaign. He married Mable McKee in December 1916 and had two children.

BIBLIOGRAPHY: Lee Allen, *The Cincinnati Reds* (New York, 1948); Stephen Jay Gould, "The Strike That Was Low and Outside," *NYT*, November 10, 1984; Babe Pinelli as told to Joe King, *Mr. Ump* (Philadelphia, PA, 1953); Babe Pinelli file, National Baseball Library, Cooperstown, NY; San Francisco (CA) *Examiner*, October 23–25, 1984; Herbert Simons, "The Babe in Blue," *BM* 68 (February 1942), pp. 401–402; *TSN*, November 5, 1984.

Larry R. Gerlach

PINIELLA, Louis Victor "Lou," "Sweet Lou" (b. August 28, 1943, West Tampa, FL), player, coach, manager, and executive, grew up in a household that included his mother, Margaret, and her Spanish immigrant parents. Piniella's father, Louis, owned a candy/tobacco distributorship and played for a men's baseball team, on which young Lou served as batboy. Basketball was Piniella's favorite sport in high school, as he played for Tampa's Jesuit High School and won Catholic All-America honors. An ankle injury, however, hampered his roundball ability. After spending a year at the University of Tampa on an athletic scholarship, the 6-foot, 187-pound Piniella signed a bonus professional baseball contract with the Cleveland Indians (AL).

Piniella batted .270 in 1962 in his first professional season for Selma, AL (AlFL). After being drafted by the Washington Senators (AL), Piniella advanced to Peninsula, VA (CL) in 1963 and hit .310 to capture CrL Rookie-of-the-Year honors. During five more minor league seasons, the fastball hitter learned to handle curveballs and sliders. In October 1968, the Seattle Pilots selected Piniella in the AL expansion draft. The Seattle Pilots traded him to the Kansas City Royals (AL) expansion club in April 1969. In his Kansas City debut, Piniella made the first hit and scored the first run in Royal history. After hitting .282 with 11 HR in 1969, he was named the AL's Rookie of the Year. Three years later, Piniella batted .312, led the AL with 33 doubles, and appeared in his only major league All-Star Game.

Piniella was traded to the New York Yankees (AL) in December 1973 and performed for 11 seasons in pinstripes, becoming one of the club's most popular players and a favorite of owner George Steinbrenner.* The outfielder–DH batted over .300 in five different seasons with New York and averaged .306 at the plate in 44 postseason games. The clutch hitter's career included a .291 major league batting average, 1,705 hits, 305 doubles, 102 HR, and 766 RBI. Piniella retired as a player in 1984 and served successively as a New York Yankee coach (1984–1985), manager (1986–1987), general manager (1988), manager (June 1988), and special adviser (1989). In November 1989, the Cincinnati Reds (NL) named him manager. Piniella piloted the 1990 Reds to a 91–71 win–loss record and the NL pennant. The Cincinnati Reds swept the Oakland A's in four games in the World Series. Piniella managed the Cincinnati Reds to a 90–72 record and second place Central Division finish in his final season in Cincinnati in 1992.

After the 1992 season, the Seattle Mariners (AL) appointed him manager. He guided the Seattle Mariners to first place in the AL West to a 79–66 record in 1995. The Seattle Mariners defeated the New York Yankees in the 1995 AL Division Series but lost to the Cleveland Indians in the AL Championship Series. The Seattle Mariners boasted a 90–72 mark and first place in the AL West in 1997, but were eliminated by the Baltimore Orioles in the AL Division Series. In 13 managerial seasons, he has compiled a 1,019–949 record and .518 winning percentage.

The sociable, temperamental Piniella, who wed former "Miss Tampa" Anita Garcia in 1967 and has three children, is a cousin of major leaguer Dave Magadan.

BIBLIOGRAPHY: S. Buckley, "Lou Piniella," *Sport* 84 (June 1993), pp. 20–21; J. Klein, "Sweet Lou," *NY* 19 (March 24, 1986), pp. 38–45; Thomas Aylesworth and Benton Minks, *The Encyclopedia of Baseball Managers* (New York, 1990); Reggie Jackson and Mike Lupica, *Reggie* (New York, 1984); Sid Bordman, *Expansion to Excellence* (Marcelline, MS, 1981); Dave Anderson et al., *The Yankees* (New York, 1979); Mark Gallagher, *The Yankee Encyclopedia*, vol. 3 (Champaign, IL, 1997); Lou Piniella file, National Baseball Library, Cooperstown, NY; *CB* (1986), pp. 433–436; Leigh Montville, "The Edge of Rage," *SI* 73 (October 1, 1990), pp. 34–37; Lou Piniella and

Maury Allen, *Sweet Lou* (New York, 1986); Mike Shatzkin, ed., *The Ballplayers* (New York, 1990); *TSN Official Baseball Register, 1998; WWA*, 45th ed. (1988–1989) vol. 2, p. 2461; *Yankees Magazine 1984*, pp. 93–94.

Thomas D. Jozwik

PINSON, Vada Edward, Jr. (b. August 11, 1938, Memphis, TN; d. October 21, 1995, Oakland, CA), player and coach, moved at age six to Oakland, CA, where his father, Vada, Sr., worked as a longshoreman. Until age 15, Pinson was influenced by his natural grandmother, Lily Perkins, to practice the trumpet as much as baseball. He attended McClymonds High School, noted for Curt Flood,* Frank Robinson,* and other professional athletes. Robinson, a senior, played on the same baseball team with Pinson. Under the tutelage of high school coach George Powles, the left-handed hitting and fielding Pinson developed baseball skills to complement his natural speed. Pinson, who married Jacqueline Garibaldi in February 1960, was timed running to first base in 3.3 seconds.

After being signed by the Cincinnati Reds (NL), Pinson hit .278 in 1956 as a first baseman for Wausau, WI (NoL). The following year at Visalia, CA (CaL), he batted .361 with 20 HR and 53 stolen bases. After batting .343 for Seattle, WA (PCL) in 1958, he finished the season as an outfielder with the Cincinnati Reds (NL) and remained there through the 1968 campaign. Pinson enjoyed his best years with the Reds, where he batted a career-high .343 in 1961. He led the NL in at-bats twice (648 in 1959, 652 in 1960), runs scored once (131 in 1959), hits twice (208 in 1961, 204 in 1963), doubles twice (47 in 1959, 37 in 1960), and triples twice (14 in 1963, 13 in 1967). At one stretch, the 5-foot 11-inch, 180 pounder played in 505 consecutive games for Cincinnati. In his one World Series, Pinson hit only .091 in 5 games in 1961 against the New York Yankees.

Pinson was traded in October 1968 to the St. Louis Cardinals (NL), where he combined with Flood and Lou Brock* to make one of baseball's fastest modern outfields. The next two years, he played with the Cleveland Indians (AL) and slugged a career-high 24 HR in 1970. He played for the California Angels (AL) in 1972 and 1973 and finished his career with the Kansas City Royals (AL) in 1974 and 1975. Pinson never achieved the superstar status of his high school classmate Robinson, nor did he take full advantage of his blinding speed in stealing bases. His lifetime statistics nevertheless included a .286 batting average, 1,366 runs scored, 1,170 RBI, 2,757 hits, 485 doubles, 127 triples, 256 HR, and 305 stolen bases. Pinson served as a hitting coach for the Seattle Mariners (AL) from 1977 through 1980 and in 1982 and 1983, Chicago White Sox (AL) in 1981, Detroit Tigers (AL) from 1985 through 1991, and Florida Marlins (NL) in 1993 and 1994.

BIBLIOGRAPHY: Vada Pinson file, National Baseball Library, Cooperstown, NY; Maury Allen, *Yesterday's Heroes* (New York, 1990); Donald Honig, *The Cincinnati Reds* (New York, 1992); Jim Brosnan, *Pennant Race* (New York, 1962); Ritter Collett, *The*

Cincinnati Reds (Virginia Beach, VA, 1976); Bob Rathgeber, *Cincinnati Reds Scrapbook* (Virginia Beach, VA, 1982); Floyd Connor and John Snyder, *This Date in Cincinnati Reds History* (West Point, NY, 1984); Furman Bisher, "Is He the Nearest-Perfect Player?" *SEP* 233 (July 16, 1960), pp. 72–78; "Cincinnati's Vada Pinson," *Look* 25 (August 25, 1961), pp. 84–86; Gene Karst and Martin J. Jones, Jr., *Who's Who in Professional Baseball* (New Rochelle, NY, 1973); Larry Moffi and Jonathan Kronstadt, *Crossing the Line* (Jefferson, NC, 1994); Ralph C. Moses, "Vada Pinson," *BRJ* 25 (1996), pp. 88–89; *NYT Biographical Service* 26 (October 1995), p. 1564; *The Baseball Encyclopedia*, 10th ed. (New York, 1996); "Rookie with a Wallop," *Newsweek* 53 (April 27, 1959), p. 100; *Who's Who Among Black Americans* (Northbrook, IL, 1976).

James K. Skipper, Jr.

PIPP, Walter Clement "Wally" (b. February 17, 1893, Chicago, IL; d. January 11, 1965, Grand Rapids, MI), player, grew up in Grand Rapids and attended Catholic University. He entered professional baseball with Kalamazoo, MI (SML) in 1912 and played first base with Providence, RI (IL) and Scranton, PA (NYSL) in 1913, debuting in the major leagues in September 1913 with the Detroit Tigers (AL). After having a good season at Rochester, NY (IL) in 1914, he was sold in January 1915 to the New York Yankees (AL).

Pipp's name has become part of the legend and lore of baseball history. To "Pipp" is to be replaced due to injury or illness and never regain one's position. On June 1, 1925, Pipp begged out of a New York Yankee game due to a headache. He was replaced in the lineup by Lou Gehrig,* who had started his 2,130 consecutive playing game streak the previous day as a pinch hitter. Miller Huggins's* famous last words to Pipp were, "The kid can replace you and you can take the day off." Pipp was beaned in practice during the 1925 season by New York Yankee rookie pitcher Charlie Caldwell (FB), later Princeton University football coach. The pitch fractured Pipp's skull, causing him to spend two weeks in the hospital. When he had recovered, his regular position with the New York Yankees was gone permanently.

Pipp showed considerable power during the dead ball era, leading the AL in 1916 in HR with 12 and recording 93 RBI. The following season, the left-handed hitter repeated as HR champion with nine. The 6-foot 1-inch, 180-pound Pipp enjoyed his best seasons as the New York Yankees won their first three AL pennants from 1921 through 1923. Pipp compiled batting averages of .296, .329, and .304 during this period.

Pipp's career was always deeply intertwined with that of Gehrig. Pipp scouted Gehrig at the suggestion of William C. Smith, the owner of the Indianapolis, IN club (AA) and offered him $500 to sign. Gehrig refused because the New York Yankees and New York Giants (NL) had offered him more money. Gehrig was not the only replacement the oft-injured Pipp had. After Pipp sprained his ankle on September 27, 1923, the New York Yankees called up Gehrig from Hartford, CT (EL) for the World Series against the

New York Giants. The New York Giants, however, refused to approve this replacement, causing the New York Yankees to play Babe Ruth* at first base the rest of the season. Pipp answered the bell for the 1923 World Series with his ankle heavily taped. He reinjured the ankle sliding in the third game. Ruth replaced him for the remainder of that contest, but Pipp returned the next day to complete the series.

In February 1926 the New York Yankees sold the sure-handed first baseman to the Cincinnati Reds (NL), where he played three seasons. Pipp finished his 15-year major league career with 1,872 games, a .281 batting average, 1,941 hits, 90 HR, and 997 RBI. In three World Series, Pipp batted .224 with 15 hits. His last professional baseball season came in 1930 with Newark, NJ (IL), where he hit .312.

Following his playing career, Pipp worked in publishing, aired a pregame show, and even wrote scripts for a Detroit announcer. He later worked as a manufacturer's representative in the automotive supply business, selling screws and bolts. Pipp spent his last days in a rest home after suffering several debilitating strokes. He was survived by his wife, Nora (Powers) Pipp, and their three sons, Tom, Ben, and Walter, Jr., and daughter, Mrs. William Bibler.

BIBLIOGRAPHY: Wally Pipp file, National Baseball Library, Cooperstown, NY; B. Anderson, "Just a Pipp of a Legend," *SI* 66 (June 29, 1987), pp. 78–82; Edward Barrow and James Kahn, *My 50 Years in Baseball* (New York, 1957); Frank Graham, *The New York Yankees* (New York, 1943); Dave Anderson et al., *The Yankees* (New York, 1979); Mark Gallagher, *The Yankee Encyclopedia*, vol. 3 (New York, 1997); Paul Dickson, *The Dickson Baseball Dictionary* (New York, 1989); Ernie Harwell, "Pipp Picks Out Highlights of His Career at Gateway," *TSN*, December 20, 1961, p. 17; Gene Karst and Martin Jones, Jr., eds., *Who's Who in Professional Baseball* (New Rochelle, NY, 1973); Obituary, *TSN*, January 23, 1965, p. 26; Mike Shatzkin, ed., *The Ballplayers* (New York, 1990); Lee Allen, *The Cincinnati Reds* (New York, 1948).
                                                                William A. Borst

PIZARRO, Juan Roman (Cordova) (b. February 7, 1937, Santurce, PR), player, is the son of Luis Pizarro, a sugar refinery worker, and Millie Pizarro and learned baseball with his 11 brothers and sisters at an early age. Pizarro's pitching skill earned him a position at age 17 on his hometown's Santurce Cangrejeros semiprofessional team. In 1956, Ben Geraghty recommended that the Milwaukee Braves (NL) purchase Pizarro from the Santurce club. The Milwaukee Braves assigned him to Jacksonville, FL (SL). The 5-foot 11-inch, 170-pound, fireballing left-hander performed sensationally in his professional debut, winning 23 games, losing just six, striking out 318 batters, and completing 27 contests. His superlative 1.77 ERA garnered him the SL's MVP.

In May 1957, Pizarro joined the Milwaukee Braves after starting the season with Wichita, KS (AA). In his first outing, Pizarro fanned nine Chicago

Cubs in a 4–1 victory. He duplicated the score against the Los Angeles Dodgers, striking out eight batters in his second major league appearance. Pizarro helped the Milwaukee Braves to a NL pennant and a World Series championship over the New York Yankees in 1957 and a second NL pennant in 1958, but inconsistency prevented him from spending a full season in the major leagues until 1960. Pizarro won six of 13 games in 1960 and was traded that December to the Cincinnati Reds (NL) and Chicago White Sox (AL).

Pizarro reached his pitching pinnacle during six seasons with the Chicago White Sox. From 1961 to 1966, he compiled a 75–47 win–loss record and 3.16 ERA. He twice threw two-hitters in 1962, finishing 16–8 with a 2.39 ERA in 1963 and 19–9 with a 2.56 ERA in 1964. Following the 1966 season, Pizarro began brief courtships with seven teams. He pitched for the Pittsburgh Pirates (NL) in 1967, 1968, and 1974, Boston Red Sox (AL) in 1968 and 1969, Cleveland Indians (AL) and Oakland Athletics (AL) in 1969, Chicago Cubs (NL) from 1970 to 1973, and Houston Astros (NL) in 1973. Pizarro was used mostly in relief during that span, winning 26 games and losing 29 contests with a 4.50 ERA. With the Chicago Cubs in 1971, Pizarro outdueled Tom Seaver* of the New York Mets, 1–0, and homered for the only run.

Pizarro pitched from 1975 to 1978 with the Puebla Pericos (MEL) and Anahuac Indios (MEL) before retiring in 1978. During 18 major league seasons, Pizarro compiled 131 wins, 105 losses, a .555 winning percentage, and a 3.43 ERA. He appeared in the 1957 and 1958 World Series and in the 1963 and 1965 All-Star games. The confirmed bachelor Pizarro served as director of youth baseball programs in San Juan, PR and has resided in Santurce, PR since 1986.

BIBLIOGRAPHY: *TSN Baseball Register*, 1967, 1969; Bob Buege, *The Milwaukee Braves: A Baseball Eulogy* (Milwaukee, WI, 1988); Bob Buege, "Milwaukee Madness," *OTBN* 6 (1994), pp. 12–14; Bob Buege, *Eddie Mathews and the National Pastime* (Milwaukee, WI, 1994); Gary Caruso, *The Braves Encyclopedia* (Philadelphia, PA, 1995); Tom Meany, *Milwaukee's Miracle Braves* (New York, 1954); *Milwaukee Braves Yearbook*, 1957–1959; Larry Moffi and Jonathan Kronstadt, *Crossing the Line* (Jefferson, NC, 1994); Richard Lindberg, *Sox* (New York, 1984); Richard Lindberg, *Who's on Third?* (South Bend, IN, 1983); Bob Vanderberg, *Sox: From Lane and Fain to Zisk and Fisk* (Chicago, IL, 1982); Eddie Gold and Art Ahrens, *The New Era Cubs, 1941–1985* (Chicago, IL, 1985); Jim Enright, *Chicago Cubs* (New York, 1975); Michael M. Oleksak and Mary Adams Oleksak, *Beisbol, Latin Americans and the Grand Old Game* (Indianapolis, IN, 1996); Juan Pizarro file, National Baseball Library, Cooperstown, NY; John Thorn et al., eds., *Total Baseball*, 5th ed. (New York, 1997).

Jerry J. Wright

PLANK, Edward Stewart "Eddie," "Gettysburg Eddie" (b. August 31, 1875, Gettysburg, PA; d. February 24, 1926, Gettysburg, PA), player, won more games than any left-handed pitcher in AL history during a 17-year major league career. The son of the David Plank, he grew up on his father's farm and attended Gettysburg Academy. He at age 21 entered Gettysburg College, where he played organized baseball for the first time. Plank was persuaded to try out for the team by coach Frank Foreman, a former major league pitcher, and became one of the top collegiate players in Pennsylvania.

Upon graduation from Gettysburg College in 1901, Plank signed with the Philadelphia Athletics (AL) in the AL's first year as a major circuit. With no minor league experience, the 25-year-old rookie won 17 and lost 13 his initial season. He remained in the major leagues until his retirement in 1918. Plank, who recorded four consecutive 20-win seasons (1902–1905), joined teammates Rube Waddell,* Chief Bender,* Jack Coombs,* and Andy Coakley to form one of the finest pitching staffs of all time. Under manager Connie Mack,* the Athletics won AL pennants in 1902, 1905, 1910–1911, 1913, and 1914 and world championships in 1910, 1911, and 1913.

Throughout his career, Plank exhibited excellent control, hurled numerous complete games and shutouts, and compiled consistently low ERAs. The 5-foot 11½-inch, 175 pounder used a fastball and curve from a sidearm delivery to baffle opposing batters. An extremely slow worker, he infuriated the opposition, umpires, and spectators with long delays between pitches. Plank pitched for the Athletics from 1901 through 1914 and won at least 20 games seven times. His season high for wins (26) came in both 1904 and 1912. He led the AL twice in shutouts (1907, 1911) and recorded the most complete games once (1905).

Plank suffered hard luck in World Series competition. He played in the 1905, 1911, 1913, and 1914 Series and appeared in seven games, winning two, losing five, and posting a 1.32 ERA. Four of his five defeats were by shutouts, while his teammates scored only eight total runs in the games. His greatest World Series performance came against the New York Giants in 1913, when he bested Christy Mathewson,* 3–1, in the fifth game to clinch the championship for Philadelphia. Plank, who had lost in the 10th inning after pitching nine scoreless frames in Game 2, allowed just two hits in this deciding contest. In two previous World Series matchups, Mathewson had defeated Plank by identical 3–0 scores.

Plank was released after the 1914 season and signed with the St. Louis Terriers (FL). The veteran hurler won 21 games and finished second in ERA with a 2.08 mark. When the FL folded in 1916, Plank was awarded to the St. Louis Browns (AL). Although past age 40, the still effective Plank compiled 16–15 and 5–6 records in his two seasons with the Browns. His 1.79 ERA in 1917 marked the second best of his career. Plank was traded to the New York Yankees (AL) in January 1918, but retired and returned to his home in Gettysburg. During off-seasons, Plank worked as a tour guide at the Gettysburg battlefield. After retiring from baseball, he farmed and also operated an automobile business until a few years before his death. For a few years, he pitched in the semiprofessional BeL. Plank married Anna Myers in 1915 and had one son.

Plank pitched in 623 major league games, won 326, lost 194 (.627 winning percentage), issued 1,072 bases on balls, and struck out 2,246 batters. He ranks fifth on the all-time list of shutout leaders (69) and compiled a 2.35 ERA. Plank holds the major league record for most complete games by a left-hander (410) and AL records for most shutouts (63) and most games won by a left-hander (305). He shares the AL record for most consecutive years of 100 or more strikeouts (13, from 1902 to 1914). In 1–0 games, Plank won 15 and lost 11 and ranks near the top in these categories. The quiet, serious Plank lacked the color of many of his contemporaries and never was a great favorite of the sportswriters. During the first two decades of this century, however, he became major league baseball's most successful left-handed pitcher. His victory total stood until 1961, when Warren Spahn* became the game's winningest left-hander. In 1946, Plank was elected to the National Baseball Hall of Fame.

BIBLIOGRAPHY: Lee Allen and Tom Meany, *Kings of the Diamond* (New York, 1965); Martin Appel and Burt Goldblatt, *Baseball's Best: The Hall of Fame Gallery* (New York, 1977); Gene Karst and Martin J. Jones, Jr., *Who's Who in Professional Baseball* (New Rochelle, NY, 1973); A. W. Laird, *Ranking Baseball's Elite* (Jefferson, NC, 1990); Connie Mack, *My 66 Years in the Big Leagues* (Philadelphia, PA, 1950); Frederick G. Lieb, *Connie Mack* (New York, 1945); Jerome C. Romanowski, *The Mackmen* (Upper Darby, PA, 1979); Bill Borst, ed., *Ables to Zoldak*, vol. 2 (St. Louis, MO, 1989); Tom Meany, *Baseball's Greatest Pitchers* (New York, 1951); *NYT*, February 25, 26, 27, 28, 1926; Edward Plank file, National Baseball Library, Cooperstown, NY.

Joseph Lawler

PODRES, John Joseph "Johnny" (b. September 30, 1932, Witherbee, NY), player and coach, is the son of a miner, a semipro pitcher who encouraged his son's athletic career by never insisting that he work during the summer, and is the oldest of five children. His mother gave birth to him while suffering from double pneumonia. On February 12, 1966, Podres married Joan Taylor. They have two sons, Joseph and John, a harness racing driver, and reside in Glens Falls, NY.

Podres graduated from Mineville High School, where he starred as a pitcher and pole vaulter. Podres signed for a modest bonus with his favorite baseball team, the Brooklyn Dodgers (NL). His first minor league season proved sensational even by Class D standards. He finished 21–3 with a 1.67 ERA and 228 strikeouts in 200 innings at Hazard, KY (MtnSL). The 5-foot 11-inch, 170-pound left-hander threw hard with excellent control and learned quickly. After spending a season with Montreal, Canada (IL) that was curtailed by a bad back, he joined the Brooklyn Dodgers in 1953 at age 20. An appendectomy disrupted his 11–7 1954 season, while a sore arm limited him to a 9–10 record in 1955. In the 1955 World Series, Podres led the Brooklyn Dodgers to their only world championship by defeating the New York Yankees twice and hurling a 2–0 shutout in Game 7.

Podres missed the 1956 season with U.S. Navy duty, but was discharged due to a recurrent back injury. After returning to the Brooklyn and Los Angeles Dodgers for nine more seasons, he spent 1967 and 1968 with the Detroit Tigers (AL) and finished his major league career with the San Diego Padres (NL) in 1969. He enjoyed wine, women, and horses. His accomplishments far exceeded the World Series triumph for which he is best known. Prodres compiled a 148–116 regular season win–loss record with a 3.68 ERA and registered four wins and a 2.11 ERA in six World Series starts. He also appeared in two All-Star games and led the NL with a 2.66 ERA and six shutouts in 1957, and a .783 winning percentage in 1961.

Podres became an outstanding minor and major league pitching coach. He coached with the San Diego Padres in 1973, Boston Red Sox (AL) in 1980, Minnesota Twins (AL) from 1981 to 1985, and Philadelphia Phillies (NL) from 1992 to 1996, turning a young, erratic staff into consistent winners and leading it to the 1993 World Series against the Toronto Blue Jays. He also worked with the Los Angeles Dodgers as a roving minor league coach. Known for a positive, supportive approach to coaching, he enjoyed excellent rapport with his pitchers. Podres stressed consistency and control and masterfully taught the change-up, the pitch most responsible for his own success.

BIBLIOGRAPHY: Tim Kurkjian, "Johnny Podres," *SI* 79 (October 25, 1993), pp. 26–27; Rich Marazzi, "Bums Win," *SCD* 22 (April 28, 1995), pp. 130–132; Rich Marazzi, "1955: The 'Boys of Summer' Have Their October," *SCD* 22 (May 12, 1995), pp. 140–142; John Podres file, National Baseball Library, Cooperstown, NY; Richard Goldstein, *Superstars and Screwballs* (New York, 1991); Peter Golenbock, *Bums* (New York, 1964); Tommy Holmes, *The Dodgers* (New York, 1975); William F. McNeil, *The Dodgers Encyclopedia* (Champaign, IL, 1997); Fred Smith, *995 Tigers* (Detroit, MI, 1981); Harold Rosenthal, "Miner Dad Saw Podres as Gem," *TSN*, October 12, 1955, pp. 3ff, Fluffy Saccucci, "Podres Pitched Brooklyn to '55 World Championship," *SCD* 25 (March 6, 1996), p. 130.

Allen E. Hye

POLES, Spottswood "Spot" (b. November 7, 1889, Winchester, VA; d. September 12, 1962, Harrisburg, PA), player, was a fleet-footed, sharp-hitting center fielder in the early 20th century Negro Leagues. He was the son of French Poles, a laborer, and Matilda Poles and played baseball with the Springdale AC of Harrisburg, PA in 1902. Poles usually batted in the leadoff position to utilize his incredible speed, rivaling that of James "Cool Papa" Bell.* Poles began his professional baseball career with the Harrisburg Colored Giants in 1906 at age 19 and three years later joined Sol White's* Philadelphia Giants. In 1911, he moved with White to the New York Lincoln Giants. Known as the black Ty Cobb,* the left-handed Poles batted .440 and .398 in 1911 and 1912, respectively, and stole 41 bases in only 60 games the former year. Superstar teammates with the Lincoln Giants included John Henry Lloyd,* Smoky Joe Williams,* Dick Redding,* Louis Santop,* and Grant "Home Run" Johnson.* John McGraw* listed Poles, Lloyd, Williams, and Redding as the players that he would have selected for the New York Giants if the major leagues had integrated then.

After the Lincolns soundly defeated Rube Foster's* Chicago American Giants in the 1913 playoff for their second consecutive championship, owner Jess McMahon boasted that his team could beat any team including major league squads. In 1914, Poles compiled an even more impressive .487 batting average. The speedster averaged .319 at bat for four winters spent in Cuba and batted .594 in frequent exhibitions against the Philadelphia Phillies, Philadelphia Athletics and other major league teams. In 1917, at age 30, Poles began his World War I military service as a member of the 369th infantry and was decorated for his combat experience in France. He played with the Lincolns and Brooklyn Royal Giants (ECL) until 1923, retiring after 15 seasons with a career batting average over .400 against top-level competition in black baseball. After ending his baseball career, Poles owned a small fleet of taxicabs and and worked at Olmsted Air Force Base in Middletown, PA.

BIBLIOGRAPHY: John Holway, "Spottswood Poles," *BRJ* 4 (1975); Robert W. Peterson, *Only the Ball Was White* (Englewood Cliffs, NJ, 1970); James A. Riley, *The All-Time All-Stars of Black Baseball* (Cocoa, FL, 1983); James A. Riley, *Biographical Encyclopedia of the Negro Baseball Leagues* (New York, 1994); James A. Riley, interviews with former Negro League players, James A. Riley Collection, Canton, GA; Spottswood Poles file, National Baseball Library, Cooperstown, NY.

James A. Riley

POLLET, Howard Joseph "Howie" (b. June 26, 1921, New Orleans, LA; d. August 8, 1974, Houston, TX), player and coach, was of French ancestry and attended Jesuit Prep High School and Fourtier High School in New Orleans. St. Louis Cardinals (NL) scout Eddie Dyer* signed Pollet, who joined New Iberia, LA (EvL) in 1939. The 6-foot ½ inch, 175-pound southpaw won 20 games for Houston, TX (TL) in 1940 and 1941. St. Louis Cardinals general manager Branch Rickey* promoted Pollet to the St. Louis Cardinals in September 1941, provided he sign a contract for 1942 at $600 per month. After signing reluctantly, Pollet in September hurled six complete games, won five contests, and pitched two shutouts. Pollet married Virginia Clark on October 18, 1941 and had seven children, including Roberta, Howard, Jr., Shirley, Christopher, and John. He divided time in 1942 between the bullpen and starting rotation, winning seven of 12 decisions. Pollet retired the only batter he faced in the fourth game of the 1942 World Series, in which the St. Louis Cardinals defeated the New York Yankees in five games.

In 1943, Pollet hurled three consecutive shutouts, led the NL with a 1.75 ERA, and raised his record to eight wins and four losses before entering the U.S. Army Air Corps on July 11. He was attached to the 58th Bomb Wing, 20th Air Force in the Pacific theater. With fellow players Enos Slaughter,* Billy Hitchcock, Birdie Tebbetts,* Joe Gordon,* and Tex Hughson,* Pollet said his purpose was "to provide recreation and entertainment for the men over there. We accomplished our mission in excellent fashion as any G.I. who witnessed the games will agree." He was discharged in November 1945, missing the St. Louis Cardinals' NL pennants in 1943 and 1944.

Pollet returned in 1946 to enjoy the finest season of his major league career, leading the NL with 21 victories, 266 innings pitched, and a 2.10 ERA. Manager Eddie Dyer's St. Louis Cardinals defeated Brooklyn Dodgers twice in the second-ever major league playoff to win the NL pennant. Pollet pitched 10 innings in the first game of the World Series against the Boston Red Sox, but lost, 3–2, when Rudy York* belted a change-up over the fence. Pollet started Game 5 with pain in his arm and could not make it through the first inning. The St. Louis Cardinals won the World Championship in seven games. After arm surgery, he won only nine of 20 decisions in 1947. Pollet recovered to win 13 of 21 decisions in 1948. He used a moving fastball, straight change-up, and slow curveball to win 20 games, hurl an NL-best five shutouts, and record a 2.77 ERA in 1949, but the St. Louis Cardinals fell one game short of the NL pennant-winning Brooklyn Dodgers. Teammate Stan Musial* described Pollet as "a class pitcher, a stylist with pitching rhythm, and a student of the game."

Pollet, who was often bothered by a bad back, won 14 contests and lost 13 games in 1950. After Pollet dropped his first three decisions in 1951, the Cardinals in June traded him with catcher Joe Garagiola* to the Pittsburgh Pirates (NL). Pollet lost 10 of 16 decisions for the Pirates in 1951 and stumbled to a 7–16 record in 1952. On June 4, 1953, the Pittsburgh Pirates sent Pollet as part of a 10-player deal to the Chicago Cubs (NL). In three seasons with the Cubs, he won 17 contests and lost 19 games. He divided the 1956 campaign between the Chicago White Sox (AL) and the Pittsburgh Pirates, compiling a 3–5 record. Pollet's 14-year major league career included 403 games, 131 victories, and 116 defeats with 20 saves and 934 strikeouts in 2,107.1 innings.

Pollet pursued the insurance business during the off-season with Eddie Dyer in Houston, TX and served as St. Louis Cardinals pitching coach from 1959 to 1964, being credited with developing Ernie Broglio, Bob Gibson,* and Ray Sadecki. He held the same position with the Houston Astros (NL) in 1965.

BIBLIOGRAPHY: Bob Broeg, *Redbirds: A Century of Cardinals' Baseball* (St. Louis, MO, 1981); Gene Karst and Martin Jones, Jr., *Who's Who in Professional Baseball* (New Rochelle, NY, 1973); Eddie Gold and Art Ahrens, *The New Era Cubs, 1941–1985* (Chicago IL, 1985); Richard L. Burtt, *The Pittsburgh Pirates, A Pictorial History* (Virginia Beach, VA, 1977); Frederick G. Lieb, *The St. Louis Cardinals* (New York, 1945);

Stan Musial as told to Bob Broeg, *Stan Musial, "The Man's" Own Story* (Garden City, NY, 1964); Howard Pollet file, National Baseball Library, Cooperstown, NY; Rob Rains, *The St. Louis Cardinals* (New York, 1992); Bob Broeg and Jerry Vickery, *St. Louis Cardinals Encyclopedia* (Grand Rapids, MI, 1998); *St. Louis Cardinals' Yearbook, 1962.*

Frank J. Olmsted

PORTER, Darrell Ray (b. January 17, 1952, Joplin, MO), player, is the son of Raymond Porter, a driver for United Transport Company, and Twila Mae (Conley) Porter, a high school cafeteria manager, and was the second of five children. Porter, the MVP in football, basketball, and baseball at Southeast High School in Oklahoma City, OK, was selected an All-State catcher in Oklahoma for 1968 and 1969. After Porter signed a football letter of intent to attend the University of Oklahoma, the Milwaukee Brewers (AL) baseball club drafted him fourth in June 1970. The 6-foot 1-inch, 200-pound Porter signed a $70,000 plus incentives contract with Milwaukee and reported to Clinton, IA (ML).

A 24-HR outburst at Danville, IL (ML) in 1971 earned the left-handed-batting Porter a September trial with the Milwaukee Brewers. After more seasoning at Evansville, IN (AA), Porter started as Milwaukee's catcher in 1973. He showed promise with the Milwaukee Brewers, but blossomed after being dealt in December 1976 to the Kansas City Royals (AL). Two fine seasons with the Kansas City Royals were followed by his best year in 1979 with 20 HR and AL-leading 121 RBI, as Porter became only the second catcher in history to exceed 100 walks, runs scored, and RBI in a season. Kansas City Royals skipper Whitey Herzog* claimed Porter should have been AL MVP.

Although Porter enjoyed success on the field, his personal life collapsed. He married Teri Brown on June 2, 1972, but they divorced in 1976. They had no children. While playing winter ball in 1970, Porter was introduced to marijuana. The next few years saw him start taking quaaludes, amphetamines, and finally cocaine. During spring training in 1980, Porter sought help from former Brooklyn Dodger great Don Newcombe* and entered a rehabilitation program. Porter, who credited his deep Christian faith in helping him through, returned to the Kansas City Royals six weeks later. He hit .249 with seven HR in 1980, batted only .100 against the New York Yankees in the AL Championship Series, and hit .143 in the World Series loss to the Philadelphia Phillies.

Over the Thanksgiving holiday in 1980, Porter married Deanne Gaulter. The following month, he agreed to a five-year deal worth $3.5 million with general manager Whitey Herzog of the St. Louis Cardinals (NL). Porter endured three months on the disabled list in 1981 and criticism of St. Louis fans, who lamented the departure of his popular predecessor Ted Simmons.* However, 1982 marked a new beginning for Porter. A daughter, Lindsey, was born in March. An excellent handler of pitchers, Porter was named 1982 NL Championship Series MVP as the St. Louis Cardinals defeated the Atlanta Braves and World Series MVP when the Cardinals downed the Milwaukee Brewers in seven games. Porter sparkled defensively and at bat in both series. He returned to postseason play a fifth time in 1985, when the St. Louis Cardinals defeated the Los Angeles Dodgers in the NL Championship Series. The St. Louis Cardinals, however, lost the World Series in seven games to Porter's former teammates, the Kansas City Royals.

The Texas Rangers (AL) in January 1986 signed Porter, who experienced two productive seasons as occasional DH and backup receiver. He retired following the 1987 season with 1,369 hits, 188 HR, 765 runs scored, 826 RBI, and .247 batting average and played on the AL All-Star team in 1978, 1979, and 1980. Porter resides in Lee's Summit, MO, where he oversees his investments and enjoys fishing.

BIBLIOGRAPHY: Darrell Porter file, National Baseball Library, Cooperstown, NY; Whitey Herzog and Kevin Horrigan, *White Rat* (New York, 1987); Arnold Irish, "He Has a Talent for Guiding Pitchers," *BD* 42 (August 1983), pp. 80–82; Kansas City Royals, *Grandslam* (Kansas City, MO, 1980); Sid Bordman, *Expansion to Excellence* (Marcelline, MS, 1981); Robert E. Kelly, *Baseball's Best* (Jefferson, NC; 1988); Darrell Porter with William Deerfield, *Snap Me Perfect* (Nashville, TN, 1984); Rob Rains, *The St. Louis Cardinals* (New York, 1992); Bob Broeg and Jerry Vickery, *St. Louis Cardinals Encyclopedia* (Grand Rapids, MI, 1998).

Frank J. Olmsted

POSEY, Cumberland Willis, Jr. "Cum" (b. June 20, 1890, Homestead, PA; d. March 28, 1946, Pittsburgh, PA), baseball player, manager, and executive, and basketball player, owned the powerful Homestead, PA Grays (NNL) team and also participated in professional basketball as an organizer and player. Posey's father, Cumberland W. Posey, Sr., worked as a riverboat engineer on the Ohio River and reputedly was the first so licensed. He later became general manager of Delta Coal Company and pursued banking and real estate interests. Posey's mother, Anna (Stevens) Posey, became the first black to graduate from and teach at Ohio State University.

After growing up in Homestead, Posey attended Pennsylvania State College in 1909 and 1910 and played basketball there both years. He also joined the then semipro Homestead Grays in 1910 as an outfielder and began a lifetime association there. In 1910, he organized a semipro basketball team and ranked among the nation's greatest basketball players. Besides working as a mail clerk in Pittsburgh, PA, Posey in 1912 became the booking agent for the Grays and put the team on a full-time schedule. Posey, who married Ethel Truman in 1913 and had five daughters, attended the University of Pittsburgh in 1913. He formed and played through 1925 for the Loendi Big Five basketball team, the nation's first great black team. Loendi played several games against the New York Original Celtics and, by 1919, claimed the national championship. The slightly built 5-foot 9-inch, 145-pound Posey enrolled at Holy Ghost College (later Duquesne University) in 1915 as Charles W. Cumbert. He led the basketball team in scoring and captained the golf team. He became field captain of the Grays that year and held that post until his retirement as a player in 1928.

From 1919 to 1935, Posey managed the Homestead Grays. The Grays dominated Pennsylvania, Virginia, and Ohio until 1922, when the Pittsburgh Keystones (NNL) attempted to raid them. Posey gained control of the team by attaining financing from Charles Walker, placed all his players on a salary basis, and made a deal for the Grays to use Forbes Field when the Pittsburgh Pirates were on the road. The Keystones eventually left town. Posey's Grays refused to join the EL in 1923 and raided many teams of their stars, including Sam Streeter, George Scales,* "Smoky Joe" Williams,* Martin Dihigo,* and Vic Harris.* These players helped the Grays compile a 140–13 record in 1926 and win 43 straight games. That fall, they defeated a major league team with stars Lefty Grove* and Goose Goslin* in three out of four games.

Nicknamed "Cum" by friends, Posey in 1927 formed the Grays basketball team and defeated the great New York Celtics in three of five games. An excellent booking agent, Posey made more money than the Negro League teams and enlisted Oscar Charleston,* Judy Johnson,* and Josh Gibson* for his baseball squad by 1930. That year, the Grays defeated the New York Lincoln Giants to claim the Negro Championship. In 1931, the Grays won 136 games and conquered Connie Mack's* All Stars twice. Gus Greenlee* formed the Pittsburgh Crawfords in 1932 and snatched Johnson, Charleston, Gibson, and others from the Grays. Posey also formed the short-lived Detroit Wolves (EWL) that year.

Financial troubles plagued Posey's Grays through the early and middle 1930s. After the Grays joined the NNL in 1935, Posey lured stars Buck Leonard,* Satchel Paige,* and even Gibson back to the Grays when the Pittsburgh Crawfords (NNL) collapsed in 1937. Posey built a powerhouse club, winning nine straight NNL pennants and Negro World Series titles in 1943 and 1944. The 1937 team won 152 games and lost only 24. In 1940, the Grays began playing many games in Washington, DC's Griffith Stadium. They drew 102,000 fans in ten games by 1942, providing a financial boon to the Grays.

Posey continued securing the best talent in Negro baseball, signing Roy Partlow, Johnny Wright, Jud Fields, and James "Cool Papa" Bell.* He also served on the Homestead school board, worked as the NNL secretary, and wrote occasionally for the Pittsburgh *Courier*. The integration of baseball in 1945 ended the great Washington-Homestead Grays teams. After losing players Luke Easter,* Wright, Partlow, Bob Thurman, and Luis Marquez, Posey protested that the major leagues did not pay for his stars. In 1946, Posey died of lung cancer.

Besides organizing both baseball and basketball teams, Posey served as a baseball player, manager, owner, talent scout, and league official, created among the finest baseball teams in history, and became one of the first black executives to pay salaries and ensure adequate meals and lodging. His move to Griffith Stadium in Washington and its consequent financial rewards demonstrated conclusively that people would pay to see black stars and provided a large boost to the integration of baseball.

BIBLIOGRAPHY: Amsterdam *News*, September 16, 1944; John B. Holway, "The Long Gray Line, Cum Posey," John B. Holway Collection, Alexandria, VA; John B. Holway, *Blackball Stars* (Westport, CT, 1988); John N. Ingham and Lynne B. Feldman, eds., *American Business Leaders* (Westport, CT, 1994); Robert W. Peterson, *Only the Ball Was White* (Englewood Cliffs, NJ, 1970); James A. Riley, *The Biographical Encyclopedia of the Negro Baseball Leagues* (New York, 1994); Jules Tygiel, *Baseball's Great Experiment* (New York, 1983).

Terry A. Baxter

POST, Walter Charles "Wally" (b. July 9, 1929, St. Wendelin, OH; d. January 6, 1982, St. Henry, OH), player, was the son of Frank Post, a successful farmer, and pitched and hit the St. Henry High School baseball team to two consecutive state championship final games. After his junior year, he signed a professional contract with the Cincinnati Reds (NL) and played two games for Middletown, OH (OSL) in 1946. In 1947 the Cincinnati Reds assigned Post to Muncie, IN (OSL), where he won 17 games and hit .338 as an outfielder. With Columbia, SC (SAL) in 1948, he posted a 8–11 won–lost record and shared outfield duties. After pitching briefly at Charleston, SC (CL) in 1949, he developed a sore arm and was converted to a full-time outfielder. Post was returned to Columbia and made his major league debut with the Cincinnati Reds at the end of the 1949 season. Post spent the next four seasons learning his trade in the minor leagues, appearing in 45 games with the Cincinnati Reds from 1951 through 1953. He performed with Tulsa, OK (TL) in 1950, Buffalo, NY (IL) in 1951, Milwaukee, WI (AA) in 1952, and Indianapolis, IN (AA) in 1953, earning All-Star team recognition in 1951 and 1953.

From 1954 to 1957 and 1960 through 1962, the 6-foot 1-inch, 203-pound right fielder performed with the Cincinnati Reds. He spent the 1958 and 1959 seasons with the Philadelphia Phillies (NL). His 40 HR in 1954 set an all-time record for a Cincinnati Reds right-handed batter, while his 109 RBI that year marked the most ever by a Reds outfielder. Post compiled the highest slugging percentage (.556) of the brief 1961 World Series against the New York Yankees, attaining 10 total bases in 18 at-bats. Post won most acclaim for his long-distance HR. His 1961 HR at Busch Stadium in St. Louis struck the scoreboard behind the left field bleachers while headed for an estimated 569 feet journey. Many of his HR at Crosley Field in Cincinnati hit the billboard atop the roof of the laundry building, situated behind the left field fence, and won him a record number of suits offered by a local clothing store.

Post finished his major league career with the Minnesota Twins (AL) in 1963 and Cleveland Indians (AL) in 1964. His 15 major league seasons included a .266 career batting average, a .485 slugging percentage, 194 doubles, 210 HR, and 699 RBI. He was elected to the Cincinnati Reds Hall of Fame in 1965.

Post returned to St. Henry, OH and worked with his father-in-law at the nearby Minster Canning Company. He married Pat Beckman in January 1949 and had three daughters and a son. His first wife died of cancer in January 1980. His second wife, Pat, and all four children survived him.

BIBLIOGRAPHY: Wally Post file, National Baseball Library, Cooperstown, NY; Al Silverman, "Everyone Wants Wally Post," *Sport* 23 (April 1956), pp. 40–41, 81–83; Harry T. Paxton, "The Redlegs' Hardest Hitter," *SEP* 228 (June 30, 1956), pp. 31ff; Donald Honig, *The Cincinnati Reds* (New York, 1992); Jim Brosnan, *Pennant Race* (New York, 1992); Ritter Collett, *The Cincinnati Reds* (Virginia Beach, VA, 1976); Bob Rathgeber, *Cincinnati Reds Scrapbook* (Virginia Beach, VA, 1982); Peter C. Bjarkman, *Baseball's Great Dynasties—The Reds* (New York, 1991).

Richard D. Miller

POWELL, John Joseph "Jack" (b. July 9, 1874, Bloomington, IL; d. October 17, 1944, Chicago, IL), player and umpire, was the son of boilermaker John W. Powell and Mary A. Powell. He spent most of his adult life in St. Louis, MO, where he pitched for both of its major league teams and operated a saloon with his former battery mate and brother-in-law, Jack O'Connor.* Powell married O'Connor's sister Nora, but the marriage ended in divorce in 1907. The Powells had one son, Jim, who played and managed in the minor leagues.

After pitching one year of minor league ball with Fort Wayne, IN (WA) in 1895, the 5-foot 11-inch, 195-pound, right-handed Powell hurled for the Cleveland Spiders (NL) in 1897 and 1898. In 1899, some Spiders moved to St. Louis to play for the Cardinals. Powell became one of the St. Louis Cardinals' pitching aces until joining the St. Louis Browns (AL) in 1902. Powell was traded to the New York Highlanders (AL) in January 1904 and won 23 games that season. He combined with Jack Chesbro* to hurl 64 victories, the all-time AL high. Powell returned to the St. Louis Browns (AL) in September 1905, and pitched for the Browns through the 1912 season. He pitched for the Louisville, KY Colonels (AA) and Venice, CA (PCL) in 1913 and 1914. He played semipro baseball (1916–1917), tried an unsuccessful comeback at age 44 with the Browns in 1918, and became an umpire for several years.

Powell, who pitched nine seasons for the Browns, placed at or near the top in several club statistical categories. He ranks first in games started (264), complete games (210), innings pitched (2,229.2), strikeouts (884), shutouts

(27), and games lost (143); second in games pitched (294) and games won (117); and fifth in ERA (2.71). In 16 major league seasons, Powell pitched in 578 games, struck out 1,621 batters, walked 1,021 hitters, and compiled a 2.97 ERA. He ranks high on the all-time major league lists for pitchers in several departments. Powell recorded 245 victories, 254 losses (8th), started 516 games, completed 422 games (14th), pitched 4,389 innings, hurled 46 shutouts, surrendered 4,319 hits, and allowed 1,976 runs. His most productive season came with Cleveland in 1898, when he recorded 23 victories and an NL-leading 6 shutouts. Powell paced the NL in games started (41) and complete games (40) in 1899 and in games pitched (45) in 1901.

BIBLIOGRAPHY: Jack Powell file, National Baseball Library, Cooperstown, NY; Bill Borst, *Still Last in the American League* (West Bloomfield, MI, 1992); Craig Carter, ed., *TSN Daguerreotypes*, 8th ed. (St. Louis, MO, 1990); Brent P. Kelley, *The Case For: Those Overlooked by the Baseball Hall of Fame* (Jefferson, NC, 1992); J. Thomas Hetrick, *The Misfits!* (Jefferson, NC, 1992); John Phillips, *The Spiders—Who Was Who* (Cabin John, MD, 1991); Frederick G. Lieb, *The St. Louis Cardinals* (New York, 1945); Bob Broeg and Jerry Vickery, *St. Louis Cardinals Encyclopedia* (Grand Rapids, MI, 1998); Bill Borst, ed., *Ables to Zoldak*, vol. 2 (St. Louis, MO, 1989); *TSN*, October 26, 1944; *TSN Official Baseball Record Book, 1998* (St. Louis, MO, 1998).

John L. Evers

POWELL, John Wesley "Boog" (b. August 17, 1941, Lakeland, FL), player, ranked among his era's most feared hitters and proved a fine defensive first baseman. His father, a car salesman, nicknamed him "Boog" or "Booger" because of his mischievous childhood pranks. The Powells moved in 1957 to Key West, FL, where Boog starred in three sports at Key West High School. Spurning several college football scholarship offers, he signed in 1958 with the Baltimore Orioles (AL) baseball club for a reported $35,000. In 1959, he began his professional baseball career with Bluefield, WV (ApL). After playing at Fox Cities, WI (3IL) in 1960, Powell slugged 32 HR and batted .321 for Rochester, NY (IL) in 1961. He joined the Baltimore Orioles in 1962 and married Janet Swinton, a Kent State University student, on July 9 of that year.

From 1962 until 1974, Powell starred for Baltimore. An outfielder and later an All-Star first baseman, he belted 39 HR and made an AL-leading .606 slugging average in 1964. In 1970, he was voted AL MVP. During his 17-year major league career, Powell made 1,776 hits, slugged 270 doubles, knocked in 1,187 runs, and hit .266. His 339 career HR ranked among the top 60 as of 1999 among lifetime batting leaders. He appeared in five AL Championship Series and the 1966, 1969, 1970, and 1971 World Series. In the 1966 World Series, Powell batted .357 to lead his team to a four-game sweep over the Los Angeles Dodgers.

The 6-foot 4½-inch, 250- to 290-pound Powell enjoyed widespread popularity among fans and fellow players and was among the biggest men ever to play major league baseball. In the mid–1960s, the Baltimore team physician, an endocrinologist, and a psychologist sought unsuccessfully to curb his eating habits. In his MVP year (1970), Powell reportedly weighed 280 pounds. He was traded to the Cleveland Indians (AL) in February 1975, where he batted .297 in 134 games. After several minor injuries, he ended his career in 1977 with the Los Angeles Dodgers (NL). The Baltimore, MD resident operates a food concession at Camden Yards.

BIBLIOGRAPHY: Boog Powell file, National Baseball Library, Cooperstown, NY; Ted Patterson, *The Baltimore Orioles* (Dallas, TX, 1995); James H. Bready, *Baseball in Baltimore* (Baltimore, MD, 1998); Phil Jackman, "The Ball's Going Pffft," *SI* 40 (May 13, 1974), p. 70; "People on the Way Up," *SEP* 23 (May 5, 1962), p. 28; J. D. Reed, "Always Ready to Chew the Fat," *SI* 39 (July 16, 1973), pp. 65–72, 74.

John Hanners

POWER, Victor Pellot "Vic" (b. November 1, 1927, Arecibo, PR), player and scout, ranked as the slickest fielding first baseman of all-time. He married Idalia Albarado on December 19, 1956. A versatile defensive player who handled several positions, the 5-foot 11-inch, 195-pound right-handed batter was purchased by the New York Yankees (AL) in October 1953 after pacing the AA with a .349 batting average for the Kansas City Blues. He and Elston Howard* were the first black players brought up to the major leagues by the New York Yankees.

The New York Yankees traded Power to the Philadelphia Athletics (AL) for Eddie Robinson* and Harry Byrd in December 1953. Power began his major league career in 1954 with the Philadelphia Athletics. He accompanied the Athletics to Kansas City in 1955 and was traded in June 1958 to the Cleveland Indians (AL). Cleveland General Manager Frank Lane* called Power "the best first baseman in baseball." The right-handed batter and thrower employed a sweeping motion with his glove that made him a favorite among fans but often drew criticism from more conservative-minded baseball followers. He once engaged in a heated debate with the legendary Ohio State University football coach Woody Hayes (FB) in Cleveland after the latter accused him of showboating. Power's six consecutive Gold Glove Awards (1958–1963), and seven altogether, demonstrated his outstanding defensive skills. He led AL first basemen in fielding percentage in 1957, 1959, and 1960.

Power also played for the Minnesota Twins (AL) from 1962 through 1964, Los Angeles Angels (AL) in 1964, and Philadelphia Phillies (NL) in 1964, and finished his 12-year major league career with the California Angels (AL) in 1965. Offensively, his career totals included a solid .284 batting average, 658 RBI, and 126 HR. He paced the AL with 10 triples in 1958. He scouted for the California Angels from 1979 through 1992, serving as supervisor in 1992. He conducts a baseball school for Puerto Rican youngsters. The mayor of Guaynabo City, PR built a stadium in Power's name.

BIBLIOGRAPHY: *The Baseball Encyclopedia*, 10th ed. (New York, 1996); Peter C. Bjarkman, *Baseball with a Latin Beat* (Jefferson, NC, 1994); Terry Pluto, *The Curse of Rocky Colavito* (New York, 1994); Jack Torry, *Endless Summers* (South Bend, IN, 1995); Ernest Mehl, *The Kansas City Athletics* (New York, 1956); Dave Mona and Dave Jarzyna, *Twenty-five Seasons* (Minneapolis, MN, 1986); Rich Marazzi, "The Yankees Passed on Slick-Fielding Vic Power," *SCD* 26 (January 15, 1999), pp 76–77; Peter Golenbock, *Dynasty* (New York, 1975); *NYT*, October 14, 1953; Larry Moffi, *This Side of Cooperstown* (Iowa City, IA, 1996); Larry Moffi and Jonathan Kronstadt, *Crossing the Line* (Jefferson, NC, 1994); Victor Power file, National Baseball Library, Cooperstown, NY; Leonard Shecter, "Vic Power's New Wonderful World," *Sport* 5 (May 5, 1963), pp. 65–71; *TSN*, November 1, 1982, July 10, 1965, September 10, 1963.

Albert J. Figone

PRATT, Derrill Burnham "Del" (b. January 10, 1888, Walhalla, SC; d. September 30, 1977, Texas City, TX), player and manager, performed for the University of Alabama from 1907 through 1909. In 1910, he debuted professionally with Montgomery, AL (SA) and batted a disappointing .232 mark in 51 games. Pratt was demoted to Hattiesburg, MS (CSL), where his .367 batting average earned him a ticket back to Montgomery the next season. After batting .310 there, he was sold to the St. Louis Browns (AL) for players and cash. With St. Louis from 1912 to 1917, Pratt became a steady performer, usually batted well, and played second base in virtually all the team's games. His best season with St. Louis came in 1912, when he hit .302. Pratt stole 37 bases in both 1913 and 1914 and pilfered 174 altogether for the Browns to rank third on their all-time list just behind George Sisler* and Burt Shotton. He also ranked high on their all-time list of doubles and triples leaders. In 1915, the 5-foot 11-inch, 175-pound right-hander appeared in 159 games, a league record until the schedule was expanded in 1961.

In 1918, Pratt and teammate Doc Lavan sued Browns owner Phil Ball for $50,000 for saying they were "lazy" and implying that they had accepted money to throw baseball games. When Ball refused to retract the statement, AL president Byron Johnson* persuaded the players to settle out of court. Lavan was traded to the Washington Senators (AL), while Pratt and pitcher Eddie Plank* were shipped to the New York Yankees (AL) in January 1918 for pitchers Urban Shocker* and Nick Cullop, catcher Les Nunamaker, infielders Joe Gedeon and Fritz Maisel, and $15,000. After a clubhouse hassle involving the disposition of the 1920 World Series shares, Pratt was traded with Muddy Ruel* to the Boston Red Sox (AL) in December for Wally Schang* and Waite Hoyt.* In October 1922, the Red Sox sold Pratt and Warren Collins to the Detroit Tigers (AL) for three players and cash.

Pratt ended his 13-year career with the Detroit Tigers following the 1924 season. He became player–manager of the Waco, TX Navigators (TL) in 1925 and stayed there through the 1930 season. He managed Galveston, TX (TL) for two seasons and Fort Worth, TX (TL) until his retirement after the 1934 season. Pratt remained in Texas thereafter. He enjoyed his best batting average in 1921 by hitting .324 in 135 games and led the AL in RBI (1916) with 103. During 13 major league seasons, he played in 1,836 games and compiled 1,996 hits, 392 doubles, 117 triples, 43 HR, 856 runs scored, 968 RBI, 247 stolen bases, and a lifetime .292 batting average. On September 1, 1914, he married Leotine Mindora Ramsauer.

BIBLIOGRAPHY: Del Pratt file, National Baseball Library, Cooperstown, NY; Bill Borst, ed., *Ables to Zoldak*, vol. 2 (St. Louis, MO, 1989); Frank Graham, *The New York Yankees* (New York, 1943); Mark Gallagher, *The Yankee Encyclopedia*, vol. 3 (Champaign, IL, 1997); Bill Borst, *Last in the American League* (St. Louis, MO, 1976); Harold Seymour, *Baseball: The Golden Age* (New York, 1971); *WWIB, 1924*, 9th ed. (New York, 1924); Frederick G. Lieb, *The Boston Red Sox* (New York, 1947); Robert Redmount, *The Red Sox Encyclopedia* (Champaign, IL, 1998); Fred Smith, *995 Tigers* (Detroit, MI, 1981).

                                                                      William A. Borst

PRIDDY, Gerald Edward "Jerry" (b. November 9, 1919, Los Angeles, CA; d. March 3, 1980, North Hollywood, CA), player, was of German-Dutch ancestry and played baseball at Washington High School in Los Angeles. New York Yankees (AL) scout Bill Essick signed Priddy, who made his professional baseball debut with Rogers, AR (AML) in 1937. Priddy batted .336 and supplied good power for a middle infielder. He spent the 1938 season with Norfolk, VA (PiL) at shortstop and second base, compiling a .323 batting average. The New York Yankees promoted the 5-foot 11-inch, 180-pound Priddy to Kansas City, MO (AA), where he hit even more impressively. At Kansas City, the right-hander played second exclusively and collaborated with shortstop Phil Rizzuto* in a double-play combination that seemed destined for major league stardom.

Both made the New York Yankees in 1941, with Rizzuto immediately starting. Priddy's path at second base, however, was blocked by Joe "Flash" Gordon,* a devastating hitter and top fielder. Priddy became a utility infielder, hitting only .213 in 56 games. He batted .280 in 1942, but displayed little power as a reserve. He hit only .100 in the 1942 World Series, which the New York Yankees lost to the St. Louis Cardinals in five games.

Priddy griped in the clubhouse, antagonizing New York Yankee manager Joe McCarthy.* New York dispatched him to the Washington Senators (AL) in January 1943. Priddy immediately started at second base, batting .277 with 62 RBI. He spent the next two years in the U.S. Army Air Force and hit .254 upon returning to the Washington Senators in 1946. His batting average dipped to .214 the following year.

The Washington Senators sold Priddy for $25,000 to the St. Louis Browns in December 1947. He rebounded with a career-high .296 batting average in 1948 and hit .290 in 1949, increasing his market value. The cash-starved St. Louis Browns sold Priddy in December 1949 to the Detroit

Tigers (AL) for $100,000. The Detroit Tigers, solid at every other position, viewed him as a key link in their AL pennant quest in 1950. Although Priddy enjoyed a good season, the Detroit Tigers faded in September and finished second to the New York Yankees. The 1951 campaign marked his last as a regular. Priddy saw only spot duty the next two years with struggling Detroit and retired following the 1953 season, ending his 11-year major league career with 1,252 hits, 541 RBI, and a .265 lifetime batting average.

Priddy, who had married Evelyn Herberger in October 1939, pursued professional golf without much success and returned to Los Angeles, where he operated a paper products distributorship. In 1973, he was arrested on extortion charges involving threats made to a shipping company. Priddy was sentenced to nine months in prison and served about half the term before being paroled.

BIBLIOGRAPHY: Jerry Priddy file, National Baseball Library, Cooperstown, NY; *WWIB, 1951*, 36th ed.; *TSN Baseball Register*, 1944; Rich Marazzi and Len Florito, *Aaron to Zuverink* (New York, 1981); Frank Graham, *The New York Yankees* (New York, 1943); Mark Gallagher, *The Yankee Encyclopedia*, vol. 3 (Champaign, IL, 1997); Shirley Povich, *The Washington Senators* (New York, 1954); Fred Smith, *995 Tigers* (Detroit, MI, 1981); Joe Falls, *Detroit Tigers* (New York, 1975).

Lloyd J. Graybar

PUCKETT, Kirby (b. March 14, 1961, Chicago, IL), player and executive, is the youngest of nine children born to William Puckett and Catherine Puckett and started playing baseball in the south Chicago projects of Robert Taylor Homes, just one mile south of Comiskey Park. At Chicago's Calumet High School, he starred as a third baseman and earned All-America honors. Following graduation in 1979, however, Puckett received no baseball offers and worked at a Ford plant. Bradley University coach Dewey Kalmer, who spotted Puckett at a Kansas City Royals (AL) free agent tryout in the summer of 1980, offered him a baseball scholarship and moved him to center field. Following his father's death in 1981, Puckett left the Peoria, IL campus to live closer to his mother and enrolled at Triton CC in River Grove, IL. In his one season for Triton CC in 1982, he hit .472, belted 16 HR, stole 42 bases, and was named 1982 Region IV Player of the Year. In 1993, Puckett was inducted into the Triton Hall of Fame.

The Minnesota Twins (AL) made the right-handed-hitting and -throwing outfielder their first selection and third overall pick in the January 1982 free agent draft and assigned him to Elizabethton, TN (ApL), where he led the ApL in batting (.382), runs scored (65), hits (105), total bases (135), and stolen bases (43). Puckett was named to the ApL All-Star team and ApL Player of the Year by *BA*. The Minnesota Twins assigned him in 1983 to Visalia, CA (CaL), where he finished second in the CaL in doubles (29), fourth in triples (7), and sixth in batting (.314), and was named to the CaL All-Star team and CaL Player of the Year.

Puckett's 1984 season began with Toledo, OH (IL), but on May 8 the Minnesota Twins promoted him to the major league club for a game with the California Angels. Puckett, only the ninth major league player to get four hits in his initial game, made the Topps' Major League All-Rookie Team and finished third to Alvin Davis of the Seattle Mariners in the AL Rookie of the Year balloting. Puckett represented the heart and soul of the Twins. Puckett appeared in ten consecutive All-Star Games (1986–1995), starting in 1986, 1989, 1992, 1993, 1994, and 1995. In All-Star contests, he batted .292 and was named 1993 MVP with a double, HR, and 2 RBI. Puckett played in the AL Championship Series against the Detroit Tigers in 1987 and Toronto Blue Jays in 1991. The Minnesota Twins won both series in five games. In 10 AL Championship Series games, the 1991 Series MVP batted .311 with three HR and nine RBI. Puckett appeared in the World Series against the St. Louis Cardinals in 1987 and Atlanta Braves in 1991, helping the Twins win both seven-game series. Puckett's World Series statistics include a .308 batting average, 16 hits, two HR, and seven RBI. In 1991, he became the ninth player to end a World Series game with a HR, belting an eleventh inning HR in Game 6 against Charlie Liebrandt.*

In 12 major league seasons, the 5-foot 9-inch, 215-pound Puckett batted .318 with 2,304 hits (the most by any major leaguer during that span), 207 HR, 1,071 runs scored, and 1,085 RBI. Puckett's best offensive year came in 1988, when he batted .356 with 234 hits, 24 HR, 109 runs scored, and 121 RBI. In 1989, Puckett won his only AL batting title with a .339 average. He led the AL four times in hits and with 112 RBI in 1994. During his career, he won six *TSN* Gold Glove (1986–1989, 1991–1992) and six *TSN* Silver Slugger (1986–1989, 1992, 1994) awards. Since 1997, he has served as executive vice president and a director for the Minnesota Twins. Puckett resides in Minneapolis, MN, with his wife, Tonya (Hudson) Puckett, one daughter, Catherine, and one son, Kirby, Jr.

BIBLIOGRAPHY: Kirby Puckett file, National Baseball Library, Cooperstown, NY; Chuck Carlson, *Puck! Kirby Puckett* (Lenexa, KS, 1997); Henry Hecht, "Cal Can Bring 'em Up Right," *SI* 61 (July 23, 1984), pp. 56–57; Kirby Puckett, *I Love the Game* (New York, 1993); Harry Hecht, "Kirby Puckett's Home Run Derby," *SI* 64 (May 12, 1986), p. 72; J. Coplon, "The Secret of My New Success," *Sport* 78 (November 1987), pp. 50–51; Kirby Puckett and Greg Brown, *Be the Best You Can Be* (Minneapolis, MN, 1993); Kirby Puckett, "With No Regrets," *PW* 47 (March 3, 1997), pp. 67–68; Wil A. Linkugel and Edward J. Pappas, *They Tasted Glory* (Jefferson, NC, 1998); Barbara Carlisle Bigelow, ed., *Contemporary Black Biography*, vol. 4 (Detroit, MI, 1993); W. Leavy, "Puckett; On a New Mission," *Ebony* 52 (October 1997), pp. 174ff; *Minnesota Twins Media Guide*, 1994; David L. Porter, ed., *African-American Sports Greats* (Westport, CT, 1995); Steve Rushin, "A Bright Outlook," *SI* 86 (May 26, 1997), pp. 74–76; Rick Telander, "Minny's Mighty Mite," *SI* 66 (June 15, 1987), pp. 46–49.

James E. Welch

PUHL, Terry Stephen (b. July 8, 1956, Melville, Canada), player, is the son of Frank Puhl and Margaret (Gulash) Puhl and performed capably with the Houston Astros (NL) for 14 seasons. Puhl, a 6-foot 2-inch, 197-pound left-handed line-drive hitter, began his professional baseball career with Covington, KY (ApL) in 1974 and played outfield with Dubuque, IA (ML) in 1975, Columbus, GA (SAL) and Memphis, TN (IL) in 1976, and Charlestown, WV (IL) in 1977. He first saw major league action with the Houston Astros in 1977. As an outfielder, Puhl batted .301 in 60 games. He quickly demonstrated his above-average fielding prowess, making just one error in 123 chances.

In 1978, Puhl became a regular fixture in the Houston Astros outfield. From 1978 through 1980, he played 447 games for the Houston Astros. Puhl never hit for power, attaining a season-high 13 HR in 1980, but consistently hit for average. He recorded batting marks of .289, .287 and .282 during the 1978–1980 period and represented the Houston Astros at the 1978 All-Star game. The following year, he tied the major league record for highest fielding percentage and fewest errors by an outfielder. When the Houston Astros won the NL West Division title in 1980, Puhl paced his club in the thrilling NL Championship Series against the Philadelphia Phillies. Although the Houston Astros were defeated, Puhl batted .526 to establish a League Championship Series record for a five-game series.

During his major league career, Puhl seldom struck out. His season-high 52 strikeouts came in 1980. A legitimate speedster, he was credited with 217 career stolen bases. After suffering a pulled hamstring in 1985 and a debilitating ankle injury in 1986, Puhl proved less daring on the basepaths. Puhl split his duties with the Houston Astros in 1987 as a pinch hitter and as an outfielder. Upon returning as an outfield regular in 1988, he posted a career-best .303 batting average. By 1990, Puhl again saw part-time action on the Houston Astros roster. He finished his major league career in 1991 with the Kansas City Royals (AL), appearing in 15 games mostly as a pinch hitter. Puhl, whose career featured a .280 batting average, 62 HR, 435 RBI, and a .993 fielding percentage in 1,531 games, was inducted into the Canadian Baseball Hall of Fame in 1995. He holds the major league record for best fielding percentage by an outfielder in 1,000 or more games and led NL outfielders in fielding percentage in 1979 and 1981.

BIBLIOGRAPHY: Terry Puhl file, National Baseball Library, Cooperstown, NY; Mike Shatzkin, ed., *The Ballplayers* (New York, 1990); Paul Burka, "Houston Astros," *TM* (December 1980), pp 156–161, 264–271; *The Baseball Encyclopedia*, 10th ed. (New York, 1996).

John Robertson

PULLIAM, Harry Clay (b. February 8, 1869, Scottsville, KY; d. July 29, 1909, New York, NY), executive, was named for his tobacco farmer father, who had three sons and two daughters. After graduating from Louisville High School, he attended law school at the University of Virginia and became a reporter and city editor for the Louisville (KY) *Commercial*. A bachelor, he was elected in 1897 to the Kentucky Assembly, wore gala colored waistcoats, and often quoted Shakespeare. *SL* described him as "an idealist, a dreamer, a lover of solitude and nature." When Barney Dreyfuss* purchased the Louisville Colonels (NL) franchise, he persuaded Pulliam to become the club's secretary. In 1900, Pulliam moved with Dreyfuss to Pittsburgh as the Pirates' secretary–treasurer. Pulliam's reputation for honesty, business-like approach to baseball, and support of Dreyfuss led NL owners to elect him NL president in 1902.

Pulliam quickly moved to smooth relationships between the NL and the rival AL and minor leagues. In January 1903, Pulliam, AL president Ban Johnson,* and a committee of owners reached the National Agreement, which established the governance of organized baseball for two decades. Pulliam quickly became frustrated with his limited authority and constant conflicts with club owners and managers, especially New York Giants (NL) president John T. Brush* and manager John McGraw.* Pulliam, however, exercised stronger leadership than his predecessor, Nicholas Young,* giving firm control of the game on the field to the umpires. He also helped sportswriters organize the BBWAA in 1908.

Bitter conflicts with the New York club and press culminated in the famous Fred Merkle* decision of 1908. Pulliam followed his established pattern of supporting the umpires and received unmerciful criticism from McGraw and the press when his decision contributed to the New York Giants' losing the NL pennant to the Chicago Cubs. A ticket scalping controversy at the 1908 World Series created a rift between Pulliam and Chicago owner Charles W. Murphy. These controversies undid Pulliam, who became paranoid, moody, and uncommunicative. He committed suicide in his New York AC apartment. Although temperamentally unsuited to be NL president, he nonetheless brought some order and respectability to the game after the turbulent 1890s.

BIBLIOGRAPHY: Harry Pulliam file, National Baseball Library, Cooperstown, NY; Lee Allen, *The National League Story* (New York, 1961); Joseph Durso, *The Days of Mr. McGraw* (New York, 1969); Frederick G. Lieb, *The Pittsburgh Pirates* (New York, 1948); Noel Hynd, *The Giants of the Polo Grounds* (New York, 1988); Charles C. Alexander, *John McGraw* (New York, 1988); Francis C. Richter, "Passing of Pulliam," *SL* (August 7, 1909); Harold Seymour, *Baseball: The Golden Age* (New York, 1971); David Quentin Voigt, *American Baseball*, vol. 1 (Norman, OK, 1966).

William E. Akin

PURKEY, Robert Thomas "Bob" (b. July 14, 1929, Pittsburgh, PA), player, is the son of Edward Dallas Purkey, a field man for the Hartford Insurance

Group, and Anna (Lippencott) Purkey and graduated from Pittsburgh's South Hills High School, where he played baseball and football.

The Pittsburgh Pirates (NL) signed the 6-foot 2-inch, 200-pound, right-handed pitcher in 1948. Purkey began his professional baseball career with Greenville, AL (ASL), where his 19 victories included a no-hitter. After pitching for Davenport, IA (3IL) and New Orleans, LA (SA) and serving a two-year hitch in the U.S. Army, he debuted with three victories for the Pittsburgh Pirates in 1954. The woeful Pittsburgh Pirates lost 101 games that season. He shuffled between Pittsburgh and the minor leagues in 1955 and 1956, but recorded 11 of 62 victories for a weak 1957 Pirate squad.

The Pittsburgh Pirates traded Purkey in December 1957 to the Cincinnati Reds (NL), where he enjoyed his best seasons. In 1958, he won 17 games and was selected for the NL All-Star team. Purkey helped the Cincinnati Reds capture the 1961 NL pennant with a 16–12 record and was named a NL All-Star for the second time. In the 1961 World Series against the New York Yankees, he lost one game and compiled a 1.64 ERA in 11 innings.

Purkey's best season came in 1962, when he won 23 games, lost only five decisions, and led the major leagues with an .821 winning percentage. Besides repeating on the NL All-Star team, he finished third in the NL Cy Young Award balloting and was named to the *TSN* All-Star team.

Purkey hurt his arm in spring training the following year and never recovered. The Cincinnati Reds traded him to the St. Louis Cardinals (NL) in December 1964. Purkey ended his major league career with the Pittsburgh Pirates in 1966. During 13 major league seasons, Purkey won 129 games and lost 115 with a 3.79 ERA.

Purkey, who married Joan Latsko in June 1952 and had two children, Robert Jr. and Candy, resides in Pittsburgh and owns an insurance agency there. He participates in the PPAA, which raises money for charity. Purkey recently said concerning baseball, "If I could still run and still throw I would be there."

BIBLIOGRAPHY: Martin Appel, *Baseball Heroes* (New York, 1988); *The Baseball Encyclopedia*, 10th ed. (New York, 1996); Richard L. Burtt, *The Pittsburgh Pirates, A Pictorial History* (Virginia Beach, VA, 1977); Jim Brosnan, *Pennant Race* (New York, 1962); Floyd Connor and John Snyder, *Day-by-Day in Cincinnati Reds History* (West Point, NY, 1984); Ritter Collett, *The Cincinnati Reds* (Virginia Beach, VA, 1976); Bob Rathgeber, *Cincinnati Reds Scrapbook* (Virginia Beach, VA, 1982); Dave Molinari, "Pirates Trade of Purkey Was Insurance for Reds," *Pittsburgh Press*, July 5, 1988; Steve Perkins, "Cincinnati's Pitching Con Man," *Sport* 34 (October 1962), pp. 30–31; Robert Purkey file, PPAA, Pittsburgh, PA; Robert Purkey file, *TSN*, St. Louis, MO; Frank W. Thackeray, interview with Robert Purkey, December 1, 1996; Robert Purkey file, National Baseball Library, Cooperstown, NY.

Frank W. Thackeray